HISTORY OF ART

HISTORY
BY H. W. JANSON

PROFESSOR OF FINE ARTS, NEW YORK UNIVERSITY

HARRY N. ABRAMS, INC., NEW YORK

OF ART

THIRD EDITION · REVISED AND EXPANDED BY ANTHONY F. JANSON

CHIEF CURATOR, THE JOHN AND MABLE RINGLING MUSEUM OF ART, SARASOTA

PRENTICE-HALL, INC., ENGLEWOOD CLIFFS, N.J.

Editor: Patricia Egan
Designer: Bob McKee
Rights and Reproductions: Barbara Lyons
Photo Research for the Third Edition: Ivan Stoler

Library of Congress Cataloging in Publication Data

Janson, H. W. (Horst Woldemar),
    History of art.

    Bibliography: p. 802
    Includes index.
    1. Art—History.   I. Janson, Anthony F.
II. Title.
N5300.J3 1986b   709   85–12406
ISBN 0–13–389388–X

Published in 1986 by Harry N. Abrams, Incorporated, New York

Printed and bound in Japan

Note on the Picture Captions
Each black-and-white figure in this volume has been placed as
close as possible to the first discussion of its subject. This discussion includes references to the figures, as well as to any related
colorplate. The colorplate captions refer the reader to the page
where the discussion is to be found.

Unless otherwise noted, all paintings are in tempera on panel, or
oil on canvas, and all sculpture is of stone. Measurements are not
given for objects that are inherently large (architecture, architectural
sculpture, wall paintings), or small (manuscript illuminations,
drawings, prints). Height precedes width. A probable measuring
error of more than one percent is indicated by "c." Dates are
based on documentary evidence, unless preceded by "c."

First Edition 1962
Revised and Enlarged in 1969
Second Edition 1977
Third Edition 1986

CONTENTS

PREFACE AND ACKNOWLEDGMENTS
TO THE FIRST EDITION

The title of this book has a dual meaning: it refers both to the events that *make* the history of art, and to the scholarly discipline that deals with these events. Perhaps it is just as well that the record and its interpretation are thus designated by the same term. For the two cannot be separated, try as we may. There are no "plain facts" in the history of art—or in the history of anything else, for that matter; only degrees of plausibility. Every statement, no matter how fully documented, is subject to doubt, and remains a "fact" only so long as nobody questions it. To doubt what has been taken for granted, and to find a more plausible interpretation of the evidence, is every scholar's task. Nevertheless, there is always a large body of "facts" in any field of study; they are the sleeping dogs whose very inertness makes them landmarks on the scholarly terrain. Fortunately, only a minority of them can be aroused at the same time, otherwise we should lose our bearings; yet all are kept under surveillance to see which ones might be stirred into wakefulness and locomotion. It is these "facts" that fascinate the scholar.

I believe they will also interest the general reader. In a survey such as this, the sleeping dogs are indispensable, but I have tried to emphasize that their condition is temporary, and to give the reader a fairly close look at some of the wakeful ones. I am under no illusion that my diagnosis is up to date in every case. The field is too vast for anyone to encompass all of it with equal competence. If the shortcomings of my account have been kept within tolerable limits, this is due to the many friends and colleagues who have permitted me to tax their kindness with inquiries, requests for favors, or discussions of doubtful points. I am particularly indebted to the following: Richard Ettinghausen, M. S. İpşiroğlu, Wolfgang Lotz, Richard Krautheimer, and Meyer Schapiro, who reviewed various aspects of the book; and Max Loehr, Florentine Mütherich, Ernest Nash, and Halldor Soehner, for generous help in securing photographic material. I must also record my gratitude to the American Academy in Rome, which made it possible for me, as art historian in residence during the spring of 1960, to write the chapters on ancient art under ideal conditions; and to the Academy's indefatigable librarian, Nina Langobardi. Irene Gordon, Celia Butler, and Patricia Egan have improved the book in countless ways. Patricia Egan also deserves the chief credit for the reading list. I should like, finally, to acknowledge the admirable skill and patience of Philip Grushkin, who is responsible for the design and layout of the volume; my thanks go to him and to Adrianne Onderdonk, his assistant.

H. W. J.
1962

PREFACE AND ACKNOWLEDGMENTS
TO THE THIRD EDITION

This, the third edition of H. W. Janson's *History of Art*, preserves most of the text of the previous one. At the same time, it presents several major changes which deserve a few words of explanation. The most conspicuous difference is the addition of two sections and one entire chapter on the history of photography; though its status is still challenged, photography now merits treatment as a legitimate field of art historical investigation. At the same time, the decision was made, with regret, to drop the Postscript on the meeting of East and West. The entire study of Third World art is presently being transformed so dramatically that a new synthesis will not be possible for at least another decade. The chapters on twentieth-century art have been updated on the 1980s and several new sections added, notably on the Russian avant-garde, which has only recently begun to be understood in the West. The Introduction to the book has been expanded, as well as given an emphasis that is admittedly more philosophical in cast. Time charts, reading list, and glossary have been suitably revised, and a separate time line displays in synoptic form the contents of the entire book. And the achievement of women artists here receives recognition, long overdue.

In making these revisions, I am mindful that changing anything in what has become an institution is not a task to be undertaken lightly. My primary aim was to preserve the humanism that provided the foundation of this book. Though differences in style and approach inevitably arise between two writers, I have tried to keep them to a minimum. In this I have been helped immeasurably by Patricia Egan, who edited the previous editions. I am grateful to Paul Gottlieb, Barbara Lyons, Ivan Stoler, Bob McKee, and Shun Yamamoto at Harry N. Abrams, Inc., and above all to Margaret Kaplan, for their supportiveness throughout the processes of this revision. I would also like to thank Michael Auping, Chief Curator of the Albright-Knox Gallery, Buffalo, for our stimulating discussions of modern art in general and of Francesco Clemente in particular. Ward Bissell of the University of Michigan was kind enough to share his thoughts on Artemisia Gentileschi. Finally, I am indebted to Arthur K. Wheelock, Curator of Dutch Art at The National Gallery of Art, Washington, D.C., for sharing his research and photographs of Vermeer's *Woman with Scales*.

A. F. J.
1985

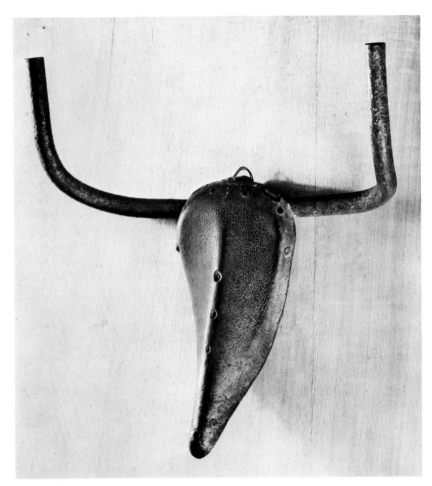

1. PABLO PICASSO. *Bull's Head*. 1943. Bronze cast of parts of a bicycle, height 16⅛". Galerie Louise Leiris, Paris

INTRODUCTION

"What is art?" Few questions provoke such heated debate, yet provide so few satisfactory answers. Without coming to any final conclusions, we can still bring some light to the problems. For art to us is first of all a *word*—one which acknowledges both the idea of art and the fact that art exists. Without the word, we might wonder whether there is art in the first place, and indeed the term does not occur in the language of every society. Yet art is *made* everywhere. Art, therefore, is also an object, but not just any kind of object. Art is an *aesthetic object*. It is meant to be looked at and appreciated for its intrinsic value. Its special qualities set art apart, so that precious examples have often been placed away from everyday life—in museums, churches, or caves. What do we mean by aesthetic? Aesthetics is defined as "that which concerns the beautiful."

Of course, not all art is beautiful to our eyes, but it is art nonetheless. However unsatisfactory, the term aesthetics will have to do, for lack of a better one. Aesthetics, as a branch of philosophy, has occupied thinkers from Plato to the present day, but like all matters philosophical, the issues raised by "beauty" are perhaps inherently unresolvable. During the past century aesthetics has also become a field of psychology, which has found equally little agreement. Why should this be so? On the one hand, people the world over make much the same fundamental judgments, since our brains and nervous systems are the same. On the other hand, our taste and choices are conditioned solely by our culture, and cultures are so varied that it is impossible to reduce art to one set of precepts that will apply everywhere. The laws of "scientific" inquiry into visual perception are only valid when the artist knows the theories too, and consciously applies them. Otherwise, laws are virtually useless in helping us to understand works of art. It would seem, therefore, that absolute qualities in art elude us, that we cannot escape viewing works of art in the context of their time and circumstance, whether past or present. How indeed could it be otherwise, so long as art is still being created all around us, opening our eyes almost daily to new experiences and thus forcing us to readjust our sights?

Imagination

We all dream. That is imagination at work. To imagine means simply to make an image—a picture—in our minds. Human beings are not the only creatures who have imagination. Even animals dream. A cat's ears and tail may twitch as he sleeps, and a sleeping dog may whine and growl and paw the air, as if he were having a fight. Even when awake, animals "see" things. For no apparent reason a cat's fur may rise on his back as he peers into a dark closet, just as you or I may get goose pimples from phantoms we neither see nor hear. Clearly, however, there is a profound difference between human and animal imagination. Men are the only creatures who can tell one another about imagination in stories or pictures. The urge to make art is unique to man. No other animal has ever been observed to draw a recognizable image spontaneously in the wild. In fact, the only images by animals have been produced under carefully controlled laboratory conditions that tell us more about the experimenter than about art.

There can be little doubt, on the other hand, that man possesses an aesthetic faculty. By the age of five every normal child has drawn a moon pie-face. The ability to make art is one of man's most distinctive features, for it separates him from all other creatures across a gap that is unbridgable.

Just as a developing embryo retraces much of man's evolutionary past, so the budding artist reinvents the first stages of art. Soon, however, he completes that process and begins to respond to the culture around him. Even the art of a child is subject to the taste and outlook of the society that shapes his personality. In fact, we tend to judge children's art according to the same criteria as adult art—only in appropriately simpler terms—and with good reason, for if we examine the successive stages, we find that the youngster must develop all the skills that go into adult art: coordination, intellect, personality, imagination, creativity, aesthetic judgment. Seen this way, the making of a youthful artist is as fragile a process as growing up itself, one that can be stunted at any step by the vicissitudes of life. No wonder that so few are fortunate enough to continue their creative aspirations into adulthood.

Given the many factors that feed into it, art must play a very special role in the artist's personality. Sigmund Freud, the father of modern psychiatry, conceived of art primarily in terms of sublimation outside of consciousness. Such a view hardly does justice to artistic creativity, since art is not simply a negative force at the mercy of our neuroses but a positive expression which integrates diverse aspects of personality. Indeed, when we look at the art of the mentally ill, we may be struck by its vividness but we instinctively sense that something is wrong, for the expression is incomplete.

Artists may sometimes be tortured by the burden of their genius, but they can never be truly creative under the thrall of psychosis. The imagination is one of the most mysterious facets of mankind. It can be regarded as the connector between the conscious and the subconscious, where most of our brain activity takes place. It is the very glue that holds man's personality, intellect, and spirituality together. Because the imagination responds to all three, it acts in lawful, if unpredictable, ways determined by the psyche and the mind. Thus, even the most private artistic statements can be understood on some level, even if only an intuitive one.

The imagination is important for allowing us to conceive of all kinds of possibilities in the future and to understand the past in a way that has real survival value. It is a fundamental part of our make-up. The ability to make art, in contrast, must have been acquired relatively recently in the course of evolution. The record of man's earliest art is lost to us. Man has been walking the earth for some three million years, but the oldest prehistoric art that we know was made only about 25,000 years ago, though it was undoubtedly the culmination of a long development no longer traceable. Even the most "primitive" ethnographic art represents a late stage of development within a stable society.

Who were the first artists? In all likelihood, they were shamans. Like the legendary Orpheus, they were believed to have divine powers of inspiration and could enter the underworld of the subconscious in a deathlike trance; but, unlike ordinary mortals, they were then able to return to the realm of the living. With the shaman's unique ability to penetrate the unknown and his rare talent for expressing it through art, he gained control over the forces hidden in man and nature. Even today the artist remains a magician whose work can mystify and move us—an embarrassing fact to civilized man, who does not readily relinquish his veneer of rational control.

Why does man create art? Surely one reason is an irresistible urge to adorn himself and decorate the world around him. Both are part of a larger desire, not to remake the world in his image but to recast himself and his environment in *ideal* form. Art is, however, much more than decoration, for it is laden with meaning, even if that content is sometimes slender or obscure. Art enables us to communicate our understanding in ways that cannot be expressed otherwise. Truly a picture is worth a thousand words, not only in its descriptive value but also in its symbolic significance. In art, as in language, man is above all an inventor of symbols to convey complex thoughts in new ways. We must think of art not in terms of everyday prose but as poetry, which is free to rearrange conventional vocabulary and syntax in order to convey new, often multiple meanings and moods. A painting likewise suggests much more than it states. And like a poem, the value of art lies equally in what it says and how it says it. It does so partly by implying meanings through allegory, pose, facial expression, and the like, or by evoking them through the visual elements: line, form, color, and composition.

But what is the *meaning* of art? What is it trying to say? Artists often provide no clear explanation, since the work is the statement itself. If they could say it in words, they would surely be writers instead. Fortunately, certain visual symbols and responses occur so regularly over time and space that they can be regarded as virtually universal. Nevertheless, their exact meaning is specific to each particular culture, giving rise to the incredible diversity of art.

Thus art, like language, requires that we learn the style and outlook of a country, period, and artist if we are to understand it properly. We are so accustomed to a naturalistic tradition of accurate reproductions that we expect art to imitate reality, yet such illusionism is but one vehicle for expressing an artist's understanding of reality. Truth, it seems, is indeed relative, for it is a matter not only of what our eyes tell us but also of the concepts through which our perceptions are filtered.

There is, then, no reason to place a premium on realism for its own sake. Instead, style need only be appropriate to the content. The advantage of realism at face value is that it *seems* easier to understand. The disadvantage is that representational art is, like prose, always bound to at least some extent by the literal meaning and appearance of the everyday world. Actually, realism is exceptional in the history of art and isn't even necessary to its purposes. We must remember that any image is a separate and self-contained reality which has its own ends and responds to its own imperatives, for the artist is bound only to his creativity. Even the most convincing illusion is the product of the artist's imagination and understanding, so that we must always ask why he chose this subject and made it this way rather than some other way.

Creativity

What do we mean by making? If, in order to simplify our problem, we concentrate on the visual arts, we might say that a work of art must be a tangible thing shaped by human hands. This definition at least eliminates the confusion of treating as works of art such natural phenomena as flowers, seashells, or sunsets. It is a far from sufficient definition, to be sure, since man makes many things other than works of art. Still, it will serve as a starting point. Now let us look at the striking *Bull's Head* by Picasso (fig. 1), which consists of nothing but the seat and handlebars of an old bicycle. How meaningful is our formula here? Of course the materials used by Picasso are man-made, but it would be absurd to insist that Picasso must share the credit with the manufacturer, since the seat and handlebars in themselves are not works of art.

While we feel a certain jolt when we first recognize the ingredients of this visual pun, we also sense that it was a stroke of genius to put them together in this unique way, and we cannot very well deny that it is a work of art. Yet the handiwork—the mounting of the seat on the handlebars—is ridiculously simple. What is far from simple is the leap of the imagination by which Picasso recognized a bull's head in these unlikely objects; that, we feel, only he could have done. Clearly, then, we must be careful not to confuse the making of a work of art with manual skill or craftsmanship. Some works of art may demand a great deal of technical discipline; others do not. And even the most painstaking piece of craft does not deserve to be called a work of art unless it involves a leap of the imagination.

But if this is true are we not forced to conclude that the real making of the *Bull's Head* took place in the artist's mind? No, that is not so, either. Suppose that, instead of actually putting the two pieces together and showing them to us, Picasso merely told us, "You know, today I saw a bicycle seat and handlebars that looked just a like a bull's head to me." Then there would be no work of art and his remark would not even strike us as an interesting bit of conversation. Moreover, Picasso himself would not feel the satisfaction of having created something on the basis of his leap of the imagination alone. Once he had conceived his visual pun, he could never be sure that it would really work unless he put it into effect.

Thus the artist's hands, however modest the task they may have to perform, play an essential part in the creative process. Our *Bull's Head* is, of course, an ideally simple case, involving only one leap of the imagination and a single manual act in response to it—once the seat had been properly placed on the handlebars, the job was done. The leap of the imagination is sometimes experienced as a flash of inspiration, but only rarely does a new idea emerge full-blown like Athena from the head of Zeus. Instead, it is usually preceded by a long gestation period in which all the hard work is done without finding the key to the solution to the problem. At the critical point, the imagination makes connections between seemingly unrelated parts and then recombines them.

Ordinarily, artists do not work with ready-made parts but with materials that have little or no shape of their own; the creative process consists of a long series of leaps of the artist's imagination and his attempts to give them form by shaping the material accordingly. The hand tries to carry out the commands of the imagination and hopefully puts down a brush stroke, but the result may not be quite what had been expected, partly because all matter resists the human will, partly because the image in the artist's mind is constantly shifting and changing, so that the commands of the imagination cannot be very precise. In fact, the mental image begins to come into focus only as the artist "draws the line somewhere." That line then becomes part—the only fixed part—of the image; the rest of the image, as yet unborn, remains fluid. And each time the artist adds another line, a new leap of the imagination is needed to incorporate that line into his ever-growing mental image. If the line cannot be incorporated, he discards it and puts down a new one.

In this way, by a constant flow of impulses back and forth between his mind and the partly shaped material before him, he gradually defines more and more of the image, until at last all of it has been given visible form. Needless to say, artistic creation is too subtle and intimate an experience to permit an exact step-by-step description; only the artist himself can observe it fully, but he is so absorbed by it that he has great difficulty explaining it to us.

Our metaphor of birth comes closer to the truth than would a description of the process in terms of a transfer or projection of the image from the artist's mind, for the making of a work of art is both joyous and painful, replete with surprises, and in no sense mechanical. We have, moreover, ample testimony that the artist himself tends to look upon his creation as a living thing. Perhaps that is why creativity was once a concept reserved for God, as only He could give material form to an idea. Indeed, the artist's labors are much like the Creation as told in the Bible, but this divine ability was not realized until Michelangelo described the anguish and glory of the creative experience more eloquently than anyone else when he spoke of "liberating the figure from the marble that imprisons it." We may translate this to mean that he started the process of carving a statue by trying to visualize a figure in the rough, rectilinear block as it came to him from the quarry. (At times he may even have done so while the marble was still part of the living rock; we know that he liked to go to the quarries and pick out his material on the spot.)

It seems fair to assume that at first he did not see the figure any more clearly than one can see an unborn child inside the womb, but we may believe that he could see isolated "signs of life" within the marble—a knee or an elbow press-ing against the surface. To get a firmer grip on this dimly felt, fluid image, he was in the habit of making numerous drawings, and sometimes small models in wax or clay, before he dared to assault the "marble prison" itself, for that, he knew, was the final contest between himself and his material. Once he started carving, every stroke of the chisel would commit him more and more to a specific conception of the figure hidden in the block, and the marble would permit him to free the figure whole only if his guess as to its shapes was correct.

Sometimes he did not guess well enough—the stone refused to give up some essential part of its prisoner, and Michelangelo, defeated, left the work unfinished, as he did

2, 3. MICHELANGELO. *St. Matthew.* 1506. Marble, height 8' 11". Academy, Florence

with *St. Matthew* (fig. 2), whose very gesture seems to record the vain struggle for liberation. Looking at the side view of the block (fig. 3), we may get some inkling of Michelangelo's difficulties here. But could he not have finished the statue in *some* fashion? Surely there is enough material left for that. Well, he probably could have, but perhaps not in the way he wanted, and in that case the defeat would have been even more stinging.

Clearly, then, the making of a work of art has little in common with what we ordinarily mean by "making." It is a strange and risky business in which the maker never quite knows what he is making until he has actually made it; or, to put it another way, it is a game of find-and-seek in which the seeker is not sure what he is looking for until he has found it. (In the case of the *Bull's Head* it is the bold "finding" that impresses us most; in the *St. Matthew*, it is the strenuous "seeking.")

The non-artist may find it hard to believe that this uncertainty, this need-to-take-a-chance, should be the essence of the artist's work. We all tend to think of "making" in terms of the craftsman or manufacturer who knows exactly what he wants to produce from the very outset, picks the tools best fitted to his task, and is sure of what he is doing at every step. Such "making" is a two-phase affair: first the craftsman makes a plan, then he acts on it. And because he—or his customer—has made all the important decisions in advance, he has to worry only about the means, rather than ends, while he carries out his plan. There is thus little risk, but also little adventure, in his handiwork, which as a consequence tends to become routine. It may even be replaced by the mechanical labor of a machine.

No machine, on the other hand, can replace the artist, for with him conception and execution go hand in hand and are so completely interdependent that he cannot separate the one from the other. Whereas the craftsman only attempts what he knows to be possible, the artist is always driven to attempt the impossible—or at least the improbable or unimaginable. Who, after all, would have imagined that a bull's head was hidden in the seat and handlebars of a bicycle until Picasso discovered it for us; did he not, almost literally, "make a silk purse out of a sow's ear"? No wonder the artist's way of working is so resistant to any set rules, while the craftsman's way encourages standardization and regularity. We acknowledge this difference when we speak of the artist as *creating* instead of merely *making* something, although the word is being done to death by overuse nowadays, when every child and every lipstick manufacturer is labeled "creative."

Needless to say, there have always been many more craftsmen than artists among us, since our need for the familiar and expected far exceeds our capacity to absorb the original but often deeply unsettling experiences we get from works of art. The urge to penetrate unknown realms, to achieve something original, may be felt by every one of us now and then; to that extent, we can all fancy ourselves potential artists—mute inglorious Miltons. What sets the real artist apart is not so much the desire to *seek*, but that mysterious ability to *find* which we call talent. We also speak of it as a "gift," implying that it is a sort of present from some higher power; or as "genius," a term which originally meant that a higher power—a kind of "good demon"—inhabits the artist's body and acts through him.

All we can really say about talent is that it must not be confused with aptitude. Aptitude is what the craftsman needs; it means a better-than-average knack for doing something that any ordinary person can do. An aptitude is fairly constant and specific; it can be measured with some success by means of tests which permit us to predict future performance. Creative talent, on the other hand, seems utterly unpredictable; we can spot it only on the basis of *past* performance. And even past performance is not enough to assure us that a given artist will continue to produce on the same level: some artists reach a creative peak quite early in their careers and then "go dry," while others, after a slow and unpromising start, may achieve astonishingly original work in middle age or even later.

Originality

Originality, then, is what distinguishes art from craft. We may say, therefore, that it is the yardstick of artistic greatness or importance. Unfortunately, it is also very hard to define; the usual synonyms—uniqueness, novelty, freshness—do not help us very much, and the dictionaries tell us only that an original work must not be a copy. Thus, if we want to rate works of art on an "originality scale" our problem does not lie in deciding whether or not a given work is original (the obvious copies and reproductions are for the most part easy enough to eliminate) but in establishing just exactly *how* original it is. To do that is not impossible. However, the difficulties besetting our task are so great that we cannot hope for more than tentative and incomplete answers. Which does not mean, of course, that we should not try; quite the contrary. For whatever the outcome of our labors in any particular case, we shall certainly learn a great deal about works of art in the process.

A straightforward copy can usually be recognized as such on internal evidence alone. If the copyist is a conscientious craftsman rather than artist, he will produce a work of craft; the execution will strike us as pedestrian and thus out of tune with the conception of the work. There are also likely to be small slip-ups and mistakes that can be spotted in much the same way as misprints in a text. But what if one great artist copies another? In using another work as his model, the artist does not really copy it in the accepted sense of that word, since he does not try to achieve the effect of a duplicate. He does it purely for his own instruction, transcribing it accurately yet with his own inimitable rhythm. In other words, he is not the least constrained or intimidated by the fact that his model, in this instance, is another work of art. Once we understand this, it becomes clear to us that the artist *represents* (he does not *copy*) the other work, and that his artistic originality does not suffer thereby.

A relationship as close as this between two works of art is not as rare as one might think. Ordinarily, though, the link is less obvious. Edouard Manet's famous painting *Luncheon on the Grass* (fig. 4) seemed so revolutionary a work when first exhibited more than a century ago that it caused a scan-

4. EDOUARD MANET. *Luncheon on the Grass (Le Déjeuner sur l'Herbe)*. 1863. Oil on canvas, 7′ × 8′ 10″. The Louvre, Paris

dal, in part because the artist had dared to show an un-dressed young woman next to two fashionably clothed men. In real life such a party might indeed get raided by the po-lice, and people assumed that Manet had intended to repre-sent an actual event. Not until many years later did an art historian discover the source of these figures: a group of classical deities from an engraving after Raphael (fig. 5). The relationship, so striking once it has been pointed out to us, had escaped attention, for Manet did not *copy* or *repre-sent* the Raphael composition—he merely *borrowed* its main outlines while translating the figures into modern terms.

Had his contemporaries known of this, the *Luncheon* would have seemed a rather less disreputable kind of outing to them, since now the hallowed shade of Raphael could be seen to hover nearby as a sort of chaperon. (Perhaps the art-ist meant to tease the conservative public, hoping that after the initial shock had passed, somebody would recognize the well-hidden quotation behind his "scandalous" group.) For us, the main effect of the comparison is to make the cool, formal quality of Manet's figures even more conspicuous. But does it decrease our respect for his originality? True, he

is "indebted" to Raphael; yet his way of bringing the forgot-ten old composition back to life is in itself so original and creative that he may be said to have more than repaid his debt. As a matter of fact, Raphael's figures are just as "de-rivative" as Manet's; they stem from still older sources which lead us back to ancient Roman art and beyond (com-pare the relief of *River Gods*, fig. 6).

Thus Manet, Raphael, and the Roman river gods form three links in a chain of relationships that arises somewhere out of the dim and distant past and continues into the fu-ture—for *Luncheon on the Grass* has in its turn served as a source for more recent works of art. Nor is this an exception-al case. All works of art anywhere—yes, even such works as Picasso's *Bull's Head*—are part of similar chains that link them to their predecessors. If it is true that "no man is an island," the same can be said of works of art. The sum total of these chains makes a web in which every work of art oc-cupies its own specific place, and which we call *tradition*. Without tradition—the word means "that which has been handed down to us"—no originality would be possible; it provides, as it were, the firm platform from which the artist makes his leap of the imagination. The place where he lands will then become part of the web and serve as a point of departure for further leaps.

And for us, too, the web of tradition is equally essential. Whether we are aware of it or not, tradition is the framework within which we inevitably form our opinions of works of art and assess their degree of originality. Let us not forget, however, that such assessments must always remain incomplete and subject to revision. For in order to arrive at a definitive view, we should be able to survey the entire length of every chain. And that we can never hope to achieve.

If originality is what distinguishes art from craft, tradition serves as the common meeting ground of the two. Every budding artist starts out on the level of craft, by imitating other works of art. In this way, he gradually absorbs the ar-

5. MARCANTONIO RAIMONDI, after RAPHAEL.
The Judgment of Paris (detail). c. 1520. Engraving

6. *River Gods* (detail of Roman sarcophagus).
3rd century A.D. Villa Medici, Rome

tistic tradition of his time and place until he has gained a firm footing in it. But only the truly gifted ever leave that stage of traditional competence and become creators in their own right. No one, after all, can be taught how to create; he can only be taught how to go through the motions of creating. With talent, he will eventually achieve the real thing. What the apprentice or art student learns are skills and techniques—established ways of drawing, painting, carving, and designing; established ways of *seeing*.

If he senses that his gifts are too modest for painting, sculpture, or architecture, he is likely to turn to one of the countless special fields known collectively as "applied art." There he can be fruitfully active on a more limited scale: he may become an illustrator, typographer, or interior decorator; he may design textile patterns, chinaware, furniture, clothing, or advertisements. All these pursuits stand somewhere between "pure" art and "mere" craft. They provide some scope for originality to their more ambitious practitioners, but the flow of creative endeavor is hemmed in by such factors as the cost and availability of materials or manufacturing processes, and accepted notions of what is useful, fitting, or desirable; for the applied arts are more deeply enmeshed in our everyday lives and thus cater to a far wider public than do painting and sculpture.

The purpose of the applied arts, as the name suggests, is to beautify the useful—an important and honorable end, but of a lesser order than that of art pure-and-simple. Nevertheless, we often find it difficult to maintain this distinction. Medieval painting, for instance, is to a large extent "applied," in the sense that it embellishes surfaces which serve another, practical purpose as well—walls, book pages, windows, furniture. The same may be said of much ancient and medieval sculpture. Greek vases, as we shall see, although technically pieces of pottery, were sometimes decorated by artists of very impressive ability. And in architecture the distinction breaks down altogether, since the design of every building, from country cottage to cathedral, reflects external limitations imposed upon it by the site, by cost factors, materials, and techniques, and by the practical purpose of the structure. (The only "pure" architecture is imaginary architecture.) Thus architecture is, almost by definition, an applied art, but it is also a major art (as against the others, which are often called the "minor arts").

Likes and Dislikes

Deciding what is art and rating a work of art are two separate problems; if we had an absolute method for distinguishing art from non-art, it would not necessarily enable us to measure quality. People have long been in the habit of compounding the two problems into one; quite often when they ask, "Why is that art?" they mean, "Why is that *good* art?" How often have we heard this question asked—or asked it ourselves, perhaps—in front of one of the strange, disquieting works that we are likely to find nowadays in museums or art exhibitions. There usually is an undertone of exasperation, for the question implies that we don't think we are looking at a work of art, but that the experts—the critics, museum curators, art historians—must suppose it to be one, or why else would they put it on public display? Clearly, their standards are very different from ours; we are at a loss to understand them and we wish they'd give us a few simple, clear-cut rules to go by. Then maybe we would learn to like what we see, we would know "why it is art." But the experts do not post exact rules, and the layman is apt to fall back upon his final line of defense: "Well, I don't know anything about art but I know what I like."

It is a formidable roadblock, this stock phrase, in the path of understanding between expert and layman. Until not so very long ago, there was no great need for the two to communicate with each other; the general public had little voice in matters of art and therefore could not challenge the judgment of the expert few. Today both sides are aware of the barrier between them (the barrier itself is nothing new, although it may be greater now than at certain times in the past) and of the need to level it. That is why books like this one are being written. Let us examine the roadblock and the various unspoken assumptions that buttress it.

Our troubled layman may be willing to grant, on the basis of our discussion so far, that art is indeed a complex and in many ways mysterious human activity about which even the experts can hope to offer only tentative and partial conclusions; but he is also likely to take this as confirming his own beliefs that "I don't know anything about art." Are there really people who know nothing about art? If we except small children and the victims of severe mental illness or deficiency, our answer must be no, for we cannot help knowing *something* about it, just as we all know something about politics and economics no matter how indifferent we may be to the issues of the day. Art is so much a part of the fabric of human living that we encounter it all the time, even if our contacts with it are limited to magazine covers, advertising posters, war memorials, television, and the buildings where we live, work, and worship.

Much of this art, to be sure, is pretty shoddy—art at third- and fourth-hand, worn out by endless repetition, representing the lowest common denominator of popular taste. Still, it is art of a sort; and since it is the only art most people ever experience, it molds their ideas on art in general. When they say, "I know what I like," they really mean, "I like what I know (and I reject whatever fails to match the things I am familiar with)"; such likes are not in truth theirs at all, but have been imposed on them by habit and circumstance, without any personal choice. To like what we know and to distrust what we do not know is an age-old human trait. We always tend to think of the past as "the good old days," while the future seems fraught with danger.

But why should so many of us cherish the illusion of having made a personal choice in art when in actual fact we have not? I suspect there is another unspoken assumption here, which goes something like this: "Since art is such an 'unruly' subject that even the experts keep disagreeing with each other, my opinion is as good as theirs—it's all a matter of subjective preference. In fact, my opinion may be *better* than theirs, because as a layman I react to art in a direct, straightforward fashion, without having my view obstructed by a lot of complicated theories. There must be something wrong with a work of art if it takes an expert to appreciate it."

7. JOHN DE ANDREA. *The Artist and His Model.* 1980. Lifesize; polyvinyl, polychromed in oil (see colorplate 1). Collection Foster Goldstrom, Dallas and San Francisco

Self-expression and Audience

All art involves self-expression. Most of us are familiar with the famous Greek myth of the sculptor Pygmalion who carved such a beautiful statue of the nymph Galatea that he fell in love with it and embraced her when Venus made his sculpture come to life. Recently the myth has been given a fresh interpretation by John De Andrea (fig. 7, colorplate 1) that tells us a good deal about creativity by reversing the roles. Now it is the artist, lost in thought, who is oblivious to the statue's gaze. She is clearly based on a real model rather than an ideal conception, and is still in the process of "coming to life" as the artist has not finished painting her white legs. The illusion is so convincing that we wonder which figure is real and which one is dreaming of the other, the artist or the sculpture? De Andrea makes us realize that to the artist, the creative act is a labor of love that brings art to life.

But can we not also say that it is the work of art which gives birth to the artist? The birth of a work of art is an intensely private experience (so much so that many artists can work only when completely alone and may refuse to show their unfinished pieces to anyone), yet it must, as a final step, be shared by the public, in order for the birth to be successful. The artist does not create merely for his own satisfaction, but wants his work approved by others. In fact, the hope for approval is what makes him want to create in the first place, and the creative process is not completed until the work has found an audience. In the end, works of art exist in order to be liked rather than to be debated.

Perhaps we can resolve the paradox once we understand what the artist means by "public." He is concerned not with *the* public as a statistical entity but with his particular public, his audience; quality matters more to him than quantity. At a minimum, this audience needs to consist of no more than one or two people whose opinions he values. If he can win them over by his work, he feels encouraged to go on; without them, he despairs of his calling. Some very great artists have had only such a minimum audience; they hardly ever sold their work or displayed it in public but continued to create with the moral support of a few friends. These, of course, are rare cases. Ordinarily, artists also need patrons who will purchase their work, thus combining moral and financial support; from the artist's point of view, patrons are always "audience" rather than "customers."

There is a vital difference between these last two terms. A customer buys the products of craftsmanship; he knows from previous experience what he will get and that he is going to like it—why else should he have formed the custom of returning to the same source of supply? We think of him as "regular" and "satisfied." An audience, in contrast, merits such adjectives as critical, fickle, receptive, enthusiastic; it is uncommitted, free to accept or reject, so that anything placed before it is on trial—nobody knows in advance how they will receive the work. Hence there is an emotional tension between artist and audience that has no counterpart in the relationship of craftsman and customer.

It is this very tension, this sense of uncertainty and challenge, that the artist needs. He must feel that his work is able to overcome the resistance of the audience, otherwise he cannot be sure that what he has brought forth is a genuine creation, a work of art in fact as well as in intention. The more ambitious and original his work, the greater the tension and the more triumphant his sense of release after the response of the audience has shown him that his leap of the imagination was successful. On a tiny scale we all have a similar experience when we happen to think up a joke: we have an irresistible urge to tell it to someone, for we can't be sure that it really *is* a joke until it strikes others as funny, too. This is a modest analogy, but it does suggest why artists need an audience to "complete" their work.

The audience whose approval looms so large in the artist's mind is a limited and special one, not the general public: the merits of the artist's work can never be determined by a popularity contest. The size and composition of the audience may vary a good deal with time and circumstance; its members may be other artists as well as patrons, friends, critics, and interested bystanders. The one qualification they all have in common is an informed love of works of art—an attitude at once discriminating and enthusiastic that lends particular weight to their judgments. They are, in a word, *experts*, people whose authority rests on experience rather than theoretical knowledge. And because experience, even within a limited field, varies from one individual to another, it is only natural that they should at times disagree among themselves. Such disagreement often stimulates new insights; far from invalidating the experts' role, it shows, rather, how passionately they care about their subject, whether this be the art of their own time or of the past.

The active minority which we have termed the artist's primary audience draws its recruits from a much larger and more passive secondary audience, whose contact with works of art is less direct and continuous. This group, in turn, shades over into the vast numbers of those who believe they "don't know anything about art," the layman pure-and-simple. What distinguishes the layman, as we have seen before, is not that he actually *is* pure and simple but that he likes to think of himself as being so. In reality, there is no sharp break, no difference in kind, between him and the expert, only a difference in degree. The road to expertness invites anyone with an open mind and a capacity to absorb new experiences. As we travel on it, as our understanding grows, we shall find ourselves liking a great many more things than we had thought possible at the start, yet at the same time we shall gradually acquire the courage of our own convictions, until—if we travel far enough—we know how to make a meaningful individual choice among works of art. We shall have joined the active minority that participates directly in shaping the course of art in our time. Then we can recognize what is a masterpiece, and we shall be able to say, with some justice, that we know what we like. The solution to this old riddle lies in the human need to understand and communicate. Art, like science, religion, and philosophy, fulfills man's strongly felt urge to comprehend himself and the universe. This function makes art especially significant and, hence, worthy of our attention.

Art has the power to penetrate to the core of man's being, which recognizes itself in the creative act. Art represents its creator's deepest understanding and highest aspirations; at the same time, the artist often plays an important role as the articulator of our shared beliefs and values, which he expresses through an ongoing tradition to us, his audience. A masterpiece is, we can say with some assurance, a work that contributes to our vision of life and leaves us profoundly moved. Moreover, it does so to many people over time and space. In other words, it can bear the closest scrutiny and withstand the test of time. That is not to say that everyone will respond to it, for limitations of personality, experience, and understanding may prevent some of us from appreciating it. We must keep an open mind by giving the artist the benefit of the doubt and making every attempt to understand his work on its own terms. If we do this, we shall discover the real value of art: the more we know about life, the more we know about art; and in turn, the more we understand art, the more we understand what it means to be a human being in the fullest sense of the term.

Looking at Art

We live in a sea of images conveying the culture and learning of modern civilization. Fostered by an unprecedented media explosion, this "visual background noise" has become so much a part of our daily lives that we take it for granted. In the process, we have become desensitized to art as well.

Anyone can buy cheap paintings and reproductions to decorate a room, where they often hang virtually unnoticed, perhaps deservedly so. It is small wonder that we also look at the art in museums with equal casualness. We pass rapidly from one object to another, sampling them like a smorgasbord. We may pause briefly before the famous masterpiece we have been told we are supposed to admire, then ignore the galleryful of equally beautiful and important works around it. We will have seen the art but not really looked at it. Looking at great art is not such an easy task, for art never reveals its secrets so readily. While the experience of a work can be immediately electrifying, we sometimes do not realize its impact until time has let it filter through the recesses of our imaginations. It even happens that something which at first repelled or confounded us emerges only many years later as one of the most important artistic events of our lives.

Because so much feeds into art, it makes many of the same demands on our faculties as it did on the person who created it. For that reason, we must be able to respond to it on many levels. If we are going to get the most out of art, we will have to learn how to look and think for ourselves in an intelligent way, which is perhaps the hardest task of all as we will not always be fortunate enough to have someone to help us. In the end, the confrontation of viewer and art remains a solitary act. Looking at a masterpiece is a complex matter. Analyzing its appearance can help us to appreciate the beauty of a great work; the danger is that it may just as well trivialize a masterpiece, so we must be careful not to use a formulaic approach. Every aesthetic "law" advanced so far has proved of dubious value, and most often gets in the way of our understanding. Even if a valid one were to be found—and none has yet been discovered—it would probably be so elementary as to be useless in the face of art's complexity. Art appreciation is more than mere enjoyment of aesthetics. It is learning to understand the meaning of a work of art. No work can be understood outside its historical context. That is why we must be wary of treating broad themes such as the "hero in art." No matter how interesting they may seem, such discussions necessarily provide a superficial overview at best.

Art has been called a visual dialogue, for it expresses its creator's imagination just as surely as if he were speaking to us, though the object itself is mute. For there to be a dialogue, however, requires our active participation. If we cannot literally talk to a work of art, we can at least learn how to respond to it and to question it. Finding the right answers usually involves asking the right questions. Even if we aren't sure which question to ask, we can always start with, "What would happen if the artist had done it another way?" And when we are through, we must question our explanation according to the same test of adequate proof that applies to any investigation: Have we taken into account *all* the evidence we have, and arranged it in a logical and coherent way? There is, alas, no step-by-step method to guide us, but this does not mean that the process is entirely mysterious. We can illustrate it by looking at some paintings together; the demonstration will help us gain courage to try the same analysis next time we enter a museum. Let us look at three examples to see how it works.

LOOKING AT AN OLD MASTER. The great Dutch painter Jan Vermeer has been called The Sphinx of Delft, and with good reason, for his paintings always retain a degree of mystery. In *Woman with Scales* (fig. 8), a young woman, richly dressed in a furred jacket and with strings of pearls and gold coins spread out on the table before her, is contemplating a balance in her hand. The canvas is painted entirely in gradations of cool, neutral tones, except for a bit of the red dress visible beneath her jacket. The soft light from the partly open window is concentrated on her face and the cap framing it. Other beads of light reflect from the pearls and from her right hand. The serene atmosphere is sustained throughout the stable composition. Vermeer places us at an intimate distance within the relatively shallow space, which has been molded around the figure. The underlying grid of horizontals and verticals is modulated by the gentle curves of the woman's form and the heap of blue drapery, as well as by the oblique angles of the mirror. The design is so perfect that we cannot move a single element without upsetting the delicate balance.

The composition is controlled in part by perspective. The vanishing point of the diagonals formed by the top of the mirror and the right side of the table lies at the juncture of the woman's little finger and the picture frame. If we look closely at the bottom of the frame, we see that it is actually lower on the right than on the left, where it lies just below her hand. The effect is so carefully calculated that the artist must have wanted to guide our eye to the painting on the back wall. Though difficult to read at first, it depicts Christ

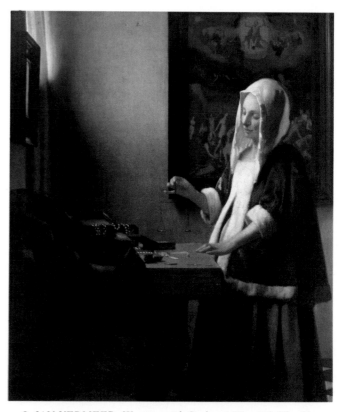

8. JAN VERMEER. *Woman with Scales.* 16¾ × 15″. The National Gallery of Art, Washington, D.C. (Widener Collection, 1942)

at the Last Judgment, when every soul is weighed. The parallel of this subject to the woman's activity tells us that, contrary to our initial impression, this cannot be simply a scene of everyday life. The meaning is nevertheless far from clear. Because Vermeer treated forms as beads of light, it was assumed until recently that the balance holds items of jewelry and that the girl is weighing the worthlessness of earthly possessions in the face of death; hence, the painting was generally called *The Pearl Weigher* or *The Gold Weigher*. When we look closer, however, we can see that the pans contain nothing (fig. 9).

What, then, is the young woman doing? If she is weighing temporal against spiritual values, it can be only in a symbolic sense, because nothing about the figure or the setting betrays a sense of conflict. What accounts for this inner peace? Perhaps it is self-knowledge, signified here by the mirror. It may also be the promise of salvation through her faith. In *Woman with Scales*, as in Caravaggio's *The Calling of St. Matthew* (fig. 693, colorplate 76), light might therefore serve not only to illuminate the scene but also to represent religious revelation. In the end, we cannot be sure, because Vermeer's approach to his subject proves as subtle as his pictorial treatment. He avoids any anecdote or symbolism that might limit us to a single interpretation. There can be no doubt, however, about his fascination with light. Vermeer's mastery of its expressive qualities elevates his concern for the reality of appearance to the level of poetry, and subsumes its visual and symbolic possibilities. Here we find the real "meaning" of Vermeer's art.

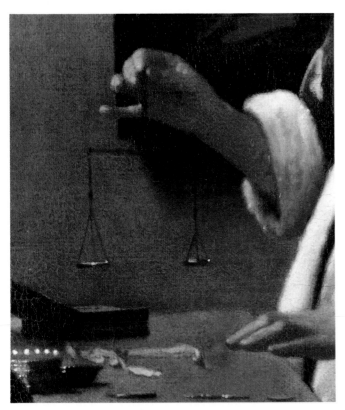

9. *Woman with Scales*, detail

LOOKING AT A NEW MASTER. The ambiguity in *Woman with Scales* serves to heighten our interest and pleasure, while the carefully organized composition expresses the artist's underlying concept with singular clarity. But what are we to do when a work seems deliberately devoid of ostensible meaning? Modern artists can pose a gap between their intention and the viewer's understanding. The gap is, however, often more apparent than real, for the meaning is usually intelligible to the imagination at some level. Still, we feel we must comprehend intellectually what we perceive intuitively. We can partially solve the personal code in Jasper Johns' *Target with Four Faces* (fig. 10) by treating it somewhat like a rebus. Where did he begin? Surely with the target, which stands alone as an object, unlike the long box at the top, particularly when its hinged door is closed. Why a target in the first place? The size, texture, and colors inform us that this is not to be interpreted as a real target. The design is nevertheless attractive in its own right, and Johns must have chosen it for that reason. When the wooden door is up, however, the assemblage is transformed from a neutral into a loaded image, bringing out the nascent connotations of the target. Johns has used the same plaster cast four times, which lends the faces a curious anonymity; then he cut them off at the eyes, "the windows of the soul," rendering them even more enigmatic; finally, he crammed them into their compartments, so that they seem to press urgently out toward us. The results are disquieting, aesthetically as well as expressively.

Something so disturbing cannot be without significance—but what? We may be reminded of prisoners trying to look out from small cell windows—or perhaps "blindfolded" targets of execution. Whatever our impression, the claustrophobic image radiates an aura of menacing danger. Unlike Picasso's joining of a bicycle seat and handlebars to form a bull's head, *Target with Four Faces* combines two disparate components in an open conflict that we cannot reconcile, no matter how hard we try. The ominous intrusion creates an extraordinary tension with the dispassionate investigation of the target's formal qualities, and this disparity between form and content must have been Johns' goal.

How do we know we are right? After all, this is merely our "personal" interpretation, so we turn to the critics for help. We find them divided about the meaning of *Target with Four Faces*, although they agree it must have one. Johns, on the other hand, has insisted that there is none! Whom are we to believe, the critics or the artist himself? The more we think about it, the more likely it seems that both sides may be right. The artist is not always aware why he has made a work. That does not mean that there were no reasons, only that a number of them were unconscious ones. Under these circumstances, a critic may know the artist's mind better than the artist does and explain his creation more clearly. We can now understand that to Johns the leap of his imagination in *Target with Four Faces* remains as mysterious as it first seemed to us. Our account reconciles the artist's aesthetic concerns and the critics' search for meaning, and while we realize that no ultimate solution is possible, we have arrived at a satisfactory explanation by looking and thinking for ourselves.

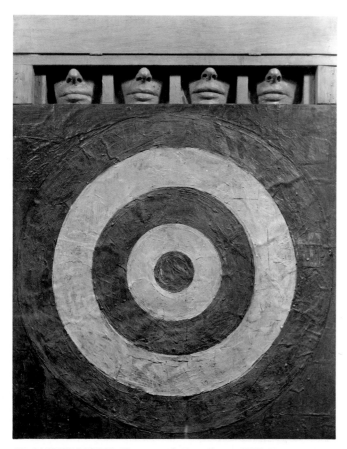

10. JASPER JOHNS. *Target with Four Faces*. 1955. Encaustic on newspaper over canvas, 26 × 26″ surmounted by four tinted plaster faces in wood box with hinged front. Box, closed, 3¾ × 26 × 3½″. Overall dimensions with box open, 33⅝ × 26 × 3″. The Museum of Modern Art, New York (Gift of Mr. and Mrs. Robert C. Scull)

PORTRAITS: THE PLEASURES OF RESEARCH. It is all too easy to overlook the obvious, and this is particularly true in looking at portraits. Those of famous people have a special appeal, for they seem to bridge a gap of time and place and to establish a personal link with us. In their faces we read a thousand insights about character which no amount of historical data can satisfy nearly as well. Our interest arises no doubt from the remnant of a primitive belief that an image captures not merely the likeness but also the soul of a sitter, though in the age of photography we have come to see portraits as mere likenesses and we readily forget that they call on all our skill to grasp their meaning. *Paul Revere* (fig. 11), painted by the American artist John Singleton Copley around 1770, gives rise to questions we cannot solve with on-the-spot observations, so we must look elsewhere to answer them. The fruits of our investigation must, however, agree with our observations; otherwise we cannot be sure that we are right.

Silversmith, printmaker, businessman, and patriot, Revere has acquired legendary status thanks to Henry Wadsworth Longfellow's famous poem about his midnight ride, and Copley's painting has become virtually an American icon. It has generally been treated as a workingman's portrait, so to speak, but by rights such a portrait ought to be more straightforward than this—and, hence, less memorable. Here Revere has a penetrating glance and thoughtful pose which are heightened by the sharp light, lending him an unusually forceful presence. He looks out at us with astonishing directness, as if he were reading us with the same intensity that we bring to bear on his strongly modeled features. Clearly, Revere is shown as a thinker possessing an active intelligence, and we will recognize the pose of hand on chin as an old device used since Antiquity to represent philosophers. This is certainly no ordinary craftsman here, and we may also wonder whether this is really his working outfit. Surely no silversmith would have carried out his craft in what are probably Revere's best business clothes. By simply looking at the picture we have raised enough doubts to challenge the traditional view of this famous painting.

At this point our questioning of the picture's surface comes to an end, for the portrait does not yield up further clues. Once we have posed the problem of this "craftsman's" portrayal, however, we feel compelled to investigate it further. The more we pursue the matter, the more fascinating it becomes. Copley, we discover, had painted only a few years earlier a portrait of another Boston silversmith, Nathaniel Hurd (fig. 12), yet from this painting we would never even guess the sitter's trade. Hurd is wearing a casual robe and turban, and before him are only two books, one of them on heraldry, from which he culled the coats of arms he needed for his work. Why, then, did Copley show Revere at a workbench with his engraving tools spread out before him, holding a teapot as the object of his contemplation and offering it to us for our inspection? In the light of Hurd's portrait, Revere's work as a silversmith hardly explains these attributes and actions, natural as they seem. Oddly enough, the question has never been raised; yet surely the differences between the two paintings cannot be accidental.

Perhaps we can find the answer in the antecedents for each. Hurd's image can be traced back to informal portraits that originated in France in the early eighteenth century; in England, where there was a rage for portraits of well-known men, such informal portraits soon became popular, and were customarily made for artists, writers, and the like. A distinctive offshoot of the type arose that showed a sculptor at work in his studio with his tools prominently displayed (fig. 13); sometimes an engraver is seen. Another possible precedent is in moralizing portraits, descendants of pictures of St. Jerome, that show men holding or pointing to skulls, much as Revere holds the teapot in his hand.

Copley was surely familiar with all of these kinds of images from the engravings of portraits that we know he collected, but his exact sources for the Revere painting remain a mystery—and may never be discovered. For after 1765 Copley freely adapted and combined motifs from different engravings in his paintings, often disguising their origins so completely that we cannot be certain which they were. Probably he conflated two or three in Revere's portrait. In any case, Copley has evidently transformed Revere from a craftsman into an artist-philosopher.

In Europe, so elevated a representation of a craftsman was almost unheard of, for the craftsman's inferior position to the artist's had been asserted since the Renaissance—except in England, where the newly founded Royal Academy

11. JOHN SINGLETON COPLEY. *Paul Revere*. 35 × 25½".
Museum of Fine Arts, Boston (Gift of Joseph W., William B., and Edward H. R. Revere)

13. FRANCIS XAVIER VISPRÉ (attr.). *Portrait of Louis-François Roubiliac*. c. 1750. Pastel, 24½ × 21½". Yale Center for British Art (Paul Mellon Collection), New Haven, Connecticut

12. JOHN SINGLETON COPLEY. *Nathaniel Hurd*. 30 × 25½".
The Cleveland Museum of Art (John Huntington Collection)

first drew the distinction in 1768, about when Copley painted Hurd's portrait. But in the Colonies, as Copley himself complained, no one differentiated between the artist's work and the craftsman's trade. Indeed, it can be argued that in America, apart from portraiture, the applied arts *were* the fine arts.

It is interesting that Copley's portrait probably dates from around the time of Revere's first political engravings, a technique rooted, suitably enough, in the decorating of late medieval metalwork. By 1770 Revere was already involved with libertarianism, a cause which Copley himself did not share. This difference in their points of view did not prevent Copley from endowing Revere's portrait with an ingenious significance and penetrating seriousness of characterization. The painter and the silversmith must have known each other well. The portrait stands as Copley's compelling tribute to a fellow artist—and as an invaluable statement about the culture of the Colonial era.

While the art historian and interested layman are plainly in the best position to undertake this kind of research, this does not mean that "there must be something wrong with a work of art if it takes an expert to appreciate it." On the contrary, these efforts have clarified and reaffirmed the portrait of Paul Revere as a masterpiece. In reacting to art in "a direct, straightforward fashion" without the benefit of additional knowledge, we deprive ourselves of the understanding that leads to a full appreciation. The critic, scholar, or curator is by no means the adversary of the layman. His role is to present what he knows to the public, and to share his expertise with all who seek it.

PART ONE

THE

ANCIENT WORLD

1
MAGIC AND RITUAL —THE ART OF PREHISTORIC MAN

THE OLD STONE AGE

When did man start creating works of art? What prompted him to do so? What did these earliest works of art look like? Every history of art must begin with these questions—and with the admission that we cannot answer them. Our earliest ancestors began to walk the earth on two feet about four million years ago, but how they were using their hands remains unknown to us. More than two million years later we meet the earliest traces of man the toolmaker. He must have been *using* tools all along; after all, even apes will pick up a stick to knock down a banana, or a stone to throw at an enemy. The *making* of tools is a more complex matter. It demands first of all the ability to think of sticks or stones as "fruit knockers" or "bone crackers," not only when they are needed for such purposes but at other times as well.

Once man was able to do that, he gradually discovered that some sticks or stones had a handier shape than others, and he put them aside for future use. He selected and "appointed" certain sticks or stones as tools because he had begun to connect *form* and *function*. The sticks, of course, have not survived, but a few of the stones have; they are large pebbles or chunks of rock that show the marks of repeated use for the same operation—whatever that may have been. The next step was for man to try chipping away at these tools-by-appointment so as to improve their shape. This is the first craft of which we have evidence, and with it we enter a phase of human development known as the Paleolithic, or Old Stone Age.

Cave Art

It is during the last stage of the Paleolithic, which began about 35,000 years ago, that we meet the earliest works of art known to us. But these already show an assurance and refinement far removed from any humble beginnings. Unless we are to believe that they came into being in a single, sudden burst, as Athena is said to have sprung full-grown from the head of Zeus, we must assume that they were preceded by thousands of years of slow growth about which we know nothing at all. At that time the last Ice Age was drawing to a close in Europe (there had been at least three previous ones, alternating with periods of subtropical warmth, at intervals of about 25,000 years), and the climate between the Alps and Scandinavia resembled that of present-day Siberia or Alaska. Huge herds of reindeer and other large herbivores roamed the plains and valleys, preyed upon by the ferocious ancestors of today's lions and tigers—and by our own ancestors. These men liked to live in caves or in the shelter of overhanging rocks wherever they could find them. Many such sites have been discovered, mostly in Spain and in southwestern France; on the basis of differences among the tools and other remains found there, scholars have divided up the "cavemen" into several groups, each named after a characteristic site, and of these it is especially the so-called Aurignacians and Magdalenians who stand out for the gifted artists they produced and for the important role art must have played in their lives.

ALTAMIRA AND LASCAUX. The most striking works of Paleolithic art are the images of animals, incised, painted, or sculptured, on the rock surfaces of caves, such as the wonderful *Wounded Bison* from the cave at Altamira in northern Spain (fig. 14). The dying animal has collapsed on the ground, its legs no longer able to carry the weight of the body, its head lowered in defense. What a vivid, lifelike picture it is! We are amazed not only by the keen observation, the assured, vigorous outlines, the subtly controlled shading that lends bulk and roundness to the forms, but even more perhaps by the power and dignity of this creature in its final agony. Equally impressive, if not quite as fine in detail, are

14. *Wounded Bison* (cave painting). c. 15,000–10,000 B.C. Altamira, Spain

the painted animals in the cave at Lascaux, in the Dordogne region of France (fig. 15, colorplate 2). Bison, deer, horses, and cattle race across walls and ceiling in wild profusion, some of them simply outlined in black, others filled in with bright earth colors, but all showing the same uncanny sense of life.

How did this extraordinary art develop? What purpose did it serve? And how did it happen to survive intact over so many thousands of years? The last question can be answered easily enough—for the pictures never occur near the mouth of a cave, where they would be open to easy view (and destruction) but only in the darkest recesses, as far from the entrance as possible. Some can be reached only by crawling on hands and knees, and the path is so intricate that one would soon be lost without an expert guide. The cave at Lascaux, characteristically enough, was discovered purely by chance in 1940 by some neighborhood boys whose dog fell into a hole that led to the underground chamber.

Hidden away as they are in the bowels of the earth, to protect them from the casual intruder, these images must have served a purpose far more serious than mere decoration. There can be little doubt, in fact, that they were produced as part of a magic ritual, perhaps to ensure a successful hunt. We gather this not only from their secret location and from the lines meant to represent spears or darts that are sometimes found pointing at the animals, but also from the peculiar, disorderly way the images are superimposed on one another (as in fig. 15). Apparently, people of the Old Stone Age made no clear distinction between image and reality; by making a picture of an animal they meant to bring the animal itself within their grasp, and in "killing" the image they thought they had killed the animal's vital spirit. Hence a "dead" image lost its potency after the killing ritual had been performed, and could be disregarded when the spell had to be renewed. The magic worked, too, we may be sure; hunters whose courage was thus fortified were bound to be more successful when slaying these formidable beasts with their primitive weapons. Nor has the emotional basis of this kind of magic been lost even today. We carry snapshots of those we love in our wallets because this gives us a sense of their presence, and people have been known to tear up the photograph of someone they have come to hate.

Even so, there remains a good deal that puzzles us about the cave paintings. Why do they have to be in such inaccessible places? Couldn't the hunting magic they serve have been performed just as well out in the open? And why are they so marvelously lifelike? Would not the magic have been equally effective if the "killing" had been practiced upon less

15. Cave Paintings (see colorplate 2). Lascaux (Dordogne), France

realistic images? We know of countless later instances of magic which require only the crudest and most schematic kind of representation, such as two crossed sticks for a human figure.

Perhaps we should regard the Magdalenian cave pictures as the final phase of a development that began as simple killing magic at a time when big game was plentiful but shifted its meaning when the animals became scarce (there is evidence that the big herds withdrew northward as the climate of Central Europe grew warmer). At Altamira and Lascaux, then, the main purpose may no longer have been to "kill" but to "make" animals—to increase their supply, perhaps through seasonal rituals repeated year after year. In some of the weapons associated with the animals (see colorplate 2) images of plants have recently been recognized. Could it be that the Magdalenians practiced their fertility magic in the bowels of the earth because they thought of the earth itself as a living thing from whose womb all other life springs? Such a notion is familiar to us from the cults of earth deities of later times; it is not impossible that its origin goes back to the Old Stone Age. If it does, it would help to explain the admirable realism of the cave paintings, for an artist who believes that he is actually "creating" an animal is more likely to strive for this quality than one who merely sets up an image for the kill.

POSSIBLE ORIGINS. Some of the cave pictures may even provide a clue to the origin of this tradition of fertility magic; in a good many instances, the shape of the animal seems to have been suggested by the natural formation of the rock, so that its body coincides with a bump or its contour follows a vein or crack as far as possible. We all know how our imagination sometimes makes us see all sorts of images in chance formations such as clouds or blots. A Stone Age hunter, his mind filled with thoughts of the big game on which he depended for survival, would have been even more likely to recognize such animals as he stared at the rock surfaces of his cave, and to attribute deep significance to his discovery. Perhaps at first he merely reinforced the outlines of such images with a charred stick from the fire, so that others, too, could see what he had found. It is tempting to think that those who proved particularly good at finding such images were given a special status as artist-magicians and relieved of the dangers of the real hunt so that they could perfect their image-hunting, until finally they learned how to make images with little or no aid from chance formations, though they continued to welcome such aid.

A striking example of this process of creation is the remarkable *Nude Woman* from the La Magdelaine Cave at Penne (fig. 16), one of the rare instances of the human figure in Paleolithic art (apparently human fertility was a less pressing problem than animal fertility.) The legs and torso have been carved from natural ledges of the rock in such a way that the shapes seem to emerge almost imperceptibly from the stone. The right arm is barely visible and the head appears to have been omitted altogether, for lack of "co-operation" on the part of the natural surface. What kind of ritual may have centered on this figure we can only guess. Yet the existence of cave rituals relating to both human and animal

16. *Nude Woman.* c. 15,000–10,000 B.C. Rock carving, lifesize. La Magdelaine Cave, Penne (Tarn), France

17. *Ritual Dance* (?). c. 10,000 B.C. Rock engraving, height of figures c. 10″. Cave of Addaura, Monte Pellegrino (Palermo)

fertility would seem to be confirmed by a unique group of Paleolithic drawings found in the 1950s on the walls of the cave of Addaura near Palermo in Sicily (fig. 17). These images, incised into the rock with quick and sure lines, show human figures in dancelike movements, along with some animals; and here, as at Lascaux, we again find several separate layers of images superimposed on one another.

Carved Objects, Painted Objects

Apart from large-scale cave art, the men of the Upper Paleolithic also produced small, hand-sized drawings and carvings in bone, horn, or stone, skillfully cut by means of flint tools. The earliest of these found so far are small figures of mammoth ivory from a cave in southwestern Germany, made 30,000 years ago. Even they, however, are already so accomplished that they must be the fruit of an artistic tradition many thousands of years old. The graceful, harmonious curves of the running horse (fig. 18) could hardly be improved upon by a more recent sculptor. Many years of handling have worn down some details of the tiny animal; but the two converging lines on the shoulder, indicating a dart or wound, were not part of the original design. In the end, then, this horse too has been "killed" or "sacrificed."

Some of these carvings suggest that the objects may have originated with the recognition and elaboration of some chance resemblance. At an earlier stage, it seems, Stone Age men were content to collect pebbles (as well as less durable small specimens) in whose natural shape they saw something that rendered them "magic"; echoes of this approach can sometimes be felt in later, more fully worked pieces. Thus the so-called *Venus of Willendorf* in Austria (fig. 19), one of many such female fertility figurines, has a bulbous roundness of form that recalls an egg-shaped "sacred pebble"; her navel, the central point of the design, is a natural cavity in the stone. And the masterful *Bison* (fig. 20) of reindeer horn owes its compact, expressive outline in part to the contours of the palm-shaped piece of antler from which it was carved. It is not an unworthy companion to the splendid beasts at Altamira and Lascaux.

The art of the Old Stone Age in Europe as we know it today marks the highest achievements of a way of life that began to decline soon after. Adapted almost perfectly to the special conditions of the receding Ice Age, it could not survive beyond them. In other parts of the world, the Old Stone Age gave way to new developments between c. 10,000 and 5000 B.C., except for a few particularly inhospitable areas where the Old Stone Age way of life continued because

19. *Venus of Willendorf.* c. 25,000–20,000 B.C. Stone, height 4⅜". Museum of Natural History, Vienna

18. *Horse,* from Vogelherd cave. c. 28,000 B.C. Mammoth ivory, length 2½". Private collection (Photograph copyright Alexander Marshack)

20. *Bison,* from La Madeleine near Les Eyzies (Dordogne). c. 15,000–10,000 B.C. Reindeer horn, length 4". Museum of National Antiquities, St.-Germain-en-Laye, France

21. *A Spirit Man Spearing Kangaroos*, aboriginal painting from Western Arnhem Land, North Australia. c. 1900. Tree bark

there was nothing to challenge or disturb it. The Bushmen of South Africa and the aborigines of Australia are—or were, until very recently—the last remnants of this primeval phase of man's development. Even their art has decidedly Paleolithic features; the painting on tree bark from North Australia (fig. 21), while far less skillful than the cave pictures of Europe, shows a similar interest in movement and a keen observation of detail (including an "X-ray view" of the inner organs), only here it is kangaroos rather than bison on which the hunting magic is being worked.

FROM HUNTING TO HUSBANDRY: THE NEW STONE AGE

What brought the Old Stone Age to a close has been termed the Neolithic Revolution. And a revolution it was indeed, although its course extended over several thousand years. It began in the Near East sometime about 8000 B.C., when men made their first successful attempts to domesticate animals and food grains—one of the truly epoch-making achievements of human history. Paleolithic man had led the unsettled life of the hunter and food gatherer, reaping where nature sowed and thus at the mercy of forces which he could neither understand nor control. But now, having learned how to assure a food supply by their own efforts, people settled down in permanent village communities; a new discipline and order entered their lives. There is, then, a very basic difference between the New Stone Age, or Neolithic, and the Old, or Paleolithic, despite the fact that all still depended on stone as the material of their main tools and weapons. The new mode of life brought forth a number of

important new crafts and inventions long before the earliest appearance of metals: pottery, weaving and spinning, basic methods of architectural construction in wood, brick, and stone.

We know all this from the tangible remains of Neolithic settlements that have been uncovered by excavation. Unfortunately, these remains tell us very little, as a rule, of the spiritual condition of Neolithic man; they include stone implements of ever greater technical refinement and beauty of shape, and an infinite variety of clay vessels covered with abstract ornamental patterns, but hardly anything comparable to the painting and sculpture of the Paleolithic. Yet the change-over from hunting to husbandry must have been accompanied by profound changes in man's view of himself and the world, and it seems impossible to believe that these did not find expression in art. There may be a vast chapter in the development of art here that is lost to us simply because Neolithic artists worked in wood or other impermanent materials. Or perhaps excavations in the future will help to fill the gap.

Jericho

A tantalizing glimpse of what lies in store for us is provided by the recent discoveries at prehistoric Jericho, which include a group of impressive sculptured heads dating from about 7000 B.C. (fig. 22). They are actual human skulls whose faces have been "reconstituted" in tinted plaster, with pieces of sea shell for the eyes. The subtlety and precision of the modeling, the fine gradation of planes and ridges, the feeling for the relationship of flesh and bone would be remarkable enough in themselves, quite apart from the amazingly early date. The features, moreover, do not conform to a single type; each has a strongly individual cast. Mysterious as they are, these Neolithic heads clearly point forward to Mesopotamian art (compare fig. 90); they are the first harbingers of a tradition of portraiture that will continue unbroken until the collapse of the Roman Empire.

Unlike Paleolithic art, which had grown from the perception of chance images, the Jericho heads are not intended to "create" life but to perpetuate it beyond death by replacing the transient flesh with a more enduring substance. From the circumstances in which these heads were found we gather that they were displayed above ground while the rest of the body was buried beneath the floor of the house; most likely they belonged to venerated ancestors whose beneficent presence was thus assured.

Paleolithic man, too, had buried his dead, but we do not know what ideas he associated with the grave: was death merely a return to the womb of mother earth, or did he have some conception of the beyond? The Jericho heads, on the other hand, suggest that Neolithic man believed in a spirit or soul, located in the head, which could survive the death of the body and assert its power over the fortunes of later generations, and thus had to be appeased or controlled. The preserved heads, apparently, were "spirit traps," designed to keep the spirit in its original dwelling place. They thus express in visible form the sense of tradition, of family or clan continuity, that sets off the settled life of husbandry from the roving existence of the hunter. And Neolithic Jericho was a settled community of the most emphatic sort: the people who treasured the skulls of their forebears lived in stone houses with neat plaster floors, within a fortified town protected by walls and towers of rough but strong masonry construction (fig. 23). Yet, amazingly enough, they had no pottery; the technique of baking clay in a kiln, it seems, was not invented until later.

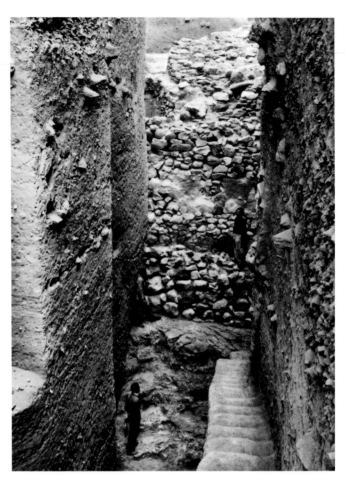

23. Early Neolithic Wall and Tower. c. 7000 B.C. Jericho, Jordan

22. Neolithic Plastered Skull, from Jericho. c. 7000 B.C. Lifesize. Archaeological Museum, Amman, Jordan

Çatal Hüyük

Since 1961, excavations at Çatal Hüyük in Anatolia have brought to light another Neolithic town, roughly a thousand years younger than Jericho. Its inhabitants lived in houses built of mud bricks and timber, clustered around open courtyards (fig. 24). There were no streets, since the houses had no doors; people apparently entered through the roof. The settlement included a number of religious shrines—the earliest found so far—and on their plaster-covered walls we encounter the earliest paintings on a man-made surface. Animal hunts, with small running figures surrounding huge bulls or stags (fig. 25, colorplate 3), evoke echoes of the Old Stone Age, an indication that the Neolithic Revolution must have been a recent event at the time. But the balance has already shifted; these hunts have the character of rituals honoring the male deity to whom the bull and stag were sacred, rather than of an everyday activity necessary for survival.

Compared to the animals of the cave paintings, these at Çatal Hüyük are simplified and immobile; it is the hunters who are in energetic motion. Animals associated with female deities display an even more rigid discipline; the two symmetrically opposed leopards (fig. 26) are mirror images of each other, and another pair of leopards forms the sides of the throne of a fertility goddess (fig. 27), one of the many

24. Houses and Shrines in terraces, Çatal Hüyük (schematic reconstruction of Level VI after Mellaart). c. 6000 B.C.

27. *Fertility Goddess*, from Shrine A.II.1, Çatal Hüyük. c. 6000 B.C. Baked clay, height 8″. Archaeological Museum, Ankara

25. *Animal Hunt*, restoration of Main Room, Shrine A.III.1, Çatal Hüyük (after Mellaart). c. 6000 B.C. (see colorplate 3)

28. *View of Town and Volcano*, wall painting, Shrine VII.14, Çatal Hüyük. c. 6000 B.C.

26. *Twin Leopards*. Painted plaster relief, Shrine VI.A., Çatal Hüyük. c. 6000 B.C. 27×65″

29. *View of Town and Volcano* (reconstruction drawing)

baked clay statuettes that betray their descent from the *Venus of Willendorf* (compare fig. 19). Among the wall paintings at Çatal Hüyük, the most surprising one is a view of the town itself, with the twin cones of an erupting volcano above it (figs. 28, 29). The densely packed rectangles of the houses are seen from above, while the mountain is shown in profile, its slope covered with dots representing blobs of lava. Such a volcano is still visible today from Çatal Hüyük. Its eruption must have been a terrifying event for the inhabitants; how could they have viewed it as other than a manifestation of the power of a deity? Nothing less could have brought forth this image, halfway between a map and a landscape.

Neolithic Europe

While the Near East became the cradle of civilization (to be civilized, after all, means to live as a citizen, a town dweller), the Neolithic Revolution progressed at a very much slower pace in Europe. About 3000 B.C., Near Eastern influences began to spread to the northern shore of the Mediterranean. Baked clay figurines of fertility goddesses found in the Balkans, such as the very striking one from Cernavoda (figs. 30, 31), have their closest relatives in Asia Minor. What makes the Cernavoda *Goddess* so memorable is the sculptor's ability to simplify the shapes of a woman's body and yet retain its salient features (which, to him, did not include the face). The smoothly concave back sets off the ballooning convexity of the front—thighs, belly, arms, and breasts—in a way that would do honor to any twentieth-century sculptor.

DOLMENS AND CROMLECHS. North of the Alps, Near Eastern influence cannot be detected until a much later time. In Central and Northern Europe a sparse population continued to lead the simple tribal life of small village communities even after the introduction of bronze and iron, until a few hundred years before the birth of Christ. Thus Neolithic Europe never reached the level of social organization that produced the masonry architecture of Jericho or the dense urban community of Çatal Hüyük. Instead we find there monumental stone structures of a different kind, called megalithic because they consist of huge blocks or boulders placed upon each other without mortar. Their purpose was religious, rather than civic or utilitarian; apparently the sustained and co-ordinated effort they required could be compelled only by the authority of religious faith—a faith that almost literally demanded the moving of mountains. Even today these megalithic monuments have an awe-inspiring, superhuman air about them, as if they were the work of a forgotten race of giants. Some, known as dolmens, are tombs, "houses of the dead" with upright stones for walls and a single giant slab for a roof (fig. 32).

Others, the so-called cromlechs, form the setting of religious observances. Stonehenge in southern England (figs. 33, 34, colorplate 4) has a great outer circle of evenly spaced uprights supporting horizontal slabs (lintels) and two inner circles similarly marked, with an altar-like stone at the center. The entire structure is oriented toward the exact point at which the sun rises on the day of the summer solstice, and therefore it must have served a sun-worshiping ritual.

30, 31. *Fertility Goddess*, from Cernavoda (Romania). c. 5000 B.C. Baked clay, height 6¼". National Museum, Bucharest (Photographs copyright Alexander Marshack)

32. Dolmen, c. 1500 B.C. Carnac, Brittany

Whether a monument such as this should be termed architecture is a matter of definition: nowadays we tend to think of architecture in terms of enclosed interiors, yet we also have landscape architects, the designers of gardens, parks, and playgrounds; nor would we want to deny the status of architecture to open-air theaters or sports stadiums. Perhaps we ought to consult the ancient Greeks, who coined the term. To them, "archi-tecture" meant something higher than ordinary "tecture" (that is, "construction" or "building")—much as an archbishop ranks above a bishop or an archfiend above a fiend—a structure distinguished from the

33. Stonehenge, air view. c. 2000 B.C. Diameter of circle 97'.
Salisbury Plain, Wiltshire, England

34. Stonehenge (see colorplate 4).
Salisbury Plain, Wiltshire, England

merely practical, everyday kind by its scale, order, permanence, or solemnity of purpose. A Greek, therefore, would certainly have acknowledged Stonehenge as architecture. And we, too, shall have no difficulty in doing so once we understand that it is not necessary to *enclose* space in order to define or articulate it. If architecture is "the art of shaping space to human needs and aspirations," then Stonehenge more than meets the test.

Neolithic America

Comparable to the megalithic monuments of Europe in terms of the effort involved is the "earth art" of the prehistoric Indians of North America, the so-called Mound Builders. The term is misleading, since these mounds vary greatly in shape and purpose as well as in date, ranging from about 2000 B.C. to the time of the white man's arrival. Of particular interest are the "effigy mounds" in the shape of animals—presumably the totems of the tribes that produced them. The most spectacular is the Great Serpent Mound (fig. 35), a snake some 1,400 feet long that slithers along the crest of a ridge by a small river in southern Ohio. The huge head, its center marked by a heap of stones that may once have been

an altar, occupies the highest point. Evidently it was the natural formation of the terrain that inspired this extraordinary work of landscape architecture, as mysterious and moving in its way as Stonehenge.

PRIMITIVE ART

There are, as we have seen, a few human groups for whom the Old Stone Age lasted until the present day. Modern survivors of the Neolithic are far easier to find. They include all the so-called primitive societies of tropical Africa, the islands of the South Pacific, and the Americas. "Primitive" is a somewhat unfortunate word: it suggests—quite wrongly—that these societies represent the original condition of mankind, and has thus come to be burdened with many conflicting emotional overtones. Still, no other single term will serve us better. Let us continue, then, to use primitive as a convenient label for a way of life that has passed through the Neolithic Revolution but shows no signs of evolving in the direction of the "historic" civilizations. What this means is that primitive societies are essentially rural and self-sufficient; their social and political units are the village and the tribe, rather than the city and the state; they perpetuate

35. Great Serpent Mound, Adams County, Ohio. c. 300 B.C.–400 A.D. Length 1400′

themselves by custom and tradition, without the aid of written records: hence they depend on oral tradition for their own history.

The entire pattern of primitive life is static rather than dynamic, without the inner drive for change and expansion that we take for granted in ours. Primitive societies tend to be strongly isolationist and defensive toward outsiders; they represent a stable but precarious balance of man and his environment, ill-equipped to survive contact with urban civilizations. Most of them have proved tragically helpless against encroachment by the West. Yet at the same time the cultural heritage of primitive man has enriched our own: his customs and beliefs, his folklore, and his music have been recorded by ethnologists, and primitive art is being avidly collected and admired throughout the Western world.

ANCESTOR WORSHIP. The rewards of this concern with the world of primitive man have been manifold. Among them is a better understanding of the origins of our own culture in the Neolithic of the Near East and Europe. Though the materials on which we base our knowledge of primitive society and its ways are almost invariably of quite recent date—very few of them go back beyond the seventeenth century—they offer striking analogies with the Neolithic of the distant past; and, of course, they are infinitely richer. Thus the meaning of the cult of skulls at Jericho (fig. 22) is illuminated by countless parallels in primitive art.

The closest parallel, astonishingly enough, is to be found in the Sepik River district of New Guinea, where until quite recently the skulls of ancestors (and of important enemies) were given features in much the same fashion, including the use of seashells for eyes (fig. 36). And here we *know* that the purpose was to "trap" and thereby to gain power over the spirit of the dead. On the other hand, the Jericho cult probably differed from the New Guinea version in some significant respects, for the sculptured skulls from the Sepik River lack the delicate, realistic modeling of those from Jericho; the painted tribal pattern on the faces, rather than any actual portrait resemblance, establishes the identity of the deceased. Their unrelieved savagery of expression makes it hard for us to think of these heads as works of art, yet they embody the same belief as the splendid wood carvings of ancestral figures produced in that area, such as the one in figure 37. The entire design is centered on the head, with its intensely staring shell-eyes, while the body—as in primitive art generally—has been reduced to the role of a mere support. The limbs suggest the embryo position in which so many primitive people like to bury their dead.

The bird emerging from behind the head with its great wings outspread represents the ancestor's vital spirit or life force; from its appearance, it must be a frigate bird or some other sea bird noted for its powers of flight. Its soaring movement, contrasted with the rigidity of the human figure, forms a compelling image—and a strangely familiar one: for our own tradition, too, includes the "soul bird," from the dove of the Holy Spirit to the albatross of the Ancient Mariner, so that we find ourselves responding, almost against our will, to a work of art that at first glance might seem to be both puzzling and repellent.

36. Plastered Skull, from the Sepik River, New Guinea. 19th century. British Museum, London

37. *Male Figure Surmounted by a Bird*, from the Sepik River, New Guinea. 19th–20th century. Wood, height 48″. Washington University Art Collection, St. Louis

GUARDIANS. Ancestor worship is the most persistent feature of primitive religions and the strongest cohesive force in primitive society, but since the primitive world consists of countless isolated tribal groups, it can take an almost infinite variety of forms, and its artistic expression varies even more. On Easter Island, for instance, we find huge ancestral figures carved from volcanic rock. Lined up on raised platforms like giant guardians, they must have cast a powerful protective spell (fig. 38). Here the carver's effort has again centered on the elongated, craggy features of the face, and the back of the head is suppressed entirely. These figures seem to reflect an impulse akin to that behind the megalithic monuments of Europe.

Among the native tribes of Gabon in Equatorial Africa, the skulls of ancestors used to be collected in large containers that were protected by a carved guardian figure, a sort of communal dwelling place of the ancestral spirits. Figure 39 shows such a guardian in the form traditional among the Bakota. This tribe, like a number of others along the west coast of Central Africa, was familiar with nonferrous metals to

some extent, so that its artists were able to sheathe their guardian images in polished brass, thus endowing them with special importance. This figure is a remarkable example of the geometric abstraction which occurs, to a greater or lesser extent, throughout the realm of primitive art. Except for the head, the entire design has been flattened into a single plane; body and limbs are contracted to a hollow diamond shape, the headdress consists of two segments of circles. The face, in contrast, is a concave oval within which two spherical eyes and a pyramid-like nose nestle as they would in the center of a dish. The effect of the whole is extraordinarily calm, disciplined, and harmonious—a finely balanced sequence of shapes so unaggressive that one might almost mistake it for mere decoration. Surely this guardian could not have been meant to frighten anybody.

Tribal secrets are not readily betrayed, hence the available accounts do not tell us very much about the exact significance of the Bakota guardians. It seems reasonable, however, to explain their extreme remoteness from nature—and the abstract tendency of primitive art generally—as an effort

38. Stone Images. 17th century or earlier. Height c. 30'. Akivi,
Easter Island

39. Guardian Figure, from the Bakota area, Gabon.
19th–20th century. Wood covered with brass, height 30".
Musée Ethnographie, Geneva

40. Guardian Figure, from the Bakota area, Gabon.
19th–20th century. Wood covered with brass and copper,
height 26½". Collection Charles Ratton, Paris

to convey the "otherness" of the spirit world, to divorce it as strictly as the artist's imagination would allow from the world of everyday appearances. Well and good—but how are we to account for the varying *degrees* of abstraction in primitive art? Must we assume that the more abstract its form, the more "spiritual" its meaning? If so, does the difference between the Bakota and Sepik River figures reflect an equally great difference in the kinds of ancestor worship from which they spring, or are there perhaps other factors to be taken into account as well?

As it happens, the Bakota guardians provide a good test for these assumptions. They have been collected in considerable numbers, and the differences among them are notable, even though they all clearly belong to a single type and must have been employed for exactly the same purpose. Our second specimen (fig. 40) is almost identical with the first, except for the head, which in comparison seems almost gruesomely realistic; its shape is strongly convex rather than concave, and every detail has an unmistakable representational meaning. This face, with its open mouth full of pointed teeth, is obviously designed to frighten. Here, we feel, is a guardian figure that does indeed live up to its function. Yet the members of the tribe failed to share our reac-

tion, for they found the more abstract guardian figure equally acceptable.

What, then, is the relation between the two guardians? They were probably made at different times, but the interval could not have been more than a century or two, inasmuch as wooden sculpture does not survive for long under tropical conditions, and European travelers, so far as we know, did not begin to bring back any Bakota guardians until the eighteenth century. In any event, given the rigidly conservative nature of primitive society, we can hardly believe that the ancestor cult of the Bakota underwent any significant change during the time span that separates figure 39 from figure 40. Which of them came first, or—to put the question more cautiously—which represents the older, more nearly original version? Figure 40, surely, since we cannot imagine how its realistic features could have evolved from the spare geometry of figure 39. The line of development thus leads from figure 40 to figure 39, from representation to abstraction (we also have a good many intermediate examples). This change seems to have taken place while the religious meaning remained the same. Must we then credit the primitive artist and his public with an interest in abstraction for its own sake? That hardly sounds plausible. There is, I think, a far easier explanation: the increasingly abstract quality of the Bakota guardians resulted from endless repetition.

We don't know how many such figures were in use at the same time, but the number must have been considerable, since each guardian presided over a container of not more than a dozen skulls. Their life expectancy being limited, they had to be replaced at frequent intervals, and the conservative temper of primitive society demanded that every new guardian follow the pattern of its predecessor. Yet, as we know, no copy is ever completely faithful to its model; so long as he repeated the basic outlines of the traditional design, the Bakota carver enjoyed a certain latitude, for no two of the many surviving guardian figures have exactly the same facial structure. Maybe these slight variations were even expected of him, so as to distinguish the newly created guardian from the one it replaced. Any gesture or shape that is endlessly repeated tends to lose its original character—it becomes ground down, simplified, more abstract. We see a good example of this in the ideographs of Chinese writing, which started out as tiny pictures but before long lost all trace of their representational origin and became mere signs. The same kind of transformation, although not nearly as far-reaching, can be traced among the Bakota guardians: they grew simpler and more abstract, since this was the only direction in which they could develop. One might term what happened to them "abstraction by inbreeding."

We have discussed the process at such length because it is a fundamental characteristic of Neolithic and primitive art, though we cannot often observe it as clearly as in the case of the Bakota figures. But let us be careful not to take a negative view of this "inbreeding." It has its dangers, to be sure, but it also leads to the creation of an infinite variety of new and distinctive designs, both in art and in nature (as witness the vast number of breeds among dogs, all of them the result of inbreeding). Finally, we should note that "abstraction by inbreeding" does have its ultimate source in the primitive artist's concern with the otherness of the spirit world; for it is this concern that makes him repeat the same designs over and over again. After all, if he sets out to create a guardian of ancestral skulls, the only model he can use is another such guardian figure, and he cannot know whether he has succeeded unless the two resemble each other.

RULERS. The inbreeding of images in primitive art can be interrupted in two ways: there may be a forcible interbreeding of different tribal traditions as the consequence of migration or conquest, or conditions may develop that favor a return to the world of visible appearances. Such conditions prevailed for a time along the coast of Equatorial Africa a few hundred miles northwest of Gabon. There, through contact with the historic civilizations of the Mediterranean, a number of native kingdoms arose, but none of them proved very enduring. A king, unlike a tribal chieftain, bases his authority on the claim that it has been given to him by supernatural forces; he rules "by the grace of God," embodying the divine will in his own person, or he may even assume the status of a deity himself. There are thus no inherent limits, ethnic, linguistic, or otherwise, to royal authority. Every king is, at least in theory, all-conquering. Hence his domain is not only larger and more complex than that of the tribal chief; he also has to exact far greater obedience from his subjects. He does so with the aid of a favored ruling elite, the aristocracy, to whom he delegates some of his authority. They enforce security and order among the rest of the population, which in return must support the aristocracy and the royal court by contributing a share of its goods and services.

The institution of kingship, then, demands a society divided into classes, rather than the loose association of family or clan groups that makes up a tribe. It means the victory of the town over the countryside, and thus runs counter to the rural tenor of primitive life. The African kingdoms never quite achieved this victory, so their instability is perhaps not surprising. The decisive factor may have been their failure to develop or adopt a system of writing. They existed, as it were, along the outer edge of the historic civilizations, and their rise and fall, therefore, are known to us only in dim and fragmentary fashion.

Artistically, the most impressive remains of these vanished native kingdoms are the portrait heads excavated at Ife, Nigeria, somewhat to the west of the lower course of the Niger River. Some are of terracotta; others, such as the splendid example in figure 41, of bronze. The casting technique, called the cire-perdue (lost-wax) process, surely had

41. *Male Portrait Head,* from Ife, Nigeria. 12th century. Bronze, height 13½". Collection the Oni of Ife

been imported from the Mediterranean, but it was used here with great skill: the actual modeling is done in wax over an earthen core, another layer of earth is firmly packed around the head, the whole is then heated to melt out the wax, and molten bronze is poured into the hollow form thus created. Even more astonishing than its technical refinement, however, is the subtle and assured realism of our Ife head. The features are thoroughly individual, yet so harmonious and noble in expression as to recall the classical art of Greece and Rome (see figs. 208, 268, and colorplate 17).

At the time this head was produced, the twelfth century A.D., nothing of comparable character can be found in Europe. Only the tribal scars on the face, and the holes for attaching hair and beard, relate it to primitive art elsewhere; these, and the purpose for which it was made: ancestor worship. Our head, together with its companions, must have formed part of a long series of portraits of dead rulers, and the use of real hair—probably hair taken from the person represented—strongly suggests that these heads were prepared as "traps" for the spirits of the deceased. But since the rulers each had individual importance, their spirits, unlike those of the tribal ancestors, could not be merged into an impersonal collective entity; in order to be an effective trap, every head had to be an authentic, clearly distinguishable portrait. It is possible, in fact, that these heads were made (if not of bronze, then at least of terracotta) while their subjects were still alive, and became spirit traps only after the ruler's death, through the addition of his hair. Clearly, each of these heads is unique and irreplaceable. It had to last forever, hence it was executed in laborious bronze rather than wood. It is no accident, then, that the Ife heads bear a closer resemblance to the Jericho skulls than to the ancestor figures of primitive art, for the rulers of Ife had indeed recaptured something of the urban quality of the Jericho ancestor cult.

The bronze technique of Ife was handed on to the kingdom of Benin, which arose in the same area and did not disappear until the early eighteenth century. In addition to ancestor heads, the artists of Benin produced a vast variety of works that had nothing to do with the spirit world but served to glorify the ruler and his court. The *Hornblower* (fig. 42) is a characteristic specimen of this art for display. By the standards of primitive sculpture as a whole, it seems exceptionally realistic, but when measured against the art of Ife it betrays its close kinship with tribal wood carvings in the emphasis on the head and the geometric simplification of every detail.

ANIMISM. That primitive man should prefer to think of the spirits of his ancestors collectively, as did the Bakota, rather than in terms of separate individuals, is not at all surprising in view of the curiously fluid nature of his religious beliefs. Such religious beliefs have been termed animism, for to the primitive mind a spirit exists in every living thing. He will feel that he must appease the spirit of a tree before he cuts it down but the spirit of any particular tree is also part of a collective "tree spirit" which in turn merges into a general "life spirit." Other spirits dwell in the earth, in rivers and lakes, in the rain, in sun and moon; still others demand to be appeased in order to promote fertility or cure disease.

42. *Hornblower,* from Benin. Late 16th–early 18th century. Bronze, height 24⅞". The Metropolitan Museum of Art, New York

43. *Kneeling Woman,* from the Baluba area, Kinshasa, Zaïre. 19th–20th century. Wood, height 18½". Royal Museum of Central Africa, Tervueren, Belgium

Colorplate 1. JOHN DE ANDREA. *The Artist and His Model* (see page 16). 1980. Lifesize; polyvinyl, polychromed in oil.
Collection Foster Goldstrom, Dallas and San Francisco

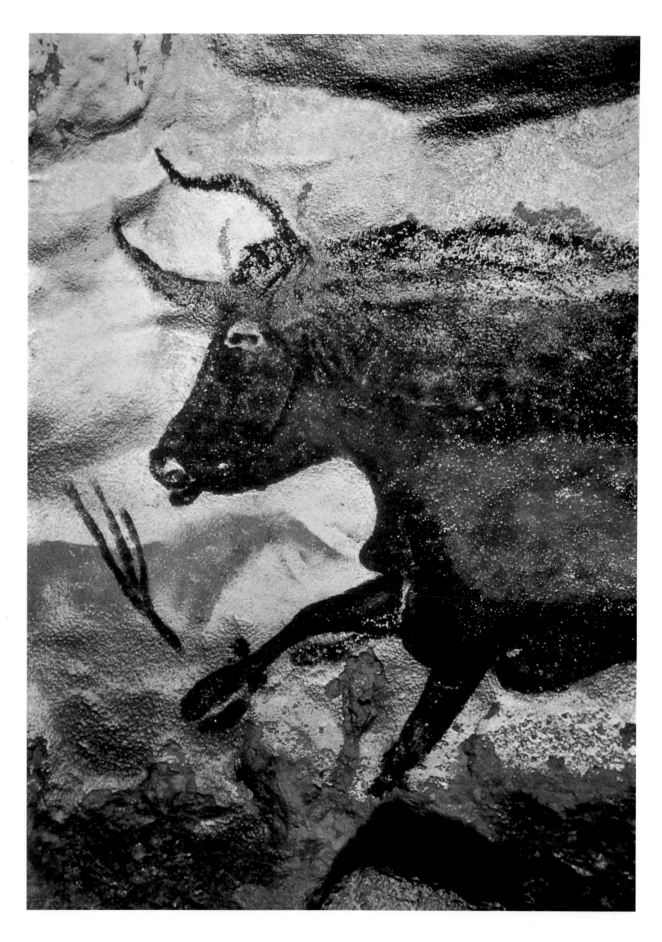

Colorplate 2. PALEOLITHIC. *Black Bull.* Portion of cave painting (see page 27).
15,000–10,000 B.C. Lascaux (Dordogne), France

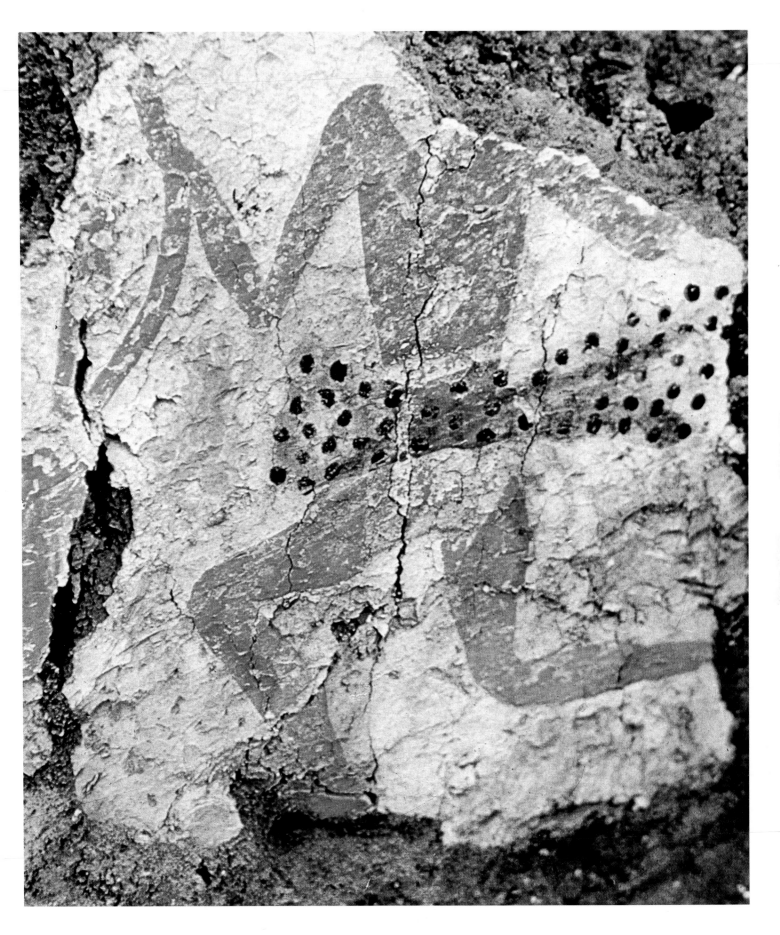

Colorplate 3. NEOLITHIC. *Hunter* or *Dancer* (see page 31). Detail of wall painting
in Main Room of Shrine A.III.I, Çatal Hüyük. About 6000 B.C.

Colorplate 4. NEOLITHIC. Stonehenge (see page 33). About 2000 B.C. Diameter of circle 97′, height of stones above ground 13½′. Salisbury Plain, Wiltshire, England

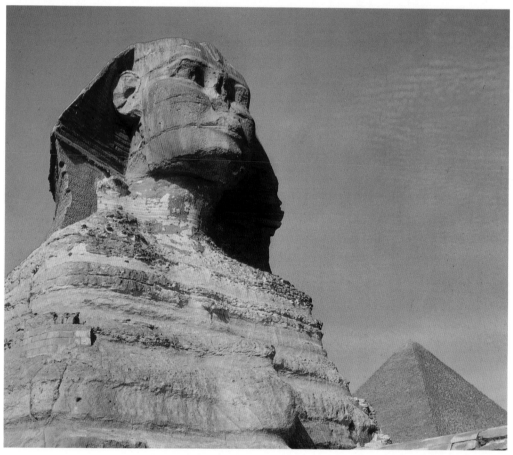

Colorplate 5. (*above*) EGYPTIAN. *The Great Sphinx* (see page 60). About 2500 B.C. Height 65′. Giza

Colorplate 6. (*right*) EGYPTIAN. *Prince Rahotep and His Wife Nofret* (see page 61). About 2580 B.C. Painted limestone, height 47¼″. Egyptian Museum, Cairo

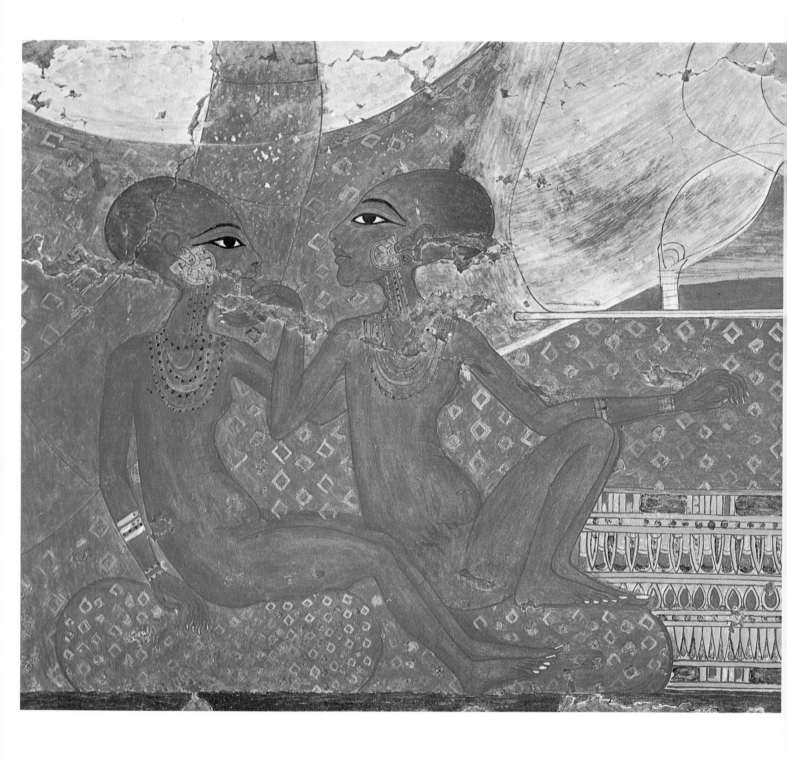

Colorplate 7. (*above*) EGYPTIAN. *The Daughters of Akhenaten*
(see page 68). Fragment of wall painting. About 1360 B.C.
11¾ × 16″. The Oriental Institute, University of Chicago

Colorplate 8. (*right*) EGYPTIAN. Cover of the Coffin of
Tutankhamen (see page 69). About 1340 B.C. Gold,
inlaid with enamel and semiprecious stones;
height of whole 72⅞″. Egyptian Museum, Cairo

Colorplate 9. SUMERIAN. *Billy Goat and Tree*, offering stand, from Ur (see page 74). About 2600 B.C.
Wood, gold, and lapis lazuli, height 20″. The University Museum, Philadelphia

Their dwelling places may be given the shape of human figures, in which case such spirits sometimes achieve enough of a stable identity to be viewed as rudimentary deities. This seems to be true of the very fine *Kneeling Woman* (fig. 43), produced by the Baluba tribe of the Congo region, though little is known about her ritual significance. The figure is among the gentlest and least abstract of all tribal carvings, and her trancelike expression, as well as the hollow bowl, suggests a ceremonial of incantation or divination.

MASKS. In dealing with the spirit world, primitive man was not content to perform rituals or to present offerings before his spirit traps; he needed to act out his relations with the spirit world through dances and similar dramatic ceremonials in which he himself could temporarily assume the role of the spirit trap by disguising himself with elaborate masks and costumes. The origin of these dance rituals goes back as far as the Old Stone Age (see fig. 17), and there are indications that animal disguises were worn even then. In primitive society, the acting-out ceremonials assumed a vast variety of patterns and purposes; and the costumes, always with a mask as the central feature, became correspondingly varied and elaborate. Nor has the fascination of the mask died out to this day. We still feel the thrill of a real change of identity when we wear one at Halloween or carnival time, and among the folk customs of the European peasantry there were, until recently, certain survivals of pre-Christian ceremonies in which the participants impersonated demons by means of carved masks of truly primitive character (fig. 44).

Masks form by far the richest chapter in primitive art; the proliferation of shapes, materials, and functions is almost limitless. Even the manner of wearing them varies surprisingly: some cover only the face, others the entire head; some rest on the shoulders; some may be worn above the head, attached to a headdress or atop a pole. There are masks of human faces, ranging from the realistic to the most fantastic, and animal masks or combinations of both in every conceivable form. There are also masks that are not made to be worn at all but to be displayed independently as images complete in themselves.

The few samples reproduced here can convey no more than the faintest suggestion of the wealth of the available material. Their meaning, more often than not, is impossible to ascertain; the ceremonies which they served usually had elements of secrecy that were jealously guarded from the uninitiated, especially if the performers themselves formed a secret society. This emphasis on the mysterious and spectacular not only heightened the dramatic impact of the ritual, it also permitted the makers of masks to strive for imaginative new effects, so that masks in general are less subject to traditional restrictions than other kinds of primitive sculpture.

African masks, such as the one in figure 45, are distinguished for symmetry of design and the precision and sharpness of their carving. In our example, the features of the human face have not been rearranged but restructured, so to speak, with the tremendous eyebrows rising above the rest like a protective canopy. The solidity of these shapes be-

44. Mask, from Kippel, Lötschental, Switzerland. 19th century. Wood, height 18″. Rietberg Museum, Zurich (E.v.d. Heydt Collection)

45. Mask, from the Bamenda area, Cameroon. 19th–20th century. Wood, height 26½″. Rietberg Museum, Zurich (E. v.d. Heydt Collection)

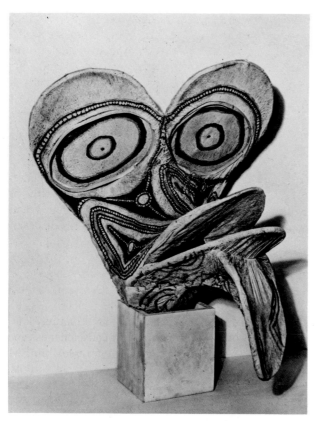

46. Mask, from the Gazelle Peninsula, New Britain. 19th–20th century. Bark cloth, height 18″. Museo Nacional de Antropología, Mexico

47. Mask (Eskimo), from southwest Alaska. Early 20th century. Wood, height 22″. Museum of the American Indian, Heye Foundation, New York

comes strikingly evident as we turn to the fluid, ghostly features of the mask from the Gazelle Peninsula on the island of New Britain in the South Pacific, made of bark cloth over a bamboo frame (fig. 46). It is meant to represent an animal spirit, said to be a crocodile, and was worn in nocturnal ceremonies by dancers carrying snakes. Even stranger is the Eskimo mask from southwest Alaska (fig. 47), with its nonsymmetrical design of seemingly unrelated elements, especially the dangling "leaves" or sticks attached to curved "branches." The single eye and the mouth full of teeth are the only recognizable details to the outsider, yet to those who know how to "read" this assembly of shapes it is the condensed representation of a tribal myth about a swan that drives white whales to the hunters. Such radical displacement of facial details is characteristic of Eskimo masks generally, though it is seldom carried as far as here.

The wooden war helmet from southeast Alaska (fig. 48), in contrast, strikes us by its powerful realism, which may be due not only to the fact that this is a work of Indian rather than Eskimo origin, but also to its function. It, too, is a kind of mask, a second face intended to disconcert the enemy by its fierce expression. Our final specimen, one of the most fascinating of all, comes from an Indian burial mound in Tennessee (fig. 49). It has been estimated as being between 400 and 1000 years old. The material is a single large sea shell, whose rim has been smoothed and whose gently convex outer surface has been transformed into a face by simple but strangely evocative carving and drilling. Shell masks such as this seem to have been placed in graves for the purpose of providing the dead with a second, permanent face to trap his spirit underground.

PAINTING. Compared to sculpture, painting plays a subordinate role in primitive society. Though the technique was widely known, its use was restricted in most areas to the coloring of wood carvings or of the human body sometimes

48. War Helmet (Tlingit), from southeast Alaska. Early 19th century. Wood, height 12″. The American Museum of Natural History, New York

with intricate ornamental designs (see fig. 37). As an independent art, however, painting could establish itself only when exceptional conditions provided suitable surfaces. Thus the Nootka Indians on Vancouver Island, off the northwest coast of North America, developed fairly large wooden houses with walls of smooth boards which they liked to decorate with scenes of tribal legend. Figure 50 shows a section of such a wall, representing a thunder bird on a killer whale flanked by a lightning snake and a wolf. The animals are clearly recognizable but they do not form a meaningful scene unless we happen to know the context of the story. The owner of the house obviously did, so the painter's main concern was how to combine the four creatures into an effective pattern filling the area at his disposal.

It is apparent that these animals, which play important parts in the tribal mythology, must have been represented countless times before; each of them is assembled in accordance with a well-established traditional formula made up of fixed ingredients—small, firmly outlined pieces of solid color that look as if they have been cut out separately and laid down one by one. The artist's pattern-consciousness goes so far that any overlapping of forms embarrasses him; where he cannot avoid it, he treats the bodies of the animals as transparent, so that the outline of the whale's back can be seen continuing right through the lower part of the bird's body, and the feathers of the right wing reveal the front legs of the wolf.

49. Mask, from the Brakebill Mound, Tennessee. c. 1000–1600. Ocean shell, height 8⅝″. Peabody Museum of Harvard University, Cambridge, Mass.

50. *Lightning Snake, Wolf, and Thunder Bird on Killer Whale* (Nootka). c. 1850. Wood, 5′ 8″ × 8′ 10″. The American Museum of Natural History, New York

51. Sand Painting Ritual for a Sick Child (Navaho). Arizona

SAND PAINTING. Formal and abstract as the Nootka wall painting may seem in comparison with the animals of the Paleolithic, it becomes downright realistic if we judge it by the standards of the sand painting visible in figure 51. That unique art grew up among the Indian tribes inhabiting the arid Southwest of the United States; its main practitioners today are the Navaho of Arizona. The technique, which demands considerable skill, consists of pouring powdered rock or earth of various colors on a flat bed of sand. Despite (or perhaps because of) the fact that they are impermanent and must be made fresh for each occasion that demands them, the designs are rigidly fixed by tradition; they can, indeed, be cited as a prime example of abstraction by inbreeding. The various compositions are rather like recipes, prescribed by the medicine man and "filled" under his supervision by the painter, for the main use of sand paintings is in ceremonies of healing.

That these ceremonies are sessions of great emotional intensity on the part of both doctor and patient is well attested by our illustration. Such a close union—or even, at times, identity—of priest, healer, and artist may be difficult to understand in modern Western terms. (Or could it be that all these qualities are present, though not to an equal degree, in the personality and work of Sigmund Freud?) But for primitive man, trying to bend nature to his needs by magic and ritual, the three functions must have appeared as different aspects of a single process. And the success or failure of this process was to him quite literally a matter of life and death.

2 EGYPTIAN ART

History, we are often told, begins with the invention of writing, some 5,000 years ago. It makes a convenient landmark, for the two events do coincide in a rough way, and the absence of written records is surely one of the key differences between prehistoric and historic societies. But as soon as we ask why this is so, we face some intriguing problems. First of all, how valid is the distinction between "prehistoric" and "historic"? Does it merely reflect a difference in our *knowledge* of the past? (Thanks to the invention of writing, we do know a great deal more about history than about prehistory.) Or was there a genuine change in the way things happened—or the kinds of things that happened—after "history" began? Obviously, prehistory was far from uneventful: the road from hunting to husbandry is a long and arduous one. Yet the changes in man's condition that mark this road, decisive though they are, seem incredibly slow-paced and

gradual when measured against the events of the past 5,000 years. The beginning of history, then, means a sudden increase in the speed of events, a shifting from low into high gear, as it were. And we shall see that it also means a change in the *kind* of events.

Perhaps it is merely a matter of perspective—things that are near to us loom larger—but I do not think so. For the problems and pressures faced by historic societies are very different from those that confronted Paleolithic or Neolithic man. Prehistory might be defined as that phase of human evolution during which mankind as a species learned how to maintain himself against a hostile environment; his achievements were responses to threats of physical extinction. With the domestication of animals and food plants, he had won a decisive victory in this battle, assuring his survival on this planet. But the Neolithic Revolution placed him on a level at which he might well have remained indefinitely; the forces of nature—at least during that geological era—would never again challenge him as they had Paleolithic man. And in many parts of the globe, as we saw in the previous chapter, man was content to stay on the "Neolithic plateau" of primitive society.

PRESSURES IN EARLY SOCIETY. In a few places, however, the Neolithic balance of man and nature was upset by a new threat, a threat posed not by nature but by man himself. The earliest monument to that threat is seen in the fortifications of Neolithic Jericho (see fig. 23), constructed almost 9,000 years ago. What was the source of the human conflict that made them necessary? Competition for grazing land among tribes of herdsmen or for arable soil among farming communities? The basic cause, we suspect, was that the Neolithic Revolution had been too successful in this area, permitting the local population to grow beyond the available food supply. This situation might have been resolved in a number of ways: constant tribal warfare could have reduced the population; or the people could have united in larger and more disciplined social units for the sake of ambitious group efforts that no loosely organized tribal society would have been able to achieve. The fortifications at Jericho were an enterprise of this kind, requiring sustained and specialized labor over a long period. We do not know the outcome of the struggle in that region (future excavations may tell us how far the urbanizing process extended) but about 3,000 years later similar conflicts, on a larger scale, arose in the Nile valley and that of the Tigris and Euphrates, and there these conflicts generated enough pressure to produce a new kind of society, very much more complex and efficient than had ever existed before.

It is at this point that we find the pace of events shifting into high gear. These societies quite literally *made* history; they not only brought forth "great men and great deeds"—the traditional definition of history—by demanding human effort on a new and larger scale, but they made these achievements *memorable*. (In order to be memorable, an event must be more than "worth remembering"; it must also be accomplished quickly enough to be grasped by human memory, and not spread over many centuries, as was the Neolithic Revolution.) From now on, first in Egypt and Mesopotamia, somewhat later in neighboring areas, and in the Indus valley and along the Yellow River in China, people were to live in a new, dynamic world, where their capacity to survive was challenged not by the forces of nature but by human forces—by tensions and conflicts arising either within society or as the result of competition between societies. These efforts to cope with his human environment have proved a far greater challenge to man than his earlier struggle with nature; they are the cause of the ever-quickening pace of events during the past 5,000 years.

The invention of writing was an early and indispensable accomplishment of the historic civilizations of Mesopotamia and Egypt. Without it, the growth we have known would have been impossible. We do not know the earliest phases of its development, but it must have taken several hundred years (between 3300 and 3000 B.C., roughly speaking, with

Mesopotamia in the lead), after the new societies were already past their first stage. History was well under way by the time writing could be used to record historic events.

THE OLD KINGDOM

Egyptian civilization has long been regarded as the most rigid and conservative ever. Plato said that Egyptian art had not changed in 10,000 years. Perhaps "enduring" and "continuous" are better terms for it, although at first glance all Egyptian art between 3000 and 500 B.C. does tend to have a certain sameness. There is a kernel of truth in this: the basic pattern of Egyptian institutions, beliefs, and artistic ideas was formed during the first few centuries of that vast span of years and kept reasserting itself until the very end. We shall see, however, that as time went on this basic pattern went through ever more severe crises that challenged its ability to survive; had it been as inflexible as supposed, it would have succumbed long before it finally did. Egyptian art alternates between conservatism and innovation, but is never static. Some of its great achievements had a decisive influence on Greek and Roman art, and thus we can still feel ourselves linked to the Egypt of 5,000 years ago by a continuous, living tradition.

DYNASTIES. The history of Egypt is divided into dynasties of rulers, in accordance with ancient Egyptian practice, beginning with the First Dynasty, shortly after 3000 B.C. (the dates of the earliest rulers are difficult to translate exactly into our calendar). The transition from prehistory to the First Dynasty is known as the predynastic period. The Old Kingdom forms the first major division after that, ending about 2155 B.C. with the overthrow of the Sixth Dynasty. This method of counting historic time conveys at once the strong Egyptian sense of continuity and the overwhelming importance of the Pharaoh (king), who was not only the supreme ruler but a god. We have had occasion to mention the main features of kingship before (see page 39); the Pharaoh transcended them all, for his kingship was not a duty or privilege derived from a superhuman source, but was absolute, divine. However absurd his status may seem to us, and however ineffective it was in practice at times of political disturbance, it remained the key feature of Egyptian civilization. For us it has particular importance because it very largely determined the character of Egyptian art. We do not know exactly the steps by which the early Pharaohs established their claim to divinity, but we know their historic achievements: molding the Nile valley from the first cataract at Assuan to the Delta into a single, effective state, and increasing its fertility by regulating the annual inundation of the river waters through dams and canals.

TOMBS AND RELIGION. Of these vast public works nothing remains today, and very little has survived of ancient Egyptian palaces and cities. Our knowledge of Egyptian civilization rests almost entirely on the tombs and their contents. This is no accident, since these tombs were built to last forever. Yet we must not make the mistake of concluding that the Egyptians viewed life on this earth mainly as a road to the grave. Their preoccupation with the cult of the dead is a link with the Neolithic past, but the meaning they gave it was quite new and different: the dark fear of the spirits of the dead which dominates primitive ancestor cults seems entirely absent. Instead, the Egyptian attitude was that each man must provide for his own happy afterlife. He would equip his tomb as a kind of shadowy replica of his daily environment for his spirit, his *ka*, to enjoy, and would make sure that his *ka* had a body to dwell in (his own mummified corpse or, if that should become destroyed, a statue of himself).

There is a curious blurring of the sharp line between life and death here, and perhaps that was the essential impulse behind these mock households; a man who knew that after death his *ka* would enjoy the same pleasures he did, and who had provided these pleasures in advance by his own efforts, could look forward to an active and happy life without being haunted by fear of the great unknown. In a sense, then, the Egyptian tomb was a kind of life insurance, an investment in peace of mind. Such, at least, is the impression one gains of Old Kingdom tombs. Later on, the serenity of this concept of death was disturbed by a tendency to subdivide the spirit or soul into two or more separate identities, and by the introduction of a sort of judgment, a weighing of souls; and it is only then that we also find expressions of the fear of death.

HIERAKONPOLIS. An early stage in the development of Egyptian funerary customs—and of Egyptian art—can be seen in the fragment of a wall painting from Hierakonpolis (fig. 52). The design is still decidedly primitive in its character—an even scattering of forms over the entire surface. It is instructive to note, however, that the human and animal figures tend to become standardized, abbreviated "signs," almost as if they were on the verge of turning into hieroglyphics (such as we see in fig. 85). The large white shapes are boats; their significance here seems to be that of funeral barges or "vehicles of the soul," since that is their role in later tombs. The black and white figures above the topmost boat are mourning women, their arms spread out in a gesture of grief. For the rest, the picture does not appear to have any coherence as a scene or any symbolic import; perhaps we ought to view it as an early attempt at those typical scenes of daily life that we meet several centuries later in Old Kingdom tombs (figs. 70, 71).

EGYPTIAN STYLE AND
THE PALETTE OF KING NARMER

At the time of the Hierakonpolis mural—about 3200 B.C.—Egypt was in process of learning the use of bronze tools. The country, we may assume, was ruled by a number of local sovereigns not too far removed from the status of tribal chiefs.

52. *Men, Boats, and Animals*. Wall Painting in Predynastic tomb. c. 3200 B.C. Hierakonpolis

The fight scenes between black-bodied and white-bodied men in the painting probably reflect local wars or raids. Out of these emerged two rival kingdoms, Upper and Lower Egypt. The struggle between them was ended when certain Upper Egyptian kings conquered Lower Eygpt and combined the two realms.

One of these was King Narmer, who appears on the strange but impressive object in figures 53 and 54, a ceremonial slate palette celebrating a victory over Lower Egypt (note the different crowns worn by the king). It, too, comes from Hierakonpolis, but otherwise it has little in common with the wall painting. In many ways, the Narmer palette can claim to be the oldest historic work of art we know: not only is it the earliest surviving image of a historic personage identified by name, but its character is clearly no longer primitive; in fact, it already shows most of the features of later Egyptian art. If only we had enough preserved material to trace step by step the evolution that led from the wall painting to this palette!

Let us first "read" the scenes on both sides. The fact that we are able to do so is another indication that we have left prehistoric art behind. For the meaning of these reliefs is made clear and explicit not only by means of hieroglyphic labels, but also through the use of a broad range of visual symbols conveying precise messages to the beholder, and—most important of all—through the disciplined, rational orderliness of the design. In figure 53 Narmer has seized a fallen enemy by the hair and is about to slay him with his mace; two more defeated enemies are placed in the bottom compartment (the small rectangular shape next to the man on the left stands for a fortified town or citadel). Facing the king in the upper right we see a complex bit of picture writing: a falcon standing above a clump of papyrus plants holds a tether attached to a human head which "grows" from the same soil as the plants. This composite image actually repeats the main scene on a symbolic level; the head and papyrus plants stand for Lower Egypt, while the victorious falcon is Horus, the local god of Upper Egypt. The parallel is plain: Horus and Narmer are the same; a god triumphs over human foes. Hence, Narmer's gesture must not be taken as representing a real fight; the enemy is helpless from th' very start, and the slaying is a ritual rather than a physical effort. We gather this from the fact that Narmer has taken off his sandals (the court official behind him carries them in his right hand), an indication that he is standing on holy ground.

53, 54. *Palette of King Narmer*, from Hierakonpolis. c. 3000 B.C. Slate, height 25″. Egyptian Museum, Cairo

On the other side of the palette (fig. 54) he again appears barefoot, followed by the sandal carrier, as he marches in solemn procession behind a group of standard-bearers to inspect the decapitated bodies of prisoners. (The same notion recurs in the Old Testament, apparently as the result of Egyptian influence, when the Lord commands Moses to remove his shoes before He appears to him in the burning bush.) The bottom compartment re-enacts the victory once again on a symbolic level, with the Pharaoh represented as a strong bull trampling an enemy and knocking down a citadel. (A bull's tail hanging down from his belt is shown in both images of Narmer; it was to remain a part of Pharaonic ceremonial garb for the next 3000 years.) Only the center section fails to convey an explicit meaning; the two long-necked beasts and their attendants have no identifying attributes and may well be a carry-over from earlier, purely ornamental palettes. In any event, they do not reappear in Egyptian art.

STYLE AND STYLES. We have discussed these reliefs at such length because we must grasp their content in order to understand their formal qualities, their *style*. We have avoided this term until now and it is necessary to comment on it briefly before we proceed. *Style* is derived from *stilus*, the writing instrument of the ancient Romans; originally, it referred to distinctive ways of writing—the shape of the letters as well as the choice of words. Nowadays, however, style is used loosely to mean the distinctive way a thing is done in any field of human endeavor. It is simply a term of praise in most cases: "to have style" means to have distinction, to stand out. But something else is implied, too, which comes to the fore if we ask ourselves what we mean when we say that something "has no style." Such a thing, we feel, is not only undistinguished but also undistinguishable; in other words, we do not know how to classify it, how to put it into its proper context, because it seems to be pointing in several directions at once. Of a thing that *has style*, then, we expect that it must not be inconsistent within itself, that it must have an inner coherence, or unity; a sense of wholeness, of being all of a piece. This is the quality we admire in things that have style, for it has a way of impressing itself upon us even if we do not know what particular *kind* of style is involved.

In the visual arts, style means the particular way in which the forms that make up any given work of art are chosen and fitted together. To art historians the study of styles is of central importance; it not only enables them to find out, by means of careful analysis and comparison, when and where (and by whom) a given work was produced, but it also leads them to understand the artist's intention as expressed through the style of his work. This intention depends on both the artist's personality and the setting in which he lives and works. Accordingly, we speak of "period styles" if we are concerned with those features which distinguish, let us say, Egyptian art as a whole from Greek art. And within these broad period styles we in turn distinguish the styles of particular phases, such as the Old Kingdom; or, wherever it seems appropriate, we differentiate national or local styles within a period, until we arrive at the personal styles of individual artists. Even these may need to be subdivided further into the various phases of an artist's development. The extent to which we are able to do all this depends on how much internal coherence, how much of a sense of continuity, there is in the material we are dealing with.

LOGIC OF EGYPTIAN STYLE. Let us now return to the Narmer palette. The new inner logic of its style becomes readily apparent in contrast to the predynastic wall painting. What strikes us first is its strong sense of order: the surface of the palette has been divided into horizontal bands (or registers), and each figure stands on a line or strip denoting the ground. The only exceptions are the attendants of the long-necked beasts, whose role seems mainly ornamental; the hieroglyphic signs, which belong to a different level of reality; and the dead enemies. The latter are seen from above, whereas the standing figures are seen from the side. Obviously, the modern notion of representing a scene as it would appear to a single observer at a single moment is as alien to the Egyptian artist as it had been to his Neolithic predecessor; he strives for clarity, not illusion, and therefore he picks the most telling view in each case.

But he imposes a strict rule on himself: when he changes his angle of vision, he must do so by 90 degrees, as if he were sighting along the edges of a cube. As a consequence, he acknowledges only three possible views: full face, strict profile, and vertically from above. Any intermediate position embarrasses him (note the oddly rubber-like figures of the fallen enemies: fig. 53, bottom). Moreover, he is faced with the fact that the standing human figure, unlike that of an animal, does not have a single main profile but two competing profiles, so that, for the sake of clarity, he must combine these views. His method of doing this—a method that was to survive unchanged for 2,500 years—is clearly shown in the large figure of Narmer in figure 53: eye and shoulders in frontal view, head and legs in profile. Apparently this formula was worked out so as to show the Pharaoh (and all persons of significance who move in the penumbra of his divinity) in the most complete way possible. And since the scenes depict solemn and, as it were, timeless rituals, our artist did not have to concern himself with the fact that this method of representing the human body made almost any kind of movement or action practically impossible. In fact, the frozen quality of the image would seem especially suited to the divine nature of the Pharaoh; ordinary mortals *act*, he simply *is*.

Whenever physical activity demanding any sort of effort or strain must be depicted, the Egyptian artist does not hesitate to abandon the composite view if necessary, for such activity is always performed by underlings whose dignity does not have to be preserved; thus, in our palette the two animal trainers and the four men carrying standards are shown in strict profile throughout (except for the eyes). The Egyptian style of representing the human figure, then, seems to have been created specifically for the purpose of conveying in visual form the majesty of the divine king; it must have originated among the artists working for the royal court. And it never lost its ceremonial, sacred flavor, even when, in later times, it had to serve other purposes as well.

55. *Portrait Panel of Hesy-ra*, from Saqqara. c. 2660 B.C.
Wood, height 45″. Egyptian Museum, Cairo

Third Dynasty

The full beauty of the style which we saw in the Narmer palette does not become apparent until about three centuries later, during the Third Dynasty, and especially under the reign of King Zoser, who was its greatest figure. From the tomb of Hesy-ra, one of Zoser's high officials, comes the masterly wooden relief (fig. 55) showing the deceased with the emblems of his rank. (These include writing materials, since the position of scribe was a highly honored one.) The view of the figure corresponds exactly to that of Narmer on the palette, but the proportions are far more balanced and harmonious, and the carving of the physical details shows keen observation as well as great delicacy of touch.

TOMBS. When we speak of the Egyptians' attitude toward death and afterlife as expressed in their tombs, we must be careful to make it clear that we do not mean the attitude of the average Egyptian but only that of the small aristocratic caste clustered around the royal court. The tombs of the members of this class of high officials (who were often relatives of the royal family) are usually found in the immediate neighborhood of the Pharaohs' tombs, and their shape and contents reflect, or are related to, the funerary monuments of the divine kings. We still have a great deal to learn about the origin and significance of Egyptian tombs, but there is reason to believe that the concept of afterlife we find in the so-called private tombs did not apply to ordinary mortals but only to the privileged few because of their association with the immortal Pharaohs.

MASTABAS. The standard form of these tombs was the mastaba, a squarish mound faced with brick or stone, above the burial chamber, which was deep underground and linked to the mound by a shaft (figs. 56, 58). Inside the mastaba is a chapel for offerings to the *ka* and a secret cubicle for the statue of the deceased. Royal mastabas grew to conspicuous size as early as the First Dynasty, and their exteriors could be elaborated to resemble a royal palace. During the Third Dynasty, they developed into step pyramids; the best known (and probably the first) is that of King Zoser (fig. 57), built over a traditional mastaba (see figs. 58, 59). The pyramid itself, unlike later examples, is a completely solid structure whose only purpose seems to have been to serve as a great landmark.

FUNERARY DISTRICTS. The modern imagination, enamored of "the silence of the pyramids," is apt to create a false picture of these monuments. They were not erected as isolated structures in the middle of the desert, but as part of vast funerary districts, with temples and other buildings which were the scene of great religious celebrations during the Pharaoh's lifetime as well as after. The most elaborate of these is the funerary district around the pyramid of Zoser: enough of its architecture has survived to make us understand why its creator, Imhotep, came to be deified in later Egyptian tradition. He is the first artist whose name has been recorded in history, and deservedly so, since his achievement is more impressive even today.

COLUMNS. Egyptian architecture had begun with structures made of mud bricks, wood, reeds, and other light materials. Imhotep used cut stone masonry, but his repertory of architectural forms still reflected shapes or devices developed for less enduring materials. Thus we find columns of several kinds—always "engaged" rather than free-standing—which echo the bundles of reeds or the wooden supports that used to be set into mud-brick walls in order to strengthen them. But the very fact that these members no longer had their original functional purpose made it possible for Imhotep and his fellow architects to redesign them so as to make them serve a new, *expressive* purpose. The notion that architectural forms can express anything may seem difficult to grasp at first; today we tend to assume that unless these forms have a clear-cut structural service to perform (such as supporting or enclosing), they are mere surface decoration. But let us look at the slender, tapering fluted columns in figure 57, or the papyrus-shaped half-columns in

56. Group of Mastabas (after A. Badawy). 4th Dynasty

58. Transverse Section of the Step Pyramid of King Zoser, Saqqara

57. Step Pyramid of King Zoser, Saqqara. 3rd Dynasty, c. 2600 B.C.

59. Plan of the Funerary District of King Zoser, Saqqara
(M. Hirmer after J. P. Lauer). 1) Pyramid (m = mastaba);
2) Funerary Temple; 3, 4, 6) Courts; 5) Entrance Hall; 7) Small
Temple; 8) Court of North Palace; (9) Court of South Palace;
10) Southern Tomb

figure 60: these do not simply decorate the walls to which they are attached, but interpret them and give them life, as it were. Their proportions, the feeling of strength or resilience they convey, their spacing, the degree to which they project, all share in this task.

We shall learn more about their expressive role when we discuss Greek architecture, which took over the Egyptian stone column and developed it further. For the time being, let us note one additional factor that may enter into the design and use of such columns: announcing the symbolic purpose of the building. The papyrus half-columns in figure 60 are linked with Lower Egypt (compare the papyrus plants in fig. 53), hence they appear in the North Palace of Zoser's funerary district. The South Palace has columns of different shape, to evoke its association with Upper Egypt.

Fourth Dynasty

PYRAMIDS OF GIZA. The development of the pyramid reaches its climax during the Fourth Dynasty in the famous triad of great pyramids at Giza (figs. 61, 62), all of them of the familiar, smooth-sided shape. They originally had an

60. Papyrus Half-Columns, North Palace, Funerary District of King Zoser, Saqqara

61. The Pyramids of Mycerinus (c. 2470 B.C.), Chefren (c. 2500 B.C.), and Cheops (c. 2530 B.C.), Giza

62. Plan of the Pyramids at Giza

63. North-South Section of Pyramid of Cheops (after L. Borchardt)

outer casing of carefully dressed stone, which has disappeared except near the top of the pyramid of Chefren. Each of the three differs slightly from the others in details of design and construction; the essential features are shown in the section of the earliest and largest, that of Cheops (fig. 63): the burial chamber is now near the center of the structure, rather than below ground as in the pyramid of Zoser. Clustered about the three great pyramids are several smaller ones and a large number of mastabas for members of the royal family and high officials, but the unified funerary district of Zoser has given way to a simpler arrangement; adjoining each of the great pyramids to the east is a funerary temple, from which a processional causeway leads to a second temple at a lower level, in the Nile valley, at a distance of about a third of a mile.

THE SPHINX. Next to the valley temple of the pyramid of Chefren stands the Great Sphinx carved from the live rock (fig. 64, colorplate 5), perhaps an even more impressive embodiment of divine kingship than the pyramids themselves. The royal head rising from the body of a lion towers to a height of 65 feet, and bore, in all probability, the features of Chefren (damage inflicted upon it during Islamic times has obscured the details of the face). Its awesome majesty is such that a thousand years later it could be regarded as an image of the sun-god.

Enterprises of this huge scale mark the high point of Pharaonic power. After the end of the Fourth Dynasty (less than two centuries after Zoser) they were never attempted again, although pyramids on a much more modest scale continued to be built. The world has always marveled at the sheer size of the great pyramids as well as at the technical accomplishment they represent; but they have also come to be regarded as symbols of slave labor—thousands of men forced by cruel masters to serve the aggrandizement of absolute rulers. Such a picture may well be unjust: certain records have been preserved indicating that the labor was paid for, so that we are probably nearer the truth if we regard these monuments as vast public works providing economic security for a good part of the population.

PORTRAITS. Apart from its architectural achievements, the chief glory of Egyptian art, during the Old Kingdom and later, are the portrait statues recovered from funerary temples and tombs. One of the finest is that of Chefren, from the valley temple of his pyramid (fig. 65). Carved of diorite, a stone of extreme hardness, it shows the king enthroned, with the falcon of the god Horus enfolding the back of the head with its wings (we encountered the association, in different form, in the Narmer palette, fig. 53). Here the Egyptian sculptor's "cubic" view of the human form appears in full force: clearly, the sculptor prepared the statue by drawing its front and side views on the faces of a rectangular block and then worked inward until these views met. The result is a figure almost overpowering in its three-dimensional firmness and immobility. Truly a magnificent vessel for the spirit! The body, well proportioned and powerfully built, is completely impersonal; only the face suggests some individual traits, as will be seen if we compare it with that of Mycerinus (fig. 66), Chefren's successor and the builder of the third and smallest pyramid at Giza.

Mycerinus, accompanied by his queen, is standing. Both have the left foot placed forward, yet there is no hint of a forward movement. Since the two are almost of the same height, they afford an interesting comparison of male and female beauty as interpreted by one of the finest of Old Kingdom sculptors, who knew not only how to contrast the structure of the two bodies but also how to emphasize the soft, swelling forms of the queen through her light and close-fitting gown.

The sculptor who carved the statues of Prince Rahotep and his wife Nofret (fig. 67, colorplate 6) was less subtle in this respect. They owe their strikingly lifelike appearance to the vivid coloring, which they must have shared with other such statues but which has survived completely intact only in a few instances. The darker body color of the prince has no individual significance; it is the standard masculine complexion in Egyptian art. The eyes have been inlaid with shining quartz to make them look as alive as possible, and the portrait character of the faces is very pronounced.

Standing and seated figures comprise the basic repertory of Egyptian large-scale sculpture in the round. At the end of the Fourth Dynasty, a third pose was added, as symmetrical and immobile as the first two: that of the scribe squatting cross-legged on the ground. The finest of these scribes dates from the beginning of the Fifth Dynasty (fig. 68). The name of the sitter (in whose tomb at Saqqara the statue was found) is unknown, but we must not think of him as a lowly secretary waiting to take dictation; rather, the figure represents a

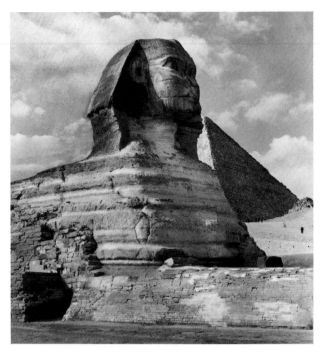

64. *The Great Sphinx* (see colorplate 5). Giza

65. *Chefren*, from Giza. c. 2500 B.C. Diorite, height 66".
Egyptian Museum, Cairo

high court official, a "master of sacred—and secret—letters," and the solid, incisive treatment of form bespeaks the dignity of his station (which in the beginning seems to have been restricted to the sons of Pharaohs). Our example stands out not only for the vividly alert expression of the face, but also for the individual handling of the torso, which records the somewhat flabby body of a man past middle age.

Another invention of Old Kingdom art was the portrait bust, a species of sculpture so familiar that we tend to take it for granted. Yet its origin is puzzling: was it simply an abbreviated statue, a cheaper substitute for a full-length figure? Or did it have a distinct purpose of its own, perhaps as a remote echo of the Neolithic custom of keeping the head of the deceased separate from the rest of his body (see page 31)?

67. *Prince Rahotep and His Wife Nofret* (detail; see colorplate 6). Egyptian Museum, Cairo

66. *Mycerinus and His Queen*, from Giza. c. 2470 B.C. Slate, height 56″. Museum of Fine Arts, Boston

68. *Seated Scribe*, from Saqqara. c. 2400 B.C. Limestone, height 21″. The Louvre, Paris

Be that as it may, the earliest of these busts (fig. 69) is also the finest—indeed, one of the great portraits of all time. In this noble head, we find a memorable image of the sitter's individual character as well as a most subtle differentiation between the solid, immutable shape of the skull and its soft, flexible covering of flesh.

TOMB DECORATION. Before we leave the Old Kingdom, let us cast a brief glance at some of the scenes of daily life from the offering chambers of nonroyal tombs, such as that of the architectural overseer Ti at Saqqara. The hippopotamus hunt in figure 70 is of special interest to us because of its landscape setting. The background of the relief is formed by a papyrus thicket; the stems of the plants make a regular, rippling pattern that erupts in the top zone into an agitated scene of nesting birds menaced by small predators. The water in the bottom zone, marked by a zigzag pattern, is equally crowded with struggling hippopotamuses and fish. All these, as well as the hunters in the first boat, are acutely observed and full of action; only Ti himself, standing in the second boat, is immobile, as if he belonged to a different world. His pose is that of the funerary portrait reliefs and statues (compare fig. 55), and he towers above the other men, since he is more important than they.

'His size also lifts him out of the context of the hunt—he neither directs nor supervises it, but simply observes. His passive role is characteristic of the representations of the deceased in all such scenes from the Old Kingdom. It seems to be a subtle way of conveying the fact that the body is dead but the spirit is alive and aware of the pleasures of this world, though the man can no longer participate in them directly. We should also note that these scenes of daily life do not represent the dead man's favorite pastimes; if they did, he would be looking back, and such nostalgia is quite alien to the spirit of Old Kingdom tombs. It has been shown, in fact, that these scenes form a seasonal cycle, a sort of perpetual calendar of recurrent human activities for the spirit of the deceased to watch year in and year out. For the artist, on the other hand, these scenes offered a welcome opportunity to widen his powers of observation, so that in details we often find astounding bits of realism.

70. *Ti Watching a Hippopotamus Hunt* (painted limestone relief). c. 2400 B.C. Tomb of Ti, Saqqara

71. *Cattle Fording a River* (detail of a painted limestone relief). c. 2400 B.C. Tomb of Ti, Saqqara

69. *Bust of Prince Ankh-haf*, from Giza. c. 2520 B.C. Limestone, lifesize. Museum of Fine Arts, Boston

Another relief from the tomb of Ti shows some cattle fording a river (fig. 71); one of the herders carries a newborn calf on his back, to keep it from drowning, and the frightened animal turns its head to look back at its mother, who answers with an equally anxious glance. Such sympathetic portrayal of an emotional relationship is as delightful as it is unexpected in Old Kingdom art. It will be some time before we encounter anything similar in the human realm. But eventually we shall even see the deceased abandoning his passive, timeless stance to participate in scenes of daily life.

THE MIDDLE KINGDOM

After the collapse of centralized Pharaonic power at the end of the Sixth Dynasty, Egypt entered a period of political disturbances and ill fortune that was to last almost 700 years. During most of this time, effective authority lay in the hands of local or regional overlords, who revived the old rivalry of North and South. Many dynasties followed one another in rapid succession, but only two, the Eleventh and Twelfth, are worthy of note. The latter constitute the Middle Kingdom (2134–1785 B.C.), when a series of able rulers managed to reassert themselves against the provincial nobility. However, the spell of divine kingship, having once been broken, never regained its old effectiveness, and the authority of the Middle Kingdom Pharaohs tended to be personal rather than institutional. Soon after the close of the Twelfth Dynasty, the weakened country was invaded by the Hyksos, a western Asiatic people of somewhat mysterious origin, who seized the Delta area and ruled it for 150 years until their expulsion by the princes of Thebes about 1570 B.C.

PORTRAITURE. The unquiet spirit of the times is well reflected in Middle Kingdom art. We find it especially in the new type of royal portrait that marks the Twelfth Dynasty, such as the one in figure 72. There is a real sense of shock on first encountering this strangely modern face; the serene assurance of the Old Kingdom has given way to a brooding, troubled expression that bespeaks a new level of self-awareness. Deprived of its royal trappings, our fragment displays so uncompromising a realism, physical as well as psychological, that at first glance the link with the sculptural tradition of the past seems broken entirely. Here is another enduring achievement of Egyptian art, destined to live on in Roman portraiture and in the portraiture of the Renaissance.

PAINTING AND RELIEF. A loosening of established rules also makes itself felt in Middle Kingdom painting and relief, where it leads to all sorts of interesting departures from convention. They occur most conspicuously in the decoration of the tombs of local princes at Beni Hasan, which have survived destruction better than most Middle Kingdom monuments because they are carved into the living rock. The mural *Feeding the Oryxes* (fig. 73) comes from one of these rock-cut tombs, that of Khnum-hotep. (As the emblem of the prince's domain, the oryx antelope seems to have been a sort of honored pet in his household.) According to the standards of Old Kingdom art, all the figures ought to share the same ground-line, or the second oryx and its attendant ought to be placed above the first; instead, the painter has introduced a secondary ground-line only slightly higher than the primary one, and as a result the two groups are related in a way that closely approximates normal appearances. His interest in exploring spatial effects can also be seen in the awkward but quite bold foreshortening of the shoulders of the two attendants. If we cover up the hieroglyphic signs, which emphasize the flatness of the wall, we can "read" the forms in depth with surprising ease.

72. *Portrait of Sesostris III.* c. 1850 B.C. Quartzite, height 6⅛". The Metropolitan Museum of Art, New York (Gift of Edward S. Harkness, 1926)

73. *Feeding the Oryxes.* c. 1920 B.C. Tomb of Khnum-hotep, Beni Hasan

THE NEW KINGDOM

The five hundred years following the expulsion of the Hyksos, and comprising the Eighteenth, Nineteenth, and Twentieth dynasties, represent the third Golden Age of Egypt. The country, once more united under strong and efficient kings, extended its frontiers far to the east, into Palestine and Syria (hence this period is also known as the Empire). During the climactic period of power and prosperity, between c. 1500 and the end of the reign of Ramesses III in 1162 B.C., tremendous architectural projects were carried out, centering on the region of the new capital, Thebes, while the royal tombs reached unequaled material splendor.

The divine kingship of the Pharaohs was now asserted in a new way: by association with the god Amun, whose identity had been fused with that of the sun-god Ra, and who became the supreme deity, ruling the lesser gods much as the Pharaoh towered above the provincial nobility. But this very development produced an unexpected threat to royal authority; the priests of Amun grew into a caste of such wealth and power that the king could maintain his position only with their consent. Amenhotep IV, the most remarkable figure of the Eighteenth Dynasty, tried to defeat them by proclaiming his faith in a single god, the sun disk Aten. He changed his name to Akhenaten, closed the Amun temples, and moved the capital to central Egypt, near the modern Tell el 'Amarna. His attempt to place himself at the head of a new monotheistic faith, however, did not outlast his reign (1365–1347 B.C.), and under his successors orthodoxy was speedily restored. During the long decline that began about 1000 B.C., the country became increasingly priest-ridden, until, under Greek and Roman rule, Egyptian civilization came to an end in a welter of esoteric religious doctrines.

New Kingdom art covers a vast range of styles and quality, from rigid conservatism to brilliant inventiveness, from oppressively massive ostentation to the most delicate refinement. Like the art of Imperial Rome fifteen hundred years later, it is almost impossible to summarize in terms of a representative sampling. Different strands are interwoven into a fabric so complex that any choice of monuments is bound to seem arbitrary. All we can hope to accomplish is to convey some of the flavor of its variety.

Architecture

TEMPLE OF HATSHEPSUT. Among the architectural enterprises that have survived from the early years of the New Kingdom, the outstanding one is the funerary temple of Queen Hatshepsut, built about 1480 B.C. against the rocky cliffs of Deir el-Bahari (figs. 74, 75) and dedicated to Amun and several other deities. The worshiper is led toward the holy of holies—a small chamber driven deep into the rock—through three large courts on ascending levels, linked by ramps among long colonnades: a processional road reminiscent of those at Giza, but with the mountain instead of a pyramid at the end. It is this magnificent union of man-made and natural architecture—note how ramps and colonnades echo the shape of the cliff—that makes Hatshepsut's temple the rival of any of the Old Kingdom monuments.

TEMPLE AT LUXOR. The later rulers of the New Kingdom continued to build funerary temples, but an ever greater share of their architectural energies was devoted to huge imperial temples of Amun, the supreme god whom the reigning monarch traditionally claimed as his father. The temple at Luxor, across the Nile from Thebes, dedicated to

74. Funerary Temple of Hatshepsut, Deir el-Bahari. 18th Dynasty, c. 1480 B.C.

75. Plan of Funerary Temple of Queen Hatshepsut (after Lange)

76. Court and Pylon of Ramesses II (c. 1260 B.C.) and Colonnade and Court of Amenhotep III
(c. 1390 B.C.), Temple of Amun-Mut-Khonsu, Luxor

77. Plan of the Temple of Amun-Mut-Khonsu, Luxor
(after N. de Garis Davies)

Amun, his wife Mut, and their son Khonsu, was begun about 1390 B.C. by Amenhotep III but was extended and completed more than a century later. Its plan is characteristic of the general pattern of later Egyptian temples. The façade consists of two massive walls, with sloping sides, flanking the entrance; this unit is known as the gateway or pylon (fig. 76, far left), and leads to the court (fig. 77, A). The court, in this case, is a parallelogram, because Ramesses II, who added it to the temple that had been planned under Amenhotep III, changed the axis of his court slightly, so as to conform with the direction of the Nile. We then enter a pillared hall, which brings us to the second court (fig. 77, B and C; fig. 76, center and right). On its far side we find another pillared hall. Beyond it, the temple proper begins: a series of symmetrically arranged halls and chapels shielding the holy of holies, a square room with four columns (fig. 77, extreme right).

The entire sequence of courts, halls, and temple was enclosed by high walls that shut off the outside world. Except for the monumental façade, such a structure is designed to be experienced from within; ordinary worshipers were confined to the courts and could but marvel at the forest of columns that screened the dark recesses of the sanctuary. The columns had to be closely spaced, for they supported the stone lintels of the ceiling, and these had to be short to keep them from breaking under their own weight. Yet the architect has consciously exploited this condition by making the columns far heavier than they need be. As a result, the beholder feels almost crushed by their sheer mass. The overawing effect is certainly impressive, but also rather vulgar when measured against the earlier masterpieces of Egyptian architecture. We need only compare the papyrus columns of the colonnade of Amenhotep III with their remote ancestors in Zoser's North Palace (fig. 60) in order to realize how little of the genius of Imhotep has survived at Luxor.

BRICK ARCHITECTURE. The massive vastness of their tombs and temples makes us think that the Egyptians built mainly in stone. Yet, except where absolute durability was essential for religious reasons, they used sun-dried mud bricks, an infinitely cheaper and more convenient material. The achievements of Egyptian brick architecture have attracted little interest so far, and much of the work has been destroyed, but the few well-preserved structures, such as the storehouses attached to the mortuary temple of Ramesses II (fig. 78), show a masterful command of brick building techniques. These barrel vaults, with a span of over 13 feet, anticipate the engineering skill of the Romans.

Akhenaten

Of the great projects built by Akhenaten hardly anything remains above ground. He must have been a revolutionary not only in his religious beliefs but in his artistic tastes as well, consciously fostering a new style and a new ideal of beauty in his choice of masters. The contrast with the past becomes

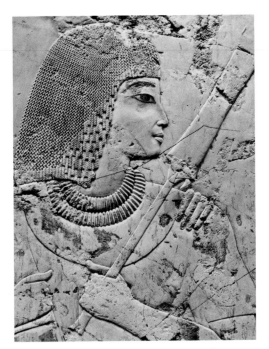

79. *The Brother of the Deceased*
(detail of a limestone relief).
c. 1375 B.C. Tomb of Ramose, Thebes

80. *Akhenaten (Amenhotep IV)*.
c. 1360 B.C. Limestone,
height 3⅛″. State Museums, Berlin

78. Brick Storehouses, Mortuary Temple of Ramesses II,
West Thebes. c. 1260 B.C.

strikingly evident if we compare a head in low relief from the Tomb of Ramose, done at the end of the reign of Amenhotep III (fig. 79), with a low-relief portrait of Akhenaten that is only about ten years later in date (fig. 80). Figure 79 shows the traditional style at its best; the wonderful subtlety of the carving—the precision and refinement of its lines—makes the head of Akhenaten seem at first glance like a brutal caricature. And the latter work is indeed an extreme statement

of the new ideal, with its oddly haggard features and overemphatic, undulating outlines. Still, we can perceive its kinship with the justly famous bust of Akhenaten's queen, Nofretete (fig. 81), one of the masterpieces of the "Akhenaten style."

What distinguishes this style is not greater realism so much as a new sense of form that seek to unfreeze the traditional immobility of Egyptian art; not only the contours but the plastic shapes, too, seem more pliable and relaxed, anti-geometric, as it were. We find these qualities again in the delightful fragment of a wall painting showing the daughters of Akhenaten (fig. 82, colorplate 7). Their playful gestures and informal poses seem in defiance of all rules of Pharaonic dignity.

The old religious tradition was quickly restored after Akhenaten's death, but the artistic innovations he encouraged could be felt in Egyptian art for some time to come. The scene of workmen struggling with a heavy beam (fig. 83), from the tomb of Horemheb at Saqqara, shows a freedom and expressiveness that would have been unthinkable in earlier times.

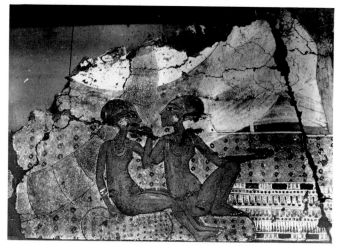

81. *Queen Nofretete.* c. 1360 B.C. Limestone, height c. 20″. State Museums, Berlin

82. *The Daughters of Akhenaten* (see colorplate 7). Oriental Institute, University of Chicago

83. *Workmen Carrying a Beam,* from the Tomb of Horemheb, Saqqara. c. 1325 B.C. Museo Civico, Bologna

Tutankhamen

Even the face of Akhenaten's successor, Tutankhamen, as it appears on his gold coffin, betrays an echo of the Akhenaten style (fig. 84, colorplate 8). Tutankhamen, who died at the age of eighteen, owes his fame entirely to the accident that his is the only Pharaonic tomb discovered in our times with most of its contents undisturbed. The sheer material value of the tombs (Tutankhamen's gold coffin alone weighs 250 pounds) makes it understandable that grave robbing has been practiced in Egypt ever since the Old Kingdom. To us, the exquisite workmanship of the coffin cover, with the rich play of colored inlays against the polished gold surfaces, is even more impressive.

84. Cover of the Coffin of Tutankhamen (detail; see colorplate 8). Egyptian Museum, Cairo

As unique in its way as the gold coffin is a painted chest from the same tomb, showing the youthful king in battle and hunting scenes (fig. 85). These had been traditional subjects since the late years of the Old Kingdom, but here they are done with astonishing freshness, at least so far as the animals are concerned. While the king and his horse-drawn chariot remain frozen against the usual blank background filled with hieroglyphics, the same background in the right-hand half of the scene suddenly turns into a desert; the surface is covered with stippled dots to suggest sand, desert plants are strewn across it in considerable variety, and the animals stampede over it helterskelter, without any ground-lines to impede their flight.

Here is an aspect of Egyptian painting that we rarely see on the walls of tombs; perhaps this lively scattering of forms against a landscape background existed only on the miniature scale of the scenes on Tutankhamen's chest and even there it became possible only as a result of the Akhenaten style. How these animals-in-landscape survived in later Egyptian painting we do not know, but they must have survived somehow, for their resemblance to Islamic miniatures done more than two thousand years later is far too striking to be ignored.

85. *Tutankhamen Hunting*, from a painted chest found in the king's tomb, Thebes, c. 1340 B.C. Length of scene c. 20″. Egyptian Museum, Cairo

3
THE ANCIENT
NEAR EAST

SUMERIAN ART

It is an odd and astonishing fact that man should have emerged into the light of history in two separate places at just about the same time. Between 3500 and 3000 B.C., when Egypt was being united under Pharaonic rule, another great civilization arose in Mesopotamia, the "land between the rivers." And for close to 3,000 years, the two rival centers retained their distinct character, even though they had contact with each other from their earliest beginnings and their destinies were interwoven in many ways. The pressures that forced the inhabitants of both regions to abandon the pattern of Neolithic village life may well have been the same (see fig. 23). But the valley of the Tigris and Euphrates, unlike that of the Nile, is not a narrow fertile strip protected by deserts on either side; it resembles a wide, shallow trough with few natural defenses, crisscrossed by two great rivers and their tributaries, and easily encroached upon from any direction.

Thus the facts of geography tended to discourage the idea of uniting the entire area under a single head. Rulers who had this ambition did not appear, so far as we know, until about a thousand years after the beginnings of Mesopotamian civilization, and they succeeded in carrying it out only for brief periods and at the cost of almost continuous warfare. As a consequence, the political history of ancient Mesopotamia has no underlying theme of the sort that divine kingship provides for Egypt; local rivalries, foreign incursions, the sudden upsurge and equally sudden collapse of military power—these are its substance. Against such a disturbed background, the continuity of cultural and artistic traditions seems all the more remarkable. This common heritage is very largely the creation of the founding fathers of Mesopotamian civilization, whom we call Sumerians after the region of Sumer, which they inhabited, near the confluence of the Tigris and Euphrates.

86. (*left*) The "White Temple" on Its Ziggurat,
Uruk (Warka). c. 3500–3000 B.C.

87. (*above*) Plan of the "White Temple"
on Its Ziggurat
(after H. Frankfort)

The origin of the Sumerians remains obscure. Their language is unrelated to any other known tongue. Sometime before 4000 B.C., they came to southern Mesopotamia from Persia, and there, within the next thousand years, they founded a number of city-states and developed their distinctive form of writing in cuneiform (wedge-shaped) characters on clay tablets. This transitional phase, corresponding to the predynastic period in Egypt, is called "protoliterate"; it leads to the early dynastic period, from about 3000 to 2340 B.C.

ARCHAEOLOGICAL CONDITIONS. Unfortunately, the tangible remains of Sumerian civilization are extremely scanty compared to those of ancient Egypt; building stone being unavailable in Mesopotamia, the Sumerians used mud brick and wood, so that almost nothing is left of their architecture except the foundations. Nor did they share the Egyptians' concern with the hereafter, although some richly endowed tombs—in the shape of vaulted chambers below ground—of the early dynastic period have been found in the city of Ur. Our knowledge of Sumerian civilization thus depends very largely on chance fragments brought to light by excavation, including vast numbers of inscribed clay tablets. Yet in recent decades we have learned enough to form a general picture of the achievements of this vigorous, inventive, and disciplined people.

RELIGION. Each Sumerian city-state had its own local god, who was regarded as its "king" and owner. It also had a human ruler, the steward of the divine sovereign, who led the people in serving the deity. The local god, in return, was expected to plead the cause of his subjects among his fellow deities who controlled the forces of nature such as wind and weather, water, fertility, and the heavenly bodies. Nor was the idea of divine ownership treated as a mere pious fiction; the god was quite literally believed to own not only the territory of the city-state but also the labor power of the population and its products. All these were subject to his commands, transmitted to the people by his human steward. The result was an economic system that has been dubbed "theocratic socialism," a planned society whose administrative center was the temple. It was the temple that controlled the pooling of labor and resources for communal enterprises, such as the building of dikes or irrigation ditches, and it collected and distributed a considerable part of the harvest. All this required the keeping of detailed written records. Hence we need not be surprised to find that the texts of early Sumerian inscriptions deal very largely with economic and administrative rather than religious matters, although writing was a priestly privilege.

ARCHITECTURE. The dominant role of the temple as the center of both spiritual and physical existence is strikingly conveyed by the layout of Sumerian cities. The houses clustered about a sacred area that was a vast architectural complex embracing not only shrines but workshops, storehouses, and scribes' quarters as well. In their midst, on a raised platform, stood the temple of the local god. These platforms soon reached the height of true man-made mountains, comparable to the pyramids of Egypt in the immensity of effort required and in their effect as great landmarks that tower above the featureless plain. They are known as ziggurats.

The most famous of them, the biblical Tower of Babel, has been completely destroyed, but a much earlier example, built shortly before 3000 B.C. and thus several centuries older

88. Interior of the Cella, "White Temple"

than the first of the pyramids, survives at Warka, the site of the Sumerian city of Uruk (called Erech in the Bible). The mound, its sloping sides reinforced by solid brick masonry, rises to a height of 40 feet; stairs and ramps lead up to the platform on which stands the sanctuary, called the "White Temple" because of its whitewashed brick exterior (figs. 86, 87). Its heavy walls, articulated by regularly spaced projections and recesses, are sufficiently well preserved to suggest something of the original appearance of the structure. The main room, or cella (fig. 88), where sacrifices were offered before the statue of the god, is a narrow hall that runs the entire length of the temple and is flanked by a series of smaller chambers. But the main entrance to the cella is on the southwest side, rather than on the side facing the stairs or on one of the narrow sides of the temple, as one might expect. In order to understand the reason for this, we must view the ziggurat and temple as a whole: the entire complex is planned in such a way that the worshiper, starting at the bottom of the stairs on the east side, is forced to go around as many corners as possible before he reaches the cella. The processional path, in other words, resembles a sort of angular spiral.

This "bent-axis approach" is a fundamental characteristic of Mesopotamian religious architecture, in contrast to the straight single axis of Egyptian temples (see fig. 77). During the following 2,500 years, it was elaborated into ever taller and more tower-like ziggurats rising in multiple stages. The one built by King Urnammu at Ur about 2500 B.C. (fig. 89) had three levels. Little is left of the upper two stages, but the bottom one, some 50 feet high, has survived fairly well, and its facing of brick has recently been restored. What was the impulse behind these structures? Certainly not the kind of pride attributed to the builders of the Tower of Babel in the Old Testament. They reflect, rather, the widespread belief that mountaintops are the dwelling places of the gods (we need only recall the Mount Olympus of the Greeks). In the plain of Sumer, men felt they could provide a fit residence for the deity only by creating their own artificial mountains.

STONE SCULPTURE. The image of the god to whom the "White Temple" was dedicated is lost—it was probably Anu, the god of the sky—but a splendid female head of white marble from the same period at Uruk (Warka) may well

89. Ziggurat of King Urnammu, Ur. c. 2500 B.C.

have belonged to another cult statue (fig. 90). The eyes and eyebrows were originally inlaid with colored materials, and the hair was covered with a "wig" of gold or copper. The rest of the figure, which must have been close to life size, probably consisted of wood. As an artistic achievement, this head is on the level of the finest works of Egyptian Old Kingdom sculpture. The softly swelling cheeks, the delicate curves of the lips, combined with the steady gaze of the huge eyes, create a balance of sensuousness and severity that seems worthy of any goddess.

It was the geometric and expressive aspects of the Uruk head, rather than the realistic ones, that survived in the stone sculpture of the early dynastic period, as seen in a group of figures from Tell Asmar (fig. 91) carved about five centuries later than the head. The tallest, about 30 inches high, represents Abu, the god of vegetation; the second largest, a mother goddess; the others, priests and worshipers. The two deities are distinguished from the rest not only by their size but by the larger diameter of the pupils of their eyes, although the eyes of all the figures are enormous. Their insistent stare is emphasized by colored inlays, which are still in place. The entire group must have stood in the cella of the Abu temple, the priests and worshipers confronting the two gods and communicating with them through their eyes.

"Representation" here had a very direct meaning: the gods were believed to be present in their images, and the statues of the worshipers served as stand-ins for the persons they portrayed, offering prayers or transmitting messages to the deity in their stead. Yet none of them indicates any at-

90. *Female Head*, from Uruk (Warka). c. 3500–3000 B.C. Marble, height 8″. The Iraq Museum, Baghdad

91. Statues, from the Abu Temple, Tell Asmar. c. 2700–2500 B.C. Marble, height of tallest figure c. 30″. The Iraq Museum, Baghdad, and The Oriental Institute, University of Chicago

92. *Billy Goat and Tree* (see colorplate 9). The University Museum, Philadelphia

has an almost demonic power of expression as it gazes at us from between the branches of the symbolic tree. And well it might, for it is sacred to the god Tammuz and thus embodies the male principle in nature.

Such an association of animals with deities is a carry-over from prehistoric times; we find it not only in Mesopotamia but in Egypt as well (see the falcon of Horus in figs. 53 and 65). What distinguishes the sacred animals of the Sumerians is the active part they play in mythology. Much of this lore, unfortunately, has not come down to us in written form, but tantalizing glimpses of it can be caught in pictorial representations such as those on an inlaid panel from a harp (fig. 93) that was recovered together with the offering stand at Ur. The hero embracing two human-headed bulls in the top compartment was so popular a subject that its design has become a rigidly symmetrical, decorative formula; the other sections, however, show animals performing a variety of human tasks in surprisingly animated and precise fashion: the wolf and the lion carry food and drink to an unseen banquet, while the ass, bear, and deer provide musical entertainment (the bull-headed harp is the same type as the instrument to which the inlaid panel was attached). At the bottom, a scorpion-man and a goat carry some objects they have taken from a large vessel.

tempt to achieve a real likeness. The bodies as well as the faces are rigorously simplified and schematic, in order to avoid distracting attention from the eyes, the "windows of the soul." If the Egyptian sculptor's sense of form was essentially cubic, that of the Sumerian was based on the cone and cylinder. Arms and legs have the roundness of pipes, and the long skirts worn by all these figures are as smoothly curved as if they had been turned on a lathe. Even in later times, when Mesopotamian sculpture had acquired a far richer repertory of shapes, this quality asserted itself again and again.

BRONZE OR ASSEMBLED SCULPTURE. The conic-cylindrical simplification of the Tell Asmar statues is characteristic of the carver, who works by cutting his forms out of a solid block. A far more flexible and realistic style prevails among the Sumerian sculpture that was made by addition rather than subtraction (that is, either modeled in soft materials for casting in bronze or put together by combining such varied substances as wood, gold leaf, and lapis lazuli). Some pieces of the latter kind, roughly contemporary with the Tell Asmar figures, have been found in the tombs at Ur which we had occasion to mention earlier. They include the fascinating object shown in colorplate 9 and figure 92, an offering stand in the shape of a billy goat rearing up against a flowering tree. The animal, marvelously alive and energetic,

93. Inlay on the Soundbox of a Harp, from Ur. c. 2600 B.C. The University Museum, Philadelphia

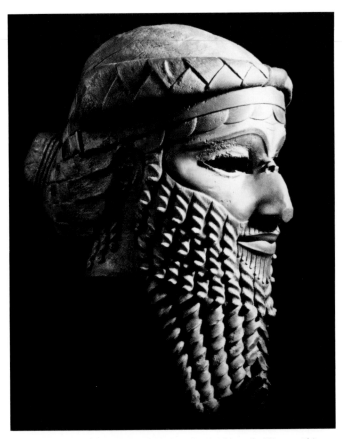

94. *Head of an Akkadian Ruler*, from Nineveh (Kuyunjik).
c. 2300–2200 B.C. Bronze, height 12″.
The Iraq Museum, Baghdad

they produced the first Mesopotamian rulers who openly called themselves kings and proclaimed their ambition to rule the entire earth.

Under these Akkadians, Sumerian art faced a new task—the personal glorification of the sovereign. The most impressive work of this kind that has survived is a magnificent royal portrait head in bronze from Nineveh (fig. 94). Despite the gouged-out eyes (once inlaid with precious materials), it remains a persuasive likeness, majestic and humanly moving at the same time. Equally admirable is the richness of the surfaces framing the face; the plaited hair and the finely curled strands of the beard are shaped with incredible precision, yet without losing their organic character and becoming mere ornament. The complex technique of casting and chasing has been handled with an assurance that bespeaks true mastery. This head could hold its own in the company of the greatest works of any period.

The skillful artist who created these scenes was far less constrained by rules than his contemporaries in Egypt; even though he, too, places his figures on ground-lines, he is not afraid of overlapping forms or foreshortened shoulders. We must be careful, however, not to misinterpret his intention—what strikes the modern eye as delightfully humorous was probably meant to be viewed with perfect seriousness. If we only knew the context in which these actors play their roles! Nevertheless, we are entitled to regard them as the earliest known ancestors of the animal fable that flourished in the West from Aesop to La Fontaine. At least one of them, the ass with the harp, survived as a fixed image, and we encounter it almost 4,000 years later in medieval sculpture.

The Akkadians

Toward the end of the early dynastic period, the theocratic socialism of the Sumerian city-states began to decay. The local "stewards of the god" had in practice become reigning monarchs, and the more ambitious among them attempted to enlarge their domain by conquering their neighbors. At the same time, the Semitic inhabitants of northern Mesopotamia drifted south in ever larger numbers, until they outweighed the Sumerian stock in many places. They had adopted Sumerian civilization but were less bound to the tradition of the city-state. So it is perhaps not surprising that in Sargon of Akkad and his successors (2340–2180 B.C.)

95. *Victory Stele of Naram-Sin*. c. 2300–2200 B.C.
Stone, height 6′ 6″. The Louvre, Paris

STELE OF NARAM-SIN. Sargon's grandson, Naram-Sin, had himself and his victorious army immortalized in relief on a large stele (fig. 95)—an upright stone slab used as a marker—which owes its survival to the fact that at a later time it was carried off as booty to Susa, where modern archaeologists discovered it. Here rigid ground-lines have been discarded; we see the king's forces advancing among the trees on a mountainside. Above them, Naram-Sin alone stands triumphant, as the defeated enemy soldiers plead for mercy. He is as vigorously active as his men, but his size and his isolated position endow him with superhuman status. Moreover, he wears the horned crown hitherto reserved for the gods. Nothing appears above him except the mountaintop and the celestial bodies, his "good stars." This is the earliest known monument to the glory of a conqueror.

Ur

The rule of the Akkadian kings came to an end when tribesmen from the northeast descended into the Mesopotamian plain and gained mastery of it for more than half a century. They were driven out in 2125 B.C. by the kings of Ur, who reestablished a united realm that was to last a hundred years.

GUDEA. During the period of foreign dominance, Lagash (the modern Telloh), one of the lesser Sumerian city-states, managed to retain local independence. Its ruler, Gudea, was careful to reserve the title of king for the city-god, whose cult he promoted by an ambitious rebuilding of his temple. Of this architectural enterprise nothing remains today, but Gudea also had numerous statues of himself placed in the shrines of Lagash, and some twenty examples, all obviously of the same general type, have been found so far. Carved of diorite, the extremely hard stone favored by Egyptian sculp-

97. *Gudea with Architectural Plan*, from Lagash (Telloh). c. 2150 B.C. Diorite, height 29". The Louvre, Paris

tors, they are much more ambitious works than their predecessors from Tell Asmar. Even Gudea, however devoted he was to the traditional pattern of the Sumerian city-state, seems to have inherited something of the sense of personal importance that we felt in the Akkadian kings, although he prided himself on his intimate relations with the gods rather than on secular power.

His portrait head (fig. 96) appears far less distinctly individualized when compared with the Akkadian ruler, yet its fleshy roundness is far removed from the geometric simplicity of the Tell Asmar statues. The stone has been worked to a high and subtly accented finish, inviting a wonderful play of light upon the features. The seated statue (fig. 97) represents Gudea with an architectural plan on his lap (perhaps the enclosing wall of a temple district), which he is offering for the god's approval; there are six entrances framed by tower-like projections, and the walls show regularly spaced buttresses of the kind we saw in the "White Temple" at Uruk (Warka). The figure makes an instructive contrast with such Egyptian statues as in figures 65, 67, and colorplate 6—the Sumerian carver has rounded off all the corners to emphasize the cylindrical quality of the forms. Equally characteristic is the muscular tension in Gudea's bare arm and shoulder, compared with the passive, relaxed limbs of Egyptian statues.

96. *Head of Gudea*, from Lagash (Telloh). c. 2150 B.C. Diorite, height 9". Museum of Fine Arts, Boston

Babylon

The second millennium B.C. was a time of almost continuous turmoil in Mesopotamia. The ethnic upheaval that brought the Hyksos to Egypt had an even more disruptive effect on the valley of the Tigris and Euphrates. Central power by native rulers prevailed only from about 1760 to 1600 B.C., when Babylon assumed the role formerly played by Akkad and Ur. Hammurabi, the founder of the Babylonian dynasty, is by far the greatest figure of the age: combining military prowess with a deep respect for Sumerian tradition, he saw himself as "the favorite shepherd" of the sun god Shamash, whose mission it was "to cause justice to prevail in the land." Under him and his successors, Babylon became the cultural center of Sumer. The city was to retain this prestige for more than a thousand years after its political power had waned.

CODE OF HAMMURABI. Hammurabi's most memorable achievement is his law code, justly famous as the earliest uniform written body of laws and amazingly rational and humane in conception. He had it engraved on a tall diorite stele whose top shows Hammurabi confronting the sun god (fig. 98). The ruler's right arm is raised in a speaking gesture, as if he were reporting his work of codification to the divine

99. The Lion Gate, Bogazköy, Anatolia. c. 1400 B.C.

king. Although this scene was carved four centuries after the Gudea statues, it is strongly related to them in both style and technique. In fact, the relief here is so high that the two figures almost give the impression of statues sliced in half when we compare them with the pictorial treatment of the Naram-Sin stele. As a result, the sculptor has been able to render the eyes in the round, so that Hammurabi and Shamash gaze at each other with a force and directness unique in representations of this kind. They make us recall the statues from Tell Asmar, whose enormous eyes indicate an attempt to establish the same relationship between man and god in an earlier phase of Sumerian civilization.

ASSYRIAN ART

The city-state of Assur on the upper course of the Tigris owed its rise to power to a strange chain of events. During the earlier half of the second millennium B.C., Asia Minor had been invaded from the east by people of Indo-European language. One group, the Mitannians, created an independent kingdom in Syria and northern Mesopotamia, including Assur, while another, the Hittites, established themselves farther north on the rocky plateau of Anatolia. Their capital, near the present-day Turkish village of Bogazköy, was protected by impressive fortifications built of large, roughly cut stones; the gates were flanked by snarling lions or other guardian figures protruding from the enormous blocks that formed the jambs of the doorway (fig. 99).

About 1360 B.C., the Hittites attacked the Mitannians, who were allies of the Egyptians. But the latter, because of the internal crisis provoked by the religious reforms of Akhenaten (see pages 66–68), could send no effective aid; the Mitannians were defeated and Assur regained its independence. Under a series of able rulers, the Assyrian domain gradually expanded until it embraced not only Mesopotamia proper but the surrounding regions as well. At the height of its power, from about 1000 to 612 B.C., the Assyrian empire stretched from the Sinai peninsula to Armenia; even Lower Egypt was successfully invaded in 671 B.C.

98. Upper Part of Stele Inscribed with the Law Code of Hammurabi. c. 1760 B.C. Diorite, height of stele c. 7', height of relief 28". The Louvre, Paris

100. Citadel of Sargon II at Dur Sharrukin
(Khorsabad). 742–706 B.C. (reconstruction by Charles Altman)

101. Gate of the Citadel of Sargon II (during excavation)

Palaces and Their Decoration

The Assyrians, it has been said, were to the Sumerians what the Romans were to the Greeks. Assyrian civilization drew on the achievements of the south but reinterpreted them to fit its own distinctive character. Thus the temples and ziggurats they built were adapted from Sumerian models while the palaces of Assyrian kings grew to unprecedented size and magnificence.

DUR SHARRUKIN. Only one of these, that of Sargon II at Dur Sharrukin (the modern Khorsabad), dating from the second half of the eighth century B.C., has been explored sufficiently to permit a reconstruction (fig. 100). It was surrounded by a citadel with turreted walls that shut if off from the rest of the town. Figure 101 shows one of the two gates of the citadel in process of excavation. Although the Assyrians, like the Sumerians, built in brick, they liked to line gateways and the lower walls of important interiors with great slabs of stone (which were less difficult to procure in northern Mesopotamia). These slabs were either decorated with low reliefs or, as in our case, elaborated into guardian demons that are an odd combination of relief and sculpture in the round. They must have been inspired by Hittite exam-

ples such as the lion gate at Bogazköy (fig. 98). Awesome in size and appearance, they were meant to impress the visitor with the power and majesty of the king.

Inside the palace, the same impression was reinforced by long series of reliefs illustrating the conquests of the royal armies. Every campaign is described in detail, with inscriptions supplying further data. The Assyrian forces, relentlessly efficient, always seem to be on the march, meeting the enemy at every frontier of the overextended empire, destroying his strong points and carrying away booty and prisoners. There is neither drama nor heroism in these scenes—the outcome of the battle is never in doubt—and they are often depressingly repetitious. Yet, as the earliest large-scale efforts at narrative in the history of art, they represent an achievement of great importance. To describe the progress of specific events in time and space had been outside the scope of both Egyptian and Sumerian art; even the scene on the stele of Naram-Sin is symbolic rather than historic. The Assyrian artist thus had to develop an entirely new set of devices in order to cope with the requirements of pictorial story-telling.

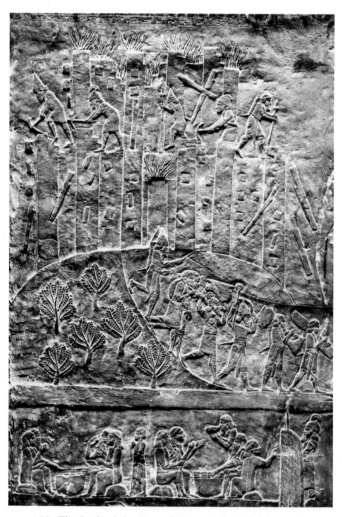

102. *The Sack of the City of Hamanu by Ashurbanipal,*
from Nineveh (Kuyunjik). c. 650 B.C.
Limestone, 36 × 24½". British Museum, London

103. *Ashurnasirpal II Killing Lions*, from Nimrud (Calah). c. 850 B.C. Limestone, 3′ 3″×8′ 4″. British Museum, London

104. *Dying Lioness*, from Nineveh (Kuyunjik).
c. 650 B.C. Limestone, height of figure 13¾″.
British Museum, London

NINEVEH. If the artist's results can hardly be called beautiful, they achieve their main purpose—to be clearly readable. This is certainly true of our example (fig. 102), from the Palace of Ashurbanipal at Nineveh (now Kuyunjik), which shows the sack of the Elamite city of Hamanu in the main register: Assyrian soldiers with pickaxes and crowbars are demolishing the fortifications—notice the falling tim- bers and bricks in mid-air—after they have set fire to the town itself; others are marching away from it, down a wood- ed hill, laden with booty. The latter group poses a particular- ly interesting problem in representation, for the road on which they walk widens visibly as it approaches the fore- ground, as if the artist had meant to render it in perspective, yet the same road also serves as a curved band that frames the marchers. An odd mixture of modes—but an effective device for linking foreground and background. Below the main scene, we observe the soldiers at camp, relaxing with food and drink, while one of them stands guard.

LION HUNTS. The mass of descriptive detail in the reliefs of military campaigns often leaves little room for the personal glorification of the king. This purpose is served more directly by another recurrent subject, the royal lion hunts. These were more in the nature of ceremonial combats than actual hunts: the animals were released from cages within a hollow square formed by troops with shields, for the king to kill. (Presumably, at a much earlier time, the hunting of lions in the field had been an important duty of Mesopotamian rulers as the "shepherds" of the communal flocks.) Here the Assyrian relief sculptor rises to his greatest heights; in figure 103, from the Palace of Ashurnasirpal II at Nimrud (Calah), the lion attacking the royal chariot from the rear is clearly the hero of the scene. Of magnificent strength and courage, the wounded animal seems to embody all the dramatic emotion that we miss in the pictorial accounts of war. The dying lion on the right is equally impressive in its agony. How differently the Egyptian artist (see fig. 85) had interpreted the same composition! We need only compare the horses—the Assyrian ones are less graceful but very much more energetic and alive as they flee from the attacking lion, their ears folded back in fear. The lion hunt reliefs from Nineveh, about two centuries later than those of Nimrud, are the finest of all. Despite the shallowness of the actual carving, the bodies have a greater sense of weight and volume because of the subtle gradations of the surface. Images such as the dying lioness (fig. 104) have an unforgettable tragic grandeur.

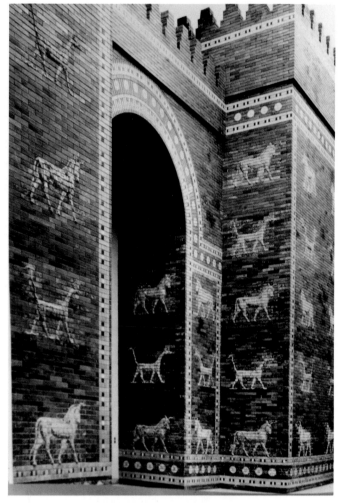

105. Ishtar Gate (restored) from Babylon, Dragon and Bull (see colorplate 10). State Museums, East Berlin

Neo-Babylonians

The Assyrian empire came to an end when Nineveh fell before the combined onslaught of Medes and Scythians from the east. At that time the commander of the Assyrian army in southern Mesopotamia made himself king of Babylon; under him and his successors the ancient city had a final brief flowering between 612 and 539 B.C., before it was conquered by the Persians. The best known of these Neo-Babylonian rulers was Nebuchadnezzar, the builder of the Tower of Babel. That famous structure represented only one part of a very large architectural complex comparable to the citadel of Sargon II at Dur Sharrukin.

Whereas the Assyrians had used carved stone slabs, the Neo-Babylonians (who were farther removed from the sources of such slabs) substituted baked and glazed brick. This technique, too, had been developed in Assyria, but now it was used on a far larger scale, both for surface ornament and for architectural reliefs. Its very distinctive effect becomes evident if we compare the gate of Sargon's citadel (fig. 101) with the Ishtar Gate of Nebuchadnezzar's sacred precinct in Babylon, which has been rebuilt from the thousands of individual glazed bricks that covered its surface (fig. 105, colorplate 10). The stately procession of bulls,

dragons, and other animals of molded brick within a framework of vividly colored ornamental bands has a grace and gaiety far removed from the ponderous guardian monsters of the Assyrians. Here, for the last time, we sense again that special genius of ancient Mesopotamian art for the portrayal of animals, which we noted in early dynastic times.

PERSIAN ART

Persia, the mountain-fringed high plateau to the east of Mesopotamia, takes its name from the people who occupied Babylon in 539 B.C. and became the heirs of what had been the Assyrian empire. Today the country is called Iran, its older and more suitable name, since the Persians, who put the area on the map of world history, were latecomers who had arrived on the scene only a few centuries before they began their epochal conquests. Inhabited continuously since prehistoric times, Iran always seems to have been a gateway for migratory tribes from the Asiatic steppes to the north as well as from India to the east. The new arrivals would settle down for a while, dominating or intermingling with the local popu-

106. Painted Beaker, from Susa. c. 5000–4000 B.C. Height 11¼". The Louvre, Paris

mountain goat) reduced to a few sweeping curves, so that the body of the animal becomes a mere appendage of the huge horns. The racing hounds above the ibex are little more than horizontal streaks, and on closer inspection the striations below the rim turn out to be long-necked birds. In the historic art of Sumer, this style soon gave way to an interest in the organic unity of animal bodies (see colorplate 9, figs. 92, 93), but in Iran it survived despite the powerful influence of Mesopotamia.

Several thousand years later, the style reappears in the small bronzes of the Luristan region, nomad's gear of a particularly resourceful kind. The pole top ornament (fig. 107) consists of a symmetrical pair of rearing ibexes, with vastly elongated necks and horns; originally, we suspect, they were pursued by a pair of lions, but the bodies of the latter have been absorbed into those of the ibexes, whose necks have been pulled out to dragon-like slenderness. By and for whom the Luristan bronzes were produced remains something of a mystery. There can be little doubt, however, that they are somehow linked with the animal-style metalwork of the Asiatic steppes, such as the splendid Scythian gold stag from southern Russia, which is only slightly later in date

lation, until they in turn were forced to move on—to Mesopotamia, to Asia Minor, to southern Russia—by the next wave of migrants. These movements form a shadowy area of historical knowledge; all available information is vague and uncertain. Since nomadic tribes leave no permanent monuments or written records, we can trace their wanderings only by a careful study of the objects they buried with their dead. Such objects, of wood, bone, or metal, represent a distinct kind of portable art which we call the nomad's gear: weapons, bridles for horses, buckles, fibulas and other articles of adornment, cups, bowls, etc. They have been found over a vast area, from Siberia to Central Europe, from Iran to Scandinavia. They have in common not only a jewel-like concentration of ornamental design but also a repertory of forms known as the "animal style." And one of the sources of this animal style appears to be ancient Iran.

ANIMAL STYLE. Its main feature, as the name suggests, is the decorative use of animal motifs, in a rather abstract and imaginative manner. We find its earliest ancestors on the prehistoric painted pottery of western Iran, such as the fine beaker in figure 106, which shows an ibex (a wild

107. Pole Top Ornament, from Luristan. 9th–7th century B.C. Bronze, height 7½". British Museum, London

108. *Stag*, from Kostromskaya. Scythian, 7th–6th century B.C. Chased gold, height c. 12". Hermitage Museum, Leningrad

(fig. 108). The animal's body here shows far less arbitrary distortion, and the smoothly curved sections divided by sharp ridges have no counterpart among Luristan bronzes, yet the way the antlers have been elaborated into an abstract openwork ornament betrays a similar feeling for form.

Whether or not this typically Scythian piece reflects Central Asiatic sources independent of the Iranian tradition, the Scythians surely learned a good deal from the bronze-casters of Luristan during their stay in Iran. They belonged to a group of nomadic Indo-European tribes, including the Medes and the Persians, that began to filter into the country soon after 1000 B.C. An alliance of Medes and Scythians, it will be recalled, had crushed Nineveh in 612 B.C. The Persians at that time were vassals of the Medes, but only sixty years later, under Cyrus the Great of the family of the Achaemenids, they reversed this situation.

Achaemenids

After conquering Babylon in 539 B.C., Cyrus assumed the title "King of Babylon" along with the ambitions of the Assyrian rulers. The empire he founded continued to expand under his successors; Egypt as well as Asia Minor fell to them, and Greece escaped the same fate only by the narrowest of margins. At its high tide, under Darius I and Xerxes (523–465 B.C.), the Persian empire was far larger than its Egyptian and Assyrian predecessors together. Moreover, this vast domain endured for two centuries—it was toppled by Alexander the Great in 331 B.C.—and during most of its life it was ruled both efficiently and humanely. For an obscure tribe of nomads to have achieved all this is little short of miraculous. Within a single generation, the Persians not only mastered the complex machinery of imperial administration but also evolved a monumental art of remarkable originality to express the grandeur of their rule.

Despite their genius for adaptation, the Persians retained their own religious belief drawn from the prophecies of Zoroaster; this was a faith based on the dualism of Good and Evil, embodied in Ahuramazda (Light) and Ahriman (Darkness). Since the cult of Ahuramazda centered on fire altars in the open air, the Persians had no religious architecture. Their palaces, on the other hand, were huge and impressive structures.

PERSEPOLIS. The most ambitious palace, at Persepolis, was begun by Darius I in 518 B.C.; its general layout—a vast number of rooms, halls, and courts assembled on a raised platform—recalls the royal residences of Assyria (see fig. 100), and Assyrian traditions are the strongest single element throughout. Yet they do not determine the character of the building, for they have been combined with influences from every corner of the empire in such a way that the result is a new, uniquely Persian style. Thus, at Persepolis columns are used on a grand scale. The Audience Hall of Darius, a room 250 feet square, had a wooden ceiling supported by 36 columns 40 feet tall, a few of which are still standing (fig. 109). Such a massing of columns suggests Egyptian architecture (compare fig. 76), and Egyptian influence does indeed appear in the ornamental detail of the bases and capitals, but the slender, fluted shaft of the Persepolis columns is derived from the Ionian Greeks in Asia Minor, who are known to have furnished artists to the Persian court. Entirely without precedent in earlier architecture is the strange "cradle" for the beams of the ceiling, composed of the front parts of two bulls or similar creatures, that crowns the Persepolis columns (fig. 110); while the animals themselves are of Assyrian origin, the way they are combined suggests nothing so much as an enormously enlarged version of the pole top ornaments of Luristan. This seems to be the only instance of Persian architects' drawing upon their native artistic heritage of nomad's gear (fig. 107).

The double stairway leading up to the Audience Hall is decorated with long rows of solemnly marching figures in low relief (fig. 109). Their repetitive, ceremonial character emphasizes a subservience to the architectural setting that is typical of all Persian sculpture. We find it even in scenes of special importance such as *Darius and Xerxes Giving Audience* (fig. 111); the expressive energy and narrative skill of Assyrian relief have been deliberately rejected.

PERSIAN STYLE. The style of these Persian carvings seems at first glance to be only a softer and more refined echo of the Mesopotamian tradition. Even here, however, we discover that the Assyrian-Babylonian heritage has been enriched in one important respect: there is no precedent in Near Eastern sculpture for the layers of overlapping garments, for the play of finely pleated folds such as we see in the Darius and Xerxes relief. Another surprising effect is the way the arms and shoulders of these figures press through the fabric of the draperies. These innovations stem from the Ionian Greeks, who had created them in the course of the sixth century B.C.

Persian art under the Achaemenids, then, is a remarkable synthesis of many diverse elements. Yet it lacked a capacity for growth; the style formulated under Darius I about 500 B.C. continued without significant change until the end of the empire. The main reason for this failure, it seems, was

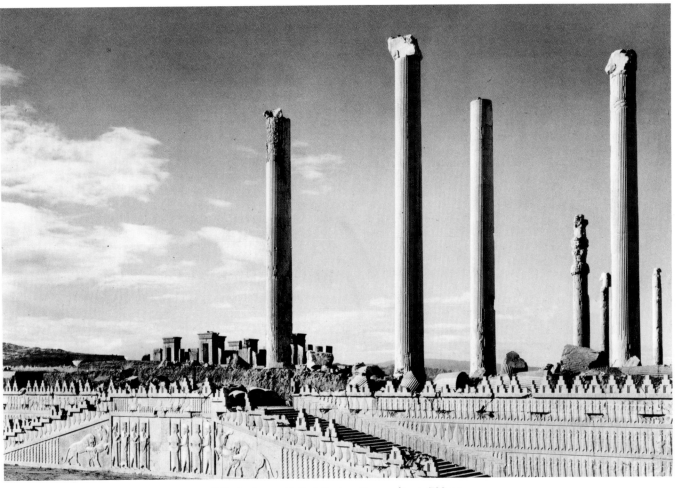

109. Audience Hall of Darius, Persepolis. c. 500 B.C.

110. Bull Capital (restored), from Persepolis.
The Oriental Institute, University of Chicago

the Persians' preoccupation with decorative effects regardless of scale, a carry-over from their nomadic past which they never sloughed off. There is no essential difference between the bull capital of figure 110 and the fine goldsmith's work (fig. 112), textiles, and other portable art of Achaemenid Persia. The latter tradition, unlike that of monumental architecture and sculpture, somehow managed to survive the more than 500 years during which the Persian empire was under Greek and Roman domination, so that it could flower once more when Persia regained its independence and seized Mesopotamia from the Romans.

Sassanians

The rulers who accomplished this feat were of the house of the Sassanians; their greatest figure, Shapur I, had the political and artistic ambitions of Darius. At Naksh-i-Rustam, the burial place of the Achaemenid kings not far from Persepolis, he commemorated his victory over two Roman emperors in an enormous relief hewn into the living rock (fig. 114). The formal source of this scene of triumph is a well-known composition in Roman sculpture—with the emperors now in the role of the humiliated barbarians—but the flattening of the volumes and the ornamental elaboration of

111. *Darius and Xerxes Giving Audience.* c. 490 B.C. Limestone, height 8′ 4″. Treasury, Persepolis

112. Gold Rhyton. Achaemenid, 5th–3rd century B.C.
Archaeological Museum, Teheran

the draperies indicate a revival of Persian qualities. The two elements hold each other in balance, and that is what makes the relief so strangely impressive. A blending of Roman and Near Eastern elements can also be observed in Shapur's palace at Ctesiphon, near Babylon, with its enormous brick-vaulted audience hall (fig. 113); the blind arcades of the façade again emphasize decorative surface pattern.

But monumental art under Sassanian rule proved as incapable of further evolution as it had under the Achaemenids. Metalwork and textiles, on the other hand, continued to flourish. The chief glory of Sassanian art—and a direct echo of the ornamental tradition reaching back more than a thousand years to the Luristan bronzes—is its woven silks, such as the splendid sample in figure 115. They were copiously exported both to Constantinople and to the Christian West, and we shall see that their wealth of colors and patterns exerted an important stimulus upon the art of the Middle Ages. And since their manufacture was resumed after the Sassanian realm fell to the Arabs in the mid-seventh century, they provided an essential treasury of design motifs for Islamic art as well.

113. Palace of Shapur I, Ctesiphon. 242–272 A.D.

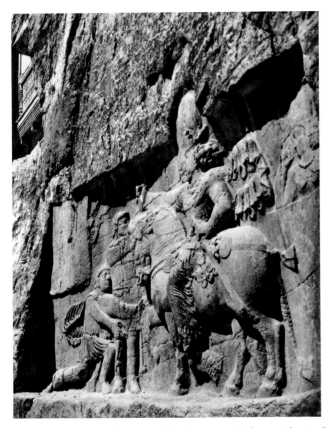

114. *Shapur I Triumphing over the Emperors Philippus the Arab and Valerian.* 260–272 A.D. Naksh-i-Rustam

115. Woven Silk. Sassanian, c. 6th century A.D.
National Museum, Florence (Franchetti Collection)

4
AEGEAN ART

If we sail from the Nile Delta northwestward across the Mediterranean, our first glimpse of Europe will be the eastern tip of Crete. Beyond it, we find a scattered group of small islands, the Cyclades, and, a little farther on, the mainland of Greece, facing the coast of Asia Minor across the Aegean Sea. To archaeologists, "Aegean" is not merely a geographical term; they have adopted it to designate the civilizations that flourished in this area during the third and second millenniums B.C., before the development of Greek civilization proper. There are three of these, closely interrelated yet distinct from each other: that of Crete, called Minoan after the legendary Cretan King Minos; that of the small islands north of Crete (Cycladic); and that of the Greek mainland (Helladic). Each of them has in turn been divided into three phases, Early, Middle, and Late, which correspond, very roughly, to the Old, Middle, and New Kingdom in Egypt. The most important remains, and the greatest artistic achievements, date from the latter part of the Middle phase and from the Late phase.

About a hundred years ago, Aegean civilization was known only from Homer's account of the Trojan War in the *Iliad* and from Greek legends centering on Crete. The earliest excavations (by Heinrich Schliemann during the 1870s in Asia Minor and Greece, by Sir Arthur Evans in Crete shortly before 1900) were undertaken to test the factual core of these tales. Since then, a great amount of fascinating material has been brought to light—far more than the literary sources would lead us to expect—but our knowledge of Aegean civilization even now is very much more limited than our knowledge of Egypt or the ancient Near East. Unfortunately, our reading of the archaeological evidence has so far received almost no aid at all from the written records of the Aegeans.

MINOAN SCRIPT AND LINEAR B. In Crete a system of writing was developed about 2000 B.C., and a late form of this Minoan script, called Linear B, which was in use about six centuries later both in Crete and on the Greek mainland, has recently been deciphered. The language of Linear B is Greek, yet this apparently was not the language for which Minoan script was used before the fifteenth century B.C., so that being able to read Linear B does not help us to understand the great mass of earlier Minoan inscriptions. Moreover, the Linear B texts are largely palace inventories and administrative records, which reveal very little about the history and religion of the people who composed them. We thus lack a great deal of the background knowledge necessary for an understanding of Aegean art. Its forms, although linked both to Egypt and the Near East on the one hand and to later Greek art on the other, are no mere transition between these two worlds; they have a haunting beauty of their own that belongs to neither. Among the many strange qualities of Aegean art, perhaps the most puzzling is its air of freshness and spontaneity, which makes us forget how little we know of its meaning.

CYCLADIC ART

The people who inhabited the Cycladic Islands between about 2600 and 1100 B.C. have left hardly any trace apart from their modest stone tombs. The things they buried with their dead are remarkable in one respect only: they include a large number of marble idols of a peculiarly impressive kind. Almost all of them represent a standing nude female figure with arms folded across the chest, presumably the mother and fertility goddess known to us from Asia Minor and the ancient Near East, whose ancestry reaches far back to the Old Stone Age (see figs. 19, 30, 31). They also share a distinctive shape, which at first glance recalls the angular, abstract qualities of primitive sculpture: the flat, wedge shape of the body, the strong, columnar neck, and the tilted, oval shield of the face, featureless except for the long, ridgelike nose. Within this narrowly defined and stable type, however, the Cycladic idols show wide variations in scale (from a few inches to lifesize) as well as form. The best of them, such as that in figure 116, have a disciplined refinement utterly beyond the range of Paleolithic or primitive art.

The longer we study this piece, the more we come to realize that its qualities can only be defined as "elegance" and "sophistication," however incongruous such terms may seem in our context. What an extraordinary feeling for the organic structure of the body there is in the delicate curves of the outline, in the hints of convexity marking the knees and abdomen. Even if we discount its deceptively modern look, the figure seems a bold departure from anything we have seen before. There is no dearth of earlier fertility idols, but almost all of them betray their descent from the bulbous, heavy-bodied "Venus" figurines of the Old Stone Age; in fact, the earliest Cycladic idols, too, were of that type. What, then, made the Cycladic sculptors suppress the traditional fertility aspects of their female idols until they arrived at the lithe, "girlish" ideal of figure 116? Was there perhaps a radical change in the meaning or the ritual purposes of these statues?

We cannot even venture a guess to explain the mystery. Suffice it to say that the Cycladic sculptors of the second millennium B.C. produced the oldest lifesize figures of the female nude we know, and that for many hundreds of years they were the only ones to do so. In Greek art, we find very few nude female statues until the middle of the fourth century B.C., when Praxiteles and others began to create cult images of the nude Venus. It can hardly be coincidence that the most famous of these Venuses were made for sanctuaries on the Aegean islands or the coast of Asia Minor, the region where the Cycladic idols had flourished.

MINOAN ART

Minoan civilization is by far the richest, as well as the strangest, of the Aegean world. What sets it apart, not only from Egypt and the Near East but also from the Classical civilization of Greece, is a lack of continuity that appears to have deeper causes than archaeological accident. In surveying the main achievements of Minoan art, we cannot really speak of growth or development; they appear and disappear

116. Idol from Amorgos.
2500–1100 B.C.
Marble, height 30".
Ashmolean Museum, Oxford

so abruptly that their fate must have been determined by external forces—sudden violent changes affecting the entire island—about which we know little or nothing. Yet the character of Minoan art, which is gay, even playful, and full of rhythmic motion, conveys no hint of such threats.

Architecture

The first of these unexpected shifts occurred about 2000 B.C. Until that time, during the eight centuries of the Early Minoan era, the Cretans had not advanced much beyond the Neolithic level of village life, even though they seem to have engaged in some overseas trade that brought them contact with Egypt. Then they created not only their own system of writing but an urban civilization as well, centering on several great palaces. At least three of them, Knossos, Phaistos, and Mallia, were built in short order. Hardly anything is left today of this sudden spurt of large-scale building activity, for the three palaces were all destroyed at the same time, about 1700 B.C.; after an interval of a hundred years, new and even larger structures began to appear on the same sites, only to suffer destruction, in their turn, about 1500 B.C.

It is these "new" palaces that are our main source of information on Minoan architecture. The one at Knossos, called the Palace of Minos, was the most ambitious, covering a vast territory and composed of so many rooms that it survived in Greek legend as the labyrinth of the Minotaur. It has been carefully excavated and partly restored. We cannot recapture the appearance of the building as a whole, but we can assume that the exterior probably did not look impressive compared with Assyrian or Persian palaces (see figs. 100, 109). There was no striving for unified, monumental effect. The individual units are generally rather small and the ceilings low (figs. 117, 118), so that even those parts of the structure that were several stories high could not have seemed very tall.

Nevertheless, the numerous porticoes, staircases, and air shafts must have given the palace a pleasantly open, airy quality; and some of the interiors, with their richly decorated walls, retain their atmosphere of intimate elegance to this very day. The masonry construction of Minoan palaces is excellent throughout, but the columns were always of wood. Although none has survived, their characteristic form (the smooth shaft tapering downward, topped by a wide, cushion-shaped capital) is known from representations in painting and sculpture. About the origins of this type of column, which in some contexts could also serve as a religious symbol, or about its possible links with Egyptian architecture, we can say nothing at all.

Who were the rulers that built these palaces? We do not know their names or deeds (except for the legendary Minos), but the archaeological evidence permits a few conjectures: they were not warrior princes, since no fortifications have been found anywhere in Minoan Crete and military subjects are almost unknown in Minoan art; nor is there any hint that they were sacred kings on the Egyptian or Mesopotamian model, although they may well have presided at religious festivals (the only parts of Minoan palaces that can be identified as places of worship are small chapels, suggesting that religious ceremonies took place out of doors). On the

117. Staircase, East Wing, Palace of Minos, Knossos, Crete. c. 1500 B.C.

other hand, the many storerooms, workshops, and "offices" at Knossos indicate that the palace was not only a royal residence but a great center of administrative and commercial activity. Since shipping and trade formed an important part of Minoan economic life (to judge from elaborate harbor installations and from Cretan export articles found in Egypt and elsewhere), perhaps the king should be viewed as the head of a merchant aristocracy.

Sculpture

The religious life of Minoan Crete is even harder to define than the political or social order. It centered on certain sacred places, such as caves or groves; and its chief deity (or deities?) was female, akin to the mother and fertility goddesses we have encountered before. Since the Minoans had no temples, we are not surprised to find that they lacked large cult statues as well, but even on a small scale religious subjects in Minoan art are few in number and of uncertain significance. Two terracotta statuettes of c. 1600 B.C. from Knossos may represent the goddess in one of her several identities; one of them (fig. 119) shows her with three long snakes wound around her arms, body, and headdress. The meaning would seem to be clear: snakes are associated with earth deities and male fertility in many ancient religions, just as the bared breasts of our statuette suggest female fertility.

But is she really a cult image? Her rigid, frontal stance would be equally fitting for a votive figure, and the snakes

118. The Queen's Megaron, Palace of Minos, Knossos, Crete

may represent a ritual of snake-handling rather than a divine attribute. Perhaps, then, our figure is a queen or priestess? She seems oddly lacking in awesomeness, and the emphasis on the costume endows her with a secular, "fashionable" air. Another paradox is the fact that Crete has few snakes, so that its snake cult was probably imported, not home-grown, yet no snake goddesses have so far been discovered outside Crete. Only the style of the statuette hints at a possible foreign source: the emphatically conical quality of the figure, the large eyes and heavy, arched eyebrows suggest a kinship—remote and indirect, perhaps through Asia Minor—with Mesopotamian art.

Paintings; Pottery; Reliefs

Our snake goddess dates from the beginning of the brief period, between 1600 and 1450 B.C., which produced almost everything we have of Minoan architecture, sculpture, and painting. After the catastrophe that had wiped out the earlier palaces, and a century of slow recovery, there was what seems to our eyes an explosive increase in wealth and an equally remarkable outpouring of creative energy.

The most surprising aspect of this sudden efflorescence, however, is its great achievement in painting. At the time of the earlier palaces, between 2000 and 1700 B.C., Crete had developed a type of pottery famous for its technical perfection and its dynamic, swirling ornament (fig. 120, colorplate 11), but in no way preparing us for the "naturalistic" murals

119. *Snake Goddess (Priestess?)*. c. 1600 B.C. Terracotta, height 13½". Museum, Heraklion, Crete

that covered the walls of the new palaces. Unfortunately, these paintings have survived only in small fragments, so that we hardly ever have a complete composition, let alone the design of an entire wall.

A great many of them were scenes from nature showing animals and birds among luxuriant vegetation, or the creatures of the sea. In the remarkable fragment in figure 121, we see a cat cautiously stalking a pheasant behind a bush. The flat forms, silhouetted against a background of solid color, recall Egyptian painting, and the acute observation of plants and animals also suggests Egyptian art. But if Minoan wall painting owes its origin to Egyptian influence, it betrays an attitude of mind, a sense of beauty, very different from that of the Nile valley: instead of permanence and stability, we find a passion for rhythmic, undulating movement, and the forms themselves have an oddly weightless quality—they seem to float, or sway, in a world without gravity, as if the scene took place under water.

Marine life (as seen in the fish and dolphin fresco in fig. 118) was a favorite subject of Minoan painting, and the marine feeling pervades everything else as well; we sense it even in the "Toreador Fresco," the largest and most dynamic Minoan mural recovered so far (fig. 122, colorplate 12); the darker patches are the original fragments on which the restoration is based). The conventional title should not mis-

121. *Cat Stalking a Pheasant,* mural fragment, Hagia Triada. c. 1600–1580 B.C. Height 21″. Museum, Heraklion, Crete

122. *"The Toreador Fresco"* (see colorplate 12). Museum, Heraklion, Crete

120. Beaked Jug (Kamares Style), from Phaistos (see colorplate 11). Museum, Heraklion, Crete

lead us: what we see here is not a bullfight but a ritual game in which the performers vault over the back of the animal. Two of the slim-waisted athletes are girls, differentiated (as in Egyptian art) mainly by their lighter skin color. That the bull was a sacred animal, and that bull-vaulting played an important role in Minoan religious life, is beyond doubt; scenes such as this still echo in the Greek legend of the youths and maidens sacrificed to the Minotaur. If we try, however, to "read" the fresco as a description of what actually went on during these performances, we find it strangely ambiguous. Do the three figures show successive phases of the same action? How did the youth in the center get onto the back of the bull, and in what direction is he moving? Scholars have even consulted rodeo experts without getting clear answers to these questions. All of which does not mean that the Minoan artist was deficient—it would be absurd to blame him for failing to accomplish what he never intended to do in the first place—but that fluid, effortless ease of movement was more important to him than factual precision or dramatic power. He has, as it were, idealized the ritual by stressing its harmonious, playful aspect to the point that the participants behave like dolphins gamboling in the sea.

The floating world of Minoan wall painting was an imaginative creation so rich and original that its influence can be felt throughout Minoan art during the era of the new palaces. In painted pottery, the abstract patterns of old (fig. 120, colorplate 11) gave way to a new repertory of designs drawn from plant and animal life. Some vessels are covered entirely with fish, shells, and octopuses, as if the ocean itself had been caught within them (fig. 123). Monumental sculpture, had there been any, might have retained its independence, but the small-scale works to which the Minoan sculptor was confined are often closely akin to the style of the murals; the splendidly observed mountain goat carved on a stone vase (fig. 124) leaps in the same "flying" movement as the bull of the "Toreador Fresco." These mountain goats, too, were sacred animals.

Even more vivid is the relief on the so-called Harvester Vase (fig. 125; the lower part is lost): a procession of slim, muscular men, nude to the waist, carrying long-handled implements that look like a combination of scythe and rake. A harvest festival? Quite probably, although here again the lively rhythm of the composition takes precedence over descriptive clarity. Our view of the scene includes three singers led by a fourth who is swinging a sistrum (a rattle of Egyptian origin); they are bellowing with all their might, especially the "choirmaster," whose chest is so distended that the ribs press through the skin. What makes the entire relief so remarkable—in fact, unique—is its emphasis on physical strain, its energetic, raucous gaiety, which combines sharp observation with a consciously humorous intent. How many works of this sort, we wonder, did Minoan art produce? Only once have we met anything at all like it: in the

124. *Leaping Mountain Goat*, on a vase from the Palace at Kato Zakro. c. 1500 B.C. Limestone (originally covered with gold foil), length of goat c. 4″. Museum, Heraklion, Crete

125. *The Harvester Vase* (detail), from Hagia Triada. c. 1550–1500 B.C. Steatite, width 4½″. Museum, Heraklion, Crete

relief of workmen carrying a beam (see fig. 83), carved almost two centuries later under the impact of the Akhenaten style. Is it possible that pieces similar to the Harvester Vase stimulated Egyptian artists during that brief but important period?

MYCENAEAN ART

Along the southeastern shores of the Greek mainland there were during Late Helladic times (c. 1600–1100 B.C.) a number of settlements that corresponded in many ways to those of Minoan Crete. They, too, were grouped around palaces. Their inhabitants have come to be called Mycenaeans, after Mycenae, the most important of these settlements. Since the works of art unearthed there by excavation often showed

123. "Octopus Vase," from Palaikastro, Crete. c. 1500 B.C. Height 11″. Museum, Heraklion, Crete

126. (*left*) Interior, Treasury of Atreus,
Mycenae, c. 1300–1250 B.C.

127. (*below*) Section, Treasury of Atreus

a strikingly Minoan character, the Mycenaeans were at first regarded as having come from Crete, but it is now agreed that they were the descendants of the earliest Greek tribes, who had entered the country soon after 2000 B.C.

TOMBS AND THEIR CONTENTS. For some 400 years these people had led an inconspicuous pastoral existence in their new homeland; their modest tombs have yielded only simple pottery and a few bronze weapons. Toward 1600 B.C., however, they suddenly began to bury their dead in deep shaft graves and, a little later, in conical stone chambers, known as beehive tombs. This development reached its height toward 1300 B.C. in such impressive structures as the one shown in figures 126 and 127, built of concentric layers of precisely cut stone blocks. Its discoverer thought it far too ambitious for a tomb and gave it the misleading name "The Treasury of Atreus." Burial places as elaborate as this can be matched only in Egypt during the same period.

The Treasury of Atreus had been robbed of its contents long ago, but other Mycenaean tombs were found intact, and what they yielded up caused even greater surprise: alongside the royal dead were placed masks of gold or silver, presumably to cover their faces. If so, these masks were similar in purpose (if not in style) to the masks found in Pharaonic tombs of the Middle and New Kingdoms (compare fig. 84, colorplate 8). There was considerable personal equipment—drinking vessels, jewelry, weapons—much of it gold and exquisite in workmanship. Some of these pieces, such as the magnificent gold vessel in the shape of a lion's head (fig. 128), show a boldly expressive style of smooth planes bounded by sharp ridges which suggests contact with the Near East, while others are so Minoan in flavor that they might be imports from Crete.

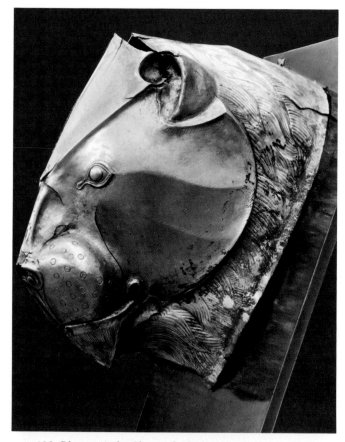

128. Rhyton in the Shape of a Lion's Head, from a shaft grave at Mycenae. c. 1550 B.C. Gold, height 8″.
National Museum, Athens

THE VAPHIO CUPS. Of the latter kind are the two famous gold cups from a tomb at Vaphio (figs. 129, 130); they must have been made about 1500 B.C., a few decades after the lion vessel, but where, for whom, and by whom? Here the problem "Minoan or Mycenaean?" becomes acute. The dispute is not as idle as it may seem, for it tests our ability to differentiate between the two neighboring cultures. It also forces us to consider every aspect of the cups: do we find anything in their style or content that is un-Minoan? Our first impulse, surely, is to note the similarity of the human figures to those on the Harvester Vase, and the similarity of the bulls to the animal in the "Toreador Fresco." On the other hand, we cannot overlook the fact that the men on the Vaphio cups are not engaged in the Cretan bull-vaulting game but in the far more mundane business of catching the animals on the range, a subject that does not occur in Minoan art, though we do find it in Mycenae. Once we realize this, we are also apt to notice that the design on the cups does not quite match the continuous rhythmic movement of Minoan compositions, and that the animals, for all their physical power, have the look of cattle rather than of sacred animals. It would seem, then, that the cups are a Mycenaean adaptation of Minoan forms, either by a mainland artist or by a Cretan working for Mycenaean patrons.

MYCENAE, CRETE, AND EGYPT. In the sixteenth century B.C., Mycenae thus presents a strange picture: what appears to be an Egyptian influence on burial customs is combined with a strong artistic influence from Crete and with an extraordinary material wealth as expressed in the lavish use of gold. Did the Mycenaeans perhaps conquer the Minoans, causing the destruction of the "new" palaces there about 1500 B.C.? This idea has now been discarded; the new palaces, it seems, were destroyed by a natural catastrophe (earthquakes and tidal waves following the eruption of a volcano). In any event, it does not account for the puzzling connection with Egypt.

What we need is a triangular explanation that involves the Mycenaeans with Crete as well as Egypt about a century before the destruction of the new palaces; and such a theory—fascinating and imaginative, if hard to confirm in detail—has been taking shape in recent years. It runs about as follows: between 1700 and 1580 B.C., the Egyptians were trying to rid themselves of the Hyksos, who had seized the Nile Delta (see page 64). For this they gained the aid of warriors from Mycenae, who returned home laden with gold (of which Egypt alone had an ample supply), and deeply impressed with Egyptian funerary customs. The Minoans, unmilitary but famous as sailors, ferried the Mycenaeans back and forth, so that they, too, had a new and closer contact with Egypt (which may help to account for their sudden prosperity toward 1600 B.C. as well as for the rapid development of naturalistic wall painting at that time). The close relations between Crete and Mycenae, once established, were to last a long time; toward 1400 B.C., when Linear B script began to appear, the Mycenaeans were the rulers of Crete, either by conquest or through dynastic marriage. In any event, their power rose as that of the Minoans declined; the great monuments of Mycenaean architecture were all built between 1400 and 1200 B.C.

ARCHITECTURE. Apart from such details as the shape of the columns or decorative motifs of various sorts, Mycenaean architecture owes little to the Minoan tradition. The palaces on the mainland were hilltop fortresses surrounded by defensive walls of huge stone blocks, a type of construction quite unknown in Crete but similar to the Hittite fortifications at Bogazköy (see fig. 99). The Lion Gate at Mycenae (fig. 131) is the most impressive remnant of these massive ramparts, which inspired such awe in the Greeks of later times that they were regarded as the work of the Cyclopes (a mythical race of one-eyed giants). Even the Treasury of Atreus, although built of smaller and more precisely shaped blocks, has a Cyclopean lintel (see fig. 126).

129, 130. *The Vaphio Cups*. c. 1500 B.C. Gold, height 3–3½″. National Museum, Athens

131. The Lion Gate, Mycenae, c. 1250 B.C.

Another aspect of the Lion Gate foreign to the Minoan tradition is the great stone relief over the doorway. The two lions flanking a symbolic Minoan column have the same grim, heraldic majesty as the golden lion's head we encountered in figure 128. Their function as guardians of the gate, their tense, muscular bodies, and their symmetrical design again suggest an influence from the ancient Near East. We may at this point recall the Trojan War, immortalized in Homer's *Iliad*, which brought the Mycenaeans to Asia Minor soon after 1200 B.C.; it seems likely, however, that they began to sally eastward across the Aegean, for trade or war, much earlier than that.

132. Plan of a Mycenean Megaron

133, 134. *Three Deities,* from Mycenae. c. 1500–1400 B.C. Ivory, height 3″. National Museum, Athens

The center of the palace, at Mycenae and other mainland sites, was the royal audience hall, called the megaron. Only its plan is known for certain: a large rectangular room with a round hearth in the middle and four columns to support the roof beams (fig. 132). It was entered through a deep porch with two columns, and an antechamber. This design is in essence no more than an enlarged version of the simple houses of earlier generations; its ancestry can be traced back to Middle Helladic times. There must have been a rich decorative scheme of wall paintings and ornamental carvings to stress its dignity as the king's abode.

SCULPTURE. No trace has been found of Mycenaean temple architecture—if it ever existed. The palaces did, however, include modest shrines, as in Crete. What gods were worshiped there is a matter of dispute; Mycenaean religion surely included Minoan elements but also influences from Asia Minor, as well as deities of Greek origin inherited from their own forebears. But gods have an odd way of merging or exchanging their identities, so that the religious images in Mycenaean art are extremely hard to interpret.

What, for instance, are we to make of the exquisite little ivory group (figs. 133, 134) unearthed at Mycenae in 1939? The style of the piece—its richly curved shapes and easy, flexible body movements—still echoes Minoan art, but the subject is strange indeed. Two kneeling women, closely united, tend a single child; whose is he? The natural interpretation would be to regard the now headless figure as the mother, since the child clings to her arm and turns toward her; the second woman, whose left hand rests on the other's shoulder, would then be the grandmother. Such three-generation family groups are a well-known subject in Christian art, in which we often find St. Anne, the Virgin Mary, and the Infant Christ combined in similar fashion.

It is the memory of these later works that colors our view of the Mycenaean ivory. Yet we search in vain for a subject in ancient religion that fits our reading of the group. On the other hand, there is a very widespread myth about the divine child (his name varies from place to place) who is abandoned by his mother and reared by nymphs, goddesses, or even animals. We are thus forced to conclude—rather reluctantly—that our ivory in all likelihood shows a motherless child god with his nurses. The real mystery, however, lies deeper; it is the tender play of gestures, the intimate human feeling, that binds the three figures together. Nowhere in the entire range of ancient art before the Greeks do we find gods—or men, for that matter—expressing affection with such warmth and eloquence.

Something quite basically new is reflected here, a familiar view of divine beings that makes even the Minoan snake goddess (fig. 119) seem awesome and remote. Was this change of attitude, and the ability to express it in art, a Mycenaean achievement? Or did they inherit it from the Minoans? However that may be, our ivory group opens up a dimension of experience that had never been accessible to Egypt or Mesopotamia.

5
GREEK ART

The works of art we have come to know so far are like fascinating strangers: we approach them fully aware of their alien background and of the "language difficulties" they present. If it turns out that, after all, we can understand something of what they have to say, we are surprised and grateful. As soon as we reach the Greeks, our attitude undergoes a change: they are not strangers but relatives, we feel, older members of our own family whom we recognize immediately. A Greek temple will remind us at a glance of the First National Bank around the corner, a Greek statue will bring to mind countless other statues we have seen somewhere, a Greek coin will make us want to reach for the small change in our own pockets. But this air of familiarity is not an unmixed blessing. We would do well to keep in mind that the continuous tradition which links us with the Greeks is a handicap as well as an advantage. If we are to get an unhampered view of Greek architecture, we must take care not to be swayed by our memories of the First National Bank, and in judging Greek sculpture we had better forget its latter-day descendants in the public park.

Another complication peculiar to the study of Greek art arises from the fact that we have three separate, and sometimes conflicting, sources of information on the subject. There are, first of all, the monuments themselves, a reliable but often woefully inadequate source. Then we have various copies made in Roman times which tell us something about

important Greek works that would otherwise be lost to us entirely. These copies, however, always pose a problem: some are of such high quality that we cannot be sure that they really *are* copies, others make us wonder how faithfully they follow their model (especially if we have several copies, all slightly different, of the same lost original).

Finally, there are the literary sources. The Greeks were the first people in history to write at length about their own artists, and their accounts were eagerly collected by the Romans, who handed them down to us. From them we learn what the Greeks themselves considered their most important achievements in architecture, sculpture, and painting. This written testimony has helped us to identify some celebrated artists and monuments, but much of it deals with works of which no visible trace remains today, while other works, which do survive and which strike us as among the greatest masterpieces of their time, are not mentioned at all. To reconcile the literary evidence with that of the copies and of the original monuments, and to weave these strands into a coherent picture of the development of Greek art, is a difficult task indeed, despite the vast amount of work that has been done since the beginnings of archaeological scholarship some two hundred years ago.

Who were the Greeks? We have met some of them before—the Mycenaeans, who had come to Greece about 2000 B.C. Other Greek-speaking tribes entered the peninsula from

Colorplate 10. NEO-BABYLONIAN. Ishtar Gate (restored), from Babylon (see page 80). About 575 B.C. Glazed brick. State Museums, East Berlin

Colorplate 11. (*left*) CRETAN. Beaked Jug (Kamares Style), from Phaistos (see page 89). About 1800 B.C. Height 10⅝″. Museum, Heraklion, Crete

Colorplate 12. (*above*) CRETAN. *"The Toreador Fresco"* (see page 90). About 1500 B.C. Height about 24½″ (including upper border). Museum, Heraklion, Crete

Colorplate 13. PSIAX. *Herakles Strangling the Nemean Lion*, detail of Attic
black-figured amphora, from Vulci (see page 110). About 525 B.C. Museo Civico, Brescia

Colorplate 14. THE FOUNDRY PAINTER. *Lapith and Centaur*, interior of an Attic
red-figured kylix (see page 110). About 490–480 B.C. Staatliche Antikensammlungen, Munich

Colorplate 15. GREEK. *Kore*, from Chios (?). About 520 B.C. (see page 114).
Marble, height 21⅞″. Acropolis Museum, Athens

Colorplate 16. THE ACHILLES PAINTER. White-ground lekythos with *Mistress and Maid* (see page 137). Attic, about 440–430 B.C. Height 16″. Staatliche Antikensammlungen, Munich

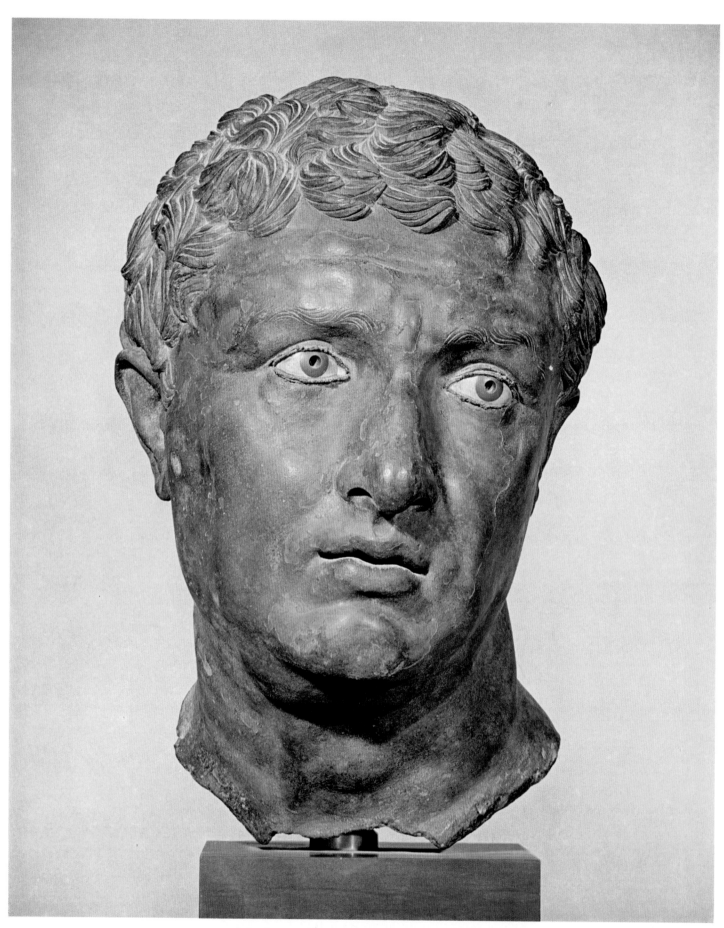

Colorplate 17. GREEK. *Portrait Head*, from Delos
(see page 147). About 80 B.C. Bronze, height 12¾". National Museum, Athens

the north, toward 1100 B.C., overwhelmed and absorbed the Mycenaean stock, and gradually spread to the Aegean islands and Asia Minor. It was these tribes who during the following centuries created the great civilization for which we now reserve the name Greek. We do not know how many separate tribal units there were in the beginning, but two main groups stand out: the Dorians, who settled mostly on the mainland, and the Ionians, who inhabited the Aegean islands and the nearby coast of Asia Minor and thus had closer contacts with the ancient Near East. Some centuries later, the Greeks also spread westward, founding important settlements in Sicily and southern Italy.

Despite a strong sense of kinship based on language and common beliefs, and expressed in such traditions as the four great Panhellenic (all-Greek) festivals, the Greeks remained divided into many small, independent city-states. The pattern may be viewed as an echo of age-old tribal loyalties, as an inheritance from the Mycenaeans, or as a response to the geography of Greece, whose mountain ranges, narrow valleys, and jagged coastline would have made political unification difficult in any event. Perhaps all of these factors reinforced one another. The intense rivalry of these states—military, political, and commercial—undoubtedly stimulated the growth of ideas and institutions.

Our own thinking about government continues to make use of a number of key terms of Greek origin which reflect the evolution of the city-state: *monarchy*, *aristocracy*, *tyranny*, *democracy*, and, most important, *politics* (derived from *polites*, the citizen of the *polis* or city-state). In the end, however, the Greeks paid dearly for their inability to broaden the concept of the state beyond the local limits of the *polis*. The Peloponnesian War (431–404 B.C.), in which the Spartans and their allies defeated the Athenians, was a catastrophe from which Greece never recovered.

135. Dipylon Vase. 8th century B.C. Height 42½".
The Metropolitan Museum of Art, New York (Rogers Fund)

Geometric Style

The formative phase of Greek civilization embraces about four hundred years, from c. 1100 to 700 B.C. Of the first three centuries of this period we know very little, but after about 800 B.C. the Greeks rapidly emerge into the full light of history. The earliest specific dates that have come down to us are from that time: 776 B.C., the founding of the Olympic Games and the starting point of Greek chronology, as well as several slightly later dates recording the foundation of various cities. That time also saw the full development of the oldest characteristically Greek style in the fine arts, the so-called Geometric. We know it only from painted pottery and small-scale sculpture (monumental architecture and sculpture in stone did not appear until the seventh century).

THE DIPYLON VASE. At first the pottery had been decorated only with abstract designs—triangles, checkers, concentric circles—but toward 800 B.C. human and animal figures began to appear within the geometric framework, and in the most mature examples these figures could form elaborate scenes. Our specimen (fig. 135), from the Dipylon cemetery in Athens, belongs to a group of very large vases that served as grave monuments; its bottom has holes

through which liquid offerings could filter down to the dead below. On the body of the vessel we see the deceased lying in state, flanked by figures with their arms raised in a gesture of mourning, and a funeral procession of chariots and warriors on foot.

The most remarkable thing about this scene is that it contains no reference to an afterlife; its purpose is purely commemorative. Here lies a worthy man, it tells us, who was mourned by many and had a splendid funeral. Did the Greeks, then, have no conception of a hereafter? They did, but the realm of the dead to them was a colorless, ill-defined region where the souls, or "shades," led a feeble and passive existence without making any demands upon the living. When Odysseus, in the Homeric poem, conjures up the shade of Achilles, all the dead hero can do is mourn his own demise: "Speak not conciliatorily of death, Odysseus. I'd rather serve on earth the poorest man . . . than lord it over all the wasted dead." If the Greeks nevertheless marked and tended their graves, and even poured libations over them, they did so in a spirit of pious remembrance, rather than to satisfy the needs of the dead. Clearly, they had refused to adopt the elaborate burial customs of the Mycenaeans (see page 92). Nor is the Geometric style an outgrowth of the Mycenaean tradition but a fresh—and in some respects quite primitive—start.

Given his limited repertory of shapes, the artist who painted our vase has achieved an astonishingly varied effect. The spacing of the bands, their width and density, show a rather subtle relationship to the structure of the vessel. His interest in representation, however, is as yet very limited: the figures or groups, repeated at regular intervals, are little more than another kind of ornament, part of the same over-all texture, so that their size varies in accordance with the area to be filled. Organic and geometric elements still coexist in the same field, and the distinction between them is often difficult: lozenges indicate legs, whether of a man, a chair, or a bier; circles with dots may or may not be human heads; and the chevrons, boxed triangles, and so on between the figures may be decorative or descriptive—we cannot tell.

Much the same could be said of figure 136, a shipwreck scene from another Geometric vase which makes an instructive contrast with the Minoan view of marine life (see fig. 123); if it were not for the fact that the boat is upside down and that the biggest fish has seized the head of one of the men, we would read the design simply as a pattern, rather than as a disaster at sea. And what of the swastikas? Are they ornamentalized starfish or abstract space fillers?

Geometric pottery has been found not only in Greece but in Italy and the Near East as well, a clear indication that Greek traders were well established throughout the eastern Mediterranean in the eighth century B.C. What is more, they had already adopted the Phoenician alphabet and reshaped it for their own use, as we know from the inscriptions on these same vases. The greatest Greek achievements of this era, however, are the two Homeric epics, the *Iliad* and the *Odyssey*. The scenes on Geometric vases contain barely a hint of the narrative power of these poems; if our knowledge of eighth-century Greece were based on the visual arts alone, we would inevitably think of it as a far simpler and more provincial society than the literary evidence suggests.

There is a paradox here that needs to be resolved. Perhaps, at this particular time, Greek civilization was so language-minded that painting and sculpture played a less important role than they were to assume in the following centuries. In that event, the Geometric style may well have been something of an anachronism in the eighth century, a

137. *The Blinding of Polyphemus* and *Gorgons* (Proto-Attic amphora). c. 675–650 B.C. Height 56". Museum, Eleusis

conservative tradition about to burst at the seams. In the shipwreck scene, its rigid order already seems in process of dissolution; representation and narrative demand greater scope than the style can provide. Toward 700 B.C., the dam finally bursts; new forms come flooding in, and Greek art enters another phase, which we call the Orientalizing style.

Orientalizing Style

As its name implies, the new style reflects powerful influences from Egypt and the Near East, stimulated by increasing trade with these regions. Between c. 725 and 650 B.C., Greek art absorbed a host of Oriental motifs and ideas, and was profoundly transformed in the process. The change becomes very evident if we compare the large amphora (a two-handled storage jar) from Eleusis (fig. 137) with the Dipylon vase of a hundred years earlier (fig. 135).

136. *Shipwreck*, drawing after a Geometric vase in the Museum at Ischia. 8th century B.C.

THE ELEUSIS AMPHORA. Geometric ornament has not disappeared from this vase altogether, but it is confined to the peripheral zones—the foot, the handles, and the lip; new, curvilinear motifs—such as spirals, interlacing bands, palmettes and rosettes—are conspicuous everywhere; on the shoulder of the vessel we see a frieze of fighting animals, derived from the repertory of Near Eastern art. The major areas, however, are given over to narrative, which has become the dominant element.

Narrative painting tapped a nearly inexhaustible source of subjects from Greek myths and legends. These tales were the result of mixing local Doric and Ionic deities and heroes into the pantheon of Olympian gods and Homeric sagas. They also represent a comprehensive attempt to understand the world. The Greeks grasped the internal meaning of events in terms of fate and human character rather than as the accidents of history, in which they had little interest before about 500 B.C. The main focus was on explaining why the legendary heroes of the past seemed incomparably greater than men of the present. Some were historical figures—Herakles, for example, was the king of Tiryns—but all were believed to be descendants of the gods, themselves often very human in behavior, who had had children with mortals. This lineage explained the hero's extraordinary powers.

Such an outlook also helps us to understand the strong appeal exerted on the Greek imagination by Oriental lions and monsters. These terrifying creatures embodied the unknown forces of life faced by the hero. This fascination is clearly seen on the Eleusis amphora. The figures have gained so much in size and descriptive precision that the decorative patterns scattered among them can no longer interfere with their actions; ornament of any sort now belongs to a separate and lesser realm, clearly distinguishable from that of representation.

As a result, the blinding of the giant Polyphemus by Odysseus and his companions—the scene on the neck of the amphora—is enacted with memorable directness and dramatic force. If these men lack the beauty we expect of epic heroes, their movements have an expressive vigor that makes them seem thoroughly alive. The slaying of another monstrous creature is depicted on the body of the vase, the main part of which has been badly damaged, so that only two figures have survived intact; they are Gorgons, the sisters of the snake-haired, terrible-faced Medusa whom Perseus killed with the aid of the gods. Even here we notice an interest in the articulation of the body far beyond the limits of the Geometric style.

The Eleusis vase belongs to a group called Proto-Attic, the ancestors of the great tradition of vase painting that was soon to develop in Attica, the region around Athens. A second family of Orientalizing vases is known as Proto-Corinthian, since it points toward the later pottery production of Corinth. These vessels, noted for their spirited animal motifs, show particularly close links with the Near East. Some of them, such as the perfume vase in figure 138, are molded in the shape of animals. The enchanting little owl, "streamlined" to fit the palm of a lady's hand and yet so animated in pose and expression, helps us to understand why Greek pottery came to be in demand throughout the Mediterranean world.

ARCHAIC VASE PAINTING

The Orientalizing phase of Greek art was a period of experiment and transition, in contrast to the stable and consistent Geometric style. Once the new elements from the East had been fully assimilated, however, there emerged another style, as well defined as the Geometric but infinitely greater in range: the Archaic, which lasted from the later seventh century to about 480 B.C., the time of the famous Greek victories over the Persians at Salamis and Plataea. During the Archaic period, we witness the unfolding of the artistic genius of Greece not only in vase painting but also in monumental architecture and sculpture. While Archaic art lacks the balance, the sense of perfection of the Classical style of the later fifth century, it has a freshness that gives it particularly strong appeal for the modern beholder. It is difficult to argue with those who regard it as the most vital phase in the development of Greek art.

Greek architecture and sculpture on a large scale must have begun to develop long before the mid-seventh century. Until that time, however, both were mainly of wood, and nothing of them has survived except the foundations of a few buildings. The desire to build and sculpt in stone, for the sake of permanence, was the most important new idea that entered Greece during the Orientalizing period. Moreover, the revolution in material and technique must have brought about decisive changes of style as well, so that we cannot safely reconstruct the appearance of the lost wooden temples or statues on the basis of later works. In vase painting, on the other hand, there was no such break in continuity. It thus seems best to deal with Archaic vases before we turn to the sculpture and architecture of the period.

138. Proto-Corinthian Perfume Vase, c. 650 B.C. Height 2″. The Louvre, Paris

139. *A Vase Painter and Assistants, Crowned by Athena and Victories* (Attic red-figured hydria, detail; composite photograph). c. 450 B.C. Private Collection

The significance of Archaic vase painting is in some ways completely unique. Decorated pottery, however great its value as an archaeologist's tool, rarely enters into the mainstream of the history of art; we think of it, in general, as a craft or industry. This remains true even of Minoan vases, despite their exceptional beauty and technical refinement, and the same may be said of the vast bulk of Greek pottery. Yet if we study such pieces as the Dipylon vase or the amphora from Eleusis, impressive not only by virtue of their sheer size but as vehicles of pictorial effort, we cannot escape the feeling that they are among the most ambitious works of art of their day.

There is no way to prove this, of course—far too much has been lost—but it seems obvious that these are objects of highly individual character, rather than routine ware produced in quantity according to set patterns. Archaic vases are generally a good deal smaller than their predecessors, since pottery vessels no longer served as grave monuments (which were now made of stone). Their painted decoration, however, shows a far greater emphasis on pictorial subjects (fig. 141, colorplate 13); scenes from mythology, legend, and everyday life appear in endless variety, and the artistic level is often very high indeed, especially among Athenian vases.

140. EXEKIAS. *Dionysus in a Boat*
(interior of an Attic black-figured kylix). c. 540 B.C.
Diameter 12″. Staatliche Antikensammlungen, Munich

141. PSIAX. *Herakles Strangling the Nemean Lion* (Attic black-figured amphora from Vulci; see color-plate 13). Height 19½". Museo Civico, Brescia

How greatly the Greeks themselves valued the beauty of these vessels is evident from figure 139, which shows Athena and two Victories bestowing wreaths on a vase painter and two male assistants, presumably because he was the winner of a contest. The scene also includes a female assistant (on the extreme right), the earliest depiction we know of a woman artist at work. She was, we may assume, a member of a family workshop. Unlike Sappho, the greatest of early Greek lyric poets, women artists in Greece never achieved individual fame; yet even the subordinate role played by our female vase painter must have been a significant step on the road to equality.

After the middle of the sixth century the finest vases frequently bear the signatures of the men who made them. This indicates not only that individual artists—potters as well as painters—took pride in their work, but also that they could become famous for their personal style. To us, such signatures in themselves do not mean a great deal; they are no more than convenient labels unless we know enough of an artist's work to gain some insight into his personality. And, remarkably enough, that is possible with a good many Archaic vase painters. Some of them have so distinctive a

style that their artistic "handwriting" can be recognized even without the aid of a signature; and in a few cases we are lucky enough to have dozens (in one instance, over 200) of vases by the same hand, so that we can trace one master's development over a considerable period. Archaic vase painting thus introduces us to the first clearly defined personalities in the entire history of art. For while it is true that signatures occur in Archaic sculpture and architecture as well, they have not helped us to identify the personalities of individual masters.

Archaic Greek painting was, of course, not confined to vases. There were murals and panels, too. Although nothing has survived of them except a few poorly preserved fragments, we can form a fair idea of what they looked like from the wall paintings in Etruscan tombs of the same period (see figs. 217, 218, and colorplate 18). How, we wonder, were these large-scale works related to the vase pictures? We do not know—but one thing seems certain: *all* Archaic painting was essentially drawing filled in with solid, flat color, and therefore murals could not have been very different in appearance from vase pictures.

According to the literary sources, Greek wall painting did not come into its own until after the Persian wars (c. 475–450 B.C.), through the gradual discovery of modeling and spatial depth. From that time on, vase painting became a lesser art, since depth and modeling were beyond its limited technical means; by the end of the fifth century, its decline was obvious. The great age of vase painting, then, was the Archaic era. Until about 475 B.C., good vase painters enjoyed as much prestige as other artists. Whether or not their work directly reflects the lost wall paintings, it deserves to be viewed as a major achievement in its own right.

BLACK-FIGURED STYLE. The difference between Orientalizing and Archaic vase painting is one of artistic discipline. In the amphora from Eleusis (fig. 137), the figures are shown partly as solid silhouettes, partly in outline, or as a combination of both. Toward the end of the seventh century, Attic vase painters resolved these inconsistencies by adopting the "black-figured" style, which means that the entire design is silhouetted in black against the reddish clay; internal details are scratched in with a needle, and white and purple may be added on top of the black to make certain areas stand out. The virtues of this procedure, which favors a decorative, two-dimensional effect, are apparent in figure 140, a kylix (drinking cup) of c. 540 B.C. by Exekias. The slender, sharp-edged forms have a lacelike delicacy, yet also resilience and strength, so that the composition adapts itself to the circular surface without becoming mere ornament. Dionysus reclines in his boat (the sail was once entirely white); it moves with the same ease as the dolphins, whose light forms are counterbalanced by the heavy clusters of grapes. But why is he at sea? What does the happy poetry of Exekias' image mean?

According to a Homeric hymn, the god of wine had once been abducted by pirates, whereupon he caused vines to grow all over the ship and frightened his captors until they jumped overboard and were turned into dolphins. We see him here on his return journey (an event to be gratefully recalled by every Greek drinker), accompanied by seven dolphins and seven bunches of grapes for good luck.

If the spare elegance of Exekias seems to retain something of the spirit of Geometric pottery (see fig. 136 for an instructive comparison), the work of the slightly younger Psiax seems more akin to the forceful Orientalizing style of the blinding of Polyphemus in the Eleusis amphora. The scene of Herakles killing the lion, on an amphora attributed to Psiax (fig. 141, colorplate 13), is all grimness and violence. The two heavy bodies are truly locked in combat, so that they almost grow together into a single, compact unit. Incised lines and subsidiary colors have been added with utmost economy in order to avoid breaking up the massive expanse of black. Yet Psiax succeeds to an extraordinary degree in conveying the three-dimensional quality of these figures; his knowledge of body structure, his ability to use foreshortening—note the way the abdomen and shoulders of Herakles are rendered!—seem little short of amazing when measured against anything we have seen before. Only in such details as the eye of Herakles do we still find the traditional combination of front and profile views.

RED-FIGURED STYLE. Psiax must have felt that the silhouette-like black-figured technique made the study of foreshortening unduly difficult, for in some of his vases he tried the reverse procedure, leaving the figures red and filling in the background. This red-figured technique gradually replaced the older method toward 500 B.C. Its advantages are

143. DOURIS. *Eos and Memnon*
(interior of an Attic red-figured kylix).
c. 490–480 B.C. Diameter 10½″. The Louvre, Paris

142. The Foundry Painter. *Lapith and Centaur* (interior of an
Attic red-figured kylix; see colorplate 14). Staatliche
Antikensammlungen, Munich

well shown in figure 142 and colorplate 14, a kylix of c. 490–480 B.C. by an unknown master nicknamed the "Foundry Painter." The details of the Lapith and Centaur are now freely drawn with the brush, rather than laboriously incised, so the artist depends far less on the profile view than before; instead, he exploits the internal lines of communication that permit him to show boldly foreshortened and overlapping limbs, precise details of costume (note the pleated skirt), and interesting facial expressions. He is so fascinated by all these new effects that he has made the figures as large as he possibly could. They almost seem to burst from their circular frame, and a piece of the Lapith's helmet has actually been cut off.

A similar striving for monumental effect, but with more harmonious results, may be seen in the *Eos and Memnon* by Douris (fig. 143), one of the masterpieces of late Archaic vase painting. It shows the goddess of dawn holding the body of her son, who had been killed and despoiled of his armor by Achilles. In this moving evocation of grief, Greek art touches a mood that seems strangely prophetic of the Christian *Pietà* (see fig. 468). Notable too is the expressive freedom of the draftsmanship; the lines are as flexible as if they had been done with a pen. Douris knows how to trace the contours of limbs beneath the drapery, how to contrast vigorous, dynamic outlines with thinner and more delicate secondary strokes, such as those indicating the anatomical details of Memnon's body. This vase also has a special interest because of its elaborate inscription, which includes the signatures of both painter and potter as well as a dedication ("Hermogenes is beautiful").

ARCHAIC SCULPTURE

The new motifs that distinguish the Orientalizing style from the Geometric—fighting animals, winged monsters, scenes of combat—had reached Greece mainly through the importation of ivory carvings and metalwork from Phoenicia or Syria which reflected Mesopotamian as well as Egyptian influences. Such objects have actually been found on Greek soil, so that we can regard this channel of transmission as well established. They do not help us, however, to explain the rise of monumental architecture and sculpture in stone about 650 B.C., which must have been based on acquaintance with Egyptian works that could be studied only on the spot. We know that small colonies of Greeks existed in Egypt at the time, but why, we wonder, did Greece suddenly develop a taste for monumentality, and how did her artists acquire so quickly the Egyptian mastery of stone carving? The mystery may never be cleared up, for the oldest surviving witnesses of Greek stone sculpture and architecture show that the Egyptian tradition had already been well assimilated and Hellenized, though their link with Egypt is still clearly visible.

Kouros and Kore

Let us consider two very early Greek statues, a female figure of c. 650–625 B.C. (fig. 144) and a nude youth of c. 600 B.C. (fig. 145), and compare them with their Egyptian predecessors (fig. 66). The similarities are certainly striking: we note the block-conscious, cubic character of all four statues, the

144. *Female Figure*, c. 650 B.C. Limestone, height 24½″. The Louvre, Paris

145. *Standing Youth (Kouros)*. c. 600 B.C. Marble, height 6′ 1½″. The Metropolitan Museum of Art, New York (Fletcher Fund, 1932)

slim, broad-shouldered silhouette of the male figures, the position of their arms, their clenched fists, the way they stand with the left leg forward, the emphatic rendering of the kneecaps. The formalized, wiglike treatment of the hair, the close-fitting garment of the female figure and her raised arm are further points of resemblance. Judged by Egyptian standards, the Archaic statues seem somewhat "primitive"—rigid, oversimplified, awkward, less close to nature. Whereas the Egyptian sculptor allows the legs and hips of the female figure to press through the skirt, the Greek shows a solid, undifferentiated mass from which only the toes protrude.

But the Greek statues also have virtues of their own that cannot be measured in Egyptian terms. First of all, they are truly free-standing—the earliest large stone images of the human form in the entire history of art of which this can be said. The Egyptian carver had never dared to liberate such figures completely from the stone; they remain immersed in it to some degree, as it were, so that the empty spaces between the legs and between the arms and the torso (or between two figures in a double statue, as in fig. 66) always remain partly filled. There are never any holes in Egyptian stone figures. In that sense, they do not rank as sculpture in the round but as an extreme case of high relief. The Greek carver, on the contrary, does not mind holes in the least; he separates the arms from the torso and the legs from each other (unless they are encased in a skirt), and goes to great lengths to cut away every bit of dead material (the only exceptions are the tiny bridges between the fists and the thighs of the nude youth). Apparently it is of the greatest importance to him that a statue consist only of stone that has representational meaning within an organic whole; the stone must be transformed, it cannot be permitted to remain inert, neutral matter.

This is not, we must insist, a question of technique but of artistic intention. The act of liberation achieved in our two figures endows them with a spirit basically different from that of any of the Egyptian statues. While the latter seem becalmed by a spell that has released them from every strain for all time to come, the Greek images are tense, full of hidden life. The direct stare of their huge eyes offers the most telling contrast to the gentle, faraway gaze of the Egyptian figures.

Whom do they represent? We call the female statues by the general name of Kore (Maiden), the male ones by that of Kouros (Youth)—noncommittal terms that gloss over the difficulty of identifying them further. Nor can we explain why the Kouros is always nude while the Kore is clothed. Whatever the reason, both types were produced in large numbers throughout the Archaic era, and their general outlines remained extraordinarily stable. Some are inscribed with the names of artists ("So-and-so made me") or with dedications to various deities. These, then, were votive offerings; but whether they represent the donor, the deity, or a divinely favored person such as a victor in athletic games remains uncertain in most cases. Others were placed on graves, yet they can be viewed as representations of the deceased only in the broadest (and completely impersonal) sense. This odd lack of differentiation seems part of the es-

146. *Kroisos (Kouros from Anavysos).* c. 525 B.C. Marble, height 6′ 4″. National Museum, Athens

sential character of these figures; they are neither gods nor men but something in between, an ideal of physical perfection and vitality shared by mortal and immortal alike, just as the heroes of the Homeric epics dwell in the realms of both history and mythology.

If the type of Kouros and Kore is narrowly circumscribed, its artistic interpretation shows the same inner dynamic we have traced in Archaic vase painting. The pace of this development becomes strikingly clear from a comparison of the Kouros of figure 145 with another carved some 75 years later (fig. 146) and identified by the inscription on its base as the funerary statue of Kroisos, who had died a hero's death in the front line of battle. Like all such figures, it was originally painted; traces of color can still be seen in the hair and the pupils of the eyes. Instead of the sharply contoured, abstract planes of the older statue, we now find swelling curves. The whole body displays a greater awareness of massive volumes, but also a new elasticity, and countless anatomical details are more functionally rendered than before. The style of the *Kroisos* thus corresponds exactly to that of Psiax's *Herakles* (colorplate 13); we witness the transition from black-figured to red-figured in sculptural terms.

There are numerous statues from the middle years of the sixth century marking previous way stations along the same road, such as the magnificent *Calf-Bearer* of c. 570 B.C. (fig. 147), a votive figure representing the donor with the sacrificial animal he is offering to Athena. Needless to say, it is not a portrait, any more than the *Kroisos* is, but it shows a type: the beard indicates a man of mature years. The *Calf-Bearer* originally had the Kouros standing pose (the legs are badly damaged), and the body conforms to the Kouros ideal of physical perfection; its vigorous, compact forms are emphasized, rather than obscured, by the thin cloak, which fits them like a second skin, detaching itself only momentarily at the elbows. The face, effectively framed by the soft curve of the animal, no longer has the masklike quality of the early Kouros; the features have, as it were, caught up with the rest of the body in that they, too, are permitted a gesture, a movement expressive of life: the lips are drawn up in a smile. We must be careful not to impute any psychological meaning to this "Archaic smile," for the same radiant expression occurs throughout sixth-century Greek sculpture (even on the face of the dead hero Kroisos). Only after 500 B.C. does it gradually fade out.

One of the most famous instances of this smile is the wonderful *Rampin Head* (fig. 148), which probably belonged to the body of a horseman. Slightly later than the *Calf-Bearer*, it shows the black-figured phase of Archaic sculpture at its highest stage of refinement. Hair and beard have the appearance of richly textured beaded embroidery that sets off the subtly accented planes of the face.

The Kore type is somewhat more variable than that of the Kouros, although it follows the same pattern of development. A clothed figure by definition, it poses a different problem—how to relate body and drapery. It is also likely to reflect changing habits or local differences of dress. Thus, the impressive statue in figure 149, carved about the same time as the *Calf-Bearer*, does not represent a more evolved stage of the Kore in figure 144 but an alternative approach to the same basic task. She was found in the Temple of Hera on the island of Samos, and may well have been an image of the goddess, because of her great size as well as her extraordinary dignity. If the earlier Kore echoes the planes of a rectangular slab, the "*Hera*" seems like a column come to life. Instead of clear-cut accents, such as the nipped-in waist in figure 144, we find here a smooth, continuous flow of lines uniting limbs and body. Yet the majestic effect of the statue depends not so much on its abstract quality as on the way the abstract form blossoms forth into the swelling softness of a living body. The great upward sweep of the lower third of the figure gradually subdivides to reveal several separate layers of garments, and its pace is slowed further (but never fully stopped) as it encounters the protruding shapes of

147. *Calf-Bearer* (upper portion). c. 570 B.C. Marble, height of entire statue 65″. Acropolis Museum, Athens

148. *The Rampin Head*. c. 560 B.C. Marble, height 11½″. The Louvre, Paris

arms, hips, and torso. In the end, the drapery, so completely architectonic up to the knee region, turns into a second skin, the kind we have seen in the *Calf-Bearer*.

The Kore of figure 150, in contrast, seems a linear descendant of our first Kore, even though she was carved a full century later. She, too, is blocklike rather than columnar, with a strongly accented waist. The simplicity of her garments, however, is new and sophisticated; the heavy cloth forms a distinct, separate layer over the body, covering but not concealing the solidly rounded shapes beneath. And the left hand, which originally was extended forward, proffering a votive gift of some sort, must have given the statue a spatial quality quite beyond the two earlier Kore figures we have discussed. Equally new is the more organic treatment of the hair, which falls over the shoulders in soft, curly strands, as compared with the massive, rigid wig in figure 144. Most

noteworthy of all, perhaps, is the full, round face with its enchantingly gay expression—a softer, more natural smile than any we have seen hitherto. Here, as in the *Kroisos*, we sense the approaching red-figured phase of Archaic art.

Our final Kore (fig. 151, colorplate 15), about a decade later, has none of the severity of figure 150, though both were found on the Acropolis of Athens. In many ways she seems more akin to the *Hera* from Samos: in fact, she probably came from Chios, another island of Ionian Greece. The architectural grandeur of her ancestress, though, has given way to an ornate, perhaps overly refined grace. The garments still loop around the body in soft diagonal curves, but the play of richly differentiated folds, pleats, and textures has almost become an end in itself. Color must have played a particularly important role in such works, and we are fortunate that so much of it survives in our example.

149. *"Hera,"* from Samos.
c. 570–560 B.C. Marble,
height 6' 4". The Louvre, Paris

150. *Kore in Dorian Peplos.*
c. 530 B.C. Marble, height 48".
Acropolis Museum, Athens

151. *Kore,* from Chios (?).
Acropolis Museum, Athens
(see colorplate 15)

152. (*above*) Central Portion of the West Pediment of the Temple
of Artemis at Corfu, c. 600–580 B.C. Limestone, height 9′ 2″.
Museum, Corfu

153. (*right*) Reconstruction Drawing of the West Front of the
Temple of Artemis at Corfu (after Rodenwaldt)

Architectural Sculpture

When the Greeks began to build their temples in stone, they
also fell heir to the age-old tradition of architectural sculpture. The Egyptians had been covering the walls (and even
the columns) of their buildings with reliefs since the time of
the Old Kingdom, but these carvings were so shallow (for
example, figs. 70, 83) that they left the continuity of the wall
surface undisturbed; they had no weight or volume of their
own, so that they were related to their architectural setting
only in the same limited sense as Egyptian wall paintings
(with which they were, in practice, interchangeable). This is
also true of the reliefs on Assyrian, Babylonian, and Persian
buildings (for example, figs. 103, 111). There existed, however, another kind of architectural sculpture in the ancient
Near East, originated, it seems, by the Hittites: the great
guardian monsters protruding from the blocks that framed
the gateways of fortresses or palaces (see figs. 99, 101). This
tradition must have inspired, although perhaps indirectly,
the carving over the Lion Gate at Mycenae (see fig. 131). We
must nevertheless note one important feature that distinguishes the Mycenaean guardian figures from their predecessors: although they are carved in high relief on a huge
slab, this slab is thin and light compared to the enormously
heavy, Cyclopean blocks around it. In building the gate, the
Mycenaean architect left an empty triangular space above
the lintel, for fear that the weight of the wall above would
crush it, and then filled the hole with the comparatively
lightweight relief panel. Here, then, we have a new kind of
architectural sculpture—a work integrated with the structure yet also a separate entity rather than a modified wall
surface or block.

TEMPLE OF ARTEMIS, CORFU. The Lion Gate relief is
indeed the direct ancestor of Greek architectural sculpture,
as will become evident when we compare it with the façade
of the early Archaic Temple of Artemis on the island of Corfu, erected soon after 600 B.C. (figs. 152, 153). Here again

the sculpture is confined to a zone that is framed by structural members but is itself structurally empty: the triangle between the horizontal ceiling and the sloping sides of the roof. This area, called the pediment, need not be filled in at all except to protect the wooden rafters behind it against moisture; it demands not a wall but merely a thin screen. And it is against this screen that the pedimental sculpture is displayed.

154. Reconstruction of the Façade of the Treasury of the Siphnians in the Sanctuary of Apollo at Delphi. Museum, Delphi

Technically, these carvings are in high relief, like the guardian lions at Mycenae. Characteristically enough, however, the bodies are strongly undercut, so as to detach them from the background. Even at this early stage of development, the Greek sculptor wanted to assert the independence of his figures from their architectural setting. The head of the central figure actually overlaps the frame. Who is this frightening creature? Not Artemis, surely, although the temple was dedicated to that goddess. As a matter of fact, we have met her before: she is a Gorgon, a descendant of those on the Eleusis amphora (fig. 137). Her purpose here was to serve as a guardian, along with the two huge lions, warding off evil from the temple and the sacred image of the goddess within. (The other pediment, of which only small fragments survive, had a similar figure.) She might be defined, therefore, as an extraordinarily monumental—and still rather frightening—hex sign. On her face, the Archaic smile appears as a hideous grin; and to emphasize further how alive and real she is, she has been represented running, or rather flying, in a pinwheel stance that conveys movement without locomotion.

The symmetrical, heraldic arrangement of the Gorgon and the two animals reflects an Oriental scheme which we know not only from the Lion Gate at Mycenae but from many earlier examples as well (see fig. 52, bottom center, and fig. 93, top). Because of its ornamental character, it fits the shape of the pediment to perfection. Yet the early Archaic designer was not content with that; he also wanted the pediment to contain narrative scenes; therefore he has added a number of smaller figures in the spaces left between or behind the huge main group. The design of the whole thus shows two conflicting purposes in uneasy balance. As we might expect, narrative will soon win out over heraldry.

Aside from the pediment, there were not many places that the Greeks deemed suitable for architectural sculpture. They might put free-standing figures—often of terracotta—above the ends and the center of the pediment, to break the

155. *Battle of the Gods and Giants*, from the north frieze of the Treasury of the Siphnians
c. 530 B.C. Marble, height 26". Museum, Delphi

severity of its outline. And they often placed reliefs in the zone immediately below the pediment. In Doric temples such as that at Corfu (fig. 153), this "frieze" consists of alternating triglyphs (blocks with three vertical markings) and metopes. The latter were originally the empty spaces between the ends of the ceiling beams; hence they, like the pediment, could be filled in with sculpture. In Ionic architecture, the triglyphs were omitted, and the frieze became what the term usually conveys to us, a continuous band of painted or sculptured decoration. The Ionians would also sometimes elaborate the columns of a porch into female statues—not a very surprising development in view of the columnar quality of the *Hera* from Samos (fig. 149).

SIPHNIAN TREASURY, DELPHI. All these possibilities are combined in the Treasury (a miniature temple for storing votive gifts) erected at Delphi shortly before 525 B.C. by the inhabitants of the Ionian island Siphnos. Although the building itself is not standing any longer, it has been convincingly reconstructed on the basis of the preserved fragments (fig. 154). Of its lavish sculptural décor, the most impressive part is the splendid frieze. The detail reproduced here (fig. 155) shows part of the battle of the Greek gods against the giants: on the extreme left, two lions (who pull the chariot of Cybele) are tearing apart an anguished giant; in front of them, Apollo and Artemis advance together, shooting their arrows; a dead giant, despoiled of his armor, lies at their feet, while three others enter from the right.

The high relief, with its deep undercutting, recalls the Corfu pediment, but the Siphnian sculptor has taken full advantage of the spatial possibilities offered by this technique. He uses the projecting ledge at the bottom of the frieze as a stage on which he can place his figures in depth. The arms and legs of those nearest the beholder are carved completely in the round; in the second and third layer, the forms become shallower, yet even those farthest removed from us are never permitted to merge with the background. The result is a limited and condensed but very convincing space that permits a dramatic relationship between the figures such as we have never seen before in narrative reliefs. Any comparison with older examples (such as figs. 71, 102, 125, 129) will show us that Archaic art has indeed conquered a new dimension here, not only in the physical but also in the expressive sense.

TEMPLE AT AEGINA. Meanwhile, in pedimental sculpture, relief has been abandoned altogether. Instead, we find separate statues placed side by side in complex dramatic sequences designed to fit the triangular frame. The most ambitious ensemble of this kind, that of the east pediment of the temple at Aegina, was created about 490 B.C., and thus brings us to the final stage in the evolution of Archaic sculpture. The figures were found in pieces on the ground and are now in the Glyptothek in Munich, stripped of their nineteenth-century restorations. The position of each within the pediment, however, can be determined almost exactly, since

156. Reconstruction Drawing of the East Pediment of the Temple at Aegina (after Furtwängler)

157. *Dying Warrior*, from the east pediment of the Temple at Aegina. c. 490 B.C. Marble, length 72″. Glyptothek, Munich

their height (but not their scale) varies with the sloping sides of the triangle (fig. 156). The center is accented by the standing goddess Athena, who calmly presides, as it were, over the battle between Greeks and Trojans that rages to either side of her in symmetrically diminishing fashion.

The correspondence in the poses of the fighters on the two halves of the pediment makes for a balanced and orderly design, yet it also forces us to see the statues as elements in an ornamental pattern and thus robs them of their individuality to some extent. They speak most strongly to us when viewed one by one. Among the most impressive are the fallen warrior from the left-hand corner (fig. 157), and the kneeling Herakles—who once held a bronze bow—from the right-hand half (fig. 158); both are lean, muscular figures whose bodies seem marvelously functional and organic. That in itself, however, does not explain their great beauty, much as we may admire the artist's command of the human form in action. What really moves us is their nobility of spirit, whether in the agony of dying or in the act of killing. These men, we sense, are suffering—or carrying out—what fate has decreed, with tremendous dignity and resolve. And this communicates itself to us in the very feel of the magnificently firm shapes of which they are composed.

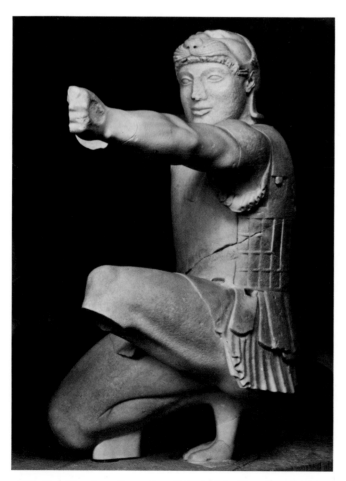

158. *Herakles*, from the east pediment of the Temple at Aegina, c. 490 B.C. Marble, height 31″. Glyptothek, Munich

ARCHITECTURE
Orders and Plans

In architecture the Greek achievement has been identified since ancient Roman times with the creation of the three classical architectural orders, Doric, Ionic, and Corinthian. Actually, there are only two, the Corinthian being a variant of the Ionic. The Doric (so named because its home is the Greek mainland) may well claim to be the basic order, since it is older and more sharply defined than the Ionic, which developed on the Aegean islands and the coast of Asia Minor.

What do we mean by "architectural order"? By common agreement, the term is used for Greek architecture only (and its descendants); and rightly so, for none of the other architectural systems known to us produced anything like it. Perhaps the simplest way to make clear the unique character of the Greek orders is this: there is no such thing as "the Egyptian temple" or "the Gothic church"—the individual buildings, however much they may have in common, are so varied that we cannot distill a generalized type from them—while "the Doric temple" is a real entity that inevitably forms in our minds as we examine the monuments themselves. We must be careful, of course, not to think of this abstraction as an ideal that permits us to measure the degree of perfection of any given Doric temple; it simply means that the elements of which a Doric temple is composed are extraordinarily constant in number, in kind, and in their relation to one another. As a result of this narrowly circumscribed repertory of forms, Doric temples all belong to the same clearly recognizable family, just as the Kouros statues do; like the Kouros statues, they show an internal consistency, a mutual adjustment of parts, that gives them a unique quality of wholeness and organic unity.

DORIC ORDER. The term Doric order refers to the standard parts, and their sequence, constituting the exterior of any Doric temple. Its general outlines are already familiar to us from the façade of the Temple of Artemis at Corfu (fig. 153): the diagram in figure 159 shows it in detail, along with names of all the parts. To the nonspecialist, the detailed terminology may seem something of a nuisance, yet a good many of these terms have become part of our general architectural vocabulary, to remind us of the fact that analytical thinking, in architecture as in countless other fields, originated with the Greeks. Let us first look at the three main divisions: the stepped platform, the columns, and the entablature (which includes everything that rests on the columns). The Doric column consists of: the shaft, marked by shallow vertical grooves known as flutes; the capital, which is made up of the flaring, cushion-like echinus, and a square tablet called the abacus. The entablature is the most complex of the three major units; it is subdivided into the architrave (a series of stone blocks directly supported by the columns), the frieze with its triglyphs and metopes, and the projecting cornice. On the long sides of the temple, the cornice is horizontal, while on the short sides (or façades), it is split open in such a way as to enclose the pediment between its upper and lower parts.

159. The Doric and Ionic Orders (after Grinnell)

160. Ground Plan of a Typical Greek Temple (after Grinnell)

The entire structure is built of stone blocks fitted together without mortar; they had to be shaped with extreme precision to achieve smooth joints. Where necessary, they were fastened together by means of metal dowels or cramps. Columns, with very rare exceptions, are composed of sections, called drums (clearly visible in fig. 162). The roof consisted of terracotta tiles supported by wooden rafters, and wooden beams were used for the ceiling; thus the threat of fire was constant.

TEMPLE PLANS. The plans of Greek temples are not directly linked to the orders (which, as we have seen, concern the elevation only). They may vary according to the size of the building or regional preferences, but their basic features are so much alike that it is useful to study them from a generalized "typical" plan (fig. 160). The nucleus is the cella or

naos (the room in which the image of the deity is placed), and the porch (pronaos) with its two columns flanked by pilasters (antae). The Siphnian Treasury shows this minimal plan (see fig. 155). Often we find a second porch added behind the cella, to make the design more symmetrical. In the larger temples, this central unit is surrounded by a colonnade, called the peristyle, and the structure is then known as peripteral. The very largest temples of Ionian Greece may even have a double colonnade.

Doric Temples

How did the Doric originate? What factors shaped the rigid and precise vocabulary of the Doric order? This is an important and fascinating problem, which has occupied archaeologists for many years but which even now can be answered only in part, for we have hardly any remains from the time when the system was still in process of formation. The earliest stone temples known to us, such as that of Artemis at Corfu, show that the essential features of the Doric order were already well established soon after 600 B.C. How these features developed, individually and in combination, why they congealed into a system as rapidly as they seem to have done, remains a puzzle to which we have few reliable clues.

The early Greek builders in stone apparently drew upon three distinct sources of inspiration: Egypt, Mycenae, and pre-Archaic Greek architecture in wood and mud brick. The Mycenaean contribution is the most tangible, although probably not the most important, of these. The central unit of the Greek temple, the cella and pronaos, clearly derives from the megaron (see fig. 132), either through a continuous tradition or by way of revival. There is something oddly symbolic about the fact that the Mycenaean royal hall should have been converted into the dwelling place of the Greek gods; for the entire Mycenaean era had become part of Greek mythology, as attested by the Homeric epics, and the walls of the Mycenaean fortresses were believed to be the work of mythical giants, the Cyclopes. The religious awe the Greeks felt before these remains also helps us to understand the relationship between the Lion Gate relief at Mycenae and the sculptured pediments on Doric temples. Finally, the flaring, cushion-like capital of the Minoan-Mycenaean column is a good deal closer to the Doric echinus and abacus than is any Egyptian capital. The shaft of the Doric column, on the other hand, tapers upward, not downward as does the Minoan-Mycenaean column, and this definitely points to Egyptian influence.

Perhaps we will recall now—with some surprise—the fluted columns (or rather half-columns) in the funerary district of Zoser at Saqqara (see fig. 57), which had approximated the Doric shaft more than 2,000 years before its appearance in Greece. Moreover, the very notion that temples ought to be built of stone, and that they required large numbers of columns, must have come from Egypt. It is true, of course, that the Egyptian temple is designed to be experienced from the inside, while the Greek temple is arranged so that the impressive exterior matters most (few were allowed to enter the dimly lit cella, and religious ceremonies usually took place at altars erected out of doors, with the temple façade as a backdrop). But might a peripteral temple not be interpreted as the columned court of an Egyptian sanctuary turned inside out? The Greeks also must have acquired much of their stone-cutting and masonry techniques from the Egyptians, along with architectural ornament and the knowledge of geometry they needed in order to lay out their temples and to fit the parts together. Yet we cannot say just how they went about all this, or exactly what they took over, technically and artistically, although there can be little doubt that they owed more to the Egyptians than to the Minoans or the Mycenaeans.

FORM FOLLOWS FUNCTION? The problem becomes acute when we consider a third factor: to what extent can the Doric order be understood as a reflection of wooden structures? Those historians of architecture who believe that form follows function—that an architectural form will inevitably reflect the purpose for which it was devised—have pursued this line of approach at great length, especially in trying to explain the details of the entablature. Up to a point, their arguments carry conviction; it seems plausible to assume that at one time the triglyphs did mask the ends of wooden beams, and that the droplike shapes below called guttae (see fig. 159) are the descendants of wooden pegs. The peculiar vertical subdivisions of the triglyphs are perhaps a bit more difficult to accept as an echo of three half-round logs. And when we come to the flutings of the column, our doubts continue to rise: were they really devel-

oped from adz marks on a tree trunk, or did the Greeks take them over ready-made from the "proto-Doric" stone columns of Egypt?

As a further test of the functional theory, we would have to ask how the Egyptians came to put flutes in their columns. They, too, after all, had once had to translate architectural forms from impermanent materials into stone. Perhaps it was they who turned adz marks into flutes? But the predynastic Egyptians had so little timber that they seem to have used it only for ceilings; the rest of their buildings consisted of mud brick, fortified by bundles of reeds. And since the proto-Doric columns at Saqqara are not free-standing but are attached to walls, their flutings might represent a sort of abstract echo of bundles of reeds (there are also columns at Saqqara with convex rather than concave flutes that come a good deal closer to the notion of a bundle of thin staves). On the other hand, the Egyptians may have developed the habit of fluting without reference to any earlier building techniques at all; perhaps they found it an effective way to disguise the horizontal joints between the drums and to stress the continuity of the shaft as a vertical unit. Even the Greeks did not flute the shafts of their columns drum by drum, but waited until the entire column was assembled and in position. Be that as it may, fluting certainly enhances the expressive character of the column: a fluted shaft looks stronger, more energetic and resilient, than a smooth one; and this, rather than its manner of origin, accounts for the persistence of the habit.

Why then did we enter at such length into an argument that seems at best inconclusive? Mainly in order to suggest the complexity—and the limitations—of the technological approach to problems of architectural form. The question, always a thorny one, of how far stylistic features can be explained on a functional basis will face us again and again. Obviously, the history of architecture cannot be fully understood if we view it only as an evolution of style in the abstract, without considering the actual purposes of building or its technological basis. But we must likewise be prepared to accept the purely aesthetic impulse as a motivating force. At the very start, Doric architects certainly imitated in stone some features of wooden temples, if only because these features were deemed necessary in order to identify a building as a temple. When they enshrined them in the Doric order, however, they did not do so from blind conservatism or force of habit, but because the wooden forms had by now been so thoroughly transformed that they were an organic part of the stone structure.

PAESTUM. We must confront the problem of function once more when we consider the best-preserved sixth-century Doric temple, the so-called Basilica at Paestum in southern Italy (fig. 161, right; fig. 162), in relation to its neighbor, the so-called Temple of Poseidon (fig. 161, left), which was built almost a century later. Both are Doric, but we at once note striking differences in their proportions. The "Basilica" seems low and sprawling (and not only because so much of the entablature is missing), while the "Temple of Poseidon" looks tall and compact. Even the columns themselves are different: those of the older temple taper far more

161. The "Temple of Poseidon" (c. 460 B.C.) and the "Basilica" (c. 550 B.C.), Paestum, Italy

162. Corner of the "Basilica," Paestum. c. 550 B.C.

emphatically, their capitals are larger and more flaring. Why the difference?

The peculiar shape of the columns of the "Basilica" (peculiar, that is, compared to fifth-century Doric) has been explained as being due to overcompensation: the architect, not yet fully familiar with the properties of stone as compared with wood, exaggerated the taper of the shaft for greater stability and enlarged the capitals so as to narrow the gaps to be spanned by the blocks of the architrave. Maybe so—but if we accept this interpretation in itself as sufficient to account for the design of these Archaic columns, do we not judge them by the standards of a later age? To label them simply "primitive," or awkward, would be to disregard the particular expressive effect that is theirs—and theirs alone.

The "Basilica's" columns seem to be more burdened by their load than those of the "Temple of Poseidon," so that the contrast between the supporting and the supported members of the order is dramatized rather than harmoniously balanced, as in the later building. Various factors contribute to this impression; the echinus of the "Basilica's" capitals is not only larger than its counterpart in the "Temple of Poseidon," it seems more elastic and hence more distended by the weight it carries, almost as if it were made of rubber. And the shafts not only show a more pronounced taper but also a particularly strong bulge or curve along the line of taper, so that they, too, convey a sense of elasticty and compression compared with the rigidly geometric blocks of the entablature. (This curve, called "entasis," is a basic feature of the Doric

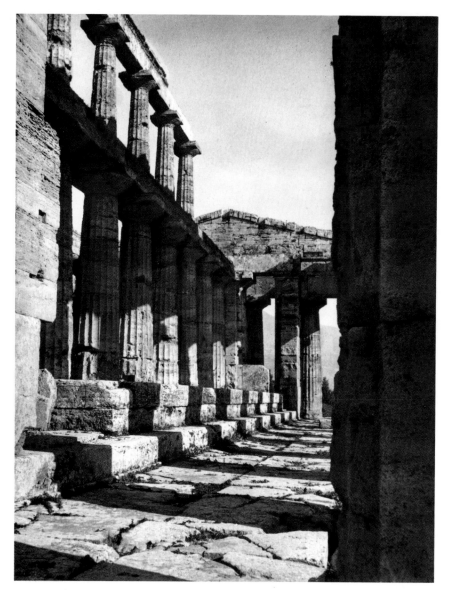

163. Interior, "Temple of Poseidon," Paestum. c. 460 B.C.

164, 165. Transverse Section and Plan
of the "Temple of Poseidon"
(after Hodge)

column; although it may be very slight, it endows the shaft with a "muscular" quality quite unknown in Egyptian or Minoan-Mycenaean columns.)

The "Temple of Poseidon" (figs. 161, 163–65)—it was probably dedicated to Hera—is among the best preserved of all Doric sanctuaries. Begun c. 475 B.C. and finished fifteen years later, it reflects the plan of the temple at Aegina. Of special interest are the interior supports of the cella ceiling (figs. 163–64), two rows of columns, each supporting a smaller set of columns in a way that makes the tapering seem continuous despite the architrave in between. Such two-story interiors had become a practical necessity for the cellas of the larger Doric temples of the fifth century.

ATHENS AND THE PARTHENON. In 480 B.C., shortly before their defeat, the Persians had destroyed the temple and statues on the Acropolis, the sacred hill above Athens

which had been a fortified site since Mycenaean times. (For modern archaeologists, this disaster has turned out to be a blessing in disguise, since the debris, which was subsequently used as fill, has yielded many fine Archaic pieces, such as those in figures 147, 148, 150, 151, and colorplate 15, that would hardly have survived otherwise.) The rebuilding of the Acropolis under the leadership of Pericles during the later fifth century, when Athens was at the height of her power, was the most ambitious enterprise in the history of Greek architecture, as well as its artistic climax. Individually and collectively, these structures represent the Classical phase of Greek art in full maturity.

The greatest temple, and the only one to be completed before the Peloponnesian War (431–404 B.C.), is the Parthenon (figs. 166, 167), dedicated to the virginal Athena, the patron deity in whose honor Athens was named. Built of gleaming white marble on the most prominent site along the southern

166. ICTINUS and CALLICRATES. The Parthenon (view from the west). 448–432 B.C. Acropolis, Athens

167. Frieze above the Western Entrance of the Cella of the Parthenon (see also fig. 188)

flank of the Acropolis, it dominates the entire city and the surrounding countryside, a brilliant landmark against the backdrop of mountains to the north of it. The history of the Parthenon is as extraordinary as its artistic significance—it is the only sanctuary we know that has served four different faiths in succession. The architects Ictinus and Callicrates erected it in 448–432 B.C., an amazingly brief span of time for a project of this size. In order to meet the huge expense of building the largest and most lavish temple on the Greek mainland, Pericles delved into funds collected from states allied with Athens for mutual defense against the Persians. He may have felt that the danger was no longer a real one, and that Athens, the chief victim and victor at the climax of the Persian War in 480–478 B.C., was justified in using the money to rebuild what the Persians had destroyed. His act did weaken the position of Athens, however (Thucydides openly reproached him for adorning the city "like a harlot with precious stones, statues and temples costing a thousand talents"), and contributed to the disastrous outcome of the Peloponnesian War. In Christian times, the Virgin Mary displaced the virginal Athena; the Parthenon became first a Byzantine church, then a Catholic cathedral; finally, under the Turks, it was a mosque. It has been a ruin since 1687, when a store of gunpowder the Turks had put into the cella exploded during a siege. Much of the sculpture was removed during the years 1801–1803 by Lord Elgin. These are today the greatest treasure of the British Museum.

As the perfect embodiment of Classical Doric architecture, the Parthenon makes an instructive contrast with the "Temple of Poseidon" (fig. 161). Despite its greater size, it seems far less massive. Rather, the dominant impression it creates is one of festive, balanced grace, within the austere scheme of the Doric order. This has been achieved by a general lightening and readjustment of the proportions: the entablature is lower in relation to its width and to the height of the columns; the cornice projects less; and the columns themselves are a good deal more slender, their tapering and entasis less pronounced and the capitals smaller and less flaring; yet the spacing of the columns has become wider. We might say that the load carried by the columns has decreased, and as a consequence the supports can fulfill their task with a new sense of ease.

"REFINEMENTS." These so-called refinements, intentional departures from the strict geometric regularity of the design for aesthetic reasons, are another feature of the Classical Doric style that can be observed in the Parthenon better than anywhere else. Thus the stepped platform and the entablature are not absolutely straight but slightly buckled, so that the center is a bit higher than the ends; the columns lean inward; and the interval between the corner column and its neighbors is smaller than the standard interval adopted for the colonnade as a whole.

A great deal has been written about these deviations from mechanical exactitude. That they are planned rather than accidental is beyond doubt, but why did the architects go to the enormous trouble of carrying them through? (Every capital of the colonnade is slightly distorted to fit the curving architrave!) They used to be regarded as optical corrections designed to produce the illusion of absolutely straight horizontals and verticals. Unfortunately, however, this functional explanation does not work: if it did, we should be unable to perceive the deviations except by careful measurement; yet the fact is that, though unobtrusive, they are visible to the naked eye, even in photographs such as our figure 166. Moreover, in temples that do not have these refinements, the columns do not give the appearance of leaning outward, nor do the horizontal lines look "dished." Plainly, then, the deviations were built into the Parthenon because they were thought to add to its beauty; they are a positive element that is meant to be noticed. And they do indeed contribute—in ways that are hard to define—to the integral, harmonious quality of the structure.

The cella of the Parthenon (see plan, fig. 168) is unusually wide and somewhat shorter than in other temples, so as to accommodate a second room behind it. The pronaos and its counterpart at the western end have almost disappeared, but there is an extra row of columns in front of either entrance. The architrave above these columns is more Ionic than Doric, since it has no triglyphs and metopes but a continuous sculptured frieze that encircles the entire cella (fig. 167).

THE PROPYLAEA. Immediately after the completion of the Parthenon, Pericles commissioned another splendid and expensive edifice, the monumental entry gate at the western end of the Acropolis, called the Propylaea (see plan, fig. 168). It was begun in 437 B.C., under the architect Mnesicles, who completed the main part in five years; the remainder had to be abandoned because of the Peloponnesian War. Again the entire structure was built of marble, and included refinements comparable to those of the Parthenon. Its main fascination for us consists in the manner in which the elements of a Doric temple have here been adapted to another task, on an irregular and steeply rising site. Mnesicles has indeed acquitted himself nobly; his design not only fits the difficult terrain but also transforms it, so that a rude passage among rocks becomes a splendid overture to the sacred precinct on which it opens.

Of the two porches (or façades) at either end, only the eastern one is in fair condition today (fig. 169); it resembles a Classical Doric temple front, except for the wide opening between the third and fourth columns. The western porch was flanked by two wings (figs. 170, 171). The one to the north, considerably larger than its companion, included a picture gallery (pinakotheke), the first known instance of a room especially designed for the display of paintings. Along the central roadway that passes through the Propylaea, we find two rows of columns which are Ionic rather than Doric. Apparently at that time the trend in Athenian architecture was toward using Ionic elements inside Doric structures (we recall the sculptured frieze of the Parthenon cella).

Ionic Temples

Athens, with its strong Aegean orientation, had shown itself hospitable to the eastern Greek style of building from the mid-fifth century on, and the finest surviving examples of the Ionic order are to be found among the structures of the

168. Plan of the Acropolis at Athens in 400 B.C. (after A. W. Lawrence)

169. MNESICLES. The Propylaea (view from the east). 437–432 B.C. Acropolis, Athens

170. The Propylaea (with *pinakotheke*), Western Entrance

171. The Propylaea (view from the west) and the Temple of Athena Nike (427–424 B.C.), Acropolis, Athens

172. Aeolian Capital, from Larissa. c. 600 B.C. Archaeological Museum, Istanbul

173. Corinthian Capital, from the Tholos at Epidaurus. c. 350 B.C. Museum, Epidaurus

Acropolis. The previous development of the order is known only in very fragmentary fashion; of the huge Ionic temples that were erected in Archaic times on Samos and at Ephesus, little has survived except the plans. Its vocabulary, however, seems to have remained fairly fluid, with strong affinities to the Near East (see figs. 109, 110), and it did not really become an order in the strict sense until the Classical period. Even then it continued to be rather more flexible than the Doric order. Its most striking feature is the Ionic column, which differs from the Doric not only in body but also, as it were, in spirit (see fig. 159). It rests on an ornately profiled base of its own; the shaft is more slender, and there is less tapering and entasis; the capital shows a large double scroll, or volute, between the echinus and abacus, which projects strongly beyond the width of the shaft.

That these details add up to an entity very distinct from the Doric column becomes clear as soon as we turn from the diagram to an actual building (fig. 174). How shall we define it? The Ionic column is, of course, lighter and more graceful than its mainland cousin; it lacks the latter's muscular quality. Instead, it evokes the echo of a growing plant, of something like a formalized palm tree. And this vegetal analogy is not sheer fancy, for we have early ancestors, or relatives, of the Ionic capital that bear it out (fig. 172). If we were to pursue these plantlike columns all the way back to their point of origin, we would eventually find ourselves at Saqqara, where we not only encounter "proto-Doric" supports but the wonderfully graceful papyrus half-columns of figure 60, with their curved, flaring capitals. It may well be, then, that the Ionic column, too, had its ultimate source in Egypt, but instead of reaching Greece by sea, as we suppose the proto-Doric column did, it traveled a slow and tortuous path by land, through Syria and Asia Minor.

In pre-Classical times, the only Ionic structures on the Greek mainland had been the small treasuries built by eastern Greek states at Delphi in the regional styles (see fig. 154). Hence the Athenian architects who took up the Ionic order about 450 B.C. thought of it, at first, as suitable only for small temples of simple plan. Such a building is the little Temple of Athena Nike on the southern flank of the Propylaea (fig. 171), probably built 427–424 B.C. from a design prepared twenty years earlier by Callicrates.

THE ERECHTHEUM. Larger and more complex is the Erechtheum (fig. 173; and plan, fig. 168), on the northern edge of the Acropolis opposite the Parthenon. It was erected in 421–405 B.C., perhaps by Mnesicles, for, like the Propylaea, it is masterfully adapted to an irregular, sloping site. The area had various associations with the mythical founding of Athens, so that the Erechtheum was actually a "portmanteau" sanctuary with several religious functions. Its name derives from Erechtheus, a legendary king of Athens; the eastern room was dedicated to Athena Polias (Athena the city goddess); and it may also have covered the spot where a contest between Athena and Poseidon was believed to have taken place. (Apparently there were four rooms, in addition to a basement on the western side, but their exact purpose is under dispute.)

174. The Erechtheum (view from the east). 421–405 B.C.. Acropolis, Athens

Instead of a west façade, the Erechtheum has two porches attached to its flanks, a very large one facing north and a small one toward the Parthenon. The latter is the famous Porch of the Maidens, its roof supported by six female figures (caryatids) on a high parapet, instead of regular columns (compare fig. 154). One wonders whether these statues were the reason why a Turkish governor chose the building to house his harem two thousand years later. We cannot altogether blame him, for here the exquisite refinement of the Ionic order does indeed convey a "feminine" quality, compared with the "masculinity" of the Parthenon across the way. Apart from the caryatids, sculptural decoration on the Erechtheum was confined to the frieze (of which very little survives). The pediments remained bare, perhaps for lack of funds at the end of the Peloponnesian War. However, the ornamental carving on the bases and capitals of the columns, and on the frames of doorways and windows, is extraordinarily delicate and rich; its cost, according to the accounts inscribed on the building, was higher than that of figure sculpture.

THE CORINTHIAN CAPITAL. Such emphasis on ornament seems characteristic of the late fifth century. It was at this time that the Corinthian capital was invented, as an elaborate substitute for the Ionic; its shape is that of an inverted bell covered with the curly shoots and leaves of the acanthus plant, which seem to sprout from the top of the column shaft (fig. 173). At first, Corinthian capitals were used only for interiors. Not until a century later do we find them replacing Ionic capitals on the exterior. The earliest known instance is the Monument of Lysicrates in Athens (fig. 175), built soon after 334 B.C. It is not really a building in the full sense of the term—the interior, though hollow, has no entrance—but an elaborate support for a tripod won by Lysicrates in a contest. The round structure, resting on a tall base, is a miniature version of a tholos, a type of circular building of which several earlier examples are known to have existed. The columns here are engaged (set into the wall) rather than free-standing, to make the monument more compact. Soon after, the Corinthian capital came to be employed on the exteriors of large buildings as well, and in Roman times it was the standard capital for almost any purpose.

TOWN PLANNING; THEATERS. During the three centuries between the end of the Peloponnesian War and the Roman conquest, Greek architecture shows little further development. Even before the time of Alexander the Great, the largest volume of building activity was to be found in the Greek cities of Asia Minor. There we do encounter some structures of a new kind, often under Oriental influence, such as the huge Tomb of Mausolus at Halicarnassus (see figs. 193–95) and the Altar of Zeus at Pergamum (see figs. 203–5); town planning on a rectangular grid pattern, first introduced at Miletus in the mid-fifth century, assumed new importance, as did the municipal halls (stoas) lining the market places where the civic and commercial life of Greek towns was centered; private houses, too, became larger and more ornate than before. Yet the architectural vocabulary, aesthetically as well as technically, remained essentially that of the temples of the late fifth century.

The basic repertory of Greek architecture was increased in one respect only: the open-air theater achieved a regular, defined shape. Before the fourth century, the auditorium had simply been a natural slope, preferably curved, equipped with stone benches; now the hillside was provided with concentric rows of seats, and with staircase-aisles at regular intervals, as at Epidaurus (figs. 176–77). At center is the orchestra, where most of the action took place. At the extreme right we see the remains of a hall-like building that formed the backdrop and supported the scenery.

176. The Theater, Epidaurus. c. 350 B.C.

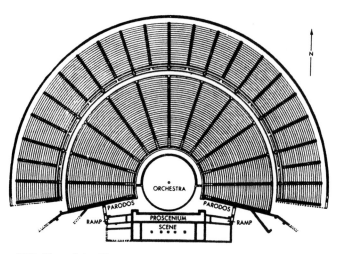

177. Plan of the Theater, Epidaurus (after Picard-Cambridge)

Limitations

How are we to account for the fact that Greek architecture did not grow significantly beyond the stage it had reached at the time of the Peloponnesian War? After all, neither intellectual life nor the work of sculptors and painters shows any tendency toward staleness during the last three hundred years of Greek civilization. Are we perhaps misjudging her architectural achievements after 400 B.C.? Or were there inherent limitations that prevented Greek architecture from continuing the pace of development it had maintained in Archaic and Classical times? A number of such limitations come to mind: the concern with monumental exteriors at the expense of interior space; the concentration of effort on temples of one particular type; the lack of interest in any structural system more advanced than the post-and-lintel (uprights supporting horizontal beams). Until the late fifth century, these had all been positive advantages; without them, the great masterpieces of the Periclean age would have been unthinkable. But the possibilities of the traditional Doric temple were nearly exhausted by then, as indicated by the attention lavished on expensive refinements.

What Greek architecture needed after the Peloponnesian War was a breakthrough, a revival of the experimental spirit

175. The Monument of Lysicrates, Athens. c. 334 B.C.

of the seventh century, which would create an interest in new building materials, vaulting, and interior space. What prevented the breakthrough? Could it have been the architectural orders, or rather the cast of mind that produced them? The suspicion will not go away that it was the very coherence and rigidity of these orders which made it impossible for Greek architects to break from the established pattern. What had been their great strength in earlier days became a tyranny. It remained for later ages to adapt the Greek orders to brick and concrete, to arched and vaulted construction, for such adaptation necessitated doing a certain amount of violence to the original character of the orders, and the Greeks, it seems, were incapable of that.

CLASSICAL SCULPTURE

THE KRITIOS BOY. Among the statues excavated from the debris the Persians had left behind on the Acropolis, there is one Kouros (fig. 178) that stands apart from the rest. It must have been carved very shortly before the fateful year 480 B.C. This remarkable work, which some have attributed to the Athenian sculptor Kritios and which therefore has come to be known as the *Kritios Boy*, differs subtly but importantly from the Archaic Kouros figures we discussed above (figs. 145, 146): it is the first statue we know that *stands* in the full sense of the word. Of course, the earlier figures also stand, but only in the sense that they are in an upright position, and are not reclining, sitting, kneeling, or running; their stance is really an arrested walk, with the weight of the body resting evenly on both legs. The *Kritios Boy*, too, has one leg placed forward, yet we never doubt for an instant that he is standing still. Why this is so becomes evident when we compare the left and right half of his body, for we then discover that the strict symmetry of the Archaic Kouros has now given way to a calculated nonsymmetry: the knee of the forward leg is lower than the other, the right hip is thrust down and inward, the left hip up and outward; and if we trace the axis of the body, we realize that it is not a straight vertical line but a faint, S-like curve (or, to be exact, a reversed S-curve). Taken together, all these small departures from symmetry tell us that the weight of the body rests mainly on the left leg, and that the right leg plays the role of an elastic prop or buttress to make sure that the body keeps its balance.

CONTRAPPOSTO. The *Kritios Boy*, then, not only stands, he stands at ease. And the artist has masterfully observed the balanced nonsymmetry of this relaxed, natural stance. To describe it, we use the Italian word *contrapposto* (counterpoise); the leg that carries the main weight is commonly called the engaged leg; the other, the free leg. These terms are a useful shorthand, for from now on we shall have frequent occasion to mention *contrapposto*. It was a very basic discovery. Only by learning how to represent the body at rest could the Greek sculptor gain the freedom to show it in motion. But is there not plenty of motion in Archaic art? There is indeed (see figs. 152, 154, 157, 158), but somewhat mechanical and inflexible in kind; we read it from the poses without really feeling it. In the *Kritios Boy*, on the other

178. *Standing Youth (The Kritios Boy)*. c. 480 B.C. Marble, height 34″. Acropolis Museum, Athens

179. *Doryphorus (Spear Bearer)*. Roman copy after an original of c. 450–440 B.C. by Polyclitus. Marble, height 6′ 6″. National Museum, Naples

180. *Charioteer*, from the Sanctuary of Apollo at Delphi. c. 470 B.C. Bronze, height 71″. Museum, Delphi

hand, we sense for the first time not only a new repose but an animation of the body structure that evokes the experience we have of our own body. Life now suffuses the entire figure, hence the Archaic smile, the "sign of life," is no longer needed. It has given way to a serious, pensive expression characteristic of the early phase of Classical sculpture (or, as it is often called, the Severe Style).

The new articulation of the body that appears in the *Kritios Boy* was to reach its full development within half a century in the mature Classical style of the Periclean era. The most famous Kouros statue of that time, the *Doryphorus (Spear Bearer)* by Polyclitus (fig. 179), is known to us only through Roman copies whose hard, dry forms convey little of the beauty of the original. Still, it makes an instructive comparison with the *Kritios Boy*. The *contrapposto* (with the engaged leg in the forward position) has now become much more emphatic; the differentiation between the left and right halves of the body can be seen in every muscle, and the turn of the head, barely hinted at in the *Kritios Boy*, is equally pronounced. This studied poise, the precise, if overexplicit, anatomical detail, and above all the harmonious proportions of the figure, made the *Doryphorus* re-

182. *Hippodamia Attacked by a Centaur*, from the west pediment of the Temple of Zeus at Olympia. c. 460 B.C. Marble, slightly over lifesize. Museum, Olympia

nowned as the standard embodiment of the Classical ideal of human beauty. According to one ancient writer, it was known simply as the Canon (rule, measure), so great was its authority.

THE SEVERE STYLE. But let us return to the Severe Style. The reason why this term was chosen to describe the character of Greek sculpture during the years between c. 480 and 450 B.C. becomes clear to us as we look at the splendid *Charioteer* from Delphi (fig. 180), one of the earliest large bronze statues in Greek art. It must have been made about a decade later than the *Kritios Boy*, as a votive offering after a race; the young victor originally stood on a chariot drawn by four horses. Despite the long, heavy garment, we sense a hint of *contrapposto* in the body—the feet are carefully differentiated so as to inform us that the left leg is the engaged one, and the shoulders and head turn slightly to the right. The garment is severely simple, yet compared with Archaic drapery the folds seem softer and more pliable; we feel (probably for the first time in the history of sculpture) that they reflect the behavior of real cloth. Not only the body but the drapery, too, has been transformed by a new understanding of functional relationships, so that every fold is shaped by the forces which act upon it—the downward pull of gravity, the shape of the body underneath, and the belts or straps that constrict its flow. The face has the pensive, somewhat faraway look we saw in the *Kritios Boy*, but the color inlay of the eyes, fortunately preserved in this instance, as well as the slightly parted lips, give it a more ani-

181. *Apollo* (portion), from the west pediment of the Temple of Zeus at Olympia. c. 460 B.C. Marble, over lifesize. Museum, Olympia

183. *Poseidon (Zeus?).* c. 460–450 B.C. Bronze, height 6′ 10″. National Museum, Athens

mated expression. The bearing of the entire figure conveys the solemnity of the event commemorated, for chariot races and similar contests at that time were competitions for divine favor, not sporting events in the modern sense.

TEMPLE OF ZEUS, OLYMPIA. The greatest sculptural ensemble of the Severe Style is the pair of pediments of the Temple of Zeus at Olympia, carved c. 460 B.C. and now reassembled in the local museum. In the west pediment, the more mature of the two, we see the victory of the Lapiths over the Centaurs under the aegis of Apollo, who forms the center of the composition (fig. 181). His commanding figure is part of the drama and yet above it; the outstretched right arm and the strong turn of the head show his active intervention—he *wills* the victory but, as befits a god, does not physically help to achieve it. Nevertheless, there is a tense-

ness, a gathering of forces, in this powerful body that makes its outward calm doubly impressive. The forms themselves are massive and simple, with soft contours and undulating, continuous surfaces. Apollo's glance is directed at a Centaur who has seized Hippodamia, bride of the king of the Lapiths (fig. 182). Here we witness another achievement of the Severe Style: the passionate struggle is expressed not only through action and gesture but through the emotions mirrored in the faces—revulsion on the face of the girl, pain and desperate effort on that of the Centaur. Nor would an Archaic artist have known how to combine the two figures into a group so compact, so full of interlocking movements.

MOVEMENT IN STATUES. Strenuous action had already been investigated in pedimental sculpture of the Late Archaic period (see figs. 157, 158). Such figures, however, although technically carved in the round, are not free-standing; they represent, rather, a kind of super-relief, since they are designed to be seen against a background and from one direction only. To infuse the same freedom of movement into genuinely free-standing statues was a far greater challenge; not only did it run counter to an age-old tradition that denied mobility to these figures, but the unfreezing had to be done in such a way as to safeguard their all-around balance and self-sufficiency. The problem could not really be tackled until the concept of *contrapposto* had been established, but once this was done the solution no longer presented serious difficulties. Large, free-standing statues in motion are the most important achievement of the Severe Style. The finest figure of this kind was recovered from the sea near the coast of Greece some thirty years ago (fig. 183): a magnificent nude bronze Poseidon (or Zeus?), almost sev-

185. *Dying Niobid.* c. 450–440 B.C. Marble, height 59″.
Museo delle Terme, Rome

184. *Discobolus (Discus Thrower).* Roman marble
copy after a bronze original of c. 450 B.C. by Myron.
Lifesize. Museo delle Terme, Rome

en feet tall, in the act of hurling his trident (or thunderbolt?). The pose is that of an athlete, yet it does not strike us as the arrested phase of a continuous succession of movements but as an awe-inspiring gesture that reveals the power of the god. Hurling a weapon is a divine attribute here, rather than a specific performance aimed at a particular adversary.

Some years after the *Poseidon*, about 450 B.C., Myron created his famous bronze statue of the *Discobolus (Discus Thrower)*, which came to enjoy a reputation comparable to that of the *Doryphorus*. Like the latter, it is known to us only from Roman copies (fig. 184). Here the problem of how to condense a sequence of movements into a single pose without freezing it is a very much more complex one, involving a violent twist of the torso in order to bring the action of the arms into the same plane as the action of the legs. We wonder whether the copy does not make the design seem harsher and less poised than it was in the original.

THE CLASSICAL STYLE. The *Discobolus* brings us to the threshold of the second half of the century, the era of the mature Classical style. The conquest of movement in a free-standing statue now exerted a liberating influence on pedimental sculpture as well, endowing it with a new spaciousness, fluidity, and balance. The *Dying Niobid* (fig. 185), a work of the 440s, was carved for the pediment of a Doric temple but is so richly three-dimensional, so self-contained, that we hardly suspect her original context. Niobe, according to legend, had humiliated the mother of Apollo and Artemis by boasting of her seven sons and seven daughters, whereupon the two gods killed all of Niobe's children. Our Niobid has been shot in the back while running; her strength broken, she sinks to the ground while trying to extract the fatal arrow. The violent movement of her arms has made her garment slip off; her nudity is thus a dramatic device, rather than a necessary part of the story. The artist's primary motive in devising it, however, was to display a beautiful female body in the kind of strenuous action hitherto reserved for the male nude. (The *Niobid* is the earliest large female nude in Greek art.) Still, we must not misread the artist's intention: it was not a detached interest in the physical aspect of the event alone but the desire to unite motion and emotion and thus to make the beholder experience the suffering of this victim of a cruel fate. Looking at the face of the Niobid, we feel that here, for the first time, human feeling is expressed as eloquently in the features as in the rest of the figure.

A brief glance backward at the wounded warrior from Aegina (fig. 157) will show us how very differently the agony of death had been conceived only half a century before. What separates the *Niobid* from the world of Archaic art is a quality summed up in the Greek word *pathos*, which means suffering, but particularly suffering conveyed with nobility and restraint so that it touches rather than horrifies us. Late Archaic art may approach it now and then, as in the Eos and Memnon group (fig. 143) yet the full force of pathos can be felt only in Classical works such as the *Niobid*. Perhaps, in order to measure the astonishing development we have witnessed since the beginnings of Greek monumental sculpture less than two centuries before, we ought to compare the *Niobid* with the earliest pedimental figure we came to know, the Gorgon from Corfu (fig. 152); and as we do so, we suddenly realize that these two, worlds apart as they may be, belong to the same artistic tradition, for the *Niobid*, too, shows the pinwheel stance, even though its meaning has been radically reinterpreted. Once we recognize the ancient origin of her pose, we understand better than before why the Niobid, despite her suffering, remains so monumentally self-contained.

PHIDIAS AND THE PARTHENON. The largest, as well as the greatest, group of Classical sculptures at our disposal consists of the remains of the marble decoration of the Parthenon, most of them, unfortunately, in battered and fragmentary condition. The centers of both pediments are gone

186. *Dionysus*, from the east pediment of the Parthenon.
c. 438–432 B.C. Marble, over lifesize. British Museum, London

187. *Three Goddesses*, from the east pediment of the Parthenon. c. 438–432 B.C. Marble, over lifesize. British Museum, London

completely, and of the figures in the corners only those from the east pediment are sufficiently well preserved to convey something of the quality of the ensemble. They represent various deities, most in sitting or reclining poses, witnessing the birth of Athena from the head of Zeus (figs. 186, 187). Here, even more than in the case of the *Niobid*, we marvel at the spaciousness, the complete ease of movement of these statues. There is neither violence nor pathos in them, indeed no specific action of any kind, only a deeply felt poetry of being. We find it equally in the relaxed masculine body of Dionysus and in the soft fullness of the three goddesses, enveloped in thin drapery that seems to share the qualities of a liquid substance as it flows and eddies around the forms underneath.

The figures are so freely conceived in depth that they create their own aura of space, as it were. How, we wonder, did they ever fit into the confined shape of a pediment? Might they not have looked a bit incongruous, as if they had been merely shelved there? The great master who designed them must have felt something of the sort, for the composition as a whole suggests that he refused to accept the triangular field as more than a purely physical limit. In the sharp angles at the corners, at the feet of Dionysus and the reclining goddesses, he has placed two horses' heads; they are meant to represent the chariots of the rising sun and the waning moon emerging into (and dipping below) the pedimental space, but visually the heads are merely two fragments arbitrarily cut off by the frame. Clearly, we are approaching the moment when the pediment will be rejected altogether as the focal point of Greek architectural sculpture.

The frieze of the Parthenon, a continuous band 525 feet long (fig. 167), shows a procession honoring Athena, in the presence of the other Olympic gods. It is of the same high rank as the pedimental sculptures. In a somewhat different way it, too, suffered from its subordination to the architectural setting, for it must have been poorly lit and difficult to

188. *Horsemen*, from the west frieze of the Parthenon. c. 440 B.C. Marble, height 43". British Museum, London (see also fig. 260)

see, placed as it was immediately below the ceiling. The depth of the carving and the concept of relief are not radically different from the frieze of the Siphnian Treasury (figs. 154, 155), although the illusion of space and of rounded form is now achieved with sovereign ease. The most remarkable quality of the Parthenon frieze is the rhythmic grace of the design, particularly striking in the spirited movement of the groups of horsemen (fig. 188).

Who was responsible for this magnificent array of sculptures? They have long been associated with the name of Phidias, the chief overseer of all artistic enterprises sponsored by Pericles. According to ancient writers, Phidias was particularly famous for a huge ivory-and-gold statue of Athena he made for the cella of the Parthenon, a colossal Zeus in the same technique for the temple of that god in Olympia, and an equally large bronze statue of Athena that stood on the Acropolis facing the Propylaea. None of these survives, and small-scale representations of them in later times are utterly inadequate to convey anything of the artist's style. It is, in any event, hard to imagine that enormous statues of this sort, burdened with the requirements of cult images and the demands of a difficult technique, shared the vitality of the Elgin Marbles. The admiration they elicited could have been due in large part to their size, the preciousness of the materials, and the aura of religious awe surrounding them. Phidias' personality thus remains oddly intangible; he may have been a great genius, or simply a very able co-ordinator and supervisor. They term "Phidian style" used to describe the Parthenon sculptures is no more than a generic label, justified by its convenience but of questionable accuracy. Undoubtedly a large number of masters were involved, since the frieze and the two pediments were executed in less than ten years (c. 440–432 B.C.). The metopes, which we have omitted here, date from the 440s.

190. *Grave Stele of Hegeso.* c. 410–400 B.C. Marble, height 59″. National Museum, Athens

189. *Nike*, from the balustrade of the Temple of Athena Nike. c. 410–407 B.C. Marble, height 42″. Acropolis Museum, Athens

THE PHIDIAN STYLE. It is hardly surprising that the Phidian style should have dominated Athenian sculpture until the end of the fifth century and beyond, even though large-scale sculptural enterprises gradually came to a halt because of the Peloponnesian War. The last of these was the balustrade erected around the small temple of Athena Nike c. 410–407 B.C. Like the Parthenon frieze, it shows a festive procession, but the participants are winged Nike figures (personifications of victory) rather than citizens of Athens. One *Nike* (fig. 189) is taking off her sandals, in conformity with an age-old tradition, indicating that she is about to step on holy ground (see page 56). Her wings—one open, the other closed—are effectively employed to help her keep her balance, so that she performs with consummate elegance of movement what is ordinarily a rather awkward act. Her figure is more strongly detached from the relief ground than are those on the Parthenon frieze, and her garments, with their deeply cut folds, cling to the body as if they were wet (we have seen an earlier phase of this treatment of drapery in the three goddesses of the Parthenon, fig. 187).

"Phidian," too, and also from the last years of the century, is the beautiful *Grave Stele of Hegeso* (fig. 190). Memorials of this kind were produced in large numbers by Athenian sculptors, and their export must have helped to spread the Phidian style throughout the Greek world. Few of them, however, can match the harmonious design and the gentle melancholy of our example. The deceased is represented in a simple domestic scene; she has picked a necklace from the box held by the girl servant and seems to be contemplating it as if it were a keepsake. The delicacy of the carving can be seen especially well in the forms farthest removed from the beholder, such as the servant's left arm supporting the lid of the jewel box, or the veil behind Hegeso's right shoulder. Here the relief merges almost imperceptibly with the background, so that the ground no longer appears as a solid surface but assumes something of the transparency of empty space. This novel effect was probably inspired by the painters of the period, who, according to the literary sources, had achieved a great breakthrough in mastering illusionistic space.

CLASSICAL PAINTING

Unhappily, we have no murals or panels to verify this claim; and vase painting by its very nature could echo the new concept of pictorial space only in rudimentary fashion. Still, there are vessels that form an exception to this general rule; we find them mostly in a special class of vases, the lekythoi (oil jugs) used as funerary offerings. These had a white coating on which the painter could draw as freely, and with the same spatial effect, as his modern successor using pen and paper. The white ground, in both cases, is treated as empty space from which the sketched forms seem to emerge—if the draftsman knows how to achieve this.

Not many lekythos painters were capable of bringing off the illusion. Foremost among them is the unknown artist, nicknamed the "Achilles Painter," who drew the woman in figure 191 and colorplate 16. Although some twenty-five years older than the Hegeso Stele, this vase shows exactly the same scene; here, too, a standing maidservant holds a box from which the deceased has just taken a piece of jewelry. There is the same mood of "Phidian" reverie, and even the chairs match almost exactly. This scene, then, was a standard subject for painted or sculptured memorials of young women.

Our chief interest, however, is in the masterly draftsmanship; with a few lines, sure, fresh, and fluid, the artist not only creates a three-dimensional figure but reveals the body beneath the drapery as well. How does he manage to persuade us that these shapes exist in depth rather than merely on the surface of the vase? First of all, by his command of foreshortening. But the "internal dynamics" of the lines are equally important, their swelling and fading, which make some contours stand out boldly while others merge with one another or disappear into the white ground. However, we must not assume that the carver of the Hegeso Stele actually knew our lekythos; more likely, they both derive from a common ancestor, which may have been a marble stele like that of Hegeso but with a *painted* representation of the jewel-box scene.

191. THE ACHILLES PAINTER. White-ground lekythos with *Mistress and Maid* (detail; see colorplate 16). Staatliche Antikensammlungen, Munich

192. THE AURORA PAINTER. *Peleus and Thetis*, detail of
a Faliscan vase. Early 4th century B.C.
Museo Nazionale di Villa Giulia, Rome

Considering its artistic advantages, we might expect a more general adoption of the white-ground technique. Such, however, was not the case. Instead, from the mid-fifth century on, the impact of monumental painting gradually transformed vase painting as a whole into a satellite art that tried to reproduce large-scale compositions in a kind of shorthand dictated by its own limited technique. The result, more often than not, was spotty and overcrowded.

Even the finest examples suffer from this defect, as we can see in figure 192, which is taken from a vase produced in central Italy—probably by a Greek master—not very long after 400 B.C. It shows Thetis, who was about to bathe under a fountain, being abducted by Peleus as her two girl servants flee in panic. Our artist, the so-called Aurora Painter, has placed three of the figures on a rocky slope (the fourth, intended to be farther away, seems suspended in mid-air) in order to suggest the spatial setting of the scene; he even shows the fountain, in the shape of two pipes coming out of a rock in the upper right-hand corner. Yet the effect remains silhouette-like, because of the obtrusive black background. He has also tried to enlarge his color range: the body of Thetis has a lighter tint than the other figures, and some details have been added in white. This expedient, too, fails to solve his problem, since his medium does not permit him to shade

or model. He thus must rely on creating a maximum of dramatic excitement to hold the scene together; and, being a spirited draftsman, he almost succeeds. Still, it is a success at second hand, for the composition must have been inspired by a mural or panel picture. He is, as it were, battling for a lost cause; in another hundred years, vase painting was to disappear altogether.

SCULPTURE OF THE FOURTH CENTURY

There is, unfortunately, no single word, like Archaic or Classical, that we can use to designate the third phase in the development of Greek art, from c. 400 to the first century B.C. The seventy-five-year span between the end of the Peloponnesian War and the rise of Alexander the Great used to be labeled "Late Classical," the remaining two centuries and a half, "Hellenistic," a term meant to convey the spread of Greek civilization southeastward through Asia Minor to Mesopotamia, Egypt, and the borders of India. It was perhaps natural to expect that the world-shaking conquests of

193. Reconstruction Drawing of
the Mausoleum at Halicarnassus
(after F. Krischen)

Here, then, is our dilemma: "Hellenistic" is a concept so closely linked with the political and cultural consequences of Alexander's conquest that we cannot very well extend it backward to the early fourth century, although there is wide agreement now that the art of the years 400–325 B.C. can be far better understood if we view it as pre-Hellenistic rather than as Late Classical. Until the right word is found and wins general acceptance, we shall have to make do with the existing terms as best we can, always keeping in mind the essential continuity of the "third phase" that we are about to examine.

THE MAUSOLEUM AND SCOPAS. The contrast between Classical and pre-Hellenistic is strikingly demonstrated by the only project of the fourth century that corresponds to the Parthenon in size and ambition. It is not a temple but a huge tomb—so huge, in fact, that its name, Mausoleum, has become a generic term for all outsized funerary monuments. It was erected at Halicarnassus in Asia Minor just before and after 350 B.C. by Mausolus, who was ruler of the area as a satrap of the Persians, and by his widow Artemisia. The structure itself is completely destroyed, but its dimensions and general appearance can be reconstructed on the basis of ancient descriptions and the fragments (including a good deal of sculpture) excavated over a hundred years ago. The drawing in figure 193 does not pretend to be exact in detail; it probably shows fewer statues than were actually there. We do know, however, that the building rose in three stages to a height of about 160 feet. A tall rectangular base 117 feet wide and 82 feet deep supported a colonnade of Ionic columns 40 feet tall, and above this rose a pyramid crowned by

Alexander in 333–323 B.C. would also effect an artistic revolution, but the history of style is not always in tune with political history, and we have come to realize that there was no decisive break in the tradition of Greek art at the end of the fourth century. The art of the Hellenistic era is the direct outgrowth of developments that occurred, not at the time of Alexander, but during the preceding fifty years.

194. SCOPAS (?). *Battle of Greeks and Amazons*, from the east frieze of the Mausoleum, Halicarnassus.
359–351 B.C. Marble, height 35″. British Museum, London

Greek Art 139

195. "*Mausolus*," from the Mausoleum, Halicarnassus. 359–351 B.C. Marble, height 9′ 10″. British Museum, London

ordinary human status. His kinship with the gods may have been hinted at. Apparently Mausolus took this view of himself as a divinely ordained sovereign from the Persians, who in turn had inherited it from the Assyrians and Egyptians, although he seems to have wanted to glorify his individual personality as much as his high office. The structure embodying these ambitions must have struck his contemporaries as impressive and monstrous at the same time, with its multiple friezes and the receding faces of a pyramid in place of pediments above the colonnade.

According to ancient sources, the sculpture on each of the four sides of the monument was entrusted to a different master, chosen from among the best of the time. Scopas, the most famous, did the main side, the one to the east. His dynamic style has been recognized in some portions of the Amazon frieze, such as the portion in figure 194. The Parthenon tradition can still be felt here, but there is also a decidedly un-Classical violence, physical as well as emotional, conveyed through strained movements and passionate facial expressions (deep-set eyes are a hallmark of Scopas' style). As a consequence, we no longer find the rhythmic flow of the Parthenon frieze; continuity and harmony have been sacrificed so that each figure may have greater scope for sweeping, impulsive gestures. Clearly, if we are to do justice to this explosive energetic style we must not judge it by Classical standards.

The "pre-Hellenistic" flavor is even more pronounced in the portrait statue presumed to represent Mausolus himself (fig. 195). The colossal figure must be the work of a man younger than Scopas and even less encumbered by Classical standards, probably Bryaxis, the master of the north side. We know, through Roman copies, of some Greek portraits of Classical times, but they seem to represent types rather than individuals, whereas the *Mausolus* is both the earliest Greek portrait to have survived in the original and the first to show a clear-cut personal character. This very fact links it with the future rather than the past, for individual likenesses were to play an important part in Hellenistic times. Nor is it merely the head, with its heavy jaws and small, sensuous mouth, that records the sitter's appearance; the thick neck and the broad, fleshy body seem equally individual. The massiveness of the forms is further emphasized by the sharp-edged and stiff-textured drapery, which might be said to *encase*, rather than merely clothe, the body. The great volumes of folds across the abdomen and below the left arm seem designed for picturesque effect more than for functional clarity.

PRAXITELES. Some of the features of the Mausoleum sculpture recur in other important works of the period. Foremost among these is the wonderful seated figure of Demeter from the temple of that goddess at Cnidus (fig. 196), a work only slightly later in date than the *Mausolus*. Here again the drapery, though more finely textured, has an impressive volume of its own; motifs such as the S-curve of folds across the chest form an effective counterpoint to the shape of the body beneath. The deep-set eyes gaze into the distance with an intensity that suggests the influence of Scopas. The modeling of the head, on the other hand, has a veiled softness that

a chariot with statues of the deceased. The sculptural program consisted of three friezes showing Lapiths battling Centaurs, Greeks fighting Amazons, and chariot races; their combined length was twice that of the Parthenon frieze. There were also rows of carved guardian lions and an unknown number of large statues, including portraits of the deceased and their ancestors.

The commemorative and retrospective character of the monument, based on the idea of human life as a glorious struggle or chariot race, is entirely Greek, yet we immediately notice the un-Greek way it has been carried out. The huge size of the tomb, and more particularly the pyramid, derive from Egypt; they imply an exaltation of the ruler far beyond

A more faithful embodiment of Praxitelean beauty is the group of Hermes with the infant Bacchus at Olympia (fig. 198); it is of such high quality that it was long regarded as Praxiteles' own work. Today some scholars believe it to be a very fine Greek copy made some three centuries later. The dispute is of little consequence for us, except perhaps in one respect: it emphasizes the unfortunate fact that we do not have a single undisputed original by any of the famous sculptors of Greece. Nevertheless, the *Hermes* is the most completely Praxitelean statue we know. The lithe proportions, the sinuous curve of the torso, the play of gentle curves, the sense of complete relaxation (enhanced by the use of an outside support for the figure to lean against), all these agree well enough with the character of the *Cnidian Aphrodite*. We also find many refinements here that are ordinarily lost in a copy, such as the caressing treatment of the

196. *Demeter*, from Cnidus. c. 340–330 B.C. Marble, height 60″. British Museum, London

points to an altogether different source: Praxiteles, the master of feminine grace and sensuous evocation of flesh.

As it happens, Praxiteles' most acclaimed statue, an Aphrodite, was likewise made for Cnidus, although probably some years later than the *Demeter*. But his reputation was well established even earlier, so that the unknown sculptor who carved the *Demeter* would have had no difficulty incorporating some Praxitelean qualities into his own work. The *Cnidian Aphrodite* by Praxiteles achieved such proverbial fame that she is often referred to in ancient literature as a synonym for absolute perfection. To what extent her renown was based on her beauty, or on the fact that she was (so far as we know) the first completely nude cult image of the goddess, is difficult to say; for the statue is known to us only through Roman copies that can be no more than pallid reflections of the original (fig. 197). She was to have countless descendants in Hellenistic and Roman art.

197. *Aphrodite of the Cnidians*. Roman copy after an original of c. 300 B.C. by PRAXITELES. Marble, height 6′ 8″ Vatican Museums, Rome

198. PRAXITELES. *Hermes.* c. 300–320 B.C. (or copy?).
Marble, height 7′ 1″. Museum, Olympia

marble, the faint smile, the meltingly soft, "veiled" modeling of the features; even the hair, left comparatively rough for contrast, shares the silky feel of the rest of the work. The bland, lyrical charm of the *Hermes* makes it easy to believe that the *Cnidian Aphrodite* was the artist's most successful accomplishment.

APOLLO BELVEDERE. The same qualities recur in many other statues, all of them Roman copies of Greek works in a more or less Praxitelean vein. The best known—one is tempted to say the most notorious—is the *Apollo Belvedere* (fig. 199); it interests us less for its own sake than because of its tremendous popularity during the eighteenth and nineteenth centuries. Winckelmann, Goethe, and other champions of the Greek Revival found it the perfect exemplar of Classical beauty; plaster casts or reproductions of it were thought indispensable for all museums, art academies, or

liberal arts colleges, and generations of students grew up in the belief that it embodied the essence of the Greek spirit. This enthusiasm tells us a good deal—not about the qualities of the *Apollo Belvedere* but about the character of the Greek Revival. Although our own time takes a rather jaundiced view of the statue, we had better refrain from scoffing at the naïveté of our forefathers. Who knows whether the tide of taste may not turn some day? Let us not discount the possibility that the *Apollo Belvedere* may again hold a message for our grandchildren.

LYSIPPUS. Besides Scopas and Praxiteles, there is yet another great name in pre-Hellenistic sculpture: Lysippus, whose long career may have begun as early as c. 370 and

199. *The Apollo Belvedere.* Roman marble copy,
probably of a Greek original of the late 4th (or 1st)
century B.C. Height 7′ 4″. Vatican Museums, Rome

continued to the end of the century. The main features of his personal style, however, are more difficult to grasp than those of his two famous contemporaries, because of the contradictory evidence of the Roman copies that are assumed to reproduce his work. Ancient authors praised him for replacing the canon of Polyclitus with a new set of proportions that produced a more slender body and a smaller head. His realism, too, was proverbial: he is said to have had no master other than nature itself. But these statements describe little more than a general trend toward the end of the fourth century. Certainly the proportions of Praxiteles' statues are Lysippic rather than "Polyclitan," nor could Lysippus have been the only artist of his time to conquer new aspects of reality.

200. *Apoxyomenos (Scraper)*. Roman marble copy, probably after a bronze original of c. 330 B.C. by LYSIPPUS. Height 6′ 9″. Vatican Museums, Rome

Even in the case of the *Apoxyomenos*, the statue most insistently linked with his name, the evidence is far from conclusive (fig. 200). It shows a young athlete cleaning himself with a scraper, a motif often represented in Greek art from Classical times on. Our version, of which only a single copy has turned up so far, is distinguished from all the others by the fact that the arms are horizontally extended in front of the body. This bold thrust into space, at the cost of obstructing the view of the torso, is a noteworthy feat, whether or not we credit it to Lysippus; it endows the figure with a new capacity for spontaneous three-dimensional movement. A similar freedom is suggested by the diagonal line of the free leg. Even the unruly hair reflects the new trend toward spontaneity.

HELLENISTIC SCULPTURE

Of the artistic enterprises sponsored by Alexander the Great, such as the numerous portraits of the great conqueror by Lysippus, no direct evidence survives. In fact, we know very little of the development of Greek sculpture as a whole during the first hundred years of the Hellenistic era. Even after that, we have few fixed points of reference; of the large number of works at our disposal only a small fraction can be securely identified as to date and place of origin. Moreover, Greek sculpture was now being produced throughout a vast territory, and the interplay of local and international currents must have formed a complex pattern, a pattern of which we can trace only some isolated strands. One of these is represented by the bronze groups dedicated by Attalus I of Pergamum (a city in northwestern Asia Minor) between c. 240 and 200 B.C. to celebrate his victories over the Gauls. The Gauls were a Celtic tribe that had entered Asia Minor and kept raiding the Greek states there until Attalus forced them to settle down; we meet them a few centuries later as the Galatians in St. Paul's Epistle.

THE DYING GAUL. The statues commemorating their defeat were reproduced in marble for the Romans (who may have had a special interest in them because of their troubles with Celtic tribes in northwestern Europe), and a number of these copies have survived, including the famous *Dying Gaul* (fig. 201). The sculptor who conceived the figure must have known the Gauls well, for he has carefully rendered the ethnic type in the facial structure and in the bristly shock of hair. The torque around the neck is another characteristically Celtic feature. Otherwise, however, the Gaul shares the heroic nudity of Greek warriors, such as those on the Aegina pediments (see fig. 157); and if his agony seems infinitely more realistic in comparison, it still has considerable dignity and pathos. Clearly, the Gauls were not considered unworthy foes. "They knew how to die, barbarians though they were," is the thought conveyed by the statue. Yet we also sense something else, an animal quality that had never before been part of the Greek image of man. Death, as we witness it here, is a very concrete physical process: no longer able to move his legs, the Gaul puts all his waning strength into his arms, as if to prevent some tremendous invisible weight from crushing him against the ground.

201. *Dying Gaul.* Roman copy after a bronze original of c. 230–220 B.C. from Pergamum. Marble, lifesize. Capitoline Museum, Rome

202. *The Barberini Faun.* Roman copy of a Greek original of c. 220 B.C. Marble, over lifesize. Glyptothek, Munich

THE BARBERINI FAUN. A similar exploration of uncontrolled bodily responses may be seen in the *Barberini Faun* (fig. 202), probably a very fine Roman copy after a Hellenistic work of the late third century B.C., contemporary with the *Dying Gaul.* A drunken satyr is sprawled on a rock, asleep in the heavy-breathing, unquiet manner of the inebriated. He is obviously dreaming, and the convulsive gesture of the right arm and the troubled expression of the face betray the passionate, disturbing nature of his dream. Here again we witness a partial uncoupling of body and mind, no less persuasive than in the *Dying Gaul.*

THE PERGAMUM ALTAR. Some decades later, we find a second sculptural style flourishing at Pergamum. About 180 B.C., the son and successor of Attalus I had a mighty altar erected on a hill above the city to commemorate his father's victories. Much of the sculptural decoration has been recovered by excavation, and the entire west front of the altar is to be seen in East Berlin (fig. 203). It is an impressive structure indeed. The altar proper occupies the center of a rectangular court surrounded by an Ionic colonnade which rises on a tall base about 100 feet square; a monumental flight of stairs leads to the court on the west side (fig. 204). Altar structures of such great size seem to have been an Ionian tradition since Archaic times, but the Pergamum Altar is the most elaborate of all, as well as the only one of which considerable portions have survived. Its boldest feature is the great frieze covering the base, 400 feet long and between 7 and 8 feet tall. The huge figures, carved to such a depth that they are almost detached from the background, have the scale and weight of pedimental statues without the confining triangular frame—a unique compound of two separate traditions that represents a thundering climax in the development of Greek architectural sculpture (fig. 205).

203. The West Front of the Altar of Zeus at Pergamum (restored). State Museums, Berlin

204. Plan of the Altar of Zeus
at Pergamum
(after J. Schrammen)

205. *Athena and Alcyoneus*, from the east side of the Great Frieze of the Altar of Zeus at Pergamum, c. 180 B.C. Marble, height 7′ 6″. State Museums, Berlin

rhythm. It is this sense of unity that disciplines the physical and emotional violence of the struggle and thus keeps it—but just barely—from exploding its architectural frame.

NIKE OF SAMOTHRACE. Equally dramatic in its impact is another great victory monument of the early second century B.C., the *Nike of Samothrace* (fig. 206). The goddess has just descended to the prow of a ship; her great wings spread wide, she is still partly air-borne by the powerful head wind against which she advances. This invisible force of onrushing air here becomes a tangible reality; it not only balances the forward movement of the figure but also shapes every fold of the wonderfully animated drapery. As a result, there is an active relationship—indeed, an interdependence—between the statue and the space that envelops it, such as we have never seen before. Nor shall we see it again for a long time to come. The *Nike of Samothrace* deserves all of her fame as the greatest masterpiece of Hellenistic sculpture.

LAOCOÖN. Until the *Nike* was discovered over a hundred years ago, the most admired work of Hellenistic statuary had been a group showing the death of Laocoön and his two sons (fig. 207). It had been found in Rome as early as 1506 and had made a tremendous impression on Michelangelo and

206. *Nike of Samothrace.* c. 200–190 B.C. Marble, height 8'. The Louvre, Paris

The subject, the battle of gods and giants, is a traditional one for Ionic friezes; we saw it before on the Siphnian Treasury (compare fig. 155). At Pergamum, however, it has a novel significance, since the victory of the gods is meant to symbolize the victories of Attalus I. Such a translation of history into mythology had been an established device in Greek art for a long time; victories over the Persians were habitually represented in terms of Lapiths battling Centaurs or Greeks fighting Amazons. But to place Attalus I in analogy with the gods themselves implies an exaltation of the ruler than is Oriental rather than Greek in origin. Since the time of Mausolus, who may have been the first to introduce it on Greek soil, the idea of divine kingship had been adopted by Alexander the Great and it continued to flourish among the lesser sovereigns who divided his realm, such as the rulers of Pergamum.

The carving of the frieze, though not very subtle in detail, has tremendous dramatic force; the heavy, muscular bodies rushing at each other, the strong accents of light and dark, the beating wings and wind-blown garments, are almost overwhelming in their dynamism. A writhing movement pervades the entire design, down to the last lock of hair, linking the victors and the vanquished in a single continuous

207. *The Laocoön Group.* Roman copy, perhaps after Agesander, Athenodorus, and Polydorus of Rhodes (present state, former restorations removed). 1st century A.D. Marble, height 7'. Vatican Museums, Rome

208. *Portrait Head*, from Delos (see colorplate 17). National Museum, Athens

the sitter is unknown. Whoever he was, we get an intensely private view of him that immediately captures our interest. The fluid modeling of the somewhat flabby features, the uncertain, plaintive mouth, the unhappy eyes under furrowed brows, reveal an individual beset by doubts and anxieties, an extremely human, unheroic personality. There are echoes of Greek pathos in these features, but it is a pathos translated into psychological terms. Men of these particular character traits had surely existed earlier in the Greek world, just as they exist today. Yet it is significant that the inner complexity of such men could be conveyed by a work of art only when Greek independence, culturally as well as politically, was about to come to an end.

STATUETTES. Before we leave Hellenistic sculpture, we must cast at least a passing glance on another aspect of it, represented by the enchanting bronze statuette of a veiled dancer (fig. 209). She introduces us to the vast variety of small-scale works produced for private ownership. Such pieces were collected in much the same way as painted vases had been in earlier times; and, like vase pictures, they show a range of subject matter far broader than that of monumental sculpture. Besides the familiar mythological themes we encounter a wealth of everyday subjects: beggars, street entertainers, peasants, young ladies of fashion.

countless others. The history of its fame is rather like that of the *Apollo Belvedere*; the two were treated as complementary, the *Apollo* exemplifying harmonious beauty, the *Laocoön* sublime tragedy. Today we tend to find the pathos of the group somewhat calculated and rhetorical; its meticulous surface finish strikes us as a display of virtuoso technique. In style, including the relief-like spread of the three figures, it clearly descends from the Pergamum frieze, although its dynamism has become uncomfortably self-conscious. It was long accepted as a Greek original and identified with a group by Agesander, Athenodorus, and Polydorus of Rhodes that the Roman writer Pliny mentions, in the palace of the Emperor Titus; now it is thought to be a Roman copy or reconstruction of a late Hellenistic work. For the Romans, the subject must have held a special meaning: the divine punishment meted out to Laocoön and his sons forewarned Aeneas of the fall of Troy and caused him to flee that city in time. Since Aeneas was believed to have come to Italy and to have been the ancestor of Romulus and Remus, the death of Laocoön could be viewed as the first link in a chain of events that ultimately led to the founding of Rome.

PORTRAITS. Portraiture, an important branch of Greek sculpture since the fourth century, continued to flourish in Hellenistic times. Its achievements, however, are known to us only indirectly for the most part, through Roman copies. One of the few originals is the very vivid bronze head from Delos, a work of the early first century B.C. (fig. 208, colorplate 17). It was not made as a bust but, in accordance with Greek custom, as part of a full-length statue. The identity of

209. *Veiled Dancer*. c. 200 B.C.? Bronze statuette, height 8½". Collection Walter C. Baker, New York

210. *Winged God*, silver coin from Peparethus.
c. 500 B.C. Diameter 1½″. British Museum, London

211. *Silenus*, silver coin from Naxos,
c. 460 B.C. Diameter 1¼″. British Museum, London

212. *Apollo*, silver coin from Catana
c. 415–400 B.C. Diameter 1⅛″. British Museum, London

213. *Alexander the Great with Amun Horns*, four-drachma
silver coin issued by Lysimachus. c. 300 B.C. Diameter 1⅛″.

214. *Antimachus of Bactria*, silver coin, c. 185 B.C.
Diameter 1¼″. British Museum, London

The grotesque, the humorous, the picturesque—qualities that rarely enter into Greek monumental art—play a conspicuous role here. At their best, as in our example, these small figures have an imaginative freedom rarely matched on a larger scale. The bold spiral twist of the veiled dancer, reinforced by the diagonal folds of the drapery, creates a multiplicity of interesting views that practically forces the beholder to turn the statuette in his hands. No less extraordinary is the rich interplay of concave and convex forms, the intriguing contrast between the compact silhouette of the figure and the mobility of the body within. If we only knew when and where this little masterpiece was made!

COINS

We rarely think of coins as works of art, and the great majority of them do not encourage us to do so. The study of their history and development, known as numismatics, offers many rewards, but visual delight is the least of these. If many Greek coins form an exception to this general rule, it is not simply because they are the earliest (the idea of stamping metal pellets of standard weight with an identifying design originated in Ionian Greece sometime before 600 B.C.); after all, the first postage stamps were no more distinguished than their present-day descendants. The reason, rather, is the persistent individualism of Greek political life. Every city-state had its own coinage, adorned with its particular emblem, and the designs were changed at frequent intervals so as to take account of treaties, victories, or other occasions for local pride. As a consequence, the number of coins struck at any one time remained relatively small, while the number of coinages was large.

The constant demand for new designs produced highly skilled specialists who took such pride in their work that they sometimes even signed it. Greek coins thus are not only an invaluable source of historical knowledge but an authentic expression of the changing Greek sense of form. Within their own compass, they illustrate the development of Greek sculpture from the sixth to the second century as faithfully as the larger works we have examined. And since they form a continuous series, with the place and date of almost every item well established, they reflect this development more fully in some respects than do the works of monumental art.

Characteristically enough, the finest coins of Archaic and Classical Greece were usually produced not by the most powerful states such as Athens, Corinth, or Sparta, but by the lesser ones along the periphery of the Greek world. Our first example (fig. 210), from the Aegean island of Peparethus, reflects the origin of coinage: a square die deeply embedded in a rather shapeless pellet, like an impression in sealing wax. The winged god, his pinwheel stance so perfectly adapted to the frame, is a summary-in-miniature of Archaic art, down to the ubiquitous smile. On the coin from Naxos in Sicily (fig. 211), almost half a century later, the die fills the entire area of the coin; the drinking Silenus fits it as tightly as if he were squatting inside a barrel. An astonishingly monumental figure, he shows the articulation and organic vitality of the Severe Style. Our third coin (fig. 212) was struck in the Sicilian town of Catana toward the end of the Peloponnesian War. It is signed with the name of its maker, Herakleidas, and it well deserves to be, for it is one of the true masterpieces of Greek coinage. Who would have thought it possible to endow the full-face view of a head in low relief with such plasticity! This radiant image of Apollo has all the swelling roundness of the mature Classical style. Its grandeur completely transcends the limitations of the tiny scale of a coin.

From the time of Alexander the Great onward, coins began to show profile portraits of rulers. The successors of Alexander at first put his features on their coins, to emphasize their link with the deified conqueror. Such a piece is shown in figure 213; Alexander here displays the horns identifying him with the ram-headed Egyptian god Amun. His "inspired" expression, conveyed by the half-open mouth and the upward-looking eyes, is as characteristic of the emotionalism of Hellenistic art as are the fluid modeling of the features and the agitated, snakelike hair. As a likeness, this head can have only the most tenuous relation to the way Alexander actually looked; yet this idealized image of the all-conquering genius projects the flavor of the new era more eloquently than do the large-scale portraits of Alexander.

Once the Hellenistic rulers started putting themselves on their coins, the likenesses became more individual. Perhaps the most astonishing of these (fig. 214) is the head of Antimachus of Bactria (present-day Afghanistan), which stands at the opposite end of the scale from the Alexander-Amun. Its mobile features show a man of sharp intelligence and wit, a bit skeptical perhaps about himself and others, and, in any event, without any desire for self-glorification. This penetratingly human portrait seems to point the way to the bronze head from Delos (fig. 206, colorplate 17) a hundred years later. It has no counterpart in the monumental sculpture of its own time, and thus helps to fill an important gap in our knowledge of Hellenistic portraiture.

6
ETRUSCAN ART

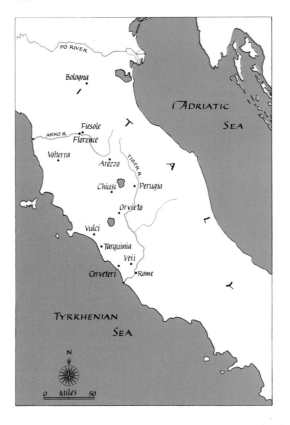

The Italian peninsula did not emerge into the light of history until fairly late. The bronze age came to an end there only in the eighth century B.C., about the time the earliest Greeks began to settle along the southern shores of Italy and in Sicily. Even earlier, if we are to believe the Classical Greek historian Herodotus, another great migration had taken place: the Etruscans had left their homeland of Lydia in Asia Minor and settled in the area between Florence and Rome which to this day is known as Tuscany, the country of the Tusci or Etrusci. Who were the Etruscans? Did they really come from Asia Minor? Strange as it may seem, Herodotus' claim is still the subject of lively debate among scholars. We know that the Etruscans borrowed their alphabet from the Greeks toward the end of the eighth century, but their language—of which our understanding is as yet very limited—has no kin among any known tongues.

Culturally and artistically, the Etruscans are strongly linked with Asia Minor and the ancient Near East, yet they also show many traits for which no parallels can be found anywhere. Might they not, then, be a people whose presence on Italian soil goes back to before the Indo-European migrations of about 2000–1200 B.C. that brought the Mycenaeans and the Dorian tribes to Greece and the ancestors of the Romans to Italy? If so, the sudden flowering of Etruscan civilization from about 700 B.C. onward could have resulted from a fusion of this prehistoric Italian stock with small but powerful groups of seafaring invaders from Lydia in the course of the eighth century. Interestingly enough, such a hypothesis comes very close to the legendary origin of Rome; the Romans believed that their city had been founded in 753 B.C. by the descendants of refugees from Troy (see page 147) in Asia Minor. Was this perhaps an Etruscan story which the Romans later made their own, along with a great many other things they took from their predecessors?

What the Etruscans themselves believed about their origin we do not know. The only Etruscan writings that have come down to us are brief funerary inscriptions and a few somewhat longer texts relating to religious ritual, though Roman authors tell us that a rich Etruscan literature once existed. We would, in fact, know practically nothing about the Etruscans at first hand were it not for their elaborate tombs, which the Romans did not molest when they destroyed or rebuilt Etruscan cities and which therefore have survived intact until modern times.

Italian bronze-age burials had been of the modest sort found elsewhere in prehistoric Europe: the remains of the deceased, contained in a pottery vessel or urn, were placed in a simple pit along with the equipment they required in afterlife (weapons for men, jewelry and household tools for women). In Mycenaean Greece, this primitive cult of the dead had been elaborated under Egyptian influence, as shown by the monumental beehive tombs. Something very similar happened eight centuries later in Tuscany. Toward 700 B.C., Etruscan tombs began to imitate, in stone, the interiors of actual dwellings, covered by great conical mounds of earth; they could be roofed by vaults or domes built of horizontal, overlapping courses of stone blocks, as was the Treasury of Atreus at Mycenae (see fig. 126). And at the same time, the pottery urns gradually took on human shape: the lid grew into the head of the deceased, and body markings appeared on the vessel itself, which could be placed on a sort of throne to indicate high rank (fig. 215). Alongside the modest beginnings of funerary sculpture, we find sudden evidence of great wealth in the form of exquisite goldsmith's work decorated with motifs familiar from the Orientalizing Greek vases of the same period, and intermingled with precious objects imported from the ancient Near East.

The seventh and sixth centuries B.C. saw the Etruscans at the height of their power. Their cities rivaled those of the Greeks, their fleet dominated the western Mediterranean and protected a vast commercial empire competing with the Greeks and Phoenicians, and their territory extended as far as Naples in the south and the lower Po valley in the north. Rome itself was ruled by Etruscan kings for about a century, until the establishing of the Republic in 510 B.C. The kings threw the first defensive wall around the seven hills, drained the swampy plain of the Forum, and built the original temple on the Capitoline Hill, thus making a city out of what had been little more than a group of villages before.

But the Etruscans, like the Greeks, never formed a unified nation; they were no more than a loose federation of individual city-states given to quarreling among themselves and slow to unite against a common enemy. During the fifth and fourth centuries B.C., one Etruscan city after another succumbed to the Romans; by the end of the third, all of them had lost their independence, although many continued to prosper, if we are to judge by the richness of their tombs during the period of political decline.

Tombs and Their Decoration

The flowering of Etruscan civilization thus coincides with the Archaic age in Greece. It was during this period, especially near the end of the sixth and the early in the fifth century B.C., that Etruscan art showed its greatest vigor. Greek Archaic influence had displaced the Orientalizing tendencies—many of the finest Greek vases have been found in Etruscan tombs of that time—but Etruscan artists did not simply imitate their Hellenic models. Working in a very different cultural setting, they retained their own clear-cut identity.

One might expect to see the Etruscan cult of the dead wane under Greek influence, but that was by no means the case. On the contrary, the tombs and their equipment grew more elaborate as the capacities of the sculptor and painter expanded. The deceased themselves could now be represented full-length, reclining on the lids of sarcophagi shaped like couches, as if they were participants in a festive repast, an Archaic smile about their lips. The monumental example in figure 216 shows a husband and wife side by side, strangely gay and majestic at the same time. The entire work is of terracotta and was once painted in bright colors. The smoothly rounded, elastic forms betray the Etruscan sculptor's preference for modeling in soft materials, in contrast to the Greek love of stone carving; there is less formal discipline here but an extraordinary directness and vivacity.

EARLY FUNERARY BELIEFS. We do not know precisely what ideas the Archaic Etruscans held about the afterlife. Effigies such as our reclining couple, which for the first time in history represent the deceased as thoroughly alive and enjoying themselves, suggest that they regarded the tomb as an abode not only for the body but for the soul as well (in contrast to the Egyptians, who thought of the soul as roaming freely and whose funerary sculpture therefore remained "inanimate"). Or perhaps the Etruscans believed that by filling the tomb with banquets, dancing, games, and similar pleasures they could induce the soul to stay put in the city of the dead and therefore not haunt the realm of the living. How else are we to understand the purpose of the wonderfully rich array of murals in these funerary chambers? Since nothing of the sort has survived in Greek territory, they are uniquely important, not only as an Etruscan achievement but also as a possible reflection of Greek wall painting.

215. Human-Headed Cinerary Urn. c. 675–650 B.C. Terracotta, height 25½". Etruscan Museum, Chiusi

TOMB OF HUNTING AND FISHING. Perhaps the most astonishing of them all is the great marine panorama of c. 520 B.C. in the Tomb of Hunting and Fishing at Tarquinia, of which figure 217 shows the best-preserved portion: a vast, continuous expanse of water and sky in which the fishermen, and the hunter with his slingshot, play only an incidental part. The free, rhythmic movement of birds and dolphins is strangely reminiscent of Minoan painting of a thousand years earlier (see fig. 118) but the weightless, floating quality of Cretan art is absent. We might also recall Exekias' *Dionysus in a Boat* (fig. 140) as the closest Greek counterpart to our scene. The differences here, however, are as revealing as the similarities, and one wonders if any Greek Archaic artist knew how to place man in a natural setting as effectively as the Etruscan painter did. Could the mural have been inspired by Egyptian scenes of hunting in the marshes, such as the one in figure 70? They seem the most convincing precedent for the general conception of our subject. If so, the Etruscan artist has brought the scene to life, just as the reclining couple in figure 216 has been brought to life compared with Egyptian funerary statues.

TOMB OF THE LIONESSES. A somewhat later example, from another tomb in Tarquinia (fig. 218, colorplate 18), shows a pair of ecstatic dancers; the passionate energy of their movements again strikes us as characteristically Etruscan rather than Greek in spirit. Of particular interest is the transparent garment of the woman, which lets the body shine through; in Greece, this differentiation appears only a few years earlier, in the final phase of Archaic vase painting. The contrasting body color of the two figures continues a practice introduced by the Egyptians more than two thousand years before (see fig. 67, colorplate 6).

LATER FUNERARY BELIEFS. During the fifth century, the Etruscan view of the hereafter must have become a good deal more complex and less festive. We notice the change immediately if we compare the group in figure 219, a cinerary container carved of soft local stone soon after 400 B.C., with its predecessor in figure 216. The woman now sits at the foot of the couch, but she is not the wife of the young man; her wings indicate that she is the demon of death, and the scroll in her left hand records the fate of the deceased.

216. Sarcophagus, from Cerveteri. c. 520 B.C. Terracotta, length 6′ 7″. Museo Nazionale di Villa Giulia, Rome

217. Wall painting, detail. c. 520 B.C. Tomb of Hunting and Fishing, Tarquinia

218. *Two Dancers*, detail of a wall painting (see colorplate 18). Tomb of the Lionesses, Tarquinia

219. *Youth and Demon of Death* (cinerary container). Early 4th century B.C. Stone (pietra fetida), length 47″. Archaeological Museum, Florence

The young man is pointing to it as if to say, "Behold, my time has come." The thoughtful, melancholy air of the two figures may be due to some extent to the influence of Classical Greek art which pervades the style of our group. At the same time, however, a new mood of uncertainty and regret is reflected: man's destiny is in the hands of inexorable supernatural forces; death is the great divide rather than a continuation, albeit on a different plane, of life on earth.

In later tombs, the demons of death gain an ever more fearful aspect; other, more terrifying demons enter the scene, often battling against benevolent spirits for possession of the soul of the deceased. One of these demons appears in the center of figure 220, a tomb of the third century B.C. at Cerveteri, richly decorated with stucco reliefs rather than paintings. The entire chamber, cut into the live rock, closely imitates the interior of a house, including the beams of the roof. The sturdy pilasters (note the capitals, which recall the Aeolian type from Asia Minor; fig. 172), as well as the wall surfaces between the niches, are covered with exact reproductions of weapons, armor, household implements, small domestic animals, and busts of the deceased. In such a setting, the snake-legged demon and his three-headed hound (whom we recognize as Cerberus, the guardian of the infernal regions) seem particularly disquieting.

Temples and Their Decoration

Only the stone foundations of Etruscan temples have survived, since the buildings themselves were wooden. Apparently the Etruscans, although they were masters of masonry construction for other purposes, rejected for religious reasons the use of stone in temple architecture. The design of their sanctuaries bears a general resemblance to the simpler Greek temples (fig. 221), but with several distinctive features, some of these later perpetuated by the Romans. The entire structure rests on a tall base, or podium, that is no wider than the cella and has steps only on the south side; these lead to a deep porch, supported by two rows of four columns each, and to the cella beyond. The cella is generally subdivided into three compartments, for Etruscan religion was dominated by a triad of gods, the predecessors of the Roman Juno, Jupiter, and Minerva. The Etruscan temple, then, must have been of a squat, squarish shape compared to the graceful Greek sanctuaries, and more closely linked with domestic architecture. Needless to say, it provided no place for stone sculpture; the plastic decoration usually consisted of terracotta plaques covering the architrave and the edges of the roof. Only after 400 B.C. do we occasionally find large-scale terracotta groups designed to fill the pediment above the porch.

VEII. We know, however, of one earlier attempt—and an astonishingly bold one—to find a place for monumental sculpture on the exterior of an Etruscan temple. The so-called Temple of Apollo at Veii, not very far north of Rome, a structure of standard type in every other respect, had four lifesize terracotta statues on the ridge of its roof (seen also in the reconstruction model, fig. 221). They formed a dramatic group of the sort we might expect in Greek pedimental

220. Burial Chamber. 3rd century B.C. Tomb of the Reliefs, Cerveteri

221. Reconstruction of an Etruscan Temple. Istituto di Etruscologia e Antichità Italiche, University of Rome

sculpture: the contest of Hercules and Apollo for the sacred hind, in the presence of other deities. The best preserved of these figures is the *Apollo* (fig. 222, colorplate 19), acknowledged to be the masterpiece of Etruscan Archaic sculpture. His massive body, completely revealed beneath the ornamental striations of the drapery; the sinewy, muscular legs; the hurried, purposeful stride—all these betray an expressive power that has no counterpart in free-standing Greek statues of the same date.

That Veii was indeed a sculptural center at the end of the sixth century seems to be confirmed by the Roman tradition that the last of the Etruscan rulers of the city called on a master from Veii to make the terracotta image of Jupiter for the temple on the Capitoline Hill. This image has disappeared, but an even more famous symbol of Rome, the bronze figure of the she-wolf that nourished Romulus and Remus, is still in existence (fig. 223). The two babes are Renaissance additions, and the early history of the statue is obscure; some scholars, therefore, have even suspected it of being a medieval work. Nevertheless, it is almost surely an Etruscan Archaic original, for the wonderful ferocity of expression, the latent physical power of the body and legs, have the same awesome quality we sense in the *Apollo* from Veii. In any event, the she-wolf as the totemic animal of Rome has the strongest links with Etruscan mythology, in which wolves seem to have played an important part from very early times.

222. *Apollo*, from Veii (see colorplate 19). Museo Nazionale di Villa Giulia, Rome

223. *She-Wolf.* c. 500 B.C. Bronze, height 33½". Capitoline Museums, Rome

224. *Portrait of a Boy.* Early 3rd century B.C.
Bronze, height 9". Archaeological Museum, Florence

Portraiture and Metalwork

The Etruscan concern with effigies of the deceased might
lead us to expect an early interest in individual portraiture.
Yet the features of such funerary images as those in figures
216 and 219 are entirely impersonal, and it was only toward
300 B.C., under the influence of Greek portraiture, that individual likenesses began to appear in Etruscan sculpture.
The finest of them are not funerary portraits, which tend to
be rather crude and perfunctory, but the heads of bronze
statues. *Portrait of a Boy* (fig. 224) is a real masterpiece of
its kind; the firmness of modeling lends a special poignancy
to the sensitive mouth and the gentle, melancholy eyes.

No less impressive is the very high quality of the casting
and finishing, which bears out the ancient fame of the
Etruscans as master craftsmen in metal. Their ability in this
respect was of long standing, for the wealth of Etruria was
founded on the exploitation of copper and iron deposits.
From the sixth century on, they produced vast quantities of
bronze statuettes, mirrors, and such, both for export and domestic consumption. The charm of these small pieces is well
displayed by the engraved design on the back of a mirror
done soon after 400 B.C. (fig. 225). Within an undulating
wreath of vines, we see a winged old man, identified as Chal-
chas, examining a roundish object. The draftsmanship is
so beautifully balanced and assured that we are tempted to
assume that Classical Greek art was the direct source of inspiration. So far as the style of our piece is concerned, this
may well be the case, but the subject is uniquely Etruscan,
for the winged genius is gazing at the liver of a sacrificial
animal.

DIVINATION. We are witnessing a practice that loomed as
large in the lives of the Etruscans as the care of the dead: the
search for omens or portents. The Etruscans believed that
the will of the gods manifested itself through signs in the
natural world, such as thunderstorms or the flight of birds,
and that by reading them man could find out whether the
gods smiled or frowned upon his enterprises. The priests
who knew the secret language of these signs enjoyed enormous prestige; even the Romans were in the habit of consulting them before any major public or private event.
Divination (as the Romans called the art of interpreting
omens) can be traced back to ancient Mesopotamia—nor
was the practice unknown in Greece—but the Etruscans
carried it further than any of their predecessors. They put
especial trust in the livers of sacrificial animals, on which,
they thought, the gods had inscribed the hoped-for divine
message. In fact, they viewed the liver as a sort of micro-
cosm, divided into regions that corresponded, in their mind,
to the regions of the sky. Weird and irrational as they were,
these practices became part of our cultural heritage, and
echoes of them persist to this day. True, we no longer try to
tell the future by watching the flight of birds or examining
animal livers, but tea leaves and horoscopes are still "ominous" to many people; and we speak of auspicious events,
that is, of events indicating a favorable future, unaware that
"auspicious" originally referred to a favorable flight of birds.
Perhaps we do not believe very seriously that four-leaf clo-
vers bring good luck and black cats bad luck, yet a surprising number of us admit to being superstitious.

225. Engraved Back of a Mirror. c. 400 B.C.
Bronze, diameter 6". Vatican Museums, Rome

226. Porta Augusta, Perugia. 2nd century B.C.

Cities

According to Roman writers, the Etruscans were masters of architectural engineering, and of town planning and surveying. That the Romans learned a good deal from them can hardly be doubted, but exactly how much the Etruscans contributed to Roman architecture is difficult to say, since hardly anything of Etruscan or early Roman architecture remains standing above ground. Roman temples certainly retained many Etruscan features, and the atrium, the central hall of the Roman house (see fig. 247), likewise originated in Etruria. In town planning and surveying, too, the Etruscans have a good claim to priority over the Greeks. The original homeland of the Etruscans, Tuscany, was too hilly to encourage geometric schemes; however, when they colonized the flatlands south of Rome in the sixth century, they laid out their newly founded cities as a network of streets centering on the intersection of two main thoroughfares, the *cardo* (which ran north and south) and the *decumanus* (which ran east and west). The four quarters thus obtained could be further subdivided or expanded, according to need. This system, which the Romans adopted for the new cities they were to found throughout Italy, western Europe, and North Africa, may have been derived from the plan of Etruscan military camps. Yet it also seems to reflect the religious beliefs that made the Etruscans divide the sky into regions according to the points of the compass and place their temples along a north-south axis.

The Etruscans must also have taught the Romans how to build fortifications, bridges, drainage systems, and aqueducts, but very little remains of their vast enterprises in these fields. The only truly impressive surviving monument is the Porta Augusta in Perugia, a fortified city gate of the second century B.C. (fig. 226). The gate itself, recessed between two massive towers, is not a mere entry but an architectural façade. The tall opening is spanned by a semi-circular arch, framed by a molding; above it is a balustrade of dwarf pilasters alternating with round shields, a pattern obviously derived from the triglyphs and metopes of the Doric frieze; it supports a second arched opening (now filled in) flanked by two larger pilasters.

THE ARCH. The arches here are true, which means they are constructed of wedge-shaped blocks, called voussoirs, each pointing toward the center of the semicircular opening. Such an arch is strong and self-sustaining, in contrast to the "false" arch composed of horizontal courses of masonry or brickwork (like the opening above the lintel of the Lion Gate at Mycenae, fig. 131). The true arch, and its extension, the barrel vault, had been discovered in Egypt as early as c. 2700 B.C., but the Egyptians had used it mainly in underground tomb structures and in utilitarian buildings (fig. 78), never in temples. Apparently they thought it unsuited to monumental architecture. In Mesopotamia, the true arch was used for city gates (see fig. 100, colorplate 10) and perhaps elsewhere as well—to what extent we cannot determine for lack of preserved examples. The Greeks knew the principle from the fifth century on, but they confined the use of the true arch to underground structures or to simple gateways, refusing to combine it with the elements of the architectural orders. And herein lies the importance of the Porta Augusta: it is the first instance we know in which arches were integrated with the vocabulary of the Greek orders into a monumental whole. The Romans were to develop this combination in a thousand ways, but the merit of having invented it, of having made the arch respectable, seems to belong to the Etruscans.

7
ROMAN ART

Among the civilizations of the ancient world, that of the Romans is far more accessible to us than any other. The growth of the Roman domain from city-state to Empire; its military and political struggles, its changing social structure, the development of its institutions; the public and private lives of its leading personalities—all these we can trace with a wealth of detail that never ceases to amaze us. Nor is this a matter of chance. The Romans themselves seem to have wanted it that way. Articulate and posterity-conscious, they have left us a vast literary legacy, from poetry and philosophy to humble inscriptions recording everyday events, and an equally huge mass of visible monuments that were scattered throughout their Empire, from England to the Persian Gulf, from Spain to Romania.

Yet, paradoxically, there are few questions more embarrassing to the art historian than "What is Roman art?" The Roman genius, so clearly recognizable in every other sphere of human activity, becomes oddly elusive when we ask whether there was a characteristic Roman style in the fine arts. Why is this so? The most obvious reason is the great admiration the Romans had for Greek art of every period and variety. Not only did they import originals of earlier date—Archaic, Classical, and Hellenistic—by the thousands, and have them copied in even greater numbers; their own production was clearly based on Greek sources, and many of their artists, from Republican times to the end of the Empire, were of Greek origin. Moreover, Roman authors show little concern with the art of their own time. They tell us a good deal about the development of Greek art as described in Greek writings on the subject, or they speak of artistic production during the early days of the Roman Republic, of which not a trace survives today, but rarely about contemporary works. While anecdotes or artists' names may be mentioned incidentally in other contexts, the Romans never developed a rich literature on the history, theory, and criticism of art such as had existed among the Greeks. Nor do we hear of Roman artists who enjoyed individual fame, although the great names of Greek art—Polyclitus, Phidias, Praxiteles, Lysippus—were praised as highly as ever.

One might well be tempted to conclude, therefore, that the Romans themselves looked upon the art of their time as being in decline compared with the great Greek past, whence all important creative impulses had come. This, indeed, was the prevalent attitude among scholars until not very long ago. Roman art, they claimed, is essentially Greek art in its final decadent phase—Greek art under Roman rule; there is no such thing as Roman style, there is only Roman subject matter. Yet the fact remains that, as a whole, the art produced under Roman auspices does look distinctly different from Greek art; otherwise our problem would not have arisen. If we insist on evaluating this difference by Greek standards, it will appear as a process of decay. If, on the other hand, we interpret it as expressing different, un-Greek intentions, we are likely to see it in a less negative light; and once we admit that art under the Romans had positive un-Greek qualities, we cannot very well regard these innovations as belonging to the final phase of Greek art, no matter how many artists of Greek origin we may find in Roman records. Actually, the Greek names of these men do not signify much; most of the artists, it seems, were thoroughly "Romanized." The Empire was a cosmopolitan society in which national or regional traits were soon absorbed into the common all-Roman pattern set by the capital, the city of Rome. In any event, the great majority of Roman works of art are unsigned, and their makers, for all we know, may have come from any part of the far-flung Roman domain.

But Roman society from the very start proved astonishingly tolerant of alien traditions; the all-Roman pattern had a way of accommodating them all, so long as they did not threaten the security of the state. The populations of newly conquered provinces were not forced into a uniform strait jacket but, rather, were put into a fairly low-temperature melting pot. Law and order, and a token reverence for the symbols of Roman rule, were imposed on them; at the same time, however, their gods and sages were hospitably received in the capital, and eventually they themselves would be given the rights of citizenship. Roman civilization—and Roman art—thus acquired not only the Greek heritage but, to a lesser extent, that of the Etruscans and of Egypt and the Near East as well. All this made for an extraordinarily complex and open society, homogeneous and diverse at the same time. The sanctuary of Mithras accidentally unearthed some years ago in the center of London offers a striking illustration of the cosmopolitan character of Roman society:

the god is Persian in origin but he had long since become a Roman "citizen," and his sanctuary, now thoroughly and uniquely Roman in form, can be matched by hundreds of others throughout the Empire.

Under such conditions, it would be little short of a miracle if Roman art were to show a consistent style such as we found in Egypt, or the clear-cut evolution that distinguishes the art of Greece. Its development—to the extent that we understand it today—might be likened to a counterpoint of divergent tendencies that may exist side by side, even within a single monument, and none of them ever emerges as overwhelmingly dominant. The "Roman-ness" of Roman art must be found in this complex pattern, rather than in a single and consistent quality of form.

ARCHITECTURE

If the autonomy of Roman sculpture and painting has been questioned, Roman architecture is a creative feat of such magnitude as to silence all doubts of this sort. Its growth, moreover, from the very start reflected a specifically Roman way of public and private life, so that whatever elements had been borrowed from Etruscans or Greeks were soon marked with an unmistakable Roman stamp. These links with the past are strongest in the temple types developed during the final century of the Republican period (510–60 B.C.), the heroic age of Roman expansion.

Religious Architecture

"TEMPLE OF FORTUNA VIRILIS." The delightful small "Temple of Fortuna Virilis" (the name is sheer fancy, for the sanctuary seems to have been dedicated to the Roman god of harbors, Portunus) is the oldest well-preserved example of its kind (fig. 227). Built during the last years of the second century B.C., it suggests, in the elegant proportions of its Ionic columns and entablature, the wave of Greek influence following the Roman conquest of Greece in 146. Yet it is no mere copy of a Greek temple, for we recognize a number of Etruscan elements: the high podium, the deep porch, and the wide cella, which engages the columns of the peristyle. On the other hand, the cella is no longer subdivided into three compartments as it had been under the Etruscans; it now encloses a single, unified space. The Romans needed spacious temple interiors, since they used them not only for the image of the deity but also for the display of trophies (statues, weapons, etc.) brought back by their conquering armies. The "Temple of Fortuna Virilis" thus represents a well-integrated new type of temple designed for Roman requirements, not a haphazard cross of Etruscan and Greek elements. It was to have a long life; numerous examples of it, usually large and with Corinthian columns, can be found as late as the second century A.D., both in Italy and in the provincial capitals of the Empire.

TEMPLE OF THE SIBYL. Another type of Republican temple is seen in the so-called Temple of the Sibyl at Tivoli (figs. 228, 229), erected a few decades later than the "Temple of Fortuna Virilis." It, too, was the result of the merging

227. "Temple of Fortuna Virilis," Rome. Late 2nd century B.C.

228. "Temple of the Sibyl," Tivoli. Early 1st century B.C.

229. Plan of the "Temple of the Sibyl"

of two separate traditions. Its original ancestor was a structure in the center of Rome in which the sacred flame of the city was kept. This building at first had the shape of the traditional round peasant huts in the Roman countryside; later on it was redesigned in stone, under the influence of Greek structures of the tholos type (see page 127), and thus became the model for the round temples of late Republican times. Here again we find the high podium, with steps only opposite the entrance, and a graceful Greek-inspired exterior.

As we look closely at the cella, however, we notice that while the door and window frames are of cut stone, the wall is built in a technique we have not encountered before. It is made of concrete—a mixture of mortar and gravel with rubble (that is, small pieces of building stone and brick)—and, in this case, faced with small, flat pieces of stone. Concrete construction had been invented in the Near East more than a thousand years earlier but had been used mainly for fortifications; it was the Romans who developed its potentialities until it became their chief building technique. Its advantages are obvious: strong, cheap, and flexible, it alone made possible the vast architectural enterprises that are still the chief mementos of "the grandeur that was Rome." The Romans knew how to hide the unattractive concrete surface behind a facing of brick, stone, or marble, or by covering it with smooth plaster. Today, this decorative skin has disappeared from the remains of most Roman buildings, leaving the concrete core exposed and thus depriving these ruins of the appeal that Greek ruins have for us. They speak to us in other ways, through massive size and boldness of conception.

SANCTUARY OF FORTUNA PRIMIGENIA. The oldest monument in which these qualities are fully in evidence is the Sanctuary of Fortuna Primigenia at Palestrina, in the foothills of the Apennines east of Rome. Here, in what had once been an important Etruscan stronghold, a strange cult had been established since early times, dedicated to Fortuna (Fate) as a mother deity and combined with a famous oracle. The Roman sanctuary dates from the early first century B.C.; its size and shape were almost completely hidden by the medieval town that had been built over it, until a bombing at-

tack in 1944 destroyed most of the later houses and thus laid bare the remains of the huge ancient temple precinct, which has been thoroughly explored during the past decades. A series of ramps and terraces (clearly visible in fig. 230) lead up to a great colonnaded court, from which we ascend, on a flight of steps arranged like the seats of a Greek theater, to the semicircular colonnade that crowned the entire structure (fig. 231). Arched openings, framed by engaged columns and entablatures, play an important part in the elevation, just as semicircular recesses do in the plan. One of these openings appears in our view of the lower terrace (fig. 232); it is covered by a barrel vault, another characteristic feature of the Roman architectural vocabulary. Except for the columns and architraves, all the surfaces now visible are of concrete, like the cella of the round temple at Tivoli, and it is indeed hard to imagine how a complex as vast as this could have been constructed otherwise.

What makes the sanctuary of Palestrina so imposing, however, is not merely its scale but the superb way it fits the site. An entire hillside, comparable to the Acropolis of Athens in its commanding position, has been transformed and articulated so that the architectural forms seem to grow out of the rock, as if man had simply completed a design laid out by nature herself. Such a molding of great open spaces had never been possible—or even desired—in the Classical Greek world; the only comparable projects are found in Egypt (see the Temple of Hatshepsut, figs. 74, 75). Nor did it express the spirit of the Roman Republic. Significantly enough, the Palestrina sanctuary dates from the time of Sulla, whose absolute dictatorship (82–79 B.C.) marked the transition from Republican government to the one-man rule of Julius Caesar and his Imperial successors. Since Sulla had won a great victory against his enemies in the civil war at Palestrina, it is tempting to assume that he personally ordered the sanctuary built, both as a thanks offering to Fortuna and as a monument to his own fame.

FORUMS. If Sulla did order it, the Palestrina complex perhaps inspired Julius Caesar, who near the end of his life sponsored a project planned on a similar scale in Rome itself: the Forum Julium, a great architecturally framed

230. Sanctuary of Fortuna Primigenia, Praeneste (Palestrina). Early 1st century B.C.

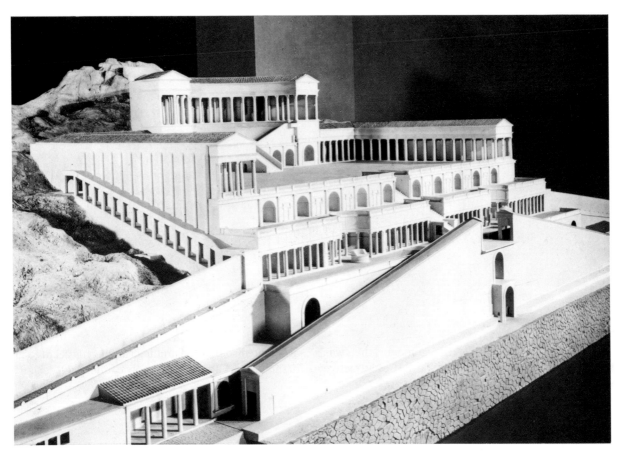

231. Reconstruction Model of the Sanctuary of Fortuna
Primigenia at Praeneste (Palestrina).
Archaeological Museum, Palestrina

232. Lower Terraces, Sanctuary of Fortuna Primigenia at Praeneste (Palestrina)

square adjoining the Temple of Venus Genetrix, the mythical ancestress of Caesar's family. Here the merging of religious cult and personal glory is even more overt. This Forum of Caesar set the pattern for all the later Imperial forums, which were linked to it by a common major axis (fig. 233), forming the most magnificent architectural sight of the Roman world. Unfortunately, nothing is left of the forums today but a stubbly field of ruins that conveys little of their original splendor.

Secular Architecture

The arch and vault, which we encountered at Palestrina as an essential part of Roman monumental architecture, also formed the basis of construction projects such as sewers, bridges, and aqueducts, designed for efficiency rather than beauty. The first enterprises of this kind were built to serve the city of Rome as early as the end of the fourth century B.C.; only traces of them survive today. There are, however, numerous others of later date throughout the Empire, such as the exceptionally well-preserved aqueduct at Nîmes in southern France known as the Pont du Gard (fig. 234). Its rugged, clean lines which span the wide valley are a tribute not only to the high quality of Roman engineering but also to the sense of order and permanence that inspired these efforts.

THE COLOSSEUM. The qualities we met here impress us again in the Colosseum, the enormous amphitheater for gladiatorial games in the center of Rome (figs. 235–37). Completed in 80 A.D., it is, in terms of mass, one of the largest single buildings anywhere; when intact, it accommodated more than 50,000 spectators. The concrete core, with its miles of vaulted corridors and stairways, is a masterpiece of engineering efficiency to ensure the smooth flow of traffic to and from the arena. It utilizes both the familiar barrel vault and a more complex form, the groined vault (see fig. 237), which results from the interpenetration of two barrel vaults at right angles. The exterior, dignified and monumental, reflects the interior articulation of the structure but clothes and accentuates it in cut stone. There is a fine balance between vertical and horizontal elements in the framework of engaged columns and entablatures that contains the endless series of arches. The three Classical orders are superimposed according to their intrinsic "weight": Doric, the oldest and most severe, on the ground floor, followed by Ionic and Corinthian. The lightening of the proportions, however, is barely noticeable; the orders, in their Roman adaptation, are almost alike. Structurally, they have become ghosts, yet their aesthetic function continues unimpaired, for it is through them that this enormous façade becomes related to the human scale.

233. (*below*) Plan of the Forums at Rome

234. (*right*) Pont du Gard, Nîmes. Early 1st century A.D.

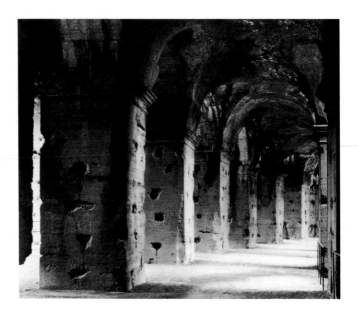

235. (*above*) The Colosseum (aerial view), Rome. 72–80 A.D.

236. (*left*) View of the outer wall of the Colosseum

237. (*below*) Interior, second floor of the Colosseum

238. (*below*) The Pantheon, Rome. 118–25 A.D.

239. (*right, above*) *The Interior of the Pantheon*, painting by Giovanni Paolo Pannini, c. 1750. The National Gallery of Art, Washington, D.C. (Kress Collection)

240. (*right, center*) Plan of the Pantheon

241. (*right, below*) Transverse Section of the Pantheon

Interiors

Arches, vaults, and the use of concrete permitted the Romans, for the first time in the history of architecture, to create vast interior spaces. These were explored especially in the great baths, or thermae, which had become important centers of social life in Imperial Rome. The experience gained there could then be applied to other, more traditional types of buildings, sometimes with revolutionary results.

THE PANTHEON. Perhaps the most striking example of this process is the famous Pantheon in Rome, a very large round temple of the early second century A.D. whose interior is the best preserved as well as the most impressive of any surviving Roman structure (figs. 238–41). There had been round temples long before that time, but their shape, well represented by the "Temple of the Sibyl" (figs. 228, 229), is so different from that of the Pantheon that the latter could not possibly have been derived from them. On the outside, the cella of the Pantheon appears as an unadorned cylindrical drum, surmounted by a gently curved dome; the entrance is emphasized by a deep porch of the kind familiar to us from Roman temples of the standard type (see fig. 227). The junction of these two elements seems rather abrupt, but we must remember that we no longer see the building as it was meant to be seen. Today the level of the surrounding streets is a good deal higher than it was in antiquity, so that the steps leading up to the porch are now submerged; moreover, the porch was designed to form part of a rectangular, colonnaded forecourt, which must have had the effect of detaching it from the rotunda. So far as the cella is concerned, therefore, the architect apparently discounted the effect of the exterior, putting all the emphasis on the great domed space that opens before us with dramatic suddenness as we step through the entrance.

The impact of this interior, awe-inspiring and harmonious at the same time, is impossible to convey in photographs; even the painting we have chosen (fig. 239) renders it only imperfectly. In any event, the effect is quite different from what the rather forbidding exterior would lead us to expect. The dome is not shallow, but is a true hemisphere; and the circular opening in its center admits an ample—and wonderfully even—flow of light. This "eye" is 143 feet above the floor, and that is also the diameter of the interior (fig. 241); dome and drum, also of equal heights, are in exact balance. On the exterior, this balance could not be achieved, for the outward thrust of the dome had to be contained by making its base considerably heavier than the top (the thickness of the dome decreases upward from 20 feet to 6 feet). Another surprise are the niches, which show that the weight of the dome does not rest uniformly on the drum but is concentrated on eight wide "pillars." The niches, of course, are closed in back, but with their screen of columns they give the effect of openings that lead to adjoining rooms and thus prevent us from feeling imprisoned inside the Pantheon. The columns, the colored marble paneling of the wall surfaces, and the floor remain essentially as they were in Roman times; the recessed coffers of the dome, too, are original, but the gilt that covered them has disappeared.

As its name suggests, the Pantheon was dedicated to "all the gods" or, more precisely, to the seven planetary gods (there are seven niches). It seems reasonable, therefore, to assume that the golden dome had a symbolic meaning, that it represented the Dome of Heaven. Yet this solemn and splendid structure grew from rather humble antecedents. The Roman architect Vitruvius, writing more than a century earlier, describes the domed steam chamber of a bathing establishment that anticipates (undoubtedly on a very much smaller scale) the essential features of the Pantheon: a hemispherical dome, a proportional relationship of height and width, and the circular opening in the center (which could be closed by a bronze shutter on chains, to adjust the temperature of the steam room).

BASILICAS. The Basilica of Constantine, of the early fourth century A.D., is a similar example, for, unlike other basilicas, of which we speak below, it derives its shape from the main hall of the public baths built by two earlier emperors, Caracalla and Diocletian. But it is built on an even vaster scale. It must have been the largest roofed interior in all of Rome. Today only the north aisle—three huge barrel-vaulted compartments—is still standing (fig. 242). The center tract, or nave, covered by three groined vaults (figs. 243, 244), rose a good deal higher. Since a groined vault resembles a canopy, with all the weight and thrust concentrated at the four corners, the upper walls of the nave (called the clerestory) could be pierced by large windows, so that the interior of the basilica must have had a light and airy quality despite its enormous size. We shall meet its echoes in many later buildings, from churches to railway stations.

242. The Basilica of Constantine, Rome. c. 310–20 A.D.

243. Reconstruction Drawing of the Basilica of Constantine (after Huelsen)

244. Plan of the Basilica of Constantine

245. Basilica, Leptis Magna, Libya. Early 3rd century A.D.

246. Plan of the Basilica, Leptis Magna

Basilicas, long halls serving a variety of civic purposes, had first been developed in Hellenistic Greece. Under the Romans, they became a standard feature of every major town, where one of their chief functions was to provide a dignified setting for the courts of law that dispensed justice in the name of the Emperor. Rome itself had a number of basilicas, but very little remains of them today. Those in the provinces have fared somewhat better. An outstanding one is that at Leptis Magna in North Africa (figs. 245, 246), which has most of the characteristics of the standard type. The long nave terminates in a semicircular niche, or apse, at either end; its walls rest on colonnades that give access to the side aisles. These are generally lower than the nave to permit clerestory windows in the upper part of the nave wall.

These basilicas had wooden ceilings instead of masonry vaults, for reasons of convenience and tradition rather than technical necessity. They were thus subject to destruction by fire; the one at Leptis Magna, sadly ruined though it is, counts among the best-preserved examples. The Basilica of Constantine in Rome was a daring attempt to create a novel, vaulted type, but the design seems to have met little public favor; it had no direct successors. Perhaps people felt that it lacked dignity, because of its obvious resemblance to the public baths. In any event, the Christian basilicas of the fourth century were modeled on the older, wooden-roofed type (see fig. 290). Not until seven hundred years later did vaulted basilican churches become common in western Europe.

Domestic Architecture

One of the delights in studying Roman architecture is that it includes not only great public edifices but also a vast variety of residential dwellings, from Imperial palaces to the quarters of the urban poor. If we disregard the extremes of this scale, we are left with two basic types that account for most of the domestic architecture that has survived. The *domus* is a single-family house based on ancient Italic tradition. Its distinguishing feature is the atrium, a square or oblong central hall lighted by an opening in the roof, around which the other rooms are grouped. In Etruscan times, it had been a rural dwelling, but the Romans "citified" and elaborated it into the typical home of the well-to-do.

Many examples of the domus, in various stages of development, have come to light at Herculaneum and Pompeii, the two famous towns near Naples that were buried under volcanic ash during an eruption of Mount Vesuvius in 79 A.D. Let us enter the so-called House of the Silver Wedding at Pompeii. The view in figure 247 is taken from the vestibule, along the main axis of the domus. Here the atrium has become a room of impressive size; the four Corinthian columns at the corners of the opening in the roof give it something of the quality of an enclosed court. There is a shallow basin in the center to catch the rain water (the roof slants inward). The atrium was the traditional place for keeping portrait images of the ancestors of the family. At its far end we see a recess, the *tablinum*, and beyond it the garden, surrounded by a colonnade, the peristyle. In addition to the chambers grouped around the atrium, there may be further rooms attached to the back of the house. The entire establishment is shut off from the street by windowless walls; obviously, privacy and self-sufficiency were important to the wealthy Roman.

Less elegant than the domus, and decidedly urban from the very start, is the *insula*, or city block, which we find mainly in Rome itself and in Ostia, the ancient port of Rome near the mouth of the Tiber. The insula anticipates many features of the modern apartment house; it is a good-sized concrete-and-brick building (or a chain of such buildings) around a small central court, with shops and taverns open to the street on the ground floor and living quarters for numerous families above. Some insulae had as many as five stories, with balconies above the second floor (fig. 248). The daily life of the craftsmen and shopkeepers who inhabited such

248. Insula of the House of Diana, Ostia. c. 150 A.D.

an insula was oriented toward the street, as it still is to a large extent in modern Italy. The privacy of the domus was reserved for the minority that could afford it.

Late Roman Architecture

In discussing the new forms based on arched, vaulted, and domed construction, we have noted the Roman architect's continued allegiance to the Classical Greek orders. If he no longer relied on them in the structural sense, he remained faithful to their spirit, acknowledging the aesthetic authority of the post-and-lintel system as an organizing and articulating principle. Column, architrave, and pediment might be merely superimposed on a vaulted brick-and-concrete core, but their shape, as well as their relationship to each other, was still determined by the original grammar of the orders.

This orthodox, reverential attitude toward the architectural vocabulary of the Greeks prevailed, generally speaking, from the Roman conquest of Greece until the end of the first century A.D. After that, we find increasing evidence of a contrary trend, of a taste for imaginative, "ungrammatical" transformations of the Greek vocabulary. Just when and where it began is still a matter of dispute; there is some evidence that it may go back to late Hellenistic times in the Near East. The tendency certainly was most pronounced in the Asiatic and African provinces of the Empire. A characteristic example is the Market Gate from Miletus, c. 160 A.D. (rebuilt in the State Museums, East Berlin; fig. 249). One might refer to it as display architecture, both in terms of its effect and of its ancestry, for the picturesque façade, with its alternating recesses and projections, derives from the architectural stage backgrounds of the Roman theater. The continuous in-and-out rhythm has even seized the pediment above the central doorway, breaking it into three parts. Equally astonishing is the small Temple of Venus at Baalbek, probably built in the early second century A.D. and refurbished in the third (figs. 250, 251). The convex curve of the cella is effectively counterbalanced by the concave niches

247. Atrium, House of the Silver Wedding, Pompeii. Early 1st century A.D.

249. The Market Gate from Miletus (restored). c. 160 A.D. State Museums, Berlin

250, 251. View and Plan of the Temple of Venus, Baalbek
(after Wiegand)

Colorplate 18. ETRUSCAN. *Two Dancers*, portion of a wall painting
(see page 152). About 480–470 B.C. Tomb of the Lionesses, Tarquinia

Colorplate 19. ETRUSCAN. *Apollo*, from Veii
(see page 155). About 510 B.C. Terracotta, height
69″. Museo Nazionale di Villa Giulia, Rome

Colorplate 20. ROMAN. *Aulus Metellus (L'Arringatore)*. Early
1st century B.C. (see page 178). Bronze, height 71″.
Archaeological Museum, Florence

Colorplate 21. ROMAN. *The Battle of Issus or Battle of Alexander and the Persians* (see page 190).
Mosaic copy from Pompeii, 1st century B.C., of a Hellenistic painting. 8' 11" × 16' 9½". National Museum, Naples

Colorplate 22. (*left*) ROMAN. *The Laestrygonians Hurling Rocks at the Fleet of Odysseus* (see page 191). Wall painting from a house on the Esquiline Hill. Late 1st century B.C. Museo Profano, The Vatican, Rome

Colorplate 23. (*above*) ROMAN. *Peaches and Glass Jar* (see page 192). Wall painting from Herculaneum. About 50 A.D. National Museum, Naples

Colorplate 24. (*above*) ROMAN. *Scenes of a Dionysiac Mystery Cult* (see page 192). Wall painting. About 50 B.C. Villa of the Mysteries, Pompeii

Colorplate 25. (*right*) EGYPTO-ROMAN. *Portrait of a Boy*, from the Faiyum, Lower Egypt (see page 194). 2nd century A.D. Encaustic on panel, 13 × 7¼″. The Metropolitan Museum of Art, New York (Gift of Edward S. Harkness, 1918)

Colorplate 26. ROMAN. *The Consecration of the Tabernacle and Its Priests*, from the Assembly Hall of the Synagogue at Dura-Europos (see page 195). 245–56 A.D. Mural, 4' 8¼" × 7' 8¼". National Museum, Damascus

252. Peristyle, Palace of Diocletian, Split, Yugoslavia. c. 300 A.D.

and the scooped-out base and entablature, introducing a new play of forces into the conventional ingredients of the round temple (compare figs. 228, 229).

By the late third century, unorthodox ideas such as these had become so well established that the traditional "grammar" of the Greek orders was in process of dissolution everywhere. In the peristyle of the Palace of Diocletian (fig. 252) at Split (Spalato), the architrave between the two center columns is curved, echoing the arch of the doorway below, and on the left we see an even more revolutionary device—a series of arches resting directly on columns. A few isolated instances of such an arcade can be found earlier, but it was only now on the eve of the victory of Christianity, that the marriage of arch and column became fully legitimate. The union, indispensable to the future development of architecture, seems so natural to us that we can hardly understand why it was ever opposed.

SCULPTURE

The dispute over the question "Is there such a thing as a Roman style?" has centered largely on the field of sculpture, and for quite understandable reasons. Even if we discount the wholesale importing and copying of Greek originals, the reputation of the Romans as imitators seems borne out by vast quantities of works that are obviously—or at least probably—adaptations and variants of Greek models of every period. While the Roman demand for sculpture was tremendous, a good deal of it may be attributed to antiquarianism, both the learned and the fashionable variety, and to a taste for sumptuous interior decoration. There are thus whole categories of sculpture produced under Roman auspices that deserve to be classified as "deactivated" echoes of Greek creations, emptied of their former meaning and reduced to the status of highly refined works of craftsmanship. At times this attitude extended to Egyptian sculpture as well, creating a vogue for pseudo-Egyptian statuary. On the other hand, there can be no doubt that some kinds of sculpture had serious and important functions in ancient Rome. They represent the living sculptural tradition, in contradistinction to the antiquarian-decorative trend. We shall concern ourselves here mainly with those aspects of Roman sculpture that are most conspicuously rooted in Roman society: portraiture and narrative relief.

Republican

We know from literary accounts that, from early Republican times on, meritorious political or military leaders were honored by having their statues put on public display. The habit

253. *Aulus Metellus (L'Arringatore).*
Archaeological Museum, Florence (see colorplate 20)

was to continue until the end of the Empire a thousand years later. Its beginnings may well have derived from the Greek custom of placing votive statues of athletic victors and other important individuals in the precincts of such sanctuaries as Delphi and Olympia (see fig. 180). Unfortunately, the first four hundred years of this Roman tradition are a closed book to us; not a single Roman portrait has yet come to light that can be dated before the first century B.C. with any degree of confidence. How were those early statues related to Etruscan or Greek sculpture? Did they ever achieve any specifically Roman qualities? Were they individual likenesses in any sense, or were their subjects identified only by pose, costume, attributes, and inscriptions?

L'ARRINGATORE. Our sole clue in answer to these questions is the lifesize bronze statue called *L'Arringatore* (fig. 253, colorplate 20), once assigned to the second century B.C. but now generally placed in the early years of the first. It comes from southern Etruscan territory and bears an Etruscan inscription which includes the name Aule Metele (Aulus Metellus in Latin), presumably the name of the official represented. He must have been a Roman, or at least a Roman-appointed official. The workmanship is evidently Etruscan, as indicated by the inscription, but the gesture, which denotes both address and salutation, recurs in hundreds of Roman statues of the same sort, and the costume, too, is Roman—an early kind of toga. One suspects, therefore, that our sculptor tried to conform to an established Roman type of portrait statue, not only in these externals but in style as well. For we find very little here of the Hellenistic flavor characteristic of the later Etruscan tradition. What makes the figure remarkable is its serious, prosaically factual quality, down to the neatly tied shoelaces. The term "uninspired" suggests itself, not as a criticism but as a way to describe the basic attitude of the artist in contrast to the attitude of Greek or Etruscan portraitists.

PORTRAITS. That seriousness was consciously intended as a positive value becomes clear when we familiarize ourselves with Roman portrait heads of the years around 75 B.C., which show it in its most pronounced form. Apparently the creation of a monumental, unmistakably Roman portrait style was achieved only in the time of Sulla, when Roman architecture, too, came of age (see page 160). We see it at its most impressive perhaps in the features of the unknown Roman of figure 254, contemporary with the fine Hellenistic portrait from Delos in figure 208 and colorplate 17. A more telling contrast could hardly be imagined; both are extremely persuasive likenesses, yet they seem worlds apart. Whereas the Hellenistic head impresses us with its subtle grasp of the sitter's psychology, the Roman may strike us at first glance as nothing but a detailed record of facial topography—the sitter's character emerges only incidentally, as it were. And yet this is not really the case: the wrinkles are true to life, no doubt, but the carver has nevertheless treated them with a selective emphasis designed to bring out a specifically Roman personality—stern, rugged, iron-willed in its devotion to duty. It is a "father image" of frightening authority, and the minutely observed facial details are like individual biographical data that differentiate this father image from others.

Its peculiar flavor reflects a Roman custom of considerable antiquity; at the death of the head of the family, a waxen image was made of his face, which was then preserved in

254. *Portrait of a Roman.* c. 80 B.C. Marble, lifesize.
Palazzo Torlonia, Rome

255. *A Roman Patrician with Busts of His Ancestors.*
c. 30 B.C. Marble, lifesize. Capitoline Museums, Rome

them in the spiritual sense as well. Nevertheless, the marble heads retained the character of records, of visual documents, which means that they could be freely duplicated; what mattered was only the facial "text," not the "handwriting" of the artist who recorded it. The impressive head in figure 254 is itself a copy, made some fifty years later than the lost original, and so are the two ancestors in figure 255 (differences in style and in the shape of the bust indicate that the original of the head on the left is about thirty years older than that of its companion). Perhaps this Roman lack of feeling for the uniqueness of the original, understandable enough in the context of their ancestor cult, also helps to explain why they developed so voracious an appetite for copies of famous Greek statues.

Imperial

PORTRAITS. As we approach the reign of the Emperor Augustus (27 B.C.–14 A.D.), we find a new trend in Roman portraiture that reaches its climax in the images of Augustus himself, as, for example, in the splendid statue from Primaporta (figs. 256, 257). At first glance, we may well be uncertain of whether it represents a god or a human being; this doubt is entirely appropriate, for the figure is meant to be both. Here, on Roman soil, we meet a concept familiar to us from Egypt and the ancient Near East: that of the divine ruler. It had entered the Greek world in the fourth century (see fig. 195); Alexander the Great had made it his own, and so did his successors, who modeled themselves after him. The latter, in turn, transmitted it to Julius Caesar and the Roman emperors, who at first encouraged the worship of themselves only in the eastern provinces, where belief in a divine ruler was a long-established tradition.

The idea of attributing superhuman stature to the Emperor, thus enhancing his authority, soon became official policy, and while Augustus did not carry it as far as his successors, the Primaporta statue clearly shows him enveloped in an air of divinity. Still, despite its heroic, idealized body, the statue has an unmistakably Roman flavor; the Emperor's gesture is familiar from *Aulus Metellus* (fig. 253, colorplate 20); the costume, including the rich allegorical program on the breastplate, has a concreteness of surface texture that conveys the actual touch of cloth, metal, and leather. The head, too, is idealized, or, better perhaps, "Hellenized"; small physiognomic details are suppressed, and the focusing of attention on the eyes gives it something of the "inspired" look we find in portraits of Alexander the Great (compare fig. 213). Nevertheless, the face is a definite likeness, elevated but clearly individual, as we can determine by comparison with the numerous other portraits of Augustus. Every Roman would have recognized it immediately, for he knew it from coins and countless other representations. In fact, the Emperor's image soon came to acquire the symbolic significance of a national flag. As a consequence of such mass production, artistic quality was rarely very high, except when portraits were produced under the ruler's direct patronage. That must have been true of the Primaporta statue, which was found in the villa of Augustus' wife, Livia.

a special shrine, or family altar. At funerals, these ancestral images were carried in the procession. We have seen the roots of this kind of ancestor worship in primitive societies (compare figs. 22, 36–41); the patrician families of Rome clung to it tenaciously, well into Imperial times. The images were, of course, records rather than works of art, and because of the perishability of wax they probably did not last more than a few decades. Thus the desire to have them duplicated in marble seems natural enough, yet the demand did not arise until the early first century B.C.; perhaps the patricians, feeling their traditional position of leadership endangered, wanted to make a greater public display of their ancestors, as a way of emphasizing their ancient lineage.

That display certainly is the purpose of the statue in figure 255, carved about half a century later than our previous example. It shows an unknown Roman holding two busts of his ancestors, presumably his father and grandfather. The work has little distinction, yet the "father-image" spirit can be felt even here. Needless to say, this quality was not present in the wax images themselves; it came to the fore when they were translated into marble, a process that not only made the ancestral images permanent but monumentalized

NARRATIVE RELIEF. Imperial art, however, was not confined to portraiture. The emperors also commemorated their outstanding achievements in narrative reliefs on monumental altars, triumphal arches, and columns. Similar scenes are familiar to us from the ancient Near East (see figs. 95, 102, 111) but not from Greece. Historic events—that is, events which occurred only once, at a specific time and in a particular place—had not been dealt with in Classical Greek sculpture; if a victory over the Persians was to be commemorated, it would be represented indirectly, as a combat of Lapiths and Centaurs, or Greeks and Amazons—a mythical event outside any space-time context. Even in Hellenistic times, this attitude persisted, although not quite as absolutely; when the kings of Pergamum celebrated their victories over the Gauls, the latter were represented faithfully (see fig. 201) but in typical poses of defeat rather than in the framework of a particular battle.

Greek painters, on the other hand, had depicted historic subjects such as the battle of Salamis as early as the mid-fifth century, although we do not know how specific these pictures were in detail. According to the Roman writer Pliny, Philoxenus of Eretria at the end of the fourth century painted the victory of Alexander the Great over Darius at Issus; an echo of that work may survive in a famous Pompeian mosaic (fig. 275, colorplate 21). In Rome, too, historic events had been depicted from the third century B.C. on; a victorious military leader would have his exploits painted on panels that were carried in his triumphal procession, or he would show such panels in public places. These pictures seem to have had the fleeting nature of posters advertising the hero's achievements. None has survived. Sometime during the late years of the Republic—we do not know exactly when—the temporary representations of such events began to assume more monumental and permanent form, no longer painted, but carved and attached to structures intended to last indefinitely. They were thus a ready tool for the glorification of Imperial rule, and the emperors did not hesitate to use them on a large scale.

256, 257. *Augustus of Primaporta.* c. 20 B.C. Marble, 6′ 8″. Vatican Museums, Rome

258. The Ara Pacis, Rome. 13–9 B.C.

259. *Imperial Procession*, portion of the
frieze of the Ara Pacis. Marble, height 63″

ARA PACIS. Since the leitmotif of his reign was peace, Augustus preferred to appear in his monuments as the "Prince of Peace" rather than as the all-conquering military hero. The most important of these monuments was the Ara Pacis (the Altar of Peace), voted by the Roman Senate in 13 B.C. and completed four years later. It is probably identical with the richly carved Augustan altar that bears this name today. (Parts of it were found as early as the sixteenth century A.D., but their reintegration was not achieved until 1938.) The

260. *Procession*, portion of east frieze, Parthenon. c. 440 B.C.
Marble, height 43″. The Louvre, Paris

entire structure (fig. 258) recalls the Pergamum Altar, though on a much smaller scale (compare figs. 203, 205). On the wall that screens the altar proper, a monumental frieze depicts allegorical and legendary scenes as well as a solemn procession led by the Emperor himself.

Here the "Hellenic," classicizing style we noted in the Primaporta statue reaches fullest expression. It is instructive, therefore, to compare the Ara Pacis frieze (fig. 259) with that of the Parthenon (figs. 167, 260). Only a direct confrontation of the two will show how different they really are, despite all surface similarities. The Parthenon frieze belongs to an ideal, timeless world; it shows a procession that took place in the remote, mythic past, beyond living memory. What holds it together is the great formal rhythm of the ritual itself, not its variable particulars. On the Ara Pacis, in contrast, we see a procession in celebration of one particular recent event—probably the founding of the altar in 13 B.C.—idealized to evoke something of the solemn, timeless air that surrounds the Parthenon procession, yet filled with concrete details of a remembered event. The participants, at least so far as they belong to the imperial family, are meant to be identifiable as portraits, including those of children dressed in miniature togas but too young to grasp the significance of the occasion: note how the little boy in the center of our group is tugging at the mantle of the young man in front of him while the somewhat older child to his left smilingly tells him to behave. The Roman artist also shows a greater concern with spatial depth than his Classical Greek predecessor; the softening of the relief background, which we first

261. Allegorical and Ornamental Panels of the Ara Pacis

chanting product of the Augustan era (fig. 262). The modeling, as suits the light material, is delicate and sketchy throughout, but the meaning of the blank surfaces to which it is applied varies a great deal. On the bottom strip of our illustration, there are two winged genii with plant ornament; here depth is carefully eschewed, since this zone belongs to the framework. Above it, we see that which is being framed; it can only be described as a "picture painted in relief," an idyllic landscape of great charm and full of atmospheric depth, despite the fact that its space is merely suggested rather than clearly defined. The whole effect echoes that of painted room decorations (see fig. 277).

ARCH OF TITUS. The spatial qualities of the Ara Pacis reliefs reached their most complete development in the two large narrative panels on the triumphal arch erected in 81 A.D. to commemorate the victories of the Emperor Titus. One of them (fig. 263) shows part of the triumphal procession celebrating the conquest of Jerusalem; the booty displayed includes the seven-branched candlestick and other sacred objects. Despite the mutilated surface, the movement of a crowd of figures in depth still appears strikingly successful. On the right, the procession turns away from us and disappears through a triumphal arch placed obliquely to the background plane so that only the nearer half actually emerges from the background—a radical but effective device.

The companion panel (fig. 264) avoids such experiments, although the number of layers of relief is equally great here. We also sense that its design has an oddly stationary quality, despite the fact that this is simply another part of the same procession. The difference must be due to the subject, which is the Emperor himself in his chariot, crowned by the

observed in the Stele of Hegeso (fig. 190), has been carried so far that the figures farthest removed from us seem partly immersed in the stone (such as the woman on the left whose face emerges behind the shoulder of the young mother in front of her).

The same interest in space appears even more strongly in the allegorical panel in figure 261, showing Mother Earth as the embodiment of human, animal, and plant fertility, flanked by two personifications of winds. Here the figures are placed in a real landscape setting of rocks, water, and vegetation, and the blank background clearly stands for the empty sky. Whether this pictorial treatment of space is a Hellenistic or Roman invention remains a matter of dispute. There can be no question, however, about the Hellenistic look of the three personifications, which thus represent not only a different level of reality but also a different—and less distinctly Roman—style from the Imperial procession. The acanthus ornament on the pilasters and the lower part of the wall, on the other hand, has no counterpart in Greek art, although the acanthus motif as such derives from Greece. The plant forms are wonderfully graceful and alive, yet the design as a whole, with its emphasis on bilateral symmetry, never violates the discipline of surface decoration and thus serves as an effective foil for the spatially conceived reliefs above.

Much the same contrast of flatness and depth occurs in the stucco decoration of a Roman house, a casual but en-

262. Stucco Decoration from the Vault of a Roman House.
Late 1st century B.C. Museo delle Terme, Rome

263. *Spoils from the Temple in Jerusalem*, relief in passageway, Arch of Titus, Rome. 81 A.D. Marble, height 7′ 10″.

264. *Triumph of Titus*, relief in passageway, Arch of Titus

winged Victory behind him. Apparently the sculptor's first concern was to display this set image, rather than to keep the procession moving. Once we try to read the Imperial chariot and the surrounding figures in terms of real space, we become aware of how strangely contradictory the spatial relationships are: four horses, shown in strict profile view, move in a direction parallel to the bottom edge of the panel, but the chariot is not where it ought to be if they were really pulling it. Moreover, the bodies of the Emperor and of most of the other figures are represented in frontal view, rather than in profile. These seem to be fixed conventions for representing the triumphant Emperor which our artist felt constrained to respect, though they were in conflict with his desire to create the kind of consistent movement in space he achieved so well in figure 263.

COLUMN OF TRAJAN. That the purposes of Imperial art, narrative or symbolic, were sometimes incompatible with a realistic treatment of space becomes fully evident in the Col-

265. Lower portion of the Column of Trajan, Rome. 106–13 A.D. Marble, height of relief band c. 50"

umn of Trajan, erected in 106–113 A.D. to celebrate that Emperor's victorious campaigns against the Dacians (the ancient inhabitants of Romania). Single, free-standing columns had been used as commemorative monuments from Hellenistic times on; their ultimate source may have been the obelisks of Egypt. The Column of Trajan is distinguished not only by its great height (125 feet, including the base) but by the continuous spiral band of relief covering its surface (fig. 265) and recounting, in epic breadth, the history of the Dacian wars. The Column was crowned by a statue of the Emperor (destroyed in the Middle Ages) and the base served as a burial chamber for his ashes. If we could unwind the relief band, we would find it to be 656 feet long, two-thirds the combined length of the three friezes of the Mausoleum at Halicarnassus and a good deal longer than the Parthenon frieze. In terms of the number of figures and the density of the narrative, however, our relief is by far the most ambitious frieze composition attempted up to that time in the ancient world. It is also the most frustrating, for the beholder must "run around in circles like a circus horse" (to borrow the apt description of one scholar) if he wants to follow the narrative; once he gets above the fourth or fifth turn, he finds himself defeated by the wealth of detail unless he is equipped with field glasses.

One wonders for whose benefit this elaborate pictorial account was intended. In Roman times, the monument formed the center of a small court flanked by public buildings at least two stories tall, but even that does not quite answer our question. Nor does it explain the evident success of our Column, which served as the model for several others of the same type. But let us take a closer look at the scenes visible in our figure 265: in the center of the bottom strip, we see the upper part of a large river god representing the Danube; to the left, there are some river boats laden with supplies, and a Roman town on the rocky bank; to the right, the Roman army crosses the river on a pontoon bridge. The second strip shows Trajan addressing his soldiers (to the left) and the building of fortifications; the third, the construction of a garrison camp and bridge as Roman cavalry (on the right) sets out on a reconnaissance mission. In the fourth strip, Trajan's foot soldiers are crossing a mountain stream (center); on the right, the Emperor addresses his troops in front of a Dacian fortress. These scenes are a fair sampling; among the more than 150 separate episodes, actual combat occurs only rarely, while the geographic, logistic, and political aspects of the campaign receive detailed attention, much as they do in Julius Caesar's famous account of his conquest of Gaul.

Only at one other time have we seen this matter-of-fact visualization of military operations—in Assyrian reliefs such as that in figure 102. Was there an indirect link between the two? And, if so, of what kind? The question is difficult to answer, especially since there are no extant copies of the Roman antecedents for our reliefs: the panels showing military conquests that were carried in triumphal processions (see page 180). At any rate, the spiral frieze on the Column of Trajan was a new and demanding framework for historic narrative which imposed a number of difficult conditions upon the sculptor: since there could be no clarifying inscriptions, the pictorial account had to be as self-sufficient and explicit as possible, which meant that the spatial setting of each episode had to be worked out with great care; visual continuity had to be preserved without destroying the inner coherence of the individual scenes; and the actual depth of the carving had to be much shallower than in reliefs such as those on the Arch of Titus, otherwise the shadows cast by the projecting parts would make the scenes unreadable from below.

Our artist has solved these problems with conspicuous success, but at the cost of sacrificing all but the merest remnants of illusionistic spatial depth. Landscape and architecture are reduced to abbreviated "stage sets," and the ground on which the figures stand is tilted upward. All these devices had already been employed in Assyrian narrative reliefs; here they asserted themselves once more, against the tradition of foreshortening and perspective space. In another two hundred years, they were to become dominant, and we shall find ourselves at the threshold of medieval art. In this respect, the relief band on the Column of Trajan is curiously prophetic of both the end of one era and the beginning of the next.

PORTRAITS. The Ara Pacis, the Arch of Titus, and the Column of Trajan are monuments of key importance for the art of Imperial Rome at the height of its power. To single out equally significant works among the portraits of the same period is very much more difficult; their production was vast, and the diversity of types and styles mirrors the ever more complex character of Roman society. If we regard the Republican ancestral image tradition and the Greek-inspired *Augustus of Primaporta* as opposite ends of the scale, we can find almost any variety of interbreeding between the two. The fine head of the Emperor Vespasian, of c. 75 A.D., is a case in point (fig. 266): he was the first of the Flavian emperors, a military man who came to power after the Julio-Claudian (Augustan) line had died out and who must have viewed the idea of emperor worship with considerable skepticism. (When he was dying, he is reported to have said, "It seems I am about to become a god.") His humble origin and simple tastes may be reflected in the anti-Augustan, Republican flavor of his portrait. The soft, veiled quality of the carving, on the other hand, with its emphasis on the texture of skin and hair, is so Greek that it immediately recalls the seductive marble technique of Praxiteles and his school. A similar refinement can be felt in the surfaces of the slightly later bust of a lady (fig. 267), probably the subtlest portrait of a woman in all of Roman sculpture. The graceful tilt of the head and the glance of the large eyes convey a gentle mood of reverie; and how effectively the silky softness of skin and lips is set off by the many corkscrew curls of the fashionable coiffure!

The wonderful head of Trajan (fig. 268), of c. 100 A.D., is another masterpiece of portraiture. Its firm, rounded forms recall the *Augustus of Primaporta*, as does the commanding look of the eyes, dramatized by the strongly projecting brows. The face radiates a strange emotional intensity that is difficult to define—a kind of Greek pathos transmuted into Roman nobility of character.

266. *Vespasian.* c. 75 A.D. Marble, lifesize. Museo delle Terme, Rome

267. *Portrait of a Lady.* c. 90 A.D. Marble, lifesize. Capitoline Museums, Rome

268. *Trajan.* c. 100 A.D. Marble, lifesize. Museum, Ostia

Trajan still conformed to age-old Roman custom by being clean-shaven. His successors, in contrast, adopted the Greek fashion of wearing beards, as an outward sign of admiration for the Hellenic heritage. It is not surprising, therefore, to find a strong neo-Augustan, classicistic trend, often of a peculiarly cool, formal sort, in the sculpture of the second century A.D., especially during the reigns of Hadrian and Marcus Aurelius, both of them introspective men deeply interested in Greek philosophy. We can sense this quality in the equestrian bronze statue of Marcus Aurelius (fig. 269), which is remarkable not only as the sole survivor of this class of monument but as one of the few Roman statues that remained on public view throughout the Middle Ages. The equestrian image of the Emperor, displaying him as the all-conquering lord of the earth, had been a firmly established tradition ever since Julius Caesar had permitted such a statue of himself to be erected in the Forum Julium. That of Marcus Aurelius, too, was meant to characterize the Emperor as ever victorious, for beneath the right front leg of the horse (according to medieval accounts) there once crouched a small figure of a bound barbarian chieftain. The wonderfully spirited and powerful horse expresses this martial spirit. But the Emperor himself, without weapons or armor, presents a picture of stoic detachment—a bringer of peace rather than a military hero. And so indeed he saw himself and his reign (161–180 A.D.).

It was the calm before the storm. The third century saw the Empire in almost perpetual crisis. Barbarians endangered its far-flung frontiers while internal conflicts under-mined the authority of the Imperial office. To retain the throne became a matter of naked force, succession by murder a regular habit; the "soldier emperors"—mercenaries from the outlying provinces of the realm—followed one another at brief intervals. The portraits of some of these men, such as Philippus the Arab (fig. 270; see fig. 114), who reigned from 244 to 249 A.D., are among the most powerful likenesses in all of art. Their facial realism is as uncompromising as that of Republican portraiture, but its aim is expressive rather than documentary: all the dark passions of the human mind—fear, suspicion, cruelty—suddenly stand revealed here, with a directness that is almost unbelievable. The face of Philippus mirrors all the violence of the time. Yet in a strange way it also moves us to pity; there is a psychological nakedness about it that recalls a brute creature doomed and cornered. Clearly, the agony of the Roman world was not only physical but spiritual. That Roman art should have been able to create an image of man embodying this crisis is a tribute to its continued vitality.

Let us note the new plastic means through which the impact of these portraits is achieved: we are struck, first of all, by the way expression centers on the eyes, which seem to gaze at some unseen but powerful threat. The engraved outline of the iris and the hollowed-out pupils, devices alien to earlier portraits, serve to fix the direction of the glance. The hair, too, is rendered in thoroughly un-Classical fashion as a close-fitting, textured cap; and the beard has been replaced by a peculiar unshaven look that results from roughing up the surfaces of the lower part of the face with short chisel strokes.

A somewhat later portrait, probably that of the late Greek philosopher Plotinus, suggests a different aspect of the third-century crisis (fig. 271). Plotinus' thinking—abstract, speculative, and strongly tinged with mysticism—marked a retreat from concern with the outer world that seems closer to the Middle Ages than to the Classical tradition of Greek philosophy. It sprang from the same mood which, on a more popular level, expressed itself in the spread of Oriental mystery cults throughout the Roman Empire. How trustworthy a likeness our head represents is hard to say; the ascetic features, the intense eyes and tall brow, may well portray inner qualities more accurately than outward appearance. According to his biographer, Plotinus was so contemptuous of the imperfections of the physical world that he refused to have any portrait made of himself. The body, he maintained, was an awkward enough likeness of the true, spiritual self; why then go to the bother of making an even more awkward "likeness of a likeness"?

Such a view presages the end of portraiture as we have known it so far. If a physical likeness is worthless, a portrait becomes meaningful only as a visible symbol of the spiritual self. It is in these terms that we must view the head of Constantine the Great, the first Christian Emperor and reorganizer of the Roman state (fig. 272). Originally, it belonged to a colossal statue which stood in the Basilica of Constantine. We may call it superhuman, not only because of its enormous size, but even more so perhaps as an image of Imperial majesty. The huge, radiant eyes, the massive, immobile features do not tell us much about Constantine's actual appear-

269. *Equestrian Statue of Marcus Aurelius*. 161–80 A.D. Bronze, over lifesize. Piazza del Campidoglio, Rome

270. *Philippus the Arab*. 244–49 A.D.
Marble, lifesize. Vatican Museums, Rome

271. *Portrait Head* (probably Plotinus).
Late 3rd century A.D. Marble, lifesize. Museum, Ostia

272. *Constantine the Great.* Early 4th century A.D.
Marble, height 8'. Capitoline Museums, Rome

The arch also contains a number of reliefs made especially for it, however, such as the friezes above the lateral openings, and these show the new Constantinian style in full force. If we compare the medallions of figure 274, carved in Hadrian's time, with the relief immediately below them, the contrast is such that they seem to belong to two different worlds. The scene represents Constantine, after his entry into Rome in 312 A.D., addressing the Senate and the people from the rostrum in the Forum.

The first thing we notice here is the avoidance of all the numerous devices developed since the fifth century B.C. for creating spatial depth; we find no oblique lines, no foreshortening, and only the barest ripple of movement in the listening crowds. The architecture has been flattened out against the relief background, which thus becomes a solid, impenetrable surface. The rostrum and the people on or beside it form a second, equally shallow layer—the second row of figures appears simply as a series of heads above those of the first. The figures themselves have an oddly doll-like quality: the heads are very large, while the bodies seem not only dwarfish (because of the thick, stubby legs) but also lacking in articulation. The mechanism of *contrapposto* has disappeared completely, so that these figures no longer stand freely and by their own muscular effort; rather, they seem to dangle from invisible strings.

All the characteristics we have described so far are essentially negative, judged from the Classical point of view: they represent the loss of many hard-won gains—a throwback to earlier, more primitive levels of expression. Yet such an approach does not really advance our understanding of the new style. The Constantinian panel cannot be explained as the result of a lack of ability, for it is far too consistent within itself to be regarded as no more than a clumsy attempt to imitate earlier Roman reliefs. Nor can it be viewed as a return to Archaic art, since there is nothing in pre-Classical times that looks like it. No, the Constantinian sculptor must have had a positive new purpose of his own. Perhaps we can approach it best by stressing one dominant feature of our relief: its sense of self-sufficiency.

The scene fills the available area, and fills it completely (note how all the background buildings are made to have the same height), but any suggestion that it continues beyond the frame is carefully avoided. It is as if our artist had asked himself, "How can I get *all* of this complicated ceremonial event into my panel?" In order to do so, he has imposed an abstract order upon the world of appearances: the middle third of the strip is given over to the rostrum with Constantine and his entourage, the rest to the listeners and the buildings that identify the Roman Forum as the scene of the action (they are all quite recognizable, even though their scale and proportions have been drastically adjusted). The symmetrical design also permits him to make clear the unique status of the Emperor. Constantine not only occupies the exact center; he is shown full-face (his head, unfortunately, has been knocked off), while all the other figures turn their heads toward him to express their dependent relationship. That the frontal pose is indeed a position of majesty reserved for sovereigns, human or divine, is nicely demonstrated by the seated figures at the corners of the rostrum,

ance; they tell us a great deal about how he viewed himself and his exalted office.

ARCH OF CONSTANTINE. Constantine's conception of his role is clearly reflected in his triumphal arch (fig. 273), erected near the Colosseum 312–315 A.D. One of the largest and most elaborate of its kind, it is decorated for the most part with sculpture taken from earlier Imperial monuments. This procedure has often been viewed as dictated by haste and by the poor condition of the sculptural workshops of Rome at that time. These may have been contributory factors, but there appears to be a conscious and carefully considered plan behind the way the earlier pieces were chosen and employed. All of them come from a related group of monuments, those dedicated to Trajan, Hadrian, and Marcus Aurelius, and the portraits of these Emperors have been systematically reworked into likenesses of Constantine. Does this not convey Constantine's view of himself as the restorer of Roman glory, the legitimate successor of the "good emperors" of the second century?

273. Arch of Constantine, Rome. 312–15 A.D.

274. Medallions (117–38 A.D.) and Frieze (early 4th century), Arch of Constantine

the only ones besides Constantine to face us directly: these figures are statues of emperors—the same "good emperors" we met elsewhere on the arch, Hadrian and Marcus Aurelius. Looked at in this way, our relief reveals itself as a bold and original creation. It is the harbinger of a new vision that will become basic to the development of Christian art.

PAINTING

The modern beholder, whether expert or amateur, is apt to find painting the most exciting as well as the most baffling aspect of art under Roman rule—exciting because it represents the only large body of ancient painting subsequent to the Etruscan murals and because much of it, having come to light only in modern times, has the charm of the unfamiliar; baffling because we know infinitely less about it than we do about Roman architecture or sculpture. The surviving material, with very few exceptions, is severely limited in range; almost all of it consists of wall paintings, and the great majority of these come from Pompeii, Herculaneum, and other settlements buried by the eruption of Mount Vesuvius in 79 A.D., or from Rome and its environs. Their dates cover a span of less than two hundred years, from the end of the first century B.C. to the late first century A.D.; what happened before or after remains largely a matter of guesswork. And since we have no Classical Greek or Hellenistic wall paintings, the problem of singling out the Roman element as against the Greek is far more difficult than in sculpture or architecture.

Greek Sources

That there was copying of Greek designs, that Greek paintings as well as painters were imported, nobody will dispute. But the number of instances in which this can be demonstrated is small indeed. Let us consider two of these. At an

275. *The Battle of Issus* or *Battle of Alexander and the Persians* (detail; see colorplate 21). National Museum, Naples

276. ALEXANDROS OF ATHENS.
The Knuckle-Bone Players. 1st century B.C.
Marble panel, 16½ × 15″. National Museum, Naples

earlier point, we mentioned Pliny's reference to a Greek picture of the late fourth century B.C. representing the battle of Issus (see page 180). The same subject—or, at any rate, another battle of Alexander's war against the Persians—is shown in an exceptionally large and technically accomplished floor mosaic from a Pompeian house of the first century B.C. Figure 275 and colorplate 21 illustrate the center and right half, with Darius and the fleeing Persians, and the badly damaged left-hand portion, with the figure of Alexander. While there is no special reason to link this mosaic with Pliny's account, we can hardly doubt that it is a copy—and an astonishingly proficient one—of a Hellenistic painting. But a Hellenistic painting of what date? The crowding, the air of frantic excitement, the powerfully modeled and foreshortened forms, the precise cast shadows—when did all these qualities reach this particular stage of development? We do not know, for even the great frieze of Pergamum seems restrained in comparison.

Our second instance is the very opposite of the first. A small marble panel from Herculaneum painted in a delicate, linear style, it shows a group of five women, two of them engaged in a game of knucklebones (fig. 276). An inscription tells us that Alexandros of Athens painted this. The style plainly recalls that of the late fifth century B.C. (compare the Attic white-ground lekythos in fig. 191, colorplate 16), yet the execution seems so much weaker than the conception that it must be a copy or, better perhaps, an imitation in the Classical manner, comparable to the copies or adaptations of Classical Greek statues manufactured for the Roman market. It belongs to a special class of "collector's items" that is no more representative of Roman painting as a whole than the Alexander mosaic. We wonder, moreover, whether anything as attenuated as this actually existed in Classical Athenian art. Was it perhaps a late "neo-Attic" invention meant to cater to the taste of some particular group of Roman connoisseurs?

Roman Illusionism

The earliest phase of Roman wall painting, known from a few examples of the second century B.C., does show a clear connection with the Hellenistic world, since it has also been found in the eastern Mediterranean. Unfortunately, it is not very informative for us, as it consists entirely of the imitation of colored marble paneling. About 100 B.C., this so-called First Style began to be displaced by a far more ambitious and elaborate style that sought to push back or open up the flat surface of the wall by means of illusionistic architectural perspectives and "window effects," including landscapes and figures. Three phases of this more elaborate style have been distinguished, known as the Second, Third, and Fourth Styles, but the differences between them are not always clear, and there seems to have been considerable overlapping in their sequence, so that we can largely disregard this classification here. The Fourth Style, which prevailed at the time of the eruption of Vesuvius in 79 A.D., is the most intricate of all; our example, a corner of the Ixion Room in the House of the Vettii at Pompeii (fig. 277), combines imitation marble paneling, conspicuously framed mythological scenes intended to give the effect of panel pictures set into the wall, and fantastic architectural vistas seen through make-believe windows. This architecture has a strangely unreal and picturesque quality that is believed to reflect the architectural backdrops of the theaters of the time; it often anticipates effects such as that of the Market Gate of Miletus (see fig. 249).

The architectural vistas of the Second Style, as represented by our figure 278, are a good deal more substantial and

277. The Ixion Room, House of the Vettii, Pompeii. 63–79 A.D.

278. *Architectural View*, wall painting from a villa at Boscoreale, near Pompeii. 1st century B.C. The Metropolitan Museum of Art, New York (Rogers Fund, 1903)

thus provide a better measure of the illusionistic devices by which the Roman painter achieved these breakthroughs. He is clearly a master of modeling and surface textures; the forms framing the vista—the lustrous, richly decorated columns, the moldings, the mask at the top—have an extraordinary degree of three-dimensional reality. They effectively set off the distant view of buildings, which is flooded with light to convey a sense of free, open-air space. But as soon as we try to penetrate this architectural maze, we find ourselves lost; the individual structures cannot be disentangled from each other, their size and relationship are obscure. And we quickly realize that the Roman painter has no systematic grasp of spatial depth, that his perspective is haphazard and inconsistent within itself. Apparently he never intended us to enter the space he has created; like a promised land, it remains forever beyond us.

When landscape takes the place of architectural vistas, exact foreshortening becomes less important, and the virtues of the Roman painter's approach outweigh his limitations. This is most strikingly demonstrated by the famous Odyssey Landscapes, a continuous stretch of landscape subdivided into eight compartments by a framework of pilasters. Each section illustrates an episode of the adventures of Odysseus (Ulysses). One of the adventures with the Laestrygonians is reproduced (fig. 279, colorplate 22). It has re-

279. *The Laestrygonians Hurling Rocks at the Fleet of Odysseus* (see colorplate 22). Museo Profano, The Vatican, Rome

cently been cleaned, so that its colors stand out in all their original brilliance. The airy, bluish tones create a wonderful feeling of atmospheric, light-filled space that envelops and binds together all the forms within this warm Mediterranean fairyland, where the human figures seem to play no more than an incidental role. Only upon further reflection do we realize how frail the illusion of coherence is even here: if we were to try mapping this landscape, we would find it just as ambiguous as the architectural perspective discussed above. Its unity is not structural but poetic, like that of the stucco landscape in figure 262.

The Odyssey Landscapes form an instructive contrast with another approach to nature, which we know from the murals in a room of the Villa of Livia at Primaporta (fig. 280). Here the architectural framework has been dispensed with altogether; the entire wall is given over to a view of a delightful garden full of flowers, fruit trees, and birds. These charming details have the same tangible quality, the same concreteness of color and texture as the architectural framework of figure 278, and their apparent distance from the beholder is also about the same—they seem to be within arm's reach. At the bottom, there is a low trellis, beyond it a narrow strip of lawn with a tree in the center, then a low wall, and immediately after that the garden proper begins. Oddly enough, however, we cannot enter it; behind the front row of trees and flowers lies an opaque mass of greenery that shuts off our view as effectively as a dense hedge. This garden, then, is another promised land made only for looking. The wall has not really been opened up but merely pushed back a few feet and replaced by a wall of plants. It is this very limitation of spatial depth that endows our mural with its unusual degree of coherence.

On a large scale, such restraint does not occur often in Roman mural decoration. We do find it, though, in the still lifes that sometimes make their appearance within the intricate architectural schemes. These usually take the form of make-believe niches or cupboards, so that the objects, which are often displayed on two levels, remain close to us.

Our example (fig. 281, colorplate 23), is particularly noteworthy for the rendering of the translucent glass jar half-filled with water. The reflections are so acutely observed that we feel the painter must have copied them from an actual jar illuminated in just this way. But if we try to determine the source and direction of the light in the picture, we find that this cannot be done, because the shadows cast by the various objects are not consistent with each other. Nor do we have the impression that the jar stands in a stream of light; instead, the light seems to be imprisoned within the jar. Clearly, the Roman artist, despite his striving for illusionistic effects, is no more systematic in his approach to the behavior of light than in his handling of perspective. However sensuously real the details, his work nearly always lacks a basic unifying element in its overall structure. In the finest examples, this lack is amply compensated for by other qualities, so that our observation must not be regarded as condemning him to an inferior status. The absence of a consistent view of the visible world should be thought of, rather, as a fundamental barrier which differentiates Roman painting from that of the Renaissance or of modern times.

The illusionistic tendencies that gained the upper hand in Roman murals during the first century B.C. may have been anticipated to some extent by Hellenistic painters, but in the form in which we know them they seem to be a specifically Roman development, as against the reproductive or imitative works we had examined before. Echoes of the latter persist in the mythological panels that occur like islands within an elaborate architectural framework (see fig. 277). While these scenes hardly ever give the impression of straightforward copies after Hellenistic originals, they often have the somewhat disjointed character of compilations of motifs from various sources.

A characteristic example is the picture of Hercules discovering the infant Telephus in Arcadia, from the Basilica at Herculaneum (fig. 282). What stamps this as the handiwork of a Roman painter is its oddly unstable style; almost everything here has the look of a "quotation," so that not only the forms, but even the brushwork varies from one figure to the next. Thus the personification of Arcadia, seated in the center, seems as cold, immobile, and tightly modeled as a statue, whereas Hercules, although his pose is equally statuesque, exhibits a broader and more luminous technique. Or compare the lion, painted in sketchy, agitated dabs, with the precise and graceful outlines of the doe. The sparkling highlights on the basket of fruit are derived from yet another source: still lifes such as figure 281 and colorplate 23. And the mischievously smiling young Pan in the upper left-hand corner is composed of quick, feathery brush strokes that have a character all their own.

VILLA OF THE MYSTERIES. There exists, however, one monument whose sweeping grandeur of design and coherence of style are unique in Roman painting: the great frieze in one of the rooms in the Villa of the Mysteries just outside Pompeii (fig. 283, colorplate 24). Like the garden view from the Villa of Livia, it dates from the latter part of the first century B.C., when the Second Style was at its height. So far as the treatment of the wall space is concerned, the two works

280. *View of a Garden*, wall painting from the Villa of Livia at Primaporta. c. 20 B.C. Museo delle Terme, Rome

281. *Peaches and Glass Jar* (see colorplate 23).
National Museum, Naples

282. *Hercules and Telephus*, wall painting from
Herculaneum. c. 70 A.D. National Museum, Naples

283. Wall Painting Frieze. c. 50 B.C.
Villa of the Mysteries, Pompeii (detail of colorplate 24)

gitimate heir in the same sense that the finest Latin poets of the Augustan age were the legitimate heirs to the Greek poetic tradition.

PORTRAITS. Portrait painting, according to Pliny, was an established custom in Republican Rome, serving the ancestor cult as did the portrait busts discussed earlier (see pages 178–79). None of these panels has survived, and the few portraits found on the walls of Roman houses in Pompeii may well derive from a different, a Hellenistic, tradition. The only coherent group of painted portraits at our disposal, strangely enough, comes from the Faiyum district in Lower Egypt. The earliest of them found so far seems to date from the second century A.D. We owe them to the survival—or revival—of an ancient Egyptian custom, that of attaching a portrait of the deceased to his wrapped, mummified body. Originally, these portraits had been sculptured (compare fig. 84, colorplate 8), but became replaced in Roman times by painted ones such as the very fine and well-preserved wooden panel reproduced in figure 284 and colorplate 25.

284. *Portrait of a Boy*, from the Faiyum, Lower Egypt (see colorplate 25). The Metropolitan Museum of Art, New York (Gift of Edward S. Harkness, 1918)

have more in common with each other than with the typical products of Second Style mural decoration, for both of them are conceived in terms of rhythmic continuity and arm's-length depth.

The artist who created the frieze in the Villa of the Mysteries has placed his figures on a narrow ledge of green against a regular pattern of red panels separated by strips of black, a kind of running stage on which they enact their strange and solemn ritual. Who are they, and what is the meaning of the cycle? Many details remain puzzling, but the program as a whole represents various aspects of the Dionysiac Mysteries, a semisecret cult of very ancient origin that had been brought to Italy from Greece. The sacred rites are performed in the presence of Dionysus and Adriadne, with their train of satyrs and sileni, so that human and mythical reality tend to merge into one.

We sense the blending of these two spheres in the qualities all the figures have in common—their dignity of bearing and expression, the wonderful firmness of body and drapery, the rapt intensity with which they participate in the drama of the ritual. Many of the poses and gestures are taken from the repertory of Classical Greek art, yet they lack the studied and self-conscious quality we call classicism. An artist of exceptional greatness of vision has filled these forms with new life. Whatever his relation to the famous masters of Greek painting whose works are lost to us forever, he was their le-

285. *Portrait of a Man.* c. 250 A.D. Glass, diameter c. 2".
Archaeological Museum, Arezzo

The amazing freshness of its colors is due to the fact that it was done in a technique of great durability called encaustic, which means that the pigments are suspended in hot wax. The mixture can be opaque and creamy, like oil paint, or thin and translucent. At their best, these portraits have an immediacy and sureness of touch that have rarely been surpassed; our dark-haired boy is as solid, sparkling, and lifelike a piece of reality as anyone might wish. The style of the picture—and it does have style, otherwise we could not tell it from a snapshot—becomes apparent only when we compare it with other Faiyum portraits. Since they were produced quickly and in large numbers, they tend to have many elements in common, such as the emphasis on the eyes, the placing of the highlights and shadows, the angle from which the face is seen. In the later examples, these conventional elements stiffen more and more into a fixed type, while in ours they merely furnish a flexible mold within which to cast the individual likeness.

Whether to call this style Roman or Hellenistic is an idle question. We do know, however, that it was not confined to Egypt, since it can be linked with some portrait miniatures on glass apparently done in Italy during the third century A.D. The finest of them is the medallion shown in its actual size in figure 285. Its power of characterization, superior to that of any Faiyum portrait, represents the same climax of Roman portraiture that produced the marble bust of Philippus the Arab (see fig. 270).

Eastern Religions

In discussing the crisis of the Roman world in the third century A.D. (see page 186), we mentioned, as characteristic of the mood of the times, the spread of Oriental mystery religions. They were of various origins—Egyptian, Persian, Semitic—and their early development naturally centered in their home territory, the southeastern provinces and border regions of the Roman Empire. Although based on traditions in effect long before the conquest of these ancient lands by Alexander the Great, the cults had been strongly influenced by Greek ideas during the Hellenistic period; it was, in fact, to this fusion of Oriental and Greek elements that they owed their vitality and appeal.

The names of most of these cults, and their doctrines, are today remembered only by specialists, even though they were powerful rivals of Christianity during the early centuries of our era. In those days, the Near East was a vast religious and cultural melting pot where all the competing faiths, including Judaism, Christianity, Mithraism, Manichaeism, Gnosticism, and many more, tended to influence each other, so that they had an astonishing number of things in common, whatever their differences of origin, ritual, or nomenclature. Most of them shared such features as an emphasis on revealed truth, the hope of salvation, a chief prophet or messiah, the dichotomy of good and evil, a ritual of purification or initiation (baptism), and the duty to seek converts among the "unbelievers." The last and, in Near Eastern terms, the most successful product of this cross-breeding process was Islam, which still dominates the entire area to this day (see pages 238–39).

The growth of the Graeco-Oriental religions under Roman rule is as yet very incompletely understood, since much of it was part of an underground movement which has left few tangible traces. Besides, the area where it took place has been a theater of war and destruction so many times that important discoveries, such as the Dead Sea Scrolls of recent memory, are rare events indeed. There is mounting evidence, however, that the new faiths also gave birth to a new style in art, and that this style, too, resulted from a fusion of Graeco-Roman and Oriental elements. The artists who struggled with the task of coining images to express the content of these faiths were not among the most gifted of their time; they were provincial craftsmen of modest ambition who drew upon whatever visual sources happened to be available to them, adapting, combining, and reshaping these as best they could. Their efforts are often clumsy, yet it is here that we find the beginnings of a tradition which was to become of basic importance for the development of medieval art.

DURA-EUROPOS. The most telling illustrations of this new compound style have been found in the Mesopotamian town of Dura-Europos on the upper Euphrates, a Roman frontier station that was captured by the resurgent Persians under Shapur I about 256 A.D. and abandoned by its population soon after. Its ruins have yielded the remains of sanctuaries of several religions, decorated with murals which all show essentially the same Graeco-Oriental character. The best preserved are those from the assembly hall of a synagogue, painted about 250 A.D.; of their numerous compartments, we illustrate the one representing the consecration of the tabernacle (fig. 286, colorplate 26).

It is characteristic of the melting-pot conditions described above that even Judaism should have been affected by them. Momentarily, at least, the age-old injunction against images was relaxed so that the walls of the assembly hall could be covered with a richly detailed visual account of the history of the Chosen People and their Covenant with the Lord. The

286. *The Consecration of the Tabernacle and Its Priests,*
from the Assembly Hall of the Synagogue at Dura-Europos
(see colorplate 26). National Museum, Damascus

new attitude seems to have been linked with a tendency to change Judaism from a national to a universal faith by missionary activity among the non-Jewish population; interestingly, some of the inscriptions on the murals (such as the name Aaron in fig. 286, colorplate 26) are in Greek. In any event, we may be sure that the artists who designed these pictures faced an unaccustomed task, just as did the painters who worked for the earliest Christian communities; they had to cast into visible form what had hitherto been expressed only in words. How did they go about it? Let us take a closer look at our illustration: we can read the details—animals, human beings, buildings, cult objects—without trouble, but their relationship eludes us. There is no action, no story, only an assembly of forms and figures confronting us in the expectation that we will be able to establish the proper links between them. The frieze in the Villa of the Mysteries presents a similar difficulty—there, too, the beholder is supposed to know—yet it strikes us as very much less puzzling, for the figures have an eloquence of gesture and expression that makes them meaningful even though we may not understand the context of the scenes.

If the synagogue painter fails to be equally persuasive, must we attribute this to his lack of competence, or are there other reasons as well? The question is rather like the one we faced when discussing the Constantinian relief of figure 274, which resembles the Dura-Europos mural in a number of ways. The synagogue painter exhibits the same sense of self-sufficiency, of condensation for the sake of completeness, but his subject is far more demanding: he had to represent a historical event of vast religious importance (the consecration of the tabernacle and its priests, which began the reconciliation of man and God) as described in detail in the Holy Scriptures, and he had to represent it in such a way as to suggest that it was also a timeless, recurrent ritual. Thus his picture is burdened with a wealth of significance

far greater and more rigidly defined than that of the Dionysiac frieze or the Constantinian relief. Nor did he have a well-established tradition of Jewish religious painting at his disposal to help him visualize the tabernacle and the consecration ceremony.

No wonder he has fallen back on a sort of symbolic shorthand composed of images borrowed from other, older traditions. The tabernacle itself, for instance, is shown as a Classical temple, simply because our artist could not imagine it, in accordance with the biblical description, as a tent-like construction of poles and goat's-hair curtains. The attendant and red heifer in the lower left-hand corner are derived from Roman scenes of animal sacrifice, hence they show remnants of foreshortening not found among the other figures. Other echoes of Roman painting appear in the perspective view of the altar table next to the figure of Aaron, in the perfunctory modeling here and there, and in the rudimentary cast shadows attached to some of the figures. Did the painter still understand the purpose of these shadows? They seem to be mere empty gestures, since the rest of the picture betrays no awareness of either light or space in the Roman sense. Even the occasional overlapping of forms appears largely accidental. The sequence of things in space is conveyed by other means: the seven-branched candlestick, the two incense burners, the altar, and Aaron are to be understood as behind, rather than on top of, the crenelated wall that shields the precinct of the tabernacle. Their size, however, is governed by their importance, not by their position in space. Aaron, as the principal figure, is not only larger than the attendants but also more rigid and abstract. His costume, because of its ritual significance, is diagramed in detail, at the cost of obliterating the body underneath. The attendants, on the other hand, still show a residue of mobility and three-dimensional existence. Their garments, surprisingly enough, are Persian, an indication not only of the odd mixture of civilizations in this border area but of possible artistic influences from Persia.

Our synagogue mural, then, combines—in none-too-skillful fashion—a considerable variety of formal elements whose only common denominator is the religious message of the whole. In the hands of a great artist, this message might have been a stronger unifying force, but even then the shapes and colors would have been no more than a humble, imperfect simile of the spiritual truth they were meant to serve. That, surely, was the outlook of the authorities who supervised the execution of the mural cycle and controlled its program. The essential quality of these pictures can no longer be understood in the framework of ancient art; they express an attitude that seems far closer to the Middle Ages. If we were to sum up their purpose in a single phrase, we could hardly do better than to quote a famous dictum justifying the pictorial representation of Christian themes: *Quod legentibus scriptura, hoc idiotis ... pictura*—translated freely: painting conveys the Word of God to the unlettered.

8
EARLY CHRISTIAN AND BYZANTINE ART

In 323 A.D. Constantine the Great made a fateful decision, the consequences of which are still felt today—he resolved to move the capital of the Roman Empire to the Greek town of Byzantium, which henceforth was to be known as Constantinople. Six years later, after an energetic building campaign, the transfer was officially completed. In taking this step, the Emperor acknowledged the growing strategic and economic importance of the eastern provinces (a development that had been going on for some time). The new capital also symbolized the new Christian basis of the Roman state, since it was in the heart of the most thoroughly Christianized region of the Empire.

Constantine could hardly have foreseen that shifting the seat of Imperial power would result in splitting the realm, yet within less than a hundred years the division had become an accomplished fact, even though the emperors at Constantinople did not relinquish their claim to the western provinces. The latter, ruled by western Roman emperors, soon fell prey to invading Germanic tribes—Visigoths, Vandals, Ostrogoths, Lombards. By the end of the sixth century, the last vestige of centralized authority had disappeared. The eastern, or Byzantine, Empire, in contrast, survived these onslaughts, and under Justinian (527–565) reached new power and stability. With the rise of Islam a hundred years later, the African and Near Eastern parts of the Empire were overrun by conquering Arab armies; in the eleventh century, the Turks occupied a large part of Asia Minor, while the last Byzantine possessions in the West (in southern Italy) fell to the Normans. Yet the Empire, with its domain reduced to the Balkans and Greece, held on until 1453, when the Turks finally conquered Constantinople itself.

The division of the Roman Empire soon led to a religious split as well. At the time of Constantine, the bishop of Rome, deriving his authority from St. Peter, was the acknowledged head, the pope, of the Christian Church. His claim to preeminence, however, soon came to be disputed by the patriarch of Constantinople, differences in doctrine began to develop, and eventually the division of Christendom into a Western, or Catholic, and an Eastern, or Orthodox, Church, became all but final. The differences between them went very deep; Roman Catholicism maintained its independence from Imperial or any other state authority and became an international institution reflecting its character as the Universal Church, while the Orthodox Church was based on the union of spiritual and secular authority in the person of the Emperor, who appointed the patriarch. It thus remained dependent on the power of the State, exacting a double allegiance from the faithful and sharing the vicissitudes of political power.

We will recognize this pattern as the Christian adaptation of a very ancient heritage, the divine kingship of Egypt and the Near East; if the Byzantine emperors, unlike their pagan predecessors, could no longer claim the status of gods, they retained an equally unique and exalted role by placing themselves at the head of the Church as well as of the State. Nor did the tradition die with the fall of Constantinople. The tsars of Russia claimed the mantle of the Byzantine emperors, Moscow became "the third Rome," and the Russian Orthodox Church was as closely tied to the State as was its Byzantine parent body.

"EARLY CHRISTIAN" AND "BYZANTINE." It is the religious even more than the political separation of East and West that makes it impossible to discuss the development of Christian art in the Roman Empire under a single heading. "Early Christian" does not, strictly speaking, designate a style; it refers, rather, to any work of art produced by or for Christians during the time prior to the splitting off of the Orthodox Church—or, roughly, the first five centuries of our era. "Byzantine art," on the other hand, designates not only the art of the eastern Roman Empire but a specific quality of style as well. Since this style grew out of certain tendencies that can be traced back to the time of Constantine or even earlier, there is no sharp dividing line between Early Christian and Byzantine art. Thus the reign of Justinian has been termed the First Golden Age of Byzantine art, yet Justinian himself was a man of strongly western, Latin orientation who almost succeeded in reuniting the Constantinian domain; and the monuments he sponsored, especially those on Italian soil, may be viewed as either Early Christian or Byzantine, depending on which frame of reference we select.

Soon after, it is true, the political and religious cleavage between East and West became an artistic cleavage as well.

In western Europe, Celtic and Germanic peoples fell heir to the civilization of late antiquity, of which Early Christian art had been a part, and transformed it into that of the Middle Ages. The East, in contrast, experienced no such break; in the Byzantine Empire, late antiquity lived on, although the Greek and Oriental elements came increasingly to the fore at the expense of the Roman heritage. As a consequence, Byzantine civilization never became wholly medieval. "The Byzantines may have been senile," one historian has observed, "but they remained Greeks to the end." The same sense of tradition, of continuity with the past, determines the development of Byzantine art. We can understand it best, therefore, if we see it in the context of the final, Christian phase of antiquity rather than in the context of the Middle Ages.

EARLY CHRISTIAN ART

When and where the first Christian works of art were produced remains a matter of conjecture. Of the surviving monuments, none can be dated earlier than about 200 A.D.; therefore, we lack all direct knowledge of art in the service of Christianity before that time. In fact, there is little we know for certain about Christian art until we reach the reign of Constantine the Great, because the third century, too, is poorly represented. The painted decorations of the Roman catacombs, the underground burial places of the Christians, provide the only sizable and coherent body of material, but these are merely one among various possible kinds of Christian art.

Before Constantine's reign, Rome did not embody the faith; older and larger Christian communities existed in the great cities of North Africa and the Near East, such as Alexandria and Antioch. They had probably developed separate artistic traditions of their own. The extraordinary murals of the synagogue at Dura-Europos (see fig. 286, colorplate 26) suggest that paintings similarly orientalizing in style may have decorated the walls of Christian places of worship in Syria and Palestine, since the earliest Christian congregations were formed by dissident members of the Jewish community. Alexandria, the home of a large and thoroughly Hellenized Jewish colony, during the first or the second century A.D. may have produced illustrations of the Old Testament in a style akin to that of Pompeian murals. We meet echoes of such scenes in Christian art later on, but we cannot be sure when or where they originated, or by what paths they entered the Christian tradition.

Catacombs

If the dearth of material from the eastern provinces of the Empire makes it difficult to judge the position of the catacomb paintings within the early development of Christian art, they nevertheless tell us a good deal about the spirit of the communities that sponsored them. The burial rite and the safeguarding of the tomb were of vital concern to the early Christian, whose faith rested on the hope of eternal life in paradise. The imagery of the catacombs, as can be seen in

287. Painted Ceiling. 4th century A.D. Catacomb of SS. Pietro e Marcellino, Rome

the painted ceiling in figure 287, clearly expresses this otherworldly outlook, although the forms are in essence still those of pre-Christian mural decoration. Thus we recognize the division of the ceiling into compartments as a late and highly simplified echo of the illusionistic architectural schemes in Pompeian painting; and the modeling of the figures, as well as the landscape settings, betray their descent from the same Roman idiom, which here, in the hands of an artist of very modest ability, has become debased by endless repetition. But the catacomb painter has used this traditional vocabulary to convey a new, symbolic content, and the original meaning of the forms is of little interest to him. Even the geometric framework shares in this task, for the great circle suggests the Dome of Heaven, inscribed with the cross, the basic symbol of the faith. In the central medallion we see a youthful shepherd, with a sheep on his shoulders, in a pose that can be traced back as far as Greek Archaic art (compare fig. 147); he stands for Christ the Saviour, the Good Shepherd who gives His life for His sheep.

The semicircular compartments tell the story of Jonah: on the left he is cast from the ship, on the right he emerges from the whale, and at the bottom he is safe again on dry land, meditating upon the mercy of the Lord. This Old Testament miracle, often juxtaposed with New Testament miracles, enjoyed immense favor in Early Christian art as proof of the Lord's power to rescue the faithful from the jaws of death. The standing figures represent members of the Church, with their hands raised in prayer, pleading for divine help. The entire scheme, though small in scale and unimpressive in execution, has a coherence and clarity that set it apart from its pagan ancestors as well as from the synagogue murals of Dura-Europos (see fig. 286, colorplate 26). Here is, if not the reality, at least the promise of a truly monumental new form (compare fig. 321).

Architecture

Constantine's decision to make Christianity the state religion of the Roman Empire had a profound impact on Christian art. Until that time, congregations had been unable to meet for worship in public; services were held inconspicuously in the houses of the wealthier members. Now, almost overnight, an impressive architectural setting had to be created for the new official faith, so that the Church might be

288. Reconstruction Drawing of Old St. Peter's, Rome (after Frazer)

289. Plan of Old St. Peter's. Begun c. 333 A.D. (after Frazer)

visible to all. Constantine himself devoted the full resources of his office to this task, and within a few years an astonishing number of large, imperially sponsored churches arose, not only in Rome but also in Constantinople, in the Holy Land, and at other important sites.

THE BASILICA. These structures were a new type, now called the Early Christian basilica, that provided the basic model for the development of church architecture in western Europe. Unfortunately, none of them has survived in its original form, but the plan of the greatest Constantinian church, St. Peter's in Rome, is known with considerable accuracy (figs. 288, 289). For an impression of the interior, we

must draw upon the slightly later basilica of St. Paul Outside the Walls, built on the same pattern, which remained essentially intact until it was wrecked by fire in 1823 (fig. 290). The Early Christian basilica, as exemplified in these two monuments, is a synthesis of assembly hall, temple, and private house. It also has the qualities of an original creation that cannot be wholly explained in terms of its sources. What it owes to the imperial basilicas of pagan times becomes obvious when we compare the plan of St. Peter's with that of the basilica at Leptis Magna, erected a hundred years earlier (fig. 246): the long nave flanked by aisles and lit by clerestory windows, the apse, the wooden roof, are familiar features of the earlier structure. The pagan basilica was indeed a uniquely suitable model for Constantinian churches, since it combined the spacious interior demanded by Christian ritual with imperial associations that proclaimed the privileged status of Christianity as the new State religion.

But a church had to be more than an assembly hall; in addition to enclosing the community of the faithful, it was the sacred House of God, the Christian successor to the temples of old. In order to express this function, the design of the pagan basilica had to be given a new focus, the altar, which was placed in front of the apse at the eastern end of the nave, and the entrances, which in pagan basilicas had usually been on the flanks, were shifted to the western end. The Christian basilica was thus oriented along a single, longitudinal axis that is curiously reminiscent of the layout of Egyptian temples (compare fig. 77). Before entering the church proper, we traverse a colonnaded court, the atrium (see page 167), the far side of which forms an entrance hall, the narthex. Only when we step through the nave portal do we gain the view presented in figure 290. The steady rhythm of the nave arcade pulls us toward the great arch at the eastern end (called the triumphal arch), which frames the altar and the vaulted apse beyond. As we come closer, we realize that the altar stands in a separate compartment of space placed at right angles to the nave and aisles, the transept (in the lesser basilican churches, this feature is frequently omitted).

290. *Interior, St. Paul Outside the Walls*, Rome. Begun 386 A.D. (etching by G.B. Piranesi, 1749)

291. S. Apollinare in Classe, Ravenna. 533–549 A.D.

292. Plan of S. Apollinare in Classe
(after De Angelis d'Ossat)

One essential aspect of Early Christian religious architecture has not yet emerged from our discussion: the contrast between exterior and interior. It is strikingly demonstrated in the sixth-century church of S. Apollinare in Classe near Ravenna, which still retains its original appearance for the most part. The plain brick exterior (figs. 291, 292) remains conspicuously unadorned; it is merely a shell whose shape reflects the interior space it encloses—the exact opposite of the Classical temple. (Our view, taken from the west, shows the narthex but not the atrium, which was torn down a long time ago; the round bell tower, or campanile, is a medieval addition.) This ascetic, antimonumental treatment of the exterior gives way to the utmost richness as we enter the church (fig. 293, colorplate 27). Here, having left the everyday world behind us, we find ourselves in a shimmering realm of light and color where precious marble surfaces and the brilliant glitter of mosaics evoke the spiritual splendor of the Kingdom of God.

DOMED STRUCTURES. Before dealing with these mosaic decorations at greater length, we must take note of another type of structure that entered the tradition of Christian architecture in Constantinian times: round or polygonal buildings crowned with a dome. They had been developed, we will recall, as part of the elaborate Roman baths; the design of the Pantheon was derived from that source (see page

293. Interior (view toward the apse), S. Apollinare in Classe
(see colorplate 27)

162). Similar structures had been built to serve as monumental tombs, or mausoleums, by the pagan emperors. In the fourth century, this type of building is given a Christian meaning in the baptisteries (where the bath becomes a sacred rite) and the funerary chapels linked with basilican churches. The finest surviving example is Sta. Costanza (figs. 294–96), the mausoleum of Constantine's daughter

Early Christian and Byzantine Art 201

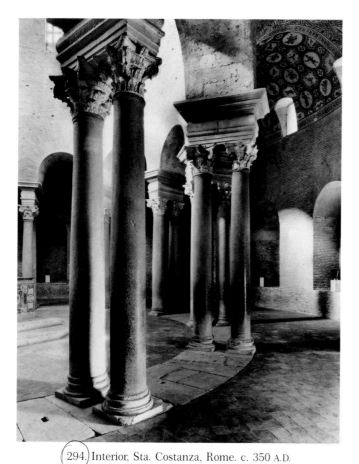

294. Interior, Sta. Costanza, Rome. c. 350 A.D.

295. Plan of Sta. Costanza

296. Section, Sta. Costanza

Constantia, originally attached to the (now ruined) Roman church of St. Agnes Outside the Walls. In contrast to its pagan predecessors, it shows a clear articulation of the interior space into a domed cylindrical core lit by clerestory windows—the counterpart of the nave of a basilican church—and a ring-shaped "aisle" or ambulatory covered by a barrel vault. Here again the mosaic decoration plays an essential part in setting the mood of the interior.

Painting and Mosaic

The rapid growth of Christian architecture on a large scale must have had a well-nigh revolutionary effect on the development of Early Christian painting. All of a sudden, huge wall surfaces had to be covered with images worthy of their monumental framework. Who was equal to this challenge? Certainly not the humble artists who had decorated the catacombs with their limited stock of types and subjects. They were superseded by masters of greater ability, recruited, we may suppose, under imperial auspices, as were the architects of the new basilicas. Unfortunately, so little has survived of the decoration of fourth-century churches that its history cannot be traced in detail. Apparently, great pictorial cycles were spread over the nave walls, the triumphal arch, and the apse from the very start. These cycles must have drawn upon a great variety of earlier sources, reflecting the whole range of Graeco-Roman painting. The heritage of the past, however, was not only absorbed but transformed so as to make it fit its new environment, physical and spiritual.

WALL MOSAICS. Out of this process, there emerged a great new art form, the Early Christian wall mosaic, which to a large extent replaced the older and cheaper technique of mural painting. Mosaics—designs composed of small pieces of colored material set in plaster—had been used by the Sumerians as early as the third millennium B.C. to embellish architectural surfaces. The Hellenistic Greeks and the Romans, employing small cubes of marble called tesserae, had refined the technique to the point that it could reproduce paintings, as in the *Battle of Issus* (see fig. 275, colorplate 21). But these were mostly floor mosaics, and the color scale, although rich in gradations, lacked brilliance, since it was limited to the various kinds of colored marble found in nature. The Romans would also produce wall mosaics occasionally, but only for special purposes and on a limited scale.

The vast and intricate wall mosaics of Early Christian art thus are essentially without precedent. The same is true of their material, for they consist of tesserae made of colored glass. These, too, were not entirely unknown to the Romans, yet their special virtues had never been exploited before; they offered colors of far greater range and intensity than marble tesserae, including gold, but lacked the fine gradations in tone necessary for imitating painted pictures. Moreover, the shiny (and slightly irregular) faces of glass tesserae act as tiny reflectors, so that the over-all effect is that of a glittering, immaterial screen rather than of a solid, continuous surface. All these qualities made glass mosaic the ideal complement of the new architectural aesthetic that confronts us in Early Christian basilicas.

297. Dome Mosaic (detail). Late 4th century A.D. St. George, Salonica

CONTRASTS WITH GRAECO-ROMAN. The guiding principle of Graeco-Roman architecture, we recall, had been to express a balance of opposing forces, rather like the balance within the *contrapposto* of a Classical statue—a muscular, physical display of active and passive, supporting and supported members, whether these were structurally real or merely superimposed on a concrete core. Viewed in such terms, Early Christian architecture is strangely inexpressive, even antimonumental. The tangible, material structure has become subservient to the creation and definition of immaterial space; walls and vaults have the quality of weightless shells, their actual thickness and solidity hidden rather than emphasized as before. The brilliant color, the light-filled, transparent brightness of gold, the severe geometric order of the images in a mosaic complex such as that of S. Apollinare in Classe (colorplate 23) fit the spirit of these interiors to perfection. One might say, in fact, that Early Christian and Byzantine churches *demand* mosaics the way Greek temples demand architectural sculpture.

Roman mural painting had developed elaborate illusionistic devices in order to suggest a reality beyond the surface of the wall. In Early Christian mosaics the flatness of the wall surface is also denied, but in order to achieve an "illusion of unreality," a luminous realm peopled by celestial beings or symbols. The difference in aim becomes particularly striking whenever these mosaics make use of the old formulas of spatial illusionism. Such is the case in figure 297, which shows a section of the magnificent dome mosaics from the church of St. George at Salonica, done at the end of the fourth century. Two saints, their hands raised in prayer, stand against a background that clearly betrays its descent from the perspective vistas of "stage architecture" in Pompeian painting; the foreshortening, to be sure, seems somewhat askew, but a surprising amount of it survives intact. Even so, the structure no longer seems real, for it lacks all physical substance: its body consists of the same gold as the background (other colors, mainly purple, blue, and green, are used only in the shaded portions and the ornament), so that the entire building becomes translucent. This is not a stage set but a piece of symbolic, otherworldly architecture meant to evoke such concepts as the Heavenly Jerusalem or the City of God.

SANTA MARIA MAGGIORE. In narrative scenes, too, we see the illusionistic tradition of ancient painting being transformed by new content. Long sequences of scenes, selected from the Old and New Testaments, adorned the nave walls of Early Christian basilicas. *The Parting of Lot and Abraham* (fig. 298) is taken from the oldest surviving cycle of this kind, executed about 430 in the church of Sta. Maria Maggiore in Rome. Abraham, his son Isaac, and the rest of his family occupy the left half of the composition; Lot and his clan, including his two small daughters, turn toward the city of Sodom on the right.

The task of the artist who designed our panel is comparable to that faced by the sculptors of the Column of Trajan (see fig. 265): how to condense complex actions into a visual form that would permit them to be read at a distance. He has, in fact, employed many of the same "shorthand" devices, such as the abbreviative formulas for house, tree, and city, or the trick of showing a crowd of people as a "grape-cluster of heads" behind the foreground figures. But in the Trajanic reliefs, these devices could be used only to the extent that they were compatible with the realistic aim of the scenes, which re-create actual historic events. "Look, this is what happened in the Dacian wars," we are told. The mosaics in Sta. Maria Maggiore, on the other hand, depict the history of salvation; the reality they illustrate is the living word of the Scriptures (in our instance, Genesis 13), which is a *present* reality shared by artist and beholder alike, rather than something that happened only once in the space-and-time context of the external world.

Our panel does not tell us, "This is what happened in Genesis 13" (we are expected to know that already), but "Behold the working of the Lord's will." Hence the artist need not clothe the scene with the concrete details of historic narrative; glances and gestures are becoming more important to him than dramatic movement or three-dimensional form. The symmetrical composition, with its cleavage in the center, makes clear the symbolic significance of this parting: the way of Abraham, which is that of righteousness and the Covenant, as against the way of Lot, destined for divine vengeance. And the contrasting fate of the two groups is further emphasized by the juxtaposition of Isaac and the daughters of Lot, whose future roles are thus called to mind.

Roll, Book, and Illustration

From what source did the designers of narrative mosaic cycles such as that of Sta. Maria Maggiore derive their compositions? Were they the first to illustrate scenes from the Bible in extensive fashion? For certain subjects, they could have found models among the catacomb murals, but their most important prototypes may have come from illustrated manuscripts, especially of the Old Testament. As a scriptural religion, founded on the Word of God as revealed in Holy Writ, the early Christian Church must have sponsored the duplicating of the sacred text on a vast scale; and every copy of it was handled with a reverence quite unlike the treatment of any book in Graeco-Roman civilization. But when did these copies become works of pictorial art as well? And what did the earliest Bible illustrations look like?

Books, unfortunately, are frail things; thus, their history in the ancient world is known to us largely from indirect evidence. It begins in Egypt—we do not know exactly when—with the discovery of a suitable material, paper-like but rather more brittle, made from the papyrus plant. Books of papyrus were in the form of rolls; they remained in use throughout antiquity. Not until late Hellenistic times did a better substance become available: parchment or vellum, thin, bleached animal hide, far more durable than papyrus. It was strong enough to be creased without breaking, and thus made possible the kind of bound book we know today, technically called a codex.

Between the first and the fourth century A.D., the vellum codex gradually replaced the roll, whether vellum or papyrus. This technological change must have had an important effect on the growth of book illustration. As long as the roll form prevailed, illustrations seem to have been mostly line drawings, since layers of pigment would soon have cracked and come off in the process of rolling and unrolling; only the vellum codex permitted the use of rich colors, including gold, that was to make book illustration—or, as we usually say, illumination—the small-scale counterpart of murals, mosaics, and panel pictures. When, where, and at what pace the development of pictorial book illumination took place, whether biblical or classical subjects were primarily depicted, how much of a carry-over there might have been from roll to codex—all these are still unsettled problems.

THE VATICAN VERGIL. There can be little question, however, that the earliest illuminations, whether Christian, Jewish, or pagan, were done in a style strongly influenced by the illusionism of Hellenistic-Roman painting of the sort we meet at Pompeii. One of the oldest illustrated manuscript books known, the *Vatican Vergil*, probably made in Italy

298. *The Parting of Lot and Abraham* (mosaic). c. 430 A.D. Sta. Maria Maggiore, Rome

about the time of the Sta. Maria Maggiore mosaics, reflects this tradition, although the quality of the miniatures is far from inspired (fig. 299); the picture, separated from the rest of the page by a heavy frame, has the effect of a window, and in the landscape we find remnants of deep space, perspective, and the play of light and shade.

The oldest illustrated Bible manuscripts so far discovered apparently belong to the early sixth century (except for one fragment of five leaves that seems related to the *Vatican Vergil*); they, too, contain echoes of the Hellenistic-Roman style, in various stages of adaptation to religious narrative, often with a Near Eastern flavor that at times recalls the Dura-Europos murals (see fig. 286, colorplate 26).

THE VIENNA GENESIS. The most important example, the *Vienna Genesis*, is a far more striking work than the rather lame *Vergil*. Written in silver (now turned black) on purple vellum and adorned with brilliantly colored miniatures, it achieves a sumptuous effect not unlike that of the mosaics we have seen. Colorplate 28 and figure 300 show a part of the story of Jacob; in the foreground, we see him wrestling with the angel and receiving the angel's benediction. The picture, then, does not show a single event but a whole sequence, strung out along a single U-shaped path, so that progression in space becomes progression in time. This method, known as continuous narration, has a complex—and much debated—history going back as far as ancient Egypt and Mesopotamia; its appearance in miniatures such as ours may reflect earlier illustrations made for books

300. Page with *Jacob Wrestling the Angel*, from the *Vienna Genesis* (detail; see colorplate 28). National Library, Vienna

in roll form. (Our picture certainly looks like a frieze turned back upon itself.)

For manuscript illustration, the continuous method offers the advantage of spatial economy; it permits the painter to pack a maximum of narrative content into the area at his disposal. Our artist apparently thought of his picture as a running account to be read like so many lines of text, rather than as a window demanding a frame. The painted forms are placed directly on the purple background that holds the letters, emphasizing the primary importance of the page as a unified field.

Sculpture

Compared to painting and architecture, sculpture played a secondary role in Early Christian art. The biblical prohibition of graven images was thought to apply with particular force to large cult statues, the idols worshiped in pagan temples; if religious sculpture was to avoid the pagan taint of idolatry, it had to eschew lifesize representations of the human figure. It thus developed from the very start in an antimonumental direction: away from the spatial depth and massive scale of Graeco-Roman sculpture toward shallow, small-scale forms and lacelike surface decoration. The earliest works of Christian sculpture are marble sarcophagi, which were produced from the middle of the third century on for the more important members of the Church. Before the time of Constantine, their decoration consisted mostly of the same limited repertory of themes familiar from catacomb murals—the Good Shepherd, Jonah and the Whale, and so forth—but within a framework borrowed from pagan sarcophagi. Not until a century later do we find a significantly broader range of subject matter and form.

SARCOPHAGUS OF JUNIUS BASSUS. A key example for those years is the richly carved sarcophagus of Junius Bassus, a prefect of Rome, who died in 359 (figs. 301, 302). Its colonnaded front, divided into ten square compartments, shows a mixture of Old and New Testament scenes: in the upper row (left to right), the Sacrifice of Isaac, St. Peter Taken Prisoner, Christ Enthroned between SS. Peter and Paul, Christ before Pontius Pilate (two compartments); in the low-

299. Miniature from the *Vatican Vergil*.
Early 5th century A.D. Vatican Library, Rome.

301. Sarcophagus of Junius Bassus. c. 359 A.D. Marble, 3' 10½" × 8'. Vatican Grottoes, Rome

302. *Christ Enthroned* (detail of fig. 301)

er, the Misery of Job, the Fall of Man, Christ's Entry into Jerusalem, Daniel in the Lions' Den, and St. Paul Led to His Martyrdom. This choice, somewhat strange to the modern beholder, is highly characteristic of the Early Christian way of thinking, which stresses the divine rather than the human nature of Christ. Hence His suffering and death are merely hinted at; He appears before Pilate as a youthful, long-haired philosopher expounding the true wisdom (note the scroll), and the martyrdom of the two apostles is represented in the same discreet, nonviolent fashion. The two central scenes are devoted to Christ the King: as Ruler of the Universe He sits enthroned above the personification of the firmament, and as an earthly sovereign He enters Jerusalem in triumph. Adam and Eve, the original sinners, denote the burden of guilt redeemed by Christ, the Sacrifice of Isaac is the Old Testament prefiguration of Christ's sacrificial death, while Job and Daniel carry the same message as Jonah— they fortify man's hope of salvation.

When measured against the anti-Classical style of the frieze on the Arch of Constantine, carved almost half a century before (see fig. 274), the sarcophagus of Junius Bassus seems decidedly classicistic. The figures in their deeply recessed niches betray a conscious attempt to recapture the statuesque dignity of the Greek tradition. Yet beneath this superimposed quality we sense a basic kinship to the Constantinian style in the doll-like bodies, the large heads, the oddly becalmed, passive air of scenes calling for dramatic action. The events and personages confronting us are no longer intended to tell their own story, physically or emotionally, but to call to our minds a higher, symbolic meaning that binds them together.

CLASSICISM. Classicizing tendencies of this sort seem to have been a recurrent phenomenon in Early Christian sculpture from the mid-fourth to the early sixth century. Their causes have been explained in various ways. On the one hand, during this period paganism still had many important adherents who may have fostered such revivals as a kind of rear-guard action; recent converts (such as Junius Bassus himself, who was not baptized until shortly before his death) often kept their allegiance to values of the past, artistic and otherwise. There were also important leaders of the Church who favored a reconciliation of Christianity with the heritage of Classical antiquity; and the imperial courts, too, both East and West, always remained aware of their institutional links with pre-Christian times, and could thus become centers for revivalist impulses. Whatever its roots in any given instance, classicism had its virtues in this age of transition, for it preserved—and thus helped to transmit to the future—a treasury of forms and an ideal of beauty that might have been irretrievably lost without it.

IVORY DIPTYCHS. All this holds true particularly for a class of objects whose artistic importance far exceeds their physical size: the ivory panels and other small-scale reliefs in precious materials. Designed for private ownership and meant to be enjoyed at close range, they often mirror a collector's taste, a refined aesthetic sensibility not found among the large, official enterprises sponsored by Church or State. Such a piece is the ivory leaf (fig. 303) forming the right half of a hinged diptych that was carved about 390–400, probably on the occasion of a wedding among the Nicomachi and Symmachi, two aristocratic Roman families. Their conservative outlook is reflected not only in the pagan subject (a priestess of Bacchus and her assistant before an altar of Jupiter) but also in the design, which harks back to the era of Augustus (compare fig. 259). At first glance, we might well mistake it for a much earlier work, until we realize, from small spatial incongruities such as the priestess's right foot overlapping the frame, that these forms are quotations, reproduced with loving care but no longer fully understood. Significantly enough, the pagan theme did not prevent our panel from being incorporated into the shrine of a saint many centuries later; its cool perfection had an appeal for the Middle Ages as well.

Our second ivory (fig. 304), done soon after 500 in the eastern Roman Empire, shows a classicism that has become an eloquent vehicle of Christian content. The majestic archangel is clearly a descendant of the winged Victories of Graeco-Roman art, down to the richly articulated drapery. Yet the power he heralds is not of this world; nor does he inhabit an earthly space. The architectural niche against which he appears has lost all three-dimensional reality; its relationship to him is purely symbolic and ornamental, so that he seems to hover rather than to stand (notice the position of the feet on the steps). It is this disembodied quality, conveyed through classically harmonious forms, that gives him so compelling a presence.

303. *Priestess of Bacchus* (leaf of a diptych). c. 390–400 A.D. Ivory, 11¾ × 5½". Victoria & Albert Museum, London (Crown Copyright Reserved)

PORTRAITURE. If monumental statuary was discouraged by the Church, it retained, for a while at least, the patronage of the State. Emperors, consuls, and high officials continued the old custom of erecting portrait statues of themselves in public places as late as the reign of Justinian, and sometimes later than that (the last recorded instance is in the late eighth century). Here, too, we find retrospective tendencies during the latter half of the fourth century and the early years of the fifth, with a revival of pre-Constantinian types and a renewed interest in individual characterization. From about 450 on, however, the outward likeness gives way to the image of a spiritual ideal, sometimes intensely expressive but increasingly impersonal; there were not to be any more portraits, in the Graeco-Roman sense of the term, for almost a thousand years to come.

The process is strikingly exemplified by the head of Eutropios from Ephesus (fig. 305), one of the most memorable of its kind. It reminds us of the strangely sorrowful features of "Plotinus" (see fig. 271) and of the masklike colossal head of Constantine (see fig. 272), but both of these have a physical concreteness that seems almost gross compared to the extreme attenuation of Eutropios. The face is frozen in visionary ecstasy, as if the sitter were a hermit saint; it looks, in fact, more like that of a specter than of a being of flesh and blood. The avoidance of solid volumes has been carried so far that the features are for the most part indicated only by thin ridges or shallow engraved lines. Their smooth curves emphasize the elongated oval of the head and thus reinforce its abstract, otherworldly character. Not only the individual person but the human body itself has ceased to be a tangible reality here; and with that the Greek tradition of sculpture in the round has reached the end of the road.

304. *The Archangel Michael* (leaf of a diptych). Early 6th century A.D. Ivory, 17 × 5½". British Museum, London

305. *Portrait of Eutropios*. c. 450 A.D. Marble, height 12½". Kunsthistorisches Museum, Vienna

Colorplate 27. BYZANTINE. Interior, view toward the apse, S. Apollinare in Classe, Ravenna (see page 201). 533–49 A.D.

Colorplate 28. BYZANTINE. Page with *Jacob Wrestling with the Angel,* from the *Vienna Genesis*
(see page 205). Early 6th century A.D. 11¾ × 9½″. National Library, Vienna

Colorplate 29. BYZANTINE. *Empress Theodora and Her Attendants*,
portion of a mosaic (see page 218). About 547 A.D. San Vitale, Ravenna

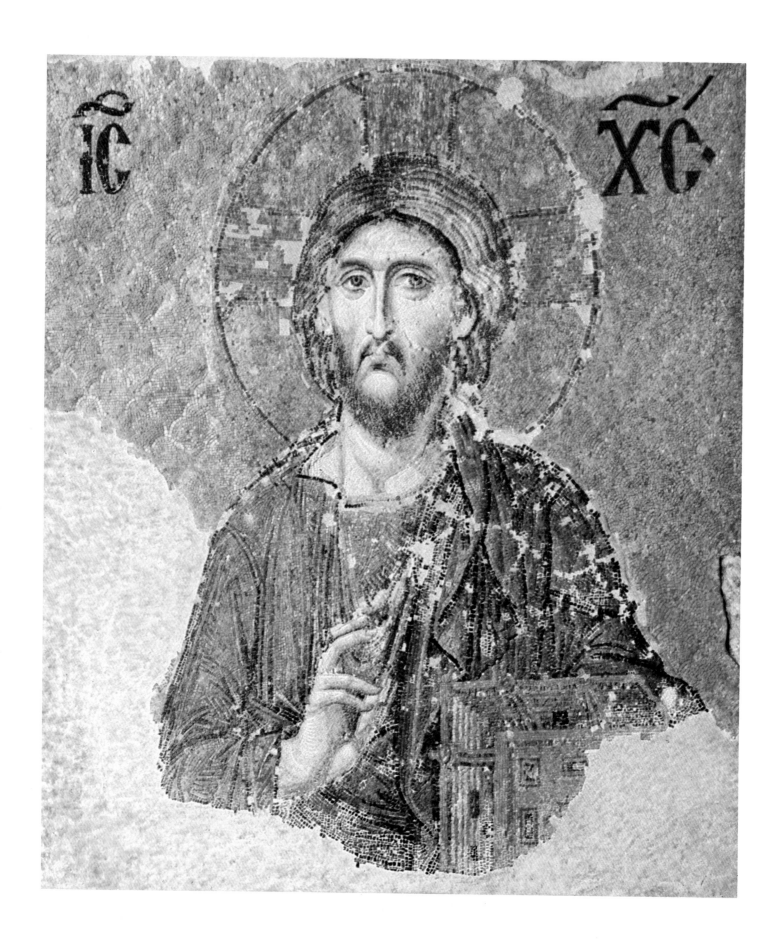

Colorplate 30. BYZANTINE. *Christ*, portion of a *Deësis* mosaic
(see page 221). 13th century. Hagia Sophia, Istanbul

Colorplate 31. BYZANTINE. Churches of the Monastery of Hosios Loukas (St. Luke of Stiris), Greece
(see page 222). Early 11th century

Colorplate 32. BYZANTINE. Interior, St. Mark's, Venice (see page 224). Begun 1063

Colorplate 33. BYZANTINE. *David Composing the Psalms*, from the *Paris Psalter*
(see page 225). c. 900 A.D. 14⅛ × 10¼″. Bibliothèque Nationale, Paris

Colorplate 34. ANDREI RUBLEV. *Old Testament Trinity* (see page 229).
About 1410–20. Panel, 55½ × 44½″. Tretyakov Gallery, Moscow

Colorplate 35. ISLAMIC. *Summer Landscape,* from the *Album of the Conqueror*
(*Sultan Mohammed II*; see page 252). Mongol, mid-14th century. Topkapu Palace Museum, Istanbul

BYZANTINE ART

There is no clear-cut line of demarcation between Early Christian and Byzantine art. It could be argued that a Byzantine style (that is, a style associated with the imperial court of Constantinople) becomes discernible within Early Christian art as early as the beginning of the fifth century, soon after the effective division of the Empire. We have avoided making this distinction, for East Roman and West Roman—or, as some scholars prefer to call them, East and West Christian—characteristics are often difficult to separate before the sixth century. Until that time, both areas contributed to the development of Early Christian art, although the leadership tended to shift more and more to the East as the position of the West declined. During the reign of Justinian (527–565) this shift was completed; Constantinople not only reasserted its political dominance over the West but became the undisputed artistic capital as well. Justinian himself was an art patron on a scale unmatched since Constantine's day; the works he sponsored or promoted have an imperial grandeur that fully justifies the acclaim of those who have termed his era a golden age. They also display an inner coherence of style which links them more strongly with the future development of Byzantine art than with the art of the preceding centuries.

First Golden Age: Architecture and Decoration

Ironically enough, the richest array of monuments of the First Golden Age survives today not in Constantinople (where much has been destroyed) but on Italian soil, in the town of Ravenna. Originally a naval station on the Adriatic, it had become the capital of the West Roman emperors in 402 and, at the end of the century, of Theodoric, king of the Ostrogoths, whose tastes were patterned after those of Constantinople. Under Justinian, Ravenna was the main stronghold of Byzantine rule in Italy.

SAN VITALE. The most important church of that time, S. Vitale, built in 526–547, is of a type derived mainly from Constantinople. We recognize its octagonal plan, with the domed central core (figs. 306–9), as a descendant of the mausoleum of Sta. Costanza in Rome (see figs. 294–96), but the intervening development seems to have taken place in the East, where domed churches of various kinds had been built during the previous century. Compared to Sta. Costanza, S. Vitale is both larger in scale and very much richer in its spatial effect; below the clerestory, the nave wall turns into a series of semicircular niches that penetrate into the aisle and thus link it to the nave in a new and intricate way. The aisle itself has been given a second story (the galleries were reserved for women). A new economy in the construction of the vaulting permits large windows on every level, which flood the interior with light. We find only the merest remnants of the longitudinal axis of the Early Christian basilica: a cross-vaulted compartment for the altar,

306. S. Vitale, Ravenna, 526–47 A.D.

307. Plan of S. Vitale

308. Transverse Section of S. Vitale

backed by an apse, toward the east, and a narthex on the other side (its odd, nonsymmetrical placement has never been fully accounted for).

Remembering S. Apollinare in Classe, built at the same time on a straightforward basilican plan, we are particularly struck by the alien character of S. Vitale. How did it happen that the East favored a type of church building (as distinct

309. Interior (view from the apse), S. Vitale

from baptisteries and mausoleums) so radically different from the basilica and—from the Western point of view—so ill-adapted to Christian ritual? After all, had not the design of the basilica been backed by the authority of Constantine himself? Many different reasons have been suggested—practical, religious, political. All of them may be relevant, yet, if the truth be told, they fall short of a really persuasive explanation. In any event, from the time of Justinian domed, central-plan churches were to dominate the world of Orthodox Christianity as thoroughly as the basilican plan dominated the architecture of the medieval West.

As for S. Vitale, its link with the Byzantine court is evidenced by the two famous mosaics flanking the altar (figs. 310, 311, and colorplate 29), whose design must have come directly from the imperial workshop. Here Justinian and his empress, Theodora, accompanied by officials, the local clergy, and ladies-in-waiting, attend the service as if this were a palace chapel. In these large panels, made shortly before the consecration of the church, we find an ideal of human beauty quite distinct from the squat, large-headed figures we encountered in the art of the fourth and fifth centuries; occasionally (figs. 297, 303, 304) we had caught a glimpse

of this emerging new ideal, but only now do we see it complete: extraordinarily tall, slim figures, with tiny feet, small, almond-shaped faces dominated by their huge, staring eyes, and bodies that seem to be capable only of slow ceremonial gestures and the display of magnificently patterned costumes. Every hint of movement or change is carefully excluded—the dimensions of time and earthly space have given way to an eternal present amid the golden translucency of Heaven, and the solemn, frontal images seem to present a celestial rather than a secular court. This union of political and spiritual authority accurately reflects the "divine kingship" of the Byzantine Emperor. We are, in fact, invited to see Justinian and Theodora as analogous to Christ and the Virgin: on the hem of Theodora's mantle (just visible in figure 311) is conspicuous embroidery showing the three Magi carrying their gifts to Mary and the newborn King; and Justinian is flanked by twelve companions—the imperial equivalent of the twelve apostles (six are soldiers, crowded behind a shield with the monogram of Christ).

If we turn from these mosaics to the interior space of the church, we discover that it, too, shares the quality of dematerialized, soaring slenderness that endows the figures with

310. *Emperor Justinian and His Attendants* (mosaic). c. 547 A.D. S. Vitale

311. *Empress Theodora and Her Attendants*, mosaic (see detail, colorplate 29). S. Vitale

312. Section of Hagia Sophia (after Gurlitt)

313. Plan of Hagia Sophia (after v. Sybel)

314. ANTHEMIUS OF TRALLES AND ISIDORUS OF MILETUS. Hagia Sophia, Istanbul. 532–37 A.D.

their air of mute exaltation. Justinian, Theodora, and their immediate neighbors were surely intended to be individual likenesses, and their features are indeed differentiated to a degree (those of the Archbishop, Maximianus, more so than the rest), but the ideal type has molded the faces as well as the bodies, so that they all have a curious family resemblance. We shall meet the same large dark eyes under curved brows, the same small mouths and long, narrow, slightly aquiline noses countless times from now on in Byzantine art.

HAGIA SOPHIA. Among the surviving monuments of Justinian's reign in Constantinople, the most important by far is Hagia Sophia (the Church of Holy Wisdom), the architectural masterpiece of that age and one of the great creative triumphs of any age (figs. 312–16). Built in 532–537, it achieved such fame that the names of the architects, too, were remembered—Anthemius of Tralles and Isidorus of Miletus. After the Turkish conquest in 1453, it became a mosque (the four minarets were added then) and the mosaic decoration was largely hidden under whitewash. Some of

315. Capital, Hagia Sophia

316. Interior, Hagia Sophia

317. *Deësis* mosaic (see detail, colorplate 30). Hagia Sophia

the mosaics were uncovered in recent years (fig. 317, color-plate 30), since the building was turned into a museum.

The design of Hagia Sophia presents a unique combination of elements: it has the longitudinal axis of an Early Christian basilica, but the central feature of the nave is a square compartment crowned by a huge dome and abutted at either end by half domes, so that the nave becomes a great oval. Attached to these half domes are semicircular niches with open arcades, similar to those in S. Vitale; one might say, then, that the dome of Hagia Sophia has been inserted between the two halves of a central-plan church. The dome rests on four arches that carry its weight to the great piers at the corners of the square, so that the walls below the arches have no supporting function at all. The transition from the square formed by these arches to the circular rim of the dome is achieved by spherical triangles called pendentives; hence we speak of the entire unit as a dome on pendentives. This device permits the construction of taller, lighter, and more economical domes than the older method (as seen in the Pantheon, Sta. Costanza, and S. Vitale) of placing the dome on a round or polygonal base. Where or when the dome on pendentives was invented we do not know; Hagia Sophia is the earliest case we have of its use on a monumental scale, and its example must have been of epoch-making importance, for from that time on the dome on pendentives became a basic feature of Byzantine architecture and, somewhat later, of Western architecture as well.

There is, however, still another element that entered into the design of Hagia Sophia. The plan, the buttressing of the main piers, and the vast scale of the whole recall the Basilica of Constantine (figs. 242–44), the most ambitious achievement of Imperial Roman vaulted architecture and the greatest monument associated with a ruler for whom Justinian had particular admiration. Hagia Sophia thus unites East and West, past and future, in a single overpowering synthesis. Its massive exterior, firmly planted upon the earth like a great mound, rises by stages to a height of 184 feet—41 feet higher than the Pantheon—and therefore its dome, although its diameter is somewhat smaller (112 feet), stands out far more boldly.

Early Christian and Byzantine Art 221

318. Churches of the Monastery of Hosios Loukas (St. Luke of Stiris), Greece (see colorplate 31)

Once we are within, all sense of weight disappears, as if the material, solid aspects of the structure had been banished to the outside; nothing remains but an expanding space that inflates, like so many sails, the apsidal recesses, the pendentives, and the dome itself. Here the architectural aesthetic we saw taking shape in Early Christian architecture (see pages 201–2) has achieved a new, magnificent dimension. Even more than previously, light plays a key role: the dome seems to float—"like the radiant heavens," according to a contemporary description of the building—because it rests upon a closely spaced ring of windows, and the nave walls are pierced by so many openings that they have the transparency of lace curtains.

The golden glitter of the mosaics must have completed the "illusion of unreality." We can sense the new aesthetic even in ornamental details such as moldings and capitals (fig. 315). The motifs—scrolls, acanthus foliage, and such —all derive from Classical architecture, but their effect is radically different; instead of actively cushioning the impact of heavy weight upon the shaft of the column, the capital has become a sort of open-work basket whose delicate surface pattern belies the strength and solidity of the stone.

Second Golden Age:
Architecture and Decoration

Byzantine architecture never produced another structure to match Hagia Sophia. The churches of the Second Golden Age (from the late ninth to the eleventh century) and after were modest in scale, and monastic rather than imperial in

319. Plan of Churches of the Monastery of Hosios Loukas (after Diehl)

spirit. Their usual plan is that of a Greek cross (that is, a cross with arms of equal length) contained in a square, with a narthex added on one side and an apse (sometimes with flanking chapels) on the other. The central feature is a dome on a square base; it often rests on a cylindrical drum with tall windows, which raises it high above the rest of the building, as in both churches of the Monastery of Hosios Loukas in Greece (figs. 318–20, colorplate 31). They also show other characteristics of later Byzantine architecture: a tendency toward more elaborate exteriors, in contrast to the extreme severity we observed earlier (compare fig. 306), and a preference for elongated proportions. The full impact of this verticality, however, strikes us only when we enter the church (fig. 320 shows the interior of the Katholikon, on the left in figs. 318, 319, colorplate 31). The tall, narrow space compartments produce a sense of crowdedness, almost of compression, which is dramatically relieved as we raise our glance toward the luminous pool of space beneath the dome.

Figure 321 shows this view as it presents itself to us in the Greek monastery church of Daphnē, where the pictorial decoration of the dome is better preserved than in the Katholikon of Hosios Loukas. Staring down from the center of the dome is an awesome mosaic image of Christ the Pantocrator (Ruler of the Universe) against a gold background, its huge scale emphasized by the much smaller figures of the sixteen Old Testament prophets between the windows. In the corners, we see four scenes revealing the divine and human natures of Christ—the Annunciation (bottom left) followed in counterclockwise order by the Birth, Baptism, and Transfiguration. The entire cycle represents a theological program so perfectly in harmony with the geometric relationship of the images that we cannot say whether the architecture has been shaped by the pictorial scheme or vice versa. A similarly strict order governs the distribution of subjects throughout the rest of the interior.

320. Interior, Katholikon, Hosios Loukas

321. Dome Mosaics. 11th century. Monastery Church, Daphnē, Greece

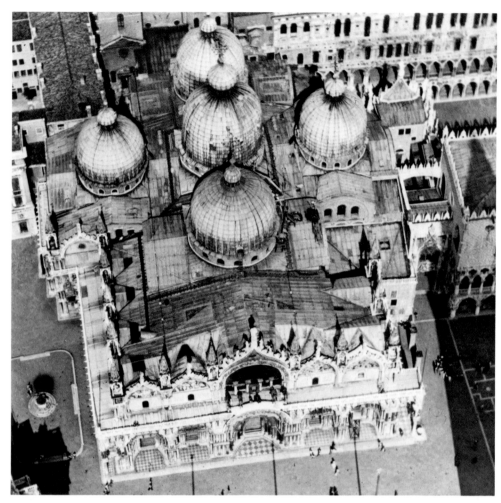

322. St. Mark's (aerial view), Venice. Begun 1063

The largest and most lavishly decorated church of the Second Golden Age surviving today is St. Mark's in Venice, begun in 1063. The Venetians had long been under Byzantine sovereignty and remained artistically dependent on the East well after they had become politically and commercially powerful in their own right. St. Mark's, too, has the Greek-cross plan inscribed within a square, but here each arm of the cross is emphasized by a dome of its own (figs. 322, 323). These domes are not raised on drums; instead, they have been encased in bulbous wooden helmets covered by gilt copper sheeting and topped by ornate lanterns, to make them appear taller and more conspicuous at a distance. They make a splendid landmark for the seafarer. The spacious interior, famous for its mosaics, shows that it was meant to receive the citizenry of a large metropolis, and not just a small monastic community as at Daphnē or Hosios Loukas (colorplate 32).

During the Second Golden Age, Byzantine architecture also spread to Russia, along with the Orthodox faith. There the basic type of the Byzantine church underwent an amazing transformation through the use of wood as a structural material. The most famous product of this native trend is the Cathedral of St. Basil adjoining the Kremlin in Moscow (fig. 324). Built during the reign of Ivan the Terrible, it seems as unmistakably Russian as that extraordinary ruler. The

323. Interior, St. Mark's (see colorplate 32)

domes, growing in amazing profusion, have become fantastic tower-like structures whose vividly patterned helmets may resemble anything from mushrooms and berries to Oriental turbans. These huge ice-cream cones have the gay unreality of a fairy tale, yet their total effect is oddly impressive; keyed as they are to the imagination of faithful peasants (who must have stared at them in open-mouthed wonder on their rare visits to the capital), they nevertheless convey a sense of the miraculous that is derived from the more austere miracles of Byzantine architecture.

ICONOCLASTS, ICONOPHILES. The development of Byzantine painting and sculpture after the age of Justinian was disrupted by the Iconoclastic Controversy, which began with an imperial edict of 726 prohibiting religious images. It raged for more than a hundred years, dividing the population into two hostile groups. The image-destroyers (Iconoclasts), led by the emperor and supported mainly in the eastern provinces of the realm, insisted on a literal interpretation of the biblical ban against graven images as conducive to idolatry; they wanted to restrict religious art to abstract symbols and plant or animal forms. Their opponents, the Iconophiles, were led by the monks and centered in the western provinces, where the imperial edict remained ineffective for the most part. The roots of the conflict went very deep: on the plane of theology they involved the basic issue of the relationship of the human and the divine in the person of Christ; socially and politically, they reflected a power struggle between State and Church. The Controversy also marked the final break between Catholicism and the Orthodox faith.

Had the edict been enforceable throughout the Empire, it might well have dealt Byzantine religious art a fatal blow. It did succeed in reducing the production of sacred images very greatly, but failed to wipe it out altogether, so that there was a fairly rapid recovery after the victory of the Iconophiles in 843. While we know little for certain about how the Byzantine artistic tradition managed to survive from the early eighth to the mid-ninth century, Iconoclasm seems to have brought about a renewed interest in secular art, which was not affected by the ban.

CLASSICAL REVIVAL. This interest may help to explain the astonishing reappearance of Late Classical motifs in the art of the Second Golden Age, as in *David Composing the Psalms* from the so-called *Paris Psalter* (fig. 325, colorplate 33). It was probably illuminated about 900, although the temptation to put it earlier is almost irresistible. Not only do we find a landscape that recalls Pompeian murals, but the figures, too, obviously derive from Classical models. David himself could well be mistaken for Orpheus charming the beasts with his music, and his companions prove even more surprising, since they are allegorical figures that have nothing to do with the Bible at all: the young woman next to David is Melody, the one coyly hiding behind a pillar is Echo, and the male figure with a tree trunk personifies the mountains of Bethlehem. The late date of the picture is evident only from certain qualities of style such as the abstract zigzag pattern of the drapery covering Melody's legs.

324. Cathedral of St. Basil, Moscow. 1554–60

325. *David Composing the Psalms*, from the *Paris Psalter* (see colorplate 33)

Early Christian and Byzantine Art 225

326. Scenes from Genesis (mosaic). c. 1200. St. Mark's, Venice

327. *The Crucifixion* (mosaic). 11th century.
Monastery Church, Daphnē

Another fascinating reflection of an early source is the sequence of scenes from Genesis among the mosaics of St. Mark's in Venice (fig. 326), which must have been adapted from an Early Christian illuminated manuscript. The squat, large-headed figures recall the art of the fourth century, as does the classical young philosopher type representing the Lord (compare fig. 302), which had been long since replaced in general usage by the more familiar bearded type (see fig. 321). Of particular interest is the scene in the upper right-hand corner. Ancient art had visualized the human soul as a tiny nude figure with butterfly wings; here this image reappears—or survives, rather—under Christian auspices as the spirit of life that the Lord breathes into Adam.

The *Paris Psalter* and the Genesis mosaics in St. Mark's betray an almost antiquarian enthusiasm for the traditions of Classical art. Such direct revivals, however, are extreme cases. The finest works of the Second Golden Age show a classicism that has been harmoniously merged with the spiritualized ideal of human beauty we encountered in the art of Justinian's reign. Among these, the *Crucifixion* mosaic at Daphnē (fig. 327) enjoys special fame. Its Classical qualities are more fundamental, and more deeply felt, than those of the *Paris Psalter*, yet also completely Christian: there is no attempt to re-create a realistic spatial setting, but the composition has a balance and clarity that are truly monumental as against the cluttered Pompeian landscape of the David miniature. Classical, too, is the statuesque dignity of the figures, which seem extraordinarily organic and graceful compared to those of the Justinian mosaics at S. Vitale (figs. 310, 311).

The most important aspect of these figures' Classical heritage, however, is emotional rather than physical; it is the gentle pathos conveyed by their gestures and facial expressions, a restrained and noble suffering of the kind we first met in Greek art of the fifth century B.C. (see page 134). Early Christian art had been quite devoid of this quality. Its view of Christ stressed the Saviour's divine wisdom and power, rather than His sacrificial death, so that the Crucifixion was depicted only rarely and in a notably unpathetic spirit. The image of the Pantocrator as we saw it on the sarcophagus of Junius Bassus and above the apse of S. Apollinare in Classe (figs. 293, 302, colorplate 27) retained its importance throughout the Second Golden Age—the majestic dome mosaic at Daphnē stems from that tradition—but alongside it we now find a new emphasis on the Christ of the Passion.

When and where this human interpretation of the Saviour made its first appearance, we cannot say for sure; it seems to have developed in the wake of the Iconoclastic Controversy. There are few examples of it earlier than the Daphnē *Crucifixion*, and none of them has so powerful an appeal to the emotions of the beholder. To have introduced this compassionate quality into sacred art was perhaps the greatest achievement of the Second Golden Age, even though its full possibilities were to be exploited not in Byzantium but in the medieval West at a later date. Yet Byzantine art, too, preserved and developed the human view of Christ in the centuries to come. The wonderful mosaic fragment from Hagia Sophia (fig. 317, colorplate 30), probably of the thirteenth century, no longer has the forbidding severity of the Daphnē *Pantocrator*: instead, we find an expression of gentle melancholy, along with a subtlety of modeling and color that perpetuates the best Classical tradition of the Second Golden Age.

Late Byzantine Painting

In 1204 Byzantium sustained an almost fatal defeat when the armies of the Fourth Crusade, instead of warring against the Turks, assaulted and took the city of Constantinople. For over fifty years, the core of the Eastern Empire remained in Latin hands. Byzantium, however, survived this catastrophe; in 1261, it once more regained its sovereignty, and the fourteenth century saw a last efflorescence of Byzantine painting, with a distinct and original flavor of its own, before the Turkish conquest in 1453.

Because of the impoverished state of the greatly shrunken Empire, mural painting often took the place of mosaics, as in the recently uncovered wall decoration of a mortuary chapel attached to the Kariye Camii (the former Church of the Saviour in Chora) in Istanbul. From this impressive cycle of pictures, done about 1310–20, we reproduce the *Anastasis* (Greek word for resurrection), in figure 328. The scene actually depicts the event just before the Resurrection—Christ's Descent into Limbo. Surrounded by a radiant glor-

328. *Anastasis*. Fresco, c. 1310–20. Kariye Camii (Church of the Saviour in Chora), Istanbul

329. *Madonna* (detail). 6th–7th century A.D.
Encaustic on wood. Sta. Francesca Romana, Rome

iole, the Saviour has vanquished Satan and battered down the gates of Hell (note the bound Satan at His feet, in the midst of an incredible profusion of hardware), and is raising Adam and Eve from the dead. What amazes us about this central group is its dramatic force, a quality we would hardly expect to find on the basis of what we have seen of Byzantine art so far. Christ here moves with extraordinary physical energy, tearing Adam and Eve from their graves, so that they appear to fly through the air—a magnificently expressive image of divine triumph. Such dynamism had been unknown in the earlier Byzantine tradition. Coming in the fourteenth century, it shows that 800 years after Justinian, Byzantine art still had its creative powers.

ICONS. During the Iconoclastic Controversy, one of the chief arguments in favor of sacred images was the claim that Christ Himself had permitted St. Luke to paint His portrait, and that other portraits of Christ or of the Virgin had miraculously appeared on earth by divine fiat. These original, "true" sacred images were supposedly the source for the later, man-made ones. Such pictures, or icons, had developed in early Christian times out of Graeco-Roman portrait panels (such as fig. 284, colorplate 25). Little is known about their origins, for examples antedating the Iconoclastic Controversy are extremely scarce.

Of the few discovered so far, perhaps the most important is the *Madonna* from Sta. Francesca Romana in Rome,

brought to light some years ago by the cleaning of a much-repainted panel. Only the Virgin's face still shows the original surface in fair condition (fig. 329). Its link with Graeco-Roman portraiture is evident not only from the painting medium, which is encaustic (see page 195), a technique that went out of use after the Iconoclastic Controversy, but also from the fine gradations of light and shade. The forms themselves, however—the heart-shaped outline of the face, the tiny mouth, the long, narrow nose, the huge eyes under strongly arched brows—reflect an ideal of human beauty as spiritualized as that of the S. Vitale mosaics, while retaining a far higher degree of three-dimensional solidity. What makes this image so singularly impressive is the geometric severity of the design, which endows the features with a monumental grandeur such as we never encounter again in Early Christian or Byzantine art. Where and when was it produced? In the sixth or seventh century, we must assume, but whether in Italy or the East we cannot say, for lack of comparable material. Be that as it may, it is a work of extraordinary power that makes us understand how people came to believe in the superhuman origin of sacred pictures.

Because of the veneration in which they were held, icons had to conform to strict formal rules, with fixed patterns repeated over and over again. As a consequence, the majority of them are more conspicuous for exacting craftsmanship than for artistic inventiveness. The *Madonna Enthroned* (fig. 330) is a work of this kind; although painted in the thirteenth century, it reflects a type several hundred years earlier. Echoes of the Classicism of the Second Golden Age abound: the graceful pose, the rich play of drapery folds, the tender melancholy of the Virgin's face, the elaborate, architectural perspective of the throne (which looks rather like a miniature replica of the Colosseum). But all these elements have become oddly abstract. The throne, despite its foreshortening, no longer functions as a three-dimensional object, and the highlights on the drapery resemble ornamental sunbursts, in strange contrast to the soft shading of hands and faces. The total effect is neither flat nor spatial but transparent, somewhat like that of a stained-glass window; the shapes look as if they were lit from behind. And this is almost literally true, for they are painted in a thin film on a highly reflecting gold surface that forms the highlights, the halos, and the background, so that even the shadows never seem wholly opaque.

This all-pervading celestial radiance, we will recall, is a quality first encountered in Early Christian mosaics. Panels such as ours, therefore, should be viewed as the aesthetic equivalent, on a smaller scale, of mosaics, and not simply as the descendants of the ancient panel painting tradition. In fact, the most precious Byzantine icons are miniature mosaics done on panels, rather than paintings.

Along with the Orthodox faith, icon painting spread throughout the Balkans and Russia, where it continued to flourish even after the disappearance of the Byzantine Empire. The shifting of the creative impulses within this tradition to the outlying areas of the Orthodox world is signalized by the work of Andrei Rublev, the finest Russian icon painter and a great artist by any standard. Colorplate 34 and figure 331 show his famous panel *Old Testament Trinity*, done about 1410–20. (The title refers to the three angels who visited Abraham at Mamre.) Although parts of it are poorly preserved—most of the background has disappeared—the picture reveals a harmonious beauty of design and a depth of lyrical feeling that vie with the most Classical products of the Second Golden Age. Rublev must have been thoroughly acquainted with the best that Byzantine art had to offer, either through contact with Greek painters in Russia or

330. *Madonna Enthroned*. Late 13th century.
Panel, 32 × 19½". National Gallery of Art,
Washington, D.C. (Mellon Collection)

331. ANDREI RUBLEV. *Old Testament Trinity*
(see colorplate 34). Tretyakov Gallery, Moscow

through a sojourn in Constantinople. The most individual element—and also the most distinctively Russian—is the color scale, brighter, more complex, and different in key from that of any Byzantine work. In the hands of a lesser master, such combinations as orange, vermilion, and turquoise might easily have a primitive garishness of the sort we often find in folk art; here, the controlled intensity of these tones is an essential part of the composition.

Sculpture

Monumental sculpture, as we saw earlier, tended to disappear completely from the fifth century on. In Byzantine art, large-scale statuary died out with the last imperial portraits, and stone carving was confined almost entirely to architectural ornament (see fig. 315). But small-scale reliefs, especially in ivory and metal, continued to be produced throughout the Second Golden Age and beyond.

Their extraordinary variety of content, style, and purpose is suggested by the two samples shown here, both of them dating from the tenth century. One is a triptych—a small portable altar shrine with two hinged wings—of the sort a high dignitary might carry for his private devotions while traveling (fig. 332); in the upper half of the center panel we see Christ Enthroned, flanked by St. John the Baptist and the Virgin—who plead for divine mercy on behalf of mankind—and five apostles below. The exquisite refinement of this icon-in-miniature recalls the style of the Daphnē *Crucifixion* (fig. 327).

Our second panel, representing the Sacrifice of Iphigenia (fig. 333), belongs to an ivory casket meant for wedding gifts and, rather surprisingly, is decorated with scenes of Greek mythology. Even more than the miniatures of the *Paris Psalter*, it illustrates the antiquarian aspects of Byzantine Classicism after the Iconoclastic Controversy, for the subject is that of a famous Greek drama by Euripides; and our composition (which is curiously shallow, despite the deep undercutting of the relief) probably derives from an illustrated Euripides manuscript, rather than from a sculptural source. Though drained of all tragic emotion and reduced to a level of ornamental playfulness, these knobby little figures form a coherent visual quotation from ancient art. It was through channels such as this that the Graeco-Roman heritage entered the mainstream of Byzantine tradition.

332. *The Harbaville Triptych.* Late 10th century. Ivory, 9½ × 11". The Louvre, Paris

333. *The Sacrifice of Iphigenia* (detail of ivory casket). 10th century. Victoria & Albert Museum, London
(Crown copyright reserved)

ILLUSTRATED TIME CHART I

POLITICAL HISTORY, RELIGION	LITERATURE, SCIENCE, TECHNOLOGY

6000

4000

Sumerians settle in lower Mesopotamia
Predynastic period in Egypt; Menes
   unites Upper and Lower Egypt c. 3100

"White Temple"
and ziggurat, Uruk

Pictographic writing, Sumer, c. 3500
Wheeled carts, Sumer, c. 3500–3000
Sailboats used on Nile c. 3500
Potter's wheel, Sumer, c. 3250

3000

Old Kingdom, Egypt (dynasties I–VI)
   c. 3100–2185
Divine Kingship of the Pharaoh
Early dynastic period, Sumer, c. 3000–
   2340; Akkadian Kings 2340–2180;
   Gudea c. 2150
Theocratic socialism in Sumer

Hieroglyphic writing, Egypt, c. 3000
Cuneiform writing, Sumer, c. 2900
First bronze tools and weapons, Sumer
Plows drawn by oxen

Sphinx, Giza

Tomb of Khnum-hotep, Beni Hasan

2000

Middle Kingdom, Egypt 2133–1786
Hammurabi founds Babylonian dynasty
   c. 1760, writes Code of Hammurabi
Hittites conquer Babylon c. 1600
Flowering of Minoan civilization
   c. 1700–1500
New Kingdom, Egypt, c. 1580–1085
Monotheism of Akhenaten (r. 1372–
   1358)
Dorians invade Greece c. 1100

Bronze tools and weapons in Egypt
Canal from Nile to Red Sea
Mathematics and astronomy flourish in
   Babylon under Hammurabi
Hittites employ iron tools and weapons
Book of the Dead, first papyrus book,
   XVIII dynasty
Hyksos bring horses and wheeled vehi-
   cles to Egypt c. 1725
China develops silk production c. 1500

Stonehenge, England

Stele of Hammurabi

Funerary temple of Hatshepsut, Deir el-Bahari

1000

Hebrews accept monotheism
Jerusalem capital of Palestine; rule of
   David; of Solomon (died 926)
Assyrian Empire c. 1000–612
Zoroaster, Persian prophet (born c. 660)
Nebuchadnezzar destroys Jerusalem 586
Gautama Buddha (563–483), India
Confucius (551–479), Chinese philos-
   opher
Persians conquer Babylon 539; Egypt
   525
Athenians expel tyrants, establish de-
   mocracy 510
Romans revolt against Etruscans, set up
   republic 509

Phoenicians develop alphabetic writing
   c. 1000; Greeks adopt it c. 800
Earliest iron tools and weapons in China
Ideographic writing in China
First Olympic games 776
Homer (fl. c. 750–700), *Iliad* and *Odyssey*
Coinage invented in Lydia (Asia Minor)
   c. 700–650; soon adopted by Greeks
Thales of Miletus calculates solar eclipse
   585; Anaximander of Miletus designs
   geographic map and celestial globe c. 560
Aeschylus, Greek playwright (525–456)
Pythagoras, Greek philosopher (fl. c. 520)

She-Wolf from Rome

500

Kylix painted by Exekias

PAINTING, SCULPTURE, ARCHITECTURE

Fortifications and Sculpture, Jericho, Jordan

Houses, Shrine, and Wall Painting, Çatal Hüyük

Plaster skull, Jericho

7000 B.C.

6000

4000

3000

2000

1000

500

Palette of Narmer

Painted beaker, Susa
Female Head from Uruk
"White Temple" and ziggurat, Uruk
Mural, Hierakonpolis

Palette of Narmer
Statues from Abu temple, Tell Asmar
Step pyramid and funerary district of Zoser,
     Saqqara, by Imhotep
Harp and offering stand from Ur
Rahotep and Nofret
Sphinx, Giza
Pyramids at Giza
Cycladic Idol from Amorgos
Ziggurat of King Urnammu
Tomb of Ti, Saqqara
Stele of Naram-Sin
Gudea statues from Lagash

Gudea statue from Lagash

Nofretete

Tomb of Khnum-hotep, Beni Hasan
Sesostris III
Stonehenge, England
Stele of Hammurabi
Cat Stalking Pheasant, Hagia Triada
Snake goddess, Crete
"Toreador Fresco"
Harvester Vase from Hagia Triada
Vaphio Cups
Palace of Minos, Knossos, Crete
Funerary temple of Hatshepsut, Deir el-Bahari
Lion Gate, Bogazköy
Temple of Amun-Mut-Khonsu, Luxor
Akhenaten and Nofretete
Tomb of Tutankhamen
Treasure of Atreus, Mycenae
Lion Gate, Mycenae

Lion Gate, Mycenae

Apollo from Veii

Dipylon vase
Citadel of Sargon II, Dur Sharrukin
Stag, Scythian
Reliefs from Nimrud and Nineveh
Temple of Artemis, Corfu
Ishtar Gate, Babylon
"Hera" from Samos
"Basilica," Paestum
Kylix painted by Exekias
"Peplos Kore"
Siphnian Treasury and sculpture, Delphi
Tomb of Hunting and Fishing, Tarquinia
Kore from Chios
Sarcophagus from Cerveteri
Apollo from Veii
She-Wolf from Rome

"Hera" from Samos

500

Persian Wars in Greece 499–478
Periclean Age in Athens c. 460–429
Peloponnesian War, Sparta against Athens, 431–404
Alexander the Great (356–323)
  occupies Egypt 333; defeats Persia
  331; conquers Near East
Rome defeats Carthage in First Punic
  War 264–241; acquires Spain 201
Gauls invade eastern Greek states; repulsed 240, 200

Parthenon

Travels of Herodotus, Greek historian
  c. 460–440
Sophocles, Greek tragic playwright
  (496–406)
Euripides, Greek tragic playwright (died 406)
Hippocrates, Greek physician (born 469)
Socrates, philosopher (died 399)
Plato, philosopher (427–347); founds
  Academy 386
Aristotle (384–322)
Theophrastus of Athens, botanist (fl. c. 300)
Euclid's books on geometry (fl. c. 300–280)
Archimedes, physicist and inventor
  (287–212)
Eratosthenes of Cyrene measures the
  globe c. 240
Plautus, Roman comedies (255–184)

Charioteer, Delphi

200

Rome dominates Asia Minor and Egypt;
  annexes Macedonia (and thereby
  Greece) 147; destroys Carthage 146

Invention of paper, China
Carneades of Cyrene, head of Academy,
  brings delegation of Greek
  philosophers to Rome 156
Terence, Roman comedies (died 159)

100

Sulla, dictator of Rome 82–79
Julius Caesar conquers Gaul 58–49;
  dictator of Rome 49–44
Emperor Augustus (r. 27 B.C.–14 A.D.)

Augustus of Primaporta

Golden Age of Roman literature: Cicero,
  Catullus, Vergil, Horace, Ovid, Livy
Earliest water wheels
Vitruvius' *De architectura*

A.D. 1

Crucifixion of Jesus c. 30
Jewish rebellion against Rome 66–70;
  destruction of Jerusalem by Emperor
  Titus
Paul (died c. 65) spreads Christianity to
  Asia Minor and Greece
Eruption of Mt. Vesuvius buries Pompeii,
  Herculaneum 79

Colosseum, Rome

Pliny the Elder, *Natural History*, dies in
  Pompeii 79
Varieties of glass blowing
Tacitus, *Germania*
Seneca, Roman statesman

100

Emperor Trajan (r. 98–117) rules
  Roman Empire at its largest extent
Emperor Marcus Aurelius (r. 161–180),
  author of *Meditations*

Ptolemy, geographer and astronomer
  (died 160)
Galen, physician and anatomist (died
  201)

200

Shapur I (r. 242–272), Sassanian king of Persia
Persecution of Christians in Roman
  Empire 250–302
Emperor Diocletian (r. 284–305) divides
  Empire
Mithraism spreads in Roman Empire

Basilica, Leptis Magna

Plotinus,
  Neo-Platonist
  philosopher (died 270)

Plotinus

300

500

Alexander the Great

Palace, Persepolis
East pediment from Aegina
Tomb of Lionesses, Tarquinia
Charioteer, Delphi
Pediments, Temple of Zeus, Olympia
"Temple of Poseidon," Paestum
Doryphorus by Polyclitus
Temples on Acropolis, Athens:
    Parthenon, Propylaea, Temple of
    Athena Nike, Erechtheum
Parthenon sculpture by Phidias
Mausoleum, Halicarnassus
Theater, Epidaurus
Monument of Lysicrates, Athens
Aphrodite and *Hermes* by Praxiteles
Apoxyomenos by Lysippus

Dying Niobid

Nike of Samothrace

200

Laocoön Group

Nike of Samothrace
Pergamum Altar
Porta Augusta, Perugia
Laocoön Group
"Temple of Fortuna Virilis," Rome

100

Aulus Metellus
"Temple of the Sibyl," Tivoli
Sanctuary of Fortuna, Praeneste
Portrait head from Delos
Villa of the Mysteries, Pompeii
Forum of Caesar, Rome
Villa of Livia, Primaporta
Augustus of Primaporta
Odyssey Landscapes
Ara Pacis (Altar of Peace), Rome

Aulus Metellus

1 A.D.

Villa of the Mysteries, Pompeii

House of the Silver Wedding, Pompeii
House of the Vettii, Pompeii
Hercules and Telephus, Herculaneum
Colosseum, Rome
Vespasian
Arch of Titus, Rome

100

Column of Trajan, Rome
Pantheon, Rome
Insula of House of Diana, Ostia
Market Gate, Miletus
Equestrian statue of Marcus Aurelius,
    Rome
Portrait of a boy, Faiyum
Temple of Venus, Baalbek

Pantheon, Rome

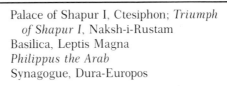

Equestrian statue of
Marcus Aurelius, Rome

200

Palace of Shapur I, Ctesiphon; *Triumph
    of Shapur I*, Naksh-i-Rustam
Basilica, Leptis Magna
Philippus the Arab
Synagogue, Dura-Europos

300

300

Christianity legalized by Edict of Milan
313; state religion 395
Emperor Constantine the Great (r. 324–
337) moves capital to Byzantium
(renamed Constantinople) 330;
recognizes Christianity; baptized on
deathbed
St. Ambrose (340–397); St. Jerome
(c. 347–420); St. Augustine (354–430)
Roman Empire split into eastern and
western branches 395

Colossal statue of Constantine

Sarcophagus of Junius Bassus

400

Rome sacked by Visigoths 410
St. Patrick (died c. 461) founds Celtic
Church in Ireland 432
Western Roman Empire falls to Goths 476
Theodoric founds Ostrogoth kingdom in
Ravenna c. 493
"Golden Age" of Justinian 527–565
St. Gregory (540–604)
St. Benedict (died 543) founds
Benedictine order
Lombard kingdom in north Italy 568

Invention of the stirrup in China
Silk cultivation brought to eastern
Mediterranean from China
Oldest illustrated Bible manuscripts,
early 6th cent.

Mosaics, S. Vitale, Ravenna

Archangel Michael, diptych leaf

Hagia Sophia, Istanbul

600

Mohammed (570–632); Hegira 622, beginning
of Moslem chronology
Byzantium loses Near Eastern and
African provinces to Moslems 642–732;
to Seljuk Turks 1071
Moslems conquer Spain 711
Iconoclastic controversy 726–843
Conversion of Russia to Orthodox Church c. 990

Koran 652

1200

Latin empire in Constantinople 1204–61
Mongols conquer China 1234–79

Madonna Enthroned, icon

Fresco, Kariye Camii, Istanbul

1400

Constantinople conquered by Ottoman
Turks 1453; Moscow assumes
leadership of Orthodox Church

Palace of Diocletian, Split
Arch of Constantine, Rome
Colossal statue of Constantine
Basilica of Constantine, Rome
Old St. Peter's, Rome
Sta. Costanza, Rome
Sarcophagus of Junius Bassus
St. Paul Outside the Walls, Rome
Catacomb of Santi Pietro e Marcellino,
    Rome
Dome mosaic, St. George, Salonica

Arch of Constantine, Rome

Interior, Sta. Costanza, Rome

— 400

Mosaics, Sta. Maria Maggiore, Rome
Eutropios
Vatican Vergil
Mosaics, S. Apollinare in Classe and
    S. Vitale, Ravenna
S. Vitale, Ravenna
Hagia Sophia, Istanbul
Vienna Genesis
Archangel Michael, diptych leaf

Capital, Hagia Sophia

Portrait of Eutropios

Plan of S. Vitale, Ravenna

— 600

Madonna, Sta. Francesca
    Romana, Rome
St. Mark's, Venice
Harbaville Triptych
Paris Psalter
Monastery churches,
    Hosios Loukas
Mosaics, Daphnē
The Sacrifice of Iphigenia

The Sacrifice of Iphigenia

Mosaics, Daphnē

— 1200

Mosaics, St. Mark's, Venice
Fresco, Kariye Camii, Istanbul
Madonna Enthroned, icon

— 1400

Old Testament Trinity by Andrei Rublev
Cathedral of St. Basil, Moscow

Old Testament Trinity by Andrei Rublev

Time Chart I   237

PART TWO

THE

INTRODUCTION

When we think of the great civilizations of our past, we tend to do so in terms of visible monuments that have come to symbolize the distinctive character of each: the pyramids of Egypt, the ziggurats of Babylon, the Parthenon of Athens, the Colosseum, Hagia Sophia. The Middle Ages, in such a review of climactic achievements, would be represented by a Gothic cathedral—Notre-Dame in Paris, perhaps, or Reims, or Salisbury. We have many to choose from, but whichever one we pick, it will be well north of the Alps, although in territory that formerly belonged to the Roman Empire. And if we were to spill a bucket of water in front of the cathedral of our choice, this water would eventually make its way to the English Channel, rather than to the Mediterranean.

Here, then, we have the most important single fact about the Middle Ages: the center of gravity of European civilization has shifted to what had been the northern boundaries of the Roman world. The Mediterranean, for so many centuries the great highway of commercial and cultural exchange binding together all the lands along its shores, has become a barrier, a border zone.

We have already observed some of the events that paved the way for this shift—the removal of the Imperial capital to Constantinople, the growing split between the Catholic and Orthodox faiths, the decay of the western half of the Roman

Empire under the impact of invasions by Germanic tribes. Yet these tribes, once they had settled down in their new environment, accepted the framework of late Roman, Christian civilization, however imperfectly; the local kingdoms they founded—the Vandals in North Africa, the Visigoths in Spain, the Franks in Gaul, the Ostrogoths and Lombards in Italy—were all Mediterranean-oriented, provincial states on the periphery of the Byzantine Empire, subject to the pull of its military, commercial, and cultural power. As late as 630, after the Byzantine armies had recovered Syria, Palestine, and Egypt from the Sassanid Persians, the reconquest of the lost western provinces remained a serious possibility.

ISLAM. Ten years later, the chance had ceased to exist, for meanwhile a tremendous and completely unforeseen new force had made itself felt in the East: the Arabs, under the banner of Islam, were overrunning the Near Eastern and African provinces of Byzantium. By 732, within a century after the death of Mohammed, they had swallowed all of North Africa as well as Spain, and threatened to add southwestern France to their conquests.

It would be difficult to exaggerate the impact of the lightning-like advance of Islam upon the Christian world. The

MIDDLE AGES

Byzantine Empire, deprived of its western Mediterranean bases, had to concentrate all its efforts on keeping Islam at bay in the East. Its impotence in the West (where it retained only a precarious foothold on Italian soil) left the European shore of the western Mediterranean, from the Pyrenees to Naples, exposed to Arabic raiders from North Africa or Spain. Western Europe was thus forced to develop its own resources, political, economic, and spiritual. The Church in Rome broke its last ties with the East and turned for support to the Germanic north, where the Frankish kingdom, under the energetic leadership of the Carolingian dynasty, rose to the status of imperial power during the eighth century.

CHARLEMAGNE. When the Pope, in the year 800, bestowed the title of Emperor upon Charlemagne, he solemnized the new order of things by placing himself and all of Western Christianity under the protection of the king of the Franks and Lombards. He did not, however, subordinate himself to the newly created Catholic emperor, whose legitimacy depended on the pope, whereas hitherto it had been the other way around (the emperor in Constantinople had formerly ratified the newly elected pope). This interdependent dualism of spiritual and political authority, of Church and State, was to distinguish the West from both the Orthodox East and the Islamic South. Its outward symbol was the fact that though the emperor had to be crowned in Rome, he did not reside there; Charlemagne built his capital at the center of his effective power, in Aachen, close to France, Germany, Belgium, and the Netherlands on the present-day map of Europe.

ISLAM AND THE WEST. Meanwhile, Islam had created a new civilization stretching from Spain in the west to the Indus Valley in the east, a civilization that reached its highest point far more rapidly than did that of the medieval West. Baghdad on the Tigris, the capital city of Charlemagne's great contemporary, Harun al-Rashid, rivaled the splendor of Byzantium. Islamic art, learning, and craftsmanship were to have a far-ranging influence on the European Middle Ages, from arabesque ornament, the manufacture of paper, and Arabic numerals to the transmission of Greek philosophy and science through the writings of Arabic scholars. (Our language records this debt in such words of Arabic origin as algebra and alcohol.) It is well, therefore, that we acquaint ourselves with some of the artistic achievements of Islam before we turn to medieval art in Western Europe.

NORWAY
Oseberg
SWEDEN

BRITISH
ISLES

SCOTLAND

BALTIC
SEA

SCANDINAVIA

Lindisfarne

NORTH SEA

IRELAND

Durham

ENGLAND

Dublin

GERMANY

ELBE R.

VISTULA R.

RO

Brunswick
Hildesheim

SAXONY

EU
RO

Sutton
Hoo

Utrecht

Naumburg

Gloucester

OXFORDSHIRE

NETHERLANDS

BELGIUM

Cologne

Dorchester

THAMES R.

Canterbury

Liège

Aachen

Prague

Salisbury

London

FLANDERS

Tournai

Huy

RHINE R.

Nuremberg

St.-Riquier

Cambrai

Avesnes

Echternach

NORTHERN FRANCE

Klosterneuburg

Abbeville

ENGLISH CHANNEL

Amiens

Corbie

St.-

Reims

RHINELAND

Speyer

Vienna

Bayeux

Rouen

Denis

Verdun

MEUSE

Strasbourg

Munich

HUNGAR

NORMANDY

Caen

ILE-DE-FRANCE

Paris

SEINE R.

Épernay

Reichenau

LAKE
CONSTANCE

ATLANTIC

OCEAN

Chartres

Troyes

Clairvaux

St.Gall

Lindau

AUSTRIA

Vézelay

Dijon

BURGUNDY

SWITZERLAND

ALPS

Cividale

LOIRE R.

Bourges

Autun

FRANCE

ALPS

Padua

BAY

Poitiers

St.-Savin-

sur-Gartempe

RHONE R.

Milan

Verona

Venice

OF BISCAY

LOMBARDY

PO VALLEY

PO R.

Fidenza

Ravenna

Genoa

Prato

Moissac

GARONNE R.

St.-Gilles-

Avignon

ARNO R.

Florence

SOUTHWESTERN

du-Gard

PROVENCE

Pisa

Siena

Assisi

ADRIATIC

FRANCE

Toulouse

VAR-MESK

TUSCANY

APENNINES

SEA

Santiago

de Compostela

Orvieto

TIBER R.

Rome

APULIA

PYRENEES

ITALY

Fossanova

SPAIN

MURCIA

IBERIAN

PENINSULA

TYRRHENIAN SEA

IONIA

Cordova

GUADALQUIVIR R.

Palermo

SICILY

Granada

MEDITERRANEAN

NORTH AFRICA

THE MIDDLE AGES

SITES AND CITIES:

ISLAMIC – EARLY MEDIEVAL – ROMANESQUE – GOTHIC

Moscow

RUSSIA

STEPPE

DNIEPER R.

CARPATHIANS

BLACK SEA

DANUBE R.

Constantinople
(Istanbul)

MT. ATHOS

AEGEAN
SEA

MT. PARNASSUS

Athens

RHODES

CYPRUS

CRETE

SEA

EGYPT

Cairo

NILE R.

RED

SEA

Mecca

ARMENIA

Erzurum

PERSIA

TURKEY

ANATOLIA

NEAR EAST

MESOPOTAMIA

TIGRIS R.

Samarra

Baghdad

EUPHRATES R.

SYRIA

Damascus

Jerusalem

Mshatta

DEAD
SEA

ARABIA

N
W   E
S

MILES
0   300
KM
0   300
palacios

Inset map (ASIA):

ASIA

BLACK SEA

CASPIAN SEA

ARAL SEA

NEAR EAST

MEDITERRANEAN
SEA

Damascus

Cairo

EGYPT

TIGRIS R.

EUPHRATES R.

PERSIA

LURISTAN

KHURASAN

AFGHANISTAN

CHINA

FAR EAST

PAKISTAN

INDUS R.

HIMALAYAS

Agra

GANGES R.

ARABIA

PERSIAN GULF

RED SEA

Mecca

INDIA

ARABIAN
SEA

BAY OF BENGAL

1
ISLAMIC ART

The incredible speed with which Islam spread throughout the Near East and North Africa remains one of the most astonishing phenomena in world history. In two generations, the new faith conquered a larger territory and greater numbers of believers than Christianity had in three centuries. How was it possible for a group of semicivilized desert tribes suddenly to burst forth from the Arab peninsula and to impose their political and religious dominance on populations far superior to them in numbers, wealth, and cultural heritage? That they had the advantage of surprise, great fighting skill, and a fanatical will to win, that both Byzantine and Persian military power was at a low ebb, has been pointed out often enough; these favorable circumstances may help to account for the initial Arab successes but not for the enduring nature of their conquests. What had begun as a triumph of force soon turned into a spiritual triumph as Islam gained the allegiance of millions of converts. Clearly, the new faith must have satisfied the needs of vast multitudes of people more fully than any of the older religions of the Hellenized Orient.

Islam owes many of its essential elements to the Judaeo-Christian tradition. The word Islam means "submission"; Moslems are those who submit to the will of Allah, the one and all-powerful God, as revealed to Mohammed in the Koran, the sacred scriptures of Islam. The Koran often draws upon the contents of the Bible and counts the Old Testament prophets as well as Jesus among the predecessors of Mohammed. Its teachings include the concepts of the Last Judgment, of Heaven and Hell, of angels and devils.

The ethical commands of Islam, too, are basically similar to those of Judaism and Christianity. As to dissimilarities, there is no ritual demanding a priesthood; every Moslem has equal access to Allah, and the observances required of him are simple: prayer at stated times of day (alone or in a mosque), almsgiving, fasting, and a pilgrimage to Mecca. All true believers, according to Mohammed, are brothers, members of one great community. During his lifetime, he was their leader not only in the religious sense but in all temporal affairs as well, so that he bequeathed to posterity a faith which was also a new pattern of society. The tradition of placing both religious and political leadership in the hands of a single ruler persisted after the Prophet's death; his successors were the caliphs, the deputies of Mohammed, whose claim to authority rested on their descent from the families of the Prophet or his early associates.

The unique quality of Islam—and the core of its tremendous appeal—is the blending of ethnic and universal elements. Like Christianity, it opened its ranks to everyone, stressing the brotherhood of the faithful before God, regardless of race or culture. Yet, like Judaism, it was also a national religion, firmly centered in Arabia. The Arab warriors under the early caliphs who set out to conquer the earth for Allah did not expect to convert the unbelievers to Islam; their aim was simply to rule, to enforce obedience to them-

334. Landscape Mosaic. 715 A.D. The Great Mosque, Damascus

selves as the servants of the One True God. Those who wanted to share this privileged status by joining Islam had to become Arabs-by-adoption: they not only had to learn Arabic in order to read the Koran (since Allah had chosen to speak in that language, his words must not be translated into lesser tongues), but also to adopt the social, legal, and political framework of the Moslem community. As a result, the Arabs, though few in numbers, were never in danger of being absorbed by the inhabitants of the regions they ruled. Instead, they absorbed the conquered populations, along with their cultural heritage, which they skillfully adapted to the requirements of Islam.

ARCHITECTURE

In art, this heritage encompassed the Early Christian and Byzantine style, with its echoes of Hellenistic and Roman forms, as well as the artistic traditions of Persia (see page 84). Pre-Islamic Arabia contributed nothing except the beautifully ornamental Arabic script; populated largely by nomadic tribes, it had no monumental architecture, and its sculptured images of local deities fell under Mohammed's ban against idolatry. Originally, Islam, like early Christianity, made no demands at all upon the visual arts. During the first fifty years after the death of the Prophet, the Moslem place of prayer could be a church taken over for the purpose,

a Persian columned hall, or even a rectangular field surrounded by a fence or a ditch. The one element these improvised mosques had in common was the marking of the *qibla* (the direction to which Moslems turn in praying): the side facing toward Mecca had to be emphasized by a colonnade, or merely by placing the entrance on the opposite side.

At the end of the seventh century, however, the Moslem rulers, now firmly established in their conquered domains, began to erect mosques and palaces on a large scale as visible symbols of their power, intended to outdo all pre-Islamic structures in size and splendor. These early monuments of Moslem architecture do not, for the most part, survive in their original form. What we know of their design and decoration shows that they were produced by craftsmen gathered from Egypt, Syria, Persia, and even Byzantium, who continued to practice the styles in which they had been trained. A distinctive Islamic tradition crystallized only in the course of the eighth century.

Eastern Islam

GREAT MOSQUE, DAMASCUS. Thus the Great Mosque at Damascus, built 706–715 within the enclosure of a Roman sanctuary, had its walls covered with wonderful glass mosaics of Byzantine origin. The surviving remnants, such as the section reproduced in figure 334, consist entirely of views of landscape and architecture framed by richly ornamented borders against a gold background. Nothing quite like them is known in Byzantine art, but their style obviously reflects an illusionism familiar to us from Pompeian painting. Apparently, ancient traditions persisted more strongly in the Near Eastern provinces of Byzantium than in Europe. Caliph al-Walid, who built the mosque, must have welcomed these Hellenistic-Roman motifs, so different from the symbolic and narrative content of Christian mosaics. A somewhat later Arabic author records that the country contained many churches "enchantingly fair and renowned for their splendor," and that the Great Mosque at Damascus was meant to keep the Moslems from being dazzled by them.

335. Portion of the Façade of the Palace at Mshatta (Jordan).
c. 743 A.D. Height of triangles 9½'. State Museums, East Berlin

PALACE AT MSHATTA. The date of the huge desert palace at Mshatta (in the present-day Kingdom of Jordan) has been much disputed; we can well understand why, for the style of the façade decoration (fig. 335) harks back to various pre-Islamic sources. According to the best available evidence, the palace was erected by one of al-Walid's successors, probably about 743. The lacelike carving and the character of the plant motifs are strongly reminiscent of Byzantine architectural ornament (compare fig. 315), and variations within the reliefs indicate that they were done by craftsmen conscripted from several provinces of the former Byzantine domain in the Near East. There is also, however, a notable Persian element, evidenced by winged lions and similar mythical animals familiar from Sassanian textiles or metalwork (see fig. 115). On the other hand, the geometric framework of zigzags and rosettes, uniformly repeated over the entire width of the façade, suggests a taste for symmetrical abstract patterns characteristic of Moslem art.

GREAT MOSQUE, SAMARRA. A striking example of the early caliphs' architectural enterprises, all of which were built on an immense scale at incredible speed, is the Great Mosque at Samarra (on the Tigris, northwest of Baghdad), built under al-Mutawakkil, 848–852. Only an aerial view (fig. 336) can convey its vast dimensions, which make it the largest mosque in the world. The basic features of the plan (fig. 337) are typical of the mosques of this period: a rectangle, its main axis pointing south (up) to Mecca, encloses a court surrounded by aisles that run toward the *qibla* side, the center of which is marked by a small niche, the *mihrab*; on the northern side rises the minaret, a tower from which the faithful were summoned to prayer by the cry of the muezzin. (This feature was derived from the towers of Early Christian churches in Syria, which may also have influenced the church towers of medieval Europe.) The floor area of the Great Mosque at Samarra is more than 45,000 square yards—almost ten acres, of which five and a half were covered by a wooden roof resting on 464 supports.

336. Mosque of Mutawakkil (view from the north), Samarra, Iraq. 848–52 A.D.

337. Plan of the
Mosque of Mutawakkil
(after Creswell)

These have all disappeared now, along with the mosaics that once covered the walls. The most spectacular aspect of the building is the minaret, linked with the mosque by a ramp. Its bold and unusual design, with a spiral staircase leading to the platform at the top, reflects the ziggurats of ancient Mesopotamia, such as the famed Tower of Babel (see pages 71–72), at that time still in a fair state of repair. Did al-Mutawakkil wish to announce to the world that the realm of the caliphs was heir to the empires of the ancient Near East?

Western Islam

MOSQUE, CORDOVA. In order to gain some notion of the interior effect of the Great Mosque at Samarra, we must turn to the mosque at Cordova in Spain, begun in 786. Although converted to Christian use after the reconquest of the city in 1236, the structure retains its Islamic character. The plan (fig. 338) was originally designed as a simpler version of the type we came to know at Samarra, the aisles being confined to the *qibla* side. Half a century later, the mosque was enlarged by extending the length of these aisles; in 961–965 they were lengthened again, and twenty years later eight more aisles were added on the east side, since a river bank barred any further extension to the south. These successive

338. Plan of the Mosque at Cordova, showing successive enlargements between 786 and 987 A.D. (after Marçais)

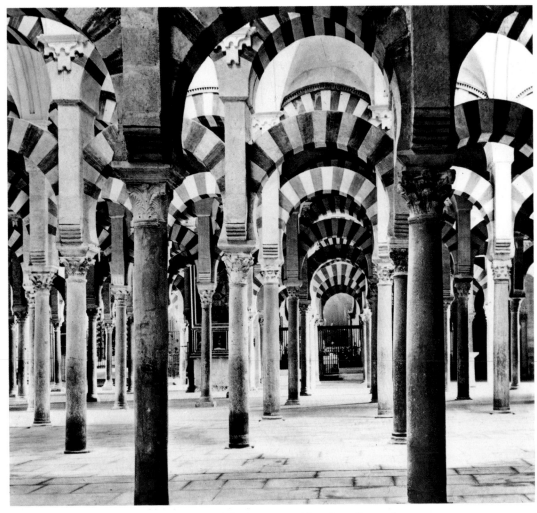

339. Interior of the Sanctuary (view from the east), Mosque, Cordova

340. Capilla de Villaviciosa, Mosque, Cordova. 961–65 A.D.

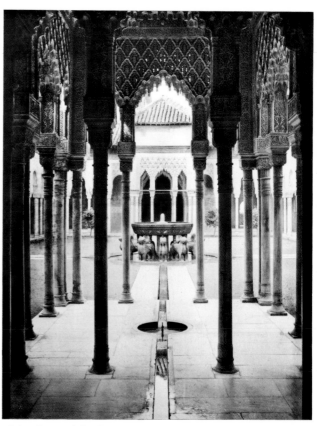

341. Court of the Lions, The Alhambra, Granada. 1354–91

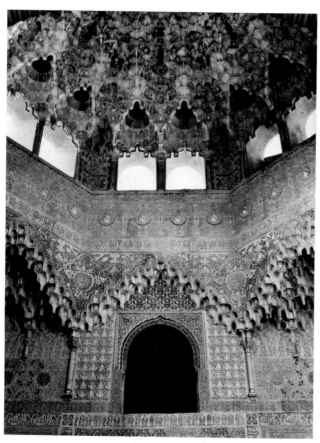

342. Stucco Decoration, Hall of the Two Sisters,
The Alhambra

stages illustrate the flexible nature of early mosque plans, which made it possible to quadruple the size of the sanctuary without departing from the original pattern. As we enter, a seemingly endless forest of columns confronts us, with nothing but the direction of the aisles to guide us toward the *qibla* side.

The sanctuary was covered by a wooden roof (now replaced by vaults) resting on double arcades of remarkable and picturesque design (fig. 339). The lower arches are horseshoe-shaped, a form that sometimes occurs in Near Eastern buildings of pre-Islamic date but which Moslem architecture made peculiarly its own. They rise from short, slender columns of a kind familiar to us from Roman and Early Christian times. These columns, however, also support stone piers that carry a second tier of arches. Was this piggy-back arrangement a practical necessity because the architect who began the building of the mosque—apparently at maximum speed—had to utilize a set of too-short columns from some earlier structure? If so, he certainly has used the device to excellent advantage, for it produces an effect far lighter and airier than a system of single arches and supports could have achieved.

A further elaboration of the same principle is found in the Capilla de Villaviciosa (fig. 340), a vaulted chamber to the north of the *mihrab*, which dates from the building campaign of 961–965. Here we meet lobed arches in three tiers, interlaced in such a way as to form a complex, ornamental screen. The vault is even more imaginative; eight slender arches, or ribs, cross each other above the square compartment, subdividing it into a network of cells. It is instructive to compare the spatial effects of the Mosque at Cordova and of a Byzantine church (fig. 316): in the latter, space always is treated as volume and has a clearly defined shape, while at Cordova its limits are purposely obscured, so that we experience it as something fluid, limitless, and mysterious. Even in the Capilla de Villaviciosa, the surfaces and cavities prevent us from perceiving walls or vaults as continuous surfaces; the space is like that of an open-work cage, screened off yet continuous with its surroundings.

This distinctively Moorish (North African and Spanish) style reaches its ultimate stage of refinement in the Alhambra Palace in Granada, the last Islamic stronghold on the Iberian peninsula during the late Middle Ages. Its richest portion, the Court of the Lions and the rooms around it, was built between 1354 and 1391 (fig. 341). The columns now have become slender as flower stalks; they support stilted arches of extravagantly complex shape, cut into walls that seem to consist of nothing more than gossamer-like webs of ornament.

On the interior surfaces (fig. 342) we find the same lacework of arabesque decoration, carried out in delicately colored stucco or tile—a limitless variety of designs, including bands of inscriptions, yet disciplined by symmetry and rhythmic order. The effect is infinitely richer than that of the Mshatta façade, but in retrospect the two monuments, separated by six centuries and the entire expanse of the Mediterranean, appear clearly linked by the same basic sense of form. Moorish vaulting has gone through a similar

process of evolution: the ribs of the Capilla de Villaviciosa have disappeared behind a honeycomb of ever-multiplying cells framed by tiny arches that hang like stalactites from the ceilings. Little wonder that the Alhambra is enshrined in the romantic imagination of the West as the visible counterpart of all the wonders of *The Thousand and One Nights*.

The Turks

From the tenth century onward, the Seljuk Turks gradually advanced into the Near East, where they adopted Islam, seized control of most of Persia, Mesopotamia, Syria, and the Holy Land, and advanced against the Byzantine Empire in Asia Minor. They were followed in the thirteenth century by the Mongols of Genghis Khan—whose armies included the Mamelukes (a people related to the Turks)—and by the Ottoman Turks. The latter not only put an end to the Byzantine Empire by their capture of Constantinople in 1453, but occupied the entire Near East and Egypt as well, thus becoming the most important power in the Moslem world. The growing weight of the Turkish element in Islamic civilization is reflected by the westward spread of a new type of mosque, the madrasah, which had been created in Persia under Seljuk domination in the eleventh century.

MADRASAH OF SULTAN HASAN, CAIRO. One of the most imposing examples is the Madrasah of Sultan Hasan in Cairo, contemporary with the Alhambra but very different in spirit. Its main feature is a square court (fig. 343), with a

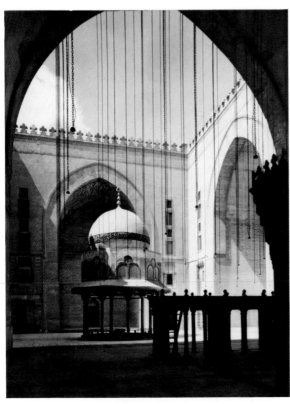

343. Court (view from the *qibla* side),
Madrasah of Sultan Hasan, Cairo. 1356–63

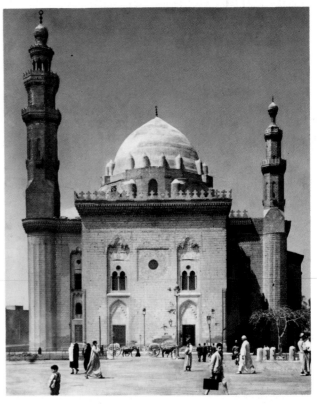

344. Mausoleum Attached to the Madrasah
of Sultan Hasan

fountain in the center. Opening onto each side of this court is a rectangular vaulted hall; that on the *qibla* side, larger than the other three, serves as the sanctuary. The monumental scale of these halls seems to echo the palace architecture of Sassanian Persia (see fig. 113), while the geometric clarity of the whole design, emphasized by the severe wall surfaces, is a Turkish contribution that we shall meet again later. It represents an attitude toward architectural space completely opposed to that of many-aisled Arabic mosques.

Attached to the *qibla* side of the Madrasah of Sultan Hasan is the Sultan's mausoleum, a large cubic structure surmounted by a dome (fig. 344). Such funerary monuments had been unknown to early Islam; they were borrowed from the West (see page 201) in the ninth century and became especially popular among the Mameluke sultans of Egypt. The dome in our example betrays its descent from Byzantine domes.

TAJ MAHAL, AGRA. The most famous mausoleum of Islamic architecture is the Taj Mahal at Agra (fig. 345), built three centuries later by one of the Moslem rulers of India, Shah Jahan, as a memorial to his wife. He belonged to the Mogul dynasty, which had come from Persia, so that the basic similarity of the Taj Mahal and the mausoleum of Sultan Hasan is less surprising than it might seem at first glance. At the same time, such a comparison emphasizes the special qualities that make the Taj Mahal a masterpiece of its kind. The massiveness of the Cairo mausoleum, with its projecting cornice and firmly anchored dome, has given way to a weightless elegance not unlike that of the Alhambra. The white marble walls, broken by deep shadowy recesses, seem paper-thin, almost translucent, and the entire building gives the impression of barely touching the ground, as if it were suspended from the balloon-like dome. Its mood of poetic reverie is greatly enhanced by the setting; the long reflecting pool lined with dark green shrubs sets off the cool whiteness of the great pavilion in truly magnificent fashion.

MOSQUES, ERZURUM AND ISTANBUL. The Turks, once they settled in Asia Minor, developed a third variety of mosque by interbreeding the Seljuk madrasah with the domed Byzantine church. Among the earliest and most astonishing results of this process is the wooden dome of the Ulu Mosque at Erzurum (see fig. 717), which has successfully withstood the earthquakes common in that region. The Turks, therefore, were well prepared to appreciate the beauty of Hagia Sophia when they entered Constantinople. It impressed them so strongly that echoes of it appear in numerous mosques built in that city and elsewhere after 1453. One of the most impressive is that of Sultan Ahmed I, erected 1609–1616 (figs. 346–48). Its plan elaborates and regularizes the design of Hagia Sophia into a square, with the main dome abutted by four half domes instead of two, and

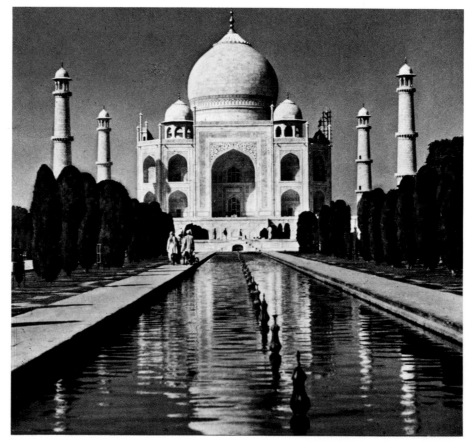

345. Taj Mahal, Agra, India. 1630–48

346. Mosque of Ahmed I, Istanbul. 1609–16

347. Plan of the Mosque
of Ahmed I (after Ünsal)

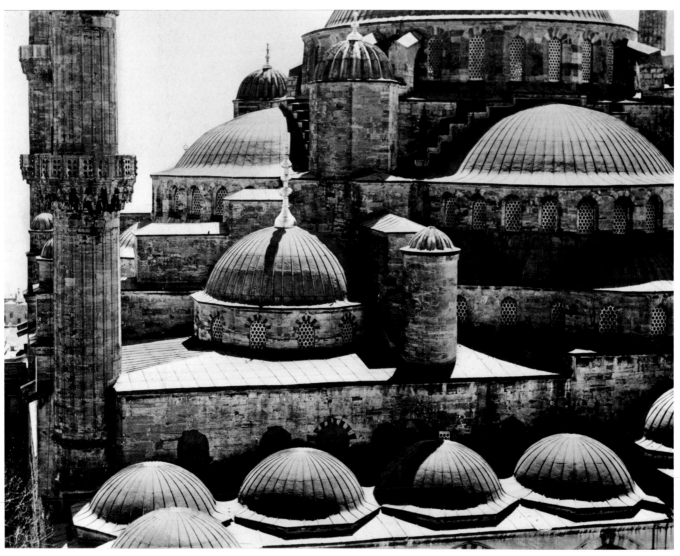

348. Detail, Mosque of Ahmed I

four smaller domes next to the minarets at the corners. The mounting sequence of these domes has been handled with marvelous logic and geometric precision, so that the exterior is far more harmonious than that of Hagia Sophia. Thus, the first half of the seventeenth century, which produced both the Taj Mahal and the Mosque of Ahmed I, marks the final flowering of Moslem architectural genius.

REPRESENTATION

Before we can enter into a discussion of Islamic painting and sculpture, we must understand the Moslem attitude toward representation. It has often been likened to that of the Byzantine Iconoclasts, but there are significant differences. The Iconoclasts, we will recall, were opposed to sacred images (that is, images of religious personages) rather than to representation as such. Mohammed, too, condemned idolatry; one of his first acts after his triumphant return to Mecca in 630 was to take over the Kaaba, an age-old Arabic sanctuary, and to remove all the idols he found there. These were always understood to have been statues, and the Koran expressly places statues among the handiwork of Satan, while painting and representation in general are not mentioned.

Mohammed's attitude toward painting seems to have been ambiguous. An early Arabic source informs us that in 630 the Kaaba also contained murals of religious (apparently biblical) subjects; the Prophet ordered them all to be destroyed, except for a picture of Mary with the Infant Jesus, which he protected with his own hands. This incident, as well as the lack of any discussion of the subject in early Moslem theology, suggests that *painted* sacred images never posed a serious problem to Mohammed and his immediate successors; since there was no pictorial tradition among the Arabs, Islamic religious painting could have been created only by borrowing from outside sources, and such a development was most unlikely as long as the authorities did not encourage it. They could afford to display indifference or even at times a certain tolerance toward the sacred pictures of other faiths. (Mohammed may have saved the *Virgin and Child* from destruction in order not to hurt the feelings of former Christians among his followers.)

This passive iconoclasm did not prevent the Arabs from accepting the nonreligious representational art they found in the newly conquered territories. Statues of any sort they surely abominated, but Hellenistic landscapes could be introduced into mosques (see fig. 334) and Sassanian animals scattered among the relief decoration of the Mshatta façade (see fig. 335). The ruins of another palace, contemporary with Mshatta, have even yielded fresco fragments with human figures. Only from about 800 on do we find strictures against representation as such in Moslem religious literature, perhaps under the influence of prominent Jewish converts. The chief argument became not the danger of idolatry but of human presumption: in making images of living things, the artist usurps a creative act that is reserved to God alone, since only He can breathe a soul into living creatures.

DECORATED OBJECTS. Theoretically, therefore, human or animal figures of any kind were forbidden by Islamic law. Yet in actual practice the ban was fully effective only against large-scale representational art for public display. There seems to have been a widespread conviction, especially at the luxury-loving courts of the caliphs and other Moslem princes, that images of living things were harmless if they did not cast a shadow, if they were on a small scale, or ap-

349. Coronation Cloak of the German Emperors. 1133–34. Red silk and gold embroidery, width 11′ 2″.
Kunsthistorisches Museum, Vienna

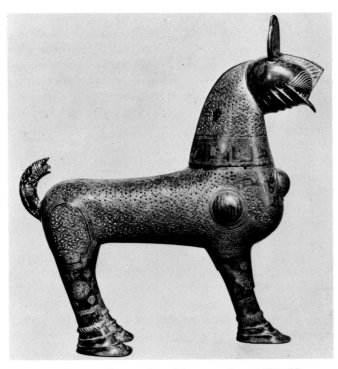

350. Incense Burner, from Khurasan, Iran. 1181–82.
Bronze, height 33½″. The Metropolitan Museum of Art,
New York (Rogers Fund, 1951)

plied to objects of daily use, such as rugs, fabrics, pottery. As a result, human and animal figures did survive in Islamic art, but they tended to become reduced to decorative motifs, intrinsically no more important than geometric or plant ornament.

We must remember, too, that this tendency was an age-old tradition; among the peoples who shaped Moslem civilization, Arabs, Persians, Turks, and Mongols all shared a love of portable, richly decorated objects as the common heritage of their nomadic past (see page 80). Islam, then, merely reinforced a taste that was natural to them. When the techniques of the nomads' arts—rugmaking, metalwork, and leathercraft—merged with the vast repertory of forms and materials accumulated by the craftsmen of Egypt, the Near East, and the Graeco-Roman world, the decorative arts of Islam reached a level of sumptuousness never equaled before or since. The few samples illustrated here can convey only the faintest suggestion of their endless variety.

Characteristically enough, a good number of the finest specimens are to be found in the churches and palaces of western Europe; whether acquired by trade, by gift, or as crusaders' booty, they were treasured throughout the Middle Ages as marvels of imaginative craftsmanship, and often imitated. Such a piece is the embroidered coronation cloak of the German emperors (fig. 349), made by Islamic artisans in Palermo for Roger II of Sicily in 1133–1134, fifty years after the Normans had captured that city from the Moslems (who had held it for 241 years). The symmetrical grouping of two lions attacking camels on either side of a symbolic tree of life is a motif whose ancestry goes back thousands of years in the ancient Near East (compare fig. 107); here, in-

scribed within quarter-circles and filled with various kinds of ornament, the animals have yielded their original fierceness to a splendid sense of pattern.

It is the element of pattern that links them with the bronze creature made fifty years later in a very different part of the Moslem world, northeast Persia (fig. 350). This one certainly casts a shadow, and a sizable one at that, since it is almost three feet tall; it is, in fact, one of the largest pieces of free-standing sculpture in all of Islamic art. Yet to call it the statue of an animal hardly does justice to its peculiar character. It is primarily a vessel, a perforated incense burner whose shape approaches that of an animal; the representational aspect of the forms seems secondary and casual. We cannot tell what kind of beast this is meant to be; if only a part of it had survived, we might even be doubtful whether it represented anything at all, so abstract and ornamental is the handling of the body. The object becomes a "living creature" only while it is serving its proper function; filled with burning incense, breathing fire and smoke, our animal might well have seemed terrifyingly real to a naïve beholder. The Seljuk prince who owned it undoubtedly enjoyed the performance of this half-comic, half-demoniacal guardian monster, which he himself could "bring to life" whenever he wished.

PAINTING. The fate of painting in the Moslem world between the eighth and thirteenth centuries remains almost entirely unknown to us. So little has survived from the five hundred years following the Damascus mosaics that we should be tempted to assume the complete disappearance of pictorial expression under Islam if literary sources did not contain evidence to the contrary. Even so, it seems clear that the tradition of painting was kept alive, not by Moslems but by artists of other faiths. Byzantine masters were imported occasionally to work for Arab rulers, and the Oriental Christian churches that survived within the Islamic empire must have included many painters who were available to Moslem art patrons. But what kind of pictures could the Moslems have wanted?

We may assume there was a more or less continuous demand for the illustration of scientific texts. The Arabs had inherited such manuscripts from the Byzantines in the Near East, and, being keenly interested in Greek science, they reproduced them in their own language. This meant that the illustrations had to be copied as well, since they formed an essential part of the content, whether they were abstract diagrams or representational images (as in zoological, medical, or botanical treatises). Works of this sort are among the earliest Islamic illuminated manuscripts known so far, although none of them can be dated before about 1200. This example (fig. 351) is from an Arabic translation, signed and dated 1224, of Dioscorides' *De Materia Medica*; it shows the Greek physician Erasistratus reclining on a couch and discoursing with an assistant. (Both are equipped with halos, to indicate their venerability.) Interestingly enough, the scribe in this instance also did the illustration; or, rather, he copied it along with the text. The ultimate source of the picture must have been a late Antique miniature with three-dimensional figures in a spatial setting, but it takes a real effort of

351. *Erasistratus and an Assistant*, from an Arabic translation of Dioscorides' *De Materia Medica*. 1224. Smithsonian Institution, Freer Gallery of Art, Washington, D.C.

352. Pen Drawing in Red Ink, from a Hariri manuscript. Mesopotamian (?). 1323. British Museum, London

the imagination to see remnants of these qualities in the present version, in which everything is flattened out and ornamentalized. The forms remain strictly on the surface of the page, like the script itself, and our artist's pen lines have a rhythmic assurance akin to that of the lettering.

It is tempting to think that manuscript illumination found its way into Islamic art through scribes who doubled as draftsmen, for to a Moslem the calling of scribe was an ancient and honorable one; a skilled calligrapher might do pictures if the text demanded them, without having to feel that this incidental activity stamped him as a painter (and an abomination in the sight of Allah). Be that as it may, the calligrapher's style of pen-drawn illustrations, with or without the addition of color, soon made its appearance in secular Arabic literature such as the *Maqamat* of Hariri. These de-

lightful stories, composed about 1100, were probably illustrated within a hundred years after they were written, since we have illuminated Hariri manuscripts from the thirteenth century on. The drawing in figure 352, from a copy dated 1323, is clearly a descendant of the style we saw in the Dioscorides illustration of a century before. The lines have the same quick, rhythmic quality, but they are handled very much more freely now, and with an extraordinary expressive power. Our artist's grasp of human character, showing the response of the eleven men to the plea of the clever rascal in the center, is so precise and witty that we must regard him as far more important than a mere copyist.

Persia

Arab merchants had been in touch with the Far East even before the advent of Islam, and occasional references to Chinese painters by early Moslem authors indicate that these contacts had brought about some acquaintance with the art of China. It was only after the Mongol invasion of the thirteenth century, however, that Chinese influence became an important factor in Islamic art. It can be felt most strongly in Persian illuminated manuscripts done under Mongol rule, from about 1300 on, such as the *Summer Landscape* in figure 353 and colorplate 35. More than three centuries earlier, under the Song Dynasty, the painters of China had created a landscape art of great atmospheric depth, mist-shrouded mountains and rushing streams embodying a poetic vision of untamed nature. Our Mongol painter must have known this tradition well; most of the essential elements recur in his own work, enhanced by a lively sense of color that made him stress the red and yellow of leaves turning in early fall. Did such landscapes reach medieval Europe? We do not know, but it may be more than coincidence that landscape painting in the West, which had been dormant since the end of Antiquity, began to revive just about this time (see figs. 496, 501).

353. *Summer Landscape* from the *Album of the Conqueror* (*Sultan Mohammed II*). Mongol (see colorplate 35). Topkapu Palace Museum, Istanbul

represented before, the artists who created them had to rely on both Christian and Buddhist art as their source of inspiration. The result was a curious mixture of elements, often far from well integrated.

Only on rare occasions does Islamic religious painting rise to a level that bears comparison with the art of older faiths. Such a picture is the wonderful miniature in figure 355 and colorplate 36, showing Mohammed's ascension to Paradise. In the Koran, we read that the Lord "caused His servant to make a journey by night...to the remote place of worship which We have encircled with blessings, that We might show him of Our signs." Later Moslem authors added elaborate details to this brief account: the ascent was made from Jerusalem, under the guidance of the angel Gabriel; Mohammed rose through the seven heavens, where he met his predecessors, including Adam, Abraham, Moses, and Jesus, before he was brought into the presence of Allah. The entire journey apparently was thought of as analogous to that of Elijah, who ascended to heaven in a fiery chariot. Mohammed, however, was said to have ridden a miraculous mount named *buraq*, "white, smaller than a mule and larger than an ass," and having a cheek—or a face—like that of a human being; some authors also gave it wings. We will rec-

354. JUNAYD. *Solitary Combat of Prince Humay and Princess Humayun*, from a Persian manuscript. 1396. British Museum, London

The extent to which Chinese influence transformed the tradition of Islamic miniature painting is well demonstrated by the combat scene of prince and princess in a landscape (fig. 354): this is no colored drawing but an ambitious pictorial composition that fills the entire page. The narrative to be illustrated has served merely as a point of departure for our artist; most of his effort is devoted to the setting, rather than to the action described in the text. He must have been a great admirer of Chinese landscapes, for the graceful and delicately shaded rocks, trees, and flowers of our picture clearly reflect their Far Eastern source. At the same time, the design has a decorative quality that is characteristically Islamic; in this respect, it seems more akin to the pattern of a Persian carpet than to the airy spaciousness of Chinese landscape painting.

Another important result of Far Eastern influence, it would seem, was the emergence of religious themes in Persian miniatures. The Mongol rulers, familiar with the rich tradition of Buddhist religious art in India and China, did not share their predecessors' horror at the very idea of pictures of Mohammed. In any event, scenes from the life of the Prophet do occur in Persian illuminated manuscripts from the early fourteenth century on. Since they had never been

355. *The Ascension of Mohammed*, from a Persian manuscript (see colorplate 36). British Library, London

ognize the ancestry of this beast: it derives from the winged, human-headed guardian monsters of ancient Mesopotamia (see fig. 101) and their kin, the sphinxes and centaurs, all of which had survived as ornamental motifs in the great melting pot of Islamic decorative art, where they lay dormant, as it were, until Moslem writers identified them with *buraq*. In our miniature, the wings are reduced to a ring of feathers around *buraq*'s neck, so as not to interfere with the saddle. The animal follows Gabriel across a deep-blue, star-studded sky; below, among scattered clouds, there is a luminous celestial body, probably the moon. The Far Eastern elements in this poetic vision are striking. We find them in the flame-like golden halos behind Gabriel and Mohammed, a familiar feature of Buddhist art; in the curly, "intestinal" stylization of the clouds; in the costumes and facial types of the angels. Yet the composition as a whole—the agitated movement of the angelic servitors converging from all sides upon the Prophet—strongly recalls Christian art. Our miniature thus represents a true, and singularly felicitous, meeting of East and West. There is only one small concession to Islamic iconoclasm: the Prophet's face has been left blank, evidently because it was thought too holy to be depicted.

Scenes such as this one occur in manuscripts of historical or literary works but not of the Koran. Even the Persians apparently did not dare to illustrate the Sacred Book directly, although—or perhaps because—illustrated copies of the Bible were not altogether unknown in the Moslem world. The Koran remained the calligraphers' domain, as it had been from the very beginning of Islam. In their hands, Arabic lettering became an amazingly flexible set of shapes, capable of an infinite variety of decorative elaborations, both geometric and curvilinear. At their best, these designs are masterpieces of the disciplined imagination that seem to anticipate, in a strange way, the abstract art of our own time. The page shown in figure 356 and colorplate 37, probably done by a Turkish calligrapher of the fifteenth century, renders the single word Allah. It is indeed a marvel of intricacy within a rigorous set of formal rules, sharing the qualities of a maze, of a rug pattern, and even of certain non-objective paintings. More than any other single object, it sums up the essence of Islamic art.

356. Calligraphic Page from the *Album of the Conqueror* (*Sultan Mohammed II*). Turkish (?) (see colorplate 37). Topkapu Palace Museum, Istanbul

2
EARLY MEDIEVAL ART

THE DARK AGES

The labels we use for historical periods tend to be like the nicknames of people: once established, they are almost impossible to change, even though they may no longer be suitable. Those who coined the term "Middle Ages" thought of the entire thousand years from the fifth to the fifteenth century as an age of darkness, an empty interval between classical Antiquity and its rebirth, the Renaissance in Italy. Since then, our view of the Middle Ages has changed completely; we no longer think of the period as "benighted" but as the "Age of Faith."

With the spread of this new, positive conception, the idea of darkness has become confined more and more to the early part of the Middle Ages. A hundred years ago, the "Dark Ages" were generally thought to extend as far as the twelfth century; they have been shrinking steadily ever since, so that today the term covers no more than the 200-year interval between the death of Justinian and the reign of Charlemagne. Perhaps we ought to pare down the Dark Ages even

further; for in the course of the century 650–750 A.D., as we have pointed out earlier, the center of gravity of European civilization shifted northward from the Mediterranean, and the economic, political, and spiritual framework of the Middle Ages began to take shape. We shall now see that the same century also gave rise to some important artistic achievements.

Celtic-Germanic Style

ANIMAL STYLE. The Germanic tribes that had entered western Europe from the east during the declining years of the Roman Empire carried with them, in the form of nomads' gear, an ancient and widespread artistic tradition, the so-called animal style. We have encountered early examples of it in the Luristan bronzes of Iran and the Scythian gold ornaments from southern Russia (see pages 76–77 and figs. 107, 108). This style, with its combination of abstract and organic shapes, of formal discipline and imaginative freedom, became an important element in the Celtic-Germanic

357. Purse Cover, from the Sutton Hoo Ship-Burial. 625–33 A.D.
Gold with garnets and enamels. British Museum, London

art of the Dark Ages, such as the gold-and-enamel purse cover (fig. 357) from the grave, at Sutton Hoo, of an East Anglian king who died between 625 and 633.

On it are four pairs of symmetrical motifs: each has its own distinctive character, an indication that the motifs have been assembled from four different sources. One motif, the standing man between confronted animals, has a very long history indeed—we first saw it in Sumerian art more than three thousand years before (see fig. 93). The eagles pouncing on ducks bring to mind similar pairings of carnivore-and-victim in Luristan bronzes. The design above them, on the other hand, is of more recent origin. It consists of fighting animals whose tails, legs, and jaws are elongated into bands forming a complex interlacing pattern. Interlacing bands as an ornamental device occur in Roman and Early Christian art, especially along the southern shore of the Mediterranean, but their combination with the animal style, as shown here, seems to be an invention of the Dark Ages, not much before the date of our purse cover.

Metalwork, in a variety of materials and techniques and often of exquisitely refined craftsmanship, had been the principal medium of the animal style. Such objects, small, durable, and eagerly sought after, account for the rapid diffusion of its repertory of forms. During the Dark Ages, however, these forms migrated not only in the geographic sense but also technically and artistically, into wood, stone, and even manuscript illumination.

Wooden specimens, as we might expect, have not survived in large numbers; most of them come from Scandinavia, where the animal style flourished longer than anywhere else. The splendid animal head in figure 358, of the early ninth century, is the terminal of a post that was found, along with much other equipment, in a buried Viking ship at Oseberg in southern Norway. Like the motifs on the Sutton Hoo

purse cover, it shows a peculiarly composite quality: the basic shape of the head is surprisingly realistic, as are certain details (teeth, gums, nostrils), but the surface has been spun over with interlacing and geometric patterns that betray their derivation from metalwork. Snarling monsters such as this used to rise from the prows of Viking ships, endowing them with the character of mythical sea dragons.

Hiberno-Saxon Style

The earliest Christian works of art that were made north of the Alps also reflected the pagan Germanic version of the animal style. In order to understand how they came to be produced, however, we must first acquaint ourselves with the important role played by the Irish, who, during the Dark Ages, assumed the spiritual and cultural leadership of western Europe. The period 600–800 A.D. deserves, in fact, to be called the Golden Age of Ireland. Unlike their English neighbors, the Irish had never been part of the Roman Empire; thus the missionaries who carried the Gospel to them from England in the fifth century found a Celtic society entirely barbarian by Roman standards. The Irish readily accepted Christianity, which brought them into contact with Mediterranean civilization, but they did not become Rome-oriented. Rather, they adapted what they had received in a spirit of vigorous local independence.

IRISH CHRISTIANITY. The institutional framework of the Roman Church, being essentially urban, was ill-suited to the rural character of Irish life. Irish Christians preferred to follow the example of the desert saints of Egypt and the Near East who had left the temptations of the city to seek spiritual perfection in the solitude of the wilderness. Groups of such hermits, sharing a common ideal of ascetic disci-

358. *Animal Head*, from the Oseberg Ship-Burial. c. 825 A.D. Wood, height c. 5″. University Museum of Antiquities, Oslo

The Cross Page in the *Lindisfarne Gospels* (fig. 359, colorplate 38) is an imaginative creation of breath-taking complexity; the miniaturist, working with a jeweler's precision, has poured into the compartments of his geometric frame an animal interlace so dense and yet so full of controlled movement that the fighting beasts on the Sutton Hoo purse cover seem childishly simple in comparison. It is as if the world of paganism, embodied in these biting and clawing monsters, had suddenly been subdued by the superior authority of the Cross. In order to achieve this effect, our artist has had to impose an extremely severe discipline upon himself. His "rules of the game" demand, for instance, that organic and geometric shapes must be kept separate; that within the animal compartments every line must turn out to be part of an animal's body, if we take the trouble to trace it back to its point of origin. There are also rules, too complex to go into here, concerning symmetry, mirror-image effects, and repetitions of shapes and colors. Only by working these out for ourselves by intense observation can we hope to enter into the spirit of this strange, mazelike world.

Of the representational images they found in Early Christian manuscripts, the Hiberno-Saxon illuminators generally retained only the symbols of the four evangelists, since these

pline, had founded the earliest monasteries. By the fifth century, monasteries had spread as far north as western Britain, but only in Ireland did monasticism take over the leadership of the Church from the bishops. Irish monasteries, unlike their Egyptian prototypes, soon became seats of learning and the arts; they also developed a missionary fervor that sent Irish monks to preach to the heathen and to found monasteries in northern Britain as well as on the European mainland, from Poitiers to Vienna. These Irishmen not only speeded the conversion to Christianity of Scotland, northern France, the Netherlands, and Germany; they also established the monastery as a cultural center throughout the European countryside. Although their Continental foundations were taken over before long by the monks of the Benedictine order, who were advancing north from Italy during the seventh and eighth centuries, Irish influence was to be felt within medieval civilization for several hundred years to come.

MANUSCRIPTS. In order to spread the Gospel, the Irish monasteries had to produce copies of the Bible and other Christian books in large numbers. Their writing workshops (scriptoria) also became centers of artistic endeavor, for a manuscript containing the Word of God was looked upon as a sacred object whose visual beauty should reflect the importance of its contents. Irish monks must have known Early Christian illuminated manuscripts, but here again, as in so many other respects, they developed an independent tradition instead of simply copying their models. While pictures illustrating biblical events held little interest for them, they devoted great effort to decorative embellishment. The finest of these manuscripts belong to the Hiberno-Saxon style, combining Celtic and Germanic elements, which flourished in the monasteries founded by Irishmen in Saxon England.

359. Cross Page from the *Lindisfarne Gospels* (see colorplate 38). British Library, London

360. *Symbol of St. Mark*, from the
Echternach Gospels (see colorplate 39).
Bibliothèque Nationale, Paris

ing bands. Clearly, there is a wide gulf between the Celtic-Germanic and the Mediterranean traditions, a gulf that the Irish artist who modeled the *Crucifixion* did not know how to bridge.

Lombard Style

The situation was much the same in Continental Europe: we even find it among the Lombards in northern Italy. The Germanic stone carver who did the marble balustrade relief in the Cathedral Baptistery at Cividale (fig. 362) was just as perplexed as his Irish contemporaries by the problem of representation. His evangelists' symbols are strange creatures indeed; all four of them have the same spidery front legs, and their bodies consist of nothing but head, wings, and (except for the angel) a little spiral tail. Apparently he did not feel he was violating their integrity by forcing them into their circular frames in this Procrustean fashion. On the other hand, he had a well-developed sense of ornament; the panel as a whole, with its flat, symmetrical pattern, is an effective piece of decoration, rather like an embroidered cloth. He may, in fact, have derived his design in part from Oriental textiles (compare fig. 115).

361. *Crucifixion* (from a book cover?).
8th century A.D. Bronze. National
Museum of Ireland, Dublin

could be translated into their ornamental idiom without much difficulty. The lion of St. Mark in the *Echternach Gospels* (fig. 360, colorplate 39), sectioned and patterned like the enamel inlays of the Sutton Hoo purse cover, is animated by the same curvilinear sense of movement we saw in the animal interlaces of the previous illustration. Here again we marvel at the masterly balance between the shape of the animal and the geometric framework on which it has been superimposed (and which, in this instance, includes the inscription, *imago leonis*).

The human figure, on the other hand, remained beyond the Celtic or Germanic artist's reach for a long time. The bronze plaque of the *Crucifixion* (fig. 361), probably made for a book cover, shows how helpless he was when faced with the image of a man. In his attempt to reproduce an Early Christian composition, he suffers from an utter inability to conceive of the human frame as an organic unit, so that the figure of Christ becomes disembodied in the most literal sense: the head, arms, and feet are all separate elements joined to a central pattern of whorls, zigzags, and interlac-

362. Balustrade Relief Inscribed by the Patriarch Sigvald, (762–776 A.D.), probably carved c. 725–50 A.D. Marble, about 3 × 5 '. Cathedral Baptistery, Cividale, Italy

CAROLINGIAN ART

The empire built by Charlemagne (see page 239) did not endure for long. His grandsons divided it into three parts, and proved incapable of effective rule even in these, so that political power reverted to the local nobility. The cultural achievements of his reign, in contrast, have proved far more lasting; this very page would look different without them, for it is printed in letters whose shape derives from the script in Carolingian manuscripts. The fact that these letters are known today as "roman" rather than Carolingian recalls another aspect of the cultural reforms sponsored by Charlemagne: the collecting and copying of ancient Roman literature. The oldest surviving texts of a great many classical Latin authors are to be found in Carolingian manuscripts, which, until not very long ago, were mistakenly regarded as Roman, hence their lettering, too, was called Roman.

This interest in preserving the classics was part of an ambitious attempt to restore ancient Roman civilization, along with the imperial title. Charlemagne himself took an active hand in this revival, through which he expected to implant the cultural traditions of a glorious past in the minds of the semibarbaric people of his realm. To an astonishing extent, he succeeded. Thus the "Carolingian revival" may be termed the first—and in some ways the most important—phase of a genuine fusion of the Celtic-Germanic spirit with that of the Mediterranean world.

Architecture

PALACE CHAPEL, AACHEN. The fine arts played an important role in Charlemagne's cultural program from the very start. On his visits to Italy, he had become familiar with the architectural monuments of the Constantinian era in Rome and with those of the reign of Justinian in Ravenna; his own capital at Aachen, he felt, must convey the majesty of empire through buildings of an equally impressive kind. His famous Palace Chapel (figs. 363–65) is, in fact, directly inspired by S. Vitale (compare figs. 306–9). To erect such a structure on Northern soil was a difficult undertaking; columns and bronze gratings had to be imported from Italy, and expert stonemasons must have been hard to find. The design, by Odo of Metz (probably the earliest architect north of the Alps known to us by name), is by no means a mere echo of S. Vitale but a vigorous reinterpretation, with piers and vaults of Roman massiveness and a geometric clarity of the spatial units very different from the fluid space of the earlier structure.

Equally significant is Odo's scheme for the western entrance (now largely obscured by later additions and rebuilding); at S. Vitale, the entrance consists of a broad, semi-detached narthex with twin stair turrets, at an odd angle to the main axis of the church, while at Aachen these elements have been molded into a tall, compact unit, in line with the main axis and closely attached to the chapel proper. This monumental entrance structure, or westwork (from the German *Westwerk*), which makes one of its first known appearances here, holds the germ of the two-tower façade familiar from so many later medieval churches.

363. (*above*) Interior of the Palace
Chapel of Charlemagne,
Aachen. 792–805 A.D.

364. (*left*) Restored Plan of the
Palace Chapel of Charlemagne

365. (*below*) Axonometric Projection of
the Palace Chapel of Charlemagne
(after Kubach)

366. Plan of the Abbey Church of St.-Riquier, France. Consecrated 799 A.D. (after Effmann, 1912)

367. Abbey Church of St.-Riquier
(engraved view by Petau, 1612, after
an 11th-century manuscript illumination)

ST.-RIQUIER. An even more elaborate westwork formed part of the greatest basilican church of Carolingian times, that of the monastery of St.-Riquier (also called Centula), near Abbeville in northeastern France. It has been completely destroyed, but its design is known in detail from drawings and descriptions (figs. 366, 367). Several innovations in the church were to become of basic importance for the future: the westwork leads into a vaulted narthex which is in effect a western transept; the crossing (the area where the transept intersects the nave) was crowned by a tower, and the same feature recurred above the crossing of the eastern transept, again with two round stair towers. The apse, unlike that of Early Christian basilicas (compare fig. 289), is separated from the eastern transept by a square compartment, called the choir. St.-Riquier was widely imitated in other Carolingian monastery churches, but these, too, have been destroyed or rebuilt in later times (a fine westwork of the tenth century is shown in figure 376).

PLAN OF A MONASTERY, ST. GALL. The importance of monasteries, and their close link with the imperial court, are vividly suggested by a unique document of the period, the large drawing of a plan for a monastery preserved in the Chapter Library at St. Gall in Switzerland (fig. 368). Its basic features seem to have been determined at a council held near Aachen in 816–817; this copy was then sent to the abbot of St. Gall for his guidance in rebuilding the monastery. We may regard it, therefore, as a standard plan, to be modified according to local needs. (Our illustration omits the explanatory titles.)

The monastery is a complex, self-contained unit, filling a rectangle about 500 by 700 feet (fig. 369). The main entrance-way, from the west, passes between stables and a hostelry toward a gate which admits the visitor to a colonnaded semicircular portico flanked by two round towers, a sort of strung-out westwork that looms impressively above the low outer buildings. It emphasizes the church as the center of the monastic community. The church is a basilica, with a transept and choir in the east but an apse and altar at either end; the nave and aisles, containing numerous other altars, do not form a single continuous space but are subdivided into compartments by screens. There are numerous entrances: two beside the western apse, others on the north and south flanks.

This entire arrangement reflects the functions of a monastery church, designed for the liturgical needs of the monks rather than for a lay congregation. Adjoining the church to the south is an arcaded cloister, around which are grouped the monks' dormitory (on the east side), a refectory and kitchen (on the south side), and a cellar. The three large buildings north of the church are a guesthouse, a school, and the abbot's house. To the east are the infirmary, a chapel and quarters for novices, the cemetery (marked by a large cross), a garden, and coops for chickens and geese. The south side is occupied by workshops, barns, and other service buildings. There is, needless to say, no monastery exactly like this anywhere—even in St. Gall the plan was not carried out as drawn—yet its layout conveys an excellent notion of such establishments throughout the Middle Ages.

368. Plan of a Monastery. c. 820 A.D. Chapter Library, St. Gall

369. Reconstruction Model (Walter Horn, 1965)

Manuscripts and Book Covers

GOSPEL BOOK OF CHARLEMAGNE. We know from literary sources that Carolingian churches contained murals, mosaics, and relief sculpture, but these have disappeared almost entirely. Illuminated manuscripts, ivories, and goldsmiths' work, on the other hand, have survived in considerable numbers. They demonstrate the impact of the Carolingian revival even more strikingly than the architectural remains of the period. The former Imperial Treasury in Vienna contains a Gospel Book said to have been found in the tomb of Charlemagne and, in any event, closely linked with his court at Aachen. As we look at the picture of St. Matthew from that manuscript (fig. 370), we find it hard to believe that such a work could have been executed in northern Europe about the year 800: if it were not for the large golden halo, the Evangelist might almost be mistaken for a classical author's portrait like the one of Menander (fig. 371), painted at Pompeii almost eight centuries earlier. Whoever the artist was—Byzantine, Italian, or Frankish—he plainly was fully conversant with the Roman tradition of painting, down to the acanthus ornament on the wide frame, which emphasizes the "window" aspect of the picture. The *St. Matthew* represents the most orthodox phase of the Carolingian revival; it is the visual counterpart of copying the text of a classical work of literature.

371. *Portrait of Menander* (wall painting).
c. 70 A.D. House of Menander, Pompeii

370. *St. Matthew*, from the *Gospel Book of Charlemagne*.
c. 800–810 A.D. Kunsthistorisches Museum, Vienna

372. *St. Mark*, from the *Gospel Book of Archbishop Ebbo of Reims* (see colorplate 40). Municipal Library, Epernay, France

GOSPEL BOOK OF ARCHBISHOP EBBO. A miniature of some three decades later for the *Gospel Book of Archbishop Ebbo of Reims* (fig. 372, colorplate 40) shows the classical model translated into a Carolingian idiom. It must have been based on an evangelist's portrait of the same style as the *St. Matthew*, but now the entire picture is filled with a vibrant energy that sets everything into motion: the drapery swirls about the figure, the hills heave upward, the vegetation seems to be tossed about by a whirlwind, and even the acanthus pattern on the frame assumes a strange, flamelike character. The Evangelist himself has been transformed from a Roman author setting down his own thoughts into a man seized with the frenzy of divine inspiration, an instrument for recording the Word of God. His gaze is fixed, not upon his book but upon his symbol (the winged lion with a scroll), which acts as the transmitter of the Sacred Text. This dependence upon the Will of the Lord, so powerfully expressed here, marks the contrast between the classical and the medieval image of man. But the *means* of expression—the dynamism of line that distinguishes our miniature from its predecessor—recalls the passionate movement we found in the ornamentation of Irish manuscripts of the Dark Ages (colorplates 38, 39).

373. Illustration to Psalm 44, from the *Utrecht Psalter*. c. 820–32 A.D. University Library, Utrecht

Colorplate 36. PERSIAN. *The Ascension of Mohammed* (see page 253),
from a Persian manuscript. 1539–43. British Library, London

Colorplate 37. ISLAMIC. Calligraphic Page, from the *Album of the Conqueror*
(*Sultan Mohammed II*; see page 254). Turkish (?), 15th century. Topkapu Palace Museum, Istanbul

Colorplate 38. ANGLO-IRISH. Cross Page, from the *Lindisfarne Gospels*
(see page 257). About 700 A.D. British Library, London

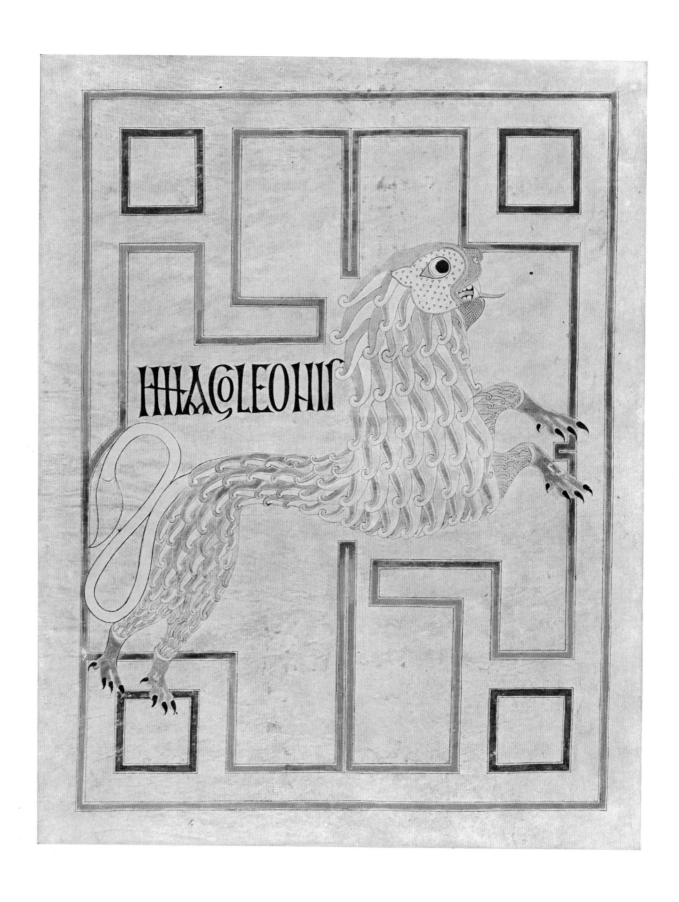

Colorplate 39. ANGLO-IRISH. *Symbol of St. Mark*, from the
Echternach Gospels (see page 258). About 700 A.D. Bibliothèque Nationale, Paris

Colorplate 40. CAROLINGIAN. *St. Mark*, from the *Gospel Book of Archbishop Ebbo of Reims* (see page 264). 816–835 A.D. Municipal Library, Épernay, France

Colorplate 41. CAROLINGIAN. Upper Cover of the Binding of the *Lindau Gospels* (see page 273). About 870 A.D. Gold and jewels, 13¾ × 10½″. The Pierpont Morgan Library, New York

Colorplate 42. OTTONIAN. *St. Luke; Christ Washing the Feet of Peter, from the Gospel Book of Otto III* (see page 276). About 1000. Bavarian State Library, Munich

Colorplate 43. ROMANESQUE. Speyer Cathedral, from the east (see page 286). Begun 1030

Colorplate 44. ROMANESQUE. Baptistery, Florence (see page 287). c. 1060–1150

Colorplate 45. ROMANESQUE. *St. John the Evangelist*, from the *Gospel
Book of Abbot Wedricus* (see page 296). Shortly before 1147. Société Archéologique, Avesnes, France

UTRECHT PSALTER. The Reims School also produced the most extraordinary of all Carolingian manuscripts, the *Utrecht Psalter* (fig. 373). It displays the style of the *Ebbo Gospels* in an even more energetic form, since the entire book is illustrated with pen drawings. Here again the artist has followed a much older model, as indicated by the architectural and landscape settings of the scenes and by the use of Roman capital lettering, which had gone out of general use several centuries before. The wonderfully rhythmic quality of his draftsmanship, however, gives to these sketches a kind of emotional coherence that could not have been present in the earlier pictures. Without it, the drawings of the *Utrecht Psalter* would carry little conviction, for the poetic language of the Psalms does not lend itself to illustration in the same sense as the narrative portions of the Bible.

The Psalms can be illustrated only by taking each phrase literally and then by visualizing it in some manner. Thus, at the top of our picture, we see the Lord reclining on a bed, flanked by pleading angels, an image based on the words, "Awake, why sleepest thou, O Lord?" On the left, the faithful crouch before the Temple, "for . . . our belly cleaveth unto the earth," and at the city gate in the foreground they are killed "as sheep for the slaughter." In the hands of a pedestrian artist, this procedure could well turn into a wearisome charade; here, it has the force of a great drama.

COVER, LINDAU GOSPELS. The style of the Reims School can still be felt in the reliefs of the jeweled front cover

374. Upper Cover of Binding, the
Lindau Gospels (see colorplate 41). The
Pierpont Morgan Library, New York

of the *Lindau Gospels* (fig. 374, colorplate 41), a work of the third quarter of the ninth century. This masterpiece of the goldsmith's art shows how splendidly the Celtic-Germanic metalwork tradition of the Dark Ages adapted itself to the Carolingian revival. The clusters of semiprecious stones are not mounted directly on the gold ground but raised on claw feet or arcaded turrets, so that the light can penetrate beneath them, to bring out their full brilliance. Interestingly enough, the crucified Christ betrays no hint of pain or death; He seems to stand rather than to hang, His arms spread out in a solemn gesture. To endow Him with the signs of human suffering was not yet conceivable, even though the means were at hand, as we can see from the eloquent expressions of grief among the small figures in the adjoining compartments.

OTTONIAN ART

In 870, about the time when the *Lindau Gospels* cover was made, the remains of Charlemagne's empire were ruled by his two surviving grandsons: Charles the Bald, the West Frankish king, and Louis the German, the East Frankish king, whose domains corresponded roughly to the France and Germany of today. Their power was so weak, however, that continental Europe once again lay exposed to attack. In the south, the Moslems resumed their depredations, Slavs and Magyars advanced from the east, and Vikings from Scandinavia ravaged the north and west.

These Norsemen (the ancestors of today's Danes and Norwegians) had been raiding Ireland and Britain by sea from the late eighth century on; now they invaded northwestern France as well, occupying the area that ever since has been called Normandy. Once established there, they soon adopted Christianity and Carolingian civilization, and, from 911 on, their leaders were recognized as dukes nominally subject to the authority of the king of France. During the eleventh century, the Normans assumed a role of major importance in shaping the political and cultural destiny of Europe, with William the Conqueror becoming king of England while other Norman nobles expelled the Arabs from Sicily and the Byzantines from South Italy.

In Germany, meanwhile, after the death of the last Carolingian monarch in 911, the center of political power had shifted north to Saxony. The Saxon kings (919–1024) reestablished an effective central government, and the greatest of them, Otto I, also revived the imperial ambitions of Charlemagne. After marrying the widow of a Lombard king, he extended his rule over most of Italy and had himself crowned emperor by the pope in 962. From then on the Holy Roman Empire was to be a German institution—or perhaps we ought to call it a German dream, for Otto's successors never managed to consolidate their claim to sovereignty south of the Alps. Yet this claim had momentous consequences, since it led the German emperors into centuries of conflict with the papacy and local Italian rulers, linking North and South in a love-hate relationship whose echoes can be felt to the present day.

Sculpture

During the Ottonian period, from the mid-tenth century to the beginning of the eleventh, Germany was the leading nation of Europe, politically as well as artistically. German achievements in both areas began as revivals of Carolingian traditions but soon developed new and original traits.

THE GERO CRUCIFIX. These changes of outlook are impressively brought home to us if we compare the Christ on the cover of the *Lindau Gospels* with the *Gero Crucifix* (fig. 375) in the Cathedral at Cologne. The two works are separated by little more than a hundred years' interval, but the contrast between them suggests a far greater span. In the *Gero Crucifix* we meet an image of the crucified Saviour new to Western art: monumental in scale, carved in powerfully rounded forms, and filled with a deep concern for the sufferings of the Lord. Particularly striking is the forward bulge of the heavy body, which makes the physical strain on arms and shoulders seem almost unbearably real. The face, with its deeply incised, angular features, has turned into a mask of agony, from which all life has fled.

How did the Ottonian sculptor arrive at this startlingly bold conception? We do not belittle his greatness by recalling that the compassionate view of Christ on the Cross had been created in Byzantine art of the Second Golden Age (see fig. 327) and that the *Gero Crucifix* clearly derives from that source. Nor need we be surprised that Byzantine influence should have been strong in Germany at that time, for Otto II had married a Byzantine princess, establishing a direct link between the two imperial courts. It remained for the Ottonian artist to translate the Byzantine image into large-scale sculptural terms and to replace its gentle pathos with an expressive realism that has been the main strength of German art ever since.

Architecture

Cologne was closely connected with the imperial house through its Archbishop, Bruno, the brother of Otto I, who left a strong mark on the city through the numerous churches he built or rebuilt. His favorite among these, the Benedictine Abbey of St. Pantaleon, became his burial place as well as that of the wife of Otto II. Only the monumental westwork (fig. 376) has retained its original shape essential-

375. *The Gero Crucifix.* c. 975–1000 A.D. Wood, height 6′ 2″. Cathedral, Cologne

376. Westwork, St. Pantaleon, Cologne. Consecrated 980 A.D.

ly unchanged until modern times; we recognize it as a massive and well-proportioned successor to Carolingian westworks, with the characteristic tower over the crossing of the western transept and a deep porch flanked by tall stair turrets.

BERNWARD, BISHOP OF HILDESHEIM. The most ambitious patron of architecture and art in the Ottonian age, however, judged in terms of surviving works, was Bernward, who, after having been one of the tutors of Otto III, became Bishop of Hildesheim. His chief monument is another Benedictine abbey church, St. Michael's (figs. 377–79). The plan, with its two choirs and lateral entrances, recalls the monastery church of the St. Gall plan (fig. 368). But in St. Michael's the symmetry is carried much further: not only are there two identical transepts, with crossing towers and stair turrets (see St.-Riquier, figs. 366, 367), but the supports of the nave arcade, instead of being uniform, consist of pairs of columns separated by square piers. This alternate system divides the arcade into three equal units of three openings each; the first and third units are correlated with the entrances, thus echoing the axis of the transepts. Since, moreover, the aisles and nave are unusually wide in relation to their length, Bernward's intention must have been to achieve a harmonious balance between the longitudinal and transverse axes throughout the structure.

The exterior, as well as the choirs, of Bernward's church have been disfigured by rebuilding, but the interior of the nave (figs. 378, 379), with its great expanse of wall space between arcade and clerestory, retained the majestic spatial feeling of the original design until World War II reduced it to ruins. (The capitals of the columns date from the twelfth century, the painted wooden ceiling from the thirteenth.) The Bernwardian western choir, as reconstructed in our plan on the basis of recent studies, is particularly interesting: its floor was raised above the level of the rest of the church, so as to accommodate a half-subterranean basement chapel, or crypt, apparently a special sanctuary of St. Michael, which could be entered both from the transept and from the west. The crypt was roofed by groined vaults resting on two rows of columns, and its walls were pierced by arched openings that linked it with the U-shaped corridor, or ambulatory, wrapped around it. This ambulatory must have been visible above ground, enriching the exterior of the western choir, since there were windows in its outer wall. Such crypts with ambulatories, usually housing the venerated tomb of a saint, had been introduced into the repertory of Western church architecture during Carolingian times; the Bernwardian design stands out for its large scale and its carefully planned integration with the rest of the building.

Metalwork

BRONZE DOORS OF BISHOP BERNWARD. How much importance Bernward himself attached to the crypt at St. Michael's can be gathered from the fact that he commissioned a pair of richly sculptured bronze doors which were probably meant for the two entrances leading from the transept to the ambulatory (they were finished in 1015, the year

377. Reconstructed Plan, St. Michael's, Hildesheim

378. Reconstructed Longitudinal Section, St. Michael's, Hildesheim (after Beseler)

379. Interior (view toward the west, before World War II), St. Michael's, Hildesheim

380. *Adam and Eve Reproached by the Lord*, from the Bronze Doors of Bishop Bernward for St. Michael's. 1015. c. 23 × 43″. Hildesheim Cathedral

the crypt was consecrated). The idea may have come to him as a result of his visit to Rome, where he could see ancient Roman—and perhaps Byzantine—bronze doors. The Bernwardian doors, however, differ from their predecessors; they are divided into broad horizontal fields rather than vertical panels, and each field contains a biblical scene in high relief.

Our detail (fig. 380) shows Adam and Eve after the Fall. Below it, in inlaid letters remarkable for their classical Roman character, is part of the dedicatory inscription, with the date and Bernward's name. In these figures we find nothing of the monumental spirit of the *Gero Crucifix:* they seem far smaller than they actually are, so that one might easily mistake them for a piece of goldsmiths' work such as the *Lindau Gospels* cover (compare fig. 374, colorplate 41). The entire composition must have been derived from an illuminated manuscript; the oddly stylized bits of vegetation have a good deal of the twisting, turning movement we recall from Irish miniatures. Yet the story is conveyed with splendid directness and expressive force. The accusing finger of the Lord, seen against a great void of blank surface, is the focal point of the drama; it points to a cringing Adam, who passes the blame to his mate, while Eve, in turn, passes it to the serpent at her feet.

Manuscripts

GOSPEL BOOK OF OTTO III. The same intensity of glance and of gesture characterizes Ottonian manuscript painting, which blends Carolingian and Byzantine elements into a new style of extraordinary scope and power. The most important center of manuscript illumination at that time was the Reichenau monastery, on an island in the Lake of Constance. Perhaps its finest achievement—and one of the great masterpieces of medieval art—is the *Gospel Book of Otto III*, from which we reproduce two full-page miniatures (figs. 381, 382, colorplate 42).

The scene of Christ washing the feet of St. Peter contains notable echoes of ancient painting, transmitted through Byzantine art; the soft pastel hues of the background recall the illusionism of Graeco-Roman landscapes, and the architectural frame around Christ is a late descendant of such architectural perspectives as the mural from Boscoreale (see fig. 278). That these elements have been misunderstood by the Ottonian artist is obvious enough; but he has also put them to a new use, so that what was once an architectural vista now becomes the Heavenly City, the House of the Lord filled with golden celestial space as against the atmospheric earthly space without. The figures have undergone a similar

381. *Christ Washing the Feet of Peter*, from the
Gospel Book of Otto III (see colorplate 42).
Bavarian State Library, Munich

transformation: in ancient art, this composition had been used to represent a doctor treating a patient. Now St. Peter takes the place of the sufferer, and Christ that of the physician (note that He is still the beardless young philosopher type here). As a consequence, the emphasis has shifted from physical to spiritual action, and this new kind of action is not only conveyed through glances and gestures, it also governs the scale of things: Christ and St. Peter, the most active figures, are larger than the rest; Christ's "active" arm is longer than His "passive" one; and the eight disciples who merely watch have been compressed into a tiny space, so that we see little more than their eyes and hands.

The other miniature, the painting of St. Luke, is a symbolic image of overwhelming grandeur. Unlike his Carolingian predecessors, the Evangelist is no longer shown writing; his Gospel lies completed on his lap. Enthroned on two rainbows, he holds aloft a huge cluster of clouds from which tongues of light radiate in every direction. Within it we see his symbol, the ox, surrounded by five Old Testament prophets and an outer circle of angels. At the bottom, two lambs drink the life-giving waters that spring from beneath the Evangelist's feet. The key to the entire design is the inscription: *Fonte patrum ductas bos agnis elicit undas*— "From the source of the fathers the ox brings forth a flow of water for the lambs"—that is, St. Luke makes the prophets' message of salvation explicit for the faithful. The Ottonian artist has truly "illuminated" the meaning of this terse and enigmatic phrase by translating it into such compelling visual terms.

382. *St. Luke*, from the *Gospel Book of Otto III*
(see colorplate 42). Bavarian State Library, Munich

3
ROMANESQUE ART

Looking back over the ground we have covered in this book so far, a thoughtful reader will be struck by the fact that almost all of our chapter headings and subheadings might serve equally well for a general history of civilization. Some are based on technology (e.g., the Old Stone Age), others on geography, ethnology, religion; whatever the source, they have been borrowed from other fields, even though in our context they also designate artistic styles. There are only two important exceptions to this rule: Archaic and Classical are primarily terms of style; they refer to qualities of form rather than to the setting in which these forms were created. Why don't we have more terms of this sort? We do, as we shall see—but only for the art of the past 900 years.

The men who first conceived the idea of viewing the history of art as an evolution of styles started out with the conviction that art in the ancient world developed toward a single climax: Greek art from the age of Pericles to that of Alexander the Great. This style they called Classical (that is, perfect). Everything that came before was labeled Archaic, to indicate that it was still old-fashioned and tradition-bound, not-yet-Classical but striving in the right direction, while the style of post-Classical times did not deserve a special term since it had no positive qualities of its own, being merely an echo or a decadence of Classical art.

The early historians of medieval art followed a similar pattern; to them, the great climax was the Gothic style, from the thirteenth century to the fifteenth. For whatever was not-yet-Gothic they adopted the label Romanesque. In doing so, they were thinking mainly of architecture; pre-Gothic churches, they noted, were round-arched, solid, and heavy (as against the pointed arches and the soaring lightness of Gothic structures), rather like the ancient Roman style of building, and the term Romanesque was meant to convey just that. In this sense, all of medieval art before 1200, insofar as it shows any link with the Mediterranean tradition, could be called Romanesque. Some scholars speak of medieval art before Charlemagne as pre-Romanesque, and of Carolingian and Ottonian as proto- or early Romanesque, and they are right to the extent that Romanesque art proper (that is, medieval art from about 1050 to 1200) would be unthinkable without the contributions of these earlier styles. On the other hand, if we follow this practice we are likely to do less than justice to those qualities that make the art of the Dark Ages and of Carolingian and Ottonian times different from the Romanesque.

Carolingian art, we will recall, was brought into being by Charlemagne and his circle, as part of a conscious revival policy; even after his death, it remained strongly linked with his imperial court. Ottonian art, too, had this sponsorship, and a correspondingly narrow base. The Romanesque, in contrast, sprang up all over western Europe at about the same time; it consists of a large variety of regional styles, distinct yet closely related in many ways, and without a central source. In this respect, it resembles the art of the Dark Ages rather than the court styles that had preceded it, although it includes the Carolingian-Ottonian tradition along with a good many other, less clearly traceable ones, such as Late Classical, Early Christian, and Byzantine elements, some Islamic influence, and the Celtic-Germanic heritage.

What welded all these different components into a coherent style during the second half of the eleventh century was not any single force but a variety of factors that made for a new burgeoning of vitality throughout the West. Christianity had at last triumphed everywhere in Europe; the Vikings, still largely pagan in the ninth and tenth centuries when their raids terrorized the British Isles and the Continent, had entered the Catholic fold, not only in Normandy but in Scandinavia as well; the Caliphate of Cordova had disintegrated in 1031 into many small Moslem states, opening the way for the reconquest of the Iberian peninsula; and the Magyars had settled down in Hungary.

There was a growing spirit of religious enthusiasm, reflected in the greatly increased pilgrimage traffic to sacred sites and culminating, from 1095 on, in the crusades to liberate the Holy Land from Moslem rule. Equally important was the reopening of Mediterranean trade routes by the navies of Venice, Genoa, and Pisa; the revival of commerce and manufacturing; and the consequent growth of city life. During the turmoil of the early Middle Ages, the towns of the West Roman Empire had shrunk greatly in size (the population of Rome, about one million in 300 A.D., fell to less than 50,000 at one point); some were deserted altogether. From the eleventh century on, they began to regain their former importance. New towns sprang up everywhere, and an urban middle class of craftsmen and merchants established itself between the peasantry and the landed nobility as an important factor in medieval society.

In many respects, then, western Europe between 1050 and 1200 became a great deal more "Roman-esque" than it had been since the sixth century, recapturing some of the international trade patterns, the urban quality, and the military strength of ancient imperial times. The central political authority was lacking, to be sure (even the Empire of Otto I did not extend much farther west than modern Germany does) but the central spiritual authority of the pope took its place to some extent as a unifying force. The international army that responded to Urban II's call for the First Crusade was more powerful than anything a secular ruler could have raised for the purpose.

ARCHITECTURE

The most conspicuous difference between Romanesque architecture and that of the preceding centuries is the amazing increase in building activity. An eleventh-century monk, Raoul Glaber, summed it up well when he triumphantly exclaimed that the world was putting on a "white mantle of churches." These churches were not only more numerous than those of the early Middle Ages, they were also generally larger, more richly articulated, and more "Roman-looking," for their naves now had vaults instead of wooden roofs, and their exteriors, unlike those of Early Christian, Byzantine, Carolingian, and Ottonian churches, were decorated with both architectural ornament and sculpture. Geographically, Romanesque monuments of the first importance are distributed over an area that might well have represented the world—the Catholic world, that is—to Raoul Glaber: from northern Spain to the Rhineland, from the Scottish-English border to central Italy. The richest crop, the greatest variety of regional types, and the most adventurous ideas are to be found in France. If we add to this group those destroyed or disfigured buildings whose original design is known to us through archaeological research, we have a wealth of architectural invention unparalleled by any previous era.

Southwestern France

ST.-SERNIN. We begin our sampling—it cannot be more than that—with St.-Sernin, in the southern French town of Toulouse (figs. 383–86), one of a group of great churches of the "pilgrimage type," so called because they were built along the roads leading to the pilgrimage center of Santiago de Compostela in northwestern Spain. The plan immediately strikes us as very much more complex and more fully integrated than those of earlier structures such as St.-Riquier, or St. Michael's at Hildesheim (see figs. 366, 377). It is an emphatic Latin cross, with the center of gravity at the eastern end. Clearly, this church was not designed to serve a monastic community only but (like Old St. Peter's in Rome) to accommodate large crowds of lay worshipers in its long nave and transept.

The nave is flanked by two aisles on either side, the inner aisle continuing around the arms of the transept and the apse and thus forming a complete ambulatory circuit anchored to the two towers of the west façade. The ambulatory, we will recall, had developed as a feature of the crypts of earlier churches (as at St. Michael's); now it has emerged above ground and it is linked with the aisles of nave and transept, and enriched with apsidal chapels that seem to radiate from the apse and continue along the eastern face of the transept. (Apse, ambulatory, and radiating chapels form a unit known as the pilgrimage choir.) The plan also shows that the aisles of St.-Sernin are groin-vaulted throughout. This, in conjunction with the features already noted, imposes a high degree of regularity upon the entire design: the aisles are made up of square bays, which serve as a basic unit, or module, for the other dimensions, so that the nave and transept bays equal two such units, the crossing and the façade towers four units.

On the exterior, this rich articulation is further enhanced by the different roof levels that set off the nave and transept against the inner and outer aisles, the apse, the ambulatory, and the radiating chapels; by the buttresses reinforcing the walls between the windows, so as to contain the outward thrust of the vaults; by the decorative framing of windows and portals; and by the great crossing tower (completed in

383. St.-Sernin, Toulouse (aerial view). c. 1080–1120

384. Plan of St.-Sernin (after Conant)

385. Axonometric Projection of Nave,
St.-Sernin (after Choisy)

386. Nave and Choir, St.-Sernin

In thus describing our experience we do not, of course, mean to suggest that the architect consciously set out to achieve this effect. For him, beauty and engineering were inseparable. Vaulting the nave so as to eliminate the fire hazard of a wooden roof was not only a practical aim; it also challenged him to make the House of the Lord grander and more impressive. And since a vault becomes the more difficult to sustain the farther it is from the ground, he strained every resource to make the nave as tall as he dared. He had, however, to sacrifice the clerestory for safety's sake. Instead, he built galleries over the inner aisles, to abut the lateral pressure of the nave vault, hoping that enough light would filter through them into the central space. St.-Sernin serves to remind us that architecture, like politics, is "the art of the possible," and that its success, here as elsewhere, is measured by the degree to which the architect has explored the limits of what was possible to him under those particular circumstances, structurally and aesthetically.

Burgundy; Western France

The builders of St.-Sernin would have been the first to admit that their answer to the problem of the nave vault was not a final one, impressive though it is in its own terms.

AUTUN CATHEDRAL. The architects of Burgundy arrived at a more elegant solution, as evidenced by the Cathedral of Autun (fig. 387), where the galleries are replaced by a

Gothic times and taller than originally intended). The two façade towers, unfortunately, have remained stumps.

As we enter the nave, we are impressed with its tall proportions, the architectural elaboration of the nave walls, and the dim, indirect lighting, all of which create a sensation very different from the ample and serene interior of St. Michael's, with its simple and clearly separated "blocks" of space (see figs. 378, 379). The contrast between these structures is such as to make the nave walls of St. Michael's look Early Christian (see fig. 290), while those of St.-Sernin seem more akin to structures such as the Colosseum (see fig. 236). The syntax of ancient Roman architecture— vaults, arches, engaged columns, and pilasters firmly knit together into a coherent order—has indeed been recaptured here to a remarkable degree; yet the forces whose interaction is expressed in the nave of St.-Sernin are no longer the physical, "muscular" forces of Graeco-Roman architecture but spiritual forces—spiritual forces of the kind we have seen governing the human body in Carolingian and Ottonian miniatures. The half columns running the entire height of the nave wall would appear just as unnaturally drawn-out to an ancient Roman beholder as the arm of Christ in colorplate 42. They seem to be driven upward by some tremendous, unseen pressure, hastening to meet the transverse arches that subdivide the barrel vault of the nave. Their insistently repeated rhythm propels us toward the eastern end of the church, with its light-filled apse and ambulatory (now obscured by a huge altar of later date).

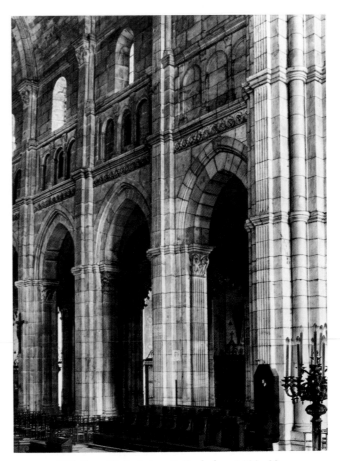

387. Nave Wall, Autun Cathedral. c. 1120–32

blind arcade (called a triforium, since it often has three openings per bay) and a clerestory. What made this three-story elevation possible was the use of the pointed arch for the nave vault, which produced a thrust more nearly downward than outward. For reasons of harmony, the pointed arch also appears in the nave arcade (it had probably reached France from Islamic architecture, where it had been employed for some time). Autun, too, comes close to straining the limits of the possible, for the upper part of the nave wall shows a slight but perceptible outward lean under the pressure of the vault, a warning against any further attempts to increase the height of the clerestory or to enlarge the windows.

HALL CHURCHES. A third alternative, with virtues of its own, appears in the west of France, in such churches as that of St.-Savin-sur-Gartempe (fig. 388). The nave vault here lacks the reinforcing arches, since it was meant to offer a continuous surface for murals (see fig. 417 for this cycle, the finest of its kind). Its great weight rests directly on the nave arcade, which is supported by a majestic set of columns. Yet the nave is fairly well lit, for the two aisles are carried almost to the same height, making it a "hall church," and their outer walls have generously sized windows. At the eastern end

389. West Façade, Notre-Dame-la-Grande, Poitiers. Early 12th century

388. Choir (c. 1060–75) and Nave (c. 1095–1115), St.-Savin-sur-Gartempe

of the nave, there is a pilgrimage choir—happily unobstructed in this case—beyond the crossing tower.

The nave and aisles of hall churches are covered by a single roof, as at St.-Savin. The west façade, too, tends to be low and wide, and may become a richly sculptured screen. That of Notre-Dame-la-Grande at Poitiers (fig. 389), due west from St.-Savin, is particularly noteworthy in this respect, with its elaborately bordered arcades housing large seated or standing figures. A wide band of relief stretches across the façade on either side of the doorway, which is deeply recessed and framed by a series of arches resting on stumpy columns. Taller bundles of columns enhance the turrets, whose conical helmets match the height of the gable in the center (which rises above the actual height of the roof behind it). The sculptural program spread out over this entire area is a visual exposition of Christian doctrine that is a feast for the eyes as well as the mind.

Normandy and England

Further north, in Normandy, the west façade evolved in an entirely different direction. That of the abbey church of St.-Etienne at Caen (fig. 390), founded by William the Conqueror a year or two after his invasion of England, offers a striking contrast with Notre-Dame-la-Grande. Decoration is at a minimum, four huge buttresses divide the front of the church into three vertical sections, and the vertical impetus continues triumphantly in the two splendid towers, whose height would be impressive enough even without the tall Early Gothic helmets. The interior is equally remarkable, but in order to understand its importance we must first turn to the extraordinary development of Anglo-Norman architecture in Britain during the last quarter of the eleventh century.

DURHAM CATHEDRAL. Its most ambitious product is the Cathedral of Durham (figs. 391–93), just south of the Scottish border, begun in 1093. Though somewhat more austere in plan, it has a nave one-third wider than St.-Sernin's, and a greater over-all length (400 feet), which places it among the largest churches of medieval Europe. The nave may have been designed to be vaulted from the start; and the vault over its eastern end had been completed by 1107;

390. West Façade, St.-Etienne, Caen. Begun c. 1068

the rest of the nave, following the same pattern, by 1130. This vault is of great interest, for it represents the earliest systematic use of a ribbed groined vault over a three-story nave, and thus marks a basic advance beyond the solution we saw at Autun. Looking at the plan, we see that the aisles consist of the usual groin-vaulted compartments closely approaching a square, while the bays of the nave, separated by strong transverse arches, are decidedly oblong and groin-vaulted in such a way that the ribs form a double-X design, dividing the vault into seven sections rather than the conventional four. Since the nave bays are twice as long as the aisle bays, the transverse arches occur only at the odd-numbered piers of the nave arcade, and the piers therefore alternate in size, the larger ones being of compound shape (that is, bundles of column and pilaster shafts attached to a square or oblong core), the others cylindrical.

Perhaps the easiest way to visualize the origin of this peculiar system is to imagine that the architect started out by designing a barrel-vaulted nave, with galleries over the aisles, and without a clerestory, as at St.-Sernin, but with the transverse reinforcing arches spaced more widely. As he was doing so, he realized that he could have a clerestory after all if the barrel vault of each nave bay were intersected by two transverse barrel vaults of *oval* shape; the result would be a pair of Siamese-twin groined vaults, and the ends of the transverse barrel vaults could become the clerestory, since the outward thrust and the weight of the whole vault would be concentrated at six securely anchored points on the gallery level. The ribs, of course, were necessary to provide a stable skeleton for the groined vault, so that the curved surfaces between them could be filled in with masonry of minimum thickness, thus reducing both weight and thrust. We do not know whether this ingenious scheme was actually invented at Durham, but it could not have been created much earlier, for it is still in an experimental stage; while the transverse arches at the crossing are round, those to the west of it are slightly pointed, indicating a continuous search for improvements in detail. Aesthetically, the nave at Durham is among the finest in all Romanesque architecture: the wonderful sturdiness of the alternating piers makes a splendid contrast with the dramatically lighted, sail-like surfaces of the vault.

ST.-ETIENNE, CAEN. Let us now return to the interior of St.-Etienne at Caen (fig. 394). The nave, it seems, had originally been planned with galleries and clerestory, and a wooden ceiling. After the experience of Durham, it became possible, in the early twelfth century, to build a groined nave vault instead, with only slight modifications of the wall design. But the bays of the nave here are approximately square, so that the double-X rib pattern could be replaced by a single X with an additional transverse rib (⊠), producing a groined vault of six sections instead of seven. These sexpartite vaults are no longer separated by heavy transverse arches but by simple ribs—another saving in weight which, besides, gives a stronger sense of continuity to the nave vault as a whole and makes for a less emphatic alternating system of piers. Compared to Durham, the nave of St.-Etienne creates an impression of graceful, airy lightness

391. Nave (looking east), Durham Cathedral. 1093–1130

392, 393. Plan and Transverse Section, Durham Cathedral (after Conant)

394. Nave (vaulted c. 1115–20), St.-Etienne, Caen

closely akin to the quality of the Gothic choir that was added in the thirteenth century. And structurally, too, we have here reached the point where Romanesque merges into Early Gothic.

Lombardy

At the time when the Normans and Anglo-Normans constructed their earliest ribbed groined nave vaults, the same problem was being explored in Lombardy, where ancient cities had once again grown large and prosperous. Lombard Romanesque architecture was both nourished and impeded by a continuous building tradition reaching back to Roman and Early Christian times and including the monuments of Ravenna.

S. AMBROGIO. We sense this background as we approach one of its most venerable and important structures, S. Ambrogio in Milan (figs. 395–97), on a site that had been occupied by a church since the fourth century. The present building was begun in the late eleventh century, except for the apse and southern tower, which date from the tenth. The brick exterior, though more ornate and far more monumental, recalls the proportions and the geometric simplicity of the Ravennate churches (compare figs. 291, 306). Upon entering the atrium, we are confronted by the severely handsome façade, with its deeply recessed arcades; just beyond it are two bell towers, separate structures just touching the outer walls of the church. We had seen a round tower of

395. (*left*) S. Ambrogio, Milan. Late 11th and 12th centuries

396. (*above*) Interior, S. Ambrogio

397. (*below*) Longitudinal Section of S. Ambrogio

this kind—probably the earliest surviving example, of the ninth or tenth century—on the north side of S. Apollinare in Classe (fig. 291); most of its successors are square, but the tradition of the free-standing bell tower, or campanile, remained so strong in Italy that they hardly ever became an integral part of the church proper.

The nave of S. Ambrogio, low and broad (it is some ten feet wider than that at Durham), consists of four square bays separated by strong transverse arches. There is no transept, but the easternmost nave bay carries an octagonal, domed crossing tower or lantern. This was an afterthought, and we can easily see why, for the nave has no clerestory and the windows of the lantern provide badly needed illumination. As at Durham, or Caen, there is an alternate system of nave piers, since the length of each nave bay equals that of two aisle bays; the latter are groin-vaulted, like the first three of the nave bays, and support galleries. The nave vaults, however, differ significantly from their northern counterparts. Constructed of brick and rubble, in a technique reminiscent of Roman groined vaults such as those in the Basilica of Constantine, they are a good deal heavier; the diagonal ribs, moreover, form true half circles (at Durham and Caen, they are flattened), so that the vaults rise to a point considerably above the transverse arches. This produces a domed effect and gives each bay the appearance of a separate entity, apart from further increasing the weight of the vault.

On a smaller scale, the Milanese architect might have attempted a clerestory instead of galleries; but the span of the nave was determined by the width of the tenth-century apse, and he shared with his patrons a taste for ample interior proportions like those of Early Christian basilicas (compare fig. 293, colorplate 27) instead of striving for height and light as his Norman contemporaries did. Under these circumstances, he saw no reason to take risks by experimenting with more economical shapes and lighter construction, so that the ribbed groined vault in Lombardy remained conservative and never approached the proto-Gothic stage.

Germany

SPEYER CATHEDRAL. German Romanesque architecture, centered in the Rhineland, was equally conservative, although its conservatism reflects the persistence of Carolingian-Ottonian rather than earlier traditions. Its finest achievement, the Imperial Cathedral of Speyer, begun about 1030, but not completed until more than a century later, has a westwork (now sheathed by a modern reconstruction) and an equally monumental eastern grouping of crossing tower and paired stair towers (fig. 398, colorplate 43). The architectural detail derives from Lombardy, long a focus of German imperial ambitions (compare S. Ambrogio), but the tall proportions are northern, and the scale is so vast as to dwarf every other church of the period. The nave, one-third taller and wider than that of Durham, has a generous clerestory, since it was planned for a wooden roof; in the early twelfth century, it was divided into square bays and covered with heavy, unribbed groined vaults akin to the Lombard rather than the Norman type.

398. Speyer Cathedral, from the east (see colorplate 43)

TOURNAI CATHEDRAL. The impressive eastern end of Speyer Cathedral is echoed in a number of churches of the Rhine Valley and the Low Countries. In the Cathedral of Tournai (fig. 399), it occurs twice, at either end of the transept—the most memorable massing of towers anywhere in Romanesque architecture. Originally, there were to have been four more: two at the west façade (later reduced to turrets) and two flanking the eastern apse (replaced by a huge Gothic choir). Such multiple towers had been firmly established in medieval church design north of the Alps since the time of Charlemagne (see St.-Riquier, fig. 367), although few complete sets were ever finished and even fewer have survived. Whatever their practical functions (as stair towers, bell towers, or watchtowers), their popularity can hardly be accounted for on this basis. In a way not easily fathomed today, they expressed medieval man's relation to the supernatural, as the ziggurats had done for the ancient Mesopotamians (the story of the Tower of Babel always fascinated the Middle Ages). Perhaps their symbolic meaning is best illustrated by a "case history." A certain count had a quarrel with the people of a nearby town, led by their bishop. He finally laid siege to the town, captured it, and, to express his triumph and humiliate his enemies, he lopped the top off their cathedral tower. Evidently, loss of tower meant loss of face, towers being architectural symbols of strength, power, and authority.

399. Tournai Cathedral. Nave 1110–71, transept and crossing c. 1165–1213

Tuscany

PISA. The most famous tower of all, however, owes its renown to an accident. It is the Leaning Tower of Pisa (or, more precisely, the campanile of Pisa Cathedral), which began to assume its present angle, because of poor foundations, even before completion (figs. 400, 401; note that its axis is slightly bent). The tower forms part of a magnificent ensemble on an open site north of the city that includes the Cathedral and the circular, domed Baptistery to the west of it. They represent the most ambitious monument of the Tuscan Romanesque, reflecting the wealth and pride of the city republic of Pisa.

Far more than Lombardy, with its strong northward connections, Tuscany retained an awareness of its classical heritage throughout the Middle Ages. The plan of Pisa Cathedral is essentially that of an Early Christian basilica, elaborated into a Latin cross by the addition of two transept arms that resemble smaller basilicas in themselves, with apses of their own; the crossing is marked by a dome but the rest of the church is wooden-roofed except for the aisles (four in the nave, two in the transept arms), which have groined vaults. The interior (fig. 402) has somewhat taller proportions than an Early Christian basilica, because there are galleries over the aisles, as well as a clerestory, yet the splendid files of classical columns supporting the nave and aisle arcades inevitably recall such Roman structures as St. Paul Outside the Walls (see fig. 290).

Pisa Cathedral and its companions are sheathed entirely in white marble inlaid with horizontal stripes and ornamental patterns in dark green marble. This practice, familiar from Imperial Roman times, survived (or was revived) only in central Italy during the Middle Ages. On the exteriors, it is combined with blind arcades and galleries, producing a lacelike richness of texture and color very different from the austerely simple Early Christian exteriors. But then the time had long passed when it might be thought undesirable for a church to compete with the outward splendor of classical temples.

BAPTISTERY, FLORENCE. In Florence, which was to outstrip Pisa commercially and artistically, the greatest achievement of the Tuscan Romanesque is the Baptistery (fig. 403, colorplate 44) opposite the Cathedral, a domed octagonal structure of impressive size. Here the marble paneling follows severe geometric lines, and the blind arcades are extraordinarily classical in proportion and detail. The entire building, in fact, exudes so classical an air that the Florentines themselves came to believe, a few hundred years later, that it had originally been a temple of Mars. And even today the controversy over its date has not yet been settled to

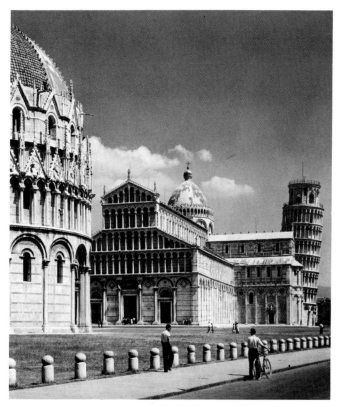

400. Pisa Cathedral, Baptistery, and Campanile.
View from the west. 1053–1272

401. Plan of Pisa Cathedral,
Baptistery, and Campanile

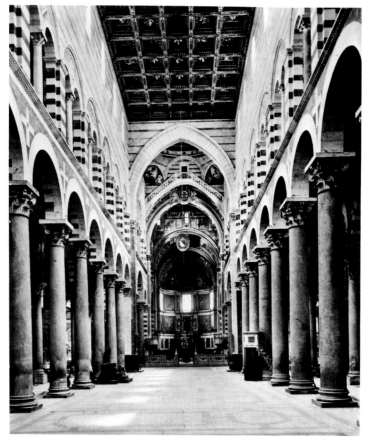

402. Interior, Pisa Cathedral

everyone's satisfaction. We shall have to return to this Baptistery a number of times, since it was destined to play an important role in the Renaissance.

SCULPTURE

The revival of monumental stone sculpture is even more astonishing than the architectural achievements of the Romanesque era, since neither Carolingian nor Ottonian art had shown any tendencies in this direction. Free-standing statues, we will recall, all but disappeared from Western art after the fifth century; stone relief survived only in the form of architectural ornament or surface decoration, with the depth of the carving reduced to a minimum. Thus the only continuous sculptural tradition in early medieval art was that of sculpture-in-miniature: small reliefs, and occasional statuettes, in metal or ivory. Ottonian art, in works such as the bronze doors of Bishop Bernward (see fig. 380), had enlarged the scale of this tradition but not its spirit; and its truly large-scale sculptural efforts, represented by the impressive *Gero Crucifix* (fig. 375), were limited almost entirely to wood. What little stone carving there was in western Europe before the mid-eleventh century hardly went beyond the artistic and technical level of the Sigvald relief (fig. 362).

403. Baptistery, Florence (see colorplate 44)

Southwestern France

Fifty years later, the situation had changed dramatically. Just when and where the revival of stone sculpture began we cannot say with assurance, but if any one area has a claim to priority it is southwestern France and northern Spain, along the pilgrimage roads leading to Santiago de Compostela. The link with the pilgrimage traffic seems logical enough, for architectural sculpture, especially when applied to the exterior of a church, is meant to appeal to the lay worshiper rather than to the members of a closed monastic community.

ST.-SERNIN. Like Romanesque architecture, the rapid development of stone sculpture between 1050 and 1100 reflects the growth of religious fervor among the lay population in the decades before the First Crusade. St.-Sernin at Toulouse contains several important examples probably carved about 1090, including the *Apostle* in figure 404. This panel is now in the ambulatory; its original location remains uncertain—perhaps it decorated the front of an altar. Be that as it may, the figure (which is somewhat more than half lifesize), was not intended for viewing at close range only. Its impressive bulk and weight "carry" over a considerable distance. This emphasis on massive volume hints at what may well have been the main impulse behind the revival of large-scale sculpture: a stone-carved image, being tangible and three-dimensional, is far more "real" than a painted one. To the mind of a cleric, steeped in the abstractions of theology, this might seem irrelevant, or even dangerous. St. Bernard of Clairvaux, writing in 1127, denounced the sculptured decoration of churches as a vain folly and diversion that tempts us "to read in the marble rather than in our books." He was a voice not very much heeded, however; for the unsophisticated layman, any large piece of sculpture inevitably had something of the quality of an idol, and it was this very fact that gave it such great appeal.

But let us return to the *Apostle* from St.-Sernin. Where have we seen its like before? The solidity of the forms has a strongly classical air, indicating that our artist must have had a close look at late Roman sculpture (of which there are considerable remains in southern France). The design as a whole, on the other hand—the solemn frontality of the figure, its placement in the architectural frame—derives from a Byzantine source, in all likelihood an ivory panel descended from the *Archangel Michael* in figure 304. Yet in enlarging such a miniature, the carver of our relief has also reinflated it: the niche is a real cavity, the hair a round, close-fitting cap, the body severe and blocklike. Our *Apostle* has, in fact, much the same dignity and directness as the sculpture of Archaic Greece.

MOISSAC. Another important early center of Romanesque sculpture was the abbey at Moissac, some distance north of Toulouse. The south portal of its church, carved a generation later than the *Apostle* from St.-Sernin, displays a richness of invention that would have made St. Bernard wince. In figure 405 we see the magnificent *trumeau* (the center post supporting the lintel) and the western jamb. Both have a scalloped profile—apparently a bit of Moorish influence

404. *Apostle*, c. 1090. St.-Sernin, Toulouse

But what of the crossed lions that form a symmetrical zigzag on the face of the *trumeau*—do they have a meaning? So far as we know, they simply "animate" the shaft as the interlacing beasts of Irish miniatures (whose descendants they are) animate the compartments assigned to them. In manuscript illumination, this tradition had never died out; our sculpture has undoubtedly been influenced by it, just as the agitated movement of the Prophet has its ultimate origin in miniature painting (see fig. 415). The crossed lions, however, reflect another source as well; we find them in Persian metalwork (although not in this tower-like formation), whence they can be traced back to the confronted animals of ancient Near Eastern art (see figs. 93, 131). Yet we cannot fully account for their presence at Moissac in terms of their effectiveness as ornament. They belong to a vast family of savage or monstrous creatures in Romanesque art that retain their demoniacal vitality even though they are com-

(see fig. 340)—and the shafts of the half-columns applied to jambs and *trumeau* follow this scalloped pattern as if they had been squeezed from a giant pastry tube. Human and animal forms are treated with the same incredible flexibility, so that the spidery Prophet on the side of the *trumeau* seems perfectly adapted to his precarious perch (notice how he, too, has been fitted into the scalloped outline). He even remains free to cross his legs in a dancelike movement and to turn his head toward the interior of the church as he unfurls his scroll.

405. South Portal (portion), St.-Pierre, Moissac. Early 12th century

406. East Flank, South Portal, St.-Pierre, Moissac
(the Angel of the *Annunciation*, bottom left, is modern)

Burgundy

AUTUN CATHEDRAL. The tympanum (the lunette above the lintel) of the main portal of Romanesque churches is usually given over to a composition centered on the Enthroned Christ, most often the Apocalyptic Vision or the Last Judgment, the most awesome scene of Christian art. At Autun Cathedral, the latter subject has been visualized with singular expressive force. Our detail (fig. 407) shows part of the right half of the tympanum, with the weighing of the souls. At the bottom, the dead rise from their graves in fear and trembling; some are already beset by snakes or gripped by huge, clawlike hands. Above, their fate quite literally hangs in the balance, with devils yanking at one end of the scales and angels at the other. The saved souls cling like children to the hem of the angel's garment for protection, while the condemned are seized by grinning devils and cast into the mouth of Hell. These devils betray the same nightmarish imagination we observed in the Romanesque animal world; they are composite creatures, human in general outline but with spidery, birdlike legs, furry thighs, tails, pointed ears, and enormous, savage mouths. But their violence, unlike that of the animal monsters, is unchecked; they enjoy themselves to the full in their grim occupation. No visitor, having "read in the marble" here (to speak with St. Bernard), could fail to enter the church in a chastened spirit.

pelled—like our lions—to perform a supporting function. (Similar examples may be seen in figs. 405 and 410). Their purpose is thus not merely decorative but expressive; they embody dark forces that have been domesticated into guardian figures or banished to a position that holds them fixed for all eternity, however much they may snarl in protest.

The portal proper at Moissac is preceded by a deep porch, with lavishly sculptured sides. On the east flank (fig. 406) we see, within the arcade, the *Annunciation* and *Visitation*, as well as the *Adoration of the Magi*. Other events from the early life of Christ are shown on the frieze above. Here we find the same thin limbs, the same eloquent gestures we saw in the Prophet on the *trumeau* (note especially the wonderful play of hands in the *Visitation* and *Annunciation*); only the proportions of the bodies and the size of the figures vary with the architectural context. What matters is the vividness of the narrative, rather than consistency of treatment.

407. *Last Judgment* (detail), west tympanum,
Autun Cathedral. c. 1130–35

408. *The Mission of the Apostles*, tympanum of center portal of narthex, Ste.-Madeleine, Vézelay. 1120–32

STE.-MADELEINE, VÉZELAY. Perhaps the most beautiful of all Romanesque tympanums is that of Vézelay, not far from Autun in Burgundy (fig. 408). Its subject, the Mission of the Apostles, had a special meaning for this age of crusades, since it proclaims the duty of every Christian to spread the Gospel to the ends of the earth. From the hands of the majestic ascending Christ we see the rays of the Holy Spirit pouring down upon the apostles, all of them equipped with copies of the Scriptures in token of their mission. The lintel and the compartments around the central group are filled with representatives of the heathen world, a veritable encyclopedia of medieval anthropology which includes all sorts of legendary races (fig. 409). On the archivolt (the arch framing the tympanum) we recognize the signs of the zodiac and the labors appropriate to every month of the year, to indicate that the preaching of the Faith is as unlimited in time as it is in space.

Romanesque Classicism

PROVENCE. The portal sculpture at Moissac, Autun, and Vézelay, although varied in style, has many qualities in common: intense expression, unbridled fantasy, and a nervous agility of form that owes more to manuscript illumination and metalwork than to the sculptural tradition of antiquity.

The *Apostle* from St.-Sernin, in contrast, had impressed us with its stoutly "Roman" flavor. The influence of classical monuments is particularly strong in the Provence, the coastal region of southeastern France (which had been part of the Graeco-Roman world far longer than the rest of the country and is full of splendid Roman remains) as well as in Italy. Perhaps for this reason, the Romanesque style persisted longer in these areas than elsewhere. Looking at the center portal of the church at St.-Gilles-du-Gard (fig. 410), one of the great masterpieces of Romanesque art, we are struck immediately by the classical flavor of the architectural framework, with its free-standing columns, meander patterns, and fleshy acanthus ornament. The two large statues, carved almost in the round, have a sense of weight and volume akin to that of the *Apostle* from St.-Sernin, although, being half a century later in date, they also display the richness of detail we have observed in the intervening monuments. They stand on brackets supported by crouching beasts of prey, and these, too, show a Roman massiveness, while the small figures on the base (Cain and Abel) recall the style of Moissac.

FIDENZA CATHEDRAL, ITALY. The two statues at St.-Gilles are akin to the splendid figure of King David from the façade of Fidenza Cathedral in Lombardy (fig. 411), by Benedetto Antelami, the greatest sculptor of Italian Romanesque art. That we should know his name is not surprising in itself—artists' signatures are far from rare in Romanesque times; what makes Antelami exceptional is the fact that his work shows a considerable degree of individuality, so that, for the first time since the ancient Greeks, we can begin to speak (though with some hesitation) of a personal style. And his *David*, too, approaches the ideal of the self-sufficient statue more closely than any medieval work we have seen so far. The *Apostle* from St.-Sernin is one of a series of figures, all of them immutably fixed to their niches, while Antelami's *David* stands physically free and even shows an attempt to recapture the Classical *contrapposto*. To be sure, he would look awkward if placed on a pedestal in isolation; he *demands* the architectural framework for which he was made, but certainly to a far lesser extent than do the two statues at St.-Gilles. Nor is he subject to the group discipline of a series; his only companion is a second niche statue on the other side of the portal. An extraordinary achievement indeed, especially if we consider that not much more than a hundred years separate it from the beginnings of the sculptural revival.

410. North Jamb, Center Portal, St.-Gilles-du-Gard.
Second quarter of 12th century

409. *Pig-Snouted Ethiopians*, portion of
tympanum, Ste.-Madeleine, Vézelay

The Meuse Valley

The emergence of distinct artistic personalities in the twelfth century is a phenomenon that is rarely acknowledged, perhaps because it contravenes the widespread assumption that all medieval art is anonymous. It does not happen very often, of course, but it is no less significant for all that. Antelami is not an isolated case; he cannot even claim to be the earliest. Nor is the revival of individuality confined to Italy. We also find it in one particular region of the north, in the valley of the Meuse River, which runs from northeastern France into Belgium and Holland. This region had been the home of the "Reims style" in Carolingian times (see figs. 372, 373, and colorplates 40, 41), and that awareness of classical sources pervades its art during the Romanesque period. Here again, then, interestingly enough, the revival of individuality is linked with the influence of ancient

411. BENEDETTO ANTELAMI. *King David.* c. 1180–90.
West façade, Fidenza Cathedral

Germany

The one monumental free-standing statue of Romanesque art—perhaps not the only one made, but the only one that has survived—is that of an animal, and in a secular rather than a religious context: the lifesized bronze lion on top of a tall shaft that Duke Henry the Lion of Saxony had placed in front of his palace at Brunswick in 1166 (fig. 413). The wonderfully ferocious beast (which, of course, personifies the duke, or at least that aspect of his personality which earned him his nickname) reminds us in a curious way of the archaic bronze she-wolf of Rome (see fig. 223). Perhaps the resemblance is not entirely coincidental, since the she-wolf was on public view in Rome at that time and must have had a strong appeal for Romanesque artists.

The more immediate relatives of the Brunswick Lion, however, are the countless bronze water ewers in the shape of lions, dragons, griffins, and such, that came into use in the twelfth century for the ritual washing of the priest's hands during Mass. These vessels—another instance of monsters doing menial service for the Lord—were of Near Eastern inspiration. The beguiling specimen reproduced in figure 414 still betrays its descent from the winged beasts of Persian art, transmitted to the West through trade with the Islamic world.

art, although this influence did not produce works on a monumental scale. "Mosan" Romanesque sculpture excelled in metalwork, such as the splendid baptismal font of 1107–1118 in Liège (fig. 412), which is also the masterpiece of the earliest among the individually known artists of the region, Renier of Huy. The vessel rests on twelve oxen (symbols of the twelve apostles), like Solomon's basin in the Temple at Jerusalem as described in the Bible. The reliefs make an instructive contrast with those of Bernward's doors (see fig. 380), since they are about the same height. Instead of the rough expressive power of the Ottonian panel, we find here a harmonious balance of design, a subtle control of the sculptured surfaces, and an understanding of organic structure that, in medieval terms, are amazingly classical. The figure seen from the back (beyond the tree on the left in our picture), with its graceful turning movement and Greek-looking drapery, might almost be taken for an ancient work.

412. RENIER OF HUY. Baptismal Font.
1107–18. Bronze, height 25″. St.-Barthélemy, Liège

413. Lion Monument. 1166. Bronze, length c. 6'.
Cathedral Square, Brunswick

414. Ewer, Mosan. c. 1130. Gilt bronze, height 7¼". Victoria
& Albert Museum, London (Crown Copyright Reserved)

PAINTING

Unlike architecture and sculpture, Romanesque painting shows no sudden revolutionary developments that set it apart immediately from Carolingian or Ottonian. Nor does it look more "Roman" than Carolingian or Ottonian painting. This does not mean, however, that in the eleventh and twelfth centuries painting was any less important than it had been during the earlier Middle Ages; it merely emphasizes the greater continuity of the pictorial tradition, especially in manuscript illumination.

France

GOSPEL BOOK, CORBIE. Nevertheless, soon after the year 1000 occur the beginnings of a painting style which corresponds to—and often anticipates—the monumental qualities of Romanesque sculpture. The new attitude is clearly evident in the *St. Mark* (fig. 415), from a Gospel Book probably done toward 1050 at the monastery of Corbie in northern France. The twisting and turning movement of the lines, which pervades not only the figure of the Evangelist but the winged lion, the scroll, and the curtain, recalls Carolingian miniatures of the Reims School such as the *Ebbo Gospels* (see fig. 372, colorplate 40). This very resemblance helps us see the differences between the two works: in the

415. *St. Mark*, from a Gospel Book produced
at Corbie. c. 1025–50. Municipal Library, Amiens

larger scale or in another medium. The Corbie miniature, on the contrary, might be translated into a mural, a stained-glass window, a tapestry, or a relief panel without losing any of its essential qualities.

BAYEUX TAPESTRY. This monumentality is the same as in the Vézelay tympanum (fig. 408), where much the same pleated drapery patterns are rendered in sculptural terms; or in the so-called Bayeux Tapestry, an embroidered frieze 230 feet long illustrating William the Conqueror's invasion of England. Our detail (fig. 416), portraying the Battle of Hastings, has stylistic kinship with the Corbie manuscript even in the lively somersaults of the falling horses, so strikingly like the pose of the lion in the miniature. Again we marvel at the ease with which the designer has integrated narrative and ornament: the main scene is enclosed by two border strips that perform their framing function equally well, although the upper one is purely decorative while the other consists of dead warriors and horses and thus forms part of the story.

ST.-SAVIN, GARTEMPE. Firm outlines and a strong sense of pattern are equally characteristic of Romanesque wall painting. *The Building of the Tower of Babel* (fig. 417) is taken from the most impressive surviving cycle, on the nave vault of the church at St.-Savin-sur-Gartempe (compare fig. 388). It is an intensely dramatic design, crowded with strenuous action; the Lord Himself, on the far left, participates directly in the narrative as He addresses the builders of the colossal structure. He is counterbalanced, on the right, by the giant Nimrod, the leader of the enterprise, who frantically hands blocks of stone to the masons atop the tower, so that the entire scene becomes a great test of strength between God and man. The heavy dark contours, the emphatic play of gestures make the composition eminently readable from a distance, yet these same qualities occur in the illuminated manuscripts of the region, which can be equally monumental despite their small scale.

The Channel Region

While Romanesque painting, like architecture and sculpture, developed a wide variety of regional styles throughout western Europe, its greatest achievements emerged from the monastic scriptoria of northern France, Belgium, and southern England. The works produced in this area are so closely related in style that it is at times impossible to be sure on which side of the English Channel a given manuscript belongs.

GOSPEL BOOK OF ABBOT WEDRICUS. Thus the style of the wonderful miniature of St. John (fig. 418, colorplate 45), has been linked with both Cambrai and Canterbury. The abstract linear draftsmanship of the Corbie manuscript (fig. 415) has been influenced by Byzantine style (note the ropelike loops of drapery, whose origin can be traced back to such works as fig. 304) but without losing its energetic rhythm. It is the precisely controlled dynamics of every

Corbie manuscript, every trace of classical illusionism has disappeared; the fluid modeling of the Reims School, with its suggestion of light and space, has been replaced by firmly drawn contours filled in with bright, solid colors, so that the three-dimensional aspects of the picture are reduced to overlapped planes. Even Ottonian painting (see figs. 381, 382, colorplate 42) seems illusionistic in comparison. Yet by sacrificing the last remnants of modeling in terms of light and shade, the Romanesque artist has endowed his work with an abstract clarity and precision that had not been possible in Carolingian or Ottonian times; only now can we truly say that the representational, the symbolic, and the decorative elements of the design are knit together into a single, unified structure.

This style of rhythmic lines and planes eschews all effects that might be termed specifically pictorial—not only tonal values but the rendering of textures and highlights such as we still find in Ottonian painting, and because of this it gains a new universality of scale. The evangelists of the *Ebbo Gospels*, the drawings of the *Utrecht Psalter*, the miniatures in the *Gospel Book of Otto III* are made up of open, spontaneous flicks and dashes of brush or pen that have an intimate,

416. *The Battle of Hastings*, detail of the *Bayeux Tapestry*. c. 1073–83. Wool embroidery on linen, height 20″.
Town Hall, Bayeux

417. *The Building of the Tower of Babel* (detail of painting on the nave vault). Early 12th century. St.-Savin-sur-Gartempe

contour, both in the main figure and in the frame, that unite the varied elements of the composition into a coherent whole. This quality of line still betrays its ultimate source, the Celtic-Germanic heritage; if we compare our miniature with the *Lindisfarne Gospels* (fig. 359, colorplate 38), we see how much the interlacing patterns of the Dark Ages have contributed to the design of the St. John page. The drapery folds, the clusters of floral ornament have an impul-

sive yet disciplined aliveness that echoes the intertwined snakelike monsters of the animal style, even though the foliage is derived from the classical acanthus and the human figures are based on Carolingian and Byzantine models. The unity of the entire page, however, is conveyed not only by the forms but by the content as well. The Evangelist "inhabits" the frame in such a way that we could not remove him from it without cutting off his ink supply (proffered by the donor of the manuscript, Abbot Wedricus), his source of inspiration (the dove of the Holy Spirit in the hand of God), or his identifying symbol, the eagle. The other medallions, less directly linked with the main figure, show scenes from the life of St. John.

PORTRAIT OF A PHYSICIAN. Soon after the middle of the twelfth century, an important change of style begins to make itself felt in Romanesque painting on either side of the English Channel. The *Portrait of a Physician* (fig. 419), from a medical manuscript of c. 1160, is surprisingly different from the St. John miniature, although it was produced in the same region. Instead of abstract patterns, we suddenly find lines that have regained the ability to describe three-dimensional shapes; the drapery folds no longer lead an ornamental life of their own but suggest the rounded volume of the body underneath; there is even a renewed interest in foreshortening. Here at last, then, we meet the pictorial counterpart of that classicism which we saw earlier in the Baptismal Font of Renier of Huy at Liège (see fig. 412). In

419. *Portrait of a Physician*, from a medical treatise.
c. 1160. British Museum, London

418. *St. John the Evangelist*, from the *Gospel Book of Abbot Wedricus* (see colorplate 45).
Société Archéologique, Avesnes, France

fact, our miniature was probably done at Liège, too, and its sharp, deliberate lines look as if they had been engraved in metal, rather than drawn with pen or brush.

NICHOLAS OF VERDUN. That a new painting style should have originated in metalwork is perhaps less strange than it might seem at first, for the style's essential qualities are sculptural rather than pictorial; moreover, metalwork (which includes not only cast or embossed sculpture but also engraving, enameling, and goldsmithing) had been a highly developed art in the Meuse valley area since Carolingian times. Its greatest practitioner after Renier of Huy was Nicholas of Verdun, in whose work the classicizing, three-dimensional style of draftsmanship reaches full maturity. The engraved and enameled plaques of the Klosterneuburg altar, which he completed in 1181 (fig. 420 shows one of them, *The Crossing of the Red Sea*), clearly belong to the same tradition as the Liège miniature, but the figures, clothed in rippling, "wet" draperies familiar to us from countless classical statues, have achieved so high a degree of organic body structure and freedom of movement that we tend to think of them as harbingers of Gothic art rather than as the final phase of the Romanesque. Whatever we choose to call it, the style of the Klosterneuburg altar was to have a profound impact upon both painting and sculpture during the next fifty years (see figs. 459, 460).

The astonishing humanity of Nicholas of Verdun's art must be understood against the background of a general reawakening of interest in man and the natural world throughout northwestern Europe. This attitude could express itself in various ways: as a new regard for classical literature and mythology, an appreciation of the beauty of ancient works of art, or simply as a greater readiness to acknowledge the enjoyment of sensuous experience.

CARMINA BURANA. The latter aspect is reflected particularly in such lighthearted poetry as the well-known *Carmina Burana*, composed during the later twelfth century and preserved in an illuminated manuscript of the early thirteenth. That a collection of verse devoted largely—and at times all too frankly—to the delights of nature, love, and drinking should have been embellished with illustrations is significant in itself. We are even more surprised, however, to find that one of the miniatures (fig. 421, colorplate 46), coupled with a poem praising spring, represents a landscape—the first, so far as we know, in Western art since late classical times.

Echoes of ancient landscape painting, derived from Early Christian and Byzantine sources, can be found in Carolingian art (see figs. 372, 373, colorplate 40), but only as background for the human figure. Later on, these remnants had been reduced still further, even when the subject required a landscape setting; the Garden of Eden on Bernward's doors (see fig. 380) is no more than a few strangely twisted stems and bits of foliage. Thus the *Carmina Burana* illustrator, called upon to depict the life of nature in springtime, must

421. Page with *Spring Landscape*, from a manuscript of *Carmina Burana* (see colorplate 46). Bavarian State Library, Munich

have found his task a rather perplexing one. He has solved it in the only way possible for him—by filling his page with a sort of anthology of Romanesque plant ornament, interspersed with birds and animals.

The trees, vines, and flowers remain so abstract that we cannot identify a single species (the birds and animals, probably copied from a zoological treatise, are far more realistic), yet they have an uncanny vitality of their own that makes them seem to sprout and unfold as if the growth of an entire season were compressed into a few frantic moments. These giant seedlings convey the exuberance of spring, of stored energy suddenly released, far more intensely than any normal vegetation could. Our artist has created a fairytale landscape, but his enchanted world nevertheless evokes essential aspects of reality.

420. NICHOLAS OF VERDUN. *The Crossing of the Red Sea*. 1181. Enamel on gold plaque, height 5½". Klosterneuburg Abbey, Austria

4
GOTHIC
ART

Time and space, we have been taught, are interdependent. Yet we tend to think of history as the unfolding of events in time without sufficient awareness of their unfolding in space—we visualize it as a stack of chronological layers, or periods, each layer having a specific depth that corresponds to its duration. For the more remote past, where our sources of information are scanty, this simple image works reasonably well. It becomes less and less adequate as we draw closer to the present and our knowledge grows more precise. Thus we cannot define the Gothic era in terms of time alone; we must consider the changing surface area of the layer as well as its depth.

At the start, about 1150, this area was small indeed. It embraced only the province known as the Île-de-France (that is, Paris and vicinity), the royal domain of the French kings. A hundred years later, most of Europe had "gone Gothic," from Sicily to Iceland, with only a few Romanesque pockets left here and there; through the Crusaders, the new style had even been introduced to the Near East. About 1450, the Gothic area had begun to shrink—no longer including Italy —and about 1550 it had disappeared almost entirely. The

Gothic layer, then, has a rather complicated shape, its depth varying from close to 400 years in some places to a minimum of 150 in others. This shape, moreover, does not emerge with equal clarity in all the visual arts.

USE OF THE TERM. The term Gothic was coined for architecture, and it is in architecture that the characteristics of the style are most easily recognized. Only during the past hundred years have we become accustomed to speak of Gothic sculpture and painting. There is, as we shall see, some uncertainty even today about the exact limits of the Gothic style in these fields. This evolution of our concept of Gothic art suggests the way the new style actually grew: it began with architecture, and for a century—from about 1150 to 1250, during the Age of the Great Cathedrals—architecture retained its dominant role. Gothic sculpture, at first severely architectural in spirit, tended to become less and less so after 1200; its greatest achievements are between the years 1220 and 1420. Painting, in turn, reached a climax of creative endeavor between 1300 and 1350 in central Italy. North of the Alps, it became the leading art from about 1400 on. We thus find, in surveying the Gothic era as a whole, a gradual shift of emphasis from architecture to painting or, better perhaps, from architectural to pictorial qualities (characteristically enough, Early Gothic sculpture and painting both reflect the discipline of their monumental setting, while Late Gothic architecture and sculpture strive for "picturesque" effects rather than clarity or firmness).

REGIONAL VARIETY. Overlaying this broad pattern there is another one: international diffusion as against regional independence. Starting as a local development in the Île-de-France, Gothic art radiates from there to the rest of France and to all Europe, where it comes to be known as *opus modernum* or *francigenum* (modern or French work). In the course of the thirteenth century, the new style gradually loses its "imported" flavor; regional variety begins to reassert itself. Toward the middle of the fourteenth century, we notice a growing tendency for these regional achievements to influence each other until, about 1400, a surprisingly homogeneous "International Gothic" style prevails almost everywhere. Shortly thereafter, this unity breaks apart: Italy, with Florence in the lead, creates a radically new art, that of the Early Renaissance, while north of the Alps, Flanders assumes an equally commanding position in the development of Late Gothic painting and sculpture. A century later, finally, the Italian Renaissance becomes the basis of another international style. With this skeleton outline to guide us, we can now explore the unfolding of Gothic art in greater detail.

ARCHITECTURE
France

ST.-DENIS AND THE ABBOT SUGER. We can pinpoint the origin of no previous style as exactly as that of Gothic. It was born between 1137 and 1144 in the rebuilding, by Abbot Suger, of the royal Abbey Church of St.-Denis just outside the city of Paris. If we are to understand how Gothic architecture happened to come into being at this particular spot, we must first acquaint ourselves with the special relationship between St.-Denis, Suger, and the French monarchy. The kings of France derived their claim to authority from the Carolingian tradition, although they belonged to the Capetian line (founded by Hugh Capet after the death of the last Carolingian in 987). But their power was eclipsed by that of the nobles who, in theory, were their vassals; the only area they ruled directly was the Île-de-France, and they often found their authority challenged even there. Not until the early twelfth century did the royal power begin to expand; and Suger, as chief adviser to Louis VI, played a key role in this process. It was he who forged the alliance between the monarchy and the Church, which brought the bishops of France (and the cities under their authority) to the King's side, while the King, in turn, supported the papacy in its struggle against the German emperors.

Suger, however, championed the monarchy not only on the plane of practical politics but on that of "spiritual politics"; by investing the royal office with religious significance, by glorifying it as the strong right arm of justice, he sought to rally the nation behind the King. His architectural plans for the Abbey of St.-Denis must be understood in this context, for the church, founded in the late eighth century, enjoyed a dual prestige that made it ideally suitable for Suger's purpose: it was the shrine of the Apostle of France, the sacred protector of the realm, as well as the chief memorial of the Carolingian dynasty (both Charlemagne and his father, Pepin, had been consecrated kings there, and it was also the burial place of Charles Martel, Pepin, and Charles the Bald). Suger wanted to make the Abbey the spiritual center of France, a pilgrimage church to outshine the splendor of all the others, the focal point of religious as well as patriotic emotion. But in order to become the visible embodiment of such a goal, the old edifice had to be enlarged and rebuilt. The great abbot himself has described the entire campaign in such eloquent detail that we know more about what he desired to achieve than we do about the final result, for the west façade and its sculpture are sadly mutilated today, and the choir, which Suger regarded as the most important part of the enterprise, retains its original appearance only in the ambulatory (figs. 422, 423).

Looking at the plan, we recognize familiar elements of the Romanesque pilgrimage choir (compare fig. 384), with an arcaded apse surrounded by an ambulatory and radiating chapels. Yet these elements have been integrated in strikingly novel fashion; the chapels, instead of remaining separate entities, are merged so as to form, in effect, a second ambulatory, and ribbed groined vaulting based on the pointed arch is employed throughout (in the Romanesque pilgrimage choir, only the ambulatory had been groin-vaulted). As a result, the entire plan is held together by a new kind of geometric order: it consists of seven identical wedge-shaped units fanning out from the center of the apse. We experience this double ambulatory not as a series of separate compartments but as a continuous (though articulated) space, whose shape is outlined for us by the network of slender arches, ribs, and columns that sustains the vaults.

What distinguishes this interior immediately from its predecessors is its lightness, in both senses; the architectural forms seem graceful, almost weightless as against the massive solidity of the Romanesque, and the windows have been enlarged to the point that they are no longer openings cut into a wall—they fill the entire wall area, so that they themselves become translucent walls. If we now examine the plan once more, we realize what makes this abundance of light possible. The outward pressure of the vaults is contained by heavy buttresses jutting out between the chapels (in the plan, they look like stubby black arrows pointing toward the center of the apse). The main weight of the masonry construction is concentrated there, visible only from the outside. No wonder, then, that the interior appears so amazingly airy and weightless, since the heaviest members of the structural skeleton are beyond our view. The same impression would be even more striking if we could see all of Suger's choir, for the upper part of the apse, rising above the double ambulatory, had very large, tall windows (the effect, from the nave, must have been similar to that of the somewhat later choir of Notre-Dame in Paris; see fig. 424).

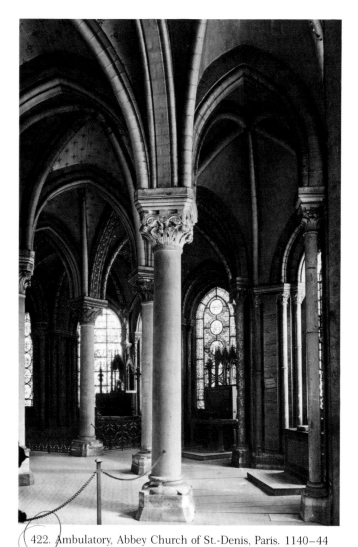

422. Ambulatory, Abbey Church of St.-Denis, Paris. 1140–44

423. Plan of Choir of St.-Denis (after Gall)

SUGER AND GOTHIC ARCHITECTURE. In describing Suger's choir, we have also described the essentials of Gothic architecture. Yet none of the individual elements that entered into its design is really new; the pilgrimage choir plan, the pointed arch, the ribbed groined vault, are familiar to us from the various regional schools of the French (and Anglo-Norman) Romanesque, even though we never encounter them all combined in the same building until St.-Denis. The Île-de-France had failed to develop a Romanesque tradition of its own, so that Suger—as he himself tells us—had to

bring together artisans from many different regions for his project. We must not conclude from this, however, that Gothic architecture originated as a mere synthesis of Romanesque traits. If it were no more than that, we would be hard pressed to explain the new spirit that strikes us so forcibly at St.-Denis: the emphasis on strict geometric planning and the quest for luminosity. Suger's account of the rebuilding of his church insistently stresses both of these as the highest values achieved in the new structure. "Harmony" (that is, the perfect relationship among parts in terms of mathematical proportions or ratios) is the source of all beauty, since it exemplifies the laws according to which divine reason has constructed the universe; the "miraculous" light that floods the choir through the "most sacred" windows becomes the Light Divine, a mystic revelation of the spirit of God.

This symbolic interpretation of light and of numerical harmony had been established over the centuries in Christian thought. It derived from the writings of a fifth-century Greek theologian who, in the Middle Ages, was believed to have been Dionysius the Areopagite, an Athenian disciple of St. Paul. Through this identification, the works of the fifth-century writer, known as the Pseudo-Dionysius, came to be vested with great authority. In Carolingian France, however, Dionysius the disciple of St. Paul was identified both with the author of the Pseudo-Dionysian writings and with St. Denis, the Apostle of France and the special protector of the realm.

The revival of monarchic power during the early twelfth century gave new importance to the theology of the Pseudo-Dionysius, attributed to St. Denis and therefore regarded as France's very own. For Suger, the light-and-number symbolism of Dionysian thought must have had a particularly strong appeal. We can well understand why his own mind was steeped in it, and why he wanted to give it visible expression when he rebuilt the church of the royal patron saint. That he succeeded is proved not only by the inherent qualities of his choir design but also by its extraordinary impact; every visitor to St.-Denis, it seems, was overwhelmed by Suger's achievement, and within a few decades the new style had spread far beyond the confines of the Île-de-France.

SUGER AND THE ARCHITECT. The how and why of his success are a good deal more difficult to explain. Here we encounter a controversy we have met several times before—that of form versus function. To the advocates of the functionalist approach, Gothic architecture has seemed the result of advances in architectural engineering, which made it possible to build more efficient vaults, to concentrate their thrust at a few critical points, and thus eliminate the solid walls of the Romanesque. Suger, they would argue, was fortunate in securing the services of an architect who evidently understood the principles of ribbed groined vaulting better than anybody else at that time. If the abbot chose to interpret the resulting structure as symbolic of Dionysian theology, he was simply expressing his enthusiasm over it in the abstract language of the churchman; his account does not help us to understand the origin of the new style.

425. Nave and Choir, Notre-Dame, Paris. 1163–c. 1200

424. Plan of Notre-Dame, Paris. 1163–c. 1250

426. West Façade, Notre-Dame, Paris

It is perfectly true, of course, that the choir of St.-Denis is more rationally planned and constructed than any Romanesque church. The pointed arch (which can be "stretched" to reach any desired height regardless of the width of its base) has now become an integral part of the ribbed groined vault. As a result, these vaults are no longer restricted to square or near-square compartments; they have gained a flexibility that permits them to cover areas of almost any shape (such as the trapezoids and pentagons of the ambulatory). The buttressing of the vaults, too, is more fully understood than before. How could the theological ideas of Suger have led to these technical advances, unless we are willing to assume that he was a professionally trained architect? If we grant that he was not, can he claim any credit at all for the style of what he so proudly calls "his" new church? Perhaps the question poses a false alternative, somewhat like the conundrum of the chicken and the egg. The function of a church, after all, is not merely to enclose a maximum of space with a minimum of material; for the master who built the choir of St.-Denis under Suger's supervision, the technical problems of vaulting must have been inextricably bound up with considerations of form (that is, of beauty, harmony, fitness, etc.). As a matter of fact, his design includes various elements that *express* function without actually performing

427. Notre-Dame (view from the southeast), Paris

it, such as the slender shafts (called "responds") that seem to carry the weight of the vaults to the church floor.

But in order to know what constituted beauty, harmony, and fitness, the medieval architect needed the guidance of ecclesiastical authority. Such guidance might be a simple directive to follow some established model or, in the case of a patron as actively concerned with architectural aesthetics as Suger, it might amount to full participation in the designing process. Thus Suger's desire to "build Dionysian theology" is likely to have been a decisive factor from the very beginning; it shaped his mental image of the kind of structure he wanted, we may assume, and determined his choice of a master of Norman background as the chief architect. This man, a great artist, must have been singularly responsive to the Abbot's ideas and instructions. Between them, the two together created the Gothic style.

NOTRE-DAME, PARIS. Although St.-Denis was an abbey, the future of Gothic architecture lay in the towns rather than in rural monastic communities. There had been a vigorous revival of urban life, we will recall, since the early eleventh century; this movement continued at an accelerated pace, and the growing weight of the cities made itself felt not only economically and politically but in countless other ways as well: bishops and the city clergy rose to new importance; cathedral schools and universities took the place of monasteries as centers of learning, while the artistic efforts of the age culminated in the great cathedrals. That of Notre-Dame ("Our Lady," the Virgin Mary) at Paris, begun in 1163, reflects the salient features of Suger's St.-Denis more directly than any other (figs. 424–27).

The plan (fig. 425), with its emphasis on the longitudinal axis, is extraordinarily compact and unified as against that of major Romanesque churches; the double ambulatory of the choir continues directly into the aisles, and the stubby transept barely exceeds the width of the façade. In the interior (fig. 424) we still find echoes of the Norman Romanesque: sexpartite nave vaults over squarish bays, and galleries above the inner aisles. The columns of the nave arcade are another conservative feature. Yet the large clerestory windows, the lightness and slenderness of the forms, create an unmistakably Gothic effect (note how thin the nave walls are made to seem). Gothic, too, is the "verticalism" of the interior space. This depends less on the actual proportions of the nave—for some Romanesque naves are equally tall, relative to their width—than on the constant accenting of the verticals and on the soaring ease with which the sense of height is attained. Romanesque interiors (such as fig. 386), by contrast, emphasize the great effort required in supporting the weight of the vaults.

In Notre-Dame, as in Suger's choir, the buttresses (the "heavy bones" of the structural skeleton) are not visible from the inside. The plan shows them as massive blocks of masonry that stick out from the building like a row of teeth. Above the aisles, these piers turn into flying buttresses—arched bridges that reach upward to the critical spots between the clerestory windows where the outward thrust of the nave vault is concentrated (fig. 427). This method of anchoring vaults, a characteristic feature of Gothic architecture, certainly owed its origin to functional considerations. Even the flying buttress, however, soon became aesthetically important as well, and its shape could express support (apart from actually providing it) in a variety of ways, according to the designer's sense of style.

The most monumental aspect of the exterior of Notre-Dame is the west façade (fig. 426). Except for its sculpture, which suffered heavily during the French Revolution and is for the most part restored, it retains its original appearance. The design reflects the general disposition of the façade of St.-Denis, which in turn had been derived from Norman Romanesque façades such as that of St.-Etienne at Caen (see fig. 390). Comparing the latter with Notre-Dame, we note the persistence of some basic features: the pier buttresses that reinforce the corners of the towers and divide the façade into three main parts; the placing of the portals; the three-story arrangement. The rich sculptural decoration, however, recalls the façades of the west of France (see fig. 389) and the elaborately carved portals of Burgundy.

Much more important than these resemblances, however, are the qualities that distinguish the façade of Notre-Dame from its Romanesque ancestors. Foremost among these is the way all the details have been integrated into a wonderfully balanced and coherent whole; the meaning of Suger's emphasis on harmony, geometric order, and proportion becomes evident here even more strikingly than in St.-Denis itself. This formal discipline also embraces the sculpture, which is no longer permitted the spontaneous (and often uncontrolled) growth so characteristic of the Romanesque but has been assigned a precisely defined role within the architectural framework. At the same time, the cubic solidity of the façade of St.-Etienne at Caen has been transformed into its very opposite; lacelike arcades, huge portals and windows dissolve the continuity of the wall surfaces, so that the total effect approximates that of a weightless openwork screen. How rapidly this tendency advanced during the first half of the thirteenth century can be seen by comparing the west façade of Notre-Dame with the somewhat later façade of the south transept, visible in figure 427. In the former the rose window in the center is still deeply recessed and, as a result, the stone tracery that subdivides the opening is clearly set off against the surrounding wall surface; on the transept façade, in contrast, we can no longer distinguish the rose window from its frame—a single network of tracery covers the entire area.

CHARTRES CATHEDRAL. Toward 1145 the Bishop of Chartres, who befriended Abbot Suger and shared his ideas, began to rebuild his cathedral in the new style. Fifty years later, all but the west façade of Chartres Cathedral was destroyed by fire (for sculpture of the west portals, see figs. 456–57, colorplate 48); a second rebuilding took place between 1194 and 1220 (fig. 428). It is the rebuilt nave that appears in figure 429. Conceived one generation after the nave of Notre-Dame in Paris, it represents the first masterpiece of the mature, or High Gothic, style. The galleries have now been reduced to a narrow passageway within the thickness of the nave wall, screened by a triforium arcade; the openings of the nave arcade are taller and narrower; responds have been added to the columnar supports, so as to stress the continuity of the vertical lines; and the nave vault is no longer sexpartite. Alone among all major Gothic cathedrals, Chartres still retains most of its original stained-glass windows. The magic of its interior space, unforgettable to anyone who has experienced it on the spot, cannot be suggested by black-and-white photographs, which inevitably exaggerate the brightness of the windows and thus make them look like "holes" instead of "translucent walls" (fig. 429). In reality, the windows admit far less light than one might expect; they act mainly as huge, multicolored diffusing filters that change the *quality* of ordinary daylight, en-

428. West Façade, Chartres Cathedral
(north spire is 16th century). 1145–1220.

429. Nave toward west, Chartres Cathedral
(see colorplate 47)

an instructive contrast with the west façade of Notre-Dame in Paris, even though its basic design was conceived only about thirty years later. Many of the same elements are common to both (as the Coronation Cathedral of the kings of France, Reims was closely linked to Paris), but in the younger structure they have been reshaped into a very different ensemble. The portals, instead of being recessed, are projected forward as gabled porches, with windows in place of tympanums above the doorways; the gallery of royal statues, which in Paris forms an incisive horizontal between the first and second stories, has been raised until it merges with the third-story arcade; every detail except the rose window has become taller and narrower than before; and a multitude of pinnacles further accentuates the restless upward-pointing movement. The sculptural decoration, by far the most lavish of its kind (see figs. 460, 461), no longer remains in clearly marked-off zones; it has now spread to so many hitherto unaccustomed perches, not only on the façade but on the flanks as well, that the exterior of the cathedral begins to look like a dovecote for statues.

LATER THIRTEENTH-CENTURY GOTHIC. The High Gothic cathedrals of France represent a concentrated expenditure of effort such as the world has rarely seen before or since. They are truly national monuments, whose immense cost was borne by donations collected all over the country and from all classes of society—the tangible expression of that merging of religious and patriotic fervor which had been the goal of Abbot Suger. As we approach the second half of the thirteenth century, we sense that this wave of enthusiasm has passed its crest: work on the vast structures begun during the first half now proceeds at a slacker pace; new projects are fewer and generally on a far less ambitious scale; and the highly organized teams of masons and sculptors that had developed at the sites of the great cathedrals during the preceding decades gradually break up into smaller units.

A characteristic church of the later years of the century, St.-Urbain in Troyes (figs. 434, 435), leaves no doubt that the "heroic age" of the Gothic style is past. Refinement of detail, rather than towering monumentality, has been the designer's chief concern; by eliminating the triforium and simplifying the plan, he has created a delicate cage of glass (in the choir, the windows begin ten feet above the floor), sustained by flying buttresses so thin as to be hardly noticeable. The same spiny, attenuated elegance can be felt in the architectural ornament.

FLAMBOYANT GOTHIC. In some respects, St.-Urbain is prophetic of the Late, or Flamboyant, phase of Gothic architecture. The beginnings of Flamboyant Gothic do indeed seem to go back to the late thirteenth century, but its growth was delayed by the Hundred Years' War with England, so that we do not meet any full-fledged examples of it until the early fifteenth. Its name, which means flamelike, refers to the undulating patterns of curve and countercurve that are a prevalent feature of Late Gothic tracery, as at St.-Maclou in Rouen (fig. 436). Structurally, Flamboyant Gothic shows no significant developments of its own; what distinguishes St.-

dowing it with the poetic and symbolic values so highly praised by Abbot Suger. Our colorplate 47, which shows the northern nave wall illuminated by sunlight shining through the windows on the south side, conveys something of the wonderfully warm and vibrant effect that prompted Suger to describe his choir as filled with "miraculous" light.

AMIENS CATHEDRAL; REIMS CATHEDRAL. The High Gothic style defined at Chartres reaches its climax a generation later in the interior of Amiens Cathedral (figs. 430–32). Breathtaking height has become the dominant aim, both technically and aesthetically; skeletal construction is carried to its most precarious limits. The inner logic of the system forcefully asserts itself in the shape of the vaults, taut and thin as membranes, and in the expanded window area, which now includes the triforium so that the entire wall above the nave arcade becomes a clerestory.

The same emphasis on verticality and translucency can be traced in the development of the High Gothic façade. The most famous of these, at Reims Cathedral (fig. 433), makes

430. Choir Vault, Amiens Cathedral. Begun 1220

431. Plan, Amiens Cathedral

432. Transverse Section, Amiens Cathedral

Maclou from such churches as St.-Urbain in Troyes is the luxuriant profusion of ornament. The architect has turned into a virtuoso who overlays the structural skeleton with a web of decoration so dense and fanciful as to obscure it almost completely. It becomes a fascinating game of hide-and-seek to locate the "bones" of the building within this picturesque tangle of lines.

SECULAR ARCHITECTURE. Since our account of medieval architecture is mainly concerned with the development of style, we have until now confined our attention to religious structures, the most ambitious as well as the most representative efforts of the age. Secular building, indeed, reflects the same general trends, but these are often obscured by the diversity of types, ranging from bridges and fortifications to royal palaces, from barns to town halls. Moreover, social, economic, and practical factors play a more important part here than in church design, so that the useful life of the buildings is apt to be much briefer and their chance of preservation correspondingly less. (Fortifications, indeed, are often made obsolete by even minor advances in the technology of warfare.) As a consequence, our knowledge of secular structures of the pre-Gothic Middle Ages remains extremely fragmentary, and most of the surviving examples from Gothic times belong to the latter half of the period. This fact, however, is not without significance; non-religious architecture, both private and public, became far

433. West Façade, Reims Cathedral. c. 1225–99

434. St.-Urbain, Troyes. 1261–75

more elaborate during the fourteenth and fifteenth centuries than it had been before.

The history of the Louvre in Paris provides a telling example: the original building, erected about 1200, followed the severely functional plan of the castles of that time—it consisted mainly of a stout tower, the donjon or keep, surrounded by a heavy wall. In the 1360s, King Charles V had it built as a sumptuous royal residence. Although this second Louvre, too, has now disappeared we know what it looked like from a fine miniature painted in the early fifteenth century (see colorplate 58). There is still a defensive outer wall, but the great structure behind it has far more the character of a palace than of a fortress. Symmetrically laid out around a square court, it provided comfortable quarters for the royal family and household (note the countless chimneys) as well as lavishly decorated halls for state occasions. (Fig. 506, another miniature from the same manuscript, conveys a good impression of such a hall.)

If the exterior of the second Louvre still has some of the forbidding qualities of a stronghold, the sides toward the court displayed a wealth of architectural ornament and sculpture. The same contrast also appears in the house of Jacques Cœur in Bourges, built in the 1440s. We speak of it as a house, not a palace, only because Jacques Cœur was a silversmith and merchant, rather than a nobleman. Since, however, he also was one of the richest men of his day, he could well afford an establishment obviously modeled on the mansions of the aristocracy. The courtyard (fig. 437), with its high-pitched roofs, its pinnacles and decorative carvings, suggests the picturesque qualities familiar to us from Flamboyant church architecture (fig. 436). That we should find an echo of the Louvre court in a merchant's residence is striking proof of the importance attained by the urban middle class during the later Middle Ages.

436. St.-Maclou, Rouen. Begun 1434

435. St.-Urbain, Troyes. Interior toward northeast. 1261–75

437. Court, House of Jacques Cœur, Bourges. 1443–51

England

Among the astonishing things about Gothic art is the enthusiastic response this "royal French style of the Paris region" evoked abroad. Even more remarkable was its ability to acclimate itself to a variety of local conditions—so much so, in fact, that the Gothic monuments of England and Germany have become objects of intense national pride in modern times, and critics in both countries have acclaimed Gothic as a peculiarly "native" style. How are we to account for the rapid spread of Gothic art? A number of factors might be cited, singly or in combination: the superior skill of French architects and stone carvers; the vast intellectual prestige of French centers of learning, such as the Cathedral School of Chartres and the University of Paris; and the influence of the Cistercians, the reformed monastic order founded by St. Bernard of Clairvaux. He, we will recall, had violently denounced the flights of fancy of Romanesque sculpture (see page 289). In conformity with his ascetic ideals, Cistercian abbey churches were a distinctive, severe type—decoration of any sort was held to a minimum, and a square choir took the place of apse, ambulatory, and radiating chapels. For that very reason, however, Cistercian architects put special emphasis on harmonious proportions and exact craftsmanship; and their "anti-Romanesque" outlook prompted them to adopt certain basic features of the Gothic style. During the latter half of the twelfth century, as the reform movement gathered momentum, this austere Cistercian Gothic came to be known throughout western Europe.

Still, one wonders whether any of the explanations we have mentioned really goes to the heart of the matter. The

439. Plan of Salisbury Cathedral

438. Salisbury Cathedral. 1220–70

440. Nave and Choir, Salisbury Cathedral

ultimate reason for the international victory of Gothic art seems to have been the extraordinary persuasive power of the style itself, its ability to kindle the imagination and to arouse religious feeling even among people far removed from the cultural climate of the Île-de-France.

That England should have proved particularly receptive to the new style is hardly surprising. Yet English Gothic did not grow directly from Anglo-Norman Romanesque but from the Gothic of the Île-de-France (introduced in 1175 by the French architect who rebuilt the choir of Canterbury Cathedral) and from that of the Cistercians. Within less than fifty years, it developed a well-defined character of its own, known as the Early English style, which dominated the second quarter of the thirteenth century. Although there was a great deal of building activity during those decades, it consisted mostly of additions to Anglo-Norman structures. A great many English cathedrals had been begun about the same time as Durham (see figs. 391–93) but remained unfinished; they were now completed or enlarged. As a consequence, we find few churches that are designed in the Early English style throughout.

SALISBURY CATHEDRAL. Among cathedrals, only Salisbury meets this requirement (figs. 438–40). Viewing the exterior, we realize immediately how different it is from its counterparts in France—and how futile it would be to judge it by French Gothic standards. Compactness and verticality have given way to a long, low, sprawling look (the great crossing tower, which provides a dramatic unifying accent, was built a century later than the rest and is much taller than originally planned). Since there is no straining after height, flying buttresses have been introduced only as an afterthought. Characteristically enough, the west façade has become a screen wall, wider than the church itself and stratified by emphatic horizontal bands of ornament and statuary, while the towers have shrunk to stubby turrets. The plan, with its strongly projecting double transept, retains the segmented quality of Romanesque structures; the square east end derives from Cistercian architecture.

As we enter the nave, we recognize the same elements familiar to us from French interiors of the time, such as Chartres (see fig. 429), but the English interpretation of these elements produces a very different total effect. As on the façade, the horizontal divisions are stressed at the expense of the vertical, so that we see the nave wall not as a succession of bays but as a continuous series of arches and supports. These supports, carved of dark marble, stand out against the rest of the interior—a method of stressing their special function that is one of the hallmarks of the Early English style. Another insular feature is the steep curve of the nave vault. The ribs ascend all the way from the triforium level, and the clerestory, as a result, gives the impression of being "tucked away" among the vaults. At Durham, more than a century earlier, the same treatment had been a technical necessity (compare fig. 391); now it has become a matter of style, thoroughly in keeping with the character of Early English Gothic as a whole. This character might be described as conservative in the positive sense: it accepts the French system but tones down its revolutionary aspects

441. Choir, Gloucester Cathedral. 1332–57

so as to maintain a strong sense of continuity with the Anglo-Norman past.

PERPENDICULAR STYLE. The contrast between the bold upward thrust of the crossing tower and the leisurely horizontal progression throughout the rest of Salisbury Cathedral suggests that English Gothic had developed in a new direction during the intervening hundred years. The change becomes very evident if we compare the interior of Salisbury with the choir of Gloucester Cathedral, built in the second quarter of the next century (fig. 441). This is a striking example of English Late Gothic, also called Pependicular. The name certainly fits, since we now find the dominant vertical accent that is so conspicuously absent in the Early English style (note the responds running in an unbroken line from the vault to the floor). In this respect Perpendicular Gothic is much more akin to French sources, yet it includes so many features we have come to know as English that it would look very much out of place on the Continent. The repetition of small uniform tracery panels recalls the bands of statuary on

442. Chapel of Henry VII, Westminster Abbey, London. 1503–19

443. Diagram of Vault Construction,
Chapel of Henry VII, Westminster Abbey,
London. 1503–19

the west façade at Salisbury; the plan simulates the square east end of earlier English churches; and the upward curve of the vault is as steep as in the nave of Salisbury.

The ribs of the vaults, on the other hand, have assumed an altogether new role—they have been multiplied until they form an ornamental network that screens the boundaries between the bays and thus makes the entire vault look like one continuous surface. This, in turn, has the effect of emphasizing the unity of the interior space. Such decorative elaboration of the "classic" quadripartite vault is characteristic of the Flamboyant style on the Continent as well, but the English started it earlier and carried it to greater lengths. The ultimate is reached in the amazing pendant vault of Henry VII's Chapel at Westminster Abbey, built in the early years of the sixteenth century (figs. 442, 443), with its lantern-like knobs hanging from conical "fans." This fantastic scheme merges ribs and tracery patterns in a dazzling display of architectural pageantry.

Germany

In Germany, Gothic architecture took root a good deal more slowly than in England. Until the mid-thirteenth century, the Romanesque tradition, with its persistent Ottonian reminiscences, remained dominant, despite the growing acceptance of Early Gothic features. From about 1250 on, the High Gothic of the Île-de-France had a strong impact on the Rhineland; Cologne Cathedral (begun in 1248) represents an ambitious attempt to carry the full-fledged French system beyond the stage of Amiens. Significantly enough, however, the building remained a fragment until it was finally completed in modern times; nor did it have any successors.

HALL CHURCHES. Far more characteristic of German Gothic is the development of the hall church, or *Hallenkirche*. Such churches—with aisles and nave of the same height—are familiar to us from Romanesque architecture (see fig. 388). For reasons not yet well understood, the type found particular favor on German soil, where its artistic possibilities were very fully explored. The large hall choir added in 1361–72 to the church of St. Sebald in Nuremberg (fig. 444) is one of many fine examples from central Germany. The space here has a fluidity and expansiveness that enfolds us as if we were standing under a huge canopy; there is no pressure, no directional command to prescribe our path. And the unbroken lines of the pillars, formed by bundles of shafts which gradually diverge as they turn into ribs, seem to echo the continuous movement that we feel in the space itself.

Italy

Italian Gothic architecture stands apart from that of the rest of Europe. Judged by the formal criteria of the Île-de-France, most of it hardly deserves to be called Gothic at all. Yet it produced structures of singular beauty and impressiveness that cannot be understood as mere continuations of the local Romanesque. We must be careful, therefore, to avoid too rigid or technical a standard in approaching these monuments, lest we fail to do justice to their unique blend of Gothic qualities and Mediterranean tradition. It was the Cistercians, rather than the cathedral builders of the Île-de-France, who provided the chief exemplars on which Italian architects based their conception of the Gothic style. As early as the end of the twelfth century, Cistercian abbeys sprang up in both north and central Italy, their designs patterned directly after those of the French abbeys of the order.

ABBEY CHURCH, FOSSANOVA. One of the finest, at Fossanova, some 60 miles south of Rome, was consecrated in 1208 (figs. 445, 446). Without knowing its location, we would be hard put to decide where to place it on a map—it might as well be Burgundian or English; the plan looks like a simplified version of Salisbury, and the finely proportioned interior bears a strong family resemblance to all Cistercian abbeys of the time. There are no façade towers, only a lantern over the crossing, as befits the Cistercian ideal of austerity. The groined vaults, although based on the pointed arch, have no diagonal ribs, the windows are small, and the architectural detail retains a good deal of Romanesque solidity, but the flavor of the whole is unmistakably Gothic nevertheless.

Churches such as the one at Fossanova made a deep impression upon the Franciscans, the monastic order founded by St. Francis of Assisi in the early thirteenth century. As mendicant friars dedicated to poverty, simplicity, and humil-

445. Nave and Choir, Abbey Church of Fossanova. Consecrated 1208

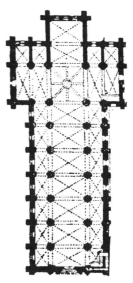

446. Plan of the Abbey Church of Fossanova

444. Choir, St. Sebald, Nuremberg. 1361–72

ity, they were the spiritual kin of St. Bernard, and the severe beauty of Cistercian Gothic must have seemed to them to express an ideal closely related to theirs. Be that as it may, their churches from the first reflected Cistercian influence and thus played a leading role in establishing Gothic architecture in Italy.

447. Nave and Choir, Sta. Croce, Florence. Begun c. 1295

448. Plan of Sta. Croce

STA. CROCE, FLORENCE. Santa Croce in Florence, begun about a century after Fossanova, may well claim to be the greatest of all Franciscan structures (figs. 447, 448); it is also a masterpiece of Gothic architecture, even though it has wooden ceilings instead of groined vaults. There can be no doubt that this was a matter of deliberate choice, rather than of technical or economic necessity—a choice made not only on the basis of local practice (we recall the wooden ceilings of the Tuscan Romanesque) but also perhaps from a desire to evoke the simplicity of Early Christian basilicas and, in doing so, to link Franciscan poverty with the traditions of the early Church. The plan, too, combines Cistercian and Early Christian features. We note, however, that it shows no trace of the Gothic structural system, except for the groin-vaulted choir; the walls remain intact as continuous surfaces (indeed, Sta. Croce owes part of its fame to its wonderful murals) and, in contrast to Fossanova, there are no longer any buttresses, since the wooden ceilings do not require them.

Why, then, do we speak of Sta. Croce as Gothic? Surely the use of the pointed arch is not sufficient to justify the term? A glance at the interior will dispel our misgivings. For we sense immediately that this space creates an effect fundamentally different from that of either Early Christian or Romanesque architecture. The nave walls have the weightless, "transparent" quality we saw in northern Gothic churches, and the dramatic massing of windows at the eastern end conveys the dominant role of light as forcefully as Abbot Suger's choir at St.-Denis. Judged in terms of its emotional impact, Sta. Croce is Gothic beyond doubt; it is also profoundly Franciscan—and Florentine—in the monumental simplicity of the means by which this impact has been achieved.

FLORENCE CATHEDRAL. If in Sta. Croce the architect's main concern was an impressive interior, Florence Cathedral was planned as a monumental landmark towering above the entire city (figs. 449–51). The original design, by Arnolfo di Cambio, dating from 1296—about the time construction was begun at Sta. Croce—is not known in detail; although somewhat smaller than the present building, it probably showed the same basic features. The most striking of these is the great octagonal dome with its subsidiary half-domes, a motif ultimately of late Roman origin (see 239, 240, 294–96). Arnolfo may have thought of it at first as an oversized dome above the crossing of nave and transept, but it soon grew into a huge central pool of space that makes the nave look like an afterthought. The actual building of the dome, and the details of its design, belong to the early fifteenth century (see page 400).

Apart from the windows and the doorways, there is nothing Gothic about the exterior of Florence Cathedral (flying buttresses to sustain the nave vault may have been planned but proved unnecessary). The solid walls, encrusted with geometric marble inlays, are a perfect match for the Romanesque Baptistery (see fig. 403, colorplate 44). Characteristically enough, a separate campanile takes the place of the façade towers familiar to us in northern Gothic churches. The interior, on the other hand, recalls Sta. Croce, even though the dominant impression is one of chill solemnity rather than lightness and grace. The ribbed groined vault of the nave rests directly on the huge nave arcade, producing an emphasis on width instead of height, and the architectural detail throughout has a massive solidity that seems more Romanesque than Gothic. Thus the unvaulted interior of Sta. Croce reflects the spirit of the new style more faithfully than does the Cathedral, which, on the basis of its structural system, ought to be the more Gothic of the two.

449. (*above*) Florence Cathedral. Begun by
Arnolfo di Cambio, 1296; dome by
Filippo Brunelleschi, 1420–36

450. (*top*) Plan of Florence Cathedral

451. (*right*) Nave and Choir, Florence Cathedral

The west façade, so dramatic a feature in French cathedrals, never achieved the same importance in Italy. It is remarkable how few Italian Gothic façades were ever carried near completion before the onset of the Renaissance (those of Sta. Croce and Florence Cathedral are both modern).

ORVIETO CATHEDRAL. Of the façades that were finished, Orvieto Cathedral has the finest (fig. 452), designed in the main by Lorenzo Maitani. It makes an instructive comparison with Tuscan Romanesque façades (such as fig. 400) on the one hand, and with French Gothic façades on the other. Many of its ingredients clearly derive from the latter source, and its screenlike lightness, too, is unmistakably Gothic. Yet we realize at once that these features have been superimposed on what is essentially a basilican façade like that of Pisa Cathedral; the towers are reduced to turrets so as not to compete in height or importance with the central gable, and, as at Pisa, the entire design has a strangely small-scale quality that has nothing to do with its actual size.

This impression may strike us as somewhat paradoxical, for the Orvieto façade is less complex and more clearly articulated than that of, say, Reims Cathedral (fig. 433). But whereas at Reims the infinite richness of detail is subordinated to the grandly simple two-tower silhouette, the Orvieto façade lacks a dominant motif, so that the elements which compose it seem "assembled" rather than merged into a single whole. One somehow feels that the entire arrangement, beautifully balanced though it is, could be folded up or taken apart if the need arose. Except for the

452. LORENZO MAITANI AND OTHERS.
Façade, Orvieto Cathedral. Begun c. 1310

453. Milan Cathedral. Begun 1386

454. Palazzo Vecchio, Florence. Begun 1298

modest-sized rose window and the doorways, the Orvieto façade has no real openings, and large parts of it consist of framed sections of wall area. Yet we experience these not as solid, material surfaces but as translucent, since they are filled with brilliantly colored mosaics—an effect equivalent to Gothic stained glass in the North.

MILAN CATHEDRAL. By far the largest Gothic church on Italian soil, as well as the one most nearly comparable to Northern structures, is Milan Cathedral (fig. 453), begun in 1386. Its design was the subject of a famous dispute between the local architects and consulting experts from France and Germany. What they achieved can hardly be termed a genuine synthesis of Northern and Southern traditions; it strikes us, rather, as an uneasy—though ambitious—compromise, burdened with overly elaborate Late Gothic decoration but devoid of any unity of feeling. The façade in particular reveals its shortcomings very plainly if we compare it with that of Orvieto. Both are composed in much the same way, yet the earlier design has a jewel-like perfection while the later one strikes us as little more than a mechanical piling-up of detail.

SECULAR ARCHITECTURE. The secular buildings of Gothic Italy convey as distinct a local flavor as the churches. There is nothing in the cities of northern Europe to match the impressive grimness of the Palazzo Vecchio (fig. 454),

the town hall of Florence. Fortress-like structures such as this reflect the factional strife—among political parties, social classes, and prominent families—so characteristic of life within the Italian city-states. The wealthy man's home (or *palazzo*, a term denoting any large urban house) was quite literally his castle, designed both to withstand armed assault and to proclaim the owner's importance. The Palazzo Vecchio, while larger and more elaborate, follows the same pattern. Behind its battlemented walls, the city government could feel well protected from the wrath of angry crowds. The tall tower not only symbolizes civic pride but has an eminently practical purpose; dominating the city as well as the surrounding countryside, it served as a lookout against enemies from without or within.

Among Italian cities Venice alone was ruled by a merchant aristocracy so firmly established that internal disturbances were the exception rather than the rule. As a consequence, Venetian *palazzi*, unhampered by defensive requirements, developed into graceful, ornate structures such as the Ca' d'Oro (fig. 455). There is more than a touch of the Orient in the delicate latticework effect of this façade, even though most of the decorative vocabulary derives from the Late Gothic of northern Europe. Its rippling patterns, ideally designed to be seen against their own reflection in the water of the Grand Canal, have the same fairy-tale quality we recall from the exterior of St. Mark's (see fig. 322).

SCULPTURE
France

Although the Abbot Suger's story of the rebuilding of St.-Denis does not deal at length with the sculptural decoration of the church, he must have attached considerable importance to this aspect of the enterprise. The three portals of his

455. Ca' d'Oro, Venice. 1422–c. 1440

456. West Portal, Chartres Cathedral (see colorplate 48)

west façade were far larger and more richly carved than those of Norman Romanesque churches. Unhappily, their condition today is so poor that they do not tell us a great deal about Suger's ideas of the role of sculpture within the total context of the structure he had envisioned.

CHARTRES: WEST PORTALS. We may assume, however, that Suger's ideas had prepared the way for the admirable west portals of Chartres Cathedral (fig. 456, colorplate 48), begun about 1145 under the influence of St.-Denis, but even more ambitious. They probably represent the oldest full-fledged example of Early Gothic sculpture. Comparing them with Romanesque portals, we are impressed first of all with a new sense of order, as if all the figures had suddenly come to attention, conscious of their responsibility to the architectural framework. The dense crowding, the frantic movement of Romanesque sculpture have given way to an emphasis on symmetry and clarity; the figures on the lintels, archivolts, and tympanums are no longer entangled with each other but stand out as separate entities, so that the entire design carries much farther than that of previous portals.

Particularly striking in this respect is the novel treatment of the jambs (fig. 457), which are lined with tall figures at-

tached to columns. Similarly elongated figures, we recall, had occurred on the jambs or *trumeaux* of Romanesque portals (see figs. 405, 410), but they had been conceived as reliefs carved into—or protruding from—the masonry of the doorway. The Chartres jamb figures, in contrast, are essentially statues, each with its own axis; they could, in theory at least, be detached from their supports. Here, then, we witness a development of truly revolutionary importance: the first basic step toward the reconquest of monumental sculpture in the round since the end of classical antiquity. Apparently, this step could be taken only by "borrowing" the rigid cylindrical shape of the column for the human figure, with the result that these statues seem more abstract than their Romanesque predecessors. Yet they will not retain their immobility and unnatural proportions for long; the very fact that they are round endows them with a more emphatic presence than anything in Romanesque sculpture, and their heads show a gentle, human quality that betokens the fundamentally realistic trend of Gothic sculpture.

Realism is, of course, a relative term whose meaning varies greatly according to circumstances. On the Chartres west portals, it appears to spring from a reaction against the fantastic and demoniacal aspects of Romanesque art, a reaction that may be seen not only in the calm, solemn spirit of

458. Jamb Statues, South Transept Portal,
Chartres Cathedral. c. 1215–20

457. Jamb Statues, West Portal, Chartres Cathedral

1145 - 70

the figures and their increased physical bulk (compare the Christ of the center tympanum with that at Vézelay, fig. 408) but in the rational discipline of the symbolic program underlying the entire scheme. While the subtler aspects of this program are accessible only to a mind fully conversant with the theology of the Chartres Cathedral School, its main elements are simple enough to be understood by the average person.

The jamb statues, a continuous sequence linking all three portals, represent the prophets, kings, and queens of the Bible; their purpose is both to acclaim the rulers of France as the spiritual descendants of Old Testament royalty and to stress the harmony of secular and spiritual rule, of priests (or bishops) and kings—an ideal insistently put forward by Abbot Suger. Christ Himself appears enthroned above the main doorway as Judge and Ruler of the Universe, flanked by the symbols of the four Evangelists, with the Apostles assembled below and the twenty-four Elders of the Apocalypse in the archivolts. The right-hand tympanum shows His incarnation—the Birth, the Presentation in the Temple, and the Infant Christ on the lap of the Virgin (who also stands for the Church)—while in the archivolts we see the personifications and representatives of the liberal arts: human wisdom paying homage to the divine wisdom of Christ. In the left-hand tympanum, finally, we see the timeless Heavenly Christ, the Christ of the Ascension, framed by the signs of the zodiac and their earthly counterparts, the labors of the twelve months—the ever-repeating cycle of the year.

GOTHIC CLASSICISM. When Chartres Cathedral was rebuilt after the fire of 1195, the Royal Portals of the west façade must have seemed rather small and old-fashioned in

459. *Death of the Virgin*, tympanum of the South
Transept Portal, Strasbourg Cathedral (see colorplate 49)

relation to the rest of the new edifice. Perhaps for that reason, the two transept façades each received three large and lavishly carved portals preceded by deep porches. The jamb statues of these portals, such as the group shown in figure 458, represent an early phase of High Gothic sculpture. By now, the symbiosis of statue and column has begun to dissolve: the columns are quite literally put in the shade by the greater width of the figures, by the strongly projecting canopies above, and by the elaborately carved bases of the statues.

In the three saints on the right, we still find echoes of the rigid cylindrical shape of Early Gothic jamb statues, but even here the heads are no longer strictly in line with the central axis of the body; and St. Theodore, the knight on the left, already stands at ease, in a semblance of Classical *contrapposto*. His feet rest on a horizontal platform, rather than on a sloping shelf as before, and the axis of his body, instead of being straight, describes a slight but perceptible S-curve. Even more astonishing is the abundance of precisely observed detail—the weapons, the texture of the tunic and chain mail—and, above all, the organic structure of the body. Not since imperial Roman times have we seen a figure as thoroughly alive as this. Yet the most impressive quality of the statue is not its realism; it is, rather, the serene, bal-

anced image of man which this realism conveys. In this ideal portrait of the Christian Soldier, the spirit of the Crusades has been cast into its most elevated form.

The style of the *St. Theodore* could not have evolved directly from the elongated columnar statues of Chartres' west façade. It incorporates another, equally important tradition: the classicism of the Meuse valley, which we traced in the previous chapter from Renier of Huy to Nicholas of Verdun (compare figs. 412, 419, 420). At the end of the twelfth century this trend, hitherto confined to metalwork and miniatures, began to appear in monumental stone sculpture as well, transforming it from Early Gothic to Classic High Gothic. The link with Nicholas of Verdun is striking in the *Death of the Virgin* (fig. 459, colorplate 49), a tympanum from Strasbourg Cathedral contemporary with the Chartres transept portals; here the draperies, the facial types, the movements and gestures have a classical flavor that immediately recalls the Klosterneuburg altar (fig. 420).

What marks it as Gothic rather than Romanesque, on the other hand, is the deeply felt tenderness pervading the entire scene. We sense a bond of shared emotion among the figures, an ability to communicate by glance and gesture such as we have never met before. This quality of pathos, too, has Classical roots—we recall its entering into Chris-

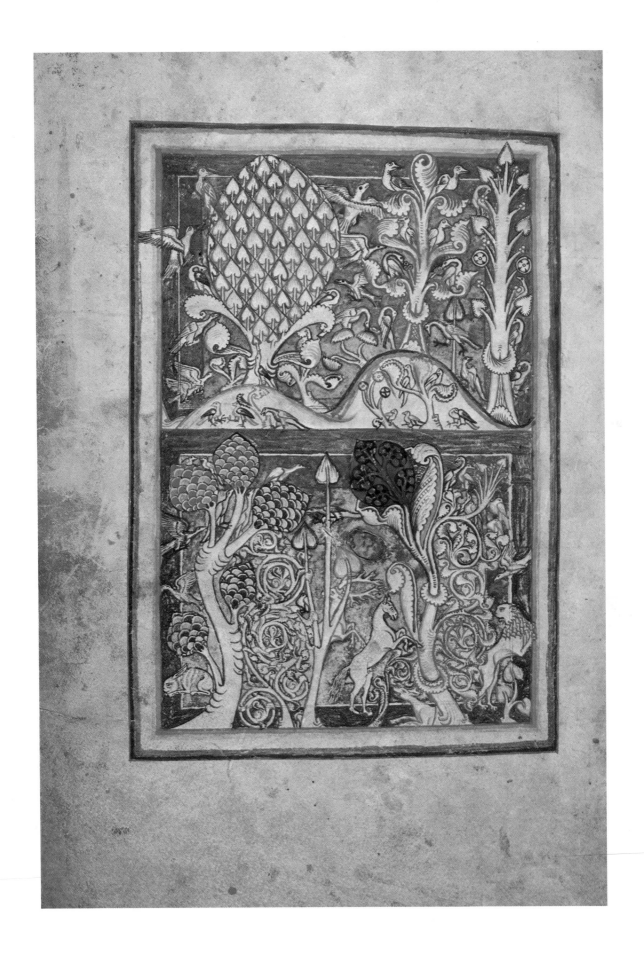

Colorplate 46. ROMANESQUE. Page with *Spring Landscape*, from a manuscript
of *Carmina Burana* (see page 299). Early 13th century. Bavarian State Library, Munich

Colorplate 47. GOTHIC. View of the North Clerestory Wall
of the Nave, Chartres Cathedral (see page 306). 1194–1220

Colorplate 48. (*above*) EARLY GOTHIC. West Portal, Chartres Cathedral (see page 318). c. 1145–70

Colorplate 49. (*right*) GOTHIC. *Death of the Virgin*, tympanum of the South Transept Portal, Strasbourg Cathedral (see page 320). c. 1220

Colorplate 50. CIMABUE. *Madonna Enthroned* (see page
342). c. 1280–90. Panel, 12′ 7½″ × 7′ 4″. Uffizi Gallery, Florence

Colorplate 51. DUCCIO. *Madonna Enthroned*, front of the *Maestà Altar*
(see page 342). 1308–11. Panel, height 6′ 10½″. Cathedral Museum, Siena

Colorplate 52. DUCCIO. *Christ Entering Jerusalem*, from back of the *Maestà
Altar* (see page 343). 1308–11. Panel, 40½ × 21⅛″. Cathedral Museum, Siena

Colorplate 53. (*above*) GIOTTO. *Christ Entering Jerusalem*
(see page 344). 1305–6. Fresco. Arena Chapel, Padua

Colorplate 54. (*right*) SIMONE MARTINI. *The Road to Calvary*
(see page 350). About 1340. Panel, 9⅞ × 6⅛″. The Louvre, Paris

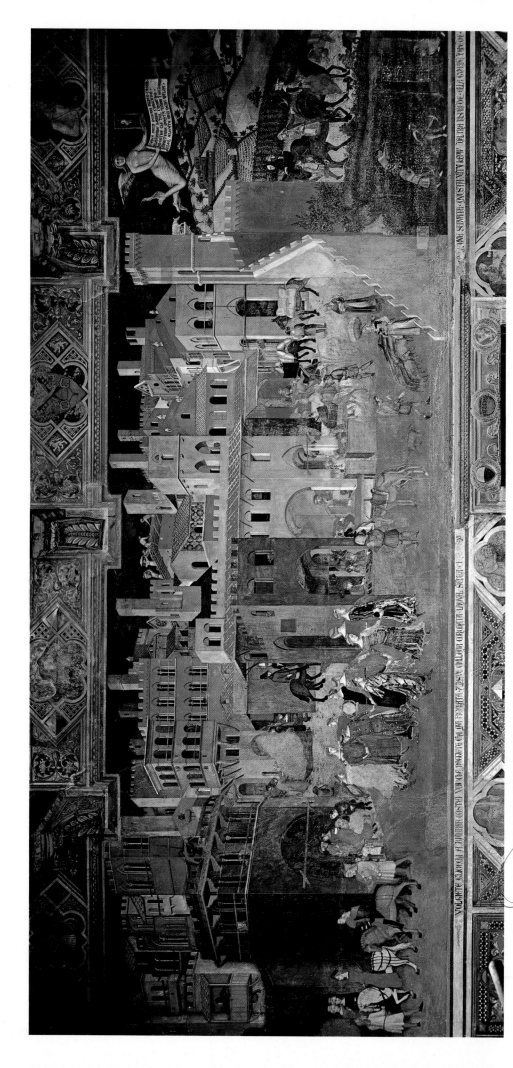

Colorplate 55. AMBROGIO LORENZETTI. *Good Government in the City* (see page 350). 1338–40. Fresco, width of entire wall 46'. Palazzo Pubblico, Siena

tian art during the Second Golden Age in Byzantium (see fig. 327). But how much warmer and more eloquent it is at Strasbourg than at Daphnē!

The climax of Gothic classicism is reached in some of the statues at Reims Cathedral, the most famous among them being the Visitation group (fig. 460, right). To have a pair of jamb figures enact a narrative scene such as this would have been unthinkable in Early Gothic sculpture; the fact that they can do so now shows how far the sustaining column has receded into the background. Characteristically enough, the S-curve, much more conspicuous than in the *St. Theodore*, dominates the side view as well as the front view, and the physical bulk of the body is further emphasized by horizontal folds pulled across the abdomen. The relationship of the two women shows the same human warmth and sympathy we found in the Strasbourg tympanum, but their classicism is of a far more monumental kind; they remind us so forcibly of ancient Roman matrons (compare fig. 259) that we wonder if the artist could have been inspired directly by large-scale Roman sculpture. The influence of Nicholas of Verdun alone could hardly have produced such firmly rounded, solid volumes.

The vast scale of the sculptural program for Reims Cathedral had made it necessary to call upon the services of masters and workshops from various other building sites, and so we encounter several distinct styles among the Reims sculpture. Two of these styles, both clearly different from the classicism of the *Visitation*, appear in the Annunciation group (fig. 460, left). The Virgin exhibits a severe manner, with a rigidly vertical body axis and straight, tubular folds meeting at sharp angles, a style probably invented about 1220 by the sculptors of the west portals of Notre-Dame in Paris; from there it traveled to Reims as well as Amiens (see fig. 463, above). The angel, in contrast, is conspicuously graceful: we note the tiny, round face framed by curly locks, the emphatic smile, the strong S-curve of the slender body, the ample, richly accented drapery. This "elegant style," created around 1240 by Parisian masters working for the royal court, was to spread far and wide during the following decades; it soon became, in fact, the standard formula for High Gothic sculpture. We shall feel its effect for many years to come, not only in France but abroad.

A characteristic instance of the "elegant style" is the fine group of Melchizedek and Abraham, carved shortly after the middle of the century for the interior west wall of Reims Cathedral (fig. 461). Abraham, in the costume of a medieval knight, still recalls the vigorous realism of the *St. Theodore* at Chartres; Melchizedek, however, shows clearly his descent from the angel of the Reims *Annunciation*—his hair and beard are even more elaborately curled, the draperies more lavishly ample, so that the body almost disappears among the rich play of folds. The deep recesses and sharply projecting ridges betray a new awareness of effects of light and shadow that seem more pictorial than sculptural; the same may be said of the way the figures are placed in their cavernous niches.

A half century later every trace of classicism has disappeared from Gothic sculpture. The human figure itself now becomes strangely cavernous and abstract. Thus the fam-

460. *Annunciation* and *Visitation*, West Portal, Reims Cathedral. c. 1225–45

461. *Melchizedek and Abraham*, interior west wall, Reims Cathedral. After 1251

462. *The Virgin of Paris*. Early 14th century.
Notre-Dame, Paris

ous *Virgin of Paris* (fig. 462) in Notre-Dame Cathedral consists largely of hollows, the projections having been reduced to the point where they are seen as lines rather than volumes. The statue is quite literally disembodied—its swaying stance no longer bears any relationship to the Classical *contrapposto*. Compared to such unearthly grace, the angel of the Reims *Annunciation* seems solid and tangible indeed, yet it contains the seed of the very qualities so strikingly expressed in the *Virgin of Paris*.

When we look back over the century and a half that separates the *Virgin of Paris* from the Chartres west portals, we cannot help wondering what brought about this retreat from the realism of Early and Classic High Gothic sculptures. Despite the fact that the new style was backed by the royal court and thus had special authority, we find it hard to explain why attenuated elegance and calligraphic, smoothly flowing lines came to dominate Gothic art throughout northern Europe from about 1250 to 1400. It is clear, nevertheless, that the *Virgin of Paris* represents neither a return to the Romanesque nor a complete repudiation of the earlier realistic trend.

Gothic realism had never been of the all-embracing, systematic sort: it had been a "realism of particulars," focused on specific details rather than on the over-all structure of the visible world. Its most characteristic products are not the classically oriented jamb statues and tympanum compositions of the early thirteenth century, but small-scale carvings such as the *Labors of the Months* in quatrefoil frames on the façade of Amiens Cathedral (fig. 463), with their delightful observation of everyday life. This intimate kind of realism survives even within the abstract formal framework of the *Virgin of Paris*; we see it in the Infant Christ, who appears here not as the Saviour-in-miniature austerely facing the beholder, but as a thoroughly human child playing with his mother's veil. Our statue thus retains an emotional appeal which links it to the Strasbourg *Death of the Virgin* and to the Reims *Visitation*. It is this appeal, not realism or classicism as such, that is the essence of Gothic art.

England

The spread of Gothic sculpture beyond the borders of France began only toward 1200—the style of the Chartres west portals had hardly any echoes abroad—but, once under way, proceeded at an astonishingly rapid pace. England may well have led the way, as it did in evolving its own version of Gothic architecture. Unfortunately, so much English Gothic sculpture was destroyed during the Reformation that we can study its development only with difficulty. Our richest materials are the tombs, which did not arouse the iconoclastic zeal of anti-Catholics. They include a type, illustrated by the splendid example in figure 464, that has no counterpart on the other side of the Channel: it shows the deceased, not in quiet repose as does the vast majority of medieval tombs, but in violent action, a fallen hero, fighting to the last breath. According to an old tradition, these dramatic figures, whose agony so oddly recalls the *Dying Gaul* (see fig. 201), honor the memory of Crusaders who died in the struggle for the Holy Land. If so, they would, as the tombs of Christian

463. *Signs of the Zodiac* and *Labors of the Months* (*July, August, September*), west façade, Amiens Cathedral. c. 1220–30

Soldiers, carry a religious meaning that might help to account for their compelling expressive power. In any event, they are among the finest achievements of English Gothic sculpture.

Germany

In Germany, the growth of Gothic sculpture can be traced more easily. From the 1220s on, German masters trained in the sculptural workshops of the great French cathedrals transplanted the new style to their homeland, although German architecture at that time was still predominantly Romanesque. However, even after the middle of the century, Germany failed to emulate the vast statuary cycles of France. As a consequence, German Gothic sculpture tended to be less closely linked with its architectural setting (the finest work was often done for the interiors rather than the exteriors of churches) and this, in turn, permitted it to develop an individuality and expressive freedom greater than that of its French models.

THE NAUMBURG MASTER. All these qualities are strikingly evident in the style of the Naumburg Master, an artist of real genius whose best-known work is the magnificent series of statues and reliefs he carved, about 1240–1250, for

464. Tomb of a Knight. c. 1260.
Dorchester Abbey, Oxfordshire

Naumburg Cathedral. The *Crucifixion* (fig. 465) forms the central feature of the choir screen; enclosed by a deep, gabled porch, the three figures frame the opening that links the nave with the sanctuary. Placing the group as he did (rather than above the screen, in accordance with the usual practice) our sculptor has brought the sacred subject down to earth both physically and emotionally: the suffering of Christ becomes a human reality because of the emphasis on the weight and volume of the Saviour's body, and Mary and

465. *Crucifixion*, on the choir screen,
Naumburg Cathedral. c. 1240–50

466. *The Kiss of Judas*, on the choir screen,
Naumburg Cathedral. c. 1240–50

John, pleading with the beholder, convey their grief more eloquently than ever before.

The pathos of these figures is heroic and dramatic, as against the lyricism of the Strasbourg tympanum or the Reims *Visitation.* If the Classic Gothic sculpture of France evokes comparison with Phidias, the Naumburg Master might be termed the temperamental kin of Scopas. The same intensity of feeling dominates the Passion scenes, such as the *Kiss of Judas* (fig. 466), with its unforgettable contrast between the meekness of Christ and the violent, sword-wielding St. Peter. Finally there are, attached to the responds inside the choir, the statues of nobles associated with the founding of the cathedral, among them the famous pair, Ekkehard and Uta (fig. 467). Although these men and women were not of the artist's own time, so that he knew them only as names in a chronicle, he has given each of them a personality as distinctive and forceful as if he had portrayed them from life. They make an instructive contrast with the *St. Theodore* at Chartres (see fig. 458).

THE PIETÀ. Gothic sculpture, as we have come to know it so far, reflects a desire to endow the traditional themes of Christian art with an ever greater emotional appeal. Toward

467. *Ekkehard and Uta*, Naumburg Cathedral. c. 1240–50

468. *Pietà*. Early 14th century.
Wood, height 34 ½ ". Provinzialmuseum, Bonn

the end of the thirteenth century, this tendency gave rise to a new kind of religious imagery, designed to serve private devotion; it is often referred to by the German term *Andachtsbild*, since Germany played a leading part in its development. The most characteristic and widespread type of *Andachtsbild* was the *Pietà* (an Italian word derived from the Latin *pietas*, the root word for both "pity" and "piety"), a representation of the Virgin grieving over the dead Christ. No such scene occurs in the scriptural account of the Passion; it was invented, rather—we do not know exactly where or when—as a tragic counterpart to the familiar motif of the Madonna and Child.

The *Pietà* reproduced in figure 468 dates from the same period as the *Virgin of Paris*; like most such groups, it is carved of wood, with a vividly painted surface to enhance its

impact. Realism here has become purely a vehicle of expression—the agonized faces; the blood-encrusted wounds of Christ that are enlarged and elaborated to an almost grotesque degree; and the bodies and limbs, puppet-like in their thinness and rigidity. The purpose of the work, clearly, is to arouse so overwhelming a sense of horror and pity that the beholder will identify his own feelings completely with those of the grief-stricken Mother of God.

At a glance, our *Pietà* would seem to have little in common with the *Virgin of Paris*. Yet they both share a lean, "deflated" quality of form that is the characteristic period flavor of Northern European art from the late thirteenth century to the mid-fourteenth. Only after 1350 do we again find an interest in weight and volume, coupled with a renewed impulse to explore tangible reality.

469. CLAUS SLUTER. Portal of the Chartreuse
de Champmol, Dijon. 1385–93

The International Style (North)

CLAUS SLUTER. The climax of this new trend came around 1400, during the period of the so-called International Style (see also page 338), and its greatest exponent was Claus Sluter, a sculptor of Netherlandish origin working for the Duke of Burgundy at Dijon. The portal of the Chartreuse de Champmol (fig. 469), which he did in 1385–93, recalls the monumental statuary on thirteenth-century cathedral portals, but the figures have grown so large and expansive that they almost overpower their architectural framework. This effect is due not only to their size and the bold three-dimensionality of the carving, but also to the fact that the jamb statues (Duke Philip the Bold and his wife, accompanied by their patron saints) are turned toward the Madonna on the *trumeau*, so that the five figures form a single, coherent unit, like the Crucifixion group at Naumburg. In both instances, the sculptural composition has simply been superimposed—however skillfully—on the shape of the doorway, not developed from it as at Chartres, Notre-Dame, or Reims. Significantly enough, the Champmol portal did not pave the way for a revival of architectural sculpture; it remained an isolated effort.

Sluter's other works belong to a different category, which for lack of a better term we must label church furniture (tombs, pulpits, etc.), combining large-scale sculpture with a small-scale architectural setting. The most impressive of these is the *Moses Well* at the Chartreuse de Champmol (fig. 470), a symbolic well surrounded by statues of Moses and other Old Testament prophets and once surmounted by a crucifix. The majestic Moses epitomizes the same qualities we find in Sluter's portal statues; soft, lavishly draped garments envelop the heavy-set body like an ample shell, the swelling forms seem to reach out into the surrounding space, determined to capture as much of it as possible (note the outward curve of the scroll).

In the Isaiah, facing left in our illustration, these aspects of our artist's style are less pronounced; what strikes us, rather, is the precise and masterful realism of every detail, from the minutiae of the costume to the texture of the wrinkled skin. The head, unlike that of Moses, has all the individuality of a portrait. Nor is this impression deceiving, for the sculptural development that culminated in Claus Sluter had produced, from about 1350 on, the first genuine portraits since late Antiquity. And Sluter himself has left us two splendid examples in the heads of the Duke and Duchess on the Chartreuse portal. It is this attachment to the tangible and specific that distinguishes his realism from that of the thirteenth century.

Italy

We have left a discussion of Italian Gothic sculpture to the last, for here, too, as in Gothic architecture, Italy stands apart from the rest of Europe. The earliest Gothic sculpture on Italian soil was probably produced in the extreme south, in Apulia and Sicily, the domain of the German Emperor Frederick II, who employed Frenchmen and Germans along with native artists at his court. Of the works he sponsored little has survived, but there is evidence that his taste favored a strongly Classic style derived from the sculpture of the Chartres transept portals and the Visitation group at Reims. This style not only provided a fitting visual language for a ruler who saw himself as the heir of the Caesars of old; it also blended easily with the classical tendencies in Italian Romanesque sculpture (see above, page 292).

470. CLAUS SLUTER. *The Moses Well.* 1395–1406.
Height of figures c. 6′. Chartreuse de Champmol, Dijon

NICOLA PISANO. Such was the background of Nicola Pisano, who came to Tuscany from southern Italy about 1250 (the year of Frederick II's death). In 1260 he completed the marble pulpit in the Baptistery of Pisa Cathedral (fig. 471). His work has been well defined as that of "the greatest— and in a sense the last—of medieval classicists." In the Pisa Baptistery pulpit the classical flavor is indeed so strong, whether we look at the architectural framework or at the sculptured parts, that the Gothic elements are hard to detect at first glance. But we do find such elements in the design of the arches, in the shape of the capitals, and in the standing figures at the corners (which look like small-scale descendants of the jamb statues on French Gothic cathedrals).

More striking, perhaps, is the Gothic quality of human feeling in the reliefs of narrative scenes such as the *Nativity* (fig. 472). The dense crowding of figures, on the other hand, has no counterpart in northern Gothic sculpture (aside from the Nativity, the panel also shows the Annunciation and the shepherds in the fields receiving the glad tidings of the birth of Christ). This treatment of the relief as a shallow box filled almost to the bursting point with solid, convex shapes tells us that Nicola Pisano must have been thoroughly familiar with Roman sarcophagi (compare fig. 301).

GIOVANNI PISANO. Half a century later Nicola's son Giovanni (1245/50–after 1314), who was an equally gifted sculptor, did a marble pulpit for Pisa Cathedral. It, too, includes a *Nativity* (fig. 473). Both panels have a good many things in common, as we might well expect, yet they also offer a sharp—and instructive—contrast. Giovanni's slender, swaying figures, with their smoothly flowing draperies, recall neither classical Antiquity nor the Visitation group at Reims; instead, they reflect the elegant style of the royal court at Paris that had become the standard Gothic formula during the later thirteenth century. And with this change there has come about a new treatment of relief: to Giovanni Pisano, space is as important as plastic form. The figures are no longer tightly packed together; they are now spaced far enough apart to let us see the landscape setting that contains them, and each figure has been allotted its own pocket of space. If Nicola's *Nativity* strikes us as essentially a sequence of bulging, rounded masses, Giovanni's appears to be made up mainly of cavities and shadows.

Giovanni Pisano, then, seems to follow the same trend toward "disembodiment" that we encountered north of the Alps around 1300. He does so, however, only within limits. Compared to the *Virgin of Paris*, his *Madonna* at Prato (figs. 474, 475) immediately evokes memories of Nicola's style. The three-dimensional firmness of the modeling is further emphasized by the strong turn of the head and the thrust-out left hip; we also note the heavy, buttress-like folds that anchor the figure to its base. Yet there can be no doubt that the Prato statue derives from a French prototype which must have been rather like the *Virgin of Paris*. (The back view, with its suggestion of "Gothic sway," reveals the connection more clearly than the front view.)

CHURCH FAÇADES. The façades of Italian Gothic churches, we will recall, do not rival those of the French ca-

471. (*above*) NICOLA PISANO. Marble
Pulpit. 1259–60. Baptistery, Pisa

472. (*upper right*) *The Nativity*, detail of the
Marble Pulpit, Baptistery, Pisa

473. (*right*) GIOVANNI PISANO.
The Nativity, detail of the Marble Pulpit.
1302–10. Pisa Cathedral

thedrals as focal points of architectural and sculptural endeavor. The French Gothic portal, with its jamb statues and richly carved tympanum, never found favor in the South. Instead, we often find a survival of Romanesque traditions of architectural sculpture, such as statues in niches or small-scale reliefs overlaying the wall surfaces (compare fig. 411).

At Orvieto Cathedral, Lorenzo Maitani (before 1270–1330) covered the wide pilasters between the portals with relief carvings of such lacelike delicacy that we become aware of them only if we see them at close range. The tortures of the damned from the *Last Judgment* on the southernmost pilaster (fig. 476) make an instructive comparison with similar scenes in Romanesque art (such as fig. 407): the hellish monsters are as vicious as ever, but the sinners now evoke compassion rather than sheer horror. Even here, then, we feel the spirit of human sympathy that distinguishes the Gothic from the Romanesque.

TOMBS. If Italian Gothic sculpture failed to emulate the vast sculptural programs of northern Europe, it excelled in the field which we have called church furniture, such as

pulpits, screens, shrines, and tombs. Among the latter, the most remarkable perhaps is the monument of Can Grande della Scala, the lord of Verona. A tall structure built out-of-doors next to the church of Sta. Maria Antica, it consists of a vaulted canopy housing the sarcophagus and surmounted by a truncated pyramid which in turn supports an equestrian statue of the deceased (fig. 477). The ruler, astride his richly caparisoned mount, is shown in full armor, sword in hand, as if he were standing on a windswept hill at the head of his troops; and, in a supreme display of self-confidence, he wears a broad grin. Clearly, this is no Christian Soldier, no crusading knight, no embodiment of the ideals of chivalry, but a frank glorification of power.

Can Grande, remembered today mainly as the friend and protector of Dante, was indeed an extraordinary figure; although he held Verona as a fief from the German emperor, he styled himself "the Great Khan," thus asserting his claim to the absolute sovereignty of an Asiatic potentate. His free-standing equestrian statue—a form of monument traditionally reserved for emperors—conveys the same ambition in visual terms.

474, 475. GIOVANNI PISANO. *Madonna*. c. 1315.
Marble, height 27". Prato Cathedral

476. LORENZO MAITANI.
The Last Judgment (detail).
c. 1320. Façade, Orvieto Cathedral

477. *Equestrian Statue of Can Grande della Scala,*
from his tomb. 1330. Castelvecchio, Verona

The International Style (South)

During the later fourteenth century, northern Italy proved particularly hospitable to artistic influences from across the Alps, not only in architecture (see Milan Cathedral, fig. 453), but in sculpture as well. The Apostles atop the choir screen of St. Mark's in Venice (fig. 478), carved by Jacobello and Pierpaolo dalle Masegne about 1394, reflect the trend toward greater realism and the renewed interest in weight and volume that culminated in the work of Claus Sluter, even though these qualities are not yet fully developed here. With the Apostles from St. Mark's, we are on the threshold of the "International Style," which flourished throughout Western Europe in about 1400 to 1420.

GHIBERTI. The style's outstanding representative in Italian sculpture was a Florentine, Lorenzo Ghiberti (c. 1381–1455), who as a youth must have had close contact with French art. We first encounter him in 1401–1402, when he won a competition for a pair of richly decorated bronze doors for the Baptistery in Florence. (It took him more than two decades to complete these doors, which fill the north portal of the building.) Each of the competing artists had to submit a trial relief, in a Gothic quatrefoil frame, representing the Sacrifice of Isaac. Ghiberti's panel (fig. 479) strikes us first of all with the perfection of its craftsmanship, which reflects his training as a goldsmith. The silky shimmer of the surfaces, the wealth of beautifully articulated detail, make it

479. LORENZO GHIBERTI. *The Sacrifice of Isaac.* 1401–02. Gilt bronze, 21 × 17″. National Museum, Florence

easy to understand why this entry was awarded the prize. If the composition seems somewhat lacking in dramatic force, that is as characteristic of Ghiberti's calm, lyrical temper as of the taste of the period, for the realism of the International Style did not extend to the realm of the emotions. The figures, in their softly draped, ample garments, retain an air of courtly elegance even when they enact scenes of violence.

However much his work may owe to French influence, Ghiberti proves himself thoroughly Italian in one respect: his admiration for ancient sculpture, as evidenced by the beautiful nude torso of Isaac. Here our artist revives a tradition of classicism that had reached its highest point in Nicola Pisano but had gradually died out during the fourteenth century.

But Ghiberti is also the heir of Giovanni Pisano. In the latter's *Nativity* panel (fig. 473) we noted a bold new emphasis on the spatial setting; the trial relief carries this same tendency a good deal further, achieving a far more natural sense of recession. For the first time since classical Antiquity, we are made to experience the background of the panel not as a flat surface but as empty space from which the sculptured forms emerge toward the beholder (note particularly the angel in the upper right-hand corner). This "pictorial" quality relates Ghiberti's work to the painting of the International Style, where we find a similar concern with spatial depth and atmosphere (see below, page 355). While not a revolutionary himself, he prepares the ground for the great revolution that will mark the second decade of the fifteenth century in Florentine art and that we call the Early Renaissance.

478. JACOBELLO and PIERPAOLO DALLE MASEGNE.
Apostles, on the choir screen.
1394. Marble, height c. 53″. St. Mark's, Venice

PAINTING

France

STAINED GLASS. Although Gothic architecture and sculpture began so dramatically at St.-Denis and Chartres, Gothic painting developed at a rather slow pace in its early stages. The new architectural style sponsored by Abbot Suger gave birth to a new conception of monumental sculpture almost at once but did not demand any radical change of style in painting. Suger's account of the rebuilding of his church, to be sure, places a great deal of emphasis on the miraculous effect of stained-glass windows, whose "continuous light" flooded the interior. Stained glass was thus an integral element of Gothic architecture from the very beginning. Yet the technique of stained-glass painting had already been perfected in Romanesque times; the "many masters from different regions" whom Suger assembled to do the choir windows at St.-Denis may have faced a larger task and a more complex pictorial program than before, but the style of their designs remained Romanesque.

During the next half century, as Gothic structures became ever more skeletal and clerestory windows grew to vast size, stained glass displaced manuscript illumination as the leading form of painting. Since the production of stained glass was so intimately linked with the great cathedral workshops, the designers came to be influenced more and more by architectural sculpture, and in this way, about the year 1200, arrived at a distinctively Gothic style of their own.

The majestic *Habakkuk* (fig. 480) of Bourges Cathedral, one of a series of windows representing Old Testament prophets, is the direct kin of the jamb statues on the Chartres transept portals and of the Visitation at Reims. All these works share a common ancestor, the classicizing style of Nicholas of Verdun (compare fig. 420), yet the *Habakkuk* resembles a statue projected onto a translucent screen rather than an enlarged figure from the enamel plaques of the Klosterneuburg altar.

Examining one of the sections of the stained glass at close range (fig. 481), we realize that the window consists not of large panes but of hundreds of small pieces of tinted glass bound together by strips of lead. The maximum size of these pieces was severely limited by the primitive methods of medieval glass manufacture, so that the artist who created this window could not simply "paint on glass"; rather, he painted *with* glass, assembling his design, somewhat the way one would a mosaic or a jigsaw puzzle, out of odd-shaped fragments which he cut to fit the contours of the forms. Only the finer details, such as eyes, hair, and drapery folds, were added by actually painting—or, better perhaps, drawing—in black or gray on the glass surfaces. While this process encourages an abstract, ornamental style, it tends to resist any attempt to render three-dimensional effects. Yet in the hands of a great master the maze of lead strips could resolve itself into figures having the looming monumentality of our *Habakkuk*.

Apart from the peculiar demands of their medium, the stained-glass workers who filled the windows of the great Gothic cathedrals also had to face the difficulties arising from the enormous scale of their work. No Romanesque

480. *Habakkuk*. c. 1220. Stained-glass window, height c. 14'. Bourges Cathedral

481. *Habakkuk*, detail of figure 480

482. VILLARD DE HONNECOURT.
Wheel of Fortune. c. 1240.
Bibliothèque Nationale, Paris

painter had ever been called upon to cover areas so vast—the *Habakkuk* window is more than 14 feet tall—or so firmly bound into an architectural framework. The task required a technique of orderly planning for which the medieval painting tradition could offer no precedent.

VILLARD DE HONNECOURT. Only architects and stone masons knew how to deal with this problem, and it was their methods that the stained-glass workers borrowed in mapping out their own compositions. Gothic architectural design, as we recall from our discussion of the choir of St.-Denis (see figs. 422, 423), uses a system of geometric relationships; the same rules could be used to control the design of a stained-glass window, or even of an individual figure.

We gain some insight into this procedure from the drawings in a notebook compiled about 1240 by the architect Villard de Honnecourt, such as the *Wheel of Fortune* (fig. 482). What we see here is not the final version of the design but the scaffolding of circles and triangles on which the image is to be constructed. The pervasiveness of these geometric schemes is well illustrated by another drawing from the same notebook, the *Front View of a Lion* (fig. 483). According to the inscription, Villard has portrayed the animal from life, but a closer look at the figure will convince us that he was able to do so only after he had laid down a geometric pattern: a circle for the face (the dot between the eyes is its center) and a second, larger circle for the body. To Villard, then, drawing from life meant something far different from what it does to us—it meant filling in an abstract framework with details based on direct observation. If we now turn back

once more to the firmly drawn, simplified outlines of the *Habakkuk*, we cannot help wondering to what extent they, too, reflect a geometric scaffolding of some sort.

The period 1200–1250 might be termed the golden age of stained glass. After that, as architectural activity declined and the demand for stained glass began to slacken, manuscript illumination gradually recaptured its former position of leadership. By then, however, miniature painting had been thoroughly affected by the influence of both stained glass and stone sculpture, the artistic pacemakers of the first half of the century.

ILLUMINATED MANUSCRIPTS. The resulting change of style is fully evident in figure 484, from a Psalter done about 1260 for King Louis IX (St. Louis) of France. The scene illustrates I Samuel 11:2, in which Nahash the Ammonite threatens the Jews at Jabesh. We notice first of all the careful symmetry of the framework, which consists of flat, ornamented panels very much like those in the *Habakkuk* window, and of an architectural setting. The latter recalls the canopies above the heads of jamb statues (see fig. 458) and the arched twin niches enclosing the relief of *Melchizedek and Abraham* at Reims (fig. 461).

Against this emphatically two-dimensional background, the figures are "relieved" by smooth and skillful modeling. But their sculptural quality stops short at the outer contours, which are defined by heavy dark lines rather like the lead strips in stained-glass windows. The figures themselves show all the characteristics of the elegant style originated about twenty years before by the sculptors of the royal court (compare the Annunciation Angel in fig. 460 and Melchiz-

483. VILLARD DE HONNECOURT.
Front View of a Lion. c. 1240.
Bibliothèque Nationale, Paris

edek in fig. 461): graceful gestures, swaying poses, smiling faces, neatly waved strands of hair. Of the expressive energy of Romanesque painting we find no trace (colorplates 36, 37); our miniature exemplifies the subtle and refined taste that made the court art of Paris the standard for all Europe.

Until the thirteenth century, the production of illuminated manuscripts had been centered in the scriptoria of monasteries. Now, along with a great many other activities once the special preserve of monasteries, it shifted ever more to urban workshops organized by laymen, the ancestors of the publishing houses of today. Here again the workshops of sculptors and stained-glass painters may have set the pattern.

Some members of this new, secular breed of illuminator are known to us by name, such as Master Honoré of Paris who, in 1295, did the miniatures in the *Prayer Book of Philip the Fair*. Our sample (fig. 485) shows him working in a style derived from the *Psalter of St. Louis*. Significantly enough, however, the framework no longer dominates the composition; the figures have become larger, and their relief-like modeling is more emphatic; they are even permitted to overlap the frame, a device that helps to detach them from the flat pattern of the background and thus introduces a certain—though very limited—spatial range into the picture.

Italy

We must now turn our attention to Italian painting, which at the end of the thirteenth century produced an explosion of creative energy as spectacular, and as far-reaching in its impact upon the future, as the rise of the Gothic cathedral in France. A single glance at Giotto's *Lamentation* (fig. 491) will convince us that we are faced with a truly revolutionary development here. How, we wonder, could a work of such intense dramatic power be conceived by a contemporary of Master Honoré? What were the conditions that made it possible? Oddly enough, as we inquire into the background of Giotto's art, we find that it arose from the same "old-fashioned" attitudes we met in Italian Gothic architecture and sculpture.

Medieval Italy, although strongly influenced by Northern art from Carolingian times on, nevertheless had always maintained close contact with Byzantine civilization. As a result, panel painting, mosaics, and murals—techniques that had never taken firm root north of the Alps—were kept alive on Italian soil; and at the very time when stained glass became the dominant pictorial art in France, a new wave of Byzantine influence overwhelmed the lingering Romanesque elements in Italian painting.

There is a certain irony in the fact that this neo-Byzantine style (or "Greek manner," as the Italians called it) made its appearance soon after the conquest of Constantinople by the armies of the Fourth Crusade in 1204—one thinks of the way Greek art had once captured the taste of the victorious Romans of old. Be that as it may, the Greek manner prevailed almost till the end of the thirteenth century, so that Italian painters were able to absorb the Byzantine tradition far more thoroughly than ever before. During this same period, we recall, Italian architects and sculptors followed a very different course; untouched by the Greek manner, they were assimilating the Gothic style. Eventually, toward 1300, Gothic influence spilled over into painting as well, and it was the interaction of this element with the neo-Byzantine that

486. CIMABUE. *Madonna Enthroned* (see colorplate 50).
Uffizi Gallery, Florence

produced the revolutionary new style of which Giotto is the greatest exponent.

CIMABUE. Among the painters of the Greek manner, the Florentine master Cimabue (c. 1250–after 1300), who may have been Giotto's teacher, enjoyed special fame. His huge altar panel, *Madonna Enthroned* (fig. 486, colorplate 50), rivals the finest Byzantine icons or mosaics (compare figs. 317, 330, and colorplate 30); what distinguishes it from them is mainly a greater severity of design and expression, which befits its huge size. Panels on such a monumental scale had never been attempted in the East. Likewise un-Byzantine is the picture's gabled shape, and the way the throne of inlaid wood seems to echo this shape. The geometric inlays—indeed, the throne's architectural style—reminds us of the Florence Baptistery (see fig. 403, colorplate 44).

DUCCIO. The *Madonna Enthroned* (fig. 487, colorplate 51), of a quarter century later by Duccio of Siena (c. 1255–before 1319) for the main altar of Siena Cathedral, makes an instructive comparison with Cimabue's. The Sienese honored this panel by calling it the *Maestà*—"majesty"—to identify the Virgin's role here as the Queen of Heaven surrounded by her celestial court of saints and angels. At first glance, the two pictures may seem much alike, since both follow the same basic scheme; yet the differences are important. They reflect not only two contrasting personalities and contrasting local tastes—the gentleness of Duccio is characteristic of Siena—but also the rapid evolution of style.

In Duccio's hands the Greek manner has become unfrozen, as it were: the rigid, angular draperies have given way to an undulating softness, the abstract shading-in-reverse with lines of gold is reduced to a minimum, and the bodies, faces, and hands are beginning to swell with a subtle three-dimensional life. Clearly, the heritage of Hellenistic-Roman illusionism that had always been part of the Byzantine tradition, however dormant or submerged, is asserting itself once more. But there is also a half-hidden Gothic element here; we sense it in the fluency of the drapery folds, the appealing naturalness of the Infant Christ, and the tender glances by which the figures communicate with each other. The chief

487. DUCCIO. *Madonna Enthroned*, center of
the *Maestà Altar* (see colorplate 51).
Cathedral Museum, Siena

488. DUCCIO. *Annunciation of the Death of the Virgin*, from the *Maestà Altar*

source of this Gothic influence must have been Giovanni Pi-sano (see page 335), who was in Siena from 1285 to 1295 as the sculptor-architect in charge of the cathedral façade.

Apart from the *Madonna*, the *Maestà* includes many small compartments with scenes from the lives of Christ and the Virgin. In these panels, the most mature works of Duc-cio's career, the cross-fertilization of Gothic and Byzantine elements has given rise to a development of fundamental importance—a new kind of picture space. The *Annuncia-tion of the Death of the Virgin* (fig. 488) shows us something we have never seen before in the history of painting: two fig-ures enclosed by an architectural interior.

Ancient painters (and their Byzantine successors) were quite unable to achieve this space; their architectural set-tings always stay *behind* the figures, so that their indoor scenes tend to look as if they were taking place in an open-air theater, on a stage without a roof. Duccio's figures, in contrast, inhabit a space that is created and defined by the architecture, as if the artist had carved a niche into his pan-el. Perhaps we will recognize the origin of this spatial frame-work: it derives from the architectural "housing" of Gothic sculpture (compare especially figs. 461, 465). Northern Gothic painters, too, had tried to reproduce these architec-tural settings, but they could do so only by flattening them out completely (as in the *Psalter of St. Louis*, fig. 484). The Italian painters of Duccio's generation, on the other hand, trained as they were in the Greek manner, had acquired enough of the devices of Hellenistic-Roman illusionism to let them render such a framework without draining it of its three-dimensional qualities. Even in the outdoor scenes on the back of the *Maestà*, such as *Christ Entering Jerusalem*

489. DUCCIO. *Christ Entering Jerusalem*, from back of the *Maestà Altar* (see colorplate 52)

(fig. 489, colorplate 52), the architecture keeps its space-creating function: the diagonal movement into depth is conveyed not by the figures—which have the same scale throughout—but by the walls on either side of the road leading to the city, by the gate that frames the welcoming crowd, and by the structures beyond. Whatever the shortcomings of Duccio's perspective, his architecture again demonstrates its capacity to contain and enclose, and for that very reason strikes us as more intelligible than similar vistas in ancient art (compare fig. 278).

GIOTTO. Turning from Duccio to Giotto (1267?–1336/7), we meet an artist of far bolder and more dramatic temper. Ten to fifteen years younger, Giotto was less close to the Greek manner from the start, despite his probable apprenticeship under Cimabue. As a Florentine, he fell heir to Cimabue's sense of monumental scale, which made him a wall painter by instinct, rather than a panel painter. Of his surviving murals, those in the Arena Chapel, Padua, done in 1305–6, are the best preserved as well as the most characteristic. They include many of the same subjects that we find on the reverse of Duccio's *Maestà*, such as *Christ Entering Jerusalem* (fig. 490, colorplate 53).

The two versions have many elements in common, since they both ultimately derive from the same Byzantine source; but where Duccio has enriched the traditional scheme, spatially as well as in narrative detail, Giotto subjects it to a radical simplification. The action proceeds parallel to the picture plane; landscape, architecture, and figures have been reduced to the essential minimum. And the sober technique of fresco painting (watercolors applied to the freshly plastered wall), with its limited range and intensity of tones, further emphasizes the austerity of Giotto's art as against the jewel-like brilliance of Duccio's picture, which is executed in egg tempera on gold ground. (Note the sparkling colors of the *Maestà* panel in colorplate 52). Yet Giotto's work has far the more powerful impact of the two; it makes us feel so close to the event that we have a sense of being participants rather than distant observers.

How does the artist achieve this extraordinary effect? He does so, first of all, by having the entire scene take place in the foreground and—even more important—by presenting it in such a way that the beholder's eye-level falls within the lower half of the picture. Thus we can imagine ourselves standing on the same ground plane as these painted figures, while Duccio makes us survey the scene from above in bird's-eye perspective. The consequences of this choice of viewpoint are truly epoch-making; choice implies conscious awareness—in this case, awareness of a relationship in space between the beholder and the picture—and Giotto may well claim to be the first to have established such a relationship. Duccio, certainly, does not yet conceive his picture space as continuous with the beholder's space (hence we have the sensation of vaguely floating above the scene, rather than of knowing where we stand), and even ancient painting at its most illusionistic provides no more than a pseudo-continuity in this respect (see page 182, discussion of figs. 259, 261, 262). Giotto, on the other hand, tells us where we stand, and he also endows his forms with a three-dimensional reality so forceful that they seem as solid and tangible as sculpture in the round.

With Giotto it is the figures, rather than the architectural framework, that create the picture space. As a result, this space is more limited than Duccio's—its depth extends no further than the combined volumes of the overlapping bodies in the picture—but within its limits it is very much more persuasive. To his contemporaries, the tactile quality of Giotto's art must have seemed a near-miracle; it was this that made them praise him as equal, or even superior, to the greatest of the ancient painters, because his forms looked so lifelike that they could be mistaken for reality itself. Equally significant are the stories linking Giotto with the claim that painting is superior to sculpture—not an idle boast, as it turned out, for Giotto does indeed mark the start of what might be called "the era of painting" in Western art. The symbolic turning point is the year 1334, when he was appointed the head of the Florence Cathedral workshop, an honor and responsibility hitherto reserved for architects or sculptors.

Yet Giotto's aim was not simply to transplant Gothic statuary into painting. By creating a radically new kind of picture space, he had also sharpened his awareness of the picture surface. When we look at a work by Duccio (or his ancient and medieval predecessors) we tend to do so in installments, as it were; our glance travels from detail to detail at a leisurely pace until we have surveyed the entire area. Giotto, on the contrary, invites us to see the whole at one glance. His large, simple forms, the strong grouping of his figures, the limited depth of his "stage," all these factors help to endow his scenes with an inner coherence such as we have never found before. Notice how dramatically the massed verticals of the "block" of Apostles on the left are contrasted with the

490. GIOTTO. *Christ Entering Jerusalem*
(see colorplate 53). Arena Chapel, Padua

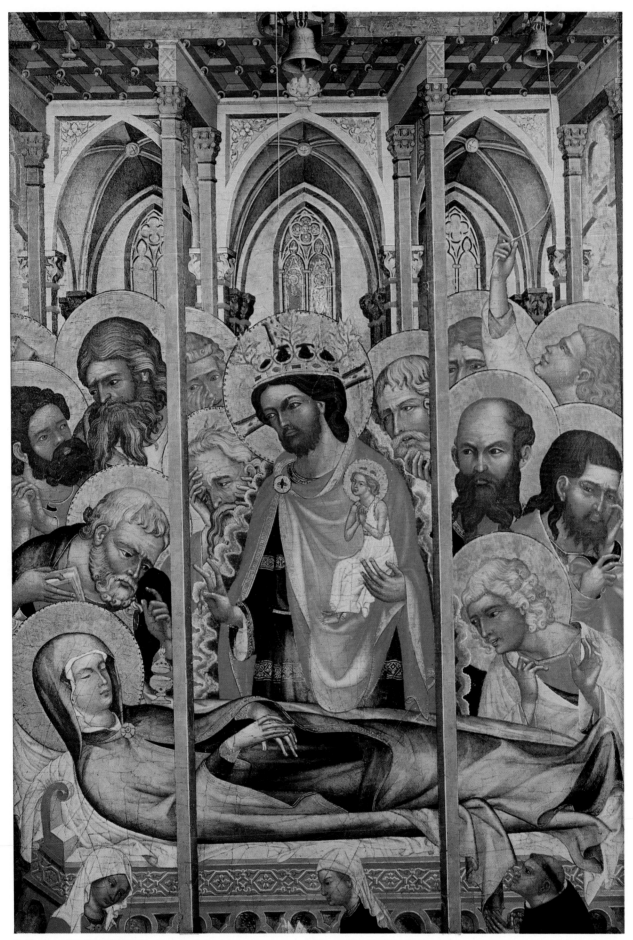

Colorplate 56. BOHEMIAN. *Death of the Virgin* (see page 354). 1350–60. Panel, 39 × 27¾″. Museum of Fine Arts, Boston

Colorplate 57. MELCHIOR BROEDERLAM. *The Presentation in the Temple* and *Flight into Egypt* (see page 355). 1394–99. Panel, 64 × 51″. Museum of Fine Arts, Dijon

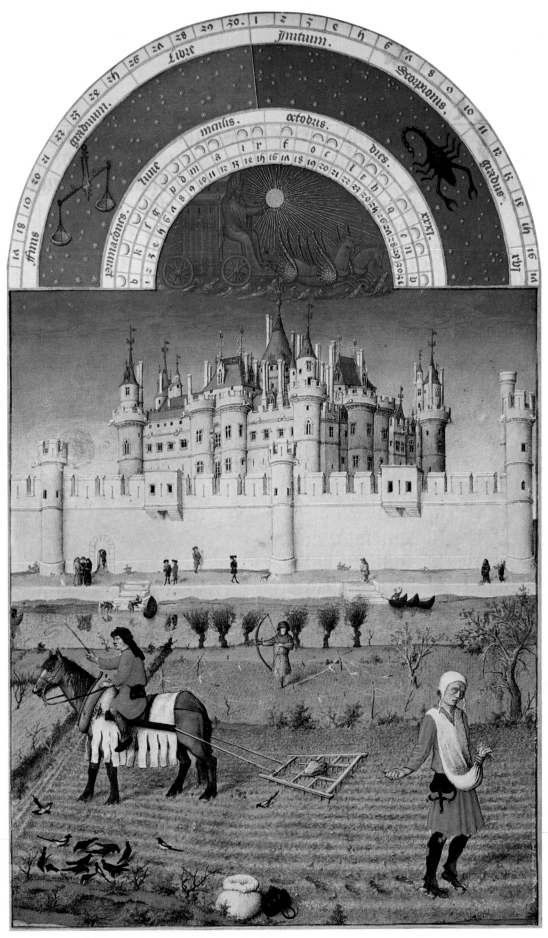

Colorplate 58. THE LIMBOURG BROTHERS. *October*, from *Les Très Riches Heures du Duc de Berry* (see page 357). 1413–16. Musée Condé, Chantilly, France

Colorplate 59. GENTILE DA FABRIANO. *The Adoration of the Magi*
(see page 359). 1423. Panel, 9′ 10⅛″ × 9′ 3″. Uffizi Gallery, Florence

upward slope formed by the welcoming crowd on the right; how Christ, alone in the center, bridges the gulf between the two groups. The more we study the composition, the more we come to realize its majestic firmness and clarity.

Giotto's achievement as a master of design does not fully emerge from any single work. Only if we compare a number of scenes from the Padua fresco cycle do we understand how perfectly the composition in each instance is attuned to the emotional content of the subject. Thus the artist has "rephrased" the traditional pattern of Christ's Entry into Jerusalem to stress the solemnity of the event as a triumphal procession of the Prince of Peace, while the tragic mood of the *Lamentation* (fig. 491) is brought home to us by the formal rhythm of the design as much as by the gestures and expressions of the participants. The very low center of gravity, the hunched, bending figures communicate the somber quality of the scene and arouse our compassion even before we have grasped the specific meaning of the event depicted. With extraordinary boldness, Giotto sets off the frozen grief of the human mourners against the frantic movement of the weeping angels among the clouds, as if the figures on the ground were restrained by their collective duty to maintain the stability of the composition while the angels, small and weightless as birds, do not share this burden.

Let us note, too, how the impact of the drama is heightened by the severely simple setting; the descending slope of the hill acts as a unifying element and at the same time directs our glance toward the heads of Christ and the Virgin, which are the focal point of the scene. Even the tree has a twin function. Its barrenness and isolation suggest that all of nature somehow shares in the Saviour's death, yet it also invites us to ponder a more precise symbolic message. For it alludes—as does Dante in a passage in the *Divine Com-*

492. GIOTTO. *Madonna Enthroned.* c. 1310. Panel, 10' 8" × 6' 8". Uffizi Gallery, Florence

edy—to the Tree of Knowledge, which the sin of Adam and Eve had caused to wither and which was to be restored to life through the sacrificial death of Christ.

The art of Giotto is so daringly original that its sources are far more difficult to trace than those of Duccio's style. Apart from his Florentine background as represented by the Greek manner of Cimabue, the young Giotto seems to have been familiar with the neo-Byzantine painters of Rome; in that city, he probably also became acquainted with older monuments—Early Christian and ancient Roman mural decoration. Classical sculpture, too, left an impression on him. More fundamental than any of these, however, was the influence of the Pisanos—Nicola, and especially Giovanni—the founding fathers of Italian Gothic sculpture. They were the chief intermediaries through whom Giotto first came in contact with the world of northern Gothic art. And the latter remains the most important of all the elements that entered into Giotto's style. Without the knowledge, direct or indirect, of Northern works such as those illustrated in figure 459 or figure 466, he could never have achieved the emotional impact of his *Lamentation*.

491. GIOTTO. *The Lamentation.* 1305–6. Fresco. Arena Chapel, Padua

What we have said of the Padua frescoes applies equally to the *Madonna Enthroned* (fig. 492), the most important among the small number of panel paintings by our master. Done about the same time as Duccio's *Maestà*, it illustrates once again the difference between Florence and Siena; its architectural severity clearly derives from Cimabue (see fig. 486). The figures, however, have the same overpowering sense of weight and volume we saw in the frescoes in the Arena Chapel, and the picture space is just as persuasive— so much so, in fact, that the golden haloes look like foreign bodies in it.

Characteristically enough, the throne, of a design based on Italian Gothic architecture, has now become a niche-like structure that encloses the Madonna on three sides and thus "insulates" her from the gold background. Its lavish ornamentation includes one feature of special interest: the colored marble surfaces of the base and of the quatrefoil within the gable. Such make-believe stone textures had been highly developed by ancient painters (see figs. 277, 278, and colorplate 24), but the tradition had died out in Early Chris-

tian times. Its sudden reappearance here offers concrete evidence of Giotto's familiarity with whatever ancient murals could still be seen in medieval Rome.

SIMONE MARTINI. There are few men in the entire history of art to equal the stature of Giotto as a radical innovator. His very greatness, however, tended to dwarf the next generation of Florentine painters, which produced only followers rather than new leaders. Their contemporaries in Siena were more fortunate in this respect, since Duccio never had the same overpowering impact. As a consequence, it was they, not the Florentines, who took the next decisive step in the development of Italian Gothic painting. Simone Martini (c. 1284–1344), who painted the tiny but intense *Road to Calvary* (fig. 493, colorplate 54) about 1340, may well claim to be the most distinguished of Duccio's disciples. He spent the last years of his life in Avignon, the town in southern France that served as the residence-in-exile of the popes during most of the fourteenth century. Our panel, originally part of a small altar, was probably done there.

In its sparkling colors, and especially in the architectural background, it still echoes the art of Duccio (see colorplate 52). The vigorous modeling of the figures, on the other hand, as well as their dramatic gestures and expressions, betray the influence of Giotto. While Simone Martini is not much concerned with spatial clarity, he proves to be an extraordinarily acute observer; the sheer variety of costumes and physical types, the wealth of human incident, create a sense of down-to-earth reality very different from both the lyricism of Duccio and the grandeur of Giotto.

THE LORENZETTI BROTHERS. This closeness to everyday life also appears in the work of the brothers Pietro and Ambrogio Lorenzetti (both died 1348?), but on a more monumental scale and coupled with a keen interest in problems of space. The boldest spatial experiment is Pietro's triptych of 1342, *The Birth of the Virgin* (fig. 494), where the painted architecture has been correlated with the real architecture of the frame in such a way that the two are seen as a single system. Moreover, the vaulted chamber where the birth takes place occupies two panels—it continues unbroken behind the column that divides the center from the right wing. The left wing represents an anteroom which leads to a vast and only partially glimpsed architectural space suggesting the interior of a Gothic church. What Pietro Lorenzetti achieved here is the outcome of a development that began three decades earlier in the work of Duccio (compare fig. 488), but only now does the picture surface assume the quality of a transparent window through which—not *on* which—we perceive the same kind of space we know from daily experience.

Yet Duccio's work alone is not sufficient to explain Pietro's astonishing breakthrough; it became possible, rather, through a combination of the *architectural* picture space of Duccio and the *sculptural* picture space of Giotto. The same procedure enabled Ambrogio Lorenzetti, in his frescoes of 1338–40 in the Siena city hall, to unfold a comprehensive view of the entire town before our eyes (fig. 495, colorplate 55). Again we marvel at the distance that separates this pre-

493. SIMONE MARTINI. *The Road to Calvary* (see colorplate 54). The Louvre, Paris

494. PIETRO LORENZETTI. *The Birth of the Virgin.* 1342.
Panel, 6' 1½" × 5' 11½". Cathedral Museum, Siena

cisely articulated "portrait" of Siena from Duccio's Jerusalem (see colorplate 52). Ambrogio's mural forms part of an elaborate allegorical program depicting the contrast of good and bad government; hence the artist, in order to show the life of a well-ordered city-state, had to fill the streets and houses with teeming activity.

The gay and busy crowd gives the architectural vista its striking reality by introducing the human scale. On the right, beyond the margin of colorplate 55, the *Good Government* fresco provides a view of the Sienese countryside, fringed by distant mountains. It is a true landscape—the first since ancient Roman times—full of sweeping depth yet distinguished from its classical predecessors (such as colorplate 22) by an ingrained orderliness, a domesticated air. Here the presence of man is not accidental; he has taken full possession of nature, terracing the hillsides with vineyards, patterning the valleys with the geometry of fields and pastures. In such a setting, Ambrogio observes the peasants at their seasonal labors (fig. 496), recording a rural Tuscan scene so characteristic that it has hardly changed during the past six hundred years.

495. AMBROGIO LORENZETTI. *Good Government in the City* (detail; see colorplate 55). Palazzo Pubblico, Siena

496. AMBROGIO LORENZETTI. *Good Government in the Country*
(detail; see colorplate 55).
Palazzo Pubblico, Siena

THE BLACK DEATH. The first four decades of the four-teenth century in Florence and Siena had been a period of political stability and economic expansion as well as of great artistic achievement. In the 1340s both cities suffered a se-ries of catastrophes whose echoes were to be felt for many years: banks and merchants went bankrupt by the score, in-ternal upheavals shook the government, there were repeat-ed crop failures, and in 1348 the epidemic of bubonic plague throughout Europe, the Black Death, wiped out more than half their urban population. The popular reaction to these calamitous events was mixed. Many people regarded them as signs of Divine wrath, warnings to a sinful humanity to forsake the pleasures of this earth; in such people the Black Death engendered a mood of otherworldly exaltation. To others, such as the gay company in Boccaccio's *Decameron*, the fear of sudden death merely intensified the desire to en-joy life while there was yet time. These conflicting attitudes are reflected in the pictorial theme of the Triumph of Death.

TRAINI. The most impressive version of this subject is an enormous fresco in the Camposanto, the cemetery building next to Pisa Cathedral. From this work, attributed to the Pi-san master Francesco Traini (doc. c. 1321–1363), we repro-duce a particularly dramatic detail (fig. 497). The elegantly costumed men and women on horseback have suddenly come upon three decaying corpses in open coffins; even the animals are terrified by the sight and smell of rotting flesh. Only the hermit, having renounced all earthly pleasures,

calmly points out the lesson of the scene. But will the living accept the lesson, or will they, like the characters of Boccac-cio, turn away from the shocking spectacle more determined than ever to pursue their own hedonistic ways? The artist's own sympathies seem curiously divided; his style, far from being otherworldly, recalls the realism of Ambrogio Loren-zetti, although the forms are harsher and more expressive.

In a fire which occurred in 1944, Traini's fresco was badly damaged and had to be detached from the wall in order to save what was left of it. This procedure exposed the first, rough coat of plaster underneath, on which the artist had sketched out his composition (fig. 498). These drawings, of the same size as the fresco itself, are done in red, hence they are called *sinopie* (an Italian word derived from ancient Si-nope, in Asia Minor, which was famous as a source of brick-red earth pigment); amazingly free and sweeping, they reveal Traini's personal style more directly than the painted version, which was carried out with the aid of assistants. *Sinopie* also serve to acquaint us with the standard tech-nique of preparing frescoes in the fourteenth century.

Traini still retains a strong link with the great masters of the second quarter of the century. More characteristic of Tuscan painting after the Black Death are the artists who reached maturity around the 1350s. None of them can com-pare with the men whose work we have discussed; their style, in comparison, seems dry and formula-ridden. Yet they were capable, at their best, of expressing the somber mood of the time with memorable intensity. Giovanni da Mi-

497. FRANCESCO TRAINI. *The Triumph of Death*
(portion). c. 1325–50. Fresco. Camposanto, Pisa

lano's (doc. 1346–1369) *Pietà* panel of 1365 (fig. 499) has all the emotional appeal of a German *Andachtsbild* (compare fig. 468), although the heritage of Giotto can be clearly felt even here.

North of the Alps

ILLUMINATED MANUSCRIPTS. We are now in a position to turn once more to Gothic painting north of the Alps. What happened there during the latter half of the fourteenth century was determined in large measure by the influence of the great Italians. Some examples of this influence can be found even earlier, such as the *Annunciation* (fig. 500) from the private prayer book—called "book of hours"—illuminated by Jean Pucelle in Paris about 1325–1328 for Jeanne d'Evreux, queen of France. The style of the figures still recalls Master Honoré (see fig. 485) but the architectural interior clearly derives from Duccio (fig. 488). It had taken less than twenty years for the fame of the *Maestà* to spread from Tuscany to the Île-de-France.

In taking over the new picture space, however, Jean Pucelle had to adapt it to the special character of a manuscript page, which lends itself far less readily than a panel to being treated as a "window." The Virgin's chamber no longer fills the entire picture surface; it has become an ethereal cage that floats on the blank parchment background (note the supporting angel on the right) like the rest of the ornamental framework, so that the entire page forms a harmonious

498. FRANCESCO TRAINI. "Sinopia" drawing for the
Triumph of Death (detail). Camposanto, Pisa

499. GIOVANNI DA MILANO. *Pietà*. 1365. Panel,
48 × 22¾". Academy, Florence

rable to the license traditionally claimed by the court jester,
that accounts for the wide appeal of *drôlerie* during the later
Middle Ages.

FRESCOES, PANEL PAINTINGS. As we approach the
middle years of the fourteenth century, Italian influence becomes ever more important in Northern Gothic painting.
Sometimes this influence was transmitted by Italian artists
working on northern soil; an example is Simone Martini
(see page 350). The delightful frescoes with scenes of country life in the Palace of the Popes at Avignon (fig. 501) were
done by one of his Italian followers, who must have been
thoroughly familiar with the pioneer explorers of landscape
and deep space in Sienese painting. His work shows many
of the qualities we recall from the *Good Government* fresco
by Ambrogio Lorenzetti (see fig. 496). Another gateway of
Italian influence was the city of Prague, which in 1347 became the residence of Emperor Charles IV and rapidly developed into an international cultural center second only to
Paris. The *Death of the Virgin* (fig. 502, colorplate 56), by an
unknown Bohemian painter of about 1360, again brings to
mind the achievements of the great Sienese masters, although these were known to our artist only at second or

500. JEAN PUCELLE. *The Annunciation*, from the *Hours of
Jeanne d'Evreux* (slightly enlarged). 1325–28.
The Metropolitan Museum of Art, New York
(The Cloisters Collection, Purchase, 1954)

unit. As we explore the details of this framework, we realize
that most of them have nothing to do with the religious purpose of the manuscript: the kneeling queen inside the initial
D is surely meant to be Jeanne d'Evreux at her devotions,
but who could be the man with the staff next to her? He
seems to be listening to the lute player perched on the ten-
dril above him. The four figures at the bottom of the page are
playing a game of tag outdoors; a rabbit peers from its bur-
row beneath the girl on the left, and among the foliage leading up to the initial we find a monkey and a squirrel.

DRÔLERIE. These fanciful marginal designs—or *drôleries*—are a characteristic feature of Northern Gothic manuscripts. They had originated more than a century before
Jean Pucelle in the regions along the English Channel,
whence they spread to Paris and all the other centers of
Gothic art. Their subject matter encompasses a vast range of
motifs: fantasy, fable, and grotesque humor, as well as
acutely observed scenes of everyday life, appear side by side
with religious themes. The essence of *drôlerie* is its playfulness, which marks it as a special domain where the artist
enjoys almost unlimited freedom. It is this freedom, compa-

501. Italian Follower of SIMONE MARTINI (MATTEO GIOVANNETTI?).
Scenes of Country Life (detail). c. 1345. Fresco. Palace of the Popes, Avignon

third hand. Its glowing richness of color recalls Simone Martini (compare colorplate 54), and the carefully articulated architectural interior betrays its descent from such works as Pietro Lorenzetti's *Birth of the Virgin* (fig. 494), although it lacks the spaciousness of its Italian models. Italian, too, is the vigorous modeling of the heads and the overlapping of the figures, which reinforces the three-dimensional quality of the design but raises the awkward question of what to do with the halos. (Giotto, we will remember, had faced the same problem in his *Madonna Enthroned*; compare fig. 492.) Still, the Bohemian master's picture is not a mere echo of Italian painting. The gestures and facial expressions convey an intensity of emotion that represents the finest heritage of Northern Gothic art. In this respect, our panel is far more akin to the *Death of the Virgin* at Strasbourg Cathedral (fig. 459, colorplate 49) than to any Italian work.

The International Style

Toward the year 1400, the merging of Northern and Italian traditions had given rise to a single dominant style throughout western Europe. This International Style was not confined to painting—we have used the same term for the sculpture of the period—but painters clearly played the main role in its development.

BROEDERLAM. Among the most important was Melchior Broederlam (fl. c. 1387–1409), a Fleming who worked for the court of the duke of Burgundy in Dijon. Figure 503 and colorplate 57, showing the panels of a pair of shutters for an

502. BOHEMIAN MASTER. *Death of the Virgin* (see colorplate 56). Museum of Fine Arts, Boston

503. MELCHIOR BROEDERLAM.
Annunciation and *Visitation*;
Presentation in the Temple and *Flight into Egypt* (see colorplate 57). Museum of Fine Arts, Dijon

altar shrine which he did in 1394–1399, are really two pictures within each frame; the temple of the *Presentation* and the landscape of the *Flight into Egypt* stand abruptly side by side, even though the artist has made a half-hearted effort to persuade us that the landscape extends around the building. Compared to Pietro and Ambrogio Lorenzetti, Broederlam's picture space still strikes us as naïve in many ways—the architecture looks like a doll's house, and the details of the landscape are quite out of scale with the figures. Yet the panels convey a far stronger feeling of depth than we have found in any previous Northern work. The reason for this is the subtlety of the modeling; the softly rounded shapes, the dark, velvety shadows create a sense of light and air that more than makes up for any shortcomings of scale or perspective. The same soft, pictorial quality—a hallmark of the International Style—appears in the ample, loosely draped garments with their fluid curvilinear patterns of folds, which remind us of Sluter and Ghiberti (see figs. 470, 479).

Our panels also exemplify another characteristic of the International Style: its "realism of particulars," the same kind of realism we encountered first in Gothic sculpture (see fig. 463) and somewhat later among the marginal *drôleries* of manuscripts. We find it in the carefully rendered foliage and flowers, in the delightful donkey (obviously drawn from life), and in the rustic figure of St. Joseph, who looks and behaves like a simple peasant and thus helps to emphasize the delicate, aristocratic beauty of the Virgin. It is this painstaking concentration on detail that gives Broederlam's work the flavor of an enlarged miniature rather than of large-scale painting, even though the panels are more than five feet tall.

THE LIMBOURG BROTHERS. That book illumination remained the leading form of painting in northern Europe at the time of the International Style, despite the growing importance of panel painting, is well attested by the miniatures of the *Très Riches Heures du Duc de Berry*. Produced for the brother of the king of France, a man of far from admirable character but the most lavish art patron of his day, this luxurious book of hours represents the most advanced phase of the International Style. The artists were Pol de Limbourg and his two brothers, a group of Flemings who, like Sluter and Broederlam, had settled in France early in the fifteenth century. They must have visited Italy as well, for their work includes a great number of motifs and whole compositions borrowed from the great masters of Tuscany.

The most remarkable pages of the *Très Riches Heures* are those of the calendar, with their elaborate depiction of the life of man and nature throughout the months of the year. Such cycles, originally consisting of twelve single figures each performing an appropriate seasonal activity, had long been an established tradition in medieval art (compare fig. 463). Jean Pucelle had enriched the margins of the calendar pages of his books of hours by emphasizing the changing aspects of nature in addition to the labors of the months. The Limbourg brothers, however, integrated all these elements into a series of panoramas of human life *in* nature. Thus the February miniature (fig. 504), the earliest snow landscape in the history of Western art, gives an enchantingly lyrical account of village life in the dead of winter, with the sheep huddled together in their fold, birds hungrily scratching in the barnyard, and a maid blowing on her frostbitten hands as she hurries to join her companions in the warm cottage (the front wall has been omitted for our benefit), while in the middle distance we see a villager cutting trees for firewood and another driving his laden donkey toward the houses

505. THE LIMBOURG BROTHERS. *October,*
from *Les Très Riches Heures du Duc de Berry* (see colorplate 58)

504. THE LIMBOURG BROTHERS. *February,* from
Les Très Riches Heures du Duc de Berry. 1413–16.
Musée Condé, Chantilly

among the hills. Here the promise of the Broederlam panels has been fulfilled, as it were: landscape, architectural interiors and exteriors are harmoniously united in deep, atmospheric space. Even such intangible, evanescent things as the frozen breath of the maid, the smoke curling from the chimney, and the clouds in the sky have become "paintable."

Our figure 505 and colorplate 58 show the sowing of winter grain during the month of October. It is a bright, sunny day, and the foreground figures—for the first time since classical Antiquity—cast visible shadows on the ground. Once more we marvel at the wealth of realistic detail such as the scarecrow in the middle distance or the footprints of the sower in the soil of the freshly plowed field. That sower is memorable in other ways was well; his tattered clothing, his unhappy mien, go beyond mere description. He is meant to be a pathetic figure, to arouse our awareness of the miserable lot of the peasantry in contrast to the life of the aristocracy, as symbolized by the splendid castle on the far bank of the river. (The castle, we will recall, is a "portrait" of the

506. THE LIMBOURG BROTHERS. *January,* from
Les Très Riches Heures du Duc de Berry

Gothic Louvre, the most lavish structure of its kind at that time; see page 309.)

Several of the calendar pages are devoted to the life of the nobility. The most interesting perhaps is the January picture, the only interior scene of the group, which shows the Duke of Berry at a banquet (fig. 506). He is seated next to a huge fireplace, with a screen to protect him and incidentally to act as a kind of secular halo that sets him off against the multitude of courtiers and attendants. His features, known to us also from other works of the period, have all the distinctive qualities of a fine portrait, but the rest of the crowd— except for the youth and the cleric on the Duke's right— displays an odd lack of individuality. They are all of the same type, in face as well as stature: aristocratic mannequins whose superhuman slenderness brings to mind their feminine counterparts in the fashion magazines of our own day. They are differentiated only by the luxuriance and variety of their clothing. Surely the gulf between them and the melancholy peasant of the October miniature could not have been greater in real life than it appears in these pictures!

507. GENTILE DA FABRIANO. *The
Adoration of the Magi*
(detail; see colorplate 59).
Uffizi Gallery, Florence

508. GENTILE DA FABRIANO. *The Nativity* (predella panel of the altarpiece; see colorplate 59). 1423. 12¼ × 29½". Uffizi Gallery, Florence

GENTILE DA FABRIANO. From the courtly throng of the January page it is but a step to the three Magi and their train in the altarpiece by Gentile da Fabriano (c. 1370–1427), the greatest Italian painter of the International Style (fig. 507, colorplate 59). The costumes here are as colorful, the draperies as ample and softly rounded, as in the North. The Holy Family on the left almost seems in danger of being overwhelmed by the gay and festive pageant pouring down upon it from the hills in the distance. Again we admire the marvelously well-observed animals, which now include not only the familiar ones but hunting leopards, camels, and monkeys (Such creatures were eagerly collected by the princes of the period, many of whom kept private zoos.) The Oriental background of the Magi is further emphasized by the Mongolian facial cast of some of their companions. It is not these exotic touches, however, that mark our picture as the work of an Italian master but something else, a greater sense of weight, of physical substance, than we could hope to find among the Northern representatives of the International Style.

Gentile, despite his love of fine detail, is obviously a painter used to working on a monumental scale, rather than a manuscript illuminator at heart. Yet he, too, had command of the delicate pictorial effects of a miniaturist, as we see on turning to the small panels decorating the base, or predella, of his altarpiece. In the *Nativity* (fig. 508) the new awareness of light that we first observed in the October page of the *Très Riches Heures*—light as an independent factor, separate from form and color—dominates the entire picture. Even though the main sources of illumination are the divine radiance of the newborn Child ("the light of the world") and of the angel bringing the glad tidings to the shepherds in the fields, their effect is as natural—note the strong cast shadows—as if the Virgin were kneeling by a campfire. The poetic intimacy of this night scene opens up a whole new world of artistic possibilities, possibilities that were not to be fully explored until two centuries later.

ILLUSTRATED TIME CHART II

POLITICAL HISTORY, RELIGION   LITERATURE, SCIENCE, TECHNOLOGY

600

Golden Age of Ireland, 600–800
Mohammed (570–632)
Omayyad caliphs (Damascus) 661–750
Moslems invade Spain 711–718; defeated
  by Franks, battle of Tours 732
Abbasid caliphate (Baghdad) begins 750
St. Boniface (died 755) converts Germans
Pepin the Short crowned king of Franks
  by St. Boniface 751; conquers Ravenna
  and donates it to papacy 756
Moslem state established in Spain 756
Viking invasions begin 794

Stirrup introduced into Western Europe c. 600
Earliest cast iron in China
Porcelain invented in China c. 700
Paper-making introduced into Near East
  from China
Isidore of Seville, encyclopedist (died 636)
The Venerable Bede, English historian
  (673–735)
Beowulf epic, England, early 8th cent.

Sigvald relief, Cividale Cathedral

800

Charlemagne (r. 768–814) crowned Holy
  Roman Emperor by Pope 800; empire
  extends from northern Spain to western
  Germany and northern Italy
Treaty of Verdun 843, split of Carolingian
  empire: France, Germany, Lorraine
Rhabanus Maurus, German encyclopedist
  (784–856)
Alfred the Great (r. 871–899?), Anglo-
  Saxon king of England, defeats Danish
  invaders

Earliest version of *1001 Nights*, Arabian stories
Earliest documented church organ, Aachen 822
Carolingian revival of Latin classics
Earliest printed book, China, 868
Horse collar adopted in Western Europe
  makes horses efficient draft animals
Vikings discover Iceland 860

Palace Chapel of Charlemagne, Aachen

Oseberg ship-burial

900

Monastic order of Cluny founded 910
Normandy awarded to Vikings by king of
  France 911
Otto I (the Great) crowned Holy Roman
  Emperor by Pope 962
Otto II (r. 973–983) defeated by Moslems
  in southern Italy
Ethelred the Unready (r. 978–1016) buys
  off Danish invaders of England
Hugh Capet (r. 987–996) founds Cape-
  tian dynasty in France

Earliest documented use of windmills, in
  Near East
Earliest application of water power to in-
  dustry
Vikings discover Greenland c. 980

1000

Bishop Bernward of Hildesheim (r. 993–
  1022)
Normans arrive in Italy 1016; conquer
  Bari, last Byzantine stronghold, 1071;
  Sicily 1072–92
Reconquest of Spain from Moslems be-
  gins 1085
William the Conqueror (Norman) defeats
  English king Harold at Battle of Has-
  tings 1066
First Crusade 1095–99 takes Jerusalem
Cistercian order founded 1098; St. Ber-
  nard of Clairvaux (1090–1153) becomes
  principal abbot

Leif Ericson sails to North America 1002
Avicenna (980–1037), chief medical au-
  thority in Middle Ages
Hariri, Arabic writer (1054–1121)
Omar Khayyam, Persian poet (fl. c. 1100)
Chanson de Roland, French epic c. 1098

Gospel Book of Otto III

Bayeux Tapestry

1100

—— 600

Lindisfarne Gospels

Sutton Hoo ship-burial treasure
Lindisfarne Gospels
Echternach Gospels
Sigvald relief, Cividale Cathedral
Palace at Mshatta, Jordan
Mosaic, Great Mosque, Damascus
Mosque at Cordova
Abbey Church of St.-Riquier

Sutton Hoo ship-burial treasure

—— 800

Mosque of Mutawakkil, Samarra, Iraq

Palace Chapel of Charlemagne, Aachen
Gospel Book of Charlemagne
Gospel Book of Ebbo of Reims
Utrecht Psalter
Monastery plan, St. Gall
Oseberg ship-burial
Mosque of Mutawakkil, Samarra, Iraq
Crucifixion relief, cover of *Lindau Gospels*

Monastery plan, St. Gall

—— 900

St. Pantaleon, Cologne

Gero Crucifix, Cologne Cathedral
St. Pantaleon, Cologne

Gero Crucifix, Cologne Cathedral

—— 1000

Baptistery, Florence

Gospel Book of Otto III
St. Michael's, Hildesheim
Bronze doors of Bernward, Hildesheim
Gospel Book of Corbie
Speyer Cathedral
Pisa Cathedral, Baptistery, Bell Tower
Baptistery, Florence
St.-Etienne, Caen
Bayeux Tapestry
St.-Sernin, Toulouse, and *Apostle*
S. Ambrogio, Milan
Durham Cathedral

St.-Sernin, Toulouse

—— 1100

Mediterranean made safe for commerce
  by Italian naval supremacy over Moslems
Knights Hospitalers founded 1113; Tem-
  plars 1118; Teutonic Knights 1190
Rivalry of Guelfs (Duke Henry the Lion)
  and Hohenstaufen emperors in Germany
Norman Kingdom of Naples and Sicily 1139–1373
Louis the Fat of France (died 1137)
  strengthens monarchy
Portugal becomes independent 1143
Frederick I Barbarossa (r. 1155–90) titles himself
  "Holy Roman Emperor," tries to dominate Italy
King Henry II founds Plantagenet line 1154

Rise of universities (Bologna, Paris, Oxford); faculties of law, medicine, theology
Peter Abelard, French philosopher and
  teacher (1079–1142)
Geoffrey of Monmouth, English historian
  (died 1154)
Crossbow gains in use over bow and arrow
St. Bernard denounces sculpture in
  churches 1127
Flowering of French vernacular literature
  (epics, fables, chansons); troubadours
Mined coal supplements charcoal as fuel
Earliest use of magnetic compass for navigation
Earliest documented windmill in Europe
  1180

Lion monument, Brunswick

Tympanum, center portal, Vézelay

1200

Fourth Crusade (1202–4) conquers Constantinople
St. Dominic (1170–1221) founds Dominican order; Inquisition established to
  combat heresy
St. Francis of Assisi (died 1226) founds
  Franciscan order
Emperor Frederick II (1194–1250) ne-
  glects Germany, resides at Palermo
Magna Carta limits power of English
  kings 1215
King Louis IX (St. Louis, r. 1226–70)
  leads Seventh and Eighth Crusades

Nibelung, German epic c. 1205; minne-
  singers
Golden Legend by Jacobus de Voragine
  written 1266–83
St. Thomas Aquinas, Italian scholastic
  philosopher (died 1274)
Albertus Magnus, scholastic philosopher
  (1193–1280)
Roger Bacon, English philosopher and
  scientist (Franciscan) (1214–1292)
Dante Alighieri (1265–1321), *Divine
  Comedy* in Italian vernacular

Sketchbook, Villard de Honnecourt

Madonna Enthroned, by Cimabue

Interior west wall sculpture, Reims Cathedral

Mongol invasion of Russia 1237
Teutonic Knights colonize Prussia
Edward I (r. 1272–1307) conquers Wales
Philip IV (the Fair, r. 1285–1314), king
  of France, humiliates Pope Boniface
  VI 1303
Moslems reconquer Acre, last Christian
  stronghold in Holy Land, 1291

Marco Polo travels to China and India
  c. 1275–93
Arabic (actually Indian) numerals introduced in Europe
Spectacles invented c. 1286
First documented use of spinning wheel
  in Europe 1298, replaces distaff and
  spindle

1300

Nave vault murals, St.-Savin-sur-
  Gartempe
South Portal, Moissac
Notre-Dame-la-Grande, Poitiers
Font, St.-Barthélemy, Liège, by Renier
  of Huy
Tournai Cathedral
Tympanum, center portal, Vézelay
Last Judgment tympanum, Autun
Coronation Cloak of German Emperors
Abbey Church of St.-Denis, Paris
Gospel Book of Wedricus
Portal sculpture, St.-Gilles-du-Gard
West portals, Chartres Cathedral
Notre-Dame, Paris
Lion monument, Brunswick
Klosterneuburg altar, by Nicholas of
  Verdun
Façade sculpture, Fidenza Cathedral, by
  Antelami
Chartres Cathedral (rebuilding after fire)
Abbey Church, Fossanova (Cistercian)

West portals, Chartres Cathedral

Notre-Dame, Paris

Stained glass, Chartres Cathedral
Carmina Burana manuscript, Munich
Transept portals, Chartres Cathedral
Stained glass, Bourges Cathedral
South transept portal, Strasbourg Cathe-
  dral
Amiens Cathedral
Salisbury Cathedral
Illustrated Arabic *Dioscorides*
Reims Cathedral
Tomb of a Knight, Dorchester Abbey
Sketchbook, Villard de Honnecourt
Choir screen and "portraits," Naumburg
  Cathedral
Interior west wall sculpture, Reims Cathe-
  dral
Pulpit, Baptistery, Pisa, by Nicola Pisano
Psalter of St. Louis
St.-Urbain, Troyes
Madonna Enthroned, by Cimabue
Prayer Book of Philip the Fair, by Master
  Honoré
Sta. Croce, Florence
Florence Cathedral
Palazzo Vecchio, Florence

Choir screen and "portraits,"
Naumburg Cathedral

Stained glass, Bourges Cathedral

Florence Cathedral

Time Chart II 363

POLITICAL HISTORY, RELIGION	LITERATURE, SCIENCE, TECHNOLOGY	PAINTING, SCULPTURE, ARCHITECTURE

1300

Exile of papacy in Avignon 1309–76
Hundred Years' War between England and France begins 1337
Black Death throughout Europe 1347–50
Jacquerie (peasant) revolt in France 1358
St. Bridget of Sweden (1303–1373)
Russians defeat Mongols at Kulikovo 1380
Wat Tyler leads peasant uprising in England 1381
John Wycliffe (died 1384) challenges church doctrine; translates Bible into English

First large-scale production of paper in Italy and Germany
Large-scale production of gunpowder; earliest known use of cannon 1326
Earliest cast iron in Europe
Master Eckhart, German mystic (died 1327)
William of Occam, English scholastic philosopher (c. 1300–1349)
Longbow replaces crossbow, Battle of Crécy, 1346
Canterbury Tales by Chaucer c. 1387
Decameron by Boccaccio 1387

Virgin of Paris, Notre Dame
Cathedral pulpit, Pisa, by Giovanni Pisano
Arena Chapel frescoes, Padua, by Giotto
Maestà altar, Siena, by Duccio
Pietà (Andachtsbild), Bonn
Façade sculpture, Orvieto Cathedral
Triumph of Death, Pisa, by Traini
Hours of Jeanne d'Evreux, by Jean Pucelle
Equestrian statue of Can Grande, Verona
Choir, Gloucester Cathedral
Good and Bad Government frescoes, Siena, by Ambrogio Lorenzetti
Country Life fresco, Avignon
Alhambra Palace, Granada
Madrasah of Sultan Hasan, Cairo
Choir, St. Sebald, Nuremberg
Portal of Chartreuse, Dijon, by Claus Sluter; Moses Well
Altar wings, Dijon, by Broederlam

Pietà (Andachtsbild), Bonn *Madonna Enthroned*, by Giotto Choir, Gloucester Cathedral

1400

Teutonic Knights beaten by Poles and Lithuanians at Tannenberg 1410
Jan Huss, Czech reformer, burned at stake for heresy 1415
Great Papal Schism (since 1378) settled by election of Martin V at Council of Constance 1417; Pope returns to Rome

Gutenberg invents printing with movable type 1446–50
Earliest account of sea quadrant in navigation 1456

Competition relief for Baptistery doors, Florence
Très Riches Heures du Duc de Berry, by Limbourg brothers
Ca' d'Oro, Venice
Adoration of the Magi altar, by Gentile da Fabriano
St.-Maclou, Rouen
House of Jacques Coeur, Bourges
Chapel of Henry VII, Westminster Abbey

Adoration of the Magi altar, by Gentile da Fabriano Ca' d'Oro, Venice

PART THREE

THE

INTRODUCTION

In discussing the transition from classical antiquity to the Middle Ages, we were able to point to a great crisis—the rise of Islam—marking the separation between the two eras. No comparable event sets off the Middle Ages from the Renaissance. The fifteenth and sixteenth centuries, to be sure, witnessed far-reaching developments: the fall of Constantinople and the Turkish conquest of southeastern Europe; the journeys of exploration that led to the founding of overseas empires in the New World, in Africa and Asia, with the subsequent rivalry of Spain and England as the foremost colonial powers; the deep spiritual crisis of Reformation and Counter Reformation.

But none of these events, however vast their effects, can be said to have produced the new era. By the time they happened, the Renaissance was well under way. Thus it is hardly surprising that the causes, the extent, and the significance of the Renaissance have long been a favorite subject of debate among historians, and that their opinions vary like those of the proverbial blind men trying to describe an elephant. Even if we disregard the minority of scholars who would deny the existence of the animal altogether, we are left with an extraordinary diversity of views on the Renaissance. Every branch of historic study has tended to develop its own image of the period. While these images overlap, they do not coincide, so that our concept of the Renaissance may vary as we focus on its fine arts, music, literature, philosophy, politics, economics, or science. Perhaps the only essential point on which most experts agree is that the Renaissance had begun when people realized they were no longer living in the Middle Ages.

This statement is not as simple-minded as it sounds; it brings out the undeniable fact that the Renaissance was the first period in history to be aware of its own existence and to coin a label for itself. (Those who believe that there was no such thing as the Renaissance admit this fact, but claim that the people who thought they were no longer living in the Middle Ages were deluded.) Medieval man did not think he belonged to an age distinct from classical antiquity; the past, to him, consisted simply of "B.C." and "A.D.," the era "under the Law" (that is, of the Old Testament) and the era "of Grace" (that is, after the birth of Christ). From his point of view, then, history was made in Heaven rather than on earth. The Renaissance, by contrast, divided the past not according to the Divine plan of salvation, but on the basis of human achievements. It saw classical antiquity as the era when man had reached the peak of his creative powers, an era brought to a sudden end by the barbarian invasions that destroyed the Roman Empire. During the thousand-year interval of "darkness" which followed, little was accomplished, but now, at last, this "time in-between" or "Middle Age" had been superseded by a revival of all those arts and sciences which flourished in classical antiquity. The present, the "New Age," could thus be fittingly labeled a "rebirth"—*rinascita* in Italian (from the Latin *renasci*, to be reborn), *renaissance* in French and, by adoption, in English.

PETRARCH. The origin of this revolutionary view of history can be traced back to the 1330s in the writings of the Italian poet Francesco Petrarca, the first of the great men who made the Renaissance. Petrarch, as we call him, thought of the new era mainly as a "revival of the classics," limited to the restoration of Latin and Greek to their former purity and the return to the original texts of ancient authors. During the next two centuries, this concept of the rebirth of antiquity grew to embrace almost the entire range of cultural endeavor, including the visual arts. The latter, in fact, came to play a particularly important part in shaping the Renaissance, for reasons that we shall have to explore later.

That the new historic orientation—to which, let us remember, we owe our concepts of the Renaissance, the Middle Ages, and classical antiquity—should have had its

RENAISSANCE

start in the mind of one man is itself a telling comment on the new era. Petrarch's plea for a revival of antiquity is extraordinary not for his veneration of the ancients—classical revivals, we recall, had been far from unknown in the Middle Ages—but, rather, for the outlook, strangely modern for his time, that underlies his plea, revealing him to be both an individualist and a humanist. Individualism—a new self-awareness and self-assurance—enabled him to proclaim, against all established authority, his own conviction that the "age of faith" was actually an era of darkness, while the "benighted pagans" of antiquity really represented the most enlightened stage of history. Such readiness to question traditional beliefs and practices was to become profoundly characteristic of the Renaissance as a whole. Humanism, to Petrarch, meant a belief in the importance of what we still call "the humanities" or "humane letters" (rather than Divine letters, or the study of Scripture); that is, the pursuit of learning in languages, literature, history, and philosophy for its own end, in a secular rather than a religious framework. Here again he set a pattern that proved to be most important, for the humanists, the new breed of scholar who followed him, became the intellectual leaders of the Renaissance.

HUMANISM AND ANTIQUITY.   We must not assume, however, that Petrarch and his successors wanted to revive classical antiquity lock, stock, and barrel. By interposing the concept of "a thousand years of darkness" between themselves and the ancients, they acknowledged—unlike the medieval classicists—that the Graeco-Roman world was irretrievably dead. Its glories could be revived only in the mind, by nostalgic and admiring contemplation across the barrier of the "dark ages," by rediscovering the full greatness of ancient achievements in art and thought, and by endeavoring to compete with these achievements on an ideal plane.

The aim of the Renaissance was not to duplicate the works of antiquity but to equal and, if possible, to surpass them. In practice, this meant that the authority granted to the ancient models was far from unlimited. Writers strove to express themselves with Ciceronian eloquence and precision, but not necessarily in Latin. Architects continued to build the churches demanded by Christian ritual, not to duplicate pagan temples; but their churches were designed *all'antica*, "in the manner of the ancients," using an architectural vocabulary based on the study of classical structures. Renaissance physicians admired the anatomical handbooks of the ancients, which they found very much more accurate than those of the Middle Ages, but they discovered discrepancies when they matched the hallowed authority of the classical texts against the direct experience of the dissection table, and learned to rely on the evidence of their own eyes. And the humanists, however great their enthusiasm for classical philosophy, did not become neo-pagans but went to great lengths trying to reconcile the heritage of the ancient thinkers with Christianity.

The men of the Renaissance, then, found themselves in the position of the legendary sorcerer's apprentice who set out to emulate his master's achievements and in the process released far greater energies than he had bargained for. But since their master was dead, rather than merely absent, they had to cope with these unfamiliar powers as best they could, until they became masters in their own right. This process of forced growth was replete with crises and tensions. The Renaissance must have been an uncomfortable, though intensely exciting, time to live in. Yet these very tensions—or so it appears in restrospect—called forth an outpouring of creative energy such as the world had never experienced before. It is a fundamental paradox that the desire to return to the classics, based on a rejection of the Middle Ages, brought to the new era not the rebirth of antiquity but the birth of Modern Man.

THE RENAISSANCE
SITES AND CITIES:
LATE GOTHIC ~ RENAISSANCE ~ MANNERIST ~ BAROQUE

BALTIC SEA

RUSSIA

Berlin

ELBE R.

SAXONY

Naumburg

Nuremberg

Vienna

DANUBE R.

Augsburg

Munich

St. Wolfgang

AUSTRIA

Melk

CARPATHIANS

PRUTH R.

TISZA R.

DANUBE R.

BLACK SEA

ALPS

Verona

Vicenza

Venice

Brescia

Padua

Mantua

PO R.

Parma

Bologna

Ravenna

Rimini

Prato

Urbino

Vinci

Florence

Arezzo

Pisa

ARNO R.

Siena

Perugia

Volterra

TUSCANY

ADRIATIC SEA

APENNINES

Orvieto

UMBRIA

Tiber R.

Rome

APULIA

Naples

ASIA MINOR

AEGEAN SEA

GREECE

Athens

TYRRHENIAN SEA

IONIAN SEA

STRAIT OF MESSINA

Messina

SEA

SICILY

CRETE

N

Miles
0   200

0   km   200

nalacios

1
"LATE GOTHIC" PAINTING, SCULPTURE, AND THE GRAPHIC ARTS

RENAISSANCE vs. "LATE GOTHIC"

As we narrow our focus from the Renaissance as a whole to the Renaissance in the fine arts, we are faced with some questions that are still under debate: When did it start? Did it, like Gothic art, originate in a specific center, or in several places at the same time? Should we think of it as one new, coherent style, or as a new attitude that might be embodied in more than one style? "Renaissance-consciousness," we know, was an Italian idea, and there can be no doubt that Italy played the leading role in the development of Renaissance art, at least until the early sixteenth century.

But when did this development get under way? So far as architecture and sculpture are concerned, modern scholarship agrees with the traditional view, first expressed more than five hundred years ago, that the Renaissance began soon after 1400. For painting, however, an even older tradition claims that the new era began with Giotto, who (as Boccaccio wrote about 1350) "restored to light this art which had been buried for many centuries." We cannot disregard such testimony, yet we hesitate to accept it at face value, for we must then assume that the Renaissance in painting dawned about 1300, a full generation before Petrarch. Nor did Giotto himself reject the past as an age of darkness; after all, the two chief sources of his own style were the Byzantine tradition and the influence of Northern Gothic. The artistic revolution he created from these elements does not necessarily place him in a new era, since revolutionary changes had occurred in medieval art before. Nor is it fair to credit this revolution to him alone, disregarding Duccio and the other great Sienese masters. Petrarch was well aware of the achievements of all these men—he wrote admiringly of both Giotto and Simone Martini—but he never claimed that they had restored to light what had been buried during the centuries of darkness.

BOCCACCIO.   How, then, do we account for Boccaccio's statement about Giotto? We must understand that Boccaccio, an ardent disciple of Petrarch, was chiefly concerned with advancing humanism in literature. In his defense of the status of poetry, he found it useful to draw analogies with painting—had not the ancients themselves proclaimed that the two arts were alike, in Horace's famous dictum, *ut pictura poesis?*—and to cast Giotto in the role of "the Petrarch of painting," taking advantage of his already legendary fame. Boccaccio's view of Giotto as a Renaissance artist is a bit of intellectual strategy, rather than a trustworthy reflection of Giotto's own attitude. Nevertheless, what he has to say interests us because he was the first to apply Petrarch's concept of "revival-after-the-dark-ages" to one of the visual arts (even though he did it somewhat prematurely), and for his way of describing Giotto's achievement. It was he who claimed that Giotto depicted every aspect of nature so truthfully that people often mistook his paintings for reality itself (see page 344). Here he implies that the revival of antiquity means for painters an uncompromising realism. And this, as we shall see, was to become a persistent theme in Renaissance thought, justifying the imitation of nature as part of the great movement "back to the classics" and tending to minimize the possible conflict between these two aims.

Boccaccio, of course, was not in a position to know how many aspects of reality Giotto and his contemporaries had failed to investigate. These aspects, we recall, were explored by the painters of the International Style, although in somewhat tentative fashion.

Flemish Painting

To advance beyond Gothic realism required a second revolution, which began simultaneously and independently in Florence and in the Netherlands, about 1420. We have to think, therefore, of two events, both linked by a common aim—the conquest of the visible world—yet sharply separated in almost every other respect. The Florentine, or Southern, revolution was the more systematic and, in the long run, the more fundamental, since it included architecture and sculpture as well as painting; we call it the Early Renaissance. The same term is not generally applied to the new style that emerged in the North, in Flanders. We have, in fact, no satisfactory name to designate the Northern focus of the revolution, for art historians are still of two minds about its scope and significance in relation to the Renaissance movement as a whole.

"LATE GOTHIC."   The customary label, "Late Gothic" (which we shall use, for the sake of convenience, with quotation marks to indicate its doubtful status), hardly does justice to the special character of Northern fifteenth-century painting. But it has some justification. It indicates, for instance, that the creators of the new style, unlike their Italian contemporaries, did not reject the International Style; rather, they took it as their point of departure, so that the break with the past was less abrupt in the North than in the South. "Late Gothic" also reminds us that fifteenth-century architecture outside Italy remained firmly rooted in the Gothic tradition.

Whatever we choose to call the style of Northern painters of this time, their artistic environment was clearly "Late Gothic" (see pages 312, 353). How could they create a genuinely post-medieval style in such a setting, one wonders; would it not be more reasonable to regard their work, despite its great importance, as the final phase of Gothic painting? If we treat them here as the Northern counterpart of the Early Renaissance, we do so for several reasons. The great Flemish masters whose work we are about to examine had an impact that went far beyond their own region. In Italy they were as admired as the leading Italian artists of the period, and their intense realism had a conspicuous influence on Early Renaissance painting. (The Italians, we will recall, had associated the exact imitation of nature in painting with a "return to the classics.") Italian Renaissance art, in contrast, made very little impression north of the Alps during the fifteenth century.

To Italian eyes, then, "Late Gothic" painting appeared definitely post-medieval. Moreover, the situation of the Flemish painters had a close parallel in the field of music. After about 1420, the Netherlands produced a school of composers so revolutionary as to dominate the development of music throughout Europe for the next hundred years. How much

509. THE MASTER OF FLÉMALLE (ROBERT CAMPIN?). *The Merode Altarpiece* (see colorplate 60).
The Metropolitan Museum of Art, New York (The Cloisters, Purchase, 1957)

the new style of these men was appreciated can be gathered from a contemporary source which states that "nothing worth listening to had been composed before their time." This remark, with its sweeping rejection of the "musical dark ages," links the attitude of the Flemish musicians with Italian "Renaissance-consciousness" (except for the absence of any reference to the revival of antiquity). We have no similar testimony concerning the new style of the Flemish painters, but from what we know of the impact of their work it seems likely that people felt "nothing worth looking at had been painted before their time."

THE MASTER OF FLÉMALLE. The first phase—and perhaps the decisive one—of the pictorial revolution in Flanders is represented by an artist whose name we do not know for certain. We call him the Master of Flémalle (after the fragments of a large altar from Flémalle, now in the Staedel Institute, Frankfurt), although he was probably identical with Robert Campin, the foremost painter of Tournai, whose career we can trace in documents from 1406 to his death in 1444. Among his finest works is the *Merode Altarpiece* (fig. 509, colorplate 60), which he must have done soon after 1425. Comparing it with its nearest relatives, the Franco-Flemish pictures of the International Style (figs. 503–6, colorplates 57, 58), we see that it belongs within that tradition; yet we also recognize in it a new pictorial experience.

Here, for the first time, we have the sensation of actually looking *through* the surface of the panel into a spatial world that has all the essential qualities of everyday reality: unlimited depth, stability, continuity, and completeness. The painters of the International Style, even at their most adventurous,

had never aimed at such consistency; their commitment to reality was far from absolute. The pictures they created have the enchanting quality of fairy tales where the scale and relationship of things can be shifted at will, where fact and fancy mingle without conflict. The Master of Flémalle, in contrast, has undertaken to tell the truth, the whole truth, and nothing but the truth. He does not yet do it with ease—his objects, overly foreshortened, tend to jostle each other in space. With a determination that seems almost obsessive, he endows every last detail with its maximum concreteness by defining every aspect: its individual shape and size; its color, material, surface textures; its degree of rigidity; and its way of responding to illumination. The artist even distinguishes between the diffused light producing soft shadows and delicate gradations of brightness, and the direct light entering through the two round windows; the latter accounts for the twin shadows sharply outlined in the upper part of the center panel, and for the twin reflections on the brass vessel and candlestick.

The *Merode Altarpiece*, in short, transports us with shocking abruptness from the aristocratic world of the International Style to the household of a Flemish burgher. The Master of Flémalle, whether or not we believe him to have been Robert Campin, was not a court painter, but a townsman catering to the tastes of such well-to-do fellow citizens as the two donors piously kneeling outside the Virgin's chamber. Characteristically, this is the earliest Annunciation in panel painting that occurs in a fully equipped domestic interior (for contrast, see figs. 488, 500), as well as the first to honor Joseph, the humble craftsman, by showing him at work next door.

This bold departure from tradition forced upon our artist a problem no one had faced before: how to transfer supernatural events from symbolic settings to an everyday environment, without making them look either trivial or incongruous. He has met this challenge by the method known as "disguised symbolism," which means that almost any detail within the picture, however casual, may carry a symbolic message. Thus the rosebush, the violets and daisies in the left wing, and the lilies in the center panel, are flowers associated with the Virgin, the roses denoting her charity, the violets her humility, and the lilies her chastity; the shiny water basin and the towel on its rack are not merely ordinary household equipment but further tributes to Mary as the "vessel most clean" and the "well of living waters." Perhaps the most intriguing symbol of this sort is the candle next to the vase of lilies. It was extinguished only moments ago, as we can tell from the glowing wick and the curl of smoke. But why, in broad daylight, had it been lit, and what made the flame go out? Has the divine radiance of the Lord's presence overcome the material light? Or did the flame of the candle itself represent the Divine light, now extinguished to show that God has become man, that in Christ "the Word was made flesh"?

Clearly, the entire wealth of medieval symbolism survives in our picture, but it is so completely immersed in the world of everyday appearances that we are often left to doubt whether a given detail demands symbolic interpretation. Observers had long wondered, for instance, about the little boxlike object on Joseph's workbench (and a similar one on the ledge outside the open window), until one scholar proposed to identify them as mousetraps intended to convey a specific theological message: according to St. Augustine, God had to appear on earth in human form so as to fool Satan—"the Cross of the Lord was the devil's mousetrap."

Since explanations of this sort require much scholarly ingenuity, we tend to think of the *Merode Altarpiece* and similar pictures as embodying a special kind of puzzle. And so they often do, to the modern beholder, although they can be enjoyed apart from knowing all their symbolic content. But what about the patrons for whom these works were painted? Did they immediately grasp the meaning of every detail? They would have had no difficulty with such well-established symbols in our picture as the flowers. Let us grant, too, that they probably understood the significance of the water basin. The message of the extinguished candle and the mousetrap could not have been common knowledge even among the well-educated, however; for these two symbols—and from their incongruity we can hardly question that they *are* symbols—make their earliest appearance in the *Merode Altarpiece*. They must be unusual ones, for St. Joseph with the mousetrap has been found in only one other picture, and the recently extinguished candle does not recur elsewhere, so far as we know. Apparently, then, the Master of Flémalle introduced these symbols into the visual arts, yet hardly any artists adopted them despite his vast influence. But if the candle and the mousetrap were difficult to understand even in the fifteenth century, why are they in our picture at all? Did the patron (who may have been exceptionally erudite) tell the artist to put them in? Possibly, if this

were the only case of its kind. Since, however, there are countless instances of equally subtle or obscure symbolism in "Late Gothic" painting, it seems more probable that the initiative came from the artists, rather than from their various patrons.

We have reason to believe, therefore, that the Master of Flémalle was either a man of unusual learning himself, or had contact with the theologians and other scholars who could supply him with the references that suggested the symbolic meanings of things like the extinguished candle and the mousetrap. In other words, our artist did not merely continue the symbolic tradition of medieval art within the framework of the new realistic style; he expanded and enriched it by his own efforts. But why, we wonder, did he pursue simultaneously what we are accustomed to regard as two opposite goals, realism and symbolism? To him, apparently, the two were interdependent, rather than in conflict. We might say that he needed a growing symbolic repertory because it encouraged him to explore features of the visible world never represented before (such as a candle immediately after it has been blown out, or the interior of a carpenter's shop, needed as the setting for the mousetraps). For him to paint everyday reality, he had to "sanctify" it with a maximum of spiritual significance.

This deeply reverential attitude toward the physical universe as a mirror of Divine truths helps us to understand why in the Merode panels the smallest and least conspicuous details are rendered with the same concentrated attention as the sacred figures; potentially at least, everything is a symbol and thus merits an equally exacting scrutiny. The disguised symbolism of the Master of Flémalle and his successors was not an external device grafted onto the new realistic style, but ingrained in the creative process. Their Italian contemporaries must have sensed this, for they praised both the miraculous realism and the "piety" of the Flemish masters.

If we compare our colorplate of the *Merode Annunciation* with those of earlier panel paintings (colorplates 54, 56, 57, 59), we see vividly that, all other differences aside, its distinctive tonality makes the Master of Flémalle's picture stand out among the rest. The jewel-like brightness of the older works, their patterns of brilliant hues and lavish use of gold, have given way to a color scheme far less decorative but much more flexible and differentiated. The subdued tints—muted greens, bluish or brownish grays—show a new subtlety, and the scale of intermediate shades is smoother and has a wider range. All these effects are essential to the realistic style of the Master of Flémalle; they were made possible by the use of oil, the medium he was among the first to exploit.

TEMPERA AND OIL TECHNIQUES. The basic technique of medieval panel painting had been tempera, in which the finely ground pigments were mixed ("tempered") with diluted egg yolk. It produced a thin, tough, quick-drying coat admirably suited to the medieval taste for high-keyed, flat color surfaces. However, in tempera the different tones on the panel cannot be smoothly blended, and the continuous progression of values necessary for three-dimensional effects was difficult to achieve; also, the darks tended to look muddy and undifferentiated. For the Master of Flémalle these were serious drawbacks, which he overcame by substituting oil for the water-and-egg-yolk mixture. In a purely material sense oil was not unfamiliar to medieval artists, but it had been used only for special purposes, such as the coating of stone surfaces or painting on metal. It was the Master of Flémalle and his contemporaries who discovered its artistic possibilities. Oil, a viscous, slow-drying medium, could produce a vast variety of effects, from thin, translucent films (called "glazes") to the thickest impasto (that is, a thick layer of creamy, heavy-bodied paint); the tones could also yield a continuous scale of hues, including rich, velvety dark shades previously unknown. Without oil, the Flemish masters' conquest of visible reality would have been much more limited. Thus, from the technical point of view, too, they deserve to be called the "fathers of modern painting," for oil has been the painter's basic medium ever since.

JAN (AND HUBERT) VAN EYCK.   Needless to say, the full range of effects made possible by oil was not discovered all at once, nor by any one man. The Master of Flémalle contributed less than Jan van Eyck, a somewhat younger and very much more famous artist, who was long credited with the actual "invention" of oil painting. About Jan's life and career we know a good deal; born about 1390, he worked in Holland from 1422 to 1424, in Lille from 1425 to 1429, and thereafter in Bruges, where he died in 1441. He was both a townsman and a court painter, highly esteemed by Duke Philip the Good of Burgundy, who occasionally sent him on confidential diplomatic errands. After 1432, we can follow Jan's career through a number of signed and dated pictures. The inscription on the frame of the great *Ghent Altarpiece* (figs. 512–14) tells us that he completed it in that year, after it had been begun by his older brother, Hubert, who died in 1426.

Jan's earlier development, however, remains disputed; there are several "Eyckian" works, obviously older than the *Ghent Altarpiece*, that may have been painted by either of the two brothers. The most fascinating of these is a pair of panels showing the Crucifixion and the Last Judgment (figs. 510, 511, colorplate 61). Scholars agree that their date is between 1420 and 1425, whichever brother, Jan or Hubert, was the author.

The style of the two panels has many qualities in common with that of the *Merode Altarpiece*—the all-embracing devotion to the visible world, the unlimited depth of space, the angular drapery folds, less graceful but far more realistic than the unbroken loops of the International Style. At the same time, however, the individual forms are not starkly tangible, like those characteristic of the Master of Flémalle, and seem less isolated, less "sculptural"; the sweeping sense of space is the result not so much of violent foreshortening as of subtle changes of light and color. If we inspect the *Crucifixion* panel slowly, from the foreground figures to the far-off city of Jerusalem and the snow-capped peaks beyond, we see a gradual decrease in the intensity of local colors and in the contrast of light and dark. Everything tends toward a uniform tint of light bluish gray, so that the farthest moun-

510. HUBERT and/or JAN VAN EYCK. *The Crucifixion* (see colorplate 61). The Metropolitan Museum of Art, New York (Fletcher Fund, 1933)

511. HUBERT and/or JAN VAN EYCK. *The Last Judgment* (see colorplate 61). The Metropolitan Museum of Art, New York (Fletcher Fund, 1933)

tain range merges imperceptibly with the color of the sky.

This optical phenomenon, which the Van Eycks were the first to utilize fully and systematically (the Limbourg brothers had already been aware of it, as is seen in fig. 504), is known as "atmospheric perspective," since it results from the fact that the atmosphere is never wholly transparent. Even on the clearest day, the air between us and the things we are looking at acts as a hazy screen that interferes with our ability to see distant shapes clearly; as we approach the limit of visibility, it swallows them altogether. Atmospheric perspective is more fundamental to our perception of deep space than linear perspective, which records the diminution in the apparent size of objects as their distance from the observer increases. It is effective not only in faraway vistas; in our *Crucifixion* panel even the foreground seems enveloped in a delicate haze that softens contours, shadows, and colors, and thus the entire scene has a continuity and harmony quite beyond the pictorial range of the Master of Flémalle. How did the Van Eycks accomplish this effect? Their exact technical procedure is difficult to reconstruct, but there can be no question that they used the oil medium with extraordinary refinement. By alternating opaque and translucent layers of pigment, they were able to impart to their pictures a soft, glowing radiance of tone that has never been equaled, probably because it depends fully as much on their individual sensibilities as it does on their skillful craftsmanship.

Viewed as a whole, the *Crucifixion* seems singularly devoid of drama, as if the scene had been gently becalmed by some magic spell. Only when we concentrate on the details do we become aware of the violent emotions in the faces of the crowd beneath the cross, and the restrained but profoundly touching grief of the Virgin Mary and her companions in the foreground. In the *Last Judgment* panel, this dual aspect of the Eyckian style takes the form of two extremes: above the horizon, all is order, symmetry, and calm, while below it—on earth and in the subterranean realm of Satan—the opposite condition prevails. The two states thus correspond to Heaven and Hell, contemplative bliss as against physical and emotional turbulence. The lower half, clearly, was the greater challenge to the artist's imaginative powers. The dead rising from their graves with frantic gestures of fear and hope, the damned being torn apart by

devilish monsters more frightful than any we have seen before, all have the awesome reality of a nightmare, but a nightmare "observed" with the same infinite care as the natural world of the *Crucifixion* panel.

The *Ghent Altarpiece* (figs. 512–14), the greatest monument of early Flemish painting, presents problems so complex that our discussion must be limited to bare essentials. We have already mentioned the inscription informing us that the work, begun by Hubert, was completed by Jan in 1432. Since Hubert died in 1426, the altarpiece was presumably made in the seven-year span between 1425 and 1432. We may expect it, therefore, to introduce to us the next phase of the new style, following that of the pictures we have discussed so far. Although its basic form is a triptych—a central body with two hinged wings—each of the three units consists of four separate panels, and since, in addition, the wings are painted on both sides, the altarpiece has a total of twenty component parts of assorted shapes and sizes. The ensemble makes what has rightly been called a "super-altar," overwhelming but far from harmonious, which could not have been planned this way from the start. Apparently Jan took over a number of panels left unfinished by Hubert,

512. HUBERT and JAN VAN EYCK. *The Ghent Altarpiece* (open). Completed 1432. Panel, 11′ 3″ × 14′ 5″. St. Bavo, Ghent

513. *Adam* and *Eve*, details of *The Ghent Altarpiece*,
left and right wings

514. *The Ghent Altarpiece* (closed)

completed them, added some of his own, and assembled them at the behest of the wealthy donor whose portrait we see on the outside of the altar.

To reconstruct this train of events, and to determine each brother's share, is a fascinating but treacherous game. Suffice it to say that Hubert remains a somewhat shadowy figure; his style, overlaid with retouches by Jan, can probably be found in the four central panels, although these did not belong together originally. The upper three, whose huge figures in the final arrangement crush the multitude of small ones below, were intended, it seems, to form a self-contained triptych: the Lord between the Virgin Mary and St. John the Baptist. The lower panel and the four flanking it probably formed a separate altarpiece, the Adoration of the Lamb, symbolizing Christ's sacrificial death. The two panels with music-making angels may have been planned by Hubert as a pair of organ shutters.

If this set of conjectures is correct, the two tall, narrow panels showing Adam and Eve (fig. 513) are the only ones added by Jan to Hubert's stock. They certainly are the most daring of all: the earliest monumental nudes of Northern panel painting (hardly less than lifesize), magnificently observed, and caressed by the most delicate play of light and shade. Their quiet dignity—and their prominent place in the altar—suggests that they should remind us not so much of Original Sin, as of man's creation in God's own image. Actual evil, by contrast, is represented in the small, violently expressive scenes above, which show the story of Cain and Abel. Still more extraordinary, however, is the fact that the Adam and Eve were designed specifically for their present positions in the ensemble. Acknowledging that they would really appear this way to the spectator whose eye-level is below the bottom of the panels, Jan van Eyck has depicted them in accordance with this abnormal viewpoint and thereby established a new, direct relationship between picture space and real space.

The outer surfaces of the two wings (fig. 514) were evidently planned by Jan as one coherent unit. Here, as we would normally expect, the largest figures are not above, but in the lower tier. The two St. Johns (painted in grays to simulate sculpture, like the scenes of Cain and Abel), the donor, and his wife, each in a separate niche, are the immediate kin of the Adam and Eve panels. The upper tier has two pairs of panels of different width; the artist has made a virtue of this awkward necessity by combining all four into one interior. Such an effect, we recall, had first been created almost a century earlier (compare fig. 494), but Jan, not content with perspective devices alone, heightens the illusion by painting the shadows cast by the frames of the panels on the floor of the Virgin's chamber. Interestingly enough, this *Annunciation* resembles, in its homely detail, the *Merode Altarpiece*, thus providing a valuable link between the two great pioneers of Flemish realism.

Donors' portraits of splendid individuality occupy conspicuous positions in both the Merode and the Ghent altarpieces. A renewed interest in realistic portraiture had developed in the mid-fourteenth century, but until about 1420 its best achievements had been in sculpture (see fig. 469), the painters usually confining themselves to silhouette-like profile views (such as the portrait of the duke of Berry in fig. 506). Not until the Master of Flémalle, the first artist since antiquity to have real command of a close-range view of the human face from a three-quarter angle, did the portrait play a major role in Northern painting.

In addition to donors' portraits, we now begin to encounter in growing numbers small, independent likenesses whose peculiar intimacy suggests that they were treasured keepsakes, pictorial substitutes for the real presence of the sitter. One of the most fascinating is Jan van Eyck's *Man in a Red Turban* of 1433 (fig. 515), which may well be a self-portrait—the slight strain about the eyes seems to come from gazing into a mirror. The sitter is bathed in the same gentle, clear light as the Adam and Eve of the *Ghent Altarpiece;* every detail of shape and texture has been recorded with almost microscopic precision. Jan does not suppress the sitter's personality, yet this face, like all of Jan's portraits, remains a psychological puzzle. It might be described as "even-tempered" in the most exact sense of the term, its character traits balanced against each other so perfectly that none can assert itself at the expense of the rest. As Jan was fully capable of expressing emotion (we need only recall the faces of the crowd in the *Crucifixion,* or the scenes of Cain and Abel in the *Ghent Altarpiece*), the stoic calm of his portraits surely reflects his conscious ideal of human character rather than his indifference or lack of insight.

The Flemish cities where the new style of painting flourished—Tournai, Ghent, Bruges—rivaled those of Italy as centers of international banking and trade. Their foreign residents included many Italian businessmen. For one of these, perhaps a member of the Arnolfini family, Jan van Eyck painted his remarkable *Wedding Portrait*, one of the major masterpieces of the period (fig. 516, colorplate 62). The young couple is solemnly exchanging marriage vows in the privacy of the bridal chamber. They seem to be quite alone, but as we scrutinize the mirror, conspicuously placed

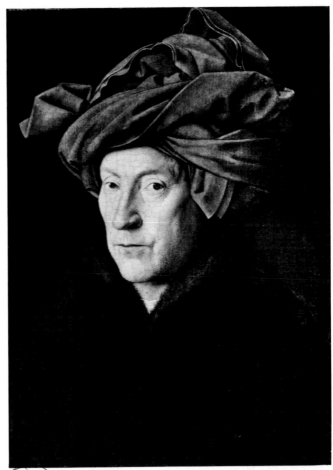

515. JAN VAN EYCK. *A Man in a Red Turban (Self-portrait?).* 1433. Panel, 10¼ × 7½". The National Gallery, London

516. JAN VAN EYCK. *Wedding Portrait* (detail; see colorplate 62). The National Gallery, London

behind them, we discover in the reflection that two other persons have entered the room. One of them must be the artist, since the words above the mirror, in florid legal lettering, tell us that "Johannes de eyck fuit hic" (Jan van Eyck was here) in the year 1434.

Jan's role, then, is that of a witness; the picture purports to show exactly what he saw and has the function of a pictorial marriage certificate. Yet the domestic setting, however persuasively realistic, is replete with disguised symbolism of the most subtle kind, conveying the sacramental nature of marriage. The single candle in the chandelier, burning in broad daylight, stands for the all-seeing Christ (note the Passion scenes of the mirror frame); the shoes which the couple has taken off remind us that they are standing on "holy ground" (for the origin of the theme, see page 56); even the little dog is an emblem of marital faith, and the furnishings of the room invite similar interpretation. The natural world, as in the *Merode Altarpiece*, is made to contain the world of the spirit in such a way that the two actually become one.

ROGIER VAN DER WEYDEN. In the work of Jan van Eyck, the exploration of the reality made visible by light and color had reached a limit that was not to be surpassed for another two centuries. Rogier van der Weyden (1399/1400–1464), the third great master of early Flemish painting, set himself a different though equally important task: to recapture, within the framework of the new style created by his predecessors, the emotional drama, the *pathos*, of the Gothic past. We can see this immediately in his early masterpiece, *The Descent from the Cross* (fig. 517, colorplate 63), which dates from about 1435, when the artist was in his mid-thirties. Here the modeling is sculpturally precise, with its brittle, angular drapery folds recalling the Master of Flémalle; and the soft half-shadows and rich, glowing colors show his knowledge of Jan van Eyck. Yet Rogier is far more than a mere follower of the two older men; whatever he owes to them—and it is obviously a great deal—he uses for ends which are not theirs but his. The outward events (in this case, the lowering of Christ's body from the cross) concern him less than the world of human feeling; this *Descent*, judged for its expressive content, could well be called a *Lamentation*.

The artistic ancestry of these grief-stricken gestures and faces is in sculpture rather than in painting—from the Strasbourg *Death of the Virgin* (fig. 459, colorplate 49) and the Naumburg *Crucifixion* (fig. 465), to the Bonn *Pietà* (fig. 468) and Claus Sluter's *Moses Well* (fig. 470). It seems peculiarly fitting, therefore, that Rogier should have staged his scene in a shallow architectural niche or shrine, as if his figures were colored statues, not seen against a landscape background. This bold device gave him a double advantage in heightening the effect of this tragic event: it focused the beholder's entire attention on the foreground, and allowed him to mold the figures into a coherent, formal group. No wonder that Rogier's art, which has been well described as "at once physically barer and spiritually richer than Jan van Eyck's," set an example for countless other artists. When he died in 1464, after thirty years of unceasing activity as the

517. ROGIER VAN DER WEYDEN.
Descent from the Cross (detail; see colorplate 63).
The Prado, Madrid

518. ROGIER VAN DER WEYDEN.
Francesco d'Este. c. 1455 Panel, 11¾ × 8".
The Metropolitan Museum of Art, New York
(The Michael Friedsam Collection, 1931)

519. HUGO VAN DER GOES. *The Portinari Altarpiece* (open). c. 1476. Panel, center 8′ 3½″ × 10′,
wings 8′ 3½″ × 4′ 7½″ each. Uffizi Gallery, Florence

520. *The Portinari Altarpiece*, detail of center panel

foremost painter of Brussels, his influence was supreme in European painting north of the Alps. Its echoes continued to be discernible almost everywhere outside Italy until the end of the century, such was the authority of his style.

What is true of Rogier's religious works applies equally well to his portraits. The likeness of Francesco d'Este (fig. 518), an Italian nobleman resident at the Burgundian court, may strike us as less lifelike than Jan van Eyck's. Modeling is reduced to a minimum; much descriptive detail has been simplified or omitted altogether; the gracefully elongated forms of the body render an aristocratic ideal rather than the sitter's individual appearance. Yet this face, compared with that of the *Man in a Red Turban* (fig. 515), conveys a more vivid sense of character. Instead of striving for the psychologically "neutral" calm of Jan's portraits, Rogier interprets the human personality by suppressing some traits and emphasizing others. In consequence, he tells us more about the inner life of his sitters, less about their outward appearance.

HUGO VAN DER GOES.   Among the artists who followed Rogier van der Weyden, few succeeded in escaping from the great master's shadow. The most dynamic of these was Hugo van der Goes (c. 1440–1482), an unhappy genius whose tragic end suggests an unstable personality peculiarly interesting to us today. After a spectacular rise to fame in the cosmopolitan atmosphere of Bruges, he decided in 1478, when he was near forty years of age, to enter a mónastery as a lay brother; for some time he continued to paint, but increasing fits of depression drove him to the verge of suicide, and four years later he was dead.

Hugo van der Goes' most ambitious work, the huge altarpiece he completed about 1476 for Tommaso Portinari, is an awesome achievement (figs. 519, 520). While we need not search it for hints of Hugo's future mental illness, it nonetheless evokes a tense, explosive personality. Or is there no strain between the artist's devotion to the natural world (the wonderfully spacious and atmospheric landscape setting, and the wealth of precise realistic detail) and his concern with the supernatural? In the wings, for instance, the kneeling members of the Portinari family are dwarfed by their patron saints, whose gigantic size characterizes them as being of a higher order, like Joseph, the Virgin Mary, and the shepherds of the *Nativity* in the center panel, who share the same huge scale. But these latter figures are not meant to be "larger-than-life," for their height is normal in relation to the architecture and to the ox and ass; the angels, which are drawn to the same scale as the donors, thus appear abnormally small.

This variation of scale, although its symbolic and expressive purpose is clear, stands outside the logic of everyday experience affirmed in the environment the artist has provided for his figures. There is another striking contrast between the frantic excitement of the shepherds (fig. 520) and the ritual solemnity of all the other figures. These field hands, gazing in breathless wonder at the newborn Child,

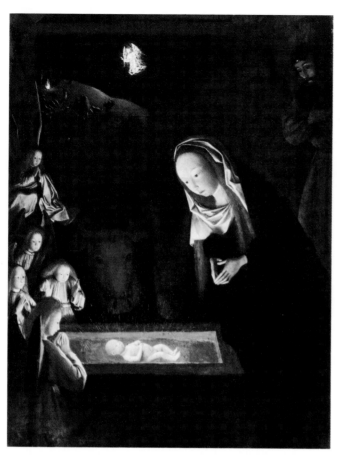

521. GEERTGEN TOT SINT JANS. *The Nativity.* c. 1490.
Panel, 13½ × 10″. The National Gallery, London

react to the dramatic miracle of the Nativity with a wide-eyed directness never attempted before. They aroused particular admiration in the Italian painters who saw the work after it arrived in Florence in 1483.

GEERTGEN TOT SINT JANS.   During the last quarter of the fifteenth century there were no painters in Flanders comparable to Hugo van der Goes, and the most original artists appeared further north, in Holland. To one of these, Geertgen tot Sint Jans of Haarlem, who died about 1495, we owe the enchanting *Nativity* reproduced in figure 521, a picture as daring, in its quiet way, as the center panel of the *Portinari Altarpiece.* The idea of a nocturnal Nativity, illuminated mainly by radiance from the Christ Child, goes back to the International Style (see fig. 508), but Geertgen, applying the pictorial discoveries of Jan van Eyck, gives new, intense reality to the theme. The magic effect of his little panel is greatly enhanced by the smooth, simplified shapes that record the impact of light with striking clarity; the manger is a rectangular trough; the heads of the angels, the Infant, and the Virgin are all as round as objects turned on a lathe.

BOSCH.   If Geertgen's uncluttered, "abstract" forms attract us specially today, another Dutch artist, Hieronymus Bosch, appeals to our interest in the world of dreams. Little is known about Bosch except that he spent his life in the provincial town of 's Hertogenbosch and that he died, an old man, in 1516. His work, full of weird and seemingly irrational imagery, has proved so difficult to interpret that much of

522. HIERONYMUS BOSCH. *The Garden of Delights.* c. 1500. Panel, center 86½ × 76¾″,
wings 86½ × 38″ each. The Prado, Madrid (see detail, colorplate 64)

Colorplate 60. THE MASTER OF FLÉMALLE (ROBERT CAMPIN?). *The Annunciation*, center panel of the *Merode Altarpiece* (see page 372). About 1425–28. Panel, 25¼ × 24⅞″. The Metropolitan Museum of Art, New York (The Cloisters Collection, Purchase)

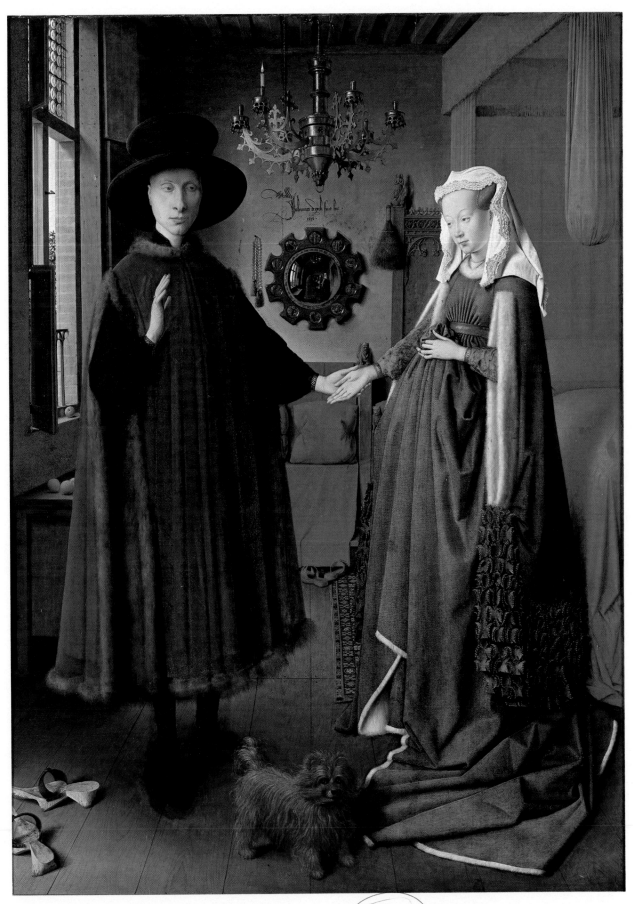

Colorplate 61. (*left*) HUBERT and/or JAN VAN EYCK.
The Crucifixion; The Last Judgment (see page 374).
About 1420–25. Canvas, transferred from panel, each panel
22¼ × 7¾". The Metropolitan Museum of Art, New York
(Fletcher Fund, 1933)

Colorplate 62. (*above*) JAN VAN EYCK. *Wedding Portrait*
(see page 377). 1434. Panel, 33 × 22½".
The National Gallery, London

523. HIERONYMUS BOSCH. *The Garden of Delights*, detail of right wing

it, despite the remarkable insights contributed by recent research, remains unsolved.

We can readily understand this problem when we study the triptych known as *The Garden of Delights* (figs. 522, 523, colorplate 64), the richest and most puzzling of Bosch's pictures. Of the three panels, only the left one has a clearly recognizable subject: the Garden of Eden, wherein the Lord introduces Adam to the newly created Eve. The landscape, almost Eyckian in its airy vastness, is filled with animals, among them such exotic creatures as an elephant and a giraffe, and also hybrid monsters of odd and sinister kinds. Behind them, the distant rock formations are equally strange. The right wing, a nightmarish scene of burning ruins and fantastic instruments of torture, surely represents Hell. But what of the center?

Here we see a landscape much like that of the Garden of Eden, populated with countless nude men and women performing a variety of peculiar actions: in the center, they parade around a circular basin on the backs of all sorts of beasts; many disport themselves in pools of water; most of them are closely linked with enormous birds, fruit, flowers, or marine animals. Only a few are openly engaged in love-making, yet there can be no doubt that the delights in this "garden" are those of carnal desire, however oddly disguised. The birds, fruit, etc., are symbols or metaphors which Bosch uses to depict man's life on earth as an unending repetition of the Original Sin of Adam and Eve, whereby we are all doomed to be the prisoners of our appetites. Nowhere does he so much as hint at the possibility of Salvation; corruption, on the animal level at least, had already asserted itself in the Garden of Eden before the Fall, and we are all destined for Hell, the Garden of Satan, with its grisly and refined instruments of torture.

So profound is Bosch's pessimism—if we read the meaning of the triptych correctly—that some scholars have refused to take it at face value; the center panel, they claim, is really an unusual vision of Paradise according to the beliefs of a secret heretical sect to which Bosch supposedly belonged. While their view has few adherents, it does point up the fundamental ambiguity of the *Garden*: there is indeed an innocence, even a haunting poetic beauty, in this panorama of sinful mankind. Consciously, Bosch was a stern moralist who intended his pictures to be visual sermons, every detail packed with didactic meaning. Unconsciously, however, he must have been so enraptured by the sensuous appeal of the world of the flesh that the images he coined with such prodigality tend to celebrate what they are meant to condemn. That, surely, is the reason why *The Garden of Delights* still evokes so strong a response today, even though we no longer understand every word of the sermon.

French, Swiss, and German Painting

We must now glance briefly at fifteenth-century art in the rest of Northern Europe. After about 1430, the new realism of the Flemish masters began to spread into France and Germany until, by the middle of the century, its influence was paramount from Spain to the Baltic. Among the countless artists (many of them still anonymous) who turned out provincial adaptations of Netherlandish painting, only a few were gifted enough to impress us today with a distinctive personality.

WITZ. One of the earliest and most original masters was Conrad Witz of Basel (1400/10–1445/46), whose altarpiece for Geneva Cathedral, painted in 1444, includes the remarkable panel shown in figure 524. To judge from the drapery, with its tubular folds and sharp, angular breaks, he must have had close contact with the Master of Flémalle. But the setting, rather than the figures, attracts our interest, and

524. CONRAD WITZ. *The Miraculous Draught of Fishes.* 1444. Panel, 51 × 61". Museum, Geneva

525. JEAN FOUQUET. *Etienne Chevalier and St. Stephen.*
c. 1450. Panel, 36½ × 33½″. Dahlem Museum, West Berlin

526. JEAN FOUQUET. *Self-Portrait.* c. 1450. Gold and
enamel on copper, diameter 3″. The Louvre, Paris

here the influence of the Van Eycks seems dominant. Witz, however, did not simply follow these great pioneers; an explorer himself, he knew more about the optical appearances of water than any other painter of his time (note especially the bottom of the lake in the foreground). The landscape, too, is an original venture, representing a specific part of the shore of the Lake of Geneva—among the earliest landscape "portraits" that have come down to us.

FOUQUET.   In France, the painter Jean Fouquet (c. 1420–1481), twenty-odd years younger than Witz, had the exceptional fortune, soon after he had completed his training, of a lengthy visit to Italy, about 1445. In consequence, his work represents a unique blend of Flemish and Early Renaissance elements, although it remains basically Northern. *Etienne Chevalier and St. Stephen* (fig. 525), painted about 1450 for the left wing of a diptych, shows his mastery as a portraitist (the head of the saint seems no less individual than that of the donor); Italian influence can be seen in the style of the architecture and, less directly, in the statuesque solidity and weight of the two figures.

The artist's self-portrait from about the same time also reflects his sojourn in the South (fig. 526); it is a tiny picture executed in gold on black enamel, which must have been inspired by a late Roman miniature like the one reproduced in figure 285. It revives a species of "portable" portrait that was to become immensely popular, especially in England, a century later. And it has the further distinction of being the earliest clearly identified self-portrait that is a separate painting, not an incidental part of a larger work. The style of the likeness is Flemish in origin, however, rather than

527. SOUTHERN FRENCH MASTER. *The Avignon Pietà.* c. 1470. Panel, 64 × 86″. The Louvre, Paris

ancient or Renaissance. In fact, the quality of the glance recalls Jan van Eyck's *Man in a Red Turban* (fig. 515) so strongly that one is tempted to cite it as evidence that Jan's picture, too, must be a self-portrait.

THE AVIGNON PIETÀ. A Flemish style, influenced by Italian art, also characterizes the most famous of all French fifteenth-century pictures, *The Avignon Pietà* (fig. 527). As its name indicates, the panel comes from the extreme south of France. It was probably painted by an artist of that region, but the name of this important master is not recorded, and we know no other works by his hand. All we can say about his background is that he must have been thoroughly familiar with the art of Rogier van der Weyden, for the figure types and the expressive content of *The Avignon Pietà* could be derived from no other source. At the same time, the design, magnificently simple and stable, is Italian rather than Northern (we first saw these qualities in the art of Giotto). Southern, too, is the bleak, featureless landscape emphasizing the monumental isolation of the figures. The distant buildings behind the donor on the left have an unmistakably Islamic flavor: did the artist mean to place the scene in an authentic Near Eastern setting? However that may be, he has created from these various features an unforgettable image of heroic pathos.

"Late Gothic" Sculpture

If we had to describe fifteenth-century art north of the Alps in a single phrase, we might label it "the first century of panel painting," for panel painting so dominated the art of the period between 1420 and 1500 that its standards apply to manuscript illumination and stained glass and even, to a large extent, to sculpture. After the later thirteenth century, we will recall, the emphasis had shifted from architectural sculpture to the more intimate scale of devotional images, tombs, pulpits, and the like. Claus Sluter, whose art is so impressive in weight and volume, had briefly recaptured the monumental spirit of the High Gothic; but he had no real successors, although echoes of his style can be felt in French art for the next fifty years.

What ended the International Style in the sculpture of Northern Europe was the influence of the Master of Flémalle and Rogier van der Weyden. The carvers (who quite often were also painters) began to reproduce in stone or wood the style of these artists, and continued to do so, in essence, until about 1500. How completely the aims of "Late Gothic" sculpture became identified with those of painting may be seen in figures 528 and 529: the *Flying Angel* from a work of the Master of Flémalle, about 1420, anticipates all the main features of a carved angel by a fine German sculptor almost a century later.

MICHAEL PACHER. The most characteristic works of the "Late Gothic" carver are wooden altar shrines, often large in size and incredibly intricate in detail. Such shrines were especially popular in the Germanic countries. One of the richest examples is the *Coronation of the Virgin* (fig. 530) by the Tyrolean sculptor and painter Michael Pacher (c.

1435–1498), in St. Wolfgang, Austria. Its lavishly gilt and colored forms make a dazzling spectacle as they emerge from the shadowy depth of the shrine under spiky Flamboyant canopies; we enjoy it—but in pictorial rather than plastic terms. We have no experience of volume, either positive or negative; the figures and setting seem to melt into a single pattern of agitated, twisting lines that permits only the heads to stand out as separate entities.

If we compare this *Coronation* with Rogier's *Descent from the Cross* (colorplate 63), we realize that the latter, paradoxically, is a far more "sculptural" scene. Did Pacher, the "Late Gothic" sculptor, feel unable to compete with the painter's rendering of three-dimensional bodies and therefore choose to meet him in the pictorial realm, by extracting the maximum of drama from contrasts of light and shade? Pacher's own work seems to support this view: some years after completing the St. Wolfgang shrine he made another altarpiece, this time with a painted center (fig. 531). Again we see large figures under ornate canopies—the equivalent of a carved

528. THE MASTER OF FLÉMALLE (ROBERT CAMPIN?).
Flying Angel, detail of the *Entombment*. c. 1420.
Panel. Collection Count Antoine Seilern, London

529. VEIT STOSZ. *Flying Angel*, detail
of the *Annunciation*. 1518. St. Lorenz, Nuremberg

530. MICHAEL PACHER. *Coronation of the Virgin* (center portion of wooden shrine). 1471–81. Figures about lifesize. Parish church, St. Wolfgang, Austria

531. MICHAEL PACHER. *St. Augustine and St. Gregory,* center panel of the *Altarpiece of the Four Latin Fathers.* c. 1483. 81 × 77″. Pinakothek, Munich

shrine—but now with far greater emphasis on space and volume. To say that Pacher is a painter when he sculpts, and a sculptor when he paints, is only a slight exaggeration: in this exchange, sculpture inevitably gets the short end of the bargain.

THE GRAPHIC ARTS
Printing

At this point we must take note of another important event north of the Alps—the development of printing, for pictures as well as books. Our earliest printed books in the modern sense were produced in the Rhineland soon after 1450 (we are not certain whether Gutenberg deserves the priority long claimed for him). The new technique quickly spread all over Europe and developed into an industry that had a profound effect on Western civilization, ushering in the era of general literacy.

Printed pictures, however, had hardly less importance, for without them, the printed book could not have replaced the work of the medieval scribe and illuminator so quickly and completely. The pictorial and the literary aspects of printing were, indeed, closely linked from the start. But where is the start? When, and by whom, was printing invented? The beginnings of the story—which will be told here in barest outline—lie in the ancient Near East five thousand years ago. Mechanically speaking, the Sumerians were the earliest "printers," for their relief impressions on clay from stone seals were carved with both pictures and inscriptions. From Mesopotamia, the use of seals spread to India and eventually to China. The Chinese applied ink to their seals in order to impress them on wood or silk, and, in the second century A.D., they invented paper. By the ninth century, they were printing pictures and books on paper from wooden blocks carved in relief, and two hundred years later they developed movable type. Some of the products of Chinese printing surely reached the medieval West—through the Arabs, the Mongols, or travelers such as Marco Polo—although we lack direct evidence.

PRINTING IN THE WEST.   The technique of manufacturing paper, too, came to Europe from the East, and Chinese silk and porcelain were imported in small quantities from the fourteenth century on. Paper and printing from wood blocks were both known in the West during the later Middle Ages, but paper, as a cheap alternative to parchment, gained ground very slowly, while printing was used only for ornamental patterns on cloth. All the more astonishing is the development, beginning about 1400, that produced within the century a printing technology which was superior to that of the Far East and of far wider cultural importance. After 1500, in fact, no basic changes were made in this field until the Industrial Revolution.

Woodcut

The idea of printing pictorial designs from wood blocks onto paper seems to have originated in Northern Europe at the very end of the fourteenth century. Many of the oldest surviv-

532. *St. Dorothy.* c. 1420. Woodcut.
Staatliche Graphische Sammlung, Munich

ing examples of such prints, called woodcuts, are German, others are Flemish, and some may be French; all show the familiar qualities of the International Style. The designs were probably furnished by painters or sculptors, but the actual carving of the wood blocks was done by the specially trained craftsmen who also produced wood blocks for textile prints. As a result, early woodcuts, such as the *St. Dorothy* in figure 532, have a flat, ornamental pattern; forms are defined by simple, heavy lines with little concern for three-dimensional effects (there is no hatching or shading). Since the outlined shapes were meant to be filled in with color, these prints often recall stained glass (compare fig. 481) more than the miniatures which they replaced.

Despite their aesthetic appeal to modern eyes, fifteenth-century woodcuts were popular art, on a level that did not attract masters of high ability until shortly before 1500. A single wood block yielded thousands of copies, to be sold for a few pennies apiece, bringing the individual ownership of pictures within everyone's reach for the first time in our history. What people did with these prints is illustrated in figure 533, a detail from a Flemish *Annunciation* panel of about 1435, where a tattered woodcut of St. Christopher is pinned up above the mantel. Perhaps it is a hint at the Virgin's journey to Bethlehem (St. Christopher is the patron of travelers), but this charmingly incongruous feature must also be understood as a disguised symbol of her humility, for only the poor would have such an object on their walls.

The St. Christopher woodcut has two lines of lettering—a short prayer, presumably—at the bottom. Inscriptions of this kind are often found among early woodcuts, the letters having been either added by hand or printed from the same block as the picture. Such woodcuts combining image and text were sometimes assembled into popular picture books, called "block books."

But to carve lines of text backward in relief on a wooden block was a wearisome and particularly risky task—a single slip could ruin an entire page. Little wonder, then, that printers soon had the idea of putting each letter on its own small block. Wooden movable type carved by hand worked well for letters of large size but not for small ones; moreover, it was too expensive to use for printing long texts such as the Bible. By 1450, this problem had been solved through the introduction of metal type cast from molds, and the stage was set for book production as we know it today.

Engraving

Whoever first thought of metal type probably had the aid of goldsmiths to work out the technical production problems. This is the more plausible since many goldsmiths, as engravers, had already entered the field of printmaking. An engraving, unlike a woodcut, is printed not from a raised design but from V-shaped grooves, cut into a metal plate (usually copper) with a steel tool known as a burin. The technique of embellishing metal surfaces with engraved pictures was developed in classical antiquity (see fig. 225) and continued to be practiced throughout the Middle Ages (see fig. 420; the engraved lines are filled in with enamel). Thus, no new skill was required to engrave a plate that was to serve as the "matrix" for a paper print; the subsequent printing was done by rubbing ink into the grooves, wiping off the surface of the plate, covering it with a damp sheet of paper, and putting it through the press.

The notion of making an engraved print apparently came from the desire for an alternative, more refined and flexible, to woodcuts. (On a wood block, let us remember, lines are ridges; hence the thinner they are, the more difficult to carve.) Engravings appealed from the first to a smaller and more sophisticated public. The oldest examples we know, dating from about 1430, already show the influence of the great Flemish painters; their forms are systematically modeled with fine hatched lines, and often convincingly foreshortened. Nor do engravings share the anonymity of early woodcuts: individual hands can be distinguished almost

533. *Woodcut of St. Christopher,* detail from an *Annunciation* by Jacques Daret (?). c. 1435. Royal Museum of Fine Arts, Brussels

534. MARTIN SCHONGAUER. *The Temptation of St. Anthony.*
c. 1480–90. Engraving. The Metropolitan Museum of Art,
New York (Rogers Fund, 1920)

535. THE MASTER OF THE HAUSBUCH. *Holy Family.*
c. 1480–90. Drypoint. Rijksmuseum, Amsterdam

from the beginning, dates and initials shortly appear, and most of the important engravers of the last third of the fifteenth century are known to us by name. Even though the early engravers were usually goldsmiths by training, their prints are so closely linked to local painting styles that we may determine their geographic origin far more easily than for woodcuts. Especially in the Upper Rhine region, we can trace a continuous tradition of fine engravers from the time of Conrad Witz to the end of the century.

SCHONGAUER.   The most accomplished of these is Martin Schongauer (c. 1430–1491), the first printmaker whom we also know as a painter, and the first to gain international fame. Schongauer might be called the Rogier van der Weyden of engraving. After learning the goldsmith's craft in his father's shop, he must have spent considerable time in Flanders, for he shows a thorough knowledge of Rogier's art. His prints are replete with Rogierian motifs and expressive devices, and reveal a deep temperamental affinity to the great Fleming. Yet Schongauer had his own impressive powers of invention; his finest engravings have a complexity of design, spatial depth, and richness of texture that make them fully equivalent to panel paintings, and lesser artists often found inspiration in them for large-scale pictures.

The Temptation of St. Anthony (fig. 534), one of Schongauer's most famous works, masterfully combines savage expressiveness and formal precision, violent movement and ornamental stability. The longer we look at it, the more we marvel at its range of tonal values, the rhythmic beauty of the engraved line, and the artist's ability to render every conceivable surface—spiky, scaly, leathery, furry—merely by

varying the burin's attack upon the plate. He was not to be surpassed by any later engraver in this respect.

MASTER OF THE HAUSBUCH.   For originality of conception and technique, Schongauer had only one rival among the printmakers of his time, the Master of the Hausbuch (so called after a book of drawings attributed to him). The very individual style of this artist, who was probably of Dutch origin, although he seems to have spent most of his career, from about 1475 to 1490, in the Rhineland, is the opposite of Schongauer's. His prints (such as the *Holy Family*, fig. 535) are small, intimate in mood, and spontaneous, almost sketchy, in execution.

Even his tools were different from the standard engraver's equipment; instead of submitting to the somewhat impersonal discipline demanded by the burin, the Master of the Hausbuch scratched his designs into the copperplate with a fine steel needle. This technique, known as "drypoint," permitted him to draw almost as freely as if he were working with a pen on a sheet of paper. The needle, of course, did not cut grooves as deep as those made by the burin, so that a drypoint plate was apt to wear out after yielding a mere handful of impressions, whereas an engraved plate lasted through hundreds of printings. But the drypoint technique preserved the artist's personal "handwriting," and permitted soft, atmospheric effects—velvety shadows, delicate, luminous distances—unattainable with the burin. The Master of the Hausbuch knew how to take full advantage of these possibilities. He was a pioneer in the use of a tool that was to become, a century and a half later, the supreme instrument of Rembrandt's graphic art.

2
THE EARLY RENAISSANCE IN ITALY

When we discussed the new style of painting that arose in Flanders about 1420, we avoided suggesting why this revolution took place at that particular time and in that particular area. This does not mean, however, that no explanation is possible. Unless we believe in sheer fate or chance, we find it difficult to place the entire burden of responsibility on the Master of Flémalle and the brothers Van Eyck; there must, we feel, be some link between their accomplishment and the social, political, and cultural setting in which they worked. But this link is as yet less apparent, and less well understood, than we might wish. Regarding the origins of Early Renaissance art, we are in a better position. Thanks to recent research, we have more insight into the special circumstances that help to explain why this style was born in Florence at the beginning of the fifteenth century, rather than elsewhere or at some other time.

In the years around 1400, Florence faced an acute threat to its independence. The powerful duke of Milan, trying to

bring all of Italy under his rule, had already subjugated the Lombard plain and most of the Central Italian city-states; Florence remained the only serious obstacle to his ambition. The city put up a vigorous and successful defense, on the military, diplomatic, and intellectual fronts. Of these three, the intellectual was by no means the least important; the duke had much eloquent support as a new Caesar, bringing peace and order to the country, whereas Florence, in its turn, rallied public opinion by proclaiming itself the champion of freedom against unchecked tyranny.

This propaganda war was waged on both sides by humanists, the heirs of Petrarch and Boccaccio, but the Florentines gave by far the better account of themselves. Their writings, such as *Praise of the City of Florence* (1402–3) by Leonardo Bruni (see fig. 582), give renewed focus to the Petrarchan ideal of a Rebirth of the Classics: the humanist, speaking as the citizen of a free republic, asks why, among all the states of Italy, Florence alone had been able to defy the superior

536. NANNI DI BANCO. *Four Saints (Quatro Coronati).* c. 1410–14. Marble, about lifesize. Or San Michele, Florenc[e]

537. *Four Saints (Quattro Coronati),* head of second figure from left (fig. 536)

power of Milan; he finds the answer in her institutions, her cultural achievements, her geographical situation, the spirit of her people, and her descent from the city-states of ancient Etruria. Does not Florence today, he concludes, assume the same role of political and intellectual leadership as that of Athens at the time of the Persian Wars?

The patriotic pride, the call to greatness, implicit in this image of Florence as the "new Athens" must have aroused a deep response throughout the city, for just when the forces of Milan threatened to engulf them, the Florentines embarked upon an ambitious campaign to finish the great artistic enterprises begun a century before, at the time of Giotto. Following the competition of 1401-2 for the bronze doors of the Baptistery (see page 338), another extensive program continued the sculptural decoration of the Cathedral and other churches, while deliberations were resumed on how to build the dome of the Cathedral, the largest and most difficult project of all. The campaign lasted more than thirty years (it gradually petered out after the completion of the dome in 1436). Its total cost, although difficult to express in present-day financial terms, was comparable to the cost of rebuilding the Acropolis in Athens (page 122). The huge investment was itself not a guarantee of artistic quality but, motivated by such civic enthusiasm, it provided a splendid opportunity for the emergence of creative talent and the coining of a new style worthy of the "new Athens."

From the start, the visual arts were considered essential to the resurgence of the Florentine spirit. They had been classed with the crafts, or "mechanical arts," throughout antiquity and the Middle Ages, and it cannot be chance that the first explicit statement claiming a place for them among the liberal arts occurs in the writings of the Florentine chronicler Filippo Villani, about 1400. A century later, this claim was to win general acceptance throughout the Western world. What does it imply? The liberal arts were defined by a tradition going back to Plato, and comprised the intellectual disciplines necessary for a gentleman's education—mathematics (including musical theory), dialectics, grammar, rhetoric, and philosophy; the fine arts were excluded because they were "handiwork" lacking a theoretical basis. Thus, when the artist gained admission to this select group, the nature of his work had to be redefined: he was acknowledged as a man of ideas, rather than a mere manipulator of materials; and the work of art came to be viewed more and more as the visible record of his creative mind. This meant that works of art need not—indeed, should not—be judged by fixed standards of craftsmanship; soon everything that bore the imprint of a great master—drawings, sketches, frag-

538. *Portrait of a Roman.* Early 3rd century A.D. Marble, lifesize. State Museums, Berlin

ments, unfinished pieces—was eagerly collected, regardless of its incompleteness.

The artist's outlook, too, underwent certain changes. Now in the company of scholars and poets, he himself often became a man of learning and literary culture; he might write poems, an autobiography, or theoretical treatises. As another consequence of this new social status, artists tended to develop into one of two contrasting personality types: the man of the world, self-controlled, polished, at ease in aristocratic society; and the solitary genius, secretive, idiosyncratic, subject to fits of melancholy, and likely to be in conflict with his patrons. It is remarkable how soon this modern view of art and artists became a living reality in the Florence of the Early Renaissance.

FLORENCE: 1400–1450
Sculpture

The first half of the fifteenth century became the heroic age of the Early Renaissance. Florentine art, dominated by the original creators of the new style, retained the undisputed leadership of the movement. To trace its beginnings, we must discuss sculpture first, for the sculptors had earlier and more plentiful opportunities than the architects and painters to meet the challenge of the "new Athens." The artistic campaign had opened with the competition for the Baptistery doors, and for some time it consisted mainly of sculptural projects. Ghiberti's trial relief, we recall, does not differ significantly from the International Gothic (see fig. 479); nor do the completed Baptistery doors, even though their execution took another twenty years. In the trial panel only Ghiberti's admiration for ancient art, evidenced by the torso of Isaac, can be linked with the classicism of the Florentine humanists around 1400. Similar instances occur in other Florentine sculpture at that time. But such "quotations" of ancient sculpture, isolated and small in scale, merely recapture what Nicola Pisano had done a century before (see fig. 472).

NANNI DI BANCO. A decade after the trial relief, we find that this limited medieval classicism has been surpassed by a somewhat younger artist, Nanni di Banco (c. 1384–1421). The four saints, called the *Quattro Coronati* (fig. 536), which he made about 1410–14 for one of the niches on the exterior of the church of Or San Michele, demand to be compared not with Nicola Pisano but with the Reims *Visitation* (see fig. 460). The figures in both groups are approximately lifesize, yet Nanni's give the impression of being a good deal larger than those at Reims; their quality of mass and monumentality seems quite beyond the range of medieval sculpture, even though Nanni depended less directly on ancient models than had the Master of the Visitation or Nicola Pisano. Only the heads of the second and third of the *Coronati* recall specific examples of Roman sculpture— those memorable portrait heads of the third century A.D. (figs. 537, 538). Nanni was obviously much impressed by their realism and their agonized expression. His ability to retain the essence of both these qualities indicates a new attitude toward ancient art, which unites classical form and content, no longer separating them as medieval classicists had done.

When Nanni carved the *Quattro Coronati*, he was still in his early thirties. He died in 1421, leaving almost finished a huge relief of the Assumption of the Virgin for the gable above the second north portal of Florence Cathedral. In the figure of one of the flying angels that carry the Virgin heavenward (fig. 539), we see how rapidly—and surprisingly—Nanni's art evolved during the interval. The style of this figure is remote from both the classicism of the *Coronati* and the International Gothic. It recalls, instead, the flying angels of "Late Gothic" art such as that by the Master of Flémalle (fig. 528). Both artists, at the same time and independently, had discovered how to visualize airborne figures persuasively: enveloping them in thin, loose draperies whose turbulent patterns and balloon-like bulges demonstrate the buoyant force of the wind. But the body of the Flemish angel tends to disappear among the folds, so that it seems essentially passive, whereas the body of Nanni's angel fills out the garments with its own vigorous action; this figure, we are convinced, propels itself, while its Northern counterpart merely floats.

539. NANNI DI BANCO. *Flying Angel*,
detail of *The Assumption*. c. 1420.
Porta della Mandorla, Florence Cathedral

DONATELLO'S EARLY WORKS. Comparing the two angels makes us see that Early Renaissance art, in contrast to "Late Gothic," sought an attitude toward the human body similar to that of classical antiquity. The man who did most to re-establish this attitude was Donatello, the greatest sculptor of his time. Born in 1386, several years after Nanni di Banco, he died in 1466, outliving Nanni by forty-five years. Among the "founding fathers" of the new style, he alone survived well past the middle of the century. Together with Nanni, Donatello spent the early part of his career working on commissions for the Cathedral and Or San Michele; they often faced the same artistic problems, yet the personalities of the two masters had little in common.

Their different approaches are strikingly illustrated in Nanni's *Quattro Coronati* and Donatello's *St. Mark* (fig. 540): both are located in deep Gothic niches, but Nanni's figures cannot be divorced from the architectural setting and still seem attached, like jamb statues, to the pilasters behind them. The *St. Mark* no longer needs such shelter; perfectly balanced and self-sustaining, he would lose nothing of his immense authority if he were deprived of his present enclosure. Here is the first statue since antiquity capable of standing by itself, or, to put it another way, the first statue to recapture the full meaning of the classical *contrapposto* (see page 129). In a performance that truly marks an epoch, the young Donatello has mastered at one stroke the central achievement of ancient sculpture. He treats the human body as an articulated structure, capable of movement, and its drapery as a separate and secondary element, determined by the shapes underneath rather than by patterns imposed from without. Unlike the *Coronati*, the *St. Mark* looks as if he could take off his clothes. And yet he is not at all classicistic; that is, ancient motifs are not quoted as they are in Nanni's

figures. Perhaps "classic" is the right word for him instead.

A few years later, about 1415–17, Donatello carved another statue for Or San Michele, the famous *St. George* (fig. 541). This niche is shallower than that of the *St. Mark*, and the young warrior saint can actually protrude from it slightly. Although encased in armor, his body and limbs are not rigid but wonderfully elastic; his stance, with the weight placed on the forward leg, conveys his readiness for combat (the right hand originally held a lance or sword). The controlled energy of his body is reflected in his eyes, which seem to scan the horizon for the approaching enemy. He is the Christian Soldier in his Early Renaissance version, spiritually akin to the *St. Theodore* at Chartres (see fig. 458), but also the proud defender of the "new Athens."

Below *St. George*'s niche is a relief panel showing the hero's best-known exploit, slaying the dragon (fig. 542; the maiden on the right is the captive princess whom the saint

540. DONATELLO. *St. Mark*. 1411–13.
Marble, 7' 9". Or San Michele, Florence

had come to liberate). Donatello has here produced another revolutionary work, devising a new kind of relief that is physically shallow (hence called *schiacciato,* "flattened-out") yet creates an illusion of infinite pictorial depth. This had already been achieved to some degree in certain Greek and Roman reliefs, and by Ghiberti (compare with figs. 190, 259–64, 479). But in all these cases, the actual carved depth is roughly proportional to the apparent depth of the space represented: the forms in the front plane are in very high relief, while those more distant become progressively lower, seemingly immersed in the background of the panel. Donatello discards this relationship; behind the figures, the amazing wind-swept landscape consists entirely of delicate surface modulations which cause the marble to catch light from varying angles. Thus every tiny ripple becomes endowed with a descriptive power infinitely greater than its real depth, and the chisel, like a painter's brush, becomes a tool for creating shades of light and dark. Yet Donatello cannot have borrowed his landscape from any painting, for no painter, at the time he did the St. George relief, had achieved so coherent and atmospheric a view of nature.

On the campanile of Florence Cathedral, when it was built in 1334–57, a row of tall Gothic niches had been designed for statues (barely visible above the rooftops in fig. 449). Half of these niches were still empty, and between 1416 and 1435 Donatello filled five of them. The most impressive statue of his series (fig. 543) is the unidentified prophet nicknamed *Zuccone* ("pumpkin-head"), made a dozen years after the *St. Mark.* The figure has long enjoyed special fame as a striking example of the master's realism, and there is no question that it is indeed realistic—far more so than any ancient statue or its nearest rivals, the prophets on the *Moses Well* (see fig. 470).

541. (*right*) DONATELLO. St. George Tabernacle. c. 1415–17. Marble (statue transferred to the National Museum, replaced by a bronze copy), height of statue 6′ 10″. Or San Michele, Florence

542. (*below*) *St. George and the Dragon*, portion of relief below *St. George* (fig. 541). Marble, height 15¾″

543. DONATELLO. *Prophet (Zuccone)*, on the campanile of Florence Cathedral. 1423–25. Marble, height 6′ 5″ (original now in the Cathedral Museum)

But, we may ask, what *kind* of realism have we here? Donatello has not followed the conventional image of a prophet (a bearded old man in Oriental-looking costume, holding a large scroll); he has invented an entirely new type, and it is difficult to account for his impulse in terms of realism. Why did he not reinterpret the old image from a realistic point of view, as Claus Sluter had done? Donatello obviously felt that the established type was inadequate for his own conception of the subject, but how did he conceive it anew? Surely not by observing the people around him. More likely, he imagined the personalities of the prophets from what he had read about them in the Old Testament. He gained an impression, we may assume, of divinely inspired orators haranguing the multitude; and this, in turn, reminded him of the Roman orators he had seen in ancient sculpture. Hence the classical costume of the *Zuccone*, whose mantle falls from one shoulder like those of the toga-clad patricians in figures 255 and 259. Hence, also, the fascinating head, ugly yet noble, like Roman portraits of the third century A.D. (compare figs. 270, 271).

To shape all these elements into a coherent whole was a revolutionary feat, an almost visible struggle. Donatello himself seems to have regarded the *Zuccone* as a particularly hard-won achievement; it is the first of his surviving works to carry his signature. He is said to have sworn "by the *Zuccone*" when he wanted to emphasize a statement, and to have shouted at the statue, during his work, "Speak, speak, or the plague take you!"

PERSPECTIVE: DONATELLO AND GHIBERTI. Donatello had learned the technique of bronze sculpture as a youth by working under Ghiberti on the first Baptistery doors. Now, in the 1420s, he began to rival his former teacher in that medium. *The Feast of Herod* (fig. 544), which he made about 1425 for the baptismal font of S. Giovanni (the Baptistery of Siena Cathedral), shows the same exquisite surface finish as Ghiberti's panels (see fig. 479), but also an expressive power that we could expect only of the master of the *Zuccone*. By classical or medieval standards, the main scene is poorly composed: the focus of the drama (the executioner presenting the head of St. John to Herod) is far to the left; the dancing Salome and most of the spectators are massed on the right; the center remains empty. Yet we see at once why Donatello created this gaping hole: it conveys, more effectively than the witnesses' gestures and expressions, the impact of the shocking sight. Moreover, the centrifugal movement of the figures helps persuade us that the picture space does not end within the panel but continues indefinitely in every direction; that the frame is merely a window through which we see this particular segment of unlimited, continuous reality. The arched openings within the panel serve to frame additional segments of the same reality, luring us further into the depths of the palace.

This architecture, with its round arches, its fluted columns and pilasters, is not Gothic but reflects the new style launched by Filippo Brunelleschi, whose architectural achievements will occupy us soon. Brunelleschi also invented the system of linear perspective, and *The Feast of Herod* is probably the earliest surviving example of a picture space constructed by this method. The details of the method need not concern us here, beyond saying that the system is a geometric procedure for projecting space onto a plane, analogous to the way the lens of a photographic camera now projects a perspective image on the film. Its central feature is the vanishing point, toward which any set of parallel lines will seem to converge. If these lines are perpendicular to the picture plane, their vanishing point will be on the horizon, corresponding exactly to the position of the beholder's eye. Brunelleschi's discovery in itself was scientific rather than artistic, but it immediately became highly important to Early Renaissance artists because, unlike the perspective practices of the past, it was objective, precise, and rational (in fact, it soon became an argument for up-grading the fine arts into the liberal arts).

While empirical methods could also yield striking results, mathematical perspective made it possible now to represent three-dimensional space on a flat surface in such a way that all the distances remained measurable—and this meant, in turn, that by reversing the procedure the plan could be derived from the perspective picture of a building. On the other hand, the scientific implications of the new perspective demanded that it be consistently applied, a requirement that artists could not always live up to, for practical as well as aesthetic reasons. Since the method presupposes that the beholder's eye occupies a fixed point in space, a perspective picture automatically tells us where we must stand to see it properly. Thus the artist who knows in advance that his work will be seen from above or below, rather than at ordinary eye-level, ought to make his perspective construction correspond to these conditions; but if these are so abnormal that he must foreshorten his entire design to an extreme degree, he may disregard them and assume instead an ideal beholder, normally located. Such is the case in *The Feast of Herod*: our eye should be on a line perpendicular to the center of the panel, but in the Baptistery we must crouch low to see it correctly, as the basin to which our relief is attached is only a few feet high. (For other problems raised by the use of scientific perspective, see page 413.)

At the same time that Donatello designed *The Feast of Herod*, Ghiberti was commissioned to do another pair of bronze doors for the Baptistery in Florence. This second set, so beautiful that they were soon dubbed the "Gates of Paradise," is decorated with ten large reliefs in square frames (not twenty-eight small panels in quatrefoil frames, as on the earlier doors) and shows the artist's successful conversion, under the influence of Donatello and the other pioneers of the new style, to the Early Renaissance point of view. *The Story of Jacob and Esau* (fig. 545) may be instructively contrasted with *The Feast of Herod*. It is about a decade later, and its perspective construction is more easy and assured; Brunelleschi's discovery had meanwhile been formulated in writing by Leone Battista Alberti, the author of the first Renaissance treatise on painting and, later, an important architect (see pages 420–22). The setting for Ghiberti's narrative is a spacious hall, a fine example of Early Renaissance architectural design reflecting the mature art of Brunelleschi, while the figures still remind us, by their gentle and graceful classicism, of the International Gothic style.

544. DONATELLO. *The Feast of Herod.* c. 1425. Gilt bronze, 23 ½″ square. Baptismal Font, S. Giovanni, Siena

545. LORENZO GHIBERTI. *The Story of Jacob and Esau*, panel of the "Gates of Paradise." c. 1435. Gilt bronze, 31¼″ square. Baptistery, Florence

546. JACOPO DELLA QUERCIA. *The Creation of Adam*. c. 1430.
Marble, 34½ × 27½". Main Portal, S. Petronio, Bologna

547. *Adam in Paradise*, detail of an ivory diptych.
c. 400 A.D. National Museum, Florence

THE CLASSICAL NUDE: JACOPO DELLA QUERCIA AND DONATELLO. Outside Florence the only major sculptor at that time was Jacopo della Quercia of Siena (c. 1374–1438). Like Ghiberti, he changed his style from Gothic to Early Renaissance in mid-career, mainly through contact with Donatello. Had he grown up in Florence, he might have been one of the great leaders of the new movement from the start, but his forcefully individual art remained outside the main trend. It had no effect on Florentine art until the very end of the century, when the young Michelangelo fell under its spell. Michelangelo's admiration was aroused by the scenes from Genesis framing the main portal of the church of S. Petronio in Bologna, among them *The Creation of Adam* (fig. 546).

The relief mode of these panels is conservative—Jacopo had little interest in pictorial depth—but the figures are daring and profoundly impressive. The figure of Adam slowly rising from the ground, as a statue brought to life might rise from its mold, recaptures the heroic beauty of a classical athlete. Here the nude body once again expresses the dignity and power of man as it did in classical antiquity. Yet we sense that man has not been freed from Original Sin. Jacopo's Adam contains a hint of incipient conflict as he faces the Lord; he will surely fall, but in pride of spirit rather than as a hapless victim of the Evil One.

It is instructive to compare Jacopo's *Adam* with the work that probably inspired it, an *Adam in Paradise* from an Early Christian ivory diptych (fig. 547). The latter figure represents a classicizing trend around 400 A.D. (compare fig. 303),

a final attempt to preserve the Greek ideal of physical beauty within a Christian context. Adam appears as the Perfect Man, divinely appointed to "have dominion...over every living thing," but the classic form has already become a formula, a mere shell. And the classical nude entered the tradition of medieval art in this desiccated condition. Whenever we meet the unclothed body, from 800 to 1400, we may be sure that it is derived, directly or indirectly, from a classical source, no matter how unlikely this may seem (as in fig. 380). We may also be sure—except for a few special cases—that such nudity has a moral significance, whether negative (Adam and Eve, or sinners in Hell) or positive (the nudity of the Christ of the Passion; of saints being martyred or mortifying the flesh; of Fortitude in the guise of Hercules). Finally, medieval nudes, even the most accomplished, are devoid of that sensual appeal which we take for granted in every nude of classical antiquity. Such appeal was purposely avoided rather than unattainable, for to the medieval mind the physical beauty of the ancient "idols," especially nude statues, embodied the insidious attraction of paganism.

The fifteenth century rediscovered the sensuous beauty of the unclothed body, but by way of two separate paths. The Adam and Eve of Jan van Eyck (fig. 513), or the nudes of Bosch (colorplate 64), have no precedent in either ancient or medieval art; they are, indeed, not "nude," but "naked"— people whose normal state is to be dressed and who for specific reasons appear stripped of their clothing. Jacopo's *Adam*, on the other hand, is clearly nude, in the full classical sense. So also is Donatello's bronze *David* (fig. 548, colorplate 65), an even more revolutionary achievement, the first lifesize nude statue since antiquity that is wholly freestanding. The Middle Ages would surely have condemned it as an idol, and Donatello's contemporaries, too, must have felt uneasy about it; for many years it remained the only work of its kind. The early history of the figure is unknown, but it must have been meant for an open space where it

549. DONATELLO. *Mary Magdalen* (see colorplate 66).
Cathedral Museum, Florence

548. DONATELLO. *David* (see colorplate 65).
National Museum, Florence

would be visible from every side, probably standing on top of a column.

The key to its significance is the elaborate helmet of Goliath with visor and wings, a unique (and implausible) feature that can only refer to the dukes of Milan, who had threatened Florence about 1400 (see page 391) and were now warring against it once more in the mid-1420s. The statue, then, must be understood as a civic-patriotic public monument identifying David—weak but favored by the Lord—with Florence, and Goliath with Milan. David's nudity is most readily explained as a reference to the classical origin of Florence, and his wreathed hat as the opposite of Goliath's helmet: peace *vs.* war. Donatello has chosen to model an adolescent boy, not a full-grown youth like the athletes of Greece, so that the skeletal structure here is less fully enveloped in swelling muscles; nor does he articulate the torso according to the classical pattern (compare figs. 178, 179). In fact his *David* resembles an ancient statue only in its beautifully poised *contrapposto*. If the figure nevertheless conveys a profoundly classical air, the reason lies beyond its anatomical perfection; as in ancient statues, the body speaks to us more eloquently than the face, which by Donatello's standards is strangely devoid of individuality.

In contrast, the wooden *Mary Magdalen* (fig. 549, color-plate 66) seems so far from Renaissance ideals that at first we are tempted to see in this statue a return to such Gothic devotional images as the Bonn *Pietà* (see fig. 468). But when we look back at the intensity of Donatello's *Zuccone* (fig. 543), we realize that the ravaged features and wasted body of his *Mary Magdalen* betray an insight into religious experience that is not basically different from his earlier work.

DONATELLO: PADUA AND LATER.   Donatello was invited to Padua in 1443 to produce the equestrian monument of Gattamelata, the recently deceased commander of the Venetian armies (fig. 550). This statue, the artist's largest free-standing work in bronze, still stands in its original position on a tall pedestal near the façade of the church dedicated to St. Anthony of Padua. We already know its two chief precedents, the mounted *Marcus Aurelius* in Rome and the *Can Grande* in Verona (see figs. 269, 477). Without directly

imitating the former, the *Gattamelata* shares its material, its impressive scale, and its sense of balance and dignity; Donatello's horse, a heavy-set animal fit to carry a man in full armor, is so large that the rider must dominate it by his authority of command, rather than by physical force. The link with the *Can Grande*, though less obvious, is equally significant: both statues stand next to a church façade, both are memorials to the military prowess of the deceased. But the *Gattamelata*, in the new Renaissance fashion, is not part of a tomb; it was designed solely to immortalize the fame of a great soldier. Nor is it the self-glorifying statue of a sovereign, but a monument authorized by the Republic of Venice, in special honor of distinguished and faithful service. To this purpose, Donatello has coined an image that is a complete union of ideal and reality; the general's armor combines modern construction with classical detail; the head is powerfully individual, and yet endowed with a truly Roman nobility of character.

When Donatello went home to Florence after a decade's absence, he must have felt like a stranger. The political and spiritual climate had changed, and so had the taste of artists and public (see page 424). His subsequent works, between 1453 and 1466, stand apart from the dominant trend; perhaps that is why their fierce expressiveness and personal quality exceed anything the master had revealed before. The extreme individualism of his late works confirms Donatello's reputation as the earliest "solitary genius" among the artists of the new age.

Architecture

BRUNELLESCHI.   Although Donatello was its greatest and most daring master, he had not created the Early Renaissance style in sculpture all by himself. The new architecture, on the other hand, did owe its existence to one man, Filippo Brunelleschi (1377–1446). Ten years older than Donatello, Brunelleschi had begun his career as a sculptor. After failing to win the competition of 1401–2 for the first Baptistery doors, he reportedly went to Rome with Donatello. He studied the architectural monuments of the ancients, and seems to have been the first to take exact measurements of these structures. His discovery of scientific perspective may well have grown out of his search for an accurate method of recording their appearance on paper. What else he did during this long "gestation period" we do not know, but in 1417–19 we again find him competing with Ghiberti, this time for the job of building the Cathedral dome (see figs. 449, 450). Its design had been established half a century earlier and could be altered only in details, but its vast size posed a difficult problem of construction. Brunelleschi's proposals, although contrary to all traditional practice, so impressed the authorities that this time he won out over his rival. Thus the dome deserves to be called the first work of post-medieval architecture, as an engineering feat if not for style.

The technical details need not concern us here. Brunelleschi's main achievement was to build the dome in two separate shells that are ingeniously linked to reinforce each other, rather than in one solid mass. As the total weight of the structure was thereby lightened, he could dispense with

550. DONATELLO. *Equestrian Monument of Gattamelata.* 1445–50. Bronze, c. 11' × 13'. Piazza del Santo, Padua

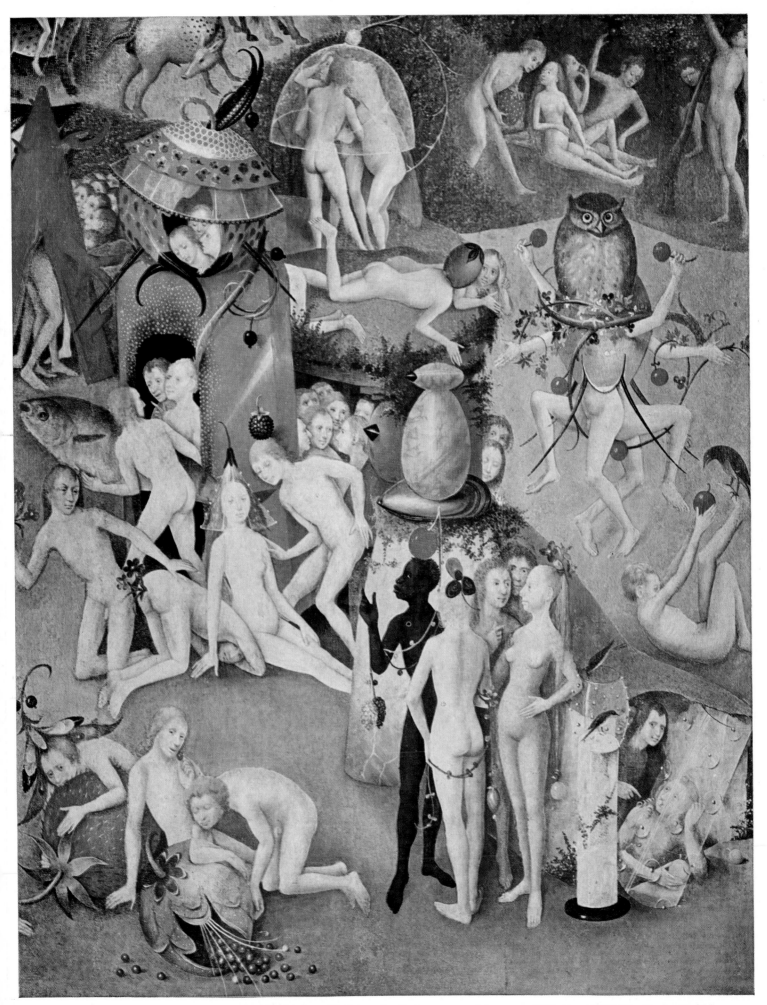

Colorplate 64. HIERONYMUS BOSCH. *The Garden of Delights*, detail of center panel (see page 385). About 1500. The Prado, Madrid

Colorplate 65. DONATELLO. *David* (see page 398). c. 1425–30.
Bronze, height 62¼″. National Museum, Florence

Colorplate 66. DONATELLO. *Mary Magdalen*
(see page 400). About 1455. Wood, partially gilded; height 74″.
Cathedral Museum, Florence

Colorplate 67. DOMENICO VENEZIANO. *Madonna and Child with Saints*
(see page 416). About 1445. Panel, 6′ 7½″ × 6′ 11⅞″. Uffizi Gallery, Florence

Colorplate 68. PIERO DELLA FRANCESCA. Portion of the *Discovery and Proving of the True Cross* (see page 417). About 1460. Fresco. S. Francesco, Arezzo

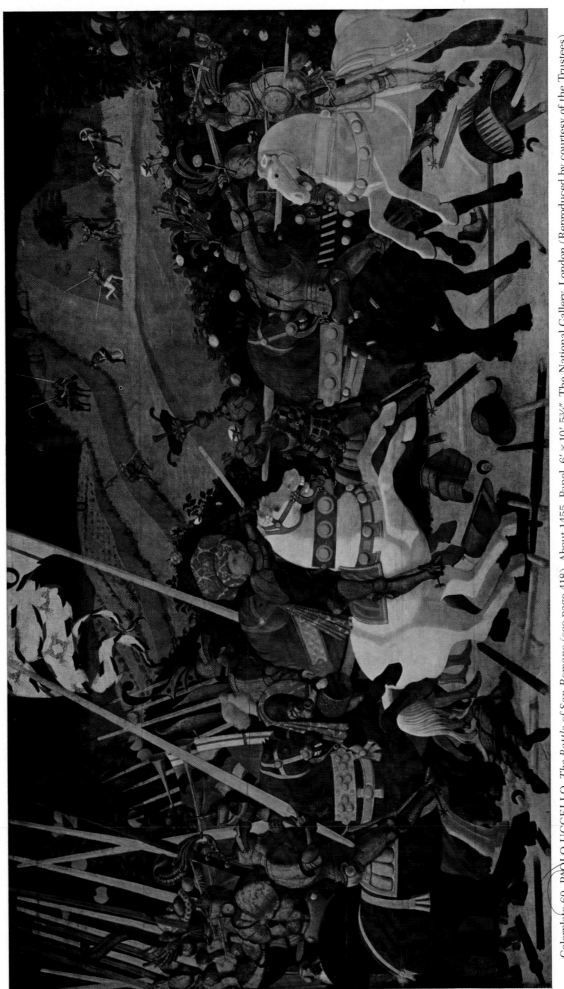

Colorplate 69. PAOLO UCCELLO. *The Battle of San Romano* (see page 418). About 1455. Panel, 6′ × 10′ 5¾″. The National Gallery, London (Reproduced by courtesy of the Trustees)

Colorplate 70. ANDREA DEL
CASTAGNO. *David* (see
page 420). About 1450–57.
Leather, surface curved; height
45½″. The National Gallery
of Art, Washington, D.C.
(Widener Collection)

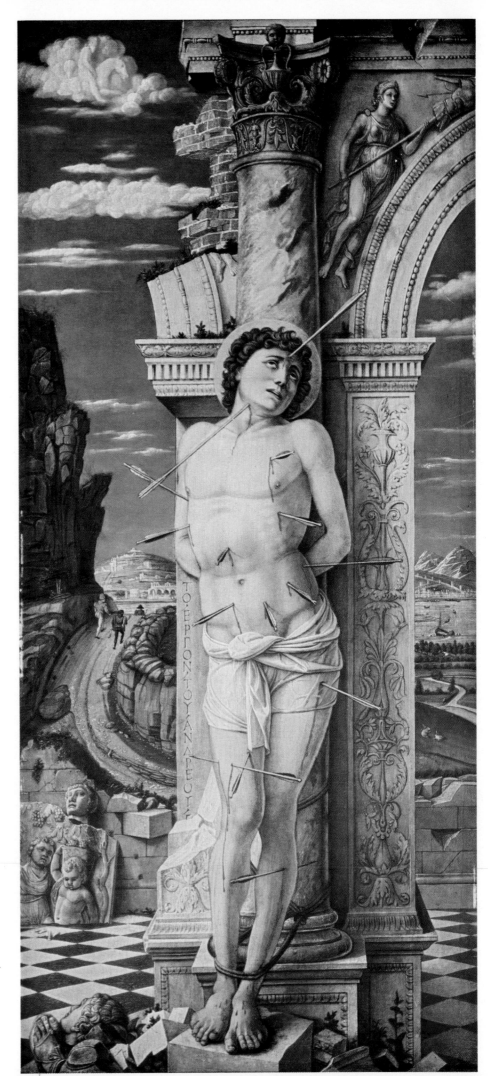

Colorplate 71. ANDREA MANTEGNA.
St. Sebastian (see page 430).
About 1455–60. Panel, 26¾ × 11⅞".
Kunsthistorisches Museum, Vienna

Colorplate 72.
GIOVANNI BELLINI.
St. Francis in Ecstasy
(see page 431).
About 1485.
Panel, 48½ × 55″.
The Frick Collection,
New York
(Copyright)

551. FILIPPO BRUNELLESCHI.
S. Lorenzo, Florence. 1421–69

552. Plan of S. Lorenzo

the massive and costly wooden trusswork required by the older method of construction. Instead of having building materials carried up on ramps to the required level, he designed hoisting machines; his entire scheme reflects a bold, analytical mind, always discarding conventional solutions if better ones could be devised. This fresh approach distinguishes Brunelleschi from the Gothic stonemason-architects, with their time-honored procedures.

San Lorenzo. In 1419, while he was working out his final plans for the dome, Brunelleschi received his first opportunity to create buildings entirely of his own design. It came from the head of the Medici family, one of the leading merchants and bankers of Florence, who commissioned him to add a sacristy to the Romanesque church of San Lorenzo. His plans for this sacristy (which was to serve also as a burial chapel for the Medici) so impressed his patron that he was immediately asked to develop a new design for the entire church. The construction, begun in 1421, was often interrupted, so that the interior was not completed until 1469, more than twenty years after the architect's death (the exterior remains unfinished to this day). Nevertheless, the building in its present form is essentially what Brunelleschi had envisioned about 1420, and thus represents the first full statement of his architectural aims (figs. 551, 552).

The plan may not seem very novel, at first glance. Its general arrangement recalls Cistercian Gothic churches (see fig. 446); the unvaulted nave and transept link it to Sta. Croce (see fig. 447). What distinguishes it is a new emphasis on symmetry and regularity. The entire design consists of square units: four large squares form the choir, the crossing, and the arms of the transept; four more are combined into the nave; other squares, one-fourth the size of the large units, make up the aisles and the chapels attached to the transept (the oblong chapels outside the aisles were not part of the original design). We notice, however, some small deviations from this scheme—the transept arms are slightly longer than they are wide, and the length of the nave is not four but four and one-half times its width.

A few simple measurements will explain these apparent inconsistencies. Brunelleschi must have first decided to make the floor area of the choir equal to four of the small square units; the nave and transept were thus to be twice as wide as the aisles or chapels. But in fixing this system, he made no allowance for the inevitable thickness of the walls between these compartments, so that the transept arms have a width of two units, and a length of two units plus one wall-thickness; the nave is seven wall-thicknesses longer than, ideally speaking, it should be. In other words, Brunelleschi conceived San Lorenzo as a grouping of abstract "space blocks," the larger ones being simple multiples of the standard unit. Once we understand this we realize how revolutionary he was, for his clearly defined, separate space compartments represent a radical departure from the Gothic architect's way of thinking.

The interior bears out our expectations. Cool, static order has replaced the emotional warmth, the flowing spatial movement of Gothic church interiors. San Lorenzo does not sweep us off our feet. It does not even draw us forward after we have entered it—we are quite content to remain near the door, for our view seems to take in the entire structure almost as if, from that vantage point, we were confronted with a particularly clear and convincing demonstration of scientific perspective (compare fig. 545). The total effect recalls the "old-fashioned" Tuscan Romanesque—such as Pisa Cathedral (see fig. 402)—and Early Christian basilicas (compare fig. 290), for these monuments, to Brunelleschi, exemplified the church architecture of classical antiquity; they inspired his return to the use of the round arch and of columns, rather than piers, in the nave arcade. Yet these earlier buildings lack the transparent lightness, the wonderfully precise articulation of San Lorenzo. Unlike Brunelleschi's, their columns are larger and more closely spaced, tending to screen off the aisles from the nave. Only the arcade of the Florentine Baptistery is as gracefully proportioned as that of San Lorenzo, but it is a *blind* arcade, without any supporting function (see fig. 403, colorplate 44; the Baptistery, we recall, was in Brunelleschi's day thought to have once been a classical temple).

But Brunelleschi did not revive the architectural vocabulary of the ancients out of mere antiquarian enthusiasm. The very quality that attracted him to the component parts of classical architecture must have seemed, from the medieval point of view, their chief drawback: their inflexibility.

A classical column, unlike a medieval column or pier, is strictly defined and self-sufficient, and its details and proportions can be varied only within narrow limits (the ancients thought of it as an organic structure comparable to the human body); the classical round arch, unlike any other arch (horseshoe, pointed, etc.), has only one possible shape, a semicircle; the classical architrave and the classical repertory of profiles and ornaments are all subject to similarly strict rules. Not that the classical vocabulary is completely inflexible—if it were, it could not have persisted from the seventh century B.C. to the fourth century A.D. in the ancient world—but the disciplined spirit of the Greek orders, which can be felt even in the most original Roman buildings, demands regularity and consistency, and discourages sudden, arbitrary departures from the norm.

Without the aid of such a "standardized" vocabulary, Brunelleschi would have found it impossible to define the shape of his "space blocks" so convincingly. With remarkable logic, he emphasizes the edges or "seams" of the units without disrupting their rhythmic sequence. To single out a particularly noteworthy example, consider the vaulting of the aisles: the transverse arches rest on pilasters attached to the outer wall (corresponding to the columns of the nave arcade), but a continuous architrave intervenes between arch and pilaster, linking all the bays. We would expect these bays to be covered by groined vaults of the classical, unribbed type (see fig. 237); instead, we find a novel kind of vault, whose curved surface is formed from the upper part of a hemispherical dome (its radius equals half the diagonal of the square compartment). Avoiding the ribs and even the groins, Brunelleschi has created a "one-piece" vault, strikingly simple and geometrically regular, that makes of each bay a distinct unit.

Architectural Proportions. At this point we may well ask: if the new architecture consists essentially of separate elements added together, be they spaces, columns, or vaults, how did Brunelleschi relate these elements to each other? What makes the interior of San Lorenzo seem so beautifully integrated? There is indeed a controlling principle that accounts for the harmonious, balanced character of his design: the secret of good architecture, Brunelleschi was convinced, lay in giving the "right" proportions—that is, proportional ratios expressed in simple whole numbers—to all the significant measurements of a building. The ancients had possessed this secret, he believed, and he tried to rediscover it by painstakingly surveying the remains of their monuments. What he found, and how he applied his theory to his own designs, we do not know for sure. He may have been the first, though, to think out what would be explicitly stated a few decades later in Leone Battista Alberti's *Treatise on Architecture*: that the arithmetical ratios determining musical harmony must also govern architecture, for they recur throughout the universe and are thus divine in origin.

Similar ideas, ultimately derived from the Greek philosopher Pythagoras, had been current during the Middle Ages (see page 302), but they had not before been expressed so radically, directly, and simply. When Gothic architects "borrowed" the ratios of musical theory, they did so with the aid of the theologians and far less consistently than their Renaissance successors. But even Brunelleschi's faith in the universal validity of harmonious proportions did not tell him how to allot these ratios to the parts of any given building. It left him many alternatives, and his choice among them was necessarily subjective. We may say, in fact, that the main reason San Lorenzo strikes us as the product of a single great mind is Brunelleschi's individual "sense of proportion" which permeates every detail.

In the revival of classical forms, Renaissance architecture found a standard vocabulary; the theory of harmonious proportions provided it with the kind of syntax that had been mostly absent in medieval architecture. Lest this comparatively inflexible order be misinterpreted as an architectural impoverishment, we might carry our linguistic analogy a bit further. It is tempting to see a parallel between the "un-classical" flexibility of medieval architecture, proliferating in regional styles, and the equally "un-classical" attitude at that time toward language, as evidenced by its barbarized Latin and the rapid growth of regional vernaculars, the ancestors of our modern Western tongues. The revival of Latin and Greek in the Renaissance did not stunt these languages; on the contrary, the classical influence made them so much more stable, precise, and articulate that Latin before long lost the dominant position it had maintained throughout the Middle Ages as the language of intellectual discourse. It is not by chance that today we can still read Renaissance literature in Italian, French, English, or German without much trouble, while texts of a century or two before can often be understood only by scholars. In a similar way, the revival of classical forms and proportions enabled Brunelleschi to transform the architectural "vernacular" of his region into a stable, precise, and articulate system. The new rationale underlying his buildings soon spread to the rest of Italy, and later to all of Northern Europe.

Pazzi Chapel. Among the surviving structures by Brunelleschi, not one exterior shows his original design unaltered by later hands. Recent research indicates that even the façade of the Pazzi Chapel (fig. 553) can no longer be regarded as an exception to this rule. The chapel was begun about 1430, but Brunelleschi (who died in 1446) could not have planned the façade in its present form. It dates from about 1460, and the top story remains incomplete. Nevertheless, it is a most original creation, totally unlike any medieval façade. A porch, reminiscent of the narthex of Early Christian churches (see fig. 289), precedes the chapel, making the façade seem to screen the main body of the structure. The central arch linking two sections of a classical colonnade is a prime innovation; it frames the portal behind, and draws attention to the dome. The plan (fig. 555) shows us that the interrupted architrave supports two barrel vaults, which in turn help to support a small dome above the central opening.

Inside the chapel, we find the same motif on a larger scale—two barrel vaults flanking the dome—and a third small dome, like that over the entrance, above the square compartment housing the altar (figs. 554, 556). Interior

553. FILIPPO BRUNELLESCHI and others.
Pazzi Chapel, Sta. Croce, Florence. Begun 1430–33

555. Plan of the Pazzi Chapel

556. Longitudinal Section
of the Pazzi Chapel

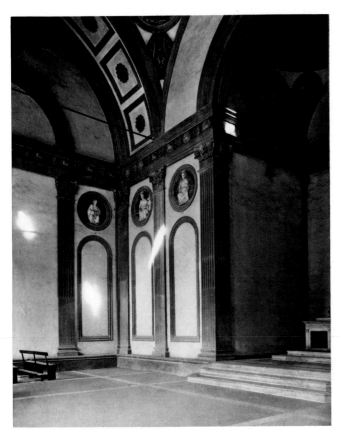

554. Interior View of the Pazzi Chapel

surfaces are articulated much as in San Lorenzo but their effect is richer and more festive. Here we also find some sculpture: large roundels on the four pendentives of the central dome, with reliefs of the evangelists (one of them is partly visible in fig. 554), and on the walls, twelve smaller ones of the apostles. These reliefs, however, are not essential to the design of the chapel; Brunelleschi provided the frames, but he need not have intended them to be filled with sculpture—the medallions may very well have been planned "blind," like the recessed panels below them. In any case, the medieval interdependence of architecture and sculpture (never as strong in Italy as in Northern Europe) had ceased to exist. Donatello had liberated the statue from its setting, and Brunelleschi's conception of architecture as the visual counterpart of musical harmonies did not permit sculpture to play a role more weighty than the roundels in the Pazzi Chapel.

Sto. Spirito, Sta. Maria degli Angeli. In the early 1430s, when the Cathedral dome was nearing completion, Brunelleschi's development as an architect entered a decisive new phase. His design for the church of Sto. Spirito (fig. 557) might be described as a perfected version of S. Lorenzo; all four arms of the cross are alike, the nave being distinguished from the others only by its greater length, the entire structure now enveloped by an unbroken sequence of aisles and chapels. These chapels are the most surprising feature of Sto. Spirito; Brunelleschi had always shunned the apsidal shape before, but now he used it to express more dynamically the relation between interior space and its boundaries (the wall seems to bulge under the outward pressure of the space).

In the church of Sta. Maria degli Angeli, which Brunelleschi began about the same time as Sto. Spirito, this new tendency reaches its ultimate conclusion (fig. 558): a domed, central-plan church—the first of the Renaissance—inspired by the round and polygonal structures of Roman and Early Christian times (compare figs. 238–41, 294–96, 306–9). Financial difficulties interfered with completing the project above the ground floor, and we cannot

557. FILIPPO
BRUNELLESCHI.
Plan of Sto. Spirito, Florence.
Begun 1434–35

558. FILIPPO
BRUNELLESCHI.
Plan of Sta. Maria
degli Angeli,
Florence. 1434–37

be sure of the design of the upper part, or even of some details in the plan. It is clear, nevertheless, that Brunelleschi here has recaptured the ancient Roman principle of the "sculptured" wall; the dome was to rest on eight heavy piers of complex shape, which belong to the same mass of masonry from which the eight chapels have been "excavated." Wall and space are both charged with energy, and the plan records the precarious balance of their pressures and counterpressures. As a conception, Sta. Maria degli Angeli was so far in advance of Brunelleschi's previous work that it must have utterly bewildered his contemporaries. It had, in fact, no echoes until the end of the century.

MICHELOZZO.   The massive "Roman" style of Sta. Maria degli Angeli may explain the great disappointment of Brunelleschi's final years: the rejection by his old patrons, the Medici, of his design for their new palace. The family had risen, since the 1420s, to such power that they were in practice, if not in theory, the rulers of Florence. For that very reason they thought it prudent to avoid any ostentation which might antagonize the public. If Brunelleschi's plan for their palace followed the style of Sta. Maria degli Angeli, it probably had such imperial Roman magnificence that the Medici could not safely afford so grand an edifice. They awarded the commission to a younger and much less distinguished architect, Michelozzo (1396–1472); actual construction began in 1444, two years before Brunelleschi's death. Michelozzo's design (fig. 559) still recalls the fortress-like Florentine palaces of old (the windows on the ground floor were added by Michelangelo seventy-five years later), but the type has been transformed by Brunelleschian principles (compare fig. 454). The three stories are in a graded sequence, each complete in itself: the lowest is built of roughhewn, "rustic" masonry like the Palazzo Vecchio;

the second of smooth-surfaced blocks with "rusticated" (that is, indented) joints; the surface of the third is unbroken. On top of the structure rests, like a lid, a strongly projecting cornice inspired by those of Roman temples, emphasizing the finality of the three stories.

Painting

MASACCIO.   Although Early Renaissance painting did not appear until the early 1420s, a decade later than Donatello's *St. Mark* and some years after Brunelleschi's first designs for S. Lorenzo, its inception is the most extraordinary of all; this new style was launched, singlehanded, by a young genius named Masaccio, who was only twenty-one years old at the time (he had been born in 1401) and who died at the age of twenty-seven. The Early Renaissance was already well established in sculpture and architecture by then, making Masaccio's task easier than it would have been otherwise; but his achievement remains stupendous, nevertheless.

The earliest of his surviving works that can be dated fairly exactly is a fresco of 1425 in Sta. Maria Novella (fig. 560) that shows the Holy Trinity accompanied by the Virgin, St. John the Evangelist, and two donors who kneel on either side. The lowest section of the fresco, linked with a tomb below, represents a skeleton lying on a sarcophagus, with

559. MICHELOZZO. Palazzo Medici-Riccardi, Florence.
Begun 1444

560. MASACCIO. *The Holy Trinity with the Virgin and St. John.* 1425. Fresco. Sta. Maria Novella, Florence

561. Ground Plan of *The Holy Trinity*

the inscription (in Italian): "What you are, I once was; what I am, you will become." Here, as in the case of the *Merode Altarpiece*, we seem to plunge into a new environment; but Masaccio's world is a realm of monumental grandeur rather than the concrete everyday reality of the Master of Flémalle. It seems hard to believe that only two years before, in this city of Florence, Gentile da Fabriano had completed one of the masterpieces of the International Gothic (see fig. 507, colorplate 59). What the *Trinity* fresco brings to mind is not the style of the immediate past, but Giotto's art, with its sense of the large scale, its compositional severity and sculptural volume. Yet Masaccio's renewed allegiance to Giotto was only a starting point. For Giotto, body and drapery form a single unit, as if both had the same substance; Masaccio's figures, like Donatello's, are "clothed nudes," their drapery falling like real fabric.

The setting, equally up-to-date, reveals a complete command of Brunelleschi's new architecture and of scientific perspective. This barrel-vaulted chamber is no mere niche, but a deep space wherein the figures could move freely if they wished. And—for the first time in history—we are given all the needed data to measure the depth of this painted interior. First we note that all the lines perpendicular to the picture plane converge upon a point below the foot of the cross, on the platform that supports the kneeling donors; to see the fresco properly, we must face this point, which is at normal eye-level, somewhat more than five feet above the floor of the church. The figures within the vaulted chamber are five feet tall, slightly less than lifesize, while the donors, who are closer to us, are fully lifesize. The exterior framework is therefore "lifesize," too, since it is directly behind the donors. The distance between the pilasters corresponds to the span of the barrel vault, and both are seven feet; the circumference of the arc over this span measures eleven feet. That arc is subdivided by eight square coffers and nine ridges, the coffers being one foot wide and the ridges four inches. Applying these measurements to the length of the barrel vault (which consists of seven coffers—the nearest one is invisible behind the entrance arch) we find that the vaulted area is nine feet deep.

We can now draw a complete floor plan (fig. 561). A puzzling feature may be the place of God the Father. His arms support the cross, close to the front plane, while His feet rest on a ledge attached to a wall. How far back is this surface? If it is the rear wall of the chamber, God would appear to be exempt from the laws of perspective. But in a universe ruled by reason, this cannot be so; hence Masaccio must have intended to locate the ledge directly behind the cross. The strong shadow that St. John casts on the wall beneath the ledge bears out our interpretation.

The largest group of Masaccio's works to come down to us are his frescoes in the Brancacci Chapel in Sta. Maria del Carmine. *The Tribute Money* (fig. 562) is the most renowned of these. It illustrates, by the age-old method known as "continuous narration" (see page 296), the story in the Gospel of Matthew (17:24–27): in the center, Christ instructs Peter to catch a fish, whose mouth will contain the tribute money for the tax collector; on the far left, in the distance, Peter takes the coin from the fish's mouth; on the right, he

562. MASACCIO. *The Tribute Money.* c. 1427. Fresco. Brancacci Chapel, Sta. Maria del Carmine, Florence

563. MASACCIO. *The Expulsion from Paradise.* c. 1427. Fresco.
Brancacci Chapel, Sta. Maria del Carmine, Florence

564. MASACCIO. *Madonna Enthroned.* 1426. Panel, 56 × 29″.
The National Gallery, London

gives it to the tax collector. Since the lower edge of the fresco is almost fourteen feet above the floor of the chapel, Masaccio could not here co-ordinate his perspective with our actual eye-level. Instead, he expects us to imagine that we are looking directly at the central vanishing point, which is located behind the head of Christ. Oddly enough, this feat is so easy that we take note of it only if we are in an analytical frame of mind. But then, pictorial illusion of any sort is always an imaginary experience; no matter how eager we are to believe in a picture, we never mistake it for reality itself, just as we are hardly in danger of confusing a statue with a living thing.

If we could see the *Tribute Money* from the top of a suitable ladder, the painted surface would be more visible, of course, but the illusion of reality would not be markedly improved. This illusion depends to only a minor degree on Brunelleschian perspective; Masaccio's weapons here are exactly those employed by the Master of Flémalle and the Van Eycks—he controls the flow of light (which comes from the right, where the window of the chapel is actually located), and he uses atmospheric perspective in the subtly changing tones of the landscape. (We recall Donatello's "preview" of such a setting, a decade earlier, in his small relief of St. George; compare fig. 542.)

The figures in the *Tribute Money*, even more than those in the *Trinity* fresco, display Masaccio's ability to merge the weight and volume of Giotto's figures with the new functional view of body and drapery. All stand in beautifully balanced *contrapposto*, and close inspection reveals fine vertical lines scratched in the plaster by the artist, establishing the gravitational axis of each figure from the head to the heel of the engaged leg. This makes the figures rather static, however; the narrative is conveyed to us by intense glances and a few emphatic gestures, rather than by physical movement. But in another fresco of the Brancacci Chapel, *The Expulsion from Paradise* (fig. 563), Masaccio proves decisively his ability to display the human body in motion. The tall, narrow format leaves little room for a spatial setting; the gate of Paradise is only indicated, and in the background are a few shadowy, barren slopes. Yet the soft, atmospheric modeling, and especially the forward-moving angel, boldly foreshortened, suffice to convey a free, unlimited space. In conception this scene is clearly akin to Jacopo della Quercia's Bolognese reliefs (fig. 546). Masaccio's grief-stricken Adam and Eve, though less dependent on ancient models, are equally striking exemplars of the beauty and power of the nude human form.

While he had a mural painter's temperament, Masaccio was equally versed in panel painting. His large polyptych, made in 1426 for the Carmelite church in Pisa, has since been dispersed among various collections. Its center panel shows a *Madonna Enthroned* (fig. 564), of the monumental Florentine type introduced by Cimabue and reshaped by Giotto (see figs. 486, 492, colorplate 50), and may be instructively compared with these. The traditional elements—including the gold ground—are still present: a large, high-backed throne dominates the composition and on either side are adoring angels (here only two). The kneeling angels in Giotto's *Madonna* have become lute players, seated on the lowest step of the throne, and the Christ Child is no longer blessing us but eating a bunch of grapes (a symbolic act alluding to the Passion and the Eucharist, the grapes referring to wine, which represents the Saviour's blood).

It is no surprise, after the *Trinity* fresco, that Masaccio replaces Giotto's ornate but frail Gothic throne with a solid and austere stone seat in the style of Brunelleschi, nor that he uses perspective expertly (note especially the two lutes). We are perhaps less prepared by the murals to find such delicacy and precision in painting the light on the surfaces. Within the picture, sunlight enters from the left—not the brilliant glare of noontime but the softer glow of the setting sun (some of the shadows on the throne permit us to determine its exact angle). There are consequently no harsh contrasts between light and shade; subtle half-shadows intervene, producing a rich scale of transitional hues. The light retains its full descriptive function, while acting as an independent force that imposes a common tonality—and a common mood—upon all the forms it touches. Clearly, Masaccio's awareness of natural light as a pictorial factor matches that of his Flemish contemporaries, but he lacked their technical means to explore it so fully.

FRA FILIPPO LIPPI. Masaccio's early death left a gap that was not filled for some time. Among his younger contemporaries only Fra Filippo Lippi (c. 1406–1469) seems to have had close contact with him. Fra Filippo's earliest dated work, the *Madonna Enthroned* of 1437 (fig. 565), evokes Masaccio's earlier *Madonna* in several important ways—the lighting, the heavy throne, the massive three-dimensional figures, the drapery folds over the Virgin's legs. Nevertheless, the picture lacks Masaccio's monumentality and severity; in fact, it seems downright cluttered by comparison. The background is a domestic interior (note the Virgin's bed on the right), and the vividly patterned marble throne displays a prayer book and a scroll inscribed with the date. Such a quantity of realistic detail, as well as the rather undisciplined perspective, indicates an artistic temperament very different from Masaccio's; it also suggests that Fra Filippo must have seen Flemish paintings (perhaps during his visit to northeastern Italy in the mid-1430s).

Finally, we must note another novel aspect of this *Madonna*: the painter's interest in movement, which is evident in the figures and, even more strikingly, in parts of the drapery (such as the curly, fluid edge of the Virgin's headdress and the curved folds of her mantle streaming to the left, accentuating her own turn to the right). These effects are found earlier in the relief sculpture of Donatello and Ghiberti—compare the dancing Salome in *The Feast of Herod* (fig. 544) and the maidens in the lower left-hand corner of *The Story of Jacob and Esau* (fig. 545). It is not surprising that these two artists should have so strongly affected Florentine painting in the decade after Masaccio's death. Age, experience, and prestige gave them authority unmatched by any painter then active in the city. Their influence, and that of the Flemish masters, modified Fra Filippo's early Masacciesque outlook in a particularly significant way, for Fra Filippo lived until 1469 and played a decisive role in setting the course of Florentine painting during the second half of the century.

FRA ANGELICO.   If Fra Filippo depended more on Donatello than on Ghiberti, the opposite is true of his slightly older contemporary Fra Angelico (c. 1400–1455). He, too, was a friar ("Fra" means "Brother"), but, unlike Fra Filippo, he took his vows seriously and rose to a responsible position within his order. When, during the years 1437–52, the monastery of S. Marco in Florence was rebuilt, Fra Angelico embellished it with numerous frescoes. The large *Annunciation* (fig. 566) from this cycle has been dated about 1440 by some scholars, about 1450 by others—either date is plausible, for this artist, like Ghiberti, developed slowly, and his style underwent no decisive changes during the 1440s. Fra Angelico preserves the very aspects of Masaccio—his dignity, directness, and spatial order—that Fra Filippo had rejected. But his figures, much as we may admire their lyrical tenderness, never achieve the physical and psychological self-assurance that characterizes the Early Renaissance image of man.

DOMENICO VENEZIANO.   In 1439 a gifted painter from Venice, Domenico Veneziano, had settled in Florence. We can only guess at his age (he was probably born about 1410 and he died in 1461), training, and previous work. He must, however, have been in sympathy with the spirit of Early Renaissance art, for he quickly became a thoroughgoing Florentine-by-choice, and a master of great importance in his new home. His *Madonna and Child with Saints*, shown in figure 567 and colorplate 67, is one of the earliest examples of a new type of altar panel that was to prove tremendously popular from the mid-fifteenth century on, the so-called *Sacra Conversazione* ("sacred conversation"). The scheme includes an enthroned Madonna, framed by architecture, and flanked by saints who may converse with her, with the beholder, or among themselves.

Looking at Domenico Veneziano's panel, we can understand the wide appeal of the *Sacra Conversazione*. The architecture and the space it defines are supremely clear and tangible, yet elevated above the everyday world; and the figures, while echoing the formal solemnity of their setting, are linked with each other and with us by a thoroughly human awareness. We are admitted to their presence, but they do not invite us to join them; like spectators in a theater, we are not allowed "on stage." (In Flemish painting, by contrast, the picture space seems a direct extension of the beholder's everyday environment; compare fig. 509, colorplate 60.)

The basic elements of our panel were already present in Masaccio's *Trinity* fresco; Domenico Veneziano must have studied it carefully, for his St. John looks at us while pointing toward the Madonna, repeating the glance and gesture of Masaccio's Virgin. Domenico's perspective setting is worthy of the older master, although the slender proportions and colored inlays of his architecture are less severely Brunelleschian. His figures, too, are balanced and dignified like Masaccio's, but without the same weight and bulk. The slim, sinewy bodies of the male saints, with their highly individualized, expressive faces, show Donatello's influence (fig. 543).

In his use of color, however, Domenico owes nothing to Masaccio; unlike the great Florentine master, he treats color as an integral part of his work, and the *Sacra Conversazione* is quite as remarkable for its color scheme as for its composition. The blond tonality, its harmony of pink, light green, and white set off by strategically placed spots of red, blue, and yellow, reconciles the decorative brightness of Gothic panel painting with the demands of perspective space and natural light. Ordinarily, a *Sacra Conversazione* is an indoor scene, but this one takes place in a kind of loggia flooded with sunlight streaming in from the right (note the cast shadow behind the Madonna). The surfaces of the architecture reflect the light so strongly that even the shadowed areas glow with color. Masaccio had achieved a similar quality of light in his *Madonna* of 1426 (which Domenico surely

565. FRA FILIPPO LIPPI. *Madonna Enthroned.* 1437. Panel, 45 × 25½". National Gallery, Rome

566. FRA ANGELICO. *The Annunciation.*
c. 1440–50. Fresco. S. Marco, Florence

knew). In this *Sacra Conversazione*, the older master's discovery is applied to a far more complex set of forms, and integrated with Domenico's exquisite color sense. The influence of its distinctive tonality can be felt throughout Florentine painting of the second half of the century.

PIERO DELLA FRANCESCA.   When Domenico Veneziano settled in Florence, he had as an assistant a young man from southeastern Tuscany named Piero della Francesca (c. 1420–1492), who became his most important disciple and one of the truly great artists of the Early Renaissance. Surprisingly enough, Piero left Florence after a few years, never to return. The Florentines seem to have regarded his work as somewhat provincial, and from their point of view they were right. Piero's style, even more strongly than Domenico's, reflected the aims of Masaccio; he retained this allegiance to the founding father of Italian Renaissance painting throughout his long career, whereas Florentine taste developed after 1450 in a different direction.

Piero's most impressive achievement is the fresco cycle in the choir of S. Francesco in Arezzo, which he painted from about 1452 to 1459. Its many scenes represent the legend of the True Cross (that is, the origin and history of the cross used for Christ's crucifixion). The section seen in figure 568 and colorplate 68 shows the Empress Helena, the mother of Constantine the Great, discovering the True Cross and the two crosses of the thieves who died beside Christ (all three had been hidden by enemies of the Faith). On the left, they are being lifted out of the ground, and on the right, the True Cross is identified by its power to bring a dead youth back to life.

567. DOMENICO VENEZIANO. *Madonna and Child with Saints*
(see colorplate 67). Uffizi Gallery, Florence

Piero's link with Domenico Veneziano is readily apparent from his colors. The tonality of this fresco, although less luminous than in Domenico's *Sacra Conversazione*, is similarly blond, evoking early morning sunlight in much the same way. Since the light enters the scene at a low angle, in

568. PIERO DELLA FRANCESCA. *The Discovery and Proving of the True Cross* (see detail; colorplate 68). S. Francesco, Arezzo

a direction almost parallel to the picture plane, it serves both to define the three-dimensional character of every shape and to lend drama to the narrative. But Piero's figures have a harsh grandeur that recalls Masaccio, or even Giotto, more than Domenico. These men and women seem to belong to a lost heroic race, beautiful and strong—and silent. Their inner life is conveyed by glances and gestures, not by facial expressions. Above all, they have a gravity, both physical and emotional, that makes them seem kin to Greek sculpture of the Severe Style (see figs. 181, 182).

How did Piero arrive at these memorable images? Using his own testimony, we may say that they were born of his passion for perspective. More than any artist of his day, Piero believed in scientific perspective as the basis of painting; in a rigorously mathematical treatise—the first of its kind—he demonstrated how it applied to stereometric bodies and architectural shapes, and to the human form. This mathematical outlook permeates all his work. When he drew a head, an arm, or a piece of drapery, he saw them as variations or compounds of spheres, cylinders, cones, cubes, and pyramids, endowing the visible world with some of the impersonal clarity and permanence of stereometric bodies. We may call him the earliest ancestor of the abstract artists of our own time, for they, too, work with systematic simplifications of natural forms. (The medieval artist, in contrast, had used the opposite procedure, building natural forms on geometric scaffoldings: fig. 482). It is not surprising that Piero's fame is greater today than ever before.

UCCELLO.   In mid-fifteenth-century Florence there was only one painter who shared—and may have helped to inspire—Piero's devotion to perspective: Paolo Uccello (1397–1475). His *Battle of San Romano* (fig. 569, colorplate 69), painted about the same time as Piero's frescoes in Arezzo, shows an extreme preoccupation with stereometric

shapes. The ground is covered with a gridlike design of discarded weapons and pieces of armor—a display of perspective studies neatly arranged to include one fallen soldier. The landscape, too, has been subjected to a process of stereometric abstraction, matching the foreground. Despite these

569. PAOLO UCCELLO. *Battle of S. Romano*
(detail; see colorplate 69). The National Gallery, London

570. ANDREA DEL CASTAGNO. *The Last Supper.* c. 1445–50. Fresco. S. Apollonia, Florence

strenuous efforts, however, the panel has none of the crystalline order and clarity of Piero della Francesca's work. In the hands of Uccello, perspective produces strangely disquieting, fantastic effects; what unites his picture is not its spatial construction but its surface pattern, decoratively reinforced by spots of brilliant color and the lavish use of gold.

Uccello had been trained in the International Gothic style of painting; it was only in the 1430s that he was "converted" to the Early Renaissance outlook by the new science of perspective. This he superimposed on his earlier style like a straitjacket. The result is a fascinating and highly unstable mixture. As we study this panel we realize that surface and space are more at war than the mounted soldiers, who get entangled with each other in all sorts of implausible ways.

CASTAGNO. The third dimension held no difficulties, however, for Andrea del Castagno (c. 1423–1457), the most gifted Florentine painter of Piero della Francesca's own generation. Less subtle but more forceful than Domenico Veneziano, Castagno recaptures something of Masaccio's monumentality in his *Last Supper* (fig. 570), one of the frescoes he painted in the refectory of the convent of S. Apollonia. The event is set in a richly paneled alcove designed as an extension of the real space of the refectory. As in medieval representations of the subject, Judas sits in isolation on the near side of the table, opposite Christ. The rigid symmetry of the architecture, emphasized by the colorful inlays, enforces a similar order among the figures and threatens to imprison them; there is so little communication among the apostles—only a glance here, a gesture there—that a brooding silence hovers over the scene.

Castagno, too, must have felt confined by a scheme imposed on him by the rigid demands of both tradition and perspective, for he used a daringly original device to break the symmetry and focus the drama of the scene. Five of the

six panels on the wall behind the table are filled with subdued varieties of colored marble, but above the heads of St. Peter, Judas, and Christ, the marble panel has a veining so garish and explosive that a bolt of lightning seems to descend on Judas' head. When Giotto revived the ancient technique

571. ANDREA DEL CASTAGNO. *David* (see colorplate 70).
The National Gallery of Art,
Washington, D.C. (Widener Collection)

of illusionistic marble textures, he hardly anticipated that it could hold such expressive significance.

Some five years after the *Last Supper*, between 1450 and 1457 (the year of his death), Castagno produced the remarkable *David* in figure 571 and colorplate 70. It is painted on a leather shield—to be used for display, not protection—and its owner probably wanted to convey an analogy between himself and the biblical hero, since David is here defiant as well as victorious. This figure differs fundamentally from the apostles of the *Last Supper*. Solid volume and statuesque immobility have given way to graceful movement, conveyed by both the pose and the windblown hair and drapery; the modeling of the earlier figures has been minimized, so that the David seems to be in relief rather than in the round, the forms now defined mainly by their outlines. This dynamic linear style has important virtues, but they are far from those of Masaccio. During the 1450s, the artistic climate of Florence changed greatly; Castagno's *David* is early evidence of the outlook that was to dominate the second half of the century.

CENTRAL AND NORTHERN ITALY: 1450–1500

As the founding fathers of Early Renaissance art and their immediate heirs disappeared one by one in the middle years of the century, a younger generation began to assert itself. At the same time, the seeds planted by Florentine masters in other regions of Italy—we recall Donatello's stay in Padua—were burgeoning; when some of these regions, notably the northeast, produced distinctive versions of the new style, Tuscany ceased to have the privileged position it had enjoyed before.

Architecture

ALBERTI.   In architecture, the death of Brunelleschi in 1446 brought to the fore Leone Battista Alberti (1404–1472), whose career as a practicing architect had been long delayed, like Brunelleschi's own. Until he was forty, Alberti seems to have been interested in the fine arts only as an antiquarian and theorist; he studied the monuments of ancient Rome, composed the earliest Renaissance treatises on sculpture and painting, and began a third treatise, far more exhaustive than the other two, on architecture. After about 1430, he was close to the leading artists of his day (the treatise *On Painting* is dedicated to Brunelleschi and refers to "our dear friend" Donatello) and began to practice art as a dilettante; eventually he became a professional architect of outstanding ability. Highly educated in classical literature and philosophy, as an artist he exemplifies both the humanist and the man of the world.

Palazzo Rucellai.   The design for the Palazzo Rucellai (fig. 572) may be Alberti's critique of the slightly earlier Medici Palace (see fig. 559). Again we meet the heavy cornice and the three-story scheme, but the articulation of the façade is more strict and more self-consciously classical. It consists of

three superimposed orders of pilasters, separated by wide architraves, in imitation of the Colosseum (see fig. 236). Yet Alberti's pilasters are so flat that they remain part of the wall, and the entire façade seems to be one surface on which the artist projects a linear diagram of the Colosseum exterior. If we are to grasp the logic of this curiously abstract and theoretical design, we must understand that Alberti has met here—perhaps for the first time—an issue which became fundamental to Renaissance architecture: how to apply a classical system of articulation to the exterior of a non-classical structure. Whether Brunelleschi ever coped with the same problem is difficult to say; only his exterior design for the Pazzi Chapel survives, but not unaltered, and too special a case to permit general conclusions. Alberti's solution acknowledges the primacy of the wall, reducing the classical system to a network of incised lines.

S. Francesco, Rimini.   For his first church exterior Alberti tried a radically different alternative. Sigismondo Malatesta, lord of the town of Rimini, engaged him toward 1450 to turn the Gothic church of S. Francesco into a "temple of fame" and a burial site for himself, his wife, and the humanists of his court. Alberti encased the older building in a Renaissance shell, the sides consisting of austere, deeply recessed niches, arched above and containing stone sarcophagi (figs. 573,

572. LEONE BATTISTA ALBERTI.
Palazzo Rucellai, Florence. 1446–51

573. LEONE BATTISTA ALBERTI. S. Francesco, Rimini. Façade designed 1450

574. Plan of S. Francesco

574). The façade has three similar niches, the large one framing the central portal, the other two (now filled in) intended to receive the sarcophagi of Sigismondo and his wife.

But the façade niches are flanked by columns, in a scheme clearly derived from the triumphal arches of ancient Rome (see fig. 273). Unlike the pilasters of the Palazzo Rucellai, these columns are not part of the wall; although partly imbedded in it, they project so strongly that we see them as separate entities. We notice, too, that they are set on separate blocks, rather than on the platform supporting the walls, and that they would have nothing to support if the entablature had not been made to project above each capital. These projections make the vertical divisions of the façade more conspicuous than the horizontal ones, and we expect each column to support some important feature of the upper story. Yet Alberti planned such a feature (an arched niche with a window, and framed by pilasters) only above the portal; the second story fails to fulfill the promise of the first. Perhaps our artist would have modified this aspect of his design in the end, but the whole enterprise was never finished, and the great dome, projected as its crowning feature, was never built. If the classical system of the Palazzo Rucellai is in danger of being devoured by the wall, that of S. Francesco retains too much of its ancient Roman character to fit the shape of a basilican façade. (See, for contrast, the medieval approach to this task in fig. 400.)

S. Andrea, Mantua. Only toward the end of his career did Alberti find a fully satisfactory answer to his problem. In the majestic façade of S. Andrea at Mantua (fig. 575), designed in 1470, he has superimposed the triumphal arch motif—now with a huge center niche—upon a classical temple front, and projected this combination onto the wall. Significantly enough, he again uses flat pilasters that acknowledge the primacy of the wall surface, but these pilasters, unlike those of the Palazzo Rucellai, are clearly differentiated from their surroundings. They are of two sizes; the larger ones are linked with the unbroken architrave and the strongly outlined pediment, and form what is known as a "colossal" order for all three stories of the façade wall, balancing exactly the horizontal and vertical impulses within the design. So intent was Alberti on stressing the inner cohesion of the façade that he made its height equal to its width, even though this height is appreciably lower than that of the nave of the church. Thus the upper portion of the west wall protrudes above the pediment. Since this part is behind the façade, it is relatively invisible from the street; Alberti's compromise is more disturbing in photographs, which must be taken from a point high above street level to avoid distortion. While the façade is thus physically distinct from the main body of the structure, artistically there is complete continuity with the interior of the church, where the same colossal order, the same proportions, and the same triumphal arch motif reappear on the nave walls (see the plan, fig. 576): the façade offers an exact "preview" of the interior.

Comparing the plan with Brunelleschi's Sto. Spirito (fig. 557), we are struck by its revolutionary compactness. Had the church been completed as planned, the difference would be even stronger, for Alberti's design had no transept, dome, or choir, only a nave terminating in an apse. The aisles are replaced by chapels alternately large and small, and there is no clerestory; the colossal pilasters and the arches of the large chapels support a barrel vault of impressive span (the nave is as wide as the façade). Alberti has here drawn upon

575. LEONE BATTISTA ALBERTI.
S. Andrea, Mantua. Designed 1470

576. Plan of S. Andrea, Mantua
(transept, dome, and choir are later additions)

his memories of the massive vaulted halls in ancient Roman baths and basilicas (compare fig. 242), yet he interprets his classical models as freely as in his façade design. They no longer embody an absolute authority that must be quoted literally, but serve as a valuable store of motifs to be utilized at will. With this sovereign attitude toward his sources, he was able to create a structure that truly deserves to be called a "Christian temple."

CENTRAL-PLAN CHURCHES.   Nevertheless, S. Andrea, which occupies the site of an older church (note the Gothic campanile next to the façade) with consequent limitations on the designer's freedom, does not conform to the ideal shape of sacred buildings defined in Alberti's *Treatise on Architecture*. There he explains that the plan of such structures should be either circular, or of a shape derived from the circle (square, hexagon, octagon, etc.), because the circle is the perfect as well as the most natural figure, and therefore a direct image of Divine reason.

This argument rests, of course, on his faith in the God-given validity of mathematically determined proportions (discussed on pages 410–412), but how could he reconcile it with the historical evidence? After all, the standard form of both ancient temples and Christian churches was longitudinal. But, he reasons, the basilican church plan became traditional only because the early Christians worshiped in private Roman basilicas. Since pagan basilicas were associated with the dispensing of justice (which originates from God), he admits that their shape has some relationship to sacred architecture, but since they cannot rival the sublime beauty of the temple, their purpose is human rather than divine.

In speaking of temples, Alberti arbitrarily disregarded the standard form and relied instead on the Pantheon (see figs. 238–41), the round temple at Tivoli (see figs. 228, 229), and the domed mausoleums (which he mistook for temples). Moreover, he asked, had not the early Christians themselves acknowledged the sacred character of these structures by converting them to their own use? Here he could point to such monuments as Sta. Costanza (see figs. 294–96), the Pantheon (which had been used as a church ever since the early Middle Ages), and the Baptistery in Florence (supposedly a former temple of Mars).

Alberti's ideal church, then, demands a design so harmonious that it would be a revelation of divinity, and would arouse pious contemplation in the worshiper. It should stand alone, elevated above the surrounding everyday life, and light should enter through openings placed high, for only the sky should be seen through them. That such an isolated, central-plan structure was ill-adapted to the requirements of Catholic ritual made no difference to Alberti; a church, he believed, must be a visible embodiment of "divine proportion," and the central plan alone permitted attainment of this aim.

When Alberti formulated these ideas in his treatise, about 1450, he could have cited only Brunelleschi's revolutionary—and unfinished—Sta. Maria degli Angeli as a modern example of a central-plan church (fig. 558). Toward the end of the century, after his treatise became widely known, the central-plan church gained general acceptance; between 1500 and 1525 it became a vogue reigning supreme in High Renaissance architecture.

GIULIANO DA SANGALLO.   It is no mere coincidence that Sta. Maria delle Carceri in Prato (figs. 577–79), an early and distinguished example of this trend, was begun in 1485, the date of the first printed edition of Alberti's treatise. Its architect, Giuliano da Sangallo (c. 1443–1516), must have been an admirer of Brunelleschi—many features of the

577. GIULIANO DA SANGALLO.
Sta. Maria delle Carceri, Prato. 1485

578. Interior, Sta. Maria delle Carceri

579. Plan of Sta. Maria delle Carceri

design recall the Pazzi Chapel—but the basic shape of his structure conforms closely to Alberti's ideal. Except for the dome, the entire church would fit neatly inside a cube, since its height (up to the drum) equals its length and width. By cutting into the corners of this cube, as it were, Giuliano has formed a Greek cross (a plan he preferred for its symbolic value). The dimensions of the four arms stand in the simplest possible ratio to those of the cube: their length is one-half their width, their width one-half their height. The arms are barrel-vaulted, and the dome rests on these vaults, yet the dark ring of the drum does not quite touch the supporting

arches, making the dome seem to hover, weightless, like the pendentive domes of Byzantine architecture (compare fig. 323). There can be no doubt that Giuliano wanted his dome to accord with the age-old tradition of the Dome of Heaven; the single round opening in the center and the twelve on the perimeter clearly refer to Christ and the apostles. Brunelleschi had anticipated this feature in the Pazzi Chapel, but Giuliano's dome, crowning a perfectly symmetrical structure, conveys its symbolic value far more strikingly.

Sculpture

Donatello left Florence for Padua in 1443; his ten-year absence had an effect similar to that of Brunelleschi's death. But whereas Alberti took Brunelleschi's place in architecture, there was no young sculptor of that stature to take Donatello's. The consequence of his absence was to bring into greater prominence the other sculptors remaining in the city. The new talents who appeared on the scene between 1443 and 1453 grew up under the influence of these men; it was they, rather than their elders, who brought about the changes Donatello must have seen with dismay upon his return.

LUCA DELLA ROBBIA. Ghiberti aside, the only significant sculptor in Florence after Donatello left was Luca della Robbia (1400–1482). He had made his reputation in the 1430s with the marble reliefs of his *Cantoria*, or singers' pulpit, in the Cathedral. The panel reproduced here (fig. 580) shows the beguiling mixture of sweetness and gravity

580. LUCA DELLA ROBBIA. *Singing Angels*, from the *Cantoria*.
c. 1435. Marble, c. 38 × 24″. Cathedral Museum, Florence

characteristic of all of Luca's work. Its style, we realize, has very little to do with Donatello; instead, it recalls the classicism of Nanni di Banco (see fig. 536), with whom Luca may have worked as a youth. We also sense a touch of Ghiberti here and there, as well as the powerful influence of classicistic Roman reliefs (such as fig. 259). But Luca, despite his great gifts, lacked a capacity for growth. He never, so far as we know, did a free-standing statue, and the *Cantoria* remained his most ambitious achievement.

For the rest of his long career, he devoted himself almost exclusively to sculpture in terracotta—a cheaper and less demanding medium than marble—which he covered with enamel-like glazes to mask its surface and make it impervious to weather. His finest works in this technique, such as the *Resurrection* in figure 581, have the dignity and charm of the *Cantoria* panels. The white glaze creates the impression of marble, with a deep blue for the background of the lunette. Other colors were confined almost entirely to the decorative framework of Luca's reliefs. This restraint, however, lasted only while he was in active charge of his workshop. Later, the quality of the modeling deteriorated and the

simple harmony of white and blue often gave way to an assortment of more vivid hues. At the end of the century, the Della Robbia shop had become a factory, turning out small Madonna panels and garish altarpieces for village churches by the score.

Because of Luca's almost complete withdrawal from the domain of marble carving, there was a real shortage of capable marble sculptors in the Florence of the 1440s. By the time Donatello returned, this gap had been filled by a group of men, most of them still in their twenties, from the little hill towns to the north and east of Florence. That region had long supplied the city with stonemasons and carvers; now, because the exceptional circumstances gave them special opportunities, the most gifted of these craftsmen developed into artists of considerable importance.

BERNARDO ROSSELLINO.   Oldest of these, Bernardo Rossellino (1409–1464) seems to have begun as a sculptor and architect in Arezzo. He established himself in Florence about 1436, but received no commissions of real consequence until some eight years later, when he was entrusted with the tomb of Leonardo Bruni (fig. 582). This great humanist and statesman had played a vital part in the city's affairs ever since the beginning of the century (see page 391). When he died in 1444, he received a grand funeral "in the manner of the ancients," and his monument, too, was probably ordered by the government. Since he had been born in Arezzo, however, his native town also wished to honor him, and its representatives may have helped to secure the commission for Bernardo, whom they knew from his earlier activity there. One wonders what chance Bernardo would have had if Donatello had been available.

Although the Bruni monument is not the earliest Renaissance tomb, nor even the earliest large-scale tomb of a humanist, it can claim to be the first memorial that fully expresses the spirit of the new era. Echoes of Bruni's funeral *all'antica* are everywhere: the deceased reclines on a bier supported by Roman eagles, his head wreathed in laurel and his hands enfolding his own volume, *History of Florence*,

581. LUCA DELLA ROBBIA. *The Resurrection*. 1442–45.
Glazed terracotta, 78¾ × 104½″. Cathedral, Florence

582. BERNARDO ROSSELLINO. Tomb of
Leonardo Bruni, c. 1445–50. Marble, height 20′
(to top of arch). Sta. Croce, Florence

rather than a prayer book—a fitting tribute to the man who, more than any other, had helped to establish the new historical perspective of the Florentine Early Renaissance. On the classically severe sarcophagus, two winged genii display an inscription very different from those on medieval tombs; instead of recording the name, rank, and age of the deceased and the date of his death, it refers only to his timeless accomplishments: "At Leonardo's passing, history grieves, eloquence is mute, and it is said that the Muses, Greek and Latin alike, cannot hold back their tears." The religious aspect of the tomb is confined to the lunette, where the Madonna is adored by angels.

The entire monument may thus be viewed as an attempt to reconcile two contrasting attitudes toward death—the retrospective, commemorative outlook of the ancients (see page 140), and the Christian concern with afterlife and salvation. Bernardo Rossellino's design is admirably suited to such a program, balancing architecture and sculpture within a compact, self-contained framework. Its dominant motif, the two pilasters supporting a round arch resting on a strongly accented architrave, suggests Alberti, who employed it repeatedly. It is derived from the entrance to the Pantheon (see fig. 239), which accounts for its use in church portals such as that of S. Andrea in Mantua (fig. 575). While Bernardo Rossellino may have adopted it for the Bruni tomb on purely aesthetic grounds, it is possible that he also meant to convey a symbolic meaning—the deceased on his bier, pausing at the gateway between one life and the next. Perhaps he even wanted us to associate the motif with the Pantheon, the "temple of the immortals" for pagans and Christians alike; once dedicated to all the gods of the Roman world, it had been rededicated to all the martyrs when it became a church, and in the High Renaissance it was to receive the remains of yet another breed of immortals—such famous artists as Raphael.

The sculptural style of the Bruni tomb is not easy to define, since its component parts vary a good deal in quality. Broadly speaking, it reflects the classicism of Ghiberti and Luca della Robbia; echoes of Donatello are few and indirect. Bernardo Rossellino surely employed assistants here, as he did in his subsequent commissions. During the later 1440s his workshop was the only training ground for ambitious young marble sculptors, such as his very gifted younger brother Antonio and other members of the same generation. Their share in Bernardo's sculptural projects is hard to identify, however, for their personalities were not distinct until they began to work independently. Nor have we yet a clear conception of Bernardo's own style as a sculptor. In any event, all the tombs, tabernacles, and Madonna reliefs produced by the younger men between 1450 and 1480 have a common ancestor in the Bruni monument, whatever other elements we may discern in them.

THE PORTRAIT BUST.   Since Bernardo Rossellino and his artistic descendants concentrated their efforts on sculptural ensembles of the kind we have labeled church furniture, free-standing statues are—with one or two possible exceptions—absent from their works. They produced only one form of large-scale sculpture in the round that was not intended for an architectural context—the marble portrait bust. The great Roman tradition of realistic portrait sculpture, we recall, had died out in late antiquity; its revival was long credited to Donatello (who certainly knew and admired Roman portraits, as we saw in the Zuccone), but the earliest examples we know all date from the 1450s, and none are by Donatello. It seems far more likely, therefore, that the Renaissance portrait bust originated among the younger marble sculptors from the circle of Bernardo Rossellino.

583. ANTONIO ROSSELLINO. *Giovanni Chellini.* 1456.
Marble, height 20″. Victoria & Albert Museum, London

The attractive example shown in figure 583 was carved in 1456 by Antonio Rossellino (1427–1479). It represents a highly esteemed Florentine physician, Giovanni Chellini, whose personality—at once sardonic and kindly—has been observed with extraordinary precision. Comparing it with Roman heads (such as figs. 254, 255, and 266–72), we cannot say the resemblance to them is striking. In fact, these Roman busts, however realistic they may seem at first, all look idealized in some respect (not always physically) beside our Florentine doctor, who radiates an individuality far beyond any attained in ancient times. He is linked to his Roman predecessors only by the idea of portrait sculpture in the round as an effective—and enduring—substitute for the sitter's real presence. Stylistically, the ancestry of Antonio's bust is to be found among the heads of effigies, such as that of Leonardo Bruni, for it was in tomb sculpture that realistic portraiture had first been revived, often with the aid of death masks. Although our piece was carved during the sitter's lifetime, its insistence on documenting every wrinkle makes it look like a death-mask portrait suddenly brought to life. Fortunately, Antonio Rossellino did not permit this preoccupation with the details of facial topography to diminish his concern with the sitter's qualities as a human being.

POLLAIUOLO. The popularity of portrait busts after about 1450 suggests a demand for works to be shown in the homes of individual art patrons. The collecting of sculpture, widely practiced in ancient times, apparently ceased during the Middle Ages; the taste of kings and feudal lords—those who could afford to collect for personal pleasure—ran to gems, jewelry, goldsmith's work, illuminated manuscripts, and precious fabrics. The habit was re-established in fifteenth-century Italy as an aspect of the "revival of antiquity." Humanists and artists first collected ancient sculpture, especially small bronzes (such as fig. 209), which were numerous and of convenient size; before long, contemporary artists began to cater to the spreading vogue, with portrait busts and with small bronzes of their own "in the manner of the ancients."

A particularly fine piece of this kind (fig. 584) is by Antonio del Pollaiuolo (1431–1498), who represents a sculptural style very different from that of the marble carvers we discussed above. Trained as a goldsmith and metalworker, probably in the Ghiberti workshop, he was deeply impressed by the late styles of both Donatello and Castagno, as well as by ancient art. From these sources, he evolved the distinctive manner that appears in our *Hercules and Antaeus*. To create a free-standing group of two figures in violent struggle, even on a small scale, was a daring idea in itself; even more astonishing is the way Pollaiuolo has endowed his composition with a centrifugal impulse: limbs seem to radiate in every direction from a common center, and we see the full complexity of their movements only when we turn the statuette before our eyes. Despite its strenuous action, the group is in perfect balance. To stress the central axis, Pollaiuolo, as it were, grafted the upper part of Antaeus onto the lower part of his adversary.

584. ANTONIO DEL POLLAIUOLO. *Hercules and Antaeus.*
c. 1475. Bronze, height 18″ (with base).
National Museum, Florence

585. ANTONIO DEL POLLAIUOLO. *Battle of Ten Naked Men.*
c. 1465–70. Engraving. The Metropolitan Museum
of Art, New York (Joseph Pulitzer Bequest, 1917)

There is no precedent for this design among earlier statuary groups of any size, ancient or Renaissance; our artist has simply given a third dimension to a composition from the field of drawing or painting. He himself was a painter and engraver as well as a bronze sculptor, and we know that about 1465 he did a large picture of Hercules and Antaeus, now lost, for the Medici Palace (our statuette also belonged to the Medici).

Few of his paintings have survived, and only a single engraving, the *Battle of Ten Naked Men* (fig. 585). This print, however, is of great importance, since it represents Pollaiuolo's most elaborate pictorial design. Its subject—undoubtedly a classical one—has not yet been convincingly identified, but that matter is not so significant; the primary purpose of the engraving, obviously, was to display Pollaiuolo's mastery of the nude body in action. About 1465–70, when the print must have been produced, this was still a novel problem, and Pollaiuolo contributed more than any other master to its solution. An interest in movement, coupled with slender proportions and an emphasis on outline rather than on modeling, had been seen in Castagno's *David*, for example (fig. 571, colorplate 70), who in these respects is clearly the progenitor of the *Ten Naked Men*. Pollaiuolo also drew upon the action poses he found in certain types of ancient painted vases (compare fig. 192). But he realized that a full understanding of bodily movement demands a detailed knowledge of anatomy, down to the last muscle and sinew.

All of these ten naked men do indeed have an oddly "flayed" appearance, as if their skin had been stripped off to reveal the play of muscles underneath, and so, to a somewhat lesser degree, do the two figures of our statuette. Equally novel are their facial expressions, as strained as the bodily movements. We have already encountered contorted features in the work of Donatello and Masaccio (see figs. 544, 549,

563, colorplate 66), but the anguish they convey does not arise from, or accompany, the extreme physical action of Pollaiuolo's struggling nudes.

NICCOLÒ DELL'ARCA.   The importance of this integration of motion and emotion is strikingly evident in figure 586, which shows one of the mourners from a lifesize group of the *Lamentation* by Niccolò dell'Arca, about 1485–90. We know of no direct link between that work and Pollaiuolo—Niccolò (c. 1435–1494) came from Apulia and lived mostly in Bologna—yet it could not have been created without his influence. The facial expression itself is not unprecedented, but coupled with the vehement forward rush, the movement of the entire figure overpowers us, as it does in the *Nike of Samothrace* (see fig. 206).

VERROCCHIO.   Although Pollaiuolo, during the late years of his career, did two monumental bronze tombs for St. Peter's in Rome, he never had an opportunity to execute a large-scale free-standing statue. For such works we must turn to his slightly younger contemporary Andrea del Verrocchio (1435–1488), the greatest sculptor of his day and the only one to share some of Donatello's range and ambition. A modeler as well as a carver—we have works of his in marble, terracotta, silver, and bronze—he combined elements from Antonio Rossellino and Antonio del Pollaiuolo into a unique synthesis. He was also a respected painter and the teacher of Leonardo da Vinci (something of a misfortune, for ever since, he has been the object of slighting comparisons).

His most popular work in Florence, because of its location in the courtyard of the Palazzo Vecchio as well as its perennial charm, is the *Putto with Dolphin* (fig. 587). It was designed as the center of a fountain—the dolphin is spouting a jet of water, as if responding to the hug it has to endure—for one of the Medici villas near Florence. The

586. NICCOLO DELL'ARCA. *The Lamentation*
(detail). c. 1485–90. Terracotta, lifesize.
Sta. Maria della Vita, Bologna

surfaces of the armored figure bestriding it. Since the horse is also smaller in relation to the rider than Gattamelata's, Colleoni looms in the saddle like the very embodiment of forceful dominance. Legs rigidly straight, one shoulder thrust forward, he surveys the scene before him with the utter concentration of Donatello's *St. George* (fig. 541), but his lip is now contemptuously curled.

Neither *Gattamelata* nor *Colleoni* is a portrait in the specific sense of the term; both project an idealization of the personality which each artist associated with successful leadership in war. If *Gattamelata* conveys steadfast purpose and nobility of character, *Colleoni* radiates an almost frightening sense of power. As an image of awesome self-assurance, he recalls the *Can Grande* (see fig. 477) rather than the Gattamelata monument. Perhaps Verrocchio visited the tomb of the Can Grande (who was well remembered in Florence as the patron of Dante), and decided to translate the wonderful arrogance of the statue into the style of his own day. In any case, Bartolommeo Colleoni got a great deal more than he had bargained for in his will.

Painting

Before we resume our discussion of Florentine painting, we must consider the growth of Early Renaissance art in Northern Italy. The International Style in painting and sculpture lingered there until the mid-century, and architecture retained a strongly Gothic flavor long after the adoption of a classical vocabulary. We shall disregard North Italian

term putto (plural, putti) designates one of the nude, often winged children that accompany more weighty subjects in ancient art; they personify spirits of various kinds (such as the spirit of love, in which case we call them cupids), usually in a gay and playful way. They were reintroduced during the Early Renaissance, both in their original identity and as child angels. The dolphin associates Verrocchio's *Putto* with the classical kind (note the small putto and dolphin in fig. 256). Artistically, however, he is closer to Pollaiuolo's *Hercules and Antaeus* than to ancient art, despite his larger size and greater sense of volume. Again the forms fly out in every direction from a central axis, but here the movement is graceful and continuous rather than jagged and broken; the stretched-out leg, the dolphin, and the arms and wings fit into an upward spiral, making the figure seem to revolve before our eyes.

By a strange coincidence, the crowning achievement of Verrocchio's career, as of Donatello's, was the bronze equestrian monument of a Venetian army commander: Bartolommeo Colleoni (fig. 588). In his will, Colleoni had requested such a statue and, by way of encouragement, had left a sizable fortune to the Republic of Venice. He obviously knew the Gattamelata monument and wanted to ensure the same honor for himself. Verrocchio, too, must have regarded Donatello's work as the prototype of his own statue. Yet he did not simply imitate his illustrious model; he reinterpreted the theme less subtly, perhaps, but no less impressively. The horse, graceful and spirited rather than robust and placid, is modeled with the same sense of anatomy-in-action that we saw in the nudes of Pollaiuolo; its thin hide reveals every vein, muscle, and sinew, in strong contrast with the rigid

587. ANDREA DEL VERROCCHIO. *Putto with Dolphin*. c. 1470.
Bronze, height 27″ (without base). Palazzo Vecchio, Florence

588. ANDREA DEL VERROCCHIO. *Equestrian Monument of Colleoni.* c. 1483–88. Bronze, height c. 13'. Campo SS. Giovanni e Paolo, Venice

architecture and sculpture between 1450 and 1500, as there are hardly any achievements of major consequence in either field. Instead, we shall focus upon painting in Venice and its dependent territories, for during these same years a great tradition was born here that was to flourish for the next three centuries. The Republic of Venice, although more oligarchic, and unique in its eastward orientation, had many ties with Florence; it is not surprising, therefore, that she, rather than the Duchy of Milan, should have become the leading center of Early Renaissance art in Northern Italy.

PADUA: MANTEGNA.   Florentine masters had been carrying the new style to Venice and to the neighboring city of Padua since the 1420s. Fra Filippo Lippi, Uccello, and Castagno had all worked there at one time or another. Still more important was Donatello's ten-year sojourn. Their presence, however, evoked only rather timid local responses until, shortly before 1450, the young Andrea Mantegna (1431–1506) emerged as an independent master. He was first trained by a minor Paduan painter, but his early development was decisively shaped by the impressions he received from locally available Florentine works and—we may assume—

by personal contact with Donatello. Next to Masaccio, Mantegna was the most important painter of the Early Renaissance. And he, too, was a precocious genius, fully capable at seventeen of executing commissions of his own. Within the next decade, he reached artistic maturity, and during the next half-century—he died at the age of seventy-five—he broadened the range of his art but never departed, in essence, from the style he had formulated in the 1450s.

His greatest achievement of that time, the frescoes in the Church of the Eremitani in Padua, was almost entirely destroyed by an accidental bomb explosion in 1944—a more grievous loss than the murals of Camposanto of Pisa (see fig. 497). The scene we reproduce in figure 589, *St. James Led to His Execution,* is the most dramatic of the cycle, because of its daring "worm's-eye view" perspective, which is based on the beholder's actual eye-level (the central vanishing point is below the bottom of the picture, somewhat to the right of center). The architectural setting consequently looms large, as in Masaccio's *Trinity* fresco (see fig. 560). Its main feature, a huge triumphal arch, although not a copy of any specific Roman monument, looks so authentic in every detail that it might as well be.

Here Mantegna's devotion to the visible remains of antiquity, almost like that of an archaeologist, shows his close association with the learned humanists at the University of Padua (who had the same reverence for every word of ancient literature). No Florentine painter or sculptor of the time could have transmitted such an attitude to him. The same desire for authenticity can be seen in the costumes of the Roman soldiers (compare fig. 256); it even extends to the use of "wet" drapery patterns, an invention of Classical Greek sculpture inherited by the Romans (see fig. 259). But the tense figures, lean and firmly constructed, and especially their dramatic interaction, clearly derive from Donatello. Mantegna's subject hardly demands this agitated staging: the saint, on the way to his execution, blesses a paralytic and commands him to walk. But the large crowd of bystanders, many of them expressing by glance and gesture how deeply the miracle has stirred them, generates an extraordinary emotional tension that erupts into real physical violence on the far right. The great spiral curl of the banner merely echoes the turbulence below.

By rare good luck, a sketch for our fresco has survived (fig. 590), the earliest instance we know of a drawing that permits us to compare the preliminary and final versions of such a design. (Among the drawings by earlier masters, none, it seems, is related to a known picture in the same way.) This sketch differs from the *sinopie,* full-scale drawings on the wall (see fig. 498), in its tentative, unsettled quality; the composition has not yet taken full shape; still growing, as it were, the image in our drawing is "unfinished" both in conception and in the sense that the forms are set down in a quick, shorthand style. We note, for example, that here the perspective is closer to normal, indicating that the artist worked out the exact scheme only on the wall. Our drawing also offers proof of what we suspected in the case of Masaccio: that Early Renaissance artists actually conceived their compositions in terms of nude figures. The group on the right is still in that first stage, and in the others the outlines

589. ANDREA MANTEGNA. *St. James Led to His Execution.*
c. 1455. Fresco. Ovetari Chapel,
Church of the Eremitani, Padua (destroyed 1944)

590. ANDREA MANTEGNA. *St. James Led to His Execution.*
c. 1455. Pen drawing, 6⅛ × 9¼″.
Collection G. M. Gathorne-Hardy,
Donnington Priory, Newbury, Berkshire, England

of the body show clearly beneath the costume. But the drawing is more than only a document; it is a work of art in its own right. The very quickness of its "handwriting" gives it an immediacy and rhythmic force that are necessarily lost in the fresco.

On the evidence of these works, we would hardly expect Mantegna to be much concerned with light and color. The

panel reproduced in figure 591 and colorplate 71, painted only a few years after the Paduan frescoes, proves that he was. In the foreground, to be sure, we find the familiar array of classical remains (including, this time, the artist's signature in Greek). The saint, too, looks more like a statue than a living body. But beyond we see a wonderfully atmospheric landscape and a deep blue sky dotted with the softest of white clouds. The entire scene is bathed in the warm

591. ANDREA MANTEGNA. *St. Sebastian* (see colorplate 71).
Kunsthistorisches Museum, Vienna

592. GIOVANNI BELLINI. *St. Francis in Ecstasy*
(see colorplate 72). The Frick Collection, New York (Copyright)

exemplified by the latest—and most monumental—member of the series, the *Madonna and Saints* of 1505 in S. Zaccaria (fig. 593). Compared to Domenico Veneziano's *Sacra Conversazione* (fig. 567, colorplate 67), the architectural setting is a good deal simpler but no less impressive: we stand in the nave of a church, near the crossing (which is partly visible), with the apse filling almost the entire panel. The figures appear in front of the apse, however, under the great vaulted canopy of the crossing. The structure is not a real church, for its sides are open and the entire scene is flooded with gentle sunlight, just as Domenico Veneziano had placed his figures in a semi-outdoors setting. The Madonna's solid, high-backed throne and the music-making angel on its lowest step are derived (through many intermediaries, no doubt) from Masaccio's *Madonna* of 1426 (fig. 564).

radiance of late afternoon sunlight, which creates a gently melancholy mood, making the pathos of the dying saint doubly poignant. The background of our panel would hardly be conceivable without the influence, direct or indirect, of the Van Eycks (compare fig. 510 and colorplate 61, left). Some works of the great Flemish masters had surely reached Florence as well as Venice between 1430 and 1450, and must have been equally admired in both cities; but in Venice they had more immediate effect, evoking the interest in lyrical, light-filled landscapes that became an ingrained part of Venetian Renaissance painting.

VENICE: BELLINI. In the painting of Giovanni Bellini (c. 1431–1516), Mantegna's brother-in-law, we trace the further growth of the Flemish tradition. Bellini was slow to mature; his finest pictures, such as *St. Francis in Ecstasy* (fig. 592, colorplate 72), date from the last decades of the century or later. The saint is here so small in comparison to the setting that he seems almost incidental, yet his mystic rapture before the beauty of the visible world sets our own response to the view that is spread out before us, ample and intimate at the same time. He has left his wooden pattens behind and stands barefoot on holy ground, like Moses in the Lord's presence (see page 57). Bellini's contours are less brittle than those of Mantegna, the colors are softer and the light more glowing, and he shares the tender regard of the great Flemings for every detail of nature. Unlike the Northerners, however, he can define the beholder's spatial relationship to the landscape—the rock formations of the foreground are structurally clear and firm, like architecture rendered by the rules of scientific perspective.

As the foremost painter of the city of Venice, Giovanni Bellini produced a number of formal altar panels of the *Sacra Conversazione* type. His compositional pattern is well

593. GIOVANNI BELLINI. *Madonna and Saints.* 1505.
Panel, 16′ 5⅛″ × 7′ 9″. S. Zaccaria, Venice

Early Renaissance in Italy 431

594. SANDRO BOTTICELLI. *The Birth
of Venus* (see colorplate 73). Uffizi
Gallery, Florence

What differentiates this altar immediately from its Florentine ancestors is not merely the ample spaciousness of the
design but its wonderfully calm, meditative mood; instead
of "conversation," we sense the figures' deep communion,
which makes all rhetorical gestures unnecessary. We shall
encounter this quality again and again in Venetian painting;
here, from the way the aged master has bathed the entire
scene in a delicate aerial haze, we see it as through a diffusing filter of atmosphere. All harsh contrasts are eliminated,
light and shadow blend in almost imperceptible gradations,
and colors glow with a new richness and depth. In this
magical moment, Giovanni Bellini becomes the true heir of
the two greatest painters of the fifteenth century, uniting the
Florentine grandeur of Masaccio with the Northern poetic
intimacy of Jan van Eyck.

FLORENCE: BOTTICELLI.   We now return once more to
Florence. The trend forecast by Castagno's *David* substitutes
energetic, graceful movement and agitated linear contours
for the stable monumentality of the Masaccio style; its climax
comes in the final quarter of the century, in the art of Sandro
Botticelli (1444/5–1510). Trained by Fra Filippo Lippi—
whose *Madonna* (fig. 565) already had undercurrents of
linear movement—and strongly influenced by Pollaiuolo,
Botticelli soon became the favorite painter of the so-called
Medici circle, those patricians, literati, scholars, and poets
surrounding Lorenzo the Magnificent, the head of the
Medici family and, for all practical purposes, the real ruler
of the city.

For one member of this group, Botticelli did *The Birth of
Venus* (fig. 594, colorplate 73), probably his most famous
picture. Its kinship with Pollaiuolo's *Battle of Ten Naked
Men* (fig. 585) is unmistakable, the shallow modeling and
the emphasis on outline producing an effect of low relief
rather than of solid, three-dimensional shapes; in both we
note a lack of concern with deep space—the ornamentalized
thicket forms a screen behind the *Naked Men* much like the
grove on the right-hand side of the *Venus*. But the differences are just as striking. Botticelli evidently does not share

Pollaiuolo's passion for anatomy; his bodies are more attenuated, and drained of all weight and muscular power; they
seem to float even when they touch the ground. All this
seems to deny the basic values of the founding fathers of
Early Renaissance art, yet the picture does not look medieval: the bodies, ethereal though they be, retain their voluptuousness; they are genuine nudes (see our discussion,
pages 398–99) enjoying full freedom of movement.

NEO-PLATONISM.   To understand this paradox, we must
consider the meaning of our picture, and the general use
of classical subjects in Early Renaissance art. During the
Middle Ages, classical form had become divorced from classical subject matter. Artists could only draw upon the ancient
repertory of poses, gestures, expressions, etc., by changing
the identity of their sources: philosophers became apostles,
Orpheus turned into Adam, Hercules into Samson. When
medieval artists had occasion to represent the pagan gods,
they based their pictures on literary descriptions rather than
visual models. This was the situation, by and large, until the
mid-fifteenth century. Only with Pollaiuolo—and Mantegna
in Northern Italy—does classical form begin to rejoin classical content. Pollaiuolo's lost paintings of the Labors of Hercules (about 1465) mark the earliest instance—so far as we
know—of large-scale subjects from classical mythology
depicted in a style inspired by ancient monuments; and *The
Birth of Venus* contains the first monumental image since
Roman times of the nude goddess in a pose derived from
classical statues of Venus (see fig. 197). Moreover, the subject of the picture is clearly meant to be serious, even solemn.

How could such images be justified in a Christian civilization, without subjecting both artist and patron to the accusation of neo-paganism? In the Middle Ages, classical myths
had at times been interpreted didactically, however remote
the analogy, as allegories of Christian precepts. Europa
abducted by the bull, for instance, could be declared to
signify the soul redeemed by Christ. But such pallid constructions were hardly an adequate excuse for reinvesting
the pagan gods with their ancient beauty and strength. To
fuse the Christian faith with ancient mythology, rather than
merely relate them, required a more sophisticated argument.
This was provided by the Neo-Platonic philosophers, whose
foremost representative, Marsilio Ficino, enjoyed tremendous prestige during the later years of the fifteenth century
and after. Ficino's thought, based as much on the mysticism
of Plotinus (see page 186) as on the authentic works of
Plato, was the very opposite of the orderly system of medieval
scholasticism. He believed that the life of the universe,
including that of man, was linked to God by a spiritual
circuit continuously ascending and descending, so that all
revelation, whether from the Bible, Plato, or classical myths,
was one. Similarly, he proclaimed that beauty, love, and beati-
tude, being phases of this same circuit, were one. Thus
Neo-Platonists could invoke the "celestial Venus" (that is,
the nude Venus born of the sea, as in our picture) inter-
changeably with the Virgin Mary, as the source of "divine
love" (meaning the cognition of divine beauty). This celestial
Venus, according to Ficino, dwells purely in the sphere of

Mind, while her twin, the ordinary Venus, engenders "human love."

Once we understand that Botticelli's picture has this quasi-religious meaning, it seems less astonishing that the two wind gods on the left look so much like angels, and that the personification of Spring on the right, who welcomes Venus ashore, recalls the traditional relation of St. John to the Saviour in the Baptism of Christ (compare fig. 412). As baptism is a "rebirth in God," the birth of Venus evokes the hope for "rebirth" from which the Renaissance takes its name. Thanks to the fluidity of Neo-Platonic doctrine, the number of possible associations to be linked with our painting is almost limitless. All of them, however, like the celestial Venus herself, "dwell in the sphere of Mind," and Botticelli's deity would hardly be a fit vessel for them if she were less ethereal.

Neo-Platonic philosophy and its expression in art were obviously too complex to become popular outside the select and highly educated circle of its devotees. In 1494, the suspicions of the man in the street were confirmed by the friar Girolamo Savonarola, an ardent advocate of religious reform, who gained a huge following with his sermons attacking the "cult of paganism" in the city's ruling circle. Botticelli himself was perhaps a follower of Savonarola and reportedly burned a number of his "pagan" pictures. In his last works—he seems to have stopped painting entirely after 1500—he returns to traditional religious themes but with no essential change in style.

FLORENCE: PIERO DI COSIMO.   Figure 595 and color-plate 74, a panel by Botticelli's younger contemporary Piero di Cosimo (1462–1521), illustrates a view of pagan mythology diametrically opposed to that of the Neo-Platonists. Instead of "spiritualizing" the pagan gods, it brings them down to earth as beings of flesh and blood. In this alternate theory, man had slowly risen from a barbaric state through the discoveries and inventions of a few exceptionally gifted indi-viduals; gratefully remembered by posterity, these men were finally accorded the status of gods. St. Augustine subscribed to such a view (which can be traced back to Hellenistic times) without facing all of the implications expressed by ancient authors. The complete theory was not revived until the late fifteenth century: it postulates a gradual evolution of man from the animal level, which thus conflicts with the scriptural account of Creation. This could be glossed over, however, by making a gay idyl out of the achievements of these pagan "culture heroes," to avoid the impression of complete seriousness—exactly what Piero di Cosimo did in our picture.

Its title, *The Discovery of Honey*, refers to the central episode, a group of satyrs busying themselves about an old willow tree. They have discovered a swarm of bees, and are making as much noise as possible with their pots and pans to induce the bees to cluster on one of the branches. The satyrs will then collect the honey, from which they will produce mead. Behind them, to the right, some of their companions are about to discover the source of another fer-mented beverage; they are climbing trees to collect wild grapes. Beyond is a barren rock, while on the left are gentle hills and a town. This contrast does not imply that the satyrs are city dwellers; it merely juxtaposes civilization, the goal of the future, with untamed nature. Here the "culture hero" is, of course, Bacchus, who appears in the lower right-hand corner, a tipsy grin on his face, next to his lady-love, Ariadne. Despite their classical appearance, Bacchus and his compa-nions do not in the least resemble the frenzied revelers of ancient mythology. They have an oddly domestic air, suggest-ing a fun-loving family clan on a picnic. The brilliant sun-light, the rich colors, and the far-ranging landscape make the scene a still more plausible extension of everyday reality. We can well believe that Piero di Cosimo, in contrast to Botticelli, admired the great Flemish realists, and this land-scape would be inconceivable without the strong influence of the *Portinari Altarpiece* (compare fig. 519).

595. PIERO DI COSIMO. *The Discovery of Honey*
(see colorplate 74). Worcester Art Museum, Massachusetts

596. DOMENICO GHIRLANDAIO.
An Old Man and His Grandson.
c. 1480. Panel, 24⅛ × 18″. The Louvre, Paris

ration of the walls of the Sistine Chapel about 1482. Among the artists who carried out this large cycle of Old and New Testament scenes we encounter most of the important painters of Central Italy, including Botticelli and Ghirlandaio, although the frescoes do not, on the whole, represent their most distinguished work.

There is, however, one exception to this rule: *The Delivery of the Keys* (fig. 597) by Pietro Perugino (c. 1450–1523) must rank as his finest achievement. Born near Perugia in Umbria (the region southeast of Tuscany), Perugino maintained close ties with Florence. His early development had been decisively influenced by Verrocchio, as the statuesque balance and solidity of the figures in *The Delivery of the Keys* still suggest. The gravely symmetrical design conveys the special importance of the subject in this particular setting (the authority of St. Peter as the first pope—and that of all his successors—rests on his having received the keys to the Kingdom of Heaven from Christ Himself). A number of contemporaries, with powerfully individualized features, witness the solemn event. Equally striking is the vast expanse of the background, its two Roman triumphal arches (both modeled on the Arch of Constantine) flanking a domed structure in which we recognize the ideal church of Alberti's *Treatise on Architecture.* The spatial clarity, the mathematically exact perspective of this view, are the heritage of Piero della Francesca, who spent much of his later life working for Umbrian clients, notably the duke of Urbino. And also from Urbino, shortly before 1500, Perugino received a pupil whose fame soon obscured his own—Raphael, the most classic master of the High Renaissance.

FLORENCE: GHIRLANDAIO. Not only Piero was receptive to the realism of the Flemings: Domenico Ghirlandaio (1449–1494), another contemporary of Botticelli, shared this attitude. Ghirlandaio's fresco cycles are so replete with portraits that they almost serve as family chronicles of the wealthy patricians who sponsored them. Among his most affecting individual portraits is the panel of an old man with his grandson (fig. 596). Lacking the pictorial delicacy of Flemish portraits, it nevertheless reflects their precise attention to surface texture and facial detail. But no Northern painter could have rendered like Ghirlandaio the tender human relationship between the little boy and his grandfather. Psychologically, our panel plainly bespeaks its Italian origin.

URBINO: PERUGINO. Rome, long neglected during the papal exile in Avignon, became once more, in the later fifteenth century, an important center of art patronage. As the papacy regained its political power on Italian soil, the occupants of the Chair of St. Peter began to beautify both the Vatican and the city, in the conviction that the monuments of Christian Rome must outshine those of the pagan past. The most ambitious pictorial project of those years was the deco-

CORTONA: SIGNORELLI. Luca Signorelli (1445/50–1523) is linked to Perugino by a similar background, although his personality is infinitely more dramatic. Of provincial Tuscan origin, he had been a disciple of Piero della Francesca before coming to Florence in the 1470s. Like Perugino, Signorelli was strongly impressed by Verrocchio, but he also admired the energy, expressiveness, and anatomic precision of Pollaiuolo's nudes. Combining these influences with Piero's cubic solidity of form and mastery of perspective foreshortening, Signorelli achieved a style of epic grandeur that later made a lasting imprint upon the mind of Michelangelo. He reached the climax of his career just before 1500 with the four monumental frescoes, representing the end of the world, on the walls of the S. Brizio Chapel in Orvieto Cathedral—especially the most dynamic of these, *The Damned Cast into Hell* (fig. 598). What most strikes us is not Signorelli's use of the nude body as an expressive instrument—even though he far surpasses his predecessors in this respect—but the deep sense of tragedy that pervades the scene. Signorelli's Hell, the exact opposite of Bosch's (compare fig. 523), is illuminated by the full light of day, without nightmarish machines of torture or grotesque monsters. The damned retain their human dignity, and the devils, too, are humanized; even in Hell, the Renaissance faith in man does not lose its force.

597. PIETRO PERUGINO. *The Delivery of the Keys.* 1482. Fresco. Sistine Chapel, The Vatican, Rome

598. LUCA SIGNORELLI. *The Damned Cast into Hell.* 1499–1500. Fresco. S. Brizio Chapel, Orvieto Cathedral

3
THE HIGH RENAISSANCE IN ITALY

It used to be taken for granted that the High Renaissance followed upon the Early Renaissance as naturally and inevitably as noon follows morning. The great masters of the sixteenth century—Leonardo, Bramante, Michelangelo, Raphael, Giorgione, Titian—were thought to have shared the ideals of their predecessors, but to have expressed them so completely that their names became synonyms for perfection. They represented the climax, the classic phase, of Renaissance art, just as Phidias seemed to have brought the art of ancient Greece to its highest point. This view could also explain why these two classic phases were so short: if art is assumed to develop along the pattern of a ballistic curve, its highest point cannot be expected to last more than a moment.

Since the 1920s, art historians have come to realize the shortcomings of this scheme. When we apply it literally, the High Renaissance becomes so absurdly brief, for example, that we wonder whether it happened at all. Moreover, we hardly increase our understanding of the Early Renaissance if we regard it as a "not-yet-perfect High Renaissance," any more than an Archaic Greek statue can be satisfactorily viewed from a Phidian standpoint. Nor is it very useful to insist that the subsequent post-Classical phase, whether Hellenistic or "Late Renaissance," must be decadent. The image of the ballistic curve has now been abandoned, and we have gained a less assured, but also less arbitrary, estimate of what, for lack of another term, we still call the High Renaissance.

In some fundamental respects, we shall find that the High Renaissance was indeed the culmination of the Early Renaissance, while in others it represented a departure. Certainly the tendency to view the artist as a sovereign genius, rather than as a devoted craftsman, was never stronger than during the first half of the sixteenth century. Plato's concept of genius—the spirit entering into the poet that causes him to compose in a "divine frenzy"—had been broadened by Marsilio Ficino and his fellow Neo-Platonists to include the architect, the sculptor, and the painter. Men of genius were thought to be set apart from ordinary mortals by the divine inspiration guiding their efforts, and worthy of being called "divine," "immortal," and "creative" (before 1500, *creating,* as distinct from *making,* was the privilege of God alone).

This cult of genius had a profound effect on the artists of the High Renaissance. It spurred them to vast and ambitious goals, and prompted their awed patrons to support such enterprises. But since these ambitions often went beyond the humanly possible, they were apt to be frustrated by external as well as internal difficulties, leaving the artist with a sense of having been defeated by a malevolent fate. At the same time, the artist's faith in the divine origin of inspiration led him to rely on subjective, rather than objective, standards of truth and beauty. If Early Renaissance artists felt bound by what they believed to be universally valid rules, such as the numerical ratios of musical harmony and the laws of scientific perspective, their High Renais-

599. LEONARDO DA VINCI. *Adoration of the Magi* (detail). 1481–82.
Panel, size of area shown c. 24 × 30". Uffizi Gallery, Florence

sance successors were less concerned with rational order than with visual effectiveness. They evolved a new drama and a new rhetoric to engage the emotions of the beholder, whether sanctioned or not by classical precedent. In fact, the works of the great High Renaissance masters immediately became classics in their own right, their authority equal to that of the most renowned monuments of antiquity.

But here we encounter a contradiction: if the creations of genius are viewed as unique by definition, they cannot be successfully imitated by lesser men, however worthy they may seem of such imitation. Unlike the founding fathers of the Early Renaissance, the leading artists of the High Renaissance did not set the pace for a broadly based "period style" that could be practiced on every level of quality. The High Renaissance produced astonishingly few minor masters; it died with the men who had created it, or even before. Of the six great personalities mentioned above, only Michelangelo and Titian lived beyond 1520.

External conditions after that date were undoubtedly less favorable to the High Renaissance style than those of the first two decades of the century. Yet the High Renaissance might well have ended soon even without the pressure of circumstances; its harmonious grandeur was inherently unstable, a balance of divergent qualities. Only these qualities, not the balance itself, could be transmitted to the artists who reached maturity after 1520. In pointing out the limited and precarious nature of the High Renaissance we do not mean to deny its tremendous impact upon later art. For most

of the next three hundred years, the great personalities of the early sixteenth century loomed so large that the achievements of their predecessors seemed to belong to a forgotten era. Even when the art of the fourteenth and fifteenth centuries was finally rediscovered, people still acknowledged the High Renaissance as the turning point, referring to all painters before Raphael as "the Primitives."

Leonardo da Vinci

One of the strangest aspects of the High Renaissance—and one important reason why, within the limitations set forth above, it rightfully deserves to be called a period—is the fact that its key monuments were all produced between 1495 and 1520, despite the great differences in age of the men creating them. Bramante, the oldest, was born in 1444, Raphael in 1483, and Titian about 1488–90. Yet the distinction of being the earliest High Renaissance master belongs to Leonardo da Vinci, not to Bramante.

Born in 1452 in the little Tuscan town of Vinci, Leonardo was trained in Florence by Verrocchio. Conditions there must not have suited him; at the age of thirty he went to work for the duke of Milan as a military engineer, and only secondarily as an architect, sculptor, and painter.

ADORATION OF THE MAGI. He left behind, unfinished, the most ambitious work he had then begun, a large *Adoration of the Magi* for which he had made many preliminary studies. Its design shows a geometric order and a precisely constructed perspective space that recall Florentine painting in the wake of Masaccio, rather than the style prevailing about 1480. The most striking—and indeed revolutionary—aspect of the panel is the way it is painted, although Leonardo had not even completed the underpainting.

Our detail (fig. 599) is taken from the area to the right of center, which is more nearly finished than the rest; the forms seem to materialize softly and gradually, never quite detaching themselves from a dusky realm. Leonardo, unlike Pollaiuolo or Botticelli, thinks not of outlines, but of three-dimensional bodies made visible, in varying degrees, by the incidence of light. In the shadows, these shapes remain incomplete; their contours are merely implied. In this method of modeling (called *chiaroscuro*, "light-and-dark") the forms no longer stand abruptly side by side but partake of a new pictorial unity, the barriers between them having been partially broken down. And there is a comparable emotional continuity as well: the gestures and faces of the crowd convey with touching eloquence the reality of the miracle they have come to behold. We will recognize the influence of both Pollaiuolo and Verrocchio in the mobile expressiveness of these figures, but Leonardo may also have been impressed by the breathless shepherds in the *Portinari Altarpiece*, then newly installed in Florence (see fig. 520).

VIRGIN OF THE ROCKS. Soon after arriving in Milan, Leonardo did *The Virgin of the Rocks* (fig. 600), another altar panel, which suggests what the *Adoration* would have looked like if it had been completed. Here the figures emerge from the semidarkness of the grotto, enveloped in a moisture-laden atmosphere that delicately veils their forms. This fine haze (called *sfumato*), more pronounced than similar effects in Flemish and Venetian painting, lends a peculiar warmth and intimacy to the scene. It also creates a remote, dreamlike quality, and makes the picture seem a poetic vision rather than an image of reality pure and simple. The subject—the infant St. John adoring the Infant Christ in the presence of the Virgin and an angel—is mysterious in many ways, without immediate precedent: the secluded, rocky setting, the pool in front, and the plant life, carefully chosen and exquisitely rendered, all hint at symbolic meanings that are somehow hard to define. And on what level, or levels, of significance are we to interpret the relationships among the four figures? Perhaps the key is the conjunction of gestures—protective, pointing, and blessing—toward the center of the group. However puzzling its content, few pictures cast a more enduring spell.

LAST SUPPER. Despite their originality, the *Adoration* and the *Virgin of the Rocks* do not yet differ clearly, in conception, from the aims of the Early Renaissance. But Leonardo's *Last Supper,* later by a dozen years, has always been recognized as the first classic statement of the ideals of High Renaissance painting (fig. 601). Unhappily, the famous mural began to deteriorate a few years after its completion; the artist, dissatisfied with the limitations of the traditional fresco technique, experimented in an oil-tempera medium that did not adhere well to the wall. We thus need

some effort to imagine its original splendor. Yet what remains is more than sufficient to account for its tremendous impact. Viewing the composition as a whole, we are struck at once by its balanced stability; only afterward do we discover that this balance has been achieved by the reconciliation of competing, even conflicting, claims such as no previous artist had attempted.

A comparison with Castagno's *Last Supper* (fig. 570), painted half a century before, is particularly instructive here: the spatial setting in both cases seems like an annex to the real interior of the refectory, but Castagno's architecture has a strangely oppressive effect on the figures while Leonardo's, despite its far greater depth, does not. The reason for this becomes clear when we realize that in the earlier work the perspective space has been conceived autonomously—it was there before the figures entered, and would equally suit another group of diners. Leonardo, in contrast, began with the figure composition, and the architecture had merely a

600. LEONARDO DA VINCI. *The Virgin of the Rocks.* c. 1485. Panel, 75 × 43½". The Louvre, Paris

601. LEONARDO DA VINCI. *The Last Supper.* c. 1495–98. Mural. Sta. Maria delle Grazie, Milan

supporting role from the start. The central vanishing point, which governs our view of the interior, is located behind the head of Christ in the exact middle of the picture, and thus becomes charged with symbolic significance. Equally plain is the symbolic function of the main opening in the back wall; its projecting pediment acts as the architectural equivalent of a halo. We thus tend to see the perspective framework of the scene almost entirely in relation to the figures, rather than as a pre-existing entity. How vital this relationship is we can easily test by covering the upper third of the picture: the composition then takes on the character of a frieze, the grouping of the apostles is less clear, and the calm triangular shape of Christ becomes merely passive, instead of acting as a physical and spiritual force.

The Saviour, presumably, has just spoken the fateful words, "One of you shall betray me," and the disciples are asking, "Lord, is it I?" We actually see nothing that contradicts this interpretation, but to view the scene as one particular moment in a psychological drama hardly does justice to Leonardo's intentions. These went well beyond a literal rendering of the biblical narrative, for he crowded together all the disciples on the far side of the table, in a space quite inadequate for so many diners. He clearly wanted to condense his subject physically by the compact, monumental grouping of the figures, and spiritually by presenting many levels of meaning at one time. Thus the gesture of Christ is one of submission to the Divine will, and of offering. It is a hint at Christ's main act at the Last Supper, the institution of the Eucharist ("And as they were eating, Jesus took bread... and gave it to the disciples, and said, Take and eat; this is my body. And he took the cup... saying, Drink ye all of it; for this is my blood..."). And the apostles do not merely react to these words; each of them reveals his own

personality, his own relationship to the Saviour. (Note that Judas is no longer segregated from the rest; his dark, defiant profile sets him apart well enough.) They exemplify what the artist wrote in one of his notebooks, that the highest and most difficult aim of painting is to depict "the intention of man's soul" through gestures and movements of the limbs—a dictum to be interpreted as referring not to momentary emotional states but to man's inner life as a whole.

BATTLE OF ANGHIARI. In 1499, the duchy of Milan fell to the French, and Leonardo, after brief trips to Mantua and Venice, returned to Florence. He must have found the cultural climate very different from his recollections of it; the Medici had been expelled, and the city was briefly a republic again, until their return. For a while, Leonardo seems to have been active mainly as an engineer and surveyor, but in 1503 the city commissioned him to do a mural for the council chamber of the Palazzo Vecchio, with some famous event from the history of Florence as its subject. Leonardo chose the Battle of Anghiari, where the Florentine forces had once defeated the Milanese army. He completed the cartoon (a full-scale drawing) and had just begun the mural itself when, in 1506, he returned once more to Milan at the request of the French, abandoning the commission. The cartoon for *The Battle of Anghiari* survived for more than a century, and enjoyed enormous fame.

Today we know it only through Leonardo's preliminary sketches and through copies of the cartoon by later artists, notably a splendid drawing by Peter Paul Rubens (fig. 602; see page 522). Leonardo had started with the historical accounts of the engagement; as his plans crystallized, however, he abandoned factual accuracy and created a monumental group of soldiers on horseback that represent a condensed, timeless image of the spirit of battle, rather than any specific event. His concern with "the intention of man's soul"—in this case, a savage fury that has seized not only the men but the animals as well—is even more evident here than in the *Last Supper. The Battle of Anghiari* stands at the opposite end of the scale from Uccello's *Battle of San Romano* (fig. 569, colorplate 69), where nothing has been omitted except the fighting itself. Yet Leonardo's battle scene is not one of uncontrolled action; its dynamism is held in check by the hexagonal outline that stabilizes this seething mass. Once again, balance has been achieved by the reconciliation of competing claims.

MONA LISA. While working on *The Battle of Anghiari*, Leonardo painted his most famous portrait, the *Mona Lisa* (fig. 603, colorplate 75). The delicate *sfumato* of the *Madonna of the Rocks* is here so perfected that it seemed miraculous to the artist's contemporaries. The forms are built from layers of glazes so gossamer-thin that the entire panel seems to glow with a gentle light from within. But the fame of the *Mona Lisa* comes not from this pictorial subtlety alone; even more intriguing is the psychological fascination of the sitter's personality. Why, among all the smiling faces ever painted, has this particular one been singled out as "mysterious"? Perhaps the reason is that, as a portrait, the picture does not fit our expectations. The features are too individual for Leonardo to have simply depicted an ideal type, yet the element of idealization is so strong that it blurs the sitter's character. Once again the artist has brought two opposites into harmonious balance. The smile, also, may be read in two ways: as the echo of a momentary mood, and as a timeless, symbolic expression (somewhat like the "Archaic smile" of the Greeks; see figures 147, 148, 150, and colorplate 15). Clearly, the Mona Lisa embodies a quality of maternal ten-

602. (*above, left*) PETER PAUL RUBENS. Drawing after Leonardo's cartoon for "*The Battle of Anghiari.*" c. 1605.
The Louvre, Paris

603. (*left*) LEONARDO DA VINCI. *Mona Lisa* (see colorplate 75).
The Louvre, Paris

604. (*below*) LEONARDO DA VINCI. *Embryo in the Womb.*
c. 1510. Pen drawing. Royal Library,
Windsor Castle (Crown copyright reserved)

Colorplate 73. SANDRO BOTTICELLI. *The Birth of Venus* (see page 432). About 1480. 5' 8⅞" × 9' 1⅞". Uffizi Gallery, Florence

Colorplate 74. PIERO DI COSIMO. *The Discovery of Honey* (see page 433). About 1498. Panel, 31¼ × 50⅝″. Worcester Art Museum, Massachusetts

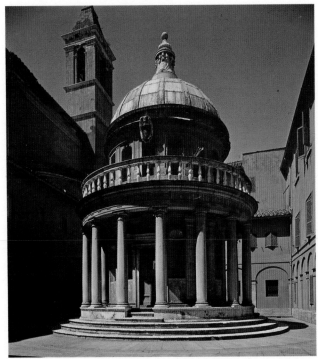

Colorplate 75. (*left*) LEONARDO DA VINCI.
Mona Lisa (see page 440). About 1503–5.
Panel, 30¼ × 21″. The Louvre, Paris

Colorplate 76. (*right*) DONATO BRAMANTE. The Tempietto
(see page 449). S. Pietro in Montorio, Rome. 1502

Colorplate 77. MICHELANGELO. *The Fall of Man and The Expulsion from
the Garden of Eden* (see page 454). 1508–12. Fresco. Ceiling of Sistine Chapel, The Vatican, Rome

Colorplate 78. RAPHAEL. *Pope Leo X with His Nephews Giulio de'Medici*
and Luigi de'Rossi (see page 461). About 1518. Panel, 60⅝ × 46⅞″. Uffizi Gallery, Florence

Colorplate 79. GIORGIONE. *The Tempest* (see page 461). About 1505. 31¼ × 28¾″. Academy, Venice

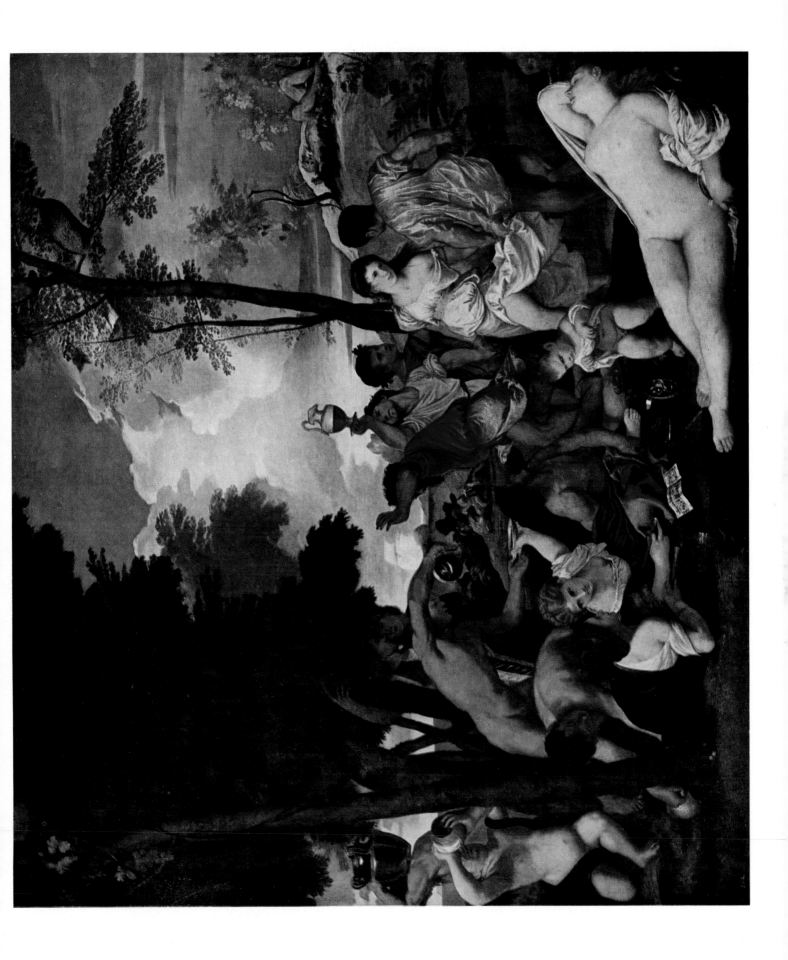

Colorplate 80. TITIAN. *Bacchanal* (see page 462). About 1518. 5′ 8⅞″ × 6′ 4″. The Prado, Madrid

Colorplate 81. ROSSO FIORENTINO. *The Descent from the Cross* (see page 465).
1521. Panel, 11′ × 6′ 5½″. Pinacoteca, Volterra

605. LEONARDO DA VINCI. *Project for a Church* (Ms. B).
c. 1490. Pen drawing. Bibliothèque de l'Arsenal, Paris

derness which was to Leonardo the essence of womanhood. Even the landscape in the background, composed mainly of rocks and water, suggests elemental generative forces.

DRAWINGS. In his later years (he died in France in 1519), Leonardo devoted himself more and more to his scientific interests. Art and science, we recall, were first united in Brunelleschi's discovery of systematic perspective; Leonardo's work is the climax of this trend. The artist, he believed, must know not only the rules of perspective but all the laws of nature, and the eye was to him the perfect instrument for gaining such knowledge. The extraordinary scope of his own inquiries is attested in the hundreds of drawings and notes that he hoped to incorporate into an encyclopedic set of treatises. How original he was as a scientist is still a matter of debate, but in one field his importance remains undisputed: he created the modern scientific illustration, an essential tool for anatomists and biologists. A drawing such as the *Embryo in the Womb* (fig. 604) combines his own vivid observation with the analytic clarity of a diagram, or—to paraphrase Leonardo's own words—sight and insight.

Contemporary sources show that Leonardo was esteemed as an architect. Actual building seems to have concerned him less, however, than basic problems of structure and design The numerous architectural projects in his drawings were intended, for the most part, to remain on paper. Yet these sketches, especially those of his Milanese period, have great historic importance, for only in them can we trace the transition from the Early to the High Renaissance in architecture.

The domed, centrally planned churches of the type illustrated in figure 605 hold particular interest for us; the plan recalls Brunelleschi's Sta. Maria degli Angeli (see fig. 558), but the new relationship of the spatial units is more complex, while the exterior, with its cluster of domes, is more monumental than any Early Renaissance structure. In conception, this design stands halfway between the dome of Florence Cathedral and the most ambitious structure of the sixteenth century, the new basilica of St. Peter's in Rome (compare figs. 449, 608, 610). It gives evidence, too, of Leonardo's close contact, during the 1490s, with the architect Donato Bramante (1444–1514), who was then also working for the duke of Milan. Bramante went to Rome after Milan fell to the French; it was in Rome, during the last fifteen years of his life, that he became the creator of High Renaissance architecture.

Bramante

THE TEMPIETTO. The new style is shown fully formed in Bramante's Tempietto at S. Pietro in Montorio (figs. 606, 607, colorplate 76), designed soon after 1500. This chapel, which marks the site of St. Peter's crucifixion, was planned to be surrounded by a circular, colonnaded courtyard. The Tempietto would then have appeared less isolated from its environment than it does today, for Bramante intended it to be set within a "molded" exterior space—a conception as bold and novel as the design of the chapel itself. Its nickname, "little temple," seems well deserved: in the three-step platform and the severe Doric order of the colonnade, Classical temple architecture is more directly recalled than in any fifteenth-century structure. Equally striking is Bramante's application of the "sculptured wall" principle, in the Tempietto itself and in the courtyard; not since Brunel-

606. DONATO BRAMANTE. The Tempietto,
S. Pietro in Montorio, Rome (see colorplate 76)

607. Plan of the Tempietto,
with projected courtyard (after Serlio)

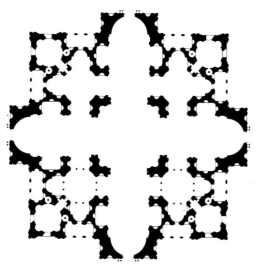

608. DONATO BRAMANTE. Original Plan for
St. Peter's, Rome. 1506 (after Geymüller)

609. Plan of Brunelleschi's S. Lorenzo,
Florence, reproduced at
the same scale as figure 608

leschi's Sta. Maria degli Angeli have we seen such deeply
recessed niches, "excavated" from heavy masses of masonry.
These cavities are counterbalanced by the convex shape of
the dome and by strongly projecting moldings and cornices.
As a result, the Tempietto has a monumental weight that
belies its modest size.

ST. PETER'S.   The Tempietto is the earliest of the great
achievements that made Rome the center of Italian art during the first quarter of the sixteenth century. Most of them
belong to the decade 1503–13, the papacy of Julius II. It was
he who decided to replace the old basilica of St. Peter's,
which had long been in precarious condition, with a church
so magnificent as to overshadow all the monuments of
ancient imperial Rome. The task naturally fell to Bramante,
the foremost architect in the city. His original design, of
1506, is known to us only from a plan (fig. 608) and from
the medal commemorating the start of the building campaign (fig. 610), which shows the exterior in rather impre-
cise perspective. These are sufficient, however, to bear out
the words Bramante reportedly used to define his aim: "I
shall place the Pantheon on top of the Basilica of
Constantine."

To surpass the two most famous structures of Roman
antiquity by a Christian edifice of unexampled grandeur—

nothing less would have satisfied Julius II, a pontiff of vast
ambition, who wanted to unite all Italy under his command
and thus to gain a temporal power matching the spiritual
authority of his office. Bramante's design is indeed of truly
imperial magnificence: a huge dome, hemispherical like that
of the Tempietto, crowns the crossing of the barrel-vaulted
arms of a Greek cross, with four lesser domes and tall corner
towers filling the angles. This plan fulfills all the demands
laid down by Alberti for sacred architecture (see page 422);
based entirely on the circle and the square, it is so rigidly
symmetrical that we cannot tell which apse was to hold the
high altar. Bramante envisioned four identical façades like
that on the medal of 1506, dominated by the same repertory
of severely classical forms we saw in the Tempietto: domes,
half domes, colonnades, pediments.

These simple geometric shapes, however, do not prevail
inside the church. Here the "sculptured wall" reigns
supreme: the plan shows no continuous surfaces, only great,
oddly shaped "islands" of masonry that have been well
described by one critic as giant pieces of toast half-eaten by
a voracious space. The actual size of these "islands" can be
visualized only if we compare the measurements of Bramante's church with those of earlier buildings. San Lorenzo
in Florence, for instance, has a length of 268 feet, less than
half that of the new St. Peter's (550 feet). Figure 609, which
reproduces the plan of S. Lorenzo on the same scale as
Bramante's plan (fig. 608), proves that Bramante's reference
to the Pantheon and the Basilica of Constantine was no idle
boast; his plan dwarfs these monuments, as well as every
Early Renaissance church (each arm of the Greek cross has
about the dimensions of the Basilica of Constantine).

How did he propose to build a structure of such overwhelming size? Cut stone and brick, the materials favored
by medieval architects, would not do, for technical and economic reasons; only construction in concrete, as used by the
Romans but largely forgotten during the Middle Ages, was
strong and cheap enough to fill Bramante's needs (see page
160). By reviving this ancient technique, he opened a new

610. CARADOSSO. Medal Showing Bramante's Design
for St. Peter's. 1506. British Museum, London

era in the history of architecture, for concrete permitted designs of far greater flexibility than the building methods of the medieval masons. The possibilities of the material, however, were not fully exploited for some time to come. The construction of St. Peter's progressed at so slow a pace that in 1514, when Bramante died, only the four crossing piers had actually been built. For the next three decades the campaign was carried on hesitantly by architects trained under Bramante, who modified his design in a number of ways. A new and decisive phase in the history of St. Peter's began only in 1546, when Michelangelo took charge; the present appearance of the church (fig. 625) is largely shaped by his ideas. But this must be considered in the context of Michelangelo's career as a whole.

Michelangelo

The concept of genius as divine inspiration, a superhuman power granted to a few rare individuals and acting through them, is nowhere exemplified more fully than in the life and work of Michelangelo (1475–1564). Not only his admirers viewed him in this light; he himself, steeped in the tradition of Neo-Platonism, accepted the idea of his genius as a living reality (see page 436), although it seemed to him at times a curse rather than a blessing. The element that brings continuity to his long and stormy career is the sovereign power of his personality, his faith in the subjective rightness of everything he created. Conventions, standards, and traditions might be observed by lesser spirits; he could acknowledge no authority higher than the dictates of his genius.

Unlike Leonardo, for whom painting was the noblest of the arts because it embraced every visible aspect of the world, Michelangelo was a sculptor—more specifically, a carver of marble statues—to the core. Art, for him, was not a science but "the making of men," analogous (however imperfectly) to divine creation; hence the limitations of sculpture that Leonardo decried were essential virtues in Michelangelo's eyes. Only the "liberation" of real, three-dimensional bodies from recalcitrant matter could satisfy his urge (for his procedure, see comment on *St. Matthew*, pages 11–12). Painting, for him, should imitate the roundness of sculptured forms, and architecture, too, must partake of the organic qualities of the human figure.

Michelangelo's faith in the image of man as the supreme vehicle of expression gave him a sense of kinship with Classical sculpture closer than that of any Renaissance artist. Among recent masters he admired Giotto, Masaccio, Donatello, and Jacopo della Quercia more than the men he knew as a youth in Florence. Yet his mind was decisively shaped by the cultural climate of Florence during the 1480s and 90s; both the Neo-Platonism of Marsilio Ficino and the religious reforms of Savonarola profoundly affected him. These conflicting influences reinforced the tensions within Michelangelo's personality, his violent changes of mood, his sense of being at odds with himself and with the world. As he conceived his statues to be human bodies released from their marble prison, so the body was the earthly prison of the soul—noble, surely, but a prison nevertheless. This dualism

611. MICHELANGELO. *David*. 1501–4. Marble, height of figure 13′ 5″. Academy, Florence

of body and spirit endows his figures with their extraordinary pathos; outwardly calm, they seem stirred by an overwhelming psychic energy that has no release in physical action.

DAVID.   The unique qualities of Michelangelo's art are fully present in the *David* (fig. 611), the earliest monumental statue of the High Renaissance. Commissioned of the artist in 1501, when he was twenty-six, the huge figure was designed to be placed high above the ground, on one of the buttresses of Florence Cathedral. The city fathers chose instead to put it in front of the Palazzo Vecchio, as the civic-patriotic symbol of the Florentine republic (see fig. 454; it has since been replaced by a modern copy).

We can well understand their decision. The head of Goliath being omitted, Michelangelo's *David* looks challenging—not a victorious hero but the champion of a just cause. Vibrant with pent-up energy, he faces the world like Donatello's *St. George* (see fig. 541), although his nudity links him to the older master's bronze *David* as well. But the style of the figure proclaims an ideal very different from the wiry slenderness of Donatello's youths. Michelangelo had just spent several years in Rome, where he had been deeply impressed with the emotion-charged, muscular bodies of Hellenistic sculpture. Although the *Laocoön* (see fig. 207), shortly to become the most famous work in this style, had not then been discovered, other Hellenistic statues were accessible to him. Their heroic scale, their superhuman beauty and power, and the swelling volume of their forms became part of Michelangelo's own style and, through him, of Renaissance art in general. Yet the *David* could never be taken for an ancient statue. In the *Laocoön* and similar works (compare fig. 205) the body "acts out" the spirit's agony, while the *David*, at once calm and tense, shows the action-in-repose so characteristic of Michelangelo.

TOMB OF JULIUS II. This trait persists in the *Moses* (fig. 612) and the two "slaves" (figs. 613, 614), carved about a decade later. They were part of the vast sculptural program for the tomb of Julius II, which would have been Michelan-

613. MICHELANGELO. *"The Dying Slave."* 1513–16. Marble, height 90″. The Louvre, Paris

614. MICHELANGELO. *"The Rebellious Slave."* 1513–16. Marble, height 84″. The Louvre, Paris

gelo's greatest achievement had he carried it out as originally planned. The majestic *Moses*, meant to be seen from below, has the awesome force which the artist's contemporaries called *terribilità*—a concept akin to the sublime. His pose, both watchful and meditative, suggests a man capable of wise leadership as well as towering wrath. The "slaves" are more difficult to interpret: they seem to have belonged to a series representing the arts, now shackled by the death of their greatest patron; later, apparently, they came to signify the territories conquered by Julius II. Be that as it may, Michelangelo has conceived the two figures as a contrasting pair, the so-called *Dying Slave* (fig. 613) yielding to his bonds, the *Rebellious Slave* (fig. 614) struggling to free himself. Perhaps their allegorical meaning mattered less to him than their expressive content, so evocative of the Neo-Platonic image of the body as the earthly prison of the soul.

THE SISTINE CEILING. The tomb of Julius II remained unfinished when the pope interrupted Michelangelo's labors on the project at an early stage, half-forcing, half-cajoling the reluctant artist to fresco the ceiling of the Sistine Chapel in the Vatican (fig. 615). Driven by his desire to resume work on the tomb, Michelangelo completed the entire ceiling in four years, 1508–12. He produced a masterpiece of truly epochal importance. The ceiling is a huge organism with hundreds of figures rhythmically distributed within the

612. MICHELANGELO. *Moses.* c. 1513–15. Marble, height 92½″. S. Pietro in Vincoli, Rome

615. Interior of the Sistine Chapel showing Michelangelo's Ceiling Fresco and *Last Judgment*. The Vatican, Rome

617. MICHELANGELO. *Fall of Man*
(detail; see colorplate 77), portion of the Sistine Ceiling

616. MICHELANGELO. *The Creation of Adam*, portion of the Sistine Ceiling. 1508–12. Fresco

painted architectural framework, dwarfing the earlier murals (fig. 597) by its size, and still more by its compelling inner unity. In the central area, subdivided by five pairs of girders, are nine scenes from Genesis, from the Creation of the World (at the far end of the chapel) to the Drunkenness of Noah.

The theological scheme behind the choice of these scenes and the rich program accompanying them—the nude youths, the medallions, the prophets and sibyls, the scenes in the spandrels—has not been fully explained, but we know that it links the early history of man and the coming of

Christ, the beginning of time and its end (the *Last Judgment* on the wall above the altar, although it was painted a quarter of a century later, must have been intended from the start). We do not know how much responsibility Michelangelo had for the program; he was not a man to submit to dictation, and the subject matter of the ceiling as a whole fits his cast of mind so perfectly that his own desires cannot have conflicted strongly with those of his patron. What greater theme could he wish than the Creation of the World, Man's Fall, and his ultimate reconciliation with the Lord?

A detailed survey of the Sistine Ceiling would fill a book; we shall have to be content with two of the four major scenes in the center portion. Of these, the *Creation of Adam* (fig. 616) must have stirred Michelangelo's imagination most deeply; it shows not the physical molding of Adam's body but the passage of the Divine spark—the soul—and thus achieves a dramatic juxtaposition of Man and God unrivaled by any other artist. Jacopo della Quercia approximated it (see fig. 546), but without the dynamism of Michelangelo's design that contrasts the earth-bound Adam and the figure of God rushing through the sky. This relationship becomes even more meaningful when we realize that Adam strains not only toward his Creator but toward Eve, whom he sees, yet unborn, in the shelter of the Lord's left arm.

Michelangelo has been called a poor colorist—unjustly, as the recently undertaken cleaning of the frescoes has revealed. *The Fall of Man* and *The Expulsion from the Garden of Eden* (fig. 617, colorplate 77) show the bold, intense hues typical of the whole ceiling. The range of his palette is astonishing. Contrary to what had been thought, the heroic figures have anything but the quality of painted sculpture. Full of life, they act out their epic roles in illusionistic "windows" that puncture the architectural setting. Michelangelo does not simply color the areas within the contours but builds up his forms from broad and vigorous brush strokes in the tradition of Giotto and Masaccio. The *Expulsion* is particularly close to Masaccio's (see fig. 563).

Colorplate 77 also permits us to glimpse the garland-bearing nude youths that accompany the main sections of the ceiling. These wonderfully animated figures, recurring at regular intervals, play an important role in Michelangelo's design; they form a kind of chain linking the Genesis scenes, yet their significance remains uncertain. Are they images of human souls? Do they represent the world of pagan antiquity? Whatever the answer, they seem to belong to the same category of being as the "slaves" from the Tomb of Julius II; again the symbolic intent is overpowered by the wealth of expression Michelangelo has poured into these figures.

LAST JUDGMENT. When Michelangelo returned to the Sistine Chapel in 1534, over twenty years later, the Western world was enduring the spiritual and political crisis of the Reformation (see page 492). We perceive with shocking directness how the mood has changed as we turn from the radiant vitality of Michelangelo's ceiling fresco to the somber vision of his *Last Judgment*. Mankind, Blessed and Damned alike, huddles together in tight clumps, pleading for mercy before a wrathful God (fig. 618). Seated on a cloud just below the Lord is the Apostle Bartholomew, holding a human

618. MICHELANGELO. *The Last Judgment* (detail, with self-portrait). 1534–41. Fresco. Sistine Chapel, The Vatican, Rome

skin to represent his martyrdom (he had been flayed). The face on that skin, however, is not the saint's but Michelangelo's own. In this grimly sardonic self-portrait (so well hidden that it was recognized only in modern times) the artist has left his personal confession of guilt and unworthiness.

THE MEDICI CHAPEL. The interval between the Sistine Ceiling and the *Last Judgment* coincides with the papacies of Leo X (1513–21) and Clement VII (1523–34); both were members of the Medici family, and preferred to employ Michelangelo in Florence. His activities centered on S. Lorenzo, the Medici church. A century after Brunelleschi's revolutionary design for the sacristy (see page 409), Leo X decided to build a matching structure—the New Sacristy—to house the tombs of Lorenzo the Magnificent, Lorenzo's brother Giuliano, and two younger members of the family, also named Lorenzo and Giuliano. Michelangelo took early charge of this project and worked on it for fourteen years, completing the architecture and two of the tombs, those for the lesser Lorenzo and Giuliano (fig. 619). The New Sacristy was thus conceived as an architectural-sculptural ensemble; it is the only work of the artist where his statues remain in the setting planned specifically for them.

The design of the two tombs still shows some kinship with such Early Renaissance tombs as that of Leonardo Bruni (see fig. 582), but the differences weigh more heavily: there is no inscription, the effigy has been replaced by two allegorical figures (*Day* on the right, *Night* on the left), and the statue of Giuliano, in classical military garb, bears no resemblance to the deceased Medici. ("A thousand years from now, nobody will know what he looked like," Michelangelo is said to have remarked.) What is the meaning of this triad? The question, put countless times, has never found a satisfactory answer. Michelangelo's plans for the Medici tombs underwent so many changes of form and program while the work was under way that the present state of the monuments can hardly be the final solution; rather, the dynamic process of design was arbitrarily halted by the artist's departure for Rome in 1534. *Day* and *Night* were certainly designed to rest on horizontal surfaces, not the curved, sloping lid of the present sarcophagus.

Perhaps they were not even intended for this particular tomb. Giuliano's niche is too narrow and too shallow to accommodate him comfortably. Other figures and reliefs were planned, but never executed. Was their omission inten-

620. MICHELANGELO. Vestibule of the Laurentian Library, Florence. Begun 1524; stairway designed 1558–59

621. Axonometric Diagram of Structural System, Vestibule Laurentian Library (after Ackerman)

619. MICHELANGELO. Tomb of Giuliano de'Medici. 1524–34. Marble, height of central figure 71″. New Sacristy, S. Lorenzo, Florence

tional or accidental? Despite all this, the tomb of Giuliano remains a compelling visual unit. The great triangle of the statues is held in place by a network of verticals and horizontals whose slender, sharp-edged forms heighten the roundness and weight of the sculpture. *Giuliano*, the ideal image of the prince, is a younger and more pensive counterpart of the *Moses;* the reclining figures contrast in mood, like the "slaves." Derived from ancient river gods (compare fig. 6), they embody the quality of action-in-repose more dramatically than any other works by Michelangelo: in the brooding menace of *Day*, and in the disturbed slumber of *Night,* the dualism of body and soul is expressed with unforgettable grandeur.

LAURENTIAN LIBRARY. Concurrently with the New Sacristy, Michelangelo built the Laurentian Library, adjoining S. Lorenzo, to house for the public the vast collection of

622. MICHELANGELO. *The Campidoglio*
(engraving by Etienne Dupérac, 1569)

623. Plan of the
Campidoglio, Rome

books and manuscripts belonging to the Medici family. In the vestibule (fig. 620) his full powers as a creator of new architectural forms are displayed for the first time. By the standards of the 1520s, based on the classical ideal of Bramante, everything here is wrong: the pediment above the door is broken; the pilasters of the niches taper downward; the columns belong to no recognizable order; the scroll brackets sustain nothing. Most paradoxical, however, from the point of view of established practice, are the recessed columns: though structurally logical—the columns support heavy piers, which in turn support the roof beams (fig. 621)—this feature upsets a hallowed rule of architectural propriety: that in the classical post-and-lintel system the columns (or pilasters) and entablature must project from the wall on which they have been superimposed, to stress their separate identities. The system could be reduced to a linear pattern (as in the Palazzo Rucellai: fig. 572), but no one before Michelangelo had dared to defy it by incorporating columns into the wall.

The entire design demonstrates what Vasari, the artist's friend and biographer, had in mind when he wrote that Michelangelo's architecture "broke the bonds and chains of... common usage." The purpose of these innovations is, of course, expressive rather than functional; the walls push inward between the columns to make of the vestibule a kind of "compression chamber" where the beholder experiences an almost physical stress. Our unease is heightened by the blank stare of the empty niches and by the nightmarish stairway, which flows downward and outward so relentlessly that we wonder if we dare brave the current by mounting the steps.

CAMPIDOGLIO. During the last thirty years of his life, architecture became Michelangelo's main preoccupation. In 1537–39, he received the most ambitious commission of his career: to reshape the Campidoglio, the top of Rome's Capitoline Hill, into a square with a monumental frame worthy of this venerable site, once the symbolic center of ancient Rome. At last he could plan on a grand scale, and he took full advantage of the opportunity. Although not com-

pleted until long after his death, the project was carried out essentially as he had designed it—the most imposing civic center ever built, and a model for countless others. Pope Paul III took the initiative by transferring the equestrian monument of Marcus Aurelius (see fig. 269) to the Campidoglio, and Michelangelo designed its base; the statue became the focal point of his entire scheme, placed at the apex of a gently rising oval mound.

Three sides of the piazza are defined by palace façades, so that the visitor, after ascending the flight of steps on the fourth side, finds himself enclosed in a huge "outdoor room." The effect of the ensemble cannot be rendered by photographs. Even the best view, an engraving based on Michelangelo's design (fig. 622), conveys it very imperfectly: it shows the complete bilateral symmetry of the scheme, and the energetic sense of progression along the main axis toward the Senators' Palace, but it distorts the shape of the piazza, which is not a rectangle but a trapezoid (the flanking façades are divergent: fig. 623). This peculiarity was imposed on Michelangelo by the existing site; the Senators' Palace, and the Conservators' Palace on the right, were older buildings which had to be preserved behind newly designed exteriors, and they were placed at an angle of 80 instead of 90 degrees. But he turned into an asset what would have hindered a less imaginative architect: the divergence of the flanks makes the Senators' Palace look larger than it is, dramatically dominating the piazza.

The whole conception has the visual effectiveness of a stage set—note that in the engraving the "New Palace" on the left is a mere show front with nothing behind it. Yet this façade and its twin on the opposite side are not shallow screens but vigorously three-dimensional structures (fig. 624) with the most "muscular" juxtaposition of voids and solids, of horizontals and verticals, of any piece of architecture since Roman antiquity. They share the striking feature of an open portico, which links the piazza and façades as a courtyard is related to the arcades of a cloister.

The columns and stone beams of the porticoes are inscribed within a colossal order of pilasters which supports a heavy cornice topped by a balustrade; the entire design is based on the classic post-and-lintel principle. We have encountered these elements on the façades of the Pazzi Chapel and Alberti's S. Andrea, and in the Tempietto of Bramante (see figs. 553, 575, 606, colorplate 76), but it was Michelangelo who welded them into a coherent system. For the Senators' Palace he employed the colossal order and balustrade above a tall basement which emphasizes the massive quality of the building. The single entrance at the top of the huge double-ramped stairway seems to gather all the spatial forces set in motion by the oval mound and the divergent flanks, and thus provides a dramatic climax for the visitor traversing the piazza.

ST. PETER'S. With the Campidoglio, the colossal order became firmly established in the repertory of monumental architecture. Michelangelo himself used it again on the exterior of St. Peter's (fig. 625), with equally impressive results. The system of the Conservators' Palace, with windows now replacing the open loggias, and an attic instead of the balustrade, could here be adapted perfectly to the jagged contour of the plan; unlike Bramante's many-layered elevation (see fig. 610) the colossal order emphasized the compact body of the structure, thus setting off the dome more dramatically. The same desire for compactness and organic unity led Michelangelo to simplify the interior, without changing its centralized character (figs. 626, 627). He brought the complex spatial sequences of Bramante's plan (see fig. 608) into one cross-and-square, and defined its main axis by modifying the exterior of the eastern apse and projecting a portico for

it. This part of his design was never carried out. The dome, however, although largely built after his death, reflects his ideas in every important respect.

Bramante had planned his dome as a stepped hemisphere above a narrow drum, which would have seemed to press down on the church below; Michelangelo's conveys the opposite sensation, a powerful thrust that draws energy upward from the main body of the structure. The high drum, the strongly projecting buttresses accented by double columns, the ribs, the raised curve of the cupola, the tall lantern—all contribute verticality at the expense of the horizontals. We may recall the Florence Cathedral dome (see fig. 449), from which Michelangelo borrowed not only the double-shell construction but the Gothic profile. Yet the effects are immensely different: the smooth planes of Brunelleschi's dome give no hint of the internal stresses, while Michelangelo finds a sculptured shape for these contending forces, and relates them to those in the rest of the building (the impulse of the paired colossal pilasters below is taken up by the double columns of the drum, continues in the ribs, and culminates in the lantern). The logic of this design is so persuasive that few domes built between 1600 and 1900 fail to acknowledge it.

MILAN PIETÀ. Michelangelo's magnificent assurance in handling such projects as the Campidoglio and St. Peter's seems to belie his portrayal of himself as a limp skin in the Last Judgment. It is indeed difficult to reconcile these contrasting aspects of his personality. Did he, perhaps,

624. MICHELANGELO. The Conservators' Palace, Campidoglio, Rome.
Designed c. 1545

625. MICHELANGELO. St. Peter's, Rome, seen from the west. 1546–64 (dome completed by Giacomo della Porta, 1590)

626. MICHELANGELO.
Plan for St. Peter's

627. Longitudinal Section of St. Peter's
(engraving by Etienne Dupérac, 1569)

628. MICHELANGELO, *Milan Pietà*. c. 1555–64.
Marble, height 77⅛". Castello Sforzesco, Milan

toward the end of his life, find greater fulfillment in architecture than in shaping human bodies? In his last piece of sculpture, the *Milan Pietà* (fig. 628), he is groping for new forms, as if his earlier work had become meaningless to him. The group is a fragment, destroyed partly by his own hand; he was still struggling with it a few days before he died. The theme—especially its emotional content—suggests that he intended it for his own tomb. These two figures have no trace of High Renaissance rhetoric; silently hovering, they evoke the devotional images of medieval art. Like the master's self-portrait (see fig. 618), the *Milan Pietà* occupies an intensely private realm. Its plea for redemption is addressed to no human audience, but to God.

Raphael

If Michelangelo exemplifies the solitary genius, Raphael belongs just as surely to the opposite type: the artist as a man of the world. The contrast between the two was as clear to their contemporaries as it is to us. Although each had his partisans, both enjoyed equal fame. Today our sympathies are less evenly divided—

> In the room the women come and go
> Talking of Michelangelo.
>
> (T. S. Eliot)

So do a lot of us, including the authors of historical novels and fictionalized biographies, while Raphael (1483–1520) is usually discussed only by historians of art. The younger master's career is too much of a success story, his work too replete with seemingly effortless grace, to match the tragic heroism of Michelangelo. As an innovator, Raphael seems to contribute less than Leonardo, Bramante, and Michelangelo, the three artists whose achievements were basic to his. Yet he is the central painter of the High Renaissance; our conception of the entire style rests more on his work than on any other master's.

The genius of Raphael was a unique power of synthesis that enabled him to merge the qualities of Leonardo and Michelangelo, creating an art at once lyric and dramatic, pictorially rich and sculpturally solid. This power is already present in the first works he made in Florence (1504–8), after he completed his apprenticeship with Perugino. The meditative calm of the *Madonna del Granduca* (fig. 629) still reflects the style of his teacher (compare fig. 597). But the forms are ampler and enveloped in Leonardesque *sfumato;* the Virgin, grave and tender, makes us think of the *Mona Lisa* without engendering any of her mystery.

SCHOOL OF ATHENS. Michelangelo's influence on Raphael asserted itself somewhat later. Its full force can be felt only in Raphael's Roman works. At the time Michelangelo began to paint the Sistine Ceiling, Julius II summoned the younger artist from Florence and commissioned him to decorate a series of rooms in the Vatican Palace. The first room, the Stanza della Segnatura, may have housed the pope's library, and Raphael's cycle of frescoes on its walls and ceiling refers to the four domains of learning—theology, philosophy, law, and the arts.

Of these frescoes, *The School of Athens* (fig. 630) has long been acknowledged as Raphael's masterpiece and the perfect embodiment of the classical spirit of the High Renaissance. Its subject is "the Athenian school of thought," a group of famous Greek philosophers gathered around Plato and Aristotle, each in a characteristic pose or activity. Raphael must have already seen the Sistine Ceiling, then nearing completion. He evidently owes to Michelangelo the expressive energy, the physical power, and the dramatic grouping of his figures. Yet Raphael has not simply borrowed Michelangelo's repertory of gestures and poses; he has absorbed it into his own style, and thereby given it different meaning.

Body and spirit, action and emotion, are now balanced harmoniously, and every member of this great assembly plays his role with magnificent, purposeful clarity. The total conception of *The School of Athens* suggests the spirit of Leonardo's *Last Supper* (fig. 601) rather than the Sistine Ceiling. This holds true of the way Raphael makes each philosopher reveal "the intention of his soul," distinguishes the relations among individuals and groups, and links them in formal rhythm. Also Leonardesque is the centralized, symmetrical design, and the interdependence of the figures and their architectural setting. But compared with the hall of the *Last Supper,* Raphael's classical edifice—its lofty dome, barrel vault, and colossal statuary—shares far more of the compositional burden. Inspired by Bramante, it seems like an advance view of the new St. Peter's. Its geometric precision and spatial grandeur bring to a climax the tradition begun by Masaccio (see fig. 560), continued by Domenico Veneziano and Piero della Francesca, and transmitted to Raphael by his teacher Perugino.

629. RAPHAEL. *Madonna del Granduca.* c. 1505.
Panel, 33 × 21½". Pitti Palace, Florence

630. (*above*) RAPHAEL. *The School of Athens*. 1510–11. Fresco.
Stanza della Segnatura, Vatican Palace, Rome

631. (*right*) RAPHAEL. *Galatea*. 1513. Fresco.
Villa Farnesina, Rome

GALATEA.   Raphael never again set so splendid an architectural stage. To create pictorial space, he relied increasingly on the movement of human figures, rather than perspective vistas. In the *Galatea* of 1513 (fig. 631) the subject is again classical—the beautiful nymph Galatea, vainly pursued by Polyphemus, belongs to Greek mythology—but here the gay and sensuous aspect of antiquity is celebrated, in contrast to the austere idealism of *The School of Athens*. Its composition recalls *The Birth of Venus* (fig. 594, colorplate 73), a picture Raphael knew from his Florentine days, yet their very resemblance emphasizes their profound dissimilarity. Raphael's full-bodied, dynamic figures take on their expansive spiral movement from the vigorous *contrapposto* of Galatea; in Botticelli's picture, the movement is not generated by the figures but imposed on them from without, so that it never detaches itself from the surface of the canvas.

632. RAPHAEL. *Pope Leo X with His Nephews Giulio de'Medici and Luigi de'Rossi* (detail; see colorplate 78). Uffizi Gallery, Florence

to the new, sixteenth century, left the orbit of Giovanni Bellini only during the final years of his short career.

THE TEMPEST. Among his very few mature works, *The Tempest* (fig. 633, colorplate 79) is both the most individual and the most enigmatic. Our first glance may show us little more than a particularly charming reflection of Bellinesque qualities, familiar from the *St. Francis in Ecstasy* (fig. 592, colorplate 72) and the S. Zaccaria altarpiece (fig. 593). The difference is one of mood—and this mood, in *The Tempest*, is subtly, pervasively pagan. Bellini's landscape is meant to be seen through the eyes of St. Francis, as a piece of God's creation. Giorgione's figures, by contrast, do not interpret the scene for us; belonging themselves to nature, they are passive witnesses—victims, almost—of the thunderstorm about to engulf them. Who are they? So far, the young soldier and the nude mother with her babe have refused to disclose their identity, and the subject of the picture remains unknown. The present title is a confession of embarrassment, yet it is not inappropriate, for the only "action" is that of the tempest. Whatever its intended meaning, the scene is like an enchanted idyl, a dream of pastoral beauty soon to be swept away. Only poets had hitherto captured this air of nostalgic reverie; now, it entered the repertory of the painter. *The Tempest* initiates what was to become an important new tradition.

PORTRAITS. Early in his career Raphael had already shown a special talent for portraiture. It is another tribute to his genius for synthesis that he combined the realism of fifteenth-century portraits (such as fig. 596) with the human ideal of the High Renaissance (which, in the *Mona Lisa*, nearly overpowers the sitter's individuality). Raphael did not flatter or conventionalize his subjects; surely Pope Leo X (fig. 632; colorplate 78) looks here no handsomer than he did in reality. His sullen, heavy-jowled features have been recorded in concrete, almost Flemish detail. Nevertheless, the pontiff has a commanding presence, his aura of power and dignity emanating more from his inner being than from his exalted office. Raphael, we feel, has not falsified the sitter's personality but ennobled and focused it, as if he had been fortunate enough to observe Leo X in his finest hour. The two cardinals, who lack this balanced strength although they are studied with equal care, enhance by contrast the sovereign quality of the main figure. Even the pictorial treatment shows a similar gradation: Leo X has been set off from his companions, his reality heightened by intensified light, color, and texture.

Giorgione

The distinction between Early and High Renaissance art, so marked in Florence and Rome, is far less sharp in Venice. Giorgione (1478–1510), the first Venetian painter to belong

633. GIORGIONE. *The Tempest* (see colorplate 79). Academy, Venice

634. TITIAN. *Bacchanal* (see colorplate 80). The Prado, Madrid

Titian

Giorgione died before he could explore in full the sensuous, lyrical world he had created in *The Tempest*. He bequeathed this task to Titian (1488/90–1576), an artist of comparable gifts who was decisively influenced by Giorgione, and who dominated Venetian painting for the next half-century.

BACCHANAL.   Titian's *Bacchanal* of about 1518 (fig. 634, colorplate 80) is frankly pagan, inspired by an ancient author's description of such a revel. The landscape, rich in contrasts of cool and warm tones, has all the poetry of Giorgione, but the figures are of another breed: active and muscular, they move with a joyous freedom that recalls Raphael's *Galatea* (fig. 631). By this time, many of Raphael's compositions had been engraved (see fig. 5), and from these reproductions Titian became familiar with the Roman High Renaissance. A number of the celebrants in his *Bacchanal* also reflect the influence of classical art. Titian's approach to antiquity, however, is very different from Raphael's; he visualizes the realm of classical myths as part of the natural world, inhabited not by animated statues but by beings of flesh and blood. The figures of the *Bacchanal* are idealized beyond everyday reality just enough to persuade us that they belong to a long-lost golden age. They invite us to share their blissful state in a way that makes Raphael's *Galatea* seem cold and remote by comparison.

THE PESARO MADONNA.   This quality of festive anima-tion reappears in many of Titian's religious paintings, such as the *Madonna with Members of the Pesaro Family* (fig. 635). Although we recognize the composition as a variant of the *Sacra Conversazione* (compare figs. 567, 593, colorplate 67), Titian has thoroughly transformed it by replacing the familiar frontal view with an oblique one. The Virgin is now enthroned in a great barrel-vaulted hall open on either side, a High Renaissance counterpart of the architectural setting

in Bellini's *Madonna and Saints* in S. Zaccharia; because the view is diagonal, open sky and clouds now fill most of the background. Except for the kneeling donors, every figure is in motion—turning, leaning, gesturing; the officer with the flag seems almost to lead a charge up the steps. Yet the design remains harmoniously self-contained despite the strong element of drama. Brilliant sunlight makes every color and texture sparkle, in keeping with the joyous spirit of the altar. The only hint of tragedy is the cross of the Passion held by two angel-putti, hidden by clouds from the participants in the *Sacra Conversazione* but not from us—a tiny note adding poignancy to the scene.

PORTRAITS.   After Raphael's death, Titian became the most sought-after portraitist of the age. His prodigious gifts, evident in the donors' portraits in the altar just discussed, are even more striking in the *Man with the Glove* (fig. 636). The dreamy intimacy of this portrait, with its soft outline and deep shadows, still reflects the style of Giorgione. Lost

635. TITIAN. *Madonna with Members of the Pesaro Family.* 1526. 16′ × 8′ 10″. Church of the Frari, Venice

636. TITIAN. *Man with the Glove.*
c. 1520. 39½ × 35″. The Louvre, Paris

637. TITIAN. *Pope Paul III and His Grandsons.*
1546. 6′ 10″ × 5′ 8″. National Museum, Naples

638. TITIAN. *Christ Crowned with Thorns.*
c. 1570. 9′ 2″ × 6′. Pinakothek, Munich

in thought, the young man seems quite unaware of us; this slight melancholy in his features conjures up the poetic appeal of *The Tempest.* The breadth and power of form, however, goes far beyond Giorgione. In Titian's hands, the possibilities of oil technique—rich, creamy highlights, deep dark tones that are yet transparent and delicately modulated—now are fully realized; the separate brush strokes, hardly visible before, become increasingly free. We can see the rapid pace of his development by turning from the *Man with the Glove* to the papal group portrait *Paul III and His Grandsons* (fig. 637), painted a quarter-century later. The quick, slashing strokes here endow the entire canvas with the spontaneity of a first sketch—some parts of it are, in fact, unfinished—even though the formal composition is derived from Raphael's *Leo X* (fig. 632, colorplate 78). In the freer technique Titian's uncanny grasp of human character also comes out: the tiny figure of the pope, shriveled with age, dominates his tall attendants with awesome authority. Comparing these two portraits by Titian, we see that a change of pictorial technique is no mere surface phenomenon. It always reflects a change of the artist's aim.

LATE WORKS. This correspondence of form and technique is even clearer in *Christ Crowned with Thorns* (fig. 638), a masterpiece of Titian's old age. The shapes emerging from the semi-darkness now consist wholly of light and color; despite the heavy impasto, the shimmering surfaces have lost every trace of material solidity and seem translucent, aglow from within. In consequence, the violent physical action has been miraculously suspended. What lingers in our minds is not the drama but the strange mood of serenity—engendered by deep religious feeling.

4 MANNERISM AND OTHER TRENDS

What happened after the High Renaissance? Fifty years ago the question would simply have been answered: after the High Renaissance came the Late Renaissance, which was dominated by shallow imitators of the great masters of the previous generation, and lasted until the Baroque style emerged at the end of the century. Although today we take a far more positive view of the artists who reached maturity after 1520, and generally discard the term Late Renaissance as misleading, we have still to agree on a name for the seventy-five years separating the High Renaissance from the Baroque. Any one label implies that the period has one style, and nobody has succeeded in defining such a style. But if there is no single style in the years 1525–1600, why should this span be regarded as a period at all, except in the negative sense of an interval between two high points, as the Renaissance viewed the Middle Ages? Perhaps this difficulty can be resolved by thinking of this period as a time of crisis that gave rise to several competing tendencies rather than one dominant ideal—or as a time full of inner contradictions, not unlike the present, and thus peculiarly fascinating to us.

PAINTING
Mannerism: Florence and Rome

Among the various trends in art after the High Renaissance, that of Mannerism is the most discussed today. But in scope and significance the term remains problematic: its original meaning was narrow and derogatory, designating a group of mid-sixteenth-century painters in Rome and Florence whose self-consciously "artificial," mannered style was derived from certain aspects of Raphael and Michelangelo. More recently, the cold and rather barren formalism of their work has been recognized as a special form of a wider movement that placed "inner vision," however subjective or fantastic, above the twin authority of nature and the ancients; some scholars have broadened the definition of Mannerism to include even the later style of Michelangelo himself—which is rather like calling Phidias a classicist.

ROSSO. The first indications of disquiet in the High Renaissance appear shortly before 1520, in the work of some

639. ROSSO FIORENTINO. *Descent from the Cross* (detail; see colorplate 81). Pinacoteca, Volterra

640. PONTORMO. *Study of a Young Girl.* c. 1526. Sanguine drawing. Uffizi Gallery, Florence

young painters in Florence. By 1521, Rosso Fiorentino (1495–1540), the most eccentric member of this group, expressed the new attitude with full conviction in *The Descent from the Cross* (fig. 639, colorplate 81). Nothing has prepared us for the shocking impact of this latticework of spidery forms spread out against the dark sky. The figures are agitated yet rigid, as if congealed by a sudden, icy blast; even the draperies have brittle, sharp-edged planes; the acid colors and the light, brilliant but unreal, reinforce the nightmarish effect of the scene. Here is what amounts to a revolt against the classical balance of High Renaissance art; a profoundly disquieting, willful, visionary style that indicates a deep-seated inner anxiety. Vasari's statement that Rosso committed suicide is probably untrue, yet seems plausible enough as we look at this picture.

PONTORMO.   Pontormo (1494–1556/7), a friend of Rosso, had an equally strange personality. Introspective and shy, he shut himself up in his quarters for weeks on end, inaccessible even to his friends. His wonderfully sensitive drawings,

such as the *Study of a Young Girl* (fig. 640), well reflect these facets of his character; the sitter, moodily gazing into space, seems to shrink from the outer world, as if scarred by the trauma of some half-remembered experience.

PARMIGIANINO.   This "anticlassical" style of Rosso and Pontormo, the first phase of Mannerism, was soon replaced by another aspect of the movement. This was less overtly anticlassical, less laden with subjective emotion, but equally far removed from the confident, stable world of the High Renaissance. The *Self-Portrait* (fig. 641) by Parmigianino (1503–1540) suggests no psychological turmoil; the artist's appearance is bland and well groomed, veiled by a delicate Leonardesque *sfumato*. The distortions, too, are objective, not arbitrary, for the picture records what Parmigianino saw as he gazed at his reflection in a convex mirror. Yet why was he so fascinated by this view "through the looking glass"? Earlier painters who used the same device as an aid to observation had "filtered out" the distortions (as in figs. 515, 526), except when the mirror image was contrasted with a

641. PARMIGIANINO. *Self-Portrait.* 1524. Panel, diameter 9⅜". Kunsthistorisches Museum, Vienna

direct view of the same scene (fig. 516, colorplate 62). But Parmigianino substitutes his painting for the mirror itself, even employing a specially prepared convex panel. Did he perhaps want to demonstrate that there is no single, "correct" reality, that distortion is as natural as the normal appearance of things?

Characteristically, his scientific detachment soon changed into its very opposite. Vasari tells us that Parmigianino, as he neared the end of his brief career (he died at thirty-seven), was obsessed with alchemy and became "a bearded, long-haired, neglected, and almost savage or wild man." Certainly his strange imagination is evident in his most famous work, *The Madonna with the Long Neck* (fig. 642, colorplate 82), painted after he had returned to his native Parma from several years' sojourn in Rome. He had been deeply impressed with the rhythmic grace of Raphael's art (compare fig. 631), but he has transformed the older master's figures into a remarkable new breed: their limbs, elongated and ivory-smooth, move with effortless languor, embodying an ideal of beauty as remote from nature as any Byzantine figure. Their setting is equally arbitrary, with a gigantic—and apparently purposeless—row of columns looming behind the tiny figure of a prophet; Parmigianino seems determined to prevent us from measuring anything in this picture by the standards of ordinary experience. Here we have approached that "artificial" style for which the term Mannerism was originally coined. *The Madonna with the Long Neck* is a vision of unearthly perfection, its cold elegance no less compelling than the violence in Rosso's *Descent.*

BRONZINO.   Keyed to a sophisticated, even rarefied taste, the elegant phase of Italian Mannerism appealed particularly to such aristocratic patrons as the grand duke of Tuscany

and the king of France, and soon became international (see fig. 679). The style produced splendid portraits, like that of Eleanora of Toledo (fig. 643), the wife of Cosimo I de'Medici, by Cosimo's court painter Agnolo Bronzino (1503–1572). The sitter here appears as the member of an exalted social caste, not as an individual personality; congealed into immobility behind the barrier of her lavishly ornate costume, Eleanora seems more akin to Parmigianino's *Madonna*—compare the hands—than to ordinary flesh and blood.

Mannerism: Venice

TINTORETTO.   Mannerism did not appear in Venice until the middle of the century. Its leading exponent, Tintoretto (1518–1594), an artist of prodigious energy and inventiveness, combined qualities of both its anticlassical and elegant phases in his work. He reportedly wanted "to paint like Titian and to design like Michelangelo," but his relationship to these two masters, though real enough, was as peculiar as Parmigianino's was to Raphael. *Christ Before Pilate* (fig. 644, colorplate 83), one of his many huge canvases for the Scuola di San Rocco, the home of the Confraternity of St. Roch, contrasts tellingly with Titian's *Christ Crowned with Thorns* (fig. 638); the bold brushwork, the glowing colors, and the sudden lights and shadows show what Tintoretto owed to the older artist, and indeed the entire composition recalls

642. PARMIGIANINO. *The Madonna with the Long Neck* (detail; see colorplate 82). Uffizi Gallery, Florence

lated on the near side of the table, but his role is so insignificant that he could almost be mistaken for an attendant).

EL GRECO. The last—and perhaps the greatest—Mannerist painter was also trained in the Venetian School. Domenikos Theotocopoulos (1541–1614), nicknamed El Greco, came from Crete, which was then under Venetian rule. His earliest training must have been from a Cretan artist still working in the Byzantine tradition. Soon after 1560 El Greco arrived in Venice and quickly absorbed the lessons of Titian, Tintoretto, and other masters. A decade later, in Rome, he came to know the art of Raphael, Michelangelo, and the Central Italian Mannerists. In 1576/77 he went to Spain, settling in Toledo for the rest of his life. Yet he remained an alien in his new homeland; although the spiritual climate of the Counter Reformation, which was especially intense in Spain, may account for the exalted emotionalism of his mature work, contemporary Spanish painting was too provincial to impress him. His style had already been formed before he arrived in Toledo, nor did he ever forget his Byzantine background—until the very end of his career, he signed his pictures in Greek.

The largest and most resplendent of El Greco's major commissions is *The Burial of Count Orgaz* (figs. 646, 647, colorplate 84); the huge canvas in the church of Santo Tomé honors a medieval benefactor so pious that St. Stephen and

643. AGNOLO BRONZINO. *Eleanora of Toledo and Her Son Giovanni de'Medici.* c. 1550
45¼ × × 37¾". Uffizi Gallery, Florence

the *Madonna with Members of the Pesaro Family* (see fig. 635). Yet the total effect is unmistakably Mannerist: the feverish emotionalism of the flickering, unreal light, and the ghostly Christ, pencil-slim and motionless among the agitated Michelangelesque figures, remind us of Rosso's *Descent.*

Even more spectacular is Tintoretto's last major work, *The Last Supper* (fig. 645). This canvas denies in every possible way the classic values of Leonardo's version (see fig. 601), painted almost exactly a century before. Christ, to be sure, still occupies the center of the composition, but now the table is placed at a sharp angle to the picture plane in exaggerated perspective; His small figure in the middle distance is distinguishable mainly by the brilliant halo. Tintoretto has gone to great lengths to give the event an everyday setting, cluttering the scene with attendants, containers of food and drink, and domestic animals. But this serves only to contrast dramatically the natural with the supernatural, for there are also celestial attendants—the smoke from the blazing oil lamp miraculously turns into clouds of angels that converge upon Christ just as He offers His body and blood, in the form of bread and wine, to the disciples. Tintoretto's main concern has been to make visible the institution of the Eucharist, the transubstantiation of earthly into Divine food; he barely hints at the human drama of Judas' betrayal, so important to Leonardo (Judas can be seen iso-

644. TINTORETTO. *Christ Before Pilate*
(see colorplate 83). Scuola di San Rocco, Venice

645. TINTORETTO. *The Last Supper.* 1592–94. 12' × 18' 8".
S. Giorgio Maggiore, Venice

St. Augustine miraculously appeared at his funeral and themselves lowered the body into its grave. The burial took place in 1323, but El Greco represents it as a contemporary event, portraying among the attendants many of the local nobility and clergy; the dazzling display of color and texture in the armor and vestments could hardly be surpassed by Titian himself. Directly above, the count's soul (a small, cloudlike figure like the angels in Tintoretto's *Last Supper*) is carried to Heaven by an angel. The celestial assembly filling the upper half of the picture is painted very differently from the lower half: every form—clouds, limbs, draperies—takes part in the sweeping, flamelike movement toward the distant figure of Christ. Here, even more than in Tintoretto's art, the various aspects of Mannerism fuse into a single ecstatic vision.

The full import of the work, however, becomes clear only when we see it in its original setting. Like an enormous window, it fills one entire wall of its chapel. The bottom of the canvas is 6 feet above the floor, and as the chapel is only about 18 feet deep, we must look sharply upward to see the upper half of the picture. El Greco's violent foreshortening is calculated to achieve an illusion of boundless space above, while the lower foreground figures appear as on a stage (their feet cut off by the molding just below the picture). The large stone plaque also belongs to the ensemble,

representing the front of the sarcophagus into which the two saints lower the body of the count; it thus explains the action within the picture. The beholder, then, perceives three levels of reality: the grave itself, supposedly set into the wall at his eye-level and closed by an actual stone slab; the contemporary re-enactment of the miraculous burial; and the vision of celestial glory witnessed by some of the participants. By sheer chance, El Greco's task here was analogous to Masaccio's in his *Trinity* mural (see fig. 560); the contrast measures the dynamic evolution of Western art since the Early Renaissance.

From El Greco's Venetian training came his mastery of portraiture. We generally know little of his relationship to his sitters, but in his memorable portrait of Fray Felix Hortensio Paravicino (fig. 648) the sitter, an important scholar and poet, was also a friend who praised El Greco's genius in several sonnets. This portrait is an artistic descendant of Titian's *Man with the Glove* and the portraits of Pontormo (see figs. 636, 640), yet the mood is not one of either reverie or withdrawal. Paravicino's frail, expressive hands and the pallid face, with its sensitive mouth and burning eyes, convey a spiritual ardor of compelling intensity. Such, we like to think, were the saints of the Counter Reformation—mystics and intellectuals at the same time.

646. Chapel with *The Burial of Count Orgaz*.
1586. S. Tomé, Toledo, Spain (compare colorplate 84)

648. EL GRECO. *Fray Felix Hortensio Paravicino.*
c. 1605. 44½ × 33¾″. Museum of Fine Arts, Boston

647. EL GRECO. *The Burial of Count Orgaz* (detail; see colorplate
84). S. Tomé, Toledo

Proto-Baroque

If Mannerism produced the personalities that today seem
most "modern"—El Greco's fame is greater now than it ever
was before—its dominance was not uncontested in the sixteenth century. Another trend that also emerged about 1520
anticipated so many features of the Baroque style that it
might be labeled Proto-Baroque.

CORREGGIO.   Correggio (1489/94–1534), the most important representative of this trend, was a phenomenally
gifted North Italian painter who spent most of his brief
career in Parma. He absorbed the influence of Leonardo and
the Venetians as a youth, then of Michelangelo and Raphael,
but their ideal of classical balance did not attract him. His
largest work, the fresco of the Assumption of the Virgin in
the dome of Parma Cathedral (fig. 649), is a masterpiece of
illusionistic perspective, a vast, luminous space filled with
soaring figures. Although they move with such exhilarating
ease that the force of gravity seems not to exist for them,
they are healthy, energetic beings of flesh and blood, not
disembodied spirits, and they frankly delight in their weightless condition.

For Correggio there was little difference between spiritual
and physical ecstasy, as we see by comparing the *Assumption
of the Virgin* with his *Jupiter and Io* (fig. 650), one canvas
in a series illustrating the Loves of the Classical Gods. The
nymph, swooning in the embrace of a cloudlike Jupiter, is the
direct kin of the jubilant angels in the fresco. Leonardesque
sfumato, combined with a Venetian sense of color and texture, produces an effect of exquisite voluptuousness that far
exceeds Titian's in his *Bacchanal* (see fig. 634, colorplate
80). Correggio had no immediate successors nor any lasting
influence on the art of his century, but toward 1600 his work
began to be widely appreciated. For the next century and a

649. CORREGGIO. *The Assumption of the Virgin*
(portion). c. 1525. Fresco. Dome, Parma Cathedral

650. CORREGGIO. *Jupiter and Io*. c. 1532.
64½ × 27¾". Kunsthistorisches Museum, Vienna

half he was admired as the equal of Raphael and Michelangelo—while the Mannerists, so important before, were largely forgotten.

Realism

A third trend in sixteenth-century painting in Italy is to be associated with the towns along the northern edge of the Lombard plain, such as Brescia and Verona. A number of artists in that region worked in a style based on Giorgione and Titian, but with a stronger interest in everyday reality.

SAVOLDO.   One of the earliest and most attractive of these North Italian Realists was Girolamo Savoldo (c. 1480–1550), from Brescia, whose *St. Matthew* (fig. 651) must be contemporary with Parmigianino's *Madonna with the Long Neck*. The broad, fluid manner of painting reflects the dominant influence of Titian, yet the great Venetian master would never have placed the Evangelist in so thoroughly domestic an environment. The humble scene in the background shows the saint's milieu to be lowly indeed, and makes the

presence of the angel doubly miraculous. This tendency to visualize sacred events among ramshackle buildings and simple people had been characteristic of "Late Gothic" painting; Savoldo must have acquired it from that source. The nocturnal lighting, too, recalls such Northern pictures as the *Nativity* by Geertgen tot Sint Jans (see fig. 521). But the main source of illumination in Geertgen's panel is the divine radiance of the Christ Child, and Savoldo uses an ordinary oil lamp for his similarly magic and intimate effect.

VERONESE.   In the work of Paolo Veronese (1528–1588), North Italian Realism takes on the splendor of a pageant. Born and trained in Verona, Veronese became, after Tintoretto, the most important painter in Venice; although utterly unlike each other in style, both found favor with the public. The contrast is strikingly evident if we compare Tintoretto's *Last Supper* and Veronese's *Christ in the House of Levi* (fig. 652, colorplate 86), both with similar subjects. Veronese avoids all reference to the supernatural. His symmetrical composition harks back to Leonardo and Raphael, the festive mood of the scene reflects Titian's work of the 1520s (compare fig. 635), and at first the picture looks like a High Renaissance work born fifty years too late. Yet we miss one essential: the elevated, ideal conception of man underlying the work of High Renaissance masters. Veronese paints a sumptuous banquet, a true feast for the eyes, but not "the intention of man's soul."

Significantly, we are not even sure which event from the life of Christ he originally meant to depict, for he gave the canvas its present title only after he had been summoned by the religious tribunal of the Inquisition, on the charge of filling his picture with "buffoons, drunkards, Germans, dwarfs, and similar vulgarities" unsuited to its sacred character. The account of this trial shows that the tribunal thought the painting represented the Last Supper; Veronese's testimony never made clear whether it was the Last Supper, or the Supper in the House of Simon. To him, apparently, this distinction made little difference; in the end, he settled on a convenient third title, the Supper in the House of Levi, which permitted him to leave the offending incidents in place. He argued that they were no more objectionable than the nudity of Christ and the Heavenly Host in Michelangelo's *Last Judgment*, but the tribunal failed to see the analogy: "…in the Last Judgment it was not necessary to paint garments, and there is nothing in those figures that is not spiritual."

The Inquisition, of course, considered only the impropriety of Veronese's art, not its unconcern with spiritual depth. His dogged refusal to admit the justice of the charge, his insistence on his right to introduce directly observed details, however "improper," and his indifference to the subject of the picture, spring from an attitude so startlingly "extroverted" that it was not generally accepted until the nineteenth century. The painter's domain, Veronese seems to say, is the entire visible world, and here he acknowledges no authority other than his senses.

652. PAOLO VERONESE. *Christ in the House of Levi* (detail; see colorplate 86). 1573. Academy, Venice

SCULPTURE

Italian sculptors of the later sixteenth century fail to match the achievements of the painters. Perhaps Michelangelo's overpowering personality discouraged new talent in this field, but the dearth of challenging new tasks is a more plausible reason. In any case, the most interesting sculpture of this period was produced outside of Italy, and in Florence, after the death of Michelangelo in 1564, the leading sculptor was a Northerner.

Mannerism, First and Second Phases

BERRUGUETE.   If the anticlassical phase of Mannerism, represented by the style of Rosso and Pontormo, has no sculptural counterpart, the work of the Spaniard Alonso Berruguete (c. 1489–1561) most closely approaches it. Berruguete had been associated with the founders of the anticlassical trend in Florence about 1520; his *St. John the Baptist* (fig. 653), one of the reliefs carved twenty years later for the choir stalls of Toledo Cathedral, still reflects this experience. The angular, emaciated body, clawlike hands, and fixed, wide-eyed stare recall the otherworldly expressiveness of Rosso's *Descent* (see fig. 639, colorplate 81). El Greco must have felt a sense of kinship with Berruguete's art.

CELLINI.   The second, elegant phase of Mannerism appears in countless sculptural examples in Italy and abroad. The best-known representative of the style is Benvenuto Cellini (1500–1571), the Florentine goldsmith and sculptor

651. GIROLAMO SAVOLDO. *St. Matthew.* c. 1535. 36¾ × 49″. The Metropolitan Museum of Art, New York (Marquand Fund, 1912)

653. ALONSO BERRUGUETE. *St. John the Baptist.* c. 1540.
Wood, 31½ × 19¼″. Toledo Cathedral, Spain

654. BENVENUTO CELLINI. *Saltcellar
of Francis I* (see other side, colorplate 87).
Kunsthistorisches Museum, Vienna

the sea and pepper from the land, Cellini placed the boat-shaped salt container under the guardianship of Neptune, while the pepper, in a tiny triumphal arch, is watched over by a personification of Earth. On the base are figures representing the four seasons and the four parts of the day.

The entire object thus reflects the cosmic significance of the Medici Tombs (compare fig. 619), but on this miniature scale Cellini's program turns into playful fancy; he wants to impress us with his ingenuity and skill, and to charm us with the grace of his figures. The allegorical significance of the design is simply a pretext for this display of virtuosity. When he tells us, for instance, that Neptune and Earth each have a bent and a straight leg to signify mountains and plains, we can only marvel at the divorce of form from content. Despite his boundless admiration for Michelangelo, Cellini's elegant figures on the saltcellar are as elongated, smooth, and languid as Parmigianino's (see fig. 642, colorplate 82).

PRIMATICCIO. Parmigianino also strongly influenced Francesco Primaticcio (1504–1570), Cellini's rival at the court of Francis I. A man of many talents, Primaticcio designed the interior decoration of some of the main rooms in the royal château of Fontainebleau, combining painted scenes and a richly sculptured stucco framework. The section shown in figure 655 and colorplate 88 caters to the same aristocratic taste that admired Cellini's saltcellar. The four maidens are not burdened with any specific allegorical significance—their role recalls the nudes of the Sistine Ceiling—but perform a task for which they seem equally ill-fitted: they reinforce the piers that sustain the ceiling. These willowy caryatids epitomize the studied nonchalance of second-phase Mannerism.

655. FRANCESCO PRIMATICCIO. Stucco Figures
(see colorplate 88). Fontainebleau

who owes much of his fame to his picaresque autobiography. The gold saltcellar for King Francis I of France (fig. 654, colorplate 87), Cellini's major work in precious metal to escape destruction, well displays the virtues and limitations of his art. To hold condiments is obviously the lesser function of this lavish conversation piece. Because salt comes from

656, 657. GIOVANNI BOLOGNA. *The Rape of
the Sabine Woman*. Completed 1583. Marble,
height 13′ 6″. Loggia dei Lanzi, Florence

GIOVANNI BOLOGNA.   Cellini, Primaticcio, and the other
Italians employed by Francis I made Mannerism the dominant style in mid-sixteenth-century France, and their influence went far beyond the royal court. It must have reached
a gifted young sculptor from Douai in northern France, Jean
de Bologne (1529–1608), who went to Italy about 1555 for
further training and stayed to become, under the Italianized
name of Giovanni Bologna, the most important sculptor in
Florence during the last third of the century. His over-lifesize
marble group, *The Rape of the Sabine Woman* (figs. 656,
657), won particular acclaim, and still has its place of honor
near the Palazzo Vecchio.

The subject, drawn from the legends of ancient Rome,
seems an odd choice for statuary; the city's founders, an
adventurous band of men from across the sea, so the story
goes, tried vainly to find wives among their neighbors, the
Sabines, and resorted at last to a trick: having invited the
entire Sabine tribe into Rome for a peaceful festival, they fell
upon them with arms, took the women away by force, and
thus ensured the future of their race. Actually, the artist
designed the group with no specific subject in mind, to
silence those critics who doubted his ability as a monumental
sculptor in marble. He selected what seemed to him the most
difficult feat, three figures of contrasting character united
in a common action. Their identities were disputed among
the learned connoisseurs of the day, who finally settled on
the Rape of the Sabine Woman as the most suitable title.

Here, then, is another artist who is noncommittal about
subject matter, although his unconcern had a different
motive from Veronese's. Giovanni Bologna's self-imposed task
was to carve in marble, on a massive scale, a sculptural
composition that was to be seen not from one but from all
sides; this had hitherto been attempted only in bronze and
on a much smaller scale (see figs. 584, 586). He has solved
this purely formal problem, but only by insulating his group
from the world of human experience. These figures, spiral-
ing upward as if confined inside a tall, narrow cylinder,
perform a well-rehearsed choreographic exercise the emotional meaning of which remains obscure. We admire their
discipline but we find no trace of genuine pathos.

ARCHITECTURE
Mannerism

The concept of Mannerism as a period style, we recall, had
been coined for painting. We have not encountered any
difficulty in applying it to sculpture. Can it usefully be
extended to architecture as well? And if so, what qualities
must we look for? These questions have arisen only recently,
so it is not surprising that we cannot yet answer them
very precisely. Some buildings, to be sure, would be called
Mannerist by almost everyone today; but this does not give
us a viable definition of Mannerism as an architectural
period style.

VASARI.   Such a Mannerist structure is the Uffizi Palace
in Florence, by Giorgio Vasari (1511–1574). It consists of
two long wings—originally intended, as its name suggests,
for offices—facing each other across a narrow court, linked
at one end by a loggia (fig. 658). Vasari's inspiration is not
far to seek: the "tired" scroll brackets and the peculiar combination of column and wall have their source in the vestibule

658. GIORGIO VASARI. Loggia of the Uffizi, Florence
(view from the Arno). Begun 1560

659. BARTOLOMMEO AMMANATI. Courtyard of
the Palazzo Pitti, Florence. 1558–70

of the Laurentian Library (on page 456 we cited Vasari's praise for Michelangelo's unorthodox use of the classical vocabulary). Yet his design lacks the sculptural power and expressiveness of its model; rather, the Uffizi loggia forms a screen as weightless as the façade of the Pazzi Chapel (see fig. 553). What is tense in Michelangelo's design becomes merely ambiguous—the architectural members seem as devoid of energy as the human figures of second-phase Mannerism, and their relationships as studiedly "artificial."

AMMANATI. The same is true of the courtyard of the Palazzo Pitti (fig. 659) by Bartolommeo Ammanati (1511–1592), despite its display of muscularity. Here the three-story scheme of superimposed orders, derived from the Colosseum, has been overlaid with an extravagant pattern of rustication that "imprisons" the columns, reducing them to an oddly passive role. These welts disguise rather than enhance the massiveness of the masonry, the overall corrugated texture making us think of the fancies of a pastry cook.

PALLADIO. If this is Mannerism in architecture, can we find it in the work of Andrea Palladio (1518–1580), the greatest architect of the later sixteenth century, second in importance only to Michelangelo? Unlike Vasari, who was a painter and historian as well as an architect (his artists' *Lives* provide the first coherent account of Italian Renaissance art), or Ammanati, who was a sculptor-architect, Palladio stands in the tradition of the humanist and theoretician Leone Battista Alberti.

Although his career centered on his native town of Vicenza, his buildings and theoretical writings soon brought him international status. Palladio insisted that architecture must be governed both by reason and by certain universal rules that were perfectly exemplified by the buildings of the ancients. He thus shared Alberti's basic outlook and his firm faith in the cosmic significance of numerical ratios (see page 410). But they differed in how each man related theory and practice. With Alberti, this relationship had been loose and flexible, whereas Palladio believed quite literally in practic-

ing what he preached. His architectural treatise is consequently more practical than Alberti's—this helps to explain its huge success—while his buildings are linked more directly with his theories. It has even been said that Palladio designed only what was, in his view, sanctioned by ancient precedent. If the results are not necessarily classic in style, we may call them "classicistic" (to denote a conscious striving for classic qualities); this is indeed the usual term for both Palladio's work and theoretical attitude.

The Villa Rotonda (figs. 660, 661), one of Palladio's finest buildings, perfectly illustrates the meaning of classicism. An aristocratic country residence near Vicenza, it consists of a square block surmounted by a dome and is faced on all four sides with identical porches in the shape of temple fronts. Alberti had defined the ideal church as such a completely symmetrical, centralized design (page 422), and it is evident that Palladio found in the same principles the ideal country house. But how could he justify a context so purely secular for the solemn motif of the temple front? Surprisingly enough, he was convinced, on the basis of ancient literary sources, that Roman private houses had porticoes like these (excavations have since disproved him; see page 167). Yet Palladio's use of the temple front here is not mere antiquari-

660. ANDREA PALLADIO. Villa Rotonda, Vicenza. c. 1567–70

661. Plan of the Villa Rotonda

662. ANDREA PALLADIO. S. Giorgio Maggiore,
Venice. Designed 1565

663. Plan of S. Giorgio Maggiore

logical and compact, did not fit the cross section of a basilica, and really circumvented the problem. Palladio—again following what he believed to be ancient precedent—found a different answer: he superimposed a tall, narrow temple front on another low and wide one to reflect the different heights of nave and aisles. Theoretically, it was a perfect solution. In practice, however, he found that he could not keep the two systems as separate as his classicistic conscience demanded, and still integrate them into a harmonious whole. This conflict makes ambiguous those parts of the design that have, as it were, a dual allegiance; this might be interpreted as a Mannerist quality. The plan (fig. 663), too, suggests a duality: the main body of the church is strongly centralized—the transept is as long as the nave—but the longitudinal axis reasserts itself in the separate compartments for the main altar and the chapel beyond.

IL GESÙ: VIGNOLA AND DELLA PORTA. Palladio's immense authority as a designer keeps the conflicting elements in the façade and plan of S. Giorgio from actually clashing. In less assured hands, such a precarious union would break apart. A more generally applicable solution was evolved just at that time in Rome by Giacomo Vignola (1507–1573) and Giacomo della Porta (c. 1540–1602), architects who had assisted Michelangelo at St. Peter's and were still using his architectural vocabulary. The church of Il Gesù (Jesus), a building whose importance for subsequent church architecture can hardly be exaggerated, is the mother church of the Jesuits; its design must have been closely supervised so as to conform to the aims of the militant new order, founded in 1540. We may thus view it as the architectural embodiment of the spirit of the Counter Reformation.

The planning stage of the structure began in 1550 (Michelangelo himself once promised a design, but apparently never furnished it); the present ground plan, by Vignola, was adopted in 1568 (fig. 665). It contrasts in almost every possible respect with Palladio's S. Giorgio: a basilica, strikingly compact, dominated by its mighty nave. The aisles have been replaced by chapels, thus "herding" the congregation quite literally into one large, hall-like space directly in view of the altar; the attention of this "audience" is positively directed toward altar and pulpit, as our view of the interior (fig. 666) confirms. (The painting shows how the church would look from the street if the center part of the façade were removed; for the later, High Baroque decoration of the nave vault, see fig. 706.) We also see here an unexpected feature which the ground plan cannot show: the dramatic contrast between the dim illumination in the nave and the abundant light beyond, in the eastern part of the church, supplied by the large windows in the drum of the dome. Light has been consciously exploited for its expressive possibilities—a novel device, "theatrical" in the best sense—to give Il Gesù a stronger emotional focus than we have yet found in a church interior.

Despite its great originality, the plan of Il Gesù is not entirely without precedent (see fig. 576). The façade, by Giacomo della Porta, is as bold as the plan (fig. 664, colorplate 89), although it, too, has its earlier sources. The paired pilasters and broken architrave of the lower story are clearly

anism; he probably persuaded himself that it was legitimate because he regarded this feature as desirable for both beauty and utility. In any case, the porches of the Villa Rotonda, beautifully correlated with the walls behind, are an organic part of his design. They lend the structure an air of serene dignity and festive grace that still appeals to us today.

The façade of S. Giorgio Maggiore in Venice (fig. 662), of about the same date as the Villa Rotonda, adds to the same effect a new sumptuousness and complexity. Palladio's problem here was how to create a classically integrated façade for a basilican church. He surely knew Alberti's solution (S. Andrea in Mantua; see fig. 575), a temple front enclosing a triumphal-arch motif; but this design, although impressively

664. GIACOMO DELLA PORTA.
Façade of Il Gesù, Rome (see colorplate 89)

665. GIACOMO VIGNOLA.
Plan of Il Gesù, Rome. 1568

broken entablature), but the horizontal divisions in turn determine the size of the vertical members (hence no colossal order). Equally important is the emphasis on the main portal: its double frame—two pediments resting on coupled pilasters and columns—projects beyond the rest of the façade and gives strong focus to the entire design. Not since Gothic architecture has the entrance to a church received such a dramatic concentration of features, attracting the attention of the beholder outside the building much as the concentrated light beneath the dome channels that of the worshiper inside.

What are we to call the style of Il Gesù? Obviously, it has little in common with Palladio, and it shares with Florentine architecture of the time only the influence of Michelangelo. But this influence reflects two very different phases of the great master's career: the contrast between the Uffizi and Il Gesù is hardly less great than that between the vestibule of the Laurentian Library and the exterior of St. Peter's. If we label the Uffizi Mannerist, the same term will not serve us for Il Gesù. As we shall see, the design of Il Gesù will become basic to Baroque architecture; by calling it "pre-Baroque," we suggest both its seminal importance for the future and its special place in relation to the past.

derived from Michelangelo's design for the exterior of St. Peter's (compare fig. 625). In the upper story the same pattern recurs on a somewhat smaller scale, with four instead of six pairs of supports; the difference in width is bridged by two scroll-shaped buttresses. A large pediment crowns the façade, which retains the classic proportions of Renaissance architecture (the height equals the width).

What is fundamentally new here is the very element that was missing in the façade of S. Giorgio: the integration of all the parts into one whole. Giacomo della Porta, freed from classicistic scruples by his allegiance to Michelangelo, gave the same vertical rhythm to both stories of the façade; this rhythm is obeyed by all the horizontal members (note the

666. ANDREA SACCHI and JAN MIEL. *Urban VIII Visiting Il Gesù*. 1639–41. National Gallery, Rome

5
THE RENAISSANCE IN THE NORTH

North of the Alps, most fifteenth-century artists had remained indifferent to Italian forms and ideas. Since the time of the Master of Flémalle and the Van Eycks they had looked to Flanders, rather than to Tuscany, for leadership. This relative isolation ends suddenly, toward the year 1500; as if a dam had burst, Italian influence flows northward in an ever wider stream, and Northern Renaissance art begins to replace "Late Gothic." That term, however, has a far less well-defined meaning than "Late Gothic," which refers to a single, clearly recognizable stylistic tradition. The diversity of trends north of the Alps is even greater than in Italy during the sixteenth century. Nor does Italian influence provide a common denominator, for this influence is itself diverse: Early Renaissance, High Renaissance, and Man-

nerist, all in regional variants from Lombardy, Venice, Florence, and Rome. Its effects, too, may vary greatly; they may be superficial or profound, direct or indirect, specific or general.

The "Late Gothic" tradition remained much alive, if no longer dominant, and its encounter with Italian art resulted in a kind of Hundred Years' War among styles which ended only when, in the early seventeenth century, the Baroque emerged as an international movement. The full history of this "war" is yet to be written; its major issues are hard to trace through all the battles, truces, and shifting alliances. Its course, moreover, was decisively affected by the Reformation, which had a far more immediate impact on art north of the Alps than in Italy. Our account, then, must be oversim-

667. MATTHIAS GRÜNEWALD. *The Crucifixion,* from the
Isenheim Altarpiece (closed). c. 1510–15. Panel, 8′ 10″ × 10′ 1″.
Musée Unterlinden, Colmar (see colorplate 85)

plified, emphasizing the heroic phases of the struggle at the expense of the lesser (but, in the long run, equally significant) skirmishes.

GERMANY
Painting and the Graphic Arts

Let us begin with Germany, the home of the Reformation, where the main battles of the "war of styles" took place during the first quarter of the century. Between 1475 and 1500, it had produced such important masters as Michael Pacher and Martin Schongauer (see figs. 530, 531, 534), but these hardly prepare us for the astonishing burst of creative energy that was to follow. The range of achievements of this period—comparable, in its brevity and brilliance, to the Italian High Renaissance—is measured by the contrasting personalities of its greatest artists: Matthias Grünewald and Albrecht Dürer. Both died in 1528, probably at about the same age, although we know only Dürer's birth date (1471). Dürer quickly became internationally famous, while Grünewald remained so obscure that his real name, Mathis Gothart Nithart, was discovered only recently.

GRÜNEWALD. Grünewald's fame, like that of El Greco, has developed almost entirely within our own century. In the Northern art of his time, he alone, in his main work, the *Isenheim Altarpiece,* overwhelms us with something like the power of the Sistine Ceiling. (Characteristically enough, this extraordinary work was long believed to be by Dürer.) The altarpiece, painted between 1509/10 and 1515 for the monastery church of the Order of St. Anthony at Isenheim, in Alsace, is now in the museum of the nearby town of Colmar; a carved shrine with two sets of movable wings, it has three stages, or "views."

The first and outermost, when all the wings are closed, shows *The Crucifixion* (fig. 667)—probably the most impressive ever painted. In one respect it is very medieval: Christ's unbearable agony and the desperate grief of the Virgin, St. John, and Mary Magdalen recall the older German *Andachtsbild* (see fig. 468). But the pitiful body on the cross, with its twisted limbs, its countless lacerations, its rivulets of blood, is on a heroic scale that raises it beyond the merely human, and thus reveals the two natures of Christ. The same message is conveyed by the flanking figures: the three historic witnesses on the left mourn Christ's death as a man, while John the Baptist, on the right, points with calm emphasis to Him as the Saviour. Even the background suggests this duality: this Golgotha is not a hill outside Jerusalem, but a mountain towering above lesser peaks. The Crucifixion, lifted from its familiar setting, thus becomes a lonely event silhouetted against a deserted, ghostly landscape and a blue-black sky. Darkness is over the land, in accordance with the Gospels, yet brilliant light bathes the foreground with the force of sudden revelation. This union of time and eternity, of reality and symbolism, gives Grünewald's *Crucifixion* its awesome grandeur.

When the outer wings are opened, the mood of the *Isenheim Altarpiece* changes dramatically (colorplate 85). All three scenes in this second "view"—the Annunciation, the Angel Concert for the Madonna and Child, and the Resurrection—celebrate events as jubilant in spirit as the Crucifixion is austere. Most striking in comparison with "Late Gothic" painting is the sense of the movement pervading these panels—everything twists and turns as though it had a life of its own. The angel of the Annunciation enters the room like a gust of wind that blows the Virgin backward; the Risen Christ shoots from His grave with explosive force; the canopy over the Angel Concert seems to writhe in response to the heavenly music. This vibrant energy has thoroughly reshaped the brittle, spiky contours and angular drapery patterns of "Late Gothic" art. Grünewald's forms are soft, elastic, fleshy. His light and color show a corresponding change: commanding all the resources of the great Flemish masters, he employs them with unexampled boldness and flexibility. His color scale is richly iridescent, its range matched only by the Venetians. And his exploitation of colored light is altogether without parallel at that time. In the luminescent angels of the Concert, the apparition of God the Father and the Heavenly Host above the Madonna, and, most spectacularly, the rainbow-hued radiance of the Risen Christ, Grünewald's genius has achieved miracles-through-light that remain unsurpassed to this day.

How much did Grünewald owe to Italian art? Nothing at all, we are first tempted to reply. Yet he must have learned from the Renaissance in more ways than one: his knowledge of perspective (note the low horizons) and the physical vigor of some of his figures cannot be explained by the "Late Gothic" tradition alone, and occasionally his pictures show architectural details of Southern origin. Perhaps the most important effect of the Renaissance on him, however, was psychological. We know little about his career, but he apparently did not lead the settled life of a craftsman-painter controlled by the rules of his guild; he was also an architect, an engineer, something of a courtier, and an entrepreneur; he worked for many different patrons and stayed nowhere for very long. He was in sympathy with Martin Luther (who frowned upon religious images as "idolatrous"), even though, as a painter, he depended on Catholic patronage.

In a word, Grünewald seems to have shared the free, individualistic spirit of Italian Renaissance artists; the daring of his pictorial vision likewise suggests a reliance on his own resources. The Renaissance, then, had a liberating influence on him but did not change the basic cast of his imagination. Instead, it helped him to epitomize the expressive aspects of the "Late Gothic" in a style of unique intensity and individuality.

DÜRER. For Dürer (1471–1528) the Renaissance held a richer meaning. Attracted to Italian art while still a young journeyman, he visited Venice in 1494/5 and returned to his native Nuremberg with a new conception of the world and the artist's place in it. The unbridled fantasy of Grünewald's art was to him "a wild, unpruned tree" (he used this phrase for painters who worked by rules-of-thumb, without theoretical foundations) which needed the discipline of the objective, rational standards of the Renaissance. Taking the Italian view that the fine arts belong among the liberal arts, he also adopted the ideal of the artist as a gentleman and humanistic scholar. By steadily cultivating his intellectual interests he came to encompass in his lifetime a vast variety of techniques and subjects. And since he was the greatest printmaker of the time, he had a wide influence on sixteenth-century art through his woodcuts and engravings, which circulated everywhere in Europe.

Dürer's youthful copies after Mantegna and other Early Renaissance masters display his eager, and intuitive grasp of the essentials of their alien style. Even more astonishing are his watercolors made on the way back from Venice, such as the one inscribed "Italian Mountains" (fig. 668). Significantly, Dürer did not record the name of the spot; the specific location had no interest for him. The title he jotted down seems exactly right, for this is not a "portrait," but a "study from the model" perceived in timeless freshness. The calm rhythm of this panorama of softly rounded slopes conveys a view of nature in its organic wholeness that was, in those years, matched only by Leonardo.

After the breadth and lyricism of the *Italian Mountains*, the expressive violence of the woodcuts illustrating the Apocalypse, Dürer's most ambitious graphic work of the years following his return from Venice, is doubly shocking. The gruesome vision of the *Four Horsemen* (fig. 669) seems at first to return completely to the "Late Gothic" world of Martin Schongauer (compare fig. 534). Yet the physical energy and solid, full-bodied volume of these figures would have been impossible without Dürer's earlier experience in

668. ALBRECHT DÜRER. *Italian Mountains.*
c. 1495. Watercolor. Ashmolean Museum, Oxford

669. ALBRECHT DÜRER. *The Four Horsemen of the Apocalypse.* c. 1497–98. Woodcut

The didactic aspect of Dürer's art is clearest perhaps in the engraving *Adam and Eve*, of 1504 (fig. 671), where the biblical subject serves as a pretext for the display of two ideal nudes: Apollo and Venus in a Northern forest (compare figs. 197, 199). No wonder they look somewhat incongruous; unlike the picturesque setting and its animal inhabitants, Adam and Eve are constructed figures—not the male and female observed from life, but exemplars of what Dürer believed to be perfect proportions.

The same approach, now applied to the body of a horse, is evident in *Knight, Death, and Devil* (fig. 672), one of the artist's finest prints. But this time there is no incongruity: the knight on his beautiful mount, poised and confident as an equestrian statue, embodies an ideal both aesthetic and moral. He is the Christian Soldier steadfast on the road of faith toward the Heavenly Jerusalem, undeterred by the hideous horseman threatening to cut him off, or the grotesque devil behind him. The dog, another symbol of virtue, loyally follows his master despite the lizards and skulls in his path. Italian Renaissance form, united with the heritage of "Late Gothic" symbolism (whether open or disguised), here takes on a new, characteristically Northern significance.

The subject of *Knight, Death, and Devil* seems to have been derived from the *Manual of the Christian Soldier* by Erasmus of Rotterdam, the greatest of Northern humanists.

copying the works of such artists as Mantegna. At this stage, Dürer's style has much in common with Grünewald's. The comparison with Schongauer's *Temptation of St. Anthony*, however, is instructive from another point of view; it shows how thoroughly Dürer has redefined his medium—the woodcut—by enriching it with the linear subtleties of engraving. In his hands, woodcuts lose their former charm as popular art, but gain the precise articulation of a fully matured graphic style. He set a standard that soon transformed the technique of woodcuts all over Europe.

The first artist to be fascinated by his own image, Dürer was in this respect more of a Renaissance personality than any Italian artist. His earliest known work, a drawing made at thirteen, is a self-portrait, and he continued to produce self-portraits throughout his career. Most impressive, and peculiarly revealing, is the panel of 1500 (fig. 670): pictorially, it belongs to the Flemish tradition (compare Jan van Eyck's *Man in a Red Turban*, fig. 515), but the solemn, frontal pose and the Christ-like idealization of the features assert an authority quite beyond the range of ordinary portraits. The picture looks, in fact, like a secularized icon (see colorplate 30), reflecting not so much Dürer's vanity as the seriousness with which he regarded his mission as an artistic reformer. (One thinks of Martin Luther's "Here I stand; I cannot do otherwise.")

670. ALBRECHT DÜRER. *Self-Portrait.* 1500. Panel, 26¼ × 19¼". Pinakothek, Munich

Colorplate 82. PARMIGIANINO. *The Madonna with the Long Neck* (see page 466).
About 1535. Panel, 7' 1" × 4' 4". Uffizi Gallery, Florence

Colorplate 83. TINTORETTO. *Christ Before Pilate* (see page 466).
1566–67. About 18′ 1″ × 13′ 3½″. Scuola di San Rocco, Venice

Colorplate 84. EL GRECO. *The Burial of Count Orgaz* (see page 467).
1586. 16′ × 11′ 10″. Santo Tomé, Toledo, Spain

Colorplate 85. MATTHIAS GRÜNEWALD. *The Annunciation; Virgin and Child with Angels; The Resurrection*,
second view of the *Isenheim Altarpiece* (see page 479). About 1510–15. Panel, each wing 8′ 10″ × 4′ 8″,
central scene 8′ 10″ × 11′ 2½″. Musée Unterlinden, Colmar

Colorplate 86. PAOLO VERONESE. *Christ in the House of Levi* (see page 470). 1573. 18′ 2″ × 42′. Academy, Venice

Colorplate 87. BENVENUTO CELLINI. *Saltcellar of Francis I* (see page 472).
1539–43. Gold with enamel, 10¼ × 13⅛″. Kunsthistorisches Museum, Vienna

Colorplate 88. FRANCESCO PRIMATICCIO. Stucco Figures (see
page 472). c. 1541–45. Fontainebleau

Colorplate 89. GIACOMO DELLA PORTA. Façade of Il
Gesù, Rome (see page 475). c. 1575–84

Colorplate 90. ALBRECHT DÜRER. *The Four Apostles* (see page 489).
1523–26. Panel, each 85 × 30″. Pinakothek, Munich

671. (*above, left*) ALBRECHT DÜRER. *Adam and Eve*. 1504. Engraving. Museum of Fine Arts, Boston

672. (*above*) ALBRECHT DÜRER. *Knight, Death, and Devil*. 1513. Engraving. Museum of Fine Arts, Boston

Dürer's own convictions were essentially those of Christian humanism; they made him an early and enthusiastic follower of Martin Luther, although, like Grünewald, he continued to work for Catholic patrons. Nevertheless, his new faith can be sensed in the growing austerity of style and subject in his religious works after 1520. The climax of this trend is represented by *The Four Apostles* (fig. 673, colorplate 90), paired panels containing what has rightly been termed Dürer's artistic testament.

Dürer presented the panels in 1526 to the city of Nuremberg, which had joined the Lutheran camp the year before. The chosen Apostles are basic to Protestant doctrine (John and Paul face one another in the foreground, with Peter and Mark behind). Quotations from their writings, inscribed below in Luther's translation, warn the city government not to mistake human error and pretense for the will of God; they plead against Catholics and ultrazealous Protestant radicals alike. But in another, more universal sense, the four figures represent the Four Temperaments (and, by implication, the other cosmic quartets—the seasons, the elements, the times of day, and the ages of man) encircling, like the cardinal points of the compass, the Deity who is at the invisible center of this "triptych." In keeping with their

673. ALBRECHT DÜRER. *The Four Apostles* (detail; see colorplate 90). Pinakothek, Munich

674. ALBRECHT DÜRER. *Demonstration of Perspective*, from the artist's treatise on geometry. 1525. Woodcut

Dürer's *Adam and Eve*. Paris is a German knight clad in fashionable armor, indistinguishable from the nobles at the court of Saxony who were the artist's patrons. The playful eroticism, small size, and precise, miniature-like detail of the picture make it plainly a collector's item, attuned to the tastes of a provincial aristocracy.

ALTDORFER.   As remote from the classic ideal, but far more impressive, is *The Battle of Issus* by Albrecht Altdorfer (c. 1480–1538), a Bavarian painter somewhat younger than Cranach (fig. 676, colorplate 91). Without the text on the tablet suspended in the sky, and the other inscriptions, we could not possibly identify the subject, Alexander's victory over Darius. The artist has tried to follow ancient descriptions of the actual number and kind of combatants in the battle, but this required him to adopt a bird's-eye view whereby the two protagonists are lost in the antlike mass of their own armies (contrast the Hellenistic representation of the same subject in fig. 275 and colorplate 21). Moreover, the soldiers' armor and the fortified town in the distance are unmistakably of the sixteenth century.

role, the Apostles have a cubic severity and grandeur such as we have not encountered since Masaccio and Piero della Francesca.

That the style of *The Four Apostles* has evoked the names of these great Italians is no coincidence, for Dürer devoted a good part of his last years to the theory of art, including a treatise on geometry based on a thorough study of Piero della Francesca's discourse on perspective. Often he went beyond his Italian sources; he invented, for instance, a device for producing an image by purely mechanical means, to demonstrate the objective validity of perspective (fig. 674). Two men "draw" the lute as it would appear to us if we looked at it from the spot on the wall marked by a little hook; the string passing through the hook substitutes for the visual rays. The man on the left attaches it to successive points on the contour of the lute; the other man marks where the string passes through the vertical frame (the picture plane) and makes corresponding dots on the drawing board hinged to the frame. Dürer, of course, knew that such an image was the record of a scientific experiment, not a work of art; neither was he really interested in a method for making pictures without human skill or judgment. Nevertheless, his device, however clumsy, is the first step toward the principle of the photographic camera (see page 614).

CRANACH.   Dürer's hope for a monumental art embodying the Protestant faith remained unfulfilled. Other German painters, notably Lucas Cranach the Elder (1472–1553), also tried to cast Luther's doctrines into visual form, but created no viable tradition. Such efforts were doomed, since the spiritual leaders of the Reformation looked upon them with indifference or, more often, outright hostility. Lucas Cranach is best remembered today for his portraits and his delightfully incongruous mythological scenes. In his *Judgment of Paris* (fig. 675) nothing could be less classical than the three coquettish damsels, whose wriggly nakedness fits the Northern background better than does the nudity of

675. LUCAS CRANACH THE ELDER.
The Judgment of Paris. 1530. Panel, 13½ × 8¾".
Staatliche Kunsthalle, Karlsruhe

676. ALBRECHT ALTDORFER. *The Battle of Issus*
(detail; see colorplate 91). Pinakothek, Munich

The picture might well show some contemporary battle, except for one feature: the spectacular sky, with the sun triumphantly breaking through the clouds and "defeating" the moon. The celestial drama above a vast Alpine landscape, obviously correlated with the human contest below, raises the scene to the cosmic level. This is strikingly similar to the vision of heavenly glory above the Virgin and Child in the *Isenheim Altarpiece* (fig. 667, colorplate 85). Altdorfer may indeed be viewed as a later, and lesser, Grünewald; although he, too, was an architect, well acquainted with perspective and the Italian stylistic vocabulary, Altdorfer's paintings show the unruly imagination already familiar from the work of the older master. But Altdorfer is also unlike Grünewald: he makes the human figure incidental to its spatial setting, whether natural or man-made. The tiny soldiers of the *Battle of Issus* have their counterpart in his other pictures, and he painted at least one landscape with no figures at all—the earliest "pure" landscape (Dürer's sketch, *Italian Mountains*, fig. 668, not being a finished work of art).

Portraiture

HOLBEIN. Gifted though they were, Cranach and Altdorfer both evaded the main challenge of the Renaissance so bravely faced—if not always mastered—by Dürer: the image of man. Their style, antimonumental and miniature-like, set the pace for dozens of lesser masters; perhaps the rapid decline of German art after Dürer's death was due to a failure of ambition, among artists and patrons alike. The career of Hans Holbein the Younger (1497–1543)—the one painter of whom this is not true—confirms the general rule. Born and raised in Augsburg, a center of international commerce in South Germany particularly open to Renaissance ideas,

he left at the age of eighteen for Switzerland. By 1520, he was firmly established in Basel as a designer of woodcuts, a splendid decorator, and an incisive portraitist. His likeness of Erasmus of Rotterdam (fig. 677), painted soon after the famous author had settled in Basel, gives us a truly memorable image of Renaissance man: intimate yet monumental, this doctor of humane letters has an intellectual authority formerly reserved for the doctors of the Church. Yet Holbein must have felt confined in Basel, for in 1523–24 he traveled to France, apparently intending to offer his services to Francis I; two years later Basel was in the throes of the Reformation crisis, and he went to England, hoping for commissions at the court of Henry VIII (Erasmus, recommending him to Thomas More, wrote: "Here [in Basel] the arts are out in the cold"). On his return in 1528, he used his English earnings to buy a house for his family. But Basel, becoming meanwhile fanatically Protestant, had iconoclastic riots; despite the entreaties of the city council, Holbein departed for London in 1532. He went back to Basel only once, in 1538, while traveling on the continent as court painter to Henry VIII. The council made a last attempt to keep him at home, but Holbein had become an artist of international fame to whom Basel now seemed provincial indeed. His style, too, had gained an international flavor. The portrait of Henry VIII (fig. 678, colorplate 92) shares with Bronzino's *Eleanora of Toledo* (fig. 643) the immobile pose, the air of unapproach-

677. HANS HOLBEIN THE YOUNGER. *Erasmus of Rotterdam.*
c. 1523. Panel, 16½ × 12½". The Louvre, Paris

678. HANS HOLBEIN THE YOUNGER. *Henry VIII*
(see colorplate 92). National Gallery, Rome

acknowledged to be his model. We see this link with the older master in the even lighting and meticulous detail of *A Young Man Among Roses* (fig. 680), but the elongated proportions and the pose of languorous grace come from Italian Mannerism, probably via Fontainebleau (compare fig. 655, colorplate 88). Our lovesick youth also strikes us as the descendant of the fashionable attendants at the court of the duke of Berry (see fig. 506). We can imagine him besieging his lady with sonnets and madrigals before presenting her with this exquisite token of devotion.

THE NETHERLANDS
Painting

The Netherlands in the sixteenth century had the most turbulent and painful history of any country north of the Alps. When the Reformation began, they were part of the far-flung empire of the Hapsburgs under Charles V, who was also king of Spain. Protestantism quickly became powerful in the Netherlands, and the attempts of the Crown to suppress it led to open revolt against foreign rule. After a bloody struggle, the northern provinces (today's Holland) emerged at the end of the century as an independent state, while the southern ones (roughly corresponding to modern Belgium) remained in Spanish hands.

ability, and the precisely rendered costume and jewels. While Holbein's picture, unlike Bronzino's, does not yet reflect the Mannerist ideal of elegance—the rigid frontality and physical bulk of Henry VIII create an overpowering sensation of the king's ruthless, commanding presence— both clearly belong to the same species of court portrait.

The link between the two may lie in such French works as Jean Clouet's *Francis I* (fig. 679), which Holbein could have seen on his travels. (For Francis I as a patron of Italian Mannerists, see page 472.) The type evidently was coined at the royal court of France, where its ancestry can be traced back as far as Jean Fouques (see fig. 525). It gained international currency between 1525 and 1550.

Although Holbein's pictures molded British taste in aristocratic portraiture for decades, he had no English disciples of real talent. The Elizabethan genius was more literary and musical than visual, and the demand for portraits in the later sixteenth century continued to be filled largely by visiting foreign artists.

HILLIARD. The most notable English painter of the period was Nicholas Hilliard (1547–1619), a goldsmith who also specialized in miniature portraits on parchment, tiny keepsakes often worn by their owners as jewelry. These "portable portraits" had been invented in antiquity (see fig. 285) and were revived in the fifteenth century (see fig. 526). Holbein, too, produced miniature portraits, which Hilliard

679. JEAN CLOUET. *Francis I.* c. 1525–30.
Panel, 37¾ × 29″. The Louvre, Paris

680. NICHOLAS HILLIARD. *A Young Man Among Roses.*
c. 1588. Parchment, 5⅜ × 2¾".
Victoria & Albert Museum, London

The religious and political strife might have had cata-strophic effects on the arts, yet this, astonishingly, did not happen. Sixteenth-century Netherlandish painting, to be sure, does not equal that of the fifteenth in brilliance, nor did it produce any pioneers of the Northern Renaissance comparable to Dürer and Holbein. This region absorbed Italian elements more slowly than Germany, but more stead-ily and systematically, so that instead of a few isolated peaks of achievement we find a continuous range. Between 1550 and 1600, their most troubled time, the Netherlands pro-duced the major painters of Northern Europe, who paved the way for the great Dutch and Flemish masters of the next century.

Two main concerns, sometimes separate, sometimes inter-woven, characterize Netherlandish sixteenth-century paint-ing: to assimilate Italian art, from Raphael to Tintoretto (in an often dry and didactic manner), and to develop a repertory supplementing, and eventually replacing, the traditional reli-gious subjects. All the secular themes that loom so large in Dutch and Flemish painting of the Baroque era—landscape, still life, genre (scenes of everyday life)—were first defined

between 1500 and 1600. The process was gradual, shaped less by the genius of individual artists than by the need to cater to popular taste as church commissions became stead-ily scarcer (Protestant iconoclastic zeal was particularly widespread in the Netherlands). Still life, landscape, and genre had been part of the Flemish tradition since the Mas-ter of Flémalle and the brothers Van Eyck—we remember the objects grouped on the Virgin's table in the *Merode Altar-piece*, and Joseph in his workshop (fig. 509, colorplate 60); or the setting of the Van Eyck *Crucifixion* (fig. 510, color-plate 61). But these had remained ancillary elements, gov-erned by the principle of disguised symbolism and subordinated to the devotional purpose of the whole. Now they became independent, or so dominant that the religious subject could be relegated to the background.

AERTSEN. *The Meat Stall* (fig. 681) by Pieter Aertsen (1508/9–1575) is such an essentially secular picture: the tiny, distant figures, representing the Flight into Egypt, are a mere pretext, almost blotted out by the avalanche of edibles in the foreground. We see little interest here in selection or formal arrangement; the objects, piled in heaps or strung from poles, are meant to overwhelm us with their sensuous reality (note the large size of the panel). Aertsen is remem-bered today mainly as a pioneer of the independent still life, but he seems to have first painted such pictures as a sideline, until he saw many of his altarpieces destroyed by iconoclasts. Perhaps still life assumed a new importance for him when he moved, about 1555, from Antwerp to Amsterdam.

BRUEGEL. Pieter Bruegel the Elder (1525/30–1569), the only genius among these Netherlandish painters, explored landscape and peasant life. Although his career was spent in Antwerp and Brussels, he may have been born near 's Hertogenbosch; certainly the work of Hieronymus Bosch deeply impressed him, and he is in many ways as puzzling to us as the older master. What were his religious convic-tions, his political sympathies? We know little about him, but his preoccupation with folk customs and the daily life of humble people seems to have sprung from a complex philosophical attitude. Bruegel was highly educated, the friend of humanists, and patronized by the Hapsburg court. Yet he apparently never worked for the Church, and when he dealt with religious subjects he did so in an oddly ambig-uous way.

His attitude toward Italian art is also hard to define: a trip to the South in 1552–53 took him to Rome, Naples, and the Strait of Messina, but the famous monuments admired by other Northerners seem not to have interested him; he returned instead with a sheaf of magnificent landscape drawings, especially Alpine views. He was probably much impressed by the landscape painting in Venice—its integra-tion of figures and scenery, and the progression in space from foreground to background (see figs. 633, 634, colorplates 79, 80).

Out of these memories came such sweeping landscapes in Bruegel's mature style as *The Return of the Hunters* (fig. 682), one of a set depicting the months. Such series, we recall, had begun with medieval calendar illustrations, and

681. PIETER AERTSEN. *The Meat Stall*. 1551. Panel, 48½ × 59".
Museum of Art, Uppsala University, Sweden

682. PIETER BRUEGEL THE ELDER. *The Return of the Hunters*. 1565. Panel, 46 × 63¾". Kunsthistorisches Museum, Vienna

683. PIETER BRUEGEL THE ELDER. *Peasant Wedding* (detail; see colorplate 93). Kunsthistorisches Museum, Vienna

Bruegel's winter scene still shows its descent from the February page in the *Très Riches Heures du Duc de Berry* (see fig. 504). Now, however, nature is more than a setting for human activities; it is the main subject of the picture. Men in their seasonal occupations are incidental to the majestic annual cycle of death and rebirth that is the breathing rhythm of the cosmos.

The *Peasant Wedding* (fig. 683, colorplate 93) is Bruegel's most memorable scene of peasant life. These are stolid, crude folk, heavy-bodied and slow, yet their very clumsiness gives them a strange gravity that commands our respect. Painted in flat colors with minimal modeling and no cast shadows,

the figures nevertheless have a weight and solidity that remind us of Giotto; space is created in assured perspective, and the entire composition is as monumental and balanced as that of any Italian master. Why, we wonder, did Bruegel endow this commonplace ceremony with the solemnity of a biblical event? Was it because he saw in the life of the peasant, free of the ambitions and vanities of city dwellers, the natural, hence the ideal, condition of man? Bruegel's philosophical detachment from religious and political fanaticism also informs one of his last pictures, *The Blind Leading the Blind* (fig. 684). Its source is the Gospels (Matt. 15: 12–19): Christ says, speaking of the Pharisees, "And if the blind lead the blind, both shall fall into the ditch." This parable of human folly recurs in humanistic literature, and we know it in at least one earlier representation, but the tragic depth of Bruegel's large and forceful image gives new urgency to the theme. Perhaps he found the biblical context of the parable specially relevant to his time: the Pharisees had asked why Christ's disciples, violating religious traditions, did not wash their hands before meals; He answered, "Not that which goeth into the mouth defileth a man; but that which cometh out of the mouth." When this offended the Pharisees, He called them the blind leading the blind, explaining that "whatsoever entereth in at the mouth goeth into the belly, and is cast out.... But those things which proceed out of the mouth come forth from the heart; and they defile the man. For out of the heart proceed evil thoughts, murders,... blasphemies." Could Bruegel have thought that this applied to the controversies then raging over details of religious ritual?

684. PIETER BRUEGEL THE ELDER. *The Blind Leading the Blind*. 1568. 34 × 66″. National Museum, Naples

685. HECTOR SOHIER. Choir of St.-Pierre, Caen. 1528–45

FRANCE
Architecture and Sculpture

We have deferred our discussion of sixteenth-century architecture and sculpture north of the Alps because in these fields Italy had no significant influence before the 1520s. France began to assimilate Italian art somewhat earlier than the other countries and was the first to achieve an integrated Renaissance style; we shall therefore confine our discussion to French monuments. As we might expect, architects still trained in the Gothic tradition could not adopt the Italian style all at once; they readily used its classical vocabulary, but its syntax gave them trouble for many years.

SOHIER.   One glance at the choir of St.-Pierre at Caen (fig. 685), built by Hector Sohier, shows that he follows the basic pattern of French Gothic church choirs (compare fig. 426), simply translating Flamboyant decoration into the vocabulary of the new language: finials become candelabra, pier buttresses are shaped like pilasters, and the round-arched windows of the ambulatory chapels have geometric tracery.

CHÂTEAU OF CHAMBORD.   The Château of Chambord (fig. 686) is stylistically more complicated. Its plan, and the turrets, high-pitched roofs, and tall chimneys, recall the

686. (above) The Château of Chambord
(north front). Begun 1519

687. (left) Plan of Center Portion,
Château of Chambord (after Du Cerceau)

688. PIERRE LESCOT. Square Court of the Louvre, Paris. Begun 1546

Gothic Louvre (see fig. 505, colorplate 58); yet the design—greatly modified by later French builders—was originally by an Italian pupil of Giuliano da Sangallo. And his was surely the plan of the center portion (fig. 687), which is quite unlike its French predecessors. This square block, developed from the keep of medieval castles (see page 309), has a central staircase fed by four corridors; these form a Greek cross dividing the interior into four square sections. Each section is further subdivided into one large and two smaller rooms, and a closet—in modern parlance, a suite or apartment. The functional grouping of these rooms, originally imported from Italy, was to become a standard pattern in France. It represents the starting point of all modern "designs for living."

LESCOT.   Francis I, who built Chambord, decided in 1546 to replace the Louvre with a new palace on the old site. He died before the project was more than begun, but his architect, Pierre Lescot (c. 1515–1578), continued it under Henry II, quadrupling the size of the court. This enlarged scheme was not completed for more than a century; Lescot built only the southern half of the court's west side (fig. 688), the finest surviving monument of the French Renaissance in its "classic" phase, so called to distinguish it from the style of such buildings as Chambord. This distinction is well warranted: the Italian vocabulary of Chambord, and St.-Pierre at Caen, is based on the Early Renaissance, while Lescot drew on the work of Bramante and his successors.

The details of Lescot's façade have indeed an astonishing classical purity, yet we would not mistake it for an Italian structure. Its distinctive quality comes not from Italian forms superficially applied, but from a genuine synthesis of the traditional château with the Renaissance palace. Italian, of course, are the superimposed classical orders (see figs. 572, 659), the pedimented window frames, and the arcade on the ground floor. But the continuity of the façade is interrupted by three projecting pavilions which have supplanted the

689, 690. JEAN GOUJON. Reliefs from the *Fontaine des Innocents*. 1548–49. Paris

château turrets, and the high-pitched roof is also traditionally French. The vertical accents thus overcome the horizontal ones (note the broken architraves), their effect reinforced
by the tall, narrow windows.

GOUJON. Equally un-Italian is the rich sculptural decoration covering almost the entire wall surface of the third story.
These reliefs, admirably adapted to the architecture, are by
Jean Goujon (c. 1510–1565?), the finest French sculptor
of the mid-century. Unfortunately, they have been much
restored. To get a more precise idea of Goujon's style we must
turn to the relief panels from the *Fontaine des Innocents*
(two are shown in figs. 689, 690), which have survived
intact, although their architectural framework is lost. These
graceful figures recall the Mannerism of Cellini (see fig.
653, colorplate 87) and, even more, Primaticcio's decorations
at Fontainebleau (see fig. 654, colorplate 88). Like Lescot's
architecture, their design combines classical details of astonishing purity with a delicate slenderness that gives them a
uniquely French air.

PILON. A more powerful sculptor—indeed, the greatest of
the later sixteenth century—was Germain Pilon (c. 1535–
1590). In his early years he, too, learned a good deal from
Primaticcio, but he soon developed his own idiom by merging
the Mannerism of Fontainebleau with elements taken from
ancient sculpture, Michelangelo, and the Gothic tradition.
His main works are monumental tombs, of which the earliest
and largest was for Henry II and Catherine de' Medici (fig.
691). Primaticcio build the architectural framework, an
oblong, free-standing chapel on a platform decorated with
bronze and marble reliefs. Four large bronze statues of
Virtues, their style reminiscent of Fontainebleau, mark the
corners. On the top of the tomb are bronze figures of the
king and queen kneeling in prayer; inside the chapel, the
couple reappear recumbent as marble *gisants*, or nude
corpses (fig. 692).

This contrast of effigies had been a characteristic feature
of Gothic tombs since the fourteenth century: the *gisant*
expressed the transient nature of the flesh, usually showing
the body in an advanced stage of decomposition, with vermin
sometimes crawling through its open cavities. How could
this gruesome image take on Renaissance form without losing its emotional significance? Pilon's solution is brilliant: by
idealizing the *gisants* he reverses their former meaning.
These figures—the recumbent queen in the pose of a classical Venus, the king in that of the Dead Christ—evoke neither
horror nor pity but, rather, the pathos of a beauty that persists even in death. The shock effect of their predecessors
has given way to a poignancy that is no less intense. Remembering our earlier distinction between the classical and medieval attitudes toward death (see page 425), this poignancy
may be defined: the Gothic *gisant*, which emphasizes physical decay, represents the future state of the body, in keeping
with the whole "prospective" character of the medieval
tomb; Pilon's *gisants*, however, are "retrospective," yet do
not deny the reality of death. In this union of opposites—
never to be achieved again, even by Pilon himself—lies the
greatness of these figures.

691. FRANCESCO PRIMATICCIO and GERMAIN PILON.
Tomb of Henry II. 1563–70. Abbey Church of St.-Denis, Paris

692. GERMAIN PILON. *Gisants* of the King and Queen,
detail of the Tomb of Henry II

6
THE BAROQUE IN ITALY AND GERMANY

Baroque has been the term used by art historians for over a century to designate the dominant style of the period 1600–1750. Its original meaning—"irregular, contorted, grotesque"—is now largely superseded. It is generally agreed that the new style was born in Rome during the final years of the sixteenth century. What remains under dispute is whether the Baroque is the final phase of the Renaissance, or an era distinct from both Renaissance and modern. We have chosen the first alternative, while admitting that a good case can be made for the second. Which of the two we adopt is perhaps less important than an understanding of the factors that must enter into our decision.

And here we run into a series of paradoxes. Thus it has been claimed that the Baroque style expresses the spirit of the Counter Reformation; yet the Counter Reformation, a dynamic movement of self-renewal within the Catholic Church, had already done its work by 1600—Protestantism was on the defensive, some important territories had been recaptured for the old faith, and neither side any longer had the power to upset the new balance. The princes of the Church who supported the growth of Baroque art were known for worldly splendor rather than piety. Besides, elements of the new style penetrated the Protestant North so quickly that we should guard against overstressing its Counter Reformation aspect.

Equally problematic is the assertion that Baroque is "the style of absolutism," reflecting the centralized state ruled by an autocrat of unlimited powers. Although absolutism reached its climax during the reign of Louis XIV in the later seventeenth century, it had been in the making since the 1520s (under Francis I in France, and the Medici dukes in Tuscany). Moreover, Baroque art flourished in bourgeois Holland no less than in the absolutist monarchies; and the style officially sponsored under Louis XIV was a notably subdued, classicistic kind of Baroque.

We encounter similar difficulties when we try to relate Baroque art to the science and philosophy of the period. Such a link did exist in the Early and High Renaissance: an artist then could also be a humanist and a scientist. But during the seventeenth century, scientific and philosophical thought became too complex, abstract, and systematic for the artist to share; gravitation, calculus, and *Cogito, ergo sum* (I think, therefore I am) could not stir his imagination. Thus Baroque art is not simply the result of religious, political, or intellectual developments. Interconnections surely existed, but we do not yet understand them very well. Until we do, let us think of the Baroque style as one among other basic features—the newly fortified Catholic faith, the absolutist state, and the new role of science—that distinguish the period 1600–1750 from what had gone before.

ROME

Around 1600 Rome became the fountainhead of the Baroque, as it had of the High Renaissance a century before, by gathering artists from other regions to perform challenging new tasks. The papacy patronized art on a large scale, with the aim of making Rome the most beautiful city of the Christian world "for the greater glory of God and the Church." This campaign had begun as early as 1585; the artists then on hand were late Mannerists of feeble distinction, but it soon attracted ambitious young masters, especially from northern Italy. These talented men created the new style.

Painting

CARAVAGGIO. Foremost among these northerners was a painter of genius, called Caravaggio after his birthplace near Milan (1571–1610), whose several monumental canvases for a chapel in the church of S. Luigi dei Francesi, from 1599 to 1602, include *The Calling of St. Matthew* (fig. 693, colorplate 94). This extraordinary picture is remote from both Mannerism and the High Renaissance; its only antecedent is the "North Italian realism" of artists like Savoldo (see fig. 651). But Caravaggio's realism is such that a new term, "naturalism," is needed to distinguish it from the earlier kind.

Never have we seen a sacred subject depicted so entirely in terms of contemporary low life. Matthew, the tax-gatherer, sits with some armed men—evidently his agents—in what is a common Roman tavern; he points questioningly at himself as two figures approach from the right. The arrivals are poor people, their bare feet and simple garments contrasting strongly with the colorful costumes of Matthew and his companions. Why do we sense a religious quality in this scene? Why do we not mistake it for an everyday event?

What identifies one of the figures as Christ? Surely it is not the Saviour's halo (the only supernatural feature in the picture), an inconspicuous gold band that we might well overlook. Our eyes fasten instead upon His commanding gesture, borrowed from Michelangelo's *Creation of Adam* (fig. 616), which bridges the gap between the two groups.

Most decisive, however, is the strong beam of sunlight above Christ that illuminates His face and hand in the gloomy interior, thus carrying His call across to Matthew. Without this light—so natural yet so charged with symbolic meaning—the picture would lose its magic, its power to make us aware of the Divine presence. Caravaggio here gives moving, direct form to an attitude shared by certain great saints of the Counter Reformation: that the mysteries of faith are revealed not by intellectual speculation but spontaneously, through an inward experience open to all men. His paintings have a "lay Christianity," untouched by theological dogma, that appealed to Protestants no less than Catholics. This quality made possible his profound—though indirect—influence on Rembrandt, the greatest religious artist of the Protestant North.

In Italy, Caravaggio fared less well. His work was acclaimed by artists and connoisseurs, but to the man in the street, for whom it was intended, it lacked propriety and reverence. He resented meeting his likes in these paintings, preferring religious imagery of a more idealized and rhetorical sort.

ARTEMISIA GENTILESCHI. We have not encountered a woman artist thus far. This does not mean that there were none, however. On the contrary, Pliny mentioned in his *Natural History* (bk. xxxv) the names and describes the work of women artists in Greece and Rome, and there are records of women's accomplishments during the Middle Ages. We must remember, however, that the vast majority of artists remained anonymous until the "Late Gothic" period, so that

693. CARAVAGGIO. *The Calling of St. Matthew*
(detail; see colorplate 94). Contarelli Chapel,
S. Luigi dei Francesi, Rome

694. ARTEMISIA GENTILESCHI. *Judith and Her Maidservant.*
c. 1610. 45⅝ × 36⅝". Pitti Palace, Florence

works specifically by women have proved difficult to identify. Women began to emerge as distinct artistic personalities around 1550, but they were largely restricted until the middle of the nineteenth century to painting portraits, genre scenes, and still lifes. Among the obstacles they encountered, they were rarely permitted to draw from the nude model in live classes, which provided the foundation of traditional academic training and the basis of narrative painting. Within those other realms, however, many women carved out successful careers, often emerging as the equals or superiors of the men in whose styles were trained. The few exceptions to this general pattern were Italian women who were members of artistic families; their major role began in the seventeenth century.

The first woman artist to occupy an important position was Artemisia Gentileschi (1593–c. 1653). The daughter of Caravaggio's disciple Orazio Gentileschi, she was born in Rome and became one of the leading painters and personalities of her day. Her characteristic subjects are Bathsheba, the unfortunate object of King David's passion, and Judith, who saved her people by beheading the Assyrian general Holofernes.

Both of these tragic biblical heroines had great popularity during the Baroque era, which delighted in erotic and violent scenes. But Artemisia's frequent choice of them as subjects throughout her turbulent, active, and widely traveled life suggests an ambivalence in her feelings: a singularly disturbing early work, *Judith and Her Maidservant* (fig. 694), can be interpreted not only as immortalizing Judith's cour-

age, but also perhaps as an expression of Artemisia's deep-seated wish for revenge against her teacher, accused and acquitted of raping her two years before. She is indebted to her father for the picture's composition and its Caravaggesque treatment, but the drama implicit in these two determined yet fearful women is unique with her, and its theatricality is no less powerful for her restraint. Artemisia's psychological tensions enabled her to render Judith's complex actions and emotions with an incomparable understanding.

ANNIBALE CARRACCI. The conservative wishes of the simpler people in Italy were met by artists less radical—and less talented—than Caravaggio, who took their lead from another newcomer among Roman painters, Annibale Carracci (1560–1609). Annibale came from Bologna, where he and two other members of his family had evolved an anti-Mannerist style since the 1580s. In 1597–1604 he produced his most ambitious work, the ceiling fresco in the gallery of the Farnese Palace, which soon became so famous that it was thought second only to the murals of Michelangelo and Raphael.

The historical significance of the Farnese Gallery is indeed great, though our enthusiasm for it as a work of art may no longer be undivided. Our detail (fig. 695) shows Annibale's rich and intricate design: the narrative scenes, like those of the Sistine Ceiling, are surrounded by painted architecture, simulated sculpture, and nude, garland-holding youths. Yet the Farnese Gallery does not merely imitate Michelangelo's masterpiece. The style of the main subjects, the Loves of the Classical Gods, is reminiscent of Raphael's *Galatea* (see fig. 631), and the whole is held together by an illusionistic scheme that reflects Annibale's knowledge of Correggio and the great Venetians. Carefully foreshortened and illuminated from below (note the shadows), the nude youths and the simulated sculpture and

695. ANNIBALE CARRACCI. Ceiling fresco (detail).
1597–1601. Gallery, Palazzo Farnese, Rome

696. GUIDO RENI. *Aurora*. Ceiling fresco. 1613. Casino Rospigliosi, Rome

architecture appear real; against this background the mythologies are presented as simulated easel pictures. Each of these levels of reality is handled with consummate skill, and the entire ceiling has an exuberance that sets it apart from both Mannerism and High Renaissance art. Annibale Carracci was a reformer rather than a revolutionary; like Caravaggio, who apparently admired him, he felt that art must return to nature, but his approach was less single-minded, balancing studies from life with a revival of the classics (which to him meant the art of antiquity, and of Raphael, Michelangelo, Titian, and Correggio). At his best, he succeeded in fusing these diverse elements, although their union always remained somewhat precarious.

GUIDO RENI; GUERCINO.   To artists who were inspired by it, the Farnese Gallery seemed to offer two alternatives: pursuing the Raphaelesque style of the mythological panels, they could arrive at a deliberate, "official" classicism; or they could take their cue from the sensuous illusionism present in the framework. The first choice is exemplified by Guido Reni's *Aurora* (fig. 696), a ceiling fresco showing Apollo in his chariot—the Sun—led by Aurora (Dawn). Despite its rhythmic grace, this relief-like design would seem like more than a pallid reflection of High Renaissance art were it not for the glowing and dramatic light which gives it an emotional impetus that the figures alone could never achieve.

Its very opposite is the *Aurora* ceiling by Guercino (fig. 697, colorplate 95). Here architectural perspective, combined with the pictorial illusionism of Correggio and the intense light and color of Titian, converts the entire surface into one limitless space; the figures sweep past as if propelled by stratospheric winds. With this work, Guercino started what soon became a veritable flood of similar visions (see figs. 706, 722).

PIETRO DA CORTONA.   The most overpowering of these is the ceiling fresco by Pietro da Cortona (1596–1669) in the great hall of the Barberini Palace in Rome, a glorification of the reign of the Barberini pope, Urban VIII (fig. 698, colorplate 96). As in the Farnese Gallery, the ceiling area is subdivided by a painted framework simulating architecture

and sculpture, but beyond it we now see the unbounded space of the sky, as in Guercino's *Aurora*. Clusters of figures, perched on clouds or soaring freely, swirl above as well as below this framework, creating a dual illusion: some figures appear to hover well inside the hall, perilously close to our heads, while others recede into a light-filled, infinite distance. Their dynamism almost literally sweeps us off our feet. Here the Baroque style reaches a thunderous climax.

LANDSCAPES.   The sculptured precision of the Farnese Gallery does not do justice to the important Venetian element in Annibale Carracci's style. This is most striking in his landscapes, such as the monumental *Landscape with the Flight into Egypt* (fig. 699). Its pastoral mood and the soft light and atmosphere hark back to Giorgione and Titian (see figs. 633, 634, colorplates 79, 80). The figures, however, play a far less conspicuous role here; they are, indeed, as small and incidental as in any Northern landscape (compare fig. 682). Nor does the character of the panorama at all suggest the Flight into Egypt—it would be equally suitable for almost any story, sacred or profane. Still, we feel that the figures could not be removed altogether (though we can imagine

697. GUERCINO. *Aurora* (detail; see colorplate 95).
Villa Ludovisi, Rome

698. PIETRO DA CORTONA. *Glorification of the Reign of Urban VIII* (see detail, colorplate 96). Palazzo Barberini, Rome

them replaced by others). This is not the untamed nature of Northern landscapes, but a "civilized," hospitable countryside. The old castle, the roads and fields, the flock of sheep, the ferryman with his boat, all show that man has been at home here for a long time. Hence the figures, however tiny, do not appear lost or dwarfed into insignificance, because their presence is implicit in the orderly, domesticated quality of the setting. This firmly constructed "ideal landscape" evokes a vision of nature that is gentle yet austere, grand but not awesome. We shall meet its descendants again and again in the next two centuries.

Architecture and Sculpture

ST. PETER'S. In architecture, the beginnings of the Baroque style cannot be defined as precisely as in painting. In the vast ecclesiastical building program that got under way in Rome toward the end of the sixteenth century, the most talented young architect to emerge was Carlo Maderno (1556–1629); in 1603 he was given the task of completing, at long last, the church of St. Peter's. The pope had decided to add a nave to Michelangelo's building (fig. 626), converting it into a basilica. The change of plan, which may have been

699. ANNIBALE CARRACCI. *Landscape with the Flight into Egypt.*
c. 1603. 48¼ × 98½″. Doria Gallery, Rome

prompted by the example of Il Gesù (see figs. 664, 665), made it possible to link St. Peter's with the Vatican Palace (fig. 700, right). Maderno's design for the façade follows the pattern established by Michelangelo for the exterior of the church—a colossal order supporting an attic—but with a dramatic emphasis on the portals. There is what can only be described as a crescendo effect from the corners toward the center: the spacing of the supports becomes closer, pilasters turn into columns, and the façade wall projects step by step.

700. Aerial View of St. Peter's, Rome.
Nave and façade by CARLO MADERNO, 1607–15;
colonnade by GIANLORENZO BERNINI,
designed 1657

This quickened rhythm, we recall, had been hinted at a generation earlier, in Giacomo della Porta's façade of Il Gesù (see fig. 664, colorplate 89). Maderno made it the dominant principle of his façade designs, not only for St. Peter's but for smaller churches as well; in so doing, he replaced the traditional notion of the church façade as one continuous wall surface—a concept not yet challenged by the façade of Il Gesù—with the "façade-in-depth," dynamically related to the open space before it. The possibilities implicit in this new concept were not to be exhausted until a hundred and fifty years later.

BERNINI. The enormous size of St. Peter's made the decoration of its interior a uniquely difficult task—how to relate its chill vastness to the human scale and imbue it with a measure of emotional warmth? That the problem was solved is very largely to the merit of Gianlorenzo Bernini (1598–1680), the greatest sculptor-architect of the century. St. Peter's occupied him at intervals during most of his long and prolific career; he began by designing the huge bronze canopy for the main altar under the dome (fig. 701).

The tabernacle is a splendid fusion of architecture and sculpture. Four ornate, spiral-shaped columns support an upper platform; at its corners are statues of angels, and vigorously curved scrolls which raise high the symbol of the victory of Christianity over the pagan world, a cross above a golden orb. The entire structure is so alive with expressive energy that it strikes us as the very epitome of Baroque style. Yet its most astonishing feature, the corkscrew columns, had been invented in late antiquity, and even employed, on a much smaller scale, in the old basilica of St. Peter's; Bernini could claim the best possible precedent for his own use of the motif. Nor is this the only instance of an affinity between Baroque and ancient art: several monuments of Roman

Colorplate 91. ALBRECHT ALTDORFER. *The Battle of Issus* (see page 490). 1529. Panel, 62 × 47″. Pinakothek, Munich

· ANNO · ÆTATIS ·   · SVÆ · XLIX ·

Colorplate 92. HANS HOLBEIN THE YOUNGER. *Henry VIII* (see page 491).
1540. Panel, 32½ × 29″. National Gallery, Rome

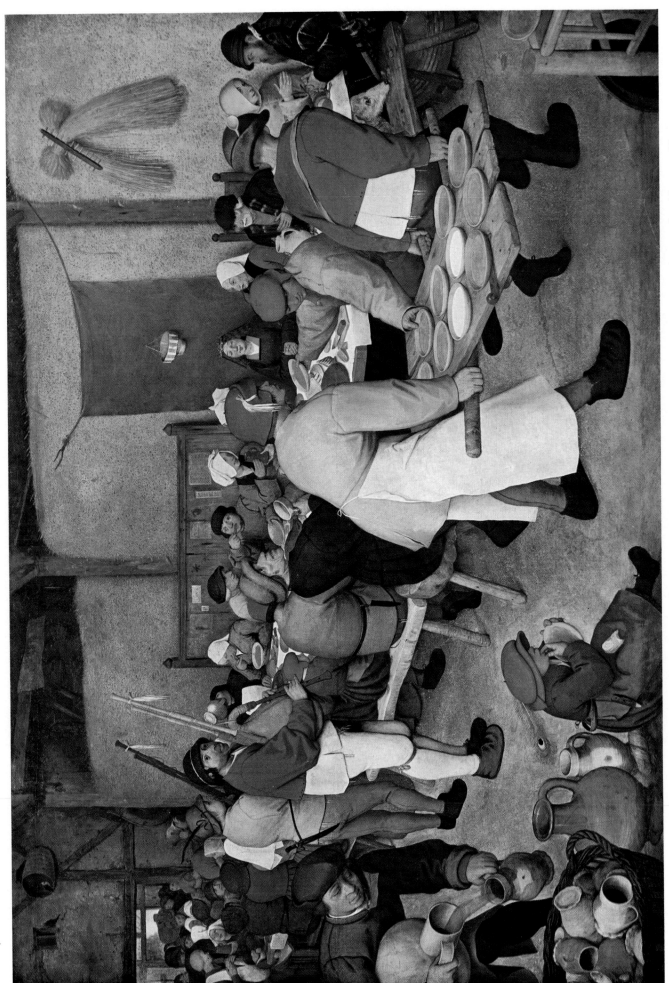

Colorplate 93. PIETER BRUEGEL THE ELDER. *Peasant Wedding* (see page 495). About 1565. Panel, 44⅞ × 64″. Kunsthistorisches Museum, Vienna

Colorplate 94. CARAVAGGIO. *The Calling of St. Matthew* (see page 500).
About 1599–1602. 11′ 1″ × 11′ 5″. Contarelli Chapel, S. Luigi dei Francesi, Rome

Colorplate 95. GUERCINO. *Aurora* (see page 502), ceiling fresco. 1621–23. Villa Ludovisi, Rome

Colorplate 96. PIETRO DA CORTONA. *Glorification of the Reign of Urban VIII* (see page 502), portion of ceiling fresco. 1633–39. Palazzo Barberini, Rome

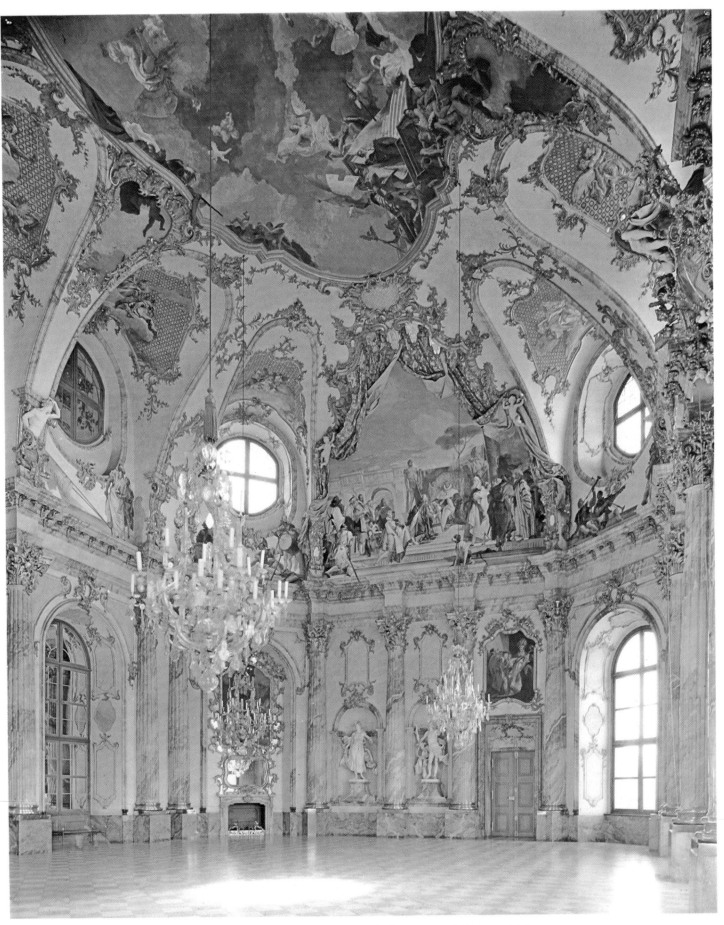

Colorplate 97. BALTHASAR NEUMANN. The Kaisersaal, Episcopal Palace,
Würzburg (see page 520). 1719–44 (frescoes by GIOVANNI BATTISTA TIEPOLO, 1751)

Colorplate 98. (*above*) PETER PAUL RUBENS.
The Garden of Love (see page 523).
About 1632–34. 6′ 6″ × 9′ 3½″. The Prado, Madrid

Colorplate 99. (*right*) ANTHONY VAN DYCK.
Portrait of Charles I Hunting (see page 523).
c. 1635. 8′ 11″ × 6′ 11½″. The Louvre, Paris

701. CARLO MADERNO. Nave, with Bernini's Tabernacle (1624–33) at crossing, St. Peter's, Rome

effects that are outside its province. The accusation is pointless, for illusion is the basis of every artistic experience, and we cannot very well regard some kinds or degrees of illusion as less legitimate than others. It is true, however, that Baroque art acknowledges no sharp distinction between sculpture and painting. The two may enter into a symbiosis previously unknown, or, more precisely, both may be combined with architecture to form a compound illusion, like that of the stage. Bernini, who had a passionate interest in the theater, was at his best when he could merge architecture, sculpture, and painting in this fashion.

His masterpiece is the Cornaro Chapel, containing the famous group called *The Ecstasy of St. Theresa* (fig. 703), in the church of Sta. Maria della Vittoria. Theresa of Avila, one of the great saints of the Counter Reformation, had described how an angel pierced her heart with a flaming golden arrow: "The pain was so great that I screamed aloud; but at the same time I felt such infinite sweetness that I wished the pain to last forever. It was not physical but psychic pain, although it affected the body as well to some degree. It was the sweetest caressing of the soul by God."

architecture of the second and third centuries A.D. seem to anticipate the style of the seventeenth (see figs. 249–52).

A similar relationship can be discovered between Hellenistic and Baroque sculpture. If we compare Bernini's *David* (fig. 702) with Michelangelo's (see fig. 611), and ask which is closer to the Pergamum Frieze or the *Laocoön Group* (see figs. 205, 207), our vote must go to Bernini. His figure shares with the Hellenistic works that unison of body and spirit, of motion and emotion, which Michelangelo so conspicuously avoids. This does not mean that Bernini is more classical than Michelangelo; it indicates, rather, that both the Baroque and the High Renaissance acknowledged the authority of ancient art, but each period drew inspiration from a different aspect of antiquity.

But Bernini's *David*, obviously, is in no sense an echo of the *Laocoön Group*. If we ask what makes it Baroque, the simplest answer would be: the implied presence of Goliath. Unlike earlier statues of David, Bernini's is conceived not as one self-contained figure but as "half of a pair," his entire action focused on his adversary. Did Bernini, we wonder, plan a statue of Goliath to complete the group? He never did, for his David tells us clearly enough where *he* sees the enemy. Consequently, the space between David and his invisible opponent is charged with energy: it "belongs" to the statue. If we stand directly in front of this formidable fighter, our first impulse is to get out of the line of fire.

Bernini's *David* shows us what distinguishes Baroque sculpture from the sculpture of the two preceding centuries: its new, active relationship with the space it inhabits. It eschews self-sufficiency for an illusion—the illusion of presences or forces that are implied by the behavior of the statue. Because it so often presents an "invisible complement" (like the Goliath of Bernini's *David*), Baroque sculpture has been denounced as a tour de force, attempting essentially pictorial

702. GIANLORENZO BERNINI. *David*. 1623. Marble, lifesize. Borghese Gallery, Rome

703. GIANLORENZO BERNINI.
The Ecstasy of St. Theresa. 1645–52. Marble, lifesize.
Cornaro Chapel, Sta. Maria della Vittoria, Rome

704. *The Cornaro Chapel.*
Eighteenth-century painting. Museum, Schwerin

Bernini has made this visionary experience as sensuously real as Correggio's *Jupiter and Io* (see fig. 650); the angel, in a different context, would be indistinguishable from Cupid, and the saint's ecstasy is palpably physical. Yet the two figures, on their floating cloud, are illuminated (from a hidden window above) in such a way as to seem almost dematerialized in their gleaming whiteness. The beholder experiences them as visionary. The "invisible complement" here, less specific than David's but equally important, is the force that carries the figures heavenward, causing the turbulence of their drapery. Its nature is suggested by the golden rays, which come from a source high above the altar: in an illusionistic fresco on the vault of the chapel, the glory of the heavens is revealed as a dazzling burst of light from which tumble clouds of jubilant angels (fig. 704). It is this celestial "explosion" that gives force to the thrusts of the angel's arrow and makes the ecstasy of the saint believable.

To complete the illusion, Bernini even provides a built-in audience for his "stage": on the sides of the chapel are balconies resembling theater boxes, where we see marble figures—members of the Cornaro family—who also witness the Ecstasy. Their space and ours are the same, and thus part of everyday reality, while the Ecstasy, housed in a strongly framed niche, occupies a space that is real but beyond our reach. The ceiling fresco, finally, represents the infinite, unfathomable space of Heaven. We may recall that *The Burial of Count Orgaz* and its setting also form a whole embracing three levels of reality (see page 468); the reader will be able to analyze for himself the profound difference between Baroque and Mannerism by contrasting these two chapels.

Some years later Bernini created another compound display, on an even grander scale, in the choir of St. Peter's (fig. 701, far background, and fig. 705)—a climax for the visitor at the very end of the church. Again the focus is a burst of heavenly light (through a real window of stained glass) that propels a mass of clouds and angels toward us. These clouds envelop the bronze *Throne of St. Peter*, which hovers weightless in mid-air, anchored to the hands of the Four Fathers of the Church.

The interior decoration of Il Gesù is further evidence of Bernini's imaginative daring (fig. 706), although his role in this case was only advisory. The commission for the ceiling frescoes went to Giovanni Battista Gaulli, his young protégé;

a talented assistant, Antonio Raggi, did the stucco sculpture. As we see the nave fresco spilling so dramatically over its frame, then turning into sculptured figures, it is clear that the plan must be Bernini's; here again we sense the spirit of the Cornaro Chapel.

While designing the *Throne of St. Peter*, Bernini also conceived as "exterior decoration" the magnificent oval piazza in front of St. Peter's (fig. 700). It acts as an immense atrium, framed by colonnades which the artist himself likened to the motherly, all-embracing arms of the Church. The basilica integrated with so grandiose a setting of "molded" open space can be compared, for sheer impressiveness, only with the ancient Roman sanctuary at Palestrina (see figs. 230–32).

BORROMINI. As a personality, Bernini represents a type we first met among the artists of the Early Renaissance— the self-assured, expansive man of the world. His great rival in architecture, Francesco Borromini (1599–1667), was the opposite type: a secretive and emotionally unstable genius, he died by suicide. The temperamental contrast between the two would be evident from their works alone, even without the testimony of contemporary witnesses. Both exemplify the climax of Baroque architecture in Rome, yet Bernini's design for the colonnade of St. Peter's is dramatically simple and unified, while Borromini's structures are extravagantly complex. Bernini himself agreed with those who denounced Borromini for flagrantly disregarding the classical tradition, enshrined in Renaissance theory and practice, that architecture must reflect the proportions of the human body.

We understand this accusation when we look at Borromini's first major project, the church of S. Carlo alle Quattro Fontane (figs. 707–9). The vocabulary is not unfamiliar, but the syntax is new and disquieting; the ceaseless play of concave and convex surfaces makes the entire structure seem elastic, "pulled out of shape" by pressures that no

705. GIANLORENZO BERNINI. *Throne of St. Peter.* 1657–66.
Gilt bronze, marble, and stucco. Apse, St. Peter's, Rome

706. GIOVANNI BATTISTA GAULLI. *Triumph of the Name of Jesus.*
Ceiling fresco. 1672–85. Il Gesù, Rome

previous building could have withstood. The plan is a pinched oval suggesting a distended and half-melted Greek cross, as if it had been drawn on rubber; the inside of the dome, too, looks "stretched"—if the tension were relaxed, it would snap back to normal. The façade was designed almost thirty years later, and the pressures and counterpressures here reach their maximum intensity. Borromini merges architecture and sculpture in a way that must have shocked Bernini; no such fusion had been ventured since Gothic art.

S. Carlo alle Quattro Fontane established Borromini's local and international fame. "Nothing similar," wrote the head of the religious order for which the church was built, "can be found anywhere in the world. This is attested by the foreigners who . . . try to procure copies of the plan. We have been asked for them by Germans, Flemings, Frenchmen, Italians, Spaniards, and even Indians. . . ." The design of Borromini's next church, S. Ivo (figs. 710, 711), is more compact and equally daring. Its plan, a star-hexagon, belongs unequivocally to the central type; Borromini may have been thinking of octagonal structures such as S. Vitale, Ravenna (compare figs. 306–9). But he did not subdivide the space into a tall, domed "nave" ringed by an ambulatory or chapels; he covered all of it with one great dome, continuing the star-hexagon pattern up to the circular base of the lantern. Again the concave-convex rhythm dominates the entire design—the structure might almost be described as

707. (*above*) FRANCESCO BORROMINI. Façade, S. Carlo alle Quattro Fontane, Rome. 1665–67

708. (*right*) Plan of S. Carlo alle Quattro Fontane. Begun 1638

709. (*far right*) Dome, S. Carlo alle Quattro Fontane

710. FRANCESCO BORROMINI.
Section, S. Ivo, Rome. Begun 1642

TURIN
Architecture

GUARINI. The wealth of new ideas that Borromini introduced was to be exploited not in Rome but in Turin, the capital of Savoy, which became the creative center of Baroque architecture in Italy toward the end of the seventeenth century. In 1666, that city attracted Borromini's most brilliant successor, Guarino Guarini (1624–1683), a Theatine monk whose architectural genius was deeply grounded in philosophy and mathematics. His design for the façade of Palazzo Carignano (figs. 713, 714) repeats on a larger scale the undulating movement of S. Carlo alle Quattro Fontane (see fig. 707), using a highly individual vocabulary. Incredibly, the exterior of the building is entirely of brick, down to the last ornamental detail.

Still more extraordinary is Guarini's dome of the Chapel of the Holy Shroud—a round structure attached to the Cathedral (figs. 715, 716). The tall drum, with alternating windows and tabernacles, consists of familiar Borrominesque motifs, but beyond it we enter a realm of pure illusion. The interior surface of the dome of S. Carlo alle Quattro Fontane, though dematerialized by light and the honeycomb of fanciful coffers, was still recognizable (see fig. 709); but here the surface has disappeared completely in a maze of segmental ribs, and we find ourselves staring into a huge

a larger version of the Temple of Venus at Baalbek, turned inside out (see figs. 250, 251).

A third project by Borromini is of special interest as a High Baroque critique of St. Peter's. Maderno had found one problem insoluble: although his new façade forms an impressive unit with Michelangelo's dome when seen from a distance, the dome is gradually hidden by the façade as we approach the church. Borromini designed the façade of S. Agnese in Piazza Navona (fig. 712) with this conflict in mind. Its lower part is adapted from the façade of St. Peter's, but curves inward, so that the dome—a tall, slender version of Michelangelo's—functions as the upper part of the façade. The dramatic juxtaposition of concave and convex, always characteristic of Borromini, is further emphasized by the two towers (such towers were also once planned for St. Peter's), which form a monumental triad with the dome. Once again Borromini joins Gothic and Renaissance features—the two-tower façade and the dome—into a remarkably "elastic" compound.

711. Dome, S. Ivo

712. FRANCESCO BORROMINI. S. Agnese in Piazza
Navona, Rome. 1653–63

creations in the history of architecture. We must be content
with a small sampling of these monuments, erected for the
glorification of princes and prelates who, generally speaking,
deserve to be remembered only as lavish patrons of the arts.

FISCHER VON ERLACH. Johann Fischer von Erlach
(1656–1723), the first great architect of the Late Baroque
in Central Europe, is linked most directly to the Italian tradition. His design for the church of St. Charles Borromaeus
in Vienna (figs. 718, 719) combines the façade of Borromini's
S. Agnese, and the Pantheon portico (figs. 712, 238), with a
pair of huge columns derived from the Column of Trajan
(see fig. 265) which here substitute for façade towers. (The
actual façade towers have become corner pavilions, reminiscent of the Louvre court—compare fig. 688.) With these
inflexible elements of Roman Imperial art embedded into
the elastic curvatures of his church, Fischer von Erlach

kaleidoscope. Above this seemingly endless funnel of space
hovers the dove of the Holy Spirit within a bright, twelve-
pointed star.

So far as we know, there is only one similar dome anywhere
in the history of art: that of the Ulu Mosque at Erzurum in
Turkish Armenia, built about 1150 (fig. 717). How could
Guarini have known about it? Or did he recapture its effect
entirely by coincidence? Guarini's dome retains the old symbolic meaning of the Dome of Heaven (see page 423, figs.
577–79). But the objective harmony of the Renaissance
has here become subjective, a compelling experience of the
infinite. If Borromini's style at times suggested a synthesis
of Gothic and Renaissance, Guarini takes the next, decisive
step; in his theoretical writings, he contrasts the "muscular"
architecture of the ancients with the opposite effect of
Gothic churches—which appear to stand only by means of
some kind of miracle—and he expresses equal admiration
for both. This attitude corresponds exactly to his own practice; by using the most advanced mathematical techniques
of his day, he achieved architectural miracles even greater
than those of the seemingly weightless Gothic structures.

Architecture

It is not surprising that the style invented by Borromini and
furthered by Guarini should achieve its climax north of the
Alps, in Austria and Southern Germany, where such a synthesis of Gothic and Renaissance was sure of a particularly
warm response. In these countries, ravaged by the Thirty
Years' War, the number of buildings remained small until
near the end of the seventeenth century; Baroque was an
imported style, practiced mainly by visiting Italians. Not
until the 1690s did native designers come to the fore. There
followed a period of intense activity that lasted more than
fifty years and gave rise to some of the most imaginative

713. GUARINO GUARINI. Façade of Palazzo
Carignano, Turin. Begun 1679

714. Plan of Palazzo Carignano

715. GUARINO GUARINI. Dome, Chapel of
the Holy Shroud, Cathedral, Turin. 1668–94

716. Plan of the Chapel
of the Holy Shroud,
and (below) of the Dome

717. Wooden Dome of the Ulu Mosque,
Erzurum. Seljuk. c. 1150

718. JOHANN FISCHER VON ERLACH.
Façade of St. Charles Borromaeus, Vienna. 1716–37

719. Plan of St. Charles Borromaeus

expresses, more boldly than any Italian Baroque architect,
the power of the Christian faith to absorb and transfigure
the splendors of antiquity.

PRANDTAUER.   Even more monumental, thanks to its
superb site, is the Monastery of Melk (fig. 720), by Jakob
Prandtauer (1660–1726). The buildings form a tightly knit
unit that centers on the church: it occupies the crest of a
promontory above the Danube, rising from the rock, not like
a fortress but like a vision of heavenly glory. The interior of
the church (fig. 721) still reflects the plan of Il Gesù, but

720. JAKOB PRANDTAUER. Monastery Church, Melk,
Austria. Begun 1702

the abundant illumination, the play of curves and counter-curves, and the weightless grace of the stucco sculpture, give it an airy lightness far removed from the Roman Baroque. The vaults and wall surfaces seem thin and pliable, like membranes easily punctured by the expansive power of space.

NEUMANN; TIEPOLO.   This tendency is carried further by the architects of the next generation, among whom Balthasar Neumann (1687–1753) was the most prominent. His largest project, the Episcopal Palace in Würzburg, includes the breath-taking Kaisersaal (colorplate 97), a great oval hall decorated in white, gold, and pastel shades—the favorite color scheme of the mid-eighteenth century. Structural members such as columns, pilasters, and architraves are now minimized; windows and vault segments are framed by continuous, ribbon-like moldings, and the white surfaces are spun over with irregular ornamental designs. This repertory of lacy, curling motifs, invented in France about 1700, is the hallmark of the Rococo style (see page 556), which is here happily combined with German Late Baroque architecture.

The membrane-like ceiling so often gives way to illusionistic openings of every sort that we no longer feel it to be a

721. PRANDTAUER, BEDUZZI, and MUNGGENAST. Interior, Monastery Church, Melk. Completed c. 1738

722. GIOVANNI BATTISTA TIEPOLO. Ceiling fresco
of the Kaisersaal (detail; see colorplate 97).
1751. Episcopal Palace, Würzburg

723. DOMINIKUS ZIMMERMAN. Interior of Die Wies,
Upper Bavaria. 1745–54

724. Plan of Die Wies

spatial boundary. These openings do not, however, reveal
avalanches of figures propelled by dramatic bursts of light,
like those of Roman ceilings (compare fig. 706), but blue
sky and sunlit clouds, and an occasional winged creature
soaring in this limitless expanse. Only along the edges are
there solid clusters of figures (fig. 722). Here the last, and
most refined, stage of illusionistic ceiling decoration is represented by its greatest master, Giovanni Battista Tiepolo
(1696–1770). Venetian by birth and training, Tiepolo
blended the tradition of High Baroque illusionism with the
pageantry of Veronese. His mastery of light and color, the
grace and felicity of his touch, made him famous far beyond
his home territory. In the Würzburg frescoes his powers are
at their height. He was afterward invited to decorate the
Royal Palace in Madrid, where he spent his final years.

ZIMMERMANN.   A contemporary of Balthasar Neumann,
Dominikus Zimmermann (1685–1766), created what may
be the finest spatial design of the mid-eighteenth century,
the Bavarian pilgrimage church nicknamed "Die Wies" (figs.
723, 724). The exterior is so plain that its interior richness
seems truly overwhelming. Like the Kaisersaal, its shape is
oval, but since the ceiling rests on paired, free-standing
supports, the spatial configuration is more complex and
fluid; despite the playful Rococo décor, we are reminded
of a German Gothic *Hallenkirche* (see fig. 444). Guarini's
prophetic revaluation of Gothic architecture has here
become reality.

7
THE BAROQUE IN FLANDERS, HOLLAND, AND SPAIN

FLANDERS

Painting

RUBENS.   Although Rome was its birthplace, the Baroque style soon became international. Among the artists who helped bring this about, the great Flemish painter Peter Paul Rubens (1577–1640) holds a place of unique importance. It might be said that he finished what Dürer had started a hundred years earlier—the breakdown of the artistic barriers between North and South. Rubens' father was a prominent Antwerp Protestant who fled to Germany to escape Spanish persecution during the war of independence (see page 492); the family returned to Antwerp after his death, when Peter Paul was ten years old, and the boy grew up a devout Catholic. Trained by local painters, Rubens became a master in 1598, but developed a personal style only when, two years later, he went to Italy.

During his eight years in the South, he eagerly studied ancient sculpture, the masterpieces of the High Renaissance (see his splendid drawing after Leonardo's *Battle of Anghiari*, fig. 602), and the work of Caravaggio and Annibale Carracci, absorbing the Italian tradition far more thoroughly than had any Northerner before him. He competed, in fact, with the best Italians of his day on even terms, and could well have made his career in Italy. When his mother's illness in 1608 brought him back to Flanders, he meant the visit to be brief. But he received a special appointment as court painter to the Spanish regent, which permitted him to establish a workshop in Antwerp, exempt from local taxes and guild regulations. Rubens thus had the best of both worlds

for he was valued at court not only as an artist, but as a confidential adviser and emissary. Diplomatic errands gave him entree to the royal households of the major powers, where he procured sales and commissions, while he was also free to carry out, aided by a growing number of assistants, a vast volume of work for the city of Antwerp, for the Church, and for private patrons.

The Raising of the Cross (fig. 725), the first major altarpiece Rubens produced after his return, shows strikingly how much he owed to Italian art. The muscular figures, modeled to display their physical power and passionate feeling, recall the Sistine Ceiling and the Farnese Gallery; the lighting suggest Caravaggio's. The panel is more heroic in scale and conception than any previous Northern work, yet Rubens is also a meticulous Flemish realist in such details as the foliage, the armor of the soldier, and the curly-haired dog in the foreground. These varied elements, integrated with sovereign mastery, form a composition of tremendous dramatic force. The unstable pyramid of bodies, swaying precariously, bursts the limits of the frame in a characteristically Baroque way, making the beholder feel that he, too, participates in the action.

In the decade of the 1620s, Rubens' dynamic style reached its climax in his huge decorative schemes for churches and palaces. The most famous, probably, is the cycle in the Luxembourg Palace in Paris, glorifying the career of Marie de' Medici, the widow of Henri IV and mother of Louis XIII. Our illustration shows the artist's oil sketch for one episode, the young queen landing in Marseilles (fig. 726). Hardly an exciting subject—yet Rubens has turned it into a spectacle of unprecedented splendor. As Marie de' Medici walks down the gangplank, Fame flies overhead sounding a triumphant blast on two trumpets, and Neptune rises from the sea with his fish-tailed crew; having guarded the queen's journey, they rejoice at her arrival. Everything flows together here in swirling movement: heaven and earth, history and allegory—even drawing and painting, for Rubens used oil sketches like this one to prepare his compositions. Unlike earlier artists, he preferred to design his pictures in terms of light and color from the very start (most of his drawings are figure studies or portrait sketches). This unified vision, adumbrated but never fully achieved by the great Venetians, was Rubens' most precious legacy to subsequent painters.

Around 1630, the turbulent drama of Rubens' preceding work changes to a late style of lyrical tenderness inspired by Titian, whom Rubens rediscovered, as it were, in the royal palace while he visited Madrid. *The Garden of Love* (fig. 727, colorplate 98) is one beautiful result of this encounter, as glowing a tribute to life's pleasures as Titian's *Bacchanal* (see fig. 634, colorplate 80). But these celebrants belong to the present, not to a golden age of the past, though they are playfully assaulted by swarms of cupids. To understand the artist's purpose, we must first realize that this subject, the

726. PETER PAUL RUBENS. *Marie de' Medici, Queen of France, Landing in Marseilles.* 1622–23. Panel, 25 × 19¾″. Pinakothek, Munich

725. PETER PAUL RUBENS. *The Raising of the Cross.* 1609–10. Panel, 15 × 11′ 2″. Antwerp Cathedral

Garden of Love, had been a feature of Northern painting ever since the courtly style of the International Gothic. The early versions, however, merely showed groups of fashionable young lovers in a garden—they were genre scenes pure and simple. By combining this tradition with Titian's classical mythologies, Rubens has created an enchanted realm where myth and reality become one.

The picture must have had special meaning for him, since he had just married a beautiful girl of sixteen (his first wife died in 1626). He also bought a country house, the Château of Steen, and led the leisurely life of a squire. This change induced a renewed interest in landscape painting, which he had practiced only intermittently before. Here, too, the power of his genius is undiminished. In the *Landscape with the Château of Steen* (fig. 728), a magnificent open space sweeps from the hunter and his prey in the foreground to the mist-veiled hills along the horizon. As a landscapist, Rubens is the heir of both Pieter Bruegel and Annibale Carracci (compare figs. 682, 699), again creating a synthesis from his Northern and Southern sources.

VAN DYCK. Besides Rubens, only one Flemish Baroque artist won international stature. Anthony van Dyck (1599–1641) was that rarity among painters, a child prodigy. Before he was twenty, he had become Rubens' most valued assistant. But he lacked the older master's vitality and inventiveness, and his fame is based mainly on his portraits, especially those he painted in England as court painter to Charles I, during 1632–41. Among the most attractive is *Charles I Hunting* (fig. 729, colorplate 99); the king stands near a horse and two grooms against a landscape backdrop. Repre-

727. PETER PAUL RUBENS. *The Garden of Love* (see colorplate 98).
The Prado, Madrid

728. PETER PAUL RUBENS. *Landscape with the Château of Steen.* 1636. Panel, 53 × 93″. The National Gallery, London

729. ANTHONY VAN DYCK. *Portrait of Charles I Hunting* (see colorplate 99). The Louvre, Paris

senting the sovereign at ease, it might be called a "dismounted equestrian portrait"—less rigid than a formal state portrait, but hardly less grand. The fluid Baroque movement of the setting contrasts oddly with the self-conscious elegance of the king's pose, which still suggests the stylized grace of Elizabethan portraits (compare fig. 680). Van Dyck has brought the Mannerist court portrait up-to-date, rephrasing it in the pictorial language of Rubens and Titian. He created a new aristocratic portrait tradition that continued in England until the late eighteenth century, and had considerable influence on the continent as well.

HOLLAND
Painting and Etching

In contrast to Flanders, where all of art was overshadowed by the majestic personality of Rubens, Holland produced a bewildering variety of masters and styles. The new nation was proud of its hard-won freedom. Though the cultural links with Flanders remained strong, several factors encouraged the quick development of Dutch artistic traditions. Unlike Flanders, where all artistic activity radiated from Antwerp, Holland had a number of flourishing local schools; besides Amsterdam, the commercial capital, we find important groups of painters in Haarlem, Utrecht, Leyden, Delft, and other towns. Holland was a nation of merchants, farmers, and seafarers, and its religion the Reformed Protestant faith; Dutch artists had not the large-scale public commissions sponsored by State and Church that were available throughout the Catholic world. While municipal authorities and civic bodies provided a certain amount of art patronage, their demands were limited, so that the private collector now became the painter's chief source of support.

This condition had already existed to some extent before (see page 493), but its full effect can be seen only after 1600. There was no shrinkage of output; on the contrary, the general public developed so insatiable an appetite for pictures that the whole country became gripped by a kind of collector's mania. John Evelyn, during a visit to Holland in 1641, noted in his diary that "it is an ordinary thing to find a common farmer lay out two or three thousand pounds in this commodity. Their houses are full of them, and they vend them at their fairs to very great gain." Pictures had indeed become a commodity, and their trade followed the law of supply and demand. Many artists produced "for the market" rather than for individual patrons.

The mechanism of the market has been said to raise a barrier between artist and public, and to degrade or falsify the "true worth" of the work of art. But such charges are unrealistic: the true worth of a work of art is always unstable, and dependent on time and circumstance; even those who believe in timeless values in art will concede that these values cannot be expressed in money. The art market reflects the dominant, rather than the most discerning, taste of the moment; works by artists now regarded as mediocre may once have been overpriced; others, highly valued today, seem once to have sold too cheaply. Yet the system in antiquity and the Middle Ages, when artists were paid on standards of craftsmanship, was hardly fairer in rewarding aesthetic merit (except, perhaps, for Alexander the Great, who is said to have ceded his mistress to the painter Apelles as a token of appreciation). The market does form a barrier between artist and patron, but there are advantages in this as well as drawbacks.

To subject the artist to the impersonal pressure of supply and demand in an egalitarian society is not necessarily worse than to make him depend on the favor of princes. The lesser men will tend to become specialists, steadily producing their marketable pictures, while artists of independent spirit, perhaps braving public indifference and economic hardship, will paint as they please and rely for support on the discerning minority. The collectors' mania in seventeenth-century Holland caused an outpouring of artistic talent comparable only to Early Renaissance Florence, although many Dutchmen were lured into becoming painters by hopes of success that failed to come true. Even the greatest masters were sometimes hard-pressed (it was not unusual for an artist to keep an inn, or run a small business on the side). Yet they survived—less secure, but freer.

UTRECHT SCHOOL. The Baroque style came to Holland from Antwerp, through the work of Rubens, and from Rome, through direct contact with Caravaggio and his followers. Although most Dutch painters did not go to Italy, in the early years of the century there were some who did, principally

730. HENDRICK TERBRUGGHEN. *The Calling
of St. Matthew.* 1621. 40 × 54″. Centraal Museum, Utrecht

731. FRANS HALS. *The Jolly Toper* (see
colorplate 100). Rijksmuseum,
Amsterdam

from Utrecht, a town with strong Catholic traditions. It is not surprising that these artists were more attracted by Caravaggio's realism and "lay Christianity" than by Annibale Carracci's classicism. *The Calling of St. Matthew* by Hendrick Terbrugghen (1588–1629), the oldest of this group (fig. 730), directly reflects Caravaggio's earlier version (fig. 693, colorplate 94): the sharp light, the dramatic timing, and the everyday detail. While the Utrecht School produced no great artists, its members were important for transmitting the style of Caravaggio to other Dutch masters who then made better use of these new Italian ideas.

HALS.   One of the first to profit from this experience was Frans Hals (1580/85-1666), the great portrait painter of Haarlem. He was born in Antwerp, and what little is known of his early work suggests the influence of Rubens. His developed style, however, seen in such pictures as *The Jolly Toper* (fig. 731, colorplate 100), combines Rubens' robustness and breadth with a concentration on the "dramatic moment" that must be derived, via Utrecht, from Caravaggio. Everything here conveys complete spontaneity: the twinkling eyes and half-open mouth, the raised hand, the teetering wineglass, and—most important of all—the quick way of setting down the forms. Hals works in dashing brush strokes, each so clearly visible as a separate entity than we can almost count the total number of "touches." With this open, split-second technique, the completed picture has the immediacy of a sketch (compare that by Rubens, fig. 726). The impression of a race against time is, of course, deceptive; Frans Hals spent hours, not minutes, on this lifesize canvas, but he maintains the illusion of having done it all in the wink of an eye.

These qualities are even more forceful in the *Malle Babbe* (fig. 732), one of the artist's genre pictures. A lower-class counterpart of *The Jolly Toper*, this folk character, half witch (note the owl), half village idiot, screams invective at other guests in a tavern. Hals seems to share their attitude toward

732. FRANS HALS. *Malle Babbe.* c. 1650.
29½ × 25″. Dahlem Museum, West Berlin

733. FRANS HALS. *The Women Regents of the Old Men's Home at Haarlem.* 1664. 67 × 98″. Frans Hals Museum, Haarlem

this benighted creature—one of cruel amusement rather than sympathy—but his characterization is masterfully sharp and his lightning-like brushwork has the bravura of incredible skill.

In the artist's last canvases these pictorial fireworks are transmuted into an austere style of great emotional depth. His group portrait, *The Women Regents of the Old Men's Home at Haarlem* (fig. 733), the institution where he spent his final years, has an insight into human character matched only in Rembrandt's late style (compare figs. 740, 741). The daily experience of suffering and death has so etched the faces of these women that they seem themselves to have become images of death—gentle, inexorable, and timeless.

LEYSTER. Hals' virtuosity was such that it could not be imitated readily, and his followers were necessarily few. The only one of importance was Judith Leyster (1609–1660). Like many women artists before modern times, her career was partially curtailed by motherhood. Leyster's enchanting *Boy with Flute* (fig. 734) is her masterpiece. In spirit it closer to Terbrugghen's than to Hals'. The rapt musician is a memorable expression of a lyrical mood. To convey this mood, she investigates the poetic quality of light with a quiet intensity that anticipates the work of Jan Vermeer a generation later (see page 534).

734. JUDITH LEYSTER. *Boy with Flute.* 1630–35. 29½ × 24¼″.
National Museum, Stockholm

735. REMBRANDT. *Tobit and Anna with the Kid.* 1626. Panel, 15½ × 11¾". Collection Baroness Thyssen-Bornemisza, Lucerne

REMBRANDT. Rembrandt (1606–1669), the greatest genius of Dutch art, was also stimulated at the beginning of his career by indirect contact with Caravaggio. His earliest pictures, from his Leyden period (1625–31), are small, sharply lit, and intensely realistic; many, such as *Tobit and Anna with the Kid* (fig. 735), deal with Old Testament subjects—a lifelong preference of the artist's. Even this little panel, filled with the homely detail of peasant life, has qualities that distinguish Rembrandt's from earlier Old Testament scenes; it shows not only his greater realism but his new emotional attitude.

Since the beginning of Christian art, episodes from the Old Testament had often been represented for the light they shed on Christian doctrine (the Sacrifice of Isaac, for example, "prefigured" the sacrificial death of Christ), rather than for their own sake. This perspective not only limited the choice of subjects, it also colored their interpretation. Rembrandt, by contrast, viewed the stories of the Old Testament in the same lay Christian spirit that governed Caravaggio's approach to the New Testament: as direct accounts of God's ways with men. How deeply they moved him is evident from the touching relationship he has created between the blind Tobit and his wife.

736. REMBRANDT. *The Blinding of Samson.* 1636. 7′ 9″ × 9′ 11″. Staedel Institute, Frankfurt

737. REMBRANDT. *The Night Watch (The Company of Captain Frans Banning Cocq).*
1642. 12′ 2″ × 14′ 7″. Rijksmuseum, Amsterdam

Ten years later, in *The Blinding of Samson* (fig. 736), Rembrandt had developed a full-blown High Baroque style. He here visualizes the Old Testament as a world of oriental splendor and violence, cruel yet seductive. The sudden flood of brilliant light pouring into the dark tent is unabashedly theatrical, heightening the drama. Rembrandt was at this time an avid collector of Near Eastern paraphernalia, which serve as props in these pictures. He was now Amsterdam's most sought-after portrait painter, as well as a man of considerable wealth.

This prosperity petered out in the 1640s; the turning point may have been his famous group portrait known as *The Night Watch* (fig. 737). The huge canvas—originally it was even larger—shows a military company, whose members had each contributed toward the cost. But Rembrandt did not do them equal justice. Anxious to avoid a mechanically regular

738. REMBRANDT. *Jacob Blessing the
Sons of Joseph* (detail; see colorplate
101). Gemäldegalerie, Kassel

739. REMBRANDT. *The Polish Rider.* c. 1655. 46 × 53".
The Frick Collection, New York (Copyright)

We cannot be sure that the rider is Polish—the title was given to him later—although his costume is of the kind worn by the local troops then fighting the Turks in eastern Europe; nor is Rembrandt's exact meaning clear. But Dürer's famous engraving, *Knight, Death, and Devil* (see fig. 672), which Rembrandt surely admired, may be the key to the picture. Is not *The Polish Rider* another Christian Soldier bravely making his way through a perilous world? The dangers in this case are ours to imagine in the gloomy landscape, but the rider's serious, alert glance suggests unseen threats. With such a relationship of form and content, the differences between the painting and the print make a rewarding study. Dürer's horseman, boxed into the composition, is balanced and stationary like an equestrian statue; Rembrandt's, slightly foreshortened and off-center, is in motion—urged on, as it were, by the light from the left. The curving path he follows will soon lead him beyond the frame.

This subtle imbalance implies a space far vaster than the compass of the picture and stamps Rembrandt's work as Baroque, despite the absence of the more obvious hallmarks of the style. The same is true of the *Self-Portrait* (fig. 740); in the sixty-odd that the artist made in his long career, his view of himself reflects every stage of his inner development—experimental in the Leyden years; theatrically disguised in the 1630s; frank and self-analytical toward the end of his life, as in our example, yet full of simple dignity.

The Return of the Prodigal Son (fig. 741), painted a few years before his death, is perhaps Rembrandt's most moving

design, he made the picture a virtuoso performance of Baroque movement and lighting; in the process some of the figures were plunged into shadow, some hidden by overlapping. Legend has it that the people whose portraits he had thus obscured were dissatisfied. There is no evidence that they were; we do know, however, that the painting was admired even then.

Like Michelangelo, Rembrandt has been the subject (one might say, the victim) of many fictionalized biographies. In these, the artist's fall from public favor is usually explained by the "catastrophe" of *The Night Watch.* Actually, his fortunes declined after 1642 less suddenly and completely than his romantic admirers would have us believe. Certain important people in Amsterdam continued to be his steadfast friends and supporters, and he received some major public commissions in the 1650s and 1660s; his financial difficulties resulted largely from poor management. Nevertheless, the years after 1642 were a period of crisis, of inner uncertainty and external troubles. Rembrandt's outlook changed profoundly: after about 1650, his style eschews the rhetoric of the High Baroque for lyric subtlety and pictorial breadth.

Such pictures as *Jacob Blessing the Sons of Joseph* (fig. 738, colorplate 101) show this new depth of feeling. Some exotic trappings from the earlier years remain, but they no longer create an alien, barbarous world. The golden light filtering from behind the curtain on the left seems as gentle as the gestures and glances. So pervasive is the mood of tender silence that the beholder, watching from the foot of the bed, senses a spontaneous kinship with this family group—our bond of shared experience is stronger and more intimate here than in any earlier work of art.

In his later years, Rembrandt often adapted, in a highly personal way, compositions of pictorial ideas from the Northern Renaissance: one instance is *The Polish Rider* (fig. 739).

740. REMBRANDT. *Self-Portrait.* c. 1660.
45 × 38". The Iveagh Bequest, Kenwood, London

741. REMBRANDT. *The Return of the Prodigal Son.*
c. 1665. 8′ 8″ × 6′ 7¾″. Hermitage Museum, Leningrad

religious picture. It is also his quietest—a moment stretching into eternity. The sensuous beauty seen in *Jacob Blessing the Sons of Joseph* has now yielded to a humble world of bare feet and ragged clothes, recalling the *Tobit and Anna* painted four decades before.

This feeling for the poor and outcast had never disappeared entirely from Rembrandt's work, although during his middle years it survived in his drawings and prints rather than in his paintings. He had a special sympathy for the Jews, as the heirs of the biblical past and as the patient victims of persecution; they were often his models, and among his prints are scenes such as *Christ Preaching* (fig. 742) that seem to take place in a corner of the Amsterdam ghetto. *The Return of the Prodigal Son* is the ultimate fruit of these studies. Rembrandt's importance as a graphic artist is second only to Dürer's, although we get no more than a hint from this single example.

ETCHINGS.   But we must add a word about etching as a new medium. By the seventeenth century, the techniques of woodcut and engraving were employed mainly to reproduce other works. The creative printmakers of the day, including Rembrandt, preferred etching, often combined with drypoint (see fig. 535). An etching is made by coating a copperplate with resin to make an acid-resistant "ground," through which the design is scratched with a needle, laying bare the metal surface underneath,. The plate is then bathed in an acid that etches (or "bites") the lines into the copper. The

742. REMBRANDT. *Christ Preaching.* c. 1652. Etching. The Metropolitan Museum of Art,
New York (Bequest of Mrs. H. O. Havemeyer, 1929)

Baroque in Flanders, Holland, Spain   531

743. JAN VAN GOYEN. *Fort on a River.* 1644. Panel, 16¾ × 29¾″. Museum of Fine Arts, Boston

depth of these grooves varies with the strength and duration of the bath. The biting is usually by stages: after a brief immersion the etcher will apply a protective coating to the plate in those areas where the lines should be faint: he then immerses the plate until it is time to protect the less delicate lines, and so on. To scratch a design into the resinous ground is, of course, an easier task than to scratch it into the copperplate itself, hence an etched line is smoother and more flexible than a drypoint line. An etched plate is also more durable; like an engraved one, it yields a far larger number of prints than a drypoint plate. Its chief virtue is its wide tonal range, including velvety dark shades not possible in other graphic media. No subsequent artist has ever exploited this tonal quality more subtly than Rembrandt.

LANDSCAPE AND STILL LIFE PAINTERS. Rembrandt's religious pictures demand an insight that was beyond the capacity of all but a few collectors. Most art buyers in Holland preferred subjects within their own experience—landscapes, architectural views, still lifes, everyday scenes. These various types, we recall, originated in the latter half of the sixteenth century (see page 493); as they became fully defined, an unheard-of specialization began. The trend was not confined to Holland. We find it everywhere to some degree, but Dutch painting was its fountainhead, in both volume and variety. There were, in fact, so many subtypes within each major division mentioned above that we can illustrate only a small sampling. *Fort on a River* (fig. 743) by Jan van Goyen (1596–1656) is a new kind of landscape which enjoyed great popularity because its elements were so familiar; the distant town under a looming gray sky, seen through a moisture-laden atmosphere across an expanse of water—this view is still characteristic of the Dutch country-

side today. No one knew better than Van Goyen how to evoke the special mood of these "nether lands," ever threatened by the sea.

Natural forces also dominate in *The Jewish Cemetery* (fig. 744) by Jacob van Ruisdael (1628/29–1682), the greatest Dutch landscape painter. The scene is frankly imaginary: the thunderclouds passing over a wild, deserted mountain valley, the medieval ruin, the torrent that has forced its way between ancient graves, all create a mood of deep melancholy. Nothing endures on this earth, the artist tells us—time, wind, and water grind all to dust, the feeble works of man as well as the trees and rocks. His signature on the gravestone nearest us is a final touch of gloomy irony. Ruisdael's vision of nature in relation to man is thus the exact opposite of Annibale Carracci's (compare fig. 699): it inspires that awe on which the Romantics, a century later, were to base their concept of the Sublime.

Nothing at first seems further removed from *The Jewish Cemetery* than the painstakingly precise architectural interior of *St. Cunera Church, Rhenen* (fig. 745), painted by Pieter Saenredam at exactly the same time. Yet it, too, is meant to invite meditation, rather than serve merely as a topographic record (these views were often freely invented). The medieval structure, stripped of all furnishings and whitewashed under Protestant auspices, is no longer a house of worship. It has become a place for the dead (note the tomb slabs in the floor), and in its crystalline spaciousness we feel the silence of a graveyard. Again we are reminded that All is Vanity.

Even still life can be tinged with this melancholy sense of the passing of all earthly pleasures; the message may lie in such established symbols as death's-heads and extinguished candles, or be conveyed by means less direct. Willem Claesz.

744. JACOB VAN RUISDAEL. *The Jewish Cemetery.*
c. 1655. 32 × 37½″. State Picture Gallery, Dresden

Heda's *Still Life* (fig. 746) belongs to a widespread type, the "breakfast piece," showing the remnants of a meal. Food and drink are less emphasized than luxury objects—crystal goblets and silver dishes—carefully juxtaposed for their contrasting shape, color, and texture.

How different this seems from the piled-up edibles of Aertsen's *Meat Stall* (see fig. 681)! But virtuosity was not Heda's only aim: his "story," the human context of these grouped objects, is suggested by the broken glass, the half-peeled lemon, the overturned silver dish; whoever sat at this table has been suddenly forced to abandon his meal. The curtain that time has lowered on the scene, as it were, invests the objects with a strange pathos. The disguised symbolism of "Late Gothic" painting lives on here in a new form.

Other types of still life, such as flower pieces, can be traced directly to their symbolic origins. How much of the older meaning survives in these examples is still being debated. Was Jan Davidsz. de Heem, the artist of the beautiful flower piece in figure 747, aware of the significance of each blossom, and of the butterflies, moths, and snails he put into the picture, and did he assemble his bouquet to this end? Or was he content to make it a feast for the eyes? Be that as it may, these flowers have such Baroque vitality that they fairly leap from their vase.

745. PIETER SAENREDAM. *St. Cunera Church, Rhenen.* 1655.
Panel, 19¾ × 27″. Mauritshuis, The Hague

746. WILLEM CLAESZ. HEDA. *Still Life*. 1634. Panel, 17 × 22⅛".
Boymans-van Beuningen Museum, Rotterdam

747. JAN DAVIDSZ. DE HEEM. *Flower Still Life*.
c. 1665. 21 × 16¼". Ashmolean Museum, Oxford

STEEN. The vast class of pictures termed genre is as varied as that of landscapes and still lifes: it ranges from tavern brawls to refined domestic interiors. *The Eve of St. Nicholas* (fig. 748), by Jan Steen (1625/26–1679), is midway between: St. Nicholas has just paid his pre-Christmas visit to the household, leaving toys, candy, and cake for the children; everybody is jolly except the bad boy on the left, who has received only a birch rod. Steen tells this story with relish, embroidering it with many delightful details. Of all the Dutch painters of daily life, he was the sharpest, and most good-humored, observer. To supplement his earnings he kept an inn, which perhaps explains his keen insight into human behavior. His sense of timing and his characterization often remind us of Frans Hals (compare fig. 732), while his story-telling stems from the tradition of Pieter Bruegel the Elder (compare fig. 683, colorplate 93).

VERMEER. In the genre scenes of Jan Vermeer, by contrast, there is hardly any narrative. Single figures, usually women, engage in simple, everyday tasks (see figs. 8, 9); when there are two, as in *The Letter* (fig. 749, colorplate 102), they do no more than exchange glances. They exist in a timeless "still life" world, seemingly calmed by some magic spell. The cool, clear light that filters in from the left is the only active element, working its miracles upon all the objects in its path. As we look at *The Letter*, we feel as if a veil had been pulled from our eyes; the everyday world shines with jewel-like freshness, beautiful as we have never seen it before. No painter since Jan van Eyck *saw* as intensely as this.

But Vermeer, unlike his predecessors, perceives reality as a mosaic of colored surfaces—or perhaps more accurately, he translates reality into a mosaic as he puts it on canvas. We see *The Letter* as a perspective "window," but also as a plane, a "field" composed of smaller fields. Rectangles predominate, carefully aligned with the picture surface, and there are no "holes," no undefined empty spaces. These interlocking shapes give to Vermeer's work a uniquely modern quality within seventeenth-century art. How did he acquire it? We know very little about him except that he was born in Delft in 1632 and lived and worked there until his death at forty-three, in 1675. Some of his works show the influence of Carel Fabritius, the most brilliant of Rembrandt's pupils; other pictures suggest his contact with the Utrecht School. But none of this really explains the genesis of his style, so daringly original that his genius was not recognized until about a century ago.

SPAIN
Painting

Spain is the last country to be surveyed in the present chapter, for Spanish Baroque painting cannot be fully understood without some knowledge of artistic events in Italy and the Netherlands. During the sixteenth century, at the height of its political and economic power, Spain had produced great saints and writers, but no artists of the first rank. Nor did El Greco's presence prove a stimulus to native talent. The

748. JAN STEEN. *The Eve of St. Nicholas.*
c. 1660–65. 32¼ × 27¾″. Rijksmuseum, Amsterdam

749. JAN VERMEER. *The Letter* (detail;
see colorplate 102). Rijksmuseum, Amsterdam

stimulus came, rather, from Caravaggio (though we do not know exactly how it was transmitted) and Flemish painting. Soon after Aertsen and his contemporaries in the Netherlands established the field of still life, Spanish masters began to develop their own versions.

SANCHEZ COTÁN. In the example by Juan Sanchez Cotán (1561–1627), who was an early and remarkable Spanish painter of still life (fig. 750), we see the distinctive character of this tradition. In contrast to the lavish display of food or luxury objects in Northern pictures, we here find an order and an austere simplicity that give a new context to these vegetables. They are so deliberately arranged in a star-and-crescent pattern that we cannot help wondering what symbolic significance the artist meant to convey. In any case, the juxtaposition of bright sunlight and impenetrable darkness, of painstaking realism and abstract form, creates a memorable image.

ZURBARÁN. Sanchez Cotán's still lives make one think of the style of Caravaggio, whose influence was certainly felt by the second decade of the century, especially in Seville, the home of the most important Spanish Baroque painters. Among them, Francisco de Zurbarán (1598–1664) stands out for the quiet intensity of his devotional pictures, such as *St. Serapion* (fig. 751, colorplate 103). Although Caravag-

750. JUAN SANCHEZ COTÁN. *Still Life*. c. 1602–3.
25 × 33½". Museum, Granada

751. FRANCISCO DE ZURBARÁN. *St. Serapion*
(see colorplate 103). Wadsworth Atheneum, Hartford, Connecticut

his powerful grasp of individual character and dignity invests this everyday scene with the solemn spirit of a ritual. A few years later, Velázquez was appointed court painter and moved to Madrid, where he spent the rest of his life, doing mainly portraits of the royal family. The earlier of these still show the precise division of light and shade and the clear outlines of his Seville period, but after the late 1620s his work acquired a new fluency and richness.

Meanwhile he had become a friend of Rubens, who probably helped him to discover the beauty of the many Titians in the king's collection, but did not influence him directly. He also traveled in Italy, where in 1650 he painted the magnificent portrait of Pope Innocent X (fig. 753). The picture is meant to evoke the great tradition of the papal portraits of Raphael (compare fig. 632, colorplate 78) but its fluid brushwork and glowing color derive from Titian. And the sitter's gaze, sharply focused on the beholder, conveys a passionate and powerful personality.

The Maids of Honor (fig. 754, colorplate 104) displays Velázquez' mature style at its fullest, at once a group portrait and a genre scene. It might be subtitled "the artist in his studio," for Velázquez shows himself at work on a huge canvas; in the center is the little Princess Margarita, who has just posed for him, among her playmates and maids of honor. The faces of her parents, the king and queen, appear in the mirror on the back wall. Have they just stepped into the room, to see the scene exactly as we do, or does the mirror reflect part of the canvas—presumably a full-length portrait of the royal family—on which the artist has been working? This ambiguity is characteristic of Velázquez' fas-

752. DIEGO VELÁZQUEZ. *The Water Carrier of Seville*.
c. 1619. 41½ × 31½". Wellington Museum, London
(Crown copyright reserved)

gesque in style, it is filled with an ascetic piety that is uniquely Spanish, and the very absence of rhetorical pathos makes this image of a martyred monk profoundly moving.

VELÁZQUEZ. Likewise, Diego Velázquez (1599–1660) painted in a Caravaggesque vein during his early years, but his interests centered on genre and still life rather than religious themes. *The Water Carrier of Seville* (fig. 752), which he did at the age of twenty, already shows his genius:

753. DIEGO VELÁZQUEZ. *Pope Innocent X.* 1650.
55 × 45 ¼″. Doria-Pamphili Gallery, Rome

cination with light. Unlike Rembrandt, he was concerned with its optical rather than its metaphysical mysteries, but these he penetrated more completely than any painter of his time except Vermeer.

The varieties of direct and reflected light in *The Maids of Honor* are almost limitless, and the artist challenges us to find them: we are expected to match the mirror image against the paintings on that wall, and against the "picture" of the man in the open doorway. Velázquez could not have known Vermeer's work, for the latter was then only twenty-four, but he may have known scenes of domestic genre by older Dutch painters. Looking at the open, sketchy brushwork in colorplate 104, we wonder if he could also have known Frans Hals (compare fig. 731, colorplate 100). Yet Velázquez' technique is far more varied and subtle, with delicate glazes setting off the impasto of the highlights. The colors, too, have a Venetian richness unmatched by Hals. Nor does Velázquez seem interested in catching time on the wing; his aim is not to show figures in motion, but the movement of light itself and the infinite range of its effects on form and color. For Velázquez, light *creates* the visible world. Not until two centuries later shall we meet painters capable of realizing the implications of this discovery.

754. DIEGO VELÁZQUEZ. *The Maids of Honor.* 1656. 10′5″ × 9′.
The Prado, Madrid (see colorplate 104)

Baroque in Flanders, Holland, Spain 537

8
THE BAROQUE
IN FRANCE
AND ENGLAND

FRANCE
Painting

Our discussion of Baroque art in Flanders, Holland, and Spain was limited to painting; architecture and sculpture in these countries, although far from negligible, are not of central importance for the history of art, so that we could afford to leave them out of our account. But in France the situation is different. Under Louis XIV France became the most powerful nation of Europe, militarily and culturally; by the late seventeenth century, Paris was vying with Rome as the world capital of the visual arts—a position it had held for centuries. How did this amazing change come about? Because of the Palace of Versailles and other vast projects glorifying the king of France, we are tempted to think of French art in the age of Louis XIV as the expression—and one of the products—of absolutism. This is true of the climactic phase of Louis' reign, 1660–85, but by that time French seventeenth-century art already had its distinctive style. Frenchmen are reluctant to call this style Baroque; to them it is the Style of Louis XIV; often they also describe the art and literature of the period as "classic."

The term "classic," so used, has three meanings: as a synonym for "highest achievement," it implies that the Style of Louis XIV corresponds to the High Renaissance in Italy, or the age of Pericles in ancient Greece; the term also refers to the emulation of the form and subject matter of classical antiquity; finally, "classic" suggests qualities of balance and restraint, like those of the classic styles of the High Renaissance and of ancient art. The second and third of these meanings describe what could be called, more accurately, "classicism." And since the Style of Louis XIV reflects Italian Baroque art, however modified, we must label it "classicistic Baroque" or "Baroque classicism."

This classicism was the official court style by 1660–85, but its origin was not political. It sprang, rather, from the persistent tradition of sixteenth-century art, which in France was more intimately linked with the Italian Renaissance than in any other northern country (page 472). Classicism was also nourished by French humanism, with its intellectual heritage of reason and Stoic virtue. These factors retarded the spread of the Baroque in France, and modified its interpretation. Rubens' Medici Cycle, for example, had no effect on French art until the very end of the century (see fig. 726); in the 1620s, the young painters in France were still assimilating the Early Baroque.

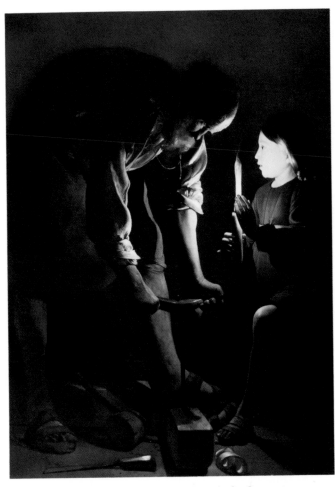

755. GEORGES DE LA TOUR. *Joseph the Carpenter.*
c. 1645. 38½ × 25½". The Louvre, Paris

GEORGES DE LA TOUR. Some of these painters were oriented toward Caravaggio, and developed astonishingly original styles; the importance of one of these men, Georges de La Tour (1593–1652), has been recognized only recently. His *Joseph the Carpenter* (fig. 755) might be mistaken for a genre scene, yet its devotional spirit has the power of Caravaggio's *Calling of St. Matthew* (see fig. 693, colorplate 94). The boy Jesus holds a candle—a favorite device with La Tour—which lights the scene with an intimacy and tenderness reminiscent of Geertgen tot Sint Jans (compare fig. 521). Strangely enough, La Tour also shares Geertgen's tendency to reduce his forms to geometric simplicity.

LE NAIN. The *Peasant Family* (fig. 756) by Louis Le Nain (1593–1648) is equally impressive. Like the peasant pictures of seventeenth-century Holland and Flanders, it stems from a tradition going back to Pieter Bruegel the Elder (see fig. 683, colorplate 93). But the Netherlandish scenes of low life are humorous or satirical (see fig. 732), whereas Louis Le Nain endows them with a human dignity and monumental weight that recall Velázquez' *Water Carrier of Seville* (see fig. 752). Like Georges de La Tour, Louis Le Nain was also rediscovered in modern times, but he did not have to wait quite so long.

POUSSIN. Why were these important painters so quickly forgotten? The reason is simple: the clarity, balance, and restraint of their art, when measured against other Caravaggesque painters, might be termed "classical," but neither was a "classicist"—and after the 1640s, classicism was supreme in France. The artist who did most to bring this about was Nicolas Poussin (1593/94–1665). The greatest French painter of the century, and the earliest French painter in history to win international fame, Poussin nevertheless spent almost his entire career in Rome. His development also was somewhat paradoxical, as we see in figures 757, 758, and colorplate 105: both works show his profound allegiance to antiquity, but in style and attitude they are much farther apart than the seven years' difference in date would suggest.

Cephalus and Aurora is inspired by Titian's warm, rich color and by his approach to classical mythology (compare fig. 634, colorplate 80). Poussin, too, visualizes antiquity here as a poetic dream world, although the unalloyed bliss of Titian's *Bacchanal* is now overcast with melancholy (his favorite subjects are tales of frustrated love). By contrast, *The Rape of the Sabine Women* must be seen altogether differently. The strongly modeled figures are "frozen in action," like statues, and many are in fact derived from Hellenistic sculpture; behind them Poussin has set reconstructions of Roman architecture that he believed to be archaeologically correct. Emotion is abundantly displayed, yet it so lacks spontaneity that it fails to touch us. Clearly, the attitude here reflected is not Titian's but Raphael's— more precisely, that of Raphael as filtered through Annibale Carracci and his school (compare figs. 695, 696). Venetian qualities have been consciously suppressed for the severe discipline of an intellectual style.

Poussin now strikes us as a man who knew his own mind only too well, an impression confirmed by the numerous letters in which he expounded his views to friends and patrons. The highest aim of painting, he believed, is to represent noble and serious human actions. These must be shown in a logical and orderly way—not as they really happened, but as they would have happened if nature were perfect. To this end, the artist must strive for the general and typical; appealing to the mind rather than the senses, he should suppress such trivialities as glowing color, and stress form and composition. In a good picture, the beholder must be able to "read" the exact emotions of each figure, and relate them to the given event. These ideas were not new—we recall Leonardo's statement that the highest aim of painting is to depict "the intention of man's soul," and the ancient dictum *ut pictura poesis* (see pages 371, 439)—but before Poussin, no one made the analogy between painting and literature so close, nor put it into practice so single-mindedly. His method accounts for the cold and over-explicit rhetoric in *The Rape of the Sabine Women* that makes the picture so much less accessible to us than his earlier *Cephalus and Aurora*.

Poussin even painted landscapes according to this theoretical view, with surprisingly impressive results. The *Landscape with the Burial of Phocion* (fig. 759) follows the tradition of Annibale Carracci's "ideal landscapes" (see fig.

756. LOUIS LE NAIN. *Peasant Family.* c. 1640. 44½ × 62½". The Louvre, Paris

757. NICOLAS POUSSIN. *Cephalus and Aurora.* c. 1630. 38 × 51". The National Gallery, London

699), but the careful order of its spaces is almost mathematically precise. Yet the effect of rational clarity has a somber calm as pervasive as the lyricism of Annibale's countryside. This mood is attuned to Poussin's theme, the burial of a Greek hero who died because he refused to conceal the truth: the landscape becomes itself a memorial to Stoic virtue. Although we may no longer read the scene so specifically, we still respond to its austere beauty.

CLAUDE LORRAINE. If Poussin developed the heroic qualities of the "ideal landscape," the great French landscapist Claude Lorraine (1600–1682) brought out its idyllic aspects. He, too, spent almost his entire career in Rome, and explored the country nearby—the Campagna—more thoroughly and affectionately than any Italian. Countless drawings made on the spot, such as the miraculously fresh and sensitive example in figure 760, bear witness to his extraordinary powers of observation. These sketches, however, were only the raw material for his paintings, which do not aim at topographic exactitude but evoke the poetic essence of a countryside filled with echoes of antiquity. Often, as in *A Pastoral* (fig. 761), the compositions are suffused with the hazy, luminous atmosphere of early morning or late afternoon; the space expands serenely, rather than receding step-by-step as in Poussin's landscapes. An air of

758. NICOLAS POUSSIN. *The Rape of the Sabine Women* (detail; see colorplate 105). The Metropolitan Museum of Art, New York

759. NICOLAS POUSSIN. *Landscape with the Burial of Phocion.* 1648. 47 × 70½". The Louvre, Paris

760. CLAUDE LORRAINE. *View of the Campagna.*
c. 1650? Wash drawing. British Museum, London

761. CLAUDE LORRAINE. *A Pastoral.* c. 1650.
Copper, 15⅞ × 21⅝". Yale University Art Gallery.
New Haven, Connecticut

The Château of Maisons near Paris, built for a newly risen administrative official, shows Mansart's mature style at its best. The vestibule leading to the grand staircase (fig. 762) has a particularly beautiful effect, severe yet festive. On seeing the classically pure articulation of the walls, one first thinks of Palladio, whose treatise Mansart certainly knew and admired. But sculpture is used here in the characteristically French way, as an integral part of architectural design; and the complex curves of the vaulting tell us that this structure, for all its classicism, belongs to the Baroque.

LOUIS XIV, COLBERT, AND THE LOUVRE. Mansart died too soon to have a share in the climactic phase of Baroque classicism, which began not long after young Louis XIV took over the reins of government in 1661. Colbert, the king's chief adviser, built the administrative apparatus supporting the power of the absolute monarch. In this system, aimed at subjecting the thoughts and actions of the entire nation to strict control from above, the visual arts had the task of glorifying the king, and the official "royal style," in both theory and practice, was classicism. That this choice was deliberate we know from the history of the first great project Colbert directed, the completion of the Louvre. Work on the palace had proceeded intermittently for over a century, along the lines of Lescot's design (see fig. 688); what remained to be done was to close the square court on the east side with an impressive façade.

Colbert, dissatisfied with the proposals of French architects, invited Bernini to Paris, hoping the most famous master of the Roman Baroque would do for the French king what he had already done so magnificently for the Church. Bernini spent several months in Paris in 1665 and submitted three designs, all on a scale that would completely engulf the extant palace. After much argument and intrigue, Louis XIV rejected these plans, and turned over the problem of a final solution to a committee of three: Louis Le Vau, his court architect, who had worked on the project before; Charles Lebrun, his court painter; and Claude Perrault, who was a

nostalgia hangs over such vistas, of past experience gilded by memory; hence they appealed especially to northerners who had seen Italy only briefly—or, perhaps, not at all.

Architecture

FRANÇOIS MANSART. In France itself, meanwhile, the foundations of Baroque classicism in architecture were laid by a group of designers whose most distinguished member was François Mansart (1598–1666). Apparently he never visited Italy, but other French architects had already imported and acclimatized some aspects of the Roman Early Baroque, especially in church design, so that Mansart was not unfamiliar with the new Italian style. What he owed to it, however, is hard to determine; his most important buildings are châteaux, and in this field the French Renaissance tradition outweighed any direct Italian Baroque influences.

762. FRANÇOIS MANSART.
Vestibule, Château of Maisons. 1642–50

763. CLAUDE PERRAULT. East Front of the Louvre, Paris. 1667–70

student of ancient architecture, not a professional architect. All three were responsible for the structure that was actually built (fig. 763), although Perrault is usually credited with the major share.

The design in some ways suggests the mind of an archaeologist, but one who knew how to select those features of classical architecture that would link Louis XIV with the glory of the Caesars and yet be compatible with the older parts of the palace. The center pavilion is a Roman temple front, and the wings look like the flanks of that temple folded outward. The temple theme demanded a single order of free-standing columns, yet the Louvre had three stories—a difficulty skillfully resolved by treating the ground story as the podium of the temple, and recessing the upper two behind the screen of the colonnade. The entire design combines grandeur and elegance in a way that fully justifies its fame.

The East Front of the Louvre signaled the victory of French classicism over Italian Baroque as the "royal style." Ironically, this great exemplar proved too pure, and Perrault soon faded from the architectural scene.

PALACE OF VERSAILLES. Baroque features, although not officially acknowledged, reappeared in the king's vastest enterprise, the Palace of Versailles. This shift corresponded to the king's own taste. Louis XIV was interested less in architectural theory and monumental exteriors than in the lavish interiors that would make suitable settings for himself and his court. Thus the man to whom he really listened was not an architect, but the painter Lebrun (1619–1690), who became supervisor of all the king's artistic projects. As chief dispenser of royal art patronage, he commanded so much power that for all practical purposes he was the dictator of the arts in France. Lebrun had spent several years studying under Poussin in Rome. But the great decorative schemes of the Roman Baroque must also have impressed him, for they stood him in good stead twenty years later, both in the Louvre and at Versailles. He became a superb decorator, utilizing the combined labors of architects, sculptors, paint-

764. HARDOUIN-MANSART, LEBRUN, and COYSEVOX. Salon de la Guerre, Palace of Versailles. Begun 1678

ers, and craftsmen for ensembles of unheard-of splendor, such as the Salon de la Guerre at Versailles (fig. 764).

To subordinate all the arts to a single goal—here, the glorification of Louis XIV—was in itself Baroque; if he went less far than Bernini, Lebrun nevertheless drew freely on his memories of Rome. The Salon de la Guerre seems in many ways closer to the Cornaro Chapel than to the vestibule at Maisons (compare figs. 704, 762). And, as in so many Italian Baroque interiors, the separate ingredients are less impressive than the effect of the whole.

The Palace of Versailles, just over eleven miles from the center of Paris, was begun in 1669 by Le Vau, who designed the elevation of the Garden Front (fig. 765). He died within a year, and the entire project, under Jules Hardouin-Mansart (1646–1708), a great-nephew of François Mansart, was vastly expanded to accommodate the ever-growing royal household. The Garden Front, intended by Le Vau to be the principal view of the palace, was stretched to an enormous length with no modification of the architectural membering; the original façade design, a less severe variant of the East Front of the Louvre, now looks repetitious and out of scale. The whole center block contains a single room, the famous Hall of Mirrors (Galerie des Glaces), with the Salon de la Guerre and its counterpart, the Salon de la Paix, at either end.

GARDENS OF VERSAILLES.   Apart from the magnificent interior, the most impressive aspect of Versailles is the park extending west of the Garden Front for several miles (the aerial view in fig. 766 shows only a small part of it). Its design, by André Le Nôtre (1613–1700), is so strictly correlated with the plan of the palace that it becomes a continuation of the architectural space. Like the interiors, these formal gardens, with their terraces, basins, clipped hedges, and statuary, were meant to provide an appropriate setting for the king's appearances in public. They form a series of "outdoor rooms" for the splendid fetes and spectacles that Louis XIV so enjoyed. The spirit of absolutism is even more striking in this geometric regularity imposed upon an entire countryside, than it is in the palace itself.

JULES HARDOUIN-MANSART.   At Versailles, Hardouin-Mansart worked as a member of a team, constrained by the design of Le Vau. His own architectural style can be better seen in the Church of the Invalides (figs. 767, 768), named

765. LOUIS LE VAU and JULES HARDOUIN-MANSART. Garden Front, Center Block, Palace of Versailles. 1669–85

766. Aerial View of the Palace of Versailles

Colorplate 100. FRANS HALS. *The Jolly Toper* (see page 526).
1627. 31⅞ × 26¼″. Rijksmuseum, Amsterdam

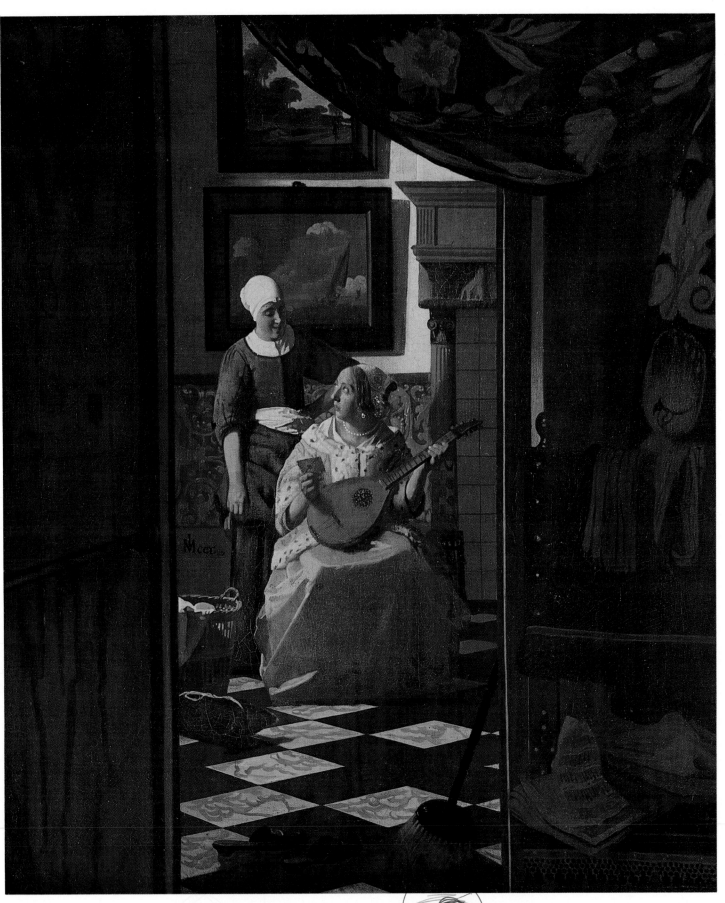

Colorplate 101. (*left*) REMBRANDT.
Jacob Blessing the Sons of Joseph (see page 530). 1656.
5′ 8½″ × 6′ 11½″. Gemäldegalerie, Kassel

Colorplate 102. (*above*) JAN VERMEER. *The Letter*
(see page 534). 1666. 17¼ × 15¼″. Rijksmuseum, Amsterdam

Colorplate 103. FRANCISCO DE ZURBARÁN. *St. Serapion* (see
page 535). 1628. 47½ × 40¾″. Wadsworth Atheneum, Hartford, Connecticut

Colorplate 104. DIEGO VELÁZQUEZ. Detail of *The Maids of Honor*
(see page 536). 1656. The Prado, Madrid

Colorplate 105. NICOLAS POUSSIN. *The Rape of the Sabine Women* (see page 539). About 1636–37. 61 × 82½″. The Metropolitan Museum of Art, New York (Dick Fund, 1946)

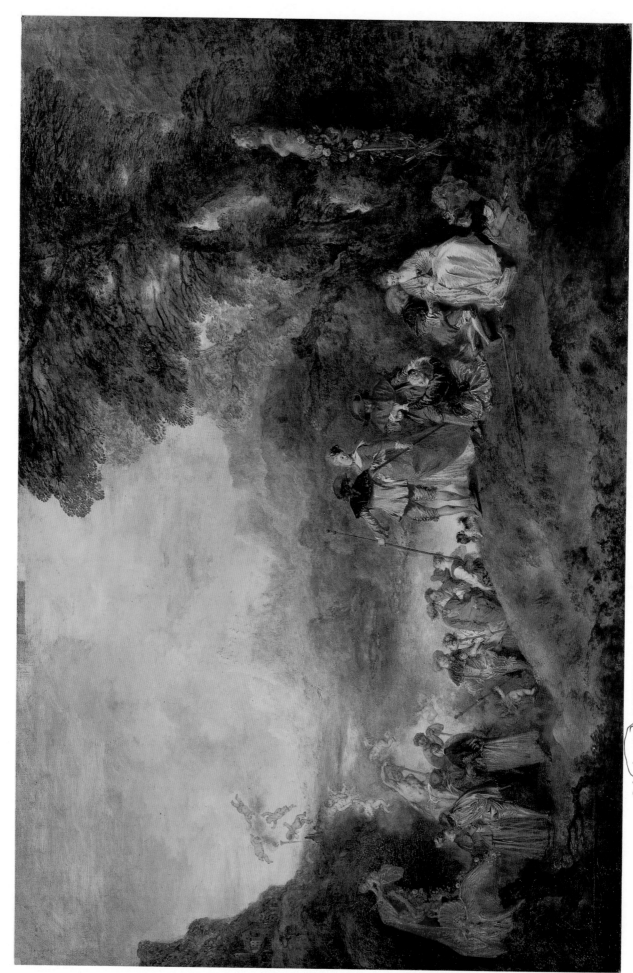

Colorplate 106. ANTOINE WATTEAU. *A Pilgrimage to Cythera* (see page 555). 1717. 4' 3" × 6' 4½". The Louvre, Paris

Colorplate 107. JEAN-HONORÉ FRAGONARD. *Bathers* (see page 557). About 1765. 25¼ × 31½". The Louvre, Paris

Colorplate 108. JEAN-BAPTISTE SIMÉON CHARDIN. *Back from the Market* (see page 557). 1739. 18½ × 14¾″. The Louvre, Paris

767. JULES HARDOUIN-MANSART.
Church of the Invalides, Paris. 1680–91

768. Plan of the
Church of the Invalides

after the institution for disabled soldiers of which it formed one part. The plan, consisting of a Greek cross with four corner chapels, is based ultimately—with various French intermediaries—on Michelangelo's plan for St. Peter's (see fig. 626); its only Baroque element is the oval choir. The dome, too, reflects the influence of Michelangelo (figs. 625, 627), and the classicistic vocabulary of the façade is reminiscent of the East Front of the Louvre. Yet the exterior as a whole is unmistakably Baroque: the façade breaks forward repeatedly in the crescendo effect introduced by Maderno (see fig. 700); and façade and dome are closely correlated (see fig. 712). The dome itself is the most original, and the most Baroque, feature of Hardouin-Mansart's design; tall and slender, it rises in one continuous curve from the base of the drum to the spire atop the lantern. On the first drum rests, surprisingly, a second, narrower drum; its windows provide light for the painted vision of heavenly glory inside the dome, but they themselves are hidden behind a "pseudo-shell" with a large opening at the top, so that the heavenly glory seems mysteriously illuminated and suspended in space; "theatrical" lighting so boldly directed would do honor to any Italian Baroque architect.

Sculpture

The official "royal style" was attained in sculpture by a process much like that in architecture. Bernini, while in Paris, had carved a marble bust of Louis XIV, and had also been commissioned to do an equestrian statue of the king. This project, for which he made a splendid terracotta model (fig. 769), shared the fate of his Louvre designs. Although he portrayed the king in classical military garb, the statue was rejected; apparently it was too dynamic to safeguard the

769. GIANLORENZO BERNINI. *Model for Equestrian Statue of Louis XIV*. 1670. Terracotta, height 30". Borghese Gallery, Rome

770. FRANCOIS GIRARDON. *Model for Equestrian Statue of Louis XIV*. 1687? Wax, height 30¼".
Yale University Art Gallery, New Haven, Connecticut
(Gift of Mr. and Mrs. James W. Fosburgh, 1933)

Lebrun (fig. 771) repeats—again with a certain restraint—the general outlines of Bernini's bust of Louis XIV. The face, however, shows a realism and a subtlety of characterization that are Coysevox' own. He is the first of a long line of distinguished French portrait sculptors.

PUGET. Coysevox approached the Baroque in sculpture as closely as Lebrun would permit. Pierre Puget, the greatest and the most Baroque of French seventeenth-century sculptors, had no success at court until after Colbert's death, when the power of Lebrun was on the decline. *Milo of Crotona* (fig. 772), Puget's finest statue, may safely be compared to one by Bernini. Its composition is more contained than that of Bernini's *David* (see fig. 702), yet the agony of the hero has such force that its impact on the beholder is almost physical; the internal tension fills every particle of marble with intense life. The figure also recalls the *Laocoön Group* (see fig. 207). That, one suspects, is what made it acceptable to Louis XIV.

The Royal Academy

Centralized control over the visual arts was exerted by Colbert and Lebrun not only through the power of the purse; it also included a new system of educating artists in the officially approved style. Throughout antiquity and the Middle Ages, artists had been trained by apprenticeship, and this time-honored practice still prevailed in the Renaissance. But as painting, sculpture, and architecture gained the status of liberal arts, artists wished to supplement their "mechanical" training with theoretical knowledge. For this purpose, "art academies" were founded, patterned on the academies of

dignity of Louis XIV. This decision was far-reaching, for equestrian statues of the king were later erected throughout France as symbols of royal authority, and Bernini's design, had it succeeded, might have set the pattern for these monuments.

GIRARDON. All the equestrian statues were destroyed in the French Revolution; we know them only from engravings, reproductions, and such models as that by François Girardon (fig. 770), who also did much garden sculpture at Versailles. Characteristically, this is an adaptation of the equestrian Marcus Aurelius on the Capitoline Hill (see fig. 269). While it may look static—lame, in fact—next to Bernini's design, its Baroque qualities show up clearly in comparison with its ancient prototype: the fluid modeling, the wind-blown movement of the king's cloak. There is even a hint at an "invisible complement"—instead of looking at us, the king raises his head and leans back as if communicating with some celestial power.

COYSEVOX. Antoine Coysevox, a less self-conscious classicist than Girardon, was another sculptor employed by Lebrun at Versailles. In his large stucco relief in the Salon de la Guerre (see fig. 764), the victorious Louis XIV retains the pose of Bernini's equestrian statue. Coysevox's bust of

771. ANTOINE COYSEVOX. *Charles Lebrun*. 1676.
Terracotta, height 26". Wallace Collection, London

overemphasized color, ranked low, and the Flemish and Dutch lower still. Subjects were similarly classified, from history (classical or biblical) at the top to still life at the bottom.

"POUSSINISTES" VS. "RUBÉNISTES." It is hardly surprising that this straitjacket system produced no significant artists. Even Lebrun, as we have seen, was far more Baroque in his practice than we would expect from his classicistic theory. The absurd rigidity of the official doctrine generated, moreover, a counterpressure that vented itself as soon as Lebrun's authority began to decline. Toward the end of the century, the members of the Academy formed two warring factions over the issue of drawing versus color: the conservatives (or "Poussinistes") against the "Rubénistes." The conservatives defended Poussin's view that drawing, which appealed to the mind, was superior to color, which appealed to the senses; the "Rubénistes" advocated color, rather than drawing, as being more true to nature. They also pointed out that drawing, admittedly based on reason, appeals only to the expert few, whereas color appeals to everyone. This argument had revolutionary implications, for it proclaimed the layman to be the ultimate judge of artistic values, and challenged the Renaissance notion that painting, as a liberal art, could be appreciated only by the educated mind. By the time Louis XIV died, in 1715, the dictatorial powers of the Academy had been overcome, and the influence of Rubens and the great Venetians was everywhere.

WATTEAU. In 1717 the "Rubénistes" scored their final triumph when the painter Antoine Watteau (1684–1721) was admitted to the Academy with his *A Pilgrimage to Cythera* (fig. 773, colorplate 106). This picture violated all academic canons, nor did its subject conform to any established category. But the Academy, now very accommodating, invented for Watteau the new category of *fêtes galantes* (elegant fetes or entertainments). The term refers less to this one canvas

773. ANTOINE WATTEAU. *A Pilgrimage to Cythera* (detail; see colorplate 106). The Louvre, Paris

772. PIERRE PUGET. *Milo of Crotona.* 1671–83. Marble, height 8′ 10½″. The Louvre, Paris

the humanists (the name is derived from the Athenian grove where Plato met with his disciples). Art academies appeared first in Italy, in the later sixteenth century; they seem to have been private associations of artists who met periodically to draw from the model and discuss questions of art theory. These academies later became formal institutions that took over some functions from the guilds, but their teaching was limited and far from systematic.

Such was the Royal Academy of Painting and Sculpture in Paris, founded in 1648; when Lebrun became its director, in 1663, he established a rigid curriculum of compulsory instruction in practice and theory, based on a system of "rules"; this set the pattern for all later academies, including their modern successors, the art schools of today. Much of this body of doctrine was derived from Poussin's views (see pages 539–541) but carried to rationalistic extremes. The Academy even devised a method for tabulating, in numerical grades, the merits of artists past and present in such categories as drawing, expression, and proportion. The ancients received the highest marks, needless to say, then came Raphael and his school, and Poussin; the Venetians, who

774. GERMAIN BOFFRAND. Salon de la Princesse,
Hôtel de Soubise, Paris. Begun 1732

than to the artist's work in general, which mainly shows scenes of elegant society, or comedy actors, in parklike settings. He characteristically interweaves theater and real life so that no clear distinction can be made between the two. The *Pilgrimage to Cythera* includes yet another element—classical mythology: these young couples have come to Cythera, the island of love, to pay homage to Venus (whose garlanded image appears on the far right). They are about to board the boat, accompanied by swarms of cupids.

The scene at once recalls Rubens' *Garden of Love* (compare fig. 727, colorplate 98), but Watteau has added a touch of poignancy, lending them a poetic subtlety reminiscent of Giorgione (see fig. 633, colorplate 79). His figures, too, have not the robust vitality of Rubens'; slim and graceful, they move with the studied assurance of actors who play their roles so superbly that they touch us more than reality ever could. They recapture in Baroque form an earlier ideal of "mannered" elegance (compare figs. 506, 680).

French Rococo

The work of Watteau gives the signal for a shift in French art and French society. After the death of Louis XIV, the centralized administrative machine that Colbert had created ground to a stop. The nobility, hitherto attached to the court at Versailles, were now freer of royal surveillance. Many of them chose not to return to their ancestral châteaux in the provinces, but to live instead in Paris, where they built elegant town houses, known as *hôtels*. Because these city sites were usually cramped and irregular, they offered scant opportunity for impressive exteriors; the layout and décor of the rooms became the architects' main concern. As state-sponsored building activity was declining, the field of "design for private living" took on a new importance. The *hôtels* demanded a style of interior decoration less grandiloquent and cumbersome than Lebrun's—an intimate, flexible style that would give greater scope to individual fancy unin-

hibited by classicistic dogma. French designers created the Rococo (or "the Style of Louis XV," as it is often called in France) in response to this need. The name fits well, although it was coined as a caricature of *rocaille* (echoing the Italian *barocco*), which meant the playful decoration of grottoes with irregular shells and stones. Rococo was a refinement in miniature of the curvilinear, "elastic" Baroque of Borromini and Guarini, and thus could be happily united with Austrian and German Late Baroque architecture (figs. 722, 723, colorplate 97).

BOFFRAND.   Most French examples of the style, such as the Salon de la Princesse in the Hôtel de Soubise, by Germain Boffrand (fig. 774), are smaller in scale and less exuberant than those in Central Europe; the ceiling frescoes and decorative sculpture in palaces and churches are unsuited to domestic interiors, however lavish. We must therefore remember that in France, Rococo painting and sculpture were less closely linked with their architectural setting than in Italy, Austria, and Germany, although they reflect the same taste that produced the Hôtel de Soubise.

CLODION.   Characteristic of Rococo sculpture are small groups like Clodion's *Satyr and Bacchante* (fig. 775), designed to be viewed at close range. Their coquettish eroticism is another form of "miniature Baroque," a playful echo of the ecstasies of Bernini and Puget (compare fig. 703).

FALCONET.   The monumental commissions for French Rococo sculptors were few, but the equestrian statue of Peter the Great, made for Catherine of Russia by Etienne Maurice Falconet (fig. 776), shows that they could recapture something of Baroque grandeur. This impressive example is a

775. CLODION. *Satyr and Bacchante*. c. 1775.
Terracotta, height 23″. The Metropolitan Museum of Art,
New York (Bequest of Benjamin Altman, 1913)

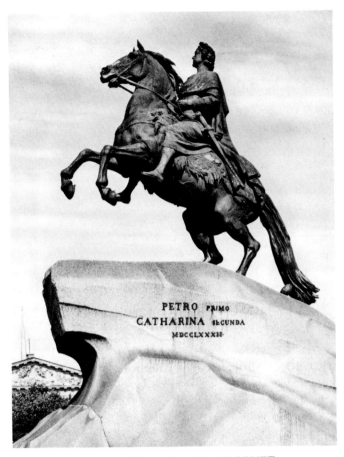

776. ETIENNE MAURICE FALCONET.
Equestrian Monument of Peter the Great.
1766–82. Bronze, over lifesize. Leningrad

splendidly energetic adaptation of Bernini's *Louis XIV* (see fig. 769).

FRAGONARD.   Much Rococo painting is the counterpart of Clodion's sculpture: intimate in scale and deliciously sensual in style and subject, it lacks the emotional depth that distinguishes Watteau's art. The finest painter in this vein was Jean-Honoré Fragonard (1732–1806); his *Bathers* (fig. 777, colorplate 107) must here suffice to represent its class. A franker "Rubéniste" than Watteau, Fragonard paints with a fluid breadth and spontaneity reminiscent of Rubens' oil sketches (see fig. 726). His figures move with a floating grace that also links him with Tiepolo, whose work he had admired in Italy (compare fig. 722). Fragonard had the misfortune to outlive his era; his pictures became outmoded as the Revolution approached. After 1789 he was reduced to poverty, and he died, forgotten, in the heyday of Napoleon. Yet the style he practiced with such mastery had not been the only alternative open to him and the other French painters of his generation.

CHARDIN.   Fragonard's art might have been different had he followed that of his first teacher, Jean-Baptiste Siméon Chardin (1699–1779), whose style can be called Rococo only with reservations. The "Rubénistes" had cleared the way for

a new interest in the Dutch masters as well, and Chardin is the finest painter of still life and genre in this trend. His genre scenes, such as *Back from the Market* (fig. 778, colorplate 108), show life in a Parisian middle-class household with such feeling for the beauty hidden in the commonplace, and so clear a sense of spatial order, that we can compare him only to Vermeer. But his remarkable technique is quite unlike any Dutch artist's. Devoid of bravura, his brushwork renders the light on colored surfaces with a creamy touch that is both analytical and subtly poetic. His still lifes usually reflect the same modest environment, eschewing the "object appeal" of their Dutch predecessors. In the example shown in figure 779, we see only the common objects that belong in any kitchen: earthenware jugs, a casserole, a copper pot, a piece of raw meat, smoked herring, two eggs. But how important they seem, each so firmly placed in relation to the rest, each so worthy of the artist's—and our—scrutiny! Despite his concern with formal problems, evident in the beautifully balanced design, Chardin treats these objects with a respect close to reverence. Beyond their shapes, colors, and textures, they are to him symbols of the life of the common man. In spirit, if not in subject matter, Chardin is more akin to Louis Le Nain and Sanchez Cotán than to any Dutch painter.

VIGÉE-LEBRUN.   It is from portraits that we can gain the clearest understanding of the French Rococo, for the transformation of the image of man lies at the heart of the era. In portraits of the aristocracy, men were endowed with the illusion of character as a natural attribute of their station in life, stemming from their noble birth. But the finest achievements of Rococo portraiture were reserved for women, hardly a surprising fact in a society that idolized the cult of love and feminine beauty. One of the finest practitioners in this vein was herself a beautiful woman: Marie-Louise-Elisabeth Vigée-Lebrun (1755–1842).

Throughout Vigée's long life she enjoyed great fame, which took her to every corner of Europe—even Russia,

777. JEAN-HONORÉ FRAGONARD. *Bathers* (see colorplate 107).
The Louvre, Paris

when she fled the French Revolution. *The Princesse de Polignac* (fig. 780) was painted a few years after Vigée had become the portraitist for Queen Marie Antoinette, and it amply demonstrates her ability. The princess has the eternally youthful loveliness of Fragonard's *Bathers* (fig. 777, colorplate 107), made all the more persuasive by the artist's ravishing treatment of her clothing. At the same time, there is a sense of transience in the engaging mood which exemplifies the Rococo's whimsical theatricality. Interrupted in her singing, the lyrical princess becomes a real-life counterpart to the poetic creatures in Watteau's *Pilgrimage to Cythera* (fig. 773, colorplate 106), by way of the delicate sentiment she shares with the girl in Chardin's *Back from the Market* (fig. 778, colorplate 108).

778. JEAN-BAPTISTE SIMÉON CHARDIN. *Back from the Market* (see colorplate 108). The Louvre, Paris

780. ELISABETH VIGÉE-LEBRUN. *The Princesse de Polignac.* 1783. 38¾ × 28″. The National Trust, Waddesdon Manor (Courtesy the Courtauld Institute of Art, London)

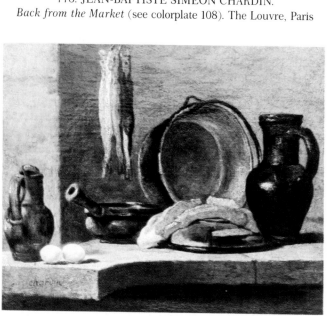

779. JEAN-BAPTISTE SIMÉON CHARDIN. *Kitchen Still Life.* c. 1730–35. 12½ × 15¼″. Ashmolean Museum, Oxford

ENGLAND
Architecture

We have not mentioned English architecture since our discussion of the Perpendicular style (see fig. 441). This insular form of "Late Gothic" proved extraordinarily persistent; it absorbed the stylistic vocabulary of the Italian Renaissance during the sixteenth century, but as late as 1600, English buildings still retained a "Perpendicular syntax"—that is to say, their stage of development corresponded to Chambord, or the choir of St.-Pierre at Caen (see figs. 685, 686).

INIGO JONES. The first architect of the English Renaissance was Inigo Jones (1573–1652). Although he went to Italy about 1600, and again in 1613, he did not bring back the Early Baroque but returned a thorough-going Palladian.

The Banqueting House he built at Whitehall in London (fig. 781) conforms in every respect to the principles in Palladio's treatise, yet does not copy any specific building by Palladio. Symmetrical and self-sufficient, it is, for its date, more like a Renaissance *palazzo* than any other building north of the Alps. Jones' style, supported by Palladio's authority as a theorist, stood as a beacon of classicist orthodoxy in England for two hundred years.

WREN.   This classicism can be seen in some parts of St. Paul's Cathedral (figs. 782–84) by Sir Christopher Wren (1632–1723), the great English architect of the late seven-

781. (*above*) INIGO JONES. West Front, Banqueting House, Whitehall Palace, London. 1619–22

782. (*below*) SIR CHRISTOPHER WREN. Façade of St. Paul's Cathedral, London. 1675–1710

783. (*right*) Plan of St. Paul's

784. (*right, below*) Interior of St. Paul's

785. SIR JOHN VANBRUGH. Blenheim Palace, Woodstock. Begun 1705

teenth century: note the second-story windows and, especially, the dome, which looks like Bramante's Tempietto (see fig. 606, colorplate 76), much enlarged. St. Paul's is otherwise an up-to-date Baroque design reflecting a thorough acquaintance with contemporary architecture in Italy and France. Sir Christopher came close to being a Baroque counterpart of the Renaissance artist-scientist. An intellectual prodigy, he first studied anatomy, then physics, mathematics, and astronomy, and was highly esteemed by Sir Isaac Newton. His serious interest in architecture did not begin until he was about thirty. However—and this seems to be characteristic of the Baroque as opposed to the Renaissance—there is apparently no direct link between his scientific and artistic ideas. (It is hard to determine whether his technological knowledge significantly affected the shape of his buildings.)

Had not the great London fire of 1666 destroyed the Gothic cathedral of St. Paul, and many lesser churches, Sir Christopher might have remained an amateur architect. But following that catastrophe, he was named to the royal commission for rebuilding the city, and a few years later he began his designs for St. Paul's. The tradition of Inigo Jones did not suffice for this task, beyond providing a starting point. On his only trip abroad, Sir Christopher had visited Paris at the time of the dispute over the completion of the Louvre, and he must have sided with Perrault, whose design for the East Front is clearly reflected in the façade of St. Paul's. Yet, despite his belief that Paris provided "the best school of architecture in Europe," Sir Christopher was not indifferent to the achievements of the Roman Baroque. He must have wanted the new St. Paul's to be the St. Peter's of the Church

of England—soberer and not so large, but equally impressive. His dome, like that of St. Peter's, has a diameter as wide as nave and aisles combined, but it rises high above the rest of the structure and dominates even our close view of the façade. The lantern and the upper part of the clock towers also suggest that he knew S. Agnese in Piazza Navona (see fig. 712), probably from drawings or engravings.

Italian Baroque elements are still more conspicuous in Blenheim Palace (fig. 785), designed by Sir John Vanbrugh (1664–1726); the grandiose structure was presented by a grateful nation to the victorious Duke of Marlborough. Vanbrugh, like Bernini, had a strong interest in the theater (he was a popular playwright). Their kinship seems even closer when we compare the façade of Blenheim, its colossal order and framing colonnade, with the piazza of St. Peter's (see fig. 700).

Painting

The development of English seventeenth-century architecture thus follows the French pattern: toward 1700, the High Baroque wins out over a classicistic tradition. Yet England never accepted the subsequent Rococo. The pomp of Blenheim soon became the object of satire, and the second quarter of the eighteenth century produced a Palladianism more rationalistic than Inigo Jones' and, at that time, unique in all Europe (see fig. 792). But French Rococo painting, from Watteau to Fragonard, had a decisive—though unacknowledged—effect across the Channel and helped, in fact, to bring about the first school of English painting since the Middle Ages that had more than local importance.

786. WILLIAM HOGARTH. *The Orgy*, Scene III of *The Rake's Progress*. c. 1734. 24½ × 29½"
Sir John Soane's Museum, London

HOGARTH. The earliest of these painters, William Hogarth (1697–1764), made his mark in the 1730s with a new kind of picture, which he described as "modern moral subjects...similar to representations on the stage." He wished to be judged as a dramatist, he said, even though his "actors" could only "exhibit a dumb show." These pictures, and the engravings he made from them for popular sale, came in sets, with details recurring in each scene to unify the sequence. Hogarth's "morality plays" teach, by horrid example, the solid middle-class virtues: they show a country girl who succumbs to the temptations of fashionable London; the evils of corrupt elections; aristocratic rakes who live only for ruinous pleasure, marrying wealthy women of lower status for their fortunes (which they soon dissipate).

In *The Orgy* (figs. 786, 787), from *The Rake's Progress*, the young wastrel is overindulging in wine and women. The scene is so full of visual clues that a full account would take pages, plus constant references to the adjoining episodes. Yet, however literal-minded, the picture has great appeal. Hogarth combines some of Watteau's sparkle with Jan Steen's narrative gusto (compare figs. 773, 748), and so entertains us that we enjoy his sermon without being overwhelmed by its message. He is probably the first artist in history to become a social critic in his own right.

787. WILLIAM HOGARTH. *He Revels (The Orgy)*, Scene III of *The Rake's Progress*. 1735. Engraving. The Metropolitan Museum of Art, New York (Harris Brisbane Dick Fund, 1932)

GAINSBOROUGH. Portraiture remained the only constant source of income for English painters. Here too, the eighteenth century produced a style that differed from the continental traditions that had dominated this field. Its greatest master, Thomas Gainsborough (1727–1788), began by painting landscapes, but ended as the favorite portraitist of British high society. His early portraits, such as *Robert Andrews and His Wife* (fig. 788, colorplate 109), have a lyrical charm that is not always found in his later pictures. Compared to Van Dyck's artifice in *Charles I Hunting* (see fig. 729, colorplate 99), this country squire and his wife are unpretentiously at home in their setting. The landscape, although derived from Ruisdael and his school, has a sunlit, hospitable air never achieved (or desired) by the Dutch masters; and the casual grace of the two figures indirectly recalls Watteau's style. Later portraits by Gainsborough, such as the very fine one of the great actress Mrs. Siddons (fig. 789), have other virtues: a cool elegance that translates Van Dyck's aristocratic poses into late-eighteenth-century terms, and a fluid, translucent technique reminiscent of Rubens.

REYNOLDS.   Gainsborough painted *Mrs. Siddons* in conscious opposition to his great rival on the London scene, Sir Joshua Reynolds (1723–1792), who just before had portrayed the same sitter as the Tragic Muse (fig. 790). Reynolds, the President of the Royal Academy since its founding in 1768, was the protagonist of the academic approach to art, which he had acquired during two years in Rome. Like his French predecessors, he formulated in his famous *Discourses* what he felt were necessary rules and theories. His views were essentially those of Lebrun, tempered by British common sense. Again like Lebrun, he found it difficult to live up to his theories in actual practice. Although he preferred history painting in the grand style, the vast majority of his works are portraits "enabled," whenever possible, by allegorical additions or disguises like those in his picture of Mrs. Siddons. His style owed a good deal more to the Venetians, the Flemish Baroque, and even to Rembrandt (note the lighting in his *Mrs. Siddons*) than he conceded in theory. The best that can be said of Reynolds is that he almost succeeded in

789. THOMAS GAINSBOROUGH. *Mrs. Siddons.* 1785.
49½ × 39″. The National Gallery, London

788. THOMAS GAINSBOROUGH.
Robert Andrews and His Wife (detail; see colorplate 109).
The National Gallery, London

making painting respectable in England as a liberal art (he received an honorary doctorate from Oxford), but at what cost! His *Discourses*, which soon became standard, inhibited the visual capacity of generations of students in England and America. He was generous enough to give praise to Gainsborough, whom he outlived by a few years, and whose instinctive talent he must have envied.

For all of the differences between them, Reynolds and Gainsborough had more in common than they cared to admit. Both of their portraits of Mrs. Siddons bear an unmistakable relationship to the Rococo style of France—note their resemblance to Vigée's *Princess* (fig. 780)—yet remain distinctly English in character.

Sculpture

English sculpture has not been discussed in these pages since that of the thirteenth century (see fig. 464). During the Reformation, it will be recalled, there was a wholesale destruction of sculpture in England. This had so chilling an effect that for two hundred years the demand for statuary of any kind was too low to sustain more than the most modest local production. With the rise of a vigorous English school of painting, however, sculptural patronage grew as well, and during the eighteenth century England set an example for the rest of Europe in creating the "monument to genius"—statues in public places honoring culture heroes such as Shakespeare, a privilege hitherto reserved for heads of state.

ROUBILIAC.   One of the earliest and most ingratiating of these statues is that of the great composer George Frederick Handel (fig. 791), by the French-born Louis-François Roubiliac (1702–1762). It was also the first to be made of a culture hero within his lifetime (the next to achieve this distinction would be Voltaire in France, a full generation later; see fig. 849). Roubiliac carved the figure in 1738 for the owner of Vauxhall Gardens in London, a pleasure park with dining facilities and an orchestra stand where Handel's music was often performed, so that the statue served two purposes: homage and advertising. Handel is in the guise of Apollo, the god of music, playing a classical lyre; a putto at his feet writes down the divine music. But Handel is a most domestic Apollo, in slippers and a worn dressing gown, a soft beret

791. LOUIS-FRANÇOIS ROUBILIAC. *George Frederick Handel.* 1738. Marble, lifesize. Victoria & Albert Museum, London (Crown copyright reserved)

on his head instead of the then customary wig. Although Roubiliac shows himself in full command of the Baroque sculptural tradition, the studied informality of his deified *Handel* seems peculiarly English: touches such as the right foot resting upon rather than inside the slipper (a hint at the composer's gouty big toe?) suggest that he sought advice from Hogarth, with whom he was on excellent terms. Be that as it may, *Handel* was Roubiliac's first big success in his adopted homeland, and it became the forebear of countless monuments to culture heroes everywhere (see fig. 891).

790. SIR JOSHUA REYNOLDS. *Mrs. Siddons as the Tragic Muse.* 1784. 93 × 57½". Henry E. Huntington Library and Art Gallery, San Marino, California

ILLUSTRATED TIME CHART III

POLITICAL HISTORY, RELIGION	LITERATURE, SCIENCE, TECHNOLOGY

1300

Papacy in Avignon 1309–76
Hundred Years War, France and England 1337–1453
Black Death throughout Europe 1347–50

Petrarch, first humanist (1304–74)
Boccaccio (1313–75)

1400

Death of Giangaleazzo Visconti of Milan (1402) removes threat to political independence of Florence
Joan of Arc burned at stake for heresy and sorcery 1431
Cosimo de'Medici, leading citizen of Florence 1434–64
Council of Florence attempts to reunite Catholic and Orthodox faiths 1439

Leonardo Bruni (c. 1374–1444); *History of Florence*
Prince Henry the Navigator of Portugal (1394–1460) promotes geographic exploration
Leon Battista Alberti (1404–72), *On Architecture; On Painting*
Earliest record of suction pump c. 1440

Masaccio, *Trinity* fresco

Master of Flémalle, *Mérode Altar*

Jan van Eyck, *Man in Red Turban*

1450

Hapsburg rule of Holy Roman Empire begins 1452
Constantinople falls to Turks 1453
Pico della Mirandola, Neo-Platonist (1463–94)
Lorenzo de'Medici, "the Magnificent," virtual ruler of Florence 1469–92
Pius II, humanist pope (r. 1458–64)
Ferdinand and Isabella unite Spain 1469
Granada, last Moslem stronghold in Spain, falls 1492
Spain and Portugal divide southern New World 1493–94
Cabot claims eastern North America for England 1497
Charles VIII of France invades Italy 1494–99
Henry VII (r. 1485–1509), first Tudor king of England
Savonarola virtual ruler of Florence 1494; burned at stake for heresy 1498

Alberti, S. Francesco, Rimini

François Villon, French poet (born c. 1431)
Marsilio Ficino, Italian Neo-Platonic philosopher (1433–99)
Refugees from Constantinople bring Greek manuscripts to Italy after 1453
Diaz rounds Cape of Good Hope 1486
Columbus discovers America 1492
Sebastian Brant, *Ship of Fools* 1494
Vasco da Gama reaches India, returns to Lisbon 1497–99

Pollaiuolo, *Battle of Ten Naked Men*

Hugo van der Goes, *Portinari Altar*

1500

— 1300

— 1400

Nanni di Banco, *Four Crowned Saints*
Donatello, *St. Mark; St. George*
Brunelleschi begins career as architect 1419,
    Florence Cathedral dome. Subsequently, all
    in Florence: S. Lorenzo; Pazzi Chapel; S. Spirito;
    Sta. Maria degli Angeli
Donatello, *Zuccone; Feast of Herod*
Masaccio, *Trinity* fresco; Brancacci
    Chapel frescoes
Master of Flémalle, *Mérode Altar*
Jacopo della Quercia, portal of S. Petronio, Bologna
Donatello, *David*
Jan van Eyck, *Ghent Altar; Man in Red
    Turban*
Rogier van der Weyden, *Descent from
    the Cross*
Ghiberti, "*Gates of Paradise,*" Baptistery,
    Florence
Luca della Robbia, *Cantoria*
Filippo Lippi, *Madonna*
Fra Angelico, S. Marco frescoes, Florence
Conrad Witz, *Geneva Altar*
Michelozzo, Palazzo Medici-Riccardi,
    Florence
Domenico Veneziano, *Madonna and Saints*
Donatello, *Gattamelata*, Padua
Bernardo Rossellino, Tomb of Leonardo
    Bruni, Sta. Croce, Florence
Castagno, *Last Supper*
Alberti, Palazzo Rucellai, Florence

Donatello, *David*

Nanni di Banco, *Four Crowned Saints*

Fra Angelico, S. Marco frescoes

— 1450

Alberti, S. Francesco, Rimini; S. Andrea,
    Mantua
Donatello, *Magdalen*
Mantegna, Ovetari Chapel frescoes,
    Padua
Antonio Rossellino, *Giovanni Chellini*
Piero della Francesca, Arezzo frescoes
Pollaiuolo, *Battle of Ten Naked Men*, en-
    graving
Pacher, *St. Wolfgang Altar*
Pollaiuolo, *Hercules and Antaeus*
Hugo van der Goes, *Portinari Altar*
Schongauer, *Temptation of St. Anthony*,
    engraving
Botticelli, *Birth of Venus*
Leonardo, *Adoration of the Magi*
Perugino, *Delivery of the Keys*, Sistine
    Chapel, Rome
Verrocchio, *Colleoni*, Venice
Giuliano da Sangallo, Sta. Maria delle
    Carceri, Prato
Giovanni Bellini, *St. Francis*
Leonardo, *Virgin of the Rocks*
Dürer, *Four Horsemen of the Apocalypse*,
    woodcut

Leonardo, *Virgin of the Rocks*

Verrocchio, *Colleoni*

— 1500

1500

Erasmus of Rotterdam, *In Praise of Folly* 1511

Martin Luther (1483–1546) posts 95 theses 1517; excommunicated 1521

Charles V elected Holy Roman Emperor 1519; Sack of Rome 1527

Cortés wins Aztec empire in Mexico for Spain 1519; Pizarro conquers Peru 1532

Suleiman the Magnificent ascends Turkish throne 1520; threatens Vienna 1525

Machiavelli, *The Prince* 1532

Henry VIII of England (r. 1509–47) founds Anglican Church 1534

Peasants' Revolt in Germany 1524–25

Ignatius of Loyola founds Jesuit order 1534

John Calvin, *Institutes of the Christian Religion* 1536

Wars of Lutheran vs. Catholic princes in Germany; Peace of Augsburg (1555) lets each sovereign decide religion of his subjects

Bramante, Tempietto

Balboa sights Pacific Ocean 1513

Thomas More, *Utopia* 1516

Portuguese reach China 1516; Japan 1543

First circumnavigation of the globe by Magellan and crew 1520–22

Castiglione, *The Courtier* 1528

François Rabelais, French writer, *Gargantua* 1532

Paracelsus, Swiss alchemist (1493–1541)

Copernicus refutes geocentric view of universe 1543

Vesalius, *De Humani Corporis Fabrica* 1543

Michelangelo, Sistine Ceiling

1550

Council of Trent for Catholic reform 1545–63

St. Francis Xavier, Jesuit missionary, dies in Goa, India 1552

Alexander Knox founds Presbyterian Church 1560

St. Theresa of Avila, Spanish saint (1515–82)

Giordano Bruno (1548–1600) burned at the stake for heresy in Venice

Ivan the Terrible of Russia (r. 1547–84)

Charles V retires 1556; son Philip II king of Spain, Netherlands, New World

Elizabeth I of England (r. 1558–1603)

Turkish sea power crushed at Lepanto 1571

Netherlands revolt against Spain 1568; northern provinces declare independence 1581

Spanish Armada defeated by English 1588

Henry IV of France (r. 1589–1610) Edict of Nantes (1598) establishes religious toleration

Lutheranism state religion in Denmark 1560

Montaigne, French essayist (1533–92)

Agricola, *De re metallica* 1556

Vasari, *Lives* 1564

Tycho Brahe, Danish astronomer (1546–1601)

Sir Philip Sidney, English poet (1554–86)

Francis Bacon, English writer (1561–1626)

Christopher Marlowe, English dramatist (1564–93)

William Shakespeare (1564–1616)

Hilliard, *Young Man Among Roses*, miniature

1600

English East India Company founded 1600; Dutch East India Company 1602

Jamestown, Virginia, founded 1607

King James Bible 1611

Romanov dynasty founded in Russia 1613

Thirty Years' War 1618–48

William Bradford (1590–1657), governor of Plymouth Colony (founded 1620)

Cardinal Richelieu, adviser to Louis XIII, consolidates power of king 1624–42

Japanese isolation against all Europeans except token Dutch begins 1639

Cardinal Mazarin governs France during minority of Louis XIV 1643–61

Charles I of England beheaded 1649; Commonwealth 1649–53

Poussin, *Cephalus and Aurora*

Cervantes, *Don Quixote* 1605–1615

Johannes Kepler establishes planetary system 1609–1619

Napier's treatise on logarithms 1614

Harvey describes circulation of blood 1628

Galileo (1564–1642) invents telescope 1609; establishes scientific method

John Donne, English poet (1572–1631)

René Descartes (1596–1650), *Discourse on Method*

Pierre Corneille, French dramatist (1606–84)

Harvard College founded 1636

Torricelli measures pressure of atmosphere 1644

Royal Academy of Paris founded 1648

1650

Bellini, *Madonna and Saints*

Bosch, *Garden of Delights*
Michelangelo, *David*
Bramante, Tempietto, new St. Peter's, Rome
Leonardo, *Mona Lisa*
Giorgione, *Tempest*
Michelangelo, Sistine Ceiling, Rome
Raphael, *School of Athens*, Rome
Grünewald, *Isenheim Altar*
Michelangelo, *Moses* and two "*Slaves*"
Titian, *Bacchanal*
Château of Chambord, France
Rosso, *Descent from the Cross*
Michelangelo, Medici tombs; Laurentian
    Library, Florence
Dürer, *Four Apostles*
Correggio, *Assumption of the Virgin*
Altdorfer, *Battle of Issus*
Parmigianino, *Madonna with Long Neck*
Clouet, *Francis I*
Holbein, *Henry VIII*
Titian, *Paul III and Grandsons*
Michelangelo begins Campidoglio, Rome
    1537–39; architect of St. Peter's 1546
Lescot, Square Court, Louvre, Paris
Goujon, *Fontaine des Innocents*, Paris

Grünewald, *Isenheim Altar*

Clouet, *Francis I*

Michelangelo, *Milan Pietà* (last work)
Ammanati, Palazzo Pitti courtyard, Florence
Hilliard, *Young Man Among Roses*, miniature
Vasari, Uffizi, Florence
Pilon, Tomb of Henry II, Paris
Bruegel, *Peasant Wedding*
Palladio, S. Giorgio Maggiore, Venice;
    Villa Rotonda, Vicenza
Vignola and Della Porta, Il Gesù, Rome
Veronese, *Christ in the House of Levi*
El Greco, *Burial of Count Orgaz*
Tintoretto, *Last Supper*
Giovanni Bologna, *Rape of Sabine
    Woman*
Caravaggio, *Calling of St. Matthew*
Annibale Carracci, Farnese Gallery ceil-
    ing, Rome

Palladio, Villa Rotonda

Rubens, *Raising of the Cross*

Maderno, nave and façade of St. Peter's,
    Rome; Bernini's colonnade
Rubens, *Raising of the Cross*
Reni, *Aurora*
Jones, Banqueting House, London
Guercino, *Aurora*
Bernini, *David*
Hals, *Jolly Toper*
Pietro da Cortona, Palazzo Barberini ceiling, Rome
Van Dyck, *Charles I Hunting*
Borromini, S. Carlo alle Quattro Fontane, Rome
Borromini, S. Ivo, Rome
Rembrandt, *Night Watch*
F. Mansart, Château of Maisons, France
Bernini, Cornaro Chapel, Rome
Poussin, *Cephalus and Aurora*

Borromini, S. Ivo, Rome

Time Chart III 567

POLITICAL HISTORY, RELIGION	LITERATURE, SCIENCE, TECHNOLOGY	PAINTING, SCULPTURE, ARCHITECTURE

1650

Charles II restores English monarchy 1660
Jacques Bossuet, French orator (1627–1704)
Spinoza, Dutch philosopher (1632–77)
Society of Friends (Quakers) founded 1668
English Parliament passes Habeas Corpus Act 1679
Frederick William, the Great Elector (r. 1640–88), founds power of Prussia
Louis XIV absolute ruler of France (r. 1661–1715); revokes Edict of Nantes 1685
Glorious Revolution against James II of England 1688; Bill of Rights

Le Vau and Hardouin-Mansart, Versailles

Thomas Hobbs, *Leviathan* 1651
Molière, French dramatist (1622–73)
Pascal, French scientist and philosopher (1623–62)

Velázquez, *Maids of Honor*

Boyle's Law of gas pressure 1662
Royal Society, London, founded 1662
Great Fire and Plague of London 1665–66
Milton, *Paradise Lost* 1667
Isaac Newton, theory of gravity 1687
John Locke, *Essay Concerning Human Understanding*, 1690
Racine, *Phèdre* 1677
Bunyan, *Pilgrim's Progress* 1678
Leibniz, German philosopher (1646–1716)

Ruisdael, *Jewish Cemetery*
Velázquez, *Maids of Honor*
Bernini, *Throne of St. Peter*
Rembrandt, *Prodigal Son*
Steen, *The Eve of St. Nicholas*
Vermeer, *The Letter*
Perrault, east front of Louvre, Paris
Bernini, Model for equestrian statue of Louis XIV
Guarini, Chapel of Holy Shroud, Turin
Puget, *Milo of Crotona*
Coysevox, *Charles Lebrun*
Wren, St. Paul's, London
Le Vau and Hardouin-Mansart, Versailles, begun 1669
Guarini, Palazzo Carignano, Turin

1700

Peter the Great (r. 1682–1725) westernizes Russia, defeats Sweden
English and allies defeat French at Blenheim 1704
Robert Walpole first prime minister 1721–42
Wesley brothers found Methodism 1738
Frederick the Great of Prussia defeats Austria 1740–45

Gainsborough, *Mrs. Siddons*

Alexander Pope, *Rape of the Lock* 1714
Defoe, *Robinson Crusoe* 1719
Swift, *Gulliver's Travels* 1726
John Gay, *The Beggar's Opera* 1728
Linnaeus, *Systema Naturae* 1737
Giovanni Battista Vico, Italian historian (1668–1744)
Pompeii and Herculaneum discovered 1745
Montesquieu, *Spirit of Laws* 1748

Prandtauer, Monastery at Melk
Vanbrugh, Blenheim Palace
Fischer von Erlach, St. Charles, Vienna
Watteau, *Pilgrimage to Cythera*
Neumann, Episcopal Palace, Würzburg
Boffrand, Hôtel de Soubise
Hogarth, *Rake's Progress*
Chardin, *Back from the Market*

Hogarth, *Rake's Progress*

1750

Seven Years' War (1756–63): England and Prussia vs. Austria and France, called French and Indian War in America; French defeated in battle of Quebec 1769
Catherine the Great (r. 1762–96) extends Russian power to Black Sea
Partition of Poland among Russia, Prussia, Austria 1772–95
American Revolution begins 1775
French Revolution begins 1789

Tiepolo, Würzburg ceiling fresco

Voltaire, *Candide* 1759
James Watt patents steam engine 1769
Edward Jenner demonstrates smallpox vaccine 1796

Tiepolo, Würzburg ceiling fresco
Fragonard, *Bathers*
Falconet, equestrian monument of Peter the Great
Vigée-Lebrun, *Princesse de Polignac*
Zimmermann, "Die Wies," Bavaria
Gainsborough, *Mrs. Siddons*

1800

PART FOUR

THE

INTRODUCTION

The era to which we ourselves belong has not yet acquired a name of its own. Perhaps this does not strike us as peculiar at first—we are, after all, still in midstream—but considering how promptly the Renaissance coined a name for itself, we may well ponder the fact that no key concept comparable to the "rebirth of antiquity" has emerged in the two hundred years since our era began. It is tempting to make "revolution" such a concept, because rapid and violent change has indeed characterized the modern world. Yet we cannot discern a common impulse behind these developments, for the modern era began with revolutions of two kinds: the industrial revolution, symbolized by the invention of the steam engine, and the political revolution, under the banner of democracy, in America and France.

Both of these revolutions are still going on; industrialization and democracy, as goals, are sought all over the world. Western science and Western political ideology (and, in their wake, all the other products of modern Western civilization—food, dress, art, music, literature) will soon belong to all mankind. These two movements are so closely linked today that we tend to think of them as different aspects of one process—with effects more far-reaching than any since the Neolithic Revolution ten thousand years ago. Still, the twin revolutions of modern times are not the same; the more we try to define their relationship, and to trace its historic roots, the more paradoxical it seems. Both are founded on the idea

MODERN WORLD

of progress, and command an emotional allegiance that once was reserved for religion; but whereas progress in science during the past two centuries has been continuous and palpable, we can hardly make this claim for man's pursuit of happiness, however we choose to define it.

Here, then, is the conflict fundamental to our era. Man today, having cast off the framework of traditional authority which confined and sustained him before, can act with a latitude both frightening and exhilarating. In a world where all values may be questioned, man searches constantly for his own identity, and for the meaning of human existence, individual and collective. His knowledge about himself is now vastly greater, but this has not reassured him as he had hoped. Modern civilization thus lacks the cohesiveness of the past; it no longer proceeds by readily identifiable periods, nor are there clear period styles to be discerned in art or in any form of endeavor.

Instead, we find a continuity of another kind, that of movements and countermovements. Spreading like waves, these "isms" defy national, ethnic, and chronological boundaries; never dominant anywhere for long, they compete or merge with each other in endlessly shifting patterns. Hence our account of modern art will be by movements rather than by countries. Only in this way can we hope to do justice to the fact that modern art, all regional differences notwithstanding, is as international as modern science.

ARCTIC OCEAN

ICELAND

NORWAY

SWEDEN

FINLAND

Oslo

Leningrad

NORTH SEA
ENGLAND

BALTIC SEA

VOLGA R.

Moscow

U. S. S. R.

RUSSIA

SIBERIA

YENISEY R.

OB R.

LENA R.

KAMCHATKA

NETHERLANDS

BELGIUM
FRANCE

BAY OF
BISCAY

ITALY

BLACK SEA

Madrid
SPAIN

Barcelona

CHIOS

TURKEY

MONGOLIA

CHINA

Peking

KOREA

JAPAN

Kyoto

Tokyo

MEDITERRANEAN SEA

NEAR EAST

SYRIA

TIGRIS R.

EUPHRATES R.

MIDDLE EAST

Teheran

AFGHANISTAN

INDUS R.

GANDHĀRA

Lahore

YELLOW R. (HWANG HO)

SZECHWAN

YANGTZE R.

Shanghai

Nara
Osaka

YELLOW SEA

EAST CHINA SEA

MOROCCO

ALGERIA

LIBYA

Cairo

EGYPT

JORDAN
ISRAEL

IRAN

PAKISTAN

Mohenjo-
Daro

Mathurā

GANGES R.

Sārnāth

FAR EAST

TAIWAN

PACIFIC OCEAN

MAURITANIA

A

F

R

NIGER R.

PERSIAN
GULF

SAUDI
ARABIA

RED SEA

NILE R.

Sānchī

Calcutta

Ajantā

Elurā

INDIA

Hong Kong

ARABIAN SEA

BAY OF
BENGAL

VIETNAM

SOUTH
CHINA SEA

PHILIPPINES

NIGERIA

Ife

BENIN

GULF OF GUINEA

CAMEROON

ETHIOPIA

SOMALIA

CEYLON

MALAYSIA

GAZELLE
PENINSULA

NEW BRITAIN

GABON

CONGO

CONGO R.

ZAÏRE

Kinshasa

KENYA

EQUATOR

INDONESIA

SEPIK R.

NEW
GUINEA

ANGOLA

ZAMBIA

TANZANIA

MOZAMBIQUE

WESTERN
ARNHEM LAND

SOUTH
AFRICA

MADAGASCAR

INDIAN OCEAN

AUSTRALIA

SOUTH
ATLANTIC
OCEAN

Perth

Sydney
Canberra
Melbourne

SCOTLAND

Glasgow

Edinburgh

Liverpool

Manchester

DENMARK

Humlebaek
Copenhagen

Neukirchen

RUSSIA

U.S.S.R.

Cambridge

Amsterdam

Hamburg

POLAND

IRELAND

Birmingham

Twickenham

The
Hague

ENGLAND

London

Hanover

Arnhem

GERMANY

Berlin

Dessau

Dresden

Weimar

CZECHOSLOVAKIA

ATLANTIC
OCEAN

Brighton

Ghent

Utrecht

Cologne

Hanau am Main

Vienna

ROMANIA

Antwerp

Brussels

Frankfurt

Munich

AUSTRIA

HUNGARY

DANUBE R.

Paris

Poissy-
sur-Seine

Barbizon

Ornans

Ronchamp

Basel Zurich

Lucerne

Bern

Arcole

SWITZERLAND

LOMBARDY

Milan

YUGOSLAVIA

Missolonghi

FRANCE

Bordeaux

Montpellier

PROVENCE

Aix Arles

Marseilles

ITALY

Herculaneum

Pompeii

Rome

Paestum

CORFU

GREECE

Athens

BAY OF
BISCAY

SPAIN

Guernica

1
NEOCLASSICISM
AND
ROMANTICISM

The history of the two movements to be dealt with in this chapter covers roughly a century, from about 1750 to 1850. Long regarded as opposites, the two seem today so interdependent that we should prefer a single name for both, if we could find a suitable one. ("Romantic Classicism" has not won wide acceptance.) The difficulty is that the two terms are unevenly matched—like "quadruped" and "carnivore." Neoclassicism is a new revival of classical antiquity, more consistent than earlier classicisms, while Romanticism refers not to a specific style but to an attitude of mind that may reveal itself in any number of ways.

Romanticism, therefore, is a far broader concept and correspondingly harder to define. The word derives from the late-eighteenth-century vogue for medieval tales of adventure (such as the legends of King Arthur or the Holy Grail, called

"romances" because they were written in a Romance language, not in Latin). But this interest in the long-neglected "Gothick" past was symptomatic of a general revulsion against the established social order and established religion—against established values of any sort—that sprang from a craving for emotional experience. Almost any experience would do, real or imaginary, provided it was sufficiently intense.

The declared aim of the Romantics, however, was to tear down the artifices barring the way to a "return to Nature"—nature the unbounded, wild and ever-changing, nature the sublime and picturesque. Were man to behave "naturally," giving his impulses free rein, evil would disappear and his happiness would be perfect. In the name of nature, the Romantic worshiped liberty, power, love, violence, the

792. LORD BURLINGTON and WILLIAM KENT.
Chiswick House, near London. Begun 1725

793. Plan of Chiswick House

Greeks, the Middle Ages, or anything that aroused his response, while actually he worshiped emotion as an end in itself. At its extreme, this attitude could be expressed only through direct action, not through works of art. (It has motivated some of the noblest—and vilest—acts of our era.) No artist, then, can be a wholehearted Romantic, for the creation of a work of art demands some detachment and self-awareness. What Wordsworth, the great Romantic poet, said of poetry in 1798—that it is "emotion recollected in tranquillity"—applies also to the visual arts.

To cast his fleeting experience into permanent form, the Romantic artist needs a style. But since he is in revolt against the old order, this cannot be the established style of his time; it must come from some phase of the past to which he feels linked by "elective affinity" (another Romantic concept). Romanticism thus favors the revival, not of one style, but of a potentially unlimited number of styles. Revivals, in fact—the rediscovery and utilization of forms hitherto neglected or disliked—became a stylistic principle: the "style" of Romanticism in art (also, to a degree, in literature and music).

Neoclassicism, seen in this context, is no more than an aspect of Romanticism. We have put it in the title of the present chapter only because, until about 1800, it loomed larger than the other Romantic revivals.

ARCHITECTURE

Given the individualistic nature of Romanticism, we might expect the range of revival styles to be widest in painting, the most personal and private of the visual arts, and least wide in architecture, the most communal and public. Yet the opposite is true. Painters and sculptors were unable to abandon Renaissance habits of representation, and never really revived medieval art, or ancient art before the classic era. Architects were not subject to this limitation, and the revival styles persisted longer in architecture than in the other arts. Let us then begin our survey with architecture, even though we shall have to omit some of the less significant architectural revivals.

Palladian England

England was the birthplace of Romanticism. The earliest sign of this attitude was the Palladian revival in the 1720s, sponsored by a wealthy amateur, Lord Burlington. Chiswick House (figs. 792, 793), adapted from the Villa Rotonda (see figs. 660, 661), is compact, simple, and geometric—the antithesis of the Baroque pomp of Blenheim Palace. What distinguishes this style from earlier classicisms is less its external appearance than its motivation: instead of merely reasserting the superior authority of the ancients, it claimed to satisfy the demands of reason, and thus to be more "natural" than the Baroque. This rationalism explains the oddly abstract, segmented look of Chiswick House—the surfaces are flat and unbroken, the ornament is meager, the temple portico juts out too abruptly from the blocklike body of the structure.

THE ENGLISH GARDEN.   Should such a villa be set in a geometric, formal garden, like Le Nôtre's at Versailles (see fig. 766)? Indeed not, Lord Burlington and his circle maintained; that would be unnatural, hence contrary to reason. So they invented what became known all over Europe as "the English landscape garden." Carefully planned to look unplanned, with winding paths, irregularly spaced clumps of trees, and little lakes and rivers instead of symmetrical

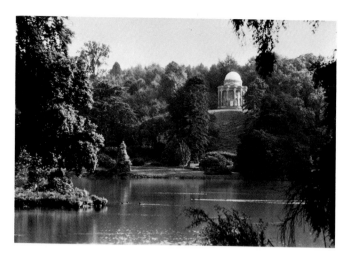

794. HENRY FLITCROFT and HENRY HOARE.
Landscape Garden with Temple of Apollo,
Stourhead, England. 1744–65

Rationalist France

SOUFFLOT. The rationalist movement against the Baroque (or, rather, against the Rococo) came somewhat later in France. Its first great monument, the Panthéon in Paris, by Jacques Germain Soufflot (1713–1780), was built as the church of Ste.-Geneviève, but secularized during the Revolution (fig. 795). Its dome, interestingly enough, is derived from St. Paul's Cathedral in London (see fig. 782), indicating England's new importance for continental architects. The smooth, sparsely decorated surfaces are abstractly severe, akin to those of Chiswick House, while the huge portico is modeled directly on ancient Roman temples. From this coolly precise exterior we would never suspect that Soufflot also had a strong interest in Gothic churches. He admired them, not for the seeming miracles they perform but for their structural elegance—a rationalist version of Guarini's point of view (see fig. 715). His ideal, in fact, was "to combine the classic orders with the lightness so

basins and canals, the "reasonable" garden must seem as unbounded, as full of surprise and variety, as nature itself. It must, in a word, be "picturesque," like the landscapes of Claude Lorraine (which English landscape architects now took as their source of inspiration), and include little temples half concealed by the shrubbery, or artificial ruins, "to draw sorrowful reflections from the soul."

Such sentiments were not new; they had often been expressed before in poetry and painting. But to project them onto nature itself, through planned irregularity, was a new idea. The landscape garden, a work of art intended *not* to look like a work of art, blurred the long-established demarcation between artifice and reality, and thus set an important precedent for the revival styles to come. After all, the landscape garden stands in the same relation to nature as a synthetic ruin to an authentic one, an imitation to a genuine folk song, or a Neoclassic or Neo-Gothic building to its ancient or medieval model. When the fashion spread to the other side of the Channel, it was welcomed not merely as a new way to lay out gardens, but as a vehicle of Romantic emotion.

Of all the landscape gardens laid out in England in the mid-eighteenth century, that at Stourhead most nearly retains its original appearance. Its creators, the banker Henry Hoare and the designer Henry Flitcroft, were both enthusiastic followers of Lord Burlington and William Kent; Stourhead is unique not only for its fine preservation but also for the owner's active role in planning every detail of its development. Our view (fig. 794) is across a small lake made by damming the river Stour; high on the far shore is the Temple of Apollo modeled on the Temple of Venus at Baalbek (see fig. 250), which became known in the West only after 1757. Occupying other focal points at Stourhead are a grotto, a Temple of Venus, a Pantheon, a genuine Gothic cross, and a neo-medieval tower built to commemorate King Alfred the Great, "the Father of His People."

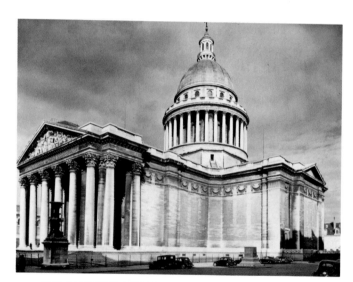

795. JACQUES GERMAIN SOUFFLOT. The Panthéon
(Ste.-Geneviève), Paris. 1755–92

796. ÉTIENNE-LOUIS BOULLÉE.
Project for a Memorial to Isaac Newton. 1784.
Ink and wash drawing, 15½ × 25½".
Bibliothèque Nationale, Paris

797. ROBERT ADAM. Front Drawing Room, Home House,
20 Portman Square, London. 1772–73

admirably displayed by certain Gothic buildings." Soufflot, however, did not yet study Gothic architecture in detail, as later generations of architects would.

BOULLÉE. Etienne-Louis Boullée (1728–1799) was half a generation younger than Soufflot and far more daring. He built little, but his teaching at the Royal Academy helped to create a tradition of visionary architecture that flourished during the last third of the century and the early years of the next. Boullée's ideal was an architecture of "majestic nobility," an effect he sought to achieve by combining huge, simple masses. Most of his designs were for structures on a scale so enormous that they could hardly be built even today.

He hailed the sphere as the perfect form, since no trick of perspective can alter its appearance (except, of course, its apparent size). Thus he projected a memorial to Isaac Newton as a gigantic hollow sphere, mirroring the universe (fig. 796). "O Newton!" he exclaimed, "I conceived the idea of surrounding you with your discovery, and thus, somehow, of surrounding you with yourself." The interior was to be bare, apart from an empty sarcophagus symbolizing the mortal remains of the great man, but the surface of its upper half was pierced by countless small holes, points of light meant to give the illusion of stars. Plans such as this have a utopian grandeur that dwarfs the boldest ambitions of earlier architects. Largely forgotten during most of the nineteenth century, Boullée and his successors were rediscovered in the early twentieth, when architects again dared to "think the unthinkable."

Archaeological Excavations

The mid-eighteenth century was greatly stirred by two experiences: the rediscovery of Greek art as the original source of classic style; and the excavations at Herculaneum and Pompeii, which for the first time revealed the daily life of the ancients and the full range of their arts and crafts. Richly illustrated books about the Acropolis at Athens, the temples at Paestum, and the finds at Herculaneum and Pompeii were published in England and France; archaeology caught everyone's imagination. From this came a new style of interior decoration, seen at its finest in the works of the Englishman Robert Adam (1728–1792), such as the front drawing room at Home House (fig. 797). Adapted from Roman stucco ornament (compare fig. 262), it echoes the delicacy of Rococo interiors but with a characteristically Neoclassic insistence on plane surfaces, symmetry, and geometric precision.

JEFFERSON. Meanwhile, the Palladianism launched by Lord Burlington had spread overseas to the American Colonies, where it became known as the Georgian style; a specimen of great distinction is Thomas Jefferson's house, Monticello (figs. 798, 799). Built of brick with wooden trim,

798. (left) THOMAS JEFFERSON.
Monticello, Charlottesville,
Virginia. 1770–84; 1796–1806

799. (above) Plan of Monticello

Neoclassicism and Romanticism 577

800. KARL LANGHANS. The Brandenburg Gate, Berlin. 1788–91

in design it is not so doctrinaire as Chiswick House (note the less compact plan and the numerous windows), and the use of the Doric order shows its later date. Jefferson (1743–1826) still preferred the Roman Doric, although the late eighteenth century came to favor the heavier and more austere Greek Doric.

This "Greek revival" phase of Neoclassicism had been pioneered in England, on a small scale; it was quickly taken up everywhere, since it was believed to embody more of the "noble simplicity and calm grandeur" of classic Greece than did the later, less "masculine" orders. Greek Doric was also the least flexible order, hence particularly difficult to adapt to modern tasks even when combined with Roman or Renaissance elements. Only rarely could Greek Doric architecture furnish a direct model for Neoclassic structures: such a case is the Brandenburg Gate in Berlin (fig. 800), derived from the Propylaea (see fig. 169).

Classic vs. Gothic, and Other Alternatives

While the classic revival between 1750 and 1800 was becoming increasingly "archaeological," the Gothic revival also got under way, again with the English in the lead. Gothic architecture had never wholly disappeared in England—for special purposes, Gothic forms were used on occasion even by Sir Christopher Wren and Sir John Vanbrugh, but these were survivals of an authentic if outmoded tradition. The conscious revival, by contrast, was linked with the cult of the picturesque, and with the vogue for medieval (and pseudo-medieval) romances.

WALPOLE.   In this spirit Horace Walpole (1717–1797), midway in the century, enlarged and "gothicized" his country house, Strawberry Hill (figs. 801, 802). Despite its studied irregularity, the rambling structure has dainty, flat surfaces that remind us strongly of Robert Adam (compare fig. 797); the interior looks almost as if decorated with lace-paper doilies. This playfulness, so free of dogma, gives Strawberry Hill its special charm. Gothic here is still an "exotic" style; it appeals because it is strange, but for that very reason

it must be "translated," like a medieval romance, or the Chinese motifs that crop up in Rococo decoration.

NASH.   The Romantic imagination saw Gothic and the mysterious East in much the same light, as John Nash's Royal Pavilion at Brighton (fig. 803) well demonstrates half a century later. The style of this "stately pleasure dome," a cream-puff version of the Taj Mahal (see fig. 345), was

801. HORACE WALPOLE, with WILLIAM ROBINSON and others. Strawberry Hill, Twickenham. 1749–77

802. Interior, Strawberry Hill

803. JOHN NASH. The Royal Pavilion, Brighton. 1815–18

804. BENJAMIN LATROBE. Catholic Cathedral,
Baltimore, Maryland. Begun 1805

then known as Indian Gothic. It is equally characteristic of Romanticism, however, that by 1800 the Gothic was a fully acceptable alternative to the Greek revival, as a style for major churches.

LATROBE. Benjamin Latrobe (1764–1820), an Anglo-American who became, under Jefferson, the most influential architect of "Federal" Neoclassicism, submitted a design in each style for the Catholic Cathedral in Baltimore; the Neoclassic one was chosen, but it might well have been the Gothic. The exterior of the present building (fig. 804) has walls that resemble Soufflot's Panthéon, a dome of more severe design, a temple front, and bell towers of disguised Gothic-Baroque ancestry (the bulbous crowns are not his work).

Far more distinguished is the interior (fig. 805). Inspired by the domed and vaulted spaces of ancient Rome, especially the Pantheon (see fig. 239), Latrobe nevertheless was not interested in archaeological correctness. The "muscularity" of Roman structures has been suppressed; moldings, profiles, and coffers are no more than linear accents that do not disturb the continuous, abstract surfaces. In this Romantic interpretation, the spatial qualities of ancient architecture become vast, pure, Sublime. The strangely weightless interior presents almost that combination of classic form and Gothic lightness first postulated by Soufflot; it also shows the free and imaginative look of the mature Neoclassic style, when handled by a gifted architect. Had the Gothic design (fig. 806) been chosen, the exterior might have been more striking, but the interior probably less impressive. Like most Romantic architects seeking the Sublime, Latrobe viewed Gothic churches "from the outside in"—as mysterious, looming structures silhouetted against the sky—but nourished his spatial fantasy on Roman monuments. Neo-Gothic interiors are usually disappointing when matched against the best of the Neoclassic.

After 1800, the choice between the classic and Gothic modes was more often resolved in favor of Gothic. Nationalist sentiments, strengthened in the Napoleonic wars, became important factors, for England, France, and Germany each

805. Interior, Catholic Cathedral, Baltimore

806. BENJAMIN LATROBE. Alternative Design for
the Catholic Cathedral, Baltimore

807. SIR CHARLES BARRY and A. WELBY PUGIN. The Houses of Parliament, London. Begun 1836

tended to think that Gothic expressed its particular national genius. Certain theorists, notably John Ruskin, also regarded Gothic as superior for ethical or religious reasons (it was "honest" and "Christian").

BARRY AND PUGIN.   All these considerations were conjoined in the design, by Sir Charles Barry and A. Welby Pugin, for the Houses of Parliament in London, the largest monument of the Gothic revival (fig. 807). As the seat of a vast and complex governmental apparatus, but at the same time as a focus of patriotic feeling, it presents a curious mixture—repetitious symmetry governs the main body of the structure, and "picturesque" irregularity its silhouette. Meanwhile the stylistic alternatives were continually increased for architects by other revivals.

GARNIER.   When, by mid-century, the Renaissance, and then the Baroque, returned to favor, the revival movement had come full circle: Neo-Renaissance and Neo-Baroque replaced the Neoclassic. This final phase of Romantic architecture, which dominated the years 1850–75 and lingered through 1900, is epitomized in the Paris Opéra (figs. 808–10), designed by Charles Garnier (1825–1898). Its Neo-Baroque quality derives more from the profusion of sculpture and ornament than from its architectural vocabulary: the paired columns of the façade, "quoted" from the East Front of the Louvre (see fig. 763), are combined with a smaller order, in a fashion suggested by Michelangelo (see fig. 624). Only the fluid curves of the Grand Staircase recall the High Baroque. The whole building looks "overdressed," its luxurious vulgarity so naïve as to be disarming. It reflects the taste of the beneficiaries of the industrial revolution, newly rich and powerful, who saw themselves as the heirs of the old aristocracy and thus found the pre-revolutionary styles more appealing than classic or Gothic.

Industrial Architecture

This "architecture of conspicuous display" was divorced, even more than the previous revival styles, from the practical demands of the industrial age—the factories, warehouses, stores, and city apartments that formed the bulk of building construction. For it is there, in the world of commercial architecture, that we find after about 1800 the gradual introduction of new materials and techniques that were to have a profound effect on architectural style by the end of the century. The most important was iron, never before used as an actual building material. Within a few decades of its first appearance, iron columns and arches had become the standard means of supporting the roofs over the large spaces required by railroad stations, exhibition halls, and public libraries.

LABROUSTE.   A famous early example is the Bibliothèque Ste.-Geneviève in Paris, by Henri Labrouste (1801–1875): in the reading room a row of cast-iron columns supports two barrel roofs resting on cast-iron arches (fig. 811). Labrouste chose to leave this iron skeleton uncovered, and to face the difficulty of relating it to the massive Renaissance revival style of his building.

If his solution does not fully integrate the two systems, it at least lets them coexist. The iron supports, shaped like Corinthian columns, are as slender as the new material permits; their collective effect is that of a space-dividing

808. (*above*) CHARLES GARNIER. The Opéra, Paris. 1861–74

809. (*left*) Plan of the Opéra

810. (*left, below*) Grand Staircase, the Opéra

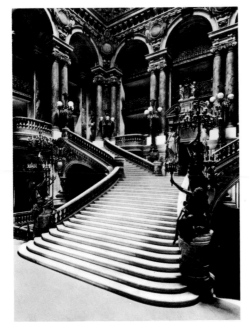

screen, belying their structural importance. To make them weightier, Labrouste has placed them on tall pedestals of solid masonry, instead of directly on the floor. Aesthetically, the arches presented greater difficulty, since there was no way to make them look as powerful as their masonry ancestors. Here Labrouste has gone to the other extreme, perforating them with lacy scrolls as if they were pure ornament. This architectural—as against merely technical—use of exposed iron members has a fanciful and delicate quality that links it, indirectly, to the Gothic revival. Later superseded by structural steel and ferroconcrete, it is a special and peculiarly appealing chapter in the history of Romantic architecture.

811. HENRI LABROUSTE. Reading Room, Bibliothèque Ste.-Geneviève, Paris. 1843–50

812. BENJAMIN WEST. *The Death of General Wolfe.*
1770. 59½ × 84″. National Gallery of Canada, Ottawa

PAINTING

In Romantic painting, as we mentioned previously, the revival of past styles had a far narrower scope than in architecture. Nonetheless, painting remains the greatest creative achievement of Romanticism in the visual arts. Less dependent than architecture or sculpture on public approval, it held a correspondingly greater appeal for the individualism of the Romantic artist; moreover, it could better accommodate the themes and ideas of Romantic literature. Romantic painting was not essentially illustrative. But literature, past and present, now became a more important source of inspiration for painters than ever before, and provided them with a new range of subjects, emotions, and attitudes. Romantic poets, in turn, often saw nature with a painter's eye. Many had a strong interest in art criticism and theory; some, notably Goethe and Victor Hugo, were capable draftsmen; and Blake cast his visions in both pictorial and literary form. Within the Romantic movement, art and literature have a complex, subtle, and by no means one-sided relationship.

Romantic painting, like architecture, began as a reaction, in the name of reason and nature, against Baroque "artificiality." The first to formulate this view was Johann Winckelmann, the German art historian and theorist who popularized the famous phrase about the "noble simplicity and calm grandeur" of Greek art (in his *Thoughts on the Imitation of Greek Works . . .* , published in 1755). His ideas deeply impressed two painters then living in Rome, the German Anton Raffael Mengs and the Scotsman Gavin Hamilton, as well as the French painter Joseph-Marie Vien. All

three had strong antiquarian leanings but otherwise limited powers—which may be why they accepted Winckelmann's doctrine so readily; their work is less important than their effect as teachers and propagators of the "Winckelmann program," during the 1760s and '70s. To these artists, a return to the classics meant the style and "academic" theory of Poussin, combined with a maximum of archaeological detail newly gleaned from ancient sculpture and the excavations of Pompeii.

America

WEST. It may seem surprising that among the first to come under their influence was Benjamin West (1738–1820), who arrived in Rome from Pennsylvania in 1760 and caused something of a sensation, since no American painter had appeared in Europe before. He relished his role of frontiersman—on being shown the *Apollo Belvedere* (see fig. 199), he reportedly exclaimed, "How like a Mohawk warrior!" He also quickly absorbed the lessons of Mengs and Hamilton; when he went to London a few years later, he was in command of the most up-to-date style, and became first a founder-member of the Royal Academy, then, after the death of Reynolds, its president. His career was thus European rather than American. Yet he always took pride in his New World background, and it enabled him to make a contribution to the growth of the Romantic movement that is summed up in his *Death of General Wolfe* (fig. 812).

Wolfe's death in 1759, occurring in the siege of Quebec during the French and Indian War, had aroused considerable feeling in London. When West, among others, decided to represent this event, two methods were open to him: he could give a factual account with the maximum of historic accuracy, or he could use "the grand manner," Poussin's ideal conception of history painting (see page 539), with figures in classical costume. Had West been a European follower of Mengs and Hamilton, he would surely have chosen the latter course; however, he knew the American locale of the scene too well for that. He merged the two approaches: his figures wear contemporary dress, and the conspicuous Indian places the event in the New World for those unfamiliar with the subject; yet all the attitudes and expressions are "heroic." The composition, in fact, recalls an old and hallowed theme, the lamentation over the dead Christ (see fig. 491), dramatized by Baroque lighting.

West thus endowed the death of a modern military hero both with the rhetorical pathos of "noble and serious human actions," as defined by academic theory, and with the trappings of a real event. He created an image that expresses a phenomenon basic to modern times: the shift of emotional allegiance from religion to nationalism. No wonder his picture had countless successors during the nineteenth century.

COPLEY. West's gifted compatriot, John Singleton Copley of Boston (1738–1815), moved to London just two years before the American Revolution. As New England's outstanding portrait painter, he had adapted the formulas of the British portrait tradition to the cultural climate of his home town (see page 20). *Mrs. Thomas Boylston* (fig. 813) makes an instructive comparison with Gainsborough's *Mrs. Siddons* (see fig. 789). The framework is much the same (note the curtain), but Gainsborough projects aristocratic coolness and fashionable elegance, while Copley's down-to-earth shrewdness of characterization and soberly exact detail seem more Dutch than English.

In Europe, Copley turned to history painting in the manner of West, thus losing his provincial virtues; most memorable as a work of art, and also a model of Romantic imagery, is his *Watson and the Shark* (fig. 814). Watson, attacked by a shark while swimming in Havana harbor, had been dramatically rescued; much later he commissioned Copley to depict this gruesome experience. Perhaps he thought that only a painter newly arrived from America would do full justice to the exotic flavor of the incident; Copley, in turn, must have been fascinated by the task of translating the story into pictorial terms. Following West's example, he made every detail as authentic as possible (here the black man has the purpose of the Indian in *The Death of General Wolfe*) and utilized all the emotional resources of Baroque painting to invite the beholder's participation. The shark becomes a monstrous embodiment of evil, the man with the boat hook resembles an Archangel Michael fighting Satan, and the nude youth flounders helplessly between the forces of doom and salvation. Copley may also have recalled representations of Jonah and the Whale: these include the elements of his scene, although the action is reversed (the prophet is thrown overboard into the jaws of the sea monster). This charging of a private adventure with the emotional and symbolic qualities of myth is highly characteristic of Romanticism.

813. JOHN SINGLETON COPLEY.
Mrs. Thomas Boylston. 1766. 50½ × 40½".
Fogg Art Museum, Harvard University,
Cambridge, Massachusetts

814. JOHN SINGLETON COPLEY. *Watson and the Shark.*
1778. 72½ × 90¼". Museum of Fine Arts, Boston

815. GEORGE STUBBS. *Lion Attacking a Horse*
(see colorplate 110). Yale University Art Gallery,
New Haven, Connecticut

England

STUBBS. The same process recurs in *Lion Attacking a Horse* (fig. 815, colorplate 110) by the Englishman George Stubbs (1724–1806), who painted portraits of race horses—and sometimes their owners—for a living. On a visit to North Africa, he had allegedly seen a horse killed by a lion; certainly this image haunted his imagination, and from it he developed a new type of animal picture full of Romantic feeling for the grandeur and violence of nature. Man has no place in this realm, "red in tooth and claw," yet the artist identifies himself emotionally with the horse, whose pure whiteness contrasts so dramatically—and symbolically—with the sinister rocks of the lion's domain. Thunderclouds racing across the sky reinforce the mood of doom; the poor horse, frightened also by the approaching storm, seems doubly defenseless against these forces of destruction. We respond to the horse as to the unfortunate Mr. Watson—with mixed fascination and horror.

FUSELI. But the Romantic quest for terrifying experiences did not pursue only physical violence. It could also lead to the dark recesses of the mind, as in *The Nightmare* (fig. 816) by John Henry Fuseli (1741–1825). This Swiss-born painter—originally named Füssli—had an extraordinary impact on his time, more perhaps because of his adventurous and forceful personality than the merits of his work. Ordained a minister at twenty, he had left the Church by 1764, and gone to London in search of freedom. Encouraged by Reynolds, he spent the 1770s in Rome. There he encountered Gavin Hamilton, but Fuseli based his style on Michelangelo and the Mannerists, not on Poussin and the antique. A German acquaintance of those years described him as "extreme in everything—Shakespeare's painter." Shakespeare and Michelangelo were indeed his twin gods; he even visualized a Sistine Chapel with Michelangelo's figures transformed into Shakespearean characters, where the Sub-

lime would be the common denominator for "classic" and "Gothic" Romanticism. In *The Nightmare* we find a similar fusion: the sleeping woman (more Mannerist than Michelangelesque) is Neoclassic, the grinning devil and the luminescent horse come from the demon-ridden world of medieval folklore. The Rembrandtesque lighting, on the other hand, reminds us of Reynolds (compare fig. 790).

What was the genesis of *Nightmare?* Nightmares usually have a strongly sexual connotation, sometimes quite openly expressed, at other times concealed behind a variety of disguises. We know that Fuseli originally conceived the subject not long after his return from Italy, when he had fallen violently in love with a friend's niece who soon married a merchant, much to the artist's distress. We can see in the picture a projection of his "dream girl," with the demon taking the artist's place while the horse, a well-known erotic symbol, looks on.

BLAKE. Later, in London, Fuseli befriended the poet-painter William Blake (1757–1827), whose personality was even stranger than his own. A recluse and visionary, Blake produced and published his own books of poems with engraved text and hand-colored illustrations. Though he never left England, he acquired a large repertory of Michelangelesque and Mannerist motifs from engravings, and through the influence of Fuseli. He also conceived a tremendous admiration for the Middle Ages, and came closer than any other Romantic artist to reviving pre-Renaissance forms

816. JOHN HENRY FUSELI. *The Nightmare.* 1785–90.
29½ × 25¼″. Goethe Museum, Frankfurt

Colorplate 109. THOMAS GAINSBOROUGH. *Robert Andrews and His Wife* (see page 561). About 1748–50. 27½ × 47″. The National Gallery, London (Reproduced by courtesy of the Trustees)

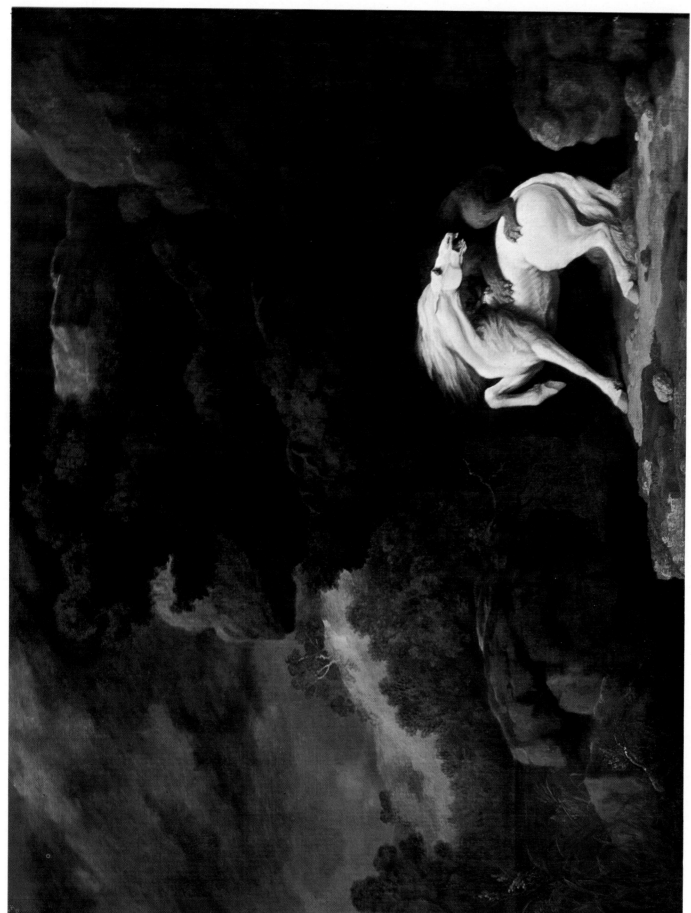

Colorplate 110. GEORGE STUBBS. *Lion Attacking a Horse* (see page 584). 1770. 40⅛ × 50½″. Yale University Art Gallery, New Haven, Connecticut

Colorplate 111. JOSEPH MALLORD WILLIAM TURNER. *The Slave Ship* (see pages 594–95). 1839. 35¾ × 48″. Museum of Fine Arts, Boston

Colorplate 112. GEORGE CALEB BINGHAM. *Fur Traders on the Missouri* (see page 596). c. 1845. 29 × 36″. The Metropolitan Museum of Art, New York (Morris K. Jessup Fund, 1933)

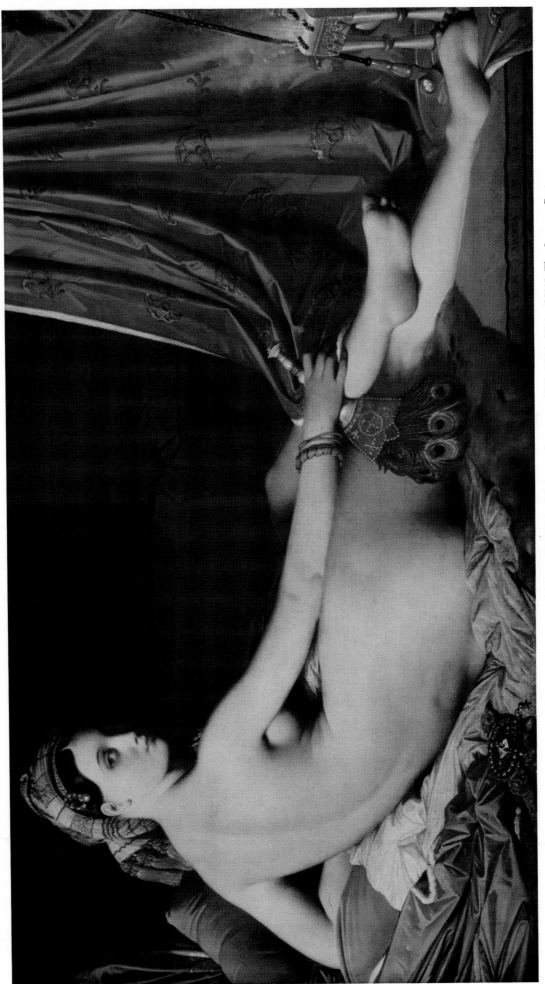

Colorplate 113. JEAN-AUGUSTE DOMINIQUE INGRES. *Odalisque* (see page 600). 1814. 35¼ × 63¾". The Louvre, Paris

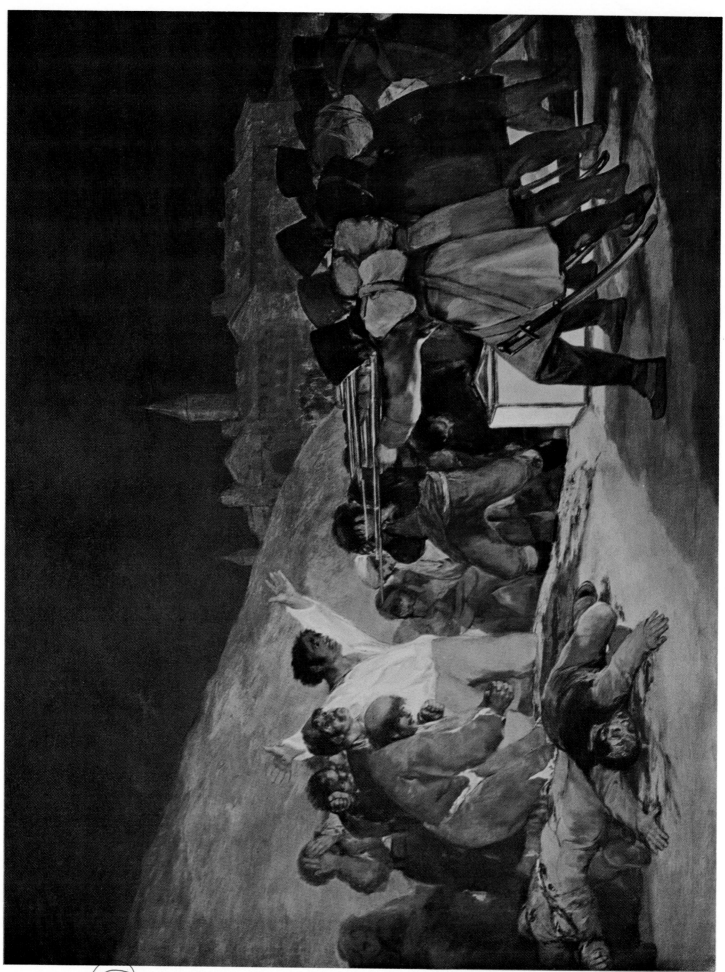

Colorplate 114. FRANCISCO GOYA. *The Third of May, 1808* (see page 602). 1814–15. 8' 9" × 13' 4". The Prado, Madrid

Colorplate 115. THÉODORE GÉRICAULT. *Mounted Officer of the Imperial Guard* (see page 602). 1812. 9′ 7″ × 6′ 4½″. The Louvre, Paris

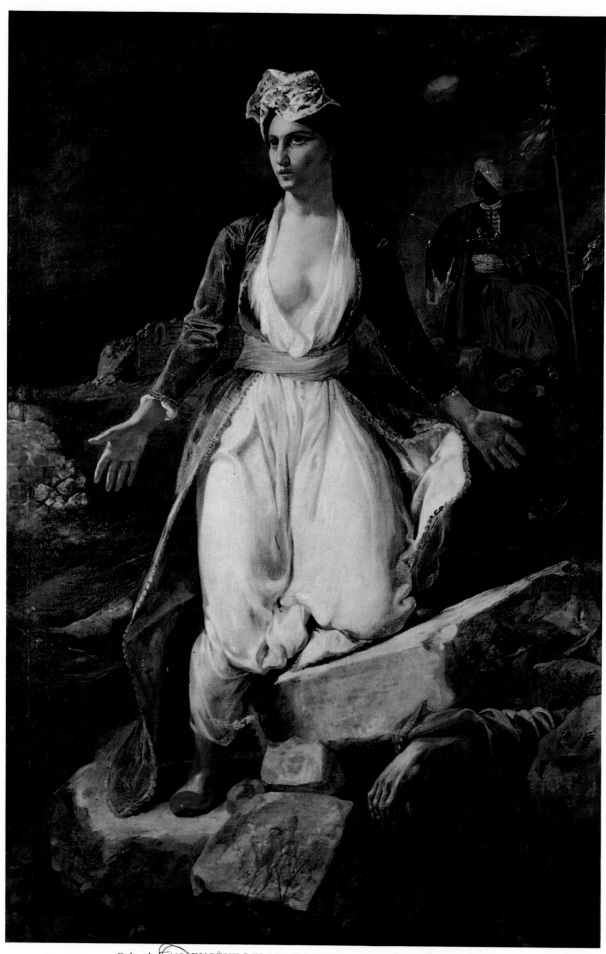

Colorplate 116. EUGÈNE DELACROIX. *Greece on the Ruins of Missolonghi*
(see page 605). 1826. 6′ 11½″ × 4′ 8¼″. Musée des Beaux-Arts, Bordeaux

817. WILLIAM BLAKE. *The Ancient of Days*, frontispiece
of *Europe, a Prophecy.* 1794. Metal relief etching,
hand-colored. The Library of Congress, Washington, D.C.
(Lessing J. Rosenwald Collection)

818. TADDEO ZUCCARI. *The Conversion of St. Paul*
(detail). c. 1555. Palazzo Doria-Pamphili, Rome

(his books were meant to be the successors of illuminated manuscripts).

These elements are all present in Blake's memorable image of *The Ancient of Days* (fig. 817). The muscular figure, radically foreshortened and fitted into a circle of light, is derived from Mannerist sources (see fig. 818), while the symbolic compasses come from medieval representations of the Lord as Architect of the Universe. With these precedents, we would expect the Ancient of Days to signify Almighty God, but in Blake's esoteric mythology, he stands rather for the power of reason, which the poet regarded as ultimately destructive, since it stifles vision and inspiration. To Blake, the "inner eye" was all-important; he felt no need to observe the visible world around him.

COZENS. It would be hard to imagine a greater contrast than that between *The Ancient of Days* and the *Landscape* (fig. 819) by Blake's older contemporary Alexander Cozens (c. 1717–1786). Yet both artists, in opposite ways, were centrally concerned with inspiration. Cozens had tired of the idyllic landscapes patterned after Claude Lorraine which were then so admired. Artists using them as a model, he felt, could produce only stereotyped variations on an established theme. The direct study of nature (important though it was) could not be the new starting point, for it did not supply the imaginative, poetic quality that for Cozens constituted the essence of landscape painting.

As a teacher, Cozens developed what he called "a new method of assisting the invention in drawing original compositions of landscapes" which he published, with illustrations such as figure 819, shortly before his death. What was this method? Leonardo da Vinci, Cozens noted, had observed that an artist could stimulate his imagination by trying to find recognizable shapes in the stains on old walls; why not produce such chance effects on purpose, to be used in the same way? Crumple a sheet of paper, smooth it; then, while thinking generally of landscape, blot it with ink, using as little conscious control as possible (our illustration is such an "ink-blot landscape"). With this as the point of departure, representational elements may be picked out in the configuration of blots, and then elaborated into a finished picture. The important difference between the two methods is that Cozens' blots are not a work of nature but a work of art—even though only half-born, they show, if nothing else, a highly individual graphic rhythm.

Needless to say, the Cozens method has far-reaching implications, theoretical as well as practical, but these could hardly have been understood by his contemporaries. If they thought Blake was mad, they regarded the "blot-master" as ridiculous. Nevertheless, the "Method" was not forgotten, its memory kept alive partly by its very notoriety. The two great masters of Romantic landscape in England, John Constable and William Turner, both profited from it, although they differed in almost every other way.

CONSTABLE. John Constable (1776–1837) admired both Ruisdael and Claude Lorraine, yet he strenuously opposed all flights of fancy. Landscape painting, he believed, must be based on observable facts; it should aim at "embodying a

819. ALEXANDER COZENS. *Landscape*, from *A New Method of Assisting the Invention in Drawing Original Compositions of Landscape.* 1784–86. Aquatint. The Metropolitan Museum of Art, New York (Rogers Fund, 1906)

pure apprehension of natural effect." All of his pictures show familiar views of the English countryside. Although he painted the final versions in his studio, he prepared them by making countless oil sketches out-of-doors. These were not the first such studies, but, unlike his predecessors, he was more concerned with the intangible qualities—conditions of sky, light, and atmosphere—than with the concrete details of the scene. Often, as in *Hampstead Heath* (fig. 820), the land serves as no more than a foil for the ever-changing drama of wind, sunlight, and clouds.

The sky, to him, was "the key note, the standard scale, and the chief organ of sentiment"; he studied it with a meteorologist's precision, the better to grasp its infinite variety as a mirror of those sweeping forces so dear to the Romantic view of nature. In endeavoring to record these fleeting effects, he arrived at a pictorial technique as broad, free, and personal as that of Cozens' "blotscapes," even though his point of departure was the exact opposite. The full-scale compositions of Constable's final years retain more and more of the quality of his oil sketches; in *Stoke-by-Nayland* (fig. 821), the earth and sky seem both to have become organs of sentiment, pulsating with the artist's poetic sensibility.

TURNER. Joseph Mallord William Turner (1775–1851) had arrived in the meantime at a style which Constable, deprecatingly but acutely, described as "airy visions, painted with tinted steam." Turner began as a watercolorist; the use of translucent tints on white paper may help to explain his preoccupation with colored light. Like Constable, he made copious studies from nature (though not in oils), but the scenery he selected satisfied the Romantic taste for the Picturesque and the Sublime—mountains, the sea, or sites linked with historic events; in his full-scale pictures he often changed these views so freely that they became quite unrecognizable.

Many of Turner's landscapes are linked with literary themes, and bear such titles as *The Destruction of Sodom*, or *Snowstorm: Hannibal Crossing the Alps*, or *Childe Harold's Pilgrimage: Italy.* When they were exhibited, he would add appropriate quotations from ancient or modern authors to the catalogue, or he would make up some lines himself and claim to be "citing" his own unpublished poem, "Fallacies of Hope." Yet these canvases are the opposite of history painting as defined by Poussin: the titles indeed indicate "noble and serious human actions," but the tiny figures, lost in the seething violence of nature, suggest the ultimate defeat of all endeavor—"the fallacies of hope."

The Slave Ship (fig. 822, colorplate 111) is one of Turner's most spectacular visions, and illustrates how he transmuted his literary sources into "tinted steam." First entitled *Slavers Throwing Overboard the Dead and Dying—Typhoon Coming On*, the painting compounds several levels of meaning. It has to do, in part, with a specific incident that Turner had recently read about: when an epidemic broke out on a slave ship, the captain jettisoned his human cargo because he was insured against the loss of slaves at sea, but not by disease. Turner also thought of a relevant passage from *The Seasons*, by the eighteenth-century poet James Thomson, that describes how sharks follow a slave ship during a typhoon, "lured by the scent of steaming crowds, or rank disease, and death." The title of the picture conjoins the slaver's action and the typhoon—but in what relation? Are the dead and dying slaves being cast into the sea against the threat of the storm (perhaps to lighten the ship)? Is the typhoon nature's retribution for the captain's greed and cruelty? Of the many storms at sea that Turner painted, none has quite this apocalyptic quality. A cosmic catastrophe seems about to engulf everything, not merely the "guilty" slaver but the sea itself with its crowds of fantastic and oddly harmless-looking fish.

820. JOHN CONSTABLE. *Hampstead Heath.* 1821. Oil sketch, 10 × 12". City Art Galleries, Manchester

821. JOHN CONSTABLE. *Stoke-by-Nayland*. 1836. 49½ × 66½". The Art Institute of Chicago

While we still feel the force of Turner's imagination, most of us today, perhaps with a twinge of guilt, enjoy the tinted steam for its own sake, rather than as a vehicle of the awesome emotions the artist meant to evoke. Even in terms of the values he himself acknowledged, Turner strikes us as "a virtuoso of the Sublime," led astray by his very exuberance. He must have been pleased by praise from Ruskin, that protagonist of the moral superiority of Gothic style, who saw in *The Slave Ship*, which he owned, "the true, the beautiful, and the intellectual"—all qualities that raised Turner above older landscape painters. Still, Turner may have come to wonder if his tinted steam had its intended effect on all beholders. Soon after finishing *The Slave Ship*, he could have read in his copy of Goethe's *Color Theory*, recently translated into English, that yellow has a "gay, softly exciting character," while orange-red suggests "warmth and gladness." Would these be the emotions aroused by *The Slave Ship* in a viewer who did not know its title?

Germany

FRIEDRICH.   In Germany, as in England, landscape was the finest achievement of Romantic painting, and the underlying ideas, too, were often strikingly similar. When Caspar David Friedrich (1774–1840), the most important German Romantic artist, painted *The Polar Sea* (fig. 823), he may have known of Turner's "Fallacies of Hope," for in an earlier picture on the same theme, now lost, he had inscribed the name "Hope" on the crushed vessel. In any case, he shared Turner's attitude toward human fate. The painting, as so

often before, was inspired by a specific event which the artist endowed with symbolic significance: a dangerous moment in William Parry's Arctic expedition of 1819–20.

One wonders how Turner might have depicted this scene—perhaps it would have been too static for him. But Friedrich was attracted by this immobility; he has visualized the piled-up slabs of ice as a kind of megalithic monument to man's defeat built by nature herself. Infinitely lonely, it is

822. JOSEPH MALLORD WILLIAM TURNER. *The Slave Ship* (see colorplate 111). Museum of Fine Arts, Boston

823. CASPAR DAVID FRIEDRICH. *The Polar Sea*. 1824. 38½ × 50½". Kunsthalle, Hamburg

a haunting reflection of the artist's own melancholy. There is no hint of tinted steam—the very air seems frozen—nor any subjective handwriting; we look right through the pigment-covered surface at a reality that seems created without the painter's intervention.

This technique, impersonal and meticulous, is peculiar to German Romantic painting. It stems from the early Neoclassicists—Mengs, Hamilton, and Vien—but the Germans, whose tradition of Baroque painting was weak, adopted it more wholeheartedly than the English or the French. About 1800, German painters rediscovered what they regarded as their native pictorial heritage: the "medieval" painters of the fifteenth and early sixteenth centuries. This "Gothic Revival," however, remained limited to subject matter and technique; the painstaking precision of the old German masters merely reinforced the Neoclassic emphasis on form at the expense of color. Although in Friedrich's hands this technique yielded extraordinary effects, it was a handicap for most of his countrymen, who lacked his compelling imagination.

America

BINGHAM.   The New World, too, had its Romantic landscape artists, even though before 1825 most Americans were far too busy carving out homesteads to pay much attention to the poetry of nature's moods. While it could be frightening, nature was everywhere, and it played a special role in the United States. Because the wilderness was believed to determine the American character, it became a symbol of the nation and its emerging civilization. *Fur Traders on the*

Missouri (fig. 824, colorplate 112) by George Caleb Bingham (1811–1879) shows this closeness with the land. The picture is both a landscape and a genre scene, and it is full of the vastness and silence of the wide-open spaces. The two trappers with a black fox chained to the prow of their dugout canoe, gliding downstream in the misty sunlight, are entirely at home in this idyllic setting. The picture carries us back to the river life of Mark Twain's childhood. At the same time, it reminds us of how much Romantic adventurousness went into the westward expansion of the United States.

824. GEORGE CALEB BINGHAM. *Fur Traders on the Missouri* (see colorplate 112). The Metropolitan Museum of Art, New York (Morris K. Jessup Fund, 1933)

France: Reform and Revolution

GREUZE. We must now catch up with events in France. There, the thinkers of the Enlightenment, who were the intellectual forefathers of the Revolution, strongly fostered the anti-Rococo trend in painting. This reform, at first a matter of content rather than style, accounts for the sudden fame, about 1760, of Jean-Baptiste Greuze (1725–1805): *The Village Bride* (fig. 825), like his other pictures of those years, is a scene of lower-class family life. What distinguishes it from earlier genre paintings (compare fig. 748, colorplate 108) is its contrived, stagelike character, borrowed from Hogarth's "dumb show" narratives (see figs. 786, 787). But Greuze has neither wit nor satire. His pictorial sermon illustrates the social gospel of Jean-Jacques Rousseau: that the poor, in contrast to the immoral aristocracy, are full of "natural" virtue and honest sentiment. Everything is intended to remind us of this, from the declamatory gestures and expressions of the actors to the smallest detail, such as the hen with her chicks in the foreground: one chick has left the brood and sits alone on a saucer, like the bride who is about to leave *her* "brood."

Strangely enough, *The Village Bride* was acclaimed a masterpiece, and the loudest praise came from Diderot, that apostle of Reason and Nature. Here at last was a painter with a social mission who appealed to the beholder's moral sense instead of merely giving him pleasure, like the frivolous artists of the Rococo! Diderot, in the first flush of enthusiasm, accepted the narrative of Greuze's pictures as "noble and serious human action" in Poussin's sense.

DAVID. Diderot modified his views later, when a far more gifted and rigorous "Neo-Poussinist" appeared on the scene—Jacques Louis David (1748–1825). A disciple of Vien, David had developed his Neoclassic style in Rome during the years 1775–81. In his *Death of Socrates* (fig. 826), of 1787, he seems more "Poussiniste" than Poussin himself (see fig. 758, colorplate 105); the composition unfolds like a relief, parallel to the picture plane, and the figures are as solid—and as immobile—as statues. Yet David has added one unexpected element: the lighting, sharply focused and casting precise shadows, is derived from Caravaggio, and so is the firmly realistic detail (note the hands and feet, the furniture, the texture of the stone surfaces). In consequence, the picture has a quality of life rather astonishing in so doctrinaire a statement of the new ideal style. The very harshness of the design suggests that its creator was passionately engaged in the issues of his age, artistic as well as political. Socrates, about to drain the poison cup, is shown here not only as an example of Ancient Virtue, but also as the founder of the "religion of Reason," a Christ-like figure (there are twelve disciples in the scene).

David took an active part in the French Revolution, and for some years he had a power over the artistic affairs of the nation comparable only to Lebrun's a century before. During this time he painted his greatest picture, *The Death of Marat* (fig. 827). David's deep emotion has made a masterpiece from a subject that would have embarrassed any lesser artist, for Marat, one of the political leaders of the Revolution, had been murdered in his bathtub. A painful skin condition

825. JEAN-BAPTISTE GREUZE. *The Village Bride.* 1761. 36 × 46½". The Louvre, Paris

826 JACQUES LOUIS DAVID. *The Death of Socrates.* 1787. 59 × 78″.
The Metropolitan Museum of Art, New York (Wolfe Fund, 1931)

827 JACQUES LOUIS DAVID. *The Death of Marat.* 1793.
65 × 50½″. Royal Museums of Fine Arts, Brussels

598   *Neoclassicism and Romanticism*

828. JACQUES LOUIS DAVID. *View of the Luxembourg Gardens.*
1794. 21½ × 30″. The Louvre, Paris

required immersion, and he did his work there, with a wooden board serving as his desk. One day a young woman named Charlotte Corday burst in with a personal petition, and plunged a knife into his chest while he read it.

David has composed the scene with a stark directness that is truly awe-inspiring. In this canvas, which was planned as a public memorial to the martyred hero, classical art coincides with devotional image and historical account. Marat's pose was derived from the sleeping figure in a mythological relief, probably of Cupid and Psyche, which was traditionally associated with the name of Polyclitus. David could have known the work in any number of versions, including engravings. But the difference in subject matter permitted classical art to offer little further guidance here, and the artist—far more than in *The Death of Socrates*—has drawn again on the Caravaggesque tradition of religious art. It is no accident that his *Marat* reminds us so strongly of Zurbarán's *St. Serapion* (see fig. 751, colorplate 103).

After the fall of Robespierre, David was imprisoned for some months in the Luxembourg Palace, and from his cell window painted his first and only landscape (fig. 828). The view of the park was predetermined by chance, and the picture thus has an astonishingly modern, casual look. That he chose to paint it at all, instead of whiling away his time with Neoclassic figure compositions, shows David's deep commitment to direct visual experience. Unencumbered for once by theory, he created a landscape of timeless, lyrical immediacy that only Constable could have rivaled.

GROS. When David met Napoleon a few years later, he became an ardent Bonapartist and painted several large pictures glorifying the emperor. But a favorite pupil, Antoine-Jean Gros (1771–1835), partially eclipsed David as the chief painter of the Napoleonic myth. Gros' first portrait of the great general shows him leading his troops at the Battle of Arcole in northern Italy (fig. 829). Painted in Milan, soon

after the series of victories that gave the French the Lombard plain, it conveys Napoleon's magic as an irresistible "man of destiny," with a Romantic enthusiasm David could never match. Much as Gros respected his teacher's doctrines, his emotional nature impelled him toward the color and drama of the Baroque. What he accomplished in this case seems especially remarkable if we consider the circumstances, recounted by an eyewitness: Napoleon, too impatient to pose, was made to sit still by his wife, who held him firmly upon her lap.

David went into exile after Napoleon's empire collapsed and turned his pupils over to Gros, urging him to return to Neoclassic orthodoxy. But Gros was torn betwen his pictorial instincts and these academic principles; he never achieved David's authority, and ended by suicide.

INGRES. The mantle of David finally descended upon another pupil, Jean-Auguste Dominique Ingres (1780–1867). Too young to share in the political passions of the Revolution, Ingres never was an enthusiastic Bonapartist; in 1806 he went to Italy and remained for eighteen years. Only after his return did he become the high priest of the Davidian tradition, defending it from the onslaughts of younger artists. What had been a revolutionary style only half a century before, now congealed into rigid dogma, endorsed by the government and backed by the weight of conservative opinion.

829. ANTOINE-JEAN GROS. *Napoleon at Arcole.*
1796. 29½ × 23″. The Louvre, Paris

830. JEAN-AUGUSTE DOMINIQUE INGRES. *Odalisque* (see colorplate 113). The Louvre, Paris

831. JEAN-AUGUSTE DOMINIQUE INGRES. *Louis Bertin.* 1832. 46 × 37½". The Louvre, Paris

Ingres is usually called a Neoclassicist, and his opponents Romantics. Actually, both factions stood for aspects of Romanticism: the Neoclassic phase, with Ingres as the last important survivor, and the Neo-Baroque, first adumbrated in Gros' *Napoleon at Arcole.* These two camps seemed to revive the old quarrel between "Poussinistes" and "Rubénistes." The original "Poussinistes" had never quite practiced what they preached, and Ingres' views, too, were far more doctrinaire than his pictures. He always held that drawing was superior to painting, yet a canvas such as his *Odalisque* (fig. 830, colorplate 113) reveals an exquisite sense of color; instead of merely tinting his design, he sets off the petal-smooth limbs of this Oriental Venus ("odalisque" is a Turkish word for a harem slave girl) with a dazzling array of rich tones and textures. The exotic subject, redolent with the enchantment of the *Thousand and One Nights,* is itself characteristic of the Romantic movement; it would be perfectly at home in the Royal Pavilion at Brighton (see fig. 803). Despite Ingres' professed worship of Raphael, this nude embodies no classical ideal of beauty. Her proportions, her languid grace, and the strange mixture of coolness and voluptuousness remind us, rather, of Parmigianino (compare fig. 642, colorplate 82).

History painting as defined by Poussin remained Ingres' life-long ambition, but he had great difficulty with it, while portraiture, which he pretended to dislike, was his strongest gift and his steadiest source of income. He was, in fact, the last great professional in a field soon to be monopolized by the camera. Although photography became a practical process only about 1840 (the earliest surviving photograph, fig. 859, dates from 1826), its experimental background goes back to the late eighteenth century (see page 614).

Ingres' *Louis Bertin* (fig. 831), at first glance looks like a kind of "super-photograph." But this impression is deceptive; comparing it with the preliminary pencil drawing (fig. 832), we realize how much of interpretation the portrait contains. The drawing, quick, sure, and precise, is a masterpiece of detached observation, while the painting, through subtle changes of emphasis and proportion, endows the sitter with a massive force of personality that has truly frightening intensity.

832. JEAN-AUGUSTE DOMINIQUE INGRES. *Louis Bertin.* 1832. Pencil drawing. The Louvre, Paris

833. FRANCISCO GOYA. *The Family of Charles IV*. 1800. 9′ 2″ × 11′. The Prado, Madrid

Only Ingres could so unify psychological depth and physical accuracy. His followers concentrated on physical accuracy alone, competing vainly with the camera; the Neo-Baroque Romantics, in contrast, emphasized the psychological aspect to such a degree that their portraits tended to become records of the artist's private emotional relationship with the sitter (see fig. 842). Often these are interesting and moving, but they are no longer portraits in the full sense of the term.

Spain

GOYA. Before pursuing the Neo-Baroque trend in France, we must take account of the great Spanish painter Francisco Goya (1746–1828), David's contemporary and the only artist of the age who may be called, unreservedly, a genius. When Goya first arrived in Madrid in 1766, he found both Mengs and Tiepolo working there. He was much impressed with Tiepolo, whom he must have recognized immediately as the greater of the two; he did not respond to the growing Neoclassic trend during his brief visit to Rome five years later. His early works, in a delightful late Rococo vein, reflect the influence of Tiepolo and the French masters (Spain had produced no painters of significance for over a century).

But during the 1780s, Goya became more of a libertarian; he surely sympathized with the Enlightenment and the Revolution, and not with the king of Spain, who had joined other monarchs in war against the young French Republic. Yet Goya was much esteemed at court, especially as a por-

834. FRANCISCO GOYA. *The Third of May, 1808* (see colorplate 114). The Prado, Madrid

trait painter. He now abandoned the Rococo for a Neo-Baroque style based on Velázquez and Rembrandt, the masters he had come to admire most.

The Family of Charles IV (fig. 833), Goya's largest royal portrait, deliberately echoes Velázquez' *The Maids of Honor* (see fig. 754, colorplate 104): the entire clan has come to visit the artist, who is painting in one of the picture galleries of the palace. As in the earlier work, shadowy canvases

835. FRANCISCO GOYA. *Bobabilicon (Los Proverbios*, No. 4).
c. 1818. Etching. The Metropolitan Museum of Art,
New York (Dick Fund, 1931)

genius, Goya created an image that has become a terrifying symbol of our era.

After the defeat of Napoleon, the restored Spanish monarchy brought a new wave of repression, and Goya withdrew more and more into a private world of nightmarish visions such as *Bobabilicon* (Big Booby), an etching from the series *Los Proverbios* (fig. 835). Although suggested by proverbs and popular superstitions, many of these scenes defy exact analysis. They belong to that realm of subjectively experienced horror which we first met in Fuseli's *Nightmare* (see fig. 816), but are infinitely more compelling. Finally, in 1824, Goya went into voluntary exile; after a brief stay in Paris, he settled in Bordeaux, where he died. His importance for the Neo-Baroque Romantic painters of France is well attested by the greatest of them, Eugène Delacroix, who said that the ideal style would be a combination of Michelangelo's art with Goya's.

France: Romantic Painting

GÉRICAULT. But Goya's influence in France began only after his death; the Neo-Baroque trend initiated by Gros had by then aroused the imagination of many talented younger men. *Mounted Officer of the Imperial Guard* (fig. 836, colorplate 115), painted by Théodore Géricault (1791–1824) at the astonishing age of twenty-one, offers the same con-

hang behind the group and the light pours in from the side, although its subtle gradations owe as much to Rembrandt as to Velázquez. The brushwork, too, has an incandescent sparkle rivaling that of *The Maids of Honor*. Measured against the Caravaggesque Neoclassicism of David, Goya's performance may seem thoroughly "pre-revolutionary," not to say anachronistic. Yet Goya has more in common with David than we might think: he, too, practices a revival style and, in his way, is equally devoted to the unvarnished truth.

Psychologically, *The Family of Charles IV* is almost shockingly modern. No longer shielded by the polite conventions of Baroque court portraiture, the inner being of these individuals has been laid bare with pitiless candor. They are like a collection of ghosts: the frightened children, the bloated vulture of a king, and—in a master stroke of sardonic humor—the grotesquely vulgar queen, posed like Velázquez' Princess Margarita (note the left arm, and the turn of the head). How, we wonder today, could the royal family tolerate this? Were they so dazzled by the splendid painting of their costumes that they failed to realize what Goya had done to them?

When Napoleon's armies occupied Spain in 1808, Goya and many of his countrymen hoped that the conquerors would bring the liberal reforms so badly needed. The savage behavior of the French troops crushed these hopes and generated a popular resistance of equal savagery. Many of Goya's works from 1810–15 reflect this bitter experience. The greatest is *The Third of May, 1808* (fig. 834, colorplate 114), commemorating the execution of a group of Madrid citizens. Here the blazing color, broad fluid brushwork, and dramatic nocturnal light are more emphatically Neo-Baroque than ever. The picture has all the emotional intensity of religious art, but these martyrs are dying for Liberty, not the Kingdom of Heaven; and their executioners are not the agents of Satan but of political tyranny—a formation of faceless automatons, impervious to their victims' despair and defiance. The same scene was to be re-enacted countless times in modern history. With the clairvoyance of

836. THÉODORE GÉRICAULT. *Mounted Officer of the Imperial Guard* (see colorplate 115). The Louvre, Paris

837. THÉODORE GÉRICAULT. *The Raft of the "Medusa."* 1818–19. 16′ 1″ × 23′ 6″. The Louvre, Paris

ception of the Romantic hero as Gros' *Napoleon at Arcole* (see fig. 829), but on a large scale and with a Rubens-like energy; ultimately, the ancestors of this splendid figure are the equestrian soldiers in Leonardo's *Battle of Anghiari* (see fig. 602). Géricault, himself an enthusiastic horseman, later became interested in the British animal painters such as George Stubbs. But his chief heroes, apart from Gros and the great Baroque masters, were David and Michelangelo.

A year's study in Italy deepened his understanding of the nude as an image of expressive power; he was then ready to begin his most ambitious work, *The Raft of the "Medusa"* (fig. 837). The *Medusa*, a government vessel, had foundered off the West African coast with hundreds of men on board; only a handful were rescued, after many days on a makeshift raft. The event attracted Géricault's attention because it was a political scandal—like many French liberals, he opposed the monarchy that was restored after Napoleon—and a modern tragedy of epic proportions. He went to extraordinary lengths in trying to achieve a maximum of authenticity: he interviewed survivors, had a model of the raft built, even studied corpses in the morgue. This search for uncompromising truth is like David's, and *The Raft* is indeed remarkable for its powerfully realistic detail.

Yet these preparations were subordinate in the end to the spirit of heroic drama that dominates the canvas. Géricault depicts the exciting moment when the men on the raft first glimpse the rescue ship. From the prostrate bodies of the

838. THÉODORE GÉRICAULT. *The Madman.* 1821–24. 24 × 20″. Museum of Fine Arts, Ghent

dead and dying in the foreground, the composition is built up to a rousing climax in the group that supports the frantically waving black, so that the forward surge of the survivors parallels the movement of the raft itself. Sensing, perhaps, that this theme of "man against the elements" would have strong appeal across the Channel (where Copley had painted *Watson and the Shark* forty years before; fig. 814), Géricault took the monumental canvas to England on a traveling exhibit in 1820.

His numerous studies for it had taught him how to explore extremes of the human condition scarcely touched by earlier artists. He went now not only to the morgue, but even to the insane asylum of Paris. There he became a friend of Dr. Georget, a pioneer in modern psychiatry, and painted for him a series of portraits of individual patients to illustrate various types of derangement, such as that in figure 838. The conception and execution of this oil sketch has an immediacy that recalls Frans Hals, but Géricault's sympathy toward his subject makes his work contrast tellingly with *Malle Babbe* (see fig. 732); this ability to see the victims of mental disease as fellow human beings, not as accursed or bewitched outcasts, is one of the noblest fruits of the Romantic movement.

DELACROIX.   The year 1824 was crucial for French painting. Géricault died (after a riding accident); Ingres returned to France from Italy, and had his first public success; the first showing in Paris of works by Constable was a revelation to many French artists; and *The Massacre at Chios* (fig. 839) established Eugène Delacroix as the foremost Neo-Baroque Romantic painter. An admirer of both Gros and Géricault, Delacroix (1798–1863) had been exhibiting for some years, but the *Massacre*—conservatives called it "the massacre of painting," others acclaimed it enthusiastically—made his reputation. For the next quarter century, he and Ingres were acknowledged rivals, and their polarity, fostered by partisan critics, dominated the artistic scene in Paris.

Like *The Raft of the "Medusa,"* the *Massacre* was inspired by a contemporary event: the Greek war of independence against the Turks, which stirred a sympathetic response throughout Western Europe (the full title is *Scenes of the Massacre at Chios: Greek Families Awaiting Death or Slavery*). Delacroix, however, aimed at "poetic truth" rather than at recapturing a specific, actual event. He shows us an intoxicating mixture of sensuousness and cruelty, but he does not succeed in forcing us to suspend our disbelief. While we revel in the sheer splendor of the painting, we do

839. EUGÈNE DELACROIX. *The Massacre at Chios.* 1822–24. 13′ 10″ × 11′ 7″. The Louvre, Paris

840. EUGÈNE DELACROIX. *Greece on the Ruins of Missolonghi* (see colorplate 116). Musée des Beaux-Arts, Bordeaux

841. EUGÈNE DELACROIX. *Odalisque*. c. 1845–50.
14⅞ × 18¼". Fitzwilliam Museum, Cambridge, England

not quite accept the human experience as authentic; we react, in other words, much as we do to Turner's *Slave Ship* (see fig. 822, colorplate 111). One reason may be the discontinuity of the foreground, with its dramatic contrasts of light and shade, and the luminous sweep of the landscape behind (Delacroix is said to have hastily repainted the latter after seeing Constable's work). Originally, the background of the *Massacre* was probably like that in Géricault's *Mounted Officer* (fig. 836, colorplate 115; the Turkish horseman directly recalls Géricault's earlier picture).

Such a dark, stormy sky also appears in Delacroix's final salute to the Greek cause, *Greece on the Ruins of Missolonghi* (fig. 840, colorplate 116). Here the complicated apparatus of the *Massacre* has been pared down to essentials, with a great gain in visual and emotional unity: a dead Greek fighter lies crushed among marble blocks in the foreground; a Turk triumphs; the defenseless maiden is fully as appealing as a martyred saint. Sonorous color—creamy whites and flesh tones set off by deep blues and reds—and the energetically fluid brushwork show Delacroix to be a "Rubéniste" of the first order. Contemporary beholders, remembering that Lord Byron had died at Missolonghi, surely found in the picture a special pathos.

Delacroix's sympathy with the Greeks did not prevent his sharing the enthusiasm of fellow Romantics for the Near East. He was enchanted by a visit to North Africa in 1832, finding there a living counterpart of the violent, chivalric, and picturesque past evoked in Romantic literature. His sketches from this trip supplied him with a large repertory of subjects for the rest of his life—harem interiors, street scenes, lion hunts. It is fascinating to compare his *Odalisque* (fig. 841) with Ingres' version (fig. 830, colorplate 113): reclining in ecstatic repose, she breathes passionate abandon and animal vitality—the exact opposite of Ingres' ideal.

This contrast persists in the portraiture of these perennial antagonists. Delacroix rarely painted portraits on commission; his finest specimens are of his personal friends and

fellow victims of the "Romantic agony," such as the famous Polish composer Frédéric Chopin (fig. 842). Here we see the image of the Romantic hero at its purest: a blend of Gros' *Napoleon* and Géricault's *Madman*, he is consumed by the fire of his genius.

DAUMIER.   The later work of Delacroix reflects the attitude that eventually doomed the Romantic movement: its growing detachment from contemporary life. History, literature, the Near East—these were the domains of the imagination where he sought refuge from the turmoil of the industrial revolution. It is ironical that Honoré Daumier (1808–1879), the one great Romantic artist who did not shrink from reality, remained in his day practically unknown as a painter; his pictures had little impact until after his death. A biting political cartoonist, Daumier contributed satirical drawings to various Paris weeklies for most of his life. He turned to painting in the 1840s, but found no public for his work. Only a few friends encouraged him and, a year before his death, arranged his first one-man show. The neat outlines and systematic crosshatching in Daumier's early cartoons (fig. 843 is a sample) show his conservative training.

He quickly developed a bolder and more personal style of draftsmanship, however, and his paintings of the 1850s and '60s have the full pictorial range of the Neo-Baroque. Their subjects vary widely; many show aspects of everyday urban

842. EUGÈNE DELACROIX. *Frédéric Chopin*.
1838. 18 × 15". The Louvre, Paris

843. HONORÉ DAUMIER. *It's Safe to Release This One!*
1834. Lithograph

life that also occur in his cartoons, now viewed from a painter's rather than a satirist's angle. *The Third-Class Carriage* (fig. 844) is such a work. Painted very freely, it must have seemed raw and "unfinished" even by Delacroix's standards. Yet its power is derived from this very freedom, and for this reason Daumier cannot be labeled a realist; his concern is not for the tangible surface of reality but the emotional meaning behind it.

In *The Third-Class Carriage* he has captured a peculiarly modern human condition, "the lonely crowd": these people have in common only that they are traveling together in one railway car. Though they are physically crowded, they take no notice of one another—each is alone with his own thoughts. Daumier explores this state with an insight into character and a breadth of human sympathy worthy of Rembrandt, whose work he revered. His feeling for the dignity of the poor also suggests Louis Le Nain, who had recently been rediscovered by French critics (compare fig. 756; the old woman on the left seems the direct ancestor of the central figure in *The Third-Class Carriage*).

Other paintings by Daumier have subjects more characteristic of Romanticism. The numerous canvases and drawings of the adventures of Don Quixote, from Cervantes'

844. HONORÉ DAUMIER. *The Third-Class Carriage.* c. 1862. 26 × 35½″.
The Metropolitan Museum of Art, New York (Bequest of Mrs. H. O. Havemeyer, 1929.
The H. O. Havemeyer Collection)

845. HONORÉ DAUMIER.
Don Quixote Attacking the Windmills. c. 1866.
22¼ × 33″. Collection Mr. Charles S. Payson, New York

sixteenth-century novel, show the perennial fascination this theme had for him. The lanky knight-errant, vainly trying to live his dream of noble deeds, and Sancho Panza, the dumpy materialist, seemed to embody for Daumier a tragic conflict within human nature that forever pits the soul against the body, ideal aspirations against harsh reality. In *Don Quixote Attacking the Windmills* (fig. 845), this polarity is forcefully realized: the mock hero dashes off in the noonday heat toward an invisible, distant goal, while Panza helplessly wrings his hands, a monument of despair. Again we marvel at the strength, the sculptured simplicity, of Daumier's shapes, and the expressive freedom of his brushwork, which make Delacroix's art seem almost tame and conventional by comparison.

MILLET. If the French public could not accept Daumier's painting style "straight," they nevertheless responded favorably to a diluted, simplified, yet powerful version of it in the work of François Millet (1814–1875). Millet was one of the artists of the Barbizon School who had settled in the village of Barbizon, near Paris, to paint landscapes and scenes of rural life. His *Sower* (fig. 846) reflects the compactness and breadth of Daumier's forms, now blurred in the hazy atmosphere. The "hero of the soil" flavor is somewhat self-conscious and quite alien to Daumier. (Could Millet have known the pathetic sower from the October page of the *Très Riches Heures du Duc de Berry?* Compare fig. 505, colorplate 58.)

popularized in, among other works, the country romances of George Sand, the equally unconventional woman novelist.

The picture shares Millet's reverence for peasant life and the dignity of labor. But the real subject, as in all of Bonheur's work, is the animals within the landscape; this she depicts here with such accuracy that one can almost smell the fertile soil in the spring sunshine. In this she was one of the originators of a strain of naturalism that endured throughout the rest of the century.

COROT. Another artist linked with the Barbizon School, though not actually a member, was Camille Corot (1796–1875). Today his finest work seems not his late landscapes, misty and poetic; it is the early ones that establish his importance for the development of modern landscape painting. In 1825 he went to Italy for two years and explored the countryside around Rome, like a latter-day Claude. But Corot did not transform his sketches into idealized pastoral visions; what Claude recorded only in his drawings—the quality of a particular place at a particular time (see fig. 760)—Corot made into paintings, small canvases done on the spot in an hour or two.

Such a work is his view of Papigno, an obscure little hill town (fig. 848). In size and immediacy, these quickly executed pictures are analogous to Constable's oil sketches (see fig. 820), yet they stem from different traditions. If Constable's view of nature, which emphasizes the sky as "the chief organ of sentiment," is derived from Dutch

846. FRANÇOIS MILLET. *The Sower.* c. 1850.
40 × 32½″. Museum of Fine Arts, Boston

847. ROSA BONHEUR. *Plowing in the Nivernais.* 1849. 5′ 9″ × 8′ 8″.
Musée National du Château de Fontainebleau

848. CAMILLE COROT. *Papigno.* 1826. 13 × 15¾″.
Collection Dr. Fritz Nathan, Zurich

seventeenth-century landscapes, Corot's instinct for architectural clarity and stability recalls Poussin and Claude. But he, too, insists on "the truth of the moment"; his exact observation, and his readiness to seize upon any view that attracted him during his excursions, shows the same commitment to direct visual experience as David's *View of the Luxembourg Gardens* (see fig. 828).

SCULPTURE

The development of sculpture, which we must discuss briefly to complete our survey of Romanticism, follows the pattern of painting. We shall find it a good deal less venturesome than either painting or architecture. The unique virtue of sculpture, its solid, space-filling reality (or, if you will, its "idol" quality), was not congenial to the Romantic temperament. The rebellious and individualistic urges of Romanticism could find expression in rough, small-scale sketches but rarely survived the laborious process of translating the sketch into a permanent, finished monument.

The sculptor was also overwhelmed by the authority accorded (since Winckelmann) to ancient statues such as the *Apollo Belvedere* (see fig. 199), praised as being supreme manifestations of the Greek genius while in actual fact most of them were mechanical Roman copies after Hellenistic pieces of no great distinction. (When Goethe saw the newly discovered Late Archaic sculpture from Aegina [figs. 157, 158] he pronounced it clumsy and inferior.) How could a modern artist rise above the quality of these works, if he was everywhere assured that they were the acme of sculptural achievement?

Finally, the new standard of uncompromising, realistic "truth" was embarrassing to the sculptor. When a painter renders clothing, anatomical detail, or furniture with photographic precision he does not produce a duplicate of reality, but a representation of it; while to do so in sculpture comes dangerously close to mechanical reproduction—a hand-

849. JEAN ANTOINE HOUDON. *Voltaire*. 1781.
Terracotta model for marble, height 47".
Fabre Museum, Montpellier, France

made equivalent of the plaster cast. Sculpture thus underwent a crisis that was resolved only toward the end of the century.

HOUDON. As we might deduce from what has just been said, portraiture proved the most viable field for Neoclassic sculpture. Its most distinguished practitioner, Jean Antoine Houdon (1741–1828), still retains the acute sense of individual character introduced by Coysevox (see fig. 771). His fine statue of Voltaire (fig. 849) does full justice to the sitter's skeptical wit and wisdom, and the classical drapery enveloping the famous sage—to stress his equivalence to ancient philosophers—is not disturbing, for he wears it as casually as a dressing gown.

Houdon was subsequently invited to America, to portray George Washington; he made two versions, one in classical and one in modern costume. Even the latter (fig. 850), though meticulously up-to-date in detail, has a classical pose and displays the fasces, a bundle of rods that symbolizes union. We can feel the chill breath of the *Apollo Belvedere*, as it were, on the becalmed, smooth surfaces.

CANOVA. Still, Washington escaped portrayal in heroic nudity during his lifetime. These representations were not unusual among younger, more doctrinaire Neoclassic sculptors: the most famous of them, Antonio Canova (1757–1822), produced a colossal nude statue of Napoleon, inspired by portraits of ancient rulers whose nudity indicates their status as divinities. Not to be outdone, Napoleon's sister Pauline Borghese permitted Canova to sculpt her as a reclining Venus (fig. 851). The statue is so obviously idealized as to still any gossip. We recognize it as a precursor, more classically proportioned, of Ingres' *Odalisque* (see fig. 830, colorplate 113). Strange to say, *Pauline Borghese* seems the less three-dimensional of the two; she is designed like a "relief in the round," for front and back view only, and her very considerable charm comes almost entirely from the fluid grace of her outlines.

Here we also encounter the problem of representation versus duplication, not in the figure itself but in the pillows, mattress, and couch. The question recurs on a larger scale in

850. JEAN ANTOINE HOUDON. *George Washington*.
1788–92. Marble, height 74".
State Capitol, Richmond, Virginia

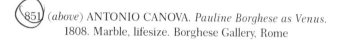
851. (above) ANTONIO CANOVA. *Pauline Borghese as Venus.* 1808. Marble, lifesize. Borghese Gallery, Rome

852. (below) ANTONIO CANOVA. Tomb of the Archduchess Maria Christina. 1798–1805. Church of the Augustinians, Vienna

853. (right) Canova's *Tomb of the Archduchess Maria Christina* (painting by Charles Swagers, 1833, based on an engraving by Pietro Bonato, 1805). 24¼ × 28¾″. The Art Museum, Princeton University

Canova's most ambitious work, the Tomb of the Archduchess Maria Christina (figs. 852, 853). Its design, again essentially linear and relief-like though the statues are carved in the round, has no precedents in earlier tombs: the deceased appears only in a portrait medallion framed by a snake biting its own tail, a symbol of eternity. Presumably, but not actually, the urn carried by the woman in the center contains her ashes. This is an ideal burial service performed by classical figures, mostly allegorical (the group on the left represents the Three Ages of Man), who are about to enter the pyramid-shaped tomb.

What troubles us is that this ensemble, in contrast to the tombs of earlier times (such as fig. 582), does not include the real burial place—the pyramid is a sham, a shallow façade built against the wall of the church. But if we must view the monument as a sort of theatrical performance in marble, we expect the artist to characterize it as such by creating a "stage space" that will set it apart from its surroundings (like Bernini's *Ecstasy of St. Theresa*; see fig. 704). Since Canova has not done this, the performance becomes confusingly realistic. Should we join the "actors" on their perfectly real marble steps? No, for we cannot follow them into a mock pyramid. What distinguishes the real from the mock architecture? To what level of reality does the cloth on the steps belong?

PRÉAULT. This dilemma could be resolved in two ways: by reviving a pre-classical style sufficiently abstract to restore the autonomous reality of sculpture, or by a return to the frankly theatrical Baroque. Only the latter alternative proved generally feasible at the time, although there were isolated attempts to explore the former. Auguste Préault (1809–1879), who was the boldest sculptor of his day and whose personality closely approached the Romantic ideal, experimented in both directions. His relief *Slaughter* (fig. 854) is brimming with a physical and emotional violence far beyond anything found in Baroque art, yet its expressive distortions, its irrational space filled to the bursting point with writhing shapes, evoke memories of Gothic sculpture (compare fig. 476). In fact, the helmeted knight's face next to that of the screaming mother hints that the subject itself is medieval: some dread apocalyptic event beyond man's control. But in true Romantic fashion Préault does not define this event. He proclaimed, "Je ne suis pas pour le fini. Je suis pour l'infini," a play on words conveying his preference for the unfinished over the finished as well as for the infinite over the finite.

RUDE. When *Slaughter* was shown to the public in 1834 it found few admirers. One of these must have been the somewhat older sculptor François Rude (1784–1855), as

854. AUGUSTE PRÉAULT. *Slaughter.*
1834. Bronze, 43 × 55″. Museum of Fine Arts, Chartres

suggested by his own masterpiece, the splendidly rhetorical *Marseillaise* (fig. 855) on one pier of the Arc de Triomphe in Paris. The soldiers, volunteers of 1792 rallying to defend the Republic, are still in classical guise, but the Genius of Liberty above them imparts her great forward-rushing movement to the entire group. She would not be unworthy of Puget (see fig. 772).

Twenty years later, Rude embodied the same *élan* in a single figure; the monument of Marshal Ney (fig. 856) claims a whole army as its invisible complement. Yet the ultimate source of the figure is pictorial (Gros' *Napoleon at Arcole*, fig. 829, and its successors).

BARYE. In a similar way, Stubbs' *Lion Attacking a Horse* (fig. 815, colorplate 110) is the sire of animal groups by Antoine-Louis Barye (1795–1875), the Romantic sculptor closest to Delacroix. The forms of his *Jaguar Devouring a Hare* (fig. 857) have energy and volume; their simplicity, for all the anatomical detail, is rare indeed in mid-nineteenth-century sculpture. However, these qualities can be found only in Barye's smaller pieces; as an architectural sculptor he is disappointingly academic.

CARPEAUX. Rude's real successor in the field of architectural sculpture was Jean-Baptiste Carpeaux (1827–1875), whose famous group for the façade of the Paris Opéra, *The Dance* (fig. 858), perfectly matches Garnier's Neo-Baroque architecture. The plaster model in our illustration is both livelier and more precise than the final stone group (visible in fig. 808, lower right). Its coquettish gaiety derives from small Rococo groups such as Clodion's (see fig. 775), and its sense of scale, too, seems at odds with its size—although the figures look smaller than life, the group is actually 15 feet tall. Nor is this the only discrepancy; Carpeaux's figures, unlike Clodion's, look undressed rather than nude. We do not accept them as legitimate denizens of the realm of mythology,

855. FRANÇOIS RUDE. *La Marseillaise*. 1833–36. c. 42 × 26'. Arc de Triomphe, Paris

856. FRANÇOIS RUDE. *Monument to Marshal Ney*. 1853. Bronze, height 8' 9". Place de l'Observatoire, Paris

and they slightly embarrass us, as if "real people" were acting out a Rococo scene. A single leg, detached from this group, might well be mistaken for a cast from nature. "Truth" here has destroyed the ideal reality that was still intact for Clodion a century before.

857. ANTOINE-LOUIS BARYE. *Jaguar Devouring a Hare.* 1850–51. Bronze, 16½ × 37½". The Louvre, Paris

858. JEAN-BAPTISTE CARPEAUX. *The Dance.* 1867–69. Plaster model, c. 15′ × 8′ 6″. Musée de l'Opéra, Paris

PHOTOGRAPHY

Is photography art? The fact that we still pose the question testifies to the continuing debate. The answers have varied with the changing definition and understanding of art. In itself, of course, photography is simply a medium, like oil paint or pastel, used to make art but having no inherent claim to being art. After all, what distinguishes an art from a craft is why, not how, it is done. But photography shares creativity with art because, by its very nature, its performance necessarily involves the imagination. Any photograph, even a casual snapshot, represents both an organization of experience and the record of a mental image. The subject and style of a photograph thus tell us about the photographer's inner and outer worlds. Furthermore, both art and photography participate in aspects of the same process of seek-and-find. The photographer may not realize what he responded to until after he sees the image that has been printed.

Like woodcut, etching, engraving, and lithography, photography is a form of printmaking that is dependent on mechanical processes. But in contrast to the other graphic media, photography has always been tainted as the product of a new technology—apart from pushing a button or lever, or setting up special effects, no active intervention is required of the artist's hand to guide an idea. For this reason, the camera has usually been considered to be little more than a recording device.

Photography, however, is by no means a neutral medium; its reproduction of reality is never completely faithful. Whether we realize it or not, the camera alters appearances; photographs reinterpret the world around us, making us literally see it in new terms.

Photography and painting are in parallel response to their times and have generally expressed the same world view. Sometimes the camera's power to extend our way of seeing has been realized first by the painter's creative vision. The two nevertheless differ fundamentally in their approach and temperament: the painter communicates his understanding through techniques that represent his cumulative response over time; the photographer recognizes the moment when the subject before him corresponds to the mental image he has formed of it.

It is hardly surprising that photography and art have enjoyed an uneasy relationship from the start. Artists have generally treated the photograph something like a preliminary sketch, as a convenient source of ideas or record of motifs to be fleshed out and incorporated into a finished work. Academic painters found the detail provided by photographs to be in keeping with their own precise naturalism; many other kinds of artists resorted to photographs, though not always admitting it. Photography has in turn been heavily influenced throughout its history by the painter's media, and photographs may still be judged according to how well they imitate paintings and drawings. To understand photography's place in the history of art, however, we must learn to recognize its particular strengths and inherent limitations.

859. NICÉPHORE NIÉPCE. *View from His Window at Le Gras.* 1826.
Heliograph, 6½ × 7⅞". Gernsheim Collection, University of Texas at Austin

The Founding Fathers

In 1822 a French inventor named Joseph Nicéphore Niépce (1765–1833) succeeded, at the age of fifty-seven, in making the first permanent photographic image, although his earliest surviving example (fig. 859) dates from four years later. He then joined forces with a younger man, Louis Jacques Mandé Daguerre (1789–1851), who had devised an improved camera. After ten more years of chemical and mechanical research, the daguerreotype, using positive exposures, was unveiled publicly in 1839 and the age of photography was born. The announcement spurred the Englishman William Henry Fox Talbot (1800–1877) to complete his own photographic process, involving a paper negative from which positives could be made, that he had been pursuing independently since 1833.

What motivated the fathers of photography? They were searching for an artistic medium, not for a device of practical utility. Though Niépce was a research chemist rather than an artist, his achievement was an outgrowth of his efforts to improve the lithographic process. Daguerre was a skilled painter, and he probably turned to the camera to heighten the illusionism in his huge painted dioramas, which were the sensation of Paris during the 1820s and '30s. Fox Talbot saw in photography a substitute for drawing, after using a camera as a tool to sketch landscapes while on a vacation.

The interest that all of these men had in the artistic potential of the medium they had created is reflected in their photographs. Daguerre's first picture (fig. 860) imitates a type of still life originated by Chardin; Fox Talbot's *Sailing Craft* (fig. 861) looks like the English marine paintings of his day.

That the new medium should have a mechanical aspect was particularly appropriate. It was as if the industrial revolution, having forever altered man's way of life, had now to

invent its own method for recording itself—although the transience of modern existence was not captured by "stopping the action" until the 1870s. Photography underwent a rapid series of improvements, including inventions for better lenses, glass plate negatives, and new chemical processes; since its initial limitations were largely overcome by mid-century, it would be misleading to tell the early history of the medium in terms of technological development.

The basic mechanics and chemistry of photography, moreover, had been known for a long time. The camera obscura, a box with a small hole in one end, dates back to antiquity; in the sixteenth century it was widely used for visual demonstrations. The camera was fitted with a mirror and then a lens in the Baroque period, which saw a revolution in optical science as part of a new world view culminating in Newtonian physics. By the 1720s it had become an aid in drawing architectural scenes; and at the same time the silver salts were discovered to be light-sensitive.

Why, then, did it take another hundred years for someone to put this knowledge together? Photography was neither inevitable in the history of technology, nor necessary to the history of art; yet it was an idea whose time had clearly come. If we try for a moment to imagine that photography was invented a hundred years earlier, we will find this to be impossible simply on artistic, apart from technological, grounds: the eighteenth century was too devoted to fantasy to be interested in the literalness of photography. Rococo portraiture, for example, was more concerned with providing a flattering image than an accurate likeness, and the camera's straightforward record would have been totally out of place. Even in architectural painting, extreme liberties were willingly taken with topographical truth.

The invention of photography was a response to the artistic urges and historical forces that underlie Romanticism. Much of the impulse came from a quest for the True and the Natural. The desire for "images made by Nature" can already be seen, on the one hand, in Cozens' ink-blot compositions (see fig. 819; "natural" because they were made by chance), and, on the other, in the late-eighteenth-century vogue for silhouette portraits (traced from the shadow of the sitter's profile), which led to attempts to record such shadows on light-sensitive materials. David's harsh realism in *The Death of Marat* and his fascination with the view from his cell window (figs. 827, 828) had already proclaimed the cause of unvarnished truth; so did Ingres' *Louis Bertin* (fig. 831), which established the standards of physical reality and character portrayal that photographers would follow.

Portraiture

Romantic art was largely art for the middle class, who replaced the aristocracy as the main patrons of culture. Like lithography, which was invented only in 1797, photography met the growing middle-class demand for images of all kinds. By 1800, large numbers of the bourgeoisie were having their likenesses painted, and it was in portraiture that photography found its readiest acceptance. Soon after the daguerreotype was introduced, photographic studios sprang up everywhere, especially in America, and multi-image *cartes de visites*, invented in 1854 by Adolphe Eugène Disdéri, became ubiquitous. Anyone could have a portrait taken cheaply and easily. In the process, the average man himself became notable. Photography thus became an outgrowth of the democratic values fostered by the American and French revolutions. There was also keen competition among photographers to get the famous to pose for portraits.

NADAR. Gaspard Félix Tournachon (1820–1910), better known as Nadar, managed to attract most of France's leading lights to his studio. Like many early photographers, he started out as an artist and initially used the camera to capture the likenesses of the 280 sitters whom he carica-

tured in an enormous lithograph *Le Panthéon Nadar;* he came to prefer the lens to the brush.

The actress Sarah Bernhardt posed for him several times, and his photographs of her (fig. 862) are the direct ancestors of modern glamour photography (compare fig. 1062). With her romantic pose and expression, she is a counterpart to the soulful maidens who inhabit much of nineteenth-century painting. Nadar has treated her in remarkably sculptural terms: indeed, the play of light and sweep of drapery are reminiscent of the sculptured portrait busts which were so popular with collectors at the time.

The Restless Spirit

Early photography reflected the outlook and temperament of Romanticism, and indeed the entire nineteenth century had a pervasive curiosity and an abiding belief that everything could be discovered. While this fascination sometimes manifested a serious interest in science—witness Darwin's voyage on the *Beagle* from 1831 to 1836—it more typically took the form of a restless quest for new experiences and places. Photography had a remarkable impact on the imagination of the period by making the rest of the world widely available, or by simply revealing it in a new way. Sometimes the search for new subjects was close to home; Nadar, for example, took aerial photographs of Paris from a hot-air balloon. This feat was wittily parodied by Daumier (fig. 863), whose caption, "Nadar Elevating Photography to the Height of Art," expresses the prevailing skepticism about the aesthetics of the new medium.

A love of the exotic was fundamental to Romantic escapism, and by 1850 photographers had begun to cart their equipment to faraway places. The same Romantic spirit that we saw in George Caleb Bingham's *Fur Traders on the Missouri* (fig. 824, colorplate 112) also drew photographers to the frontier, where they documented the westward expansion of the United States, with pictures that have primarily historical interest today.

860. LOUIS JACQUES MANDÉ DAGUERRE. *Still Life*. 1837. Daguerreotype, 6½ × 8½". Société française de photographie, Paris

861. WILLIAM HENRY FOX TALBOT. *Sailing Craft*. c. 1845. Science Museum, London.

862. NADAR. *Sarah Bernhardt*. 1859.
George Eastman House, Rochester, N.Y.

time photography's potential to enlarge man's vision. Curiously enough, this success waned, except for special uses: people were simply too habituated to viewing pictures as if with one eye.

Later on, when the half-tone plate was invented in the 1880s for reproducing pictures on a printed page, stereophotographs revealed another drawback: as our illustration shows, they were unsuitable for this process of reproduction. From then on, single-lens photography was inextricably linked with the mass media of the day.

Photojournalism

Fundamental to the rise of photography was the pervasive nineteenth-century sense that the present was already history in the making. Only with the advent of the Romantic hero did great acts other than martyrdom become popular subjects for contemporary painters and sculptors, and it can hardly be surprising that photography was invented a year after the death of Napoleon, who had been the subject of more paintings than any secular leader ever before.

At about the same time, Géricault's *Raft of the "Medusa"* (fig. 837) and Delacroix's *Massacre at Chios* (fig. 839) signaled a decisive shift in the Romantic attitude, toward representing contemporary events. This outlook brought with it a new kind of photography: photojournalism.

BRADY; GARDNER.   The first great photojournalist was Mathew Brady (1823–1896), who covered the Civil War. Other wars had already been photographed, but Brady and his twenty assistants (including Timothy O'Sullivan), using cameras too slow and cumbersome to show actual combat, nevertheless brought home its horrors with unprecedented

O'SULLIVAN.   An exception is the landscape photography of Timothy O'Sullivan (c. 1841–1882), who often preferred scenery that contemporary painters had overlooked. He practically invented his own aesthetic in photographing the *Cañon de Chelley* (fig. 864), for it conforms to no established pictorial type. The view fills the entire photograph, allowing no visual relief and lending it awesome force. The composition is held together by the play of lines of the displaced strata of the rock, which creates a striking abstract design. O'Sullivan's control of tonal relations is so masterful that even color photographs taken since of the same site have far less impact.

Stereophotography

The unquenchable thirst for vicarious experiences accounts for the expanding popularity of stereoscopic daguerreotypes. Invented in 1849, the two-lens camera produced two photographs that correspond to the slightly different images perceived by our two eyes; when seen through a special viewer called a stereoscope, the stereoptic photographs fuse to create a remarkable illusion of three-dimensional depth. Two years later stereoscopes became the rage at the Crystal Palace exposition in London (see fig. 1018). Countless thousands of double views were taken, such as that in figure 865; virtually every corner of the earth became accessible to practically any household, with a vividness second only to being there.

Stereophotography was an important breakthrough, for its binocular vision marked a distinct departure from perspective in the pictorial tradition and demonstrated for the first

863. HONORÉ DAUMIER. *Nadar Elevating Photography to the Height of Art*. 1862. Lithograph. George Eastman House, Rochester, N.Y

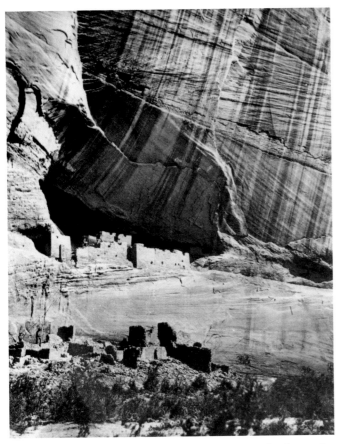

directness. *Home of a Rebel Sharpshooter* (fig. 866) by Alexander Gardner (1821–1882), who left Brady to form his own team, is a landmark in the history of art, conveying inexorably both the grim reality and the significance of death on the battlefield in a single image. Compared with the heroic act celebrated by Benjamin West (see fig. 812), this tragedy is as anonymous as the slain soldier himself. The photograph is all the more persuasive for having the same harsh realism found in David's *Death of Marat* (see fig. 827), and the limp figure, hardly visible between the rocks framing the scene, is no less poignant. In contrast, the paintings and engravings by the artists—notably Winslow Homer—who illustrated the Civil War for magazines and newspapers were mostly genre scenes that kept the reality of combat safely at arm's length.

864. TIMOTHY O'SULLIVAN. *Ancient Ruins in the Cañon de Chelle, N.M. In a Niche 50 Feet above the Present Cañon Bed* (now Canyon de Chelly National Monument, Arizona). 1873. Albumen print. George Eastman House, Rochester, N.Y.

865. *Tsar Cannon Outside the Spassky Gate, Moscow* (cast 1586; world's largest caliber, 890 mm; presently inside Kremlin). Second half 19th century. Stereophotograph (courtesy Culver Photos)

866. ALEXANDER GARDNER. *Home of a Rebel Sharpshooter, Gettysburg.* 1863. Wet-plate photograph. Chicago Historical Society

2
REALISM AND IMPRESSIONISM

PAINTING
France

"Can Jupiter survive the lightning rod?" asked Karl Marx, not long after the middle of the century. The question, implying that the ancient god of thunder and lightning was now in jeopardy through science, sums up the dilemma we felt in Carpeaux's *The Dance*. The French poet and art critic Charles Baudelaire was addressing himself to the same problem when, in 1846, he called for paintings that expressed "the heroism of modern life." At that time only one painter was willing to make an artistic creed of this demand: Baudelaire's friend Gustave Courbet (1819–1877).

COURBET AND REALISM. Proud of his rural background—he was born in Ornans, a village near the French-Swiss border—and a socialist in politics, Courbet had begun as a Neo-Baroque Romantic in the early 1840s; but by 1848, under the impact of the revolutionary upheavals then sweeping over Europe, he had come to believe that the Romantic emphasis on feeling and imagination was merely an escape from the realities of the time. The modern artist must rely on his own direct experience ("I cannot paint an angel because I have never seen one," he said); he must be a Realist. As a descriptive term, "realism" is not very precise. For Courbet, it meant something akin to the "naturalism" of Caravaggio (fig. 693, colorplate 94). As an admirer of Louis Le Nain and Rembrandt he had, in fact, strong links with the Caravaggio tradition, and his work, like Caravaggio's, was denounced for its supposed vulgarity and lack of spiritual content.

The storm broke in 1849, when he exhibited *The Stone Breakers* (fig. 867), the first canvas fully embodying his programmatic Realism. Courbet had seen two men working on a road, and had asked them to pose for him in his studio. He painted them lifesize, solidly and matter-of-factly, with none of Millet's overt pathos or sentiment: the young man's face is averted, the old one's half hidden by a hat. Yet he cannot have picked them casually: their contrast in age is significant—one is too old for such heavy work, the other too young. Endowed with the dignity of their symbolic status, they do not turn to us for sympathy. Courbet's friend, the socialist Proudhon, likened them to a parable from the Gospels.

At the Paris Exposition of 1855, works by Ingres and Delacroix were prominently displayed, while Courbet failed to gain entry for his pictures. He brought them to public attention by organizing a private exhibition in a large wooden shed and by distributing a "manifesto of Realism." The show centered on a huge canvas, the most ambitious of his career, entitled: *Interior of My Studio, a Real Allegory Summing Up Seven Years of My Life as an Artist* (fig. 868, colorplate 117). "Real allegory" is something of a teaser (allegories, after all, are unreal by definition); Courbet meant either an allegory couched in the terms of his particular Realism, or one that did not conflict with the "real" identity of the figures or objects embodying it.

The framework is familiar; Courbet's composition clearly belongs to the type of Velázquez' *Maids of Honor* and Goya's *Family of Charles IV* (see figs. 754, 833). But now the artist has moved to the center; his visitors are here his guests,

867 GUSTAVE COURBET. *The Stone Breakers.*
1849 (destroyed 1945). 63 × 102″. State Picture Gallery, Dresden

not royal patrons who enter whenever they wish. He has invited them specially, for a purpose that becomes evident only upon thoughtful reflection; the picture does not yield its full meaning unless we take the title seriously and inquire into Courbet's relation to this assembly.

There are two main groups: on the left are "the people"— types rather than individuals, drawn largely from the artist's home environment at Ornans—hunters, peasants, workers, a Jew, a priest, a young mother with her baby. On the right, in contrast, we see groups of portraits representing the Parisian side of Courbet's life—clients, critics, intellectuals (the man reading is Baudelaire). All of these people are strangely passive, as if they were waiting for we know not what. Some are quietly conversing among themselves, others seem immersed in thought; hardly anybody looks at Courbet. They are not his audience, but a representative sampling of his human environment.

Only two people watch the artist at work: a small boy, intended to suggest "the innocent eye," and the nude model. What is her role? In a more conventional picture, we would identify her as Inspiration, or Courbet's Muse, but she is no less "real" than the others here; Courbet probably meant her to be Nature, or that undisguised Truth which he proclaimed the guiding principle of his art (note the emphasis on the clothing she has just taken off). Significantly enough, the center group is illuminated by clear, sharp daylight but the background and the lateral figures are veiled in semi-darkness, to underline the contrast between the artist—the active creator—and the world around him that waits to be brought to life.

868. GUSTAVE COURBET. *Interior of My Studio,
a Real Allegory Summing Up Seven Years of My Life as an Artist*
(detail; see colorplate 117). The Louvre, Paris

869. ÉDOUARD MANET. *The Fifer*
(detail; see colorplate 118). The Louvre, Paris

MANET AND THE "REVOLUTION OF THE COLOR
PATCH." Courbet's *Studio* helps us to understand a picture
that shocked the public even more: Manet's *Luncheon on
the Grass* (fig. 4), showing a nude model accompanied by
two gentlemen in frock coats. Edouard Manet (1832–1883)
was the first to grasp Courbet's full importance—his *Luncheon*, among other things, is a tribute to the older artist. He
particularly offended contemporary morality by juxtaposing
the nude and clothed figures in an outdoor setting, the
more so since the noncommittal title offered no "higher"
significance. Yet the group has so formal a pose (for its
classical source, see figs. 5, 6) that Manet certainly did not
intend to depict an actual event. Perhaps the meaning of the
canvas lies in this denial of plausibility, for the scene fits
neither the plane of everyday experience nor that of allegory.

The *Luncheon*, as a visual manifesto of artistic freedom,
is much more revolutionary than Courbet's; it asserts the
painter's privilege to combine whatever elements he pleases
for aesthetic effect alone. The nudity of the model is
"explained" by the contrast between her warm, creamy flesh
tones and the cool black-and-gray of the men's attire. Or, to
put it another way, the world of painting has "natural laws"
that are distinct from those of familiar reality, and the painter's first loyalty is to his canvas, not to the outside world.
Here begins an attitude that was later summed up in the
doctrine of Art for Art's Sake, and became a bone of conten-
tion between progressives and conservatives for the rest of
the century (see page 634). Manet himself disdained such
controversies, but his work attests his lifelong devotion to

"pure painting"—to the belief that brush strokes and color
patches themselves, not what they stand for, are the artist's
primary reality. Among painters of the past, he found that
Hals, Velázquez, and Goya had come closest to this ideal. He
admired their broad, open technique, their preoccupation
with light and color values. Many of his canvases are, in
fact, "pictures of pictures"—they translate into modern
terms those older works that particularly challenged him.
Yet he always took care to filter out the expressive or symbolic
content of his models, lest the beholder's attention be dis-
tracted from the pictorial structure itself. His paintings,
whatever their subject, have an emotional reticence that can
easily be mistaken for emptiness unless we understand
its purpose.

Courbet is said to have remarked that Manet's pictures
were as flat as playing cards. Looking at *The Fifer* (fig. 869,
colorplate 118), we can see what he meant. Done three years
after the *Luncheon*, it is a painting without shadows (there
are a few, actually, but it takes a real effort to find them),
hardly any modeling, and no depth. The figure looks three-
dimensional only because its contour renders the forms in
realistic foreshortening; otherwise, Manet eschews all the
methods devised since Giotto's time for transmuting a flat
surface into a pictorial space. The undifferentiated light-gray
background seems as near to us as the figure, and just as
solid; if the fifer stepped out of the picture, he would leave
a hole, like the cut-out shape of a stencil.

Here, then, the canvas itself has been redefined—it is no
longer a "window," but a screen made up of flat patches of
color. How radical a step this was can be readily seen if
we match *The Fifer* against Delacroix's *Greece* (fig. 840,
colorplate 116) and a Cubist work such as Picasso's *Three
Dancers* of 1925 (fig. 947, colorplate 137). The structure
of Manet's painting obviously resembles that of Picasso's,
whereas Delacroix—or even Courbet—still follows the
"window" tradition of the Renaissance. In retrospect, we

870. CLAUDE MONET. *The River* (see colorplate 119).
The Art Institute of Chicago (Potter Palmer Collection)

871. ÉDOUARD MANET. *A Bar at the Folies-Bergères.* 1881–82. 37½ × 51″. The Courtauld Collection, London

realize that the revolutionary qualities of Manet's art were already to be seen, if not yet so obvious, in the *Luncheon*. The three figures lifted from Raphael's group of river gods form a unit nearly as shadowless and stencil-like as the fifer; they would be more at home on a flat screen, for the chiaroscuro of their present setting, which is inspired by the landscapes of Courbet, no longer fits them.

MONET AND IMPRESSIONISM. What brought about this "revolution of the color patch"? We do not know, and Manet himself surely did not reason it out beforehand. It is tempting to think that he was impelled to create the new style by the challenge of photography. The "pencil of nature," then known for a quarter century, had vindicated the objective truth of Renaissance perspective, but it established a standard of representational accuracy that no hand-made image could hope to rival. Painting needed to be rescued from competition with the camera. This Manet accomplished by insisting that a painted canvas is, above all, a material surface covered with pigments—that we must look *at* it, not *through* it. Unlike Courbet, he gave no name to the style he had created; when his followers began calling themselves Impressionists, he refused to accept the term for his own work.

The word Impressionism had been coined in 1874, after a hostile critic had looked at a picture entitled *Impression:*

Sunrise, by Claude Monet (1840–1926), and it certainly fits Monet better than it does Manet. Monet had adopted Manet's concept of painting and applied it to landscapes done out-of-doors. Monet's *The River*, of 1868 (fig. 870, colorplate 119), is flooded with sunlight so bright that conservative critics claimed it made their eyes smart; in this flickering network of color patches, the reflections on the water are as "real" as the banks of the Seine. Even more than *The Fifer*, Monet's painting is a "playing card"; were it not for the woman and the boat in the foreground, the picture could hang upside-down with hardly any difference of effect. The mirror image here serves a purpose contrary to that of earlier mirror images (compare fig. 524): instead of adding to the illusion of real space, it strengthens the unity of the actual painted surface. This inner coherence sets *The River* apart from Romantic "impressions" like Constable's *Hampstead Heath* (see fig. 820), or Corot's *Papigno* (see fig. 848), even though all three share the same on-the-spot immediacy and fresh perception.

MANET AND IMPRESSIONISM. These latter qualities came less easily to the austere and deliberate Manet; they appear in his work only after about 1870, under Monet's influence. Manet's last major picture, *A Bar at the Folies-Bergères*, of 1881–82 (fig. 871), shows a single figure as calm—and as firmly set within the rectangle of the canvas—

872. BERTHE MORISOT. *The Artist's Sister Edma and Their Mother*. 1869–70. 39½ × 32″. The National Gallery of Art, Washington, D.C. (Chester Dale Collection)

couples in *Le Moulin de la Galette* (fig. 873, colorplate 120), dappled with sunlight and shadow, radiate a human warmth that is utterly entrancing, even though the artist permits us no more than a fleeting glance at any of them. Our role is that of the casual stroller, who takes in this slice of life as he passes.

DEGAS. By contrast, Edgar Degas (1834–1917) makes us look steadily at the disenchanted pair in his café scene (fig. 874), but, so to speak, out of the corner of our eye. The design of this picture at first seems as unstudied as a snapshot (indeed Degas practiced photography), yet a longer look shows us that everything here dovetails precisely—that the zigzag of empty tables between us and the luckless couple reinforces their brooding loneliness. Compositions as boldly calculated as this set Degas apart from his fellow Impressionists. A wealthy aristocrat by birth, he had been trained in the tradition of Ingres, whom he greatly admired. Like Ingres, he despised portraiture as a trade but, unlike him, he acted on his conviction and portrayed only friends and relatives—individuals with whom he had emotional ties. His profound sense of human character lends weight even to seemingly casual scenes such as that in *Glass of Absinthe*.

When he joined the Impressionists, Degas did not abandon his early allegiance to draftsmanship. His finest works were often done in pastel (powdered pigments molded into sticks), a medium that had a strong appeal for him since it yielded effects of line, tone, and color simultaneously. *Prima Ballerina* (fig. 875) well demonstrates this flexible tech-

as the fifer, but the background is no longer neutral. A huge shimmering mirror image now reflects the whole interior of the nightclub, but deprives it of three-dimensional reality. (The mirror, close behind the barmaid, fills four-fifths of the picture.) The barmaid's attitude, detached and touched with melancholy, contrasts poignantly with the sparkling gaiety of her setting, which she is not permitted to share. For all its urbanity, the mood of the canvas reminds us oddly of Daumier's *Third-Class Carriage* (see fig. 844).

MORISOT. A similar introspection is found in the portrait of her mother and sister by Berthe Morisot (1841–1895), who concentrated on such images of family members (fig. 872). It was painted a year after she met Manet (whose brother she later married). In fact, he partly reworked the mother's dark dress, but the picture remains Morisot's creation. The scene is deceptive in its repose. Distinctive to her early work is the subtle aura of alienation. Here it is not the heroism, but the pathos, of modern life that is revealed, yet with a delicacy of sentiment that is characteristic of Morisot's art.

RENOIR. Scenes from the world of entertainment—dance halls, cafés, concerts, the theater—were favorite subjects for Impressionist painters. Auguste Renoir (1841–1919), another important member of the group, filled his with the *joie de vivre* of a singularly happy temperament. The flirting

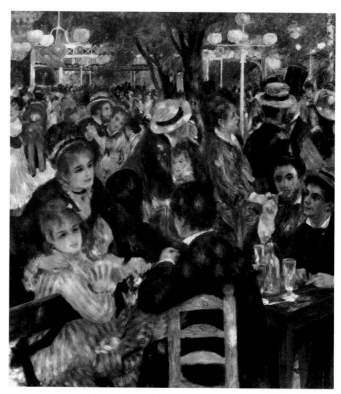

873. AUGUSTE RENOIR. *Le Moulin de la Galette* (detail; see colorplate 120). The Louvre, Paris

874. EDGAR DEGAS. *The Glass of Absinthe.*
1876. 36 × 27″. The Louvre, Paris

875. EDGAR DEGAS. *Prima Ballerina.* c. 1876.
Pastel, 23 × 16½″. The Louvre, Paris

nique. The oblique view of the stage, from a box near the proscenium arch, has been shaped into another deliberately off-center composition; the dancer floats above the steeply tilted floor like a butterfly caught in the glare of the footlights.

A decade later, *The Tub* (fig. 876, colorplate 121) is again an oblique view, but now severe, almost geometric in design: the tub and the crouching woman, both vigorously outlined, form a circle within a square, and the rest of the rectangular format is filled by a shelf so sharply tilted that it almost shares the plane of the picture; yet on this shelf Degas has placed two pitchers (note how the curve of the small one fits the handle of the other!) that are hardly foreshortened at all. Here the tension between "two-D" and "three-D," surface and depth, comes close to the breaking point.

The Tub is Impressionist only in its shimmering, luminous colors. Its other qualities are more characteristic of the 1880s, the first post-Impressionist decade, when many artists showed a renewed concern with problems of form (see Chapter 3).

MONET'S LATER WORKS. Among the major figures of the movement, Monet alone remained faithful to the Impressionist view of nature. About 1890, he began to paint pictures in series, showing the same subject under various conditions of light and atmosphere. These tended increasingly to resem-

876. EDGAR DEGAS. *The Tub*
(see colorplate 121). The Louvre, Paris

ble Turner's "airy visions, painted with tinted steam" as Monet concentrated on effects of colored light (see page 594; he had visited London, and knew Turner's work). But Monet never ventured into subjective fantasy, nor did he abandon the basic approach of his earlier work. His *Water Lilies, Giverny* (fig. 877) is a consistent sequel to *The River,*

877. CLAUDE MONET. *Water Lilies, Giverny.* 1907.
36½ × 29″. Collection Jocelyn Walker, London

contrast between the brooding young couple in the foreground and the "good riddance" gesture of the man at the
upper left—we recognize its source in the "dumb shows" of
Hogarth, whom Brown revered (see fig. 786).

Brown's style, however, has nothing in common with
Hogarth's; its impersonal precision of detail strikes us as
almost photographic; no hint of subjective "handwriting" is
permitted to intervene between us and the scene depicted.
Brown had acquired this painstaking technique some years
earlier, after he met a group of German painters in Rome
who practiced what they regarded as a "medieval" style (see
above, page 596). He in turn transmitted it to the painter
and poet Dante Gabriel Rossetti (1828–1882), who in 1848
helped to found an artists' society called the Pre-Raphaelite
Brotherhood.

THE PRE-RAPHAELITES.   Brown himself never actually
joined the Pre-Raphaelites, but he shared their basic aim:
to do battle against the frivolous art of the day by producing
"pure transcripts . . . from nature" and by having "genuine
ideas to express." As the name of the Brotherhood proclaims,
its members took their inspiration from the "primitive" masters of the fifteenth century; to that extent, they belong to
the Gothic revival, which had long been an important aspect
of the Romantic movement. What set the Pre-Raphaelites
apart from Romanticism pure and simple was an urge to
reform the ills of modern civilization through their art; thus
the emigrants in *The Last of England* dramatize the conditions that made them decide to leave England.

across a span of almost forty years. The pond surface now
takes up the entire canvas, so that the effect of a weightless
screen is stronger than ever; the artist's brushwork has
greater variety and a more personal rhythm; the theme,
however, is still the endlessly fascinating interplay of reflection and reality.

England

REALISM.   By the time Monet came to admire his work,
Turner's reputation was at a low ebb in his own country.
Toward 1850, when Courbet launched his revolutionary doctrine of Realism, a concern with "the heroism of modern
life" asserted itself quite independently in English painting
as well, although the movement lacked a leader of Courbet's
stature and assertiveness. Perhaps best known is *The Last
of England* (fig. 878, colorplate 122), by Ford Madox Brown
(1821–1893), a picture that enjoyed vast popularity throughout the latter half of the century in the English-speaking
world. The subject—a group of emigrants watching the
coast of their homeland disappear as they set out on their
long overseas journey—may be less obvious today than it
once was, and does not carry the same emotional charge.
Nonetheless, there can be no question that the artist has
treated an important theme taken from modern experience,
and that he has done so with touching seriousness. If the
pathos of the scene strikes us as a bit theatrical—note the

878. FORD MADOX BROWN. *The Last
of England* (see colorplate 122). City
Museum and Art Gallery, Birmingham, England

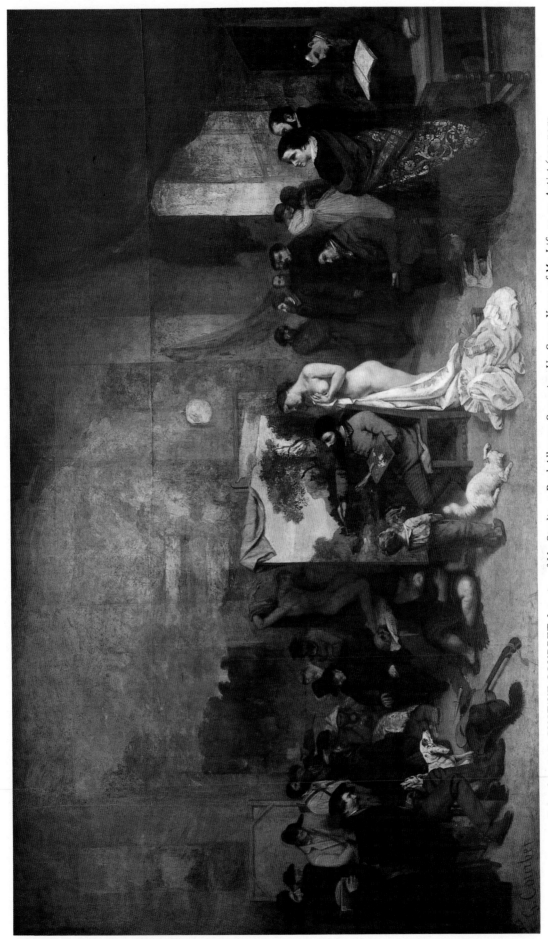

Colorplate 117. GUSTAVE COURBET. *Interior of My Studio, a Real Allegory Summing Up Seven Years of My Life as an Artist* (see page 618). 1854–55. 11' 10" × 19' 7". The Louvre, Paris

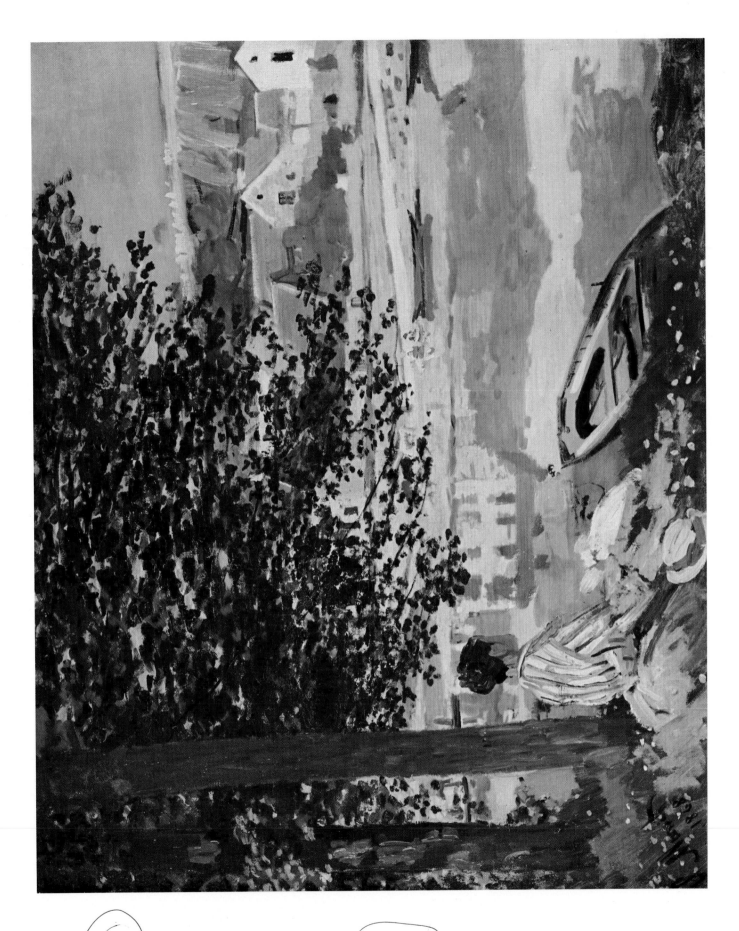

Colorplate 118. (*left*) EDOUARD MANET. *The Fifer*
(see page 620). 1866. 63 × 38¼″. The Louvre, Paris

Colorplate 119. (*above*) CLAUDE MONET. *The River* (see page 621).
1868. 32 × 39½″. The Art Institute of Chicago
(Potter Palmer Collection)

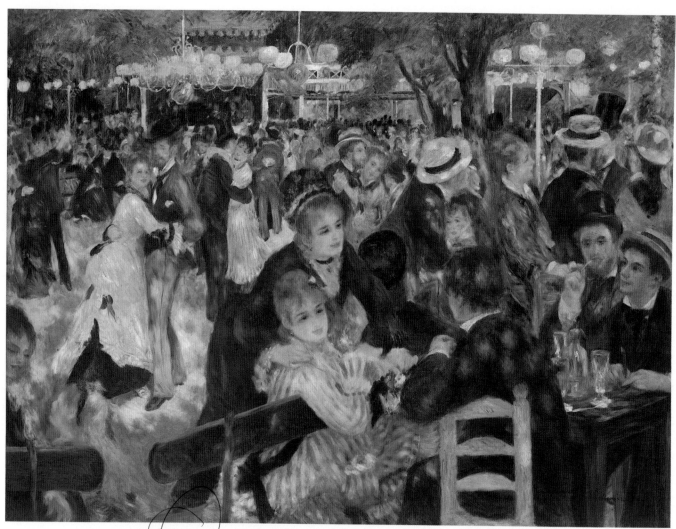

Colorplate 120. AUGUSTE RENOIR. *Le Moulin de la Galette* (see page 622). 1876.
51½ × 69″. The Louvre, Paris

Colorplate 121. EDGAR DEGAS. *The Tub* (see page 623). 1886. Pastel, 23½ × 32⅓″.
The Louvre, Paris

Colorplate 122. FORD MADOX BROWN. *The Last of England* (see page 624). 1852–55.
Panel, 32½ × 29½″. City Museum and Art Gallery, Birmingham, England

Colorplate 123. (*above*) JAMES WHISTLER.
Nocturne in Black and Gold: the Falling Rocket (see page 634).
About 1874. 23¾ × 18⅜″. The Detroit Institute of Arts

Colorplate 124. (*right*) PAUL CÉZANNE. *Self-Portrait*
(see page 641). About 1879. 13¾ × 10⅝″. The Tate Gallery,
London (By courtesy of the Trustees)

Colorplate 125. GEORGES SEURAT. *Side Show* (*La Parade*). 1887–88. 39½ × 59¼" (see page 643).
The Metropolitan Museum of Art, New York (Bequest of Stephen C. Clark, 1960)

879. DANTE GABRIEL ROSSETTI. *Ecce Ancilla Domini.*
1850. 28½ × 16½". The Tate Gallery, London

MORRIS. The link between Rossetti and Crane's cartoon was William Morris (1834–1896), who started out as a Pre-Raphaelite painter but soon shifted his interest to "art for use"—domestic architecture and interior decoration such as furniture, tapestries, and wallpapers. He wanted to displace the shoddy products of the machine age by reviving the handicrafts of the pre-industrial past, an art "made by the people, and for the people, as a happiness to the maker and the user."

Morris was an apostle of simplicity: architecture and furniture ought to be designed in accordance with the nature of their materials and working processes; surface decoration ought to be flat rather than illusionistic. Our sample of one of his wallpapers (fig. 881) exemplifies the latter principle in its rhythmic movement of fluid, sinuous lines. Despite Morris' self-proclaimed championship of the medieval tradition, this pattern does not represent the revival of any past style but is an independent creation. He invented the first original system of ornament since the Rococo—no small achievement.

Through the many enterprises he sponsored, as well as his skill as a writer and publicist, Morris became a tastemaker without peer in his day. Toward the end of the century, his influence had spread throughout Europe and America. Nor was he content to reform the arts of design alone; he saw them, rather, as a lever by which to reform modern society as a whole. As a consequence, he played an important part

880. WALTER CRANE. Political cartoon from
Cartoons for the Cause. 1886. Woodcut

But Rossetti, unlike Brown, was not concerned with social problems; he thought of himself, rather, as a reformer of aesthetic sensibility. His early masterpiece, *Ecce Ancilla Domini* (fig. 879), though realistic in detail, is full of self-conscious archaisms such as the pale tonality, the limited range of colors, the awkward perspective, and the stress on the verticals, not to mention the title in Latin. At the same time, this Annunciation radiates an aura of repressed eroticism that became the hallmark of Rossetti's work and exerted a powerful influence on other Pre-Raphaelites.

We can sense it even in the political cartoon (fig. 880) by the illustrator and book designer Walter Crane (1845–1915), which shows another kind of "annunciation"; the genius of Liberty, strongly reminiscent of the style of Botticelli (see fig. 594, colorplate 73), brings the glad tidings of socialism to a sleeping worker who is being oppressed by Capitalism in the shape of a nightmarish vampire. Shades of Henry Fuseli! (Compare fig. 816.)

881. WILLIAM MORRIS. Detail of "Pimpernel" Wallpaper.
1876. Victoria & Albert Museum, London

austere precision of Degas' portraits. Its rise to fame as a symbol of our latter-day "mother cult" is a paradox of popular psychology that would have dismayed Whistler: he wanted the canvas to be appreciated for its formal qualities alone.

A witty, sharp-tongued advocate of Art for Art's Sake he thought of his pictures as analogous to pieces of music, calling them "symphonies" or "nocturnes." The boldest example, painted about 1874, is *Nocturne in Black and Gold: The Falling Rocket* (fig. 883, colorplate 123); without an explanatory subtitle, we would have real difficulty making it out. No French painter had yet dared to produce a picture so "non-representational," so reminiscent of Cozens' blot-scapes and Turner's "tinted steam" (see figs. 819, 822, color-plate 111). It was this canvas, more than any other, that prompted John Ruskin to accuse Whistler of "flinging a pot of paint in the public's face." Since the same critic had highly praised Turner's *Slave Ship*, we must conclude that what Ruskin really liked was not the tinted steam itself but the Romantic sentiment behind it.

During Whistler's subsequent suit for libel, he offered a definition of his aims that seems to be particularly applicable to *The Falling Rocket:* "I have perhaps meant rather to indicate an artistic interest alone in my work, divesting the picture from any outside sort of interest.... It is an arrangement of line, form, and color, first, and I make use of any incident of it which shall bring about a symmetrical result." The last phrase has special significance, since Whistler acknowledges that in utilizing chance effects, he does not look for resemblances but for a purely formal harmony. While he rarely practiced what he preached to quite the same extent as he did in *The Falling Rocket*, his statement reads like a prophecy of American abstract painting today (see fig. 967, colorplate 146).

in the early history of Fabian socialism (the gradualist variety invented in England as an alternative to the revolutionary socialism of the Continent). Many of his artist friends, including Walter Crane, came to share his convictions, and some contributed their artistic talents to the cause. Such, then, is the background of our cartoon.

America

WHISTLER. Courbet, during the later years of his life, enjoyed considerable fame and influence abroad; the Impressionists gained international recognition more slowly. Surprisingly, Americans were their first patrons, responding to the new style sooner than Europeans did. At a time when no French museum would have them, Impressionist works entered public collections in the United States, and American painters were among the earliest followers of Manet and his circle. James McNeill Whistler (1834–1903) came to Paris in 1855 to study painting; four years later he moved to London to spend the rest of his life, but he visited France during the 1860s and was in close touch with the rising Impressionist movement.

His best-known picture, *Arrangement in Black and Gray: The Artist's Mother* (fig. 882), reflects the influence of Manet in its emphasis on flat areas, and the likeness has the

882. JAMES WHISTLER. *Arrangement in Black and Gray: The Artist's Mother.* 1871. 57 × 64½". The Louvre, Paris

883. JAMES WHISTLER. *Nocturne in Black and Gold:*
The Falling Rocket (see colorplate 123).
The Detroit Institute of Arts

HOMER. Whistler's gifted contemporary in America, Winslow Homer (1836–1910), also came to Paris as a young man, but left too soon to receive the full impact of Impressionism. He was a pictorial reporter throughout the Civil War and continued as a magazine illustrator until 1875. Yet he did some of his most remarkable paintings in the 1860s. Such a work is *The Morning Bell* (fig. 884); the fresh delicacy of the sunlit scene might be called "pre-Impressionist"—halfway between Corot and Monet (compare figs. 848, 870, colorplate 119). The picture has an extraordinarily subtle design as well: the dog, the center girl, and those at the right turn the footpath into a seesaw, its upward slant balanced by the descending line of treetops.

EAKINS. Thomas Eakins (1844–1916) arrived in Paris from Philadelphia about the time Homer painted *The Morning Bell;* he went home four years later with decisive impressions of Courbet, Manet, and Velázquez. Elements from these three artists are combined in *The Gross Clinic* (fig. 885), the most imposing work of American nineteenth-century painting. A powerfully realistic canvas, it is a lifesize view of an operation in progress, glossing over none of the gruesome detail. Conservative critics denounced it as a "degradation of art," but to us it seems a splendid fulfillment of Baudelaire's demand for pictures that express the "heroism of modern life."

TANNER. Eakins encouraged both women and blacks to study art seriously at a time when professional careers were closed to them. African-Americans had had no chance to enter the arts before Emancipation, and after the Civil War the situation improved only gradually. Henry O. Tanner (1859–1937), the first important black painter, studied with Eakins in the early 1880s. Tanner's masterpiece, *The Banjo Lesson* (fig. 886), painted after he moved permanently to

884. WINSLOW HOMER. *The Morning Bell.* c. 1866. 24 × 38″. Yale University Art Gallery,
New Haven, Connecticut (Stephen C. Clark Collection)

885. THOMAS EAKINS. *The Gross Clinic.* 1875. 96 × 78".
Jefferson Medical College, Philadelphia

Paris, bears Eakins' unmistakable impress: avoiding the sentimentality in similar subjects by other American painters, the scene is rendered with a light-filled realism based on personal experience, like *The Gross Clinic.*

CASSATT. Thanks in large part to Eakins' enlightened attitude, Philadelphia became the leading center of minority artists in the United States, but they had to struggle to overcome traditional barriers. Mary Cassatt's (1845–1926) early training there was very similar to Eakins', but like Tanner she elected to settle in Paris, where she joined the Impressionists in 1877. Although her family objected to her vocation, she was able to pursue her career as an artist, at a time when it was frowned on as an occupation for women, only because she was independently wealthy (like Berthe Morisot, another member of the group; see page 622). A tireless champion of the Impressionists, Cassatt was instrumental in gaining early acceptance of their paintings in the United States through her social contacts with rich private collectors. She was never married, yet maternity provided her with the thematic material and formal focus of most of her work, which reached its maturity around 1890. In its oblique view, simplified color forms, and flat composition, *The Bath* (fig. 887) reflects Cassatt's debt to her colleagues Degas (fig. 874) and Manet (fig. 869, colorplate 118), as well as her study of Japanese prints. These influences, however, have been assimilated into an individual and highly accomplished manner which made her America's leading Impressionist.

886. HENRY O. TANNER. *The Banjo Lesson.* c. 1893.
48 × 35". Hampton Institute, Hampton, Virginia.

887. MARY CASSATT. *The Bath.* 1891. 39½ × 26″. The Art
Institute of Chicago (Robert A. Woller Collection)

dimensional form into flickering patches of light and dark?
These fiercely exaggerated shapes pulsate with sculptural
energy, and they retain this quality under whatever conditions the piece is viewed. For Rodin did not work directly in
bronze; he modeled in wax or clay. How could he calculate
in advance the reflections on the bronze surfaces of the casts
that would ultimately be made from these models?

He worked as he did, we must assume, for an altogether
different reason: not to capture elusive optical effects, but
to emphasize the process of "growth"—the miracle of dead
matter coming to life in the artist's hands. As the color patch,
for Manet and Monet, is the primary reality, so are the malleable lumps from which Rodin builds his forms. And conservative critics rejected *The Man with the Broken Nose* and
Impressionist painting on the same grounds—it was
"unfinished," a mere sketch.

Sculptors, of course, had always made small, informal
sketches (the plastic counterpart of drawings), but these
were for the artist's private use, not for public display. Rodin
was the first to make of unfinishedness an aesthetic principle
that governed both his handling of surfaces and the whole
shape of the work (*The Man with the Broken Nose* is not a
bust, but a head "broken off" at the neck). By discovering
what might be called the autonomy of the fragment, he
rescued sculpture from mechanical verisimilitude just as
Manet rescued painting from photographic realism.

This sculptural revolution, proclaimed with such daring
by Rodin at twenty-four, did not reach full force until the
late 1870s. For his living, the young artist had to collaborate

SCULPTURE
Rodin

Impressionism, it is often said, revitalized sculpture no less
than painting. The statement is at once true and misleading.
Auguste Rodin (1840–1917), the first sculptor of genius
since Bernini, redefined sculpture during the same years
that Manet and Monet redefined painting; in so doing, however, he did not follow these artists' lead. How indeed could
the effect of such pictures as *The Fifer* or *The River* be
reproduced in three dimensions and without color?

THE MAN WITH THE BROKEN NOSE.   What Rodin did
accomplish is already visible in the first piece he tried to
exhibit (it was rejected, as we might expect), *The Man with
the Broken Nose* of 1864 (fig. 888). Earlier, he had worked
briefly under Barye, whose influence may help to explain
the vigorously creased surface (compare fig. 857). These
welts and wrinkles produce, in polished bronze, an ever-
changing pattern of reflections. But is this effect borrowed
from Impressionist painting? Does Rodin dissolve three-

888. AUGUSTE RODIN. *The Man with the Broken Nose.*
1864. Bronze, height 9½″. Rodin Museum,
Philadelphia Museum of Art

889. AUGUSTE RODIN. *The Thinker*. 1879–89. Bronze,
height 27½". The Metropolitan Museum of Art,
New York (Gift of Thomas F. Ryan, 1910)

890. AUGUSTE RODIN. *The Kiss*. 1886–98.
Marble, over lifesize. Rodin Museum, Paris

with officially recognized sculptors on their public commissions, mostly memorials and architectural sculpture in the Neo-Baroque style of Carpeaux. In 1879 he was at last entrusted with a major task, the entrance of the Museum of Decorative Arts in Paris.

THE GATES OF HELL.   Rodin elaborated the commission into an ambitious ensemble called *The Gates of Hell*, its symbolic program inspired by Dante's *Inferno*. He never finished the *Gates*, but they served as a matrix for countless smaller pieces that he eventually made into independent works.

The most famous of these autonomous fragments is *The Thinker* (fig. 889), intended for the lintel of the *Gates*, whence the figure was to contemplate the panorama of despair below. The ancestry of *The Thinker* goes back, indirectly, to the first phase of Christian art (the pensive man seated at the left in a Byzantine ivory [fig. 333] reflects an Early Christian source); it also includes the action-in-repose

of Michelangelo's superhuman bodies (see figs. 614, 617, 619, colorplate 77), the tension in Puget's *Milo* (see fig. 772, especially the feet), and the expressive dynamism of *The Man with the Broken Nose*. Who is *The Thinker*? Partly Adam, no doubt (though there is also a different Adam by Rodin, another "outgrowth" of the *Gates*), partly Prometheus, and partly the brute imprisoned by the passions of the flesh. Rodin wisely refrained from giving him a specific name, for the statue fits no preconceived identity. In this new image of man, form and meaning are one, instead of cleaving apart as in Carpeaux's *Dance*. Carpeaux produced naked figures that pretend to be nude, while *The Thinker*, like the nudes of Michelangelo, is free from subservience to the undressed model.

The Kiss (fig. 890), an over-lifesize group in marble, also derives from the *Gates*. Less powerful than *The Thinker*, it exploits another kind of artful unfinishedness. Rodin had been impressed by the struggle of Michelangelo's "Slaves" against the remnants of the blocks that imprison them; *The*

891. AUGUSTE RODIN. *Balzac* (portion). 1892–97.
Plaster, 9' 10". Rodin Museum, Paris

Kiss was planned from the start to include the mass of roughhewn marble to which the lovers are attached, and which thus becomes symbolic of their earthbound passion. The contrast of textures emphasizes the veiled, sensuous softness of the bodies.

BALZAC MONUMENT.   But Rodin was by instinct a modeler, not a carver like Michelangelo. His greatest works were intended to be cast in bronze. Even these, however, reveal their full strength only when we see them in plaster casts made directly from Rodin's clay originals. The *Balzac Monument*, his most daring creation, remained in plaster for many years, rejected by the committee that had commissioned it (fig. 891).

The figure is larger than life, physically and spiritually; it has the overpowering presence of a specter. Like a huge monolith, the man of genius towers above the crowd; he shares "the sublime egotism of the gods" (as the Romantics put it). Rodin has minimized the articulation of the body, so that from a distance we see only its great bulk. As we approach, we become aware that Balzac is wrapped in a long, shroud-like cloak. From this mass the head thrusts upward— one is tempted to say, erupts—with elemental force. When we are close enough to make out the features clearly, we sense beneath the disdain an inner agony that stamps *Balzac* as the kin of *The Man with the Broken Nose*.

3
POST-IMPRESSIONISM

PAINTING

In 1882, just before his death, Manet was made a chevalier of the Legion of Honor by the French government. Four years later, the Impressionists, who had been exhibiting together since 1874, held their last group show. These two events mark the turn of the tide—Impressionism had gained wide acceptance among artists and the public, but by the same token it was no longer a pioneering movement. The future now belonged to the "Post-Impressionists."

Taken literally, this colorless label applies to all painters of significance since the 1880s; in a more specific sense, it designates a group of artists who passed through an Impressionist phase but became dissatisfied with the limitations of the style and went beyond it in various directions. As they did not share one common goal, it is difficult to find a more descriptive term for them than Post-Impressionists. In any event, they were not "anti-Impressionists." Far from trying to undo the effects of the "Manet Revolution," they wanted to carry it further; Post-Impressionism is in essence just a later stage—though a very important one—of the development that had begun in the 1870s with such pictures as Manet's *Luncheon on the Grass.*

CÉZANNE. Paul Cézanne (1839–1906), the oldest of the Post-Impressionists, was born in Aix-en-Provence, near the Mediterranean coast. A man of intensely emotional temperament, he came to Paris in 1861 imbued with enthusiasm for the Romantics; Delacroix was his first love among painters, and he never lost his admiration for him. *Christ in Limbo* (fig. 892) has the heavy impasto and highly personal, expressive brushwork of this "Neo-Baroque" phase of Cézanne's development. Yet the painting also shows how well the young artist had grasped the nature of the "Manet Revolution": it is a "picture of a picture" like those Manet had painted, and is based on an Italian sixteenth-century work which Cézanne knew only from a reproduction (fig. 893). What fascinated him here was the problem of translating the Renaissance composition into the style of Manet's *Fifer* (see fig. 869, colorplate 118): to reconcile, by "closing" the cav-

892. PAUL CÉZANNE, after SEBASTIANO DEL PIOMBO.
Christ in Limbo. c. 1868–70. 66 × 40".
Collection René Lecomte, Paris

so as to produce "chords" of warm and cool tones that reverberate throughout the canvas.

In Cézanne's still lifes, such as *Fruit Bowl, Glass, and Apples* (fig. 895), this quest for the "solid and durable" can be seen even more clearly. Not since Chardin have simple everyday objects assumed such importance in a painter's eye. Again the ornamental backdrop is integrated with the three-dimensional shapes, and the brush strokes have a rhythmic pattern that gives the canvas its shimmering texture. We also notice another aspect of Cézanne's mature style that is more conspicuous here than in the *Self-Portrait* and may puzzle us at first: the forms are deliberately simplified, and outlined with dark contours; and the perspective is "incorrect" for both the fruit bowl and the horizontal surfaces, which seem to tilt upward. The longer we study the picture, the more we realize the rightness of these apparently arbitrary distortions. When Cézanne takes these liberties with reality, his purpose is to uncover the permanent qualities beneath the accidents of appearance (all forms in nature, he believed, are based on the cone, the sphere, and the cylinder). This order underlying the external world was the true subject of his pictures, but he had to interpret it to fit the separate, closed world of the canvas. One detail of our painting is particularly instructive in this respect—the stem of the fruit bowl is slightly off-center, as if the oval shape of the bowl, in response to the pressure of the other objects, were expanding toward the left.

893. SEBASTIANO DEL PIOMBO.
Christ in Limbo. c. 1530. 89 × 45″.
The Prado, Madrid

ernous space, the claims of surface and depth. Like Manet, Cézanne accomplishes this by resolutely refusing to abide by the traditional rules of chiaroscuro: instead of modeling in a continuous scale of tones from dark to light, he treats the shadows as shapes in their own right, solid and clearly bounded. And he is bolder than Manet in his disregard of the logic of external appearance for the sake of the inner logic of the design.

Cézanne soon began to paint bright outdoor scenes, but he never shared his fellow Impressionists' interest in "slice-of-life" subjects, in movement and change. About 1879, when he painted the *Self-Portrait* in our figure 894 and colorplate 124, he had decided "to make of Impressionism something solid and durable, like the art of the museums." His Romantic impulsiveness of the 1860s has now given way to a patient, disciplined search for harmony of form and color: every brush stroke is like a building block, firmly placed within the pictorial architecture; the balance of "two-D" and "three-D" is less harsh than before (note how the pattern of wallpaper in the background frames the rounded shape of the head); and the colors are deliberately controlled

894. PAUL CÉZANNE. *Self-Portrait*
(see colorplate 124). The Tate Gallery,
London

895. PAUL CÉZANNE. *Fruit Bowl, Glass, and Apples.*
1879–82. 18 × 21½″. Collection René Lecomte, Paris

896. PAUL CÉZANNE. *Mont Sainte-Victoire Seen from Bibemus Quarry.*
c. 1898–1900. 25½ × 32″. The Baltimore Museum of Art
(The Cone Collection)

To apply this method to landscape became the greatest challenge of Cézanne's career. From 1882 on, he lived in isolation near his home town of Aix-en-Provence, exploring its environs as Claude Lorraine and Corot had explored the Roman countryside. One motif, the distinctive shape of a mountain called Mont Sainte-Victoire, seemed almost to obsess him; its craggy profile looming against the blue Mediterranean sky appears in a long series of compositions, such as the very monumental late work in figure 896. There are no hints of a man's presence here—houses and roads would only disturb the lonely grandeur of this view. Above the wall of rocky cliffs that bar our way like a chain of fortifications, the mountain rises in triumphant clarity, infinitely remote yet as solid and palpable as the shapes in the foreground. For all its architectural stability, the scene is alive with movement; but the forces at work here have been brought into equilibrium, subdued by the greater power of the artist's will. This disciplined energy, distilled from the trials of a stormy youth, gives the mature style of Cézanne its enduring strength.

SEURAT. Georges Seurat (1859–1891) shared Cézanne's aim to make Impressionism "solid and durable," but he went about it very differently. His career was as brief as those of Masaccio, Giorgione, and Géricault, and his achievement just as astonishing. Seurat devoted his main efforts to a few very large paintings, spending a year or more on each of them: he made endless series of preliminary studies before he felt sure enough to tackle the definitive version. This painstaking method reflects his belief that art must be based on a system; like Degas, he had studied with a follower of Ingres, and his theoretical interests came from this experience. But, as with all artists of genius, Seurat's theories do not really explain his pictures; it is the pictures, rather, that explain the theories.

The subject of his first large-scale composition, the *Bathers* of 1883–84 (fig. 897), is of the sort that had long been popular among Impressionist painters. Impressionist, too, are the brilliant colors and the effect of intense sunlight. Otherwise, however, the picture is the very opposite of a quick "impression"; the firm, simple contours and the relaxed, immobile figures give the scene a timeless stability that recalls Piero della Francesca (see fig. 568, colorplate 68). Even the brushwork shows Seurat's passion for order and permanence: the canvas surface is covered with systematic, impersonal "flicks" that make Cézanne's architectural brush strokes seem temperamental and dynamic by comparison.

In Seurat's later works such as *Side Show (La Parade*; fig. 898, colorplate 125), the flicks become tiny dots of brilliant color that were supposed to merge in the beholder's eye and produce intermediary tints more luminous than those obtainable from pigments mixed on the palette. This procedure was variously known as Neo-Impressionism, Pointillism, or Divisionism (the term preferred by Seurat). The

897. GEORGES SEURAT. *Bathers*. 1883–84.
79½ × 118½". The Tate Gallery, London

actual result, however, did not conform to the theory. Looking at *Side Show* from a comfortable distance (12–15″ for the colorplate, 7–10′ for the original), we find that the mixing of colors in the eye remains incomplete; the dots do not disappear, but remain as clearly visible as the tesserae of a mosaic (compare colorplate 30). Seurat himself must have liked this unexpected effect—had he not, he would have reduced the size of the dots—which gives the canvas the quality of a shimmering, translucent screen.

In *Side Show*, the bodies do not have the weight and bulk they had in the *Bathers*; modeling and foreshortening are reduced to a minimum, and the figures appear mostly in either strict profile or frontal views, as if Seurat had adopted the rules of ancient Egyptian art (see page 57). Moreover, he has fitted them very precisely into a system of vertical and horizontal coordinates that holds them in place and defines the canvas as a self-contained rectilinear field. Only in the work of Vermeer have we encountered a similar "area-consciousness" (compare fig. 749, colorplate 102).

VAN GOGH.   While Cézanne and Seurat were converting Impressionism into a more severe, classical style, Vincent van Gogh (1853–1890) pursued the opposite direction. He believed that Impressionism did not provide the artist with enough freedom to express his emotions. Since this was his main concern, he is sometimes called an Expressionist, but the term ought to be reserved for certain later painters (see the next chapter). Van Gogh, the first great Dutch master since the seventeenth century, did not become an artist until 1880; as he died only ten years later, his career was even briefer than that of Seurat. His early interests were in literature and religion; profoundly dissatisfied with the values of industrial society and imbued with a strong sense of mission, he worked for a while as a lay preacher among poverty-stricken coal miners. This same intense feeling for the poor dominates the paintings of his pre-Impressionist period, 1880–85. In *The Potato Eaters* (fig. 899), the last and most ambitious work of those years, there remains a naïve clumsiness that comes from his lack of conventional training, but

899. VINCENT VAN GOGH. *The Potato Eaters*. 1885. 32¼ × 45″. National Museum Vincent van Gogh, Amsterdam

this only adds to the expressive power of his style. We are reminded of Daumier and Millet (see figs. 844, 846), of Rembrandt and Louis Le Nain (see figs. 735, 741, 756). For this peasant family, the evening meal has the solemn importance of a ritual.

When he painted *The Potato Eaters*, Van Gogh had not yet discovered the importance of color. A year later in Paris, where his brother Theo had a gallery devoted to modern art, he met Degas, Seurat, and other leading French artists. Their effect on him was electrifying: his pictures now blazed with color, and he even experimented briefly with the Divisionist technique of Seurat. This Impressionist phase, however, lasted less than two years. Although it was vitally important for his development, he had to integrate it with the style of his earlier years before his genius could fully unfold. Paris had opened his eyes to the sensuous beauty of the visible world and had taught him the pictorial language of the color patch, but painting continued to be nevertheless a vessel for his personal emotions. To investigate this spiritual reality with the new means at his command, he went to Arles, in the south of France. It was there, between 1888 and 1890, that he produced his greatest pictures.

Like Cézanne, Van Gogh now devoted his main energies to landscape painting, but the sun-drenched Mediterranean countryside evoked a very different response in him: he saw it filled with ecstatic movement, not architectural stability and permanence. In *Wheat Field and Cypress Trees* (fig. 900, colorplate 126), both earth and sky show an overpowering turbulence—the wheat field resembles a stormy sea, the trees spring flamelike from the ground, and the hills and clouds heave with the same undulant motion. The dynamism contained in every brush stroke makes of each one not merely a deposit of color, but an incisive graphic gesture. The artist's personal "handwriting" is here an even more dominant factor than in the canvases of Daumier (compare figs. 844, 845). Yet to Van Gogh himself it was the color, not the form, that determined the expressive content of his pictures. The letters he wrote to his brother include many eloquent descriptions of his choice of hues and the emotional

898. GEORGES SEURAT. *Side Show* (*La Parade;* see colorplate 125). The Metropolitan Museum of Art, New York (Bequest of Stephen C. Clark, 1960)

meanings he attached to them. Although he acknowledged that his desire "to exaggerate the essential and to leave the obvious vague" made his colors look arbitrary by Impressionist standards, he nevertheless remained deeply committed to the visible world.

Compared to Monet's *The River* (see fig. 870, colorplate 119), the colors of *Wheat Field and Cypress Trees* are stronger, simpler, and more vibrant, but in no sense "unnatural." They speak to us of that "kingdom of light" Van Gogh had found in the South, and of his mystic faith in a creative force animating all forms of life—a faith no less ardent than the sectarian Christianity of his early years. The missionary had now become a prophet. We see him in that role in the *Self-Portrait* (fig. 901), his emaciated, luminous head with its burning eyes set off against a whirlpool of darkness. "I want to paint men and women with that something of the eternal which the halo used to symbolize," Van Gogh had written, groping to define for his brother the human essence that was his aim in pictures such as this. At the time of the *Self-Portrait*, he had already begun to suffer fits of a mental illness that made painting increasingly difficult for him. Despairing of a cure, he committed suicide a year later, for he felt very deeply that art alone made his life worth living.

GAUGUIN AND SYMBOLISM. The quest for religious experience also played an important part in the work—if not in the life—of another great Post-Impressionist, Paul Gauguin (1848–1903). He began as a prosperous stockbroker in Paris and an amateur painter and collector of modern pictures (he once owned Cézanne's *Fruit Bowl, Glass, and Apples;* see fig. 895). At the age of thirty-five, however, he became convinced that he must devote himself entirely to art; he abandoned his business career, separated from his family, and by 1889 was the central figure of a new movement called Synthetism or Symbolism.

His style, though less intensely personal than Van Gogh's, was in some ways an even bolder advance beyond Impres-

901. VINCENT VAN GOGH. *Self-Portrait.* 1889. 22½ × 17″
Collection Mr. and Mrs. John Hay Whitney, New York

sionism. Gauguin believed that Western civilization was "out of joint," that industrial society had forced men into an incomplete life dedicated to material gain, while their emotions lay neglected. To rediscover for himself this hidden world of feeling, Gauguin left Paris for western France to live among the peasants of Brittany. He noticed particularly that religion was still part of the everyday life of the country people, and in pictures such as *The Vision After the Sermon (Jacob Wrestling with the Angel;* fig. 902, colorplate 127), he tried to depict their simple, direct faith. Here at last is what no Romantic painter had achieved: a style based on pre-Renaissance sources.

Modeling and perspective have given way to flat, simplified shapes outlined heavily in black, and the brilliant colors are equally "un-natural." This style, inspired by folk art and medieval stained glass, is meant to re-create both the imagined reality of the vision, and the trancelike rapture of the peasant women. Yet we sense that Gauguin, although he tried to share this experience, remains an outsider; he could paint pictures *about* faith, but not *from* faith.

Two years later, Gauguin's search for the unspoiled life led him even farther afield. He voyaged to Tahiti as a sort of "missionary in reverse," to learn from the natives instead of teaching them. Although he spent the rest of his life in the South Pacific (he returned home only once, in 1893–95), none of his Tahitian canvases is as daring as those he had

900. VINCENT VAN GOGH. *Wheat Field and Cypress Trees* (see colorplate 126). The National Gallery, London

902. PAUL GAUGUIN. *The Vision After the Sermon*
(*Jacob Wrestling with the Angel*; see colorplate 127).
National Gallery of Scotland, Edinburgh

painted in Brittany. His strongest works of this period are woodcuts; *Offerings of Gratitude* (fig. 903) again presents the theme of religious worship, but the image of a local god now replaces the biblical subject of the *Vision*. In its frankly "carved" look and its bold white-on-black pattern, we can feel the influences of the native art of the South Seas and of other non-European styles. The renewal of Western art and Western civilization as a whole, Gauguin believed, must come from "the Primitives"; he advised his fellow Symbolists to shun the Greek tradition and to turn instead to Persia, the Far East, and ancient Egypt.

The idea of primitivism itself was not new. It stems from the Romantic myth of the Noble Savage, propagated by the thinkers of the Enlightenment more than a century before, and its ultimate source is the age-old tradition of an earthly paradise where man once lived—and might perhaps live again—in a state of nature and innocence. But no one before Gauguin had gone as far to put the doctrine of primitivism into practice. His pilgrimage to the South Pacific had more than a purely private meaning: it symbolizes the end of the four hundred years of colonial expansion which had brought the entire globe under Western domination. The "white man's burden," once so cheerfully—and ruthlessly—shouldered by the empire builders, was becoming unbearable.

Symbolists: the Nabis

Gauguin's Symbolist followers, who called themselves Nabis (from the Hebrew word for "prophet"), were less remarkable for creative talent than for their ability to spell out and justify the aims of Post-Impressionism in theoretical form. One of them, Maurice Denis, coined the statement that was to become the First Article of Faith for twentieth-century painters: "A picture—before being a war horse, a female nude, or some anecdote—is essentially a flat surface covered with colors in a particular order." The Symbolists also discovered that there were some older artists, descendants of the Romantics, whose work, like their own, placed inner vision above the observation of nature.

MOREAU.   One of these, Gustave Moreau (1826–1898), a strange recluse who admired Delacroix, created a world of personal fantasy that has much in common with the medieval reveries of some of the English Pre-Raphaelites. *The*

903. PAUL GAUGUIN. *Offerings of Gratitude*. c. 1891–93. Woodcut

Apparition (fig. 904) shows one of his favorite themes: the head of John the Baptist, in a blinding radiance of light, appears to the dancing Salome. Her odalisque-like sensuousness, the stream of blood pouring from the severed head, the vast, mysterious space of the setting—suggestive of an exotic temple rather than of Herod's palace—summon up all the dreams of oriental splendor and cruelty so dear to the Romantic imagination, commingled with an insistence on the reality of the supernatural.

Only late in life did Moreau achieve a measure of recognition; suddenly, his art was in tune with the times. During his last six years, he even held a professorship at the conservative École des Beaux-Arts, the successor of the official art academy founded under Louis XIV (see above, pages 554f). There he attracted the most gifted students, among them such future leaders as Matisse and Rouault.

BEARDSLEY. How prophetic Moreau's work was of the taste prevailing at the end of the century is evident from a comparison with Aubrey Beardsley (1872–1898), a gifted young Englishman whose elegantly "decadent" black-and-white drawings were the very epitome of that taste. They include a *Salome* illustration (fig. 905) that might well be the final scene of the drama depicted by Moreau: Salome has taken up John's severed head and triumphantly kissed

905. AUBREY BEARDSLEY. *Salome.* 1892. Pen drawing. Princeton University Library, Princeton, New Jersey

904. GUSTAVE MOREAU. *The Apparition (Dance of Salome).* c. 1876. 21¼ × 17½″. Fogg Art Museum, Harvard University, Cambridge, Massachusetts (Grenville L. Winthrop Bequest)

it. Whereas Beardsley's erotic meaning is plain—Salome is passionately in love with John and has asked for his head because she could not have him in any other way—Moreau's remains ambiguous: did his Salome perhaps conjure up the vision of the head? is she, too, in love with John? Nevertheless, the parallel is striking, and there are formal similarities as well, such as the "stem" of trickling blood from which John's head rises like a flower. Yet Beardsley's *Salome* cannot be said to derive from Moreau's. The sources of his style are English—the graphic art of the Pre-Raphaelites and the curvilinear ornament of William Morris (see figs. 880, 881)—with a strong admixture of Japanese influence.

REDON. Another solitary artist whom the Symbolists discovered and claimed as one of their own was Odilon Redon (1840–1916). Like Moreau, he had a haunted imagination, but his imagery was even more personal and disturbing. A master of etching and lithography, he drew inspiration from

906. ODILON REDON. *The Balloon Eye*, from the series
À Edgar Poe. 1882. Lithograph

(fig. 902, colorplate 127) with the shimmering Divisionist "color mosaic" and the geometric surface organization of Seurat (see fig. 898, colorplate 125). This seemingly casual view of a corner of the artist's apartment has a delicate balance of "two-D" and "three-D" effects, and a quiet magic that makes us think of Vermeer and Chardin (compare figs. 749, 778, colorplates 102, 108), masters of the past whom Vuillard must have loved. Such economy of means became an important precedent for Matisse a decade later (see fig. 928, colorplate 130). By then, however, Vuillard's own style had grown more conservative. He never recaptured the delicacy and daring of his early canvases.

TOULOUSE-LAUTREC.   Van Gogh's and Gauguin's discontent with the spiritual ills of Western civilization was part of a sentiment widely shared at the end of the nineteenth century. A self-conscious preoccupation with decadence, evil, and darkness pervaded the artistic and literary climate. Even those who saw no escape analyzed their predicament in fascinated horror. Yet, somewhat paradoxically, this very awareness proved to be a source of strength (the truly decadent, we may assume, are unable to realize their plight). The most remarkable instance of this strength was Henri de Toulouse-Lautrec (1864–1901); physically an ugly dwarf, he was an artist of superb talent who led a dissolute life in the night spots of Paris and died of alcoholism.

He was a great admirer of Degas, and his *At the Moulin Rouge* (fig. 908, colorplate 128) recalls the zigzag form of

the fantastic visions of Goya (see fig. 835) as well as Romantic literature. The lithograph shown in figure 906 is one of a set he issued in 1882 and dedicated to Edgar Allan Poe. The American poet had been dead for 33 years; but his tormented life and his equally tormented imagination made him the very model of the *poète maudit*, the doomed poet, and his works, excellently translated by Baudelaire and Mallarmé, were greatly admired in France. Redon's lithographs do not illustrate Poe; they are, rather, "visual poems" in their own right, evoking the macabre, hallucinatory world of Poe's imagination. In our example, the artist has revived a very ancient device, the single eye representing the all-seeing mind of God. But, in contrast to the traditional form of the symbol, Redon shows the whole eyeball removed from its socket and converted into a balloon that drifts aimlessly in the sky. Disquieting visual paradoxes of this kind were to be exploited on a large scale by the Dadaists and Surrealists in our own century (see figs. 960, 961, 964).

VUILLARD.   Oddly enough, the most gifted member of the Nabis, Edouard Vuillard (1868–1940), was more influenced by Seurat than by Gauguin. In his pictures of the 1890s—mainly domestic scenes, small in scale and intimate in effect, like the *Interior* (fig. 907)—he combines into a remarkable new entity the flat planes and emphatic contours of Gauguin

907. ÉDOUARD VUILLARD. *Interior.* 1898. 19¾ × 16¼".
Private Collection, Paris

Colorplate 126. VINCENT VAN GOGH. *Wheat Field and Cypress Trees* (see page 644). 1889. 28½ × 36″. The National Gallery, London
(Reproduced by courtesy of the Trustees)

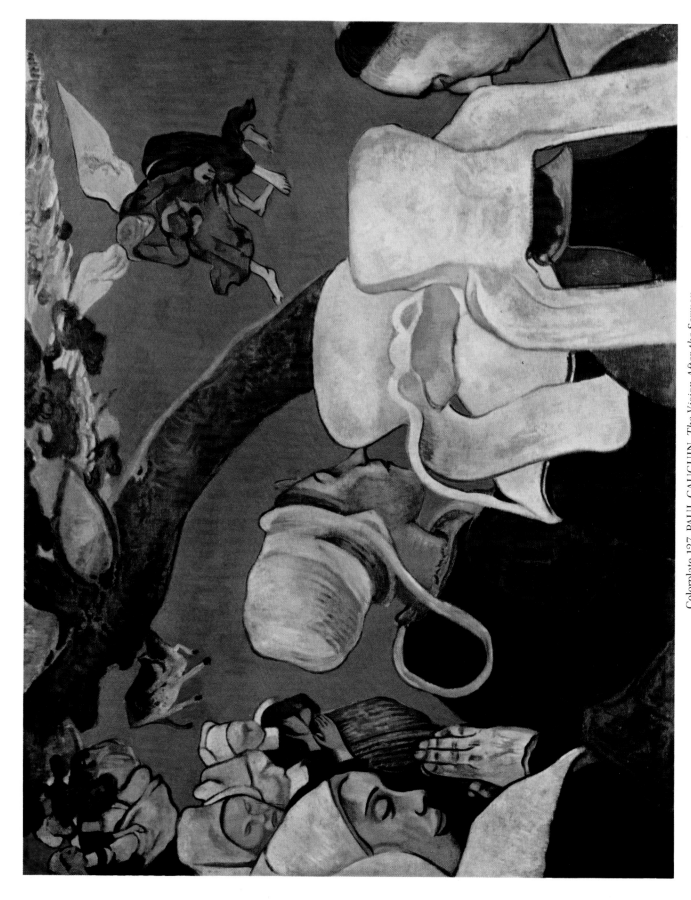

Colorplate 127. PAUL GAUGUIN. *The Vision After the Sermon*
(Jacob Wrestling with the Angel; see page 645). 1888. 28¾ × 36½″. National Gallery of Scotland, Edinburgh

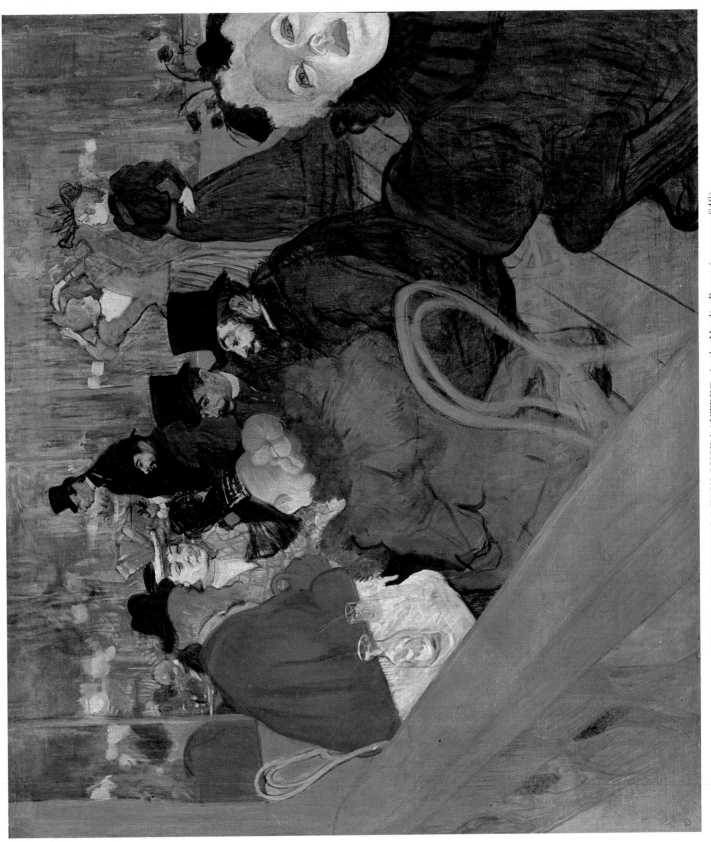

Colorplate 128. HENRI DE TOULOUSE-LAUTREC. *At the Moulin Rouge* (see page 648).
1892. 48⅜ × 55¼". The Art Institute of Chicago (Helen Birch Bartlett Memorial Collection)

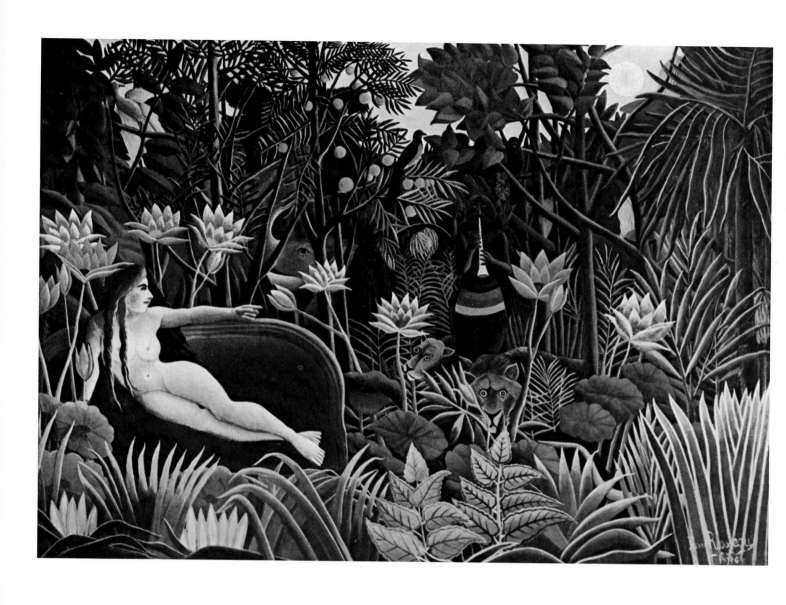

Colorplate 129. (*above*) HENRI ROUSSEAU. *The Dream*
(see page 658). 1910. 6′ 8½″ × 9′ 9½″. The Museum of Modern Art,
New York (Gift of Nelson A. Rockefeller)

Colorplate 130. (*right*) HENRI MATISSE. *Harmony in Red*
(*Red Room*; see page 668). 1908–9. 69¾ × 85⅞″.
The Hermitage Museum, Leningrad

Colorplate 131. GEORGES ROUAULT. *The Old King*
(see page 668). 1916–37. 30¼ × 21¼″. Carnegie Institute, Pittsburgh

Colorplate 132. CHAIM SOUTINE. *Dead Fowl* (see page 668). c. 1926.
38½ × 24½″. The Art Institute of Chicago (Joseph Winterbotham Collection)

Colorplate 133. FRANCIS BACON. *Figure with Meat* (see page 668). 1954.
50¾ × 48″. The Art Institute of Chicago (Harriott A. Fox Fund)

Degas' *The Glass of Absinthe* (see fig. 874). Yet this view of the well-known nightclub is no Impressionist "slice of life"; Toulouse-Lautrec sees through the gay surface of the scene, viewing performers and customers with a pitilessly sharp eye for their character (including his own: he is the tiny bearded man next to the very tall one in the back of the room). The large areas of flat color, however, and the emphatic, smoothly curving outlines, reflect the influence of Gauguin. Although Toulouse-Lautrec was no Symbolist, the Moulin Rouge that he shows here has an atmosphere so joyless and oppressive that we cannot but regard it as a place of evil.

ENSOR; MUNCH.   In the art of the Belgian painter James Ensor (1860–1949), this pessimistic view of the human condition reaches obsessive intensity. *Intrigue* (fig. 909) is a grotesque carnival, but as we scrutinize these masks we become aware that they are the mummers' true faces, revealing the depravity ordinarily hidden behind the façade of everyday appearances. The demon-ridden world of Bosch and Schongauer has come to life again, in modern guise (compare figs. 523, 534).

Something of the same macabre quality pervades the early work of Edvard Munch (1863–1944), a gifted Norwegian who came to Paris in 1889 and based his starkly expressive style on Toulouse-Lautrec, Van Gogh, and Gauguin. *The Scream* (fig. 910) shows the influences of all three; it is an image of fear, the terrifying, unreasoned fear we feel in a nightmare. Unlike Fuseli and Goya (see figs. 816, 835), Munch visualizes this experience without the aid of frightening apparitions, and his achievement is the more persuasive for that very reason. The rhythm of the long, wavy lines seems to carry the echo of the scream into every corner of the picture, making of earth and sky one great sounding board of fear.

908. HENRI DE TOULOUSE-LAUTREC. *At the Moulin Rouge* (see colorplate 128). The Art Institute of Chicago (Helen Birch Bartlett Memorial Collection)

909. JAMES ENSOR. *Intrigue*. 1890. 35½ × 59".
Royal Museum of Fine Arts, Antwerp

THE SECESSION. Munch's works generated such controversy when they were exhibited in Berlin in 1892 that a number of young radicals broke from the artists' association and formed the Berlin Secession, which took its name from a similar group that had been founded in Munich earlier that year. The Secession quickly became a loosely allied international movement. In 1897 it spread to Austria, where Gustav Klimt (1862–1918) established the Vienna Secession with the purpose of raising the level of the arts and crafts in Austria through close ties to *Art Nouveau* (see page 749; there called *Jugendstil*—literally Young Style). *The Kiss* (fig. 911) by Klimt expresses a different kind of anxiety from Munch's *The Scream*. The image will remind us of Beardsley's *Salome* (fig. 905), but here the barely suppressed eroticism has burst into desire. Engulfed in mosaic-like robes that create an illusion of rich beauty, the angular figures steal a moment of passion whose brevity emphasizes their joyless existence.

PICASSO: BLUE PERIOD. Pablo Picasso (1881–1974), coming to Paris in 1900, felt the spell of the same artistic atmosphere that had generated the style of Munch. His so-called Blue Period (the term refers to the prevailing color of his canvases as well as to their mood) consists almost exclusively of pictures of beggars and derelicts such as *The Old Guitarist* (fig. 912)—outcasts or victims of society

911. GUSTAVE KLIMT. *The Kiss*. 1907–8. 70⅞ × 72".
Österreichische Galerie, Vienna

whose pathos reflects the artist's own sense of isolation. Yet these figures convey poetic melancholy more than outright despair. The aged musician accepts his fate with a resignation that seems almost saintly, and the attenuated grace of his limbs reminds us of El Greco (compare fig. 647, colorplate 84). *The Old Guitarist* is a strange amalgam of Mannerism and of the art of Gauguin and Toulouse-Lautrec (note the smoothly curved contours), imbued with the personal gloom of a twenty-two-year-old genius.

ROUSSEAU. A few years later, Picasso and his friends discovered a painter who until then had attracted no attention, although he had been exhibiting his work since 1886. He was Henri Rousseau (1844–1910), a retired customs collector who had started to paint in his middle age without training of any sort. His ideal—which, fortunately, he never achieved—was the arid academic style of the followers of Ingres. Rousseau is that paradox, a folk artist of genius. How else could he have done a picture like *The Dream* (fig. 913, colorplate 129)? What goes on in the enchanted world of this canvas needs no explanation, because none is possible, but perhaps for that very reason its magic becomes unbelievably real to us. Rousseau himself described the scene in a little poem:

> Yadwigha, peacefully asleep
> Enjoys a lovely dream:
> She hears a kind snake charmer
> Playing upon his reed.
> On stream and foliage glisten
> The silvery beams of the moon.
> And savage serpents listen
> To the gay, entrancing tune.

910. EDVARD MUNCH. *The Scream*. 1893.
36 × 29". National Museum, Oslo

Here at last is that innocent directness of feeling which Gauguin thought was so necessary for the age, and traveled so far to find. Picasso and his friends were the first to recognize this quality in Rousseau's work. They revered him, quite justifiably, as the godfather of twentieth-century painting.

SCULPTURE

France

MAILLOL. No tendencies to be equated with Post-Impressionism appear in sculpture until about 1900. Sculptors of a younger generation had by then been trained under the dominant influence of Rodin, and were ready to go their own ways. The finest of these, Aristide Maillol (1861–1944), began as a Symbolist painter, although he did not share Gauguin's anti-Greek attitude. Maillol might be called a "classic primitivist"; admiring the simplified strength of early Greek sculpture, he rejected its later phases. The

913. HENRI ROUSSEAU. *The Dream*
(see colorplate 129). The Museum of Modern Art,
New York (Gift of Nelson A. Rockefeller)

Seated Woman (fig. 914) evokes memories of the Archaic and Severe styles (compare figs. 146, 157–58, 178–82) rather than of Phidias and Praxiteles. The solid forms and clearly defined volumes also recall Cézanne's statement that all natural forms are based on the cone, the sphere, and the cylinder. But the most notable quality of the figure is its harmonious, self-sufficient repose, which the outside world cannot disturb.

A statue, Maillol thought, must above all be "static," structurally balanced like a piece of architecture; it must represent a state of being that is detached from the stress of circumstance, with none of the restless, thrusting energy of Rodin's work. In this respect, the *Seated Woman* is the exact opposite of *The Thinker* (see fig. 889). Maillol later gave it the title *Méditerranée*—The Mediterranean—to suggest the source from which he drew the timeless serenity of his figure.

Belgium

MINNE. The *Kneeling Boy* (fig. 915) by the Belgian sculptor George Minne (1866–1941) also shows a state of brooding calm, but the haggard, angular limbs reflect Gothic, not classical, influence and the trancelike rigidity of the pose suggests religious meditation. The statue is part of a fountain design that consists of five identical kneeling boys, grouped around a circular basin as if engaged in a solemn ritual. We must see this figure as one anonymous member of a rhythmically repeated sequence, if we are to understand its mood of ascetic withdrawal. Minne's art attracted little notice in France, but was admired in Germany.

Germany

LEHMBRUCK. Minne's influence is apparent in *Standing Youth* (fig. 916) by Wilhelm Lehmbruck (1881–1919); here a Gothic elongation and angularity are conjoined with a fine balance derived from Maillol's art, and also with some of Rodin's expressive energy. The total effect is a looming monumental figure well anchored in space, yet partaking of that poetic melancholy we observed in Picasso's Blue Period.

912. PABLO PICASSO. *The Old Guitarist*. 1903.
Oil on panel, 47¾ × 32½". The Art Institute of Chicago
(Helen Birch Bartlett Memorial Collection)

914. (*left*) ARISTIDE MAILLOL. *Seated Woman (Méditerranée)*.
c. 1901. Height 41″.
Collection Oskar Reinhart, Winterthur, Switzerland

915. (*left, below*) GEORGE MINNE. *Kneeling Boy.* 1898. Marble,
height 31″. Museum of Fine Arts, Ghent

916. (*below*) WILHELM LEHMBRUCK. *Standing Youth.* 1913.
Cast stone, height 92″, base 36 × 26¾″. The Museum of Modern
Art, New York (Gift of Abby Aldrich Rockefeller)

917. ERNST BARLACH. *Man Drawing a Sword.*
1911. Wood, height 31".
Museum, Cranbrook Academy of Art, Bloomfield Hills, Michigan

camera became an important instrument of reform through the photodocumentary, which tells the story of people's lives in a pictorial essay. It responded to the same conditions that had stirred Courbet (see page 618), and its factual reportage likewise fell within the Realist tradition. Before then, photographers had been content to present the romanticized image of the poor like those in genre paintings of the day. The first photodocumentary was John Thomson's illustrated sociological study *Street Life in London*, published in 1877. To get his pictures, he had to pose his figures.

RIIS. The invention of gunpowder flash ten years later allowed Jacob Riis (1849–1914) to rely for the most part on the element of surprise. Riis was a police reporter in New York City, where he learned at first hand about the crime-infested slums and their appalling living conditions. He kept up a steady campaign of illustrated newspaper exposés, books, and lectures which in some cases led to major revisions of the city's housing codes and labor laws. His photographs' unflinching realism has lost none of its force. Certainly it would be difficult to imagine a more nightmarish scene than *Bandits' Roost* (fig. 918). With good reason we sense a pervasive air of danger in the eerie light. The Lower East Side's notorious gangs sought their victims by night, killing them without hesitation. The motionless figures seem to look us over with the practiced casualness of hunters coldly sizing up potential prey.

BARLACH. Ernst Barlach (1870–1938), another important German sculptor who reached maturity in the years before World War I, seems the very opposite of Wilhelm Lehmbruck; he is a "Gothic primitivist," and more akin to Munch than to the Western Symbolist tradition. What Gauguin had experienced in Brittany and the tropics, Barlach found by going to Russia: the simple humanity of a pre-industrial age. His figures, such as the *Man Drawing a Sword* (fig. 917), embody elementary emotions—wrath, fear, grief—that seem imposed upon them by invisible presences. When they act they are like somnambulists, unaware of their own impulses.

Man, to Barlach, is a humble creature at the mercy of forces beyond his control; he is never the master of his fate. Characteristically, these figures do not fully emerge from the material substance (often, as here, a massive block of wood) of which they are made; their clothing is like a hard chrysalis that hides the body, as in medieval sculpture. Barlach's art has a range that is severely restricted in both form and emotion, yet its mute intensity within these limits is not easily forgotten.

PHOTOGRAPHY
Documentary Photography

During the second half of the nineteenth century, the press played a leading role in the social movement which brought the harsh realities of poverty to the public's attention. The

918. JACOB RIIS. *Bandits' Roost.* c. 1888. Gelatin-silver print.
Museum of the City of New York

919. OSCAR REJLANDER. *The Two Paths of Life*. 1857. Combination albumen print, 16 × 31″.
George Eastman House, Rochester, N.Y.

Pictorialism

The raw subject matter and realism of documentary photography had little impact on art and were shunned by most other photographers as well. England, through such organizations as the Photographic Society of London, founded in 1853, became the leader of the movement to convince doubting critics that photography, by imitating painting and printmaking, could indeed be art. To Victorian England, beauty above all meant art with a high moral purpose or noble sentiment, preferably in a classical style.

REJLANDER. *The Two Paths of Life* (fig. 919) by Oscar Rejlander (1818–1875) fulfills these ends by presenting an allegory clearly descended from Hogarth's *Rake's Progress* series (figs. 786, 787). This tour de force, almost three feet wide, combines thirty negatives through composite printing:

920. HENRY PEACH ROBINSON. *Fading Away*. 1858.
Combination print. Royal Photographic Society, London

a young man (in two images) is choosing between the paths of virtue or of vice, the latter represented by a half dozen nudes. The picture created a sensation in 1857 and Queen Victoria herself purchased a print. Rejlander, however, never enjoyed the same success again. He was the most adventurous photographer of his time and soon turned to other subjects less in keeping with prevailing taste.

ROBINSON. The mantle of art photography fell to Henry Peach Robinson (1830–1901), who became the most famous photographer in the world. He established his reputation with *Fading Away* (fig. 920), which appeared a year after Rejlander's *Two Paths of Life*. With six lines from Shelley's "Queen Mab" printed below on the mat, it is typical of Robinson's sentimental scenes. Like the *Two Paths of Life* it is a photomontage, but of only five negatives, and the scene is as carefully staged as any Victorian melodrama. At first Robinson made detailed drawings of his scenes before photographing the individual components; he later renounced multiple-negative photography, but still contrived to imitate contemporary genre painting in his pictures. When treating elevated subject matter, he continued to distinguish between fact and truth, which to him was a mixture of the real and the artificial.

CAMERON. The photographer who pursued ideal beauty with the greatest passion was Julia Margaret Cameron (1815–1879). An intimate of leading poets, scientists, and artists, she took up photography at age forty-eight when given a camera, and went on to create a remarkable body of work. In her own day Cameron was known for her allegorical and narrative pictures, but now she is remembered primarily for her portraits of the men who shaped Victorian England. Her finest photographs, however, are of the women who were married to her closest friends. An early study of the actress

921. JULIA MARGARET CAMERON.
Portrait of Ellen Terry. 1864. Albumen print.
The Metropolitan Museum of Art, New York

922. PETER HENRY EMERSON.
Haymaking in the Norfolk Broads. c. 1890. Platinum print.
Société française de photographie, Paris

Ellen Terry (fig. 921), the young wife of the painter G. F. Watts, has the lyricism and grace of the Pre-Raphaelite aesthetic that shaped Cameron's style (compare fig. 879).

Naturalistic Photography

EMERSON. The cudgel against art photography was taken up by Peter Henry Emerson (1856–1936), who became Robinson's bitter enemy. Emerson espoused what he called Naturalistic Photography, based on scientific principles and Constable's landscapes. Nevertheless, he too contrasted realism with truth, defining truth in terms of sentiment, aesthetics, and the selective arrangement of nature. Using a single negative, Emerson composed his scenes with the greatest care, producing results that were sometimes similar to Robinson's, though of course he never acknowledged this. Most of Emerson's work was devoted to scenes of rural and coastal life which are not far removed from early documentary photographs.

In his best prints nature predominates. He was a master at distributing tonal masses across a scene, and his photographs (fig. 922) are equivalent to fine English landscape paintings of the period. Although the effect is rarely apparent in his work, Emerson advocated putting the lens slightly out of focus, in the belief that the eye sees sharply only the central area of a scene. When he gave up this idea a few years later, he decided that photography was indeed science instead of art because it was machine-made, not personal.

Photo-Secession

The issue of whether photography could be art came to a head in the early 1890s with the Secession movement (see page 658), which was spearheaded in 1893 by the founding in London of the Linked Ring, a rival group to the renamed Royal Photographic Society of Great Britain. Stimulated by Emerson's ideas, the Secessionists sought a pictorialism independent of science and technology. They steered a course between academicism and naturalism by imitating every form of late Romantic art that did not involve narrative. Equally antithetical to their aims were Realist and Post-Impressionist painting, then at its zenith. In the group's approach to photography as Art for Art's Sake, the Secession had the most in common with Whistler's aestheticism.

To resolve the dilemma between art and mechanics, the Secessionists tried to make their photographs look as much like paintings as possible. Rather than resorting to composite or multiple images, however, they exercised total control over the printing process, chiefly by adding special materials to their printing paper to create different effects. Pigmented gum brushed on coarse drawing paper yielded a warm-toned, highly textured print that in its way approximated Impressionist painting. Paper impregnated with platinum salts was especially popular among the Secessionists for the clear grays in their prints. Their subtlety and depth lend a remarkable ethereality to *The Magic Crystal* (fig. 923) by Gertrude Käsebier (1854–1934), in which spiritual forces are almost visibly sweeping across the photograph.

Through Käsebier and Alfred Stieglitz, the Linked Ring had close ties with America, where Stieglitz opened his Photo-Secession gallery in New York in 1902. Among his protégés was the young Edward Steichen (1879–1973), whose photograph of Rodin in his sculpture studio (fig. 924) is without doubt the finest achievement of the entire Photo-Secession movement. The head in profile contemplating *The Thinker* expresses the essence of the confrontation between the sculptor and his work of art. His brooding introspection hides the inner turmoil evoked by the ghostlike monument to Victor Hugo that rises dramatically like a genius in the background. Not since *The Creation of Adam*

923. GERTRUDE KÄSEBIER. *The Magic Crystal.* Platinum print.
Royal Photographic Society, Bath

by Michelangelo (fig. 616), who was Rodin's ideal, have we seen a more telling use of space or an image that penetrates the mystery of creativity so deeply.

The Photo-Secession achieved its goal of gaining wide recognition for photography as an art form, but by 1907 its artifices were regarded as stilted. Though the movement lasted for a few more years, it was becoming clear that the future of photography did not lie in the imitation of painting, for painting was then being drastically reformed by modernists (see page 666). Yet the legacy of the Photo-Secession was valuable, its limitations notwithstanding, for it taught photographers much about the control of composition and response to light.

Motion Photography

MUYBRIDGE.   An entirely new direction was charted by Eadweard Muybridge (1830–1904), father of motion photography. He wedded two different technologies, devising a set of cameras capable of photographing action at successive points. Photography had grown from such marriages; another instance had occurred earlier when Nadar used a hot-air balloon to take aerial shots of Paris (fig. 863). After some trial efforts, Muybridge managed in 1877 to get a set of pictures of a trotting horse which forever changed artistic depictions of the horse in movement. Of the 100,000 photographs he devoted to the study of animal and human locomotion, the most astonishing were those taken from several vantage points at once (fig. 925). The idea was surely in

924. EDWARD STEICHEN. *Rodin with His Sculptures "Victor Hugo" and "The Thinker."* 1902. Gum print.
The Art Institute of Chicago (Alfred Stieglitz Collection)

925. EADWEARD MUYBRIDGE.
Female Semi-nude in Motion.
from *Human and Animal Locomotion,*
vol. 2, pl. 271. 1887.
George Eastman House, Rochester, N.Y.

926 a, b. ÉTIENNE-JULES MAREY. *Man in black suit with white*
stripes down arms and legs, walking in front of a black wall.
c. 1884. Chronophotograph

the air, for the art of the period occasionally shows similar experiments, but Muybridge's photographs must nevertheless have come as a revelation to artists. The simultaneous views present an entirely new treatment of motion across time and space which challenges the imagination. Like a complex visual puzzle, they can be combined in any number of ways that are endlessly fascinating.

Muybridge left it to others to pursue these possibilities further. Much of his later work was conducted at the University of Pennsylvania in Philadelphia with the support of Eakins, then the head of the Academy of the Fine Arts. Eakins was already adept at using a camera, and it provided the subjects for several of his paintings; soon his interest in science—we will recall his admiration for Dr. Gross (fig. 885)—led him to take up motion photography. Unlike Muybridge's succession of static images, Eakins' multiple exposures show sequential motion on one plate. In the end, photography for Eakins was simply a means of depicting figures more realistically.

MAREY. It was Etienne-Jules Marey (1830–1904) who developed motion photography into an art. A noted French physiologist, Marey, like Muybridge, with whom he was in direct contact, saw the camera as a tool for demonstrating the mechanics of bodily movement, but he soon began to use it so creatively that his photographs have a perfection not equaled for another sixty years (compare fig. 1072). Indeed, his multiple exposure of a man walking (fig. 926) satisfies both scientific and aesthetic truth in a way that Emerson and the Secessionists never imagined.

The photographs of Muybridge and Marey convey a peculiarly modern sense of dynamics reflecting the new tempo of life in the machine age. However, because the gap was then so great between scientific fact on the one hand and visual perception and artistic representation on the other, their far-reaching aesthetic implications were to be realized only by the Futurists (see page 686).

4
TWENTIETH-CENTURY PAINTING AND SCULPTURE

PAINTING BEFORE WORLD WAR II

In our account of modern art we have already discussed a succession of "isms": Neoclassicism, Romanticism, Realism, Impressionism, Post-Impressionism, Divisionism, Symbolism. There are many more to be found in twentieth-century art—so many, in fact, that nobody has made an exact count. These "isms" can form a serious obstacle to understanding: they may make us feel that we cannot hope to comprehend the art of our time unless we immerse ourselves in a welter of esoteric doctrines. Actually, we can disregard all but the most important "isms"; like the terms we have used for the styles of earlier periods, they are merely labels to help us put things in their proper place. If an "ism" fails the test of usefulness, we need not retain it. This is true of many "isms" in contemporary art; the movements they designate either cannot be seen very clearly as separate entities, or have so little importance that they can interest only the specialist. It has always been easier to invent new labels than to create a movement in art that truly deserves a new name.

Still, we cannot do without "isms" altogether. Since the start of the modern era, the Western world—and, increasingly, the non-Western world—has faced the same basic problems everywhere, and local artistic traditions have steadily given way to international trends. Among these we can distinguish three main currents, each comprising a number of "isms," that began among the Post-Impressionists, and have developed greatly in our own century: Expression, Abstraction, and Fantasy. The first stresses the artist's emotional attitude toward himself and the world; the second, the formal structure of the work of art; the third explores the realm of the imagination, especially its spontaneous and irrational qualities. We must not forget, however, that feeling, order, and imagination are all present in *every* work of art: without imagination, it would be deadly dull; without some degree of order, it would be chaotic; without feeling, it would leave us unmoved.

These currents, then, are not mutually exclusive. We shall find them interrelated in many ways, and the work of one artist may well belong to more than one current. Moreover, each current embraces a wide range of approaches, from the realistic to the completely non-representational (or non-objective). Thus these three currents do not correspond to specific styles, but to general attitudes. The primary concern of the Expressionist is the human community; of the Abstractionist, the structure of reality; and of the artist of Fantasy, the labyrinth of the individual human mind.

In addition, we will encounter modernism, a concept peculiar to the twentieth century, though its roots can be traced to Romanticism. To the artist it is a trumpet call which both asserts his freedom to create in a new style and provides him with the mission to define the meaning of his times—and even to reshape society through his art. This is a role for which the problematic term "avant-garde" (literally, vanguard) is hardly sufficient. Of course artists have always responded to the changing world around them, but rarely have they risen to the challenge as now, with so fervent a sense of personal cause.

927. HENRI MATISSE. *The Joy of Life*. 1905–6. 68½ × 93¾".
Copyright Barnes Foundation, Merion, Pennsylvania

The Fauves; Expressionism

The twentieth century may be said, so far as painting is concerned, to have begun five years late. Between 1901 and 1906, several comprehensive exhibitions of the work of Van Gogh, Gauguin, and Cézanne were held in Paris. Thus, for the first time the achievements of these masters became accessible to a broad public.

The young painters who had grown up in the "decadent," morbid mood of the 1890s (see page 648) were profoundly impressed, and several of them developed a radical new style, full of violent color and bold distortions. On their first public appearance, in 1905, they so shocked critical opinion that they were dubbed the *Fauves* (the wild beasts), a label they wore with pride. Actually, it was not a common program that brought them together, but their shared sense of liberation and experiment. As a movement, Fauvism comprised numerous loosely related, individual styles, and the group dissolved after a few years.

MATISSE. Its leading member was Henri Matisse (1869–1954), the oldest of the founding fathers of twentieth-century painting. *The Joy of Life* (fig. 927), probably the most important picture of his long career, sums up the spirit of Fauvism better than any other single work. It obviously derives its flat planes of color, heavy undulating outlines, and the "primitive" flavor of its forms from Gauguin (see fig. 902, colorplate 127); even its subject suggests the vision of

Man in a state of Nature that Gauguin had pursued in Tahiti (see fig. 903). But we soon realize that these figures are not Noble Savages under the spell of a native god; the subject is a pagan scene in the classical sense—a bacchanal, like Titian's (compare fig. 634, colorplate 80). Even the poses of the figures have for the most part a classical origin, and in the apparently careless draftsmanship resides a profound knowledge of the human body (Matisse had been trained in the academic tradition). What makes the picture so revolutionary is its radical simplicity, its "genius of omission": everything that possibly can be, has been left out or stated by implication only, yet the scene retains the essentials of plastic form and spatial depth.

Painting, Matisse seems to say, is the rhythmic arrangement of line and color on a flat plane, but it is not *only* that; how far can the image of nature be pared down without destroying its basic properties and thus reducing it to mere surface ornament? "What I am after, above all," he once explained, "is expression…[But]…expression does not consist of the passion mirrored upon a human face.…The whole arrangement of my picture is expressive. The placement of figures or objects, the empty spaces around them, the proportions, everything plays a part." But what, we wonder, does *The Joy of Life* express? Exactly what its title says. Whatever his debt to Gauguin, Matisse was never stirred by the same agonized discontent with the "decadence" of our civilization. He had strong feelings about only one thing—the act of painting: this to him was an experience so profoundly joyous that he wanted to transmit it to the beholder

928. HENRI MATISSE. *Harmony in Red*
(*Red Room*; see colorplate 130).
The Hermitage, Leningrad

in all its freshness and immediacy. The purpose of his pictures, he always asserted, was to give pleasure.

The radical new balance Matisse struck between the "2-D" and "3-D" aspects of painting is particularly evident in his *Harmony in Red* (fig. 928, colorplate 130); he spreads the same flat blue-on-red pattern on the tablecloth and on the wall, yet he distinguishes the horizontal from the vertical planes with complete assurance. Cézanne had pioneered this integration of surface ornament into the design of a picture (see fig. 894, colorplate 124), but Matisse here makes it the mainstay of his composition. Equally bold—but perfectly readable—is the view of a garden with flowering trees, seen through the window; the house in the distance is painted the same bright pink as the interior, and is thereby brought into relation with the rest of the picture. Likewise the blue of the sky, the greens of the foliage, and the bright yellow dots (for flowers) all recur in the foreground. Matisse's "genius of omission" is again at work: by reducing the number of tints to a minimum, he makes of color an independent structural element. It has such importance that *Harmony in Red* is less meaningful in a black-and-white reproduction.

ROUAULT. Another member of the *Fauves*, Georges Rouault (1871–1958), would not have used Matisse's definition of "expression." For him this had still to include, as it had in the past, "the passion mirrored upon a human face"; we need only look at his *Head of Christ* (fig. 929). But the expressiveness does not reside only in the "image quality" of the face. The savage slashing strokes of the brush speak equally eloquently of the artist's rage and compassion. (If we cover the upper third of the picture, it is no longer a recognizable image, yet the expressive effect is hardly diminished.) Rouault is the true heir of Van Gogh's and Gauguin's concern for the corrupt state of the world. He, however, hoped for spiritual renewal through a revitalized Catholic faith. His pictures, whatever their subject, are personal statements of that ardent hope. Trained in his youth as a

stained-glass worker, he was better prepared than the other *Fauves* to share Gauguin's enthusiasm for medieval art. Rouault's later work, such as *The Old King* (fig. 930, colorplate 131), has glowing colors and compartmented, black-bordered shapes inspired by Gothic stained-glass windows (compare fig. 481). Yet within this framework he retains a good deal of the pictorial freedom we saw in the *Head of Christ*, and the old king's face conveys a mood of resignation and inner suffering that reminds us of Rembrandt and Daumier.

SOUTINE. Rouault's expressionism was unique among French painters. The only artist in Paris to follow his lead was Chaim Soutine (1894–1943), an immigrant from Eastern Europe. The rich impasto and the tempestuous, violent brushwork in *The Dead Fowl* (fig. 931, colorplate 132) clearly reflect the older master's influence. Although the picture belongs conventionally to the class of still life, the dead bird is a terrifying symbol of death. As we look at the plucked, creamy-white body, we realize with sudden horror its close resemblance to a human shape. It evokes the earthward plunge of Icarus, or it is, perhaps, a cruelly direct image of Plato's definition of Man as a "featherless biped."

BACON. For his power to transmute sheer anguish into visual form, Soutine had no equal among twentieth-century artists unless it be the Englishman Francis Bacon (born 1909). *Figure with Meat* (fig. 932, colorplate 133) reflects

929. GEORGES ROUAULT. *Head of Christ*.
1905. Oil on paper, mounted on canvas, 45 × 31″.
Collection Walter P. Chrysler, Jr., New York

930. GEORGES ROUAULT. *The Old King* (see colorplate 131). Carnegie Institute, Pittsburgh

NOLDE. One *Brücke* artist, Emil Nolde (1867–1956), stands somewhat apart; older than the rest, he shared Rouault's predilection for religious themes, although he was a far less articulate painter. The thickly encrusted surfaces and deliberately clumsy draftsmanship of his *Last Supper* (fig. 934, colorplate 134) show that Nolde rejected pictorial refinement in favor of a primeval, direct expression inspired by Gauguin. Ensor's grotesque masks, too, come to mind (see fig. 909), and the mute intensity of Barlach's peasants (see fig. 917).

KOKOSCHKA. Another artist of highly individual talent, related to the *Brücke* although not a member of it, was the Austrian painter Oskar Kokoschka (1886–1980). His most memorable works are his portraits painted before World War I, such as the moving *Self-Portrait* (fig. 935). Like Van Gogh, Kokoschka saw himself as a visionary, a witness to the truth and reality of his inner experiences (compare fig. 901); the hypersensitive features seem lacerated by a

Bacon's obsession with Velázquez' *Innocent X* (compare fig. 753), a picture that haunted him for some years. It is, of course, no longer Innocent X we see here but a screaming ghost that is materializing out of a black void in the company of two luminescent sides of beef. The canvas invites comparison with such earlier works as Grünewald's *Crucifixion*, Fuseli's *Nightmare*, Ensor's *Intrigue*, or Munch's *Scream* (see figs. 667, 816, 909, 910), yet none of these really helps us to understand it. Bacon is a compulsive gambler, a taker of risks, in real life as well as in the way he works; he competes with Velázquez here, but on his own terms, which are to set up an almost unbearable tension between the shocking violence of his vision and the luminous beauty of his brushwork. What he seeks are images that, in his own words, "unlock the deeper possibilities of sensation."

DIE BRÜCKE. It was in Germany that Fauvism had its most enduring impact, especially among the members of a society called *Die Brücke* (The Bridge), a group of like-minded painters who lived in Dresden in 1905. Their early works, such as Ernst Ludwig Kirchner's *Street* (fig. 933), not only reflect Matisse's simplified, rhythmic line and loud color, but also clearly reveal the direct influence of Van Gogh and Gauguin. *Street* also shows elements derived from Munch (compare fig. 910), who was then living in Berlin and deeply impressed the German Expressionists.

931. CHAIM SOUTINE. *Dead Fowl* (see colorplate 132). The Art Institute of Chicago (Joseph Winterbotham Collection)

932. FRANCIS BACON. *Figure with Meat* (see colorplate 133). The Art Institute of Chicago (Harriet A. Fox Fund)

great ordeal of the imagination. It may not be fanciful to find in this tortured psyche an echo of the cultural climate that also produced Sigmund Freud.

BECKMANN. A more robust descendant of the *Brücke* artists was Max Beckmann (1884–1950), who did not become an Expressionist until after he had lived through World War I, which filled him with a deep despair at the state of modern civilization. *The Dream* (fig. 936) is a mocking nightmare, a tilted, zigzag world crammed with puppet-like figures, as disquieting as those in Bosch's *Hell* (see fig. 523). Its symbolism, however, is even more difficult to interpret, since it is necessarily subjective, though no one would deny its evocative power.

How indeed could Beckmann have expressed the chaos in Germany after that war with the worn-out language of traditional symbols? "These are the creatures that haunt my imagination," he seems to say. "They show the true nature of modern man—how weak we are, how helpless against ourselves in this proud era of so-called progress." Many elements from this grotesque and sinister sideshow recur more than a decade later in the lateral panels of Beckmann's triptych *Departure* (fig. 937, colorplate 135), completed when, under Nazi pressure, he was on the point of leaving his homeland. In the hindsight of today, the topsy-turvy

933. ERNST LUDWIG KIRCHNER. *Street, Dresden.* 1908, dated 1907 on painting. 59¼ × 78⅞".
The Museum of Modern Art, New York (Purchase)

934. EMIL NOLDE. *The Last Supper* (see colorplate 134). Stiftung Seebüll Ada und Emil Nolde, Neukirchen (Schleswig), Germany

quality of these two scenes, full of mutilations and meaningless rituals, has acquired the force of prophecy. The stable design of the center panel, in contrast, with its expanse of blue sea and its sunlit brightness, conveys the hopeful spirit of an embarkation for distant shores. After living through World War II in occupied Holland, under the most trying conditions, Beckmann spent the final three years of his career in America.

NON-OBJECTIVE PAINTING: KANDINSKY. But the most daring and original step beyond Fauvism was taken in Germany by a Russian, Wassily Kandinsky (1866–1944), the leading member of a group of Munich artists called *Der Blaue Reiter* (The Blue Horseman). From 1910 on, Kandinsky abandoned representation altogether. Using the rainbow colors and the free, dynamic brushwork of the Paris *Fauves*, he created a completely non-objective style. These works have titles as abstract as their forms; our example, one of the most striking, is called *Sketch I for "Composition VII"* (fig. 938, colorplate 136).

Perhaps we should avoid the term "abstract," because it is so often taken to mean that the artist has analyzed and simplified the shapes of visible reality (compare Cézanne's dictum that all natural forms are based on the cone, sphere, and cylinder). This was not the method of Kandinsky. What-

935. OSKAR KOKOSCHKA.
Self-Portrait. 1913. 32 × 19½".
The Museum of Modern Art,
New York (Purchase)

936. MAX BECKMANN.
The Dream. 1921. 71 × 35".
Collection Morton D. May,
St. Louis, Missouri

937. MAX BECKMANN.
Departure (right panel; see colorplate 135).
The Museum of Modern Art,
New York (Given anonymously by exchange)

938. WASSILY KANDINSKY. *Sketch I for "Composition VII"* (see colorplate 136). Collection Felix Klee, Bern

ever traces of representation his work contains are quite involuntary—his aim was to charge form and color with a purely spiritual meaning (as he put it) by eliminating all resemblance to the physical world. Whistler, too, had spoken of "divesting the picture from any outside sort of interest"; he even anticipated Kandinsky's "musical" titles (fig. 883, colorplate 123). But it was the liberating influence of the *Fauves* that permitted Kandinsky to put this theory into practice. The possibility was clearly implicit in Fauvism from the start, as shown in our experiment with Rouault's *Head of Christ*: when the upper third of the picture is covered, the rest becomes a non-representational composition strangely similar to Kandinsky's.

How valid is the analogy between painting and music? When a painter like Kandinsky carries it through so uncompromisingly, does he really lift his art to another plane? Or could it be that his declared independence from representational images now forces him instead to "represent music," which limits him even more severely? Kandinsky's advocates like to point out that representational painting has a "literary" content, and to deplore such dependence on another art, but they do not explain why the "musical" content of non-objective painting should be more desirable. Is painting less alien to music than to literature? They seem to think music is a higher art than literature or painting because it is inherently non-representational—a point of view with an ancient tradition that goes back to Plato, and includes Plotinus, St. Augustine, and their medieval successors. The attitude of the non-objectivists might thus be termed "secular iconoclasm": they do not condemn images as wicked, but denounce them as non-art.

The case is difficult to argue, nor does it matter whether this theory is right or wrong; the proof of the pudding is in the eating, not in the recipe. Kandinsky's—or any artist's—ideas are not important to us unless we are convinced of the importance of his pictures. Did he create a viable style? Admittedly, his work demands an intuitive response that may

be hard for some of us, yet the painting here reproduced has density and vitality, and a radiant freshness of feeling that impresses us even though we are uncertain what exactly the artist has expressed.

UNITED STATES. Americans became familiar with the *Fauves* through exhibitions from 1908 on, and after World War I there was a growing interest in the German Expressionists as well. The driving force behind the modernist movement in the United States was the photographer Alfred Stieglitz (see page 771), who almost single-handedly supported many of its early members. To him, modernism meant abstraction and its related concepts. The modern movement proved short-lived, largely because the utopian ideals associated with abstraction were dashed by "the war to end all wars." After 1920, most of the painters in the Stieglitz circle concentrated on landscapes, which they treated in representational styles indebted chiefly to Expressionism.

The most original members of the Stieglitz group, Arthur Dove (1880–1946) and Georgia O'Keeffe (1887–1986), practiced forms of abstraction that owed a great deal to Kandinsky. Throughout her long career, O'Keeffe (who married Stieglitz in 1924) covered a wide range of subjects and styles, but all embodied the same personal approach: as she assimilated a subject into her imagination, she altered and simplified its appearance. Among her finest works are the

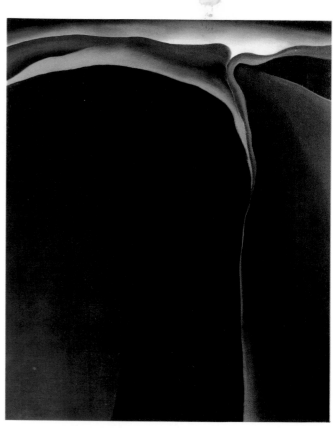

939. GEORGIA O'KEEFFE. *Dark Abstraction*. 1924.
24⅞ × 20⅞". St. Louis Art Museum (Gift of Charles E. and Mary Merrill)

Colorplate 134. EMIL NOLDE. *The Last Supper* (see page 669). 1909. 32½ × 41¾″.
Stiftung Seebüll Ada und Emil Nolde, Neukirchen (Schleswig), Germany

Colorplate 135. MAX BECKMANN. *Departure* (see page 670). 1932–33. Center panel 84¾ × 45⅜",
side panels each 84¾ × 39¼". The Museum of Modern Art, New York (Given anonymously, by exchange)

Colorplate 136. WASSILY KANDINSKY. *Sketch I for*
"*Composition VII*" (see page 671). 1913. 30¼ × 39⅜". Collection Felix Klee, Bern

Colorplate 137. PABLO PICASSO. *Three Dancers* (see page 684).
1925. 84½ × 56¼". The Tate Gallery, London

Colorplate 138. JOSEPH STELLA. *Brooklyn Bridge* (see page 687). 1917. 84 × 76″.
Yale University Art Gallery, New Haven, Connecticut (Collection of the Société Anonyme)

Colorplate 139. FERNAND LÉGER. *The City* (see page 687). 1919. 91 × 117½″. The Philadelphia Museum of Art (The A. E. Gallatin Collection)

Colorplate 140. PIET MONDRIAN. *Composition with Red, Blue, and Yellow* (see page 689).
1930. 20 × 20″. Collection Mr. and Mrs. Armand P. Bartos, New York

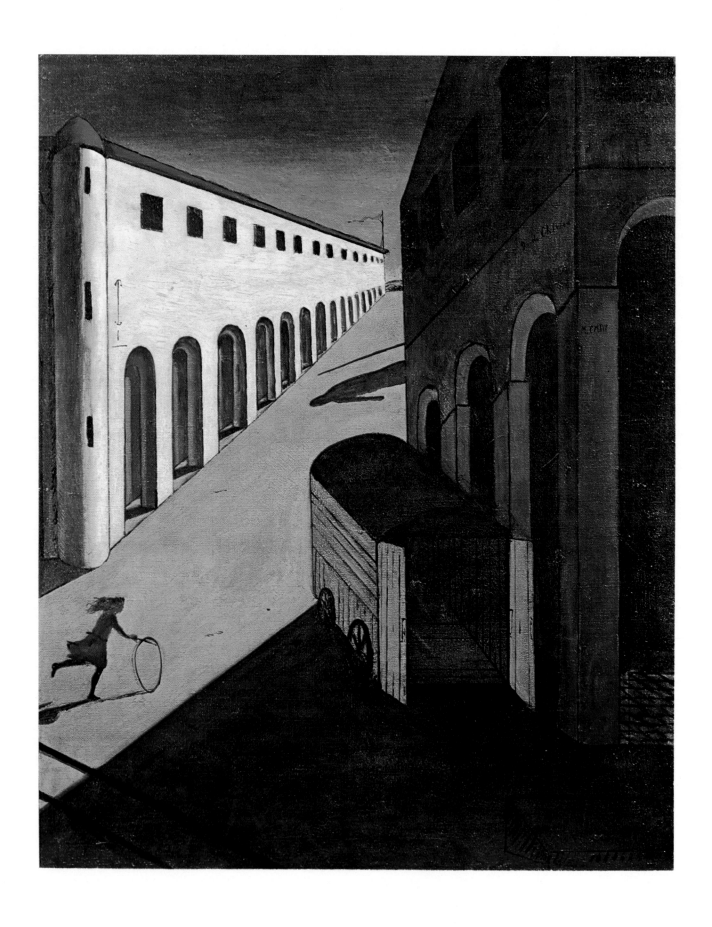

Colorplate 141. GIORGIO DE CHIRICO. *Mystery and Melancholy of a Street* (see page 690).
1914. 33½ × 27¼″. Resor Collection, New Canaan, Connecticut

940. JOSÉ CLEMENTE OROZCO. *Victims* (detail from a mural cycle). 1936. University of Guadalajara, Mexico

organic abstractions from the mid-1920s (fig. 939). Part plant, part landscape, they seem to reveal the secret life of nature from within. These paintings have a monumental spirit that belies their often modest size.

MEXICO. By the 1930s, the center of Expressionism in the New World was Mexico, rather than the United States. The Mexican Revolution began in 1911 with the fall of the dictator Porfirio Díaz, and continued for more than two decades; it inspired a group of young painters to search for a national style incorporating the great native heritage of pre-Columbian art. They also felt that their art must be "of the people," expressing the spirit of the Revolution in vast mural cycles in public buildings. Although each developed his own distinctive style, they shared a common point of departure: the Symbolist art of Gauguin. This art had shown how non-Western forms could be integrated with the Western tradition, and the flat, decorative quality was moreover particularly suited to murals. The involvement of these

artists in the political turmoil of the day often led them to overburden their works with ideological significance.

The artist least subject to this imbalance of form and subject matter was José Clemente Orozco (1883–1949), a passionately independent artist who refused to get embroiled in factional politics. Our detail from the mural cycle at the University of Guadalajara (fig. 940) illustrates his most powerful trait, a deep humanitarian sympathy with the silent, suffering masses.

Abstraction

The second of our main currents is the one we called Abstraction. When discussing Kandinsky, we said that the term is usually taken to mean the process (or the result) of analyzing and simplifying observed reality. Literally, it means "to draw away from, to separate." If we have ten apples, and then separate the ten from the apples, we get an "abstract number," a number that no longer refers to particular things. But "apples," too, is an abstraction, since it places ten apples in one class, without regard for their individual qualities. The artist who sets out to paint ten apples will find no two of them alike, yet he cannot possibly take account of all their differences: even the most painstakingly realistic portrayal of these particular pieces of fruit is bound to be some sort of an abstraction. Abstraction, then, goes into the making of any work of art, whether the artist knows it or not. The process was not conscious and controlled, however, until the Early Renaissance, when artists first analyzed the shapes of nature in terms of mathematical bodies (see page 418). Cézanne and Seurat revitalized this approach and explored it further; they are the direct ancestors of the abstract movement in twentieth-century art. Its real creator, however, was Pablo Picasso.

PICASSO'S DEMOISELLES D'AVIGNON. About 1905, stimulated as much by the *Fauves* as by the retrospective exhibitions of the great Post-Impressionists, Picasso gradually abandoned the melancholy lyricism of his Blue Period for a more robust style. He shared Matisse's enthusiasm for Gauguin and Cézanne, but he viewed these masters very differently; in 1906–7 he produced his own counterpart to *The Joy of Life*, a monumental canvas so challenging that it outraged even Matisse (fig. 941). The title, *Les Demoiselles d'Avignon* ("The Young Ladies of Avignon"), does not refer to the town of that name, but to Avignon Street in a notorious section of Barcelona; when Picasso started the picture, it was to be a temptation scene in a brothel, but he ended up with a composition of five nudes and a still life. But what nudes! Matisse's generalized figures in *The Joy of Life* (see fig. 927) seem utterly innocuous compared to this savage aggressiveness.

The three on the left are angular distortions of classical figures, but the violently dislocated features and bodies of the other two have all the barbaric qualities of primitive art (compare figs. 38, 39, 43–46). Following Gauguin's lead, the *Fauves* had discovered the aesthetic appeal of African and Oceanic sculpture, and had introduced Picasso to this mate-

941. PABLO PICASSO. *Les Demoiselles d'Avignon.* 1906–7. 96 × 92".
The Museum of Modern Art, New York (Acquired through the Lillie P. Bliss Bequest)

rial; yet it was he, rather than they, who used primitive art as a battering ram against the classical conception of beauty. Not only the proportions, but the organic integrity and continuity of the human body are denied here, so that the canvas (in the apt description of one critic) "resembles a field of broken glass."

Picasso, then, has destroyed a great deal; what has he gained in the process? Once we recover from the initial shock, we begin to see that the destruction is quite methodical: everything—the figures as well as their setting—is broken up into angular wedges or facets; these, we will note, are not flat, but shaded in a way that gives them a certain three-dimensionality. We cannot always be sure whether they are concave or convex; some look like chunks of solidified space, others like fragments of translucent bodies. They constitute a unique kind of matter, which imposes a new integrity and continuity on the entire canvas. The *Demoiselles*, unlike *The Joy of Life*, can no longer be read as an image of the external world; its world is its own, analogous to nature but constructed along different principles. Picasso's revolutionary "building material," compounded of voids and solids, is hard to describe with any precision. The early critics, who saw only the prevalence of sharp edges and angles, dubbed the new style Cubism.

FACET CUBISM.   That the *Demoiselles* owes anything to Cézanne may at first seem incredible. Nevertheless, Picasso had studied Cézanne's late work (such as fig. 896) with great care, finding in Cézanne's abstract treatment of volume and space the translucent structural units from which to derive the facets of Cubism. The link is clearer in Picasso's portrait of Ambroise Vollard (fig. 942), painted four years later: the facets are now small and precise, more like prisms, and the canvas has the balance and refinement of a fully mature style.

Contrasts of color and texture, so pronounced in the *Demoiselles*, are now reduced to a minimum (the subdued tonality of the picture approaches monochrome), so as not to compete with the design. And the structure has become so complex and systematic that it would seem wholly cerebral if the "imprismed" sitter's face did not emerge with such dramatic force. Of the "barbaric" distortions in the *Demoiselles* there is no trace; they had served their purpose. Cubism has become an abstract style within the purely Western sense. But its distance from observed reality has not significantly increased—Picasso may be playing an elaborate game of hide-and-seek with nature, but he still needs the visible world to challenge his creative powers. The non-objective realm held no appeal for him, then or later.

their work at that time is difficult to tell apart. Both of them—it is not clear to whom the chief credit belongs—initiated the next phase of Cubism, which was even bolder than the first. We see its beginnings in Picasso's *Still Life* of 1911–12 (fig. 943). Most of the painting shows the now-familiar facets, except for the letters; these, being already abstract signs, could not be translated into prismatic shapes, but from beneath the still life emerges a piece of imitation chair caning, which has been pasted onto the canvas, and the picture is "framed" by a piece of rope. This intrusion of alien materials has a most remarkable effect: the abstract still life appears to rest on a real surface (the chair caning) as on a tray, and the substantiality of this tray is further emphasized by the rope.

Within a year, Picasso and Braque were producing still lifes composed almost entirely of cut and pasted scraps of material, with only a few lines added to complete the design. In one fine example by Braque (fig. 944) we recognize strips of imitation wood graining, part of a tobacco wrapper with a contrasting stamp, half the masthead of a newspaper, and a bit of newsprint made into a playing card (the ace of hearts). The technique came to be known as *collage* (the French word for "paste-up"). Why did Picasso and Braque suddenly prefer the contents of the wastepaper basket to brush and paint? Because, wanting to explore the new concept of the picture-as-a-tray, they found the best way was to put real things on the tray. The ingredients of a collage actually play a double role; they have been shaped and combined, then drawn or painted upon to give them a representational meaning, but they do not lose their original identity as scraps of material, "outsiders" in the world of art. Thus their function is both to *represent* (to be a part of an image) and to *present* (to be themselves). In this latter capacity, they endow the collage with a self-sufficiency that no facet-Cubist picture

942. PABLO PICASSO. *Ambroise Vollard.* 1909–10. 36 × 25½″. Pushkin Museum, Moscow

943. PABLO PICASSO. *Still Life with Chair Caning.* 1911–12. 10½ × 13¾″. Collection the artist's estate

COLLAGE CUBISM.

By 1910, Cubism was well established as an alternative to Fauvism, and Picasso had been joined by a number of other artists, notably Georges Braque (1882–1963), with whom he collaborated so intimately that

944. GEORGES BRAQUE. *Le Courrier.* 1913. Collage, 20 × 22½″. The Philadelphia Museum of Art (A. E. Gallatin Collection)

945. PABLO PICASSO. *Three Musicians.* 1921.
79 × 87¾". The Museum of Modern Art, New York
(Mrs. Simon Guggenheim Fund)

can have. A tray, after all, is a self-contained area, detached from the rest of the physical world; unlike a painting, it cannot show more than is actually on it.

The difference between the two phases of Cubism may also be defined in terms of picture space: facet Cubism retains a certain kind of depth, the painted surface acting as a window through which we still perceive the remnants of the familiar perspective space of the Renaissance. Though fragmented and redefined, this space lies behind the picture plane and has no visible limits; potentially, it may contain objects that are hidden from our view. In collage Cubism, on the contrary, the picture space lies in front of the plane of the "tray"; space is not created by illusionistic devices, such as modeling and foreshortening, but by the actual overlapping of layers of pasted materials. When, as in figure 944, the apparent thickness of these materials, and their distance from each other, is increased by a bit of shading here and there, this does not affect the integrity of the non-perspective space. Collage Cubism, then, offers a basically new space concept, the first since Masaccio: it is a true landmark in the history of painting.

Before long Picasso and Braque discovered that they could retain this new pictorial space without the use of pasted materials; they had only to paint as if they were making collages. Picasso's *Three Musicians* (fig. 945) shows this "cut-paper style" so consistently that we cannot tell from the reproduction whether it is painted or pasted. It is, in any event, one of the great masterpieces of collage Cubism, monumental in size and conception. The separate pieces are fitted together as firmly as architectural blocks, yet the artist's primary concern is not with the surface pattern (if it were, the painting would resemble a patchwork quilt), but with the image of the three musicians, traditional figures

of the comedy stage. Their human presence, solemn and even sinister, may be sensed behind the screen of costumes and masks.

POST-CUBIST PICASSO.   By now, Picasso was internationally famous. Cubism had spread throughout the Western world; it influenced not only other painters, but sculptors and even architects. Picasso himself, however, was already striking out in a new direction. Soon after the invention of collage Cubism, he had begun to do drawings in a painstakingly realistic manner reminiscent of Ingres, and by 1920 he was working simultaneously in two quite separate styles: that of the *Three Musicians*, and a Neoclassic style of strongly modeled, heavy-bodied figures such as his *Mother and Child* (fig. 946). To many of his admirers, this seemed a kind of betrayal, but in retrospect the reason for Picasso's double-track performance is clear: chafing under the limitations of collage Cubism, he needed to resume contact with the classical tradition, the "art of the museums." The figures in *Mother and Child* have a mock-monumental quality that suggests colossal statues rather than flesh-and-blood human beings, yet the theme is treated with surprising tenderness. The forms, however, are carefully dovetailed within the frame, not unlike the way the *Three Musicians* is put together.

A few years later the two tracks of Picasso's style began to converge, making an extraordinary synthesis that was to become the basis of his art. The *Three Dancers* of 1925

946. PABLO PICASSO. *Mother and Child.* 1921–22.
38 × 28". The Alex L. Hillman Family Foundation, New York

(fig. 947, colorplate 137) shows how he accomplished this seemingly impossible feat. Structurally, the picture is pure collage Cubism; it even includes painted imitations of specific materials—patterned wallpaper, and samples of various fabrics cut out with pinking shears. But the figures, a wildly fantastic version of a classical scheme (compare the dancers in Matisse's *The Joy of Life*; fig. 927), are an even more violent assault on convention than the figures in the *Demoiselles d'Avignon*. Human anatomy is here simply the raw material for Picasso's incredibly fertile inventiveness; limbs, breasts, and faces are handled with the same sovereign freedom as the fragments of external reality in Braque's *Le Courrier* (fig. 944). Their original identity no longer matters—breasts may turn into eyes, profiles merge with frontal views, shadows become substance, and vice versa, in an endless flow of metamorphoses. They are "visual puns," offering wholly unexpected possibilities of expression— humorous, grotesque, macabre, even tragic.

GUERNICA. That Picasso's new style may have truly monumental grandeur is evident in his mural *Guernica* (fig. 948), painted in 1937. As a citizen of a neutral nation, Picasso had not been greatly affected by World War I, nor did he show any interest in politics during the 1920s. But the Spanish Civil War stirred him to ardent partisanship with the Loyalists. The mural, executed for the Pavilion of the Spanish Republic at the Paris International Exposition, was inspired by the terror-bombing of Guernica, the ancient capital of the Basques in northern Spain. It does not represent the event itself; rather, with a series of powerful images, it evokes the agony of total war.

The destruction of Guernica was the first demonstration of the technique of saturation bombing which was later employed on a huge scale in the course of World War II; the mural was thus a prophetic vision of doom—the doom that

947. PABLO PICASSO. *Three Dancers* (see colorplate 137)
The Tate Gallery, London

948. PABLO PICASSO. *Guernica*. 1937. 11′ 6″ × 25′ 8″. The Prado, Madrid

949. UMBERTO BOCCIONI. *Dynamism of a Cyclist.*
1913. 27⅝ × 37⅜". Collection Gianni Mattioli, Milan

threatens us even more in this age of nuclear warfare. The symbolism of the scene resists precise interpretation, despite its several traditional elements: the mother and her dead child are the descendants of the Pietà (see fig. 468), the woman with the lamp recalls the Statue of Liberty, and the dead fighter's hand, still clutching a broken sword, is a familiar emblem of heroic resistance. We also sense the contrast between the menacing, human-headed bull, surely intended to represent the forces of darkness, and the dying horse.

These figures owe their terrifying eloquence to what they *are,* not to what they *mean;* the anatomical dislocations, fragmentations and metamorphoses, which in the *Three Dancers* seemed willful and fantastic, now express a stark reality, the reality of unbearable pain. The ultimate test of the validity of collage construction (here in superimposed flat "cutouts" restricted to black, white, and gray) is that it could serve as the vehicle of such overpowering emotions.

Variants of Cubism

FUTURISM AND DYNAMISM. As originally conceived by Picasso and Braque, Cubism was a formal discipline of subtle balance applied to traditional subjects—still life, portraiture, the nude. Other painters, however, saw in the new style a special affinity with the geometric precision of engineering that made it uniquely attuned to the dynamism of modern life. The short-lived Futurist movement in Italy exemplifies this attitude; in 1910 its founders issued a manifesto violently rejecting the past, and exalting the beauty of the machine.

At first they used techniques developed from Post-Impressionism to convey in otherwise static compositions, still dependent upon representational images, the surge of

industrial society. But by adopting the simultaneous views of facet Cubism in *Dynamism of a Cyclist* (fig. 949), Umberto Boccioni (1882–1916), the most original of the Futurists, was able to communicate the look of furious pedaling across time and space far more tellingly than if he had

950. JOSEPH STELLA. *Brooklyn Bridge* (see colorplate 138). Yale University Art Gallery, New Haven (Collection of the Société Anonyme)

actually depicted the human figure, which could be seen in only one time and place in traditional art. In the flexible vocabulary provided by Cubism, Boccioni found the means of expressing the twentieth century's new sense of time, space, and energy that Albert Einstein had defined in 1905 in his theory of relativity. Moreover, Boccioni suggests the unique quality of the modern experience. With his pulsating movement, the cyclist has become an extension of his environment, from which he is now indistinguishable.

Futurism literally died out in World War I; its leaders were killed by the same vehicles of destruction they had glorified only a few years earlier in their revolutionary manifesto. But strong echoes of Futurism appear in *Brooklyn Bridge* (fig. 950, colorplate 138), by the Italo-American Joseph Stella (1880–1946), with its maze of luminescent cables, vigorous diagonal thrusts, and crystalline "cells" of space.

Cubism in a dynamized form is also to be seen in the early work of George Grosz (1893–1959), a German painter and graphic artist who had studied in Paris in 1913. At the end of World War I, he developed a bitter, savagely satiric style to express the disillusionment of his generation. In *Germany, a Winter's Tale* (fig. 951), the city of Berlin forms the kaleidoscopic—and chaotic—background for several large figures, which are superimposed on it as in a collage: the marionette-like, timid "good citizen" at his table, and the sinister forces that molded him (a hypocritical clergyman, a general, and a schoolmaster).

In contrast, *The City* (fig. 952, colorplate 139), by the Frenchman Fernand Léger (1881–1955), is a beautifully controlled industrial landscape that is stable without being static, and reflects the clean geometric shapes of modern machinery. Buoyant with optimism and pleasurable excitement, it conjures up a mechanized utopia. In this instance, the term "abstraction" applies more to the choice of design elements and their manner of combination than to the shapes themselves, since these (except for the two figures on the staircase) are "pre-fabricated" entities.

RUSSIA. As its name implies, Cubo-Futurism, which arose in Russia a few years before World War I as the result of close contacts with the leading European art centers, took

952. FERNAND LÉGER. *The City* (see colorplate 139).
The Philadelphia Museum of Art (A. E. Gallatin Collection)

951. GEORGE GROSZ. *Germany, a Winter's Tale*. 1918.
Formerly Collection Garvens, Hanover, Germany

its style from Picasso and based its theories on Futurist tracts. The Russian Futurists were above all modernists. They welcomed industry, which was spreading rapidly throughout Russia, as the foundation of a new society and the means for conquering that old Russian enemy, nature. Unlike the Italian Futurists, however, the Russians never glorified the machine, least of all as an instrument of war.

Central to Cubo-Futurist thinking was the concept of *zaum*, a term which has no counterpart in the West: invented by Russian poets, *zaum* was a trans-sense (as opposed to the Dadaists' non-sense; see page 692) language based on new word forms and syntax. In theory, *zaum* could be understood universally, since it was thought that meaning was

At the same time, the strong modeling draws attention to the surface, lending it a relief-like quality which is enhanced by the vigorous texture.

The first purely Russian art of the twentieth century, however, was that of Suprematism. In one of the greatest leaps of the symbolic and spatial imagination in the history of art, Kazimir Malevich (1878–1935) invented the *Black Quadrilateral* seen in figure 954. How is it that such a disarmingly simple image should be so important? By reducing art to the fewest possible elements—a single shape repeated in two tones and fixed firmly to the picture plane—he emphasized the painting as a painting even more radically than had his predecessors. At the same time, he transformed it into a concentrated symbol having multiple layers of meaning, thereby providing the content missing from Cubo-Futurism. The inspiration for *Black Quadrilateral* came in 1913 while Malevich was working on designs for the opera "Victory over the Sun," a production that was one of the important collaborations in the modern era. In the context of the opera, the black quadrilateral represents the eclipse of the sun of Western painting and of everything based upon it. Further, the work can be seen as the triumph of the new order over the old, of the East over the West, man

953. LIUBOV POPOVA. *The Traveler*. 1915. 56 × 41½".
Norton Simon Museum, Pasadena

implicit in the basic sounds and patterns of speech. When applied to painting, *zaum* provided the artist with complete freedom to redefine the style and content of art. The picture surface was now seen as the sole conveyer of meaning through its appearance; hence, the subject of a work of art became the visual elements and their formal arrangement. However, because Cubo-Futurism was concerned with means, not ends, it failed to provide the actual content that is found in modernism.

Although the Cubo-Futurists were more important as theorists than artists, they provided the springboard for later Russian movements. The new world envisioned by the Russian modernists led to a broad redefinition of the roles of man and woman, and the finest painter of the group was Liubov Popova (1889–1924). For the first time in history women emerged as artistic equals to an extent not achieved in Europe or America until considerably later. Popova studied in Paris in 1912 and visited Italy in 1914. The combination of Cubism and Futurism that she absorbed abroad is seen in *The Traveler* (fig. 953). The treatment of forms remains essentially Cubist, but the painting shares the Futurist obsession with representing dynamic motion in time and space. The jumble of image fragments creates the impression of objects seen in rapid succession; across the plane the furious interaction of forms with their environment threatens to extend the painting into the surrounding space.

954. KAZIMIR MALEVICH. *Black Quadrilateral*.
c. 1913–15. 24 × 17".
Copyright The George Costakis Collection, Athens

over nature, idea over matter. The black quadrilateral (which is not even a true rectangle) was intended to stand as a modern icon, superseding the traditional Christian trinity and symbolizing a "supreme" reality, because geometry is an independent abstraction in itself: hence the movement's name, Suprematism.

According to Malevich, Suprematism was also a philosophical color system constructed in time and space. His space was an intuitive one, having both scientific and mystical overtones. The flat plane replaces volume, depth, and perspective as a means of defining space; each side or point represents one of the three dimensions, the fourth side standing for the fourth dimension, time. Like the universe itself, the black surface would be infinite were it not delimited by an outer boundary which is the white border and shape of the canvas. *Black Quadrilateral* thus constitutes the first satisfactory redefinition, visually and conceptually, of time and space in modern art. Like Einstein's formula $E = mc^2$ for the theory of relativity, of which Malevich was certainly aware, it has an elegant simplicity that belies the intense effort required to synthesize a complex set of ideas and reduce them to a fundamental "law." When it appeared for the first time, Suprematism had much the same impact on Russian artists that Einstein's theory had on scientists: it unveiled a world never seen before, one that was unequivocally modern.

The heyday of Suprematism was over by the early 1920s. Reflecting the growing diversity and fragmentation of Russian art, its followers defected to other movements, above all to the Constructivism led by Vladimir Tatlin (see page 738).

DE STIJL: MONDRIAN. The most radical abstractionist of our time was, strangely enough, a Dutch painter nine years older than Picasso, Piet Mondrian (1872–1944). He came to Paris in 1912 as a mature Expressionist in the tradition of Van Gogh and the *Fauves*. Under the impact of facet Cubism, his work soon underwent a complete change, and within the next decade Mondrian developed an entirely non-representational style that he called Neo-Plasticism (the movement as a whole is also known as *De Stijl*, after the Dutch magazine advocating his ideas). *Composition with Red, Blue, and Yellow* (colorplate 140) shows Mondrian's style at its most severe: he restricts his design to horizontals and verticals and his colors to the three primary hues, plus black and white. Every possibility of representation is thereby eliminated, and his work also has no meaning in black-and-white reproduction. Yet Mondrian sometimes gave to his works such titles as *Trafalgar Square*, or *Broadway Boogie-Woogie*, that hint at some degree of relationship, however indirect, with observed reality. Unlike Kandinsky, Mondrian did not strive for pure, lyrical emotion; his goal, he asserted, was "pure reality," and he defined this as equilibrium "through the balance of unequal but equivalent oppositions."

Perhaps we can best understand what he meant if we think of his work as "abstract collage" that uses black bands and colored rectangles instead of recognizable fragments of chair caning and newsprint. He was interested solely in relationships, and wanted no distracting elements or fortuitous associations. But, by establishing the "right" relationship among his bands and rectangles, he transforms them as thoroughly as Braque transformed the snippets of pasted paper in *Le Courrier* (fig. 944). How did he discover the "right" relationship? And how did he determine the shape and number for the bands and rectangles? In Braque's *Le Courrier*, the ingredients are to some extent "given" by chance; Mondrian, apart from his self-imposed rules, constantly faced the dilemma of unlimited possibilities. He could not change the relationship of the bands to the rectangles without changing the bands and rectangles themselves. When we consider his task, we begin to realize its infinite complexity.

Looking again at *Composition with Red, Blue, and Yellow*, we find that when we measure the various units, only the proportions of the canvas itself are truly rational, an exact square; Mondrian has arrived at all the rest "by feel," and must have undergone agonies of trial and error. How often, we wonder, did he change the dimensions of the red rectangle, to bring it and the other elements into self-contained equilibrium? Strange as it may seem, Mondrian's exquisite sense for non-symmetrical balance is so specific that critics well acquainted with his work have no difficulty telling fakes from genuine pictures. Designers who work with non-figurative shapes, such as architects and typographers, are likely to be most sensitive to this quality, and Mondrian has had a greater influence among them than among painters (see Chapter 5).

Fantasy

The third current, which we termed Fantasy, follows a course less clear-cut than the other two, since it depends on a state of mind more than on any particular style. The one thing all painters of fantasy have in common is the belief that imagination, "the inner eye," is more important than the outside world. And since every artist's imagination is his own private domain, the images it provides for him are likely to be equally private, unless he subjects them to a deliberate process of selection. But how can such "uncontrolled" images have meaning to the beholder, whose own inner world is not the same as the artist's? Psychoanalysis has taught us that we are not so different from each other in this respect as we like to think. Our minds are all built on the same basic pattern, and the same is true of our imagination and memory. These belong to the unconscious part of the mind where experiences are stored, whether we want to remember them or not. At night, or whenever conscious thought relaxes its vigilance, our experiences come back to us and we seem to live through them again.

However, the unconscious mind does not usually reproduce our experiences as they actually happened. They will often be admitted into the conscious part of the mind in the guise of "dream images"—in this form they seem less vivid, and we can live with our memories more easily. This digesting of experience by the unconscious mind is surprisingly alike in all of us, although the process works better with some individuals than with others. Hence we are always interested in imaginary things, provided they are presented to us in such a way that they *seem* real. What happens in a fairy tale, for example, would be absurd in the matter-of-fact language of a news report, but when it is told to us as it should be told, we are enchanted. The same thing is true of paintings—we recall *The Dream* by Henri Rousseau (see fig. 913, colorplate 129).

But why, we may ask, does private fantasy loom so large in present-day art? We saw the trend beginning at the end of the eighteenth century in the art of Fuseli and Goya (see figs. 816, 835); perhaps they suggest part of the answer. There seem to be several interlocking causes: first, the cleavage that developed between reason and imagination in the wake of rationalism, which tended to dissolve the heritage of myth and legend that had been the common channel of private fantasy in earlier times; second, the artist's greater freedom—and insecurity—within the social fabric, giving him a sense of isolation and favoring an introspective attitude; and, finally, the Romantic cult of emotion that prompted the artist to seek out subjective experience, and to accept its validity. In nineteenth-century painting, private fantasy was still a minor current. After 1900, it became a major one.

NOSTALGIA: DE CHIRICO; CHAGALL. The heritage of Romanticism can be seen most clearly in the astonishing pictures painted in Paris just before World War I by Giorgio

956. MARC CHAGALL. *I and the Village*
(see colorplate 142). The Museum of Modern Art,
New York (Mrs. Simon Guggenheim Fund)

955. GIORGIO DE CHIRICO.
Mystery and Melancholy of a Street (see colorplate 141).
Resor Collection, New Canaan, Connecticut

de Chirico (1888–1978), such as *Mystery and Melancholy of a Street* (fig. 955, colorplate 141). This deserted square with endless diminishing arcades, nocturnally illuminated by the cold full moon, has all the poetry of Romantic reverie. But it has also a strangely sinister air; this is an "ominous" scene in the full sense of that term—everything here suggests an omen, a portent of unknown and disquieting significance. De Chirico himself could not explain the incongruities in these paintings—the empty furniture van, or the girl with the hoop—that trouble and fascinate us. Later, after he had returned to Italy, he adopted a conservative style and repudiated his early work, as if he were embarrassed at having put his dream world on public display.

The power of nostalgia, so evident in *Mystery and Melancholy of a Street*, also dominates the fantasies of Marc Chagall (1887–1985), a Russian Jew who came to Paris in 1910. *I and the Village* (fig. 956, colorplate 142) is a Cubist fairy tale, weaving dreamlike memories of Russian folk tales, Jewish proverbs, and the look of Russia into one glowing vision. Here, as in many later works, Chagall relives the experiences of his childhood; these were so important to him that his imagination shaped and reshaped them for years without their persistence being diminished.

957. PAUL KLEE. *Twittering Machine.* 1922.
Watercolor, pen and ink, 16¼ × 12".
The Museum of Modern Art, New York (Purchase)

958. PAUL KLEE. *Park near L(ucerne)*
(see colorplate 143).
Klee Foundation, Bern

KLEE. The "fairy tales" of the German-Swiss painter Paul Klee (1879–1940) are more purposeful and controlled than Chagall's, although at first they may strike us as more childlike. Klee, too, had been influenced by Cubism; but primitive art, and the drawings of small children, held an equally vital interest for him. During World War I, he molded from these disparate elements a pictorial language of his own, marvelously economical and precise.

Twittering Machine (fig. 957), a delicate pen drawing tinted with watercolor, demonstrates the unique flavor of Klee's art: with a few simple lines, he had created a ghostly mechanism that imitates the sound of birds, simultaneously mocking our faith in the miracles of the machine age and our sentimental appreciation of bird song. The little contraption (which is not without its sinister aspect: the heads of the four sham birds look like fishermen's lures, as if they might entrap real birds) thus condenses into one striking invention a complex of ideas about present-day civilization.

The title has an indispensable role; it is characteristic of the way Klee works that the picture itself, however visually appealing, does not reveal its full evocative quality unless the artist tells us what it means. The title, in turn, needs the picture—the witty concept of a twittering machine does not kindle our imagination until we are shown such a thing. This interdependence is familiar to us from cartoons; Klee lifts it to the level of high art without relinquishing the playful character of these verbal-visual puns. To him art was a "language of signs," of shapes that are images of ideas as the shape of a letter is the image of a specific sound, or an arrow the image of the command, "This way only." But he also realized that in any conventional system the sign is no more than a "trigger"; the instant we perceive it, we automatically invest it with its meaning, without stopping to ponder its shape. Klee wanted *his* signs to impinge upon our awareness as visual facts, yet also to share the quality of "triggers."

Toward the end of his life, he immersed himself in the study of ideographs of all kinds, such as hieroglyphics, hex signs, and the mysterious markings in prehistoric caves— "boiled-down" representational images that appealed to him because they had the twin quality he strove for in his own graphic language. This "ideographic style" is very pronounced in figure 958 and colorplate 143, *Park near L(ucerne);* as a lyric poet may use the plainest words, these deceptively simple shapes sum up a wealth of experience and sensation: the innocent gaiety of spring, the clipped orderliness peculiar to captive plant life in a park. Has it not also a relationship, in spirit if not in fact, with the Romanesque *Spring Landscape* in the manuscript of *Carmina Burana* (fig. 421, colorplate 46)?

DADA: DUCHAMP.   In Paris on the eve of World War I, we encounter yet another painter of fantasy, the Frenchman Marcel Duchamp (1887–1968). After basing his early style on Cézanne, he initiated a dynamic version of facet Cubism, similar to Futurism, by superimposing successive phases of movement on each other, as in multiple-exposure photography (see fig. 926). His *Nude Descending a Staircase*, done in this vein, caused a scandal at the Armory Show of modern art in New York in 1913 (fig. 959).

Very soon, however, Duchamp's development took a far more disturbing turn. In *The Bride* (fig. 960) we will look in vain for any resemblance, however remote, to the human form; what we see is a mechanism that seems part motor, part distilling apparatus; the antithesis of Klee's twittering

960. MARCEL DUCHAMP. *The Bride.* 1912.
34¾ × 21½″. The Philadelphia Museum of Art
(Louise and Walter Arensberg Collection)

machine, it is beautifully engineered to serve no purpose whatever. Its title, which cannot be irrelevant (Duchamp, by lettering it right onto the canvas, has emphasized its importance), causes us real perplexity. Did he intend to satirize the scientific outlook on man, by "analyzing" the bride until she is reduced to a complicated piece of plumbing? If so, the picture may be the negative counterpart of the glorification of the machine, so stridently proclaimed by the Futurists.

It is hardly surprising that the mechanized mass killing of World War I should have driven Duchamp to despair. Together with a number of others who shared his attitude, he launched in protest a movement called Dada (or Dadaism). The term, meaning "hobbyhorse" in French, was reportedly picked at random from a dictionary, but as an infantile "all-purpose word," it perfectly fitted the spirit of the movement. Dada has often been called nihilistic, and its declared purpose was indeed to make clear to the public at large that all established values, moral or aesthetic, had been rendered meaningless by the catastrophe of the great war.

959. MARCEL DUCHAMP. *Nude Descending a Staircase,*
No. 2. 1912. 58 × 35″. The Philadelphia Museum of Art
(Louise and Walter Arensberg Collection)

During its short life (c. 1916–22) Dada preached nonsense and anti-art with a vengeance; Duchamp would put his signature, and a provocative title, on ready-made objects such as bottle racks and snow shovels, and exhibit them as works of art; once he "improved" a reproduction of Leonardo's *Mona Lisa* with a mustache and the letters LHOOQ, which when pronounced in French, make an off-color pun. Not even modern art was safe from the Dadaists' assaults; one of them exhibited a toy monkey inside a frame with the title "Portrait of Cézanne."

ERNST. The Dadaists, however, adopted the technique of collage Cubism for their own purposes: figure 961, by the German Dadaist Max Ernst (1891–1976), an associate of Duchamp, is largely composed of snippets from illustrations of machinery. The caption pretends to enumerate these mechanical ingredients, which include (or add up to?) "1 Piping Man." Actually there is also a "piping woman." These offspring of Duchamp's prewar *Bride* stare at us blindly through their goggles.

Yet Dada was not a completely negative movement. In its calculated irrationality there was also liberation, a voyage into unknown provinces of the creative mind. The only law respected by the Dadaists was that of chance, and the only reality, that of their own imaginations.

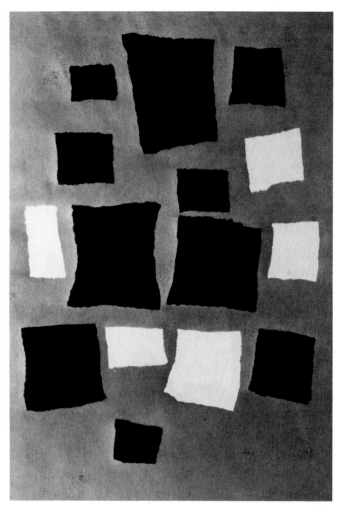

962. HANS (JEAN) ARP. *Collage with Squares Arranged According to the Laws of Chance.* 1916–17. Collage of colored papers, 19⅛ × 13⅝″. The Museum of Modern Art, New York (Purchase)

961. MAX ERNST. *1 Copper Plate 1 Zinc Plate 1 Rubber Cloth 2 Calipers 1 Drainpipe Telescope 1 Piping Man.* 1920. Collage, 12 × 9″. Estate of Hans Arp

ARP. Thus Hans Arp (1887–1966), another early member of the movement, invented a new kind of collage (fig. 962) whose elements—colored pieces of paper that had been shaped by tearing rather than by cutting—were arranged "according to the laws of chance." Arp started these compositions by dropping the bits of paper on a larger sheet, and then cautiously adjusted this "natural" configuration. The artist's task, he believed, was to "court the Muse of Chance," eliciting from her what he called "organic concretions" (he disliked the term "abstraction," which implies discipline and conscious purpose, not reliance on the happy accident).

Playfulness and spontaneity are also the impulses behind Duchamp's Ready-Mades, which the artist created simply by shifting their context from the utilitarian to the aesthetic. They are certainly extreme demonstrations of a principle. But the principle itself—that artistic creation depends neither on established rules nor on manual craftsmanship—is an important discovery, as we recall from our discussion of Picasso's *Bull's Head* in the Introduction (see fig. 1).

963. MAX ERNST. *Swamp Angel.* 1940. 26½ × 32½".
Collection Kenneth MacPherson, Rome

SURREALISM.   In 1924, after Duchamp's retirement from Dada, a group of his fellow "chance-takers" founded Dada's successor, Surrealism. They defined their aim as "pure psychic automatism…intended to express…the true process of thought…free from the exercise of reason and from any aesthetic or moral purpose." Surrealist theory was heavily larded with concepts borrowed from psychoanalysis, and its overwrought rhetoric is not always to be taken seriously. The notion that a dream can be transposed directly from the unconscious mind to the canvas, by-passing the conscious awareness of the artist, did not work in practice: some degree of control was simply unavoidable. Nevertheless, Surrealism stimulated several novel techniques for soliciting and exploiting chance effects.

Max Ernst, the most inventive member of the group, often combined collage with "frottage" (rubbings from pieces of wood, pressed flowers, and other relief surfaces—the process we all know from the children's pastime of rubbing with a pencil on a piece of paper covering a coin). In *Swamp Angel* (fig. 963) he has obtained fascinating shapes and textures by "decalcomania" (the transfer, by pressure, of oil paint to the canvas from some other surface). This procedure is in essence another variant of those recommended by Alexander Cozens (see fig. 819) and Leonardo da Vinci, and Ernst has certainly found, and elaborated upon, an extraordinary wealth of images among his stains. The end result does have some of the qualities of a dream, but it is a dream born of a strikingly Romantic imagination.

DALI.   The same can be said of *The Persistence of Memory* (fig. 964) by Salvador Dali (born 1904). The most notorious of the Surrealists, Dali uses the meticulous verism of De Chirico (see page 690) to render a "paranoid" dream in which time, forms, and space have been distorted in a frighteningly real way.

964. SALVADOR DALI. *The Persistence of Memory.* 1931.
9½ × 13". The Museum of Modern Art, New York
(Given anonymously)

965. JOAN MIRÓ. *Composition*
(see colorplate 144). Wadsworth Atheneum,
Hartford, Connecticut

MIRÓ.   Surrealism, however, has a more boldly imaginative branch: some works by Picasso, such as *Three Dancers* (fig. 947, colorplate 137), have affinities with it, and its greatest exponent was also Spanish, Joan Miró (1893–1983), who painted the striking *Composition* (fig. 965, colorplate 144). His style has been labeled "biomorphic abstraction," since his designs are fluid and curvilinear rather than geometric. Actually, "biomorphic concretion" might be a more suitable name, for the shapes in Miró's pictures have their own vigorous life. They seem to change before our eyes, expanding and contracting like amoebas until they approach human individuality closely enough to please the artist. Their spontaneous "becoming" is the very opposite of abstraction as we defined it above (see page 681), though Miró's formal discipline is no less rigorous than that of Cubism (he began as a Cubist).

PAINTING SINCE WORLD WAR II

Abstract Expressionism (Action Painting)

Equally misleading as "Surrealism" is the term Abstract Expressionism, which is often applied to the style of painting that prevailed for about a dozen years following the end of World War II. It was initiated by artists of the New York school in reaction to the anxiety brought on by the nuclear age and subsequent cold war. Under the influence of existentialist philosophy, the Abstract Expressionists or Action Painters developed from Surrealism a new approach to art. Painting became a counterpart to life itself: an ongoing process in which the artist faces comparable risks and overcomes the dilemmas confronting him through a series of conscious and unconscious decisions in response to both inner and external demands. The Color Field painters (see

page 715) later coalesced the frenetic gestures and violent hues of the Action Painters into broad forms of poetic color that partly reflect the spirituality of oriental mysticism. In a sense, Color Field painting resolved the conflicts expressed by Action Painting. They are, however, two sides of the same coin, separated by the thinnest differences of approach.

GORKY.   Arshile Gorky (1904–1948), an Armenian who came to America at sixteen, was the pioneer of the movement and the single most important influence on its other members. It took him twenty years—painting first in the vein of Cézanne, then in that of Picasso—to arrive at his mature style as we see it in *The Liver Is the Cock's Comb* (fig. 966, colorplate 145). The enigmatic title suggests Gorky's close contact with André Breton, the Surrealist poet who found refuge in New York during the war, as well as his own experience in camouflage, gained from a class he conducted earlier. Everything here is in the process of turning into something else. The biomorphic shapes clearly owe much to Miró, while their spontaneous handling and the glowing color reflect Gorky's enthusiasm for Kandinsky (figs. 938, 965, colorplates 136, 144). Yet the dynamic interlocking of the forms, their aggressive power of attraction and repulsion, are uniquely his own.

Had Gorky lived into the 1950s, he would surely have been the leading figure among the Abstract Expressionists.

POLLOCK.   Gorky's principal heir proved to be Jackson Pollock (1912–1956), who in 1950 did the huge and original picture entitled *One* (fig. 967) mainly by pouring and spattering his colors, instead of applying them with the brush. The result, especially when viewed at close range (colorplate 146), suggests both Kandinsky and Max Ernst (compare colorplate 136, fig. 963). Kandinsky's non-representational Expressionism, and the Surrealists' exploitation of chance effects, are indeed the main sources of Pollock's work, but they do not sufficiently account for his revolutionary tech-

966. ARSHILE GORKY. *The Liver Is the Cock's Comb*
(see colorplate 145). The Albright-Knox Art Gallery,
Buffalo (Gift of Seymour H. Knox)

967. (*above*) JACKSON POLLOCK. *One* (*#31, 1950*). 1950. Oil and enamel paint on canvas, 8' 10" × 17' 5⅝" (see detail, colorplate 146). The Museum of Modern Art, New York (Sidney and Harriet Janis Collection Fund)

968. (*right*) LEE KRASNER. *Celebration*. 1959–60. 7' 8¼" × 16' 4½". Private Collection, New York

nique and the emotional appeal of his art. Why did Pollock "fling a pot of paint in the public's face" (as Ruskin had accused Whistler of doing)? Not, surely, to be more abstract than his predecessors, for the strict control implied by abstraction is exactly what Pollock relinquished when he began to dribble and spatter. A more plausible explanation is that he came to regard paint itself, not as a passive substance to be manipulated at will, but as a storehouse of pent-up forces for him to release.

The actual shapes visible in our colorplate are largely determined by the internal dynamics of his material and his process: the viscosity of the paint, the speed and direction of its impact upon the canvas, its interaction with other layers of pigment. The result is a surface so alive, so sensuously rich, that all earlier painting looks pallid in comparison. But when he releases the forces within the paint by giving it a momentum of its own—or, if you will, by "aiming" it at the canvas instead of "carrying" it on the tip of his brush—Pollock does not simply "let go" and leave the rest to chance. He is himself the ultimate source of energy for these forces,

and he "rides" them as a cowboy might ride a wild horse, in a frenzy of psychophysical action. He does not always stay in the saddle, yet the exhilaration of this contest, that strains every fiber of his being, is well worth the risk. Our simile, though crude, points up the main difference between Pollock and his predecessors: his total commitment to the *act* of painting. Hence his preference for huge canvases that provide a "field of combat" large enough for him to paint not merely with his arms, but with the motion of his whole body.

Action Painting, the term coined some years ago for this style, conveys its essence far better than does Abstract Expressionism. To those who complain that Pollock is not sufficiently in control of his medium, we reply that this loss is more than offset by a gain—the new continuity and expansiveness of the creative process that gave his work its distinctive mid-twentieth-century stamp.

KRASNER. Pollock's drip technique, however, was not in itself essential to Action Painting, and he stopped using it in 1953. Lee Krasner (1908–1984), his wife, never abandoned

Colorplate 142. MARC CHAGALL. *I and the Village* (see page 690). 1911.
75½ × 59½″. The Museum of Modern Art, New York (Mrs. Simon Guggenheim Fund)

Colorplate 143. PAUL KLEE. *Park near L(ucerne).* 1938 (see page 691). 39½ × 27½". Klee Foundation, Bern

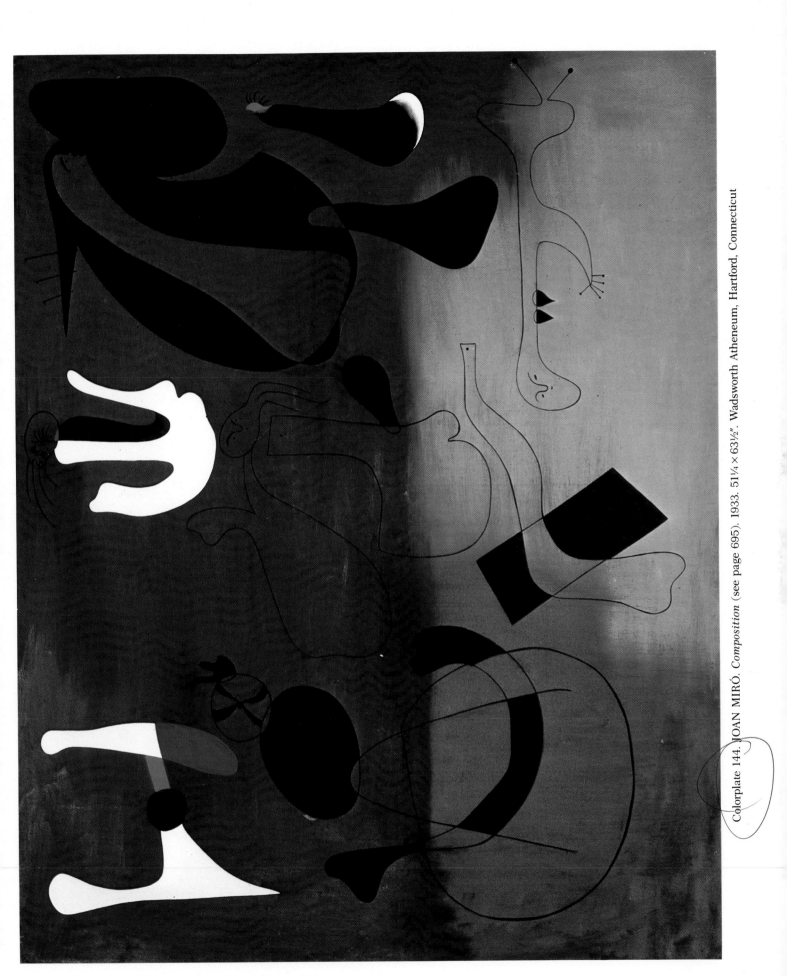

Colorplate 144. JOAN MIRÓ. *Composition* (see page 695). 1933. 51¼ × 63½". Wadsworth Atheneum, Hartford, Connecticut

Colorplate 145. ARSHILE GORKY. *The Liver Is the Cock's Comb* (see page 695). 1944. 72 × 98". The Albright-Knox Art Gallery, Buffalo (Gift of Seymour H. Knox)

Colorplate 146. JACKSON POLLOCK. Detail of *One* (*#31, 1950*). 1950 (see page 695). The Museum of Modern Art, New York (Sidney and Harriet Janis Collection Fund)

Colorplate 147. WILLEM DE KOONING. *Woman II* (see page 713). 1952.
59 × 43″. The Museum of Modern Art, New York (Gift of Mrs. John D. Rockefeller, III)

Colorplate 148. MARK ROTHKO. *Earth and Green* (see page 713).
1955. 90¼ × 73½". Collection Gallery Beyeler, Basel

Colorplate 149. KAREL APPEL. *Burned Face* (see page 715). 1961. 9' 10" × 6' 6¾". Private Collection

Colorplate 150. MORRIS LOUIS. *Beth Feh* (see page 715). 1958. Acrylic on canvas, 7′ 6″ × 10′ 8″. Collection Andrew Crispo, New York

Colorplate 151. PAUL JENKINS. *Phenomena Astral Signal* (see page 715). 1964. Acrylic on canvas, 9′ 8″ × 6′ 8″.
Collection Mr. and Mrs. Harry W. Anderson, New York (Courtesy of the Martha Jackson Gallery, New York)

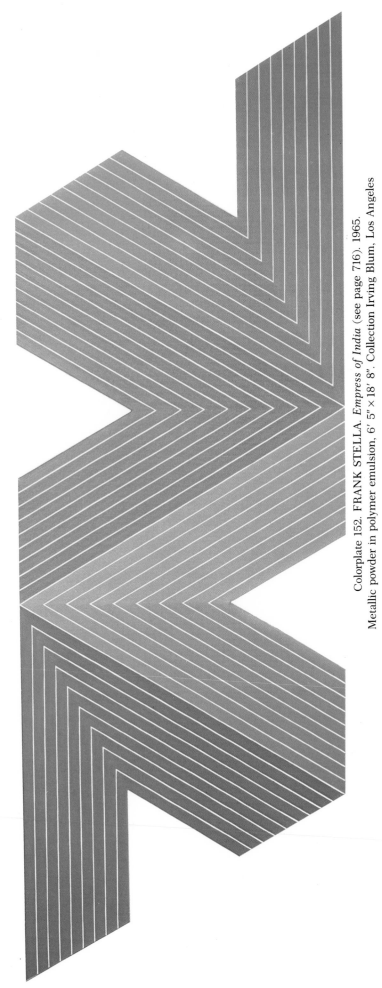

Colorplate 152. FRANK STELLA. *Empress of India* (see page 716). 1965.
Metallic powder in polymer emulsion, 6' 5" × 18' 8". Collection Irving Blum, Los Angeles

Colorplate 153. WILLIAM T. WILLIAMS. *Batman* (see page 717). 1979.
Acrylic on canvas, 80 × 60″. Collection the artist

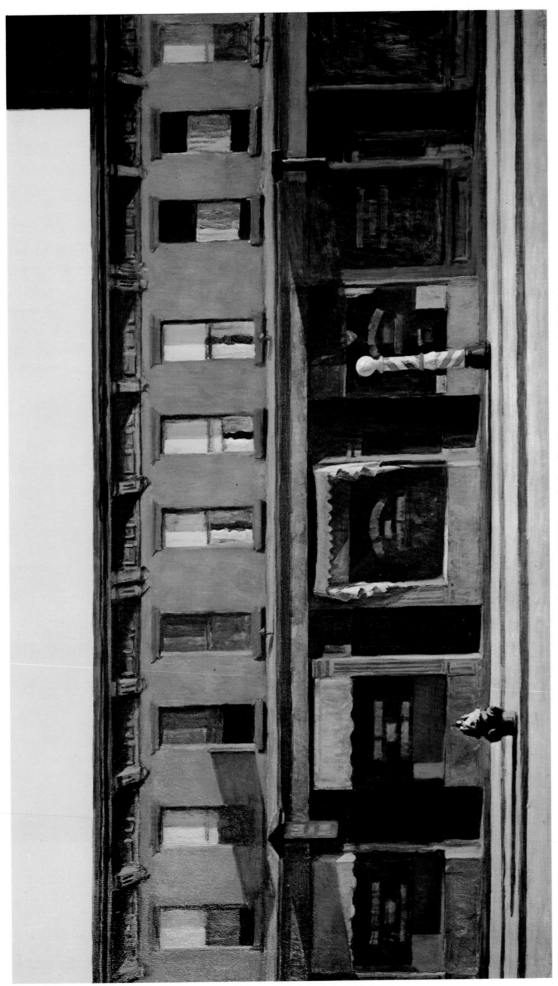

Colorplate 154. EDWARD HOPPER. *Early Sunday Morning* (see page 718). 1930.
35 × 60″. Whitney Museum of American Art, New York

Colorplate 155. LARRY RIVERS. *Europe II* (see page 718). 1956.
54 × 48″. Collection Copyright Mrs. Donald M. Weisberger, New York

Colorplate 156. JASPER JOHNS. *Three Flags* (see page 718). 1958. Encaustic on canvas, 30⅞ × 45¼″. Collection Mr. and Mrs. Burton Tremaine, Meriden, Connecticut

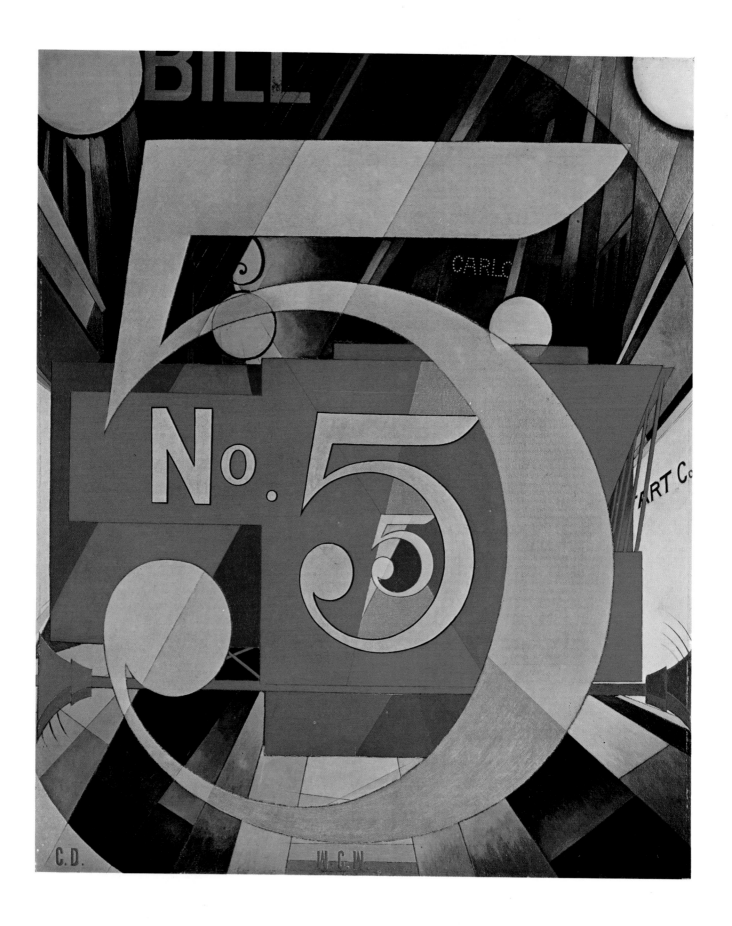

Colorplate 157. CHARLES DEMUTH. *I Saw the Figure 5 in Gold* (see page 719). 1928. Composition board,
35½ × 30″. The Metropolitan Museum of Art, New York (The Alfred Stieglitz Collection, 1949)

969. WILLEM DE KOONING. *Woman II*
(see colorplate 147). The Museum of Modern Art,
New York (Gift of Mrs. John D. Rockefeller, III)

the image emerges from the jagged welter of brush strokes as insistently as it does in Rouault's *Head of Christ* (see fig. 929). What De Kooning has in common with Pollock is the furious energy of the process of painting, the sense of risk, of a challenge successfully—but barely—met.

ROTHKO.   Mark Rothko (1903–1973) presents a challenge of the opposite kind. In the mid-1940s he too had worked in a style derived from Gorky, yet within less than a decade he subdued the aggressiveness of Action Painting so completely that his pictures breathe the purest contemplative stillness.

Earth and Green (fig. 970, colorplate 148) consists of two rectangles with blurred edges—one dark red, the other green—on a purplish blue ground; the canvas is very large, over seven and one-half feet tall, and the thin washes of paint permit the texture of the cloth to be seen throughout. But to use such bare factual terms to describe what we see hardly touches the essence of the work, or the reasons for its mysterious power to move us. These are to be found in the delicate equilibrium of the two shapes, their strange interdependence, the subtle variations of hue (note how the dark blue "halo" around the upper rectangle seems to immerse it in the blue ground, while the green rectangle stands out more assertively in front of the blue). Not every beholder responds to the works of this withdrawn, introspective artist; for those who do, the experience is akin to a trancelike rapture.

970. MARK ROTHKO. *Earth and Green* (see colorplate 148).
Collection Gallery Beyeler, Basel

the brush. She struggled to establish her artistic identity, and emerged from his long shadow only after undergoing several changes in direction and destroying much of her early work. After Pollock's death, she succeeded in doing what he had been attempting to do for the last three years of his life: to reintroduce the figure into Abstract Expressionism while retaining its automatic handwriting. The potential had always been there in Pollock's work; in *One* (fig. 967), we can easily imagine people dancing wildly. In *Celebration* (fig. 968) Krasner defines these nascent shapes from within the tangled network of lines by using the broad gestures of Action Painting to suggest human forms without actually depicting them.

DE KOONING.   The work of Willem De Kooning (born 1904), another prominent member of the group and a close friend of Gorky, always retains a link with the world of images, whether or not it has a recognizable subject. In some paintings, such as *Woman II* (fig. 969, colorplate 147),

971. HELEN FRANKENTHALER. *Blue Causeway.* 1963.
57¾ × 72″. Collection Dr. and Mrs. Max Garber, Southfield,
Michigan

FRANKENTHALER. The stained canvas was also pioneered by Helen Frankenthaler (born 1928). In *Blue Causeway* (fig. 971) she uses the same biomorphic forms basic to
early Action Painting but eliminates the personal handwriting found in the brushwork of Gorky and De Kooning, with
results that are at once more lyrical and more decorative but
no less impressive than theirs. The image will remind us of
an inkblot—the associations it conjures are entirely individual. The shapes may mean one thing to the artist, as is
indicated by the title, but may suggest something totally
different to us.

DUBUFFET. Action Painting marked the international
coming-of-age for American art. The movement had a powerful impact on European art, which in those years had nothing to show of comparable force and conviction. One French
artist, however, was of such prodigal originality as to constitute a movement all by himself: Jean Dubuffet (1901–1985),
whose first exhibition soon after the Liberation electrified—
and antagonized—the art world of Paris. As a young man
Dubuffet had formal instruction in painting, but he responded to none of the various trends he saw around him
nor to the art of the museums; all struck him as divorced
from real life, and he turned to other pursuits. Only in middle
age did he experience the breakthrough that permitted him
to discover his creative gifts: he suddenly realized that for
him true art had to come from outside the ideas and traditions
of the artistic elite, and he found inspiration in the art of
children and of the insane. The distinction between "normal" and "abnormal" struck him as no more tenable than
established notions of "beauty" and "ugliness." Not since
Marcel Duchamp (see page 692) had anyone ventured so
radical a critique of the nature of art.

Dubuffet made himself the champion of what he called
l'art brut, "art-in-the-raw," but he created something of a
paradox besides: while extolling the directness and spontaneity of the amateur as against the refinement of professional
artists, he became a professional artist himself. Duchamp's
questioning of established values had led him to cease artistic activity altogether, but Dubuffet became incredibly prolific, second only to Picasso in output. Compared with Paul
Klee, who had first utilized the style of children's drawings
(see page 691), Dubuffet's art is "raw" indeed; its stark
immediacy, its explosive, defiant presence, are the opposite
of the older painter's formal discipline and economy of
means. Did Dubuffet perhaps fall into a trap of his own
making? If his work merely imitated the *art brut* of children
and the insane, would not these self-chosen conventions
limit him as much as those of the artistic elite?

We may be tempted to think so at our first sight of *Le
Metafisyx* (fig. 972) from his *Corps de Dame* series—even
De Kooning's wildly distorted *Woman II* (fig. 969, colorplate
147) seems gentle when matched against this shocking
assault on our inherited sensibilities. The paint is as heavy
and opaque as a rough coating of plaster, and the lines
articulating the blocklike body are scratched into this surface
like graffiti made by an untrained hand. But appearances
can deceive; the fury and concentration of Dubuffet's attack

972. JEAN DUBUFFET. *Le Metafisyx (Corps de Dame).* 1950.
45¾ × 35¼″. Collection Mr. and Mrs. Arnold Maremont,
Winnetka, Illinois

973. KAREL APPEL. *Burned Face* (see colorplate 149).
Private Collection

should convince us that his demonic female is not "something any child can do." In an eloquent statement the artist has explained the purpose of images such as this: "The female body...has long...been associated with a very specious notion of beauty which I find miserable and most depressing. Surely I am for beauty, but not that one.... I intend to sweep away everything we have been taught to consider—without question—as grace and beauty [and to] substitute another and vaster beauty, touching all objects and beings, not excluding the most despised.... I would like people to look at my work as an enterprise for the rehabilitation of scorned values, and...a work of ardent celebration."

APPEL. *L'Art brut* and Abstract Expressionism provided the mainsprings for the COBRA group in Denmark, Belgium and Holland which took its name from Copenhagen, Brussels, and Amsterdam, the capitals of those countries. The Dutch artist Karel Appel (born 1921), one of the group's co-founders, soon distinguished himself as the finest pure painter of his generation in post-war Europe. To the subject matter of Dubuffet he added the slashing brushwork and vivid colors of De Kooning.

In the late 1950s and early '60s, after several extended visits to the United States, his palette became even more sonorous, the texture more sensuous, and the space more complex, the results of being directly exposed to the Action Painters and inspired by jazz musicians. *Burned Face* (fig. 973, colorplate 149), one of the personages that inhabit Appel's work from that period, is an explosion of color applied with a brilliant technique which at first hides the figural elements lurking within the painting. In maintaining the importance of content while thoroughly integrating it with the style of Abstract Expressionism, Appel established a precedent which was followed by many other European artists, as well as by a number of American painters who have recently become preoccupied with the same problem.

Color Field Painting

After the mid-1950s, Action Painting gradually lost its dominant position, but its force was far from spent. A number of artists who had been in the movement transformed it into the style called Color Field painting, in which the canvas is stained with thin, translucent color washes.

LOUIS; JENKINS.   Among the most gifted of these was Morris Louis (1912–1962). The successive veils of color in *Beth Feh* (fig. 974, colorplate 150; the title is composed of two Hebrew letters) appear to have been "floated on" without visible marks of the brush, mysteriously beautiful like the aurora borealis. It is their harmonious interaction, their delicately shifting balance, that gives the picture enduring appeal.

Other artists such as Paul Jenkins (born 1923) have developed distinctive variations on the theme of Color Field painting. In *Phenomena Astral Signal* (fig. 975, colorplate 151) the liquid medium has been made to flow in currents of varying speed and density. The resulting veils of color may be gossamer-thin or have the rich depth of stained glass. No spattering, no dribbling betrays the painter's "action"; the forces that give rise to these shapes seem to be of the same kind as those governing the cloud formations in a windswept sky and the pattern of veins in a leaf.

974. MORRIS LOUIS. *Beth Feh* (see colorplate
150). Collection Andrew Crispo, New York

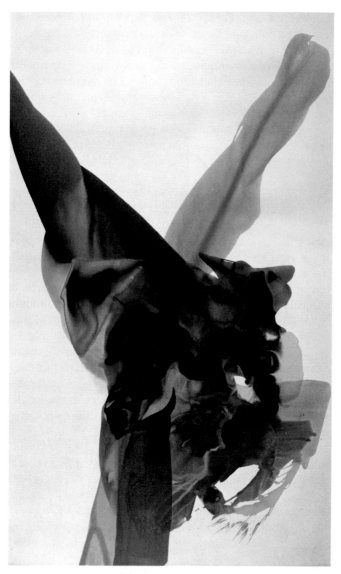

975. PAUL JENKINS. *Phenomena Astral Signal*
(see colorplate 151). Collection Mr. and
Mrs. Harry W. Anderson, New York
(Courtesy of the Martha Jackson Gallery, New York)

976. Installation view of Frank Stella exhibition at
Leo Castelli Gallery, New York, 1962 (see colorplate 152)

FRANK STELLA. Many artists who came to maturity in the 1950s, however, turned away from Action Painting altogether. The brilliant and precocious Frank Stella (born 1936), having conceived an early enthusiasm for Mondrian, soon evolved a non-figurative style that was even more self-contained; unlike Mondrian (see page 689 and colorplate 140), Stella did not concern himself with the vertical-horizontal balance which relates the older artist's work to the world of nature. Logically enough, he also abandoned the traditional rectangular format, so as to make quite sure that his pictures bore no resemblance to windows. The shape of the canvas had now become an integral part of the design (fig. 976).

In one of his largest works, the majestic *Empress of India* (colorplate 152), this shape is determined by the thrust and counterthrust of four huge chevrons, identical in size and shape but sharply differentiated in color and in their relationship to the whole. The paint, moreover, contains powdered metal which gives it an iridescent sheen—yet another way to stress the impersonal precision of the surfaces and to remove the work from any comparison with the "hand-made" look of easel pictures. In fact, to speak of *Empress of India* as a picture seems decidedly awkward. It demands to be called an object, sufficient unto itself.

Black Artists

The legacy of the Expressionist trend can still be seen in one of the most significant developments in contemporary American art, and one that has received little attention: the growth of black art since 1970. This development is all the more remarkable in the light of the African-American history in the United States.

In the 1920s, the Harlem Renaissance produced a cultural revival that unfortunately was short lived, its promise blocked by the economics of the Depression. Following World War II, however, blacks began to attend art schools in growing numbers, at the very time that Abstract Expressionism marked the coming of age of American art. The civil rights movement helped blacks to establish their artistic identities and to find appropriate styles for expressing them. The turning point proved to be the assassinations of Malcolm X in 1965 and of Martin Luther King, Jr., in 1968, which provoked an outpouring of black art. At the same time the generation of African-Americans born around 1940 were bringing black painting and sculpture to artistic maturity.

Since then, black artists have pursued three major tendencies. Mainstream abstractionists, particularly those of the older generation, tend to be concerned primarily with seeking a personal aesthetic, maintaining that there is no such thing as black art, only good art. Consequently, they have been denounced by activist artists, who, stirred by social consciousness as well as by political ideology, have adopted highly expressive representational styles as the means for communicating a distinctive black perspective directly to the people in their communities. Mediating between these two approaches is a very decorative form of art that frequently incorporates African, Caribbean, and sometimes Mexican motifs.

No hard-and-fast principles separate these alternatives, and aspects of each have been successfully combined into separate individual styles. Abstraction has nevertheless proved the most fruitful path, for it has opened up avenues of expression that allow the black artist, however private his concerns may be, to achieve a universal, not merely an ethnic, appeal.

WILLIAMS.   Faced with these aesthetic, personal, and social issues, many artists such as William T. Williams (born 1942) have withdrawn from the conflicting demands of critics, white and black alike, into the privacy of their studios. Williams belongs to the generation of lyrical Expressionists from the early 1970s whose contribution has been largely overlooked. After a period of intense self-scrutiny, he developed the extremely sophisticated technique seen in *Batman* (reproduced only in colorplate 153). His method can be compared to jazz improvisation, a debt the artist himself has acknowledged. He interweaves his color and brushwork within a clear two-part structure that permits endless variations on the central theme. Although Williams is concerned primarily with the presentation of the encrusted surface, the patterns, light, and space evoke a landscape. Instead of depicting nature, however, the painting uses color and texture to capture an evanescent memory of the artist's past.

Pop Art

Other artists who made a name for themselves in the mid-1950s rediscovered what the layman continued to take for granted despite all efforts to persuade him otherwise: that a picture is not "essentially a flat surface covered with colors" (as Maurice Denis had insisted) but an image wanting to be recognized. If art was by its very nature representational, then the modern movement, from Manet to Pollock, was based on a fallacy, no matter how impressive its achievements. Could it be that painting had been on a kind of voluntary starvation diet for the past hundred years, feeding upon itself rather than on the world around us? Wasn't it time to give in to the "image-hunger" thus built up—a hunger from which the public at large had never suffered, since its demand for images was abundantly supplied by photography, advertising, magazine illustrations, and comic strips?

The artists who felt this way seized upon these products of commercial art catering to "low-brow," popular taste. Here, they realized, was an essential aspect of our present-day visual environment that had been entirely disregarded as vulgar and anti-aesthetic by the representatives of "high-brow" culture, and cried out to be examined. Only Marcel Duchamp and some of his fellow Dadaists, with their contempt for all orthodox opinion, had dared to penetrate this realm (see page 692). It was they who now became the patron saints of "Pop Art," as the new movement came to be called.

Pop Art actually began in London in the mid-1950s, but from the very start its imagery was largely based on American mass media, which had been flooding England ever since

the end of World War II. It is not surprising, therefore, that the new art had a special appeal for America, and that it reached its fullest development here during the following decade. Unlike Dada, Pop is not motivated by despair or disgust at present-day civilization; it views commercial culture as its raw material, an endless source of pictorial subject matter, rather than as an evil to be attacked. Nor does Pop share Dada's aggressive attitude toward the established values of modern art.

THE ASH CAN SCHOOL.   In America, Pop Art could also draw on the tradition of the Ash Can School, which flourished in New York just before World War I. Centering on Robert Henri, who had studied with a pupil of Thomas Eakins at the Pennsylvania Academy, and consisting mainly of former illustrators for Philadelphia and New York newspapers, this group of artists was fascinated with the teeming life of the city slums. They found an endless source of subjects in the everyday urban scene, to which they brought the reporter's eye for color and drama. Despite the socialist philosophy that many of them shared, theirs was not an art of social commentary, but one that felt the pulse of city life, discovering its vitality and richness while ignoring the poverty and squalor of the poor. To capture these qualities they relied on rapid execution, inspired by Baroque and Post-Impressionist painting, which lends their canvases the immediacy of spontaneous observation.

Although not a founding member of the Ash Can School, George Bellows (1882–1925) became a leading representative of the group in its heyday. His masterpiece, *Stag at Sharkey's* (fig. 977), shows why: no painter in America before Jackson Pollock had expressed such heroic energy. *Stag at Sharkey's* will remind us of Eakins' *The Gross Clinic* (see fig. 885), for it continues the same Realist tradition. Both place us in the scene as if we were present, and both use the play of light to pick out the main figures against a dark background. Bellows' paintings were fully as shocking

977. GEORGE BELLOWS. *Stag at Sharkey's*. 1909. 36¼ × 48¼".
The Cleveland Museum of Art (Hinman B. Hurlbut Collection)

as Eakins' had been. Most late-nineteenth-century American artists had all but ignored urban life in favor of landscapes, and compared with these, the subjects and surfaces of the Ash Can pictures had a disturbing rawness.

The Ash Can School was soon eclipsed by the rush toward a more radical modernism set off by the Armory Show in 1913 (see page 692), but its influence was felt once again in the 1930s. During the Depression, most American artists split into two camps, the Regionalists and the Social Realists. The Regionalists sought to revive idealism by updating the American myth, defined, however, largely in Midwestern terms. The Social Realists, on the other hand, captured in their pictures the dislocation and despair of the Depression era, and were often concerned with social reform. But both movements, although bitterly opposed, drew freely on the Ash Can School.

HOPPER.   The one artist who appealed to all factions alike, including that of the few remaining modernists, was a former Henri pupil, Edward Hopper (1882–1967). He focused on what has since become known as the "vernacular architecture" of American cities—store fronts, movie houses, all-night diners—which no one else had thought worthy of an artist's attention. *Early Sunday Morning* (fig. 978, colorplate 154) distills a haunting sense of loneliness from the all-too-familiar elements of an ordinary street. Its quietness, we realize, is temporary; there is hidden life behind these façades. We almost expect to see one of the window shades raised as we look at them. But apart from its poetic appeal, the picture also shows an impressive formal discipline: we note the strategy in placing the fireplug and barber pole, the subtle variations in the treatment of the row of windows, the precisely calculated slant of sunlight, the delicate balance of verticals and horizontals. Obviously, Hopper was not unaware of Mondrian.

RIVERS.   The transition from Action Painting to Pop in the mid-1950s may be seen in *Europe II* (colorplate 155) by Larry Rivers (born 1923). With its energetic gestures of the brush, its boldly abbreviated shapes, it still speaks a language akin

979. Photograph of Great Uncle and Cousins of Larry Rivers in Poland. c. 1928 (compare colorplate 155)

to that of De Kooning. At the same time, however, we sense that the picture is *about* something, that it has been built on an older image which keeps asserting itself underneath. In this instance we happen to know the image: a photograph taken of members of the artist's family in Poland a generation earlier (fig. 979). Even if we did not, we would recognize its kind, for such frontal, stiffly posed pictures have been made ever since photography was invented, and form part of everyone's family album. Rivers has taken this visual commonplace seriously; he is moved by its solemn air commemorating some special occasion, now long forgotten, that momentarily brought these people together. In his painting the group has begun to dissolve, the divergent personalities to regain their separateness; the family icon is about to fall apart. Yet it remains a meaningful whole, a shared experience made new by the painter's intense scrutiny of it.

JOHNS.   Among the pioneers of Pop Art in America perhaps the most important is Jasper Johns (born 1930), who began by painting, meticulously and with great precision, such familiar objects as flags, targets, numerals, and maps (see fig. 10). His *Three Flags* (fig. 980, colorplate 156) presents an intriguing problem: just what is the difference between image and reality? We instantly recognize the Stars and Stripes, but if we try to define what we actually see here, we find that the answer eludes us. These flags behave "unnaturally"—instead of waving or flapping they stand at attention, as it were, rigidly aligned with each other in a kind of reverse perspective. Yet there is movement of another sort: the reds, whites, and blues are not areas of solid color but subtly modulated. Can we really say, then, that this is an image of three flags? Clearly, no such flags can exist anywhere except

978. EDWARD HOPPER. *Early Sunday Morning* (see colorplate 154). Whitney Museum of American Art, New York

980. JASPER JOHNS. *Three Flags* (see colorplate 156).
Collection Mr. and Mrs. Burton Tremaine, Meriden, Connecticut

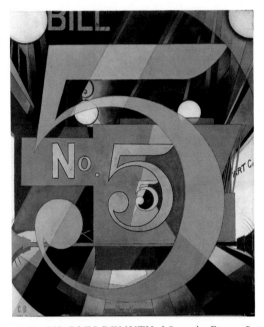

981. CHARLES DEMUTH. *I Saw the Figure 5
in Gold* (see colorplate 157). The Metropolitan Museum
of Art, New York (The Alfred Stieglitz Collection)

982. ROBERT INDIANA. *The Demuth Five.* 1963. 68″ square.
Collection Mr. and Mrs. Robert C. Scull, New York

in the artist's head. And we begin to marvel at the picture as a feat of the imagination—probably the last thing we expected to do when we first looked at it.

DEMUTH; INDIANA.   Revolutionary though it was, Johns' use of flags, numerals, and similar elements as pictorial themes had to some extent been anticipated thirty years before by another American painter, Charles Demuth (1883–1935), in such pictures as *I Saw the Figure 5 in Gold* (fig. 981, colorplate 157). A member of the Stieglitz group (see page 771), Demuth had been friendly with Duchamp and exiled Cubists in New York during World War I. A few years later, under the impact of Futurism, he developed a style known as Precisionism to depict urban and industrial architecture. We can detect influences from all of these movements in *I Saw the Figure 5 in Gold*, but the dynamic treatment of the background most directly recalls Joseph Stella's *Brooklyn Bridge* (fig. 950, colorplate 138). The title is taken from a poem by Demuth's friend William Carlos Williams, whose name—as "Bill," "Carlos," and "W.C.W."—also forms part of the design. In the poem the figure 5 appears on a red fire truck, while in the painting it has become the dominant feature, thrice repeated to reinforce its echo in our memory as the fire truck rushes on through the night.

That the canvas was an ancestor of Pop is attested by Robert Indiana (born 1928), who paid homage to it in *The Demuth Five* (fig. 982). Here, however, the format has been changed to that of a highway sign connoting danger; the numerals have been superimposed on a five-pointed star suggestive of a sheriff's badge; and the pentagonal field behind the star (a reference to the Pentagon in Washington?) carries five "commands" in big stenciled letters—an indictment of American society in capsule form. Such bitter messages are rare in Pop. Indiana has devised a uniquely

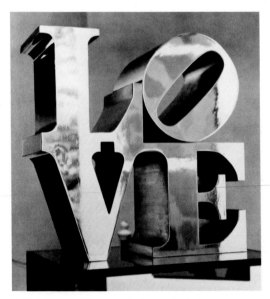

983. ROBERT INDIANA. *Love.* 1966. Aluminum,
12 × 12 × 6″ (edition of 6)

effective pictorial code for conveying them. Obsessed with word images, he even gives them three-dimensional shape: *Love* (fig. 983), in gleaming aluminum, is a tribute not only to his formal precision but to his faith in the power of what must be the most abused word in present-day English.

LICHTENSTEIN. Roy Lichtenstein (born 1923), in contrast, has seized upon comic strips—or, more precisely, upon the standardized imagery of the traditional strips devoted to violent action and sentimental love, rather than those bearing the stamp of an individual creator. His paintings, such as *Girl at Piano* (fig. 984, colorplate 158), are greatly enlarged copies of single frames, including the balloons, the impersonal, simplified black outlines, and the dots used for printing colors on cheap paper.

These pictures are perhaps the most paradoxical in the entire field of Pop Art: unlike any other paintings past or present, they cannot be reproduced on the pages of this book, for they then become indistinguishable from the comic strip on which they are based. Only a full-size detail in color enables us to see what the artist has accomplished. Enlarging a design meant for an area about six inches square to one no less than 3,264 square inches must have given rise

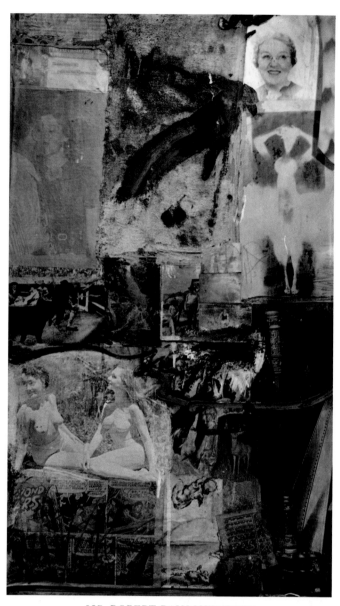

985. ROBERT RAUSCHENBERG.
Odalisk (detail; see colorplate 159).
Museum Ludwig, Cologne

984. ROY LICHTENSTEIN. *Girl at Piano.* 1963.
Magna on canvas, 68 × 48″ (see detail, colorplate 158).
Harry N. Abrams Family Collection, New York

to a host of formal problems that could be solved only by the most intense scrutiny: how, for example, to draw the girl's nose so it would look "right" in comic-strips terms, or how to space the colored dots so they would have the proper weight in relation to the outlines.

Clearly, our picture is not a mechanical copy, but an interpretation which remains faithful to the spirit of the original only because of the countless changes and adjustments of detail that the artist has introduced. What fascinates Lichtenstein about comic strips—and what he makes us see for the first time—are the rigid conventions of their style, as firmly set and as remote from life as those of Byzantine art. How is it possible for images of this sort to be so instantly communicable? Why are they so "real" to millions of people? Lichtenstein has since applied the technique to other kinds of images, reinterpreting paintings by Picasso and Mondrian, and even Abstract Expressionist works, in terms of the formal conventions of comic strips. Perhaps these experiments, often astonishingly effective, point the way to an eventual reconciliation between Pop and the classics of modern art.

Environments; Assemblages; Installations

Although Pop Art was sometimes referred to as "the new realism," the term hardly seems to fit the painters we have discussed. They are, to be sure, sharply observant of their sources; but the material chosen—flags, numerals, lettering, signs, badges, comic strips—is itself rather abstract. Other artists associated with Pop have a less narrowly selective attitude, and some embrace in their work the entire range of their physical environment, including the people. They usually find the flat surface of a canvas too confining; in order to bridge the gap between image and reality, they often introduce three-dimensional objects into their pictures, or they may even construct full-scale models of everyday things and real-life situations, utilizing every conceivable kind of material. These "environments" or "assemblages" combine the qualities of painting, sculpture, collage, and stagecraft.

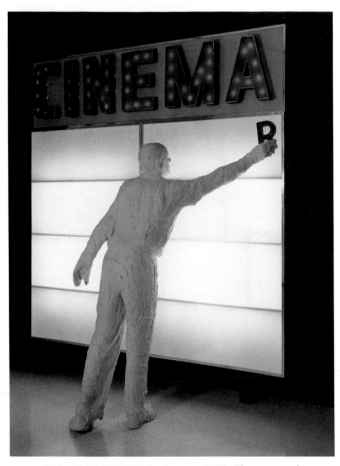

986. GEORGE SEGAL. *Cinema*. 1963. Plaster, metal, Plexiglas, and fluorescent light, 9' 10" × 8' × 3' 3". The Albright-Knox Art Gallery, Buffalo (Gift of Seymour H. Knox)

RAUSCHENBERG. Robert Rauschenberg (born 1925) pioneered this approach as early as the mid-1950s. Like a composer making music out of the noises of everyday life, he constructed works of art from the trash of urban civilization. *Odalisk* (fig. 985, colorplate 159) is a box covered with a miscellany of pasted images—comic strips, photos, clippings from picture magazines—held together only by the skein of brush strokes the artist has superimposed on them; the box perches on a foot improbably anchored to a pillow on a wooden platform, and is surmounted by a stuffed chicken.

The title, a witty blend of "odalisque" and "obelisk," refers both to the nude girls among the collage of clippings (for the original meaning of "odalisque," see page 600) and to the shape of the construction as a whole: the box shares its verticality and slightly tapering sides with real obelisks, slender four-sided pillars of stone erected by the ancient Egyptians. The Romans brought many obelisks to Italy (one marks the center of the colonnaded piazza of St. Peter's; see fig. 700), and these inspired a number of later monuments in Europe and America. Rauschenberg's unlikely "monument" has at least one element in common with its predecessors—compactness and self-sufficiency.

SEGAL. George Segal (born 1924), in contrast, creates "environments," lifesize three-dimensional pictures showing real people and real objects in everyday situations, such as *Cinema* (fig. 986). The subject is ordinary enough to be instantly recognizable: a man changing the letters on a movie theater marquee. Yet the relation of image and reality is far more subtle and complex than the obvious authenticity of the scene suggests. The man's figure is cast from a live model by a technique of Segal's invention, and retains its ghostly white plaster surface. Thus it is one crucial step removed from our world of daily experience, and the neon-lit sign has been carefully designed to complement and set off the shadowed figure. Moreover, the scene is brought down from its natural context, high above the entrance to the theater where we might have glimpsed it in passing, and presented at eye-level, in isolation, so that we grasp it completely for the first time.

HANSON; DE ANDREA. Stunningly realistic figures have been cast from models by Duane Hanson (born 1925), using a similar technique in painted polyester and fiber glass. His subjects, however, are types of people so familiar that we take them for granted. Be they satires of tourists in gaudy attire (fig. 987) or sympathetic renderings of elderly persons and of workers, Hanson's sculptures, taken collectively, represent the failure of the American dream. But by isolating them from their usual contexts he makes us see—and understand—their condition in life as if for the first time.

Hanson's main disciple, John De Andrea (born 1941), pursues very different ends. Though his sculptures sometimes create a certain tension through the choice of sitter, pose, and expression, *The Artist and His Model* (fig. 7, colorplate 1) is more typical of the subtle content and composition of his work. This conceptual integrity and almost

987. DUANE HANSON. *Tourists*. 1970. Fiber glass and polychromed polyester, 64 × 65 × 67″. Glasgow Art Gallery

classical purity make him a worthy successor to Antonio Canova, but with a difference (see pages 609–611). Here the Romantic sculptor's dilemma of representation versus duplication is reversed: without confusing the two, De Andrea's hyper-realism expresses an ideal, while leaving us in just enough doubt to make the illusion convincing.

KIENHOLZ.   Some "environments" can have a shattering impact on the beholder. This is certainly true of *The State Hospital* (fig. 988, colorplate 160) by the West Coast artist Edward Kienholz (born 1927), which shows a cell in a ward for senile patients, with a naked old man strapped to the lower bunk. He is the victim of physical cruelty—his body is little more than a skeleton covered with leathery, discolored skin—which has reduced what little he had in him of mental life almost to the vanishing point: his head is a glass bowl with live goldfish, of whom we catch an occasional glimpse. The horrifying realism of the scene even has an olfactory dimension: when the work was displayed at the Los Angeles County Museum, it exuded a sickly hospital smell. But what of the figure in the upper bunk? It almost duplicates the one below, with one important difference: it is a mental image, since it is enclosed in the outline of a comic-strip balloon rising from the goldfish bowl. It represents, then, the patient's awareness of himself. The abstract devices of the balloon and the metaphoric goldfish bowl are both alien to

the realism of the scene as a whole, yet they play an essential part in it, for they help to break the grip of horror and pity— they make us think as well as feel. Kienholz' means may be Pop, but his aim is that of Greek tragedy. As a witness to the unseen miseries beneath the surface of modern life, he has no equal anywhere today.

PFAFF.   "Installations" are expansions of environments into room-size settings. Judy Pfaff (born 1946) uses painting together with sculptural and other materials to activate architectural space. Her works can be likened to exotic indoor landscapes. The inspiration of nature is apparent in the jungle-like density of *Dragons* (fig. 989, colorplate 161), aptly named for its fiery forms and colors. The treatment of the wall surface will remind us of the collage on *Odalisk* (fig. 985, colorplate 159), but Pfaff's playfulness is closer to Calder's whimsy (fig. 1007, colorplate 168) than to Rauschenberg's ironic wit. The nearest equivalent to Pfaff's spontaneous energy is the Action Painting of Jackson Pollock. It is as if the poured paint had been released from the canvas and left free to roam in space. The swirling profusion around the viewer makes for an experience that is at once pleasurable and disorienting.

Conceptual Art

A later trend, Conceptual Art, has the same "patron saint" as Pop Art: Marcel Duchamp. It arose during the 1960s out of the Happenings staged by Alan Kaprow, in which the event itself became the art. Conceptual Art challenges our definition of art more radically than Pop, insisting that the leap of the imagination, not the execution, is art. Since the works of art are incidental by-products of the imaginative leap, they can be dispensed with althogether; so too can galleries and, by extension, even the artist's public. The creative process need only be documented in some way— usually in verbal form, or by still photography or cinema.

988. EDWARD KIENHOLZ. *The State Hospital*
(see colorplate 160). Museum of Modern Art, Stockholm

989. JUDY PFAFF. *Dragons*
(see colorplate 161). Installation view,
Whitney Museum of American Art, New York

tury painters soon after the "pencil of nature" was invented—one of the earliest to do so, surprisingly, was Delacroix—but they were no more than a convenient substitute for reality. When Larry Rivers used an old family photograph (fig. 980), he freely translated the camera image into the personal idiom of his brush. For the Photo Realists, in contrast, the photograph itself is the reality on which they build their pictures.

EDDY. At its best, their work, as in *New Shoes for H* by Don Eddy (born 1944; colorplate 162), has a visual complexity that challenges the most acute observer. Eddy grew up in southern California; as a teen-ager he learned to do fancy paint jobs on cars and surfboards with an air brush, then worked as a photographer for several years. When he became a painter, he used both earlier skills. In preparing *New Shoes for H*, Eddy took a series of pictures of the window display of a shoe store on Union Square in Manhattan. One photograph (fig. 991) served as the basis for the painting. What intrigued him, clearly, was the way glass filters (and transforms) everyday reality. Only a narrow strip along the left-hand edge offers an unobstructed view: everything

KOSUTH. This deliberately anti-art approach, stemming from Dada (see page 692), poses a number of stimulating paradoxes. As soon as the documentation takes on visible form, it begins to come perilously close to more traditional forms of art (especially if it is placed in a gallery where it can be seen by an audience), since it is impossible fully to divorce the imagination from aesthetic matters. We see this in *One and Three Chairs* (fig. 990) by Joseph Kosuth (born 1945), which is clearly indebted to Duchamp's Ready-Mades: it "describes" a chair by combining in one installation an actual chair, a full-scale photograph of that chair, and a printed dictionary definition of a chair.

Whatever the Conceptual artist's intention, this making of his work of art, no matter how minimal the process, is as essential as it was for Michelangelo (see page 12). In the end, all art is the final document of the creative process, because without execution, no idea can ever be fully realized. Without such "proof of performance," the Conceptual artist becomes like the emperor wearing his new clothes which no one else can see. And, in fact, Conceptual Art has embraced all of the media in one form or another.

Photo Realism

Another, more recent, offshoot of Pop Art is the trend called Photo Realism because of its fascination with camera images. Photographs had been utilized by nineteenth-cen-

990. JOSEPH KOSUTH. *One and Three Chairs*. 1965. Photograph of chair, 36 × 24⅛"; wood folding chair, 32⅜ × 14⅞ × 20⅞"; photographic enlargement of dictionary definition of chair, 24⅛ × 24½". The Museum of Modern Art, New York (Larry Aldrich Foundation Fund)

else—shoes, bystanders, street traffic, buildings—is seen through two or more layers of glass, all of them at oblique angles to the picture surface. The combined effect of these panes—displacement, distortion, and reflection—is the transformation of a familiar scene into a dazzlingly rich and novel visual experience.

When we compare the painting with the photograph, we realize that they are related in much the same way as Lichtenstein's *Girl at Piano* (fig. 984, colorplate 158) is to the comic-strip frame from which it derives. Unlike Eddy's photograph, his canvas shows everything in uniformly sharp focus, articulating details lost in the shadows; most important of all, he gives pictorial coherence to the scene through a brilliant color scheme whose pulsating rhythm plays over the entire surface. At the time he painted *New Shoes for H,* color had become newly important in Eddy's thinking; the H of the title pays homage to Henri Matisse and to Hans Hoffmann, the latter a painter linked to Abstract Expressionism whom Eddy had come to admire.

Photo Realism was part of a general tendency that marked American painting in the 1970s: the resurgence of realism. It has taken on a wide range of themes and techniques, from the most personal to the most detached, depending on the artist's vision of objective reality and its subjective significance; its flexibility made realism a sensitive vehicle for the feminist movement that came to the fore in the same decade. Beyond the organizing of groups dedicated to a wider recognition for women artists, feminism in art has shown little of the unity that characterizes the social movement. Many feminists, for example, turned to "traditional" women's crafts, particularly textiles, or incorporated crafts

992. AUDREY FLACK. *Queen* (see colorplate 163). Private Collection

into a collage approach known as Pattern and Decoration. In painting, however, the majority have pursued different forms of realism for a variety of ends.

FLACK. If the latitude of realism precludes a uniform content or style, women artists such as Audrey Flack (born 1931) have used realism to explore the world around them and their relation to it from a personal as well as a feminist viewpoint. Like most of Flack's paintings, *Queen* (fig. 992, colorplate 163) is an extended allegory. The queen is the most powerful figure on the chessboard yet she remains expendable in defense of the king. Equally apparent is the meaning inherent to the queen of hearts, but here the card also refers to the passion for gambling in members of the artist's family, who are present in the locket with photos of Flack's mother and sister; the contrast of youth and age is central to *Queen.* The watch is a traditional emblem of life's brevity, and the dewy rose stands for the transience of beauty, which is further conveyed by the makeup on the dressing table. The shapes of the flower and fruits can also be taken as symbols of feminine sexuality.

Queen is successful not so much for its provocative statement, however, as for its compelling imagery. Flack creates a purely artistic reality by superimposing two separate photographs. Critical to the illusion is the gray border, which acts as a framing device and also establishes the central space and color of the painting. The objects that seem to project from the picture plane are shown in a different perspective from those on the tilted tabletop behind. The picture space is made all the more active by the play of its colors within the neutral gray. For all of its liveliness, the careful composition prevents the picture from being cluttered.

991. DON EDDY. Photograph for *New Shoes for H* (see colorplate 162). 1973. 6¼ × 6½". The Cleveland Museum of Art (Gift of the artist)

Op Art

Pop Art may be said to have matured within a decade of its inception. Another direction that gathered force about the same time, in the mid-1950s, took longer to come of age: the trend known as "Op Art" because of its concern with optics (that is, the physical and psychological process of vision). There are several reasons for its slower development. Op Art does not have the topical impetus and the emotional appeal of Pop; by comparison it seems overly cerebral and systematic, more akin to the sciences than to the humanities. As a consequence it has attracted less attention and public support. Yet its possibilities appear to be as unlimited as those of science and technology. At the same time, because of its very eagerness to take advantage of the new materials and processes constantly supplied by science, Op Art has never been fully in command of its own goals. Perhaps that is why so few of its creations have an air of finality about them.

Op Art is devoted primarily to optical illusions, and to these man-made illusions we react with pleasure, whether or not they really succeed in deceiving us. If they don't, we are more than willing to give them the benefit of the doubt. Why this should be so is a difficult question which we must leave to the psychologist, perhaps to the philosopher as well. Suffice it to say that all representational art from the Old Stone Age onward has been involved with optical illusion in one sense or another. What is new about Op Art is that it is rigorously non-representational, while seeking to extend the realm of optical illusion in every possible way. Much of it consists of constructions or "environments" dependent for their effect on light and motion. These cannot be reproduced in photographs, since they exploit those aspects of our visual apparatus that are least like the camera. We must confine ourselves in this book to the kind of Op Art which does not lose all of its essential qualities when illustrated.

VASARELY.   The ancestry of Op Art can be traced back to Mondrian (see page 689). Its present development, however, stems largely from the work of Victor Vasarely (born 1908), a Hungarian long domiciled in France, who has been its chief theoretician as well as its most inventive practitioner. Many of his paintings, drawings, and constructions are in stark black-and-white, such as the large canvas, *Vega* (fig. 993), named after the brightest star in the constellation Lyra. It is a huge checkerboard whose regularity has been disturbed by bending the lines that make the squares.

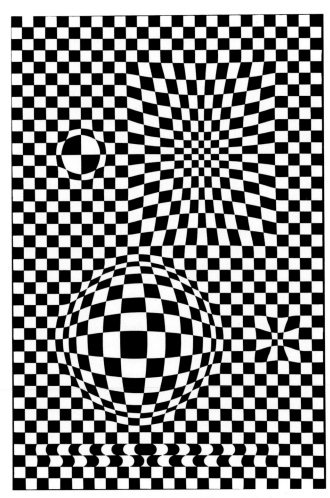

993. VICTOR VASARELY. *Vega.* 1957.
77 × 51". Collection the artist

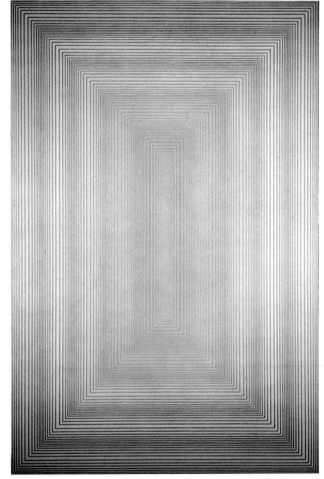

994. RICHARD ANUSZKIEWICZ. *Entrance to Green*
(see colorplate 164). Collection Sidney Janis Gallery, New York

Such a description is no more than a list of ingredients—it does not tell us what we actually see. The size of the standard squares in relation to that of the entire field has been carefully chosen so as to tempt us to link the black squares into a network of diagonals when we view the picture from a distance (about arm's length for our reproduction). But since many of these squares have been subjected to distortion, their sizes vary considerably, the largest having over ten times the area of the smallest. As a consequence, no matter what our viewing distance, our eyes receive contradictory data: we read parts of the field in terms of diagonals, others in terms of verticals and horizontals. The picture thus practically forces us to move back and forth, and as we do so, the field itself seems to move, expanding, undulating, contracting. If *Vega* were a three-dimensional object, the variety of effects to be observed as we move in relation to it would be greater still, for we would then receive different sets of contradictory data from each eye.

ANUSZKIEWICZ. Op Art, then, involves the beholder with the work of art in a truly novel, dynamic way. In America Josef Albers, who came here after 1933, when Hitler closed the Bauhaus school at Dessau (see page 761), became the founding father of another, more austere kind of Op Art based on subtle color relations among simple geometric shapes. His gifted pupil Richard Anuszkiewicz (born 1930) paints in the same vein, but his self-imposed restrictions are less severe. In *Entrance to Green* (fig. 994, colorplate 164) the ever-decreasing series of rectangles creates a sense of infinite recession toward the center; this is counterbalanced by the color pattern which brings the center close to us by the gradual shift from cool to warm tones as we move inward from the periphery.

Painting in the 1980s

Since 1980 our culture has been undergoing rapid change. An indication of the state of flux is the re-emergence of many traditional European and regional American art centers. For all the recent ferment, the direction of art has yet to appear in sufficient clarity to let us chart the future. Having received a rich heritage, artists are sorting through a wide variety of alternatives without yet arriving at durable conclusions. The first sign of this transition occurred in the early 1970s with the widespread use of "Neo-" to describe the current tendencies. Art in the 1980s has been called more simply Post-Modern. The term is, of course, incongruous: modernity can never be outdated, because it is simply whatever is contemporary.

It is true, though, that modernism as an ideal defining twentieth-century art as we have known it has reached a crisis. The principal symptoms are a ubiquitous eclecticism and a bewildering array of styles reflecting narrow causes and personal concerns. Taken together, these pieces provide a jigsaw puzzle of our times, but it is doubtful whether any of them makes a major contribution to the history of art. We are, in this sense, the new Victorians. Painting seems in particular disarray, but we need not despair of the future. A century ago, Impressionism underwent a like crisis, from

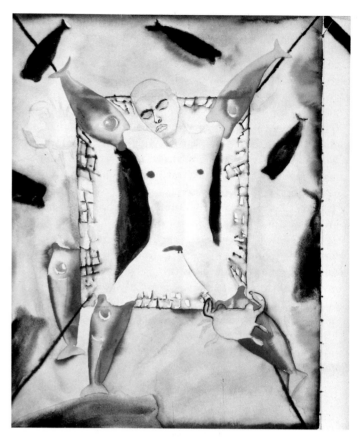

995. FRANCESCO CLEMENTE. *Untitled*, from *White Shroud* (see colorplate 165). Kunsthalle, Basel

which Post-Impressionism emerged as the direction for the next twenty years. Doubtless a new Seurat will somewhere soon proclaim a bold style and outlook that will constitute the next phase of modernism.

CLEMENTE. An artist who seems on the verge of such a breakthrough is the young Italian Francesco Clemente (born 1952). In many respects he is symptomatic of his artistic generation. Without the certitudes of abstraction, he has been forced back upon himself and has developed a potent Neo-Expressionism. Clemente is fearless in recording urges and memories that the rest of us repress. Thus art becomes for him an act of cathartic necessity which releases, but never resolves, the impulses that assault his acute self-awareness. Alternately fascinating and repellent, his images place extreme demands on the viewer, yet their expressiveness is riveting. Since his work responds to fleeting states of mind, he utilizes any style that is appropriate to the moment without, however, losing his individuality. He has an extraordinary talent for watercolor; the fluidity and speed of that medium seem perfectly suited to capturing the transient phenomena of his inner world.

Clemente's career took a decisive turn in 1982 when he decided to devote himself to oil and fresco, and came to New York in order "to be where the great painters have been." His canvases and wall paintings have an ambitiousness that seemingly points to the next phase of contemporary art.

Partly inspired by Hinduism, they can assume the form of allegorical cycles addressed directly to the Italian painters who worked on a grand scale, starting with Giotto. His most compelling paintings are those having as their subject matter the artist's moods, fantasies, and appetites. These remain curiously unsensual. A recent self-portrait (fig. 995, colorplate 165) suggests a soul crucified on drives and sensations that can never be truly enjoyed. Clemente is unusual among Italians in being influenced heavily by northern European Symbolism and Expressionism, with an occasional reminiscence of Surrealism. Here indeed is his vivid nightmare, having the masklike features of Ensor, the psychological terror of Munch, and the haunted vision of De Chirico.

ANSELM KIEFER. The German artist Anselm Kiefer (born 1945) is the direct heir to northern Expressionism, but rather than investigating personal moods he confronts moral issues posed by Nazism that have been evaded by other postwar artists in his country. By exploring from a modern perspective the major themes of German Romanticism, he has attempted to reweave the threads broken by history. That tradition, which began as a noble ideal based on a similar longing for the mythical past, ended as a perversion at the hands of Hitler and his followers because it lent itself readily to abuse.

To the Unknown Painter (fig. 996) is a powerful statement of the human and cultural catastrophe presented by World War II. Conceptually as well as compositionally it was inspired by the paintings of Caspar David Friedrich (see page 595), of which it is a worthy successor. To express the tragic proportions of the Holocaust, Kiefer works on an appropriately epic scale. Painted in jagged strokes of predominantly earth and black tones, the charred landscape is made tangible by the inclusion of pieces of straw. Amid this destruction stands a somber ruin; it is shown in woodcut to proclaim Kiefer's allegiance to the German Renaissance and to Expressionism. Recalling the tombs and temples of ancient civilizations (see figs. 57, 89), the fortress-like structure is a suitable monument for heroes. But instead of being dedicated to soldiers who died in combat, it is a memorial to the painters whose art was equally a casualty of Fascism.

SCULPTURE

The main currents we have followed in painting may be found also in sculpture. The parallelism, however, should not be overstressed. While painting has been the richer and more adventurous of the two arts, its leadership has not remained unchallenged in the last half century, and the development of sculpture has often followed its own path.

BRANCUSI. Expressionism, for instance, is a much less important current in sculpture than in painting—which is rather surprising, since the rediscovery of primitive sculpture by the *Fauves* might have been expected to evoke a strong response among sculptors. Only one important sculptor shared in this rediscovery: Constantin Brancusi (1876–1957), a Romanian who came to Paris in 1904. But he was more interested in the formal simplicity and coherence of primitive carvings than in their savage expressiveness: this is evident in *The Kiss* (fig. 997), executed in 1909 and now placed over a tomb in a Parisian cemetery.

The compactness and self-sufficiency of this group is a radical step beyond Maillol's *Seated Woman* (see fig. 914), to which it is related much as are the *Fauves* to Post-Impressionism. Brancusi has a "genius of omission" not unlike Matisse's; to him, a monument is an upright slab, symmetrical and immobile—a permanent marker, like the steles of the ancients—and he disturbs this basic shape as little as possible. The embracing lovers are differentiated just enough to be separately identifiable, and seem more primeval than primitive. They are a timeless symbol of generation, innocent and anonymous—the exact opposite of Rodin's *Kiss* (see fig. 890), where the contrast of flesh and stone mirrors the dualism of guilt and desire.

MOORE. Brancusi's "Primevalism" was the starting point of a sculptural tradition that still continues today. It has appealed particularly to English sculptors, as we may see in the early works of Henry Moore (1898–1986): his majestic *Two Forms* of 1936 (fig. 998) are, as it were, the second-generation offspring of Brancusi's *Kiss*. More abstract and subtle in shape, they are nevertheless "persons," even though they can be called "images" only in the metaphoric sense. This family group—the forked slab evolved from the artist's studies of the mother-and-child theme—is mysteri-

996. ANSELM KIEFER. *To the Unknown Painter*. 1983. Oil, emulsion, woodcut, shellac, latex, and straw on canvas, 9′ 2″ square. Carnegie Museum of Art, Pittsburgh (Richard M. Scaife Fund; A. W. Mellon Endowment Fund)

997. CONSTANTIN BRANCUSI. *The Kiss.* 1909.
Height 35¼". Tomb of T. Rachevskaia,
Montparnasse Cemetery, Paris

998. HENRY MOORE. *Two Forms.* 1936.
Height c. 42". Collection Mrs. H. Gates Lloyd,
Haverford, Pennsylvania

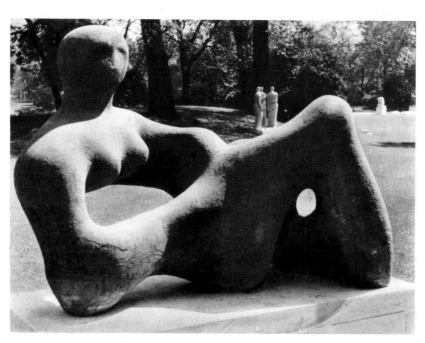

999. HENRY MOORE. *Recumbent Figure.* 1938.
Green Hornton stone, length c. 54".
The Tate Gallery, London

Colorplate 158. ROY LICHTENSTEIN. Detail, actual size, of *Girl at Piano* (see page 720).
1963. Harry N. Abrams Family Collection, New York

Colorplate 159. ROBERT RAUSCHENBERG. *Odalisk*
(see page 721). 1955–58. Construction, $81 \times 25 \times 25''$.
Museum Ludwig, Cologne

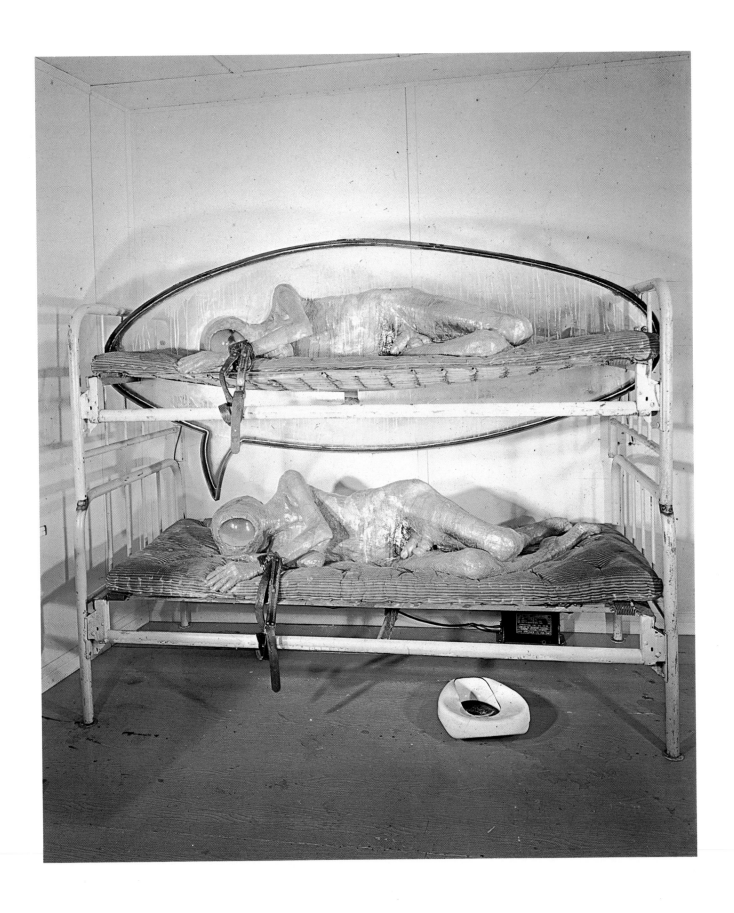

Colorplate 160. EDWARD KIENHOLZ. *The State Hospital* (see page 722).
1966. Mixed mediums, 8 × 12 × 10′. Museum of Modern Art, Stockholm

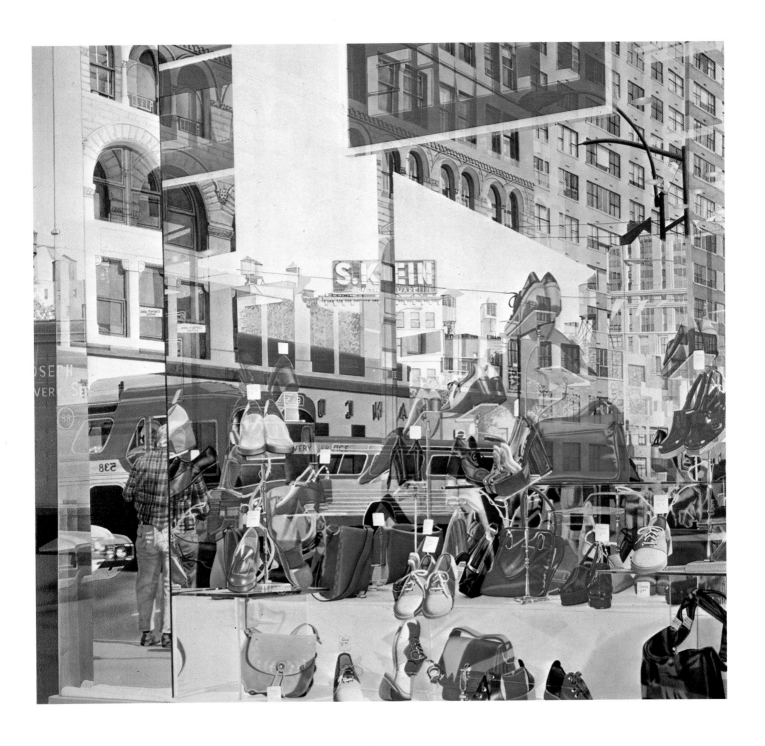

Colorplate 161. (*left*) JUDY PFAFF. *Dragons* (see page 722).
Mixed mediums. Installation view at 1981 Biennial,
Whitney Museum of American Art, New York

Colorplate 162. (*above*) DON EDDY. *New Shoes for H* (see page 723).
1973–74. Acrylic on canvas, 44 × 48″. The Cleveland Museum of Art
(Purchased with a grant from the National Endowment for the Arts
matched by gifts from members of
The Cleveland Society for Contemporary Art)

Colorplate 163. (*above*) AUDREY FLACK. *Queen* (see page 724).
1975–76. Acrylic on canvas, 80 × 80″. Private Collection

Colorplate 164. (*right*) RICHARD ANUSZKIEWICZ.
Entrance to Green (see page 726).
1970. Acrylic on canvas, 108 × 72″.
Collection Sidney Janis Gallery, New York

Colorplate 165. FRANCESCO CLEMENTE. *Untitled*, from *White Shroud*
(see page 727). 1983. Watercolor. Kunsthalle, Basel

1000. BARBARA HEPWORTH. *Sculpture with Color (Oval Form)*, *Pale Blue and Red*. 1943, Wood with strings, length 18″. Collection Mrs. N. Gray

1001. CONSTANTIN BRANCUSI.
Bird in Space (see colorplate 166).
The Museum of Modern Art, New York (Anonymous Gift)

ous and remote like the monoliths of Stonehenge, which greatly impressed the sculptor (see fig. 34, colorplate 4). His *Recumbent Figure* (fig. 999) retains both a classical motif—one thinks of a reclining river god—and a primeval look, as if the forms had resulted from slow erosion over a thousand years. The design of the figure is in complete harmony with the natural striations of the stone.

HEPWORTH.   Barbara Hepworth (1903–1975), for long the preeminent woman sculptor of modern times, was closely associated with Moore during the early 1930s; they became leaders of the modern movement in England and influenced one another. Like Moore's, her sculpture originally had a biological foundation, but during World War II she initiated an individual style that emerged fully in 1943. *Oval Form* (fig. 1000) flawlessly synthesizes painting and sculpture, Surrealist biomorphism and organic abstraction, molding of space and shaping of mass. Carved from wood and immaculately finished, Hepworth's sculpture reduces the natural shape of an egg to a timeless ideal that has the lucid perfection of a classical head, yet the elemental expressiveness of the face of a primitive mask (compare fig. 49). The colors accentuate the play between the interior and exterior of the hollowed-out form, the strings seeming to suggest a life force within.

Kinetic Sculpture

Hepworth's egg undoubtedly owes something to Brancusi, although their work is very different in appearance. About 1910, he began to produce non-representational pieces in marble or metal, reserving his "primeval" style for wood and stone. The former fall into two groups: variations on the egg shape, with such titles as *The Newborn* or *The Beginning of the World*; and soaring vertical "bird" motifs (*Bird in Space*, figure 1001, colorplate 166, is one of these).

Because he concentrated on two basic forms of such uncompromising simplicity, Brancusi has at times been called the Mondrian of sculpture; this comparison is misleading, however, for Brancusi strove for essences, not for relationships. He was fascinated by the antithesis of life as potential and as kinetic energy—the self-contained perfection of the egg, which hides the mystery of all creation, and the pure dynamics of the creature released from this shell. *Bird in Space* is not the abstract image of a bird; rather, it is flight itself, made visible and concrete. Its disembodied quality is emphasized by the high polish that gives the surface the reflectivity of a mirror, and thus establishes a new continuity between the molded space within and the free space without.

BOCCIONI.   Other sculptors at that time were tackling the problem of body-space relationships with the formal tools of Cubism. The running figure entitled *Unique Forms of Continuity in Space* (fig. 1002, colorplate 167), by the Futurist Umberto Boccioni (see page 686), is as breathtaking in its complexity as *Bird in Space* is simple. Boccioni has attempted to represent not the human form itself, but the imprint of its motion upon the medium in which it moves;

the figure remains concealed behind its "garment" of aerial turbulence. The statue recalls the famous Futurist statement that "the roaring automobile is more beautiful than the Winged Victory," although it obviously owes more to the Winged Victory (the *Nike of Samothrace*, fig. 206) than to the design of motor cars (fins and streamlining, in 1931, were still to come). Or perhaps Boccioni's source of inspiration was closer at hand—he could have seen the work of Niccolò dell'Arca (compare fig. 586).

DUCHAMP-VILLON. Raymond Duchamp-Villon (1876–1916), an elder brother of Marcel Duchamp, achieved a bolder solution in *The Great Horse* (fig. 1003). He began with abstract studies of the animal, but his final version is an image of "horsepower," wherein the body has become a coiled spring and the legs resemble piston rods. Because of this very remoteness from their anatomical model, these quasi-mechanical shapes have a dynamism that is more persuasive—if less picturesque—than that of Boccioni's figure.

1002. UMBERTO BOCCIONI. *Unique Forms of Continuity in Space* (see colorplate 167). The Museum of Modern Art, New York (Acquired through the Lillie P. Bliss Bequest)

1003. RAYMOND DUCHAMP-VILLON. *The Great Horse.* 1914. Bronze, height 39⅜". The Art Institute of Chicago (Gift of Miss Margaret Fisher)

Constructivism

In facet Cubism, we recall, concave and convex were postulated as equivalents; all volumes, whether positive or negative, were "pockets of space." The Constructivists, a group of Russian artists led by Vladimir Tatlin, applied this principle to sculpture and arrived at what might be called three-dimensional collage. Eventually the final step was taken of making the works free-standing. According to Tatlin and his followers, these "constructions" were actually four-dimensional: since they implied motion, they also implied time. Suprematism (see page 688) and Constructivism were therefore closely related, and in fact overlapped, for both had their origins in Cubo-Futurism, but they were nonetheless separated by a fundamental difference in approach. For Tatlin, art was not the Suprematists' spiritual contemplation but an active process of formation that was based on material and technique. He believed that each material dictates specific forms which are inherent in it, and that these must be followed if the work of art was to be valid according to the laws of life itself. In the end, Constructivism won out over Suprematism because it was better suited to the post-Revolution temperament of Russia, when great deeds, not great thoughts, were needed.

Cut off from artistic contact with Europe during World War I, Constructivism developed into a uniquely Russian art that was little affected by the return of some of the country's most important artists, such as Kandinsky and Chagall. The Revolution galvanized the modernists, who celebrated the overthrow of the old regime with a creative outpouring throughout Russia. Tatlin's model for a *Monument to the Third International* (fig. 1004) captures the dynamism of the technological utopia envisioned under communism: pure energy is expressed as lines of force that establish new time-space relationships as well. The work also implies a new social structure, for the Constructivists believed in the power of art literally to reshape society. This extraordinary tower revolving at three speeds was conceived on a monumental scale, complete with Communist Party offices; like other such projects, it was wildly impractical in a society still recovering from the ravages of war and revolution, and was never built.

Constructivism subsequently proceeded to a Productivist phase, which ignored any contradiction between true artistic creativity and purely utilitarian production. After the movement had been suppressed as "bourgeois formalism," some of its members emigrated to the West and joined forces with the Dutch group, De Stijl (see page 689).

Surrealism

Dada uncompromisingly rejected formal discipline in sculpture, as it did in the other arts—perhaps even more so, since only three-dimensional objects could become Ready-Mades, the sculpture of Dada. Some of Duchamp's examples consist of combinations of found objects: these "assisted" Ready-Mades approach the status of constructions, or three-dimensional collage. This technique, later baptized "assemblage," proved to have unlimited possibilities. It has produced such striking pieces as Picasso's *Bull's Head* (see fig. 1), and numerous younger artists have explored it since, especially in junk-ridden America (see fig. 1008, colorplate 169). The Surrealist contribution to sculpture is harder to define: it was difficult to apply the theory of "pure psychic automatism" to painting, but still harder to live up to it in sculpture. How indeed could solid, durable materials be given shape without the sculptor being consciously aware of the process? Thus, apart from the devotees of the Ready-Made, few sculptors were associated with the movement, and the effect produced by those who were cannot be directly compared with Surrealist painting.

GIACOMETTI. One of the exceptions is *The Palace at 4 A.M.* (fig. 1005), by Alberto Giacometti (1901–1966), a Swiss sculptor and painter who lived in Paris. The materials—wood, glass, wire, and string—suggest Constructivism, but Giacometti's concern is not with structural problems. This airy cage is the three-dimensional equivalent of a Surrealist picture; unlike earlier pieces of sculpture, it creates its own spatial environment that clings to it as though this eerie miniature world were protected from everyday reality by an invisible glass bell. The space thus trapped is mysterious and corrosive, and gnaws away at the forms until only their skeletons are left; and even they, we feel, will disappear before long.

GONZALEZ. Surrealism may also have contributed to the astonishing sculptural imagination of Julio Gonzalez (1872–1942). Trained as a wrought-iron craftsman in his native Catalonia, Gonzalez had come to Paris in 1900. Although he was a friend of both Brancusi and Picasso, he produced little of consequence until the 1930s, when his creative energies suddenly came into focus. It was Gonzalez who established

1004. VLADIMIR TATLIN. Project for *Monument to the Third International*. 1919–20. Wood, iron, and glass, height 20'. Destroyed; contemporary photograph

1005. ALBERTO GIACOMETTI. *The Palace at 4 A.M.* 1932–33. Construction in wood, glass, wire, and string, 25 × 28¼ × 15¾". The Museum of Modern Art, New York (Purchase)

1006. JULIO GONZALEZ. *Head.* c. 1935.
Wrought iron, 17¾ × 15¾". The Museum of Modern Art,
New York (Purchase)

stems, foliage quivering in the breeze, marine animals float-ing in the sea. Such mobiles are infinitely responsive to their environment. Unpredictable and ever-changing, they incorporate the fourth dimension as an essential element of their structure. Within their limited sphere, they are more truly alive than any other man-made thing.

Sculptural Materials and Assemblage

Pop Art, we recall, has produced not only paintings but constructions and "environments" (figs. 986, 988, colorplate 160). Being three-dimensional, the latter two can claim to be considered sculpture, but the claim rests on a convention which Pop itself has helped to make obsolete. According to this convention, a work of art consisting of a flat or smoothly curved surface covered with colors is a painting (or, if the surface is not covered, a drawing), while sculpture is every-thing else, whether or not the surface is colored and regard-less of the material, size, or degree of relief (unless we can enter it, in which case we call it architecture).

Our habit of using "sculpture" in this sense is only a few hundred years old. Antiquity and the Middle Ages had

wrought iron as an important medium for sculpture, taking advantage of the very difficulties that had discouraged its use before. The *Head* (fig. 1006) combines extreme economy of form with an aggressive reinterpretation of anatomy that is derived from Picasso's work after the mid-1920s (see fig. 947 and colorplate 137, especially the head of the figure on the left): the mouth is an oval cavity with spike-like teeth, the eyes two rods that converge upon an "optic nerve" link-ing them to the tangled mass of the "brain." Similar grue-somely expressive metaphors have since been created by a whole generation of younger sculptors, in wrought iron and welded steel, as if the violence of their working process mirrored the violence of modern life.

MOBILES: CALDER. The early 1930s, which brought Giacometti and Gonzalez to the fore, produced still another important development, the mobile sculpture—mobiles, for short—of the American Alexander Calder (1898–1976): these are delicately balanced constructions of metal wire, hinged together and weighted so as to move with the slight-est breath of air. They may be of any size, from tiny tabletop models to the huge *Lobster Trap and Fish Tail* (fig. 1007, colorplate 168). Kinetic sculpture had been conceived by the Constructivists, and their influence is evident in Calder's earliest mobiles; these were motor-driven, and tended toward abstract geometric configurations. It was Calder's contact with Surrealism that made him realize the poetic possibilities of "natural" rather than fully controlled movement; he bor-rowed biomorphic shapes from Miró, and began to think of mobiles as similes of organic structures—flowers on flexible

1007. ALEXANDER CALDER. *Lobster Trap and Fish Tail*
(see colorplate 168). The Museum of Modern Art, New York
(Gift of the Advisory Committee)

1008. JOHN CHAMBERLAIN. *Essex* (see colorplate 169).
The Museum of Modern Art, New York
(Gift of Mr. and Mrs. Robert C. Scull and Purchase)

separate terms to denote various kinds of sculpture according to the materials and working processes involved, but no single one that covered them all. Maybe it is time to revive such distinctions. Let us, then, modify our all-too-inclusive definition of sculpture by acknowledging "environments" as a separate category, distinct from both painting and sculpture in its use of heterogeneous materials ("mixed mediums") and its blurring of the borderline between image and reality.

Constructions present a more difficult problem. If we agree to restrict the term "sculpture" to objects made of a single substance, then we must put "assemblages" (that is, constructions using mixed mediums) in a class of their own—probably a useful distinction, because of their kinship with Ready-Mades. But what of Picasso's *Bull's Head* (fig. 1)? Is it not an instance of assemblage, and have we not called it a piece of sculpture? Actually, there is no inconsistency here; the *Bull's Head* is a bronze cast, even though we cannot tell this by looking at a photograph of it. Had Picasso wished to display the actual handlebars and bicycle seat, he would surely have done so. If he chose to have them cast in bronze, this must have been because he wanted to "dematerialize" the ingredients of the work by having them reproduced in a single material. Apparently he felt it necessary to clarify the relation of image to reality in this way— the sculptor's way—and the same procedure was his general custom whenever he utilized ready-made objects.

Nevertheless, we must not apply the "single-material" rule too strictly. Calder's mobiles, for instance, often combine metal, string, wood, and other substances, yet they do not strike us as being assemblages, because these materials are not made to assert their separate identities. Conversely, an object may deserve to be called an assemblage even though composed of essentially homogeneous material. Such is often true of the works known as "junk sculpture," made of fragments of old machinery, parts of wrecked automobiles, and similar discards.

CHAMBERLAIN. A most successful example—and a puzzling borderline case—is *Essex* (fig. 1008, colorplate 169) by John Chamberlain (born 1927). The title refers to a make of car that has not been on the market for many years, suggesting that the object is a kind of homage to a vanished species. But we may well doubt that these pieces of enameled tin ever had so specific an origin. They have been carefully selected for their shape and color, and composed in such a way that they form a new entity, evoking a gigantic multicolored rose rather than the crumpled automobiles to which they once belonged. Whether we prefer to call *Essex* assemblage or sculpture is of little importance, but in trying to reach a decision we gain a better insight into the qualities that constitute its appeal.

The New Scale; Primary Structures

Scale has assumed even greater significance for a recent sculptural movement that extends the scope—indeed, the very concept—of sculpture in a fundamentally new direction. "Primary Structure," the most suitable name so far suggested for this type, conveys its two salient characteristics: extreme simplicity of shapes, and a kinship with architecture. The radical abstraction of form is known as "Minimalism," which implies an equal reduction of content. Another term, "Environmental Sculpture" (not to be confused with the mixed-medium "environments" of Pop), refers to the fact that many Primary Structures are designed to envelop the beholder, who is invited to enter or walk through them. It is this space-articulating function that distinguishes Primary Structures from all previous sculpture and relates them to architecture. They are, as it were, the modern successors, in structural steel and concrete, to such prehistoric monuments as Stonehenge (see figs. 33, 34, colorplate 4).

GOERITZ; BLADEN. The first to explore these possibilities was Mathias Goeritz (born 1915), a German working in Mexico City. As early as 1952–53, he established an experimental museum, The Echo, for the display of massive geometric compositions, some of them so large as to occupy an entire patio (fig. 1009). His ideas have since been taken up on either side of the Atlantic. Often, these sculptors limit themselves to the role of designer and leave the execution to others, to emphasize the impersonality and duplicability of their invention. If no patron is found to foot the bill for carrying out these very costly structures, they remain on paper, like unbuilt architecture.

1009. MATHIAS GOERITZ. Steel Structure. 1952–53.
Height 14′ 9″. The Echo (Experimental Museum), Mexico City

1010. RONALD BLADEN. *The X* (in the Corcoran Gallery,
Washington, D.C.). 1967. Painted wood, to be constructed in steel,
22′ 8″ × 24′ 6″ × 12′ 6″. Fischbach Gallery, New York

Sometimes these works reach the mock-up stage, with
painted wood substituting for metal, as in *The X* (fig. 1010),
by the Canadian Ronald Bladen (born 1918), which was built
for an exhibition inside the two-story hall of the Corcoran
Gallery in Washington. Its commanding presence, dwarfing
the Neoclassic colonnade of the hall, seems doubly awesome
in such a setting.

EARTH ART; SMITHSON.   The ultimate medium for
Environmental Sculpture is the earth itself, since it provides
complete freedom from the limitations of the human scale.
Some designers of Primary Structures have, logically
enough, turned to "Earth Art," inventing projects that
stretch over many miles. These latter-day successors to the
mound-building Indians of the Neolithic (see fig. 35) have
the advantage of modern earth-moving machinery, but this
is more than outweighed by the problem of cost and the
difficulty of finding suitable sites on our crowded planet.

The few projects of theirs that have actually been carried
out are mostly found—and the finding is itself often difficult
enough—in the more remote corners of western America.
Spiral Jetty, the work of Robert Smithson (1938–1973), jut-
ted out into Great Salt Lake in Utah (fig. 1011, colorplate
170) and is now much eroded. Its appeal rests in part on the
Surrealist irony of the concept: a spiral jetty is as self-
contradictory as a straight corkscrew. But it can hardly be
said to have grown out of the natural formation of the terrain
like the Great Serpent Mound. No wonder it has not endured
long, nor was it intended to—the process of erosion by which
nature is reclaiming *Spiral Jetty*, already twice submerged,
was integral to Smithson's design from the start. The project
nevertheless lives on in photographs.

1011. ROBERT SMITHSON. *Spiral Jetty* (see colorplate 170).
Great Salt Lake, Utah

1012. CHRISTO (CHRISTO JAVACHEFF). *Surrounded Islands, Biscayne Bay, Miami* (see colorplate 171). Private Collection, New York

CHRISTO. By way of contrast, the projects of Christo (Christo Javacheff, born 1935), who specializes in wrapping things, are deliberately short-lived; they enhance the environment only temporarily instead of altering it permanently. *Surrounded Islands, Biscayne Bay, Miami* (fig. 1012, colorplate 171), his most satisfying project to date, was installed for all of two weeks in the spring of 1983. Part Conceptual Art, part Happening, this ambitious repackaging of nature was a public event involving a small army of assistants and volunteers. While the emphasis was on the campaign itself, the outcome was a triumph of epic fantasy.

Photographs hardly do justice to the results. Our collage of Christo's drawings, an aesthetic object in its own right, gives a clearer picture of the artist's intention by presenting the project in different ways and conveying the complexity of the experience it provided. In effect, Christo turned the islands into inverse man-made lily pads of pink fabric. If Smithson's *Spiral Jetty* suggests the futility of man's grandiose undertakings, this visual pun is as festive and decorative as Monet's waterlily paintings (fig. 877), an inspiration the artist has acknowledged.

SMITH. The American sculptor David Smith (1906–1965), whose earlier work had been strongly influenced by the wrought-iron constructions of Julio Gonzalez (fig. 1006), evolved during the last years of his life a singularly impressive form of Primary Structure in his *Cubi* series. Figure 1013 shows three of these against the open sky and rolling hills of the artist's farm at Bolton Landing, New York (all are now in major museums). Only two basic components are employed—cubes (or multiples of them) and cylinders—yet Smith has created a seemingly endless variety of configurations. The units which make up the structures are poised one upon the other as if they were held in place by magnetic force, so that each represents a fresh triumph over gravity. Unlike the younger members of the Primary Structure movement, Smith executed these pieces himself, welding them of sheets of stainless steel whose shiny surfaces he finished and controlled with exquisite care. As a result, his work displays an "old-fashioned" subtlety of touch that reminds us of the polished bronzes of Brancusi.

NEVELSON. In twentieth-century America there had not been any important woman sculptors until Louise Nevelson (born 1900); sculpture had traditionally been reserved for men, because of the manual labor involved. Thanks to the

1013. DAVID SMITH. *Cubi* Series. Stainless steel. (left) *Cubi XVIII*. 1964.
Height 9′ 8″. Museum of Fine Arts, Boston. (center) *Cubi XVII*. 1963. Height 9′.
Dallas Museum of Fine Arts. (right) *Cubi XIX*. 1964. Height 9′ 5″. The Tate Gallery, London

woman's suffrage movement in the second half of the nineteenth century, Harriet Hosmer (1830–1908) and her "White Marmorean Flock" (as the novelist Henry James called her and her followers in Rome) had succeeded in legitimizing sculpture as "women's work." This school of sculpture lapsed, however, when the sentimental, idealizing Neoclassical style fell out of favor after the Philadelphia Centennial of 1876.

Nevelson, unhappy with external reality, began in the 1950s to construct her separate realities, using her collection of found pieces of wood, both carved and rough. These self-contained realms were at first miniature cityscapes; they soon grew into large environments of free-standing "buildings," encrusted with decorations that were inspired by the sculpture on Mayan ruins. Nevelson's work has generally taken the form of large wall units which flatten her architecture into reliefs (fig. 1014). Assembled from individual compartments, the whole is always painted a single color, usually a matte black to suggest the shadowy world of dreams. Each compartment is elegantly designed, and is itself a metaphor of thought or experience. While the organization of the ensemble is governed by an inner logic, the whole statement remains an enigmatic monument to the artist's fertile imagination.

OLDENBURG. Primary Structures are obviously monuments. But just as obviously they are not monuments commemorating or celebrating anything except their designer's imagination. To the man in the street they offer no ready frame of reference, nothing to be reminded of, even though the original meaning of "monument" is "a reminder." Presumably, monuments in this traditional sense died out when contemporary society lost its consensus of what ought to be publicly remembered. Yet the belief in the possibility of such

1015. CLAES OLDENBURG. *Giant Ice Bag*. 1969–70. Plastic and metal, with interior motor; extended height 15′ 6″, diameter 18′. Thomas Segal Gallery, Boston

monuments has not been abandoned altogether. One artist, Claes Oldenburg (born 1929), has proposed a number of unexpected and imaginative solutions to the problem; he is, moreover, an exceptionally precise and eloquent commentator on his ideas. All his monuments are heroic in size, though not in subject matter; all share one common feature, their origin in humble objects of everyday use.

In 1969 Oldenburg conceived and executed a work shaped like a gigantic ice bag (fig. 1015) with a mechanism inside to make it move—"movements caused by an invisible hand," as the artist described them. For a piece of outdoor sculpture he wanted a form that combined hard and soft and did not need a base. An ice bag met these demands, so he bought one and started playing with it. He soon realized, he says, that the object was made for manipulation, "that movement was part of its identity and should be used." He sent the *Giant Ice Bag* to the U.S. Pavilion at EXPO 70 in Osaka, Japan, where crowds were endlessly fascinated to watch it heave, rise, and twist like a living thing, then relax with an almost audible sigh.

What do such monuments celebrate? What is the secret of their appeal? Part of it, which they share with Pop Art, is that they reveal the aesthetic potential of the ordinary and all-too-familiar. But they also have an undeniable grandeur. We might say, with Baudelaire, that they express "the heroism of modern life."

1014. LOUISE NEVELSON. *Black Chord*. 1964. Painted wood, 96 × 120 × 11½″. Collection Joel Ehrenkranz

NEWMAN. There is one dimension, however, that is missing in Oldenburg's monuments. They delight, astonish, amuse—but they do not move us. Wholly secular, wedded to the here and now, they fail to touch our deepest emotions. In our time, one monument has been successful in this: *Broken Obelisk* (fig. 1016) by Barnett Newman (1905–1970). An artist beset by profound religious and philosophical concerns which he struggled throughout his life to translate into visual form, Newman conceived *Broken Obelisk* in 1963 but could not have it executed until four years later, when he found the right steel fabricator. It consists of a square base plate beneath a four-sided pyramid whose tip meets and supports that of the up-ended broken obelisk. The two tips have exactly the same angle (53°, borrowed from that of the Egyptian pyramids, which had long fascinated the artist) so that their juncture forms a perfect X. Why this monument has such power to stir our feelings is difficult to put into words. Is it the daring juxtaposition of two age-old shapes that have contrary meanings, the one symbolizing timeless stability, the other a thrust toward the heavens? Surely—but what if the obelisk were intact? Would that not reduce the whole to an improbable balancing feat? The brokenness of the obelisk, then, is essential to the pathos of the monument. It speaks to us of our unfulfilled spiritual yearnings, of a quest for the infinite and universal that persists today as it did thousands of years ago.

1017. ELLSWORTH KELLY. *Untitled*. 1982. Aluminum, 1″ thick: (left) 105 × 29¾″; (center) 85 × 93½″; (right) 85 × 89¼″. Blum Helman Gallery, New York

KELLY. The spiritual restlessness of Newman's *Broken Obelisk* seems to find a resolution in the timeless serenity of Ellsworth Kelly's sculpture. An early leader of hard-edge Color Field painting, Kelly (born 1923) began with sculptures which adopted the same geometric shapes and primary hues. After moving to shaped canvases to escape the limitations of the rectangular format, he became interested in the two-dimensional plane as object, freed from the wall, and he largely abandoned color in favor of polished metal surfaces. His achievement is clear in the only sculptural group he has created to date (fig. 1017). Surprisingly, it centers on a true rectangle, whose straight edges, however, seem to bend in response to the curves of the totemic "Venus figure," as he calls it, and the finlike quarter circle on either side. In itself, each piece is strikingly beautiful for a subtlety and elegance equaling Brancusi's. The perfection of Kelly's contours reveals his obsession with edges and how they cut into space. When juxtaposed, the forms further articulate their surroundings; at the same time, they are transformed from monolithic slabs into mythological presences. Like Henry Moore's *Two Forms* (fig 998), they seem almost preternaturally alive, but the air of mute expectancy recalls statues from Tell Asmar (fig. 91).

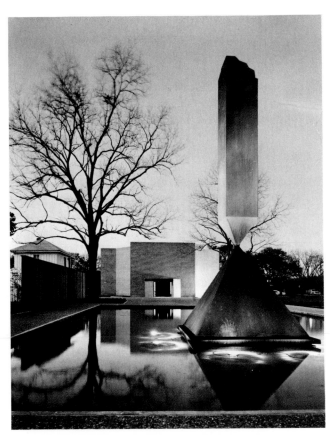

1016. BARNETT NEWMAN. *Broken Obelisk*. 1963–67. Steel, height 25′ 1″. Rothko Chapel, Houston

5
TWENTIETH-CENTURY ARCHITECTURE

For more than a century, from the mid-eighteenth to the late nineteenth, architecture had been dominated by a succession of "revival styles" (see pages 575–81). This term, we will recall, does not imply that earlier forms were slavishly copied; the best work of the time has both individuality and high distinction. Yet the architectural wisdom of the past, however freely interpreted, proved in the long run to be inadequate for the needs of the present. The authority of historic modes had to be broken if the industrial era was to produce a truly contemporary style.

England and France

This authority proved extraordinarily persistent. Even a pioneer of cast-iron construction such as Labrouste could not think of architectural supports as anything but columns having proper capitals and bases, rather than as metal rods or pipes (see page 580). It was only in structures which were not considered "architecture" at all that new building materials and techniques could be explored without these inhibitions.

THE CRYSTAL PALACE.   Within a year of the completion of the Bibliothèque Ste.-Geneviève (see fig. 811), there was built in London the Crystal Palace (fig. 1018), a pioneering achievement far bolder in conception, designed to house the first of the great international expositions that continue in our day. Its designer, Sir Joseph Paxton (1801–1865), was an engineer and builder of greenhouses; and the Crystal Palace was indeed a gigantic greenhouse—so large that it enclosed some old trees growing on the site—with its iron skeleton freely on display. Still, the notion that there might be beauty, and not merely utility, in the products of engineering made headway very slowly, even though the doctrine "form follows function" found an ever greater number of advocates from the mid-nineteenth century on.

OTHER FIELDS.   Among the earliest harbingers of "machine aesthetic" are certain jewelry designs of the 1860s in France and Germany; these are composed of screw heads, nuts, bolts, wrenches, and other symbols of the age (fig. 1019). They might have been intended to appeal to prosperous factory owners, since the materials indicated are gold and precious stones (the era of cheap mass-produced "costume jewelry" was yet to come). Be that as it may, they have a clean-cut, uncluttered quality that Fernand Léger would have liked (see fig. 952, colorplate 139).

In England, in the same decade, the reform ideas of William Morris began to bear fruit in domestic architecture and decoration (see page 633). The boldest innovations, however, came not from members of his immediate circle but from Edward William Godwin (1833–1886), a friend of Whistler, who designed the remarkable sideboard illustrated in figure 1020. Godwin had been much impressed with the simplicity of Japanese interior furnishings, which he knew mainly from the colored woodcuts recently available in the West. His sideboard, composed of "boxes" within a framework of straight "sticks," owes its elegance almost entirely to its finely balanced proportions, since applied ornament has been kept to a bare minimum. At the same time, it has been planned for ease and low cost of manufacture (the material is cheap wood, painted black). In its geometric austerity, it seems oddly prophetic of Mondrian (compare colorplate 140).

United States

Despite such forays into new territory, the search for a truly modern style did not begin in earnest until about 1880. It demanded far more than a reform of architectural grammar and vocabulary: to take advantage of the expressive qualities of the new building techniques and materials that the engineer had placed at his disposal, the architect needed a new philosophy. The leaders of modern architecture have characteristically been vigorous and articulate thinkers, in whose minds architectural theory is closely linked with ideas of social reform. It is equally significant that the movement began in commercial architecture (stores, offices, apartments), outside the range of established building types; that its symbol was the skyscraper; and that its first home was Chicago, then a burgeoning metropolis not yet encumbered by any allegiance to the styles of the past.

RICHARDSON. The great Chicago fire of 1871 had opened vast opportunities to architects from older cities such as Boston and New York. Among them was Henry Hobson Richardson (1838–1886), who profited as a young man from contact with Labrouste in Paris (see fig. 811). Most of his work along the Eastern seaboard shows a massive neo-Romanesque style. There are still echoes of this in his last major project for Chicago, the Marshall Field Wholesale Store, designed in 1885 (fig. 1021). The huge structure filled an entire city block. In its symmetry, and the treatment of masonry, it may remind us of Italian Early Renaissance palaces (see fig. 559). Yet the complete lack of ornament proclaims its utilitarian purpose.

Warehouses and factories as commercial building types had a history of their own going back to the later eighteenth century. Richardson must have been familiar with this tradition, which on occasion had produced remarkably impressive "stripped-down" designs such as those of the warehouses on New Quay, Liverpool (fig. 1022). In contrast to these earlier structures, however, the walls of the Marshall Field Wholestore Store do not present a continuous surface pierced by windows; except for the corners, which have the effect of heavy piers, they show a series of superimposed arcades, like a Roman aqueduct (see fig. 234), an impression strengthened by the absence of ornament and the thickness of the masonry (note how deeply the windows are recessed). These arcaded walls are as functional and self-sustaining as

1018. SIR JOSEPH PAXTON.
The Crystal Palace, London,
interior view looking north. 1851
(lithograph by Joseph Nash).
Victoria & Albert Museum, London
(Crown copyright reserved)

1019. STUDIO OF CARL MICHEL.
Jewelry Designs. c. 1865.
Watercolor. Staatliche
Zeichenakademie,
Hanau am Main, Germany

1020. (*left*) EDWARD WILLIAM GODWIN. Sideboard. c. 1867. Ebonized wood with silver hardware and imitation leather panels, height 71″. Victoria & Albert Museum, London (Crown copyright reserved)

1021. (*left, below*) HENRY HOBSON RICHARDSON. Marshall Field Wholesale Store (demolished 1930), Chicago. 1885–87

1022. (*below*) Warehouses on New Quay, Liverpool. 1835–40

their ancient predecessors. They invest the building with a strength and dignity unrivaled in any earlier commercial structure. Behind them is an iron skeleton that actually supports the seven floors, but the exterior does not depend on it, either structurally or aesthetically.

SULLIVAN. Richardson's Field Store thus stands midway between the old and the new: it embodies, with utmost severity and logic, a concept of monumentality derived from the past, but its opened-up walls, divided into vertical "bays," look forward to the work of Louis Sullivan (1856–1924), the first indisputably modern architect. The Wainwright Building in St. Louis (fig. 1023, colorplate 172), his first skyscraper, is only five years after the Field Store. It, too, is

monumental, but in a very untraditional way. The organization of the exterior both reflects and expresses the internal steel skeleton, in the slender, continuous brick piers that rise between the windows from the base to the attic. Their collective effect is that of a vertical grating encased by the corner piers and by the emphatic horizontals of attic and mezzanine.

This is, of course, only one of the many possible "skins" that could be stretched over the structural frame; what counts is that we immediately feel that this wall is derived from the skeleton underneath, that it is not self-sustaining. "Skin" is perhaps too weak a term to describe this brick sheathing; to Sullivan, who often thought of buildings as analogous to the human body, it was more like the "flesh"

1023. (*below*) LOUIS SULLIVAN. Wainwright Building,
St. Louis, Missouri (see colorplate 172)

1024. (*right*) LOUIS SULLIVAN. Carson Pirie Scott & Company
Department Store, Chicago. 1899–1904

1025. (*right, below*) Detail, Carson Pirie Scott & Company

and "muscle" that is organically attached to the "bone" yet capable of an infinite variety of expressive effects. When he insisted that "form follows function" he meant a flexible relationship, not rigid dependence.

The range of Sullivan's invention becomes evident if we compare the Wainwright Building with his last skyscraper, the department store of Carson Pirie Scott & Company in Chicago, begun nine years later (figs. 1024, 1025). The sheathing of white terracotta here follows the grid of the steel frame far more closely, and the over-all effect is one of lightness and crispness rather than of harnessed energy. Yet the contrast between the horizontal continuity of the flanks and the vertical accent at the corner has been subtly calculated.

Art Nouveau

In Europe, meanwhile, the authority of the "revival styles" was being undermined by a movement now usually called by its French name, *Art Nouveau*, although it was known by various other names as well. It was primarily a new style of decoration, based on linear patterns of sinuous curves that often suggest water lilies. Its ancestor was the ornament of William Morris (see fig. 881). It is also related to the styles of such artists as Gauguin, Beardsley, and Munch (see fig. 902, colorplate 127, figs. 905, 910). During the 1890s and early 1900s its pervasive influence on the applied arts may be seen in wrought-iron work, furniture, jewelry, glass, typography, and even women's fashions; it had a profound effect on public taste, but did not lend itself easily to architectural designs on a large scale.

1026. ANTONÍ GAUDÍ. Casa Milá Apartment House, Barcelona. 1905–7

1027. Typical Floor Plan, Casa Milá

GAUDÍ.   The most remarkable instance is the Casa Milá in Barcelona (figs. 1026, 1027), a large apartment house by Antoní Gaudí (1852–1926). It shows an almost maniacal avoidance of all flat surfaces, straight lines, and symmetry of any kind, so that the building looks as if it had been freely modeled of some malleable substance. (The material is not stucco or cement, as we might suppose, but cut stone.) The softly rounded openings anticipate the "eroded" shapes of Henry Moore's sculpture (see fig. 999); the roof has the rhythmic motion of a wave; and the chimneys seem to have been squeezed from a pastry tube. The Casa Milá expresses one man's fanatical devotion to the ideal of "natural" form; it could never be repeated, let alone developed further. Structurally, it is a tour de force of old-fashioned craftsmanship, an attempt at architectural reform from the periphery, rather than from the center. Gaudí and Sullivan stand at opposite poles, although both strove for the same goal—a contemporary style independent of the past.

MACKINTOSH.   Gaudí represents one extreme of *Art Nouveau* architecture; the Scotsman Charles Rennie Mackintosh (1868–1928) represents another. His basic outlook is so close to the functionalism of Sullivan that at first glance his work hardly seems to belong to *Art Nouveau* at all. The north façade of the Glasgow School of Art (fig. 1028) was designed as early as 1896, but might be mistaken for a building done thirty years later. Huge, deeply recessed studio windows have replaced the walls, leaving only a framework of massive, unadorned cut-stone surfaces except in the center

bay; this bay is "sculptured" in a style not unrelated to Gaudí's, despite its preference for angles over curves. Another *Art Nouveau* feature is the wrought-iron grillwork (here with a minimum of ornament).

Even more surprising than the exterior is the two-story library (fig. 1029), with its rectangular wooden posts and lintels supporting the balcony. The entire room has been designed in the spirit of Godwin's sideboard (see fig. 1020), as it were, but Mackintosh shows an even finer sense of balance in the matching of voids and solids.

VAN DE VELDE.   Through architectural magazines and exhibitions, Mackintosh's work came to be widely known abroad. Its structural clarity and force had a profound effect on one of the founding fathers of *Art Nouveau*, the Belgian Henry van de Velde (1863–1957). Trained as a painter, Van de Velde, under the influence of William Morris, had become a designer of posters, furniture, silverware, and glass; after 1900, he worked mainly as an architect. It was he who founded the Weimar School of Arts and Crafts in Germany, which became famous after World War I as the Bauhaus (see page 761). His most ambitious building (figs. 1030, 1031), the theater he designed in Cologne for an exhibition sponsored by the Werkbund (arts-and-crafts association) in 1914, makes a telling contrast with the Paris Opéra (figs. 808, 809). Whereas the older building tries to evoke the splendors of the Louvre Palace, Van de Velde's exterior is a tautly stretched "skin" that covers—and reveals—the individual units of which the internal space is composed. It

1028. CHARLES RENNIE MACKINTOSH. North façade, Glasgow School of Art. 1896–1910

1029. Interior of Library, Glasgow School of Art

seems almost incredible that the Opéra should have been completed only forty years before.

The Werkbund exhibition of 1914 was a showcase for a whole generation of young German architects who were to achieve prominence after the hiatus of World War I. Many of the buildings they designed for the fairgrounds anticipate ideas of the 1920s. Among the most adventurous is the staircase of the "Glass House" (fig. 1032) by Bruno Taut (1880–1938), made magically translucent by the use of glass bricks, then a novel material. Its structural steel skeleton is as thin and unobtrusive as the great strength of the metal permits. The total effect suggests Stella's Futurist *Brooklyn Bridge* (fig. 950, colorplate 138) translated into three dimensions.

1030. HENRY VAN DE VELDE. Theater, Werkbund Exhibition, Cologne (destroyed). 1914

1031. Plan of Theater, Werkbund Exhibition

1032. BRUNO TAUT. Staircase of the "Glass House,"
Werkbund Exhibition, Cologne. 1914

WRIGHT. If Sullivan, Gaudí, Mackintosh, and Van de Velde could be called the Post-Impressionists of modern architecture, Sullivan's great disciple, Frank Lloyd Wright (1867–1959), was the first to reach its Cubist phase. This is certainly true of his brilliant early style, between 1900 and 1910, which had vast international influence. (His late work, beginning with the 1930s, will be omitted from this account.) During that first decade, Wright's main activity was the design of suburban houses in the Chicago area; these were known as "Prairie Houses," because their low, horizontal lines were meant to blend with the flat land around them.

Frank Lloyd Wright's last, and his most accomplished, example in this series is the Robie House of 1909 (figs. 1033, 1034). Its "Cubism" is not merely a matter of the clean-cut rectangular elements composing the structure, but of Wright's handling of space. It is designed as a number of "space blocks" grouped around a central core, the chimney; some of the blocks are closed and others are open, yet all are defined with equal precision. Thus the space that has been architecturally shaped includes the balconies, terrace, court, and garden, as well as the house itself: voids and solids are regarded as equivalents, analogous in their way to facet Cubism in painting, and the entire complex enters into active and dramatic relationship with its surroundings.

Wright did not aim simply to design a house, but to create a complete environment. He even took command of the details of the interior, and designed stained glass, fabrics,

1033. (above) FRANK LLOYD WRIGHT.
Robie House, Chicago. 1909

1034. (right) Plan of the Robie House

Colorplate 167. UMBERTO BOCCIONI. *Unique Forms of Continuity in Space* (see page 737). 1913. Bronze, 43⅞ × 34⅞ × 15¾". The Museum of Modern Art, New York (Acquired through the Lillie P. Bliss Bequest)

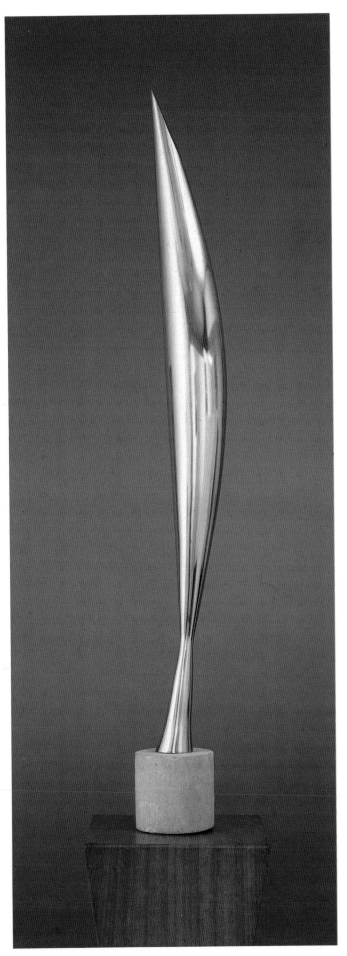

Colorplate 166. CONSTANTIN BRANCUSI. *Bird in Space* (see page 737). 1928?. Bronze, height 54". The Museum of Modern Art, New York (Anonymous Gift)

Colorplate 168. ALEXANDER CALDER. *Lobster Trap and Fish Tail*, mobile (see page 740). 1939. Steel wire and sheet aluminum, c. 8′ 6″ × 9′ 6″. The Museum of Modern Art, New York (Gift of the Advisory Committee)

Colorplate 169. JOHN CHAMBERLAIN. *Essex* (see page 741). 1960. Automobile parts and other metal, 9′ × 6′ 8″ × 43″ (relief).
The Museum of Modern Art, New York (Gift of Mr. and Mrs. Robert C. Scull and Purchase)

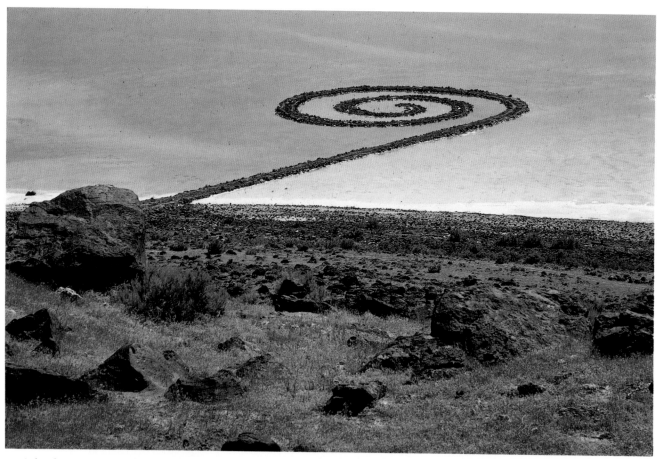

Colorplate 170. ROBERT SMITHSON. *Spiral Jetty* (see page 742). As built in 1970. Total length 1,500′; width of jetty 15′.
Great Salt Lake, Utah

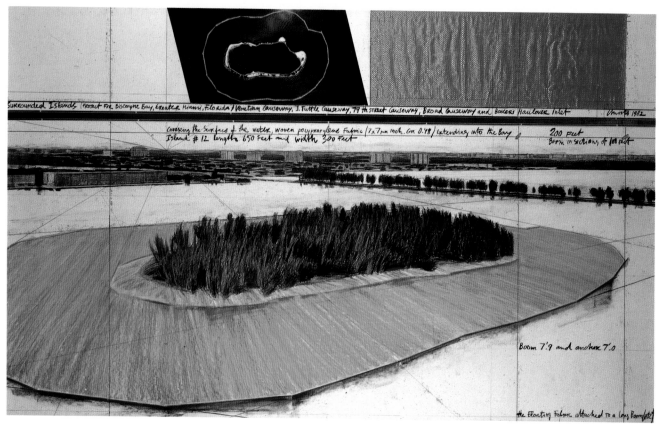

Colorplate 171. CHRISTO (CHRISTO JAVACHEFF). *Surrounded Islands, Biscayne Bay, Miami* (see page 743). 1983.
Mixed mediums; (upper) 15 × 95⅝″, (lower) 41½ × 95⅝″. Private Collection, New York

Colorplate 172. (*right*) LOUIS SULLIVAN. Wainwright Building, St. Louis, Missouri (see page 748). 1890–91

Colorplate 173. (*below*) GERRIT RIETVELD. Schröder House, Utrecht (see page 761). 1924

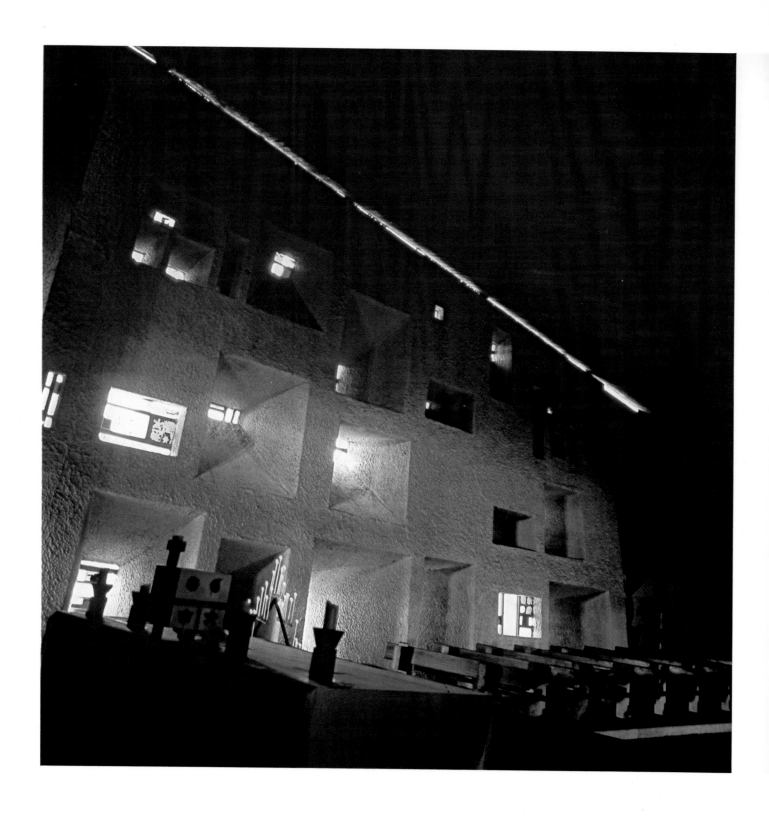

Colorplate 174. LE CORBUSIER. Interior, toward south.
Notre-Dame-du-Haut, Ronchamp, France (see page 763). 1950–55

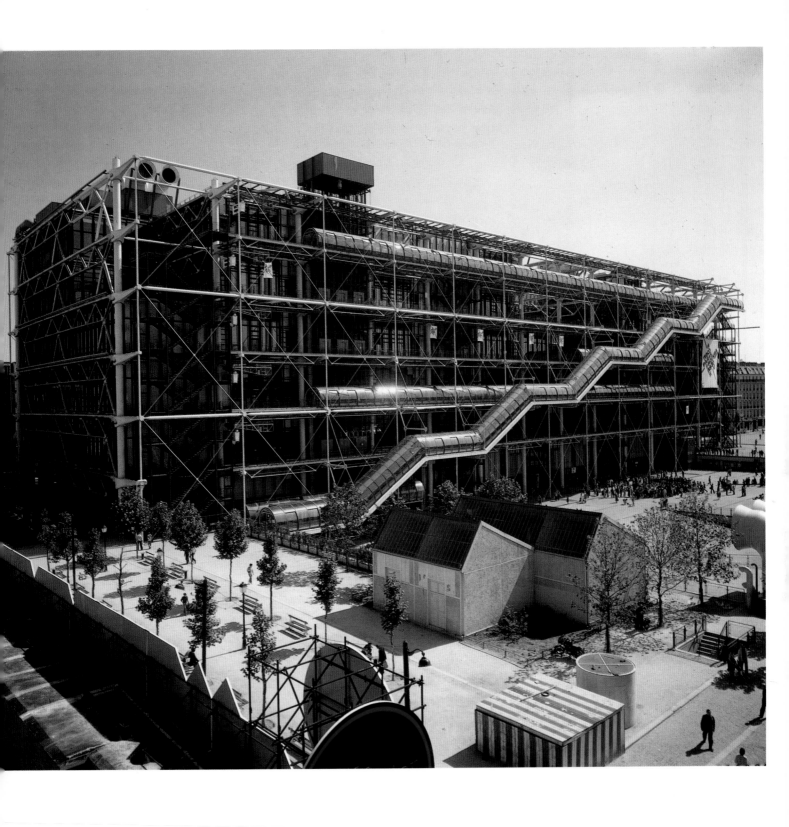

Colorplate 175. RENZO PIANO and RICHARD ROGERS. Georges Pompidou National Arts
and Cultural Center, Paris (see page 766). 1971–77

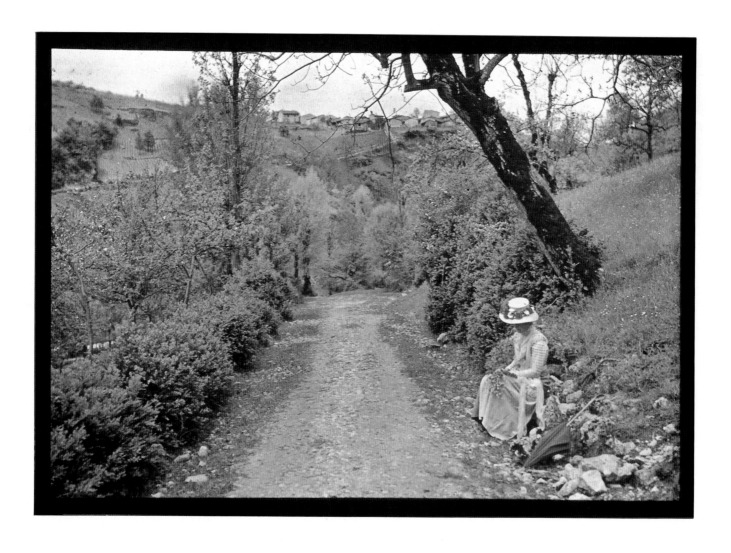

Colorplate 176. LOUIS LUMIÈRE. *Young Lady with an Umbrella* (see page 769). 1906–10. Autochrome

1035. GERRIT RIETVELD. Schröder House, Utrecht (see colorplate 173)

1036. Plan of the Schröder House

and furniture. The controlling factor here was not so much the individual client and his special wishes as Wright's conviction that buildings have a profound influence on the poeple who live, work, or worship in them, so that the architect is really a molder of men, whether or not he consciously assumes this responsibility.

RIETVELD. The work of Frank Lloyd Wright had attracted much attention in Europe by 1914. Among the first to recognize its importance were some young Dutch architects who, a few years later, joined forces with Mondrian in the De Stijl movement (see page 689). The Schröder House in Utrecht (figs. 1035, 1036, colorplate 173), by Gerrit Rietveld (1888–1964), has a number of Wrightian features—the slablike, overhanging roof and the juxtaposition of closed and open blocks of space—combined with a façade that looks like a painting by Mondrian transposed into three dimensions (compare colorplate 140). At the end of World War I, the De Stijl group represented the most advanced ideas in European architecture. Its austerely geometric designs, based on Mondrian's principle of an equilibrium achieved through the balance of unequal but equivalent oppositions, had a decisive influence on so many architects abroad that the movement soon became international.

International Style

THE BAUHAUS. The largest and most complex example of this "International Style of the 1920s" is the group of buildings created in 1925–26 by Walter Gropius (1883–1969) for the Bauhaus transferred to Dessau, the famous art school of which he was the director. (Its curriculum embraced all the visual arts, linked by the root concept of "structure," *Bau.*) The plant consists of three major blocks (fig. 1037), for classrooms, shops, and studios, the first two

linked by a bridge of ferroconcrete containing offices (fig. 1038, extreme left).

The most dramatic is the shop block, a four-story box with walls that are a continuous surface of glass. This radical step had been possible ever since the introduction of the structural steel skeleton several decades before, which relieved the wall of any bearing function; Sullivan had approached it in the Carson Pirie Scott & Co. store (fig. 1024), but he could not yet free himself from the traditional notion of the window as a "hole in the wall." Gropius frankly acknowledges, at last, that in modern architecture the wall is no more than a curtain or climate barrier, which may consist entirely of glass if maximum daylight is desirable.

A quarter century later, the same principle was used on a much larger scale for the two main faces of the great slab that houses the Secretariat of the United Nations (fig. 1039). The effect is rather surprising: since such walls reflect as well as transmit light, their appearance depends on the interplay of these two effects. They respond, as it were, to any change of conditions without and within, and thus introduce a strange quality of life into the structure. (The mirror-like finish of Brancusi's *Bird in Space* serves a similar purpose.)

EARLY WORK OF LE CORBUSIER. In France, the most distinguished representative of the "International Style" during the 1920s was the Swiss-born architect Le Corbusier (Charles Edouard Jeanneret, 1886–1965). At that time he built only private houses—from necessity, not choice—but these are as important as Wright's "Prairie Houses." Le Corbusier called them *machines à habiter* (machines to be lived in), a term intended to suggest his admiration for the clean, precise shapes of machinery, not a desire for "mechanized living." (The paintings of his friend Fernand Léger during those years reflect the same attitude: fig. 952, colorplate 139.) Perhaps he also wanted to imply that his houses

1037. WALTER GROPIUS. Shop Block, the Bauhaus,
Dessau, Germany. 1925–26

1038. Plan of the Bauhaus

1039. WALLACE K. HARRISON and an International Advisory Committee
of Architects (LE CORBUSIER, OSCAR NIEMEYER, and others).
United Nations Buildings, New York. 1949–51

were so different from conventional homes as to constitute a new species.

Such is indeed our impression as we approach the most famous of them, the Savoye House at Poissy-sur-Seine (fig. 1040): it resembles a low, square box resting on stilts—pillars of reinforced concrete that form part of the structural skeleton and reappear to divide the "ribbon-windows" run-

ning along each side of the box. The flat, smooth surfaces, denying all sense of weight, stress Le Corbusier's preoccupation with abstract "space blocks."

In order to find out how the box is subdivided, we must enter it (fig. 1041): we then realize that this simple "package" contains living spaces that are open as well as closed, separated by glass walls. Within the house, we are still in

1040. LE CORBUSIER. Savoye House,
Poissy-sur-Seine, France. 1929–30

1041. Interior, Savoye House

Chicago as a practicing architect. The Lake Shore Drive apartment houses (fig. 1043), two severely elegant slabs placed at right angles to each other, exemplify Mies van der Rohe's dictum that "less is more." He is the great spiritual heir of Mondrian among contemporary designers, possessed of the same "absolute pitch" in determining proportions and spatial relationships.

LATER WORK OF LE CORBUSIER. Abandoning the abstract purism of the "International Style," Le Corbusier's postwar work shows a growing preoccupation with sculptural, even anthropomorphic effects. Thus the Unité d'Habitation, a large apartment house in Marseilles (fig. 1044), is a "box on stilts" like the Savoye House, but the pillars are not thin rods; their shape now expresses their muscular strength in a way that makes us think of Doric columns. The exposed staircase on the flank, too, is vigorously sculptural, and the flat plane of the all-glass façade has a honeycomb-screen of louvers and balconies that forms a sun-break but also enhances the three-dimensional quality of the structure. This projecting screen has proved to be an invention of great importance, practically and aesthetically; it is now a standard feature of modern architecture throughout the tropics (Le Corbusier himself introduced it in India and Brazil).

The most revolutionary building of the mid-twentieth century, however, is Le Corbusier's church of Notre-Dame-du-Haut at Ronchamp in eastern France (figs. 1045, 1046, colorplate 174). Rising like a medieval fortress from a mountain crest, its design is so irrational that it defies analysis,

communication with the outdoors (views of the sky and the surrounding terrain are everywhere to be seen). Yet we enjoy complete privacy, since an observer on the ground cannot see us unless we stand next to a window. The functionalism of the Savoye House thus is governed by a "design for living," not by mechanical efficiency.

UNITED STATES. America, despite its early position of leadership, did not share the exciting growth that took place in European architecture during the 1920s. The impact of the "International Style" did not begin to be felt on this side of the Atlantic until the very end of the decade. A pioneer example is the Philadelphia Savings Fund Society Building of 1931–32 (fig. 1042), by George Howe (1886–1954) and William E. Lescaze (1896–1969), a skyscraper in the tradition of Sullivan that incorporates in its design many features evolved in Europe since the end of World War I.

During the following years, the best German architects, whose work Hitler condemned as "un-German," came to this country and greatly stimulated the development of American architecture. Gropius, who was appointed chairman of the architecture department at Harvard University, had an important educational influence; Ludwig Mies van der Rohe (1886–1969), his former colleague at Dessau, settled in

1042. GEORGE HOWE and WILLIAM E. LESCAZE.
Philadelphia Savings Fund Society Building,
Philadelphia. 1931–32

even with the aid of perspective diagrams. The play of curves and countercurves is here as insistent as in Gaudí's Casa Milá, though the shapes are now simple and more dynamic: the massive walls seem to obey an unseen force that makes them slant and curl like paper; and the overhanging roof suggests the brim of an enormous hat, or the bottom of a ship split lengthwise by the sharp-edged buttress from which it is suspended. If the Casa Milá brings to mind the "eroded"

1043. LUDWIG MIES VAN DER ROHE.
Lake Shore Drive Apartment Houses, Chicago. 1950–52

1044. LE CORBUSIER. Unité d'Habitation
Apartment House, Marseilles. 1947–52

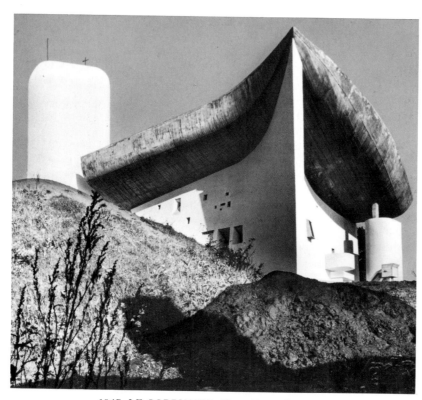

1045. LE CORBUSIER. Notre-Dame-du-Haut,
from the southeast, Ronchamp, France (see colorplate 174)

1046. Perspective diagram, Notre-Dame-du-Haut,
from the northeast

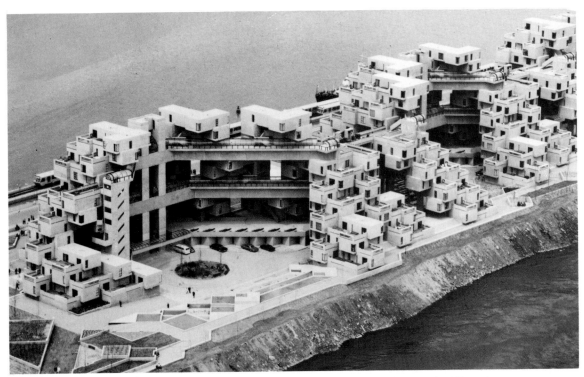

1047. MOSHE SAFDIE and others. Habitat, EXPO 67, Montreal. 1967

softness of Henry Moore's *Recumbent Figure*, Ronchamp has the megalithic quality of the same artist's *Two Forms* (see figs. 998, 999).

This evocation of the dim, prehistoric past is quite intentional: asked to create a sanctuary on a mountain top, Le Corbusier must have felt that this was the primeval task of architecture, placing him in a direct line of succession with the men who had built Stonehenge, the ziggurats of Mesopotamia, and the Greek temples. Hence, he also consciously avoids any correlation between exterior and interior. The doors are concealed: we must seek them out like clefts in a mountainside, and to pass through them is much like entering a secret—and sacred—cave.

Only inside do we sense the specifically Christian aspect of Ronchamp. The light, channeled through stained-glass windows so tiny that they seem hardly more than slits or pinpricks on the exterior, cuts widening paths through the thickness of the wall, and thus becomes once more what it had been in medieval architecture—the visible counterpart of the Light Divine. There is true magic in the interior of Ronchamp, but also a strangely disquieting quality, a nostalgia for the certainties of a faith that is no longer unquestioned. Ronchamp mirrors the spiritual condition of modern man—which is a measure of its greatness as a work of art.

Urban Planning

Le Corbusier belongs to the same heroic generation as Gropius, Rietveld, and Mies van der Rohe, all born in the 1880s. It was these men who in the course of their long, fruitful careers coined the language of twentieth-century architecture. Their successors continue to use many aspects of its

1048. Detail, Habitat

vocabulary in new building types and materials, and do not forget its fundamental logic.

To younger architects today, the greatest challenge is not the individual structure but urban design: replacing the slums of our decaying cities with housing that will provide a socially healthful environment for very large numbers of people. Urban planning is probably as old as civilization itself (which, we recall, means "city life"). We have caught only occasional glimpses of it in this book (see pages 157, 162, 352), since its history is difficult to trace by direct visual evidence: cities, like living organisms, are ever-changing, and to reconstruct their past from their present appearance is a laborious task. With the advent of the industrial era two centuries ago, cities began to grow explosively, and have continued to do so ever since.

Much of this growth was uncontrolled beyond the laying out of a network of streets; housing standards were poor or poorly enforced. The unfortunate result can be seen in the overcrowded, crumbling apartment blocks that are the blight of vast urban areas everywhere. They were taken over by the poor, while those who could afford it fled to the dormitory towns of suburbia. This exodus, accelerated by the automobile, has produced the dangerous tensions that lend urgency to the cry for urban renewal today.

Such renewal, needless to say, must involve the political, social, and economic forces of our entire society, rather than the architect alone. Yet the architect has an essential role in the process, for it is he—and he only—who will have to translate the schemes of the planning agencies into reality.

HABITAT. One problem engaging his attention is how to develop an alternative to the conventional high-rise apartment block in densely populated areas: a housing pattern that will be less deadeningly uniform (but no more expensive), and provide more light and air, safer access, and a multitude of other desirable features. A promising solution, by the Israeli architect Moshe Safdie (born 1938) and his associates (figs. 1047, 1048), was demonstrated in the Habitat complex at the Montreal EXPO 67. The individual apartments consist of prefabricated "boxes" that can be combined into units of several sizes and shapes, attached to a zigzagging concrete framework which can be extended to fit any site. If the result looks a bit like a Chinese puzzle, this impression disappears as we enter the complex and enjoy its openness, its fascinating variety of perspectives.

Post-Modern

Spurred by more radical social theories, Post-Modern architecture (as its name suggests; see page 726) also constitutes a far broader repudiation of the mainstream of modern architecture. It rejects not only the formal harmony of Gropius and his followers, but also the social and ethical ideals implicit in their lucid proportions. Among the freshest, as well as most controversial, results is the Georges Pompidou National Arts and Cultural Center in Paris (fig. 1049, colorplate 175). Selected in an international competition, the design by an Anglo-Italian team looks like the Bauhaus (fig. 1037) turned inside out. The architects have eliminated any trace of Le Corbusier's elegant façades (fig. 1040), exposing the building's inner mechanics while disguising the underlying structure. The interior itself has no fixed walls, so that temporary dividers can be arranged to meet any need. This stark utilitarianism reflects the populist sentiment current in France. Yet it is enlivened by eye-catching colors, each keyed to a different function. The festive display is as vivacious and imaginative as Léger's *The City* (fig. 952, colorplate 139), which, with Paris' Eiffel Tower, can be regarded as the Pompidou Center's true ancestor. The Pompidou Center represents a reaction against the "International Style" without abandoning its functionalism.

To create more human environments, Post-Modern architects have reverted to what can only be called pre-modernist architecture by adopting styles that were in vogue before the "International Style." The Neue Staatsgalerie in Stuttgart (fig. 1050) by the Englishman James Stirling (born 1925) has the grandiose scale befitting a "palace" of the arts, but instead of the monolithic cube of the Pompidou Center, it incorporates more varied shapes and more complex spatial

1049. RENZO PIANO and RICHARD ROGERS.
Georges Pompidou National Arts and Cultural Center, Paris
(see colorplate 175)

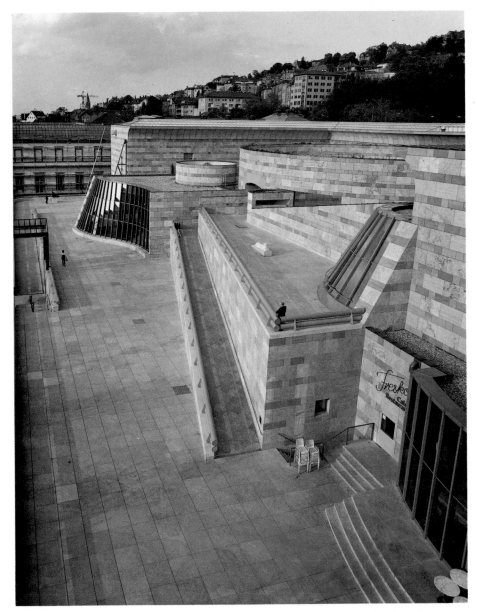

1050. JAMES STIRLING. Neue Staatsgalerie, Stuttgart. Completed 1984

relationships. There is, too, an overtly decorative quality that will remind us, however indirectly, of Garnier's Paris Opéra (fig. 808). The similarity does not stop there. Beginning with the primly Neoclassical masonry façade, Stirling has also invoked a form of historicism through paraphrase which is far more subtle than Garnier's opulent revivalism, but no less self-conscious. This eclecticism is more than a veneer—it lies at the heart of the building's success. The site, centering on a circular sculpture court, is designed along the lines of ancient temple complexes from Egypt through Rome, complete with a monumental entrance stairway. This plan enabled Stirling to solve a wide range of practical problems with ingenuity and to provide a stream of changing vistas which fascinate and delight the visitor.

6
TWENTIETH-CENTURY PHOTOGRAPHY

THE FIRST HALF CENTURY

During the nineteenth century, photography struggled to establish itself as art but failed to find an identity. Only under extraordinary conditions of political upheaval and social reform did it address the most basic subject of art, which is life itself. In developing an independent vision, photography would combine the aesthetic principles of the Secession and the documentary approach of photojournalism with lessons learned from motion photography. At the same time, modern painting, with which it soon became allied, forced a decisive change in photography by undermining its aesthetic assumptions and posing a new challenge to its credentials

as one of the arts. Like the other arts, photography responded to the three principal currents of our time: expressionism, abstraction, and fantasy. But because it has continued to be devoted for the most part to the world around us, modern photography has adhered largely to realism and, hence, has followed a separate development. We must therefore discuss twentieth-century photography primarily in terms of different schools and how they have dealt with those often conflicting currents.

The course pursued by modern photography was facilitated by technological advances. It must be emphasized, however, that these have enlarged but never dictated the photographer's options. George Eastman's invention of the

1051. LOUIS LUMIÈRE. *Young Lady with an Umbrella* (see colorplate 176)

1052. EUGÈNE ATGET. *Pool, Versailles*. 1924. Gold-toned printing-out paper, 7 × 9⅜".
The Museum of Modern Art, New York (The Abbott-Levy Collection. Partial gift of Shirley C. Burden)

hand-held camera in 1888 and the advent of 35mm photography with the Leica camera in 1924 simply made it easier to take pictures that had been difficult but by no means impossible to take with the traditional view camera.

Surprisingly, even color photography did not have such revolutionary importance as might be expected. It began in 1907 with the introduction of the "autochrome" by Louis Lumière (1864–1948). The autochrome was a glass plate covered with grains of potato starch dyed in three colors which acted as color filters, and over this the coating of silver bromide emulsion; it yielded a positive color transparency upon development and was not superseded until Kodak began to make color film in 1932, using the same principles but more advanced materials. The autochrome was based on the Divisionist color theories of Seurat and even achieved similar effects, as we can see if we look hard enough at *Young Lady with an Umbrella* (fig. 1051, colorplate 176), an early effort. Except for its color, the picture differs little from photographs by the Photo-Secessionists, who were the first to turn to the new process. Color, in fact, had relatively little impact on the content, outlook, or aesthetic of photography, even though it removed the last barrier cited by nineteenth-century critics of photography as an art.

Photography did create one new art form, the cinema. An outgrowth of motion photography, it too was first perfected in 1894 by Lumière and his brother, but the principle had been known for more than 60 years. Unfortunately, we cannot treat it in our survey, because the printed page cannot reproduce continuous action or sound.

The School of Paris

ATGET. Modern photography began quietly in Paris with Eugène Atget, who turned to the camera only in 1898 at the age of forty-two. From then until his death in 1927, he toted his heavy equipment around Paris, recording the city in all its variety. Atget was all but ignored by the art photographers, for whom his commonplace subjects had little interest. He himself was a humble man whose studio sign read simply "Atget—Documents for Artists," and indeed, he was patronized by the fathers of modern art—Braque, Picasso, Duchamp, and Man Ray, to name only the best known. It is no accident that these artists were also admirers of Henri Rousseau, for Rousseau and Atget had in common a naive vision, though Atget found inspiration in unexpected corners of his environment rather than in magical realms of the imagination.

Atget's pictures are marked by a subtle intensity and technical perfection that heighten the reality, and hence the significance, of even the most mundane subject. Few photographers have equaled his ability to compose simultaneously in two- and three-dimensional space. Like *Pool, Versailles* (fig. 1052), his scenes are often desolate, bespeaking a strange and individual outlook. The viewer has the haunting sensation that time has been transfixed in the past by the stately composition and the photographer's obsession with textures. While Atget's work participates marginally in the journalistic tradition of Nadar, Brady, and Riis (see page 661), its distinct departure from that earlier photography can only be explained in relation to late nineteenth-century art. His pictures of neighborhood shops and street vendors, for example, are virtually identical with slightly earlier paintings by minor realists whose names are all but forgotten today. Moreover, his photographs are directly related to a strain of magic realism that was a forerunner of Surrealism. Atget has sometimes been called a Surrealist, and while this characterization is misleading, one can easily understand why he was rediscovered by Man Ray, the Dada and Surrealist artist-photographer, and championed by Man Ray's assistant, Berenice Abbott (see page 779). As a whole, however, Atget's work is simply too varied to permit convenient classification.

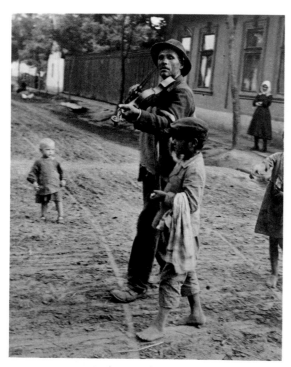

1053. ANDRÉ KERTÉSZ. *Blind Musician.*
1921. Gelatin-silver print, 16⅜ × 13¼.
The Museum of Modern Art, New York (Gift of the artist)

Kertész, and even by the cinema, he soon developed into the most influential photojournalist of his time, and he still thinks of himself primarily as one. His purpose and technique are nevertheless those of an artist.

Cartier-Bresson is the master of what he has termed "the decisive moment." This to him means the instant recognition and visual organization of an event at the most intense moment of action and emotion, in order to reveal its inner meaning, not simply to record its occurrence. Unlike other members of the Paris school, he seems to feel at home anywhere in the world and always to be in sympathy with his subjects, so that his photographs have a nearly universal appeal. His work is distinguished by an interest in composition for its own sake, derived from modern abstract art. He also has a particular fascination with motion, which he invests with all the dynamism of Futurism and the irony of Dada.

The key to his work is his use of space to establish relations which are suggestive and often astonishing. Indeed, for all that he deals with reality, Cartier-Bresson is a Surrealist at heart and has admitted as much. The results can be disturbing, as in *Mexico, 1934* (fig. 1055). By omitting the man's face, Cartier-Bresson prevents us from identifying the meaning of the gesture, yet we respond to its tension no less powerfully.

KERTÉSZ. Atget's direct successors were two East Europeans. The older of them, André Kertész (1894–1985), began photographing in his native Hungary as early as 1915, and his style was already defined when he came to Paris ten years later. *Blind Musician* (fig. 1053), made in Hungary in 1921, is the kind of picture Atget sometimes took, and it uses much the same devices, above all the careful composition that isolates the subject within just enough of its surroundings to set the scene.

BRASSAÏ. The photographic style of Gyula Halasz, known simply as Brassaï (1899–1984), Atget's other successor, was also conditioned by Paris, its views and its habits. He was born in Transylvania and studied art in Budapest, but was already a Frenchman at heart even before arriving in Paris in 1923. Several years later, while working there as a journalist, he borrowed a camera from Kertész and took a series of evocative photographs of the city by night. He soon turned to the night life of the Parisian cafés, where he had an unerring eye for the exotic characters who haunt them. *"Bijou" of Montmartre* (fig. 1054) shows the same sense of the typically aberrant as *At the Moulin Rouge* (see fig. 908, colorplate 128) by Toulouse-Lautrec, whose art certainly influenced him.

CARTIER-BRESSON. The culmination of this Paris school is no doubt Henri Cartier-Bresson (born 1908), the son of a wealthy thread manufacturer. He studied under a Cubist painter in the late 1920s before taking up photography in 1932. Strongly effected at first by Atget, Man Ray,

1054. BRASSAÏ. *"Bijou" of Montmartre.* 1933. 11⅞ × 9¼".
The Museum of Modern Art, New York. (The Ben Schultz
Memorial Collection; Gift of the artist)

1055. HENRI CARTIER-BRESSON. *Mexico, 1934*. 1934. Gelatin-silver print

1056. ROBERT DOISNEAU. *Side Glance*. 1953.
Gelatin-silver print

DOISNEAU. If Cartier-Bresson has a peer in any area, it is in the ironic wit of Robert Doisneau (born 1912). His subject matter is mankind's foibles, which he unmasks with the best of humor. Who cannot identify with the man in *Side Glance* (fig. 1056), sneaking a glimpse of the delicious nude while his wife comments on the more serious painting before them?

The Stieglitz School

STIEGLITZ. The father of modern photography in the United States was Alfred Stieglitz, whose influence continued dominant throughout his life (1864–1946). From his involvement with the Photo-Secession (see page 663), he was a tireless spokesman for photography-as-art, although he defined this more broadly than did other members of the movement. He backed his words by publishing the magazine *Camera Work* and supporting the other pioneers of American photography through exhibiting their work in his New York galleries, especially the first one, known as "291." The bulk of his early work adheres to Secessionist conventions, treating photography as a pictorial equivalent to painting. During the mid-1890s, however, he took some pictures of street scenes that are harbingers of his mature photographs.

His classic statement, and the one he regarded as his finest effort, is *The Steerage* (fig. 1057), taken in 1907 on a trip to Europe. Like Ford Madox Brown's *The Last of England* (see fig. 878, colorplate 122), painted more than a half century earlier, it captures the feeling of a voyage, but does so

1057. ALFRED STIEGLITZ. *The Steerage.* 1907. The Art Institute of Chicago (Alfred Stieglitz Collection)

by letting the shapes and composition tell the story. The gangway bridge divides the scene visually, emphasizing the contrasting activities of the people below in the steerage, which was reserved for the cheapest fares, and the observers on the upper deck. If the photograph lacks the obvious sentiment of Brown's painting, it possesses an equal drama by remaining true to life.

This kind of "straight" photography is deceptive in its simplicity, for the image mirrors the feelings that stirred Stieglitz. For that reason, it marks an important step in his evolution and a turning point in the history of photography. Its importance emerges only in comparison with earlier photographs such as Steichen's *Rodin* (see fig. 924) and Riis' *The Bandits' Roost* (see fig. 918). *The Steerage* is a pictorial statement independent of painting on the one hand and free from social commentary on the other. It represents the first time that documentary photography achieved the level of art in America.

Stieglitz' "straight" photography formed the basis of the American school. It is therefore ironic that it was Stieglitz, with Steichen's encouragement, who became the champion of abstract art against the urban realism of the Ash Can School (see page 717), whose paintings were at face value

1058. ALFRED STIEGLITZ. *Equivalent.*
1930. Chloride print. The Art Institute of Chicago
(Alfred Stieglitz Collection)

often similar in content and appearance to his photographs. The resemblance is misleading; for Stieglitz, photography was less a means of recording things than of expressing his experience and philosophy of life, much as a painter does.

This attitude culminated in his "Equivalents"; in 1922 Stieglitz began to photograph clouds to show that his work was independent of subject and personality. Like O'Keeffe's paintings (see fig. 939), these are akin to Expressionism in their intent, for their power lies outside of representation. A remarkably lyrical cloud photograph from 1930 (fig. 1058) corresponds to a state of mind waiting to find full expression rather than merely responding to the moonlit scene. The study of clouds is as old as Romanticism itself, but no one before Stieglitz had made them a major theme in photography. As in Käsebier's *The Crystal Ball* (see fig. 923), unseen forces are evoked that make *Equivalent* a counterpart to Kandinsky's *Composition VII* (see fig. 938, colorplate 136).

WESTON. Stieglitz' concept of the Equivalent opened the way to "pure" photography as an alternative to "straight" photography. The leader of this new approach was Edward Weston (1886–1958), who, although not Stieglitz' protégé, was decisively influenced by him. During the 1920s he pursued abstraction and realism as separate paths, but by 1930 he fused them both in images which are wonderful in their design and miraculous for their detail.

Pepper (fig. 1059) is a splendid example which is anything but a straightforward record of this familiar fruit. Like Stieglitz' clouds, Weston's photography makes us see the mundane with new eyes. The pepper is shown with preternatural sharpness and so close up that it seems larger than life. Thanks to the tightly cropped composition, we are forced to contemplate the form, whose every undulation is revealed by the dramatic lighting. *Pepper* possesses the inner life of O'Keeffe's *Dark Abstraction* (see fig. 939), but with a surprising sensuousness that lends the Equivalent a new meaning. Here the shapes are intentionally suggestive of the photographs of the female nude that Weston also pioneered.

ADAMS. To achieve uniform detail and depth, Weston worked with the smallest possible camera lens openings, and his success led to the formation in 1932 of the West Coast society known as Group *f*/64, for the small lens opening. Among the founding members was Ansel Adams (1902–1984), who soon became the foremost nature photographer in America. He can rightly be regarded as the successor to O'Sullivan (see fig. 864), for his landscapes hark back to nineteenth-century American painting and photography.

Adams was a meticulous technician, beginning with the composition and exposure and continuing through the final printing. His justifiably famous work *Moonrise, Hernandez, New Mexico* (fig. 1060) came from pure serendipity which could never be repeated, a perfect marriage of straight and Equivalent photography. As in all of Adams' pictures, there is a full range of tonal nuances, from clear whites to inky blacks. The key to the photograph lies in the low cloud that divides the scene into three zones, so that the moon appears to hover effortlessly in the early evening sky.

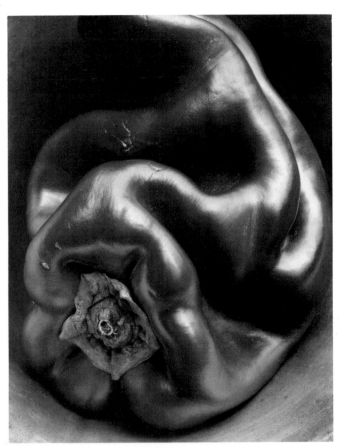

1059. EDWARD WESTON. *Pepper.* 1930. Center for Creative Photography, Tucson

BOURKE-WHITE. Stieglitz was among the first to photograph skyscrapers, the new architecture that came to dominate the horizon of America's growing cities. In turn, he championed the Precisionist painters (see page 719) who, inspired by Futurism, began to depict urban and industrial architecture around 1925. Several of them soon took up the camera as well. Thus, painting and photography once again became closely linked. Both were responding to the revitalized economy after World War I which led to an unprecedented industrial expansion on either side of the Atlantic. During the subsequent Depression, industrial photography continued surprisingly to grow with the new mass-circulation magazines that ushered in the great age of photojournalism and, with it, of commercial photography. In the United States, most of the important photographers were employed by the leading journals and corporations.

Margaret Bourke-White (1904–1971) was the first staff photographer hired by *Fortune* magazine and then by *Life* magazine, both published by Henry Luce; her cover photograph of Fort Peck Dam in Montana for *Life*'s inaugural issue on November 23, 1936, remains a classic example of the new photojournalism (fig. 1061). The decade was witnessing enormous building campaigns, and with her keen eye for composition, Bourke-White draws a visual parallel between the dam and the massive constructions of ancient Egypt (compare fig. 76), an idea that had already appeared in a painting of 1927 by Charles Demuth (see page

719), *My Egypt.* In addition to their architectural power, Bourke-White's columnar forms have a remarkable sculptural quality and an almost human presence, looming like colossal statues at the entrance to a temple. But unlike the pharaohs' passive timelessness, these "guardian figures" have the spectral alertness of Henry Moore's abstract monoliths (see fig. 998). Bourke-White's rare ability to suggest multiple levels of meaning made this cover and her accompanying photo essay an astonishing revelation.

STEICHEN; MILLER. The flourishing magazine business also gave rise to fashion and glamour photography, which was developed into an art in its own right by Edward Steichen, America's most complete photographer to date. Steichen's talent for portraiture, seen in his early Photo-Secession photograph of Rodin (see fig. 924), makes *Greta Garbo* (fig. 1062) a worthy successor to Nadar's *Sarah Bernhardt* (see fig. 862). The young film actress would have her picture taken countless times despite her desire "to be alone," but none captures better the magnetic presence and complex character seen in her movies. The photograph owes much to its abstract black-and-white design, which focuses attention on her wonderfully expressive face. But Steichen's stroke of genius was to have Garbo put her arms around her head in order to suggest her enigmatic personality.

One of Steichen's contributions to photography was to organize the "Family of Man" exhibition, which opened in New York in 1955. Wayne Miller's picture of childbirth (fig. 1063) from this epoch-making show captures the miracle of life in one dramatic image. It records with shocking honesty the newborn infant's abrupt entry into the world we all share. At the same time, the hands that reach out to help him are a moving affirmation of human existence.

Germany

With the New Objectivity movement in Germany during the late 1920s and early '30s, photography achieved a degree of excellence that has never been surpassed. Fostered by the invention of superior German cameras and the boom in pub-

1060. ANSEL ADAMS. *Moonrise, Hernandez, New Mexico.* 1941. Gelatin silver print, 15 × 18½".
The Museum of Modern Art, New York (Gift of the artist)

1061. MARGARET BOURKE-WHITE. *Fort Peck Dam, Montana.*
1936 (first cover of *Life* magazine). Time-Life

lishing everywhere, this German version of straight photography emphasized materiality at a time when many other photographers were turning away from the real world. The intrinsic beauty of things was brought out through the clarity of form and structure in their photographs. This approach accorded with Bauhaus principles except with regard to function (see page 761).

RENGER-PATZSCH; SANDER.   The *Potter's Hands* (fig. 1064) by Albert Renger-Patzsch (1897–1966), its leading exponent, is a marvel of technique and design which deliberately avoids any personal statement by reducing the image to an abstraction; the content lies solely in the cool perfection of the presentation and the orderly world it implies.

When applied to people rather than things, the New Objectivity could have deceptive results: August Sander (1876–1964), whose *Face of Our Time*, published in 1929, concealed the book's intentions behind a disarmingly straightforward surface; the sixty portraits provide a devastating survey of Germany during the rise of the Nazis, who later suppressed the book. Clearly proud of his position,

1062. EDWARD STEICHEN. *Greta Garbo.* 1928 (for *Vanity Fair* magazine).
The Museum of Modern Art, New York (Gift of the artist)

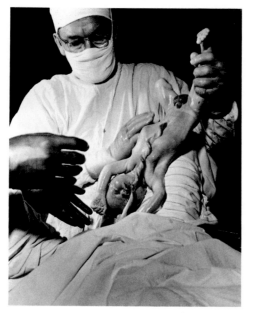

1063. WAYNE MILLER. *Childbirth.*
"Family of Man" exhibition, 1955

1064. ALBERT RENGER-PATZSCH. *Potter's Hands.*
1925. Gelatin-silver print, 15⅛ × 11¾".
The Museum of Modern Art, New York (Gift of the artist)

1065. AUGUST SANDER. *Pastry Cook, Cologne.* 1928 (Courtesy of August Sander Archive and Sander Gallery, Inc., New York)

Sander's *Pastry Cook* (fig. 1065) is the very opposite of the timid figure in George Grosz' *Germany, a Winter's Tale* (see fig. 951); despite their curious resemblance, this "good citizen" seems oblivious to the evil that Grosz has depicted so vividly. While the photograph passes no individual judgment, the subject's unconcern stands as a strong indictment, particularly in light of later history.

The Heroic Age of Photography

CAPA.   The years from 1930 to 1945 can be called the heroic age of photography for its photographers' notable response to the challenges of their times. Their physical bravery was exemplified by the combat photographer Robert Capa (1913–1954), who covered wars around the world for twenty years before being killed by a land mine in Vietnam. While barely adequate technically, his picture of a Loyalist soldier being shot during the Spanish Civil War (fig. 1066) captures fully the horror of death at the moment of impact. Had it been taken by someone else, it might seem a freak photograph, but it is altogether typical of Capa's battle close-ups, for he was as fearless as Mathew Brady.

LANGE.   Photography in those difficult times demonstrated moral courage as well. Under Roy Stryker, staff photographers of the Farm Security Administration compiled a comprehensive photodocumentary archive of rural America during the Depression. While the FSA photographers presented a balanced and objective view, most of them were also reformers whose work responded to the social problems they confronted daily in the field. The concern of Dorothea Lange (1895–1965) for people and her sensitivity to their dignity made her the finest documentary photographer of the time in America.

1066. ROBERT CAPA. *Death of a Loyalist Soldier.* 1936

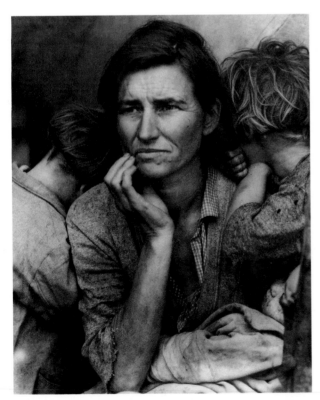

1067. DOROTHEA LANGE. *Migrant Mother, California.* 1936.
Library of Congress, Washington, D.C.

At a pea-pickers' camp in Nipomo, California, Lange discovered 2,500 virtually starving migrant workers and took several pictures of a young widow with her children, much later identified as Florence Thompson; when *Migrant Mother* (fig. 1067) was published in a news story on their plight the government rushed in food, and eventually migrant relief camps were opened. More than any Social Realist or Regionalist painting (see page 718), *Migrant Mother, California* has come to stand for that entire era. Unposed and uncropped, this photograph has an unforgettable immediacy no other medium can match.

Fantasy and Abstraction

"Impersonality," the very liability that had precluded the acceptance of photography in the eyes of many critics, became a virtue in the 1920s. Precisely because photographs are produced by mechanical devices, the camera's images now seemed to some artists the perfect means for expressing the modern era. This change in attitude did not stem from the Futurists, who contrary to what might be expected, never fully grasped the camera's importance for modern art, despite Marey's influence on their paintings (see page 686). The new view of photography arose as part of the Berlin Dadaists' assault on traditional art.

Toward the end of World War I, the Dadaists "invented" the photomontage and the photogram, although these completely different processes had been practiced early in the history of photography. In the service of anti-art they lent themselves equally well to Fantasy and to Abstraction, despite the apparent opposition of the two modes.

THE PHOTOMONTAGE. Photomontages are simply parts of photographs cut out and recombined into new images. Composite negatives originated with the art photography of Rejlander and Robinson (see page 662), but by the 1870s they were already being used in France to create witty impos-

1068. HERBERT BAYER. *lonely metropolitan.* 1932.
Photomontage, 14 × 11″. Collection the artist (copyright)

POSTERS. Photomontages were soon incorporated into carefully designed posters as well. In Germany, posters became a double-edged sword in political propaganda, used by Hitler's sympathizers and enemies alike. The most acerbic anti-Nazi commentaries were provided by John Heartfield (1891–1968), who changed his name from the German Herzfeld as a sign of protest. His horrific poster (fig. 1069) of a Nazi victim crucified on a swastika appropriates a Gothic image of mankind punished for its sins on the wheel of divine judgment. Obviously, Heartfield was not concerned about misinterpreting the original meaning in his montage, which communicates its new message to powerful effect.

THE PHOTOGRAM. The photogram does not take pictures but makes them; objects are placed directly onto photographic paper and exposed to light. This technique, too, was not new; Fox Talbot (see page 614) had used it to make negative images of plants which he called "photogenic drawings." The Dadaists' photograms, however, like their photomontages, were intended to alter nature's forms, not to record them, and to substitute impersonal technology for the work of the individual. Since the results in the photogram are so unpredictable, making one involves even greater risks than does a photomontage.

sibilities that are the ancestors of Dada photomontages. Like *1 Piping Man* (see fig. 961) by Max Ernst (who, not surprisingly, became a master of the genre), Dadaist photomontages utilize the techniques of collage Cubism to ridicule social and aesthetic conventions.

These imaginative parodies destroy all pictorial illusionism and therefore stand in direct opposition to straight photographs, which use the camera to record and probe the meaning of reality. Dada photomontages might be called Ready-Images, after Duchamp's Ready-Mades. Like other collages, they are literally torn from popular culture and given new meaning. Although the photomontage relies more on the laws of chance (see page 593), the Surrealists later claimed it to be a form of automatic handwriting, on the grounds that it responds to a stream of consciousness.

Most Surrealist photographers have been influenced by the Belgian painter René Magritte, whose mystifying fantasies are treated with a magic realism that is the opposite of automatic handwriting. Since Magritte's pictorial style was already highly naturalistic, he only experimented with the camera. His impact on photography was nevertheless considerable, because his illusionistic paradoxes can be readily emulated in photographs, such as the photomontage *lonely metropolitan* (fig. 1068) by Herbert Bayer (born 1900, in Germany). The purpose of such visual riddles is to challenge our conception of reality, showing up the discrepancy between our perception of the world and our irrational understanding of its significance.

1069. JOHN HEARTFIELD. *As in the Middle Ages,*
so in the Third Reich. 1934. Poster, photomontage.
Akademie der Künste, Heartfield Archive, West Berlin

1070. MAN RAY. *Rayograph 1928*. 1928.
Gelatin-silver print, 15½ × 11⅝″. The Museum of Modern Art,
New York (Gift of James Thrall Soby)

Man Ray (1890–1976), an American working in Paris, was not the first to make photograms, but his name is the most closely linked to them through his "Rayographs." Fittingly enough, he discovered the process by accident. The amusing face in figure 1070, like Arp's *Collage with Squares* (see fig. 962), was made according to the laws of chance by dropping a string, two strips of paper and a few pieces of cotton onto the photographic paper, then coaxing them here and there before exposure. The resulting image is a witty creation that shows the playful, spontaneous side of Dada and Surrealism as against Heartfield's grim satire.

THE CONSTRUCTIVISTS. Because the Russian Constructivists had a comparably mechanistic conception of man and society, they soon followed Dada's lead in using photograms and photomontages as a means to integrate industry and art, albeit for quite different purposes. László Moholy-Nagy, a Hungarian teaching at the Bauhaus who was deeply affected by Constructivism, successfully combined the best features of both approaches. By removing the lens to make photograms, he transformed his camera from a reproductive into a productive instrument; photography could now become, in theory if not in practice, a technological tool for fostering creativity in mass education.

Like many of the Russian artists in the 1920s, Moholy-Nagy also saw light as the embodiment of dynamic energy in space. The effects conjured up by the superimposition and

interpenetration of forms in his photographs are fascinating (fig. 1071). We feel transported in time and space to the edges of the universe, where the future takes shape in the play of cosmic forces created by a supreme cosmic will that has arisen from within the artist's imagination.

ABBOTT. One of the principal educational purposes of Moholy-Nagy's images was to extend sense perception in new ways. Similar goals have been achieved by taking pictures through microscopes and telescopes. Such photographs have helped to open our eyes to the invisibly small and the infinitely far. Wondrous scientific photographs were taken from 1939 to 1958 by Berenice Abbott (born 1898), Man Ray's former pupil and assistant, to demonstrate the laws of physics (fig. 1072). Like Marey's motion photographs of fifty years earlier (see fig. 926), they are arresting images, literally and visually. Their formal perfection makes them aesthetically compelling and scientifically valid, and they have proved to be even more educational than Moholy-Nagy's photograms.

PHOTOGRAPHY TODAY
Abstraction

SISKIND; WHITE. Photography after World War II was marked by abstraction for nearly two decades, particularly in the United States. Aaron Siskind, a close friend of the

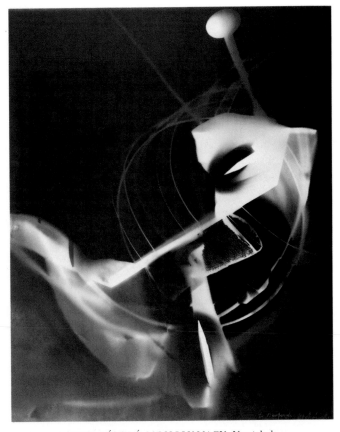

1071. LÁSZLÓ MOHOLY-NAGY. *Untitled*.
Photogram, silver bromide print, 19½ × 15¾″.
The Art Institute of Chicago (Gift of George Bancroft, 1968)

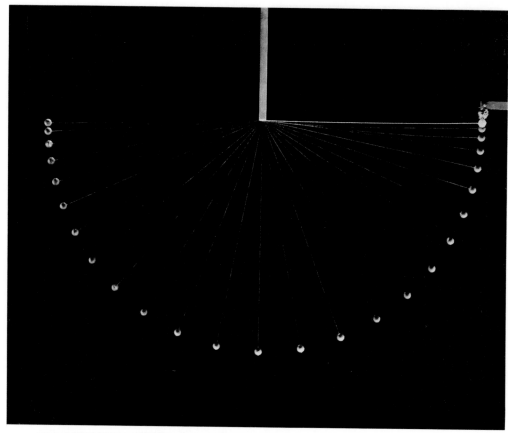

1072. BERENICE ABBOTT. *Transformation of Energy.* 1939–58 (Courtesy Parasol Press)

1073. AARON SISKIND. *New York 2.* 1951. Collection the artist

Abstract Expressionist painters, recorded modern society's debris and decaying signs. Hidden in these details he discovered cipher-like figures (fig. 1073) which are ironically similar to the ideographs of some forgotten civilization that is no longer intelligible to us.

Minor White (1908–1976) approached even closer to the spirit of Abstract Expressionism. An associate of Adams and Weston, he was decisively influenced by Stieglitz' concept of the Equivalent. During his most productive period, from the mid-1950s to the mid-'60s, he worked in a highly individual style, using the alchemy of the dark room to transform reality into a mystical metaphor. His *Ritual Branch* (fig. 1074) evokes a primordial image: what it shows is not so important as what it stands for, but the meaning that we sense there remains elusive.

Fantasy

Fantasy gradually reasserted itself on both sides of the Atlantic in the mid-1950s. Photographers first manipulated the camera for the sake of extreme visual effects by using special lenses and filters to alter appearances, sometimes virtually beyond recognition. Since about 1970, however, they have employed mainly printing techniques, with results that are frequently even more startling.

UELSMANN.   The American Jerry Uelsmann (born 1934), a leader of this movement, was inspired by Oscar Rejlander's multiple-negative photographs, as well as by Stieglitz'

1074. MINOR WHITE. *Ritual Branch.* 1958. George Eastman House, Rochester, N.Y. Reproduction courtesy
The Minor White Archive, Princeton University. Copyright © 1982 Trustees of Princeton University

Equivalents. While Uelsmann's work has a playful side close
to Pop Art, for the most part he strives to express archetypal
images from deep within the subconscious. The nude lying
within the earth in *Untitled* (fig. 1075) seemingly conveys
a dream in which the psyche retreats into the womblike
sanctuary of primal nature. Each part of the photograph is
a faithful record; it is their juxtaposition that gives the image
a new reality.

Uelsmann once participated in one of White's classes,
and their photographs are not as far removed visually or
expressively from each other's as they might seem. The principal difference lies in their approach to the Equivalent as
a means for achieving a poetical inner truth: White, like
Stieglitz, recognizes his symbols in nature, whereas
Uelsmann creates his symbols from his imagination. Paradoxically, it is Uelsmann's untitled print, not *Ritual Branch*,
that is instantly recognizable, but neither yields an ultimate
meaning.

LEONARD. Photographers have increasingly turned to
fantasy as autobiographical expression. Both the image and
the title of *Romanticism Is Ultimately Fatal* (fig. 1076)
by Joanne Leonard (born 1940) suggest a meaning that is
personal in its reference. We will recognize in this disturbing
vision something of the tortured eroticism of Fuseli's *Nightmare* (see fig. 816). The clarity of the presentation turns the
apparition at the window into a real and terrifying personification of despair. This is no romantic knight in shining armor

1075. JERRY UELSMANN. *Untitled.* 1972? Collection the artist

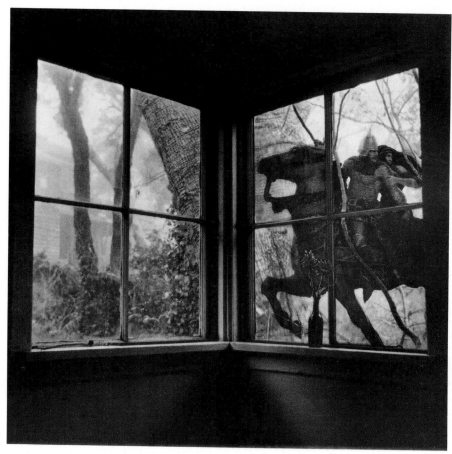

1076. JOANNE LEONARD. *Romanticism Is Ultimately Fatal,*
from "Dreams and Nightmares." 1982. Positive transparency selectively
opaqued with collage, 9¾ × 9¼″. Collection M. Neri, Benica, Cal.

1077. W. EUGENE SMITH. *Tomoko in Her Bath.* 1972.
Gelatin-silver print. Aileen and W. Eugene Smith—Black Star

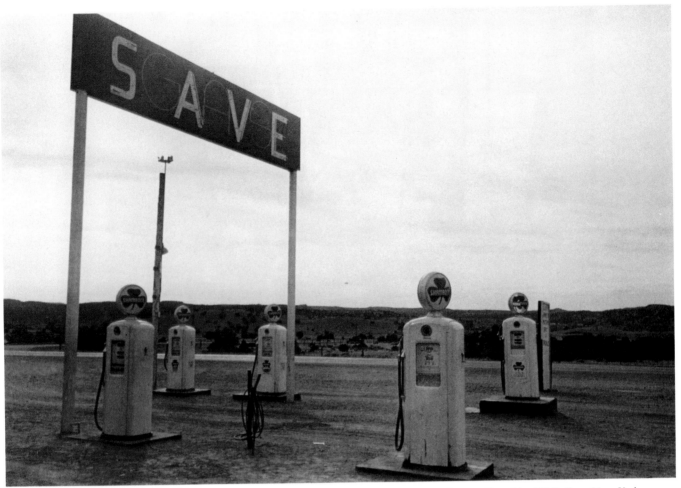

1078. ROBERT FRANK. *Santa Fe, New Mexico*. 1955–56. Gelatin-silver print. Collection Pace-MacGill Gallery, New York

but a grim reaper whose ancestors can be found in Dürer's woodcut *The Four Horsemen of the Apocalypse* (see fig. 669).

Documentary Photography

SMITH.   The continuing record of misery that photography provides has often been the vehicle for making strong personal statements. W. Eugene Smith (1918–1978), the foremost photojournalist of our time, was a compassionate cynic who commented on the human condition with "reasoned passion," as he put it. *Tomoko in Her Bath* (fig. 1077), taken in 1972 in the Japanese fishing village of Minamata, shows a child crippled by mercury poisoning being bathed by her mother. Not simply the subject itself but Smith's treatment of it makes this an intensely moving work. The imagery lies deep in our heritage: the mother holding her child's body goes back to the theme of the German Gothic *Pietà* (see fig. 468), while the dramatic lighting and vivid realism recall a painting of another martyr in his bath, Jacques Louis David's *Death of Marat* (see fig. 827). But what engages our emo-

tions above all in making the photograph memorable is the infinite love conveyed by the mother's tender expression.

FRANK.   The birth of a new form of straight photography in the United States was largely the responsibility of one man, Robert Frank (born 1924). His book *The Americans*, compiled from a cross-country odyssey in 1955–56, created a sensation upon its publication in 1959, for it expressed the same restlessness and alienation as *On the Road* by his traveling companion, the Beat poet Jack Kerouac, published in 1957. This friendship suggests that words have an important role in Frank's photographs, which are as loaded in their meaning as are Demuth's and Indiana's paintings (figs. 981, 982, colorplate 134); yet Frank's social point of view is often hidden behind a façade of disarming neutrality. It is with shock that we finally recognize the ironic intent of *Santa Fe* (fig. 1078): the gas pumps face the sign SAVE in the barren landscape like members of a religious cult vainly seeking salvation at a revival meeting. Frank, who subsequently turned to film, holds up an image of American culture that is as sterile as it is joyless. Even spiritual values, he tells us, become meaningless in the face of vulgar materialism.

1079. DAVID HOCKNEY. *Gregory Watching the Snow Fall,*
Kyoto, Feb. 1983. Photographic collage, 43½ × 46½".
Collection the artist

HOCKNEY. The most recent demonstration of photography's power to extend our vision has come, fittingly enough, from an artist. The photographic collages that the English painter David Hockney has been making since 1982 are like revelations that overcome the traditional limitations of a unified image, fixed in time and place, by closely approximating how we actually see. In *Gregory Watching the Snow Fall, Kyoto, Feb. 1983* (fig. 1079), each frame is analogous to a discrete eye movement containing a piece of visual data that must be stored in our memory and synthesized by the brain. Just as we process only essential information, so there are gaps in the matrix of the image, which becomes more fragmentary toward its edge, though without the loss of acuity experienced in vision itself. The resulting shape of the collage is a masterpiece of design. The scene appears to bow curiously as it comes toward us. This ebb and flow is more than simply the result of optical physics. In the perceptual process, space and its corollary, time, are not linear but fluid. Moreover, by including his own feet as reference points to establish our position clearly, Hockney helps us to realize that vision is less a matter of looking outward than an egocentric act which defines the viewer's visual and psychological relationship to the world around him. The picture is as expressive as it is opulent. Hockney has recorded his friend several times to suggest his reactions to the serene landscape outside the door.

Hockney's approach is embedded in the history of modern painting, for it shows a self-conscious awareness of earlier art. It combines the faceted views of Picasso (see fig. 942) and the sequential action of Duchamp (see fig. 959) with the dynamic energy of Popova (see fig. 953). *Gregory Watching the Snow Fall* is nonetheless a distinctly contemporary work, for it incorporates the fascinating effects of Photo Realism (see colorplate 162) and the illusionistic potential of Op Art (see fig. 993). Hockney has begun to explore further implications inherent in these photo collages, such as continuous narrative. No doubt others will be discovered as well. Among these is the possibility of showing an object or scene simultaneously from multiple vantage points to let us see it completely for the first time.

ILLUSTRATED TIME CHART IV

POLITICAL HISTORY, RELIGION	LITERATURE, SCIENCE, TECHNOLOGY	PAINTING, SCULPTURE, ARCHITECTURE

1750

Edmund Burke, English reformer
  (1729–97)

Soufflot, Panthéon, Paris

Gray's *Elegy* 1750
Benjamin Franklin's experiments
  with electricity c. 1750
Diderot, *Encyclopedia* 1751–72
Johnson, *Dictionary* 1755
Winckelmann, *Thoughts on Greek Art* 1755
Rousseau, *Social Contract* and *Emile* 1762
Mechanization of textile spinning 1764–69
Priestley discovers oxygen 1774
Goethe, *Sorrows of Young Werther* 1774
Coke-fed blast furnaces for iron smelting
  perfected c. 1760–75

Horace Walpole, Strawberry Hill
Soufflot, Panthéon, Paris
Greuze, *Village Bride*
West, *Death of Wolfe*
Stubbs, *Lion Attacking Horse*
Robert Adam, Home
  House, London

Stubbs, *Lion Attacking Horse*

1775

American Revolution 1775–85; Constitu-
  tion adopted 1789
French Revolution 1789–1802; Louis
  XVI beheaded, Reign of Terror under
  Robespierre 1793
Consulate of Napoleon 1799–1804

David, *Death of Marat*

Gibbon, *Decline and Fall of the
  Roman Empire* 1776–87
Adam Smith, *Wealth of Nations* 1776
Kant, *Critique of Pure Reason* 1781
Crossing of English Channel in hydrogen-
  filled balloon 1785
Paine, *The Rights of Man* 1790
Power loom 1785; cotton gin 1793
Lavoisier, French chemist (1743–94)
Hutton, *Theory of the Earth* 1795
Laplace's nebular hypothesis 1796
Jenner's smallpox vaccine 1796
Wordsworth and Coleridge,
  Lyrical Ballads 1798

Langhans, Brandenburg Gate

Jefferson, Monticello,
  Charlottesville
Copley, *Watson and the Shark*
Houdon, *Voltaire*
Cozens, *A New Method...*
Fuseli, *Nightmare*
David, *Death of Socrates*
Langhans, Brandenburg
  Gate, Berlin
Houdon, *Washington*
David, *Death of Marat*
David, *View of Luxembourg
  Gardens*
Blake, *The Ancient of Days*
Gros, *Napoleon at Arcole*
Canova, Tomb of Maria
  Christina, Vienna

1800

First child labor laws 1802
Jefferson negotiates Louisiana Purchase
  1803
Napoleon (1769–1821) crowns himself
  emperor 1804; fails in Russian campaign 1812; exiled to Elba 1814; defeated at Waterloo, exiled to St.
  Helena 1815
War of 1812
Congress of Vienna, 1814–15
Bolivar leads revolution in Latin America, six countries gain independence 1822
Greeks declare independence
  from Turks 1822
Monroe Doctrine proclaimed
  by U.S. 1823

Canova, *Pauline Borghese*

Volta invents electric battery 1800
Lewis and Clark expedition
  to Pacific 1803–6
First voyage of Fulton's steamship 1807;
  first Atlantic crossing 1819
Hegel, *Phenomenology of Mind* 1807
Goethe, *Faust*: Part I, 1808; Part II, 1833
Byron, *Childe Harold's Pilgrimage* 1812–18
Saint-Simon's ideals for the reorganization
  of European society 1814
Stephenson's first steam locomotive 1814
Cuvier's work on paleontology 1815
Shelley, *Prometheus Unbound* 1820
Faraday discovers principle of electric
  dynamo 1821
Keats (1795–1821) dies in Rome
Walter Scott, Waverley novels 1814–25

Goya, *Family of Charles IV*
Latrobe, Catholic Cathedral,
  Baltimore
Canova, *Pauline Borghese*
Géricault, *Mounted Officer*
Ingres, *Odalisque*
Goya, *Third of May...1808*
Nash, Brighton Pavilion
Géricault, *Raft of the "Medusa"*
Delacroix, *Massacre at Chios*
Friedrich, *Polar Sea*

Géricault, *Raft of the "Medusa"*

1825

1825

July Revolution of 1830 in France

Political and social reforms in England 1832–35

France conquers Algeria 1830–47

Queen Victoria crowned 1837

British win Hong Kong 1841

Oregon Trail opens western settlement 1842

U.S. treaty with China opens ports 1844

U.S. annexes western land areas 1845–60

Famine in Ireland, mass emigration 1845

Proudhon founds anarchism 1846

Parliament repeals Corn Laws 1846

Marx and Engels, *Communist Manifesto* 1848

Revolution of 1848: fails in Germany, Hungary, Austria, Italy; France sets up Second Republic (Louis Napoleon)

Gold discovered in California 1848

Daumier, *It's Safe to Release This One!*

Erie Canal opened 1825

First railroad in England 1825; in U.S. 1829

Pushkin, *Eugene Onegin* 1825–31

Lyell, *Principles of Geology* 1830

Stendhal, *The Red and The Black* 1831

McCormick invents reaper 1831; John Deere perfects steel plow 1837

Balzac writes the 92 novels and stories that comprise *La Comédie Humaine* 1832–50

Gogol's satirical drama *The Inspector General* 1836

Dickens, *Oliver Twist* 1838

Daguerre's process of photography, Fox Talbot's negative-positive process 1839

Emerson, *Essays* 1841, 1844

Kierkegaard, *Either/Or* 1843

Morse perfects telegraphy 1844

A. Dumas, *The Three Musketeers* 1844

Poe, *The Raven and Other Poems* 1845

Elias Howe invents sewing machine 1846

Morton demonstrates ether anaesthesia 1846

Joule formulates First Law of Thermodynamics 1847

Margaret Fuller, American writer and lecturer (1810–50)

Courbet, *Stone Breakers*

1850

Louis Napoleon takes title of Napoleon III 1852

Crimean War 1853–55; England and France halt Russia's advance into Balkans

Commodore Perry opens Japan 1854

Unification of Italy by Garibaldi 1860–70

Russia abolishes serfdom 1861

Frederick Douglass (c. 1817–95) becomes American abolitionist leader

Civil War (1861–65) ends slavery in U.S.; Lincoln assassinated 1865

Russia sells Alaska to U.S. 1867

Canada granted dominion status 1867

Marx, *Das Kapital* 1867–94

Susan B. Anthony (with Elizabeth Cady Stanton) organizes National Woman Suffrage Association 1869

Franco-Prussian War 1870–71; Third Republic in France; Bismarck becomes first chancellor of German empire

Disraeli, British prime minister 1874–80

Brown, *The Last of England*

Whistler, *The Artist's Mother*

Stowe, *Uncle Tom's Cabin* 1851

Lord Kelvin states Second Law of Thermodynamics 1851

Melville, *Moby Dick* 1851

Thoreau, *Walden* 1854

Whitman, *Leaves of Grass* 1855

Flaubert, *Madame Bovary* 1856

Baudelaire, *Les Fleurs du Mal* 1857

First transatlantic cable laid 1858–66

Darwin, *Origin of Species* 1859

First oil well drilled (Pennsylvania) 1859

Bessemer patents tilting converter for steel manufacture 1860

Victor Hugo, *Les Misérables* 1862

Pasteur develops germ theory 1864

Tolstoy, *War and Peace* 1864–69

Mendel publishes first experiments in genetics 1865

Lewis Carroll, *Alice in Wonderland* 1865

Dostoyevsky, *Crime and Punishment* 1867

Nobel invents dynamite 1867

First transcontinental railroad in U.S. 1869

Suez Canal opened 1869

Celluloid, first plastic, discovered c. 1869

Mendelijeff's periodic law of elements 1869

Schliemann excavates at Troy 1872

Maxwell, *Electricity and Magnetism* 1873

1875

Corot, *View of Papigno*
Daumier, *It's Safe to Release This One!*
Ingres, *Louis Bertin*
Préault, *Slaughter*
Rude, *La Marseillaise*
Barry and Pugin, Houses of Parliament, London
Constable, *Stoke-by-Nayland*
Turner, *Slave Ship*
Daguerre, *Still Life*
Labrouste, Bibliothèque Ste.-Geneviève, Paris
Bingham, *Fur Traders*
Bonheur, *Plowing in the Nivernais*
Courbet, *Stone Breakers*
Rossetti, *Ecce Ancilla Domini*
Delacroix, *Odalisque*
Fox Talbot, *Sailing Craft*

Rude, *La Marseillaise*

Constable, *Stoke-by-Nayland*

Delacroix, *Odalisque*

Barry and Pugin, Houses of Parliament

Millet, *The Sower*
Barye, *Jaguar Devouring a Hare*
Paxton, Crystal Palace, London
Brown, *The Last of England*
Courbet, *Interior of My Studio...*
Rude, *Marshal Ney*
Nadar, *Sarah Bernhardt*
Rejlander, *The Two Paths of Life*
Garnier, Opéra, Paris
Carpeaux, *The Dance*
Daumier, *Third-Class Carriage*
Manet, *Luncheon on the Grass*
Rodin, *Man with Broken Nose*
Julia Cameron, *Portrait of Ellen Terry*
Homer, *Morning Bell*
Monet, *The River*
Morisot, *The Artist's Sister...*
Whistler, *The Artist's Mother*

Paxton, Crystal Palace

Manet, *Luncheon on the Grass*

Garnier, Opéra, Paris

Rodin, *Man with Broken Nose*

1875

Peak of colonialism worldwide 1876–1914

First pogroms in Russia 1881–82

Labor unrest in U.S.: Haymarket riot, Chicago 1886; Carnegie steel strike, Homestead, Pa. 1892

"Dreyfus affair" (false treason charge), France, 1894–1906

First Zionist Congress called by Theodor Hertzl 1897

Spanish-American War 1898; U.S. gains Philippines, Guam, Puerto Rico, annexes Hawaii

Boxer Rebellion, China, against Western interests 1899–1900

Boer War, British defeat South Africans, 1899–1902

Eakins, *Gross Clinic*

Seurat, *Bathers*

Bell patents the telephone 1876

Mark Twain, *Tom Sawyer* 1876

Ibsen, *A Doll's House* 1879

Edison invents phonograph 1877; incandescent bulb 1879

Zola, *Nana* 1880

Henry James, *Portrait of a Lady* 1881

Internal combustion engines for gasoline 1885

Research on germ-caused diseases at Pasteur Institute, Paris (founded 1888); at Robert Koch's Institute of Infectious Diseases, Berlin (1891)

Emily Dickinson (1830–86), poetry published 1890, 1891

Oscar Wilde, *Lady Windermere's Fan* 1892

Edison invents motion picture 1894

Roentgen discovers X-rays 1895

Marconi invents wireless telegraphy (precursor of radio) 1895

G. B. Shaw, *Plays Pleasant and Unpleasant* 1898

Pierre and Marie Curie discover radium 1898

Anton Chekhov, *Uncle Vanya* 1899

1900

8,800,000 immigrate to U.S., 1901–10

Theodore Roosevelt (pres. 1901–9) attacks trusts, promotes Panama Canal (opened 1914)

William James, *The Varieties of Religious Experience* 1902

Internal strife, reforms in Russia 1905

Revolution in China, republic led by Sun Yat-sen set up 1911

First World War 1914–18; U.S. enters 1917

Bolshevik Revolution in Russia 1917

Armistice signed 1918; League of Nations founded in Geneva 1919

Woman suffrage enacted in U.S. 1920; in England 1928; in France 1945

Poland, Czechoslovakia, Austria, Germany become republics 1918; Finland 1919; Irish Free State 1921; Turkey 1923; Lebanon 1926

Gandhi leads Indian National Congress 1920s

Mussolini's Fascists seize Italian government 1922

Adolf Hitler writes *Mein Kampf* 1924

Gaudí, Casa Milá, Barcelona

Duchamp-Villon, *Great Horse*

Planck formulates quantum theory 1900

Freud, *Interpretation of Dreams* 1900

Pavlov experiments with conditioned reflexes in dogs 1900

Nobel Prizes initiated 1901

Walter Reed pinpoints mosquito in spread of yellow fever 1901

Maxim Gorky, *Lower Depths* 1902

Wright brothers' first flight 1903

Einstein's relativity theory, $E = mc^2$, 1905

Ford begins assembly-line automobile manufacture 1909

Gertrude Stein, *Three Lives* 1909

Russell and Whitehead, *Principia Mathematica* 1910–13

Rutherford's theory of positively charged atomic nucleus 1911

D. H. Lawrence, *Sons and Lovers* 1913

Marcel Proust, *Remembrance of Things Past* 1913–27

James Joyce, *Ulysses* 1914–21

Margaret Sanger leads birth-control movement c. 1915

John Dewey (1859–1952), philosopher, influences progressive education

First regular radio station broadcasts 1920

Sinclair Lewis, *Main Street* 1920

Maria Montessori (1870–1952) pioneers in children's education

Insulin developed by Banting and Best 1921–22

T. S. Eliot, *The Waste Land* 1922

1925

Richardson, Marshall Field
Wholesale Store

Cézanne, *Fruit Bowl, Glass, and Apples*

Eakins, *Gross Clinic*
Moreau, *The Apparition*
Renoir, *Moulin de la Galette*
Degas, *Glass of Absinthe*
Cézanne, *Fruit Bowl, Glass, and Apples*
Redon, *À Edgar Poe*
Seurat, *Bathers*
Marey, *Man in black suit...*
Richardson, Marshall Field Wholesale
    Store, Chicago
Muybridge, *Human and Animal Locomo-*
    tion
Gauguin, *Vision after the Sermon*
Riis, *Bandits' Roost*
Van Gogh, *Self-Portrait*
Ensor, *Intrigue*
Sullivan, Wainwright Building, St. Louis
Cassatt, *The Bath*
Toulouse-Lautrec, *Moulin Rouge*
Beardsley, *Salome*
Rodin, *Balzac*
Munch, *The Scream*
Tanner, *The Banjo Lesson*
Mackintosh, Glasgow School of Art
Vuillard, *Interior*

Toulouse-Lautrec, *Moulin Rouge*

Van Gogh, *Self-Portrait*

— 1900

Brancusi, *The Kiss*

Steichen, *Rodin with His Sculptures*
Matisse, *Joy of Life*
Lumière, *Young Lady with an Umbrella*
Gaudí, Casa Milá, Barcelona
Stieglitz, *The Steerage*
Picasso, *Les demoiselles d'Avignon*
Brancusi, *The Kiss*
Nolde, *Last Supper*
Bellows, *Stag at Sharkey's*
Rousseau, *The Dream*
Chagall, *I and the Village*
Barlach, *Man Drawing Sword*
Duchamp, *The Bride*
Kandinsky, *Sketch I for Composition VII*
Malevich, *Black Quadrilateral*
Boccioni, *Unique Forms...*
Popova, *The Traveler*
De Chirico, *Mystery and Melancholy...*
Duchamp-Villon, *Great Horse*
Arp, *Collage with Squares...*
Stella, *Brooklyn Bridge*
Tatlin, Project for *Monument to the*
    Third International
Léger, *The City*
Brancusi, *Bird in Space*
Kertész, *Wandering Violinist*
O'Keeffe, *Dark Abstraction*
Ernst, *1 Copper Plate...*
Klee, *Twittering Machine*
Atget, *Pool, Versailles*
Rietveld, Schröder House, Utrecht

Matisse, *Joy of Life*

De Chirico, *Mystery and Melancholy...*

Klee, *Twittering Machine*

— 1925

1925

Chiang Kai-shek unites Nationalist
China 1927–28

Stock-market crash in U.S. 1929; worldwide economic depression

Japan invades Manchuria 1931

Spain becomes republic 1931

Hitler seizes power in Germany 1933

Roosevelt proclaims New Deal 1933

Spanish Civil War 1936–39; won by Franco

Hitler annexes Austria 1938; seizes
Czechoslovakia, signs nonaggression
pact with Russia 1939

Germany invades Poland, initiating
World War II 1939

Japan bombs Pearl Harbor: U.S. enters
World War II 1941

Atomic bomb dropped on Hiroshima 1945

United Nations Charter signed 1945

Philippine independence 1946

British rule ends in India 1947

U.S. starts Marshall Plan 1947

Apartheid becomes government policy in
South Africa 1948

Israel achieves nationhood 1948

NATO founded 1949

West Germany becomes Federal Republic 1949

People's Republic of China founded 1949

Miró, *Composition*

Gropius, Bauhaus, Dessau

Ezra Pound, *Cantos* 1925–72

Lindbergh flies solo, nonstop from New
York to Paris 1927

Berthold Brecht, *Three-Penny Opera* 1928

Margaret Mead, *Coming of Age in
Samoa* 1928

Ernest Hemingway, *A Farewell to Arms* 1929

William Faulkner, *Sanctuary* 1931

Eugene O'Neill, *Mourning Becomes Electra* 1931

Radar developed, Watson-Watt 1934–35

C. F. Richter devises scale for measuring
earthquakes 1935

DDT invented 1939; banned 1972

Antibiotics discovered: penicillin 1939;
streptomycin 1944

First large-scale atomic explosion (fis-
sion), Los Alamos 1943

Jean-Paul Sartre formulates existential-
ism, *Being and Nothingness* 1943

Computer technology developed 1944

Television licensed for commercial use 1945

Xerography invented 1946; commercial
use 1958

Dead Sea scrolls discovered 1947

Norman Mailer, *The Naked and the Dead* 1948

Alfred Kinsey, *Sexual Behavior in the
Human Male* 1948; *Female* 1953

1950

Korean War 1950–53

U.S. Supreme Court outlaws racial seg-
regation in public schools 1954

Warsaw pact signed by East European
countries 1955

Common Market in Europe 1957

U.S. tests first ICBM 1957

Castro takes over Cuba 1959

De Kooning, *Woman II*

Rachel Carson, *The Sea Around Us* 1951

First hydrogen bomb (atomic fusion) 1952

Samuel Beckett, *Waiting for Godot* 1952

Double helix of DNA established 1953;
genetic code determined

Sputnik, first satellite, launched 1957

Jack Kerouac, *On the Road* 1957

Vladimir Nabokov, *Lolita* 1958

Jet planes adopted commercially 1959

1960

Sit-ins protest racial discrimination 1960

17 African countries independent 1960

Berlin Wall built 1961

John F. Kennedy assassinated 1963

U.S. intervention in Vietnam begins
1965

Martin Luther King assassinated 1968

Lichtenstein, *Girl at Piano*

Oral birth-control pill 1960

Laser device invented in U.S. 1960

Weather and communications satellites
launched 1960–61

First manned space flight 1961

Rise of the Beatles 1963

Planetary probes begin with Mars, 1965;
five probed, more planned

First manned moon landing 1969

1970

Nixon opens relations with People's Republic of China 1972

Supreme Court legalizes abortion 1973

Vietnam war ends 1973

Nixon resigns presidency 1974

Margaret Thatcher elected British Prime
Minister 1979

Ayatollah Khomeini proclaims Islamic
republic in Iran 1979

Piano and Rogers, Pompidou Center

Three "test tube" babies born in England 1973

Eudora Welty, *The Optimist's Daughter*
1973

Viking II lands on Mars 1976

Saul Bellow, *Humboldt's Gift* 1976

Personal computers become available
1978

1980

Socialization of French banks 1981

Lech Walesa, Polish Solidarity leader,
wins Nobel Peace Prize 1983

Space shuttle initiated by U.S. 1981

First artificial heart implanted 1982

Alice Walker, *The Color Purple* 1983

Picasso, *Three Dancers*
Gropius, Bauhaus, Dessau
Demuth, *I Saw the Figure 5 in Gold*
Sander, *Pastry Cook, Cologne*
Le Corbusier, Savoye House, Poissy
Howe and Lescaze, Philadelphia Savings
  Fund Society Building
Hopper, *Early Sunday Morning*
Giacometti, *Palace at 4 A.M.*
Brassaï, *"Bijou" of Montmartre*
Miró, *Composition*
Heartfield, *As in the Middle Ages...*
González, *Head*
Moore, *Two Forms*
Bourke-White, *Fort Peck Dam*
Capa, *Death of a Loyalist Soldier*
Picasso, *Guernica*
Moore, *Recumbent Figure*
Abbott, *Transformation of Energy*
Calder, *Lobster Trap and Fish Tail*
Hepworth, *Oval Form*
A. Adams, *Moonrise...*
Gorky, *The Liver Is the Cock's Comb*
Mondrian, *Composition*
Harrison, U.N. Buildings, New York
Siskind, *New York 2*

Bourke-White, *Fort Peck Dam*

Picasso, *Guernica*

Hopper, *Early Sunday Morning*

Moore, *Recumbent Figure*

— 1950

Pollock, *One*
Dubuffet, *Le Metafisyx*
Mies van der Rohe, Lake Shore
  Drive Apartments, Chicago
Le Corbusier, Notre-Dame-
  du-Haut, Ronchamp
De Kooning, *Woman II*

Rothko, *Earth and Green*
Frank, *Santa Fe...*
Rauschenberg, *Odalisk*
Vasarely, *Vega*
Johns, *Three Flags*
Appel, *Burned Face*
Krasner, *Celebration*

Rauschenberg, *Odalisk*

— 1960

Lichtenstein, *Girl at Piano*
George Segal, *Cinema*
Barnett Newman, *Broken Obelisk*
D. Smith, *Cubi* series
Nevelson, *Black Chord*
Kosuth, *One and Three Chairs*
Kienholz, *State Hospital*

George Segal, *Cinema*

— 1970

Hanson, *Tourists*
Piano and Rogers, Pompidou Center
W. E. Smith, *Tomoko in Her Bath*
Eddy, *New Shoes for H*
Flack, *Queen*

Eddy, *New Shoes for H*

— 1980

Pfaff, *Dragons*
Kiefer, *To the Unknown Painter*
Hockney, *Gregory Watching...*

Hockney, *Gregory Watching...*

GLOSSARY

ABACUS. A slab of stone at the top of a classical CAPITAL, just beneath the ARCHITRAVE (figs. 159, 161).

ABBEY. 1) A religious community headed by an abbot or abbess. 2) The buildings which house the community. An abbey church often has an especially large CHOIR to provide space for the monks or nuns (fig. 422).

ACADEMY. A place of study, the word coming from the Greek name of a garden near Athens where Plato and, later, Platonic philosophers held philosophical discussions from the 5th century B.C. to the 6th century A.D. The first Academy of Fine Arts, properly speaking, was the Academy of Drawing founded 1563 in Florence by Giorgio Vasari. Important later academies were the Royal Academy of Painting and Sculpture in Paris, founded 1648, and the Royal Academy of Arts in London, founded 1768. Their purpose was to foster the arts by systematic teaching, exhibitions, discussion, and occasionally by financial assistance.

ACANTHUS. 1) A Mediterranean plant having spiny or toothed leaves. 2) An architectural ornament resembling the leaves of this plant, used on MOLDINGS, FRIEZES, and Corinthian CAPITALS (figs. 151, 164).

ACRYLIC. A plastic binder MEDIUM for PIGMENTS that is soluble in water. Developed about 1960 (colorplates 151, 164).

AERIAL PERSPECTIVE. See PERSPECTIVE.

AISLE. See SIDE AISLE.

ALLA PRIMA. A painting technique in which PIGMENTS are laid on in one application with little or no UNDERPAINTING.

ALLAH. The unique and personal God of the MOSLEM faith.

ALTAR. 1) A mound or structure on which sacrifices or offerings are made in the worship of a deity. 2) In a Catholic church, a table-like structure used in celebrating the Mass.

ALTARPIECE. A painted or carved work of art placed behind and above the ALTAR of a Christian church. It may be a single panel (colorplate 59) or a TRIPTYCH or a POLYPTYCH having hinged wings painted on both sides (figs. 512, 514). Also called a reredos or retable.

ALTERNATE SYSTEM. A system developed in Romanesque church architecture to provide adequate support for a GROIN-VAULTED NAVE having BAYS twice as long as the SIDE-AISLE bays. The PIERS of the nave ARCADE alternate in size; the heavier COMPOUND piers support the main nave vaults where the THRUST is concentrated, and smaller, usually cylindrical piers support the side-aisle vaults (figs. 391, 396).

AMAZON. One of a tribe of female warriors said in Greek legend to dwell near the Black Sea (fig. 194).

AMBULATORY. A covered walkway. 1) In a BASILICAN church, the semicircular passage around the APSE (fig. 422). 2) In a CENTRAL-PLAN church, the ring-shaped AISLE around the central space (fig. 307). 3) In a CLOISTER, the covered COLONNADED or ARCADED walk around the open courtyard.

AMPHITHEATER. A double THEATER. A building, usually oval in plan, consisting of tiers of seats and access corridors around the central theater area (fig. 235).

AMPHORA (pl. AMPHORAE). A large Greek storage vase with an oval body usually tapering toward the base; two handles extend from just below the lip to the shoulder (fig. 137).

ANDACHTSBILD. German for devotional picture. A picture or sculpture with a type of imagery intended for private devotion, first developed in northern Europe.

ANNULAR. From the Latin word for ring. Signifies a ring-shaped form, especially an annular barrel VAULT.

ANTA (pl. ANTAE). The front end of a wall of a Greek temple, thickened to produce a PILASTER-like member. Temples having COLUMNS between the antae are said to be "in antis" (fig. 160).

APOCALYPSE. The Book of Revelation, the last book of the New Testament. In it St. John the Evangelist describes his visions, experienced on the island of Patmos, of heaven, the future of mankind, and the Last Judgment.

APOSTLE. One of the twelve disciples chosen by Christ to accompany him in his lifetime, and to spread the GOSPEL after his death. The traditional list in Matt. 10:1-4 includes Andrew, Bartholomew, James the Greater (son of Zebedee), James the Less (son of Alphaeus), John, Judas Iscariot, Matthew, Peter, Philip, Simon the Canaanite, Thaddeus (or Jude), and Thomas. In art, however, the same twelve are not always represented since "apostle" was sometimes applied to other early Christians, such as St. Paul.

APSE. 1) A semicircular or polygonal niche terminating one or both ends of the NAVE in a Roman BASILICA (fig. 246). 2) In a Christian church, it is usually placed at the east end of the nave beyond the TRANSEPT or CHOIR (fig. 289); it is also sometimes used at the end of transept arms.

AQUATINT. A print processed like an ETCHING, except that the ground or certain areas are covered with a solution of asphalt, resin, or salts which, when heated, produces a granular surface on the plate and rich gray tones in the final print (fig. 819). Etched lines are usually added to the plate after the aquatint ground is laid.

AQUEDUCT. Latin for duct of water. 1) An artificial channel or conduit for transporting water from a distant source. 2) The overground structure which carries the conduit across valleys, rivers, etc. (fig. 234).

ARCADE. A series of ARCHES supported by PIERS or COLUMNS (fig. 290). When attached to a wall, these form a blind arcade (fig. 403).

ARCH. A curved structure used to span an opening. Masonry arches are built of wedge-shaped blocks, called voussoirs, set with their narrow side toward the opening so that they lock together (figs. 226, 234). The topmost voussoir is called the keystone. Arches may take different shapes, as in the pointed Gothic arch (fig. 440), or the STILTED Islamic arch (fig. 341), but all require support from other arches or BUTTRESSES.

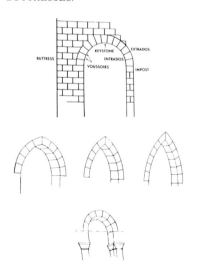

ARCHBISHOP. The chief BISHOP of an ecclesiastical district.

ARCHITRAVE. The lowermost member of a classical ENTABLATURE, i.e., a series of stone blocks that rest directly on the COLUMNS (figs. 159, 161).

ARCHIVOLT. A molded band framing an ARCH, or a series of such bands framing a TYMPANUM, often decorated with sculpture (fig. 408).

ARRICCIO. See SINOPIA.

ATMOSPHERIC PERSPECTIVE. See PERSPECTIVE.

ATRIUM. 1) The central court of a Roman house (fig. 247), or its open entrance court. 2) An open court, sometimes COLONNADED or ARCADED, in front of a church (figs. 289, 395).

ATTIC. A low upper story placed above the main CORNICE or ENTABLATURE of a building, and often decorated with windows and PILASTERS (figs. 625, 763).

AURIGNACIAN. An adjective used for describing artifacts of an Upper PALEOLITHIC culture preceding the MAGDALENIAN; the word comes from Aurignac (Haute-Garonne), a site in southern France where such work was found.

AUTOCHROME. A color photograph invented by Louis Lumière in 1903, using a glass plate covered with grains of starch dyed in three colors to act as filters, then a silver bromide emulsion (colorplate 176).

BACCHANT (fem. BACCHANTE). A priest or priestess of the wine god, Bacchus (in Greek mythology, Dionysus), or one of his ecstatic female followers, who were sometimes called maenads (colorplate 80, fig. 303).

BALUSTRADE. 1) A railing supported by short pillars called balusters (fig. 620). 2) Occasionally applied to any low parapet (figs. 189, 362).

BAPTISTERY. A building or a part of a church, often round or octagonal, in which the sacrament of baptism is administered (fig. 403). It contains a baptismal font, a receptacle of stone or metal which holds the water for the rite (fig. 412).

BARREL VAULT. See VAULT.

BASE. 1) The lowermost portion of a COLUMN or PIER, beneath the SHAFT (figs. 159, 174). 2) The lowest element of a wall, DOME, or building, or occasionally of a statue or painting (see PREDELLA).

BASILICA. 1) In ancient Roman architecture, a large, oblong building used as a hall of justice and public meeting place, generally having a NAVE, SIDE AISLES, and one or more APSES (fig. 246). 2) In Christian architecture, a longitudinal church derived from the Roman basilica, and having a nave, apse, two or four side aisles or side chapels, and sometimes a NARTHEX. 3) One of the seven main churches of Rome (St. Peter's, St. Paul Outside the Walls, St. John Lateran, etc.), or another church accorded the same religious privileges.

BATTLEMENT. A parapet consisting of alternating solid parts and open spaces designed originally for defense and later used for decoration (fig. 454).

BAY. A subdivision of the interior space of a building, usually in a series bounded by consecutive architectural supports.

BENEDICTINE ORDER. Founded at Subiaco near Rome in 529 A.D. by St. Benedict of Nursia (c. 480–c. 543). Less austere than other early ORDERS, it spread throughout much of western Europe and England in the next two centuries.

BISHOP. The spiritual overseer of a number of churches or a diocese. His throne or cathedra, placed in the principal church of the diocese, designates it as a cathedral.

BLIND ARCADE. See ARCADE.

BLOCKBOOKS. Books, often religious, of the 15th century, containing WOODCUT prints in which picture and text were usually cut into the same block (compare fig. 533).

BOOK. A written work of some length on consecutive sheets of PAPER, PARCHMENT, etc., fastened or bound together in a volume. See CODEX.

BOOK COVER. The stiff outer covers protecting the bound pages of a BOOK. In the medieval period, frequently covered with precious metal and elaborately embellished with jewels, embossed decoration, etc. (colorplate 41).

BOOK OF HOURS. A private prayer book containing the devotions for the seven canonical hours of the Roman Catholic church (matins, vespers, etc.), liturgies for local saints, and sometimes a calendar (colorplate 58). They were often elaborately ILLUMINATED for persons of high rank, whose names are attached to certain extant examples (fig. 500).

BRACKET. A stone, wooden, or metal support projecting from a wall and having a flat top to bear the weight of a statue, CORNICE, beam, etc. (fig. 410). The lower part may take the form of a SCROLL: it is then called a scroll bracket (fig. 620).

BROKEN PEDIMENT. See PEDIMENT.

BRONZE. An alloy of copper and tin, used since early times for sculpture. See BRONZE AGE, CIRE PERDU.

BRONZE AGE. The earliest period in which BRONZE was used for tools and weapons. In the Middle East, the Bronze Age succeeded the NEOLITHIC period in c. 3500 B.C., and preceded the Iron Age, which commenced c. 1900 B.C.

BRUSH DRAWING. See DRAWING.

BURIN. See ENGRAVING.

BUTTRESS. 1) A projecting support built against an external wall, usually to counteract the lateral THRUST of a VAULT or ARCH within (fig. 425). 2) FLYING BUTTRESS. An arched bridge above the aisle roof that extends from the upper nave wall, where the lateral thrust of the main vault is greatest, down to a solid pier (fig. 427).

BYZANTIUM. City on the Sea of Marmara, founded by the ancient Greeks and renamed Constantinople in 330 A.D. Today called Istanbul.

CAESAR. The surname of the Roman dictator, Caius Julius Caesar, subsequently used as the title of an emperor; hence the German *Kaiser*, and the Russian *czar (tsar)*.

CALIPH. A Moslem ruler; the first *caliph* succeeded MOHAMMED and claimed political and religious authority by his descent from the Prophet. Subsequently three caliphates were recognized: Omayyids, Abbasids, and Fatimids.

CALLIGRAPHY. From the Greek word for beautiful writing. 1) Decorative or formal handwriting executed with a quill or reed pen, or with a brush (colorplates 28, 39; figs. 299, 351). 2) A design derived from or resembling letters, and used to form a pattern (colorplates 37, 38).

CALVARY. The hill originally outside Jerusalem where Christ was crucified, the name being taken from the Latin word *calvaris*, meaning skull (Golgotha is the Greek transliteration of skull in Aramaic). The hill was thought to be the spot where Adam was buried, and was thus traditionally known as "the place of the skull."

CAMERA OBSCURA. Latin for dark room. A darkened enclosure or box with a small opening or lens on one wall through which light enters to form an inverted image on the opposite wall. The principle had long been known, but was not used as an aid in picture making until the 16th century.

CAMPAGNA. Italian word for countryside. When capitalized, it usually refers to the countryside near Rome.

CAMPANILE. From the Italian word *campana* meaning bell. A bell tower, either round or square in plan, and sometimes freestanding (figs. 291, 395).

CAMPOSANTO. Italian word for holy field. A cemetery near a church, and often enclosed.

CANOPY. In architecture, an ornamental, roof-like projection or cover above a statue or sacred object (figs. 458, 701).

CAPITAL. The uppermost member of a COLUMN or PILLAR supporting the ARCHITRAVE (figs. 159, 173).

CARDINAL. In the Roman Catholic church, a member of the Sacred College, the ecclesiastical body which elects the Pope and constitutes his advisory council.

CARMELITE ORDER. Originally a 12th-century hermitage claimed to descend from a community of hermits established by the Prophet Elijah on Mt. Carmel, Palestine. In the early 13th century it spread to Europe and England, where it was reformed by St. Simon Stock and became one of the three great mendicant orders (see FRANCISCAN, DOMINICAN).

CARTHUSIAN ORDER. See CHARTREUSE.

CARTOON. From the Italian word *cartone*, meaning cardboard. 1) A full-scale DRAWING for a picture or design intended to be transferred to a wall, panel, tapestry, etc. (fig. 602). 2) A drawing, usually humorous or satirical, calling attention to some action or person of popular interest (fig. 843).

CARVING. 1) The cutting of a figure or design out of a solid material such as stone or wood, as contrasted to the additive technique of MODELING. 2) A work executed in this technique (figs. 613, 614).

CARYATID. A sculptured female figure used as an architectural support (figs. 154, 174). A similar male figure is an atlas (pl. atlantes).

CASTING. A method of duplicating a work of sculpture by pouring a hardening substance such as plaster or molten metal into a mold. See CIRE-PERDU.

CAST IRON. A hard, brittle iron produced commercially in blast furnaces by pouring it into molds where it cools and hardens. Extensively used as a building material in the early 19th century (figs. 811, 1018), it was superseded by STEEL and FERROCONCRETE.

CATACOMBS. The underground burial places of the early Christians, consisting of passages with niches for tombs, and small chapels for commemorative services.

CATHEDRA, CATHEDRAL. See BISHOP.

CELLA. 1) The principal enclosed room of a temple, to house an image (fig. 160). Also called the naos. 2) The entire body of a temple as distinct from its external parts.

CENTERING. A wooden framework built to support an ARCH, VAULT, or DOME during its construction.

CENTRAL-PLAN CHURCH. 1) A church having four arms of equal length (fig. 579). The CROSSING is often covered with a DOME. Also called a Greek-cross church. 2) A church having a circular or polygonal plan.

CHALK. Calcium carbonate, either natural or artificially prepared, finely ground to make a white substance used in GESSO. It may be pressed in sticks and used in its white form, or mixed with colored pigments to make PASTELS.

CHANCEL. See CHOIR.

CHAPEL. 1) A private or subordinate place of worship (figs. 553–56). 2) A place of worship that is part of a church, but separately dedicated (fig. 615).

CHARTREUSE. French word for a Carthusian monastery (in Italian, *Certosa*). The Carthusian ORDER was founded by St. Bruno (c. 1030–1101) at Chartreuse near Grenoble in 1084. It is an eremetic order, the life of the monks being one of silence, prayer, and austerity.

CHASING. 1) A technique of ornamenting a metal surface by the use of various tools. 2) The procedure used to finish a raw bronze cast.

CHÂTEAU (pl. CHÂTEAUX). French word for castle, now used to designate a large country house as well (fig. 686).

CHEVET. In Gothic architecture, the term for the developed and unified east end of a church, including choir, apse, ambulatory, and radiating chapels (fig. 431).

CHIAROSCURO. Italian word for light and dark. In painting, a method of modeling form primarily by the use of light and shade (fig. 599, colorplates 80, 94).

CHOIR. In church architecture, a square or rectangular area between the APSE and the NAVE or TRANSEPT. It is reserved for the clergy and the singing choir, and is usually marked off by steps, a railing, or a CHOIR SCREEN. Also called the chancel. See PILGRIMAGE CHOIR.

CHOIR SCREEN. A screen, frequently ornamented with sculpture, separating the CHOIR of a church from the NAVE or TRANSEPT (figs. 323, 465). In Orthodox Christian churches it is decorated with ICONS, and thus called an iconostasis (fig. 320).

CIRE-PERDU PROCESS. The lost-wax process of CASTING. A method in which an original is MODELED in wax or coated with wax, then covered with clay. When the wax is melted out, the resulting mold is filled with molten metal (often BRONZE) or liquid plaster.

CISTERCIAN ORDER. Founded at Cîteaux in France in 1098 by Robert of Molesme with the objective of reforming the BENEDICTINE ORDER, and reasserting its original ideals of a life of severe simplicity.

CITY-STATE. An autonomous political unit comprising a city and the surrounding countryside.

CLERESTORY. A row of windows in the upper part of a wall that rises above an adjoining roof; built to provide direct lighting, as in a BASILICA or church (colorplate 47).

CLOISTER. 1) A place of religious seclusion such as a monastery or nunnery. 2) An open court attached to a church or monastery and surrounded by a covered ARCADED walk or AMBULATORY, as in Salisbury Cathedral. Used for study, meditation, and exercise.

CODEX (pl. CODICES). A manuscript in BOOK form made possible by the use of PARCHMENT instead of PAPYRUS. During the 1st to 4th centuries A.D., it gradually replaced the ROLL or SCROLL previously used for written documents.

COFFER. 1) A small chest or casket. 2) A recessed, geometrically shaped panel in a ceiling. A ceiling decorated with these panels is said to be coffered (figs. 239, 709, 805).

COLLAGE. A composition made of cut and pasted scraps of materials, sometimes with lines or forms added by the artist (figs. 944, 962).

COLONNADE. A series of regularly spaced COLUMNS supporting a LINTEL or ENTABLATURE (figs. 76, 700).

COLOSSAL ORDER. COLUMNS, PIERS, or PILASTERS which extend through two or more stories (figs. 573, 624).

COLUMN. An approximately cylindrical, upright architectural support, usually consisting of a long, relatively slender SHAFT, a BASE, and a CAPITAL (figs. 159, 161). When imbedded in a wall, it is called an engaged column (fig. 175). Columns decorated with spiral RELIEFS were used occasionally as free-standing commemorative monuments (fig. 265).

COMPOUND PIER. See PIER.

CONCRETE. A mixture of sand or gravel with mortar and rubble, invented in the ancient Near East and further developed by the Romans (figs. 235, 236). Largely ignored during the Middle Ages, it was revived by Bramante in the early 16th century for St. Peter's (fig. 610). Reinforced concrete: see FERROCONCRETE.

CONFRATERNITY. See SCUOLA.

CONTRAPPOSTO. Italian word for set against. A method developed by the Greeks to represent freedom of movement in a figure. The parts of the body are placed asymmetrically in opposition to each other around a central axis, and careful attention is paid to the distribution of the weight (figs. 178, 179).

CORINTHIAN ORDER. See ORDER, ARCHITECTURAL.

CORNICE. 1) The projecting, framing members of a classical PEDIMENT, including the horizontal one beneath and the two sloping or "raking" ones above (figs. 159, 161). 2) Any projecting, horizontal element surmounting a wall or other structure, or dividing it horizontally for decorative purposes (fig. 559).

COUNTER REFORMATION. The movement of self-renewal and reform within the Roman Catholic church following the Protestant REFORMATION of the early 16th century, and attempting to combat its influence. Also known as the Catholic Reform. Its principles were formulated and adopted at the Council of Trent, 1545–63.

CRENELATED. See BATTLEMENT.

CROMLECH. From the Welsh for concave stone. A circle of large upright stones, or DOLMENS, probably the setting for religious ceremonies in prehistoric England (figs. 33, 34).

CROSSHATCHING. See HATCHING.

CROSSING. The area in a church where the TRANSEPT crosses the NAVE, frequently emphasized by a DOME (fig. 400), or crossing tower (fig. 383).

CROSS SECTION. See SECTION.

CRYPT. In a church, a VAULTED space beneath the CHOIR, causing the floor of the choir to be raised above the level of that of the NAVE (fig. 379).

CUNEIFORM. Describes the wedge-shaped characters written on clay by the ancient Mesopotamians.

CYCLOPEAN. An adjective describing masonry with large, unhewn stones, thought by the Greeks to have been built by the Cyclopes, a legendary race of one-eyed giants (fig. 131).

DAGUERREOTYPE. Originally, a photograph on a silver-plated sheet of copper which had been treated with fumes of iodine to form silver iodide on its surface and, after exposure, was developed by fumes of mercury. The process, invented by L. J. M. Daguerre and made public in 1839 (fig. 857), was modified and accelerated as daguerreotypes gained worldwide popularity.

DEËSIS. From the Greek word for entreaty. The representation of Christ enthroned between the Virgin Mary and St. John the Baptist, frequent in Byzantine MOSAICS (colorplate 30) and depictions of the Last Judgment (colorplate 61); refers to the roles of the Virgin Mary and St. John as intercessors for mankind.

DIORITE. An igneous rock, extremely hard and usually black or dark gray in color (fig. 97).

DIPTYCH. 1) Originally a hinged two-leaved tablet used for writing. 2) A pair of ivory CARVINGS or PANEL paintings, usually hinged together (fig. 303).

DIPYLON VASE. A Greek funerary vase with holes in the bottom through which libations were poured to the dead (fig. 135). Named for the cemetery near Athens where the vases were found.

DOLMEN. A structure formed by two or more large, upright stones capped by a horizontal slab; thought to be a prehistoric tomb (fig. 32).

DOME. 1) A true dome is a VAULTED roof of circular, polygonal, or elliptical plan, formed with hemispherical or ovoidal curvature (figs. 606, 709). May be supported by a circular wall or DRUM (fig. 324), and by PENDENTIVES (fig. 309) or related constructions. Domical coverings of many other sorts have been devised (figs. 449, 556, 715).

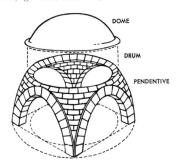

DOMINICAN ORDER. Founded as a mendicant ORDER by St. Dominic in Toulouse about 1206–16.

DOMUS. Latin word for house. A Roman detached, one-family house with rooms grouped around one, or frequently two, open courts. The first, the ATRIUM, was used for entertaining and conducting business; the second, usually with a garden and surrounded by a PERISTYLE or COLONNADE, was for the private family (fig. 247).

DONJON. See KEEP.

DONOR. The patron or client at whose order a work of art was executed; the donor may be depicted in the work (figs. 509, 525).

DORIC ORDER. See ORDER, ARCHITECTURAL.

DRAWING. 1) A work in pencil, pen and ink, charcoal, etc., often on paper (fig. 905). 2) A similar work in ink or WASH, etc., made with a brush and often called a brush drawing (fig. 760). 3) A work combining these or other techniques.

A drawing may be large or small, a quick sketch or an elaborate work. Among its various forms are: a record of something seen (figs.

602, 640); a study for all or part of another work (figs. 590, 832; see also OIL SKETCH; SINOPIA); an illustration associated with a text (figs. 482, 604); a technical aid.

DRÔLERIES. French word for jests. Used to describe the lively animals and small figures in the margins of late medieval manuscripts (fig. 500), and occasionally in wood CARVINGS on furniture.

DRUM. 1) A section of the SHAFT of a COLUMN (figs. 169, 245). 2) A wall supporting a DOME (figs. 322, 625).

DRYPOINT. See ENGRAVING.

ECHINUS. In the Doric or Tuscan ORDER, the round, cushion-like element between the top of the SHAFT and the ABACUS (figs. 159, 162).

ELDERS, TWENTY-FOUR. The twenty-four elders frequently represented on the PORTALS of Romanesque and Gothic churches (fig. 456) are those described by St. John the Evangelist in his vision of heaven, clad in white and seated around the throne of God (Rev. 4:4, 10).

ELEVATION. 1) An architectural drawing presenting a building as if projected on a vertical plane parallel to one of its sides. 2) Term used in describing the vertical plane of a building.

ENAMEL. 1) Colored glassy substances, either opaque or translucent, applied in powder form to a metal surface and fused to it by firing. Two main techniques developed: "champlevé" (from the French for raised field), in which the areas to be treated are dug out of the metal surface; and "cloisonné" (from the French for partitioned), in which compartments or "cloisons" to be filled are made on the surface with thin metal strips. 2) A work executed in either technique (figs. 357, 420).

ENCAUSTIC. A technique of painting with PIGMENTS dissolved in hot wax (colorplate 25).

ENGAGED COLUMN. See COLUMN.

ENGRAVING. 1) A means of embellishing metal surfaces or gem stones by incising a design on the surface. 2) A PRINT made by cutting a design into a metal plate (usually copper) with a pointed steel tool known as a burin. The burr raised on either side of the incised line is removed; ink is then rubbed into the V-shaped grooves and wiped off the surface; the plate, covered with a damp sheet of paper, is run through a heavy press (fig. 534). The image on the paper is the reverse of that on the plate (figs. 786, 787). When a fine steel needle is used instead of a burin and the burr is retained, a drypoint engraving results, characterized by a softer line (fig. 535). 3) These techniques are called respectively engraving and drypoint.

ENTABLATURE. 1) In a classical order, the entire structure above the COLUMNS; this usually includes ARCHITRAVE, FRIEZE, and CORNICE (figs. 159, 161). 2) The same structure in any building of a classical style (fig. 794).

ENTASIS. A swelling of the SHAFT of a COLUMN (figs. 162, 166).

ETCHING. 1) A PRINT made by coating a copper plate with an acid-resistant resin and drawing through this ground, exposing the metal with a sharp instrument called a STYLUS. The plate is bathed in acid, which eats into the lines; it is then heated to remove the resin, and

finally inked and printed on paper (fig. 742). 2) The technique itself is also called etching.

EUCHARIST. 1) The sacrament of Holy Communion, the celebration in commemoration of the Last Supper. 2) The consecrated bread and wine used in the ceremony.

EVANGELISTS. Matthew, Mark, Luke, and John, traditionally thought to be the authors of the GOSPELS, the first four books of the New Testament, which recount the life and death of Christ. They are usually shown with their symbols, which are probably derived from the four beasts surrounding the throne of the Lamb in the Book of Revelation (4:7) or from those in the vision of Ezekiel (1:4-14): a winged man or angel for Matthew (fig. 651), a winged lion for Mark (fig. 372), a winged ox for Luke (colorplate 42), and an eagle for John (colorplate 45). These symbols may also represent the Evangelists (colorplate 27, fig. 362).

FAÇADE. The principal face or the front of a building.

FALISCAN WARE. Pottery made in the Etruscan city of Falerii (the present Città Castellana), its inhabitants known as the Falisci (fig. 192).

FATHERS OF THE CHURCH. Early teachers and defenders of the Christian faith. Those most frequently represented are the four Latin fathers: St. Jerome, St. Ambrose, and St. Augustine, all of the 4th century, and St. Gregory of the 6th.

FERROCONCRETE. Reinforced CONCRETE, strengthened by STEEL rods and mesh placed it before hardening. Introduced in France c. 1900, and widely used today (colorplate 174, figs. 1037, 1040, 1047).

FIBULA. A clasp, buckle, or brooch, often ornamented.

FINIAL. A relatively small, decorative element terminating a GABLE, PINNACLE, or the like (fig. 685).

FLUTING. In architecture, the ornamental grooves channeled vertically into the SHAFT of a COLUMN or PILASTER (fig. 169). They may meet in a sharp edge as in the Doric ORDER, or be separated by a narrow strip or fillet, as in the Ionic, Corinthian, and Composite orders.

FLYING BUTTRESS. See BUTTRESS.

FONT. See BAPTISTERY.

FORESHORTENING. A method of reducing or distorting the parts of a represented object which are not parallel to the PICTURE PLANE, in order to convey the impression of three dimensions as perceived by the human eye (colorplate 105, fig. 831).

FORUM (pl. FORA). In an ancient Roman city, the main, public square which was the center of judicial and business activity, and a public gathering place (fig. 233).

FRANCISCAN ORDER. Founded as a mendicant ORDER by St. Francis of Assisi (Giovanni di Bernardone, 1181/82–1226). The monks' aim was to imitate the life of Christ in its poverty and humility, to preach, and to minister to the spiritual needs of the poor.

FRESCO. Italian word for fresh. 1) True fresco is the technique of painting on moist plaster with PIGMENTS ground in water so that the paint is absorbed by the plaster and becomes part of the wall itself (colorplate 53). Fresco secco is the technique of painting with the same colors on dry plaster. 2) A painting done in either of these techniques.

FRIEZE. 1) A continuous band of painted or sculptured decoration (figs. 154, 259). 2) In a classical building, the part of the ENTABLATURE between the ARCHITRAVE and the CORNICE. A Doric frieze consists of alternating TRIGLYPHS and METOPES, the latter often sculptured (fig. 166). An Ionic frieze is usually decorated with continuous RELIEF sculpture (fig. 159).

FROTTAGE. See RUBBING.

GABLE. 1) The triangular area framed by the CORNICE or eaves of a building and the sloping sides of a pitched roof (fig. 376). In classical architecture, it is called a PEDIMENT. 2) A decorative element of similar shape, such as the triangular structures above the PORTALS of a Gothic church (fig. 433), and sometimes at the top of a Gothic picture frame.

GALLERY. A second story placed over the SIDE AISLES of a church and below the CLERESTORY (fig. 425), or, in a church with a four-part ELEVATION, below the TRIFORIUM and above the NAVE ARCADE which supports it on its open side.

GENIUS (pl. GENII). A winged semi-nude figure, often purely decorative (fig. 582) but frequently representing the guardian spirit of a person or place, or personifying an abstract concept (fig. 852).

GENRE. French word for kind or sort. A work of art, usually a painting, showing a scene from everyday life that is represented for its own sake (colorplate 108).

GESSO. A smooth mixture of ground CHALK or plaster and glue, used as the basis for TEMPERA PAINTING and for OIL PAINTING on PANEL.

GILDING. 1) A coat of gold or of a gold-colored substance that is applied mechanically or chemically to surfaces of a painting, sculpture, or architectural decoration (colorplates 59, 66, 97). 2) The process of applying same.

GISANT. From the French verb gésir, meaning to lie helpless or dead. A recumbent statue on a tomb (fig. 692).

GLAZE. 1) A thin layer of translucent oil color applied to a painted surface or to parts of it in order to modify the tone. 2) A glassy coating applied to a piece of ceramic work before firing in the kiln, as a protective seal and often as decoration.

GLORIOLE or GLORY. The circle of radiant light around the head or figures of God, Christ,

the Virgin Mary, or a saint. When it surrounds the head only, it is called a halo or nimbus (colorplate 56); when it surrounds the entire figure with a large oval (figs. 328, 456), it is called a mandorla (the Italian word for almond). It indicates divinity or holiness, though originally it was placed around the heads of kings and gods as a mark of distinction.

GOLD LEAF, SILVER LEAF. 1) Gold beaten into very thin sheets or "leaves," and applied to ILLUMINATED MANUSCRIPTS and PANEL paintings (colorplates 45, 56, 59), to sculpture (colorplate 66), or to the back of the glass TESSERAE used in MOSAICS (colorplates 27, 29). 2) Silver leaf is also used, though ultimately it tarnishes (colorplate 28). Sometimes called gold foil, silver foil.

GOLGOTHA. See CALVARY.

GORGON. In Greek mythology, one of three hideous, female monsters with large heads, and snakes for hair (fig. 152). Their glance turned men to stone. Medusa, the most famous of the Gorgons, was killed by Perseus only with help from the gods.

GOSPEL. 1) The first four books of the New Testament. They tell the story of Christ's life and death, and are ascribed to the EVANGELISTS Matthew, Mark, Luke, and John. 2) A copy of these, usually called a Gospel Book, often richly ILLUMINATED (figs. 370, 372).

GREEK-CROSS CHURCH. See CENTRAL-PLAN CHURCH.

GROIN VAULT. See VAULT.

GROUND PLAN. An architectural drawing presenting a building as if cut horizontally at the floor level.

GUTTAE. In a Doric ENTABLATURE, small peglike projections above the FRIEZE; possibly derived from pegs originally used in wooden construction (figs. 159, 161).

HALL CHURCH, HALL CHOIR. See HALLENKIRCHE.

HALLENKIRCHE. German word for hall church. A church in which the NAVE and the SIDE AISLES are of the same height. The type was developed in Romanesque architecture, and occurs especially frequently in German Gothic churches (figs. 388, 444).

HALO. See GLORIOLE.

HATCHING. A series of parallel lines used as shading in PRINTS and DRAWINGS (fig. 590). When two sets of crossing parallel lines are used, it is called crosshatching (fig. 674).

HIEROGLYPH. A picture of a figure, animal, or object, standing for a word, syllable, or sound. These symbols are found on ancient Egyptian monuments as well as in their written records (fig. 73).

HIGH RELIEF. See RELIEF.

HÔTEL. French word for hotel, but used also to designate an elegant town house (fig. 774).

ICON. From the Greek word for image. A PANEL painting of one or more sacred personages such as Christ, the Virgin, a saint, etc., particularly venerated in the ORTHODOX Catholic church (colorplate 34).

ICONOSTASIS. See CHOIR SCREEN.

ILLUMINATED MANUSCRIPT. A MANUSCRIPT decorated with drawings (fig. 373) or with paintings in TEMPERA colors (colorplates 42, 45).

ILLUSIONISM. In artistic terms, the technique of manipulating pictorial or other means in order to cause the eye to perceive a particular reality. May be used in architecture (fig. 715) and sculpture (figs. 703, 704), as well as in painting (colorplates 23, 96; figs. 278, 706).

IMPASTO. From the Italian word meaning "in paste." Paint, usually OIL PAINT, applied very thickly (colorplates 104, 124).

IN ANTIS. See ANTA.

INQUISITION. A religious tribunal of the Catholic church for the suppression of heresy, first administered by the DOMINICAN ORDER in the 13th century. In the 16th century the Spanish Inquisition was particularly active, and was controlled independently by the Spanish kings.

INSULA (pl. INSULAE). Latin word for island. 1) An ancient Roman city block. 2) A Roman "apartment house": a CONCRETE and brick building or chain of buildings around a central court, up to five stories high. The ground floor contained shops, and above were living quarters (fig. 248).

IONIC ORDER. See ORDER, ARCHITECTURAL.

ISLAM. The religion of the MOSLEMS, based on the submission of the faithful to the will of ALLAH as this was revealed to the Prophet MOHAMMED and recorded in the KORAN. The adjectival form is Islamic.

JAMBS. The vertical sides of an opening. In Romanesque and Gothic churches, the jambs of doors and windows are often cut on a slant outward, or "splayed," thus providing a broader surface for sculptural decoration (figs. 456, 457).

JESUIT ORDER. The "Society of Jesus" was founded in 1540 by Ignatius Loyola (1491–1556), and especially devoted to the service of the pope. The order was a powerful influence in the struggle of the Catholic COUNTER REFORMATION with the Protestant REFORMATION, and also very important for its missionary work, disseminating Christianity in the Far East and the New World. The mother church in Rome, Il Gesù (figs. 664–66), conforms in design to the preaching aims of the new order.

KAABA. An ancient Arabic SANCTUARY in the Great Mosque at Mecca which became the most sacred shrine of the MOSLEMS. The small building in the mosque contains a stone which is said to have been turned black either by the tears of pilgrims, or by the sins of those who have touched it.

KEEP. 1) The innermost and strongest structure or central tower of a medieval castle, sometimes used as living quarters, as well as for defense. Also called a donjon (colorplate 58). 2) A fortified medieval castle.

KEYSTONE. See ARCH.

KORAN. The scriptures of the MOSLEMS, revealed by ALLAH to MOHAMMED at Mecca and Medina, and transcribed by the Prophet himself, or by one of his associates. The text was established 651–52 A.D.

KORE (pl. KORAI). Greek word for maiden. An archaic Greek statue of a clothed, standing female (fig. 150).

KOUROS (pl. KOUROI). Greek word for male youth. An archaic Greek statue of a standing, nude youth (fig. 146).

KYLIX. In Greek and Roman antiquity, a shallow drinking cup with two horizontal handles, often set on a stem terminating in a foot (fig. 140).

LABORS OF THE MONTHS. The various occupations suitable to the months of the year. Scenes or figures illustrating these were frequently represented in ILLUMINATED manuscripts (colorplate 58, fig. 504); sometimes with the symbols of the ZODIAC signs, CARVED around the PORTALS of Romanesque and Gothic churches (figs. 456, 463).

LANTERN. A relatively small structure crowning a DOME, roof, or tower, frequently open to admit light to an enclosed area below (figs. 322, 625).

LAPIS LAZULI. From the Latin for stone of blue. A deep-blue stone used first for ornamental purposes (colorplate 9), or, after the 12th century, for preparing the blue PIGMENT known as ultramarine.

LAPITH. A member of a mythical Greek tribe that defeated the centaurs in a battle, scenes from which are frequently represented in vase painting and sculpture (colorplate 14, fig. 182).

LAY BROTHER. One who has joined a monastic ORDER but has not taken monastic vows, and therefore belongs still to the people or laity, as distinguished from the clergy or religious.

LEKYTHOS (pl. LEKYTHOI). A Greek oil jug with an ellipsoidal body, a narrow neck, a flanged mouth, a curved handle extending from below the lip to the shoulder, and a narrow base terminating in a foot. It was used chiefly for ointments and funerary offerings (colorplate 16).

LIBERAL ARTS. Traditionally thought to go back to Plato, they comprised the intellectual disciplines considered suitable or necessary to a complete education, and included Grammar, Rhetoric, Logic, Arithmetic, Music, Geometry, and Astronomy. During the Middle Ages and the Renaissance, they were often represented allegorically in painting, engravings, and sculpture (fig. 456).

LINTEL. See POST AND LINTEL.

LITHOGRAPH. A PRINT made by drawing a design with an oily crayon or other greasy substance on a porous stone or, later, a metal plate; the design is then fixed, the entire surface is moistened, and the printing ink which is applied adheres only to the oily lines of the drawing. The design can then be transferred easily in a press to a piece of paper. The technique was invented c. 1796 by Aloys Senefelder, and quickly became popular (figs. 843, 906). It is also widely used commercially, since many impressions can be taken from a single plate.

LOGGIA. A covered GALLERY or ARCADE open to the air on at least one side. It may stand alone or be part of a building (colorplate 84, fig. 658).

LONGITUDINAL SECTION. See SECTION.

LOUVERS. One slat or a series of overlapping boards or slats which can be opened to admit air, but are slanted so as to exclude sun and rain (fig. 1044).

LOW RELIEF. See RELIEF.

LUNETTE. 1) A semicircular or pointed wall area, as under a VAULT (fig. 554) or above a door or window. When it is above the PORTAL of a medieval church, it is called a TYMPANUM (fig. 408). 2) A painting (fig. 699), relief sculpture (fig. 581), or window of the same shape (fig. 792).

MADRASAH. Arabic for place of study. A combination of a Mohammedan mosque and theological school, with living quarters for students (fig. 343).

MAESTÀ. Italian word for majesty, applied in the 14th and 15th centuries to representations of the Madonna and Child enthroned, and surrounded by her celestial court of saints and angels (fig. 487).

MAGDALENIAN. An adjective used for describing artifacts of the latest culture of the Upper PALEOLITHIC; the word comes from La Madeleine (Dordogne), a site in southwestern France where such work was found.

MAGNA. Paint in the form of PIGMENT ground in an ACRYLIC resin with solvents and plasticizer (fig. 984, colorplate 158).

MAGUS (pl. MAGI). A member of the priestly caste of ancient Media and Persia. In Christian literature (Matt. 2:1–12), one of the three Wise Men or Kings who came from the East bearing gifts to the newborn Jesus (fig. 507, colorplate 59).

MANDORLA. See GLORIOLE.

MANUSCRIPT. From the Latin word for handwritten. 1) A document, scroll, or book written by hand, as distinguished from such a work in print (i.e., after c. 1450). 2) A book produced in the Middle Ages, frequently ILLUMINATED.

MASTABA. An ancient Egyptian tomb, rectangular in shape, with sloping sides and a flat roof. It covered a chapel for offerings and a shaft to the burial chamber (fig. 56).

MAUSOLEUM. 1) The huge tomb erected at Halicarnassus in Asia Minor in the 4th century B.C. by King Mausolus and his wife Artemisia (fig. 193). 2) A generic term for any large funerary monument.

MEANDER. From the name Maeander (modern Menderes), a winding river in western Turkey that flows into the Aegean Sea. A decorative motif of intricate, rectilinear character, applied to architecture and sculpture (figs. 261, 410).

MEDIUM (pl. MEDIUMS). 1) The material or technique in which an artist works. 2) The vehicle in which PIGMENTS are carried in PAINT, PASTEL, etc.

MEGALITH. A huge stone such as those used in CROMLECHS and DOLMENS.

MEGARON (pl. MEGARONS, or MEGARA). From the Greek word for large. The central audience hall in a Minoan or Mycenaean palace or home (fig. 118).

MESOLITHIC. Transitional period of the Stone Age, between the PALEOLITHIC and the NEOLITHIC.

METOPE. In a Doric FRIEZE, one of the panels, either decorated or plain, between the TRIGLYPHS. Originally it probably covered the empty spaces between the ends of the wooden ceiling beams (figs. 159–66).

MIHRAB. The small niche which marks the QIBLA wall of a mosque showing the direction of Mecca.

MINARET. A tall, slender tower with balconies from which Moslems are summoned to prayer by the chant of the MUEZZIN (fig. 346).

MINIATURE. 1) A single illustration in an ILLUMINATED manuscript (colorplates 36–39). 2) A very small painting, especially a portrait on ivory, glass, or metal (figs. 285, 526).

MINOTAUR. In Greek mythology, a monster having the head of a bull and the body of a man, who lived in the Labyrinth of the palace of Knossos on Crete.

MODEL. 1) The preliminary form of a sculpture, often finished in itself but preceding the final CASTING or CARVING (figs. 769, 771, 858). 2) Preliminary or reconstructed form of a building, made to scale (figs. 231, 369). 3) A person who poses for an artist.

MODELING. 1) In sculpture, the building up of a figure or design in a soft substance such as clay or wax (fig. 775). 2) In painting and drawing, producing a three-dimensional effect by changes in color, the use of light and shade, etc.

MOHAMMED (also Muhammad). Arab prophet and the founder of ISLAM (c. 570–632). His first revelations were c. 610 and continued throughout his lifetime; collected and recorded, these form the basis of the KORAN. Mohammed was forced to flee from Mecca, his birthplace, to Medina in 622; the date of this "Hegira" marks the beginning of the Islamic calendar.

MOLDING. In architecture, any of various long, narrow, ornamental bands having a distinctive profile, which project from the surface of the structure and give variety to the surface by means of their patterned contrasts of light and shade (figs. 154, 262).

MOSAIC. Decorative work for walls, VAULTS, ceilings, or floors, composed of small pieces of colored materials (called TESSERAE) set in plaster or CONCRETE. The Romans, whose work was mostly for floors, used regularly shaped pieces of marble in its natural colors (colorplate 21). The early Christians used pieces of glass whose brilliant hues, including gold, and slightly irregular surfaces produced an entirely different, glittering effect (colorplates 27, 29). See also GOLD LEAF.

MOSLEM (also Muslim). 1) One who has embraced ISLAM: a follower of MOHAMMED. 2) An adjective for the religion, law, or civilization of Islam.

MOUNDS. Enormous piles of earth erected by the Indians of the central United States, the so-called Mound Builders, as a grave and/or BASE for a temple or other structure. Sometimes in the form of an animal (fig. 35).

MUEZZIN. In Mohammedan countries, a crier who calls the faithful to prayer from a MINARET or high part of a building.

MURAL. From the Latin word for wall, *murus*. A large painting or decoration, either executed directly on a wall (FRESCO) or done separately and affixed to it.

MUSES. In Greek mythology, the nine goddesses who presided over various arts and sciences. They are led by Apollo as god of music and poetry, and usually include Calliope, Muse of Epic Poetry; Clio, Muse of History; Erato, Muse of Love Poetry; Euterpe, Muse of Music; Melpomene, Muse of Tragedy; Polyhymnia, Muse of Sacred Music; Terpsichore, Muse of Dancing; Thalia, Muse of Comedy; and Urania, Muse of Astronomy.

NAOS. See CELLA.

NARTHEX. The transverse entrance hall of a church, sometimes enclosed but often open on one side to a preceding ATRIUM (fig. 289).

NAVE. 1) The central aisle of a Roman BASILICA, as distinguished from the SIDE AISLES (fig. 246). 2) The same section of a Christian basilican church extending from the entrance to the APSE or TRANSEPT (fig. 289).

NEOLITHIC. The New Stone Age, thought to have begun c. 9000–8000 B.C. The first society to live in settled communities, to domesticate animals, and to cultivate crops, it saw the beginning of many new skills such as spinning, weaving, and building (fig. 23).

NEW STONE AGE. See NEOLITHIC.

NIKE. The ancient Greek goddess of victory, often identified with Athena, and by the Romans with Victoria. She is usually represented as a winged woman with windblown draperies (figs. 139, 189, 206).

NIMBUS. See GLORIOLE.

OBELISK. A tall, tapering, four-sided stone shaft with a pyramidal top. First constructed as MEGALITHS in ancient Egypt (fig. 76); certain examples since exported to other countries (figs. 700, 712).

ODALISQUE. Turkish word for a harem slave girl or concubine (colorplate 113, fig. 841).

OIL. In art, the MEDIUM for pigments used in OIL PAINTING. Among numerous vegetable oils, the traditional favorite is refined linseed oil, which dries to a tough, solid film.

OIL PAINTING. 1) A painting executed with PIGMENTS mixed with OIL, first applied either to a panel prepared with a coat of GESSO (as also in TEMPERA PAINTING), later to a stretched canvas primed with a coat of white paint and glue. The latter method has been usual since the late 15th century. Oil painting also may be executed on paper, parchment, copper, etc. 2) The technique of executing such a painting.

OIL SKETCH. A work in oil painting of an informal character, sometimes preparatory to a finished work (figs. 726, 820, 841).

OLD STONE AGE. See PALEOLITHIC.

ORCHESTRA. 1) In an ancient Greek theater, the round space in front of the stage and below the tiers of seats, reserved for the chorus (fig. 176). 2) In a Roman theater, a similar space usually reserved for important guests.

ORDER, ARCHITECTURAL. An architectural system based on the COLUMN and its ENTABLATURE, in which the form of the elements themselves (CAPITAL, SHAFT, BASE, etc.) and their relationships to each other are specifically defined. The five classical orders are the Doric, Ionic, Corinthian, Tuscan, and Composite (fig. 159). See also COLOSSAL ORDER, SUPERIMPOSED ORDER.

ORDER, MONASTIC. A religious society whose members live together under an established set of rules. See BENEDICTINE, CARMELITE, CISTERCIAN, DOMINICAN, FRANCISCAN, JESUIT, THEATINE.

ORTHODOX. From the Greek word for right in opinion. The Eastern Orthodox Church, which split from the Western Catholic Church during the 5th century A.D. and transferred its allegiance from the pope in Rome to the Byzantine emperor in Constantinople and his appointed patriarch. Sometimes called the Byzantine Church.

PAINT. See ACRYLIC, ENCAUSTIC, FRESCO, MAGNA, OIL PAINTING, TEMPERA PAINTING, WATERCOLOR.

PALAZZO (pl. PALAZZI). Italian word for palace (in French, *palais*). Refers either to large, official buildings (fig. 454), or to important private town houses (fig. 559).

PALEOLITHIC. The Old Stone Age: usually divided into Lower, Middle, and Upper (which began about 35,000 B.C.). A society of nomadic hunters who used stone implements, later developing ones of bone and flint. Some lived in caves, which they decorated during the latter stages of the age (colorplate 2, fig. 15), at which time they also produced small CARVINGS in bone, horn, and stone (figs. 19, 20).

PALETTE. 1) A thin, usually oval or oblong board with a thumb hole at one end, used by painters to hold and mix their colors. 2) The range of colors used by a particular painter. 3) In Egyptian art, a slate slab, usually decorated with sculpture in low RELIEF. The small ones with a recessed circular area on one side are thought to have been used for eye makeup. The larger ones were commemorative objects (figs. 53, 54).

PANEL. 1) A wooden surface used for painting, usually in TEMPERA and prepared beforehand with a layer of GESSO. Large ALTARPIECES require the joining together of two or more boards (colorplate 63). 2) Recently panels of masonite or other composite material have come into use (colorplate 158).

PANTHEON. A temple dedicated to all the gods (figs. 238, 239), or housing tombs of the illustrious dead of a nation, or memorials to them (fig. 795).

PANTOCRATOR. A representation of Christ as ruler of the universe which appears frequently in the DOME or APSE MOSAICS of Byzantine churches (fig. 321).

PAPER. General name for a writing material made from various fibrous substances. Invented in China in the 2nd century A.D., it was known in Europe in the Middle Ages, but its possibilities as a cheap substitute for PARCHMENT were not fully realized until the development of printing in northern Europe in the 15th century.

PAPYRUS. 1) A tall aquatic plant that grows abundantly in the Near East, Egypt, and Abyssinia. 2) A paper-like material made by laying together thin strips of the pith of this plant, and then soaking, pressing, and drying the whole. The resultant sheets were used as writing material by the ancient Egyptians, Greeks, and Romans. 3) An ancient document or SCROLL written on this material.

PARCHMENT. From Pergamum, the name of a Greek city in Asia Minor where parchment was invented in the 2nd century B.C. 1) A paper-like material made from thin bleached animal hides, used extensively in the Middle Ages for MANUSCRIPTS (colorplates 39, 42, 45). Vellum is a superior type of parchment, made from calfskin. 2) A document or miniature on this material.

PASSION. 1) In ecclesiastic terms, the events of Christ's last week on earth. 2) The representation of these events in pictorial, literary, theatrical, or musical form (colorplates 53, 54, 63; figs. 570, 638, 725).

PASTEL. 1) A color of a soft, subdued shade. 2) A drawing stick made from PIGMENTS ground with CHALK and mixed with gum water. 3) A drawing executed with these sticks (figs. 875, 876).

PEDESTAL. An architectural support for a statue, vase, etc.

PEDIMENT. 1) In classical architecture, a low GABLE, typically triangular, framed by a horizontal CORNICE below and two raking cornices above; frequently filled with relief sculpture (fig. 156). 2) A similar architectural member, either round or triangular, used over a door, window, or niche (fig. 619). When pieces of the cornice are either turned at an angle or broken, it is called a broken pediment (fig. 249).

PENDENTIVE. One of the spherical triangles which achieve the transition from a square or polygonal opening to the round BASE of a DOME or the supporting DRUM (figs. 316, 320, 578).

PEPLOS. An outer garment worn draped in folds by women in ancient Greece (fig. 150).

PERIPTERAL. An adjective describing a building surrounded by a single row of COLUMNS or COLONNADE (figs. 160, 166).

PERISTYLE. 1) In a Roman house or DOMUS, an open garden court surrounded by a COLONNADE (fig. 252). 2) A colonnade around a building or court (figs. 160, 607).

PERSPECTIVE. A technique for representing spatial relationships and three-dimensional objects on a flat surface so as to produce an effect similar to that perceived by the human eye. In "atmospheric" or aerial perspective, this is accomplished by a gradual decrease in the intensity of local color and in the contrast of light and dark, so that everything in the far distance tends toward a light bluish-gray tone (colorplate 61). In one-point linear perspective, developed in Italy in the 15th century, a mathematical system is used, based on orthogonals (all lines receding at right angles to the picture plane) that converge on a single vanishing point on the horizon. Since this presupposes an absolutely stationary viewer and imposes rigid restrictions on the artist, it is seldom applied with complete consistency (colorplate 69, fig. 544).

PHOTOGRAM. A shadow-like photograph made without a camera by placing objects on light-sensitive paper and exposing them to a light source (fig. 1070).

PHOTOGRAPH. The relatively permanent or "fixed" form of an image made by light that passes through the lens of a camera and acts upon light-sensitive substances. Often called a PRINT.

PHOTOJOURNALISM. Journalism in which written copy is subordinate to photography.

PHOTOMONTAGE. A photograph in which prints in whole or in part are combined to form a new image (fig. 1069). A technique much practiced by the Dada group in the 1920s.

PIAZZA (pl. PIAZZE). Italian word for public square (in French, *place*; in German, *Platz*).

PICTURE PLANE. The flat surface on which a picture is painted.

PICTURESQUE. Visually interesting or pleasing, as if resembling a picture (fig. 794).

PIER. An upright architectural support, usually rectangular, and sometimes with CAPITAL and BASE (fig. 220). When COLUMNS, PILASTERS, or SHAFTS are attached to it, as in many Romanesque and Gothic churches, it is called a compound pier (fig. 391).

PIETÀ. Italian word for both pity and piety. A representation of the Virgin grieving over the dead Christ (fig. 468). When used in a scene recording a specific moment after the Crucifixion, it is usually called a "Lamentation" (fig. 491).

PIGMENT. Colored substances found in organic and inorganic sources; many are now prepared synthetically. 1) Pigment finely divided and suspended in a liquid medium becomes a paint, ink, etc. See OIL PAINTING, TEMPERA PAINTING, WATERCOLOR, FRESCO. 2) Pigment suspended in a solid medium becomes CRAYON, PASTEL, etc.

PILASTER. A flat, vertical element projecting from a wall surface, and normally having a BASE, SHAFT, and CAPITAL. It has generally a decorative rather than structural purpose (figs. 575, 577).

PILGRIMAGE CHOIR. The unit in a Romanesque church composed of the APSE, AMBULATORY, and RADIATING CHAPELS (figs. 384, 423).

PILLAR. A general term for a vertical architectural support which includes COLUMNS, PIERS, and PILASTERS.

PINNACLE. A small, decorative structure capping a tower, PIER BUTTRESS, or other architectural member, and used especially in Gothic buildings (figs. 434, 436).

PLAN. See GROUND PLAN.

PODIUM. 1) The tall base upon which rests an Etruscan or Roman temple (fig. 227). 2) The ground floor of a building made to resemble such a base (fig. 763).

POLYPTYCH. An ALTARPIECE or devotional work of art made of several panels joined together (fig. 512), often hinged.

PORCH. General term for an exterior appendage to a building which forms a covered approach to a doorway (fig. 433). See PORTICO for porches consisting of columns.

PORTA. Latin word for door or gate (fig. 226).

PORTAL. A door or gate, usually a monumental one with elaborate sculptural decoration (figs. 456, 469).

PORTICO. A porch supporting a roof or an ENTABLATURE and PEDIMENT, often approached by a number of steps (figs. 227, 622). It provides a monumental covered entrance to a building, and a link with the space surrounding it.

POST AND LINTEL. A basic system of construction in which two or more uprights, the "posts," support a horizontal member, the "lintel." The lintel may be the topmost element (figs. 33, 34), or support a wall or roof (figs. 131, 1029).

PREDELLA. The base of an ALTARPIECE, often decorated with small scenes which are related in subject to that of the main panel or panels (colorplate 59).

PRINT. A picture or design reproduced, usually on paper and often in numerous copies, from a prepared wood block, metal plate, or stone slab, or by photography. See AQUATINT, ENGRAVING, ETCHING, LITHOGRAPH, PHOTOGRAPH, WOODCUT.

PRONAOS. In a Greek or Roman temple, an open vestibule in front of the CELLA (fig. 160).

PROPYLAEUM (pl. PROPYLAEA). 1) The entrance to a temple or other enclosure, especially when it is an elaborate structure. 2) The monumental entry gate at the western end of the Acropolis in Athens (figs. 169).

PSALTER. 1) The book of Psalms in the Old Testament, thought to have been written in part by David, king of ancient Israel. 2) A copy of the Psalms, sometimes arranged for liturgical or devotional use, and often richly ILLUMINATED (colorplate 33).

PULPIT. A raised platform in a church from which the clergyman delivers a sermon or conducts the service. Its railing or enclosing wall may be elaborately decorated (fig. 471).

PUTTO (pl. PUTTI). A nude, male child, usually winged, often represented in classical and Renaissance art (colorplate 95, fig. 587). Also called a cupid or *amoretto* when he carries a bow and arrow and personifies Love (colorplate 98, fig. 631).

PYLON. Greek word for gateway. 1) The monumental entrance building to an Egyptian temple or forecourt, consisting either of a massive wall with sloping sides pierced by a doorway, or of two such walls flanking a central gateway (fig. 76). 2) A tall structure at either side of a gate, bridge, or avenue, marking an approach or entrance.

QIBLA. The direction of Mecca, toward which Moslems turn when praying. It is indicated in a mosque by the MIHRAB (niche) in the "qibla wall."

QUARTZITE. An extremely compact, granular rock, consisting essentially of quartz (fig. 72).

QUATREFOIL. An ornamental element composed of four lobes radiating from a common center (figs. 463, 479).

RADIATING CHAPELS. Term for CHAPELS arranged around the AMBULATORY (and sometimes the TRANSEPT) of a medieval church (figs. 383, 423, 434).

REFECTORY. 1) A room for refreshment. 2) The dining hall of a monastery, college, or other large institution.

REFORMATION. The religious movement in the early 16th century which had for its object the reform of the Catholic Church, and led to the establishment of Protestant churches. See also COUNTER REFORMATION.

REINFORCED CONCRETE. See FERROCONCRETE.

RELIEF. 1) The projection of a figure or part of a design from the background or plane on which it is CARVED or MODELED. Sculpture done in this manner is described as "high relief" or "low relief" depending on the height of the projection (figs. 55, 265). When it is very shallow, it is called *schiacciato*, the Italian word for flattened out (fig. 542). 2) The apparent projection of forms represented in a painting or drawing.

RESPOND. 1) A half-PIER, PILASTER, or similar element projecting from a wall to support a LINTEL, or an ARCH whose other side is supported by a free-standing COLUMN or pier, as at the end of an ARCADE (colorplate 27). 2) One of several pilasters on a wall behind a COLONNADE (figs. 249, 551) which echo or "respond to" the columns, but are largely decorative. 3) One of the slender shafts of a COMPOUND PIER in a medieval church which seems to carry the weight of the VAULT (figs. 394, 430).

RHYTON. An ancient drinking horn made from pottery or metal, and frequently having a base formed by a human or animal head (fig. 112).

RIB. A slender, projecting archlike member which supports a VAULT either transversely (fig. 386), or at the GROINS, thus dividing the surface into sections (fig. 394). In late Gothic architecture, its purpose is often primarily ornamental (fig. 441).

RIBBED VAULT. See VAULT.

ROLL. A long sheet of PAPYRUS or PARCHMENT with a written text, sometimes illustrated, used as a book before the introduction of the CODEX. Also called a SCROLL, and, in Latin, a *rotulus* (fig. 219).

ROOD SCREEN. See CHOIR SCREEN.

ROSE WINDOW. A large, circular window with stained glass and stone TRACERY, frequently used on FAÇADES and at the ends of TRANSEPTS of Gothic churches (figs. 426, 429).

ROSTRUM. 1) A beak-like projection from the prow of an ancient warship, used for ramming the enemy. 2) In the Roman FORUM, the raised platform decorated with the beaks of captured ships, from which speeches were delivered (fig. 274). 3) A platform, stage, or the like used for public speaking.

RUBBING. A reproduction of a relief surface made by covering it with paper and rubbing with pencil, chalk, etc. Also called "frottage."

RUSTICATION. A masonry technique of laying beveled stones with sharply indented joints (figs. 559, 659).

SACRA CONVERSAZIONE. Italian for holy conversation. A composition of the Madonna and Child with Saints in which the figures all occupy the same spatial setting, and appear to be conversing or communing with each other (figs. 593, 635).

SACRISTY. A room near the main altar of a church, or a small building attached to a church, where the vessels and vestments required for the service are kept. Also called a vestry.

SALON. 1) A large, elegant drawing or reception room in a palace or a private house (fig. 774). 2) Official government-sponsored exhibition of paintings and sculpture by living artists held in the Louvre at Paris, first biennially, then annually. 3) Any large public exhibition patterned after the Paris Salon.

SANCTUARY. 1) A sacred or holy place or building. 2) An especially holy place within a building, such as the CELLA of a temple, or the part of a church around the altar.

SANGUINE. A reddish-brown CHALK stick used for DRAWING (fig. 640).

SARCOPHAGUS (pl. SARCOPHAGI). A large stone coffin usually decorated with sculpture and/or inscriptions (figs. 216, 301). The term is derived from two Greek words meaning flesh and eating, which were applied to a kind of limestone in ancient Greece, since the stone was said to turn flesh to dust.

SATYR. One of a class of woodland gods thought to be the lascivious companions of Dionysus, the Greek god of wine (or of Bacchus, his Roman counterpart). They are represented as having the legs and tail of a goat, the body of a man, and a head with horns and pointed ears. A youthful satyr is also called a faun (colorplate 74, fig. 202).

SCRIPTORIUM (pl. SCRIPTORIA). A workroom in a monastery reserved for copying and illustrating MANUSCRIPTS.

SCROLL. 1) An architectural ornament with the form of a partially unrolled spiral, as on the CAPITALS of the Ionic and Corinthian ORDERS (figs. 159, 174). 2) A form of written text: see ROLL.

SCROLL BRACKET. See BRACKET.

SCUOLA. Italian word for school. In Renaissance Venice it designated a fraternal organization or confraternity, dedicated to good works, usually under ecclesiastical auspices.

SECTION. An architectural drawing presenting a building as if cut across the vertical plane, at right angles to the horizontal plane. Cross section: a cut along the transverse axis. Longitudinal section: a cut along the longitudinal axis.

SEXPARTITE VAULT. See VAULT.

SFUMATO. Italian word meaning gone up in smoke, used to describe very delicate gradations of light and shade in the MODELING of figures; applied especially to the work of Leonardo da Vinci and his followers (fig. 600).

SHAFT. In architecture, the part of a COLUMN between the BASE and the CAPITAL (fig. 159).

SIBYLS. In Greek and Roman mythology, any of numerous women who were thought to possess powers of divination and prophecy. They appear in Christian representations, notably in Michelangelo's Sistine Ceiling, because they were believed to have foretold the coming of Christ.

SIDE AISLE. A passageway running parallel to the NAVE of a Roman BASILICA or Christian church, separated from it by an ARCADE or COLONNADE (figs. 246, 289). There may be one on either side of the nave, or two, an inner and outer.

SILENI. A class of minor woodland gods in the entourage of the wine god, Dionysus (or Bacchus). Like Silenus, the wine god's tutor and drinking companion, they are thick-lipped and snub-nosed, and fond of wine. Similar to SATYRS, they are basically human in form except for horse's tails and ears (colorplate 24).

SILVER LEAF. See GOLD LEAF.

SILVER SALTS. Compounds of silver—bromide, chloride, and iodide—which are sensitive to light and are used in the preparation of photographic materials. This sensitivity was first observed by Johann Heinrich Schulze in 1727.

SINOPIA (pl. SINOPIE). Italian word taken from Sinope, the ancient city in Asia Minor which was famous for its brick-red PIGMENT. In FRESCO paintings, a full-sized, preliminary sketch done in this color on the first rough coat of plaster or "arriccio" (fig. 498).

SKENE. See THEATER.

SKETCH. See DRAWING, OIL SKETCH.

SPANDREL. The area between the exterior curves of two adjoining ARCHES, or, in the case of a single arch, the area around its outside curve from its springing to its keystone (colorplate 71, figs. 273, 304).

SPHINX. 1) In ancient Egypt, a creature having the head of a man, animal, or bird, and the body of a lion; frequently sculpted in monumental form (fig. 64). 2) In Greek mythology, a creature usually represented as having the head and breasts of a woman, the body of a lion, and the wings of an eagle. It appears in classical, Renaissance, and Neoclassical art.

STANZA (pl. STANZE). Italian word for room.

STEATITE. Soapstone, commonly gray or grayish-green in color (fig. 125).

STEEL. Iron modified chemically to have qualities of great hardness, elasticity, and strength. For use in sculpture, see figs. 1013, 1016. For architectural use, see STRUCTURAL STEEL.

STELE. From the Greek word for standing block. An upright stone slab or pillar with a CARVED commemorative design or inscription (figs. 95, 190).

STEREOBATE. The substructure of a classical building, especially a Greek temple (fig. 159).

STEREOSCOPE. An optical instrument which enables the user to combine two pictures taken from points of view corresponding to those of the two eyes into a single image having the depth and solidity of ordinary binocular vision (fig. 865). First demonstrated by Sir Charles Wheatstone in 1838.

STILTS. Term for pillars or posts supporting a superstructure; in 20th-century architecture, these are usually of FERROCONCRETE (figs. 1040, 1044). Stilted, as in stilted arches, refers to tall supports beneath an architectural member (fig. 339).

STOA. In Greek architecture, a covered COLONNADE, sometimes detached and of considerable length, used as a meeting place or promenade.

STOIC. A school of philosophy founded by Zeno about 300 B.C., and named after the STOA in Athens where he taught. Its main thesis is that man should be free of all passions.

STRUCTURAL STEEL. STEEL used as an architectural building material either invisibly (fig. 1023) or exposed (figs. 1032, 1039). See FERROCONCRETE.

STUCCO. 1) A CONCRETE or cement used to coat the walls of a building. 2) A kind of plaster used for architectural decorations such as CORNICES, MOLDINGS, etc., or for sculptured RELIEFS (figs. 220, 342).

STUDY. See DRAWING.

STYLOBATE. A platform or masonry floor above the STEREOBATE forming the foundation for the COLUMNS of a classical temple (fig. 159).

STYLUS. From the Latin word *stilus*, the writing instrument of the Romans. 1) A pointed instrument used in ancient times for writing on tablets of a soft material such as clay. 2) The needle-like instrument used in drypoint or etching. See ENGRAVING, ETCHING.

SUPERIMPOSED ORDERS. Two or more rows of COLUMNS, PIERS, or PILASTERS placed above each other on the wall of a building (figs. 236, 572).

TABERNACLE. 1) A place or house of worship. 2) A CANOPIED niche or recess built for an image (fig. 540). 3) The portable shrine used by the Jews to house the Ark of the Covenant (colorplate 26).

TABLINUM. From the Latin word meaning writing tablet, or written record. In a Roman house, a small room at the far end of the ATRIUM, or between it and the second courtyard. It was used for keeping family records.

TEMPERA PAINTING. 1) A painting made with PIGMENTS mixed with egg yolk and water. In the 14th and 15th centuries, it was applied to PANELS which had been prepared with a coating of GESSO; the application of GOLD LEAF and of underpainting in green or brown preceded the actual tempera painting (colorplates 54, 59). 2) The technique of executing such a painting.

TERRACOTTA. Italian word for cooked earth. 1) Earthenware, naturally reddish-brown but often GLAZED in various colors and fired. Used for pottery, sculpture, or as a building material or decoration. 2) An object made of this material. 3) Color of the natural material.

TESSERA (pl. TESSERAE). A small piece of colored stone, marble, glass, or gold-backed glass used in a MOSAIC.

THEATER. In ancient Greece, an outdoor place for dramatic performances, usually semicircular in plan and provided with tiers of seats, the ORCHESTRA, and the *skene*, or support for scenery (fig. 176). See also AMPHITHEATER.

THEATINE ORDER. Founded in Rome in the 16th century by members of the recently dissolved Oratory of Divine Love. Its aim was to reform the Catholic church, and its members were pledged to cultivate their spiritual lives and to perform charitable works.

THERMAE. A public bathing establishment of the ancient Romans which consisted of various types of baths and social and gymnastic facilities.

THOLOS. In classical architecture, a circular building ultimately derived from early tombs (fig. 175).

THRUST. The lateral pressure exerted by an ARCH, VAULT, or DOME, which must be counteracted at its point of greatest concentration either by the thickness of the wall or by some form of BUTTRESS.

TOGA. A garment worn by ancient Roman citizens when appearing in public. It consisted of a single, long piece of material which could be draped in a variety of ways (fig. 255).

TOTEM. Among the Indians of North America, a natural object or animal assumed as the emblem of a tribe or family, or the representation of it, such as those CARVED on the posts or "totem poles" in front of their dwellings.

TRACERY. 1) Ornamental stone work in Gothic windows. In the earlier or "plate tracery," the windows appear to have been cut through the solid stone (colorplate 47). In "bar tracery" the glass predominates, the slender pieces of stone having been added within the windows (fig. 434). 2) Similar ornamentation using various materials and applied to walls, shrines, etc. (fig. 530).

TRANSEPT. A cross arm in a BASILICAN church, placed at right angles to the NAVE, and usually separating it from the CHOIR or APSE (fig. 289).

TREE OF KNOWLEDGE. The tree in the Garden of Eden from which Adam and Eve ate the forbidden fruit which destroyed their innocence (Gen. 2:9, 17).

TREE OF LIFE. A tree in the Garden of Eden whose fruit was reputed to give everlasting life; in medieval art it was frequently used as a symbol of Christ (Gen. 2:9; 3:22).

TRIFORIUM. The section of a NAVE wall above the ARCADE and below the CLERESTORY (colorplate 47). It frequently consists of a BLIND ARCADE with three openings in each bay. When the GALLERY is also present, a four-story ELEVATION results, the triforium being between the gallery and clerestory. It may also occur in the TRANSEPT and the CHOIR walls.

TRIGLYPH. The element of a Doric FRIEZE separating two consecutive METOPES, and being divided by channels (or glyphs) into three sections. Probably an imitation in stone of wooden ceiling beam ends (figs. 159, 166).

TRIPTYCH. An ALTARPIECE or devotional picture, either CARVED or painted, with one central panel and two hinged wings (figs. 332, 522).

TRIUMPHAL ARCH. 1) A monumental ARCH, sometimes a combination of three arches, erected by a Roman emperor in commemoration of his military exploits, and usually decorated with scenes of these deeds in RELIEF sculpture (fig. 273). 2) The great transverse arch at the eastern end of a church which frames ALTAR and APSE and separates them from the main body of the church. It is frequently decorated with MOSAICS or MURAL paintings (colorplate 27, fig. 290).

TROPHY. 1) In ancient Rome, arms or other spoils taken from a defeated enemy and publicly displayed on a tree, PILLAR, etc. 2) A representation of these objects, and others symbolic of victory, as a commemoration or decoration.

TRUMEAU. A central post supporting the LINTEL of a large doorway, as in a Romanesque or Gothic PORTAL, where it was frequently decorated with sculpture (figs. 405, 469).

TRUSS. A triangular wooden or metal support for a roof which may be left exposed in the interior (figs. 290, 447), or be covered by a ceiling (figs. 379, 402).

TUNIC. In classical Greece and Rome, a loose, knee-length garment worn by both sexes. It could have sleeves or not, and was generally worn unbelted.

TURRET. 1) A small tower, part of a larger structure. 2) A small tower at an angle of a building, frequently beginning some distance from the ground.

TYMPANUM. 1) In classical architecture, the recessed, usually triangular area, also called a PEDIMENT, often decorated with sculpture (fig. 161). 2) In medieval architecture, an arched area between an ARCH and the LINTEL of a door or window, frequently carved with RELIEF sculpture (figs. 408, 459).

UNDERPAINTING. See TEMPERA PAINTING.

VAULT. An arched roof or ceiling usually made of stone, brick, or CONCRETE. Several distinct varieties have been developed; all need BUTTRESSING at the point where the lateral THRUST is concentrated. 1) A barrel vault is a semicylindrical structure made up of successive ARCHES (fig. 388). It may be straight or ANNULAR in plan (fig. 294). 2) A groin vault is the result of the intersection of two barrel vaults of equal size which produces a BAY of four compartments with sharp edges, or "groins," where the two meet (fig. 237). 3) A ribbed groin vault is one in which RIBS are added to the groins, for structural strength and for decoration (fig. 391). When the diagonal ribs are constructed as half circles, the resulting form is a domical ribbed vault (fig. 396). 4) Sexpartite vault: a ribbed groin vault in which each bay is divided into six compartments by the addition of a transverse rib across the center (fig. 394). 5) The normal Gothic vault is quadripartite with all the arches pointed to some degree (fig. 420). 6) A fan vault is an elaboration of a ribbed groin vault, with elements of TRACERY using conelike forms. It was developed by the English in the 15th century, and was employed for decorative purposes (figs. 442, 443).

VELLUM. See PARCHMENT.

VESTRY. See SACRISTY.

VICES. Often represented allegorically in conjunction with the seven VIRTUES, they include Pride, Avarice, Wrath, Gluttony, Unchastity (Luxury), Folly, and Inconstancy, though others such as Injustice are sometimes substituted.

VICTORY, see NIKE.

VILLA. Originally a large country house (fig. 660), but in modern usage, also a detached house or suburban residence.

VIRTUES. The three theological virtues, Faith, Hope, and Charity, and the four cardinal ones, Prudence, Justice, Fortitude, and Temperance, were frequently represented allegorically, particularly in medieval manuscripts and sculpture.

VOLUTE. A spiral architectural element found notably on Ionic and Composite CAPITALS (figs. 174, 227), but also used decoratively on building FAÇADES and interiors (fig. 664, colorplate 89).

VOUSSOIR. See ARCH.

WASH. A thin layer of translucent color or ink used in WATERCOLOR PAINTING and BRUSH DRAWING (fig. 760), and occasionally in OIL PAINTING.

WATERCOLOR PAINTING. Painting, usually on paper, in PIGMENTS suspended in water (figs. 668, 957).

WESTWORK. From the German word Westwerk. In Carolingian, Ottonian, and German Romanesque architecture, a monumental western front of a church, treated as a tower or combination of towers, and containing an entrance and vestibule below, and a CHAPEL and GALLERIES above. Later examples often added a TRANSEPT and a CROSSING tower (fig. 376).

WING. The side panel of an ALTARPIECE which is frequently decorated on both sides, and also hinged, so that it may be shown either open or closed (figs. 512, 514).

WOODCUT. A PRINT made by carving out a design on a wood block cut along the grain, applying ink to the raised surfaces which remain, and printing from those (figs. 532, 669, 674).

WROUGHT IRON. A comparatively pure form of iron which is easily forged and does not harden quickly, so that it can be shaped or hammered by hand (fig. 1006), in contrast to molded CAST IRON.

ZIGGURAT. From the Assyrian word ziqquratu meaning mountain top or height. In ancient Assyria and Babylonia, a pyramidal tower built of mud brick and forming the BASE of a temple; it was either stepped or had a broad ascent winding around it, which gave it the appearance of being stepped (figs. 86, 89).

ZODIAC. 1) An imaginary belt circling the heavens, including the paths of the sun, moon, and major planets, and containing twelve constellations and thus twelve divisions called signs, which have been associated with the months. The signs are: Aries, the ram; Taurus, the bull; Gemini, the twins; Cancer, the crab; Leo, the lion; Virgo, the virgin; Libra, the balance; Scorpio, the scorpion; Sagittarius, the archer; Capricorn, the goat; Aquarius, the water-bearer; and Pisces, the fish. They are frequently represented around the PORTALS of Romanesque and Gothic churches in conjunction with the LABORS OF THE MONTHS (figs. 408, 463).

This list includes standard works and the most recent and comprehensive studies available in English. Books with material relevant to several chapters are cited under the first heading only. Many of these works contain bibliographies that may be consulted for information on more specialized topics. Two excellent general bibliographies are *Guide to the Literature of Art History* by Etta Arntzen and Robert Rainwater (American Library Association, 1980) and *Art Books: A Basic Bibliography* by E. Louise Lucas (New York Graphic Society, 1968). An excellent guide to art historical research is *Art Research: Methods and Resources: A Guide to Finding Art Information* by Lois Swan Jones (2d ed., rev. & enl., Kendall/Hunt Publishing Co., 1984). Asterisks (*) indicate that titles are available in paperback; for publishers and dates, consult *Paperbound Books in Print*.

INTRODUCTION

*ARNHEIM, R., *Art and Visual Perception*, 2d ed., Univ. of California Press, Berkeley, 1974

———, *Visual Thinking*, Univ. of California Press, Berkeley, 1970

BAUMGART, F., *A History of Architectural Styles*, Praeger, N.Y., 1970

BERNHEIMER, R., *The Nature of Representation*, New York Univ. Press, 1961

CAHN, W., *Masterpieces: Chapters on the History of an Idea*, Princeton Univ. Press, 1979

*DIENHARD, H., *Meaning and Expression: Toward a Sociology of Art*, Beacon Press, Boston, 1970

DICKIE, G., *Art and the Aesthetic: An Institutional Analysis*, Cornell Univ. Press, Ithaca, 1974

*ELSEN, A. E., *Purposes of Art*, 3d ed., Holt, Rinehart, Winston, 1972

FEIBELMAN, J. K., *The Quiet Rebellion: The Making and Meaning of the Arts*, Horizon, N.Y., 1972

*GOLDWATER, R., & M. Treves, *Artists on Art*, 3d ed., Pantheon Books, N.Y., 1974

GOMBRICH, E. H., *Art and Illusion*, 4th ed., Pantheon Books, N.Y., 1972

———, *Ideals and Icons: Essays on Value in History and in Art*, Phaidon, Oxford, 1979

*HOLT, E. G., *A Documentary History of Art*, 2d ed., 2 vols., Doubleday, Garden City, 1981

KEPES, G., ed., *The Man-Made Object*, Braziller, N.Y., 1966

*KUBLER, G., *The Shape of Time*, Yale Univ. Press, New Haven, 1962

LANG, B., ed., *The Concept of Style*, Univ. of Pennsylvania Press, Philadelphia, 1979

*PANOFSKY, E., *Meaning in the Visual Arts*, Doubleday, Garden City, 1955; reprint, Overlook Press, Woodstock, 1974

PODRO, M., *The Manifold in Perception: Theories of Art from Kant to Hildebrand*, Clarendon Press, Oxford, 1972

READ, H. E., *Art and Alienation: The Role of the Artist in Society*, Horizon, N.Y., 1967

———, *Icon and Idea*, Schocken Books, N.Y., 1965

*ROSENBERG, H., *The Anxious Object: Art Today and Its Audience*, 2d ed., Horizon, N.Y., 1966

SIRCELLO, G., *Mind and Art*, Princeton Univ. Press, 1972

PART ONE
THE ANCIENT WORLD
1. MAGIC AND RITUAL—
THE ART OF PREHISTORIC MAN

*BASCOM, W. R., *African Art in Cultural Perspective*, Norton, N.Y., 1973

BÜHLER, A., T. BARROW, & C. T. MOUNTFORD, *The Art of the South Sea Islands*, Crown, N.Y., 1962

CHILDE, V. G., *The Dawn of European Civilization*, 6th ed., Knopf, N.Y., 1958

CORNET, J., *Art of Africa*, Phaidon, N.Y., 1971

DAVIES, O., *West Africa Before the Europeans: Archaeology and Prehistory*, Methuen, London, 1967

FEDER, N., *American Indian Art*, Abrams, N.Y., 1971

GIMBUTAS, M. A., *The Gods and Goddesses of Old Europe, 7000–3500 B.C.: Myths, Legends and Cult Images*, Univ. of California Press, Berkeley, 1974

GRAND, P. M., *Prehistoric Art: Paleolithic Painting and Sculpture*, New York Graphic Society, Greenwich, 1967

GRAZIOSI, P., *Paleolithic Art*, McGraw-Hill, N.Y., 1960

GUNDON, E., *Primitive Architecture*, Abrams, N.Y., 1978

*LAUDE, J., *The Arts of Black Africa*, Univ. of California Press, Berkeley, 1971

LEROI-GOURHAN, A., *Treasures of Prehistoric Art*, Abrams, N.Y., 1967

*LEUZINGER, E., *The Art of Black Africa*, Rizzoli, N.Y., 1979

LLOYD, S., *Mounds of the Near East*, Edinburgh Univ. Press, 1963

LOMMEL, A., *Shamanism, The Beginnings of Art*, McGraw-Hill, N.Y., 1967

MARSHACK, A., *The Roots of Civilization: The Cognitive Beginnings of Man's First Art, Symbol and Notation*, McGraw-Hill, N.Y., 1971

MEGAW, J. V. S., *Art of the European Iron Age*, Harper & Row, N.Y., 1970

MELLAART, J., *Çatal Hüyük: A Neolithic Town in Anatolia*, McGraw-Hill, N.Y., 1967

———, *The Neolithic of the Near East*, Scribner, N.Y., 1975

PIGGOTT, S., *Ancient Europe*, Aldine, Chicago, 1966

*POWELL, T. G. E., *Prehistoric Art*, Praeger, N.Y., 1966

RENFROW, C., *Before Civilization: The Radiocarbon Revolution and Prehistoric Europe*, Knopf, N.Y., 1973

SANDARS, N. K., *Prehistoric Art in Europe*, Pelican History of Art, Penguin, Baltimore, 1968

SILVERBERG, R., *Mound Builders of Ancient America: The Archaeology of a Myth*, New York Graphic Society, Greenwich, 1968

THOM, A., *Megalithic Sites in Britain*, Clarendon Press, Oxford, 1967

TRACHTENBERG, M., & I. HYMAN, *Architecture: From Prehistory to Post-Modernism*, Abrams, N.Y., 1985

*WILLETT, F., *African Art*, Praeger, N.Y., 1971

WINGERT, P., *Primitive Art: Its Traditions and Styles*, Oxford Univ. Press, N.Y., 1962

2. EGYPTIAN ART

ALFRED, C., *Akhenaten and Nefertiti*, Brooklyn Museum/Viking Press, 1973

———, *Art of Ancient Egypt*, 3 vols, Transatlantic, N.Y., 1974

———, *Development of Ancient Egyptian Art from 3200 to 1315 B.C.*, Transatlantic, N.Y., 1975

BADAWY, A., *A History of Egyptian Architecture*, Vol. I, Sh. Studio Misr., Giza, 1954; Vols. II–III, Univ. of California Press, Berkeley, 1966–68

DESROCHES-NOBLECOURT, C., *Tutankhamen*, New York Graphic Society, Greenwich, 1964

*FAKHRY, A., *The Pyramids*, 2d ed., Univ. of Chicago Press, 1962

FLETCHER, B., *A History of Architecture*, 18th ed., rev. R. A. Cordingley, Scribner, N.Y., 1975

GROENEWEGEN-FRANKFORT, H. A., *Arrest and Movement*, Univ. of Chicago Press, 1951

———, & B. ASHMOLE, *Art of the Ancient World*, Abrams, N.Y., 1975

HAYES, W. C., *The Scepter of Egypt*, 2 vols., Harper, in cooperation with the Metropolitan Museum of Art, N.Y., 1953–59

LANGE, K., & M. HIRMER, *Egypt: Architecture, Sculpture, Painting in Three Thousand Years*, 4th ed., Phaidon, London, 1968

*MEKHITARIAN, A., *Egyptian Painting*, Skira, N.Y., 1954/Rizzoli, N.Y., 1977

MICHALOWSKI, K., *Art of Ancient Egypt*, Abrams, N.Y., 1969; reprint 1985

*PANOFSKY, E., *Tomb Sculpture: Its Aspects from Ancient Egypt to Bernini*, Abrams, N.Y., 1969

PORTER, B., & R. L. B. MOSS, *Topographical Bibliography of Ancient Egyptian Hieroglyphic Texts, Reliefs and Paintings*, 7 vols., Oxford Univ. Press, N.Y., 1927–51; 2d ed., Vol. 1 (2 parts), 2–3, 1960–74

POULSEN, V., *Egyptian Art*, New York Graphic Society, Greenwich, 1968

SCHÄFER, H., *Principles of Egyptian Art*, Clarendon Press, Oxford, 1974

*SMITH, W. S., & W. K. SIMPSON, *The Art and Architecture of Ancient Egypt*, rev. with additions, Pelican History of Art, Penguin, N.Y., 1981

WOLF, W., *The Origins of Western Art: Egypt, Mesopotamia, the Aegean*, Universe Books, N.Y., 1971

3. THE ANCIENT NEAR EAST

AKURGAL, E., *Art of the Hittites*, Abrams, N.Y., 1962

AMIET, P., *Art of the Ancient Near East*, Abrams, N.Y., 1980

*FRANKFORT, H., *The Art and Architecture of the Ancient Orient*, 4th rev. impression with additional bibliography, Pelican History of Art, Penguin, Baltimore, 1969

———, *Cylinder Seals: A Documentary Essay on the Art and Religion of the Ancient Near East*, Gregg, London, 1968

GHIRSHMAN, R., *Iran from the Earliest Times to the Islamic Conquest*, Penguin, Harmondsworth, N.Y., 1978

GOFF, B. L., *Symbols of Prehistoric Mesopotamia*, Yale Univ. Press, New Haven, 1963

KRAMER, S. N., *The Sumerians: Their History, Culture and Characteristics*, Univ. of Chicago Press, 1963

LLOYD, S., *The Archaeology of Mesopotamia: From the Old Stone Age to the Persian Conquest*, Thames & Hudson, London, 1978

———, H. W. MÜLLER, & R. MARTIN, *Ancient Architecture: Mesopotamia, Egypt, Greece*, Abrams, N.Y., 1974

MADHLOOM, T. A., *The Chronology of Neo-Assyrian Art*, Athlone Press, London, 1970

*MELLAART, J., *Earliest Civilizations of the Near East*, McGraw-Hill, N.Y., 1965

MOOREY, P. R. S., *Ancient Iraq: Assyria and Babylonia*, Ashmolean Museum, Oxford, 1976

MOORTGAT, A., *The Art of Ancient Mesopotamia*, Phaidon, N.Y., 1969

PARROT, A., *The Arts of Assyria*, Braziller, N.Y., 1961

PORADA, E., *The Art of Ancient Iran: Pre-Islamic Cultures*, Crown, N.Y., 1965

*SAGGS, H. W. F., *The Greatness That Was Babylon*, Praeger, N.Y., 1968

SMITH, W. S., *Interconnections in the Ancient Near East*, Yale Univ. Press, New Haven, 1965

STROMMENGER, E., & M. HIRMER, *5000 Years of the Art of Mesopotamia*, Abrams, N.Y., 1964

*WOOLLEY, C. L., *Ur of the Chaldees*, Norton, N.Y., 1965

4. AEGEAN ART

BLEGEN, C. W., & M. RAWSON, eds., *The Palace of Nestor at Pylos in Western Messenia*, 3 vols, Princeton Univ. Press, 1966–73

BRANIGAN, K., *The Foundations of Palatial Crete: A Survey of Crete in the Early Bronze Age*, Praeger, N.Y., 1970

FOSTER, K. P., *Aegean Faience of the Bronze Age*, Yale Univ. Press, New Haven, 1977

*GRAHAM, J. W., *The Palaces of Crete*, Princeton Univ. Press, 1962

HAMPE, R., & E. SIMON, *The Birth of Greek Art from the Mycenaean to the Archaic Period*, Oxford Univ. Press, N.Y., 1981

HOOD, S., *The Minoans: The Story of Bronze Age Crete*, Praeger, N.Y., 1981

MARINATOS, S. N., & M. HIRMER, *Crete and Mycenae*, Abrams, N.Y., 1960

MYLONAS, G. E., *Mycenae and the Mycenaean Age*, Princeton Univ. Press, 1966

PEROWNE, S., *The Archaeology of Greece and the Aegean*, Viking, N.Y., 1974

RENFREW, C., *The Emergence of Civilization: The Cyclades and the Aegean in the Third Millennium B.C.*, Methuen, London, 1972

*VERMEULE, E., *Greece in the Bronze Age*, Univ. of Chicago Press, 1972

5. GREEK ART

ADAM, S., *The Technique of Greek Sculpture in the Archaic and Classical Periods*, Thames & Hudson, London, 1967

ARIAS, P. E., & M. HIRMER, *History of 1000 Years of Greek Vase Painting*, Abrams, N.Y., 1963

ASHMOLE, B., *Architect and Sculptor in Classical Greece*, New York Univ. Press, 1972

_____, & N. YALOURIS, *Olympia: The Sculptures of the Temple of Zeus*, Phaidon, London, 1967

BEAZLEY, J. D., *Attic Red-Figure Vase-Painters*, 2d ed., 3 vols., Oxford Univ. Press, London, 1963

_____, *The Development of Attic Black-Figure*, Univ. of California Press, Berkeley, 1964

_____, & B. ASHMOLE, *Sculpture and Painting to the End of the Hellenistic Period*, Cambridge Univ. Press, 1966

BERVÉ, H., G. GRUBEN, & M. HIRMER, *Greek Temples, Theatres, and Shrines*, Abrams, N.Y., 1963

BIEBER, M., *Laocoön: The Influence of the Group Since Its Discovery*, Wayne State Univ. Press, Detroit, 1967

*BOARDMAN, J., *Athenian Black-Figure Vases*, Oxford Univ. Press, N.Y., 1974

*_____, *Pre-Classical: From Crete to Archaic Greece*, Penguin, Baltimore, 1967

_____, *Greek Sculpture: The Archaic Period*, Oxford Univ. Press, N.Y., 1978

BRILLIANT, R., *Arts of the Ancient Greeks*, McGraw-Hill, N.Y., 1973

*CARPENTER, R., *The Architects of the Parthenon*, Penguin Books, Baltimore, 1970

CHARBONNEAUX, J., R. MARTIN, & F. VILLARD, *Classical Greek Art*, Braziller, N.Y., 1972

_____, *Hellenistic Greek Art*, Braziller, N.Y., 1973

*COOK, R. M., *Greek Art: Its Development, Character and Influence*, Farrar, Straus & Giroux, N.Y., 1973

*DINSMOOR, W. B., *The Architecture of Ancient Greece: An Account of Its Historic Development*, Norton, N.Y., London, 1975 (reprint of the 1950 ed. [3d rev.] augmented)

HAVELOCK, C. M., *Hellenistic Art*, New York Graphic Society, Greenwich, 1970

HILL, G. F., *Ancient Greek and Roman Coins: A Handbook*, new & enl. ed. (1st Amer. ed.), Argonaut, Chicago, 1964

*HOOD, S., *The Arts in Prehistoric Greece*, Pelican History of Art, Penguin, Harmondsworth, N.Y., 1978

KRAAY, C. M., & M. HIRMER, *Greek Coins*, Abrams, N.Y., 1966

LAWRENCE, A. W., *Greek and Roman Sculpture*, Harper & Row, N.Y., 1972

_____, *Greek Architecture*, 4th ed. rev., Pelican History of Art, Penguin, N.Y., 1983

*LULLIES, R., & M. HIRMER, *Greek Sculpture*, Abrams, N.Y., 1960

PFUHL, E., *Masterpieces of Greek Drawing and Painting*, 2d ed., Macmillan, N.Y., 1955

POLLITT, J. J., *The Ancient View of Greek Art: Criticism, History and Terminology*, Yale Univ. Press, New Haven, 1974

*_____, *The Art of Greece: Sources and Documents*, Prentice-Hall, Englewood Cliffs, 1965

RICHTER, G. M. A., *A Handbook of Greek Art*, 6th ed., redesigned, Phaidon, London, 1969

_____, *Kouroi*, 3d ed., Phaidon, N.Y., 1970

_____, *The Sculpture and Sculptors of the Greeks*, 4th ed., rev., Yale Univ. Press, New Haven, 1970

ROBERTSON, M., *Greek Painting*, Skira, Geneva, 1959

_____, *History of Greek Art*, 2 vols., Cambridge Univ. Press, 1975

SCHWEITZER, B., *Greek Geometric Art*, Phaidon, N.Y., 1971

*SCRANTON, R. L., *Greek Architecture*, Braziller, N.Y., 1962

*STERLING, C., *Still Life Painting from Antiquity to the Twentieth Century*, 2d rev. ed., Harper & Row, N.Y., 1981

WARD-PERKINS, J. B., *The Cities of Ancient Greece and Italy: Planning in Classical Antiquity*, Braziller, N.Y., 1974

WEBSTER, T. B. L., *Potter and Painter in Classical Athens*, Methuen, London, 1972

6. ETRUSCAN ART

BANTI, L., *Etruscan Cities and Their Culture*, Univ. of California Press, Berkeley, 1973

*BOETHIUS, A., *Etruscan and Early Roman Architecture*, 2d integrated ed., rev., Pelican History of Art, Penguin, Harmondsworth, N.Y., 1978

*BRENDEL, O. J., *Etruscan Art*, Pelican History of Art, Penguin, Harmondsworth, N.Y., 1978

_____, *Prolegomena to the Study of Roman Art*, Yale Univ. Press, New Haven, 1979

MORETTI, M., *New Monuments of Etruscan Painting*, Pennsylvania State Univ. Press, University Park, 1970

PALLOTTINO, M., *Etruscan Painting*, Skira, Geneva, 1953

RICHARDSON, E., *The Etruscans: Their Art and Civilization*, Univ. of Chicago Press, 1964

SPRENGER, M., G. BARTOLINI, & M. & A. HIRMER, *The Etruscans, Their History, Art, and Architecture*, Abrams, N.Y., 1983

7. ROMAN ART

ANDREAE, B., *The Art of Rome*, Abrams, N.Y., 1977

BIANCHI-BANDINELLI, R., *Rome: The Center of Power*, Braziller, N.Y., 1970

_____, *Rome: The Late Empire, A.D. 200–400*, Braziller, N.Y., 1971

BRILLIANT, R., *Roman Art from the Republic to Constantine*, Phaidon, N.Y., 1974

*BROWN, F. E., *Roman Architecture*, Braziller, N.Y., 1961

CHARLES-PICARD, G., *Roman Painting*, New York Graphic Society, Greenwich, 1970

HEINTZE, H. VON, *Roman Art*, Universe Books, N.Y., 1971

*L'ORANGE, H. P., *Art Forms and Civic Life in the Late Roman Empire*, Princeton Univ. Press, 1965

MacCORMACK, S., *Art and Ceremony in Late Antiquity*, Univ. of California Press, Berkeley, 1981

MACDONALD, W. L., *The Architecture of the Roman Empire*, Vol. I, rev. ed., Yale Univ. Press, New Haven, 1982

_____, *The Pantheon: Design, Meaning and Progeny*, Harvard Univ. Press, Cambridge, 1976

MAIURI, A., *Roman Painting*, Geneva, Skira, 1953

NASH, E., *Pictorial Dictionary of Ancient Rome*, 2 vols, 2d ed., rev., Praeger, N.Y., 1968

PERCIVAL, J., *The Roman Villa: An Historical Introduction*, Univ. of California Press, Berkeley, 1976

PERKINS, A., *The Art of Dura-Europas*, Clarendon Press, Oxford, 1963

POBÉ, M., & J. ROUBIER, *The Art of Roman Gaul*, Univ. of Toronto Press, 1961

*POLLITT, J. J., *The Art of Rome and Late Antiquity: Sources and Documents*, Prentice-Hall, Englewood Cliffs, 1966

*STRONG, D. E., *Roman Art*, Pelican History of Art, Penguin, Harmondsworth, Baltimore, 1976

TOYNBEE, J. M. C., *Roman Historical Portraits*, Thames & Hudson, N.Y., 1978

VERMEULE, C. C., III, *Greek Sculpture and Roman Taste*, Univ. of Michigan Press, Ann Arbor, 1977

_____, *Roman Imperial Art in Greece and Asia Minor*, Belknap Press, Cambridge, 1968

WARD-PERKINS, J. B., *Roman Architecture*, Abrams, N.Y., 1977

*_____, *Roman Imperial Architecture*, Pelican History of Art, Penguin, Harmondsworth, N.Y., 1981

8. EARLY CHRISTIAN AND BYZANTINE ART

*ALEXANDER, J. J. G., *The Decorated Letter*, Braziller, N.Y., 1978

BECKWITH, J., *The Art of Constantinople: An Introduction to Byzantine Art (330–1453)*, 2d ed., Phaidon, N.Y., 1968

*_____, *Early Christian and Byzantine Art*, 2d integrated ed., Pelican History of Art, Penguin, Harmondsworth, N.Y., 1979

BOVINI, G., & L. VON MATT, *Ravenna*, Abrams, N.Y., 1971

DEMUS, O., *Byzantine Art and the West*, New York Univ. Press, 1970

GALVARIS, G., *The Icon in the Life of the Church: Doctrine, Liturgy, Devotion*, Brill, Leiden, 1981

GRABAR, A., *The Beginnings of Christian Art, 200–395*, Thames & Hudson, London, 1967

_____, *Early Christian Art*, Braziller, N.Y., 1971

_____, *The Golden Age of Justinian, from the Death of Theodosius to the Rise of Islam*, Braziller, N.Y., 1971

*HAMILTON, G. H., *The Art and Architecture of Russia*, 3d integrated ed., Pelican History of Art, Penguin, N.Y., 1983

KÄHLER, H., & C. MANGO, *Hagia Sophia*, Praeger, N.Y., 1967

*KRAUTHEIMER, R., *Early Christian and Byzantine Architecture*, Pelican History of Art, Penguin, Baltimore, 1965

*_____, *Rome: Profile of a City, 312–1308*, Princeton Univ. Press, 1980

*LOWRIE, W., *Art in the Early Church*, Norton, N.Y., 1969

MACDONALD, W. L., *Early Christian and Byzantine Architecture*, Penguin, Baltimore, 1965

MAGUIRE, H., *Art and Eloquence in Byzantium*, Princeton Univ. Press, 1981

*MANGO, C., *The Art of the Byzantine Empire, 312–1453: Sources and Documents*, Prentice-Hall, Englewood Cliffs, 1972

_____, *Byzantine Architecture*, Abrams, N.Y., 1976

MATHEWS, T. J., *Byzantine Churches of Istanbul: A Photographic Survey*, Pennsylvania State Univ. Press, University Park, 1976

RICE, D. T., *The Appreciation of Byzantine Art*, Oxford Univ. Press, London, 1972

*RUNCIMAN, S., *Byzantine*, Style and Civilization, Penguin, Harmondsworth, Baltimore, 1975

WEITZMANN, K., *Byzantine Book Illumination and Ivories*, Variorum Reprints, London, 1980

*_____, *Late Antique and Early Christian Book Illumination*, Braziller, N.Y., 1977

ZARNECKI, G., *Art of the Medieval World*, Abrams, N.Y., 1976

PART TWO
THE MIDDLE AGES
1. ISLAMIC ART

ATIL, E., ed., *Turkish Art*, Smithsonian Institution Press, Washington, D.C., Abrams, N.Y., 1980

CRESWELL, K. A. C., *Early Muslim Architecture*, 2 vols., 3 parts (reprint, 1932 ed.), Hacker, N.Y., 1976

_____, *Muslim Architecture in Egypt*, 2 vols. (reprint, 1952–59 ed.), Hacker, N.Y., 1976

*ETTINGHAUSEN, R., *Arab Painting* (reprint, Skira, Geneva, 1962, ed.), Rizzoli, N.Y., 1977

GOODWIN, G., *A History of Ottoman Architecture*, Johns Hopkins Univ. Press, Baltimore, 1971

GRABAR, O., *The Formation of Islamic Art*, Yale Univ. Press, New Haven, 1973

HILL, D., *Islamic Architecture and Its Decoration: A.D. 800–1500*, Univ. of Chicago Press, 1964

HOAG, J. D., *Islamic Architecture*, Abrams, N.Y., 1977

PAPADOPOULO, A., *Islam and Muslim Art*, Abrams, N.Y., 1979

POPE, A. U., *Persian Architecture: The Triumph of Form and Color*, Braziller, N.Y., 1965

RICE, D. T., *Islamic Painting: A Survey*, Edinburgh Univ. Press, 1971

ROBINSON, B. W., *et al.*, *Islamic Painting and the Arts of the Book*, Faber & Faber, London, 1976

UNSAL, B., *Turkish Islamic Architecture in Seljuk and Ottoman Times*, St. Martin's Press, London, N.Y., 1973

2. EARLY MEDIEVAL ART

ALEXANDER, J. J. G., *Insular Manuscripts, 6th to the 9th Century* (A Survey of Manuscript Illumination in the British Isles, I), Miller, London, 1979

BUSCH, H., & B. LOHSE, *Pre-Romanesque Art*, Macmillan, N.Y., 1966

*CONANT, K. J., *Carolingian and Romanesque Architecture, 800–1200*, new ed., Pelican History of Art, Penguin, Norwich, 1974

*DAVIS-WEYER, C., *Early Medieval Art: 300–1150: Sources and Documents*, Prentice-Hall, Englewood Cliffs, 1971

DODWELL, C. R., *Painting in Europe: 800–1200*, Pelican History of Art, Penguin, Harmondsworth, Baltimore, 1971

FINLAY, I., *Celtic Art: An Introduction*, Faber & Faber, London, 1973

*GRABAR, A., & C. NORDENFALK, *Early Medieval Painting*, Skira, Geneva, 1957

*GROHSKOPF, B., *The Treasure of Sutton Hoo: Ship Burial for an Anglo-Saxon King*, Atheneum, N.Y., 1970

*HENDERSON, G. D. S., *Early Medieval*, Style and Civilization, Penguin, Baltimore, 1972

HENRY, F., ed., *The Book of Kells*, Knopf, N.Y., 1974

_____, *Irish Art During the Viking Invasions, 800–1020 A.D.*, Cornell Univ. Press, Ithaca, 1967

_____, *Irish Art in the Early Christian Period, to 800 A.D.*, Cornell Univ. Press, Ithaca, 1965

*HINKS, R. P., *Carolingian Art*, Univ. of Michigan Press, Ann Arbor, 1962

HUBERT, J., *The Carolingian Renaissance*, Braziller, N.Y., 1970

_____, J. PORCHER, & W. VOLBACH, *Europe of the Invasions*, Braziller, N.Y., 1969

*KITZINGER, E., *Early Medieval Art in the British Museum*, Indiana Univ. Press, Bloomington, 1964

KLINGENDER, F. D., *Animals in Art and Thought to the End of the Middle Ages*, MIT Press, Cambridge, 1971

LASKO, P., *Ars Sacra, 800–1200*, Pelican History of Art, Penguin, Baltimore, 1972

*MARTINDALE, A., *The Rise of the Artist in the Middle Ages and Early Renaissance*, McGraw-Hill, N.Y., 1972

*MUTHERICH, F., & J. E. GAEHDE, *Carolingian Painting*, Braziller, N.Y., 1976

*PEVSNER, N., *An Outline of European Architecture*, 6th ed., Penguin, Baltimore, 1960

RUSSELL, J. B., *Dissent and Reform in the Early Middle Ages*, Univ. of California Press, Berkeley, 1965

*SAALMAN, H., *Medieval Architecture*, Braziller, N.Y., 1962

3. ROMANESQUE ART

AUBERT, M., *Romanesque Cathedrals and Abbeys of France*, Vane, London, 1966

BOLOGNA, F., *Early Italian Painting: Romanesque and Early Medieval Art*, Van Nostrand, Princeton, 1964

BRAUNFELS, W., *Monasteries of Western Europe: The Architecture of the Orders*, 3d ed., Princeton Univ. Press, 1972

CAHN, W., *Romanesque Bible Illumination*, Cornell Univ. Press, Ithaca, 1982

COLLON-GEVAERT, S., J. LEJEUNE, & J. STIENNON, *A Treasury of Romanesque Art, Metalwork, Illumination and Sculpture from the Valley of the Meuse*, Phaidon, N.Y., 1972

DEMUS, O., *Romanesque Mural Painting*, Abrams, N.Y., 1971

DUBY, G., *The Age of the Cathedrals: Art and Society, 980–1420*, Univ. of Chicago Press, 1981

EVANS, J., *The Romanesque Architecture of the Order of Cluny*, 2d ed., AMS Press, N.Y., 1972

FOCILLON, H., *The Art of the West in the Middle Ages*, ed. by Jean Bony, 2 vols., Phaidon, N.Y., 1963

*GRABAR, A., *Romanesque Painting from the Eleventh to the Thirteenth Century: Mural Painting*, Skira, Geneva, 1958

HAZARD, H., ed., *The Art and Architecture of the Crusader States*, Univ. of Wisconsin Press, Madison, 1977

KAUFMANN, C. M., *Romanesque Manuscripts 1066–1190* (Survey of Manuscripts Illuminated in the British Isles, III), New York Graphic Society, Boston, 1978

KUBACH, H. E., *Romanesque Architecture*, Abrams, N.Y., 1975

*SAALMAN, H., *Medieval Cities*, Braziller, N.Y., 1968

SCHAPIRO, M., *Romanesque Art*, Braziller, N.Y., 1977

STODDARD, W. S., *Art and Architecture in Medieval France*, Harper & Row, N.Y., 1972

*SWARZENSKI, H., *Monuments of Romanesque Art: The Art of Church Treasures in North-Western Europe*, 2d ed., Univ. of Chicago Press, 1967

WEBB, G. F., *Architecture in Britain: The Middle Ages*, 2d ed., Pelican History of Art, Penguin, Baltimore, 1965

ZARNECKI, G., *Romanesque Art*, Universe Books, N.Y., 1971

4. GOTHIC ART

Abbot Suger on the Abbey Church of St.-Denis and Its Art Treasures, tr. by E. Panofsky, Princeton Univ. Press, 1946

ACKLAND, J. H., *Medieval Structure: The Gothic Vault*, Univ. of Toronto Press, 1972

*AVRIL, F., *Manuscript Painting at the Court of France: The Fourteenth Century, 1310–1380*, Braziller, N.Y., 1978

BATTISTI, E., *Cimabue*, Pennsylvania State Univ. Press, University Park, 1967

BAXANDALL, M., *Giotto and the Orators: Humanist Observers of Painting in Italy and the Discovery of Pictorial Composition, 1350–1450*, Clarendon Press, Oxford, 1971

BONY, J., *The English Decorated Style: Gothic Architecture Transformed, 1250–1350*, Cornell Univ. Press, Ithaca, 1979

_____, *French Gothic Architecture of the 12th and 13th Centuries*, Univ. of California Press, Berkeley, 1983

*BOWIE, T., ed., *The Sketchbook of Villard de Honnecourt*, 3d ed., Indiana Univ. Press, Bloomington, 1968

BRANNER, R., *Chartres Cathedral*, Norton, N.Y., 1969

*_____, *Gothic Architecture*, Braziller, N.Y., 1961

*CENNINI, C., *The Craftsman's Handbook (Il Libro dell'-Arte)*, Dover, N.Y., 1954

COLE, B., *Giotto and Florentine Painting, 1280–1375*, Harper & Row, N.Y., 1976

DEUCHLER, F., *Gothic Art*, Universe Books, N.Y., 1973

*DUPONT, J., & C. GNUDI, *Gothic Painting*, Rizzoli, N.Y., 1977

FRANKL, P., *Gothic Architecture*, Pelican History of Art, Penguin, Baltimore, 1962

*FRISCH, T. G., *Gothic Art: 1140–1450: Sources and Documents*, Prentice-Hall, Englewood Cliffs, 1971

GRODECKI, L., *Gothic Architecture*, Abrams, N.Y., 1977

HARVEY, J. H., *Medieval Craftsmen*, Batsford, London, 1978

*HENDERSON, G. D. S., *Gothic*, Style and Civilization, Penguin, Baltimore, 1967

*HOLT, E. G., ed., *A Documentary History of Art*: Vol. I, The Middle Ages and the Renaissance, 2d ed., Doubleday, Garden City, 1957

*JANTZEN, H., *High Gothic: The Classic Cathedrals of Chartres, Rheims, and Amiens*, Pantheon, N.Y., 1962

KRAUTHEIMER, R., & T. KRAUTHEIMER-HESS, *Lorenzo Ghiberti*, 2d ed., Princeton Univ. Press, 1970

LARNER, L., *Culture and Society in Italy, 1290–1420*, Scribner, N.Y., 1971

*MÂLE, E., *The Gothic Image: Religious Art in France of the Thirteenth Century*, Harper, N.Y., 1958

MARLE, R. VAN, *The Development of the Italian Schools of Painting*, 19 vols. (reprint, 1923–38 ed.), Hacker, N.Y., 1971

*MARTINDALE, A., *Gothic Art*, Praeger, N.Y., 1967

*MEISS, M., *Giotto and Assisi*, Norton, N.Y., 1967

*_____, *Painting in Florence and Siena after the Black Death*, Princeton Univ. Press, 1951

*PETERSEN, K., & J. J. WILSON, *Women Artists: Recognition and Reappraisal from the Early Middle Ages to the Twentieth Century*, Harper & Row, N.Y., 1976

POPE-HENNESSY, J. W., *Italian Gothic Sculpture*, 2d ed., Phaidon, N.Y., 1970

ROWLEY, G., *Ambrogio Lorenzetti*, 2 vols., Princeton Univ. Press, 1958

SAUERLÄNDER, W., *Gothic Sculpture in France, 1140–1270*, Abrams, N.Y., 1973

STUBBLEBINE, J. H., *Duccio di Buoninsegna and His School*, 2 vols., Princeton Univ. Press, 1979

*WATSON, P., *Building the Medieval Cathedrals*, Cambridge Univ. Press, 1976

WHITE, J., *Art and Architecture in Italy, 1250–1400*, Pelican History of Art, Penguin, Baltimore, 1966

_____, *Duccio: Tuscan Art and the Medieval Workshop*, Thames & Hudson, N.Y., 1979

PART THREE
THE RENAISSANCE
1. "LATE GOTHIC" PAINTING, SCULPTURE, AND THE GRAPHIC ARTS

BLUM, S. N., *Early Netherlandish Triptychs: A Study in Patronage*, Univ. of California Press, Berkeley, 1969

CHÂTELET, A., *Early Dutch Painting*, Rizzoli, N.Y., 1981

*CUTTLER, C. D., *Northern Painting: From Pucelle to Bruegel*, Holt, Rinehart & Winston, N.Y., 1968

DAVIES, M., *Rogier van der Weyden, an Essay with a Critical Catalogue of Paintings*, Phaidon, N.Y., 1972

DHANENS, E., *Hubert and Jan van Eyck*, Alpine Fine Arts Collection, N.Y., 1980

EICHENBERG, F., *The Art of the Print: Masterpieces, History, and Techniques*, Abrams, N.Y., 1976

FRAENGER, W., *Hieronymus Bosch*, 1st Amer. ed., Putnam, N.Y., 1983

FRIEDLÄNDER, M. J., *Early Netherlandish Painting*, 14 vols., Praeger, N.Y., 1967–73

*_____, *From Van Eyck to Bruegel: Early Netherlandish Painting*, Phaidon, N.Y., 1969

FRINTA, M. S., *The Genius of Robert Campin*, Mouton & Co., The Hague, 1966

GIBSON, W. S., *Hieronymus Bosch*, Praeger, N.Y., 1973

*HIND, A. M., *History of Engraving and Etching*, 3d ed. rev., Houghton, Mifflin, Boston, 1923

*_____, *An Introduction to a History of Woodcut*, 2 vols., Houghton, Mifflin, Boston, 1935

*IVINS, W. M., JR., *How Prints Look*, Metropolitan Museum of Art, N.Y., 1943

MEISS, M., *French Painting in the Time of Jean de Berry: The Limbourgs and Their Contemporaries*, 2 vols., Braziller, N.Y., 1974

MULLER, T., *Sculpture in the Netherlands, Germany, France and Spain, 1400–1500*, Pelican History of Art, Penguin, Harmondsworth, Baltimore, 1966

*PANOFSKY, E., *Early Netherlandish Painting*, 2 vols., Harvard Univ. Press, Cambridge, 1958

PURTLE, C. J., *The Marian Painting of Jan van Eyck*, Princeton Univ. Press, 1982

PUYVELDE, L. VAN, *Flemish Painting from the van Eycks to Metsys*, McGraw-Hill, N.Y., 1970

SNYDER, J., *Northern Renaissance Art*, Abrams, N.Y., 1985

2. THE EARLY RENAISSANCE IN ITALY

*ALAZARD, J., *The Florentine Portrait*, Schocken, N.Y., 1969

*ALBERTI, L. B., *On Painting and On Sculpture*, Phaidon, N.Y., 1972

*_____, *Ten Books on Architecture*, ed. by J. Rykwert, Tiranti, London, 1955

*ANTAL, F., *Florentine Painting and Its Social Background*, Boston Book & Art Shop, 1965

ARGAN, G. C., *The Renaissance City*, Braziller, N.Y., 1969

*AVERY, C., *Florentine Renaissance Sculpture*, Harper & Row, N.Y., 1970

BATTISTI, E., *Brunelleschi: The Complete Work*, Rizzoli, N.Y., 1981

*BAXANDALL, M., *Painting and Experience in Fifteenth-Century Italy*, Clarendon Press, Oxford, 1972

*BECK, J., *Italian Renaissance Painting*, Harper & Row, N.Y., 1981

BERENSON, B., *The Drawings of the Florentine Painters*, 3 vols. (reprint, 1938 ed.), Univ. of Chicago Press, 1973

*_____, *Italian Painters of the Renaissance*, rev. ed., Phaidon, London, 1967

_____, *Italian Pictures of the Renaissance: Central and North Italian Schools*, 3 vols., Phaidon, London, 1968

_____, *Italian Pictures of the Renaissance: Florentine School*, 2 vols., Phaidon, London, 1963

*BLUNT, A., *Artistic Theory in Italy, 1450–1600*, Oxford Univ. Press, N.Y., 1956

*BURCKHARDT, J. C., *The Civilization of the Renaissance in Italy*, 3d ed., rev., Phaidon, London, 1950

CHASTEL, A., *The Age of Humanism: Europe, 1480–1530*, McGraw-Hill, N.Y., 1964

_____, *Studios and Styles of the Italian Renaissance, 1460–1500*, Braziller, N.Y., 1971

CLARK, K. M., *Piero della Francesco*, 2d ed., Phaidon, London, 1969

COLE, B., *Masaccio and the Art of Early Renaissance Florence*, Indiana Univ. Press, Bloomington, 1980

EDGERTON, S. Y., jr., *The Renaissance: Rediscovery of Linear Perspective*, Basic Books, N.Y., 1975

FINE, E. H., *Women and Art: A History of Women Painters and Sculptors From the Renaissance to the 20th Century*, Allanheld & Schram, Montclair, 1978

GILBERT, C., *History of Renaissance Art Throughout Europe: Painting, Sculpture, Architecture*, Abrams, N.Y., 1973

*_____, *Italian Art, 1400–1500: Sources and Documents*, Prentice-Hall, Englewood Cliffs, 1980

GOMBRICH, E. H., *The Heritage of Apelles: Studies in the Art of the Renaissance*, Phaidon, Oxford Univ. Press, 1976

*_____, *Norm and Form: Studies in the Art of the Renaissance*, Phaidon, London, 1966

GREENHALGH, M., *Donatello and His Sources*, Duckworth, London, 1982

HARTT, F., *History of Italian Renaissance Art*, 2d ed., Abrams, N.Y., 1980

HENDY, P., *Piero della Francesco and the Early Renaissance*, Macmillan, N.Y., 1968

HERSEY, G. L., *Pythagorean Palaces: Magic and Architecture in the Italian Renaissance*, Cornell Univ. Press, Ithaca, 1976

HEYDENREICH, L. H., & W. LOTZ, *Architecture in Italy, 1400–1600*, Pelican History of Art, Penguin, Harmondsworth, Baltimore, 1974

JANSON, H. W., *The Sculpture of Donatello*, 2 vols., Princeton Univ. Press, 1957

KATZ, M. B., *Leon Battista Alberti and the Humanist Theory of the Arts*, Univ. Press of America, Washington, D.C., 1978

*LEE, R. W., *Ut Pictura Poesis: The Humanistic Theory of Painting*, Norton, N.Y., 1967

*LEVEY, M., *Early Renaissance*, Penguin, Harmondsworth, 1967

*LOWRY, B., *Renaissance Architecture*, Braziller, N.Y., 1962

MANETTI, A. de T., *The Life of Brunelleschi*, Pennsylvania State Univ. Press, University Park, 1970

*MURRAY, P., *Renaissance Architecture*, Abrams, N.Y., 1976

*PANOFSKY, E., *Renaissance and Renascences in Western Art*, Humanities Press, N.Y., 1970

POPE-HENNESSY, J., *Fra Angelico*, Phaidon, London, 1952

_____, *Italian Renaissance Sculpture*, Phaidon, N.Y., 1971

_____, *Paolo Uccello: Complete Edition*, 2d ed., Phaidon, N.Y., 1969

SEYMOUR, C., jr., *Sculpture in Italy, 1400–1500*, Pelican History of Art, Penguin, Baltimore, 1966

*SEZNEC, J., *The Survival of the Pagan Gods*, Reprint by Bollingen Foundation & Pantheon Books, Princeton Univ. Press, 1972

STEINBERG, R. W., *Fra Girolamo Savonarola, Florentine Art and Renaissance Historiography*, Ohio Univ. Press, Athens, 1977

TURNER, A. R., *The Vision of Landscape in Renaissance Italy*, Princeton Univ. Press, 1974

VASARI, G., *The Lives of the Painters, Sculptors and Architects*, tr. by Gaston Du C. De Vere, 4 vols., Abrams, N.Y., 1977

WACKERNAGEL, M., *The World of the Florentine Renaissance Artist: Projects and Patrons, Workshop and Art Market*, Princeton Univ. Press, 1981

WILDE, J., *Venetian Art from Bellini to Titian*, Clarendon Press, Oxford, 1974

*WITTKOWER, R., *Architectural Principles in the Age of Humanism*, 3d ed., Random House, N.Y., 1965

3. THE HIGH RENAISSANCE
IN ITALY

*ACKERMAN, J. S., & J. NEWMAN, *The Architecture of Michelangelo, With a Catalogue of Michelangelo's Works*, Penguin, Harmondsworth, Baltimore, 1971
BECK, J. H., *Raphael*, Abrams, N.Y., 1976
BRUSCHI, A., *Bramante*, Thames & Hudson, London, 1977
CLARK, K. M., *Leonardo da Vinci*, rev. ed., Penguin, Baltimore, 1967
DE TOLNAY, C., *Michelangelo*, 5 vols., 2d ed., rev., Princeton Univ. Press, 1969–71
FISCHEL, O., *Raphael*, Spring Books, London, 1964
*FREEDBERG, S. J., *Painting in Italy, 1500 to 1600*, 1st rev. ed., Pelican History of Art, Penguin, Harmondsworth, Baltimore, 1975
———, *Painting of the High Renaissance in Rome and Florence*, 2 vols., Harvard Univ. Press, Cambridge, 1961
HARTT, F., *Michelangelo*, 3 vols., Abrams, N.Y., 1965–76
*HIBBARD, H. *Michelangelo*, new ed., Penguin, Harmondsworth, 1978
*KLEIN, R., & H. ZERNER, *Italian Art, 1500–1600: Sources and Documents*, Prentice-Hall, Englewood Cliffs, 1966
*LEVEY, M., *High Renaissance*, Style and Civilization, Penguin, Baltimore, 1975
MURRAY, L., *The High Renaissance and Mannerism: Italy, The North and Spain, 1500–1600*, Oxford Univ. Press, N.Y., 1977 (Published in 1967 under 2 titles: *The High Renaissance* and *The Late Renaissance and Mannerism*)
PANOFSKY, E., *Problems in Titian, Mostly Iconographic*, New York Univ. Press, 1969
*———, *Studies in Iconology: Humanistic Theories in the Art of the Renaissance*, Harper & Row, N.Y., 1972
PIGNATTI, T., *Giorgione*, Phaidon, N.Y., 1971
POPE-HENNESSY, J., *Italian High Renaissance and Baroque Sculpture*, 3 vols, Phaidon, London, 1963
PORTOGHESI, P., *Rome of the Renaissance*, Phaidon, London, 1972
ROSAND, D., *Titian*, Abrams, N.Y., 1978
———, *Painting in Cinquecento Venice: Titian, Veronese, Tintoretto*, Yale Univ. Press, New Haven, London, 1982
WETHEY, H. E., *The Paintings of Titian*, 2 vols., Phaidon, London, 1969–71
*WÖLFFLIN, H., *Classic Art: An Introduction to the Italian Renaissance*, 3d ed., Phaidon, N.Y., 1968

4. MANNERISM AND OTHER
TRENDS

*ACKERMAN, J. S., *Palladio*, Penguin, Harmondsworth, 1966
BOSQUET, J., *Mannerism, the Painting and Style of the Late Renaissance*, Braziller, N.Y., 1964
*CELLINI, B., *Autobiography*, ed. by J. Pope-Hennessy, Phaidon, London, 1960
*FRIEDLAENDER, W. F., *Mannerism and Anti-Mannerism in Italian Painting*, Columbia Univ. Press, N.Y., 1957
GUDIOL, J., *Domenikos Theotokopoulos, El Greco, 1541–1614*, Viking, N.Y., 1973
HARRIS, A. S., & L. NOCHLIN, *Women Artists, 1550–1950*, Knopf, N.Y., 1976
*HOLT, E. G., ed., *A Documentary History of Art*, Vol. II, *Michelangelo and the Mannerists: The Baroque and the Eighteenth Century*, 2d ed., Doubleday, Garden City, 1957
*SHEARMAN, J. K. G., *Mannerism*, Style and Civilization, Penguin, Baltimore, 1967
SMYTH, C. H., *Mannerism and Maniera*, Augustin, Locust Valley, 1963
VALCANOVER, F., & T. PIGNATTI, *Tintoretto*, Abrams, N.Y., 1984
WETHEY, H. E., *El Greco and His School*, 2 vols., Princeton Univ. Press, 1962
WÜRTENBERGER, F., *Mannerism, the European Style of the Sixteenth Century*, Holt, Rinehart & Winston, 1963

5. THE RENAISSANCE IN
THE NORTH

*BENESCH, O., *The Art of the Renaissance in Northern Europe*, rev. ed., Phaidon, London, 1965
*BLUNT, A., *Art and Architecture in France, 1500–1700*, 4th ed., Pelican History of Art, Penguin, Harmondsworth, N.Y., 1981
CHRISTENSEN, C. C., *Art and the Reformation in Germany*, Ohio Univ. Press, Athens, 1979
GANZ, P., *The Paintings of Hans Holbein the Younger*, 1st comp. ed., Phaidon, London, 1956
GIBSON, W. S., *Bruegel*, Oxford Univ. Press, N.Y., 1977
LEYMARIE, J., *Dutch Painting*, Skira, Geneva, 1956
OSTEN, G. VON DER, & H. VEY, *Painting and Sculpture in Germany and the Netherlands, 1500–1600*, Pelican History of Art, Penguin, Baltimore, 1969

PANOFSKY, E., *The Life and Art of Albrecht Dürer*, 4th ed., Princeton Univ. Press, 1955
PEVSNER, N., & M. MEIER, *Gruenewald*, Abrams, N.Y., 1958
STECHOW, W., *Pieter Bruegel the Elder*, Abrams, N.Y., 1969
*———, *Northern Renaissance Art, 1400–1600: Sources and Documents*, Prentice-Hall, Englewood Cliffs 1966
STRIEDER, P., *Albrecht Dürer: Paintings, Prints, Drawings*, Eng. ed., Abaris, N.Y., 1982
*WATERHOUSE, E. K., *Painting in Britain, 1530–1790*, 4th ed., Pelican History of Art, Penguin, Baltimore, 1978

6. THE BAROQUE IN ITALY
AND GERMANY

CONNORS, J., *Borromini and the Roman Oratory: Style and Society*, MIT Press, Cambridge, and the Architectural History Foundation, N.Y., 1980
ENGASS, R., & J. BROWN, *Italy and Spain, 1600–1750: Sources and Documents*, Prentice-Hall, Englewood Cliffs, 1970
FREEDBERG, S. J., *Circa 1600: A Revolution of Style in Italian Painting*, Harvard Univ. Press, Cambridge, 1983
*FRIEDLAENDER, W. F., *Caravaggio Studies*, Princeton Univ. Press, 1955
HASKELL, F., *Patrons and Painters: A Study in the Relations Between Italian Art and Society in the Age of the Baroque*, rev. & enl. ed., Yale Univ. Press, New Haven, 1980
HELD, J., & D. POSNER, *Seventeenth and Eighteenth Century: Baroque Painting, Sculpture, Architecture*, Abrams, N.Y., 1971
HEMPEL, E., *Baroque Art and Architecture in Central Europe*, Pelican History of Art, Penguin, Baltimore, 1977
*HIBBARD, H., *Carlo Maderno and Roman Architecture: 1580–1630*, Pennsylvania State Univ. Press, University Park, 1971
HITCHCOCK, H.-R., *Rococo Architecture in Southern Germany*, Phaidon, London, 1968
MAGNUSON, T., *Rome in the Age of Bernini*, Alqvist & Wiksell, Stockholm; Humanities Press, Atlantic Highlands, 1982
*MILLON, H. A., *Baroque and Rococo Architecture*, Braziller, N.Y., 1961
MOIR, A., *Caravaggio*, Abrams, N.Y., 1982
———, *The Italian Followers of Caravaggio*, 2 vols., Harvard Univ. Press, Cambridge, 1967
MORASSI, A., *Complete Catalogue of the Paintings of G. B. Tiepolo*, Phaidon, London, 1962
NORBERG-SCHULTZ, C., *Baroque Architecture*, Abrams, N.Y., 1971
*———, *Late Baroque and Rococo Architecture*, Abrams, N.Y., 1983
PORTOGHESI, P., *Roma Barocca: The History of an Architectonic Culture*, MIT Press, Cambridge, 1970
POSNER, D., *Annibale Carracci*, 2 vols., Phaidon, London, 1971
SPEAR, R. E., *Domenichino*, 2 vols., Yale Univ. Press, New Haven, 1982
*WITTKOWER, R., *Art and Architecture in Italy, 1600 to 1750*, 3d rev. ed., with corrections and augmented bibliography, Pelican History of Art, Penguin, Harmondsworth, N.Y., 1980
———, *Gian Lorenzo Bernini: The Sculptor of the Roman Baroque*, 3d rev. ed., Cornell Univ. Press, Ithaca, 1981

7. THE BAROQUE IN FLANDERS,
HOLLAND, AND SPAIN

BAARD, H. P., *Frans Hals*, Abrams, N.Y., 1981
BAUDOUIN, F., *Pietro Paolo Rubens*, Abrams, N.Y., 1977
BROWN, J., *Francisco de Zurbaran*, Abrams, N.Y., 1974
GÁLLEGO, J., & J. GUDIOL, *Zurbaran, 1598–1664: Biography and Critical Analysis*, Rizzoli, N.Y., 1977
GERSON, H., & E. H. TER KUILE, *Art and Architecture in Belgium, 1600–1800*, Pelican History of Art, Penguin, Baltimore, 1978
HAAK, B., *The Golden Age: Dutch Painters of the Seventeenth Century*, Abrams, N.Y., 1984
KAHR, M. M., *Velazquez: The Art of Painting*, Harper & Row, N.Y., 1976
KUBLER, G. A., & M. SORIA, *Art and Architecture in Spain and Portugal and Their American Dominions, 1500–1800*, Pelican History of Art, Penguin, Baltimore, 1959
LÓPEZ-REY, J., *Velazquez' Work and World*, New York Graphic Society, Greenwich, 1968
NASH, J. M., *The Age of Rembrandt and Vermeer: Dutch Painting in the Seventeenth Century*, Holt, Rinehart & Winston, N.Y., 1972
NICOLSON, B., *Hendrick Terbrugghen*, Lund Humphries, London, 1958

*ROSENBERG, J., *Rembrandt, Life and Work*, rev. ed., Cornell Univ. Press, Ithaca, 1980
———, S. SLIVE, & E. H. TER KUILE, *Dutch Art and Architecture, 1600–1800*, 3d (2d integrated) ed., Pelican History of Art, Penguin, Harmondsworth, N.Y., 1977
SÉRULLAZ, M., & C. POUILLON, *Velazquez*, Abrams, N.Y., 1981
SLATKES, L. J., *Vermeer and His Contemporaries*, Abbeville, N.Y., 1981
SLIVE, S., *Frans Hals*, 3 vols., Phaidon, N.Y., 1970–74
———, *Jacob Van Ruisdael*, Abbeville, N.Y., 1981
*STECHOW, W., *Dutch Landscape Painting of the Seventeenth Century*, reprint of 1966 ed., Cornell Univ. Press, Ithaca, 1980
WHEELOCK, A. K., *Jan Vermeer*, Abrams, N.Y., 1981
WHITE, C., *Rembrandt as an Etcher*, 2 vols., Pennsylvania State Univ. Press, University Park, 1969

8. THE BAROQUE IN FRANCE
AND ENGLAND

BLUNT, A., *Nicolas Poussin*, 2 vols., Bollingen Foundation/Pantheon Books, 1967
FRIEDLAENDER, W. F., *Nicolas Poussin, A New Approach*, Abrams, N.Y., 1966
GAUNT, W., *The Great Century of British Painting: Hogarth to Turner*, Phaidon, London, 1971
GOULD, C. A. M., *Bernini in France*, Princeton Univ. Press, 1982
HERRMANN, L., *British Landscape Painting of the 18th Century*, Oxford Univ. Press, N.Y., 1974
*KALNEIN, W. GRAF, & M. LEVEY, *Art and Architecture of the Eighteenth Century in France*, Pelican History of Art, Penguin, Harmondsworth, Baltimore, 1972
*LEVEY, M., *Rococo to Revolution: Major Trends in Eighteenth Century Painting*, Oxford Univ. Press, N.Y., 1977
NICOLSON, B., & C. WRIGHT, *Georges de La Tour*, Phaidon, London, 1974
PARRY, E., *The Image of the Indian and the Black Man in American Art, 1590–1900*, new ed., Braziller, N.Y., 1974
PAULSON, R., *Hogarth, His Life, Art and Times*, 2 vols., Yale Univ. Press, New Haven, 1971
POSNER, D., *Antoine Watteau*, Cornell Univ. Press, Ithaca, 1984
RÖTHLISBERGER, M., *Claude Lorrain: The Paintings*, 2 vols., Yale Univ. Press, New Haven, 1961
SCHÖNBERGER, A., & H. SOEHNER, *The Rococo Age: Art and Civilization of the 18th Century*, McGraw-Hill, N.Y. 1960
*SUMMERSON, J. N., *Architecture in Britain, 1530–1830*, 6th rev. ed., Pelican History of Art, Penguin, Baltimore, 1977
WILDENSTEIN, G., & D. WILDENSTEIN, *Chardin*, rev. & enl. ed., New York Graphic Society, Greenwich, 1969
———, *The Paintings of Fragonard: Complete Edition*, Phaidon, London, 1960

PART FOUR
THE MODERN WORLD
1. NEOCLASSICISM
AND ROMANTICISM

BOIMÉ, A., *The Academy and French Painting in the 19th Century*, Phaidon, N.Y., 1970
BROWN, M. W., *American Art to 1900*, Abrams, N.Y., 1977
BUCKLAND, G., *Fox Talbot and the Invention of Photography*, Godine, Boston, 1980
*CLARK, K. M., *The Gothic Revival*, Humanities Press, N.Y., 1970
———, *The Romantic Rebellion: Romantic Versus Classical*, Harper & Row, N.Y., 1974
CRAVEN, W., *Sculpture in America*, Crowell, N.Y., 1968
DAVAL, J. L., *Photography: History of an Art*, Skira/Rizzoli, N.Y., 1982
DAVIS, L. G., & J. SIMS, *Black Artists in the United States: An Annotated Bibliography of Books, Articles and Dissertations on Black Artists, 1779–1979*, Greenwood Press, Westport, 1980
*DIXON, R., & S. MUTHESIUS, *Victorian Architecture*, Oxford Univ. Press, N.Y., 1978
DRISKELL, D. C., *Two Centuries of Black American Art*, Los Angeles County Museum of Art/Knopf, N.Y., 1976
EITNER, L. E., *Géricault: His Life and Works*, Cornell Univ. Press, Ithaca, 1982
*———, *Neoclassicism and Romanticism, 1750–1850: Sources and Documents*, 2 vols., Prentice-Hall, Englewood Cliffs, 1970

ESSICK, R. N., *William Blake, Printmaker*, Princeton Univ. Press, 1980

FINBERG, A. J., *The Life of J. M. W. Turner, R.A.*, 2d rev. ed., Clarendon Press, Oxford, 1961

*FRIEDLAENDER, W. F., *From David to Delacroix*, Harvard Univ. Press, Cambridge, 1952

GAUNT, W., *The Restless Century: Painting in Britain, 1800–1900*, Phaidon, London, 1972

GERNSHEIM, H., *Julia Margaret Cameron, Her Life and Photographic Work*, 2d ed., Aperture, Millerton, N.Y., 1975

GERNSHEIM, H. & A., *The History of Photography from the Camera Obscura to the Beginning of the Modern Era*, 2d ed., McGraw-Hill, N.Y., 1969

———, *L. J. M. Daguerre: The History of the Diorama and the Daguerreotype*, Dover, N.Y., 1968

GOSLING, N., *Nadar*, Knopf, N.Y., 1976

GUDIOL, J., *Goya*, Abrams, N.Y., 1965

HAMILTON, G. H., *Nineteenth and Twentieth Century Art: Painting, Sculpture, Architecture*, Abrams, N.Y., 1970

HERRMANN, L., *Turner: Paintings, Watercolors, Prints and Drawings*, New York Graphic Society, Boston, 1975

*HITCHCOCK, H.-R., *Architecture: Nineteenth and Twentieth Centuries*, 2d ed., Pelican History of Art, Penguin, Baltimore, 1971

*HONOUR, H., *Neoclassicism*, Style and Civilization, Penguin, Harmondsworth, 1968

JANSON, H. W., *19th Century Sculpture*, Abrams, N.Y., 1985

*JEFFREY, I., *Photography: A Concise History*, Oxford Univ. Press, N.Y., 1982

JOHNSON, L., *The Paintings of Eugène Delacroix: A Critical Catalogue, 1816–1831*, 2 vols., Clarendon Press, N.Y., 1981

LAFUENTE-FERRARI, E. L., ed., *Goya: His Complete Etchings, Aquatints, and Lithographs*, Abrams, N.Y., 1962

LICHT, F., *Canova*, Abbeville, N.Y., 1983

———, *Sculpture, 19th and 20th Century*, New York Graphic Society, Greenwich, 1967

MAISON, K. E., *Honoré Daumier: Catalogue Raisonné of the Paintings, Watercolors and Drawings*, 2 vols., New York Graphic Society, Greenwich, 1968

*McCOUBREY, J., *American Art, 1700–1960: Sources and Documents*, Prentice-Hall, Englewood Cliffs, 1965

MIDDLETON, R., & D. WATKIN, *Neoclassical and Nineteenth Century Architecture*, Abrams, N.Y., 1980

NANTEUIL, L. DE, *David*, Abrams, N.Y., 1985

*NEWHALL, B., *The History of Photography from 1830 to the Present Day*, 5th rev. ed., New York Graphic Society, Boston, 1982

*NOVOTNY, F., *Painting and Sculpture in Europe, 1780–1880*, Pelican History of Art, Penguin, Baltimore, 1971

*PIERSON, W., & W. H. JORDY, *American Buildings and Their Architects*, 4 vols., Doubleday, Garden City, 1970–78

*POLLACK, P., *Picture History of Photography*, rev. ed., Abrams, N.Y., 1970

REYNOLDS, G., *Constable, the Natural Painter*, Schocken, N.Y., 1969

ROSEN, C., & H. ZERNER, *Romanticism and Realism: The Mythology of Nineteenth-Century Art*, Viking, N.Y., 1984

ROSENBLUM, R., *Jean-Auguste-Dominique Ingres*, new ed., Abrams, N.Y., 1985

———, & H. W., JANSON, *Nineteenth Century Art*, Abrams, N.Y., 1984

*———, *Transformations in Late Eighteenth Century Art*, Princeton Univ. Press, 1967

*SCHAPIRO, M., *Modern Art: Nineteenth and Twentieth Centuries*, 2 vols., Braziller, N.Y., 1968

SNYDER, J., *American Frontiers: The Photographs of Timothy H. O'Sullivan, 1867–1874*, Aperture, Millerton, N.Y., 1981

VINCENT, H. P., *Daumier and His World*, Northwestern Univ. Press, Evanston, 1968

WELLING, W., *Photography in America: The Formative Years, 1839–1900*, Crowell, N.Y., 1978

WILDENSTEIN, G., *Ingres*, 2d rev. ed., Phaidon, London, 1956

WILTON, A., *J. M. W. Turner: His Life and Art*, Rizzoli, N.Y., 1979

2. REALISM AND IMPRESSIONISM

BREESKIN, A. D., *Mary Cassatt: A Catalogue Raisonné of the Oils, Pastels, Watercolors and Drawings*, National Gallery of Art, Washington, D.C., 1970

ELSEN, A. E., *Origins of Modern Sculpture: Pioneers and Premises*, Braziller, N.Y., 1974

*———, *Rodin*, Doubleday, Garden City, for the Museum of Modern Art, N.Y., 1963

FLEMING, G. H., *Rossetti and the Pre-Raphaelite Brotherhood*, Hart-Davies, London, 1967

GOODRICH, G. C., *Thomas Eakins*, 2 vols., Harvard Univ. Press, Cambridge, for the National Gallery of Art, Washington, D.C., 1982

GORDON, R., & A. FORGE, *Monet*, Abrams, N.Y., 1983

GREENFIELD, H., *The Impressionist Revolution*, Doubleday, Garden City, 1972

HANSEN, A. C., *Manet and the Modern Tradition*, Yale Univ. Press, New Haven, 1977

HENDRICKS, G., *The Life and Work of Winslow Homer*, Abrams, N.Y., 1979

*HILTON, T., *The Pre-Raphaelites*, Abrams, N.Y., 1971

KELDER, D., *The French Impressionists and Their Century*, Praeger, N.Y., 1970

*KLINGENDER, F. D., *Art and the Industrial Revolution*, rev. & enl. ed., Evelyn, Adams & MacKay, Chatham, 1968

NICOLL, J., *Dante Gabriel Rossetti*, 1st Amer. ed., Macmillan, N.Y., 1976, c. 1975

*NOCHLIN, L., *Impressionism and Post-Impressionism, 1874–1904: Sources and Documents*, Prentice-Hall, Englewood Cliffs, 1976

*———, *Realism*, Style and Civilization, Penguin, Harmondsworth, Baltimore, 1971

*———, *Realism and Tradition in Art, 1848–1900: Sources and Documents*, Prentice-Hall, Englewood Cliffs, 1966

REWALD, J., *The History of Impressionism*, 4th rev. ed., New York Graphic Society, Greenwich, for the Museum of Modern Art, N.Y., 1973

REYNOLDS, G., *Victorian Painting*, Macmillan, N.Y., 1966

WEISBERG, G. P., *The Realist Tradition: French Painting and Drawing, 1830–1900*, Cleveland Museum of Art, 1981

WHITE, B. E., *Renoir, His Life, Art, and Letters*, Abrams, N.Y., 1984

*WILMERDING, J., *American Art*, Pelican History of Art, Penguin, Harmondsworth, N.Y., 1976

3. POST-IMPRESSIONISM

ALLAND, A., sr., *Jacob A. Riis, Photographer and Citizen*, Aperture, Millerton, N.Y., 1974

BADT, K., *The Art of Cézanne*, Univ. of California Press, Berkeley, 1965

BUNNELL, P., ed., *A Photographic Vision: Pictorial Photography 1889–1923*, Peregrine Smith, Salt Lake City, 1980

CHASSÉ, C., *The Nabis and Their Period*, Praeger, N.Y., 1969

*CHIPP, H. B., *Theories of Modern Art*, Univ. of California Press, Berkeley, 1968

*DELEVOY, R. L., *Symbolists and Symbolism*, Rizzoli, N.Y., 1982

DOTY, R., *Photo-Secession: Stieglitz and the Fine Arts Movement in Photography*, Dover, N.Y., 1978

HAAS, R. B., *Muybridge, Man in Motion*, Univ. of California Press, Berkeley, 1976

*HAMILTON, G. H., *Painting and Sculpture in Europe, 1880–1940*, 3d ed., Pelican History of Art, Penguin, Harmondsworth, Baltimore, 1981

*HODIN, J. P., *Edward Munch*, Praeger, N.Y., 1972

HOMER, W. I., *Seurat and the Science of Painting*, MIT Press, Cambridge, 1964

HUISMAN, P., & M. G. DORTU, *Toulouse-Lautrec*, Doubleday, Garden City, 1973

HULSKER, J., *The Complete Van Gogh*, Abrams, N.Y., 1980

JAWORSKA, W., *Gauguin and the Pont-Aven School*, New York Graphic Society, Greenwich, 1972

JOHNSON, D. C., *American Art Nouveau*, Abrams, N.Y., 1979

JONES, E. Y., *Father of Art Photography: O. E. Rejlander, 1813–1875*, New York Graphic Society, Greenwich, 1973

*MADSEN, S. T., *Art Nouveau*, McGraw-Hill, N.Y., 1967

REWALD, J., *Post-Impressionism: From Van Gogh to Gauguin*, 2d ed., Museum of Modern Art, N.Y., 1962

*ROOKMAAKER, H. R., *Gauguin and 19th Century Art Theory*, Swets & Zeitlinger, Amsterdam, 1972

ROSKILL, M., *Van Gogh, Gauguin, and the Impressionist Circle*, New York Graphic Society, Greenwich, 1970

RUBIN, W., ed., *Cézanne: The Late Work-Essays*, New York Graphic Society, Boston, for the Museum of Modern Art, N.Y., 1977

SCHAPIRO, M., *Paul Cézanne*, 3d ed., Abrams, N.Y., 1965

———, *Van Gogh*, rev. ed., Abrams, N.Y., 1982

SCHARF, A., *Art and Photography*, Penguin Books, Baltimore, 1974

SCHMUTZLER, R., *Art Nouveau*, Abrams, N.Y., 1962

SELZ, P., *Art in Our Times: A Pictorial History 1890–1980*, Abrams, N.Y., 1981

SUTTER, J., ed., *The Neo-Impressionists*, New York Graphic Society, Greenwich, 1970

4. TWENTIETH-CENTURY PAINTING AND SCULPTURE

*ALLOWAY, L., *Roy Lichtenstein*, Abbeville, N.Y., 1983

ARGAN, G. C., *Henry Moore*, Abrams, N.Y., 1973

ARNASON, H. H., *History of Modern Art: Painting, Sculpture, Architecture*, 3d ed., Abrams, N.Y., 1986

ARP, H., *Arp on Arp: Poems, Essays, Memories*, Viking, N.Y., 1972

BARR, A. H., jr., ed., *Cubism and Abstract Art*, reprint, 1936 ed. of the Museum of Modern Art, Arno Press, N.Y., 1966

———, *Fantastic Art, Dada, Surrealism*, reprint of 1936 ed. of the Museum of Modern Art, Arno Press, N.Y., 1969

———, *Matisse, His Art and His Public*, reprint of 1951 ed. of the Museum of Modern Art, Arno Press, N.Y., 1966

———, *Picasso, Fifty Years of His Art*, reprint of 1946 ed. of the Museum of Modern Art, Arno Press, N.Y., 1966

*BARRON, S., & M. TUCHMAN, eds., *Avant-Garde in Russia, 1910–1930: New Perspectives*, MIT Press, Cambridge, 1980

*BATTCOCK, G., *Idea Art: A Critique*, new ed., Dutton, N.Y., 1973

*———, *Minimal Art: A Critical Anthology*, Dutton, N.Y., 1968

*———, *The New Art: A Critical Anthology*, rev. ed., Dutton, N.Y., 1973

*———, *Superrealism: A Critical Anthology*, Dutton, N.Y., 1975

*———, *Why Art: Casual Notes on the Aesthetics of the Immediate Past*, Dutton, N.Y., 1977

BOWNESS, A., *Modern European Art*, Harcourt, Brace, Jovanovich, N.Y., 1972

*BROUDE, N. & M. D. GARRARD, eds., *Feminism and Art History: Questioning the Litany*, Harper & Row, N.Y., 1982

BROWN, M. W., *American Painting from the Armory Show to the Depression*, Princeton Univ. Press, 1955

*BURNHAM, J., *Beyond Modern Sculpture*, Braziller, N.Y., 1968

*———, *Great Western Saltworks: Essays on the Meaning of Post-Formalist Art*, Braziller, N.Y., 1974

*CALAS, N., & E., *Icons and Images of the Sixties*, Dutton, N.Y., 1971

CORK, R., *Vorticism and Abstract Art in the First Machine Age*, 2 vols., Univ. of California Press, Berkeley, 1976–77

CRESPELLE, J.-P., *The Fauves*, New York Graphic Society, Greenwich, 1962

CHRICHTON, M., *Jasper Johns*, Abrams, for the Whitney Museum of American Art, N.Y., 1977

DAIX, P., *Cubists and Cubism*, Rizzoli, N.Y., 1982

DE FRANCIA, P., *Fernand Leger*, Yale Univ. Press, New Haven, 1983

DOESBURG, T. VAN, *Principles of Neo-Plastic Art*, New York Graphic Society, Greenwich, 1968

DOTY, R., ed., *Contemporary Black Artists in America*, Whitney Museum of American Art, N.Y., 1971

DUBE, W.-D., *Expressionists and Expressionism*, Rizzoli, N.Y., 1983

*DUTHUIT, G., *The Fauvist Painters*, Wittenborn, Schultz, N.Y., 1950

*FINCH, C., *Pop Art: The Object and the Image*, Dutton, N.Y., 1968

FINE, E. H., *The Afro-American Artist: A Search for Identity*, Holt, Rinehart & Winston, N.Y., 1973

FLACK, A., *Audrey Flack on Painting*, Abrams, N.Y., 1981

*FRANCIS, R. H., *Jasper Johns*, Abbeville, N.Y., 1984

*FRANK, E., *Jackson Pollock*, Abbeville, N.Y., 1983

GEIST, S., *Brancusi: The Sculpture and Drawings*, Abrams, N.Y., 1975

*GELDZAHLER, H., *American Painting in the Twentieth Century*, Metropolitan Museum of Art, N.Y., 1965

GIBIAN, G., & H. W. TJALSMA, eds., *Russian Modernism: Culture and the Avant-Garde, 1900–1930*, Cornell Univ. Press, Ithaca, 1976

*GOLDWATER, R., *Primitivism in Modern Art*, rev. ed., Vintage, N.Y., 1967

*GOWING, L., *Matisse*, Oxford Univ. Press, N.Y., 1979

*GRAY, C., *The Russian Experiment in Art, 1863–1922*, Abrams, N.Y., 1970

GREEN, C., *Leger and the Avant Garde*, Yale Univ. Press, New Haven, 1976

GROHMANN, W., *Paul Klee*, Abrams, N.Y., 1955

*HERBERT, R. L., ed., *Modern Artists on Art*, Prentice-Hall, Englewood Cliffs, 1965

HOMER, W. I., & V. ORGAN, *Robert Henri and His Circle*, Cornell Univ. Press, Ithaca, 1969

HUNTER, S., & J. JACOBUS, *American Art of the Twentieth Century: Painting, Sculpture, Architecture*, Abrams, N.Y., 1974

JAFFE, H. L. C., *De Stijl, 1917–1931: Visions of Utopia*, Abbeville, N.Y., 1982

———, *Piet Mondrian*, Abrams, N.Y., 1970

KAHNWEILER, D.-H., *Juan Gris: His Life and Work*, rev. ed., Abrams, N.Y., 1969

KRAUSS, R. E., *Terminal Ironworks: The Sculpture of David Smith*, MIT Press, Cambridge, 1971

KULTERMANN, U., *The New Sculpture, Environments and Assemblages*, Praeger, N.Y., 1968

LALIBERTE, N. & A. MOGELSON, *Collage, Montage, Assemblage: History and Contemporary Techniques*, Van Nostrand-Reinhold, N.Y., 1972

LAMBERT, J.-C., *Cobra*, Abbeville, N.Y., 1984

LEVIN, G., *Edward Hopper, The Art and the Artist*, Whitney Museum of American Art, N.Y., 1980

LIPPARD, L. R., *Dadas on Art*, Prentice-Hall, Englewood Cliffs, 1971

*_____, *From the Center: Feminist Essays on Women's Art*, Dutton, N.Y., 1976

*_____, *Pop Art*, Praeger, N.Y., 1966

*_____, *Surrealists on Art*, Prentice-Hall, Englewood Cliffs, 1970

LODDER, C., *Russian Constructivism*, Yale Univ. Press, New Haven, 1983

LUCIE-SMITH, E., *Art Now*, Morrow, N.Y., 1977

*_____, *Late Modern: The Visual Arts Since 1945*, Oxford Univ. Press, N.Y., 1975

MARCUS, S. E., *David Smith: The Sculptor and His Work*, Cornell Univ. Press, Ithaca, 1983

MARTIN, M. W., *Futurist Art and Theory, 1909–1915*, Clarendon Press, Oxford, 1968

MATTHEWS, J. H., *An Introduction to Surrealism*, Pennsylvania State Univ. Press, University Park, 1965

MELVILLE, R., *Henry Moore: Sculpture and Drawings, 1921–1969*, Abrams, N.Y., 1970

*MONTE, J. K., *22 Realists*, Whitney Museum of American Art, N.Y., 1970

MOTHERWELL, R., *The Dada Painters and Poets*, Wittenborn, Schultz, N.Y., 1951

*MULLER, J.-E., *Fauvism*, Praeger, N.Y., 1967

MUNRO, E., *Originals: Women Artists*, Simon & Schuster, N.Y., 1979

*O'KEEFFE, G., *Georgia O'Keeffe*, Viking, Penguin, N.Y., 1977

Phaidon Dictionary of Twentieth-Century Art, Phaidon, N.Y., 1973

POPPER, F., *Origins and Development of Kinetic Art*, New York Graphic Society, Greenwich, 1968

RICHTER, H., *Dada: Art and Anti-Art*, McGraw-Hill, N.Y., 1965

RICKEY, G., *Constructivism: Origins and Evolution*, Braziller, N.Y., 1967

ROETHEL, H. K., *The Blue Rider . . . in the Municipal Gallery, Munich*, Praeger, N.Y., 1971

*ROSE, B., *American Art Since 1900*, rev. ed., Praeger, N.Y., 1975

_____, *Jackson Pollock: Drawing Into Painting*, Museum of Modern Art, N.Y., 1980

ROSENBERG, H., *The De-Definition of Art: Action Art to Pop to Earthworks*, Horizon, N.Y., 1972

*ROSENBLUM, R., *Cubism and Twentieth-Century Art*, rev. ed., Abrams, N.Y., 1976

*_____, *Modern Painting and the Northern Tradition: Friedrich to Rothko*, Harper & Row, N.Y., 1975

ROSENTHAL, N., *Robert Rauschenberg*, Abbeville, N.Y., 1984

ROTERS, E., *Painters of the Bauhaus*, Praeger, N.Y., 1969

RUBIN, W., *Dada and Surrealist Art*, Abrams, N.Y., 1968

_____, ed., *Pablo Picasso, A Retrospective*, New York Graphic Society, Boston, for the Museum of Modern Art, N.Y., 1980

RUDENSTINE, A. Z., ed., *Russian Avant-Garde Art: The George Costakis Collection*, Abrams, N.Y., 1981

*SCHNEEDE, U. M., *Surrealism*, Abrams, N.Y., 1974

SCHNEIDER, P., *Matisse*, Rizzoli, N.Y., 1984

*SPIES, W., *Max Ernst*, Abrams, N.Y., 1969

_____, *Vasarely*, Abrams, N.Y., 1969

STIEGLITZ, A., *Georgia O'Keeffe: A Portrait*, Viking, N.Y., 1979

TRIER, E., *Form and Space: The Sculpture of the Twentieth Century*, rev. ed., Praeger, N.Y., 1968

TUCHMAN, M., *New York School: The First Generation*, New York Graphic Society, Greenwich, for the Los Angeles County Museum of Art, 1971

*VERGO, P., *Art in Vienna, 1898–1918: Klimt, Kokoschka, Schiele and Their Contemporaries*, Cornell Univ. Press, Ithaca, 1981

VOGT, P., *Contemporary Painting*, Abrams, N.Y., 1981

_____, *Expressionism: German Painting, 1905–1920*, Abrams, N.Y., 1980

WALDMAN, D., *Mark Rothko, 1903–1970: A Retrospective*, Abrams, N.Y., 1978

WERNER, A., *Chaim Soutine*, Abrams, N.Y., 1977

WITHERS, J., *Julio Gonzalez, Sculpture in Iron*, New York Univ. Press, 1978

5. TWENTIETH-CENTURY ARCHITECTURE

BANHAM, R., *Theory and Design in the First Machine Age*, 2d ed., Praeger, N.Y., 1960

*BAYER, H., *Bauhaus 1919–1928*, New York Graphic Society, Greenwich, for the Museum of Modern Art, N.Y., 1976

BRANZI, A., *The Hot House: Italian New Wave Design*, MIT Press, Cambridge, 1984

BUSH-BROWN, A., *Louis Sullivan*, Braziller, N.Y., 1960

*COLE, D., *From Tipi to Skyscraper: A History of Women in Architecture*, MIT Press, Cambridge, 1978

COLLINS, G., *Antonio Gaudi*, Braziller, N.Y., 1960

*DREXLER, A. L., *Ludwig Mies van der Rohe*, Braziller, N.Y., 1960

*_____, *Transformations in Modern Architecture*, New York Graphic Society, Boston, 1980

Encyclopedia of 20th-Century Architecture, rev. ed., Abrams, N.Y., 1985

FISHMAN, R., *Urban Utopias in the Twentieth Century: Ebenezer Howard, Frank Lloyd Wright and Le Corbusier*, Basic Books, N.Y., 1977

FITCH, J. M., *American Building*, 2d ed., 2 vols., Houghton, Mifflin, Boston, 1966–72

*_____, *Walter Gropius*, Braziller, N.Y., 1960

FRAMPTON, K., *Modern Architecture, 1851–1945*, 2 vols., Rizzoli, N.Y., 1983

GIEDION, S., *Space, Time and Architecture*, 5th rev. & enl. ed., Harvard Univ. Press, Cambridge, 1967

*HITCHCOCK, H.-R., & P. C. JOHNSON, *The International Style*, Norton, N.Y., 1966

*JENCKS, C., *Post-Modern Classicism*, Rizzoli, N.Y., 1981

JOHNSON, P. C., *Mies van der Rohe*, 3d ed., rev., New York Graphic Society, Boston, for the Museum of Modern Art, N.Y., 1978

OCHSNER, J. K., *H. H. Richardson: Complete Architectural Works*, MIT Press, Cambridge, 1982

*PEVSNER, N., *The Sources of Modern Architecture and Design*, Oxford Univ. Press, N.Y., 1977

*PORTOGHESI, P., *Postmodern: The Architecture of the Post-Industrial Society*, Rizzoli, N.Y., 1983

PULOS, A. J., *American Design Ethic: A History of Industrial Design*, MIT Press, Cambridge, 1983

RISEBERO, B., *Modern Architecture and Design: An Alternative History*, MIT Press, Cambridge, 1983

RUSSELL, J., *Art Nouveau Architecture*, Rizzoli, N.Y., 1979

SCULLY, V. J., *Modern Architecture*, rev. ed., Braziller, N.Y., 1974

SHARP, D., *Modern Architecture and Expressionism*, Braziller, N.Y., 1966

_____, *The Rationalists: Theory and Design in the Modern Movement*, Architectural Press, London, 1979

TAFURI, M., *Contemporary Architecture*, Abrams, N.Y., 1977

_____, & F. DAL CO, *Modern Architecture*, Abrams, N.Y., 1979

TROY, N. J., *The De Stijl Environment*, MIT Press, Cambridge, 1983

TUNNARD, C., *The City of Man*, 2d ed., Scribner, N.Y., 1970

*WINGLER, H., *Bauhaus: Weimar, Dessau, Berlin, Chicago*, MIT Press, Cambridge, 1969

6. TWENTIETH-CENTURY PHOTOGRAPHY

ADES, D., *Photomontage*, Pantheon Books, N.Y., 1976

August Sander: Photographs of an Epoch, 1904–1959. Preface by Beaumont Newhall, commentary by Robert Kramer, Aperture, Millerton, N.Y., 1980

BERNARD, B., *Photodiscovery: Masterworks of Photography 1840–1940*, Abrams, N.Y., 1980

BUCKLAND, G., *Reality Recorded: Early Documentary Photography*, New York Graphic Society, Greenwich, 1974

CALLAHAN, S., ed., *The Photographs of Margaret Bourke-White*, New York Graphic Society, Greenwich, 1972

CARTIER-BRESSON, H., *The Decisive Moment*, Simon & Schuster, N.Y., 1952

COKE, V. D., *The Painter and the Photograph from Delacroix to Warhol*, rev. ed., Univ. of New Mexico Press, Albuquerque, 1972

FREUND, G., *Photography and Society*, Godine, Boston, 1980

GIDAL, T. N., *Modern Photojournalism: Origins and Evolution 1910–33*, Macmillan, N.Y., 1973

GOLDBERG, V., ed., *Photography in Print*, Simon & Schuster, N.Y., 1981

GREEN, J., *American Photography: A Critical History, 1945 to the Present*, Abrams, N.Y., 1984

HAUS, A., *Moholy-Nagy: Photographs and Photograms*, Pantheon, N.Y., 1980

HEARTFIELD, J., *Photomontages of the Nazi Period*, Universe Books, N.Y., 1977

HOMER, W. I., *Alfred Stieglitz and the American Avant-Garde*, New York Graphic Society, Greenwich, 1977

HURLEY, F. J., *Portrait of a Decade: Roy Stryker and the Development of Documentary Photography in the Thirties*, Louisiana State Univ. Press, Baton Rouge, 1972

Life Library of Photography, 17 vols., rev. ed., Time-Life Books, Alexandria, Va., 1983

LYONS, N., ed., *Aaron Siskind Photographer*, George Eastman House, Rochester, N.Y., 1965

MADDOW, B., *Edward Weston, His Life and Photographs*, rev. ed., Aperture, Millerton, N.Y., 1979

METZKER, M., *Dorothea Lange, A Photographer's Life*, Farrar, Straus & Giroux, N.Y., 1978

NAEF, W. J., *The Collection of Alfred Stieglitz: Fifty Pioneers of Modern Photography*, The Metropolitan Museum of Art/Viking, N.Y., 1979

NEWHALL, N., *Ansel Adams: The Eloquent Light*, Aperture, Millerton, N.Y., 1980

Paul Strand: Sixty Years of Photographs, profile by Calvin Tompkins, Aperture, Millerton, N.Y., 1976

PETRUCK, P. R., ed., *The Camera Viewed: Writings on Twentieth-Century Photography*, 2 vols., Dutton, N.Y., 1979

Photographs by Man Ray: 1920 Paris 1934, 1935, reprint, Dover, N.Y., 1979

SIPLEY, L. W., *A Half Century of Color*, Macmillan, N.Y., 1951

SOUTHALL, T. W., *Diane Arbus: Magazine Work*, Aperture, Millerton, N.Y., 1984

STEICHEN, E., *A Life in Photography*, Doubleday, Garden City, 1984

STRYKER, R., & N. WOOD, *In This Proud Land: America 1935–43 as Seen in the FSA Photographs*, New York Graphic Society, Greenwich, 1973

SZARKOWSKI, J., *Mirrors and Windows: American Photography since 1960*, Museum of Modern Art, N.Y., 1978

_____, and H., and M. MORRIS, *The Work of Atget*, 4 vols., Museum of Modern Art, N.Y., 1981–84

INDEX

Vikings, 256, 273, 279
Village Bride, see Greuze
Villani, Filippo, 392
VILLARD DE HONNECOURT, *Front View of a Lion*, 340; *483*; *Wheel of Fortune*, 340, 418; *482*
Virgin and Child with Angels, see Grünewald
Virgin of Paris, Notre-Dame, 329–30, 333, 335; *462*
Virgin of the Rocks, see Leonardo da Vinci
Visigoths, 197, 238
Vision After the Sermon, see Gauguin
Visitation, see Broederlam; Moissac; Reims, Cathedral
VISPRÉ, FRANCIS XAVIER, *Portrait of Louis-François Roubiliac* (attr.), 20; *13*
Vitruvius, 165
Vogelherd, Germany, cave art, *Horse*, 29; *18*
Voltaire, 563; portrait of, *see* Houdon
VUILLARD, ÉDOUARD, 648; *Interior*, 648; *907*

Wainwright Building, St. Louis, *see* Sullivan
wallpaper, "Pimpernel," *see* Morris
WALPOLE, HORACE (with WILLIAM ROBINSON and others), Strawberry Hill, Twickenham, 578; *801, 802*
War Helmet, Tlingit, 50; *48*
Warka, *see* Uruk
Washington, George, 609; portrait of, *see* Houdon
Water Carrier of Seville, see Velázquez
Water Lilies, Giverny, see Monet
Watson and the Shark, see Copley
WATTEAU, ANTOINE, 555, 557, 560, 562; *Pilgrimage to Cythera*, 555–56, 558, 561; *773*, cp. 106
Wedding Portrait, see Eyck, J.
Wedricus, Abbot, see *Gospel Book of*
Weimar, East Germany, School of Arts and Crafts (Bauhaus), 750
Werkbund Exhibition, Cologne, *see* Taut; Velde
WEST, BENJAMIN, 582, 583; *Death of General*

Wolfe, 582–83, 617; *812*
Westminster Abbey, *see* London
WESTON, EDWARD, 773, 780; *Pepper*, 773; *1059*
westwork, 259, 261, 274–75; *376*
WEYDEN, ROGIER VAN DER, 378–79, 387, 390; *Descent from the Cross*, 378, 387; *517*, cp. 63; *Francesco d'Este*, 379; *518*
Wheat Field and Cypress Trees, see Gogh
Wheel of Fortune, see Villard de Honnecourt
WHISTLER, JAMES McNEILL, 634, 635, 663, 696, 746; *Arrangement in Black and Gray: The Artist's Mother*, 634; *882*; *Nocturne in Black and Gold: The Falling Rocket*, 634, 672; *883*, cp. 123
WHITE, MINOR, 780, 781; *Ritual Branch*, 780, 781; *1074*
White Shroud, see Clemente
"White Temple," *see* Uruk
Whitehall Palace, London, *see* Jones
"Wies, Die," West Germany, pilgrimage church, *see* Zimmermann
Willendorf, Austria, see *Venus of*
William the Conqueror, 273, 282, 296
Williams, William Carlos, 719
WILLIAMS, WILLIAM T., 717; *Batman*, 717; cp. 153
Winckelmann, Johann, 142, 582, 608
Winged God, silver coin, from Peparethus, 149; *210*
Winged Victory, see *Nike of Samothrace*
WITZ, CONRAD, 385–86, 390; *Miraculous Draught of Fishes*, altarpiece, Geneva Cathedral, 385–86, 621; *524*
Woman II, see De Kooning
Woman with Scales, see Vermeer
women artists, 109, 500–501, 527, 557–58, 607, 622, 635, 636, 688, 696, 713, 714, 724, 737, 743–44
Women Regents of the Old Men's Home at Haarlem, *see* Hals
woodcut, 388–89, 479–80, 491, 531, 613
Wordsworth, William, 575

Workmen Carrying a Beam, see Saqqara
World War I, 670, 672, 685, 687, 690, 692, 719, 738, 777
World War II, 275, 670–71, 685, 727, 737
Wounded Bison, see Altamira
WREN, SIR CHRISTOPHER, 560–61, 578; St. Paul's Cathedral, London, 560–61, 576; *782–84*
WRIGHT, FRANK LLOYD, 752, 761; Robie House, Chicago, 752; *1033, 1034*
Würzburg, West Germany, Episcopal Palace, *see:* Neumann; Tiepolo

X, The, see Bladen
Xerxes, king of Persia, 82

Young Lady with an Umbrella, see Lumière
Young Man Among Roses, see Hilliard
Youth and Demon of Death, cinerary container, Etruscan, 152–53, 156; *219*

zaum, 687–88
Zeus: Altar of, *see* Pergamum; Temple of, *see* Olympia
ziggurats, 71–72, 78, 245, 286, 765; of King Urnammu, *see* Ur; "White Temple," *see* Uruk
ZIMMERMANN, DOMINIKUS, 521; "Die Wies," pilgrimage church, Upper Bavaria, 521, 556; *723, 724*
Zoroaster, 82
Zoser, king of Egypt, 58, 60; Funerary District of, Step Pyramid of, *see* Saqqara
ZUCCARI, TADDEO, *Conversion of St. Paul*, 593; *818*
Zuccone, see Donatello
ZURBARÁN, FRANCISCO DE, 535; *St. Serapion*, 535–36, 599; *751*, cp. 103

LIST OF CREDITS

The author and publisher wish to thank the libraries, museums, and private collectors for permitting the reproduction in black-and-white and in color of paintings, prints, and drawings in their collections. Photographs have been supplied by the following, whose courtesy is gratefully acknowledged. Figure numbers in roman type refer to black-and-white illustrations; those in italics signify colorplates:

A.C.L., Brussels, Copyright: 399, 412, 512–14, 533, 725, 827, 845, 909, 915; Akademie der Kunst der D.D.R., Berlin: 1069; Albertina, Vienna: 710; Albright-Knox Art Gallery, Buffalo: 986; *145*; Alinari, Florence: 2, 3, 115, 179, 201, 215, 217, 219, 224, 226, 228, 247, 253, 255, 259, 262–64, 269, 273–77, 280, 282, 283, 298, 310, 323, 395, 396, 402, 403, 449, 451, 452, 454, 455, 471–73, 477–79, 486, 487, 491, 492, 494, 497, 508, 520, 536, 540–45, 547, 548, 550, 552, 553, 559, 562, 563, 566, 570, 572, 577, 578, 580–82, 584, 587–89, 596–99, 603, 611, 615, 616, 618–20, 629–31, 635–37, 643, 649, 656–59, 684, 696, 699, 703, 705, 707–9, 818, 851, 857, 890; *53, 55, 68*; Altarocca, Terni: 220; American Museum of Natural History, N.Y.: 48, 50, 51; Andrews, Wayne, Grosse Pointe, Mich.: 712, 774, 798; Anker, Peter, Oslo: 358; Archaeological Museum, Teheran: 112; Art Institute of Chicago: 821, 886, 912, 1003, 1057; *119, 128, 132, 133*; Arts Council of Great Britain, London: 877; Arts et Métiers Graphiques, Paris, from G. Marçais, *L'Architecture Musulmane d'Occident*: 338; Ashmolean Museum, Oxford: 82, 116, 668, 747; The Baltimore Museum of Art: 896; The Barnes Foundation, Merion, Pa., Copyright: 927; Barsotti, Florence: 474, 475; Bavarian State Library, Munich: *42, 46*; Bavarian State Museums, Munich: 531, 638, 670, 726, 762; *91*; Bayer, Herbert, Montecito, Cal., Copyright: 1068; Beseler (after): 377, 378; Beyeler Gallery, Basel: 148; Biblioteca Laurenziana, from Christian Huelsen, *Il Libro di Giuliano da Sangallo*: 556; Bibliothèque Nationale, Paris: 367, 482–85, 796; *33, 39*; Bitjebier, Paul, Brussels: 942; Bongers Verlag, Aurel, Recklinghausen: *34*; Borchardt, L. (after): 63; Borsig, Arnold, Berlin: 447; Bott, Dr. Gerhard, Darmstadt: 1019; Bowness, Alan, London, Copyright: 1000; Boymans-van Beuningen Museum, Rotterdam: 746; Braunfels, W., *Mittelalterliche . . . Toscana*, pl. III: 401; Brera Gallery, Milan: 601; Brisighelli-Udine, Cividale: 362; British Library, London: 354; *36, 38*; British Museum, London: 16, 304, 352, 354–57, 419, 610, 760; Brogi di Laurati, G., Florence: 546; Bruckmann, F., Munich: 641, 667, 744, 867; Bryan and Shear, Glasgow: 1028; Bulloz, Paris: 407, 408, 410, 689, 690, 755, 832, 838, 854, 855, 873, 892; Bundesamt für Denkmalspflege, Vienna: 420; Burstein, Barney, Boston: 929; Byzantine Institute of America, Dumbarton Oaks, Washington, D.C. (courtesy Paul A. Underwood): 328; Caisse Nationale des Monuments Historiques, Paris: 4, 20, 32, 68, 106, 138, 405, 415, 437, 469, 470, 480, 481, 501, 526, 613, 677, 692, 729, 759, 772, 773, 825, 858, 875, 876; Cameraphoto, Venice: 83; Canali, Ludovico, Rome: *19, 32, 50–52, 59, 65, 67, 73, 78, 86, 94, 95*; Castelli, Leo, N.Y.: 976; *152*; Centraal Museum, Utrecht, Copyright: 730; Chapman, William, N.Y. from: *Cradle of Man's Art*: 15; Chevojon, Paris: 808; Chicago Historical Society: 866; Choisy, A. (after): 385; Cinémathèque Française, Paris: 926; City Museums and Art Gallery, Birmingham: *122*; Clarendon Press, Oxford, from K. A. C. Creswell, *Early Muslim Architecture*: 334, 336, 337; Clements, Geoffrey, N.Y.: 984; *125, 151, 157, 158, 164*; Cleveland Museum of Art: 12, 977, 991; *162*; Commissione Pontificale d'Archeologia Sacra, Rome: 287; Compagnie Aerienne Française, Suresmes: 776; Cooper, A. C., Ltd., London: 820; Costakis Coll., George, Copyright 1981, George Costakis, Athens: 954; *Country Life*, England, Copyright: 787, 797, 802; Courtauld Institute, London: 780, 871; Davies, N. de Garis, Chicago: 77; De Angelis d'Ossat, G. (after): 292; De Dartien, F., *Etude . . . lombarde*, pl. 29: 397; De Francovich, Geza, Rome: 411; De Maré, Eric, Copyright Gordon Fraser Gallery, Ltd., London: 1022; Detroit Institute of Arts: *123*; Deutscher Kunstverlag, Munich: 19, 175, 249, 363, 379, 398, 444, 465, 800; Devinoy, Pierre, Paris: 417, 422, 856; Diehl, C. (after): 319; Dingjan, A., The Hague: 745; Dräyer, Walter, Zurich: 225; *Du-Atlantis*, Sept. 1965, Zurich: 880; Du Cerceau, Etienne, *Les Plus Excellents Batiments . . .*: 687; Dwan Gallery, N.Y.: *160*; Editions d'Art Lucien Mazenod, Paris: 58; Editions Arthaud, Paris, from S. N.

Kramer, *History Begins at Sumer*: 94, 97; Editions Cercle d'Art, Paris: *130*; Editions Tel, Paris: 95, 98, 655; Effman 1912 (after): 366; Elisofon, Eliot (Copyright Time, Inc., N.Y.): 41; Emmerich Gallery, André, N.Y.: 974; Fiorentini, Venice: 593; Fischbach Gallery, N.Y.: 1010; Florions, Lam, Hollandische Rading, The Netherlands: *173*; Fogg Art Museum, Harvard University, Cambridge, Mass.: 813, 904; Fondazione Giorgio Cini, Istituto di Storia dell'Arte (Foto Rossi), Venice: 645, 662, 663; Fotocielo, Rome: 235, 291, 322, 700; Fototeca Unione, Rome: 163, 227, 230–33, 237–38, 248, 250, 258, 261, 371, 453, 625, 753; Foto Marburg, Marburg/Lahn: 173, 375, 406, 433, 435, 456, 459, 461, 462, 466, 530, 612, 614, 685, 721, 811; Frantz, Alison, Princeton, N.J.: 119, 123, 131, 137, 166, 169, 171, 174, 176, 318, 320; Fratelli Fabbri Editore, Milan: *96*; Freeman, John R., Ltd., London: 590; Freer Gallery of Art, Smithsonian Institution, Washington, D.C.: 351; French Tourist Office, N.Y.: 767; The Frick Collection, Copyright, N.Y.: 739; *72*; Furtwängler, A. (after): 156; Gabinetto Fotografico Nazionale, Rome: 216, 223, 271, 329, 565, 606, 627, 694, 695, 702, 769; Gabinetto Nazionale delle Stampe, Rome: 622, 666; Gemäldegalerie, Kassel: *101*; George Eastman House, Rochester, N.Y.: 919, 924, 925; German Archaeological Institute, Rome: 6, 222, 245, 254, 266, 267, 281, 309; Baghdad: 86, 90; Berlin: 88; Athens: 129, 130, 152; Geymüller (after): 608; Giraudon, Paris: 416, 436, 457, 504, 506, 527, 600, 602, 605, 679, 688, 691, 756, 810, 828, 829, 831, 837, 839, 842, 849, 868, 874; *45*; Goethe Museum, Frankfurt: 816; Gorgoni, Gianfranco, N.Y.: 1011; *170*; Grinnell (after): 159, 160; Gundermann, Würzburg: 97; Gurlitt (after): 313; Hals Museum, Frans, Haarlem: 733; Hampton Institute, Hampton, Virginia: 887; Harrier, Richard, N.Y.: 194; Harris, O. K., N.Y.: *1*; Hedrich-Blessing, Chicago: 1033, (Bill Engdahl) 1043; Held, André, Ecublens: 23; Herdeg's Erban, Hugo P., Zurich: 39; Hermitage Museum, Leningrad: 108, 741; Hervé, Lucien, Paris: 1040, 1041, 1045; *174*; Hirmer Verlag, Max, Munich: 55, 57, 60, 61, 64, 65, 70, 71, 74, 76, 79, 81, 84, 89, 118, 120, 122, 125, 126, 128, 133, 134, 139–44, 146–51, 153, 155, 167, 170, 172, 178, 180–83, 185–92, 195, 196, 198, 202, 206, 208, 210–13, 218, 260, 272, 294, 297, 301, 302, 311, 315, 316, 722, 723; *6, 11–13, 15, 17, 18, 27, 29, 30, 49*; Hodge (after): 165; Holton, George, N.Y.: 38; Horn, Walter (courtesy Schmolz & Ulrich, Cologne): 369; Huelsen, C. (after): 243; Huntington Library, San Marino: 790; Hurault, St.-Germain-en-Laye, courtesy Jean M. Porcher: 404; Hürlimann, Martin, from *Moscow and Leningrad*: 324; from *France*: 389, 434, 776; Hursley, Timothy, Little Rock, Ark.: 1050; Istituto Centrale del Restauro, Rome: 488; Istituto di Etruscologia e Antichità Italiche, University of Rome: 221; The Iveagh Bequest, the trustees of Kenwood, Copyright: 740; *Jahrbuch des Deutschen Werkbundes* (1915): 1030, 1032; Janson, H. W., N.Y.: 445, 561, 997; from *Key Monuments in the History of Art*, Abrams, N.Y.: 446, 551, 574, 626, 1031; Janson, Peter A., Austin, Texas: 686; Josse, Paris: 120; Kaufmann, F., Munich: 184; Kennedy, Clarence, Northampton, Mass.: 519; Kenyon, S. W., Wellington, England: 22, 23; Kersting, A. F., London: 293, 391, 441, 442, 763, 781, 782, 795, 801; Kidder-Smith, G. E., N.Y.: 161, 162, 236, 242, 265, 306, 312, 339, 341, 344, 346, 348, 400, 426, 554, 701, 706, 711, 713, 715, 1044; Klee, Felix, Bern: *136*; Klee Foundation, Bern: *143*; Knoedler, M., and Co., N.Y.: 901; Korab, Balthazar, Trot, Mich.: 1016; Koziowski, Julius (courtesy of Holly Solomon Gallery, N.Y.): 989; Krischen, F. (after): 193; Kubach, H. E. (after): 365; Kuhn, Herbert, Mainz: 14; Kunsthalle, Hamburg: 823; Kunsthistorisches Museum, Vienna: 305, 349, 370, 650, 682; *71*; Lange, Kurt, Obersdorf/Allgau: 53, 54, 75, 537; Lauer, J. P. (after): 59; Leiris, Galerie Louise, Paris: 1; Lescaze, William, N.Y.: 1042; Library of Congress, Washington, D.C.: 817; Linck, Tony, Fort Lee, N.J.: 35; Lomeli, Juan Arauz, Guadalajara, courtesy Laurence Schmeckebier, Syracuse, N.Y.: 940; Lotz, Hilde, Florence: 587; McKenna, Rollie, Stonington, Conn.: 557, 575, 660; Magasins St.-Bernard, Vézelay: 409; Magnum, N.Y.: 1055, 1063, 1066; Mansell Collection, London: 102, 103; Marlborough Gallery, N.Y.: 1013; Marshack, Alexander, N.Y., Copyright: 18, 30, 31; Maryland Historical Society, Baltimore: 806; Marzari, P., Milan: 22; Mas, Barcelona: 340, 342, 653, 754, 843, 893, 1026; *63, 64, 80, 84, 98, 104, 114*; Mazenod, Jean: 5; Meisel Gallery, Louis K., N.Y.: 1̂63; Mellaart, James, London (from *Çatal-Hüyük*): 25–29; *3*; The Metropolitan Museum of Art,

N.Y.: 5, 42, 72, 85 (from Harry Burton), 121, 135, 145, 278, 284, 350, 500, 509, 518, 534, 585, 651, 669, 674, 742, 775, 787, 819, 826, 835, 843, 844, 889; *25, 60, 61, 105, 112*; Miller Gallery, Robert, N.Y.: 968; Millon, Henry, from *Key Monuments in the History of Architecture*; Abrams, N.Y.: 609, 714, 1046; Ministry of Works, London, Crown Copyright: 33, 34, 792, 793; Moore, Henry: 998, 999; Morgan Library, Pierpont, N.Y.: *41*; Müller, Christof, Nuremberg: 529; Multiples, Inc., N.Y.: 983; Municipal Library, Epernay: 372; *40*; Musée Condé, Chantilly: *58*; Museo Nacional de Antropología, Mexico City: 46; Museum, Geneva: 524; Museum, Schwerin: 704; Museum of Fine Arts, Boston: 11, 66, 69, 96, 648, 671, 672, 743, 814, 846; *56, 111*; The Museum of Modern Art, N.Y.: 10, 914, 916, 933, 935, 937, 941, 943, 945, 946, 948, 957, 961, 964, 967, 972, 990, 1001, 1002, 1005–8, 1037, 1038, 1052, 1053, 1054, 1058, 1062, 1064, 1070; *129, 135, 141, 142, 146, 147, 166–69*; Museum of the American Indian–Heye Foundation, N.Y.: 47; National Buildings Record, London, Copyright: 440 (F. H. Crossley), 807; National Gallery, London: 515, 516, 521, 564, 728, 757, 789; The National Gallery of Art, Washington, D.C.: 8, 9, 239, 330, 872; *70*; National Gallery of Canada, Ottawa: 812; National Gallery of Scotland, Edinburgh: *127*; National Library, Vienna: *28*; National Monuments Record, Glasgow, Crown Copyright: 1029; National Museum, Oslo: 910; National Museum, Stockholm: 734; National Museum of Ireland, Dublin: 361; National Museum Vincent van Gogh, Amsterdam: 899; Nelson, Otto, N.Y.: *153*; Nickel, Richard, Chicago: 1023–25; Österreichische Galerie, Vienna: 911; Oldenberg, Claes, Copyright, courtesy Gemini Gel, Los Angeles: 1015; Oriental Institute, University of Chicago: 73, 91, 99 (Hans G. Güterbock), 100, 101, 109–11, 114; from Davies & Gardiner, *Ancient Egyptian Paintings*: 7; Pantheon Books, N.Y., from Otto von Simson, *The Gothic Cathedral*: 423; Parasol Press, N.Y.: 1072; Peabody Museum, Harvard University, Cambridge, Mass.: 49; Pedicini, Rocco, Naples: *21*; Penguin Press, Baltimore, from K. J. Conant, *Carolingian and Romanesque Architecture, 850–1200*: 384, 392, 393; from H. Frankfort, *The Art and Architecture of the Ancient Orient*: 87; from H.-R. Hitchcock, *Architecture: Nineteenth and Twentieth Centuries*: 809, 1027; from: R. Krautheimer, *Early Christian and Byzantine Architecture*: 288, 289; from A. W. Lawrence, *Greek Architecture*: 168; from N. Pevsner, *Outline Of European Architecture*: 448, 450, 558, 768; Perron, Robert, N.Y.: 1047; Philadelphia Museum of Art: 885, 888, 944, 952, 959, 960; *139*; Photo Meyer, Vienna: 87, 93; Picard, C., Cambridge, England: 177; Pollitzer, Eric, N.Y.: 431, 432; *159*; Powell, Josephine, Rome: 321, 327, 496; Princeton University Art Museum: 853, 905; Princeton University Library: 905; Raffaeli, Armoni, and Moretti, Orvieto: 476; Rapho Agency, Paris: 1056; Rheinisches Bildarchiv, Stadtmuseum, Cologne: 376, 468; Richter, E., Rome: 268; Rietberg Museum, Zurich: 44, 45; Rijksmuseum, Amsterdam: 535, 731, 737; *100, 102*; Riter, Carl: 717; Rivers, Larry, N.Y.: 979; Roubier, Jean, Paris: 234, 386–88, 390, 394, 425, 458, 460, 463; Routhier, Paris: *121*; Royal Library, Windsor Castle, Crown Copyright: 640; Royal Museum of Central Africa, Terveuren, Belgium: 43; Royal Museum of Fine Arts, Copenhagen: *134*; St. Louis Art Museum: 939; Salas, Armando, Portugal: 1009; Scala, Florence: 77, *81, 82*; Schaeffer, J. H., Baltimore: 804, 805; Schmidt-Glassner, Helga, Stuttgart: 467, 718–20; Schnellbacher, Pittsburgh: *131*; Schram, J. (after): 204; Science Museum, London: 861; Seilern, Count Antoine, London: 528; Service Photographique Réunion des Musées Nationaux, Paris: 847; *54, 75, 99, 106–8, 113, 115, 117, 118*; Sh. Studio Misr, Giza, from A. Badawy, *A History of Egyptian Architecture*: 56; Sibbelee, Hans, Amsterdam: 429; Smith, Edwin, Saffron Walden, England: 104, 107, 438, 784, 803; Soane's Museum, Sir John, London, Copyright: 786; Soehner, Halldor, Pinakothek, Munich: 646; Solomon Gallery, Holly, N.Y.: *161*; Soprintendenza ai Monumenti, Pisa: 498; Soprintendenza all'Antichità, Palermo: 17; Florence: 285, 499; Soprintendenza alle Galerie, Florence: 539, 560, 640; *66* (Foto Studio Quattrone, Mario); Spearman, Jerry, N.Y.: 1048; Sperone-Westwater Gallery, N.Y.: *165*; Staatliche Antikensammlungen und Glyptothek, Munich: 157, 158; *14, 16*; Staatliche Graphische Sammlung, Munich: 532; Staatliche Kunsthalle, Karlsruhe: 675; Staedel Kunstinstitut, Frankfurt: 736; State Museums, East Berlin: 80, 105, 203, 205, 335, 538; *10*; State Museums, West Berlin: 532, 732;

Stearn and Sons, Cambridge, England: 841; Stoedtner, Dr. Franz, Düsseldorf: 154; Stratton, A., from *Life...Wren*: 783; Studio R. Rémy, Dijon: 57; Studios Puytorac, Bordeaux: 750; Studly, Adolph, Pennsburg, Pa.: 917; Sunami, Soichi, N.Y.: 37, 962; Sybel, von (after): 314; The Tate Gallery, London: 879, 897; *124*; Thames & Hudson, Ltd., London (from Costa and Lockhart, *Persia*): 113; Thomas, J. W., Oxford: 464; Thyssen-Bornemiza Collection, Lucerne: 735; Tiers, from Monkmeyer Press Photo Service, N.Y.: 345; Time/Life, London: *176*; Tiranti, London, from B. Ünsal, *Turkish Islamic Architecture*: 347; Trachtenberg, Marvin, N.Y.: *4, 31, 43, 44, 89*; UNESCO, from UNESCO World Art Series, *Australia*, plate XXII: 21; United Nations, N.Y.: 1039; University Museum, Philadelphia: 92, 93; *9*; University of Oxford, Copyright Reserved: 779; University of Utrecht, Library: 373;

Uppsala University, Sweden: 681; Vatican Archives, Vatican Museum, Rome: 197, 199, 200, 207, 256, 257, 270, 279; Vatican Library, Rome: 299; Versnel, Jan, Amsterdam: 1035, 1036; Vertut, Jean, from *Préhistoire de l'Art Occidental* by André Leroi-Gourhan, courtesy Editions d'Art Lucien Mazenod, Paris: 2; Victoria & Albert Museum, London, Crown Copyright: 303, 333, 414, 583, 680, 791, 1018, 1020; Vincent, John B., Berkeley, California: 573, 624, 664, 665; Vizzanova, Paris: 764, 765, 882, 891, 895; Von Matt, Leonard, Buochs, Switzerland: 124; *48*; Wadsworth Atheneum, Hartford: 751; *103, 144*; Wallace Collection, London: 771; Warburg Institute, University of London: 413; Ward, Clarence, Oberlin, Ohio: 424, 427, 430; Ware (after): 661; Webb, John, London: *62, 69, 109, 126, 137*; Wehmeyer, Hildesheim: 380; Weill, Etienne, Paris: *175*; Wellington Museum, London,

Crown Copyright: 752; Whitaker Studios, Richmond: 850; Whitney Museum of American Art, N.Y.: *154*; Wiegand, T. (after): 251; Witty, Derrick E., Sunbury-on-Thames: 881; Worcester Art Museum, Mass.: 74; Yale Center for British Art, Paul Mellon Collection, New Haven: 13; Yale University Art Gallery, New Haven: 761, 770, 884; *110, 138*; Yan Photo Reportage, Toulouse; 16, 383; Yugoslav State Tourist Office, N.Y.: 252; Zwemmer, A., Ltd., London, from J. S. Ackerman, *The Architecture of Michelangelo*: 621

Acknowledgment is made with thanks to Harcourt, Brace & Jovanovich, Inc., N.Y., for permission to use the quotation on page 459 from "The Love Song of J. Alfred Prufrock" by T. S. Eliot from his volume *Collected Poems 1909–1935*, copyright, 1936, by Harcourt, Brace & World, Inc.